PUBLIC ADMINISTRATION

EIGHTH EDITION

PUBLIC ADMINISTRATION

Concepts and Cases

EIGHTH EDITION

Richard J. Stillman II
University of Colorado

Houghton Mifflin Company   **Boston**   **New York**

For my wife, Kathleen
my daughter, Shannon
my son, Rick

Publisher: Charles Hartford
Sponsoring Editor: Katherine Meisenheimer
Assistant Editor: Christina Lembo
Senior Project Editor: Margaret Park Bridges
Senior Manufacturing Coordinator: Priscilla Bailey
Executive Marketing Manager: Nicola Poser
Marketing Assistant: Kathleen Mellon

Cover image: Michael Townsend/Getty Images
Photos on pages 48, 218 and 436: Michael Townsend/Getty Images

Printed in the U.S.A.

Library of Congress Control Number: 2002109679

ISBN: 0-618-31045-2

56789—MV—08 07

Contents

4 The Political Environment: The Concept of Administrative Power   *104*

5 Intergovernmental Relations (IGR): The Concept of IGR as Interdependence, Complexity, and Bargaining   *124*

6 Internal Dynamics: The Concept of the Informal Group   *154*

7 Key Decision Makers Inside Public Administration: The Concept of Competing Bureaucratic Subsystems   *179*

PART TWO

The Multiple Functions of Public Administrators: Their Major Activities, Responsibilities, and Roles *218*

Topical Contents

Budget and Finance

Bureaucracy

Citizens' Rights and Participation

Communications in Administration

Congress, State Legislatures, County Boards, or City Councils

Decision Making

Ethical and Moral Issues of Public Administration

Health and Human Services

Implementation

Intergovernmental Programs and Policies

National Defense and International Relations

Organizational Behavior

Organization and Management

Personnel and Civil Service

Planning and Policy Development

Power and Politics in Administration

The Presidency, Governors, Mayors, or County Commissioners

Regulation, Rule Enforcement, and Law Enforcement

State and Local Government

The Study of Public Administration as a Discipline

Third-Party Government

Women, Minority, and Gay Issues

Preface

The publication of this eighth edition marks nearly thirty years since this text's first appearance in print. When the first edition was published, I hoped that this text would offer an improved way to teach the "basics" of public administration that would be both exciting and challenging for students. Over the intervening three decades, it has succeeded more than I could have imagined. I hope that readers of this eighth edition will find that this edition continues to meet their needs for a different and better way of introducing the field of public administration to both new students and "old hands."

Format and Approach

The methodological format and design of the first seven editions remain intact in the eighth edition. The approach seeks to interrelate many of the authoritative conceptual works in public administration with contemporary case studies.

By pairing a reading with a case study in each chapter, the text serves four important purposes:

1. The concept-case study method permits students to read firsthand the work of leading administrative theorists who have shaped the modern study of public administration. This method aims at developing in students a critical appreciation of the classic administrative ideas that are the basis of modern public administration.
2. The text encourages a careful examination of practical administrative problems through the presentation of contemporary cases—often involving major national events—that demonstrate the complexity, the centrality, and the challenge of the current administrative processes of public organizations.
3. The book seeks to promote a deeper understanding of the relationship between the theory and practice of public administration by allowing readers to test for themselves the validity of major ideas about public administration in the context of actual situations.
4. Finally, the concept-case method develops a keener appreciation of the eclectic breadth and interdisciplinary dimensions of public administration by presenting articles—both conceptual and case writings—from a wide variety of sources, using many materials not available in the average library.

The immense quantity of literature in the field has always made selecting the writings a challenge. My final choice of writings is based on affirmative answers to the following four central questions:

1. Do the writings focus on the central issues confronting public administrators?
2. Do the writings, individually and collectively, give a realistic view of the contemporary practice of public administration?
3. Do the individual conceptual readings and case studies relate logically to one another?

4. Are the writings interesting and long enough to convey the true sense and spirit intended by the authors?

The arrangement of the selections follows an order of topics used by many instructors in the field, moving from a definition of public administration to increasingly specific issues and problems. Many subjects (such as headquarters-field relationships, position classification, enforcement, government regulation, productivity, and personnel recruitment), though not treated separately, are discussed within various chapters under other headings (refer to the topic index for additional cross-references).

This diagram may help readers to understand the design of the book more clearly.

At the center of this schematic figure is chapter 1, which discusses "The Scope and Purpose of Public Administration," perhaps the most difficult, central intellectual problem in public administration today. The first ring outward is Part One, "The Pattern of Public Administration in America." These six chapters present concepts and cases pertaining to the broad environment surrounding public administration and the work of public administrators. The second ring is Part Two, "The Multiple Functions of Public Administrators." These six chapters focus on the major activities, roles, and responsibilities of practicing administrators in the public sector. The exterior ring is Part Three; these three chapters discuss "Enduring and Unresolved Relationships" in public administration, ones especially critical during the dawn of the 21st century for the field as a whole.

New Material in the Eighth Edition

Readings and cases have been carefully selected with an eye to readability and contemporary appeal to ensure that the text stays current and continues to reflect the ideas and events shaping public administration today. In this edition, special attention has been paid to ensuring the accessibility of writings for students: contemporary topics and issues that students want and need to know about are addressed in the new selections.

Ten new cases (or nearly two-thirds of the total case studies) appear in this edition:

Case Study 3: Dr. Helene Gayle and the AIDS Epidemic (Norma M. Riccucci)

Case Study 4: The *Columbia* Accident (Maureen Hogan Casamayou)

Case Study 6: American Ground: Unbuilding the World Trade Center (William Langewiesche)

Case Study 7: The Decision to Go to War with Iraq (James P. Pfiffner)

Case Study 9: The Shootings at Columbine High School: The Law Enforcement Response (Susan Rosegrant)

Case Study 11: Who Brought Bernadine Healy Down? (Deborah Sontag)

Case Study 12: Wisconsin's Budget Deficit (James K. Conant)

Case Study 13: They Had a Plan (Michael Elliott)

Case Study 15: The Human Genome Project (W. Henry Lambright)

Case Study 16: The Case of the Butterfly Ballot (Robert S. Montjoy and Christa Daryl Slaton)

Revised introductions, alerting students to the main ideas that follow, open each selection. Also updated are the review questions, key terms, and suggestions for further reading that conclude each chapter, as well as the subject index and topic correlation chart.

The Instructor's Guide

The *Instructor's Guide* complements the text by offering insights, practical suggestions, and resources for teaching introductory and graduate students. The guide is organized as a set of memoranda from myself to the instructor. Each memo addresses a separate important topic, such as "How to use case studies in the classroom." The guide also includes sample quizzes, exams, and course evaluation forms, as well as helpful student handouts such as the Federalist Papers, nos. 10 and 51.

Acknowledgments

Various people have contributed to this book either by helping to shape its focus in the early stages or by reviewing the finished manuscript. Special thanks are due to the following persons:

Lois R. Wise, Indiana University

Richard D. White, Jr., Louisiana State University

Michael D. Downey, Western Nevada Community College

Paul Mavima, Grand Valley State University

Marilyn A. Davis, Spelman College

Thanks must also go to my editors at Houghton Mifflin for their generous support and enthusiastic encouragement throughout this difficult writing and editing assignment, particularly Jean Woy, Margaret Park Bridges, and Betty Duncan. Both Professor James Garnett at the Department of Public Policy and Administration, Rutgers University, Camden and Professor Michael Milakovich, Public Administration Program at the University of Miami, offered excellent ideas for improving the instruction manual in more ways than I can calculate—or thank them for. To these and many others, I owe a debt of gratitude for their assistance.

R.J.S. II

CHAPTER 1

The Search for the Scope and Purpose of Public Administration

O ur own politics must be the touchstone for all theories. The principles on which to base a science of administration for America must be principles which have democratic policy very much at heart.

Woodrow Wilson

Introduction

A definition of the parameters of a field of study, that is, the boundaries, landmarks, and terrain that distinguish it from other scientific and humanistic disciplines, is normally considered a good place to begin any academic subject. Unfortunately, as yet, no one has produced a simple definition of the study of public administration—at least one on which most practitioners and scholars agree. Attempting to define the core values and focus of twentieth-century public administration provides lively debates and even deep divisions among students of the field.

A major difficulty in arriving at a precise and universally acceptable definition arises in part from the rapid growth in the twentieth century of public administration, which today seems to be all-encompassing. Public administrators are engaged in technical, although not necessarily mundane details: they prepare budgets for a city government, classify jobs in a post office, have potholes patched and mail delivered, or evaluate the performance of a city's drug treatment centers. At the same time, they are also concerned with the major goals of society and with the development of resources for achieving those goals within the context of a rapidly changing political environment. For instance, if an engineering staff of a state agency proposes to build a highway, this decision appears at first glance to be a purely administrative activity. However, it involves a wide range of social values related to pressing concerns such as community land-use patterns, energy consumption, pollution control, and mass transit planning. Race relations, the general economic well-being of a community, and the allocation of scarce physical and human resources affect even simple administrative decisions about highway construction.

Public administration does not operate in a vacuum but is deeply intertwined with the critical dilemmas confronting an entire society. The issue then becomes: How can a theorist reasonably and concisely define a field so interrelated with all of society?

The rapidly increasing number and scope of activities involving public administration have led theorists to develop a variety of definitions. Consider fifteen offered during the past two decades by leading textbook writers:

Public Administration is the production of goods and services designed to serve the needs of citizens-consumers.

Marshall Dimock, Gladys Dimock, and Douglas Fox,
Public Administration (Fifth Edition, 1983)

We suggest a new conceptual framework that emphasizes the perception of public administration as *design,* with attendant emphasis on participative decision making and learning, purpose and action, innovation, imagination and creativity, and social interaction and "coproduction."

Jong S. Jun,
Public Administration (1986)

In ordinary usage, public administration is a generic expression for the entire bundle of activities that are involved in the establishment and implementation of public policies.

Cole Blease Graham, Jr., and
Steven W. Hays,
Managing the Public Organization (1986)

Public administration:

1. is a cooperative group effort in a public setting.
2. covers all three branches—executive, legislative, and judicial—and their interrelationships.
3. has an important role in the formulation of public policy, and is thus part of the political process.
4. is different in significant ways from private administration.
5. is closely associated with numerous private groups and individuals in providing services to the community.

Felix A. Nigro and Lloyd G. Nigro,
Modern Public Administration (Seventh Edition, 1989)

. . . Public administration is centrally concerned with the organization of government policies and programs as well as the behavior of officials (usually nonelected) formally responsible for their conduct.

Charles H. Levine, B. Guy Peters, and Frank J. Thompson,
Public Administration: Challenges, Choices, Consequences (1990)

The practice of public administration involves the dynamic reconciliation of various forces in government's efforts to manage public policies and programs.

Melvin J. Dubnick and Barbara S. Romzek,
American Public Administration: Politics and the Management of Expectations (1991)

Public administration is concerned with the management of public programs.

Robert B. Denhardt,
Public Administration: An Action Orientation (1995)

Public Administration can be portrayed as a wheel of relationships focused on the implementation of public policy.

William C. Johnson,
Public Administration: Policy, Politics and Practice (Second Edition, 1995)

Public Administration in all modern nations is identified with the executive branch.

James W. Fesler and Donald F. Kettl
The Politics of the Administrative Process (Second Edition, 1996)

Public administration is the use of managerial, political, and legal theories and processes to fulfill legislative, executive, and judicial governmental mandates for the provision of regulatory and service functions for the society as a whole or for some segments of it.

David H. Rosenbloom and Deborah D. Goldman,
Public Administration: Understanding Management, Politics, and Law in the Public Sector (Fourth Edition, 1997)

Public administration may be defined as all processes, organizations, and individuals (the latter acting in official positions and roles) associated with carrying out laws and other rules adopted or issued by legislatures, executives, and courts.

Michael E. Milakovich,
Public Administration in America (Seventh Edition, 2000).

Traditionally, public administration is thought of as the accomplishing side of government. It is supposed to comprise all those activities involved in carrying out the policies of elected officials and some activities associated with the development of those policies. Public administration is . . . all that comes after the last campaign promise and election-night cheer.

Grover Starling,
Managing the Public Sector (Sixth Edition, 2001)

Public service is service, and as such must always be seen in personal terms. . . . This is what public administration means to me . . . the only path along which personal human development can proceed.

O. C. McSuite,
Invitation to Public Administration (2002)

All administration, including public administration, depends on the cooperative effort of the individuals who make up the administration. Therefore, administration is affected by all the complexities of human nature.

N. Joseph Cayer, and Louis Weschler,
Public Administration: Social Change and Adaptive Management (Second Edition, 2002)

> Public administration is not only instrumental—public sector decisions and actions are often complex, involve multiple possibilities, and change with time; and public sector practitioners are involved with determining what government does in addition to how it does it.
>
> Richard C. Box,
> *Public Administration and Society* (2004)

Generally, these attempts at defining public administration seem to identify it with the following: (1) the executive branch of government (yet it is related in important ways to the legislative and judicial branches); (2) the formulation and implementation of public policies; (3) the involvement in a considerable range of problems concerning human behavior and cooperative human effort; (4) a field that can be differentiated in several ways from private administration; (5) the production of public goods and services; and (6) rooted in the law as well as concerned with carrying out laws. However, trying to pin down public administration in more specific detail becomes, according to specialists such as Harold Stein, a fruitless endeavor. The many variables and complexities of public administration make almost every administrative situation a unique event, eluding any highly systematic categorization. As Harold Stein writes: "public administration is a field in which every man is his own codifier and categorizer and the categories adopted must be looked on as relatively evanescent."[1]

For some writers like Frederick C. Mosher, the elusiveness of a disciplinary core for public administration gives the subject its strength and fascination, for students must draw upon many fields and disciplines, as well as their own resources, to solve a particular administrative problem. As Mosher writes: "Perhaps it is best that it [public administration] not be defined. It is more an area of interest than a discipline, more a focus than a separate science. . . . It is necessarily cross-disciplinary. The overlapping and vague boundaries should be viewed as a resource, even though they are irritating to some with orderly minds."[2]

But for others like Robert S. Parker, the frustrations of dealing with such a disorderly discipline mitigate against its being a mature, rewarding academic field of study. "There is really no such subject as 'public administration,'" writes Parker. "No science or art can be identified by this title, least of all any single skill or coherent intellectual discipline. The term has no relation to the world of systematic thought. . . . It does not, in itself, offer any promising opportunity to widen or make more precise any single aspect of scientific knowledge."[3]

Despite Parker's pessimistic assessment of the present and future status of public administration, the search for a commonly accepted definition of the field, both in its academic and professional applications, continues by many scholars.

Indeed, defining public administration—its boundaries, scope, and purpose—has become, in recent decades, a preoccupation and difficulty confronting public administration theorists. The field's "identity crisis," as Dwight Waldo once labeled the dilemma, has now become especially acute because a plethora of models, approaches, and theories now purport to define what public administration is all about.

To help us understand public administration today, it is useful to study the rationale for creating this field, as outlined in an essay written in 1887 by Woodrow Wilson, a young political

---

[1]Harold Stein, *Public Administration and Policy Development: A Case Book* (New York: Harcourt Brace Jovanovich, 1952), xxv.

[2]Frederick C. Mosher, "Research in Public Administration," *Public Administration Review,* 16 (Summer 1956): 177.

[3]Robert S. Parker, "The End of Public Administration," *Public Administration,* 34 (June 1965): 99.

scientist at the time. Wilson (1856–1924) is better known as the twenty-eighth President of the United States (1913–1921), father of the League of Nations, Commander-in-Chief during World War I, and author of much of the "New Freedom" progressive reform legislation. Wilson is also credited by scholars with writing the first essay on public administration in the United States and therefore is considered by many as its American founder. His short but distinguished essay, "The Study of Administration," was published a century after the U.S. Constitution's birth. Wilson had just begun his academic career, teaching political science at Bryn Mawr College in Pennsylvania, after earning his Ph.D. at Johns Hopkins University. The editor of a new journal *(Political Science Quarterly)* asked Wilson to contribute an essay on this developing subject. At that time, public administration had been a well-established discipline in Europe, but was largely unknown in America.

Geographic isolation, agrarian self-sufficiency, the absence of threats to national security, and limited demands for public services, among other things, had allowed the United States to get along reasonably well during its first century of existence without the self-conscious study of public administration. However, many events were forcing Americans to take notice of the need for public administration. By the late nineteenth century, technologic innovations such as the automobile, telephone, and light bulb and growing international involvement in the Spanish-American War, combined with increasing public participation in a democratic government, created urgent needs for expanded, effective administrative services. As a consequence, we also required an established field of administrative study. Wilson wrote his essay at the time when civil service reform had been instituted in the federal government (the Civil Service Act or "the Pendleton Act," named for its legislative sponsor, had been passed in 1883). Much of Wilson's centennial essay was, not surprisingly, a plea for recognizing the central importance of administrative machinery, especially a well-trained civil service based on merit, rather than politics, to operate a modern democratic government.

Just as the *Federalist Papers,* authored by James Madison, Alexander Hamilton, and John Jay had a century before advocated the passage of the U.S. Constitution, Wilson called in 1887 for the necessity of this new field "to run a constitution" during its second century. His essay strived to encourage the development of public administration and to underscore the importance of effective administration for the Constitution's survival in the future.

But how could Americans graft public administration into their Constitution, which had not mentioned this subject? For Wilson—and modern students of the field—this was the critical issue. In developing public administration—both practically and academically—Wilson's basic difficulty was to reconcile the notions of constitutional democracy with inherent concerns for popular control and participation with theories of efficient, professional administration, and their stress on systematic rules and internal procedures as distinct from democratic oversight and influence. For Wilson, this inevitable conflict could be settled by dividing government into two spheres—"politics," in which choices regarding what government should do are determined by a majority of elected representatives, and "administration," which serves to carry out the dictates of the populace through efficient procedures relatively free from political meddling.

Although modern administrative scholars generally reject the possibility or desirability of drawing any hard-or-fast line between politics and administration, or what most call "the politics-administration dichotomy," the issues Wilson raised are enduring and important. Read the essay for yourself and see how you judge the validity of Wilson's arguments.

How did Wilson define public administration, and why did he believe it was so critical to the future of the United States? Are his arguments for its basic rationale and value still valid?

Why did Wilson distinguish between "politics" and "administration" as important terms for creating public administration? In your opinion, is such a "politics-administration dichotomy" practical and workable? What are the advantages and disadvantages of using such a dichotomy today as a way to advance this field of study?

What sources did Wilson believe the United States should draw on in developing this new field? And what sources should Americans avoid in shaping their administrative enterprise? And why?

What issues and challenges did Wilson pose for administrative study and practice? Are these still priorities today?

The Study of Administration

WOODROW WILSON

I suppose that no practical science is ever studied where there is no need to know it. The very fact, therefore, that the eminently practical science of administration is finding its way into college courses in this country would prove that this country needs to know more about administration, were such proof of the fact required to make out a case. It need not be said, however, that we do not look into college programmes for proof of this fact. It is a thing almost taken for granted among us, that the present movement called civil service reform must, after the accomplishment of its first purpose, expand into efforts to improve, not the *personnel* only, but also the organization and methods of our government offices: because it is plain that their organization and methods need improvement only less than their *personnel*. It is the object of administrative study to discover, first, what government can properly and successfully do, and, secondly, how it can do these proper things with the utmost possible efficiency and at the least possible cost either of money or of energy. On both these points there is obviously much need of light among us; and only careful study can supply that light.

Reprinted with permission from *Political Science Quarterly,* 2 (June 1887): 197–222.

Before entering on that study, however, it is needful:

I. To take some account of what others have done in the same line; that is to say, of the history of the study.
II. To ascertain just what is its subject-matter.
III. To determine just what are the best methods by which to develop it, and the most clarifying political conceptions to carry with us into it.

Unless we know and settle these things, we shall set out without chart or compass.

I.

The science of administration is the latest fruit of that study of the science of politics which was begun some twenty-two hundred years ago. It is a birth of our own century, almost of our own generation.

Why was it so late in coming? Why did it wait till this too busy century of ours to demand attention for itself? Administration is the most obvious part of government; it is government in action; it is the executive, the operative, the most visible side of government, and is of course as old as government itself. It is government in action, and one might very naturally expect to find that government in action had arrested the attention and provoked the scrutiny of writers of politics very early in the history of systematic thought.

But such was not the case. No one wrote systematically of administration as a branch of the science of government until the present century had passed its first youth and had begun to put forth its characteristic flower of systematic knowledge. Up to our own day all the political writers whom we now read had thought, argued, dogmatized only about the *constitution* of government; about the nature of the state, the essence and seat of sovereignty, popular power and kingly prerogative; about the greatest meanings lying at the heart of government, and the high ends set before the purpose of government by man's nature and man's aims. The central field of controversy was that great field of theory in which monarchy rode tilt against democracy, in which oligarchy would have built for itself strongholds of privilege, and in which tyranny sought opportunity to make good its claim to receive submission from all competitors. Amidst this high warfare of principles, administration could command no pause for its own consideration. The question was always: Who shall make law, and what shall that law be? The other question, how law should be administered with enlightenment, with equity, with speed, and without friction, was put aside as "practical detail" which clerks could arrange after doctors had agreed upon principles.

That political philosophy took this direction was of course no accident, no chance preference or perverse whim of political philosophers. The philosophy of any time is, as Hegel says, "nothing but the spirit of that time expressed in abstract thought"; and political philosophy, like philosophy of every other kind, has only held up the mirror to contemporary affairs. The trouble in early times was almost altogether about the constitution of government; and consequently that was what engrossed men's thoughts. There was little or no trouble about administration,—at least little that was heeded by administrators. The functions of government were simple, because life itself was simple. Government went about imperatively and compelled men, without

thought of consulting their wishes. There was no complex system of public revenues and public debts to puzzle financiers; there were, consequently, no financiers to be puzzled. No one who possessed power was long at a loss how to use it. The great and only question was: Who shall possess it? Populations were of manageable numbers; property was of simple sorts. There were plenty of farms, but no stocks and bonds; more cattle than vested interests.

• • •

There is scarcely a single duty of government which was once simple which is not now complex; government once had but a few masters; it now has scores of masters. Majorities formerly only underwent government; they now conduct government. Where government once might follow the whims of a court, it must now follow the views of a nation.

And those views are steadily widening to new conceptions of state duty; so that, at the same time that the functions of government are every day becoming more complex and difficult, they are also vastly multiplying in number. Administration is everywhere putting its hands to new undertakings. The utility, cheapness, and success of the government's postal service, for instance, point towards the early establishment of governmental control of the telegraph system. Or, even if our government is not to follow the lead of the governments of Europe in buying or building both telegraph and railroad lines, no one can doubt that in some way it must make itself master of masterful corporations. The creation of national commissioners of railroads, in addition to the older state commissions, involves a very important and delicate extension of administrative functions. Whatever hold of authority state or federal governments are to take upon corporations, there must follow cares and responsibilities which will require not a little wisdom, knowledge, and experience. Such things must be studied in order to be well done. And these, as I have said, are only a few of the doors which are being opened to offices of government. The idea of the state and the consequent ideal of its duty are undergoing noteworthy change; and "the idea of the state is the conscience of administration." Seeing every day new things which the state ought to do, the next thing is to see clearly how it ought to do them.

This is why there should be a science of administration which shall seek to straighten the paths of government, to make its business less unbusinesslike; to strengthen and purify its organization, and to crown its duties with dutifulness. This is one reason why there is such a science.

But where has this science grown up? Surely not on this side of the sea. Not much impartial scientific method is to be discerned in our administrative practices. The poisonous atmosphere of city government, the crooked secrets of state administration, the confusion, sinecurism, and corruption ever and again discovered in the bureaus at Washington forbid us to believe that any clear conceptions of what constitutes good administration are as yet very widely current in the United States. No; American writers have hitherto taken no very important part in the advancement of this science. It has found its doctors in Europe. It is not of our making; it is a foreign science, speaking very little of the language of English or American principle. It employs only foreign tongues; it utters none but what are to our minds alien ideas. Its aims, its examples, its conditions, are almost exclusively grounded in the histories of foreign races, in the precedents of foreign systems, in the lessons of foreign revolutions. It has been developed by French and German professors, and is consequently in all parts adapted to the needs of a compact state, and made to fit highly centralized forms of government; whereas, to answer our purposes, it must be adapted, not to a simple and compact, but to a complex and multiform state, and made to fit highly decentralized forms of government. If we would employ it, we must Americanize it, and that not formally, in language merely, but radically, in thought, principle, and aim as well. It must learn our constitutions by heart; must get the bureaucratic fever out of its veins; must inhale much free American air.

If an explanation be sought why a science manifestly so susceptible of being made useful to all governments alike should have received attention first in Europe, where government has long been a monopoly, rather than in England or the United States, where government has long been a common

franchise, the reason will doubtless be found to be twofold: first, that in Europe, just because government was independent of popular assent, there was more governing to be done; and, second, that the desire to keep government a monopoly made the monopolists interested in discovering the least irritating means of governing. They were, besides, few enough to adopt means promptly.

• • •

The English race . . . has long and successfully studied the art of curbing executive power to the constant neglect of the art of perfecting executive methods. It has exercised itself much more in controlling than in energizing government. It has been more concerned to render government just and moderate than to make it facile, well-ordered, and effective. English and American political history has been a history, not of administrative development, but of legislative oversight,—not of progress in governmental organization, but of advance in law-making and political criticism. Consequently, we have reached a time when administrative study and creation are imperatively necessary to the well-being of our governments saddled with the habits of a long period of constitution-making. That period has practically closed, so far as the establishment of essential principles is concerned, but we cannot shake off its atmosphere. We go on criticizing when we ought to be creating. We have reached the third of the periods I have mentioned,—the period, namely, when the people have to develop administration in accordance with the constitutions they won for themselves in a previous period of struggle with absolute power; but we are not prepared for the tasks of the new period.

Such an explanation seems to afford the only escape from blank astonishment at the fact that, in spite of our vast advantages in point of political liberty, and above all in point of practical political skill and sagacity, so many nations are ahead of us in administrative organization and administrative skill. Why, for instance, have we but just begun purifying a civil service which was rotten full fifty years ago? To say that slavery diverted us is but to repeat what I have said—that flaws in our Constitution delayed us.

Of course all reasonable preference would declare for this English and American course of politics rather than for that of any European country. We should not like to have had Prussia's history for the sake of having Prussia's administrative skill; and Prussia's particular system of administration would quite suffocate us. It is better to be untrained and free than to be servile and systematic. Still there is no denying that it would be better yet to be both free in spirit and proficient in practice. It is this even more reasonable preference which impels us to discover what there may be to hinder or delay us in naturalizing this much-to-be desired science of administration.

What, then, is there to prevent?

Well, principally, popular sovereignty. It is harder for democracy to organize administration than for monarchy. The very completeness of our most cherished political successes in the past embarrasses us. We have enthroned public opinion; and it is forbidden us to hope during its reign for any quick schooling of the sovereign in executive expertness or in the conditions of perfect functional balance in government. The very fact that we have realized popular rule in its fullness has made the task of *organizing* that rule just so much the more difficult. In order to make any advance at all we must instruct and persuade a multitudinous monarch called public opinion,—a much less feasible undertaking than to influence a single monarch called a king. An individual sovereign will adopt a simple plan and carry it out directly; he will have but one opinion, and he will embody that one opinion in one command. But this other sovereign, the people, will have a score of differing opinions. They can agree upon nothing simple: advance must be made through compromise, by a compounding of differences, by a trimming of plans and a suppression of too straightforward principles. There will be a succession of resolves running through a course of years, a dropping fire of commands running through a whole gamut of modifications.

In government, as in virtue, the hardest of hard things is to make progress. Formerly the reason for this was that the single person who was sovereign was generally either selfish, ignorant, timid, or a fool,—albeit there was now and again one who was

wise. Nowadays the reason is that the many, the people, who are sovereign have no single ear which one can approach, and are selfish, ignorant, timid, stubborn, or foolish with the selfishnesses, the ignorances, the stubbornnesses, the timidities, or the follies of several thousand persons,—albeit there are hundreds who are wise. Once the advantage of the reformer was that the sovereign's mind had a definite locality, that it was contained in one man's head, and that consequently it could be gotten at; though it was his disadvantage that that mind learned only reluctantly or only in small quantities, or was under the influence of someone who let it learn only the wrong things. Now, on the contrary, the reformer is bewildered by the fact that the sovereign's mind has no definite locality, but is contained in a voting majority of several million heads; and embarrassed by the fact that the mind of this sovereign also is under the influence of favorites, who are none the less favorites in a good old-fashioned sense of the word because they are not persons but preconceived opinions; *i.e.,* prejudices which are not to be reasoned with because they are not the children of reason.

Wherever regard for public opinion is a first principle of government, practical reform must be slow and all reform must be full of compromises. For wherever public opinion exists it must rule. This is now an axiom half the world over, and will presently come to be believed even in Russia. Whoever would effect a change in a modern constitutional government must first educate his fellow-citizens to want *some* change. That done, he must persuade them to want the particular change he wants. He must first make public opinion willing to listen and then see to it that it listen to the right things. He must stir it up to search for an opinion, and then manage to put the right opinion in its way.

The first step is not less difficult than the second. With opinions, possession is more than nine points of the law. It is next to impossible to dislodge them. Institutions which one generation regards as only a makeshift approximation to the realization of a principle, the next generation honors as the nearest possible approximation to that principle, and the next worships as the principle itself. It takes scarcely three generations for the apotheosis. The grandson accepts his grandfather's hesitating experiment as an integral part of the fixed constitution of nature.

Even if we had clear insight into all the political past, and could form out of perfectly instructed heads a few steady, infallible, placidly wise maxims of government into which all sound political doctrine would be ultimately resolvable, *would the country act on them?* That is the question. The bulk of mankind is rigidly unphilosophical, and nowadays the bulk of mankind votes. A truth must become not only plain but also commonplace before it will be seen by the people who go to their work very early in the morning; and not to act upon it must involve great and pinching inconveniences before these same people will make up their minds to act upon it.

And where is this unphilosophical bulk of mankind more multifarious in its composition than in the United States? To know the public mind of this country, one must know the mind, not of Americans of the older stocks only, but also of Irishmen, of Germans, of Negroes. In order to get a footing for new doctrine, one must influence minds cast in every mould of race, minds inheriting every bias of environment, warped by the histories of a score of different nations, warmed or chilled, closed or expanded by almost every climate of the globe.

• • •

II.

The field of administration is a field of business. It is removed from the hurry and strife of politics; it at most points stands apart even from the debatable ground of constitutional study. It is a part of political life only as the methods of the counting-house are a part of the life of society; only as machinery is part of the manufactured product. But it is, at the same time, raised very far above the dull level of mere technical detail by the fact that through its greater principles it is directly connected with the lasting maxims of political wisdom, the permanent truths of political progress.

The object of administrative study is to rescue executive methods from the confusion and costliness of empirical experiment and set them upon foundations laid deep in stable principle.

It is for this reason that we must regard civil service reform in its present stages as but a prelude to a fuller administrative reform. We are now rectifying methods of appointment; we must go on to adjust executive functions more fitly and to prescribe better methods of executive organization and action. Civil service reform is thus but a moral preparation for what is to follow. It is clearing the moral atmosphere of official life by establishing the sanctity of public office as a public trust, and, by making the service unpartisan, it is opening the way for making it businesslike. By sweetening its motives it is rendering it capable of improving its methods of work.

Let me expand a little what I have said of the province of administration. Most important to be observed is the truth already so much and so fortunately insisted upon by our civil service reformers; namely, that administration lies outside the proper sphere of *politics*. Administrative questions are not political questions. Although politics sets the tasks for administration, it should not be suffered to manipulate its offices.

This is distinction of high authority; eminent German writers insist upon it as of course. Bluntschli, for instance, bids us separate administration alike from politics and from law. Politics, he says, is state activity "in things great and universal," while "administration, on the other hand," is "the activity of the state in individual and small things. Politics is thus the special province of the statesman, administration of the technical official." "Policy does nothing without the aid of administration"; but administration is not therefore politics. But we do not require German authority for this position; this discrimination between administration and politics is now, happily, too obvious to need further discussion.

There is another distinction which must be worked into all our conclusions, which, though but another side of that between administration and politics, is not quite so easy to keep sight of; I mean the distinction between *constitutional* and administrative questions, between those governmental adjustments which are essential to constitutional principle and those which are merely instrumental to the possibly changing purposes of a wisely adapting convenience.

One cannot easily make clear to every one just where administration resides in the various departments of any practicable government without entering upon particulars so numerous as to confuse and distinctions so minute as to distract. No lines of demarcation, setting apart administrative from non-administrative functions, can be run between this and that department of government without being run up hill and down dale, over dizzy heights of distinction and through dense jungles of statutory enactment, hither and thither around "ifs" and "buts," "whens" and "howevers," until they become altogether lost to the common eye not accustomed to this sort of surveying, and consequently not acquainted with the use of the theodolite of logical discernment. A great deal of administration goes about *incognito* to most of the world, being confounded now with political "management," and again with constitutional principle.

Perhaps this case of confusion may explain such utterances as that of Niebuhr's: "Liberty," he says, "depends incomparably more upon administration than upon constitution." At first sight this appears to be largely true. Apparently facility in the actual exercise of liberty does depend more upon administrative arrangements than upon constitutional guarantees; although constitutional guarantees alone secure the existence of liberty. But—upon second thought—is even so much as this true? Liberty no more consists in easy functional movement than intelligence consists in the ease and vigor with which the limbs of a strong man move. The principles that rule within the man, or the constitution, are the vital springs of liberty or servitude. Because dependence and subjection are without chains, are lightened by every easy-working device of considerate, paternal government, they are not thereby transformed into liberty. Liberty cannot live apart from constitutional principle; and no administration, however perfect and liberal its methods, can give men more than a poor counterfeit of liberty if it rest upon illiberal principles of government.

A clear view of the difference between the province of constitutional law and the province of administrative function ought to leave no room for misconception; and it is possible to name some roughly definite criteria upon which such a view can be built. Public administration is detailed and systematic execution of public law. Every particular application of general law is an act of administration. The assessment and raising of taxes, for instance, the hanging of a criminal, the transportation and delivery of the mails, the equipment and recruiting of the army and navy, etc., are all obviously acts of administration; but the general laws which direct these things to be done are as obviously outside of and above administration. The broad plans of governmental action are not administrative; the detailed execution of such plans is administrative. Constitutions, therefore, properly concern themselves only with those instrumentalities of government which are to control general law. Our federal Constitution observes this principle in saying nothing of even the greatest of the purely executive offices, and speaking only of that President of the Union who was to share the legislative and policy-making functions of government, only of those judges of highest jurisdiction who were to interpret and guard its principles, and not of those who were merely to give utterance to them.

This is not quite the distinction between Will and answering Deed, because the administrator should have and does have a will of his own in the choice of means for accomplishing his work. He is not and ought not to be a mere passive instrument. The distinction is between general plans and special means.

There is, indeed, one point at which administrative studies trench on constitutional ground—or at least upon what seems constitutional ground. The study of administration, philosophically viewed, is closely connected with the study of the proper distribution of constitutional authority. To be efficient it must discover the simplest arrangements by which responsibility can be unmistakably fixed upon officials; the best way of dividing authority without hampering it, and responsibility without obscuring it. And this question of the distribution of authority, when taken into the sphere of the higher, the originating functions of government, is obviously a central constitutional question. If administrative study can discover the best principles upon which to base such distributions, it will have done constitutional study an invaluable service. Montesquieu did not, I am convinced, say the last word on this head.

To discover the best principle for the distribution of authority is of greater importance, possibly, under a democratic system, where officials serve many matters, than under others where they serve but a few. All sovereigns are suspicious of their servants, and the sovereign people is no exception to the rule; but how is its suspicion to be allayed by *knowledge?* If that suspicion could but be clarified into wise vigilance, it would be altogether salutary; if that vigilance could be aided by the unmistakable placing of responsibility, it would be altogether beneficent. Suspicion in itself is never healthful either in the private or in the public mind. *Trust is strength* in all relations of life; and, as it is the office of the constitutional reformer to create conditions of trustfulness, so it is the office of the administrative organizer to fit administration with conditions of clear-cut responsibility which shall insure trustworthiness.

And let me say that large powers and unhampered discretion seem to me the indispensable conditions of responsibility. Public attention must be easily directed, in each case of good or bad administration, to just the man deserving of praise or blame. There is no danger in power, if only it be not irresponsible. If it be divided, dealt only in shares to many, it is obscured; and if it be obscured, it is made irresponsible. But if it be centred in heads of the service and in heads of branches of the service, it is easily watched and brought to book. If to keep his office a man must achieve open and honest success, and if at the same time he feels himself entrusted with large freedom of discretion, the greater his power the less likely is he to abuse it, the more is he nerved and sobered and elevated by it. The less his power, the more safely obscure and unnoticed does he feel his position to be, and the more readily does he relapse into remissness.

Just here we manifestly emerge upon the field of that still larger question,—the proper relations between public opinion and administration.

To whom is official trustworthiness to be disclosed, and by whom is it to be rewarded? Is the official to look to the public for his meed of praise and his push of promotion, or only to his superior in office? Are the people to be called in to settle administrative discipline as they are called in to settle constitutional principles? These questions evidently find their root in what is undoubtedly the fundamental problem of this whole study. That problem is: What part shall public opinion take in the conduct of administration?

The right answer seems to be, that public opinion shall play the part of authoritative critic.

But the *method* by which its authority shall be made to tell? Our peculiar American difficulty in organizing administration is not the danger of losing liberty, but the danger of not being able or willing to separate its essentials from its accidents. Our success is made doubtful by that besetting error of ours, the error of trying to do too much by vote. Self-government does not consist in having a hand in everything, any more than housekeeping consists necessarily in cooking dinner with one's own hands. The cook must be trusted with a large discretion as to the management of the fires and the ovens.

In those countries in which public opinion has yet to be instructed in its privileges, yet to be accustomed to having its own way, this question as to the province of public opinion is much more readily soluble than in this country, where public opinion is wide awake and quite intent upon having its own way anyhow. It is pathetic to see a whole book written by a German professor of political science for the purpose of saying to his countrymen, "Please try to have an opinion about national affairs"; but a public which is so modest may at least be expected to be very docile and acquiescent in learning what things it has *not* a right to think and speak about imperatively. It may be sluggish, but it will not be meddlesome. It will submit to be instructed before it tries to instruct. Its political education will come before its political activity. In trying to instruct our own public opinion, we are dealing with a pupil apt to think itself quite sufficiently instructed beforehand.

The problem is to make public opinion efficient without suffering it to be meddlesome. Directly exercised, in the oversight of the daily details and in the choice of the daily means of government, public criticism is of course a clumsy nuisance, a rustic handling delicate machinery. But as super-intending the greater forces of formative policy alike in politics and administration, public criticism is altogether safe and beneficent, altogether indispensable. Let administrative study find the best means for giving public criticism this control and for shutting it out from all other interference.

But is the whole duty of administrative study done when it has taught the people what sort of administration to desire and demand, and how to get what they demand? Ought it not to go on to drill candidates for the public service?

There is an admirable movement towards universal political education now afoot in this country. The time will soon come when no college of respectability can afford to do without a well-filled chair of political science. But the education thus imparted will go but a certain length. It will multiply the number of intelligent critics of government, but it will create no competent body of administrators. It will prepare the way for the development of a sure-footed understanding of the general principles of government, but it will not necessarily foster skill in conducting government. It is an education which will equip legislators, perhaps, but not executive officials. If we are to improve public opinion, which is the motive power of government, we must prepare better officials as the *apparatus* of government. If we are to put in new boilers and to mend the fires which drive our governmental machinery, we must not leave the old wheels and joints and valves and bands to creak and buzz and clatter on as the best they may at bidding of the new force. We must put in new running parts wherever there is the least lack of strength or adjustment. It will be necessary to organize democracy by sending up to the competitive examinations for the civil service men definitely prepared for standing liberal tests as to technical knowledge. A technically schooled civil service will presently have become indispensable.

I know that a corps of civil servants prepared by a special schooling and drilled, after appointment, into a perfected organization, with appropriate hierarchy and characteristic discipline, seems to a great many very thoughtful persons to contain elements which might combine to make an offensive official class,— a distinct, semi-corporate body with sympathies divorced from those of a progressive, free-spirited people, and with hearts narrowed to the meanness of a bigoted officialism. Certainly such a class would be altogether hateful and harmful in the United States. Any measures calculated to produce it would for us be measures of reaction and of folly.

But to fear the creation of a domineering, illiberal officialism as a result of the studies I am here proposing is to miss altogether the principle upon which I wish most to insist. That principle is, that administration in the United States must be at all points sensitive to public opinion. A body of thoroughly trained officials serving during good behavior we must have in any case: that is a plain business necessity. But the apprehension that such a body will be anything un-American clears away the moment it is asked, What is to constitute good behavior? For that question obviously carries its own answer on its face. Steady, hearty allegiance to the policy of the government they serve will constitute good behavior. That *policy* will have no taint of officialism about it. It will not be the creation of permanent officials, but of statesmen whose responsibility to public opinion will be direct and inevitable. Bureaucracy can exist only where the whole service of the state is removed from the common political life of the people, its chiefs as well as its rank and file. Its motives, its objects, its policy, its standards, must be bureaucratic. It would be difficult to point out any examples of impudent exclusiveness and arbitrariness on the part of officials doing service under a chief of department who really served the people, as all our chiefs of departments must be made to do.

• • •

The ideal for us is a civil service cultured and self-sufficient enough to act with sense and vigor, and yet so intimately connected with the popular thought, by means of elections and constant public counsel, as to find arbitrariness or class spirit quite out of the question.

III.

Having thus viewed in some sort the subject-matter and the objects of this study of administration, what are we to conclude as to the methods best suited to it—the points of view most advantageous for it?

Government is so near us, as much a thing of our daily familiar handling, that we can with difficulty see the need of any philosophical study of it, or the exact point of such study, should it be undertaken. We have been on our feet too long to study now the art of walking. We are a practical people, made so apt, so adept in self-government by centuries of experimental drill that we are scarcely any longer capable of perceiving the awkwardness of the particular system we may be using, just because it is so easy for us to use any system. We do not study the art of governing: we govern. But mere unschooled genius for affairs will not save us from sad blunders in administration. Though democrats by long inheritance and repeated choice, we are still rather crude democrats. Old as democracy is, its organization on a basis of modern ideas and conditions is still an unaccomplished work. The democratic state has yet to be equipped for carrying those enormous burdens of administration which the needs of this industrial and trading age are so fast accumulating. Without comparative studies in government we cannot rid ourselves of the misconception that administration stands upon an essentially different basis in a democratic state from that on which it stands in a non-democratic state.

After such study we could grant democracy the sufficient honor of ultimately determining by debate all essential questions affecting the public weal, of basing all structures of policy upon the major will; but we would have found but one rule of good administration for all governments alike. So far as administrative functions are concerned, all governments have a strong structural likeness; more than that, if they are to be uniformly useful and efficient, they *must* have a strong structural likeness. A free man has the same bodily organs, the same executive parts, as the slave, however different may be his motives, his services, his energies. Monarchies and democracies, radically different as they are in other respects, have in reality much the same business to look to.

It is abundantly safe nowadays to insist upon this actual likeness of all governments, because these are days when abuses of power are easily exposed and arrested, in countries like our own, by a bold, alert, inquisitive, detective public thought and a sturdy popular self-dependence such as never existed before. We are slow to appreciate this; but it is easy to appreciate it. Try to imagine personal government in the United States. It is like trying to imagine a national

worship of Zeus. Our imaginations are too modern for the feat.

But, besides being safe, it is necessary to see that for all governments alike the legitimate ends of administration are the same, in order not to be frightened at the idea of looking into foreign systems of administration for instruction and suggestion; in order to get rid of the apprehension that we might perchance blindly borrow something incompatible with our principles. That man is blindly astray who denounces attempts to transplant foreign systems into this country. It is impossible: they simply would not grow here. But why should we not use such parts of foreign contrivances as we want, if they be in any way serviceable? We are in no danger of using them in a foreign way. We borrowed rice, but we do not eat it with chopsticks. We borrowed our whole political language from England, but we leave the words "king" and "lords" out of it. What did we ever originate, except the action of the federal government upon individuals and some of the functions of the federal supreme court?

We can borrow the science of administration with safety and profit if only we read all fundamental differences of condition into its essential tenets. We have only to filter it through our constitutions, only to put it over a slow fire of criticism and distill away its foreign gases.

• • •

Let it be noted that it is the distinction, already drawn, between administration and politics which makes the comparative method so safe in the field of administration. When we study the administrative systems of France and Germany, knowing that we are not in search of *political* principles, we need not care a peppercorn for the constitutional or political reasons which Frenchmen or Germans give for their practices when explaining them to us. If I see a murderous fellow sharpening a knife cleverly, I can borrow his way of sharpening the knife without borrowing his probable intention to commit murder with it; and so, if I see a monarchist dyed in the wool managing a public bureau well, I can learn his business methods without changing one of my republican spots. He may serve his king; I will continue to serve the people; but I should like to serve my sovereign as well as he serves his. By keeping this distinction in view,—that is, by studying administration as a means of putting our own politics into convenient practice, as a means of making what is democratically politic towards all administratively possible towards each,—we are on perfectly safe ground, and can learn without error what foreign systems have to teach us. We thus devise an adjusted weight for our comparative method of study. We can thus scrutinize the anatomy of foreign governments without fear of getting any of their diseases into our veins; dissect alien systems without apprehension of blood-poisoning.

Our own politics must be the touchstone for all theories. The principles on which to base a science of administration for America must be principles which have democratic policy very much at heart. And, to suit American habit, all general theories must, as theories, keep modestly in the background, not in open argument only, but even in our own minds,— lest opinions satisfactory only to the standards of the library should be dogmatically used, as if they must be quite as satisfactory to the standards of practical politics as well. Doctrinaire devices must be postponed to tested practices. Arrangements not only sanctioned by conclusive experience elsewhere but also congenial to American habit must be preferred without hesitation to theoretical perfection. In a word, steady, practical statesmanship must come first, closet doctrine second. The cosmopolitan what-to-do must always be commanded by the American how-to-do-it.

Our duty is, to supply the best possible life to a *federal* organization, to systems within systems; to make town, city, county, state, and federal governments live with a like strength and an equally assured healthfulness, keeping each unquestionably its own master and yet making all interdependent and cooperative, combining independence with mutual helpfulness. The task is great and important enough to attract the best minds.

This interlacing of local self-government with federal self-government is quite a modern conception.

It is not like the arrangements of imperial federation in Germany. There local government is not yet, fully, local *self*-government. The bureaucrat is everywhere busy. His efficiency springs out of *esprit de corps,* out of care to make ingratiating obeisance to the authority of a superior, or, at best, out of the soil of a sensitive conscience. He serves, not the public, but an irresponsible minister. The question for us is, how shall our series of governments within governments be so administered that it shall always be to the interest of the public officer to serve, not his superior alone but the community also, with the best efforts of his talents and the soberest service of his conscience? How shall such service be made to his commonest interest by contributing abundantly to his sustenance, to his dearest interest by furthering his ambition, and to his highest interest by advancing his honor and establishing his character? And how shall this be done alike for the local part and for the national whole?

If we solve this problem we shall again pilot the world. There is a tendency—is there not?—a tendency as yet dim, but already steadily impulsive and clearly destined to prevail, towards, first the confederation of parts of empires like the British, and finally of great states themselves. Instead of centralization of power, there is to be wide union with tolerated divisions of prerogative. This is a tendency towards the American type—of governments joined with governments for the pursuit of common purposes, in honorary equality and honorable subordination. Like principles of civil liberty are everywhere fostering like methods of government; and if comparative studies of the ways and means of government should enable us to offer suggestions which will practically combine openness and vigor in the administration of such governments with ready docility to all serious, well-sustained public criticism, they will have approved themselves worthy to be ranked among the highest and most fruitful of the great departments of political study. That they will issue in such suggestions I confidently hope.

▇▇▇ **READING 1.2**

Introduction

Before going on to the case study, as normally happens in this text's concept-case methodology, which pairs concepts with cases throughout this book, let's look at one more conceptual overview that attempts to define what is the nature and substance of the study of public administration (as opposed to its practice). Unlike the Wilson essay, which is an argument for its development in 1887, the following piece by the author of this textbook tries to sketch the academic study of public administration from the vantage point of its broad historical evolution in America. He argues that public administration as a field of study is a product of a unique political tradition that he labels as "antistatist." This "antistatist" tradition permitted America to ignore this field until the late nineteenth century, but it arose as a response to the rapidly changing socio-political-economic environment throughout the twentieth century.

Because much of the following essay attempts to define the field of American Public Administration by arguing that its outlook and values were—and still are—pervasively dominated by antistatism, it is worth briefly defining "statism" and "antistatism" as an introduction to this essay. What do those two terms mean?

As one leading expert on this topic recently defined "state":

A state is any set of relatively differentiated organizations that claims sovereignty and coercive control over a territory and its population, defending and perhaps extending that claim in competition with other states. The core organizations that make up a state include administrative, judicial, and policing organizations that collect and dispense revenues, enforce the constitutive rules of the state and society, and maintain some modicum of domestic order, especially to protect the state's own claims and activities.[1]

"Statism" therefore is doctrines and ideas that advocate strengthening the role and sovereignty of the state institutions in society. "Antistatism" is the opposite, namely, ideas and doctrines expressly hostile to these central governing institutions in society, which argue for reducing, limiting, even eliminating their role(s) and activities.

As you read this "dragnet overview" of the study of Public Administration, you might ask yourself these questions:

How does the field define itself today in contrast with Wilson's 1887 perspective? What are its basic values and outlooks?

What are the central problems Public Administration is trying to address now in comparison to Wilson's era?

How does the field today view the problem of relating politics and administration, by contrast to Wilson's essay?

[1]Theda Skocpol, *Protecting Soldiers and Mothers: The Political Origins of Social Policy in the United States* (Cambridge, MA: Harvard University Press, 1995), 43. Skocpol's conceptualization of "state," as she indicates in a footnote, draws heavily from the writings of Max Weber and Otto Hintz.

Do you agree that "The Refounding Movement" is the correct label to describe Public Administration currently? If so, what are the implications for the *practice* of public administration?

The Study of Public Administration in the United States: "The Eminently Practical Science"

RICHARD J. STILLMAN II

The study of Public Administration* in the United States, unlike other nations, can be understood only within the context of a radically antistatist political tradition. The U.S. Constitution, the core framing document, says nothing about civil service, budgets, executive departments, planning, and yes, public administration, all essential to promoting effective government performance. Rather, the Great Charter of 1787 places a tangle of limits upon government action by means of federalism, separation of powers, periodic elections, enumerated powers, a bill of rights, and so forth—mainly aimed at negating public power, not enhancing it, in order to secure, in Thomas Jefferson's ringing words of the Declaration of Independence, "life, liberty and the pursuit of happiness."

The Founders, to paraphrase Louis Hartz, were "locked into John Locke" (Hartz 1955). They framed the American Constitution premised on erecting a "night watchman"–style government by means of a strict "social contract" with the people to provide for only defense, courts, foreign affairs, trade relations, coin money, and little else.

In turn, this new governing edifice was firmly founded upon a rock-hard Calvinism that viewed human nature as sinful due to Adam's fall so that no one can be

trusted with power for very long. Or in Madison's apt sentence coined to support the separation of powers in *Federalist No. 51,* "Ambition must be made to counteract ambition" (Hamilton, Madison, and Jay 1961).

An eighteenth-century enlightenment-inspired Constitution, based upon seventeenth-century Lockean politics and sixteenth-century Calvinist religion, makes it hard to accommodate twenty-first-century "positive" administrative action or thought. Indeed, the framers sought to stamp out anything that smelled of the slightest whiff of European-style statism, for their opponents, the antifederalists, were even more rabid on that subject—and they nearly won!

America's belief in antistatism was further soundly reinforced over more than three centuries by waves of immigrants fleeing all sorts of oppressive regimes, from the Puritans in 1620 to the twentieth-century's escapees from fascism, communism, and numerous other varieties of "isms," all carrying a peculiarly virulent hostility towards statism. There were no stout advocates of Machiavelli's "Prince," Bodin's "divine right of kings," or Hobbes's "Leviathan." If there were any British Tories, the Revolutionary War chased them off to Canada or back to England for good in 1776!

Quite by accident and no thanks to Adam Smith, the first century of American national life conspired to underscore that the notion "state" was not only "evil" but also unnecessary. Geographic isolation, a largely self-supporting rural populace, the absence of significant external threats, little need for sizable armed forces or social services, the frontier mentality, and the

---

*This essay was written especially for this volume. Because the English language does not differentiate between administrative institutional practice versus theory, the author follows Dwight Waldo's approach throughout this essay by capitalizing "Public Administration" when referring to ideas or theory of the study of this field, as opposed to lowercase for describing its practice and institutions.

lack of an industrial revolution created a unique hot-house environment where antistatism flourished with little challenge as the political norm. Perhaps Harvard sociologist Theda Skocpol most aptly characterized this odd situation: just as Prussia in the eighteenth century was less a state with an army than an army with a state, the early United States was "not so much a country with a post office, as a post office that gave popular reality to a fledging nation" (Skocpol 1996). During the 1830s and 1840s, three-quarters of all federal employees were postal workers, and until the Civil War, 85 percent of growth in the entire federal government occurred within that single department.

The Uniqueness of American Public Administration Thought

What does all this unrelenting antistatism have to do with the study of Public Administration in America? First, it explains why this academic field arrived so late on this side of the Atlantic. Without much necessity for public administration or its institutions and practices, why bother with Public Administration or its study and ideas? It took a century *after* the Constitution was written—in 1887, to be precise—for the first article to appear that merely *advocated* its study: Woodrow Wilson's now famous centennial essay, "The Study of Administration." It took another nearly four decades for the publication of the first American textbook: Leonard White's *An Introduction to the Study of Public Administration* (1926). Indeed, the growth of public administrative research and training of any significance was not until the 1930s and 1940s, or more than a century after the subject had been well established on the European continent.

Contextual forces in the late nineteenth and early twentieth century forced Americans to build an administrative enterprise, like it or not, in response to the closing of the frontier; massive migration from abroad; rapid technological, urbanized, industrial change with concomitant jarring "economic booms and busts"; clashes between management and labor, and the drive for international markets abroad. Only then did the development of a professional civil service, military, and diplomatic corps become urgent new priorities.

Suddenly a prophetic phrase in Wilson's 1887 essay became meaningful: "It is getting harder to run a Constitution than frame one." Up to roughly the dawn of the new century, even well into the 1920s, Americans studied government as law, proper constitutional design, and political philosophy, largely salted with Lockean-Calvinistic-Jeffersonian-antistatism. Thus, its second unique quality: U.S. Public Administration appeared well after the U.S. administrative state became an established reality and "running the Constitution" a necessity. Most scholars date the building of the American State between 1877 and 1920 (Skowronek 1982), and administrative ideas gelled only later. Again by stark contrast to continental Europe, where the development of both state and administrative sciences preceded democratic constitution-making, intense antistatism reversed the process in America and so, as a result, first its constitution, next its state and *then* its study emerged.

Third, unlike Europe's Public Administration, where top-down state-building fostered top-down, rational administrative sciences, American Public Administration "bubbled up" quietly and haphazardly from grassroots reforms, imbued with protestant "moral uplift" and "democratic idealism." It evolved in bits and pieces through the experimentation by a variety of local reform groups such as the National Civil Service League, National Municipal League, New York Bureau of Municipal Research, and more generally across the nation through the "bureau movement." To this day, American Public Administration Thought remains considerably more experimental, fragmented, inductive, applied, and reformist in caste and character compared with other countries. Again missing a sense of state, indeed vigorously opposed to it, any kind of top-down, rationalized administrative way of thinking would, for Americans, be out of the question, even inconceivable. Thus, *both* U.S. public administration as well as its Public Administration literally had to be built from the ground up by adding a civil service system here, an executive budget there, a council-manager plan over there, moving upward to the federal levels *and* toward a unique way of administrative thought that gelled under a label that today is called Public Administration.

Fourth, unlike many nations, where the positive law tradition became a basic methodology for teaching and research, particularly to create and expand welfare states on the Continent during the nineteenth century (Raadschelders and Rutgers 1999), Americans, rooted in a common law tradition as well as in the fundamental law of its Constitution that largely negated public power, had to look elsewhere to find the substance and scope of, not to mention legitimacy for, its administrative ideas. Rather, the field of management along with scientific methods founded upon a sharp differentiation between politics and administration became its early intellectual framework, unique identity, as well as its "meat and potatoes" content.

The two most important writings that so profoundly influenced early students, akin to Old and New Testaments for field, were Frank Goodnow's *Politics and Administration* (1900) and Frederick W. Taylor's *The Principles of Scientific Management* (1911). The former, as its title suggests, offered up a rationale for a clear-cut dichotomy upon which to found the new field. The latter, also as its title emphasizes, gave the emerging field both rational managerial methodology as well as "solid" scientific legitimacy to "do good" public administration, buttressed neatly by the popularity of business symbols during the progressive reform era.

Again without a sense of state, Americans had little choice but to advance a clear dichotomy that would free up "clean" administration from messy and corrupt "machine politics" while pressing for "respectable" business and scientific methods. Though Goodnow's and Taylor's ideas may seem quaint, even far-fetched, today, they in fact provided necessary answers to very real, complex empirical issues of the times. As Frederick C. Mosher astutely observed: the developments that created "the management movement were in a considerable degree, *a response* [author's emphasis] to the conditions . . . [of] fragmentation of responsibilities; lack of unified leadership; political corruption and spoils. They were spawned in an era of reform, of progressivism, of growing professionalism and occupational specialization and faith in rationality and applied sciences" (Mosher 1976).

Finally, public administration as well as Public Administration's origins and growth after the dawn of the twentieth century were directly related to the rapid expansion of democracy in all phases of public life. The twentieth century saw successful progressive challenges to "boss rule" and machine politics, by the passage of women's suffrage, direct election of senators, initiative, referendum and recall measures, combined with the rising public demands for government regulation of business, social services, and the like. In turn, these powerful democratic forces only heightened existing issues of governance. In the words of historian Robert Wiebe, America became a "distended society" (Wiebe 1967) that, in response, demanded more, not less, administrative thought, research, and training in order to knit together an increasingly fragmented or segmented society.

Whether these administrative ideas worked all that well, let alone economically, efficiently, and effectively, is another matter, but again unlike other countries, American Public Administration Thought became—and remains—a handmaiden of constitutional and democratic values. For without a preexisting stable state, its administrative ideas and institutions always had to be open for adjustment as well as to immediate shifting public interests. Therefore, U.S. administrative thought has never been—nor can ever be—defined as a fixed doctrine or set of doctrines but instead stays in flux, always chasing the shifting constitutional-democratic priorities of each new American generation. Thus too, Public Administration seems to transform itself into a new intellectual construct every generation, or every twenty years, often through highly innovative and creative methods, in order to respond to the pressing demands of the moment. Four eras of Public Administration, in retrospect, are apparent during the twentieth century, each with its distinct doctrines, ideals, theories, frameworks, methodologies, and agendas, largely shaped by the particular generational needs of that era: 1926–46, 1947–67, 1968–88, and 1989 to the present.

POSDCORB Orthodoxy, 1926–1946

The precise date for the intellectual birthing of American Public Administration can be considered 1926. In that year, the first American textbook appeared:

Leonard White's *Introduction to the Study of Public Administration* (1926). To be sure, after the turn of the century numerous basic texts were published on various functional fields such as city management, military administration, school administration, and business, but White's book stands out as a remarkable achievement. Here was the earliest volume offering Americans a subject labeled Public Administration. White's book succeeded as no other at gluing together various functional specializations as well as disparate ideas of Taylorism, Goodnow's dichotomy, and other administrative innovations under the rubric that we term today Public Administration.

At the heart of White's theoretical synthesis was a POSDCORB way of thought that Luther Gulick, a decade later, most forcefully and fully articulated in *The Papers on the Science of Administration* (1937). The acronym stood for a logical sequence of steps for practicing "good" administration, ideally in the order in which they should be accomplished, namely, planning, organizing, staffing, directing, coordinating, reporting, and budgeting. In many aspects, it reflected an efficient military model of "good management" that White applied universally throughout American civilian government.

POSDCORB certainly arrived at the right moment. Not only were the first graduate M.P.A. programs emerging and needing a basic text, beginning at the The Maxwell School, Syracuse University (1924) and University of Southern California (1928), but far more important, POSDCORB addressed as well as any alternative the twin crises of that era, the Great Depression and World War II. In the most turbulent period of the twentieth century, the nation confronted its worst economic and military conflicts back-to-back. How to plan, organize, staff, and so on, in order to cope with these unprecedented emergencies was indeed very real, and POSDCORB orthodoxy was near at hand for "the cure." Of course, what POSDCORB provided was a pretty stiff cure based upon a sharp separation of politics and administration, a no-nonsense Taylorism, applied in lockstep military fashion, ultimately raised to the highest levels of government, for reorganizing the presidency, thanks to the Brownlow Report or The Report of The President's Committee on Administrative Management

in 1937 (Karl 1963). Because Public Administration reached such visibility and prominence at the top levels of public life to deal successfully with the most pressing problems of those times, some later would envision it as "the golden age" for the field (Newland 1984).

Perhaps an exaggeration, though on a deeper level, POSDCORB indeed did knit together a respectable intellectual framework for the new academic field. It also gave a common outlook and clear cause for a small but creative and committed band of academics who founded such key institutions as the Public Administration Clearing House (1930), the American Society for Public Administration (1939), and the *Public Administration Review* (1940), which significantly advanced research and teaching agendas for the field. POSDCORB further provided a cohesive and comprehensive academic rationale for setting up graduate programs advancing research as well as its applications throughout all levels of government, federal, state, local. In short, POSDCORB, as both an idea and a practice for doing "good" administration, allowed the field to begin, grow, and even flourish in national prominence in a manner that it never quite has achieved since. Yet, to the next generation of students, POSDCORB hardly seemed heroic, but rather full of contradictions—unscientific, value-laden, time-bound, and rigid, and hardly the best means to meet the needs of the postwar era. Of course, there were some persistent critics of the POSDCORB orthodoxy during the 1930s, such as Chester Barnard, Mary Parker Follett, Elton Mayo, Fritz Roethisberger, Ordway Tead, W. W. Willoughby, and "The Brookings Group." Yet, they remained distinct "outsiders" who were only later "discovered" in the postwar era by Public Administration Scholarship.

Social Science Heterodoxy, 1947–1967

Having won dual victories over the Great Depression and fascism, the United States by default became the postwar free world leader and over the next four decades engaged in a fierce Cold War with communism, at times turning into hot flash-points in Korea, Vietnam, and elsewhere. In James Fesler's fitting aphorism, "America rapidly shifted its concern from the Fascist Axis to the Communist Nexus" (Fesler 1975).

In retrospect, it is hard to overestimate the profound influence of the Cold War in shaping American society as a whole as well as its public administration and its Administrative Sciences in particular. Just as the ancient Egyptian pyramids were products of slave labor harnessed for the greater glory of the Pharaoh's "hereafter," likewise fearful demons from abroad, fanned by popular press and political paranoia, drove postwar Americans into a self-protectionist frenzy of administrative state-building. Not only did a massive military-industrial complex emerge, as symbolized by the Pentagon, but also a host of domestic administrative activities were justified by national security needs such as the space program, educational assistance, scientific research, and even the largest public works project in the nation's history, the National Defense Highway Act (1955)—all in the name of beating the Russians!

American Administrative Sciences became the direct beneficiary of public largess through the new necessities for government training programs to staff the civil service at all levels, as well by expanded funding for scientific and applied administrative research. American universities, driven by exploding enrollment of returning veterans, opened their doors to talented young professors, themselves often fresh from New Deal and wartime work, to teach, research, and rethink the field. Thus, teaching and research opportunities grew rapidly in higher education, particularly with the wider range of demands for international scholarship. For many administrative academics, especially those who had experienced public administration firsthand during the Great Depression and World War II and now were confronted with entirely different administrative challenges in the postwar world, prewar POSDCORB orthodoxy suddenly seemed ill-equipped to grasp the new administrative realities and deal with their essentials.

In 1947 a young Yale political scientist, Robert Dahl, wrote a seminal *Public Administration Review* essay that perceptively and prophetically pointed out three central intellectual problems of prewar orthodoxy (Dahl 1947). In "The Science of Public Administration: Three Problems," Dahl challenged Public Administration, first, to rethink its normative assumptions that had been based on the sharp dichotomy between politics and administration; second, to expand its conception of human behavior, beyond a view of a narrow, technical "rational man," in order to comprehend "the whole man" and thus explain more realistically how humans act within organizations; third, to embrace broader historical, economic, and social conditions, not merely techniques or technicians, as influential factors that affect administrative results. Dahl's orientation, or rather reorientation, of the field, by contrast to prewar orthodox values, stressed values of "realism," "behavioralism," and "scientific rigor."

Herbert Simon's book *Administrative Behavior: A Study of Decision-Making Process in Administrative Organization,* also published in the same year (1947), made, however, the most profound and original theoretical impact on postwar administrative sciences in the United States (Simon 1947). For Simon, drawing upon logical-positivist, continental analytic philosophy, POSDCORB failed to live up to "true scientific methodology." His first chapter began with a slashing, if not dramatic, attack on POSDCORB principles, which he concluded were little more than "folk wisdom" or "proverbs" that confused "facts with values." Simon then set out ambitiously to refound the entire field on an entirely new interdisciplinary decision-making model, one he called "bounded rationality," to explain, as the book's title indicates, "administrative behavior." POSDCORB orthodoxy, as a result, would never look quite the same to anyone who read Simon's text.

Under the withering intellectual crossfire of Dahl, Simon, and others of that generation, Dwight Waldo, Norton Long, James Fesler, Carl Friedrich, and Herman Finer, POSDCORB rapidly faded as the commonly accepted orthodoxy and soon became simply "posdcorb," or one among many competing ideas to explain the field. By the 1950s a rich infusion of a new variety of social sciences into Public Administration from economics, political sciences, psychology, comparative studies, decision-sciences, business, and elsewhere turned the field into a dizzying array of heterodoxies in order to *both* comprehend and to cope with enormous administrative challenges at home and overseas. In the process, American Public Administration became far broader, less parochial, more theoretical, even academically more respectable, enriched by multiple doctrines, methodologies, ideas, new data, as well as factual information. The field also gravitated increasingly into formal university settings, especially within the social sciences, as opposed to prewar dominance by practitioners or academics with mostly applied backgrounds. Furthermore, its way of thinking and its dominant values became more dynamic and process-oriented, again emphasizing "realism," "behavioralism," and "science," by comparison to its prewar values, with more stable, Newtonian-like application of fixed POSDCORB Principles for understanding *and* doing "good" public administration. Indeed, what was "good" public administration turned out to be less certain, more problematic, and relative, no longer confined to promoting only twin *E*s of economy and efficiency. "Effectiveness," at best a slippery value, found favor at the core of many heterodoxies, either as part of a new trilogy of *E*s that combined the old *E*s and a new *E,* or as a standalone value orientation. One does not have to dig very deeply into the writings of several of the leading scholars during this period—Frederick Mosher, Paul Appleby, Don Price, and others—to find their value emphasis on "institutional effectiveness," not to mention "realism," "behavioralism," and "rigor." Likewise, the basic texts in the 1950s, such as those authored by John Pfiffner or Felix Nigro, or even Leonard White's textbook, then in its fourth edition, echoed such thinking and were popular no doubt because they spoke forcefully and thoughtfully to the continuing administrative demands of state-building during the Cold War.

The Reassertion of Democratic Idealism, 1968–1988

As this essay has underscored from the outset, rejection of statism has deep roots in American soil, yet no era during the twentieth century of U.S. Public Administration witnessed a more intense outpouring of antistatism literature than from the late 1960s to the late 1980s. The reasons for the outbreak of rabid antistatism during that generation remain unclear even

today. Perhaps it was caused by a backlash to perceived administrative misdeeds in Vietnam or Watergate—or later, Irangate? Was it due to the popularity of the counterculture? The widespread media criticisms of government? Growth of the civil rights, environmental, consumer, feminist, and gay movements? Assassinations of charismatic figures like President John F. Kennedy and the Reverend Martin Luther King, Jr.? Dashed hopes from program failures in the New Frontier and the Great Society? Or Presidents Jimmy Carter and Ronald Reagan waging successful campaigns against Washington, D.C. and Big Government?

Whatever the causes, Herbert Kaufman characterized this period by the title of a lead essay in the *Public Administration Review,* "Fear of Bureaucracy: A Raging Pandemic" (Kaufman 1981). Or in the words of Samuel P. Huntington, the 1960s and early 1970s inaugurated "a democratic surge" that was similar to the eras of Jefferson-Jacksonian democracy and Progressive Reform, in which "there was a vital reassertion of democratic idealism in all phases of American public life" (Huntington 1975).

The 1968 Minnowbrook Conference best symbolized the starting point of this shift toward democratic idealism within Public Administration. It was named for Syracuse University's Minnowbrook Conference Center, where the meeting took place during the warm summer of 1968, ironically not too distant from Woodstock, an even more noteworthy symbol of a generational gathering of that era. Minnowbrook involved mostly under-thirty-year-old academics, largely from political science. Their conference papers that were later published argued for the field to adopt fresh intellectual perspectives, or for a "new public administration," based on ideals of participation, consensus-building, sharing ideas, mutual trust, and even "love of mankind" (Marini 1971). These "young turks" exhibited particular hostility toward traditional public administration aimed at state-building and toward enhancing administrative efficiency, economy, and effectiveness as embodied in POSDCORB, as well as newer rational techniques such as operations research, decision-sciences, systems theory, PPBS, MBO, or other techno-professional inventions stressing rationality, science, behaviorism, realism, or any sort of hard empirical quantitative methodologies. Unlike the "young turks" in the late 1940s, Dahl, Simon, and others, who had revolted against POSDCORB precisely because they saw it had failed to accurately describe postwar administration sciences and deal with what they believed were new postwar administrative priorities, these late-1960s "young turks" (few of whom had worked in or even had held degrees in public administration) saw POSDCORB as all *too* real, *too* powerful, *too* much the embodiment of *the* establishment and therefore fundamentally detrimental to egalitarian, democratic, humane values.

If the New Public Administration challenged the prior generational way of thinking from the left, public choice economics did so even more fiercely and profoundly from the right. In the same year as Minnowbrook, Indiana University Professor Vincent Ostrom began writing *The Intellectual Crisis in American Public Administration* (Ostrom 1973). More than any other single book, Ostrom introduced and advanced public choice doctrines throughout the field. Much like the Minnowbrookers, but using a far different vocabulary and scientific paradigm, Ostrom frontally assaulted older state-building ideas that he labeled as "The Wilson-Weber Paradigm" with its "single-centered administration," "hierarchical structures," and "sharp separation of politics and administration." Based on his reading, or rather rereading, of *The Federalist Papers,* Alexis de Tocqueville's *Democracy in America,* and the growing literature in a new economic subfield of public choice, Ostrom advocated a radically antistatist alternative, one he called "the Democratic Administrative Paradigm." Here was the very reverse of "Wilson-Weber" featuring "diverse decision-making centers," "popular participation," and "fragmented, overlapping, decentralized authority." In brief, Ostrom sought to enhance "public choice"—or read it as "individual choice"—using economic language and economic methods applied with fierce antigovernmental zeal.

So if Minnowbrook and Ostrom best symbolized the "democratic temper of the times"—or was it distemper?—what distinctive marks did such literature leave on the field? Briefly, seven legacies come to mind:

1. *Clashing moral absolutes:* No longer did science, realism and behaviorism hold the dominant intellectual center, but new ideological stridency appeared throughout Public Administration thought as epitomized by the clashing moral absolutes of democratic ideals inherent in Minnowbrook and Public Choice thinking.

2. *The new two Es and one L:* If the two prior generations had promoted economy, efficiency and effectiveness, new key values emerged as dominant, mainly aimed to limit or control bureaucratic discretion and broaden democratic participation. Thus, ethical, legal, and economizing constraints on government due to "fear of bureaucracy" became paramount concerns and spawned a new infusion of ethics, law, and economics classes and texts throughout Public Administration Education.

3. *A cry for relevancy:* Both *Minnowbrook* and *The Intellectual Crisis* began by attacking the old orthodoxies as irrelevant for addressing the pressing problem of the late 1960s and early 1970s. Public Administration, its label and content, suddenly appeared old-fashioned and out of touch for many in this new generation. Alternative labels, often with far different connotations and implications, grew increasingly into favor—for example, public management, public affairs, public policy, and implementation, under which "bread and butter" Administration Sciences came to be taught.

4. *The fragmentation—or decline?—of generalist Public Administration:* Concomitant with the rise of more specialized approaches often emphasizing policy implementation and management, generalist Public Administration education and research declined in academic status, especially at major universities that had been longtime leaders, like Harvard, Berkeley, or Chicago. They shifted to becoming "policy schools" with their own professional associations and journals. Generalist associations, like the American Society for Public Administration, that had served as the focus for academic-practitioner exchange since 1940, no longer were dominant or were active at the forefront of the field. ASPA increasingly seemed to be

displaced by narrower, more specialized groups dealing with aspects of Public Administration, such as the National Academy of Public Administration, or the National Association of Schools of Public Administration.

5. *The proliferation of subfields and techniques:* As specialization grew, new subfields and sub-subfields emerged as important to teach and train public administrators, often under functional fields like criminal justice, health, or public works. Techniques such as ZBB, MBO, or OD were popularized and proliferated into a vast hodgepodge of often faddish, unrelated techniques with problematic aims.

6. *A field in intellectual crisis?* Ostrom's book title perhaps most succinctly captured the mood of the times (no doubt why, in large part, it became such a popular text), for indeed many academics felt that the field was on the verge of "flying apart" and experiencing "a profound intellectual crisis." With the combination of declining status, increasing specialization, and faddishness, what was unique about "public administration," even what defined "public" or the study of government, became more problematic, a murky enigma, at least to many old hands, not to mention those new to the field.

7. *A widening gap between theory and practice:* If the pre– and post–World War II eras mingled and mixed administrative academics and practitioners with relative ease, due to a degree of shared purposes between both, this era by contrast, 1968 to 1988, saw a much sharper differentiation. As the academic enterprise grew larger, more diverse, and more predicated on "publish or perish," with little or no common concerns for public service or for the advancement of the public interest, "the academy" became more remote, often devoting itself more to theory, with limited exposure to practice and the immediate needs of practitioners. This widening gap served to enrich theory as well as various specializations, yet it also created vexing distances, divisions, and debates over just what is Public Administration: a field or focus? theory or practice? art or science? craft or profession? or what?

The Refounding Movement, 1989 to the Present Day

As the twenty-first century was about to dawn, once more the socio-political-economic-military landscape of the United States, indeed the world, dramatically changed. The fall of the Berlin Wall in 1989 signaled the end of the Cold War and the collapse of communism. America suddenly assumed the unique role as the last global superpower, with far-flung security responsibilities. Along with the U.S. hegemony, or possibly because of it, a borderless, global economy prospered, along with the explosion of new information technologies, while serious environmental threats involving air, water, and solid waste also appeared on a worldwide, at times life-threatening scale. The lengthy list of such changes profoundly reshapes America's complexities and challenges of government. Certainly public administration, and its people, processes, and institutions, stand at the heart of helping *or* hindering the nation's present capacity to govern and to deal with this new policy agenda effectively.

In response, Public Administration likewise seems to be entering a new era of refounding its basics. During the last decade or so, several clusters of academics have emerged to rethink fundamental questions such as, What is Public Administration? What is the meaning of the "good life" and "good society"? Who should govern, and how? What are the criteria for proper administrative actions—and what defines improper or unethical action? Should public administration be centralized and/or decentralized? What should be its size and scope within society? Should public administrators behave as servants of the people, or as free-wheeling entrepreneurs? Indeed, how can old concepts like the "public interest," "accountability," "responsibility," and "public welfare" be reframed and recast to respond to twenty-first–century needs?

Right now the field seems to be in the midst of a yeasty debate over these and other seminal administrative questions. While the answers remain unclear, seven identifiable clusters or schools of thought with shared perspectives—frequently expressed through their own publications, associations and leading academics—are evident and influential today:

1. *The Reinventors:* During the early 1990s clearly the first and most significant group to suggest fundamental alternatives was that associated with the ideas put forward by David Osborne and Ted Gaebler's *Reinventing Government* (1992). Their book, which became a popular best-seller and a major part of President Bill Clinton's plan to reform the federal government, advocated "a third way" or a challenge to what was referred to as "old-style big bureaucracy" and "free-market methods" for doing the "public's business." Rather, the authors suggest building the "entrepreneurial spirit" throughout government as their "answer." While the enthusiasm for "reinventing" had markedly declined by the late 1990s for various reasons, it nonetheless has had profound effects on the size, scope, methods, *and way of thinking* about public administration at all levels of government.

2. *The communitarians:* Communitarian ideas also became popular and influential in many quarters during the 1990s, largely due to the writings of academic sociologists such as Amatai Etzioni, William Galston, David Chrislip, and Philip Selznick. Unlike the "reinventors," made up mostly of consultants and practitioners focused on advancing pragmatic administrative reforms to enhance "efficient, entrepreneurial" government operations for "customers," communitarians wrestle with larger issues of rebuilding "community" and "citizenship." While they touch on few explicit administrative reforms, most of their voluminous writings do implicitly suggest administrative arrangements to nurture moral ties of family, strengthen bonds in neighborhoods and in the workplace, and encourage wider citizen participation as well as public service.

3. *The VPI refounders:* By contrast to the two aforementioned schools, the Virginia Polytechnic Institution (VPI) refounders are largely composed of senior scholars who have been closely associated throughout their careers with American Administrative Sciences: Gary L. Wamsley, Robert N. Bacher, Charles T. Goodsell, Philip S. Kronenberg, John A. Rohr, Camilla M. Stivers, Orion F. White, and James F. Wolf. Their twin multiauthored books *Refounding Public Administration* (1990) and *Refounding Democratic Public Administration* (1996), while containing often contradictory and complex themes, seek nothing less than a fundamental philosophical, institutional, and theoretical refounding of the entire field (as both titles stress). Or in the words of Gary L. Wamsley, they sought to develop "a new normative theory of American public administration and . . . a theory of the American state . . ." (1990, p. 4). The authors provoke and challenge stereotypes as well as advance ambitious agenda for the entire field, but by no means do they offer clear-cut convincing strategies or alternative doctrines necessary to resolve deep issues of legitimacy or securing a stable place for public administration within the context of an antistatist society, at least so far.

4. *The interpretivists:* As direct heirs of the New Public Administration movement, interpretivists are oriented toward phenomenology, or "subjective-intersubjective relations, which they see undergirding the social constructions of reality." As their name suggests, they explore and interpret values, assumptions, and ideas concerning the very nature of being or human existence—that is, the study of ontology. Unquestionably these administrative theorists probe some of the deepest and most profound questions confronting the field. They also have some of the liveliest and most interesting debates over these questions, as represented within the pages of their peer-reviewed journal, *Administrative Theory and Praxis;* or as reflected in their well-attended annual PAT-NET conferences; or as found in several new books: Jay White, *Taking Language Seriously* (1999); Camilla Stivers, *Bureau Men, Settlement Women* (2000); Michael L. Spicer, *Public Administration and the State* (2001); Jun Jung, *Rethinking Administrative Theory* (2002); Hugh Miller, *Postmodern Public Policy* (2002); O. C. McSuite, *Invitation to Public Administration* (2002); and Richard Box, *Public Administration and Society* (2004). While probing and provoking, more than any other cluster of current administrative scholars, interpretivists remain the most removed from the mainline day-to-day world of practitioners.

5. *The tools-makers:* Technologists and technology have played major roles in shaping the field from its origins, as discussed before in this essay with Taylorism. Though due to the rise of implementation theory and policy studies, newer "hard" quantitative, analytical methodologies have appeared and have been applied throughout Public Administration research and training in recent years to better understand government programs theoretically and to better run them practically. One of the most innovative examples of this line of thinking was the creative product of several policy analysts, mainly associated with the Urban Institute, *Beyond Privatization* (1989), edited by Lester Salamon, and as further elaborated in his more recent edited work, *The Tools of Government* (2002). The authors offer a "new analytical framework" for understanding and evaluating government programs. Chapter by chapter, both books analyze various "tools of service delivery" by government. These authors advance new "analytic methods" with no right or wrong answers, only methods for weighing the costs and benefits of various service delivery alternatives.

6. *New bureaucratic analysts:* A rich vibrant stream of ideas and literature continues to advance Public Administration, largely from the pens of political scientists, on a broad range of political and policy issues associated with public bureaucracy, such as public accountability, oversight, control, power, institutional performance, and responsiveness to democracy and to interest groups. Prominent books from this "cluster" of contributors today include Paul Light, *The Tides of Reform* (1997); Sally Selden, *The Promise of Representative Bureaucracy* (1997); Robert Behn, *Rethinking Democratic Accountability* (2001); Martha Derthick, *Up in Smoke* (2002); Beryl Radin, *The Accountable Juggler* (2002); and Phillip Cooper, *Governing by Contract* (2003). These and numerous other junior and senior scholars thoughtfully continue to influence the field just as the young political scientist Woodrow Wilson once did beginning in 1887 with the very first American essay advocating the study of Public Administration. Their writings individually and collectively tend to address the broadest and most profound political issues of the field: What is the relationship between politics and administration? What is the role of ethics in administration? How are good and correct policies made? Is the policy process for dealing with the pressing issues of today meeting "public needs" and securing "the public interest?" How best can bureacracy be held accountable?

7. *From management to governance:* Finally, many of the old themes of management have reappeared in writings by leading administrative scholars. Although no longer narrowly focused on advancing economy/efficiency, this literature emphasizes the vital importance of managerial effectiveness for delivering "public goods" within today's complicated political context. These works are often based upon extensive empirical evidence, drawing upon diverse contemporary literature and data, with far less rigid generic "models" recommended for "best practices" compared to early POSDCORB formulations [e.g., Norma Riccucci, *Unsung Heroes* (1995); Mark Moore, *Creating Public Value* (1995); Laurence Lynn, *Public Management as Art, Science and Profession* (1996); Patricia Ingraham et al., *Government Performance* (2003); and Hal Rainey, *Understanding and Managing Public Organizations* (1997).] Especially since the 9/11 terrorist attacks, flexible yet top-down management and organization models drawn from business and military command experiences have returned to favor in developing sound administrative practices, such as for the formation of the new federal Department of Homeland Security in 2002 or throughout the prosecution of the war in Iraq in 2003. Concomitantly, renewed popularity of applied management training through case analysis and other "how-to" techniques is evident in James M. Banovetz, ed., *Managing Local Government,* 2nd ed. (1998). Also, the shift of interest into international comparative public management has resurfaced, often under the label of "governance" rather than the older categories of comparative/international Public Administration—for instance, Don Kettl, *The Transformation of Governance* (2001), and B. Guy Peters, *The Future of Governing,* 2nd ed. (2001). Within such influential

writings, Public Administration is depicted as operating in a much broader global context, often using open "networks," flexible "steering" instruments, high technologies, and specialized expertise from around the world, "outsourced" to numerous public, private, and nonprofit entities. Such trends clearly transform the field into a more complicated and expanded subject, yet one that remains central and significant for the future of twenty-first century government.

Conclusion: Public Administration As "The Eminently Practical Science"

What will the future hold for American Administration Sciences? If the past is any guide to the present—and to the future—U.S. Public Administration, unlike Public Administration elsewhere, will remain dominated by its own unique brand of inductive, experimental, reformist mindset, closely interconnected to the practicalities of coping with the immediate needs of democratic governance. Or in the best sense of Woodrow Wilson's opening lines of his famous 1887 essay, it will remain "the eminently practical science." Within a radically antistatist culture, U.S. Administrative Sciences have no alternative but to steadfastly persist at being open to change, elusive in form, pragmatic in content, a servant of democracy, and above all, keep a low profile. Born without a sense of state, as this essay repeatedly stressed, Americans only reluctantly bought into administrative state-building—and Administrative Sciences—roughly a century *after* the U.S. Constitution was written. Thus, neither its administrative institutions nor academic enterprise seems quite legitimate, even today. Their deep-seated *positive* government prescriptions never fit well—or at all—with the *negative* government values embedded at the core of the Great Charter of 1787.

Debates still rage in the serious literature about whether Public Administration as a field of study exists and what "it" is. Of course it exists, but with a sort of protean cast and character, as Table 1 summarizes, that seems to transform itself into new shapes and purposes every generation, or on twenty-year cycles, to respond to the particular needs of the times. This unobtrusive adaptability to deal with the immediate public demands of the moment may well be U.S. Public Administration's greatest strength. Administrative study must always chase—and cope with—the elusive, shifting public priorities, yet remain a low-keyed, catch-as-catch-can field. Whether it "catches" up and then copes successfully, or at all adequately with the pressing issues of society, is another matter, but certainly today in the present period of the Refounding Movement, it continues to try.

And so here within its very strength, one finds also the chief downside readily apparent: its very elusiveness and adaptability makes the field a questionable, indeed suspect, academic enterprise, one that continues to defy, even at the dawn of the twenty-first century, authoritative definition or a settled place within higher education. Is it a subfield of political science? Part of business? Policy sciences? A separate field? Or what? One can certainly hear the refrains of all these value accents and methodological emphases from earlier eras in the current refounding movement: the business values apparent within the reinventors; Taylorite themes within the tools-makers; New Public Administration idealism within the interpretivists, political science within the new bureaucratic analysts, or POSDCORB within management proponents. Within each school, new administrative concepts are therefore emerging and then gelling, while old ones are declining or disappearing according to contemporary and quickly shifting societal needs—much like a bubbling brew where some bubbles rise whereas others fall seemingly at random. Possibly the various levels of external necessities (state-building needs of society) determine the internal intensity of the boiling bubbles (concept-creation by the academy)? In essence, the field's potential genius may well be that it is continuously "bubbling up" with multiple new perspectives for understanding, defining, and dealing with salient public issues of the here-and-now by means of its own brand of interdisciplinary hands-on conceptual creativity, while frequently being maligned as a marginal, unscientific academic player within contemporary American higher education.

Table 1 Four Eras of U.S. Public Administration Thought

Eras and Dates	POSDCORB Orthodoxy 1926–46	Social Science Heterodoxy 1947–67	Reassertion of Democratic Idealism 1968–88	Refounding Movement 1989 to Present
Key Shaping Events	Depression and World War II	Cold War abroad; prosperity at home	Vietnam, Watergate, "fear of bureaucracy"	America as last global superpower, end of cold war and fall of Berlin Wall
Intellecual Benchmark Event and Date	Leonard White's textbook (1926)	Dahl's essay and Simon's book (1947)	Minnowbrook (1968) and Ostrom's book	First "refounding books" published (1989)
Framing Administrative Idea	POSDCORB	Social sciences heterodoxy	Democratic idealism	Refounding movement
Leading Administrative Theorist(s)	Leonard White and Luther Gulick	Robert Dahl, Herbert Simon, Dwight Waldo, Frederick Mosher, and Don Price	New PA and public choice scholars	Multiple "refounding" schools
Major Institution(s) Promoting Ideas within Public Administration	"The Chicago School," PACH, ASPA, *PAR*, White's text	The Maxwell School, USC, and other "generalist" programs	"Policy schools" at Harvard or Berkeley, and "think tanks" at Heritage, AEI and CATO	Professional associations such as NASPAA, ASPA, APSA, APPAM or PAT-NET
Central Values of the Field	POSDCORB Principles rooted in "economy and efficiency," as well as politics-administration dichotomy	Applied "realistic and rigorous," interdisciplinary perspectives promoting institutional effectiveness	"Two *Es* and One *L*"	In search of new legitimacy, conceptual framework and values
Main Orientation of Administrative Sciences	Dealing with depression and wartime issues	National/international issues of the Cold War	Ethical, economic, legal, oversight/control issues of bureaucracy	In search of a new overall orientation
Key Theoretical Question	How to build and apply Administrative Sciences?	What is Public Administration?	Where is Public Administration?	What will be the field's new identity?
Education Methods	Learning generalist management functions of POSDCORB	Applying ideas from business, economics, politics, history, and social sciences	Training in numerous administrative techniques, concepts, and technologies	"All depends" on a particular school's methods, perspectives, and theories
Lasting Contributions	Birth of field; highest visibility; creation of key institutions like ASPA and *PAR*	Rich infusion of social sciences; global influence; expanded views and ideas about the field	New ideas of law, economics, implementation theory; analytical methods; rapid growth in size of field	Fundamental rethinking of "basics" like PA's legitimacy, purposes, etc.

References

Banovetz, J.M., ed. 1998. *Managing Local Government,* 2nd ed. Washington, D.C.: ICMA.

Behn, R. 2001. *Rethinking Democratic Accountability.* Washington, D.C.: Brookings.

Box, R.C., ed. 2004. *Public Administration and Society.* Armonk, N.Y.: M. E. Sharpe.

Cooper, P.J. 2003. *Governing by Contract.* Washington, D.C.: CQ Press.

Dahl, R.A. 1947. "The Science of Public Administration: Three Problems." *Public Administration Review* 7:1.

Derthick, M. 2002. *Up in Smoke.* Washington, D.C.: CQ Press.

Fesler, J.W. 1975. "Public Administration and the Social Sciences: 1946 to 1960." p. 98 in *American Public Administration: Past, Present, Future,* ed. F. C. Mosher. Tuscaloosa, Ala.: University of Alabama Press.

Goodnow, F.J. 1900. *Politics and Administration.* New York: Macmillan.

Gulick, L. 1937. "Notes on the Theory of Organization." p. 13 in *Paper on the Source of Administration,* ed. L. Gulick and L. Urwick. New York: Institute of Public Administration.

Hamilton, A., J. Madison, and J. John. 1961. *The Federalist Papers.* New York: Mentor.

Hartz, L. 1955. *The Liberal Tradition in America.* New York: Harcourt, Brace.

Huntington, S.P. 1975. "The United States." pp. 74–75 in *The Crisis of Democracy,* ed. M. Crozier et al. New York: New York University Press.

Ingraham, P.W., et al. 2003. *Government Performance.* Baltimore, Md.: Johns Hopkins Press.

Jung, J. 2002. *Rethinking Administrative Theory.* Westport, Conn.: Praeger.

Karl, B.D. 1963. *Executive Reorganization and Reform in the New Deal.* Chicago: University of Chicago Press.

Kaufman, H. 1981. "Fear of Bureaucracy: A Raging Pandemic." *Public Administration Review* 41(1): 1–9.

Kettl, D. F. 2002. *The Transformation of Governance.* Baltimore, Md.: Johns Hopkins Press.

Light, P. 1997. *The Tides of Reform.* New Haven, Conn.: Yale University Press.

Lynn, L.E., Jr. 1996. *Public Management as Art, Science and Profession.* Chatham, N.J.: Chatham House.

Marini, F., ed. 1971. *Toward a New Public Administration: The Minnowbrook Perspective.* Scranton, Penn.: Chandler.

McSuite, O.C. 2002. *Invitation to Public Administration.* Armonk, N.Y.: M. E. Sharpe.

Miller, H. 2002. *Postmodern Public Policy.* Albany, N.Y.: State University of New York Press.

Moore, M. 1995. *Creating Public Value.* Cambridge, Mass.: Harvard University Press.

Mosher, F.C. 1956. "Research in Public Administration." *Public Administration Review* 16 (Summer): 177.

———, ed. 1976. *Basic Documents of American Public Administration, 1776–1950.* New York: Holmes & Meier.

Newland, C.A. 1984. *Public Administration and Community: Realism in the Practice of Ideals.* McLean, Va.: Public Administration Service.

Osborne, T., and T. Gaebler. 1992. *Reinventing Government: How the Entrepreneurial Spirit Is Transforming the Public Sector from the Schoolhouse to Statehouse, City Hall to the Pentagon.* Reading, Mass.: Addison-Wesley.

Ostrom, V. 1973. *The Intellectual Crisis in American Public Administration.* Tuscaloosa, Ala.: University of Alabama Press.

Peters, B.G. 2001. *The Future of Governing,* 2nd ed. Lawrence Kans.: University Press of Kansas.

Raadschelders, J.C.N., and M.R. Rutgers. 1999. "The Waxing and Waning of the State and Its Study," in *The Modern State and Its Study*, ed. W. J. M. Kickert and R. Stillman. London: Edward Elgar, Chapter 2.

Radin, B. 2002. *The Accountable Juggler.* Washington, D.C.: CQ Press.

Rainey, H. 1997. *Understanding and Managing Public Organizations,* 2nd ed. San Francisco, Jossey-Bass Publishers.

Riccucci, N. 1995. *Unsung Heroes.* Washington, D.C.: Georgetown University Press.

Salamon, L.M., ed. 1989. *Beyond Privatization: The Tools of Government Action.* Washington, D.C.: Urban Institute Press.

Salamon, L.M., ed. 2002. *The Tools of Government.* New York: Oxford University Press.

Selden, S. 1997. *The Promise of Representative Bureaucracy.* Armonk, N.Y.: M. E. Sharpe.

Simon, H.A. 1947. *Administrative Behavior: A Study of Decision-Making Process in Administrative Organization.* New York: Macmillan.

Skocpol, T. 1996. "Presidential Address for the Annual Meeting of Social Science History Association," unpublished manuscript, p. 10.

Skowronek, S. 1982. *Building a New American State: The Expansion of National Administrative Capacities, 1877–1920.* Cambridge: Cambridge University Press.

Spicer, M.W. 2001. *Public Administration and the State.* Tuscaloosa, Ala.: University of Alabama Press.

Stivers, C. 2000. *Bureau Men, Settlement Women.* Lawrence, Kans.: University Press of Kansas.

Taylor, F.W. 1911. *The Principles of Scientific Management.* New York: W.W. Norton.

Waldo, D. 1948. *The Administrative State: A Study of the Political Theory of American Public Administration.* New York: Ronald Press.

Wamsley, G., et. al. 1990. *Refounding Public Administration.* Newbury Park, Calif.: Sage.

Wamsley, G., et al. 1996. *Refounding Democratic Public Administration.* Newbury Park, Calif.: Sage.

White, J. 1999. *Taking Language Seriously.* Washington, D.C.: Georgetown University Press.

White, L.D. 1926. *Introduction to the Study of Public Administration.* New York: Macmillan.

Wiebe, R.H. 1967. *The Search for Order, 1877–1920.* New York: Hill and Wang.

Wilson, W. 1887. "The Study of Administration." *Political Science Quarterly* 2 (June): 197–222.

☐ CASE STUDY 1

Introduction

The following story may shed some further insight into the role of public administration in modern society. The story, "The Blast in Centralia No. 5: A Mine Disaster No One Stopped," is an excellent account of a mine disaster that occurred three generations ago in Centralia, Illinois, killing 111 miners. This article is an unusual case study in public administration; not only does the author, John Bartlow Martin, carefully recount the facts of the catastrophe, but he also attempts to understand the reasons behind the disaster. In his search for clues, the writer reveals much about the inner complexities of the administrative framework of our modern society—a coal company sensitive only to profit incentives; state regulatory agencies inadequately enforcing mine safety legislation; federal officials and mine unions complacent about a growing problem; and the miners incapable of protecting themselves against the impending disaster.

This is an example of administrative reality that, for some, will only confirm their suspicions about the inherent corruption of modern administrative enterprises. The victims died, they might argue, because the mine owners were only interested in profits, not in human lives. But is this the correct interpretation? Martin does not blame any one individual or even a group of individuals but stresses the ineffectiveness of the administrative structure on which all the disaster victims were dependent for survival.

After reading this story you will probably be struck by how much modern society depends on the proper functioning of unseen administrative arrangements—for safeguarding our environment; for protecting the purity of our food; for transporting us safely by road, rail, or air; for sending us our mail; or for negotiating an arms limitations agreement at some distant diplomatic conference. All of us, like the miners in Centralia No. 5, rely throughout our lives on the immovable juggernaut of impersonal administrative systems. A functioning, ordered public administration, as this story illustrates, is an inescapable necessity for maintaining the requisites of a civilized modern society.

As you read this selection, keep the following questions in mind:

What does this case study tell us are the central problems and issues facing public administrators in their work? Why is government administration such a complex and difficult task, according to this study?

Given the themes and problems in this case study, how would you frame a suitable definition of the field of public administration? Does it "square" with Woodrow Wilson's or any of the more recent theories put forth in Stillman's prior essay?

What does the case say about the special *public* obligations of public administrators compared to the obligations of those engaged in private administration?

Finally, if you had actually been one of the leading administrative officials in the case— Driscoll O. Scanlan, Dwight Green, or Robert Medill—what would have been your view of public administration, and how might such a perspective on administration have helped to shape the outcome of the story?

The Blast in Centralia No. 5: A Mine Disaster No One Stopped

JOHN BARTLOW MARTIN

Already the crowd had gathered. Cars clogged the short, black rock road from the highway to the mine, cars bearing curious spectators and relatives and friends of the men entombed. State troopers and deputy sheriffs and the prosecuting attorney came, and officials from the company, the Federal Bureau of Mines, the Illinois Department of Mines and Minerals. Ambulances arrived, and doctors and nurses and Red Cross workers and soldiers with stretchers from Scott Field. Mine rescue teams came, and a federal rescue unit, experts burdened with masks and oxygen tanks and other awkward paraphernalia of disaster. . . .

One hundred and eleven men were killed in that explosion. Killed needlessly, for almost everybody concerned had known for months, even years, that the mine was dangerous. Yet nobody had done anything effective about it. Why not? Let us examine the background of the explosion. Let us study the mine and the miners, Joe Bryant and Bill Rowekamp and some others, and also the numerous people who might have saved the miners' lives but did not. The miners had appealed in various directions for help but got none, not from their state government nor

their federal government nor their employer nor their own union. (In threading the maze of officialdom we must bear in mind four agencies in authority: The State of Illinois, the United States Government, the Centralia Coal Company, and the United Mine Workers of America, that is, the UMWA of John L. Lewis.) Let us seek to fix responsibility for the disaster. . . .

The Centralia Mine No. 5 was opened two miles south of Centralia in 1907. Because of its age, its maze of underground workings is extensive, covering perhaps six square miles, but it is regarded as a medium-small mine since it employs but 250 men and produces but 2,000 tons of coal daily. It was owned by the Centralia Coal Company, an appendage of the Bell & Zoller empire, one of the Big Six among Illinois coal operators. . . . The Bell & Zoller home office was in Chicago (most of the big coal operators' home offices are in Chicago or St. Louis); no Bell & Zoller officers or directors lived at Centralia.

There are in coal mines two main explosion hazards—coal dust and gas. Coal dust is unhealthy to breathe and highly explosive. Some of the dust raised by machines in cutting and loading coal stays in suspension in the air. Some subsides to the floor and walls of the tunnels, and a local explosion will kick it back into the air where it will explode and, in turn, throw more dust into the air, which will explode; and as this chain reaction continues the explosion will propagate throughout the mine or until it reaches something that will stop it.

The best method of stopping it, a method in use for some twenty-five years, is rock dusting. Rock dusting is simply applying pulverized stone to the walls and roof of the passageways; when a local explosion occurs it will throw a cloud of rock dust into the air along with the coal dust, and since rock dust is incombustible the explosion will die. Rock dusting will not prevent an explosion but it will localize one. Illinois law requires rock dusting in a dangerously dusty mine. Authorities disagreed as to whether the Centralia mine was gassy but everyone agreed it was exceedingly dry and dusty. The men who worked in it had been complaining about the dust for a long time—one recalls "the dust was over your shoetops," another that "I used to cough up chunks of coal dust like walnuts after work"—and indeed by 1944, more than two years before the disaster, so widespread had dissatisfaction become that William Rowekamp, as recording secretary of Local Union 52, prepared an official complaint. But even earlier, both state and federal inspectors had recognized the danger.

Let us trace the history of these warnings of disaster to come. For in the end it was this dust which did explode and kill one hundred and eleven men, and seldom has a major catastrophe of any kind been blueprinted so accurately so far in advance.

Driscoll O. Scanlan (who led the rescue work after the disaster) went to work in a mine near Centralia when he was 16, studied engineering at night school, and worked 13 years as a mine examiner for a coal company until, in 1941, he was appointed one of 16 Illinois state mine inspectors by Governor Green upon recommendation of the state representative from Scanlan's district. Speaking broadly, the job of a state inspector is to police the mine operators—to see that they comply with the state mining law, including its numerous safety provisions. But an inspector's job is a political patronage job. Coal has always been deeply enmeshed in Illinois politics.

Dwight H. Green, running for Governor the preceding fall, had promised the miners that he would enforce the mining laws "to the letter of the law," and however far below this lofty aim his administration fell (as we shall see), Scanlan apparently took the promise literally. Scanlan is a stubborn, righteous, zealous man of fierce integrity. Other inspectors, arriving to inspect a mine, would go into the office and chat with the

company officials. Not Scanlan; he waited outside, and down in the mine he talked with the miners, not the bosses. Other inspectors, emerging, would write their reports in the company office at the company typewriter. Not Scanlan; he wrote on a portable in his car. Widespread rumor had it that some inspectors spent most of their inspection visits drinking amiably with company officials in the hotel in town. Not Scanlan. Other inspectors wrote the briefest reports possible, making few recommendations and enumerating only major violations of the mining law. Scanlan's reports were longer than any others (owing in part to a prolix prose style), he listed every violation however minor, and he made numerous recommendations for improvements even though they were not explicitly required by law.

Scanlan came to consider the Centralia No. 5 mine the worst in his district. In his first report on it he made numerous recommendations, including these: "That haulage roads be cleaned and sprinkled. . . . That tamping of shots with coal dust be discontinued and that clay be used. . . ." Remember those criticisms, for they were made February 7, 1942, more than five years before the mine blew up as a result (at least in part) of those very malpractices.

Every three months throughout 1942, 1943, and 1944 Scanlan inspected the mine and repeated his recommendations, adding new ones: "That the mine be sufficiently rock dusted." And what became of his reports? He mailed them to the Department of Mines and Minerals at Springfield, the agency which supervises coal mines and miners. Springfield is dominated by the Statehouse, an ancient structure of spires and towers and balconies, of colonnades and domes; on its broad front steps Lincoln stands in stone. Inside all is gloom and shabby gilt. The Department of Mines and Minerals occupies three high-ceilinged rooms in a back corner of the second floor. The Director of the Department uses the small, comfortable, innermost office, its windows brushed by the leaves of trees on the Statehouse lawn, and here too the Mining Board meets. In theory, the Mining Board makes policy to implement the mining law, the Director executes its dictates; in practice, the Director possesses considerable discretionary power of his own.

In 1941 Governor Green appointed as Director Robert M. Medill, a genial, paunchy, red-faced man of about sixty-five. Medill had gone to work in a mine at sixteen; he rose rapidly in management. He had a talent for making money and he enjoyed spending it.

He entered Republican politics in 1920, served a few years as director of the Department of Mines and Minerals, then returned to business (mostly managing mines); and then, after working for Green's election in 1940, was rewarded once more with the directorship. Green reappointed him in 1944 with, says Medill, the approval of "a multitude of bankers and business men all over the state. And miners. I had the endorsement of all four factions." By this he means the United Mine Workers and its smaller rival, the Progressive Mine Workers, and the two associations of big and little operators; to obtain the endorsement of all four of these jealous, power-seeking groups is no small feat. As Director, Medill received $6,000 a year (since raised to $8,000) plus expenses of $300 or $400 a month. He lived in a sizable country house at Lake Springfield, with spacious grounds and a tree-lined driveway.

To Medill's department, then, came Driscoll Scanlan's inspection reports on Centralia Mine No. 5. Medill, however, did not see the first thirteen reports (1942–44); they were handled as "routine" by Robert Weir, an unimaginative, harassed little man who had come up through the ranks of the miners' union and on recommendation of the union had been appointed Assistant Director of the Department by Green (at $4,000 a year, now $5,200). When the mail brought an inspector's report, it went first to Medill's secretary who shared the office next to Medill's with Weir. She stamped the report [with date of receipt] . . . and put it on Weir's desk. Sometimes, but by no means always, Weir read the report. He gave it to one of a half-dozen girl typists in the large outer office. She edited the inspector's recommendations for errors in grammar and spelling, and incorporated them into a form letter to the owner of the mine, closing:

"The Department endorses the recommendations made by Inspector Scanlan and requests that you comply with same.

"Will you please advise the Department upon the completion of the recommendations set forth above?

"Thanking you . . ."

When the typist placed this letter upon his desk, Weir signed it and it was mailed to the mine operator.

But the Centralia company did not comply with the major recommendations Scanlan made. In fact, it did not even bother to answer Weir's thirteen letters based on Scanlan's reports. And Weir did nothing about this. Once, early in the game, Weir considered the dusty condition of the mine so serious that he requested the company to correct it within ten days; but there is no evidence that the company even replied.

This continued for nearly three years. And during the same period the federal government entered the picture. In 1941 Congress authorized the U.S. Bureau of Mines to make periodic inspections of coal mines. But the federal government had no enforcement power whatever; the inspections served only research. The first federal inspection of Centralia Mine No. 5 was made in September of 1942. In general, the federal recommendations duplicated Scanlan's—rock dusting, improving ventilation, wetting the coal to reduce dust—and the federal inspectors noted that "coal dust . . . at this mine is highly explosive, and would readily propagate an explosion." In all, they made 106 recommendations, including 33 "major" ones (a government official has defined a "major" hazard as one that "could . . . result in a disaster"). Four months passed before a copy of this report filtered through the administrative machinery at Washington and reached the Illinois Department at Springfield, but this mattered little: the Department did nothing anyway. Subsequent federal reports in 1943 and 1944 showed that the "major" recommendations had not been complied with. The federal bureau lacked the power to force compliance; the Illinois Department possessed the power but failed to act.

What of the men working in the mine during these three years? On November 4, 1944, on instructions from Local 52 at Centralia, William Rowekamp, the recording secretary, composed a letter to Medill: "At the present the condition of those roadways are very dirty and dusty . . . they are getting dangerous. . . . But the Coal Co. has ignored [Scanlan's recommendations]. And we beg your prompt action on this matter."

The Department received this letter November 6, and four days later Weir sent Inspector Scanlan to investigate. Scanlan reported immediately:

"The haulage roads in this mine are awful dusty, and much dust is kept in suspension all day. . . . The miners have complained to me . . . and I have wrote it up pretty strong on my inspection reports. . . . But to date they have not done any adequate sprinkling. . . . Today . . . [Superintendent Norman] Prudent said he would fix the water tank and sprinkle the roads within a week, said that he would have had this work done sooner, but that they have 20 to 30 men absent each day." (This last is a claim by the company that its cleanup efforts were handicapped by a wartime manpower shortage. This is controversial. Men of fifty-nine—the average wartime age at the mine—do not feel like spending weekends removing coal dust or rock dusting, a disagreeable task;

winter colds caused absenteeism and miners are always laying off anyway. On the other hand, the company was interested in production and profits: as Mine Manager Brown has said, "In the winter you can sell all the coal you can get out. So you want top production, you don't want to stop to rock dust.")

At any rate, Rowekamp's complaint got results. On December 2, 1944, he wrote Scanlan: "Well I am proud to tell you that they have sprinkled the 18th North Entry & 21st So. Entry and the main haulage road. . . . Myself and the Members of Local Union #52 appreciate it very much what you have done for us." It is apparent from this first direct move by Local 52 that Scanlan was working pretty closely with the Local to get something done.

But by the end of that month, December 1944, the mine once more had become so dirty that Scanlan ended his regular inspection report, ". . . if necessary the mine should discontinue hoisting coal for a few days until the [cleanup] work can be done." But all Weir said to the company was the routine "The Department endorses. . . ."

Early in 1945 it appeared that something might be accomplished. Scanlan, emerging from his regular inspection, took the unusual step of telephoning Medill at Springfield. Medill told him to write him a letter so Scanlan did:

"The haulage roads in this mine are in a terrible condition. If a person did not see it he would not believe. . . . Two months ago . . . the local officers [of Local Union 52] told me that . . . if [the mine manager] did not clean the mine up they were going to prefer charges against him before the mining board and have his certificate canceled. I talked them out of it and told them I thought we could get them to clean up the mine. But on this inspection I find that practically nothing has been done. . . . The mine should discontinue hoisting coal . . . until the mine is placed in a safe condition. . . . The coal dust in this mine is highly explosive. . . ."

This stiff letter was duly stamped "Received" at Springfield on February 23, 1945. A few days earlier a bad report had come in from Federal Inspector Perz. And now at last Medill himself entered the picture. What did he do? The Superintendent at Centralia had told Scanlan that, in order to clean up the mine, he would have to stop producing coal, a step he was not empowered to take. So Medill bypassed him, forwarding Scanlan's letter and report to William P. Young, Bell & Zoller's operating vice-president at Chicago: "Dear Bill. . . . Please let me have any comments you wish to make. . . . Very kindest personal regards." From his

quiet, well-furnished office near the top of the Bell Building overlooking Michigan Avenue, Young replied immediately to "Dear Bob" [Medill]: "As you know we have been working under a very severe handicap for the past months. The war demand for coal . . . we are short of men. . . . I am hopeful that the urgent demand of coal will ease up in another month so that we may have available both the time and labor to give proper attention to the recommendations of Inspector Scanlan. With kindest personal regards. . . ."

A week later, on March 7, 1945, Medill forwarded copies of this correspondence to Scanlan, adding: "I also talked with Mr. Young on the phone, and I feel quite sure that he is ready and willing. . . . I would suggest that you ask the mine committee [of Local 52] to be patient a little longer, inasmuch as the coal is badly needed at this time."

The miners told Scanlan they'd wait till the first of April but no longer. On March 14 Medill was to attend a safety meeting in Belleville. Scanlan went there to discuss Centralia No. 5 with him. According to Scanlan, "When I went up to his room he was surrounded with coal operators . . . all having whiskey, drinking, having a good time, and I couldn't talk to him then, and we attended the safety meeting [then] went . . . down to Otis Miller's saloon, and I stayed in the background drinking a few cokes and waited until the crowd thinned out, and went back up to his hotel room with him. . . . I told him that the mine was in such condition that if the dust became ignited that it would sweep from one end of the mine to the other and probably kill every man in the mine, and his reply to me was, 'We will just have to take that chance.' " (Medill has denied these words but not the meeting.)

On the first of April the president of Local Union 52 asked Scanlan to attend the Local's meeting on April 4. The miners complained that the company had not cleaned up the mine and, further, that one of the face bosses, or foreman, had fired explosive charges while the entire shift of men was in the mine. There can be little doubt that to fire explosives on-shift in a mine so dusty was to invite trouble—in fact, this turned out to be what later caused the disaster—and now in April 1945 the union filed charges against Mine Manager Brown, asking the State Mining Board to revoke his certificate of competency (this would cost him his job and prevent his getting another in Illinois as a mine manager). Rowekamp wrote up the charges: ". . . And being the Mine is so dry and dusty it could of caused an explosion. . . ."

Weir went to Centralia on April 17, 1945, but only to investigate the charges against Brown, not to inquire into the condition of the mine. He told the miners they should have taken their charges to the state's attorney. Nearly a month passed before, on May 11, Weir wrote a memorandum to the Mining Board saying that the company's superintendent had admitted the shots had been fired on-shift but that this was done "in an emergency" and it wouldn't happen again; and the Board refused to revoke Manager Brown's certificate.

Meanwhile, on April 12 and 13, Scanlan had made his regular inspection and found conditions worse than in February. He told the Superintendent: "Now, Norman, you claim Chicago won't give you the time to shut your mine down and clean it up. Now, I am going to get you some time," and he gave him the choice of shutting the mine down completely or spending three days a week cleaning up. The Superintendent, he said, replied that he didn't know, he'd have to "contact Chicago," but Scanlan replied: "I can't possibly wait for you to contact Chicago. It is about time that you fellows who operate the mines get big enough to operate your mines without contacting Chicago." So on Scanlan's recommendation the mine produced coal only four days a week and spent the remaining days cleaning up. For a time Scanlan was well satisfied with the results, but by June 25 he was again reporting excessive dust and Federal Inspector Perz was concurring: "No means are used to allay the dust." Following his October inspection Scanlan once more was moved to write a letter to Medill; but the only result was another routine letter from Weir to the company, unanswered.

Now, one must understand that, to be effective, both rock dusting and cleanup work must be maintained continuously. They were not at Centralia No. 5. By December of 1945 matters again came to a head. Scanlan wrote to Medill, saying that Local 52 wanted a sprinkling system installed to wet the coal, that Mine Manager Brown had said he could not order so "unusual" an expenditure, and that Brown's superior, Superintendent Prudent, "would not talk to me about it, walked away and left me standing." And Local 52 again attempted to take matters into its own hands. At a special meeting on December 12 the membership voted to prefer charges against both Mine Manager Brown and Superintendent Prudent. Rowekamp's official charge, typed on stationery of the Local, was followed next day by a letter, written in longhand on two sheets of dime-store notepaper, and signed by 28 miners. . . . At Springfield this communication too

was duly stamped "Received." And another Scanlan report arrived.

Confronted with so many documents, Medill called a meeting of the Mining Board on December 21. Moreover, he called Scanlan to Springfield and told him to go early to the Leland Hotel, the gathering place of Republican politicians, and see Ben H. Schull, a coal operator and one of the operators' two men on the Mining Board. In his hotel room, Schull (according to Scanlan) said he wanted to discuss privately Scanlan's report on Centralia No. 5, tried to persuade him to withdraw his recommendation of a sprinkling system, and, when Scanlan refused, told him, "you can come before the board." But when the Mining Board met in Medill's inner office, Scanlan was not called before it though he waited all day, and after the meeting he was told that the Board was appointing a special commission to go to Centralia and investigate.

On this commission were Weir, two state inspectors, and two members of the Mining Board itself, Schull and Murrell Reak. Reak, a miner himself, represented the United Mine Workers of America on the Mining Board. And Weir, too, owed his job to the UMWA but, oddly, he had worked for Bell & Zoller for twenty years before joining the Department, the last three as a boss, so his position was rather ambiguous. In fact, so unanimous were the rulings of the Mining Board that one cannot discern any management-labor cleavage at all but only what would be called in party politics bipartisan deals.

The commission had before it a letter from Superintendent Prudent and Manager Brown setting forth in detail the company's "absentee experience" and concluding with a veiled suggestion that the mine might be forced to close for good (once before, according to an inspector, the same company had abandoned a mine rather than go to the expense entailed in an inspector's safety recommendation). Weir wrote to Prudent, notifying him that the commission would visit Centralia on December 28 to investigate the charges against him and Brown; Medill wrote to the company's vice-president, Young, at Chicago ("You are being notified of this date so that you will have an opportunity to be present or designate some member of your staff to be present"); but Medill only told Rowekamp, "The committee has been appointed and after the investigation you will be advised of their findings and the action of the board"— he did not tell the Local when the commission would visit Centralia nor offer it opportunity to prove its charges.

Rowekamp, a motorman, recalls how he first learned of the special commission's visit. He was working in the mine and "Prudent told me to set out an empty and I did and they rode out." Prudent—remember, the commission was investigating charges against Prudent—led the commission through the mine. Rowekamp says, "They didn't see nothing. They didn't get back in the buggy runs where the dust was the worst; they stayed on the mainline." Even there they rode, they did not walk through the dust. Riding in a mine car, one must keep one's head down. In the washhouse that afternoon the men were angry. They waited a week or two, then wrote to Medill asking what had been done. On January 22, 1946, Medill replied: the Mining Board, adopting the views of the special commission, had found "insufficient evidence" to revoke the certificates of Prudent and Brown.

He did not elaborate. Next day, however, he sent to Scanlan a copy of the commission's report. It listed several important violations of the mining law: inadequate rock dusting, illegal practice in opening rooms, insufficient or improperly placed telephones, more than a hundred men working on a single split, or current, of air. In fact, the commission generally concurred with Scanlan, except that it did not emphasize dust nor recommend a sprinkling system. Thus in effect it overruled Scanlan on his sprinkling recommendation, a point to remember. It did find that the law was being violated yet it refused to revoke the certificates of the Superintendent and the Mine Manager, another point to remember. Weir has explained that the board felt that improvements requiring construction, such as splitting the airstream, would be made and that anyway "conditions there were no different than at most mines in the state." And this is a refrain that the company and the Department repeated in extenuation after the disaster. But actually could anything be more damning? The mine was no worse than most others; the mine blew up; therefore any might blow up!

The miners at Centralia were not satisfied. "It come up at the meeting," Rowekamp recalls. Local 52 met two Wednesday nights a month in its bare upstairs hall. The officers sat at a big heavy table up front; the members faced them, sitting on folding chairs which the Local had bought second-hand from an undertaker. Attendance was heavier now than usual, the men were aroused, some were even telling their wives that the mine was dangerous. They wanted to do something. But what? The state had rebuffed them. Well, why did they not go now to the higher officials

of their own union, the UMWA? Why not to John L. Lewis himself?

One of them has said, "You have to go through the real procedure to get to the right man, you got to start at the bottom and start climbing up, you see? If we write to Lewis, he'll refer us right back to Spud White." Spud White is Hugh White, the thick-necked president of the UMWA in Illinois (District 12), appointed by Lewis. Now, Lewis had suspended District 12's right to elect its own officers during the bloody strife of the early 1930s, when the members, disgusted with what they called his "dictator" methods and complaining of secret payrolls, expulsions, missing funds, stolen ballots, and leaders who turned up on operators' payrolls, had rebelled; in the end the Progressive Mine Workers was formed and Lewis retained tight control of the UMWA. A decade later the Illinois officers of UMWA demanded that he restore their self-government, but Lewis managed to replace them with his own men, including Spud White. By 1946 President White, a coal miner from the South, was consulting at high levels with Lewis, he was receiving $10,000 a year plus expenses (which usually equal salary), and he was maintaining a spacious house on a winding lane in the finest residential suburb of Springfield, a white house reached by a circular drive through weeping willows and evergreens.

Evidently the perplexed miners at Centralia already had appealed to District 12 for help, that is to White. Certainly Murrell Reak, the UMWA's man on the Mining Board and a close associate of White's, had asked Weir to furnish him with a copy of the findings of the special commission: "I want them so I may show the district UMWA. So they in turn may write Local Union down there, and show them that their charges are unfounded or rather not of a nature as to warrant the revocation of mine mgr. Certificate. . . ." Jack Ripon, the bulky vice-president of District 12 and White's right-hand man, said recently, "We heard there'd been complaints but we couldn't do a thing about it; it was up to the Mining Department to take care of it."

And yet in the past the UMWA has stepped in when the state failed to act. One unionist has said, "White could have closed that mine in twenty-four hours. All he'd have had to do was call up Medill and tell him he was going to pull every miner in the state if they didn't clean it up. It's the union's basic responsibility—if you don't protect your own wife and daughter, your neighbor down the street's not going to do it."

Perhaps the miners of Local 52 knew they must go it alone. They continued to address their official complaints to the State of Illinois. On February 26 Rowekamp wrote once more to Medill: "Dear Sir: At our regular meeting of Local Union 52. Motion made and second which carried for rec. secy. write you that the members of local union 52 are dissatisfied with the report of the special investigation commission. . . ." No answer. And so the members of Local 52 instructed Rowekamp to write to higher authority, to their Governor, Dwight H. Green.

It took him a long time. Elmer Moss kept asking if he'd finished it and Rowekamp recalls, "I'd tell him, Elmer, I can't do that fast, that's a serious letter, that'll take me a while." He wrote it out first in pencil and showed it to a couple of the boys and they thought it sounded fine. Then, sitting big and awkward at his cluttered little oak desk in the living room of his home outside town, he typed it, slowly and carefully—"anything important as that I take my time so I don't make mistakes, it looks too sloppified." He used the official stationery of the Local, bearing in one corner the device of the union—crossed shovels and picks—and in the other "Our Motto—Justice for One and All." He impressed upon it the official seal—"I can write a letter on my own hook but I dassen't use the seal without it's official"—and in the washhouse the Local officers signed it. Rowekamp made a special trip to the post office to mail it. It was a two-page letter saying, in part:

Dear Governor Green:

We, the officers of Local Union No. 52, U. M. W. of A., have been instructed by the members . . . to write a letter to you in protest against the negligence and unfair practices of your department of mines and minerals . . . we want you to know that this is not a protest against Mr. Driscoll Scanlan . . . the best inspector that ever came to our mine. . . . But your mining board will not let him enforce the law or take the necessary action to protect our lives and health. This protest is against the men above Mr. Scanlan in your department of mines and minerals. In fact, Governor Green this is a plea to you, to please save our lives, to please make the department of mines and minerals enforce the laws at the No. 5 mine of the Centralia Coal Co. . . . before we have a dust explosion at this mine like just happened in Kentucky and West Virginia. For the last couple of years the policy of the department of

mines and minerals toward us has been one of ignoring us. [The letter then recited the story of the useless special commission.] We are writing you, Governor Green, because we believe you want to give the people an honest administration and that you do not know how unfair your mining department is toward the men in this mine. Several years ago after a disaster at Gillespie we seen your pictures in the papers going down in the mine to make a personal investigation of the accident. We are giving you a chance to correct the conditions at this time that may cause a much worse disaster. . . . We will appreciate an early personal reply from you, stating your position in regard to the above and the enforcement of the state mining laws.

The letter closed "Very respectfully yours" and was signed by Jake Schmidt, president; Rowekamp, recording secretary; and Thomas Bush and Elmer Moss, mine committee. Today, of these, only Rowekamp is alive; all the others were killed in the disaster they foretold.

And now let us trace the remarkable course of this letter at Springfield. It was stamped in red ink "Received March 9, 1946, Governor's Office." In his ornate thick-carpeted offices, Governor Green has three male secretaries (each of whom in turn has a secretary) and it was to one of these, John William Chapman, that the "save our lives" letter, as it came to be called, was routed. Two days later Chapman dictated a memorandum to Medill: ". . . it is my opinion that the Governor may be subjected to very severe criticism in the event that the facts complained of are true and that as a result of this condition some serious accident occurs at the mine. Will you kindly have this complaint carefully investigated so I can call the report of the investigation to the Governor's attention at the same time I show him this letter?" Chapman fastened this small yellow memo to the miners' letter and sent both to Medill. Although Medill's office is only about sixty yards from the Governor's, the message consumed two days in traversing the distance.

The messenger arrived at the Department of Mines and Minerals at 9:00 a.m. on March 13 and handed the "save our lives" letter and Chapman's memorandum to Medill's secretary. She duly stamped both "Received" and handed them to Medill. He and Weir discussed the matter, then Medill sent the original letter back to the Governor's office and dictated his reply to Chapman, blaming the war, recounting the activities of the special commission, saying: "The complaint sounds a good deal worse than it really is. The present condition at the mine is not any different than it has been during the past ten or fifteen years. . . . I would suggest the Governor advise Local Union No. 52, U. M. W. of A., that he is calling the matter to the attention of the State Mining Board with instructions that it be given full and complete consideration at their next meeting."

This apparently satisfied Chapman for, in the Governor's name, he dictated a letter to Rowekamp and Schmidt: "I [i.e., Governor Green] am calling your letter to the attention of the Director of the Department of Mines and Minerals with the request that he see that your complaint is taken up at the next meeting of the State Mining Board. . . ." This was signed with Governor Green's name but it is probable that Green himself never saw the "save our lives" letter until after the disaster more than a year later. Nor is there any evidence that the Mining Board ever considered the letter. In fact, nothing further came of it.

One of the most remarkable aspects of the whole affair was this: An aggrieved party (the miners) accused a second party (Medill's department) of acting wrongfully, and the higher authority to which it addressed its grievance simply, in effect, asked the accused if he were guilty and, when he replied he was not, dropped the matter. A logic, the logic of the administrative mind, attaches to Chapman's sending the complaint to the Department—the administrative mind has a pigeonhole for everything, matters which relate to law go to the Attorney General, matters which relate to mines go to the Department of Mines and Minerals, and that is that—but it is scarcely a useful logic when one of the agencies is itself accused of malfunction. Apparently it did not occur to Chapman to consult Inspector Scanlan or to make any other independent investigation.

And Jack Ripon, Spud White's second-in-command at the District UMWA, said recently, "If I get a letter here I turn it over to the department that's supposed to take care of it, and the same with Governor Green— he got some damn bad publicity he shouldn't have had, he can't know everything that's going on." Ripon's sympathy with Green is understandable—he must have known how Green felt, for he and Spud White received a copy of the same letter. Ripon says, "Oh, we got a copy of it. But it wasn't none of ours, it didn't tell us to do anything. So our hands was tied. What'd we do with it? I think we gave it to Reak." Perhaps Murrell Reak, the UMWA's man on the Mining Board, felt he already had dealt with this matter (it was

Reak who, to Scanlan's astonishment, had joined the other members of the special commission in upholding the Superintendent and Mine Manager in their violations of the law and then had been so anxious to help White convince the members of Local 52 "that their charges are unfounded"). At any rate, Reak apparently did not call the Board's attention to the "save our lives" letter, even though it was a local of his own union which felt itself aggrieved. And White took no action either.

As for Medill, on the day he received the letter he called Scanlan to Springfield and, says Scanlan, "severely reprimanded" him. According to Scanlan, Medill "ordered me to cut down the size of my inspection report," because Medill thought that such long reports might alarm the miners, "those damn hunks" who couldn't read English (Medill denied the phrase); but Scanlan took this order to mean that Medill wanted him to "go easy" on the operators—"it is the same thing as ordering you to pass up certain things." And one day during this long controversy, Medill buttonholed Scanlan's political sponsor in a corridor of the Statehouse and said he intended to fire Scanlan; Scanlan's sponsor refused to sanction it and but for this, Scanlan was convinced, he would surely have lost his job.

But now hundreds of miles away larger events were occurring which were to affect the fate of the miners at Centralia. In Washington, D.C., John L. Lewis and the nation's bituminous coal operators failed to reach an agreement and the miners struck, and on May 21, 1946, President Truman ordered the mines seized for government operation. Eight days later Lewis and Julius A. Krug, Secretary of the Interior, signed the famous Krug-Lewis Agreement. Despite strenuous protests by the operators, this agreement included a federal safety code. It was drawn up by the Bureau of Mines (a part of the U.S. Department of the Interior). And now for the first time in history the federal government could exercise police power over coal mine safety.

Thus far the efforts of the miners of Local 52 to thread the administrative maze in their own state had produced nothing but a snowfall of memoranda, reports, letters, and special findings. Let us now observe this new federal machinery in action. We shall learn nothing about how to prevent a disaster but we may learn a good deal about the administrative process.

"Government operation of the mines" meant simply that the operators bossed their own mines for their own profit as usual but the UMWA had a work contract with the government, not the operators. To keep the 2,500 mines running, Secretary Krug created a new agency, the Coal Mines Administration. CMA was staffed with only 245 persons, nearly all naval personnel ignorant of coal mining. Theirs was paper work. For technical advice they relied upon the Bureau of Mines plus a handful of outside experts. More than two months passed before the code was put into effect, on July 29, 1946, and not until November 4 did Federal Inspector Perz reach Centralia to make his first enforceable inspection of Centralia No. 5. Observe, now, the results.

After three days at the mine, Perz went home and wrote out a "preliminary report" on a mimeographed form, listing 13 "major violations" of the safety code. He mailed this to the regional office of the Bureau of Mines at Vincennes, Indiana. There it was corrected for grammar, spelling, etc., and typed; copies then were mailed out to the Superintendent of the mine (to be posted on the bulletin board), the CMA in Washington, the CMA's regional office at Chicago, the District 12 office of the UMWA at Springfield, the UMWA international headquarters at Washington, the Bureau of Mines in Washington, and the Illinois Department at Springfield. While all this was going on, Perz was at home, preparing his final report, a lengthy document listing 57 violations of the safety code, 21 of them major and 36 minor. This handwritten final report likewise went to the Bureau at Vincennes where it was corrected, typed, and forwarded to the Bureau's office in College Park, Maryland. Here the report was "reviewed," then sent to the Director of the Bureau at Washington. He made any changes he deemed necessary, approved it, and ordered it processed. Copies were then distributed to the same seven places that had received the preliminary report, except that the UMWA at Springfield received two copies so that it could forward one to Local 52. (All this was so complicated that the Bureau devised a "flow sheet" to keep track of the report's passage from hand to hand.)

We must not lose sight of the fact that in the end everybody involved was apprised of Perz's findings: that the Centralia Company was violating the safety code and that hazards resulted. The company, the state, and the union had known this all along and done nothing, but what action now did the new enforcing agency take, the CMA?

Naval Captain N. H. Collison, the Coal Mines Administrator, said that the copy of the inspector's preliminary report was received at his office in Washington "by the head of the Production and Operations Department of my headquarters staff . . . Lieutenant Commander

Stull. . . . Lieutenant Commander Stull would review such a report, discuss the matter with the Bureau of Mines as to the importance of the findings, and then . . . await the final report"—unless the preliminary report showed that "imminent danger" existed, in which case he would go immediately to Captain Collison and, presumably, take "immediate action." And during all this activity in Washington, out in Chicago at the CMA's area office a Captain Yates also "would receive a copy of the report. His duty would be to acquaint himself with the findings there. If there was a red check mark indicating it fell within one of the three categories which I shall discuss later, he would detail a man immediately to the mine. If it indicated imminent danger . . . he would move immediately." The three categories deemed sufficiently important to be marked with "a red check mark" were all major hazards but the one which killed 111 men at Centralia No. 5 was not among them.

These, of course, were only CMA's first moves as it bestirred itself. But to encompass all its procedures is almost beyond the mind of man. Let us skip a few and see what actually resulted. The CMA in Washington received Perz's preliminary report November 14. Eleven days later it wrote to the company ordering it to correct one of the 13 major violations Perz found (why it said nothing about the others is not clear). On November 26 the CMA received Perz's final report and on November 29 it again wrote to the company, ordering it to correct promptly all violations and sending copies of the directive to the Bureau of Mines and the UMWA. Almost simultaneously it received from Superintendent Niermann a reply to its first order (Niermann had replaced Prudent, who had left the company's employ): "Dear Sir: In answer to your CMA8-gz of November 25, 1946, work has been started to correct the violation of article 5, section 3c, of the Federal Mine Safety Code, but has been discontinued, due to . . . a strike. . . ." This of course did not answer the CMA's second letter ordering correction of all 57 violations, nor was any answer forthcoming, but not until two months later, on January 29, 1947, did the CMA repeat its order and tell the company to report its progress by February 14.

This brought a reply from the company official who had been designated "operating manager" during the period of government operation, H. F. McDonald. McDonald, whose office was in Chicago, had risen to the presidency of the Centralia Coal Company and of the Bell & Zoller Coal Company through the sales department; after the Centralia disaster he told a reporter, "Hell, I don't know anything about a coal mine." Now he reported to CMA that "a substantial number of reported violations have been corrected and others are receiving our attention and should be corrected as materials and manpower become available." For obvious reasons, CMA considered this reply inadequate and on February 21 told McDonald to supply detailed information. Three days later McDonald replied ("Re file CMA81-swr"): He submitted a detailed report—he got it from Vice-President Young, who got it from the new General Superintendent, Walter J. Johnson—but McDonald told the CMA that this report was a couple of weeks old and he promised to furnish further details as soon as he could get them. The CMA on March 7 acknowledged this promise but before any other correspondence arrived to enrich file CMA81-swr, the mine blew up.

Now, the Krug-Lewis Agreement set up two methods of circumventing this cumbersome administrative machinery. If Inspector Perz had found what the legalese of the Agreement called "imminent danger," he could have ordered the men removed from the mine immediately (this power was weakened since it was also vested in the Coal Mines Administrator, the same division of authority that hobbled the state enforcers). But Perz did not report "imminent danger." And indeed how could he? The same hazardous conditions had obtained for perhaps twenty years and the mine hadn't blown up. The phrase is stultifying.

In addition, the Krug-Lewis Agreement provided for a safety committee of miners, selected by each local union and empowered to inspect the mine, to make safety recommendations to the management, and, again in case of "an immediate danger," to order the men out of the mine (subject to CMA review). But at Centralia No. 5 several months elapsed before Local 52 so much as appointed a safety committee, and even after the disaster the only surviving member of the committee didn't know what his powers were. The UMWA District officers at Springfield had failed to instruct their Locals in the rights which had been won for them. And confusion was compounded because two separate sets of safety rules were in use—the federal and the state—and in some instances one was the more stringent, in other instances, the other.

Meanwhile another faraway event laid another burden upon the men in the mine. John L. Lewis' combat with Secretary Krug. It ended, as everyone knows, in a federal injunction sought at President Truman's order and upheld by the U.S. Supreme Court, which forbade Lewis to order his miners to strike while the government was operating the mines. (Subsequently Lewis and the UMWA were fined heavily.) The members of Local 52 thought, correctly or not, that the injunction deprived them of their last weapon in their fight to get the mine cleaned up—a wildcat strike. A leader of Local 52 has said, "Sure we could've wildcatted it—and we'd have had the Supreme Court and the government and the whole public down on our necks."

The miners tried the state once more: Medill received a letter December 10, 1946, from an individual miner who charged that the company's mine examiner (a safety man) was not doing what the law required. Earlier Medill had ignored Scanlan's complaint about this but now he sent a department investigator, who reported that the charges were true and that Mine Manager Brown knew it, that Superintendent Niermann promised to consult Vice-President Young in Chicago, that other hazards existed, including dust. Weir wrote a routine letter and this time Niermann replied: The examiner would do his job properly. He said nothing about dust. This letter and one other about the same time, plus Young's earlier equivocal response to Medill's direct appeal, are the only company compliance letters on record.

There was yet time for the miners to make one more try. On February 24, 1947, the safety committee, composed of three miners, wrote a short letter to the Chicago area office of the Coal Mines Administration: "The biggest grievance is dust. . . ." It was written in longhand by Paul Compers (or so it is believed: Compers and one of the two other committee members were killed in the disaster a month later) and Compers handed it to Mine Manager Brown on February 27. But Brown did not forward it to the CMA; in fact he did nothing at all about it.

And now almost at the last moment, only six days before the mine blew up, some wholly new facts transpired. Throughout this whole history one thing has seemed inexplicable: the weakness of the pressure put on the company by Medill's Department of Mines and Minerals. On March 19, 1947, the St. Louis *Post-Dispatch* broke a story that seemed to throw some light upon it. An Illinois coal operator had been told by the state inspector who inspected his mine that Medill had instructed him to solicit money for the Republican Chicago mayoralty campaign. And soon more facts became known about this political shakedown.

Governor Dwight H. Green, a handsome, likeable politician, had first made his reputation as the young man who prosecuted Al Capone. By 1940 he looked like the white hope of Illinois Republicans. Campaigning for the governorship, Green promised to rid the state of the Democratic machine ("there will never be a Green machine"). He polled more votes in Illinois than Roosevelt; national Republican leaders began to watch him. Forthwith he set about building one of the most formidable machines in the nation. This task, together with the concomitant plans of Colonel Robert R. McCormick of the Chicago *Tribune* and others to make him President or Vice-President, has kept him occupied ever since. He has governed but little, permitting subordinates to run things. Reelected in 1944, he reached the peak of his power in 1946 when his machine succeeded in reducing the control of the Democratic machine over Chicago. Jubilant, Governor Green handpicked a ward leader to run for mayor in April of 1947 and backed him hard.

And it was only natural that Green's henchmen helped. Among these was Medill. "Somebody," says Medill, told him he was expected to raise "$15,000 or $20,000." On January 31, 1947, he called all his mine inspectors to the state mine rescue station in Springfield (at state expense), and told them—according to Inspector Scanlan who was present—that the money must be raised among the coal operators "and that he had called up four operators the previous day and two of them had already come through with a thousand dollars . . . and that he was going to contact the major companies, and we was to contact the independent companies and the small companies." Medill's version varied slightly: he said he told the inspectors that, as a Republican, he was interested in defeating the Democrats in Washington and Chicago, that if they found anybody of like mind it would be all right to tell them where to send their money, that all contributions must be voluntary.

After the meeting Scanlan felt like resigning but he thought perhaps Governor Green did not know about the plan and he recalled that once he had received a letter from Green (as did all state employees) asking his aid in giving the people an honest administration: Scanlan had replied to the Governor "that I had always been opposed to corrupt, grafting politicians and that I wasn't going to be one myself; and I received a nice acknowledgement . . . the Governor . . . told me that it was such letters as mine that gave him courage to carry on. . . ." Scanlan solicited no contributions from the coal operators.

But other inspectors did, and so did a party leader in Chicago. So did Medill: he says that his old friend David H. Devonald, operating vice-president of the huge Peabody Coal Company, gave him $1,000 and John E. Jones, a leading safety engineer, contributed $50 (Jones works for another of the Big Six operators and of him more later). No accounting ever has been made of the total

collected. The shakedown did not last long. According to Medill, another of Governor Green's "close advisers" told Medill that the coal operators were complaining that he and his inspectors were putting pressure on them for donations and if so he'd better stop it. He did, at another conference of the inspectors on March 7.

Since no Illinois law forbids a company or an individual to contribute secretly to a political campaign, we are dealing with a question of political morality, not legality. The Department of Mines and Minerals long has been a political agency. An inspector is a political appointee and during campaigns he is expected to contribute personally, tack up candidates' posters, and haul voters to the polls. Should he refuse, his local political boss would have him fired. (Soliciting money from the coal operators, however, apparently was something new for inspectors.) Today sympathetic Springfield politicians say: "Medill was just doing what every other department was doing and always has done, but he got a tough break." But one must point out that Medill's inspectors were charged with safeguarding lives, a more serious duty than that of most state employees, and that in order to perform this duty they had to police the coal operators, and that it was from these very operators that Medill suggested they might obtain money. A United States Senator who investigated the affair termed it "reprehensible."

What bearing, now, did this have on the Centralia disaster? Nobody, probably, collected from the Centralia Coal Company. But the shakedown is one more proof—stronger than most—that Governor Green's department had reason to stay on friendly terms with the coal operators when, as their policemen, it should have been aloof. As a miner at Centralia said recently: "If a coal company gives you a thousand dollars, they're gonna expect something in return."

Here lies Green's responsibility—not that, through a secretary's fumble, he failed to act on the miners' appeal to "save our lives" but rather that, while the kingmakers were shunting him around the nation making speeches, back home his loyal followers were busier building a rich political machine for him than in administering the state for him. Moreover, enriching the Green machine dovetailed nicely with the personal ambitions of Medill and others, and Green did not restrain them. By getting along with his old friends, the wealthy operators, Medill enhanced his personal standing. Evidence exists that Bell & Zoller had had a hand in getting him appointed Director, and remember, Weir had worked as a Bell & Zoller boss. By nature Medill was no zealous enforcer of laws. As for the inspectors, few of them went out of their way to look for trouble; some inspectors after leaving the Department have obtained good jobs as coal company executives. Anyway, as one inspector has said, "If you tried to ride 'em, they'd laugh at you and say, 'Go ahead, I'll just call up Springfield.'" As one man has said, "It was a cozy combination that worked for everybody's benefit, everybody except the miners." And the miners' man on the Board, Murrell Reak of the UMWA, did not oppose the combination. Nor did Green question it.

As the Chicago campaign ground to a close, down at Centralia on March 18 Federal Inspector Perz was making another routine inspection. General Superintendent Johnson told him the company had ordered pipe for a sprinkler system months earlier but it hadn't arrived, "that there would be a large expenditure involved there . . . they had no definite arrangements just yet . . . but he would take it up with the higher officials of the company" in Chicago. Scanlan and Superintendent Niermann were there too; they stayed in the bare little mine office, with its rickety furniture and torn window shades, till 7:30 that night. No rock dusting had been done for nearly a year but now the company had a carload of rock dust underground and Scanlan got the impression it would be applied over the next weekend. (It wasn't.) Perz, too, thought Johnson "very conscientious . . . very competent." Scanlan typed out his report—he had resorted wearily to listing a few major recommendations and adding that previous recommendations "should be complied with"—and mailed it to Springfield. Perz went home and wrote out his own report, acknowledging that 17 hazards had been corrected but making 52 recommendations most of which he had made in November (the company and the CMA were still corresponding over that November report). Perz finished writing on Saturday morning and mailed the report to the Vincennes office, which presumably began processing it Monday.

The wheels had been turning at Springfield, too, and on Tuesday, March 25, Weir signed a form letter to Brown setting forth Scanlan's latest recommendations: "The Department endorses. . . ." But that day, at 3:26 p.m., before the outgoing-mail box in the Department was emptied, Centralia Mine No. 5 blew up. . . .

The last of the bodies was recovered at 5:30 a.m. on the fifth day after the explosion. On "Black Monday" the flag on the new city hall flew at half staff and all the businesses in town closed. Already the funerals had begun, 111 of them. John L. Lewis cried that the

111 were "murdered by the criminal negligence" of Secretary Krug and declared a national six-day "mourning period" during this Holy Week, and though some said he was only achieving by subterfuge what the courts had forbidden him—a strike and defiance of Krug—nonetheless he made the point that in the entire nation only two soft coal mines had been complying with the safety code; and so Krug closed the mines.

Six separate investigations began, two to determine what had happened, and four to find out why. Federal and state experts agreed, in general, that the ignition probably had occurred at the extreme end, or face, of the First West Entry, that it was strictly a coal-dust explosion, that the dust probably was ignited by an explosive charge which had been tamped and fired in a dangerous manner—fired by an openflame fuse, tamped with coal dust—and that the resulting local explosion was propagated by coal dust throughout four working sections of the mine, subsiding when it reached rock-dusted areas. . . .

And what resulted from all the investigations into the Centralia disaster? The Washington County Grand Jury returned no-bills—that is, refused to indict Inspector Scanlan and five company officials ranging upward in authority through Brown, Niermann, Johnson, Young, and McDonald. The Grand Jury did indict the Centralia Coal Company, as a corporation, on two counts of "willful neglect" to comply with the mining law—failing to rock dust and working more than 100 men on a single split of air—and it also indicted Medill and Weir for "palpable omission of duty." The company pleaded nolo contendere—it did not wish to dispute the charge—and was fined the maximum: $300 on each count, a total of $1,000 (or less than $10 per miner's life lost). The law also provides a jail sentence of up to six months but of course you can't put a corporation in jail.

At this writing the indictments against Medill and Weir are still pending, and amid interesting circumstances. Bail for Medill was provided by Charles E. Jones, John W. Spence, G. C. Curtis, and H. B. Thompson; and all of these men, oddly enough, are connected with the oil and gas division of the Department from which Medill was fired. And one of them is also one of Medill's defense attorneys. But this is not all. Medill and Weir filed a petition for a change of venue, supported by numerous affidavits of Washington County residents that prejudice existed. These affidavits were collected by three inspectors for the oil and gas division. They succeeded in getting the trial transferred to

Wayne County, which is dominated by a segment of Governor Green's political organization led locally by one of these men, Spence. Not in recent memory in Illinois has the conviction of a Department head on a similar charge been sustained, and there is little reason to suppose that Medill or Weir will be convicted. Medill performed an act of great political loyalty when he shouldered most of the blame at Centralia, in effect stopping the investigation before it reached others above him, and this may be his reward.

Why did nobody close the Centralia mine before it exploded? A difficult question. Medill's position (and some investigators') was that Inspector Scanlan could have closed it. And, legally, this is true: The mining law expressly provided that an inspector could close a mine which persisted in violating the law. But inspectors have done so very rarely, only in exceptional circumstances, and almost always in consultation with the Department. Scanlan felt that had he closed the Centralia mine Medill simply would have fired him and appointed a more tractable inspector. Moreover, the power to close was not his exclusively: it also belonged to the Mining Board. (And is not this divided authority one of the chief factors that produced the disaster?) Robert Weir has said, "We honestly didn't think the mine was dangerous enough to close." This seems fantastic, yet one must credit it. For if Scanlan really had thought so, surely he would have closed it, even though a more pliable inspector reopened it. So would the federal authorities, Medill, or the company itself. And surely the miners would not have gone to work in it.

Governor Green's own fact-finding committee laid blame for the disaster upon the Department, Scanlan, and the company. The Democrats in the Illinois joint legislative committee submitted a minority report blaming the company, Medill, Weir, and Green's administration for "the industrial and political crime . . ."; the Republican majority confessed itself unable to fix blame. After a tremendous pulling and hauling by every special interest, some new state legislation was passed as a result of the accident, but nothing to put teeth into the laws: violations still are misdemeanors (except campaign solicitation by inspectors, a felony); it is scarcely a serious blow to a million-dollar corporation to be fined $1,000. Nor does the law yet charge specific officers of the companies—rather than the abstract corporations—with legal responsibility, so it is still easy for a company official to hide behind a nebulous chain of command

reaching up to the stratosphere of corporate finance in Chicago or St. Louis. It is hard to believe that compliance with any law can be enforced unless violators can be jailed.

As for the Congress of the United States, it did next to nothing. The Senate subcommittee recommended that Congress raise safety standards and give the federal government power to enforce that standard—"Immediate and affirmative action is imperative." But Congress only ordered the Bureau of Mines to report next session on whether mine operators were complying voluntarily with federal inspectors' recommendations. . . .

After the Centralia disaster each man responsible had his private hell, and to escape it each found his private scapegoat—the wartime manpower shortage, the material shortage, another official, the miners, or, in the most pitiable cases, "human frailty." Surely a strange destiny took Dwight Green from a federal courtroom where, a young crusader, he overthrew Capone to a hotel in Centralia where, fifteen years older, he came face to face with William Rowekamp, who wanted to know why Green had done nothing about the miners' plea to "save our lives." But actually responsibility here transcends individuals. The miners at Centralia, seeking somebody who would heed their conviction that their lives were in danger, found themselves confronted with officialdom, a huge organism scarcely mortal. The State Inspector, the Federal Inspector, the State Board, the Federal CMA, the company officials—all these forever invoked "higher authority," they forever passed from hand to hand a stream of memoranda and letters, decisions and laws and rulings, and they lost their own identities. As one strives to fix responsibility for the disaster, again and again one is confronted, as were the miners, not with any individual but with a host of individuals fused into a vast, unapproachable, insensate organism. Perhaps this immovable juggernaut is the true villain in the piece. Certainly all those in authority were too remote from the persons whose lives they controlled. And this is only to confess once more that in making our society complex we have made it unmanageable.

Author's Epilogue

Illinois Governor Dwight Green was ruined politically by the Centralia disaster. He had been mentioned as a possible Republican vice-presidential candidate in 1948 and had all the makings of a successful national political figure, but in 1948 he even lost his bid for re-election to the governorship. One of the issues that his opponent, Adlai Stevenson, raised during the campaign was mine safety. Governor Stevenson eventually became a national political figure, running twice—unsuccessfully—for U.S. president in 1952 and 1956.

Robert M. Medill, director of the Illinois Bureau of Mines and Minerals, was asked to resign his post and did so, April 1, 1947. His assistant, Robert Weir, though indicted, remained in his post until his retirement.

The mine owners, Bell and Zoller Coal Company, paid the fine of $1000, but none of the company's officers were indicted or imprisoned.

Despite the six separate investigations of the disaster that were undertaken by various state and federal authorities, neither the state of Illinois nor the federal government changed its mine safety laws or enforcement policies. Only after the 1952 West Frankfurt, Kentucky, coal mine disaster was a stricter federal mine safety code enacted and enforcement procedures improved.

The Centralia blast created 99 widows and 76 fatherless children under the age of 18, which prompted the United Mine Workers Union to change its welfare death benefits from lump sum payouts to monthly stipends. The union used the disaster to press for higher wages and benefits for miners elsewhere.

The Centralia Mine was sold to the Peabody Coal Company and reopened on July 21, 1947, with sixty miners, including many of the survivors, but was closed in two years due to the high costs of production. The mine was abandoned and sealed with concrete. In 1980 a solid waste disposal company bought the property, bulldozed the remaining buildings and plans someday to grind up solid waste and deposit it in the mine shafts. Today coal fragments and slate can be found around the grounds, along with foundations of the old mine and rusting equipment overgrown with weeds. In the nearby Centralia Foundation Park and in the Village of Wamac, plaques recently were dedicated to the miners who lost their lives in Centralia.

Chapter 1 Review Questions

1. How did Woodrow Wilson justify the creation of the new field of public administration? Why does he view public administration as being so critical to the future of the United States? Do you agree? What does Wilson conclude are the best ways to develop this new field? Are these ideas still valid? By contrast, based on your reading of Stillman's essay, how is the field evolving today? Is it evolving along the lines Wilson's essay envisioned?

2. Why does Wilson stress throughout his essay the importance of finding the appropriate relationship between democracy and public administration? What does he mean by that? For example? According to Stillman's essay, how does the field now deal with this issue?

3. Did the case, "The Blast in Centralia No. 5," help you to formulate your own view of what the scope and purpose of the field are or should be today? Does the case contradict or support the conclusions about the importance of this field made in the Wilson essay? Or in Stillman's essay?

4. Based on your reading of the case, what do you see as the central causes of the tragedy in "The Blast in Centralia No. 5"? Why did these problems develop?

5. What reforms would you recommend to prevent the tragedy from reoccurring elsewhere? How could such reforms be implemented?

6. Based on your analysis of "The Blast in Centralia No. 5," can you generalize about the importance of public administration for society? Can you list some of the pros *and* cons of having a strong and effective administrative system to perform essential services in society?

Key Terms

public administration
politics-administration dichotomy
Reinventing Government
communitarians
the refounding movement
democratic idealism

POSDCORB
social sciences heterodoxy
VPI refounders
tools approach
antistatism
public choice theory
Minnowbrook Conference

Suggestions for Further Reading

The seminal book on the origins and growth of public administration in America remains Dwight Waldo, *The Administrative State: A Study of the Political Theory of American Public Administration* (New York: Ronald Press, 1948), which was reissued in 1984, with a new preface, by Holmes and Meier Publishers. For other writings by Waldo, see "The Administrative State Revisited," *Public Administration Review,* 25 (March 1965), pp. 5–37, and *The Enterprise of Public Administration: A Summary View* (Novato, Calif.: Chandler and Sharp Publishers, 1980). For a helpful commentary on Waldo's ideas and career, see Brack Brown and Richard J. Stillman II, *A Search for Public Administration* (College Station: Texas A&M University Press, 1986). Also for insightful review of Dwight Waldo's contributions, read Frank Marini, "Leaders in the Field: Dwight Waldo," *Public Administration Review,* 53 (Sept./Oct. 1993), pp. 409–18. For two excellent reassessments of Woodrow Wilson and his influence on the field, read Paul P. Van Riper, ed., *The Wilson Influence on Public Administration: From Theory to Practice* (Washington, D.C.: American Society for Public Administration, 1990); and Daniel W. Martin, "The Fading Legacy of Woodrow Wilson," *Public Administration Review* (March/April 1988), pp. 631–36.

Much can be learned from the writings of important contributors to the field, like Woodrow Wilson, Frederick Taylor, Luther Gulick, Louis Brownlow, Herbert Simon, and Charles Lindblom. For a thoughtful reassessment of early theorists, read Laurence F. Lynn, Jr., "The Myth of the Bureaucratic Paradigm: What Traditional Public Administration Really Stood For," *Public Administration Review* 61 (March/April 2001), pp. 144–61, and also in the same issue, be sure to read the commentaries on Lynn's essay by David Rosenbloom, J. Patrick Dobel, Norma Riccucci, and James Savara. For an excellent collection of many of those classic writings with insightful commentary, see Frederick C. Mosher, ed., *Basic Literature of American Public Administration 1787–1950* (New York: Holmes and Meier, 1981), and for recent selections of key theorists, read Frederick S. Lane, ed., *Current Issues in Public Administration,* 6th ed. (New York: St. Martin's Press, 1999); Camilla Stivers, ed., *Democracy, Bureaucracy and the Study of Administration* (Boulder, Co.: Westview, 2001); and Richard Box, ed. *Public Administration and Society* (New York: Sharpe, 2004). Equally valuable is the four-volume history of public administration prior to 1900 by Leonard D. White: *The Federalists* (1948); *The Jeffersonians* (1951); *The Jacksonians* (1954); and *The Republican Era* (1958), all published by Macmillan. Michael W. Spicer, *The Founders, the Constitution, and Public Administration: A Conflict in World Views* (Washington, D.C.: Georgetown Press, 1995), offers a recent study of the constitutional origins of the field. Some of the important books that document the rise of public administration in the twentieth century are Jane Dahlberg, *The New York Bureau of Municipal Research* (New York: New York University Press, 1966); Robert H. Wiebe, *The Search for Order, 1877–1920* (New York: Hill & Wang, 1967); Don K. Price, *America's Unwritten Constitution* (Baton Rouge, La.: Louisiana State University Press, 1983); John A. Rohr, *To Run a Constitution: The Legitimacy of the Administrative State* (Lawrence: University of Kansas Press,

1986); Barry Karl, *Executive Reorganization and Reform in the New Deal* (Cambridge, Mass.: Harvard University Press, 1963); and Stephen Skowronek, *Building a New American State: The Expansion of National Administrative Capacities, 1877–1920* (New York: Cambridge University Press, 1982). Any thorough understanding of how American Public Administration since the early 1970s was decidedly shaped by Minnowbrook ideas and Public Choice theory and must be based on reading both Frank Marini (ed.), *Toward a New Public Administration: The Minnowbrook Perspective* (Scranton, Penn.: Chandler Publishing, 1971); and Vincent Ostrom, *The Intellectual Crisis in American Public Administration,* 2d ed. (Tuscaloosa, Ala.: The University of Alabama Press, 1973, revised ed., 1974). For a fine critique of public choice theory, read Peter Self, *Government by the Market?* (Boulder, Co.: Westview Press, 1993).

Because Frederick Taylor was so critical to the early development of the field, two noteworthy biographies of his life and work are Robert Kanigel, *The One Best Way* (New York: Penguin, 1999); and Hindy Lauer Schachter, *Frederick Taylor and the Public Administration Community: A Reevaluation* (Albany, N.Y.: State University of New York Press, 1989). For Taylor's postwar influences, see Stephen P. Waring, *Taylorism Transformed: Scientific Management Theory Since 1945* (Chapel Hill: University of North Carolina Press, 1991). For a broader biographical treatment of the field's major figures, see Brian R. Fry, *Mastering Public Administration: From Max Weber to Dwight Waldo* (Chatham, N.Y.: Chatham House, 1989).

In addition, several other impressive retrospectives on key founders of the field have appeared in recent years: James A. Stever, "Marshall Dimock: An Intellectual Portrait," *Public Administration Review,* 50 (Nov./Dec. 1990), pp. 615–622; Lyle C. Fitch, "Luther Gulick," *Public Administration Review,* 50 (November/ December 1990), pp. 604–638; Max O. Stephenson, Jr., and Jeremy F. Plant, "The Legacy of Frederick C. Mosher," *Public Administration Review,* 51 (March/ April 1991), pp. 97–113; L. R. Jones, "Aaron Wildavsky: A Man and Scholar for All Seasons," *Public Administration Review,* 55 (January/February 1995), pp. 3–16, as well as the entire issue of the *Public Administration Quarterly* (Fall 1988) devoted

to an appraisal of Herbert Simon's work. For excellent insights into Simon's life and work, read his autobiography: Herbert A. Simon, *Models of My Life* (New York: Basic Books, 1991).

Numerous shorter interpretative essays on the development of the field include Herbert Kaufman, "Emerging Conflicts in the Doctrines of Public Administration," *American Political Science Review* (December 1956), pp. 1057–1073; David H. Rosenbloom, "Public Administration Theory and the Separation of Powers," *Public Administration Review,* 43 (May/June 1983), pp. 213–227; Luther H. Gulick, "Reflections on Public Administration, Past and Present," *Public Administration Review,* 50 (November/ December 1990); and Laurence J. O'Toole, Jr., "Harry F. Byrd, Sr. and the New York Bureau of Municipal Research: Lessons from an Ironic Alliance," *Public Administration Review,* 46 (March/April 1986), pp. 113–123.

The past two decades or more have witnessed an outpouring of new, rich, and diverse perspectives on what public administration is and ought to be. Among the recent, more challenging points of view, which attempt to "reformulate the basics" of the field, are: James A. Stever, *The End of Public Administration* (Ardley-on-the-Hudson, N.Y.: Transnational Publishers, 1988); Lester M. Salamon, ed., *Beyond Privatization* (Washington, D.C.: The Urban Institute Press, 1989); Gary L. Wamsley et al., *Refounding Public Administration* (Newbury Park, Calif.: Sage, 1990) as well as *Refounding Democratic Public Administration* (Sage, 1996); Henry D. Kass and Bayard L. Catron, eds., *Images and Identities in Public Administration* (Newbury Park, Calif.: Sage, 1990); Richard J. Stillman II, *Preface to Public Administration: A Search for Themes and Direction,* 2nd ed., (Burke, VA: Chatelaine Press, 1998), Camilla Stivers, *Gender Images in Public Administration: Legitimacy and the Administrative State* (Newbury Park, Calif.: Sage, 1993); Charles J. Fox and Hugh T. Miller, *Postmodern Public Administration: Toward a Discourse* (Newbury Park, Calif.: Sage, 1995); Jong S. Jun, *Philosophy of Administration* (Seoul, Korea: Daeyoung Moonhwa International, 1994); Jay D. White and Guy B. Adams, eds., *Research in Public Administration* (Newbury

Park, Calif.: Sage, 1994); and O.C. McSuite, *Legitimacy in Public Administration: A Discourse Analysis* (Thousand Oaks, Calif.: Sage, 1997); and David Farmer, *Language of Public Administration* (Tuscaloosa, Ala.: University of Alabama Press, 2003). For the most useful comprehensive guide to public administration literature, see Daniel W. Martin, *The Guide to the Foundations of Public Administration* (New York: Marcel Dekker, 1989); also for the best analysis of critical theoretical issues facing the field today, see Mark R. Rutgers, ed., *Retracing Public Administration* (Oxford, U.K.: Elsevier, 2003). For a comparative view of European and American administrative thinking, see Walter J. M. Kickert and Richard Stillman (eds.), *The Modern State and Its Study* (London: Elgar, 2000). The four outstanding journals that cover administrative theory today are the *Public Admininstration Review, Administrative Theory and Praxis, Journal of Public Administration Research and Theory,* and *Administration and Society.*

PART ONE

The Pattern of Public Administration in America: Its Environment, Structure, and People

Public administrators are surrounded by multiple environments that serve to shape decisively what they do and how well (or how poorly) they do it. Part One discusses the major conceptual ideas about the key environmental factors that profoundly influence the nature, scope, and direction of contemporary public administration. Each reading in Part One outlines one of these important environmental concepts, and each case study illustrates that concept. The significant environmental concepts featured in Part One include:

CHAPTER 2
The Formal Structure: *The Concept of Bureaucracy*
What are the formal elements of the bureaucratic structure that serve as core building blocks in the administrative processes?

CHAPTER 3
The General Environment: *The Concept of Ecology*
How does the general administrative environment significantly influence the formulation, implementation, and outcomes of public programs?

CHAPTER 4
The Political Environment: *The Concept of Administrative Power*   What is the nature of the political landscape in which public agencies operate, and why is administrative power key to their survival, growth, or demise?

CHAPTER 5
Intergovernmental Relations (IGR): *The Concept of IGR as Interdependence, Complexity, and Bargaining*
Why do intergovernmental relationships create complex problems for modern American public administrators? What is the structure of these relationships at the dawn of the 21st century?

CHAPTER 6
Internal Dynamics: *The Concept of the Informal Group*   How does the internal environment of organizations affect the "outcomes" of the administrative processes? Can administrators identify them and then cope with "internal groups"?

CHAPTER 7
Key Decision Makers Inside Public Administration: *The Concept of Competing Bureaucratic Subsystems*
Who are the key decision makers in public agencies today? Why are they so vital to shaping public policy?

CHAPTER 2

The Formal Structure: The Concept of Bureaucracy

*U*nder normal conditions, the power position of a fully developed bureaucracy is always overtowering. The "political master" finds himself in the position of the "dilettante" who stands opposite the "expert." . . .

Max Weber

Introduction

To most Americans, "bureaucracy" is a fighting word. Few things are more disliked than bureaucracy, few occupations held in lower esteem than the bureaucrat. Both are subjected to repeated criticism in the press and damned regularly by political soap box orators and ordinary citizens. "Inefficiency," "red tape," "stupidity," "secrecy," "smugness," "aggressiveness," and "self-interest" are only a few of the emotionally charged words used to castigate bureaucrats.

There may be considerable truth to our dim view of bureaucrats. We also may be justified in venting our spleens occasionally at the irritating aspects of bureaucracy that arise almost daily—we may even experience a healthy catharsis in the process. But this understandably testy outlook should not prevent us from grasping the central importance and meaning of this phenomenon of bureaucracy.

From the standpoint of public administration and social science literature in general, "bureaucracy" means much more than the various bothersome characteristics of modern organizations. The term in serious administrative literature denotes the general, formal structural elements of a type of human organization, particularly a governmental organization. In this sense bureaucracy has both good *and* bad qualities; it is a neutral term rather than one referring to only the negative traits of organizations. It is a lens through which we may dispassionately view what Carl Friedrich has appropriately tagged "the core of modern government."

The German social scientist, Max Weber (1864–1920), is generally acknowledged to have developed the most comprehensive, classic formulation of the characteristics of bureaucracy. Weber not only pioneered ideas about bureaucracy but ranged across a whole spectrum of historical, political, economic, and social thought. As Reinhard Bendix observed, Weber was "like a man of the Renaissance who took in all humanity for his province." In his study of Hindu religion, Old Testament theology, ancient Roman land surveying, Junker politics, medieval trading companies, and the Chinese civil service, he sought to analyze objectively the nature of human institutions and to show how ideas are linked with the evolution of political, economic, and social systems. One of his best works, *The Protestant Ethic and the Spirit of Capitalism,* established the critical intellectual ties between the rise of Protestantism and capitalism in the sixteenth and seventeenth centuries. He constantly pressed for answers to enormously complex problems. What is the interplay between ideas and institutions? What distinguishes the Western culture and its ideas? Why has a particular society evolved the way it has?

We cannot summarize here the numerous ideas formulated by Max Weber's fertile mind, but we can examine a few aspects of his thought that bear directly on his conception of bureaucracy. Weber believed that civilization evolved from the primitive and mystical to the rational and complex. He thought that human nature progressed slowly from primitive religions and mythologies to an increasing theoretical and technical sophistication. World evolution was a one-way street in Weber's nineteenth-century view: he visualized a progressive "demystification" of humanity and humanity's ideas about the surrounding environment.

In keeping with his demystification view of progress, Weber describes three "ideal-types" of authority that explain why individuals throughout history have obeyed their rulers. One of the earliest, the "traditional" authority of primitive societies, rested on the established belief in the sanctity of tradition. Because a family of rulers has always ruled, people judge them to be just and right and obey them. Time, precedent, and tradition gave rulers their legitimacy in the eyes of the ruled.

A second ideal-type of authority, according to Weber, is "charismatic" authority, which is based on the personal qualities and the attractiveness of leaders. Charismatic figures are self-appointed leaders who inspire belief because of their extraordinary, almost superhuman, qualifications. Military leaders, warrior chiefs, popular party leaders, and founders of religions are examples of individuals whose heroic feats or miracles attract followers.

Weber postulated a third ideal-type of authority that is the foundation of modern civilizations, namely, "legal-rational" authority. It is based on "a belief in the legitimacy of the pattern of normative rules and the rights of those elevated to authority under such rules to issue commands." Obedience is owed to a legally established, impersonal set of rules, rather than to a personal ruler. Legal-rational authority vests power in the office rather than in the person who occupies the office; thus anyone can rule as long as he or she comes to office "according to the rules."

This third type of authority forms the basis for Weber's concept of bureaucracy. According to Weber, bureaucracy is the normal way that "legal-rational" authority appears in institutional form; it holds a central role in ordering and controlling modern societies. "It is," says Weber, "superior to any other form in precision, in stability, in stringency of its discipline, and in its reliability. It thus makes possible a particularly high degree of calculability of results for the heads of organizations and for those acting in relation to it." It is finally superior in its operational efficiency and "is formally capable of application to all kinds of administrative tasks." For Weber, bureaucracy is indispensable to maintaining civilization in modern society. In his view, "however much people may complain about the evils of bureaucracy it would be sheer illusion to think for a moment that continuous administrative work can be carried out in any field except by means of officials working in offices."

A great deal of Weber's analysis of bureaucracy dealt with its historical development. According to Weber, modern bureaucracy in the Western world arose during the Middle Ages when royal domains grew and required bodies of officials to oversee them. Out of necessity, princes devised rational administrative techniques to extend their authority, frequently borrowing ideas from the church, whose territories at that time encompassed most of Europe. "The proper soil for bureaucratization of administration," writes Weber, "has always been the development of administrative tasks." Bureaucracy grew because society needed to do things—to build roads, to educate students, to collect taxes, to fight battles, and to dispense justice. Work was divided and specialized to achieve the goals of a society.

Weber also identified a monied economy as an important ingredient for the development of bureaucracy. "Bureaucracy as a permanent structure is knit to the presupposition of a constant income for maintenancy. . . . A stable system of taxation is the precondition for the permanent existence of bureaucratic administration." Other cultural factors contributing to the rise of highly structured bureaucracies were the growth of education, the development of higher religions, and the burgeoning of science and rationality.

Weber listed in a detailed fashion the major elements of the formal structure of bureaucracy. Three of the most important attributes in his concept of bureaucracy were the division of labor, hierarchical order, and impersonal rules—keystones to any functioning bureaucracy. The first, specialization of labor, meant that all work in a bureaucracy is rationally divided into units that can be undertaken by an individual or group of individuals competent to perform those tasks. Unlike traditional rulers, workers do not *own* their offices in bureaucracy but enjoy tenure based on their abilities to perform the work assigned. Second, the hierarchical order of bureaucracy separates superiors from subordinates; on the basis of this hierarchy, remuneration for work is dispensed, authority recognized, privileges allotted, and promotions awarded. Finally, impersonal rules form the life-blood of the bureaucratic world. Bureaucrats, according to Weber, are not free to act in any way they please because their choices are confined to prescribed patterns of conduct imposed by legal rules. In contrast to "traditional" or "charismatic" authority, bureaucratic rules provide for the systematic control of subordinates by superiors, thus limiting the opportunities for arbitrariness and personal favoritism.

Weber theorized that the only way for a modern society to operate effectively was by organizing expertly trained, functional specialists in bureaucracies. Although Max Weber saw bureaucracy as permanent and indispensable in the modern world, he was horrified by what he believed was an irreversible trend toward loss of human freedom and dignity:

> It is horrible to think that the world could one day be filled with nothing but those little cogs, little men clinging to little jobs and striving towards bigger ones—a state of affairs which is to be seen once more, as in the Egyptian records, playing an ever-increasing part in the spirit of our present administrative system and especially of its offspring, the students. This passion for bureaucracy . . . is enough to drive one to despair.[1]

---

[1]As quoted in Reinhard Bendix, *Max Weber: An Intellectual Portrait* (New York: Doubleday and Co., 1960), p. 464.

And although he despaired over the increasing trend toward bureaucratization in the modern world, Weber also observed the leveling or democratizing effect of bureaucracy on society. As Reinhard Bendix wrote of Weber's idea: "The development of bureaucracy does away with . . . plutocratic privileges, replacing unpaid, avocational administration by notables with paid, full-time administration by professionals, regardless of their social and economic position. . . . Authority is exercised in accordance with rules, and everyone subject to that authority is legally equal."[2]

Over the last fifty years, certain elements in Max Weber's conception of bureaucracy have fueled repeated academic debate and scholarly criticism.[3] There are those social scientists who criticize his "ideal-type" formulations as misleading. They contend that it offers neither a desirable state *nor* an empirical reality. Others suggest that he overemphasizes the *formal* elements of bureaucracy—i.e., specialization, hierarchy, rules, division of labor, etc.—and does not appreciate the *informal* dimensions—such as human relationships, leadership, communication networks, etc.—as equally, if not more important, for influencing bureaucratic performance and efficiency. Still others say that Weber neglects the deficiencies of large-scale bureaucracies that can encourage alienation of workers and citizens alike, in contrast to the stimulating creativity that small, fluid networks of specialists can enhance. Some scholars charge Weber's concept as being both time-bound and culture-bound to the late nineteenth and early twentieth-century German "scientific" heritage. They say he idealized the German bureaucratic state that dominated that era. This list of social science criticisms could go on, and they are all to some degree telling criticisms.

Nevertheless, the main outline of Weber's classic formulation is generally accepted as true and significant. For students of public administration, his concept forms one of the essential intellectual building blocks in our understanding of the formal institutional structure of public administration.

As you read this selection, keep the following questions in mind:

Where can you see evidence of Weber's concept of bureaucracy within familiar organizations?

In what respects does Weber's characterization of bureaucracy as a theoretical "ideal-type" miss the mark in describing the practical reality? In what respects is it on target?

How is Weber's bureaucratic model relevant to the previous case, "The Blast in Centralia No. 5"? On the basis of that case as well as your own observations, can you describe some positive and negative features of modern bureaucracy?

---

[2]Ibid., p. 429.

[3]For an excellent discussion of general academic criticism and revision of Weber's ideas, read either Alfred Diamant, "The Bureaucratic Model: Max Weber Rejected, Rediscovered, Reformed," in Ferrel Heady and Sybil L. Stokes, *Papers in Comparative Public Administration* (Ann Arbor, Mich.: Institute of Public Administration, 1962), or Peter M. Blau and Marshall W. Meyer, *Bureaucracy in Modern Society* (New York: Random House, 1971). For a recent bold and different interpretation of Weber, see the essay on Weber by Robert Leivesley, Adrian Carr, and Alexander Kauzmin, in Ali Farazmand, ed., *Handbook of Bureaucracy* (New York: Marcel Dekker, 1994).

Bureaucracy[1]

MAX WEBER

1. Characteristics of Bureaucracy

Modern officialdom functions in the following specific manner:

I. There is the principle of fixed and official jurisdictional areas, which are generally ordered by rules, that is, by laws or administrative regulations.

1. The regular activities required for the purposes of the bureaucratically governed structure are distributed in a fixed way as official duties.
2. The authority to give the commands required for the discharge of these duties is distributed in a stable way and is strictly delimited by rules concerning the coercive means, physical, sacerdotal, or otherwise, which may be placed at the disposal of officials.
3. Methodical provision is made for the regular and continuous fulfilment of these duties and for the execution of the corresponding rights; only persons who have the generally regulated qualifications to serve are employed.

In public and lawful government these three elements constitute "bureaucratic authority." In private economic domination, they constitute bureaucratic "management." Bureaucracy, thus understood, is fully developed in political and ecclesiastical communities only in the modern state, and, in the private economy, only in the most advanced institutions of capitalism. Permanent and public office authority, with fixed jurisdiction, is not the historical rule but rather the exception. This is so even in large political structures such as those of the ancient Orient, the Germanic and Mongolian empires of conquest, or of many feudal structures of state. In all these cases, the ruler executes the most important measures through personal trustees, table-companions, or court-servants. Their commissions and authority are not precisely delimited and are temporarily called into being for each case.

II. The principles of office hierarchy and of levels of graded authority mean a firmly ordered system of super- and subordination in which there is a supervision of the lower offices by the higher ones. Such a system offers the governed the possibility of appealing the decision of a lower office to its higher authority, in a definitely regulated manner. With the full development of the bureaucratic type, the office hierarchy is monocratically organized. The principle of hierarchical office authority is found in all bureaucratic structures: in state and ecclesiastical structures as well as in large party organizations and private enterprises. It does not matter for the character of bureaucracy whether its authority is called "private" or "public."

When the principle of jurisdictional "competency" is fully carried through, hierarchical subordination—at least in public office—does not mean that the "higher" authority is simply authorized to take over the business of the "lower." Indeed, the opposite is the rule. Once established and having fulfilled its task, an office tends to continue in existence and be held by another incumbent.

III. The management of the modern office is based upon written documents ("the files"), which are preserved in their original or draught form. There is, therefore, a staff of subaltern officials and scribes of all sorts. The body of officials actively engaged in a "public" office, along with the respective apparatus of material implements and the files, make up a "bureau." In private enterprise, "the bureau" is often called "the office."

In principle, the modern organization of the civil service separates the bureau from the private domicile of the official, and, in general, bureaucracy segregates official activity as something distinct from the sphere of private life. Public monies and equipment are divorced from the private property of the official. This condition is everywhere the product of a long development. Nowadays, it is found in public as well as in private enterprises; in the latter, the principle extends even to the leading entrepreneur. In principle, the executive office is separated from the household, business from private correspondence, and business assets from private fortunes. The more consistently the modern type of business management has been carried through the more are these separations the case. The beginnings of this process are to be found as early as the Middle Ages.

It is the peculiarity of the modern entrepreneur that he conducts himself as the "first official" of his enterprise, in the very same way in which the ruler of a specifically modern bureaucratic state spoke of himself as "the first servant" of the state. The idea that the bureau activities of the state are intrinsically different in character from the management of private economic offices is a continental European notion and, by way of contrast, is totally foreign to the American way.

IV. Office management, at least all specialized office management—and such management is distinctly modern—usually presupposes thorough and expert training. This increasingly holds for the modern executive and employee of private enterprises, in the same manner as it holds for the state official.

V. When the office is fully developed, official activity demands the full working capacity of the official, irrespective of the fact that his obligatory time in the bureau may be firmly delimited. In the normal case, this is only the product of a long development, in the public as well as in the private office. Formerly, in all cases, the normal state of affairs was reversed: official business was discharged as a secondary activity.

VI. The management of the office follows general rules, which are more or less stable, more or less exhaustive, and which can be learned. Knowledge of these rules represents a special technical learning which the officials possess. It involves jurisprudence, or administrative or business management.

The reduction of modern office management to rules is deeply embedded in its very nature. The theory of modern public administration, for instance, assumes that the authority to order certain matters by decree—which has been legally granted to public authorities—does not entitle the bureau to regulate the matter by commands given for each case, but only to regulate the matter abstractly. This stands in extreme contrast to the regulation of all relationships through individual privileges and bestowals of favor, which is absolutely dominant in patrimonialism, at least in so far as such relationships are not fixed by sacred tradition.

2. The Position of the Official

All this results in the following for the internal and external position of the official:

I. Office holding is a "vocation." This is shown, first, in the requirement of a firmly prescribed course of training, which demands the entire capacity for work for a long period of time, and in the generally prescribed and special examinations which are prerequisites of employment. Furthermore, the position of the official is in the nature of a duty. This determines the internal structure of his relations, in the following manner: Legally and actually, office holding is not considered a source to be exploited for rents or emoluments, as was normally the case during the Middle Ages and frequently up to the threshold of recent times. Nor is office holding considered a usual exchange of services for equivalents, as is the case with free labor contracts. Entrance into an office, including one in the private economy, is considered an acceptance of a specific obligation of faithful management in return for a secure existence. It is decisive for the specific nature of modern loyalty to an office that, in the pure type, it does not establish a relationship to a *person,* like the vassal's or disciple's faith in feudal or in patrimonial relations of authority. Modern loyalty is devoted to impersonal and functional purposes. Behind the functional purposes, of course, "ideas of culture-values" usually stand. These are *ersatz* for the earthly or supra-mundane personal master: ideas such as "state," "church," "community," "party," or "enterprise" are thought of as being realized in a community; they provide an ideological halo for the master.

The political official—at least in the fully developed modern state—is not considered the personal servant of a ruler. Today, the bishop, the priest, and the preacher are in fact no longer, as in early Christian times, holders of purely personal charisma. The supra-mundane and sacred values which they offer are given to everybody who seems to be worthy of them and who asks for them. In former times, such leaders acted upon the personal command of their master; in principle, they were responsible only to him. Nowadays, in spite of the partial survival of the old theory, such religious leaders are officials in the service of a functional purpose, which in the present-day "church" has become routinized and, in turn, ideologically hallowed.

II. The personal position of the official is patterned in the following way:

1. Whether he is in a private office or a public bureau, the modern official always strives and usually enjoys a distinct *social esteem* as compared with the governed. His social position is guaranteed by the prescriptive rules of rank order and, for the political official, by special definitions of the criminal code against "insults of officials" and "contempt" of state and church authorities.

   The actual social position of the official is normally highest where, as in old civilized countries, the following conditions prevail: a strong demand for administration by trained experts; a strong and stable social differentiation, where the official predominantly derives from socially and economically privileged strata because of the social distribution of power; or where the costliness of the required training and status conventions are binding upon him. The possession of educational certificates—to be

discussed elsewhere—are usually linked with qualification for office. Naturally, such certificates or patents enhance the "status element" in the social position of the official. For the rest this status factor in individual cases is explicitly and impassively acknowledged; for example, in the prescription that the acceptance or rejection of an aspirant to an official career depends upon the consent ("election") of the members of the official body. This is the case in the German army with the officer corps. Similar phenomena, which promote this guild-like closure of officialdom, are typically found in patrimonial and, particularly, in prebendal officialdoms of the past. The desire to resurrect such phenomena in changed forms is by no means infrequent among modern bureaucrats. For instance, they have played a role among the demands of the quite proletarian and expert officials (the *tretyj* element) during the Russian revolution.

Usually the social esteem of the officials as such is especially low where the demand for expert administration and the dominance of status conventions are weak. This is especially the case in the United States; it is often the case in new settlements by virtue of their wide fields for profitmaking and the great instability of their social stratification.

2. The pure type of bureaucratic official is *appointed* by a superior authority. An official elected by the governed is not a purely bureaucratic figure. Of course, the formal existence of an election does not by itself mean that no appointment hides behind the election—in the state, especially, appointment by party chiefs. Whether or not this is the case does not depend upon legal statutes but upon the way in which the party mechanism functions. Once firmly organized, the parties can turn a formally free election into the mere acclamation of a candidate designated by the party chief. As a rule, however, a formally free election is turned into a fight, conducted according to definite rules, for votes in favor of one of two designated candidates.

   In all circumstances, the designation of officials by means of an election among the governed modifies the strictness of hierarchical subordination. In principle, an official who is so elected has an autonomous position opposite the superordinate official. The elected official does not derive his position "from above" but "from below," or at least not from a superior authority of the official hierarchy but from powerful party men ("bosses"), who also determine his further career. The career of the elected official is not, or at least not primarily, dependent upon his chief in the administration. The official who is not elected but appointed by a chief normally functions more exactly, from a technical point of view, because, all other circumstances being equal, it is more likely that purely functional points of consideration and qualities will determine his selection and career. As laymen, the governed can become acquainted with the extent to which a candidate is expertly qualified for office only in terms of experience, and hence only after his service. Moreover, in every sort of selection of officials by election, parties quite naturally give decisive weight not to expert considerations but to the services a follower renders to the party boss. This holds for all kinds of procurement of officials by elections, for the designation of formally free, elected officials by party bosses when they determine the slate of candidates, or the free appointment by a chief who has himself been elected. The contrast, however, is relative: Substantially similar conditions hold where legitimate monarchs and their subordinates appoint officials, except that the influence of the followings are then less controllable.

Where the demand for administration by trained experts is considerable, and the party followings have to recognize an intellectually developed, educated, and freely moving "public opinion," the use of unqualified officials falls back upon the party in power at the next election. Naturally, this is more likely to happen when the officials are appointed by the chief. The demand for a trained administration now exists in the United States, but in the large cities, where immigrant votes are "corraled," there is, of course, no educated public opinion. Therefore, popular elections of the administrative chief and also of his subordinate officials usually endanger the expert qualification of the official as well as the precise functioning of the bureaucratic mechanism. It also weakens the dependence of the officials upon the hierarchy. This holds at least for the large administrative bodies that are difficult to supervise. The superior qualification and integrity of federal judges, appointed by the President, as over against elected judges in the United States is well known, although both types of officials have been selected primarily in terms of party considerations. The great changes in American metropolitan administrations demanded by reformers have proceeded essentially from elected mayors working with an apparatus of officials who were appointed by them. These reforms have thus come about in a "Caesarist" fashion. Viewed technically, as an organized form of authority, the efficiency of "Caesarism," which often grows out of democracy, rests in general upon the position of the "Caesar" as a free trustee of the masses (of the army or of the citizenry), who is unfettered by tradition. The "Caesar" is thus the unrestrained master of a body of highly qualified military officers and officials whom he selects freely and personally without regard to tradition or to any other considerations. This "rule of the personal genius," however, stands in contradiction to the formally "democratic" principle of a universally elected officialdom.

3. Normally, the position of the official is held for life, at least in public bureaucracies; and this is increasingly the case for all similar structures. As a factual rule, *tenure for life* is presupposed, even where the giving of notice or periodic reappointment occurs. In contrast to the worker in a private enterprise, the official normally holds tenure. Legal or actual life-tenure, however, is not recognized as the official's right to the possession of office, as was the case with many structures of authority in the past. Where legal guarantees against arbitrary dismissal or transfer are developed, they merely serve to guarantee a strictly objective discharge of specific office duties free from all personal considerations. In Germany, this is the case for all juridical and, increasingly, for all administrative officials.

Within the bureaucracy, therefore, the measure of "independence," legally guaranteed by tenure, is not always a source of increased status for the official whose position is thus secured. Indeed, often the reverse holds, especially in old cultures and communities that are highly differentiated. In such communities, the stricter the subordination under the arbitrary rule of the master, the more it guarantees the maintenance of the conventional seigneurial style of living for the official. Because of the very absence of these legal guarantees of tenure, the conventional esteem for the official may rise in the same way as, during the Middle Ages, the esteem of the nobility of office rose at the expense of esteem for the freemen, and as the king's judge surpassed that of the people's judge. In Germany, the military officer or the administrative official can be removed from office at any time, or at least far more readily than the "independent judge," who never pays with loss of his office for even the grossest offense against the "code of honor" or against social conventions of the salon. For this very reason, if other things are equal, in the eyes of the master stratum the judge is considered less qualified for social intercourse than are officers and administrative officials, whose greater dependence on the master is a greater guarantee of their conformity with status conventions. Of course, the average official strives for a civil-service law, which would materially secure his old age and provide increased guarantees against his arbitrary removal from office. This striving, however, has its limits. A very strong development of the "right to the office" naturally makes it more difficult to staff them with regard to technical efficiency, for such a development decreases the career-opportunities of ambitious candidates for office. This makes for the fact that officials, on the whole, do not feel their dependency upon those at the top. This lack of a feeling of dependency, however, rests primarily upon the inclination to depend upon one's equals rather than upon the socially inferior and governed strata. The present conservative movement among the Badenia clergy, occasioned by the anxiety of a presumably threatening separation of church and state, has been expressly determined by the desire not to be turned "from a master into a servant of the parish."

4. The official receives the regular *pecuniary* compensation of a normally fixed *salary* and the old age security provided by a pension. The salary is not measured like a wage in terms of work done, but according to "status," that is, according to the kind of function (the "rank") and, in addition, possibly, according to the length of service. The relatively great security of the official's income, as well as the rewards of social esteem, make the office a sought-after position, especially in countries which no longer provide opportunities for colonial profits. In such countries, this situation permits relatively low salaries for officials.

5. The official is set for a *"career"* within the hierarchical order of the public service. He moves from the lower, less important, and lower paid to the higher positions. The average official naturally desires a mechanical fixing of the conditions of promotion: if not of the offices, at least of the salary levels. He wants these conditions fixed in terms of "seniority," or possibly according to grades achieved in a developed system of expert examinations. Here and there, such examinations actually form a character *indelebilis* of the official and have lifelong effects on his career. To this is joined the desire to qualify the right to office and the increasing tendency toward status group closure and economic security. All of this makes for a tendency to consider the offices as "prebends" of those who are qualified by educational certificates. The necessity of taking general personal and intellectual qualifications into consideration, irrespective of the often subaltern character of the educational certificate, has led to a condition in which the highest political offices, especially the positions of "ministers," are principally filled without reference to such certificates. . . . [pp. 202–204]

6. Technical Advantages of Bureaucratic Organization

The decisive reason for the advance of bureaucratic organization has always been its purely technical superiority over any other form of organization. The fully developed bureaucratic mechanism compares with other organizations exactly as does the machine with the nonmechanical modes of production.

Precision, speed, unambiguity, knowledge of the files, continuity, discretion, unity, strict subordination, reduction of friction and of material and personal costs—these are raised to the optimum point in the strictly bureaucratic administration, and especially in its monocratic form. As compared with all collegiate, honorific, and avocational forms of administration, trained bureaucracy is superior on all these points. And as far as complicated tasks are concerned, paid bureaucratic work is not only more precise but, in the last analysis, it is often cheaper than even formally unremunerated honorific service.

Honorific arrangements make administrative work an avocation and, for this reason alone, honorific service normally functions more slowly; being less bound to schemata and being more formless. Hence it is less precise and less unified than bureaucratic work because it is less dependent upon superiors and because the establishment and exploitation of the apparatus of subordinate officials and filing services are almost unavoidably less economical. Honorific service is less continuous than bureaucratic and frequently quite expensive. This is especially the case if one thinks not only of the money costs to the public treasury—costs which bureaucratic administration, in comparison with administration by notables, usually substantially increases—but also of the frequent economic losses of the governed caused by delays and lack of precision. The possibility of administration by notables normally and permanently exists only where official management can be satisfactorily discharged as an avocation. With the qualitative increase of tasks the administration has to face, administration by notables reaches its limits—today, even in England. Work organized by collegiate bodies causes friction and delay and requires compromises between colliding interests and views. The administration, therefore, runs less precisely and is more independent of superiors; hence, it is less unified and slower. All advances of the Prussian administrative organization have been and will in the future be advances of the bureaucratic, and especially of the monocratic, principle.

Today, it is primarily the capitalist market economy which demands that the official business of the administration be discharged precisely, unambiguously, continuously, and with as much speed as possible. Normally, the very large, modern capitalist enterprises are themselves unequalled models of strict bureaucratic organization. Business management throughout rests on increasing precision, steadiness, and, above all, the speed of operations. This, in turn, is determined by the peculiar nature of the modern means of communication, including, among other things, the news service of the press. The extraordinary increase in the speed by which public announcements, as well as economic and political facts, are transmitted exerts a steady and sharp pressure in the direction of speeding up the tempo of administrative reaction towards various situations. The optimum of such reaction time is normally attained only by a strictly bureaucratic organization.[2]

Bureaucratization offers above all the optimum possibility for carrying through the principle of specializing administrative functions according to purely objective considerations. Individual performances are allocated to functionaries who have specialized training and who by constant practice learn more and more. The "objective" discharge of business primarily means a discharge of business according to *calculable rules* and "without regard for persons."

"Without regard for persons" is also the watchword of the "market" and, in general, of all pursuits of naked economic interests. A consistent execution of bureaucratic domination means the leveling of status "honor." Hence, if the principle of the free-market is not at the same time restricted, it means the universal domination of the "class situation." That this consequence of bureaucratic domination has not set in everywhere, parallel to the extent of bureaucratization, is due to the differences among possible principles by which polities may meet their demands.

The second element mentioned, "calculable rules," also is of paramount importance for modern bureaucracy. The peculiarity of modern culture, and specifically of its technical and economic basis, demands this very "calculability" of results. When fully developed, bureaucracy also stands, in a specific sense, under the principle of *sine ira ac studio.* Its specific nature, which is welcomed by capitalism, develops the more perfectly the more the bureaucracy is "dehumanized," the more completely it succeeds in eliminating from official business love, hatred, and all purely personal, irrational, and emotional elements which escape calculation. This is the specific nature of bureaucracy and it is appraised as its special virtue.

The more complicated and specialized modern culture becomes, the more its external supporting apparatus demands the personally detached and strictly "objective" *expert,* in lieu of the master of older social structures, who was moved by personal sympathy and favor, by grace and gratitude. Bureaucracy offers the attitudes demanded by the external apparatus of modern culture in the most favorable combination. As a rule, only bureaucracy has established the foundation for the administration of a rational law conceptually systematized on the basis of such enactments as the latter Roman imperial period first created with a high degree of technical perfection. During the Middle Ages, this law was received along with the bureaucratization of legal administration, that is to say, with the displacement of the old trial procedure which was bound to tradition or to irrational presuppositions, by the rationally trained and specialized expert. . . . [pp. 214–216]

10. The Permanent Character of the Bureaucratic Machine

Once it is fully established, bureaucracy is among those social structures which are the hardest to destroy. Bureaucracy is *the* means of carrying "community action" over into rationally ordered "societal action." Therefore, as an instrument for "societalizing" relations of power, bureaucracy has been and is a power instrument of the first order—for the one who controls the bureaucratic apparatus.

Under otherwise equal conditions, a "societal action," which is methodically ordered and led, is superior to every resistance of "mass" or even of "communal action." And where the bureaucratization of administration has been completely carried through,

a form of power relation is established that is practically unshatterable.

The individual bureaucrat cannot squirm out of the apparatus in which he is harnessed. In contrast to the honorific or avocational "notable," the professional bureaucrat is chained to his activity by his entire material and ideal existence. In the great majority of cases, he is only a single cog in an evermoving mechanism which prescribes to him an essentially fixed route of march. The official is entrusted with specialized tasks and normally the mechanism cannot be put into motion or arrested by him, but only from the very top. The individual bureaucrat is thus forged to the community of all the functionaries who are integrated into the mechanism. They have a common interest in seeing that the mechanism continues its functions and that the societally exercised authority carries on.

The ruled, for their part, cannot dispense with or replace the bureaucratic apparatus of authority once it exists. For this bureaucracy rests upon expert training, a functional specialization of work, and an attitude set for habitual and virtuoso-like mastery of single yet methodically integrated functions. If the official stops working, or if his work is forcefully interrupted, chaos results, and it is difficult to improvise replacements from among the governed who are fit to master such chaos. This holds for public administration as well as for private economic management. More and more the material fate of the masses depends upon the steady and correct functioning of the increasingly bureaucratic organizations of private capitalism. The idea of eliminating these organizations becomes more and more utopian.

The discipline of officialdom refers to the attitude-set of the official for precise obedience within his *habitual* activity, in public as well as in private organizations. This discipline increasingly becomes the basis of all order, however great the practical importance of administration on the basis of the filed documents may be. The naive idea of Bakuninism of destroying the basis of "acquired rights" and "domination" by destroying public documents overlooks the settled orientation of *man* for keeping to the habitual rules and regulations that continue to exist independently of the documents. Every reorganization of beaten or dissolved troops, as well as the restoration of administrative orders destroyed by revolt, panic, or other catastrophes, is realized by appealing to the trained orientation of obedient compliance to such orders. Such compliance has been conditioned into the officials, on the one hand, and, on the other hand, into the governed. If such an appeal is successful it brings, as it were, the disturbed mechanism into gear again.

The objective indispensability of the once-existing apparatus, with its peculiar, "impersonal" character, means that the mechanism—in contrast to feudal orders based upon personal piety—is easily made to work for anybody who knows how to gain control over it. A rationally ordered system of officials continues to function smoothly after the enemy has occupied the area; he merely needs to change the top officials. This body of officials continues to operate because it is to the vital interest of everyone concerned, including above all the enemy.

During the course of his long years in power, Bismarck brought his ministerial colleagues into unconditional bureaucratic dependence by eliminating all independent statesmen. Upon his retirement, he saw to his surprise that they continued to manage their offices unconcerned and undismayed, as if he had not been the master mind and creator of these creatures, but rather as if some single figure had been exchanged for some other figure in the bureaucratic machine. With all the changes of masters in France since the time of the First Empire, the power machine has remained essentially the same. Such a machine makes "revolution," in the sense of the forceful creation of entirely new formations of authority, technically more and more impossible, especially when the apparatus controls the modern means of communication (telegraph, et cetera) and also by virtue of its internal rationalized structure. In classic fashion, France has demonstrated how this process has substituted *coups d'état* for "revolutions": all successful transformations in France have amounted to *coups d'état*.

11. Economic and Social Consequences of Bureaucracy

It is clear that the bureaucratic organization of a social structure, and especially of a political one, can and

regularly does have far-reaching economic consequences. But what sort of consequences? Of course in any individual case it depends upon the distribution of economic and social power, and especially upon the sphere that is occupied by the emerging bureaucratic mechanism. The consequences of bureaucracy depend therefore upon the direction which the powers using the apparatus give to it. And very frequently a crypto-plutocratic distribution of power has been the result.

In England, but especially in the United States, party donors regularly stand behind the bureaucratic party organizations. They have financed these parties and have been able to influence them to a large extent. The breweries in England, the so-called "heavy industry," and in Germany the Hansa League with their voting funds are well enough known as political donors to parties. In modern times bureaucratization and social leveling within political, and particularly within state organizations in connection with the destruction of feudal and local privileges, have very frequently benefited the interests of capitalism. Often bureaucratization has been carried out in direct alliance with capitalist interests, for example, the great historical alliance of the power of the absolute prince with capitalist interests. In general, a legal leveling and destruction of firmly established local structures ruled by notables has usually made for a wider range of capitalist activity. Yet one may expect as an effect of bureaucratization, a policy that meets the petty bourgeois interest in a secured traditional "subsistence," or even a state socialist policy that strangles opportunities for private profit. This has occurred in several cases of historical and far-reaching importance, specifically during antiquity; it is undoubtedly to be expected as a future development. Perhaps it will occur in Germany.

The very different effects of political organizations which were, at least in principle, quite similar—in Egypt under the Pharaohs and in Hellenic and Roman times—show the very different economic significances of bureaucratization which are possible according to the direction of other factors. The mere fact of bureaucratic organization does not unambiguously tell us about the concrete direction of its economic effects, which are always in some manner present. At least it does not tell us as much as can be told about its relatively leveling effect socially. In this respect, one has to remember that bureaucracy as such is a precision instrument which can put itself at the disposal of quite varied—purely political as well as purely economic, or any other sort—of interests in domination. Therefore, the measure of its parallelism with democratization must not be exaggerated, however typical it may be. Under certain conditions, strata of feudal lords have also put bureaucracy into their service. There is also the possibility—and often it has become a fact, for instance, in the Roman principate and in some forms of absolutist state structures—that a bureaucratization of administration is deliberately connected with the formation of *estates,* or is entangled with them by the force of the existing groupings of social power. The express reservation of offices for certain status groups is very frequent, and actual reservations are even more frequent. The democratization of society in its totality, and in the *modern* sense of the term, whether actual or perhaps merely formal, is an especially favorable basis of bureaucratization, but by no means the only possible one. After all, bureaucracy strives merely to level those powers that stand in its way and in those areas that, in the individual case, it seeks to occupy. We must remember this fact—which we have encountered several times and which we shall have to discuss repeatedly: that "democracy" as such is opposed to the "rule" of bureaucracy, in spite and perhaps because of its unavoidable yet unintended promotion of bureaucratization. Under certain conditions, democracy creates obvious ruptures and blockages to bureaucratic organization. Hence, in every individual historical case, one must observe in what special direction bureaucratization has developed.

12. The Power Position of Bureaucracy

Everywhere the modern state is undergoing bureaucratization. But whether the *power* of bureaucracy within the polity is universally increasing must here remain an open question.

The fact that bureaucratic organization is technically the most highly developed means of power in the hands of the man who controls it does not determine the weight that bureaucracy as such is capable of having in a particular social structure. The ever-increasing "indispensability" of the officialdom, swollen to millions, is no more decisive for this question than is the view of some representatives of the proletarian movement that the economic indispensability of the proletarians is decisive for the measure of their social and political power position. If "indispensability" were decisive, then where slave labor prevailed and where freemen usually abhor work as a dishonor, the "indispensable" slaves ought to have held the positions of power, for they were at least as indispensable as officials and proletarians are today. Whether the power of bureaucracy as such increases cannot be decided *a priori* from such reasons. The drawing in of economic interest groups or other non-official experts, or the drawing in of non-expert lay representatives, the establishment of local, inter-local, or central parliamentary or other representative bodies, or of occupational associations—these *seem* to run directly against the bureaucratic tendency. How far this appearance is the truth must be discussed in another chapter rather than in this purely formal and typological discussion. In general, only the following can be said here:

Under normal conditions, the power position of a fully developed bureaucracy is always overtowering. The "political master" finds himself in the position of the "dilettante" who stands opposite the "expert," facing the trained official who stands within the management of administration. This holds whether the "master" whom the bureaucracy serves is a "people," equipped with the weapons of "legislative initiative," the "referendum," and the right to remove officials, or a parliament, elected on a more aristocratic or more "democratic" basis and equipped with the right to vote a lack of confidence, or with the actual authority to vote it. It holds whether the master is an aristocratic, collegiate body, legally or actually based on self-recruitment, or whether he is a popularly elected president, a hereditary and "absolute" or a "constitutional" monarch. . . . [pp. 228–233]

Notes

1. *Wirtschaft und Gesellschaft,* part III, chap. 6, pp. 650–78.

2. Here we cannot discuss in detail how the bureaucratic apparatus may, and actually does, produce definite obstacles to the discharge of business in a manner suitable for the single case.

☐ CASE STUDY 2

Introduction

At first glance, the following story may seem out of place—or odd—to follow such a highly abstract and theoretical essay by Max Weber. It is a personal story told by a father, George Lardner, who recounts the details of the shooting death of his 21-year-old daughter Kristin on May 30, 1992. She had been raised in Washington, D.C., and was living in Boston, studying in a fine arts program, jointly sponsored by the Museum of Fine Arts and Tufts University. For two and a half months she had been dating 22-year-old Michael Cartier, a local nightclub bouncer, but had broken up with him on April 16. That night he became violent, beating her up a few blocks from her apartment. Increasingly he became obsessed by her rejection of him.

What follows is a sorry tale of Kristin's attempts to rely on the bureaucratic system and the subsequent breakdown of that system to protect her from a brutal "stalker." Although it is about the worst nightmares of women—and their parents and friends—the study dispassionately probes the background of Cartier and the reasons why "the system" left him "on the street," which ultimately led to Kristin's death as well as Cartier's. In the process of recounting the events surrounding this tragedy, the author, perhaps unconsciously, underscores the importance of a well-functioning, effective bureaucracy, one containing many of the key elements outlined in the foregoing essay by Max Weber, in order to protect the lives and safety of all of us.

As you read this selection, try to reflect on the following:

What were the chief elements in the overall bureaucratic system that failed to protect Kristin?

What caused their breakdown?

How does Weber's conceptualization of bureaucracy help us to understand bureaucracy, its role in society and sources of failure—as well as strengths?

Does this story "square" with Weber's conception of bureaucracy and the vital role he believed it fulfilled in modern society?

Do Weber's generalizations fit or fail to fit the American experience as portrayed by this case? The basic design of bureaucracy? Its formal scope and powers? Its informal influence on our lives? Sources of problems of modern bureaucracy?

How Kristin Died

GEORGE LARDNER, JR.

The phone was ringing insistently, hurrying me back to my desk. My daughter Helen was on the line, sobbing so hard she could barely catch her breath. "Dad," she shouted. "Come home! Right away!"

I was stunned. I had never heard her like this before. "What's wrong?" I asked. "What happened?"

"It's—it's Kristin. She's been shot . . . and killed."

Kristin? My Kristin? Our Kristin? I'd talked to her the afternoon before. Her last words to me were, "I love you Dad." Suddenly I had trouble breathing myself.

It was 7:30 p.m. on Saturday, May 30. In Boston, where Kristin Lardner was an art student, police were cordoning off an apartment building a couple of blocks from the busy, sunlit sidewalk where she'd been killed 90 minutes earlier. She had been shot in the head and face by an ex-boyfriend who was under court order to stay away from her. When police burst into his apartment, they found him sprawled on his bed, dead from a final act of self-pity.

This was a crime that could and should have been prevented. I write about it as a sort of cautionary tale, in anger at a system of justice that failed to protect my daughter, a system that is addicted to looking the other way, especially at the evil done to women.

But first let me tell you about my daughter.

She was, at 21, the youngest of our five children, born in Washington, D.C., and educated in the city's public schools, where not much harm befell her unless you count her taste for rock music, lots of jewelry, and funky clothes from Value Village. She loved books, went trick-or-treating dressed as Greta Garbo, played one of the witches in "Macbeth" and had a grand time in tap-dancing class even in her sneakers. She made life sparkle.

When she was small, she always got up in time for Saturday morning cartoons at the Chevy Chase library, and she took cheerful care of a succession of cats, mice, gerbils, hamsters and guinea pigs. Her biggest fault may have been that she took too long in the shower—and you never knew what color her hair was going to be

when she emerged. She was compassionate, and strong-minded too; when a boy from high school dropped his pants in front of her, Kristin knocked out one of his front teeth.

"She didn't back down from anything," said Amber Lynch, a close friend from Boston University. "You could tell that basically from her art, the way she dressed, the opinions she had. If you said something stupid, she'd tell you."

Midway through high school, Kristin began thinking of becoming an artist. She'd been taking art and photography classes each summer at the Corcoran School of Art and was encouraged when an art teacher at Wilson High decided two of her paintings were good enough to go on display at a little gallery there. She began studies at Boston University's art school and transferred after two years to a fine arts program run jointly by the School of the Museum of Fine Arts and Tufts University. She particularly liked to sculpt and make jewelry and, in the words of one faculty member, "showed great promise and was extremely talented."

In her apartment were scattered signs of that talent. Three wide-banded silver and brass rings, one filigreed with what looked like barbed wire. Some striking sculptures of bound figures. A Madonna, painstakingly gilded. A nude self-portrait in angry reds, oranges and yellows, showing a large leg bruise her ex-boyfriend had given her on their last date in April.

"It felt as though she was telling all her secrets to the world," she wrote of her art in an essay she left behind. "Why would anyone want to know them anyway? But making things was all she wanted to do. . . . She always had questions, but never any answers, just frustration and confusion, and a need to get out whatever lay inside of her, hoping to be meaningful."

Kristin wrote that essay last November for a course at Tufts taught by Ross Ellenhorn, who also happens to be a counselor at Emerge, an educational program for abusive men. He had once mentioned this to his students. He would hear from my daughter in April, after she met Michael Cartier.

By then, Kristin had been dating Cartier, a 22-year-old bouncer, for about two and a half months. She broke

"The Stalking of Kristin: The Law Made It Easy for My Daughter's Killer," George Lardner, Jr., *The Washington Post*, November 22, 1992. Reprinted by permission.

off with him on the early morning of April 16. On that night, a few blocks from her apartment, he beat her up.

They "became involved in an argument and he knocked her to the ground and started kicking her over and over," reads a Brookline, Mass., police report. "She remembers him saying, 'Get up or I'll kill you.' She staggered to her feet, a car stopped and two men assisted her home.

"Since that night," the report continues, "she has refused to see him, but he repeatedly calls her, sometimes 10 or 11 times a day. He has told her that if she reports him to the police, he might have to do six months in jail, but she better not be around when he gets out.

"She also stated the injuries she suffered were hematomas to her legs and recurring headaches from the kicks."

Kristin didn't call the police right away. But she did call Ellenhorn in hopes of getting Cartier into Emerge. "I made clear to her that Emerge isn't a panacea, that there was still a chance of him abusing her," Ellenhorn says. "I told her that he could kill her . . . because she was leaving him and that's when things get dangerous."

Cartier showed up at Emerge's offices in Cambridge, around April 28 by Ellenhorn's calculations. Ellenhorn, on duty that night, realized who Cartier was when he wrote down Kristin's name under victim on the intake form.

"I said, 'Are you on probation?' " Ellenhorn remembers. "He said yes. I said, 'I'm going to need the name of the probation officer.' He said, '[Expletive] this. No way.' "

With that, Cartier ripped up the contract he was required to sign, ripped up the intake form, put the tattered papers in his pocket and walked out.

"He knew," Ellenhorn says. "He knew what kind of connection would be made." Michael Cartier was, of course, on probation for attacking another woman.

Cartier preyed on women. Clearly disturbed, he once talked of killing his mother. When he was 5 or 6, he dismembered a pet rabbit. When he was 21, he tortured and killed a kitten. In a bizarre 1989 incident at an Andover restaurant, he injected a syringe of blood into a ketchup bottle. To his girlfriends, he could be appallingly brutal.

Rose Ryan could tell you that. When Kristin's murder was reported on TV—the newscaster described the killing as "another case of domestic violence"—she said to a friend, "That sounds like Mike." It was. Hearing the newscaster say his name, she recalls, "I almost dropped."

When Ryan met Cartier at a party in Boston in the late summer of 1990, she was an honors graduate of Lynn East High School, preparing to attend Suffolk University. She was 17, a lovely, courageous girl with brown hair and brown eyes like Kristin's.

"He was really my first boyfriend," she told me. "I was supposed to work that summer and save my money, but I got caught up with the scene in Boston and hanging out with all the kids. . . . At first, everything was fine."

Cartier was a familiar face on the Boston Common, thanks to his career as a freelance nightclub bouncer. He had scraped up enough money to share a Commonwealth Avenue apartment with a Museum School student named Kara Boettger. They dated a few times, then settled down into a sort of strained coexistence.

"He didn't like me very much," Boettger said. "He liked music loud. I'd tell him to turn it down."

Rose Ryan liked him better. She thought he was handsome—blue eyes, black hair, a tall and muscular frame—with a vulnerability that belied his strength. To make him happy, she quit work and postponed the college education it was going to pay for. "He had me thinking that he'd had a bad deal his whole life," she said, "that nobody loved him and I was the only one who could help him."

Cartier also knew how to behave when he was supposed to. Ryan said he made a good first impression on her parents. As with Kristin, it took just about two months before Cartier beat Ryan up. She got angry with him for "kidding around" and dumping her into a barrel on the Common. When she walked away, he punched her in the head; when she kept going, he punched her again.

"I'd never been hit by any man before and I was just shocked," she said. But what aggravated her the most, and still does, is that "every time something happened, it was in public, and nobody stopped to help."

Cartier ended the scene with "his usual thing," breaking into tears and telling her, "'Oh, why do I always hurt the people I love? What can I do? My mother didn't love me. I need your help.' "

Shortly after they started dating, Ryan spent a few days at the Cartier-Boetgger apartment. He presented her with a gray kitten, then left it alone all day without a litter box. The kitten did what it needed to do on Cartier's jacket.

"He threw the kitten in the shower and turned the hot water on and kept it there under the hot water," Ryan remembers in a dull monotone. "And he shaved all its hair off with a man's shaving razor."

The kitten spent most of its wretched life hiding under a bed. On the night of Oct. 4, 1990, Cartier began drinking with two friends and went on a rampage. He took a sledgehammer and smashed through his bedroom wall into a neighbor's apartment. And he killed the kitten, hurling it out a fourth-floor window.

"I'd left the apartment without telling them," Ryan said. "When I came back, the police were in the hallway. . . . They said, 'Get out. This guy's crazy.' They were taking him out in handcuffs."

Three months later, Cartier, already on probation, plea-bargained his way to probation again—pleading guilty to malicious destruction. Charges of burglary and cruelty to animals were dismissed; the court saw nothing wrong with putting him back on the street.

"I thought he was going to jail because he violated probation," Kara Boettger said. So did Cartier. "[But after the January hearing] he told me . . . 'Oh yeah, nothing happened. They slapped my wrist.' "

When Michael Cartier was born in Newburyport, Mass., his mother was 17. Her husband, then 19, left them six months later; Gene Cartier has since remarried twice. Her son, Penny Cartier says, was a problem from the first.

"He'd take a bottle away from his [step]sister. He'd light matches behind a gas stove. He was born that way," Penny Cartier asserted. "When he was five or six, he had a rabbit. He ripped its legs out of its sockets."

"None of this," she added in loud tones, "had anything to do with what he did to Kristin. . . . Michael's childhood had nothing to do with anything."

Life with mother, in any case, ended at age 7, when she sent him to the New England Home for Little Wanderers, a state-supported residential treatment center for troubled children. Staff there remember him—although Penny Cartier denies this—as a child abused at an early age. "That's the worst childhood I've ever seen," agrees Rich DeAngelis, one of Cartier's probation officers. "This didn't just happen in the last couple of years."

Cartier stayed at the New England Home until he was 12. In October 1982, he was put in the Harbor School in Amesbury, a treatment center for disturbed teenagers. He stayed there for almost four years and was turned over to his father, a facilities maintenance mechanic in Lawrence.

Michael Cartier was bitter about his mother. "I just know he hated her," Kara Boettger said. "He said he wanted to get a tattoo, I think maybe on his arm, of her hanging from a tree with animals ripping at her body."

Penny Cartier didn't seem surprised when I told her this. In fact, she added, after he turned 18, "he asked my daughter if she wanted him to kill me."

Cartier entered Lawrence High School but dropped out after a couple of years. "He was just getting frustrated. He couldn't keep up," said his father. By his second semester, he was facing the first of nearly 20 criminal charges that he piled up in courthouses from Lawrence to Brighton over a four-year period.

Along the way, he enjoyed brief notoriety as a self-avowed skinhead, sauntering into the newsroom of the Lawrence Eagle-Tribune with his bald friends in June 1989 to complain of the bad press and "neo-Nazi" labels skinheads usually got. "The state supported me all my life, with free doctors and dentists and everything," Cartier told columnist Kathie Neff. "My parents never had anything to do with that because they got rid of me. This is like my way of saying thanks [to them]."

Neff said Cartier cut an especially striking figure, walking on crutches and wearing a patch on one eye. He had just survived a serious car accident that produced what seems to have been a magic purse for him. He told friends he had a big insurance settlement coming and would get periodic advances on it from his lawyer. Gene Cartier said his son got a final payment late last year of $17,000 and "went through $14,000" of it before he murdered Kristin.

The high-ceilinged main courtroom in Brighton has a huge, wide-barred cell built into a wall. On busy days, it is a page from Dickens, crowded with yelling, cursing prisoners waiting for their cases to be called.

Cartier turned up in the cage April 29, 1991, finally arrested for violating probation. Ten days earlier, when Rose Ryan was coming home from a friend's house on the "T," Boston's trolley train and subway system, Cartier followed her—and accosted her at the Government Center station with a pair of scissors. She ducked the scissors and Cartier punched her in the mouth.

Even before that, Ryan and her older sister Tina had become alarmed. After a party in December, Cartier got annoyed with Rose for not wanting to eat pizza he'd just bought. She began walking back to the party when he back-handed her in the face so hard she fell down. "And I'm lying on the ground, screaming, and then he finally stopped kicking me after I don't know how long, and then he said, 'You better get up or I'll kill you.' "

The same words he would use with Kristin. And how many other young women?

Rose Ryan said Cartier threatened to kill her several times after they broke up in December and, in a chance encounter in March, told her he had a gun. The Ryan sisters called his probation officer in Brighton, Tom Casey. He told Rose to get a restraining order and, on March 28, he obtained a warrant for Cartier's arrest. It took a month for police to pick him up even though Cartier had, in between, attacked Rose in the subway and been arraigned on charges for that assault in Boston Municipal Court.

"Probation warrants have to be served by the police, who don't take them seriously enough," said another probation officer. "Probationers know . . . they can skip court appearances with impunity."

When Cartier turned up in Brighton, "he was very quiet. Sullen and withdrawn," Casey said. "It was obvious he had problems, deeper than I could ever get to." Yet a court psychiatrist, Dr. Mike Annunziata, filed a report stating that Cartier had "no acute mental disorder, no suicidal or homicidal ideas, plans or intents." The April 29, 1991, report noted that Cartier was being treated by the Tri-City Mental Health and Retardation Center in Malden and was taking 300 milligrams of lithium a day to control depression.

Cartier, the report said, had also spent four days in January 1991 at the Massachusetts Mental Health Center in Boston. He was brought there on a "Section 12," a law providing for emergency restraint of dangerous persons, because of "suicidal ideation" and an overdose of some sort. On April 2, 1991, he was admitted to the Center on another "Section 12," this time for talking about killing Rose Ryan with a gun "within two weeks." He denied making the threats and was released the next day.

Tom Casey wanted to get him off the streets this time, and a like-minded visiting magistrate ordered Cartier held on bail for a full hearing in Brighton later in the week. When the Ryan sisters arrived in court, they found themselves five feet away from Cartier in the cell. "Soon as he saw me," Tina Ryan said, "he said, 'I know who you are, I'm going to kill you too,' all these filthy words, calling me everything he could. . . ."

After listening to what the Ryans had to say, the judge sent Cartier to jail on Deer Island for three months for violating probation. The next month, he was given a year for the subway attack, but was committed for only six months.

That didn't stop the harassment. Cartier began making collect calls to Ryan from prison and he enlisted other inmates to write obscene letters. The district attorney's office advised the Ryans to keep a record of the calls so they could be used against Cartier later.

Despite all that, Cartier was released early, on Nov. 5, 1991. "'He's been a very good prisoner and we're overcrowded,'" the Ryans say they were told.

Authorities in Essex County didn't want to see him out on the streets even if officials in Boston didn't care. As soon as he was released from Deer Island, Cartier was picked up for violating his probation on the ketchup-bottle incident and sentenced to 59 days in the Essex County jail. But a six-month suspended sentence that was hanging over him for a 1988 burglary—which would have meant at least three months in jail—was wiped off the books.

"That's amazing," said another probation officer who looked at the record. "They dropped the more serious charges."

Cartier was released after serving 49 of the 59 days.

Ryan had already been taking precautions. She carried Mace in her pocketbook, put a baseball bat in her car and laid out a bunch of knives next to her bed each night before going to sleep. "I always thought that he would come back and try to get me," she said.

Kristin loved to go out with friends until all hours of the morning, but she didn't have many steady boyfriends. Most men, she said more than once, "are dogs" because of the way they treated girls she knew.

She was always ready for adventure, hopping on the back of brother Charles's motorcycle for rides; curling up with Circe, a pet ball-python she kept in her room; and flying down for a few weeks almost every August to Jekyll Island, Ga., to be with her family, a tradition started when she was less than a week old. Last year she caught a small shark from the drawbridge over the Jekyll River.

"I think she'd give anything a go," said Jason Corkin, the young man she dated the longest, before he returned last year to his native New Zealand. "When she set her mind to something, she wouldn't give it up for anything."

She could also become easily depressed, especially about what she was going to do after graduation. As she once wrote, her favorite pastime was "morbid self-reflection." Despite that, laughter came easily and she was always ready for a conversation about art, religion, philosophy, music. "I don't really remember any time we were together that we didn't have a good time," said Bekky Elstad, a close friend from Boston University.

Left in her bedroom at her death was a turntable with Stravinsky's "Rites of Spring" on it and a tape player with a punk tune by Suicidal Tendencies. Her books, paperbacks mostly, included Alice Walker's "The Color Purple" and Margaret Atwood's "The Handmaid's Tale," along with favorites by Sinclair Lewis, Dickens and E.B. White and a book about upper- and middle-caste women in Hindu families in Calcutta.

Her essays for school, lucid and well-written, showed a great deal of thought about art, religion and the relationship between men and women. She saw her art as an expression of parts of her hidden deep inside, waiting to be pulled out, but still to be guarded closely: "Art could be such a selfish thing. Everything she made, she made for herself and not one bit of it could she bear to be parted with. Whether she loved it, despised it or was painfully ashamed of it . . . she couldn't stand the thought of these little parts of her being taken away and put into someone else's possession."

Buddhism appealed to her, and once she wrote this: "Pain only comes when you try to hang on to what is impermanent. So all life need not be suffering. You can enjoy life if you do not expect anything from it."

She met Cartier last Jan. 30 at a Boston nightclub called Axis, having gone there with Lauren Mace, Kristin's roommate and best friend, and Lauren's boyfriend. At Axis, Kristin recognized Cartier as someone she'd seen at Bunratty's, a hard-rock club where Cartier had been a bouncer. Cartier was easily recognizable; he had a large tattoo of a castle on his neck.

What did she see in him? It's a question her parents keep asking themselves. But some things are fairly obvious. He reminded her of Jason, her friend from New Zealand. He could be charming. "People felt a great deal of empathy for him," said Octavia Ossola, director of the child care center at the home where Cartier grew up, "because it was reasonably easy to want things to be better for him." At the Harbor School, said executive director Art DiMauro, "he was quite endearing. The staff felt warmly about Michael."

So, at first, did Kristin. "She called me up, really excited and happy," said Christian Dupre, a friend since childhood. "She said 'I met this good guy, he's really nice.' "

Kristin told her oldest sister, Helen, and her youngest brother, Charlie, too. But Helen paused when Kristin told her that Cartier was a bouncer at Bunratty's and had a tattoo.

"Well, ah, is he nice?" Helen asked.

"Well, he's nice to me," Kristin said.

Charlie, who had just entered college after a few years of blue-collar jobs, was not impressed. "Get rid of him," he advised his sister. "He's a zero."

Her friends say they got along well at first. He told Kristin he'd been in jail for hitting a girlfriend, but called it a bum rap. She did not know he'd attacked Rose Ryan with scissors, that he had a rap sheet three pages long.

Kristin, friends say, often made excuses for his behavior. But they soon started to argue. Cartier was irrationally jealous, accusing her of going out with men who stopped by just to talk. During one argument, apparently over her art, Cartier hit her, then did his "usual thing" and started crying.

Cartier, meanwhile, was still bothering Ryan. A warrant for violating probation had been issued out of Boston Municipal Court on Dec. 19, in part for trying to contact her by mail while he was in jail. But when he finally turned up in court, a few days before he met Kristin, he got kid-glove treatment. Rather than being sentenced to complete the one-year term he'd gotten for the scissors attack, he was ordered instead to attend a once-a-week class at the courthouse for six weeks called "Alternatives to Violence."

"It's not a therapy program, it's more educational," said John Tobin, chief probation officer at Boston Municipal Court. "It's for people who react to stress in violent ways, not just for batterers. Cartier . . . showed up each time. You don't send probationers away when they do what they're supposed to do."

What Tobin didn't mention was that Cartier had actually dropped out of his Alternatives to Violence course—and, incredibly, was allowed to sign up for it again. According to a chronology I obtained elsewhere, Cartier attended the first meeting of the group on Feb. 5 and skipped the class Feb. 12. His probation was revoked two days later. But instead of sending him back to jail, the court allowed him to start the course over, beginning April 1.

Cartier's probation officer, Diane Barrett Moeller, a "certified batterer specialist" who helps run the program, declined to talk to me, citing "legal limitations" that she did not spell out. Her boss, Tobin, said she was "a ferocious probation officer."

"We tend to be a punitive department," Tobin asserted. "We are not a bunch of social rehabilitators."

However that may be, it is a department that seems to operate in a vacuum. Cartier's record of psychiatric problems, his admissions to the Boston mental health center in January and April 1991 and his reliance on a drug to control manic-depression should have disqualified him from the court-run violence program.

"If we had information that he had a prior history of mental illness, or that he was treated in a clinic or that he had been hospitalized, then what we probably would have done is recommend that a full-scale psychological evaluation be done for him," Tobin told the Boston Herald last June following Kristin's murder. "We didn't know about it."

Probation officer Tom Casey in Brighton knew. All Tobin's office had to do was pick up the phone to find out what a menace Cartier was. Meanwhile, in Salem, where she had moved to work with her sister at a family-run business, Rose Ryan remained fearful. But she had a new boyfriend, Sean Casey, 23, and, as Rose puts it, "I think he intimidated Mike because he had more tattoos. Mike knew Sean from before."

Around March 1, Sean went to Boston to tell Cartier to leave Rose alone. As they were talking, Kristin walked by. Sean didn't know who she was, but recognized her later, from newspaper photos.

Cartier nodded at Kristin as she passed. "He said, 'I don't need Rose any more,'" Casey recalled. "'I have my own girlfriend.'"

Cartier was a frequent visitor at the six-room flat Kristin shared with Lauren Mace and another BU student, Matt Newton, but he didn't have much to say to them or the other students who were always stopping by. He told Kristin they "intimidated" him because they were college-educated.

As the weeks wore on, they started to argue. When he hit her the first time, probably in early March, Kristin told friends about it, but not Lauren. She was probably too embarrassed. She had always been outspoken in her disdain for men who hit women.

"He hit her once. She freaked out on that . . . ," Bekky Elstad said. "She wanted him to get counseling. . . . He told her he was sorry. He was all broken up. She wanted to believe him."

Kristin came home to Washington in mid-March, outwardly bright and cheerful. She was more enthusiastic than ever about her art. She was "really getting it together," she said. She had yet to tell her parents that she had a boyfriend, much less a boyfriend who hit her.

When she got back to Boston, Cartier tried to make up with her. He gave her a kitten. "It was really cute—black with a little white triangle on its nose," Amber Lynch said. "It was teeny. It just wobbled around."

It didn't last long. Over Kristin's protests, Cartier put the kitten on top of a door jamb. It fell off, landing on its head. She had to have it destroyed.

Devastated, Kristin called home in tears and told her parents, for the first time, about her new boyfriend. Part of her conversation with her mother was picked up by a malfunctioning answering machine.

Rosemary: What does Mike do?
Kristin: Well, he does the same thing Jason did actually. He works at Bunratty's.
Rosemary: He does what?
Kristin: He works at Bunratty's.
Rosemary: Oh. Is he an artist also?
Kristin: No.
Rosemary: Well, that's what I was asking. What does he—? Is he a student?
Kristin: No. He just—he works. He's a bouncer.

"Oh," Rosemary said, asking after a long pause why she was going out with a boy with no education. Kristin told her that she wanted to have a boyfriend "just like everyone else does."

When I came home, Rosemary said, "Call your daughter." When I did, Kristin began crying again as she told me about the kitten. She was also upset because she had given Cartier a piece of jewelry she wanted to use for her annual evaluation at the Museum School. He told her he'd lost it.

Gently, perhaps too gently, I said I didn't think she should be wasting her time going out with a boy who did such stupid things. We talked about school and classes for a few minutes more and said goodnight.

She went out with him for the last time on April 16, the day after one of his Alternatives to Violence classes. He pushed her down onto the sidewalk in front of a fast-food place, cutting her hand. She told him several times to "go home and leave me alone," but he kept following her to a side street in Allston.

"Kristin said something like, 'Get away from me, I never want to see you again,'" Bekky Elstad remembers. But when Kristin tried to run, he caught up with her, threw her down and kicked her repeatedly in the head and legs. She was crying hysterically when she got home with the help of a passing motorist. She refused to see him again.

But Cartier kept trying to get her on the phone. He warned her not to go to the police and, for a while, she didn't. She felt sorry for him. She even agreed to take a once-a-week phone call from him the day he went to his Alternatives to Violence class.

He was rated somewhat passive at the meetings, but he got through the course on May 6 without more truancy. The next day, he walked into Gay's Flowers and Gifts on Commonwealth Avenue and bought a dozen red roses for Kristin. He brought in a card to be delivered with them.

Leslie North, a dark-haired, puffy-faced woman who had known Cartier for years, had helped him fill it out in advance. "He always called me when he had a fight with his girlfriends," she said. "He said that he was trying to change, that he needed help, that he wanted to be a better person. He said, 'I'm trying to get back with her.' "

Flower shop proprietor Alan Najarian made the delivery to Kristin's flat. "One of her roommates took them," Najarian remembers. "He was kind of reluctant. . . . I think he must have known who they were from."

Police think Cartier may have gotten his gun the day of the murder, but Leslie North remembers his showing it to her "shortly after [he and Kristin] broke up," probably in early May.

Why did he get the gun? "He said, 'Ah, just to have one,' " North says. "I asked him, 'What do you need a gun for?' He said, 'You never know.' I didn't realize you're not supposed to get a gun if you've been in jail. I didn't tell anyone he had it."

"He told me he paid $750 for it," she continues. "I showed him just a little bit of safety . . . how to hold it when you shoot. . . . It looked kind of old to me."

The gun found in Cartier's apartment after he killed Kristin and himself was 61 years old, a Colt .38 Super, serial number 13645, one of about a 100 million handguns loose in the United States. It was shipped brand new on Jan. 12, 1932, to a hardware store in Knoxville, Tenn., where all traces of it disappeared.

North remembered something else she says Cartier told her after he got the gun. "He goes, 'If I kill Kristin, are you going to tell anyone?'

"I said, 'Of course, I'm going to tell.' I didn't take him seriously. . . . He said that once or twice to me."

On May 7, the same day Cartier sent flowers to Kristin, he told her that he was going to cheat her out of the $1,000 Nordic Flex machine she'd let him charge to her Discover card. When she told him over the phone that she expected him to return the device, he laughed and said, "I guess you're out the $1,000."

Kristin was furious. She promptly called Cartier's probation officer, Diane Barrett Moeller, and gave her an earful: the exercise machine, the beating.

Kristin's call for help was another of the probation office's secrets. Tobin said nothing about it to the Boston press in the days after Kristin's murder, when it grew clear that there was something desperately wrong with the criminal justice system. Tobin told me only after I found out about it from Kristin's friends.

"Your daughter was concerned," Tobin said. "She put a lot of emphasis on the weight machine. Mrs. Moeller said, 'Get your priorities straight. You should not be worrying about the weight machine. You should be worrying about your safety. . . . Get to Brookline court, seek an assault complaint, a larceny complaint, whatever it takes . . . and get a restraining order.' "

According to Tobin, Kristin wouldn't give her name even though Moeller asked for it twice. "We can't revoke someone's probation on an anonymous phone call," he said. Kristin, he added, "did say she didn't want this man arrested and put behind bars."

Tobin also claimed that his office could have taken no action because Kristin was "not the woman in the case we were supervising," which is like saying that probationers in Boston Municipal Court should only take care not to rob the same bank twice.

The next day, Friday, May 8, instead of moving to revoke Cartier's probation, Moeller called Cartier and, in effect, told him what was up. Tobin recalled the conversation. "She told him to get the exercise machine back to her. She told him she didn't want to hear about it anymore. And she ordered a full-scale psychiatric evaluation of him. She also ordered him to report to her every week until the evaluation is completed."

Cartier did all that while planning Kristin's murder.

When Cartier called Kristin again, she told him that if he didn't return the exercise machine, she was going to take court action. "He called back 10 minutes later from a pay phone," remembers Brian Fazekas, Lauren's boyfriend. "He said, 'Okay, okay, I'll return the stupid machine.' "

Kristin was skeptical about that. And she was worried about more violence. The warnings of her friends, her brother Charlie, her teacher Ross Ellenhorn and now Cartier's probation officer rang in her ears. Her art reflected her anguish. She had painted her own self-portrait, showing some of the ugly bruises Cartier had left. Hanging sculptures showed a male, arms flexed and fists clenched. The female hung defensively, arms protecting her head.

By Monday, May 11, she had made up her mind. She was going to rely on the system. She decided to ask the courts for help. She talked about it afterwards with her big sister, Helen, a lawyer and her lifelong best friend. Kristin told her, sparingly, about the beating and, angrily, about the exercise machine. Helen kept the news to herself, as Kristin requested. "She said she found out what a loser he was. She said, 'He's even been taking drugs behind my back,' " Helen recalls. He was snorting heroin, confirms Leslie North—it helped him stay calm, she remembers him saying.

Late in the day, Kristin went to the Brookline police station, Lauren Mace and Brian Fazekas beside her.

"The courts were closed by the time we got there. We waited outside," Lauren said. "An officer showed her [Cartier's] arrest record. When she came out, she said, 'You won't believe the size of this guy's police record. He's killed cats. He's beat up ex-girlfriends. Breaking and enterings.' The officer just sort of flashed the length of it at her and said, 'Look at what you're dealing with.' "

Brookline police sergeant Robert G. Simmons found Kristin "very intelligent, very articulate"—and scared. Simmons asked if she wanted to press charges, and she replied that she wanted to think about that. Simmons, afraid she might not come back, made out an "application for complaint" himself and got a judge on night duty to approve issuance of a one-day emergency restraining order over the phone. The next day, Kristin had to appear before Brookline District Judge Lawrence Shubow to ask for a temporary order—one that would last a week.

Other paperwork that Simmons sent over to the courthouse, right next door to the police station, called for a complaint charging Cartier with assault and battery, larceny, intimidation of a witness and violation of the domestic abuse law. It was signed by Lt. George Finnegan, the police liaison officer on duty at the courthouse that day, and turned over to clerk-magistrate John Connors for issuance of a summons.

The summons was never issued. Inexcusably, the application for it was still sitting on a desk in the clerk's office the day Kristin was killed, almost three weeks later.

Other officials I spoke with were amazed by the lapse. Connors shrugged it off. "We don't have the help," he said. "It was waiting to be typed."

Shubow was unaware of the criminal charges hanging over Cartier's head at the May 12 hearing. And Shubow didn't bother to ask about his criminal record. Restraining orders in Massachusetts, as in other states, have been treated for years by most judges as distasteful "civil matters." Until Kristin was killed, any thug in the Commonwealth accused under the domestic abuse law of beating up his wife or girlfriend or ex-wife or ex-girlfriend could walk into court without much fear that his criminal record would catch up with him. Shubow later told The Boston Globe, "If there is one lesson I learned from this case, it was to ask myself whether this is a case where I should review his record. In a case that has an immediate level of danger, I could press for a warrant and immediate arrest."

Instead, Shubow treated Docket No. 92-RO-060 as a routine matter. He issued a temporary restraining order

telling Cartier to stay away from Kristin's school, her apartment and her place of work for a week, until another hearing could be held by another judge on a permanent order, good for a year.

"The system failed her completely," Shubow told me after Kristin's death. "There is no such thing as a routine case. I don't live that, but I believe that. All bureaucrats should be reminded of that."

Downtown, in Boston Municipal Court, chief probation officer Tobin said that "if we had found out about the restraining order, we would have moved immediately." But Tobin's office made no effort to find out. Cartier's probation officer knew that the anonymous female caller lived in Brookline; a call to officials there would have made clear that Cartier had once again violated probation by beating up an ex-girlfriend. No such call was made.

Apparently, the probation officer didn't ask Cartier for the details either. According to a state official who asked not to be identified, Diane Moeller met with Cartier on May 14, just eight days after he completed her Alternatives to Violence course and three days after Kristin obtained her first restraining order. Moeller did nothing to get him off the streets.

"She was concerned about getting additional assistance for this guy," the state official said of the May 14 meeting. "No charges were filed."

In Brookline, Lt. Finnegan said he sensed something was wrong. He walked up to Kristin outside the courthouse on May 12. "I had this gut feeling," he said. "I asked her, 'Are you really afraid of him?' She said, 'Yeah.' I asked her if he had a gun. She said, 'He may.' "

Finnegan told her to call the police if she saw Cartier hanging around.

The phone rang at the Brookline Police Station shortly after midnight on May 19; Kristin's request for a permanent restraining order was coming up for a hearing that morning. Now, in plain violation of the May 12 order, Cartier had called around midnight, got Kristin on the line and asked her not to go back to court. She called the cops.

Sgt. Simmons, on duty that night as shift commander, advised Kristin to file a complaint and sent officer Kevin Mealy to talk to her; Mealy arrived at her apartment at 1:10 a.m. "Ms. Lardner said that Mr. Cartier attempted to persuade her not to file for an extension of the order," Mealy wrote in his report, which he filed as soon as he got back to the station house. "A criminal complaint application has been made out against Mr. Cartier for violating the existing restraining order."

Sgt. Simmons says, "I told Kevin, 'They've got a hearing in the morning.' The documents went over there. But who reads them?"

Kristin arrived at the courthouse around 11:30 a.m. May 19, accompanied by Lauren Mace and Amber Lynch.

"He [Cartier] was out in front of the courthouse when we got there," Lynch said. "We all just walked in quickly. We waited a long time. He kept walking in and out of the courtroom. I think he was staring at her."

There was no one in the courtroom from the Norfolk County D.A.'s office to advise Kristin. Brookline probation officials didn't talk to her either. They had no idea Cartier was on probation for beating up another woman.

Neither did District Judge Paul McGill, a visiting magistrate from Roxbury. Like Shubow, he didn't check Cartier's criminal record. Unlike Shubow, it didn't trouble him. To him, it was a routine hearing. Kristin was looking for protection. She was processed like a slice of cheese.

"She thought he was going to be arrested," Lauren said. Brian Fazekas said, "It was her understanding that as soon as he got the permanent restraining order, he was going to be surrendered" for violating probation.

"What he [Cartier] did on the 19th was a crime," David Lowy, legal adviser to Gov. William Weld and a former prosecutor, said of the midnight call. "He should have been placed under arrest right then and there."

The hearing lasted five minutes. It would have been shorter except for a typical bit of arrogance from Cartier, trying to stay in control in the face of his third restraining order in 18 months. He agreed not to contact Kristin for a year and to stay away from her apartment and school. But he said he had a problem staying away from Marty's Liquors, where Kristin had just started working as a cashier. "I happen to live right around the corner from there," Cartier complained, according to a tape of the hearing.

The judge told him to patronize some other liquor store, but not before more argument from Cartier about how he would have to "walk further down the street" and about how close it was to Bunratty's, only half a block away. McGill ended the hearing by ordering Cartier to avoid any contact with Kristin, to stay at least 200 yards away from her and not to talk to her if he had to come closer when entering his home or the nightclub.

And with that, Cartier walked out scot-free. Yet, Massachusetts law, enacted in 1990, provides for mandatory arrest of anyone a law enforcement officer has probable cause to believe violated a temporary or permanent restraining order. In addition, a state law making "stalking" a crime, especially in violation of a restraining order, had been signed by Gov. Weld just the day before, May 18, effective immediately.

McGill later said that if he'd known Cartier had violated his restraining order by calling Kristin that morning, he would have turned the hearing into a criminal session.

The application for a complaint charging Cartier with violating the order was moldering in clerk John Connors's offices. Like the earlier complaint accusing him of assault and battery, it was still there the day Kristin was killed.

"Kristin could have said something [in court], I suppose," Lauren said. "But she just figured that after that, he would be out of her life. She said, 'Let's go home.' She felt very relieved that she had this restraining order."

Kristin, who now had 11 days to live, talked enthusiastically about going to Europe after graduation, only a year away. After that she was hoping to go to graduate school. She had lost interest in boys, wanting to concentrate on her art.

"I spoke to her the night before [she was killed]," Chris Dupre said. "She was like the most optimistic and happiest she'd been in months. She knew what she wanted to do with herself, with her art."

She even had a new kitten, named Stubby because its tail was broken in two places. She was working part-time in the liquor store and hoping for more hours as summer approached. But she liked to stay home and paint or just hang out with friends now that classes were over.

Cartier was still skulking about, even after issuance of the permanent restraining order. One afternoon, Kristin stepped out of the liquor store to take a break. She saw Cartier staring at her from the doorway of Bunratty's.

On the afternoon of May 28, she and Robert Hyde, a friend who had just graduated from BU, decided to get something to eat after playing Scrabble (Kristin won) and chess (Robert won) at Kristin's flat. The two hopped on the back of his Yamaha and were off. First stop was the Bay Bank branch on Commonwealth Avenue, two doors from Marty's Liquors. As they turned a corner, Kristin saw Cartier looking in Marty's window. "Did you see that?" she asked Hyde moments later as they got off the bike. "Mike was peeking in the window. What a weirdo!"

Hyde didn't think that Cartier saw them, but later that night, after taking Kristin home, he went over to Bunratty's to play pinball. Cartier was there, and he began an awkward conversation to find out where Hyde lived.

"I thought it was kind of weird, but I didn't think too much of it," Hyde said. He shuddered about it after the shooting.

Cartier had always been disturbingly jealous—and unpredictable. "He'd get under pressure, he'd start breathing heavy and start talking all wild," a longtime friend, Timothy McKernan, told the Lawrence Eagle-Tribune.

He couldn't handle rejection either. Cartier "told his friends that she broke up with him because she wanted to see other people," Bekky Elstad said. "That's not true. But that's why he killed her, I think. If he couldn't have her, no one else was going to."

If Kristin was bothered by the stalking incident that Thursday, she seemed to put it out of her mind. The usual stream of friends moved through the flat all day. She called me that afternoon in an upbeat mood. We talked about summer school, her Museum School evaluation and a half dozen other things, including the next month's check from home. I assured her it was in the mail. She had a big smile in her voice. All I knew about Cartier was that she had gotten rid of the creep. When I made some grumpy reference to boyfriends in general, she laughed and said, "That's because you're my dad."

Cartier called his father that day, too.

Gene Cartier knew about Kristin and about the restraining order. "I asked him what happened," the older Cartier said. "He said, 'Well, me and my girlfriend had a fight.' I figured they argued. . . . He loved animals, he loved children. He wouldn't hurt a fly."

A man with a persistent drinking problem, Gene Cartier at times seemed to confuse Kristin with other girlfriends his son had, but his son's last call about her stuck firmly in his mind. "He said, 'She's busting my balls again,' " Cartier recalled. "I think she was seeing another guy—in front of Michael—to get him jealous. . . . He was obsessed with her."

Kristin went to bed that night with a smile. It had been Lauren's last day at Marty's and some of the students who worked there stopped by the flat. "We were having a really, really good time," Lauren Mace said. "I remember, I said, 'Good night, Kristin.' I gave her a hug. The next morning, I saw her taking her bike down the street, on the way to work. I did not see her again."

Saturday, May 30, was a beautiful spring day in Boston, a light breeze rustling the trees on Winchester Street below the flat. Kristin was looking forward to a full day's work; Lauren was supposed to meet her at 6, when she was done at Marty's. Lauren had just graduated from BU; they were going to buy a keg for a big going-away party at the flat on Sunday.

One of the managers at the liquor store, David Bergman, was having lunch across the street at the Inbound Pizza when Kristin walked in. He waved her over to his table. She had a slice of Sicilian pizza and then, as he remembers, two more. "We talked for half an hour," Bergman said. "She was going to travel to Europe with her friend, Lauren. She had all these plans laid on."

After lunch, the day turned sour. Leslie North walked into Marty's with another girl. So, clerks say, did a man in his thirties with rotting teeth and thinning hair—North's boyfriend. He got in Kristin's checkout line and started cursing at her.

Not long after North and her friend left Marty's, J.D. Crump, the manager at Bunratty's, walked in for a sandwich from the deli counter. He'd known Kristin since she had dated Jason. "She said she was having a tough day," he told the Globe. "The customers were being mean. I told her it would get better."

When Crump spoke with Kristin on May 30, it was about 4:30. Cartier, meanwhile, was at a noisy show at the Rathskellar on Kenmore Square. Friends told the Lawrence Eagle-Tribune that he was acting strangely, greeting people with long hugs instead of the usual punch in the arm or a handshake.

"He wasn't the hugging type," Timothy McKernan told the Eagle-Tribune. "I think he knew what he was going to do." Cartier left suddenly, running out the door.

Kristin was scheduled to work until 6, but at 5 p.m., she was told, to her chagrin, to leave early, losing an hour's pay. "We had other cashiers coming in," the manager explained. Instead of hanging around to wait for Lauren, Kristin decided to go to Bekky Elstad's apartment and return at 6. It was a decision that seems to have cost her her life.

Lauren had come by around 5:40 p.m., and left when told Kristin had already gone. Kristin was still at Bekky's, keeping her eye on the clock and by now recounting how this "disgusting . . . slimy person" had been cursing at her at the cash register.

"She was laughing about how gross he was and then his being with these two girls—friends of Michael's—who were so gross," Bekky Elstad said. "She seemed pretty much in a good mood."

It was getting close to 6. By now, Cartier was back in the neighborhood, looking for a crowbar. He first asked for one at the Reading Room, a smoke shop about a block away, "maybe 20 minutes before it happened," said the proprietor. "I asked him why he wanted a crowbar. He said he had to go help somebody." Then he went over to Bunratty's, in a fruitless search for the same thing.

At one minute to 6, Kristin was heading down Commonwealth Avenue toward Marty's. Cartier, approaching from the other direction, stopped at a Store 24 convenience shop on the other side of Harvard Avenue. J.D. Crump was there, buying a pack of cigarettes. According to the police report: "Crump stated that while in Store 24 . . . he saw Michael and asked him [whether] he was going to work that night. Mike said that he was but had [to] shoot someone first. Crump stated that he did not take him seriously and walked away from him."

The shots rang out seconds later. Mike Dillon, a clerk at Marty's who clocked out at 6, had just stepped onto the sidewalk when he heard the first shattering noise.

"It was very loud," he said. "I looked up immediately. I saw Kristin fall."

Dressed all in black, she dropped instantly to the pavement outside the Soap-A-Rama, a combination laundromat, tanning salon and video rental store four doors from Marty's.

"She was lying on her right side, curled up in kind of a fetal position," Mike Dillon said. "I kind of froze dead in my tracks."

Cartier must have seen her and hid in a doorway or alley until she passed by him. Witnesses said he came at her from behind and shot into the rear of her head from a distance of 15 or 20 feet. Then he ran into a nearby alley.

Al Silva, a restaurant worker, started to walk towards Kristin to see if he could help when Cartier darted back out of the alley, rushed past Silva, and leaned down over her.

"He shot her twice more in the left side of the head," Mike Dillon said. "Then I saw him run down the alley again. . . . I was still in shock. I didn't know what to do. I took one of her hands for a second or so, I don't know why. Then I ran back to call the police, but I saw a woman in the flower shop. She was already on the phone."

Chris Toher, the proprietor at Soap-A-Rama, heard the first shot from the back of his store and hurried up to the doorway. "I saw him fire the final shots," Toher said. "It happened so fast she never had a chance. She was completely unconscious at the point he ran up to her. Her eyes were shut."

A brave young woman was dead.

The killer fled down the alley, which took him to Glenville Avenue where he lived in a red brick apartment building. Back on Commonwealth Avenue, police and an ambulance arrived within minutes. But the ambulance was no longer necessary.

Police questioned Crump at the Soap-A-Rama and learned where Cartier lived. Brooke Mezo, a clerk from Marty's who witnessed the interrogation, heard Crump say "that Michael had spoken to him in the past couple of weeks and said he couldn't live without her, that he was going to kill her. And he talked about where to get a gun."

That made at least two people who knew Cartier had or wanted a gun and was talking about killing Kristin. How many others should have known she was in grave danger?

Police quickly sealed off the area around Cartier's apartment. "He had apparently made statements to several people that he hated policemen and had no reservations about shooting a cop," homicide detective Billy Dwyer said in his report. "He stated that he would never go to prison again."

A police operations team entered Cartier's apartment at 8:30 p.m. He was dead, lying on his bed with the gun he used to kill Kristin in his right hand. He had put it to his head and fired once. Police recovered the spent bullet from the bedroom wall. They found three other shell casings in the area where he murdered Kristin.

Later that night, Leslie North walked into Bunratty's, looking for Cartier. "I said, 'He shot Kristin,' " said J.D. Crump. "She didn't look surprised. I said, 'Then he went and shot himself.' At that point, she lost it. She started screaming, 'What a waste! What a waste! He's dead!' "

Crump later said, "I've had to live the past couple of weeks feeling I could have stopped him. I should have called his probation officer."

It's doubtful that would have done any good. The system is so mindless that when the dead Cartier failed to show up in Boston Municipal Court as scheduled on June 19, a warrant was issued for his arrest.

It is still outstanding.

Author's Epilogue

Starting in 1994, Congress passed a series of laws collectively known as the Violence Against Women Act (VAWA). These laws make certain behaviors a crime and set up the punishment for some offenses. Some states have moved to improve their methods for tracking abusers. Massachusetts, where Kristin was killed, now has a computerized, statewide domestic-violence registry that judges are required to consult. Although Massachusetts is still the only state to require this, almost half of the states now have, or are in the process of setting up, similar registries. Also, the FBI recently started a nationwide system that should eventually allow officials to access data from all those states at once.

Very few prosecutions under VAWA's criminal provisions have been undertaken over the last three years. A major reason why is the difficulty in getting states to cooperate effectively to enforce a provision of VAWA in which a woman who obtains a protective order in one state should receive the same protection in any other state.

There seems to be legal questions as well. In one example from Washington D.C., a woman named Deborah Fulton has been to court more than twenty times since she first got a protection order in February 1995. Her estranged husband lives across the state line and continues to harass her. When he was finally locked up, he was charged with misdemeanors for assault and violating the D.C. protective order. Even though at the time of his arrest he was awaiting trial in a D.C. court on an earlier charge of violating the same order, federal officials say it is unclear whether they can move the case up to federal court.

Another problem is that women seeking protection also face continued resistance by judges unwilling to take these cases seriously. Many judges give the benefit of the doubt to men and blame female victims for instigating or causing violence against them. Some judges exclude evidence of past behaviors. By the time most batterers come before them, they generally are not first-time offenders.

Finally, it remains uncertain what policies work best to protect female victims. Some thwarted abusers simply direct their wrath elsewhere, and therefore many experts say protective orders could be strengthened to deal with these men. Other experts believe violators should get automatic jail time. Some believe "permanent" orders should be truly permanent and available in more than just a few states. Still others also suggest treatment programs should last longer. According to Andrew Klein, the chief probation officer for the Quincy, Massachusetts, District Court, "A lot of guys can hold anything together for six months, but this is chronic behavior."

Despite these problems, experts generally agree that in most cases a protective order is a woman's best defense—when properly crafted and enforced. Protective orders succeed in keeping many abusive men away from their victims, and according to a 1994 study, make more than 80 percent of women feel safer.

Chapter 2 Review Questions

1. What are the formal elements of Weber's model of bureaucracy? Based on your reading of the case or your own experiences with public bureaucracies, did Weber fail to mention any important attributes of bureaucracy in his description?
2. What were Kristin's reasons for relying on public bureaucracy for protection? Why did the system fail to protect her?
3. Does this case in your view support or contradict Weber's arguments about the monolithic power position of bureaucracy in society? About the nature of bureaucratic rationality? Its hierarchy? Specialization? Narrow latitude of bureaucratic rule enforcement? High degree of efficiency?
4. After reading the foregoing case study, where would you modify Weber's model to account more accurately for the pattern and the characteristics of America's bureaucracy?
5. According to the case, what are the sources of bureaucratic failure? What do you recommend to remedy the problems outlined in this case? Are there comparisons with the previous case, "The Blast in Centralia No. 5," as related to this failure?
6. Think about the case and what it says about the value of bureaucracy in modern society. Why are bureaucracies important? And yet so disliked? In your view, can anything be done about the fundamental public hostility toward bureaucracy, particularly to strengthen bureaucratic effectiveness and responsiveness in serving the public?

Key Terms

ideal-types
traditional authority
charismatic authority
legal-rational authority
bureaucratic hierarchy
tenure in office

objective experts
bureaucratic rules
monied economy
bureaucratic power
bureaucratic secrecy

Suggestions for Further Reading

For a thoughtful understanding of Weber's background, his intellectual development, and continuing influence, read the introduction of H. H. Gerth and C. Wright Mills, eds., *From Max Weber: Essays in Sociology* (New York: Oxford University Press, 1946); Reinhard Bendix, *Max Weber: An Intellectual Portrait* (New York: Doubleday, 1960); John Patrick Diggins, *Max Weber* (New York: Basic Books, 1996); and Marianne Weber, *Max Weber: A Biography* (New York: John Wiley, 1975). For a short but insightful piece, see Alfred Diamant, "The Bureaucratic Model: Max Weber Rejected, Rediscovered, and Reformed," in *Papers in Comparative Administration,* edited by Ferrel Heady and Sybil L. Stokes (Ann Arbor, Mich.: The University of Michigan Press, 1962).

The current literature on bureaucracy is vast but uneven and should be read selectively. Some of the better introductions include Graham Allison, *Essence of Decision: Explaining the Cuban Missile Crisis* (Boston: Little, Brown, 1971); Peter M. Blau and Marshall W. Meyer, *Bureaucracy in Modern Society,* 2nd ed. (New York: Random House, 1971); Francis E. Rourke, *Bureaucracy, Politics and Public Policy,* 3rd ed. (Boston: Little, Brown, 1984); Peter Woll, *American Bureaucracy,* 2nd ed. (New York: W. W. Norton, 1977); Kenneth J. Meier, *Politics and the Bureaucracy: Policy Making in the Fourth Branch of Government,* 4th ed. (Belmont, Calif.: Wadsworth, 1999); Douglas Yates, *Bureaucratic Democracy: The Search for Democracy and Efficiency in American Government* (Cambridge, Mass.: Harvard University Press, 1982); Harold Seidman, *Politics, Position, and Power,* 5th ed. (New York:

Oxford University Press, 1997); Gary C. Bryner, *Bureaucratic Discretion* (New York: Pergamon Press, 1987); Richard J. Stillman II, *The American Bureaucracy,* 3rd ed. (Belmont, Calif.: Wadsworth, 2004); James Q. Wilson, *Bureaucracy: What Government Agencies Do and Why They Do It* (New York: Basic Books, 1989); and Maureen Hogan Casamayou, *Bureaucracy in Crisis* (Boulder, Colo.: Westview Press, 1993). Francis E. Rourke's *Bureaucratic Power in National Politics,* 4th ed. (Boston: Little, Brown, 1986), offers a useful collection of various excerpts from seminal writings on this subject as well as Ali Farazmand, ed., *Handbook of Bureaucracy* (New York: Marcel Dekker, 1994); and Larry B. Hill, ed., *The State of Public Bureaucracy* (New York: M. E. Sharpe, 1992).

For five historic treatments of the rise of bureaucratic institutions, see the two volumes of E. N. Gladden, *A History of Public Administration* (London: Frank Cass, 1972); Ernest Barker, *The Development of Public Services in Western Europe, 1660–1930* (New York: Oxford University Press, 1944); William D. Richardson, *Democracy, Bureaucracy, and Character* (Lawrence: University of Kansas Press, 1997); Paul Light, *The Tides of Reform* (New Haven, Conn.: Yale University Press, 1997); and Frederick C. Mosher, *Democracy and the Public Service,* 2nd ed. (New York: Oxford University Press, 1982). Leonard D. White's four-volume history of American public administration up to 1900 (cited in the previous chapter's "Suggestions for Further Reading") is certainly valuable reading on this topic. Martin Albrow, *Bureaucracy* (New York: Praeger, 1970); Stephen Skowronek, *Building a New American State: The Expansion of National*

Administrative Capacities, 1877–1920 (New York: Cambridge University Press, 1982); Don K. Price, *America's Unwritten Constitution* (Baton Rouge, La.: Louisiana University Press, 1983); Martin J. Schiesl, *The Politics of Efficiency* (Berkeley, Calif.: University of California Press, 1977); Guy Benveniste, *The Politics of Expertise,* 2nd ed. (San Francisco: Boyd & Fraser, 1977); Thomas K. McCraw, *Prophets of Regulation* (Cambridge, Mass.: Harvard University Press, 1984); Richard J. Stillman II, *Creating the American State* (Tuscaloosa, Ala.: University of Alabama Press, 1998); Christopher Hood, *The Art of the State* (Oxford: Oxford University Press, 1998); Frederick C. Mosher, *A Tale of Two Agencies* (Baton Rouge, La.: Louisiana University Press, 1984); Theda Skocpol, *Protecting Soldiers and Mothers* (Cambridge, Mass.: Harvard University Press, 1992); Jerry Mitchell, *The American Experiment in Government Corporation* (Armonk, NY: M.E. Sharpe, 1998); and Mathew Crenson, *The Federal Machine* (Baltimore: Johns Hopkins University Press, 1975) offer unique, original conceptual and historical perspectives, as well as James Q. Wilson's essay, "The Rise of the Bureaucratic State," in *The Public Interest* (Fall 1975).

Serious students of bureaucracy should examine primary materials—executive orders, legislative acts, and official reports. Many key materials are contained in Frederick C. Mosher, ed., *Basic Documents of American Public Administration, 1776–1950* (New York: Holmes and Meier, 1976), and Richard J. Stillman II, ed., *Basic Documents of American Public Administration Since 1950* (New York: Holmes and Meier, 1982).

Five books that depict very different contemporary views of this topic since 1990 are Gerald Gavey, *Facing the Bureaucracy* (San Francisco: Jossey-Bass, 1993); B. Dan Wood and Richard W. Waterman, *Bureaucratic Dynamics* (Boulder, Colo.: Westview Press, 1994); Paul C. Light, *Thickening Government* (Washington, D.C.: Brookings, 1995); Sally Coleman Selden, *The Promise of Representative Bureaucracy* (New York: M.E. Sharpe, 1997); and Charles T. Goodsell, *The Case for Bureaucracy,* 4th ed. (New York: Seven Bridges, 2001).

Works that attempt to view bureaucracy from a comparative perspective are Joel D. Aberbach, Robert D. Putnam, and Bert Rockman, *Bureaucrats and Politicians in Western Democracies* (Cambridge, Mass.: Harvard University Press, 1981); Metin Heper, ed., *The State and Public Bureaucracy* (New York: Greenwood, 1987); B. Guy Peters, *The Politics of Bureaucracy,* Fourth Edition (White Plains, N.Y.: Longman, 1995); Ali Farazmand, ed., *Handbook of Comparative and Development Public Administration,* 2nd ed. (New York: Marcel Dekker, 2001), as well as his edited *Handbook of Bureaucracy* (New York: Marcel Dekker, 1991); World Bank, *The State in a Changing World* (Washington, D.C.: The World Bank, 1997); and Ferrel Heady, *Public Administration: A Comparative Perspective,* 6th ed. (New York: Marcel Dekker, 2001).

For a helpful, up-to-date, comprehensive guide through the history of this vast literature, see Jos C. N. Raadschelders, *Handbook of Administrative History* (Brunswick, N.J.: Transaction Books, 1998). The best American journals covering public bureaucracy include *Public Administration Review, The Bureaucrat, Administration and Society, Journal of Public Administration Research and Theory, Governing,* and *The American Review of Public Administration.*

CHAPTER 3

The General Environment: The Concept of Ecology

A n ecological approach to public administration builds, then, quite literally from the ground up. . . .

John M. Gaus

■■■■ **READING 3**

Introduction

Ecology entered the lexicon of social science and public administration literature long before it became popular in the media and on college campuses in the 1970s as a word synonymous with protecting the natural beauty of the landscape. Originally, the term was derived from the ancient Greek word *oikos,* meaning "living place," and was used extensively by nineteenth-century Darwinian botanists and zoologists to describe how organisms live and adapt to their environments. Sociologists during the 1920s borrowed the ideas of plant and animal ecology and applied the concept to human life; they emphasized the *interdependence* of human life within an increasingly complex organic system and the tendency of living systems to move toward an *equilibrium,* or stabilization of life forms in relation to the surrounding environment.

Ecology was introduced into the public administration vocabulary primarily through the writings of the late Harvard Professor John M. Gaus (1894–1969), one of the early pioneers of public administration; he elaborated on ecology in a series of famous lectures at the University of Alabama in 1945, later published as *Reflections on Public Administration.*

In this work, as well as in his other writings, Gaus was particularly adept at weaving the patterns and ideas of public administration into the total fabric of the issues and events of modern American society. Better than most observers, he showed how public administration, its development, and its activities were influenced by its setting, or its ecology. In his words, ecology "deals with all interrelationships of living organisms and their environment." Thus, "an ecological approach to public administration builds . . . quite literally from the ground up; from the elements of a place—soils, climate, location, for example—to the people who live there—their numbers and ages and knowledge, and the ways of physical and social technology by which from the place and in relationships with one another, they get their living." For Gaus, administrative systems were inextricably intertwined with the fabric of society. In particular, he delineated several important elements that he found useful "for explaining the ebb and flow of the functions of government: people, place, physical technology, social technology, wishes and ideas, catastrophe, and personality." He addressed himself to the importance of these ecological factors in the following selection abridged from his *Reflections on Public Administration.*

Gaus began teaching political science shortly after World War I (prior to Harvard, he taught at the University of Wisconsin) with an early interest in public administration. He interspersed teaching with numerous state and national administrative assignments, and he brought these practical experiences to his classes. Throughout his career, Gaus was fascinated by the interplay of forces between public administration and the larger society.

Gaus shared much in common with Frederick Jackson Turner, an early twentieth-century American historian who pored over maps, soil samples, statistical data of regions, and voting records in his empirical study of the growth of the American nation. Similarly, Gaus asked students of public administration to observe the environment of administration so as to understand how the characteristics of its ecology influence the development of administrative institutions. For Gaus, the term *ecology* was relevant not only to cloistered scholars of administration at work on universal theories of the administrative process, but also to on-the-line practitioners of administration. A conscious awareness of ecological factors permits administrators to respond more wisely to the demands and challenges of the external environment of their organizations. Thus, in the hands of the practitioner, ecology can become a diagnostic tool; it can help in visualizing the major elements in the administrative processes and provide a yardstick for measuring their impact on an organization. However, Gaus was aware that prediction would not be simple: "The task of predicting the consequences of contemporary action, of providing the requisite adjustment, is immensely difficult with the individual or in family life. The difficulty increases with the size and complexity of the unit and expansion and range of variables."

Gaus's concern with ecology of administration was prompted by a special concern with "change." He was a member of the generation rocked by the hardships of a catastrophic economic depression in the 1930s, and he saw the American landscape rapidly being transformed in myriad ways. As he observed, "Change which we have found to be so characteristic of American life, change that has disrupted neighborhoods, that has destroyed cultural stabilities, that has reflected the sweep across the continent, the restless migration to city and back to farm, from one job to another, has brought widely hailed merits. Its merits have been so spectacular, indeed, that we speak of it as progress. . . . Its costs are also becoming clearer, registered in the great dramatic collapses of the depression, more subtly in the defeat, disintegration and frustration of individuals. . . ." Gaus looked to public administration "to find some new source of content, of opportunity for the individual to assert some influence on the situation in which he finds himself." In one essay, "American Society and Public Administration," he stated: "My thesis is that through public instruments some new institutional bases which will enable the individual to find development and satisfaction can be created and some sense of purpose may flower again."*

Gaus was both pessimistic and optimistic about the condition of human society. His pessimism welled up when he saw change destroying the patterns of existence familiar to his generation,

*John Gaus, "American Society and Public Administration," in John M. Gaus, Leonard D. White, and Marshall E. Dimock, *The Frontiers of Public Administration* (Chicago: University of Chicago Press, 1936).

breaking down the stabilizing institutional arrangements, and confronting individuals with se-rious economic and personal hardships. Yet Gaus perceived a bright hope in applied social science: through an ecological approach to public administration he believed that new and re-newed institutional patterns could be devised for individuals living in an age of change. Ecol-ogy in public administration became for Gaus a vital instrument for comprehending, directing, and modulating the forceful shocks of change in contemporary life. In the almost 60 years that have passed since Gaus's studies of ecology were published, younger scholars in the field, such as Fred Riggs, have been active in the wider application of the ecological approach, especially in the newer areas of developmental and comparative public administration.

As you read this selection, keep the following questions in mind:

Why does Gaus argue that knowledge of the general environment is so critical for ad-ministrators?

If you were to revise this essay for today's readers, what other environmental factors that affect modern public administration might you add to Gaus's list? (You might include, for example, computers or ethnic and racial problems or media factors.)

In what ways can administrators recognize changes in the general environment?

What might be the price paid for the failure of organizations to respond swiftly and cor-rectly to external environmental change?

As you read Gaus's essay, reflect on its relevance to Case Study 1, "The Blast in Cen-tralia No. 5." How did ecological factors influence the outcome of that case?

The Ecology of Public Administration

JOHN M. GAUS

The study of public administration must include its ecology. "Ecology," states the Webster Dictionary, "is the mutual relations, collectively, between organisms and their environment." J. W. Bews points out that "the word itself is derived from the Greek *oikos,* a house or home, the same root word as occurs in econ-omy and economics. Economics is a subject with which ecology has much in common, but ecology is much wider. It deals with all the interrelationships

Abridged material from *Reflections on Public Administration* by John M. Gaus, pp. 6–19. Copyright © 1947 by University of Alabama Press. Reprinted with permission.

of living organisms and their environment."[1] Some social scientists have been returning to the use of the term, chiefly employed by the biologist and botanist, especially under the stimulus of studies of anthro-pologists, sociologists, and pioneers who defy easy classification, such as the late Sir Patrick Geddes in Britain. In the lecture of Frankfurter's already quoted, the linkage between physical area, population, transport and government is concretely indicated. More recently, Charles A. Beard formulated some axioms of gov-ernment in which environmental change is linked with resulting public administration. "I present," he stated, "for what it is worth, and may prove to be worth, the following bill of axioms or aphorisms on public administration, as fitting this important occasion.

1. The continuous and fairly efficient discharge of certain functions by government, central and local, is a necessary condition for the existence of any great society.
2. As a society becomes more complicated, as its division of labor ramifies more widely, as its commerce extends, as technology takes the place of handicrafts and local self-sufficiency, the functions of government increase in number and in their vital relationships to the fortunes of society and individuals.
3. Any government in such a complicated society, consequently any such society itself, is strong in proportion to its capacity to administer the functions that are brought into being.
4. Legislation respecting these functions, difficult as it is, is relatively easy as compared with the enforcement of legislation, that is, the effective discharge of these functions in their most minute ramifications and for the public welfare.
5. When a form of government, such as ours, provides for legal changes, by the process of discussion and open decision, to fit social changes, the effective and wise administration becomes the central prerequisite for the perdurance of government and society—to use a metaphor, becomes a foundation of government as a going concern.
6. Unless the members of an administrative system are drawn from various classes and regions, unless careers are open in it to talents, unless the way is prepared by an appropriate scheme of general education, unless public officials are subjected to internal and external criticism of a constructive nature, then the public personnel will become a bureaucracy dangerous to society and to popular government.
7. Unless, as David Lilienthal has recently pointed out in an address on the Tennessee Valley Authority, an administrative system is so constructed and operated as to keep alive local and individual responsibilities, it is likely to destroy the basic well-springs of activity, hope, and enthusiasm necessary to popular government and to the following of a democratic civilization."[2]

An ecological approach to public administration builds, then, quite literally from the ground up; from the elements of a place—soils, climate, location, for example—to the people who live there—their numbers and ages and knowledge, and the ways of physical and social technology by which from the place and in relationships with one another, they get their living. It is within this setting that their instruments and practices of public housekeeping should be studied so that they may better understand what they are doing, and appraise reasonably how they are doing it. Such an approach is of particular interest to us as students seeking to cooperate in our studies; for it invites—indeed is dependent upon—careful observation by many people in different environments of the roots of government functions, civic attitudes, and operating problems.

With no claim to originality, therefore, and indeed with every emphasis on the collaborative nature of the task, I put before you a list of the factors which I have found useful as explaining the ebb and flow of the functions of government. They are: people, place, physical technology, social technology, wishes and ideas, catastrophe, and personality. I have over many years built up a kind of flexible textbook in a collection of clippings, articles and books illustrative of each, as any one can do for himself. Such illustrations of the "raw material of politics" and hence administration are in themselves the raw material of a science of administration, of that part of the science which describes and interprets why particular activities are undertaken through government and the problems of policy, organization and management generally that result from such origins.[3]

By illustrating concretely the relation of these environmental factors, a cooperative testing of the theory will be facilitated. The changes in the distribution of the people of a governmental unit by time, age and place throw light on the origins of public policy and administration. At our first census, we were a people 80 per cent of whom lived on farms; at our last census, one hundred and fifty years later, 80 per cent of us did

not live on farms. Over a third are now living in a relatively few metropolitan areas; but the growth of these
areas is not in the core or mother city; it is in the surrounding suburbs, separate political entities, frequently
also separate economic-status and cultural entities, yet
sharing with the mother city, which is often absolutely
declining in population, the public housekeeping problems of a metropolitan organism for which no—or no
adequate—political organization exists. Our population
is increasingly one with a larger proportion distributed
among the older age classes. These raw facts—too little known and appreciated by citizens, which should
be at once placed before them in discussing many of
our public questions—in themselves explain much
about our functions of government. Coupled with factors of place and technology, they clarify many an issue
that is usually expressed in sterile conflicts. For example, the old people in the more frequent large family
on a farm of a century ago, where more goods and
services were provided on the farm, had a function
still to perform and a more meaningful place in the
lives of younger generations of the family. In a more
pecuniary economy, separated from the family-sub-
sistence economy, ignored in the allocation of the
work and rewards of an industrial society, the demand for pensions became irresistible.

The movement of people (by characteristic age
and income groups) from the mother city to suburbs (as guided by factors of time-space and cost
in the journey to work, the dispersal of shopping
centers, the search of industry for land space for
straight-line production facilitated by paved roads,
trucks and distribution of power by wires, and other
technological changes, and changes in what we
wish for in residential environment) produces its
repercussion in the values of land and buildings, in
the tax basis for public services already existent in
older areas and demanded in the new, in the differ-
ential requirements and capacities-to-pay of people
for housing (including the site and neighborhood
equipment) and in the adjustment of transport and
utility requirements for the ever-changing metropolitan organism.

Thus the factors of people and place are inextricably interwoven. And not merely in crowded urban
centers. I have watched the same process of change
in sparsely settled areas of farm and forest, and its
potent effect on government.

Where there are extensive cut-over areas in the
Lake States, where the older farm lands of New
England or New York are no longer profitable to
agriculture and reforestation is too recent to yield
timber crops, in the Great Plains where lands best
suited to grazing and with limited rainfall have been
subjected to the plough, in the cut-over and eroded
lands of the Southern Piedmont, or in the anthracite
region of Pennsylvania, physical conditions—the ex-
haustion of the resource which originally brought
settlement—have produced a chain of institutional
consequences. Land values and tax payments decline, tax delinquent land reverts to county or state,
public schools, roads and other services can no
longer be locally financed. Immediate relief through
state financial aids or state administered services in
turn are inadequate when widespread catastrophic
economic depression undermines state revenues. Efforts aimed at restoring a source of production, such
as encouragement of cropping timber through favoring taxation or the building up of public forests
adequate for permanent wood-using industries, or
the restoration of soil, will require a long period of
time for efficacy, and equally require an atmosphere
in which political leadership, the careful integration
of national, state, local, and individual and corporate
policies, and skilled technical personnel can be established and supported steadily. Such an atmosphere, however, is not likely to be present among the
frustrate population of such areas, or the better-pro-
vided populations of other areas called upon to tax
themselves for local units of government in areas
which they have never seen or whose problems they
do not understand. Thus changes in place, or the use
of the resources and products of a place, are coercive
in their effect upon public administration.[4]

My own generation has had a great lesson in the
importance of change in physical technology in witnessing the adoption of the automobile and the role
it has come to play. It may be noted that its widespread use was made possible by the development of
paved highways provided necessarily as a public
service. Highway expansion and design have been affected by the coercion of political forces created by

the physical invention. Groups of automobile users, manufacturers, hotel proprietors, road builders, road machinery and materials suppliers, persons seeking jobs in highway construction and administration and many others, have contended with those using horses, carriage and harness makers and persons opposed to the increased taxation that paved roads would require. The original causes—a combination of physical inventions such as the internal combustion engine and the vulcanization of rubber—get obscured in the ultimate disputes over taxation, jurisdiction, requirement of liability insurance and examination for drivers' licenses, or over the merits or defects of systems of traffic control or the financing of overhead crossings or express highways. The citizen blames "bureaucrats" and "politicians" because the basic ecological causes have not been clarified for him. This process of public function adoption may also be reversed by other changes—as we see, for example, in the abandonment of many publicly financed and constructed canals, when new technologies of transport rendered them obsolete.

Changes in physical technology, however slowly their institutional influences may spread, are more obvious even to the point of being dramatic, to the citizen. But he sometimes forgets the importance of the invention of social institutions or devices, and their continuing influences which coerce us. Thus the pooling and application of the savings of many through the invention of the corporation has set new forces to ripple through the social order, disarranging human relationships and creating new possibilities of large scale enterprise financially capable of utilizing extensive equipment and personnel and creating new relationships between buyer and seller, employer and employee—from which coercions for a new balance of forces, through consumer, labor and investor standards, have resulted.

You will have noted how interrelated all of these factors are in their operation. Perhaps the subtlest one is that for which I have difficulty in finding a satisfactory term. I have used the words "wishes and ideas." What you don't know, it is said, won't hurt you. I wonder whether this is true. If you do know that some new drug, or method of treatment of disease, will prevent the illness or perhaps death of those dear to

you, you will have a new imperative for action, even if that action requires a public program. If you know or think you know that a combination of legislative and administrative measures will safeguard your bank deposit or insurance from destruction, that idea will have a coercive effect upon your political action. If you think that public officials are corrupt, that a tariff act or a regulation of a trade is a "racket," that too will influence the political decisions of your time. If you value material well-being, and if that desire takes so definite a form as a house and yard and garden, there are inevitable consequences in standards of public services that will facilitate the realization of your desire. Down that long road one will find the public insurance of mortgages to achieve lower interest rates and longer-term financing and zoning ordinances.

The originators of ideas and of social as well as physical invention are persons. We students of public administration will do well to study the elements in the influences which Bentham, the Webbs, the city planner Burnham, the health officer Biggs, the pioneers in the New York Bureau of Municipal Research and its Training School for Public Service have wielded. Relevant preparation, longevity, personal or institutional resources for research, sympathetic disciples, frequently some catastrophic situation in which prevailing attitudes were sufficiently blasted to permit the new ideas to be applied, channels of publication and of communication generally, as well as inner qualities of industry and integrity all, or nearly all in some combination, will be found. We each will have touched some one of this kind, perhaps, in our own community; if not a pioneer in original invention, an enlightened civic interpreter, agitator, or organizer. Thus the late Governor Alfred E. Smith had a genius for relating his sense of people's needs, his experience in party and legislative processes and his position as Governor to a political and administrative program in which the special knowledge of many persons was most effectively used in the service of the State of New York.

Catastrophe, especially when leadership and knowledge are prepared with long-time programs into which the immediate hurried relief action can be fitted, has its place in the ecology of administration.

It not only is destructive, so that relief and repair are required on a scale so large that collective action is necessary, but it also disrupts, jostles or challenges views and attitudes, and affords to the inner self as well as to others a respectable and face-saving reason for changing one's views as to policy. The atomic bomb gave to many, perhaps, a determining reason for a change of attitude toward international organization. But I incline to the view that the effects of catastrophe on our thinking are relatively short-lived, and confined to relatively smaller institutional changes, and that older forces flood back with great strength to cancel most of the first reaction. A frightened and frustrated society is not one in which really significant changes will take root, unless careful preparation and wise administration of the relief period are available. The night club fire in Boston in recent years in which so many service men from various parts of the country were killed is a tragic example of one role of catastrophe. In the lurid glare of that fire, weaknesses in building codes and the administration of them were revealed. So many vested interests of materials, construction and crafts center in building codes that they are difficult to keep in tune with invention and changing social needs. The fact that many in the fire were from remote places, and were men in the armed services, gave unusually wide reporting of the tragedy for some days, especially as many victims lingered on in hospitals. One result of the shock of the catastrophe was therefore action in cities throughout the world to inspect their places of public amusement and survey their fire-prevention legislation and administration. On a vaster scale, the catastrophe of economic world depression led to a varied array of responses through collective action in which there was much similarity despite regional and ideological differences among the various states of the world, since there were also like ecological factors, common to modern power industry and the price system. World wars illustrate the extent to which a large area of collective action is necessarily adopted under modern conditions of total war—and equally illustrate the tremendous pull of older customary views at the close, when the pressure

to remove the controls rises, and individuals in office are held responsible for the frustrations once borne as a patriotic offering. Wise and fortunate indeed is that community that has so analyzed its problems and needs, and has so prepared to make use of catastrophe should it come by plans for carrying out programs of improvements, that the aftermath of tragedy finds its victims as well cared for as humanly possible and in addition some tangible new advance in the equipment and life of the community. I have seen some communities which, because they had equipped themselves with personnel capable of fresh thinking, had obtained from depression work-relief programs recreation facilities that were their first amenities.

Such an approach as this to our study of public administration is difficult, in that it makes demands upon our powers to observe, upon a sensitive awareness of changes and maladjustment and upon our willingness to face the political—that is, the public-housekeeping—basis of administration. These factors—you may improve upon my selection—in various combinations lie behind a public agency. In their combination will be found the reasons for its existence, and the reasons for attack upon it as well. Only in so far as we can find some essentially public core in the combination can we hope to have an agency free from spoils or abuse of power. The process of growth and formulation of a public policy out of these environmental materials links environment and administration. We may be too responsive to change, or we may fail to achieve our best selves by ignoring what we might do to advantage ourselves by collective action, if we perform this task of politics badly.

"When I pay taxes," wrote Justice Holmes to his friend Sir Frederick Pollock, "I buy civilization." It is no easy task of the citizen in this complicated world to get fair value in what he buys. That task is one of discovery of the causes of problems, of the communication of possible remedies, of the organizing of citizens, of the formulation of law. It is the task, in short, of politics. The task will be more fruitfully performed if the citizen, and his agents in public offices, understand the ecology of government.

Notes

1. J. W. Bews, *Human Ecology* (London: Oxford University Press, 1935), p. 1.
2. From "Administration, A Foundation of Government," by Charles A. Beard, in *American Political Science Review,* XXXIV, No. 2 (April, 1940), p. 232. Reprinted by permission of the American Political Science Association.
3. The methods as well as the substantive interpretations of Frederick Jackson Turner should be familiar to students of public administration so far as the printed page permits. It was a rich experience to be present as he worked over maps and statistical data of a county, state or region, putting geology, soils, land values, origins of residents, and voting records together for light on the resulting social action.
4. A reverse picture is the sudden demand on the use of ores in the Adirondack region during the world war because of changes in the conditions of ocean shipment. In one remote village a public housing project, to take care of the expanded work force, was a consequence, again, of the catastrophe of war.

⎯⎯⎯ CASE STUDY 3

Introduction

The concept *ecology of administration* can be well illustrated by most case studies on public administration, for it would be a rare public administrator who was *not* influenced by at least a few of the major ecological factors that John Gaus outlined in the preceding essay. The theme of ecology runs throughout administrative activities, serving to shape and reshape the course and direction of public policy. The following case study, "Dr. Helene Gayle and The AIDS Epidemic" is a good example of how ecological factors can affect public administration and why an administrator can succeed brilliantly when she takes these external factors into account before and during initiating a public program.

In many respects the following case involves all the ecological factors discussed by John Gaus, though in remarkably different ways: first, "the people" inflicted with AIDS faced certain death, and as their numbers grew they became a significant collective force favoring public policies that responded to the epidemic. Second, "place" decisively shaped what happened because of the epidemic's seemingly narrow confines, at least in its beginning stages. For several years AIDS was seen as mainly a gay man's disease, which most Americans felt immune from and thus could easily neglect as a peril to their own health. Third and fourth, "physical and social technologies" were directly influential because medical causes, cures, and even the means for institutionally coping with AIDS were unknown. So local health-care providers were at first swamped with massive health problems that they were ill-equipped to deal with, let alone even comprehend the magnitude of in lives and costs. Fifth, "wishes and ideas" of the general public were also critical to the government's response. Not only did most Americans at first believe the epidemic was simply "a gay problem," but also some even welcomed it as "a gay plague" or "the Lord's revenge" for a deviant lifestyle, which in turn implied little or nothing should be done about it. Sixth, of course, it became "a catastrophe," not only of immense national but also international significance, one that likewise demanded national as well as large-scale, international organization responses. Finally, "personality" was vitally important in addressing AIDS, especially the managerial leadership of Dr. Helene Gayle as the following case study by Professor Norma Riccucci ably recounts. Her case is not like the typical case in this text that more or less tells a straightforward story with a clear-cut beginning, middle, and ending. Rather, it is more of an analytical biography that probes Gayle's background, her motivations for public service, and why she took on the huge challenge of AIDS and tackled a medical and social crisis that many wanted to avoid altogether. In the end Riccucci draws some fascinating general lessons from Helene Gayle's work about effective managerial leadership in public service.

As you read Riccucci's thoughtful analysis, try to reflect on what this case tells us about the "ecological factors" outlined by John Gaus and how "personality" or the leadership talents of a single manager can make a difference in what happens:

> How had Gayle's background so admirably prepared her to deal with AIDS? In thinking about your own preparation for a public service career, are there important lessons that one can learn from Gayle's career training?

> Did being a black woman give her a special edge in assuming leadership during this crisis? Or, for example, could a straight, white male have exercised the same sort of leadership?

> Why was it so critical for her to "reframe" the issues prior to dealing with them? How did she succeed in reframing AIDS as a public issue?

> What key stakeholders were most critical to developing public policies that addressed AIDS? How did Gayle identify these groups? Understand them? Partner with them and devise common strategies to combat AIDS?

> Of the eleven lessons that Riccucci lists at the end, which three do you regard as the most valuable for exercising effective public managerial leadership, and why? Do you believe such attributes can be learned? Or are they simply innate individual talents that are impossible to acquire in school or on the job?

Dr. Helene Gayle and the AIDS Epidemic

NORMA M. RICCUCCI

Dr. Helene D. Gayle was director of the National Center for HIV, STD, and TB Prevention (NCHSTP) at the U.S. Centers for Disease Control and Prevention (CDC) from 1995 until August of 2001. In September of 2001, she was detailed to the Bill and Melinda

From Norma M. Riccucci, "Managing Across Boundaries: A Case Study of Dr. Helene Gayle and the AIDS Epidemic." Transforming Organizations Series, The IBM Center for The Business of Government (January 2002), pp. 8–26. Reprinted with permission of the IBM Center for The Business of Government.

Gates Foundation because of her vast experience and success at coordinating efforts across global public-private lines to combat the spread of HIV/AIDS and other infectious diseases. She has devoted her entire professional career to the public by combating such diseases.

Born on August 16, 1955, in Buffalo, New York, Helene Doris Gayle is the third of five children. She was very much influenced and inspired by her hard-working parents—Jacob, a small business owner, and Marietta, a social worker. Reflecting on the values they instilled in her, Gayle said that "both of my parents felt strongly that to make a contribution to the world around us is one of the greatest things you can do." What a presage this would be for Gayle, who would eventually go on to impact the global war against one of the deadliest diseases of the 20th century.

Gayle's parents were very active in the civil rights movement, because they, as well as their children, witnessed firsthand the impact of discrimination against African Americans in this country. Gayle's experiences here encouraged her to pursue undergraduate studies in psychology at Barnard College. Likewise, she would later pursue a medical degree at the University of Pennsylvania because she was interested in having an impact on issues affecting underserved and disenfranchised communities. And medicine—and, more broadly, public health—would provide that opportunity.

At the same time she was working on her medical degree at the University of Pennsylvania, Dr. Gayle went on to earn a Masters of Public Health (MPH) at Johns Hopkins University. Her interest in public health was sparked by a desire to be involved in the social as well as political aspects of medicine stemming from early involvement in social and political issues. Years earlier, when she was a medical student, she heard a speech by Dr. D. A. Henderson on the worldwide efforts to eradicate smallpox. That speech helped to cement her goal of pursuing a career in public health.

By 1981, Gayle had earned both an M.D. and an MPH. She was but 25 years young and about to begin a pediatric residency at the Children's Hospital National Medical Center in Washington, D.C. As a resident at Children's Hospital, she rotated on a monthly basis through all the different specialties within pediatric medicine to gain expertise as a pediatrician. Three years later, Dr. Gayle was selected to participate in the CDC's very prestigious two-year epidemiology training program, the Epidemic Intelligence Service (EIS). This program is an apprenticeship of sorts, in that the participants go through hands-on training in epidemiology. Dr. Gayle's main focus was on prevention of malnutrition in children in the United States and Africa.

She subsequently completed an additional year of training in preventive medicine focusing on diarrheal diseases of children in developing countries. Upon completion of her training in epidemiology and preventive medicine, Dr. Gayle joined CDC's Division of HIV/AIDS. Her early work at CDC involved examining the risks of HIV transmission from mother to child, and the risks for adolescents, college students, and U.S.

racial and ethnic minorities. Knowledge gained from these types of studies served to focus the development of HIV/AIDS prevention strategies.

Dr. Gayle points out that "AIDS became the focus of my work at the CDC because it is so very central to public health and policy, and it is, in fact, a way of addressing broader public health issues related to children, women, and underserved populations throughout the world. And these are all issues that I am very committed to. . . . But I maintain that if we can do something about AIDS in this country, as well as in the rest of the world, then we will have moved forward as a society in dealing with much more than just a public health issue."

Dr. Gayle's work eventually took on a more international focus, as she was promoted to chief of International Activity within the Division of HIV/AIDS. In this capacity, she was involved in epidemiological research in such countries as the former Zaire, Jamaica, South Africa, the Ivory Coast, and Thailand.

Because of her outstanding achievements in the international AIDS arena, Dr. Gayle was detailed to the U.S. Agency for International Development (USAID) in the early 1990s, where she served as the agency's AIDS coordinator and chief of the HIV/AIDS Division. Working with other countries and international organizations to develop global AIDS policies, Dr. Gayle was USAID's chief representative on international HIV/AIDS issues.

In June of 1994, Dr. Gayle returned to the CDC and served as the director of the Washington, D.C. office, representing CDC on legislative, policy, program management, and intergovernmental matters. She also acted as liaison with other high-level department officials in the federal government. It was during this period of time that Dr. Gayle was asked to participate in the group that ultimately recommended the creation of a new center, the National Center for HIV, STD, and TB Prevention (NCHSTP).

Dr. Helene Gayle was in fact a key player in the effort to create this new center. Through an examination of the broader managerial and organizational functions of the CDC as they pertained to disease prevention and control, she and her working group assessed the feasibility of reorganizing and consolidating major organizational units working on HIV/AIDS and two related areas—other STDs and TB—within CDC. Integrating these activities under one structure not only improved the coordination of HIV efforts, but also provided a more integrated approach to diseases that share behavioral and biological interactions.

Career Highlights of Dr. Helene Gayle

1976:	B.A. in Psychology, Cum Laude, Barnard College, Columbia University
1981:	M.D., University of Pennsylvania
1981:	M.P.H., School of Hygiene and Public Health, Johns Hopkins University
1981–1984:	Pediatric Internship and Residency, Children's Hospital, National Medical Center, Washington, D.C.
1984–1986:	Epidemic Intelligence Service, Centers for Disease Control and Prevention
1985–1987:	Preventive Medicine Residency, Centers for Disease Control and Prevention
1987–1989:	Medical Epidemiologist, Pediatric and Family Studies Section, AIDS Program, Centers for Disease Control and Prevention
1988–1989:	Acting Special Assistant for Minority HIV Policy Coordination, Office of Deputy Director (HIV), Centers for Disease Control and Prevention
1989–1992:	Assistant Director, Preventive Medicine Residency Program, Centers for Disease Control and Prevention
1989–1990:	Assistant Chief for Science, International Activity, Division of HIV/AIDS, Centers for Disease Control and Prevention
1990–1992:	Chief, International Activity, Division of HIV/AIDS, Centers for Disease Control and Prevention
1992–1994:	Chief, HIV/AIDS Division, Agency AIDS Coordinator, U.S. Agency for International Development (USAID)
1994–1995:	Associate Director, Washington, D.C. Office, Centers for Disease Control and Prevention
Feb. 1995:	Interim Director, National Center for HIV, STD, and TB Prevention (NCHSTP), Centers for Disease Control and Prevention
May 1995– Aug. 2001:	Director, National Center for HIV/AIDS, STD, and TB Prevention, Centers for Disease Control and Prevention
Sept. 2001– present:	Senior Advisor for HIV/AIDS, Bill and Melinda Gates Foundation

On September 21, 1995, Dr. Donna Shalala, then Secretary of the Department of Health and Human Services, named Dr. Gayle director of the new National Center for HIV, STD, and TB Prevention. Dr. Gayle had served as interim director of NCHSTP since its creation in February of 1995. The CDC director at the time, Dr. David Satcher, noted that Dr. Gayle was the obvious person to run the Center, not only because she helped create it, but also because of her proven track record in managing and leading efforts to prevent and control infectious diseases, in particular her successful accomplishments in combating one of the most deadly epidemics of the 20th century—HIV/AIDS. He said: "Dr. Gayle provided impressive leadership for the Center's reorganization efforts. In addition, [she] has been instrumental in providing a thorough analysis of future prevention needs and implementing organizational solutions that will improve the visibility and accountability of CDC's HIV/AIDS programs and integrate HIV/STD/TB prevention efforts."

The NCHSTP is the largest of CDC's 11 centers, institutes, and offices. It has five divisions, which are responsible for public health surveillance, prevention research, the development of programs to prevent and control HIV infection, other sexually transmitted diseases, and tuberculosis, and evaluation of these programs.

As a recognized world leader in the fight against HIV/AIDS, Dr. Gayle is currently on loan from the CDC to the Bill and Melinda Gates Foundation, where she serves as senior advisor for HIV/AIDS. The foundation's major mission is to help improve the lives of people globally through health and learning. Dr. Gayle's primary responsibilities are managing and overseeing programs and policies aimed at preventing the spread of HIV/AIDS and other communicable diseases throughout the world.

The Five Divisions of the NCHSTP

1. **Division of HIV/AIDS Prevention: Intervention, Research, and Support:** conducts behavioral intervention and operations research and evaluation and provides financial and technical assistance for HIV prevention programs conducted by state, local, and territorial health departments, national and regional minority organizations, community-based organizations, business, labor, faith-based organizations, and training agencies.

2. **Division of HIV/AIDS Prevention: Surveillance and Epidemiology:** conducts surveillance and epidemiologic and behavioral research to monitor trends and risk behaviors and provide a basis for targeting prevention resources.

3. **Division of STD Prevention:** works to prevent STDs, including syphilis, gonorrhea, chlamydia, human papillomavirus, genital herpes, and hepatitis B.

4. **Division of Tuberculosis Elimination:** works to prevent, control, and eliminate TB.

5. **Global AIDS Program:** works closely with the U.S. Agency for International Development (USAID) and other federal and international agencies to prevent the spread of HIV/AIDS throughout the world.

When Secretary of Health and Human Services Tommy G. Thompson announced that Dr. Gayle would be detailed from the CDC to the Gates Foundation, he stated in his press release that "Dr. Gayle will provide an invaluable depth of knowledge and the ability to coordinate efforts across public and private sector lines, *and across boundaries,* to make the fullest possible use of our resources against this scourge."

Dr. Gayle looked forward to the post with the Gates Foundation, commenting, "it is my profound belief that solutions to this pandemic, both in the United States and around the world, will come only through strong public/private partnerships."

Dr. Gayle has certainly had innumerable opportunities to leave the federal service and work in the private sector as a physician, where she would earn a higher salary. Yet, she opted to remain with the government because she feels that it is still an important place where she can make a positive contribution to society. She says, "I don't regret having placed a high priority on a career that enables me to make a contribution to humankind."

The Setting

It has been almost two decades since the HIV/AIDS crisis surfaced. Very early on, the U.S. Centers for Disease Control and Prevention, an agency of the U.S. Department of Health and Human Services and the lead federal agency for protecting the health and safety of Americans, became involved in the battle against this deadly disease. The HIV/AIDS epidemic continues to ravage the world's population, and the CDC is still at the forefront of the battle. As of December 2000, the CDC reports that 774,467 Americans are estimated to have AIDS, with the estimated annual rate of HIV infections in the U.S. remaining roughly constant at 40,000 since the early 1990s. In South Africa alone, statistics indicate that 4.7 million people are infected with the virus, and more than half a million were infected with HIV last year alone. Experts say that AIDS is wiping out an entire generation in South Africa—a major portion of that country's national workforce, including doctors, teachers, and engineers. "There will be, for the first time, more people in their 60s and 70s than people in their 30s and 40s," said Dr. Peter Piot, director of the United Nations AIDS program. South Africa has one of the highest rates of HIV/AIDS infections in the world. Because there is currently no cure for AIDS, the importance of prevention is monumental.

Other sexually transmitted diseases also continued to occur at high rates in the 1980s and 1990s as well. Syphilis, gonorrhea, chlamydia, and genital human papillomavirus (HPV) infection have been widespread public health concerns, and represent a serious threat to reproductive health. Moreover, certain genital HPV types are related to cervical, vulvar, anal, and penile cancers. With an estimated 340 million people worldwide being infected with an STD, the challenge for pre-

---

Current Worldwide Statistics on HIV/AIDS

5.3 million people newly infected with HIV in 2000:

- 4.7 million adults,
- including 2.2 million women;
- 600,000 children under age 15.

  80% of all adult infections have resulted from heterosexual intercourse.

At the end of 2000, 36.1 million people living with HIV/AIDS:

- 34.7 million adults,
- including 16.4 million women;
- 1.4 million children under age 15.

  25.3 million reside in sub-Saharan Africa;
  5.8 million live in South and Southeast Asia.

In 2000, there were 3 million deaths due to HIV/AIDS:

- 2.5 million adults,
- including 1.3 million women;
- 500,000 children under age 15.

Since the beginning of the epidemic, an estimated 21.8 million people have died:

- 17.5 million adults,
- including 9.7 million women;
- 4.3 million children under age 15.

There have been 13.2 million orphans since the beginning of the epidemic.

Source: UNAIDS Joint United Nations Programme on HIV/AIDS, www.avert.org/worldstats.htm.

---

vention is great. The largest number of new cases is occurring in South and Southeast Asia, sub-Saharan Africa, Latin America, and the Caribbean. However, over 14 million cases occur in North America. Again, it is clear that collaborative efforts to build and improve the public health infrastructure in surveillance, treatment, and prevention are imperative and cost effective.

From 1985 to 1992, the nation also experienced a resurgence of TB. One of the reasons was the disappearance of public health funds specifically targeted for TB programs, which subsequently led to the dismantling of these services. Both TB and HIV are issues that require extensive collaborations in prevention, treatment, and care. It is estimated that approximately 34.3 million people living with HIV also have Myco-bacterium tuberculosis. According to the World Health Organization (WHO), "tuberculosis kills 2 million people each year." The "breakdown in health services, the spread of HIV/AIDS, and the resurgence of multidrug-resistant TB are contributing to the worsening impact of this disease." It is further estimated that one-third of the world's population is currently infected with the TB bacillus. The overall importance of identifying those with TB, assuring access to care and drugs, and working to ensure that patients maintain their prescribed drug regimen are all crucial issues in the field of TB elimination.

Additionally, according to WHO, "since 70 percent of those co-infected live in sub-Saharan Africa, this region also bears the overwhelming brunt of the global epidemic of HIV-associated TB." The lack of sufficient surveillance, access to drugs, and public health infrastructures in this region make for what seems an insurmountable task. It is also estimated that more than 16,000 new U.S. cases occur annually.

HIV/AIDS, other sexually transmitted diseases, and TB have all proved to be devastating global epidemics in the 1980s and 1990s, and continue to represent a growing threat to public health in the 21st century. One of the people who has been most instrumental in combating these diseases worldwide is Dr. Helene Gayle. In fact, in an effort to better manage and coordinate the various activities, programs, and arsenals aimed at reducing and preventing the spread of these diseases, the CDC created, through a major reorganization effort spearheaded and led by Dr. Helene Gayle, the National Center for HIV, STD, and TB Prevention in 1995.

Let's take a closer look at the career of Dr. Helene Gayle and why she has become a recognized world leader in the fight against AIDS and other communicable and sexually transmitted diseases.

Current Statistics on HIV/AIDS, other STDs, and TB in the United States

- As of December 2000, 774,467 Americans were reported to have AIDS:

  640,022 reported to be male
  134,441 reported to be female
  8,908 reported to be children under age 13

- Approximately 40,000 new HIV infections occur each year.
- In 2000, 16,377 cases of active TB among Americans reported.
- In 1999, 659,441 cases of genital chlamydial infection among Americans reported.
- In 1999, 360,076 cases of gonorrhea among Americans reported.

Source: Surveillance reports published online by the U.S. Centers for Disease Control and Prevention, www.cdc.gov.

The Case Study

Dr. Gayle can be credited with innumerable accomplishments in the battle against HIV/AIDS and other contagious diseases not only in the United States but globally as well. Her accomplishments can be characterized as a combination of skills, talents, and strategies, including her expertise as a public health official, her managerial skills within the organizations she has directed, and her strong leadership skills in the external national and international communities in the fight against deadly diseases.

Reframing the Issues

In recent years, Dr. Gayle has worked very hard within the United States to reframe the issues and concerns surrounding HIV/AIDS and other STDs. She points out that in the early stages of the AIDS epidemic, there was a perception that the disease affected primarily the white gay community, which lulled people into thinking this was the only population at risk. Clearly, HIV/AIDS is not a white gay disease. In fact, today AIDS and other STDs have the greatest impact on populations of color.

Dr. Gayle notes, "It is the African American and Latino communities that are currently at the greatest risk."

Prevention messages often miss the mark in communities of color, Dr. Gayle points out. For example, in communities of color, "for far too long, the assumption was that the impact on gay and bisexual men was only among whites; this is not the case." Dr. Gayle points out that in a study of 8,700 HIV-positive men who said they were infected by having sex with other men, one-quarter of the African Americans identified themselves as heterosexual. Only 6 percent of white men, in contrast, identified themselves as heterosexual. Men who have sex with men do not always identify themselves as gay or bisexual. They may live outwardly heterosexual lives, often married with children, but continue having sex with men. This is characteristic of men of all races, but the phenomenon appears to be more prevalent among African Americans. The phenomenon has been called having sex "on the down low" or "the D.L." She further notes that "programs for black men must address the stigma of homosexuality, which prevents many of these men from identifying themselves as gay and bisexual and may keep them from accessing needed prevention and treatment services."

In addition, needle sharing associated with injection drug use has been identified as one of the leading causes in the spread of HIV/AIDS today. In particular, injection drug use and needle sharing in African American communities has been reported to be one of the reasons for the higher rates of HIV/AIDS cases among African Americans in the United States.

The upshot is that the issues had to be reframed. One of Dr. Gayle's greatest challenges, then, has been to not only make people aware that populations of color are at the greatest risk, but to tailor and adapt the various strategies and methods for prevention to the persons (e.g., those who don't self-identify as gay) who may be less receptive and accessible to prevention messages relevant to the white gay community, yet are contributing to the rate of HIV/AIDS in communities of color. Besides reframing messages, it was also important to make sure that the appropriate messengers were also part of the equation. This requires greater collaboration and support for organizations that can effectively represent and reach communities at risk.

Creating Partnerships

Dr. Gayle stresses that linking prevention efforts with the organizations and people involved in the care and treatment of HIV/AIDS and other STDs is pivotal to success, so that there is a continuum between prevention and care. Linking and integrating the various services and strategies to assure coordination of resources, as well as cost and program effectiveness, in its efforts to control HIV/AIDS and other STDs must be accorded higher priority.

Dr. Gayle also explains that much of her work depends upon successful collaboration with community, state, national, and international partners in efforts to stop the spread of diseases such as TB, HIV/AIDS, and other STDs. As Dr. Gayle readily acknowledges, "We are not the sole players, nor will we ever have all the resources to fix all these problems on our own. Developing collaborations is key." For example, under her direction, NCHSTP works diligently to assure such coordination by developing partnerships with other agencies within its parent organization, the Department of Health and Human Services, including the National Institutes of Health, the Health Resources and Services Administration, the Food and Drug Administration, and the Substance Abuse and Mental Health Services Administration. The recently released CDC "HIV Prevention Strategic Plan" highlights the need for collaboration among government agencies, universities, state and local health departments, and community-based organizations so that relevant scientists, epidemiologists, and policy makers can come together to form a unified front in the fight against diseases such as HIV/AIDS, STDs, and TB.

Dr. Gayle points out that collaborating with private sector organizations, in particular faith-based institutions, may be one of the most important strategies for combating HIV/AIDS and other STDs in communities of color. She notes that "it has been critical to involve and have the faith communities work with us on some of these more controversial issues because of the key role they play in helping shape opinions and attitudes and, especially in the African American community, serving as agents of social change." So developing partnerships with faith-based organizations such as churches is a key strategy in controlling and preventing the spread of HIV/AIDS and other sexually transmitted diseases in the United States as well as other countries.

Dr. Gayle is an acclaimed pioneer in the creation of community-based prevention activities, especially among minority and underserved communities. She has been particularly successful in getting disparate groups, including minority, gay, and church communities, involved so that they have a better understanding of what the government does related to HIV/AIDS and other STDs. She notes that "many of the issues around AIDS have led to a good deal of mistrust between communities at risk, as well as communities at large, and I have tried to facilitate bringing a broad cross-section of people more into the process and create more open communications among them. The AIDS epidemic has stimulated us to be much more inclusive as public health officials."

Dr. David Satcher, who is currently the U.S. Surgeon General and who directed the CDC from 1993 to 1998, commented on Dr. Gayle's extraordinary ability to work effectively in local communities. He points out that "Helene gets to know and works with people locally. I think she took the concept of government-funded programs to the local community as it has never been done before. Working and helping to plan at a local level and assuring that there are planning committees in each local community—we've never really done this before in government the way it's been done for the AIDS prevention program. It's one of the most innovative strategies ever developed in terms of involving local communities, and Helene was responsible for implementing this."

Dr. Satcher went on to say, "Another thing about Helene that makes her effective in her work with different groups or communities is that she is a likable person. She doesn't take herself too seriously, and this makes it easier for people to work with her. She has a genuine interest in other people, and people recognize this; she also has a sense of humor. And I think that all this makes for a better working relationship when you are working on difficult issues. You have to create an environment where people are comfortable, and she does this very effectively."

Working to improve access to HIV care for people in poor countries is also important for Dr. Gayle, because currently treatment for HIV is still very limited in poor countries, which bear the greatest burden of HIV/AIDS. The cost of providing anti-retroviral drugs for HIV has become a particularly serious problem in developing countries, where even simple medications are out of reach for much of the population. Dr. Gayle points out that the CDC works with over 20 countries worldwide to address the issues of prevention, access, and availability of care. After years of multinational-partnered efforts, in 2001 pharmaceutical companies finally began slashing the cost of AIDS treatment drugs for Africa, which will provide great relief to those infected with the virus. However, even with lower prices, access to relatively complex anti-retroviral therapy will still be limited in the short run because of weak health infrastructure.

Some of the Key Policy Players in Dr. Gayle's Policy Arena

Dr. Kenneth Castro, Director of the TB Division of the National Center for HIV, STD, and TB Prevention (NCHSTP)

Dr. David Holtgrave, former Director of the NCHSTP's Division of HIV/AIDS Prevention: Intervention, Research and Support

Dr. David Satcher, U.S. Surgeon General and former Director of the U.S. Centers for Disease Control and Prevention (CDC)

Todd Summer, former Deputy Director of the White House Office of National AIDS Policy

Dr. Judy Wasserheit, former Director, NCHSTP's STD Division

The CDC also collaborates with private sector firms not only in the United States but also in other parts of the world, including working to set up work-site HIV prevention programs. The CDC has been involved in a program called Business Responds to AIDS (BRTA), working with major corporations for over 10 years to have employers educate and disseminate information to their workers about the causes of HIV/AIDS and how it spreads. The CDC also works with U.S. multinational corporations such as the Ford Motor Company in countries like South Africa, where education and other services are provided not only to employees but also to the neighborhoods and the communities around their plants.

In the international arena, the CDC collaborates with a number of other critical partners, including the U.S. Agency for International Development, the Joint United Nations Program on HIV/AIDS (UNAIDS), the World Health Organization, the United Nations Children's Fund (UNICEF), and the World Bank, to name a few. And, obviously, working with the countries themselves is key.

Building Relationships

One of the reasons why Dr. Gayle has been so successful at collaboration—building bridges and fostering communications between the federal government, various communities, and global partners—is her skillful interpersonal relations. As she herself admits, "I very much enjoy working with people. Also, I have tried not

to divorce myself from who I am, and the many people and communities that have contributed to my sense of self. So, I can usually see commonalities in people, [and] at the same time recognize and appreciate diversity and differences. I feel that by listening to others and relying on my own experiences, I can find these commonalities, which serve to break down barriers with groups."

Dr. Satcher, U.S. Surgeon General and former CDC director, said, "People are willing to work with her because they trust her and have confidence in her. Inside and outside of government, people have a lot of confidence and trust in her, because they trust her motivation: She really cares about people and helping them."

Todd Summer, former deputy director of the White House Office of National AIDS Policy, notes that "Helene does very well at developing relationships. . . . She is very personable, and I have never met anyone that doesn't like Helene. And sometimes when people [or outside groups] feel like blasting the CDC, it's because of affection for her that they tone down their words or hold their criticisms altogether."

Perhaps the key to Dr. Gayle's efficacy is her ability to foster dialogue between and among diverse people and groups. This means, says Dr. Gayle, "believing in what they do. If you can understand *their* position and *their* thought processes and believe they are justified in their respective positions, you can work effectively with disparate groups and people. It is then important to get people to see the similarities in their positions—that is, to make them understand that we *do* all think differently, but this is part of who we are and it doesn't make us right or wrong. When people can accept the fact that there are other equally plausible perspectives, then you can make some progress in your efforts to fold or incorporate these groups into the public policy process, in this case around AIDS."

Dr. David Holtgrave, former director of NCHSTP's Division of HIV/AIDS Prevention: Intervention, Research and Support, said that Dr. Gayle is good at collaborating because she "has been absolutely committed to HIV prevention not only in the United States but globally, especially in developing countries, and she has made international HIV/AIDS work a priority of the Center. To do this really requires collaborating with the leaders of the various countries as well as the health ministers, and then all of the international organizations such as the World Health Organization and UNAIDS to get that work done. This requires effective collaborating skills." He went on to say that "Helene has extensive knowledge about how governments function, country by country, and how we function," and she believes in "really interacting with other countries, where we are truly collaborating and not trying to impose our programs on them."

The Politics of Public Health

Obviously, developing coalitions and collaborating with governmental and nongovernmental partners at community, state, national, and international levels requires a certain degree of political savvy and acumen. Indeed, because of the political as well as social challenges that have imbued the HIV/AIDS epidemic, possessing a high degree of diplomacy is essential. Her interpersonal skills as well as her technical expertise have served her well here. This latter attribute has been especially helpful in her interactions in political arenas, because technical or public health justifications are necessary for agency decisions. As she points out, "As a 'technocrat,' I have responsibilities for assisting in the formulation of public health policy, using the best available data to do so. As I help to shape the direction of research efforts for HIV prevention programs, I try to provide justification for policy options based on what we know and what we think will have the greatest positive benefit. While this seems obvious, it often isn't, because of the political considerations which underlie diseases such as HIV/AIDS."

Dr. Judy Wasserheit, former director of the STD Division of the NCHSTP, points out that Dr. Gayle "is politically very savvy and she networks well with people. . . . and she pays attention to the care and feeding of networks and people." Dr. Wasserheit went on to say that "Helene is very skilled in interacting with people. She is very intuitive in her understanding about how political systems and individuals work. She has a very good appreciation of this, which allows her to make the system work constructively."

Dr. Gayle has also been very successful in working with political appointees across government agencies. Dr. James Curran, former associate director for HIV/AIDS at CDC, has commented on Dr. Gayle's ability to work effectively with different political and policy players. He said: "Helene has the unique capacity to get people to work together, in part, because she is so willing to go the extra mile herself in getting the job done and, in part, because she understands not only the scientific issues but she is also able to see other people's points of view; she is able to walk in their shoes and this is a very valuable asset. It is also important that

she is not politically motivated. She is committed to the public's health and not any particular philosophy of government. She is just doing her job and doing it very effectively, and this is quite laudable. . . . Also, she works so well with people because she likes interacting with them. People recognize this and so they like working with her. . . . She is very upbeat about her work, which is difficult and unusual when you are working with a fatal disease such as AIDS."

Dr. Gayle has also been successful working in a highly charged political environment, which, when working in an area such as HIV prevention, sets up a number of obstacles. Still, she has been effective, as Todd Summer points out, because "she is unflappable. Helene can take a two-by-four between the eyes and keep going. She, more than a lot of people I have ever met, is able to let a lot of things roll off her back and keep focused on what it is she is seeking to do within the limitations she faces. . . . She continues to push the edges," which is somewhat difficult for "an African American woman working in a predominately white male environment."

Dr. Gayle must also strike a careful balance between working in a political environment and in a government setting. That is to say, Dr. Gayle faces certain constraints as a public servant, indeed a career official, that serve as obstacles in her efforts to combat polemical diseases such as HIV and other STDs. Summer pointed out that, "Helene is a bureaucrat within a larger system. And there are limits to what she can do and what she can say. She tries to push to the end of those limits, but she is also appropriately cautious not to cross them, unless she's ready to leave the government. . . . When you work in government, there are always challenges against what you professionally and personally believe and what you are able to do as a government employee. And particularly in an area like HIV prevention, you rub against these limits all the time, while trying to maintain your sense of personal dignity and professional integrity in the face of bureaucratic pressures. Helene has been able to do this."

Setting Goals and Targeting Strategies

Another important aspect of her lifetime commitment to combating contagious diseases such as HIV/AIDS is having a vision. Dr. Gayle has always had a vision of what is needed to advance as well as augment existing efforts to combat infectious diseases. But, recognizing the importance of a shared vision, Dr. Gayle has always relied heavily on the input of her senior staff. As one of her division directors (the TB Division), Dr. Kenneth Castro, points out, "Helene isn't the type of person that would come in and say, 'This is my vision and you'll have to accept it.' Instead, she invited us to help develop that vision, which helped to bring all of us on board. . . . This way, it didn't come down from above and was forced on us."

Once a shared vision is developed, Dr. Gayle then moves to a series of actionable steps to guide her staff in reaching organizational goals. For instance, as director of the NCHSTP, her first step was to develop a broad strategic view of all the program areas—HIV/AIDS, other STDs, and TB. Setting long-term goals around what the Center seeks to accomplish in these areas is perhaps one of the most critical elements. In addition, under the lead of NCHSTP, the CDC recently finished a phase of long-term goal setting in the area of HIV/AIDS, where it seeks to reduce by 50 percent new HIV infections in the United States by the year 2005.

Besides setting long-term goals, Dr. Gayle also sees the importance of setting short-term actionable items that could be achieved incrementally. Setting small, attainable, and pragmatic goals enables her agency to reach overall goals on an incremental basis. She points out that "we try to determine what steps on the ladder will get us to our long-range goals, and then ask what are the processes and activities that we need to put in place to ensure that we will reach our goal. Measuring how well we do a particular sub-goal or short-term actionable goal isn't going to tell us whether we have reduced the spread of a given disease; but these short-term actionable goals are necessary steps in order to reach our long-term or end goal."

As Dr. Gayle goes on to say, "If our goal is ultimately to stop the spread of any of the diseases we deal with, certain processes need to be put in place. For example, we ask whether we are targeting the appropriate or correct areas for funding. If the epidemics are hitting the communities of color disproportionately, we have to ensure that we have processes in place to get the resources to those communities. So, we develop strategies around the people or communities who should be getting resources. This is an actionable step and will help us achieve our end goal of stopping the spread of a given disease."

U.S. Surgeon General Satcher discussed the strong sense of vision that Dr. Gayle has for leadership of the Center and for the battle against HIV/AIDS and other STDs. In fact, he noted that "Helene has an unusual *global* vision [his emphasis] for public health, which is really critical because many of us believe that in order for public health to be successful, it must be global in perspective. It's important to think globally and then act locally, and Helene exemplifies this better than anyone I know. . . . She has the global vision of the problem and then she also has a vision as to how to respond to local challenges and needs."

In addition to a shared vision, a commitment to values and engendering a commitment from staff is critical to her work in the public health arena. As a public health official, particularly one involved in areas such as HIV/AIDS and other STDs, Dr. Gayle is necessarily immersed in the social as well as political aspects of medicine. But she has a serious and dedicated commitment to the goals and values of the CDC and specifically the NCHSTP, and places its mission above *all* other interests. She points out that "clearly, it's important to be realistic and mindful of the political realities but at the same time hope that our policies can be directed by our knowledge and our commitment to the health of the populations we serve. And I hope my position would be consistent regardless of the administration in office, because it is the right thing to do from the standpoint of developing effective strategies to prevent the spread of HIV, STDs, and TB."

One representative of a community-based group points out that Dr. Gayle is so effective at her job "because, first and foremost, she has a personal commitment to the issue areas, which goes beyond her government job." Dr. Gayle, it was noted, truly has a "commitment to the health of the populations [she] serves." Her leadership in steering her Center to achieve and maintain a strong commitment to the Center's values has by all accounts proven to be successful.

Former Deputy Director of the White House Office of National AIDS Policy Todd Summer points out that "you appreciate very quickly after working with Helene that this is far more than just a job to her. She cares about the issue, she struggles within and against an environment that would probably have moved a number of people away; she's been at the CDC for 17 years, and this is a significant contribution."

The Challenges of Bureaucracy

Dr. Gayle has had to overcome a number of formidable obstacles in her work to combat HIV and other STDs, but her sheer commitment has helped her succeed. For example, Summer noted that Dr. Gayle has been very effective in "her ability to manage a system that was not designed for her to succeed." Summer was referring to the organizational structure of the CDC, where "the [various] center directors are more or less autonomous rulers of their fiefdoms." And funding for HIV programs was distributed across the CDC's centers without very much prioritization. Dr. Gayle, Summer pointed out, had a potential battle on her hands, because as she sought to set priorities for the distribution of funding to better target the areas of need, she would have to gain buy-in from the other center directors.

Another significant barrier that Dr. Gayle faced, Summer said, was "the white boys network." Dr. Gayle is the first African American and second woman Center director at the Centers for Disease Control. Summer notes that "there is a culture [at the CDC] that is not always supportive of having an African American woman Center director. And as you can see, there aren't too many colleagues like her at CDC. So, on all levels, she is battling to try to organize funds without authority and she is battling in an environment that is not necessarily supportive of her as an African American woman and in an epidemic where congressional scrutiny . . . into what [CDC] can do around prevention is always looming over her head."

Dr. Gayle agrees. She notes that being a woman and African American is often challenging. "I function in a white-male-dominated professional environment. This obviously presents many challenges. For instance, I am never sure when I walk into a room for the first time how I will be perceived. In its most productive sense, as an African American and a woman, I should not be thought of as just another statistic but hopefully as adding to the diversity that enriches our work environment and brings different perspectives, experiences, and styles of communication. I think that people who work in public health, by virtue of the issues we focus on, are often more enlightened about race and gender issues. However, many of the manifestations of racism and sexism are subtle and even unconscious based on one's lifetime experiences. Many very well-intentioned colleagues often unknowingly demonstrate an ignorance of important race and gender sensitivities."

She went on to say: "Being black and female carries some additional burdens both externally and probably internally generated as well. I hope I do a reasonable job of trying to balance those issues, choosing battles wisely and not being totally preoccupied with, but at the same time commanding respect for, my race and gender. . . . Not being white or male can certainly be a challenge. There are still times that because of my race and gender, people at first glance may perceive me as not being credible or competent. But I have to say

that people are trying hard to get past the old way of doing business, and this ultimately creates opportunities."

Leadership: Building Trust and Confidence

Dr. Gayle's approach to leadership accounts for her vast success as a public health official within the United States and globally. As Dr. Castro stresses, "Helene is viewed as an effective leader because she ensures that we are *collectively* [his emphasis] working to achieve [the Center's] common goal." In addition, as Dr. Satcher pointed out, "Leadership means developing people's trust . . . From speaking with people around the world, I learned that Helene has garnered a lot of confidence from people. And even today, I would say that she is probably the most trusted American among African countries . . . She has developed a lot of credibility because of her *knowledge* and insight into public health as it relates to AIDS and also because she really *cares* about the issues, and people see this [his emphasis]. And this, to me, translates into strong leadership."

The level of confidence and trust accorded to Dr. Gayle is clearly evident in her appointment by South African President Thabo Mbeki to his AIDS Advisory Panel. President Mbeki, at the 13th World AIDS Conference held in Durban, South Africa, in 2000, caused a great stir when he suggested during his address that, while HIV is linked to AIDS, it was not the lone cause of the syndrome. He went on to say that the world's biggest killer and the greatest cause of ill health and suffering across the globe, including in South Africa, is poverty, and that poverty is to blame for the quick spread of AIDS in his country.

Hundreds of conference delegates, dignitaries, and other participants walked out on President Mbeki's opening address, suggesting that his comments were tantamount to a claim that HIV doesn't cause AIDS. Others claimed that this was a gross misinterpretation of President Mbeki's comments and that Mbeki was merely stating that HIV and AIDS are exacerbated by poverty, poor nutrition, and certain socioeconomic conditions.

Prior to the conference, President Mbeki had appointed an AIDS Advisory Panel to help assuage the growing public dismay and consternation that would inevitably hinder his efforts to battle HIV/AIDS in South Africa. Recognized top leaders in the field of HIV/AIDS from around the world were appointed to the panel. As Dr. Holtgrave pointed out, Dr. Gayle was appointed to the panel because of her skills in diplomacy and consensus building and her ability to build trust and confidence among people. He noted that the panel was set up to address a very difficult area of public health, which demands collaboration. And, Dr. Holtgrave went on to say, President Mbeki's comments at the World AIDS Conference threatened existing international collaborations to combat HIV/AIDS. He said President Mbeki was confident that "Helene would be able to figure out a way to keep everyone together enough so that the programs could move forward. . . . Helene would be able to keep the process from breaking down and becoming divisive, which is what prevents public health programs from moving forward."

Most recently, Dr. Gayle was invited to China to provide input to that country's government on developing their efforts to battle the HIV epidemic. In a country that has avoided any public attention on its growing AIDS problem, Dr. Gayle noted that if China did not address the epidemic, the United Nations estimates there could be over 20 million Chinese carrying the AIDS virus by 2010.

Another important attribute of effective leadership, which explains why Dr. Gayle is highly sought after for her skills and professional counsel, is acting responsibly, even in the face of criticism. Todd Summer notes that even when outside groups don't agree with what the CDC is doing, "Helene doesn't point fingers. She doesn't move the blame aside and say, 'Well, that's not my fault.' She takes it and goes."

Moreover, Dr. Gayle is viewed as someone who has an unwavering, steadfast commitment to the issues. Dr. Wasserheit points out that "Helene cares very deeply about what she works on, particularly HIV prevention. That level of commitment comes through, and that's an important component of leadership."

Managing within the Bureaucracy

Dr. Gayle points out that she has always viewed staff as the backbone of her organizations and thus critical to every strategic organizational effort. In her most recent directorship of the NCHSTP, Dr. Gayle oversaw a staff of approximately 1,400 employees, and every one of them was considered important to the mission of the Center; successfully managing her own staff members has always been seen as key to accomplishing any agency goal. Dr. Wasserheit extolled Dr. Gayle's human resources management capabilities. She points out that Dr. Gayle is "a good manager because she has a pretty good sense of people. She's very insightful about people's strengths and weaknesses."

Dr. Gayle is a very strong proponent of open, shared leadership. "If anything," she points out, "I err on the side of providing more information, being open. And I believe the more teamwork you build, the more effective your organization will be. It builds more confidence among your staff and tends to cut down on uncertainties that inevitably occur in large organizations when information is missing or not readily available. It also increases morale and people's enjoyment of their jobs. If you don't empower your staff, it takes away people's purpose as organizational members."

Dr. Gayle further notes that "shared leadership is critical. I have an organization of 1,400 people, and if I didn't delegate and share power, we would fail as an organization. And to me as a decision maker, [shared leadership] helps me make better decisions, because it provides me with a wider range of knowledge and information."

Certainly, however, there must be an understanding of what information can be shared with staff. Dr. Gayle notes that "some information can only be shared with my senior staff, both because of the nature of the information and the relevance of the information at different levels. What may be relevant at the Center or Division level, for example, may not be relevant at other units within our organization levels."

Dr. Gayle's division directors point out that she does provide the flexibility needed to run their units. Dr. Wasserheit, former director of the STD Division, said that "I've had the luxury of tremendous flexibility and laissez faire," which, she further notes, has enabled her to run her division more effectively. Likewise, Dr. Castro, director of the TB Division, said: "Helene provides a very clear sense of direction, but then she has given me a very long leash to exercise my expertise and skills. So, in terms of style, she has been able to provide a sense of direction but also not be in the way of her senior staff. Some leaders tend to be very much hands-on. She has been appropriately hands-on when she has had to be there to represent us to the higher levels within the administration. But I feel very much at ease in that she has enabled her directors to contribute and is also very receptive to our own views. . . . Instead of just providing marching orders, she is very much receptive to the feedback received by her senior staff."

Dr. Gayle also stresses that risk-taking is key. "You have to be willing to take risks in leadership positions, and it means you have to take chances on the things that you believe are the right thing to do, even if it's not politically expedient. I have found that it is important not to be risk averse; taking chances and trying some things in new ways is crucial if you really want to do best for your organization and for your mission."

Dr. Castro attested to Dr. Gayle's willingness to take risks. He said, "Helene will take risks, but not recklessly. There is a balancing act here; you can't afford to take a risk that's going to bring the whole agency down." Dr. Castro pointed to a recent example of where "Helene put her neck on the line." He noted that there is a recognition among public health officials around the world that AIDS in Africa is a monumental problem with several unmet needs and that the United States is in a unique position to do something about it. Dr. Gayle, he said, "has spearheaded an effort that has resulted in resources assigned for the direct involvement of the CDC, the U.S. Agency for International Development, and other international partners to work directly with several of the sub-Saharan African countries that have an almost unmitigated AIDS problem. Her efforts have made sure we are working in partnership with the authorities there, the appropriate ministries, et cetera, to arrive at some common goals and to have us working together, shoulder to shoulder. . . . And this came at a high risk politically, because you could ask, 'Why should the U.S. taxpayers be spending money in Africa?' Well, from a public health standpoint, we should be, because, as Helene has passionately striven to demonstrate, these diseases don't stop at our borders and neither can our intervention efforts."

In sum, Dr. Gayle has been a world leader in efforts to prevent and contain the spread of infectious diseases such as HIV/AIDS. She has devoted her entire career to this. By examining her extraordinary work in the national and international arenas, we can discern what it takes to be a successful, effective manager and leader in the public service.

Lessons Learned about Effective Managerial Leadership

What are some of the factors and attributes that contribute to or characterize Dr. Gayle's success in the fight against deadly diseases such as HIV/AIDS, other STDs, and TB? Some of the factors of effective leadership correspond with Robert Denhardt's findings (1993). The following represent a summary of several lessons to be drawn.

Lesson 1: Developing Integrative, Targeted Strategies

The issues or concerns being addressed by an organization and its leaders need to be continually identified and reassessed so that there is a clear understanding of what responses and strategies can be mounted to help remedy the problems or concerns. Once the issues are clearly identified or reidentified, linking and integrating organizational resources and strategies to develop solutions is key.

In the case of Dr. Gayle and the NCHSTP, reassessment of the populations most affected today by HIV/AIDS led to a finding that people of color, in particular African Americans and Latinos—and not white gays, as popular wisdom might have it—are at the greatest risk of contracting HIV/AIDS today. The next step was to link with the individuals, organizations, and community groups involved in the prevention and treatment of HIV/AIDS to help prevent it from spreading among all populations at risk. This, as noted, requires developing and then working closely with various coalitions, which serves to leverage other resources and other key players in combating such diseases.

Lesson 2: Developing Broad Coalitions

A vital aspect of effective managerial performance is collaborating within and across governmental agencies, as well as with private sector organizations. No policy maker operates in a vacuum, and so success hinges on the extent to which government leaders develop and nurture affiliations and networks with community, state, national, international, and private sector partners. Perhaps even more important is a clear recognition of the types of resources that need to be leveraged.

For example, in the domestic arena, Dr. Gayle has found that not only are other governmental agencies instrumental in combating infectious diseases, but so, too, are faith-based and other community organizations. In her vast number of years studying these issues, Dr. Gayle has found that community-based organizations may be the most effective in helping to stop the spread of infectious diseases. Therefore, she has targeted organizations to develop community partnerships, including churches and other established organizations as important resources in helping to combat such diseases as HIV/AIDS.

In the international arena, Dr. Gayle has found that it is critical to work closely not only with global leaders, but particularly with private sector firms based in the countries being ravaged by the AIDS virus. Thus, leveraging the appropriate resources and players for the clearly identified problem or concern is key to effective management in government agencies.

Lesson 3: Possessing and Demonstrating Interpersonal Skills

Good interpersonal skills were consistently named as a key element in Dr. Gayle's ability to effectively achieve her goals, and they cut across many of the other factors attributable to successful managerial performance. Qualities such as honesty, integrity, and uncompromising commitment to one's work and agency mission significantly affect a manager's ability to be successful. In addition, a good sense of humor and the ability to appropriately inject humor can make a difference in terms of effective communication and ultimately cultivating linkages with individuals or groups.

As many noted, Dr. Gayle's outstanding interpersonal skills helped to build good working relationships across national and international boundaries and created an environment where people were comfortable addressing difficult issues such as HIV/AIDS. And her interpersonal skills go beyond good communication skills to include strengths in facilitating, coaching, moderating, and coordinating. Perhaps one of the NCHSTP division directors said it best when she said that Dr. Gayle "is politically very savvy and she networks well with people . . . and she pays attention to the care and feeding of networks and people. . . . Helene is very skilled in interacting with people."

Lesson 4: Exercising Political Skills

It seems axiomatic that political skills are critical to effective performance in government. The environment, by its very nature, is highly political. And so a high degree of diplomacy and political astuteness is essential. Dr. Wasserheit points out that Dr. Gayle "is very intuitive in her understanding about how political systems and individuals work. She has a very good appreciation of this, which allows her to make the system work constructively."

Effectively working with different political and policy players requires political savvy and good interpersonal skills. But, as was pointed out by several people, effectiveness depends on acting politically but not being politically motivated. As Dr. Curran succinctly stated, Dr. Gayle is "committed to the public's

health and not any particular philosophy of government." She has not let politics get in the way of her commitment to fighting the battle against the spread of infectious diseases.

Lesson 5: Possessing and Exercising Technical Expertise

Possessing technical expertise is critical not only because of the knowledge necessary for the substantive aspects of a policy field such as public health, but also because it provides credibility when interacting with other agencies, community groups, or policy players. The ability to engender trust and commitment from the very people, groups, and organizations that must be relied upon to achieve one's goals heavily depends on expertise.

However, technical expertise alone may be insufficient. Drive and dedication are also key. As seen here, Dr. Gayle not only has technical expertise in the epidemiology of infectious diseases, but she is also personally and professionally committed to combating them. Her life's work has been devoted to this issue, particularly around HIV/AIDS, and she has not let anything or anyone deter her in her efforts. Her dedication has been repeatedly praised and identified as one of the most important factors in her successful achievements.

Lesson 6: Setting a Vision

Having not just a vision but a *shared* vision of what is needed to advance and further develop existing efforts to combat infectious diseases is vital for effective managerial performance in government. Dr. Gayle sought out and welcomed input and participation from her senior staff, not only because of the substantive value, but also because it helped establish a sense of ownership and commitment on the part of senior policy makers and managers.

Lesson 7: Fostering Pragmatic Incrementalism

Ensuring that everyone is on board facilitates another important factor in effectively leading and managing a government agency: developing pragmatic incremental goals. Dr. Gayle recognized the importance of not only developing long-term goals, but also setting short-term actionable steps that could be achieved incrementally. Setting small, attainable goals enables her agency to reach overall goals and at the same time provides a sense of accomplishment and satisfaction. The ability to witness the positive outcomes associated with one's work provides a tremendous sense of reinforcement and job satisfaction and also helps to further workers' commitment to achieving long-range goals.

And, as Dr. David Satcher, the U.S. Surgeon General and former director of the CDC states, Dr. Gayle's *global* vision for public health is critical, because for public health to be successful in the United States, it must be global in perspective. "It's important to think globally and then act locally, and Helene exemplifies this better than anyone I know," said Dr. Satcher.

Lesson 8: Committing to Values

A commitment to values requires a serious dedication to the goals and values of your agency, placing them above all other interests. In essence, it requires *valuing* the values. Dr. Gayle formally enumerated for her agency and staff a set of values that she herself strives to maintain for her agency and works hard to instill in her staff. These values include working unyieldingly to combat infectious diseases in the United States and globally because it is the right and humane thing to do; acknowledging the hard work, dedication, focus, and intelligence of all the individuals who make up the NCHSTP; and recognizing the importance of collaborations globally and across government agencies and communities.

Lesson 9: Empowering Staff and Sharing Leadership

Sharing leadership responsibilities empowers staff. This, in turn, is likely to enhance workers' investment in their work, enhance the work's significance, promote self-determination, and increase workers' motivation and satisfaction. In addition, empowerment not only redistributes power, but it also provides a mechanism by which accountability or responsibility for outcomes is placed with individuals or teams. By making the workplace more participatory, democratic, and accountable, empowerment creates an organizational culture that promotes a sense of commitment to goal attainment and, ultimately, significantly enhances organizational productivity.

Empowering her staff comes naturally to Dr. Gayle, who has a very open, participative style of management.

This has proven to be effective for her organization, where experienced, highly trained workers, with medical or social science doctoral degrees, run the various units of the NCHSTP. She has found that by empowering her staff, they have developed a vested interest in the work of their individual units and in the integrated efforts of each unit in achieving the overall agency goals. Most importantly, Dr. Gayle emphasizes that empowerment and shared leadership are not "one-shot" processes but a way of organizational life aimed at discovering and utilizing the full potential of every member of the organization.

Lesson 10: Taking Risks

Taking responsible risks is also a critical management strategy that can promote effective managerial performance. New ideas and innovation tend to be the byproducts of risk taking, and so taking responsible risks—risks driven by a sense of ethics, honesty, and legal responsibility—is an effective managerial strategy. So, too, is encouraging staff to take risks, while working with them to help them understand the reason for mistakes and reducing their recurrence. Effective leaders also ensure that risk taking is not punished.

Dr. Gayle has found that taking risks is crucial for achieving your agency's mission. As Dr. Castro stated, "Helene will take risks, but not recklessly." Responsible risk taking can foster positive change and lead to successful organizational performance.

Lesson 11: Exercising Management and Leadership Skills

Certainly, all the factors mentioned above are important attributes of effective leadership and managerial performance, which requires flexibility, openness, dedication, commitment, and patience, to mention only a few characteristics. Effective managers and leaders in government also must have the ability to plan, organize, communicate clearly, motivate staff, and set realistic goals. They must also be honest, fair, understanding, expert in their field, and knowledgeable of the politics surrounding the environments within which they operate. And as Dr. Gayle clearly exhibits, they are goal-oriented and exhibit good interpersonal skills. Finally, an effective leader is able to create followership, which connotes not mastery but synergy. It is a relationship marked by trust, confidence, and an *intertwining* of interests.

Chapter 3 Review Questions

1. What were the chief elements from John Gaus's administrative ecology that Dr. Gayle drew on to develop public policy to combat AIDS? Explain why these elements were so critical to achieving her goals.

2. What was the role of stakeholders in supporting her work? Who were they? Which ones were most influential? What strategies did she employ to gain their support? Can you generalize about the impact of such groups on administrative programs?

3. Can you point out the ecological factors that prevented federal programs from combating AIDS aggressively at its early stages in the 1980s? What reforms would you recommend to enhance early detection and program planning in the future?

4. Compare Case Study 1, "The Blast in Centralia No. 5," with this case. How did the geographical distances in both cases influence the administrative decisions that were made or not made? Can you generalize about the difficulties of undertaking effective administrative actions as the *distances* between the administrator and "the clientele" expand?

5. Why were there various public points of view about AIDS that inhibited dealing with the epidemic? What were these competing viewpoints? Can you generalize about the difficulties of initiating effective administrative actions as public differences over an issue intensify? How did this case compare with Case Study 2, "How Kristin Died," particularly in terms of lack of public interest versus divided public support for taking administrative action?

6. After reviewing this case study, would you modify Gaus's ideas about the nature of modern administrative ecology? In your view, for instance, does he adequately include ethnic, racial, or gender differences (i.e., Dr. Gayle's leadership influence based on her being a black woman)? Media influence? Fragmented government oversight? Particularly after reviewing the eleven lessons outlined by Norma Riccucci from Dr. Gayle's public service career, would you amend or add to Gaus's list?

Key Terms

administrative ecology

physical technology

social technology

general environment

wishes and ideas

catastrophe

Suggestions for Further Reading

Gaus spent much of his life thinking about the ecology of public administration; therefore you would do well to begin by reading the entire book from which the reading in this chapter was reprinted, *Reflections on Public Administration* (Tuscaloosa, Ala.: University of Alabama Press, 1947). For an excellent summary of current literature in this field, see Chapter 4 in Hal Rainey, *Understanding and Managing Public*

Organizations (San Francisco; Jossey-Bass, 1997). In recent years comparative administrative scholars are perhaps the ablest group carrying on Gaus's investigations in this area; see Fred Riggs, *The Ecology of Administration* (New York: Asia Publishing House, 1967), as well as Ferrel Heady, *Public Administration: A Comparative Perspective,* 6th ed. (New York: Marcel Dekker, 2001). For an insightful retrospective on the comparative movement, read Ferrel Heady, *One Time Around* (Albuquerque: School of Public Administration, University of New Mexico, 1999). For other recent comparativist writings, see Jamil Jreisat, *Comparative Public Administration and Policy* (Boulder: Westview, 2002). Jon Pierre and B. Guy Peters, eds., *Handbook of Public Administration* (Thousand Oaks, Calif: Sage, 2004); B. Guy Peters, *Governing,* 2nd ed. (Lawrence: University of Kansas Press, 2001); Don Kettl, *The Transformation of Governance* (Baltimore: Johns Hopkins University Press, 2002), and Ali Farazmandy, ed., *Handbook of Comparative and Development Public Administration,* 2nd ed. (New York: Dekker, 2001).

Biographies and autobiographies offer some of the finest observations on the interplay between social forces and public administration, and the most outstanding ones are Louis Brownlow, *A Passion for Anonymity* (Chicago: University of Chicago Press, 1958); Robert Caro, *The Power Broker: Robert Moses and the Fall of New York City* (New York: Random House, 1974); Leroy F. Harlow, *Without Fear or Favor: Odyssey of a City Manager* (Provo, Utah: Brigham Young University Press, 1977); Thomas K. McCraw, *Prophets of Regulation* (Cambridge, Mass.: Harvard University Press, 1984); David Stockman, *The Triumph of Politics: The Inside Story of the Reagan Revolution* (New York: Harper & Row, 1986); Bob Woodward, *Maestro* (New York: Simon & Schuster, 2000); David Kessler, *A Question of Intent* (Washington, D.C.: Public Affairs Press, 2001); Wesley K. Clark, *Waging Modern War* (Washington, D.C.: Public Affairs Press, 2001); Deborah Shapley, *Promise and Power: The Life and Times of Robert McNamara* (Boston: Little, Brown, 1993); Daniel Patrick Moynihan, *Miles to Go* (Cambridge, Mass.: Harvard University Press, 1997), as well as several biographies in Jameson W. Doig and Erwin C. Hargrove, eds., *Leadership and Innovation* (Baltimore: Johns Hopkins University Press, 1987) and in Norma Riccucci, *Unsung Heroes* (Washington, D.C.: Georgetown University Press, 1995). There are several classic social science studies of this subject, including Philip Selznick, *TVA and the Grass Roots: A Study of the Sociology of Formal Organization* (Berkeley: University of California Press, 1949);

Herbert Kaufman, *The Forest Ranger—A Study in Administrative Behavior* (Baltimore: Johns Hopkins University Press, 1960); Arthur Maass, *The Army Engineers and the Nation's Rivers* (Cambridge, Mass.: Harvard University Press, 1951); Milton D. Morris, *Immigration: The Beleaguered Bureaucracy* (Washington, D.C.: Brookings Institute, 1985); Martha Derthick, *Up in Smoke* (Washington, D.C.: CQ Press, 2002); and Paul Light, *Artful Work: The Politics of Social Security Reform* (New York: Random House, 1985). For an excellent set of insightful cases at the local level, read James H. Svara and associates, *Facilitative Leadership in Local Government* (San Francisco: Jossey-Bass, 1994); and James M. Banovetz, ed., *Managing Local Government: Cases in Decision Making,* 2nd ed. (Washington, D.C.: ICMA, 1998).

You should not overlook the rich case studies available through the Inter-University Case Program (P.O. Box 229, Syracuse, N.Y. 13210) as well as the John F. Kennedy School of Government Case Program (Kennedy School of Government, Case Program, Harvard University, 79 JFK Street, Cambridge, Mass. 02138), most of which explore and highlight various dimensions of administrative ecology. The first ICP case book, Harold Stein, ed., *Public Administration and Policy Development: A Casebook* (New York: Harcourt Brace Jovanovich, 1952), contains an especially good introduction by Stein focusing on this topic. Also, cases available through the Electronic Hallway (halltalk@u.Washington.edu) are well worth examining.

Two short but useful pieces that should be read as well are Herbert G. Wilcox, "The Culture Trait of Hierarchy in Middle Class Children," *Public Administration Review* (March/April 1968), pp. 222–232, and F. E. Emery and E. L. Trist, "The Causal Texture of Organizational Environments," *Human Relations,* 18 (February 1965), pp. 21–32.

Of course, the most profound ecological impact on public administration in recent decades has come from technological change. A useful overview of these institutional effects can be found in Jane E. Fountain, *Building the Virtual State* (Washington, D.C.: Brookings, 2001); Manuel Castells, *The Rise of the Network Society* (Oxford:

Blackwell, 1996); P. H. A. Frissen, *Politics, Governance, and Technology* (Northampton, Mass.: Edward Elgar, 1999); as well as a fine case study, Barry Bozeman, *Government Management of Information Mega-Technology* (Arlington, Va.: Pricewaterhouse Coopers Endowment for the Business of Government, 2002).

Certainly *must* reading for comprehending the whole cultural-social milieu within which American public administration operates remains the two volumes of Alexis de Tocqueville, *Democracy in America* (New York: Vintage, 1945), or for that matter, several of the other historical treatments of the American Experience: James Bryce, *The American Commonwealth,* 2 volumes (New York: Macmillan, 1888); Richard Hofstadter, *The American Political Tradition* (New York: Vintage Books, 1948); Michael Kammen, *People of Paradox* (New York: Vintage Books, 1972); Henry Steele Commanger, *The Empire of Reason* (New York: Doubleday, 1977); and Samuel P. Huntington, *American Politics: The Promise of Disharmony* (Cambridge, Mass.: Harvard University Press, 1981), as well as his *The Clash of Civilizations and the Remaking of World Order* (New York: Simon & Schuster, 1996).

For a theoretical look at why culture matters, read Lawrence E. Harrison and Samuel P. Huntington, eds., *Culture Matters* (New York: Basic Books, 2000).

CHAPTER 4

The Political Environment: The Concept of Administrative Power

*T*he lifeblood of administration is power.

Norton E. Long

READING 4

Introduction

While John Gaus stressed the broad evolutionary perspective of administrative ecology, Norton E. Long (1910–1994), a distinguished American political scientist and former New Deal civil servant, zeroes in on the immediate environment of public administration, namely, that of administrative power. In his classic essay, "Power and Administration," Long argues that administrative institutions—public agencies, departments, bureaus, and field offices— are engaged in a continual battle for political survival. In this fierce administrative contest bureaucrats contend for limited power resources from clientele and constituent groups, the legislative and executive branches, and the general public to sustain their organizations. As he writes, "The lifeblood of administration is power. Its attainment, maintenance, increase, and losses are subjects the practitioner and student can ill afford to neglect." And yet, "it is the most overlooked in theory and the most dangerous to overlook in practice."

For Long, the concept of power cannot be bottled in a jar and kept safely tucked away for future use; nor can its nature be revealed by simply examining the U.S. Constitution, the legislative mandates, or the formal hierarchy of an organizational chart. It is, rather, an ephemeral substance that is part of the disorderly, fragmented, decentralized landscape of American public administration—a landscape reminiscent more of tenth-century warring medieval fiefs than of twentieth-century modern government. Power in this chaotic terrain is everywhere, flowing "in from the sides of an organization, as it were; it also flows up the organization to the center from the constituent parts."

This fluid situation arises partly, in Long's view, from the failure of the American party system to protect administrators from political pressures and to provide adequate direction and support for government bureaus and agencies. The American party system "fails to develop a consensus on a leadership and a program that makes possible administration on the basis of acceptable decisional premises." Left to their own devices and discretion, public agencies are forced to enter the "business of building, maintaining and increasing their political support."

Administrators seek to build strong public relations and mobilize political support by developing a "wide range of activities designed to secure enough 'customer' acceptance to survive and, if fortunate, develop a consensus adequate to program formulation and execution." If public servants are to succeed, they must understand the political environment in which they operate and the political resources at their disposal. On this point, Long has direct relevance to some of the central political problems faced by administrators in Case Study 1, "The Blast in Centralia No. 5."

How can Long's disorderly array of narrow interests weld itself together to develop an overall scheme of the national purpose? Rational schemes of coordination always run counter to "the self-centered demands of primary groups for funds and personnel." Again Long visualizes the power factor as significant in any reorganization plan for government. Improved coordination through any governmental reorganization plan will "require a political power at least as great as that which tamed the earlier feudalism." "Attempts to solve administrative reorganization in isolation from the structure of power and purpose in the polity are bound to prove illusory" and have "the academic air of South American Constitution-making."

In his perceptive essay, Long raises another important issue, namely, that because the decentralized nature of the American political system puts administrators in the midst of numerous competing interest groups, they are plagued with the continual problem, "To whom is one loyal—unit, section, branch, division, bureau, department, administration, government, country, people, world history, or what?" A precise consensus on what should be done and who should be obeyed rarely exists and will not so long as the American system fails to establish organized, disciplined political parties or so long as presidents are unable to find firm and continuing majorities in Congress for their legislative programs. Unlike the Parliamentary system, according to Long, each agency in the American executive branch must fend for itself in the political arena, grasping for its own share of political resources to sustain its programs. Therefore, Long advises American administrators to read Machiavelli, La Rochefoucauld, Duc de Saint Simon, or Madison on the reality of power rather than the classic texts on public administration that often stress only the formal components of public organizations.

The following excerpt from Long's essay, "Power and Administration," is based on his perceptive understanding, his training in classical political philosophy, as well as his practical administrative experiences while working at the local, state, and national levels during the Depression, World War II, and the postwar period, particularly his experience at the National Housing Administration in New York City and the Office of Price Administration in Washington. Long's perspectives on power were also significantly shaped by the "new realism" of such insightful students of governmental administration during the 1930s and 1940s as E. Pendleton Herring, Paul Appleby, and Herbert Simon who, like Long, were sober realists about the nature and substance of administrative power. For some traditionalists, Long may seem uncomfortably iconoclastic and politically cynical in his thinking, offering few simple answers to the questions he poses. Nevertheless, his essay raises several perplexing problems that are still critical in public administration today.

As you read this selection, keep the following questions in mind:

How does Long define administrative power? Why is it important? Are there any differences between political power and administrative power? How is administrative power attained and maintained?

What are the appropriate "ends" or "purposes" of the contest for power in administration?

Will the administrative struggle necessarily, if left unchecked, produce a coordinated, effective, and responsible public policy?

How can better planning and rationality be incorporated into the administrative system?

How does Long's approach differ from Weber's or Gaus's approach?

Power and Administration

NORTON E. LONG

There is no more forlorn spectacle in the administrative world than an agency and a program possessed of statutory life, armed with executive orders, sustained in the courts, yet stricken with paralysis and deprived of power. An object of contempt to its enemies and of despair to its friends.

The lifeblood of administration is power. Its attainment, maintenance, increase, dissipation, and loss are subjects the practitioner and student can ill afford to neglect. Loss of realism and failure are almost certain consequences. This is not to deny that important parts of public administration are so deeply entrenched in the habits of the community, so firmly supported by the public, or so clearly necessary as to be able to take their power base for granted and concentrate on the purely professional side of their problems. But even these islands of the blessed are not immune from the plague of politics. . . . To stay healthy one needs to recognize that health is a fruit, not a birthright. Power is only one of the considerations

that must be weighed in administration, but of all it is the most overlooked in theory and the most dangerous to overlook in practice.

The power resources of an administrator or an agency are not disclosed by a legal search of titles and court decisions or by examining appropriations or budgetary allotments. Legal authority and a treasury balance are necessary but politically insufficient bases of administration. Administrative rationality requires a critical evaluation of the whole range of complex and shifting forces on whose support, acquiescence, or temporary impotence the power to act depends.

Analysis of the sources from which power is derived and the limitations they impose is as much a dictate of prudent administration as sound budgetary procedure. The bankruptcy that comes from an unbalanced power budget has consequences far more disastrous than the necessity of seeking a deficiency appropriation. The budgeting of power is a basic subject matter of a realistic science of administration.

It may be urged that for all but the top hierarchy of the administrative structure the question of power is irrelevant. Legislative authority and administrative orders suffice. Power adequate to the function to be performed flows down the chain of command.

Neither statute nor executive order, however, confers more than legal authority to act. Whether Congress or President can impart the substance of power as well as the form depends upon the line-up of forces in the particular case. A price control law wrung from a reluctant Congress by an amorphous and unstable combination of consumer and labor groups is formally the same as a law enacting a support price program for agriculture backed by the disciplined organizations of farmers and their Congressmen. The differences for the scope and effectiveness of administration are obvious. The presidency, like Congress, responds to and translates the pressures that play upon it. The real mandate contained in an executive order varies with the political strength of the group demand embodied in it, and in the context of other group demands.

Both Congress and President do focus the general political energies of the community and so are considerably more than mere means for transmitting organized pressures. Yet power is not concentrated by the structure of government or politics into the hands of a leadership with a capacity to budget it among a diverse set of administrative activities. A picture of the presidency as a reservoir of authority from which the lower echelons of administration draw life and vigor is an idealized distortion of reality.

A similar criticism applies to any like claim for an agency head in his agency. Only in varying degrees can the powers of subordinate officials be explained as resulting from the chain of command. Rarely is such an explanation a satisfactory account of the sources of power.

To deny that power is derived exclusively from superiors in the hierarchy is to assert that subordinates stand in a feudal relation in which to a degree they fend for themselves and acquire support peculiarly their own. A structure of interests friendly or hostile, vague and general or compact and well-defined, encloses each significant center of administrative discretion. This structure is an important determinant of the scope of possible action. As a source of power and authority it is a competitor of the formal hierarchy.

Not only does political power flow in from the sides of an organization, as it were; it also flows up the organization to the center from the constituent parts. When the staff of the Office of War Mobilization and Reconversion advised a hard-pressed agency to go out and get itself some popular support so that the President could afford to support it, their action reflected the realities of power rather than political cynicism.

It is clear that the American system of politics does not generate enough power at any focal point of leadership to provide the conditions for an even partially successful divorce of politics from administration. Subordinates cannot depend on the formal chain of command to deliver enough political power to permit them to do their jobs. Accordingly they must supplement the resources available through the hierarchy with those they can muster on their own, or accept the consequences in frustration—a course itself not without danger. Administrative rationality demands that objectives be determined and sights set in conformity with a realistic appraisal of power position and potential. . . .

The theory of administration has neglected the problem of the sources and adequacy of power, in all probability because of a distaste for the disorderliness of American political life and a belief that this disorderliness is transitory. An idealized picture of the British parliamentary system as a Platonic form to be realized or approximated has exerted a baneful fascination in the field. The majority party with a mandate at the polls and a firmly seated leadership in the cabinets seems to solve adequately the problem of the supply of power necessary to permit administration to concentrate on the fulfillment of accepted objectives. It is a commonplace that the American party system provides neither a mandate for a platform nor a mandate for a leadership.

Accordingly, the election over, its political meaning must be explored by the diverse leaders in the executive and legislative branches. Since the parties have failed to discuss issues, mobilize majorities in their terms, and create a working political consensus on measures to be carried out, the task is left for others—most prominently the agencies concerned. Legislation passed and powers granted are frequently politically premature. Thus the Council of Economic Advisors was given legislative birth before political acceptance of its functions existed. The agencies to which tasks are assigned must devote themselves to the creation of an adequate consensus to permit administration. The mandate that the parties do not supply must be attained through public relations and the mobilization of group support. Pendleton Herring and others have shown just how vital this support is for agency action.

The theory that agencies should confine themselves to communicating policy suggestions to executive and legislature, and refrain from appealing to their clientele and the public, neglects the failure of the parties to provide either a clear-cut decision as to what they should do or an adequately mobilized political support for a course of action. The bureaucracy under the American political system has a large share of responsibility for the public promotion of policy and even more in organizing the political basis for its survival and growth. It is generally recognized that the agencies have a special competence in the technical aspects of their fields which of necessity gives them a rightful policy initiative. In addition, they have or develop a shrewd understanding of the politically feasible in the group structure within which they work. Above all, in the eyes of their supporters and their enemies they represent the institutionalized embodiment of policy, an enduring organization actually or potentially capable of mobilizing power behind policy. The survival interests and creative drives of administrative organizations combine with clientele pressures to compel such mobilization. The party system provides no enduring institutional representation for group interest at all comparable to that of the bureaus of the Department of Agriculture. Even the subject matter committees of Congress function in the shadow of agency permanency.

The bureaucracy is recognized by all interested groups as a major channel of representation to such an extent that Congress rightly feels the competition of a rival. The weakness in party structure both permits and makes necessary the present dimensions of the political activities of the administrative branch—permits because it fails to protect administration from pressures and fails to provide adequate direction and support, makes necessary because it fails to develop a consensus on a leadership and a program that makes possible administration on the basis of accepted decisional premises.

Agencies and bureaus more or less perforce are in the business of building, maintaining, and increasing their political support. They lead and in large part are led by the diverse groups whose influence sustains them. Frequently they lead and are themselves led in conflicting directions. This is not due to a dull-witted incapacity to see the contradictions in their behavior but is an almost inevitable result of the contradictory nature of their support.

Herbert Simon has shown that administrative rationality depends on the establishment of uniform value premises in the decisional centers of organization. Unfortunately, the value premises of those forming vital elements of political support are often far from uniform. These elements are in Barnard's and Simon's sense "customers" of the organization and therefore parts of the organization whose wishes are clothed with a very real authority. A major and most time-consuming aspect of administration consists of the wide range of activities designed to secure enough "customer" acceptance to survive and, if fortunate, develop a consensus adequate to program formulation and execution.

To varying degrees, dependent on the breadth of acceptance of their programs, officials at every level of significant discretion must make their estimates of the situation, take stock of their resources, and plan accordingly. A keen appreciation of the real components of their organization is the beginning of wisdom. These components will be found to stretch far beyond the government payroll. Within the government they will encompass Congress, Congressmen, committees, courts, other agencies, presidential advisors, and the President. The Aristotelian analysis of constitutions is equally applicable and equally necessary to an understanding of administrative organization.

The broad alliance of conflicting groups that makes up presidential majorities scarcely coheres about any definite pattern of objectives, nor has it by the alchemy of the party system had its collective power concentrated in an accepted leadership with a personal mandate. The conciliation and maintenance of this support is a necessary condition of the attainment and retention of office involving, as Madison so well saw, "the spirit of party and faction in the necessary and ordinary operations of government."

The President must in large part be, if not all things to all men, at least many things to many men. As a consequence, the contradictions in his power base invade administration. The often criticized apparent cross-purposes of the Roosevelt regime cannot be put down to inept administration until the political facts are weighed. Were these apparently self-defeating measures reasonably related to the general maintenance of the composite majority of the administration? The first objective—ultimate patriotism apart—of the administrator is the attainment and retention of the power on which his tenure of office depends. This is the necessary pre-condition for the accomplishment of all other objectives.

The same ambiguities that arouse the scorn of the naive in the electoral campaigns of the parties are equally inevitable in administration and for the same reasons. Victory at the polls does not yield either a clear-cut grant of power or a unified majority support for a coherent program. The task of the presidency lies in feeling out the alternatives of policy which are consistent with the retention and increase of the group support on which the administration rests. The lack of a budgetary theory (so frequently deplored) is not due to any incapacity to apply rational analysis to the comparative contribution of the various activities of government to a determinate hierarchy of purposes. It more probably stems from a fastidious distaste for the frank recognition of the budget as a politically expedient allocation of resources. Appraisal in terms of their political contribution to the administration provides almost a sole common denominator between the Forest Service and the Bureau of Engraving.

Integration of the administrative structure through an overall purpose in terms of which tasks and priorities can be established is an emergency phenomenon. Its realization, only partial at best, has been limited to war and the extremity of depression. Even in wartime the Farm Bureau Federation, the American Federation of Labor, the Congress of Industrial Organizations, the National Association of Manufacturers, the Chamber of Commerce, and a host of lesser interests resisted coordination of themselves and the agencies concerned with their interests. A presidency temporarily empowered by intense mass popular support acting in behalf of a generally accepted and simplified

purpose can, with great difficulty, bribe, cajole, and coerce a real measure of joint action. . . . Only in crises are the powers of the executive nearly adequate to impose a common plan of action on the executive branch, let alone the economy.

In ordinary times the manifold pressures of our pluralistic society work themselves out in accordance with the balance of forces prevailing in Congress and the agencies. Only to a limited degree is the process subject to responsible direction or review by President or party leadership. . . .

The difficulty of coordinating government agencies lies not only in the fact that bureaucratic organizations are institutions having survival interests which may conflict with their rational adaptation to overall purpose, but even more in their having roots in society. Coordination of the varied activities of a modern government almost of necessity involves a substantial degree of coordination of the economy. Coordination of government agencies involves far more than changing the behavior and offices of officials in Washington and the field. It involves the publics that are implicated in their normal functioning. To coordinate fiscal policy, agricultural policy, labor policy, foreign policy, and military policy, to name a few major areas, moves beyond the range of government charts and the habitat of the bureaucrats to the marketplace and to where the people live and work. This suggests that the reason why government reorganization is so difficult is that far more than government in the formal sense is involved in reorganization. One could overlook this in the limited government of the nineteenth century but the multibillion dollar government of the mid-twentieth permits no facile dichotomy between government and economy. Economy and efficiency are the two objectives a laissez faire society can prescribe in peacetime as over-all government objectives. Their inadequacy either as motivation or standards has long been obvious. A planned economy clearly requires a planned government. But, if one can afford an unplanned economy, apart from gross extravagance, there seems no compelling and therefore, perhaps, no sufficiently powerful reason for a planned government.

Basic to the problem of administrative rationality is that of organizational identification and point of view. To whom is one loyal—unit, section, branch, division, bureau, department, administration, government, country, people, world history, or what? Administrative analysis frequently assumes that organizational identification should occur in such a way as to merge primary organization loyalty in a larger synthesis. The good of the part is to give way to the reasoned good of the whole. This is most frequently illustrated in the rationalizations used to counter self-centered demands of primary groups for funds and personnel. Actually the competition between governmental power centers, rather than the rationalizations, is the effective instrument of coordination.

Where there is a clear common product on whose successful production the subgroups depend for the attainment of their own satisfaction, it is possible to demonstrate to almost all participants the desirability of cooperation. The shoe factory produces shoes, or else, for all concerned. But the government as a whole and many of its component parts have no such identifiable common product on which all depend. Like the proverbial Heinz, there are fifty-seven or more varieties unified, if at all, by a common political profit and loss account.

Administration is faced by somewhat the same dilemma as economics. There are propositions about the behavior pattern conducive to full employment—welfare economics. On the other hand, there are propositions about the economics of the individual firm—the counsel of the business schools. It is possible to show with considerable persuasiveness that sound considerations for the individual firm may lead to a depression if generally adopted, a result desired by none of the participants. However, no single firm can afford by itself to adopt the course of collective wisdom; in the absence of a common power capable of enforcing decisions premised on the supremacy of the collective interest, *sauve qui peut* is common sense.

The position of administrative organizations is not unlike the position of particular firms. Just as the decisions of the firms could be coordinated by the imposition of a planned economy, so could those of the component parts of the government. But just as it is possible to operate a formally unplanned economy by the loose coordination of the market, in the same fashion it is possible to operate a government by the loose coordination of the play of political forces through its institutions.

The unseen hand of Adam Smith may be little in evidence in either case. One need not believe in a doctrine of social or administrative harmony to believe that formal centralized planning—while perhaps desirable and in some cases necessary—is not a must. The complicated logistics of supplying the city of New York runs smoothly down the grooves of millions of well adapted habits projected from a distant past. It seems naive on the one hand to believe in the possibility of a vast, intricate, and delicate economy operating with a minimum of formal overall direction, and on the other to doubt that a relatively simple mechanism such as the government can be controlled largely by the same play of forces. . . .

It is highly appropriate to consider how administrators should behave to meet the test of efficiency in a planned polity; but in the absence of such a polity and while, if we like, struggling to get it, a realistic science of administration will teach administrative behavior appropriate to the existing political system.

A close examination of the presidential system may well bring one to conclude that administrative rationality in it is a different matter from that applicable to the British ideal. The American presidency is an office that has significant monarchical characteristics despite its limited term and elective nature. The literature on court and palace has many an insight applicable to the White House. Access to the President, reigning favorites, even the court jester, are topics that show the continuity of institutions. The maxims of La Rochefoucauld and the memoirs of the Duc de Saint Simon have a refreshing realism for the operator on the Potomac.

The problem of rival factions in the President's family is as old as the famous struggle between Jefferson and Hamilton. . . . Experience seems to show that this personal and factional struggle for the President's favor is a vital part of the process of representation. The vanity, personal ambition, or patriotism of the contestants soon clothes itself in the generalities of principle and the clique aligns itself with groups beyond the capital. Subordinate rivalry is tolerated if not encouraged by so many able executives that it can scarcely be attributed to administrative ineptitude. The wrangling tests opinion, uncovers information that would otherwise never rise to the top, and provides effective opportunity for decision rather than mere ratification of prearranged plans. Like most judges, the executive needs to hear argument for his own instruction. The alternatives presented by subordinates in large part determine the freedom and the creative opportunity of their superiors. The danger of becoming a Merovingian is a powerful incentive to the maintenance of fluidity in the structure of power.

The fixed character of presidential tenure makes it necessary that subordinates be politically expendable. The President's men must be willing to accept the blame for failures not their own. Machiavelli's teaching on how princes must keep the faith bears rereading. Collective responsibility is incompatible with a fixed term of office. As it tests the currents of public opinion, the situation on the Hill, and the varying strength of the organized pressures, the White House alters and adapts the complexion of the administration. Loyalties to programs or to groups and personal pride and interest frequently conflict with whole-souled devotion to the presidency. In fact, since such devotion is not made mandatory by custom, institutions, or the facts of power, the problem is perpetually perplexing to those who must choose.

The balance of power between executive and legislature is constantly subject to the shifts of public and group support. The latent tendency of the American Congress is to follow the age-old parliamentary precedents and to try to reduce the President to the role of constitutional monarch. Against this threat and to secure his own initiative, the President's resources are primarily demagogic, with the weaknesses and strengths that dependence on mass popular appeal implies. The unanswered question of American government—"who is boss?"—constantly plagues administration.

⬚ CASE STUDY 4

Introduction

In the foregoing essay, Norton Long discusses how critically important it is for public administrators at all levels of government to understand the dynamics and realities of administrative power—its sources, influence, impacts on their programs, as well as the methods for enhancing and maintaining their power bases. He argues that "power" is the most frequently overlooked, misunderstood, or ignored aspect of public administration. Recall his opening lines: "There is no more forlorn spectacle in the administrative world than an agency and a program possessed of statutory life, armed with executive orders, sustained in the courts, yet stricken with paralysis and deprived of power." Long's realism about the central importance and nature of administrative power for practicing public administrators is underscored poignantly throughout his writings.

Yet Long's essay was written over a half century ago, and so is today's problem of relating politics and administration the same? Or, as some suggest, is it indeed the reverse of what Long's essay outlines? Rather than neglecting "power," do contemporary public administrators suffer from "too much political involvement" or too much "micromanagement" by their political superiors that prevents them from fulfilling their responsibilities effectively—or at all?

The following case, "The Columbia Accident" by Maureen Hogan Casamayou, currently teaching at George Mason University, describes the events leading up to one of the worst recent disasters experienced by America's space program. Dramatic international headlines publicized the deaths of the seven-member crew of the *Columbia* during its reentry on February 1, 2003.

This case is an original contribution prepared for the 8th edition by Professor Maureen Hogan Casamayou, George Mason University, Fairfax, Virginia.

Replayed over and over before a worldwide television audience of an estimated billion people, the *Columbia* disintegrated during what was thought of as a routine return, sixteen minutes prior to its scheduled landing at Kennedy Space Center in Florida, in a fireball of debris that spread over several southern states. The immediate cause of the accident, in the words of the Columbia Accident Investigation Board Report: "A breach in the Thermal Protection System on the leading edge of the left wing. The breach was initiated by a piece of insulating foam that separated from the left bipod ramp of the External Tank and struck the wing in the vicinity of the lower half of Reinforced Carbon-Carbon panel 8 at 81.9 seconds after launch. During reentry, this breach in the Thermal Protection System allowed superheated air to penetrate the leading edge insulation and progressively melt the aluminum structure of the left wing resulting in a weakening of the structure until increasing aero-dynamic forces caused loss of control, failure of the wing, and breakup of the Orbiter."* In plain language, the immediate cause of the accident was a small fragment of foam insulation that broke off the left tank and struck the wing, causing superheating of the orbiter's wing, loss of control, and breakup during reentry.

Or was the foam strike responsible for the *Columbia* disaster?

Professor Casamayou probes the causes behind the disaster and according to her, rather than focusing on the technical flaw of the foam debris as the reason for the accident, or what might be called "the technical fix," she argues that it is far more important to develop an appreciation of the external and internal pressures on NASA that influenced the Shuttle Disaster. In elaborating on the details of this terrible event, the author reveals by the end of this case how the enormous external political influences placed upon NASA led to a chain of flawed internal decisions to ignore the long-standing foam problems. Top NASA officials and managers sought to maintain congressional funding as well as "the can-do" PR image for NASA. They suppressed repeated warnings by professional engineers who were close to the foam problem. At the end of her thought-provoking case, the author draws several standing parallels between *Columbia*'s accident and what happened to *Challenger* seventeen years earlier.

As you read this case, you might reflect on several issues:

Where did the external political pressures come from, according to Professor Casamayou?

Why were the views of the engineers who were concerned about the foam problem not fully considered or ignored entirely?

Do you agree with the author that the *Columbia* accident could have been prevented because its causes stem from those "eerily similar to *Challenger*'s in 1986"?

Does this case support or contradict, in your view, Long's central thesis that it is dangerous for administrators to neglect power and politics?

The *Columbia* Accident

MAUREEN HOGAN CASAMAYOU

On February 1, 2003, space shuttle *Columbia* (STS-107) disintegrated during reentry, shedding debris across California, Arizona, Utah, New Mexico, and Texas, just sixteen minutes before its scheduled landing at the Kennedy Space Center (KSC). Thought of as a routine return, exchanges before touchdown between the

Columbia Accident Investigation Board Report (Washington, D.C.: Government Printing Office, (Limited First Printing), August 2003).

Flight Director (Flight) and the Maintenance, Mechanical, and Crew Systems (MMACS) at KSC point out malfunctions on the left side of the orbiter:

MMACS: Flight—MMACS.

Flight: Go ahead, MMACS.

MMACS: "FYI, I've just lost four separate temperature transducers on the left side of the vehicle, hydraulic return temperatures. Two of them on system one and one in each of systems two and three.

Flight: Four hyd (hydraulic) return temps?

MMACS: To the left outboard and left inboard elevon.

Flight: Okay, is there anything common to them? DSC [discrete signal conditioner] or MDM [multiplexer-demultiplexer] or anything? I mean you're telling me you lost them all at exactly the same time?

MMACS: No, not exactly. They were within probably four or five seconds of each other.

Flight: Okay, where are those, where is the instrumentation located?

MMACS: All four of them are located in the aft part of the left wing, right in front of the elevons, elevon actuators. And there is no commonality.

Flight: No commonality.[1]

"No commonality" refers to the issue of whether the temperature transducers were on the same electrical circuit. The inference here is that a random malfunction in the electrical circuit caused these readings. Two minutes later, at 8:58 a.m., after further discussion on the integrity of *Columbia*'s hydraulic system with other personnel at Mission Control at Johnson Space Center (JSC) in Houston, new developments happened that did not augur well for the *Columbia*.

Columbia's commander, Rick Husband, replied to ground control, "And ugh, Hou . . . "

Immediately afterwards, Mission Control was informed, that the *Columbia* had "lost tire pressure on the left outboard and left inboard [on] both tires."[2] The flight director next told the crew, "*Columbia*, Houston, we see your tire pressure messages and we did not copy your last call."[3]

As the *Columbia* approached Dallas, a response of "Roger, [cut off in midsentence]," was Commander Husband's final word to Mission Control.[4]

Once again, the flight director asked if there was a "commonality between all these tire pressure instrumentations and hydraulic return instrumentations."[5]

Once again, he was told by Mission Control at Houston Space Center that there was none. Then more bad news: "We've also lost the nose gear down talkback and the right main gear down talkback."[6] Eighteen seconds after 9:00 a.m., the orbiter broke up. According to *Columbia*'s accident report,

> The postflight video and imagery analyses [showed] that a catastrophic event occurred. Bright flashes suddenly enveloped the Orbiter, [sic] followed by a dramatic change in the trail of superheated air. This is considered the most likely time of the main breakup of Columbia. Because the loss of signal had occurred 46 seconds earlier, Mission Control had no insight into this event.[7]

Personnel at both KSC and JSC (see Table 1) "had just seen live television coverage of Columbia breaking up during re-entry."[8] America had lost another orbiter and crew to a catastrophic accident, the first since *Challenger,* January 26, 1986.

Table 1
Key NASA Personnel

Name	Position
Sean O'Keefe	NASA administrator 2001–present
Ron Dittemore	Shuttle program manager
Linda Ham	Chair of Mission Management Team
Rodney Rocha	Chief engineer for the Thermal Protection System
Daniel S. Goldin	NASA administrator 1992–2001

Like *Challenger,* first reactions blamed flawed technology. Horrific tragedies of this sort are inevitable, so the popular theory ran, when dealing with state-of-the-art, complex "hi-tech." After seven months studying its cause, the Columbia Accident Investigation Board (CAIB) appeared to confirm that assumption:

> [There was] a breach in the Thermal Protection System on the leading edge of the left wing. The breach was initiated by a piece of insulating foam that separated from the left bipod ramp of the External Tank and struck the wing in the vicinity of the lower half of Reinforced Carbon-Carbon panel 8 at 81.9 seconds after

launch. During re-entry, this breach in the Thermal Protection System allowed superheated air to penetrate the leading edge insulation and progressively melt the aluminum structure of the left wing resulting in a weakening of the structure until increasing aerodynamic forces caused loss of control, failure of the wing, and breakup of the Orbiter.[sic][9]

The reason for this tragic accident, however, turned out to be far more than simply a technical failure. To begin with, NASA already knew about the foam strikes. In 72 of 113 imaged flights of liftoff and ascent, seven showed foam loss from the bipod ramp of the external tank. The first one went as far back as *Challenger*'s second mission when foam debris (19 inches by 12 inches) broke off the orbiter. This was categorized as an "In-Flight Anomaly" (that is, before the next flight the problem had to be resolved, "or prove[d] that it [did] not threaten the safety of the vehicle or crew.")[10] In other words, the "symptom" of foam loss was fixed, but its cause or permanent correction never addressed.[11] So, why did the shuttle program managers allow this oversight to continue? Why was the problem never investigated nor permanently resolved? First, external forces within the Space Shuttle Program at NASA decisively shaped higher-management perceptions of risks.

External Forces

Separation of powers and checks and balances shape U.S. government constitutional principles crafted by the Framers to guard against tyranny. Today the byproduct is a fragmented, porous bureaucracy, beholden to myriad outside forces. Or, as Norton E. Long explains, political power flows into bureaucratic organizations from the sides as well as from the top down—a characteristic that contrasts sharply with the highly centralized executive branch of parliamentary democracies such as the United Kingdom. James Q. Wilson notes, "In Great Britain, . . . accountability and responsiveness are one and the same thing, owed to one person and the same person."[12] U.S. government agencies are susceptible to the slightest shifts in their external environment. NASA's political support is particularly vulnerable to the dictates of Congress, the White House, client groups (such as the aerospace industry), and the American public, who feels a strong sense of patriotism and pride from the nation's superiority in space exploration. How well did NASA balance these pressures from its

constitutional overseers, the White House, which demands accountability, and Congress, which demands responsiveness?[13] The problem for NASA was actually not so much one of being pulled in different directions by its rival masters, but one of how to adapt to new external constraints imposed upon it by both the White House and Congress, that generated new launch pressures.

For example, in 1990, a review of NASA and its programs by aerospace executive Norman Augustine concluded that NASA's budget was grossly underfunded when comparing its program obligations to its available resources. Augustine recommended a reinvigorated space program with a "peak spending level" of $30 billion a year (in constant 1990 dollars) by 2000,[14] but this recommendation fell on deaf ears. NASA's budget remained flat, as the White House and Congress preferred that NASA

produce valuable scientific and symbolic payoffs for the nation without a need for increased budgets. Recent budget allocations reflect this continuing policy reality. Between 1993 and 2002, the government's discretionary spending grew in purchasing power by more than 25 percent, defense spending by 15 percent, and non-defense spending by 40 percent. NASA's budget, in comparison, showed little change, going from $14.31 billion in fiscal year 1993 to a low of $13.6 billion in fiscal year 2000, and increasing to $14.87 billion in fiscal year 2002. This represented a loss of 13 percent in purchasing power over the decade.[15] (See Table 2.)

Added congressional pressure on NASA's budget came in the form of earmarks defined as "congressional additions to the NASA budget request that reflect targeted Members' interests."[16] According to the CAIB, the fiscal year 2002 budget had "a net total of $540 million in reductions to ongoing NASA programs" that drained away valuable resources from the core tasks of the agency, including the Space Shuttle Program.[17] Moreover, NASA's Space Shuttle Program was not only competing for resources to build and maintain the International Space Station, but also with Bill Clinton's initiative to purchase Russian hardware and services to promote U.S.–Russian space cooperation.[18] In sum, the Space Shuttle Program, NASA's single most expensive activity over the three decades, was hardest hit by Clinton-Bush budget constraints.

After *Challenger*, certain "reforms" for promoting flight safety in NASA's management structure were im-

Table 2
NASA's Budget, 1965–2004

Fiscal Year	Real Dollars (in millions)	Constant Dollars (in FY 2002 millions)	Change in Constant Dollars (%)
1965	5,250	24,696	
1975	3,229	10,079	−59%
1985	7,573	11,643	+16%
1993	14,310	17,060	+47%
1994	14,570	16,965	−1%
1995	13,854	15,790	−7%
1996	13,884	15,489	−2%
1997	13,709	14,994	−3%
1998	13,648	14,641	−2%
1999	13,653	14,443	−1%
2000	13,601	14,202	−2%
2001	14,230	14,559	+3%
2002	14,868	14,868	+2%
2003	15,335	NA	
2004	(requested) 15,255	NA	

Source: NASA and Office of Management and Budget.

plemented, but following the *Columbia* accident, the CAIB discovered that these "reforms" had disappeared entirely. Most notably, the centralized program management and structure in the post-*Challenger* days that elevated JSC to level 2, responsible for the technical oversight of the shuttle program, was abandoned.[19] Its aim: to ensure better communications and control between the headquarters in Washington, D.C, and the field offices, while reducing the intercenter rivalry among Marshall, Johnson, and Kennedy Space Centers.

Six years later, in 1992, Daniel S. Goldin replaced Admiral Richard H. Truly, a former astronaut, as NASA's Administrator. A self-proclaimed "agent of change" who held office from April 1, 1992, to November 17, 2001, Goldin's leadership underscored the management principles of W. Edwards Deming.[20] Deming had developed a series of widely acclaimed management principles based on his work in Japan during the "economic miracle" of the 1980s. Goldin attempted to apply some of the principles to NASA, including the notion that a corporate headquarters should not attempt to exert bureaucratic control over a complex organization, but rather set strategic directions and provide operating units with the authority and resources needed to pursue those directions. Another Deming principle was that checks and balances in an organization were unnecessary and counterproductive, and those carrying out the work should bear primary responsibility for its quality.[21]

Goldin enthusiastically applied Deming's management principles to revitalizing NASA's human space program. As he promoted long-term exploration of Mars and the building of the International Space Station with the shuttle playing an integral role, Goldin became identified by his motto, "faster, better, cheaper." Such a mantra also reflected the Clinton White House initiative "to reinvent government" by improving efficiency while reducing costs. Indeed, Goldin viewed NASA as a prime candidate for such "reform"—it was bloated and bureaucratic, and he would fix these problems while rejecting "the criticism that he was sacrificing safety in the name of efficiency. In 1994 he told an audience at the Jet Propulsion Laboratory, 'When I ask for the budget to be cut I'm told it's going to impact safety on the Space Shuttle . . . I think that's a bunch of crap.' "[22]

Accordingly, drastic reductions in the workforce and increased use of contractors began while NASA remained committed to the space center's prior programs. Because of outside pressures from Congress and the aerospace companies, NASA avoided personnel downsizing at the space centers themselves. Instead, NASA targeted the Space Shuttle budget for cuts that included those jobs that dealt with the safety inspections of the preflight reviews (which were created during the *Challenger* aftermath). From 1991 to 1994, the Shuttle program's operating budget dropped 21 percent with drastic cuts in both contractor personnel and shuttle staff. *Columbia*'s Report stresses: "Contractor personnel working on the Shuttle declined from 28,394 to 22,387 in these three years, and NASA Shuttle staff decreased from 4,031 to 2,959."[23] 5900 additional jobs were cut from the shuttle program during fiscal years of 1996 and 1997, and all the while, NASA claimed that these reductions—totaling "just under 13 percent of the total (workforce)"—would not impact the safety of the operation.[24]

Another Goldin initiative decentralized NASA's management structure, so JSC again became the "lead center" for the Space Shuttle Program, as it had been before *Challenger*. The CAIB Report pointed out that

> Among other things, this change meant that Johnson Space Center managers would have authority over the funding and management of Shuttle activities at the Marshall and Kennedy Centers. Johnson and Marshall had been rivals since the days of Apollo, and long-term Marshall employees and managers did not easily accept the return of Johnson to this lead role.

The report went on to explain that

> The shift of Space Shuttle Program management to Johnson was worrisome to some. The head of the Space Shuttle Program at NASA Headquarters, Bryan O'Connor, argued that transfer of the management function to the Johnson Space Center would return the Shuttle Program management to the flawed structure that was in place before the Challenger accident. "It is a safety issue," he said, "we ran it that way [with program management at Headquarters, as recommended by the Rogers Commission] for 10 years without a mishap and I didn't see any reason why we should go back to the way we operated in the pre-Challenger days." Goldin gave O'Connor several opportunities to present his arguments against a transfer of management responsibility, but ultimately decided to proceed. O'Connor felt he had no choice but to resign. (O'Connor returned to NASA in 2002 as Associate Administrator for Safety and Mission Assurance.)[25]

Internal Launch Pressures

During this period of drastic personnel reductions along with unchanged, even expanding, program responsibilities, unrelenting internal pressures pushed NASA to meet its launch date of Node 2 of the space station section, February 19, 2003. As William Langwiesche explains it, "[Sean] O'Keefe (the new Administrator) had made it clear that meeting this deadline was a test, and that the very future of NASA's human space-flight was on the line."[26] In mid-2001, NASA developed a plan to regain its credibility by proving to Congress and the White House that it could "meet schedules and budgets" by focusing on the February 19, 2003, deadline. The gravity of the situation was such that, "if this goal was not met, NASA would risk losing support from the White House and Congress for subsequent Space Station growth."[27]

In plain English, overbudget and behind schedule in assembling the Space Station, NASA was "on probation." Thus, the February 19 launch acquired a serious political message to NASA that reverberated to every level of the organization. As the CAIB states,

> The importance of this date was stressed from the very top. The Space Shuttle and Space Station Program Managers briefed the new NASA administrator monthly on the status of their programs, and a significant part of their briefings was the days of margin remaining in the schedule to the launch of Node 2—still well over a year away. The Node 2 schedule margin typically accounted for more than half of the briefing slides . . . .
>
> NASA Headquarters stressed the importance of this date in other ways. A screen saver was mailed to managers in NASA's human space flight program that depicted a clock counting down to February 19, 2003—U.S. Core Complete.
>
> While employees found this amusing because they saw it as a date that could not be met, it also reinforced the message that NASA headquarters was focused on and promoting achievement of that date. This schedule was on the minds of the Shuttle managers in the months leading up to [*Columbia*'s January 16, 2003 launch..][28]

Such not-so-subtle internal pressure explains why shuttle managers ignored the seriousness of the foam strikes from the "bipod ramp" on the external tank of the shuttle during the *Atlantis* launch (STS-112) on October 7, 2002. According to the CAIB report, this event was "significant, both in size and in the damage it caused and because it occurred only two flights before STS-107."[29] Normally categorized as an "In-Flight Anomaly," the initial recommendation at the meeting of the Program Requirements Control Board, "the incident was assigned as 'an action' with a due date after the next launch." The CAIB pondered this decision, wondering

> Why NASA would treat the STS-112 foam loss differently than all others. What drove managers to reject the recommendation that the foam loss be

deemed an In-Flight Anomaly? Why did they take the unprecedented step of scheduling not one but eventually two missions to fly before the External Tank Project was to report back on foam losses? *It seems that shuttle managers had become conditioned over time to not regard foam loss or debris as a safety-of-flight concern. The need to adhere to the Node 2 launch schedule also appears to have influenced their decision. . . . Aggressive schedules by themselves are often a sign of a healthy institution. However, other institutional goals, such as safety, sometimes compete with schedules, so the effects of schedule pressure in an organization must be carefully monitored.*[30] [Italics added]

According to the *Columbia* report, NASA management denied existence of any undue launch-schedule pressures influencing their decisions. However, when both space shuttle and space station personnel were asked about their opinions, the response was different. In the words of the CAIB,

The workforce within both programs thought there was considerable pressure to hold firm to that launch date, and individuals were becoming concerned that safety might be compromised. The weight of evidence supports the workforce view. . . .

By December 2002, every bit of padding in the schedule had disappeared . . . . Even with work scheduled on holidays, a third shift of workers being hired and trained, future crew rotations drifting beyond 180 days, and some tests previously deemed "requirements" being skipped or deferred, Program Managers estimated that Node 2 launch would be one or two months late. They were slowly accepting additional risk in trying to meet a schedule that probably could not be met.[31]

Given an ambitious launch schedule and an organizational mind-set that lulled them into complacency, shuttle managers convinced themselves that the foam shedding was no real safety hazard, since the shuttle kept coming back. Yet others in the shuttle program did not share this perception of the risk. On January 16, shortly after *Columbia*'s liftoff, engineers examined the implications of suspicious debris that fell off the bipod ramp on the left side of the external tank and hit the left wing of the orbiter. What they discovered was interpreted in remarkably divergent ways by engineers and managers.

Two Worlds: Two Perceptions of Risk

Film covering *Columbia*'s liftoff recorded the foam strike. A "large object" from the left bipod ramp of the External Tank struck the Orbiter on "the underside of the left wing."[32] However, the damage was difficult to assess. The photo lab engineers from the Intercenter Photo Working Group (IPWG) at JSC voiced concern about the "size of the object and the apparent momentum of the strike."[33] In addition, NASA and contractor engineers were equally anxious about the potential damage from this particular foam strike. Yet, Linda Ham, Chair of the Mission Management Team, Ron Dittemore, Space Shuttle Program Manager, and other senior managers responded differently. The two groups worked closely together and saw the same evidence, yet perceived risk associated with the foam strike from the external tank in distinctly opposite ways. The CAIB report concludes that

The opinions of Shuttle Program managers and debris and photo analysts on the potential severity of the debris strike diverged early in the mission and continued to diverge as the mission progressed, making it increasingly difficult for the Debris Assessment Team to have concerns heard by those in a decision-making capacity. In the face of the Mission managers' low level of concern and desire to get on with the mission, Debris Assessment Team members had to prove unequivocally that a safety-in-flight issue existed before the Shuttle Program Management would move to obtain images of the left wing. The engineers found themselves in the unusual position of having to prove that the situation was *unsafe*—a reversal of the usual requirement to prove that a situation *is safe*.[34]

While engineers wanted a photo of *Columbia*'s left wing on-orbit, upper-level managers believed the strike was no serious risk to the orbiter. It was a holiday weekend, so a meeting was scheduled for the next Tuesday, January 21. Surprisingly, the contractor engineers did meet before then to calculate the potential size of the debris, its speed, and assess potential damage to the left wing by using a mathematical model known as Crater. Designated as a "conservative tool," the model "predicted more damage in previous tests than was (actually) observed."[35] However, since it was calibrated from much smaller pieces of debris than the one believed to have hit the left wing, Crater's predictive accuracy could very well be compromised, and so the engineers remained intent on acquiring photos of the left wing. The results of the Crater modeling would be presented at a meeting on January 24. In the meantime, one account of Ham's attitude at the January 21 MMT meeting characterized her as both efficient and focused: "Ham responded to news of the foam strike as if it were just another item to be efficiently handled and then checked off the list . . . . She was decisive, and very sure of her sense for what was important and what was not."[36]

Ham did inquire about the foam strike, but:

not to determine what action to take during *Columbia*'s mission, *but to understand the implications for STS-114* [italic added]. During a Mission Management Team meeting on January 21, she asked about the rationale put forward at the STS-113 Flight Readiness Review, which she had attended. Later that morning she reviewed the charts presented at that Flight Readiness Review. Her assessment, which she e-mailed to Shuttle Program Manager Ron Dittemore on January 21, was "Rationale was lousy and still is . . . ."[37]

Clearly, keen to get the next flight off the ground, Ham argued the flight rationales in the Flight Readiness review passed muster not because of their inherent validity (and hence greater safety for the crew) but simply to launch another shuttle into space on schedule. As the CAIB report states,

Ham's focus on examining the rationale for continuing to fly after foam problems with STS-87 and STS-112 indicates that her attention had already shifted from the threat of the foam posed to STS-107 to the downstream implications of the foam strike. Ham was due to serve . . . as the launch integration manager for the next mission, STS-114. If the Shuttle Program's rationale to fly with foam loss was found to be flawed, the flight, due to be launched in about a month, would have to be delayed per NASA rules that require serious problems to be resolved before the next flight. An STS-114 delay could in turn delay completion of the International Space Station's Node 2, which was a high priority goal for NASA managers.[38]

Further evidence of her preoccupation with meeting the designated launch schedule was reflected in Ham's concern about the length of time to process photos of the *Columbia* on-orbit. According to the CAIB, on January 23rd:

Ham raised concerns that the extra time spent maneuvering *Columbia* to make the left wing visible for imaging would unduly impact the mission schedule; for example, science experiments would have to stop while imagery was taken. According to personal notes obtained by the Board: "Linda Ham said it was no longer being pursued since even if we saw something, we couldn't do anything about it. The Program didn't want to spend the resources."

Shuttle managers, including Ham, also said they were looking for very small areas on the Orbiter and that past imagery resolution was not very good. The Board notes that no individuals in the STS-107 operational chain of command had the security clearance necessary to know about national imaging capabilities. Additionally, no evidence has been uncovered that anyone from NASA, United Space Alliance, or Boeing sought to determine the expected quality of images and the difficulty and costs of obtaining Department of Defense assistance. Therefore members of the Mission Management Team were making decisions about imagery capabilities based on little or no knowledge.[39]

On January 24, results of the Crater modeling were presented to the Mission Management Team, with a standing-room-only crowd of engineers. From that briefing given to Ham, the foam strike was assessed as no threat to flight safety. Concerns were only raised about handling any press queries, as well as whether or not the alleged localized damage repair (handled by tile replacement) would affect shuttle turnaround time.[40]

So what were the engineers thinking and doing while these events took place? Concerned and aware of the uncertainty about potential damage that the foam strike had inflicted on the left wing, they wanted to view firsthand by means of air force precise imaging. That weekend an engineering group headed by Rodney Rocha, the chief engineer for the Thermal Protection System, e-mailed JSC Engineering Directorate requesting that the *Columbia* crew "visually inspect the left wing for damage." It turned out that "Rocha never received an answer."[41]

Engineers also pursued other options. Through informal channels, they made three "imagery requests" to the air force for photos of the *Columbia*—especially the left wing on-orbit.[42] Not realizing these requests were from her own engineers, Ham, according to one account, simply terminated the request with the Department of Defense. This appears to have been a purely bureaucratic reaction. Months later one of the CAIB investigators . . . [seethed]with anger at what had occurred. He said, "Because the problem was not identified in the traditional way—Houston, we have a problem!—well, then, Houston, we don't have a problem! Because Houston didn't identify the problem![43]

By this time IPWG had become the Debris Assessment Team (DAT), but their efforts also were unsuccessful:

When Ham officially terminated the actions that the Department of Defense had begun, she effectively terminated both the Intercenter Photo Working Group request and the Debris Assessment Team request. While Ham has publicly stated she did not know of the Debris Assessment team members' desire for imagery, she never asked them directly if the request was theirs, even though they were the team analyzing the foam strike.[44]

A vibrant safety culture highlighted by an independent and effective safety organization would have encouraged personnel to address the issue right from the start.[45] But such an environment did not exist at NASA at that time. Safety personnel, supposedly reflecting a risk-averse philosophy, were too few and too passive. Two high-ranking safety officers contacted about the Department of Defense imaging request "took no action to obtain imagery."[46] The CAIB report summed up their role:

Shuttle program safety personnel failed to adequately assess anomalies and frequently accepted critical risks without qualitative or quantitative support, even when the tools to provide more comprehensive assessments were available.

Similarly, the Board expected to find NASA's Safety and Mission Assurance organization deeply engaged at every level of Shuttle Management. . . . This was not the case. In briefing after briefing, interview after interview, NASA remained in denial: in the agency's eyes, "there were no safety-of-flight issues," and no safety compromises in the long history of debris strikes in the Thermal Protection System. The silence of Program-level safety processes undermined oversight: when they did not speak up, safety personnel could not fulfill their stated mission to prove "checks and balances." A pattern of acceptance prevailed throughout the organization that

tolerated foam problems without sufficient engineering justification for doing so.[47]

And why didn't the engineers discuss their misgivings directly with their supervisors?[48] A major explanation for this is found in the culture at NASA that frowned on anyone holding up production by voicing safety concerns. Indeed, such a person could be deterred by "the fear of reprisals for criticism," a policy apparently considered "an agency hallmark for years and [one that] is deeply ingrained in its culture."[49] Indeed, when questioned by CAIB, members of the DAT "opined that by raising contrary points of view about Shuttle mission safety, they would be singled out for possible ridicule by their peers and managers."[50] By the same token, shuttle managers never asked the engineers if they had any concerns. As the CAIB report stated: "[Managers] didn't hear their [engineers'] concerns . . . due in part to their not asking or listening."[51] In addition, organizational culture also helped to explain the apparent silence of safety officers both at Headquarters and at the Space Centers: "Safety personnel did not serve as a channel for the voicing of concerns or dissenting views . . . safety representatives were in attendance at all of the meetings but were not rigorously challenging the shuttle managers on their assumptions and decisions. The highest ranking safety officer deferred to the shuttle managers on imaging the Columbia."[52]

The *Columbia* Accident: Déjà Vu All Over Again?

In retrospect, this accident could have been avoided; that is, early warnings of safety problems that ultimately caused the accident were repeatedly ignored. Equally troubling is the revelation that the causes of the *Columbia* accident are eerily similar to *Challenger*'s in 1986. Seven crew members perished, billions of dollars were lost to the taxpayer, and the entire NASA program reeled from its apparent inability to cope or confront its own deadly pathologies. The names of mechanisms and players inside and outside of NASA may have changed since 1986, but the mistakes that brought down the *Columbia* were virtually the same ones that brought down the *Challenger* seventeen years before. While examining the evidence on the *Columbia* accident, Sally Ride, a CAIB member and former astronaut who served on the Rogers Commission, exclaimed, "I think I'm hearing an echo here."[53] In essence, these mistakes were rooted in the complex relationship between NASA's external environment and its internal decision-making behavior.

Thus, the immediate question: whether or not NASA can learn from this accident to prevent a *third* recurrence of this magnitude in the future. "In the near term, the recent memory of the *Columbia* accident will motivate the entire NASA organization to scrupulous attention to detail and vigorous efforts to resolve elusive technical problems." The larger question involves NASA's *long-term capability* to maintain this level of energy and vigilance.[54] Can NASA learn from the two previous accidents to ensure "no return of bad habits"?

First, and probably most important, the answers to such questions depend on the long-term commitment and dedication of political forces outside of NASA to human space exploration. Such a commitment transcends the most current political "fix" or "fad" that accompanies a change in administration and congressional turnover. Adequate resources affect NASA's ability to cope with its launch schedule and its commitment to ensuring a robust safety organization.

Second, and related to the first, NASA needs to realistically adjust its launch schedules according to available resources. The specific reasons to launch *Columbia* on schedule were different from those affecting the *Challenger* launch, but in both cases the shuttle program had immense pressures to meet its tight launch deadline for commercial, foreign, and defense payloads. In the end, the overall problems of insufficient resources coupled with heavy operating pressures were identical.

Third, effective leadership that nurtures a risk-averse culture through every level of the organization is essential. Such a culture must blend openness and trust with a "can do" approach for getting the job done. A return to the earlier practice of appointing former astronauts in management—even as agency administrator—was thought to be a wise recommendation by the Rogers Commission. In the Commission's estimation, it "brought . . . flight experience and a keen appreciation of operations and flight safety" to their positions.[55] A nonastronaut, TRW Executive Daniel S. Goldin, replaced former astronaut Admiral Richard Truly in 1992. Likewise in 2003, Sean O'Keefe, a seasoned Washington bureaucrat rather than an astronaut, headed NASA.

Fourth, a robust safety organization, independent of the space centers and with a centralized authority, would provide critical checks essential for taking program managers to task on risk levels associated with

flight safety issues. Poor communications between agency engineers and shuttle program managers took several forms. Engineers were fearful of raising their concerns with shuttle managers, and when they did convey early warnings on the safety items that caused the accidents, line managers downgraded them as acceptable risks by using flawed rationales and quick fixes. When *Challenger* shuttle managers did not want to hear concerns voiced by engineers regarding the impact of cold temperatures on the solid rocket booster O rings, *Challenger* engineers found themselves in the same predicament in January 1986 as the *Columbia* engineers in January 2003; namely, they had to argue from the premise that the situation was safe, and therefore their job was to convince others the situation was unsafe. Normally, the reverse is what characterizes an organization with a healthy risk-averse culture.

The CAIB Report criticized NASA for falling down on the Rogers Commission recommendation to maintain an independent robust safety organization with clout. It recommended a "Technical Engineering Authority [TEA] that is responsible for technical requirements and all waivers to them, and [that] will build a disciplined, systematic approach to identifying, analyzing, and controlling hazards throughout the life cycle of the Shuttle System."[56] The report details the functions of the TEA and particularly argues that it should be independent of the Space Centers with funding coming from headquarters "with no connection to or responsibility for schedule or program costs."[57] Equally important, the existing Office of Safety and Mission should "have direct line authority over the entire Space Shuttle Program safety organization and should be independently resourced."[58]

Fifth, a return to centralized management would pull level 2 out of JSC and locate it at headquarters. This reform would create better communication and control over field offices and simultaneously reduce the intercenter rivalry among MSC, JSC, and KSC. This recommendation was another Rogers Commission idea adopted but then reversed after Goldin replaced Truly as administrator in 1992.

Can organizations dealing with high risk technology ever learn from their mistakes, especially those operating like NASA with an external environment that is particularly turbulent and sensitive to short-term political expediency? Is catastrophe the only real restraint on excessive risk taking, even though neglected safety problems are repeatedly brought to the attention of the bureaucrats, contractors, and the public? Are there any guarantees that those postaccident remedies for such organizational failures can become effective? Are we merely destined to "tirelessly tinker" with various short-term remedies both inside and outside NASA, hoping they might prevent future disasters?[59] Or, will demo-

cratic processes decide that the costs of these tragedies are too prohibitive and thus end NASA's future in human space flight? Within the uncertain state of current affairs, only time can determine the shuttle program's ultimate fate.

Notes

[1] *Columbia Accident Investigation Board Report* (Washington, D.C.: Government Printing Office, Limited First Printing, August 2003), 1: 42.

[2] Ibid.

[3] Ibid., 43.

[4] Ibid.

[5] Ibid.

[6] Ibid.

[7] Ibid.

[8] Ibid., 44.

[9] Ibid., 9.

[10] Ibid., 123.

[11] Two most recent works on the causes of the *Columbia* accident and the overall organizational health of NASA are Greg Klerkx, *Lost in Space*: *The Fall of NASA and the Dream of a New Space Age* (New York: Pantheon Press, 2004); Michael Cabbage and William Harwood, *Comm Check: The Final Flight of the Shuttle* Columbia (New York: Free Press, 2004).

[12] James Q. Wilson, *Bureaucracy: What Government Agencies Do and Why They Do It,* 2nd ed. (New York: Basic Books, 2000), 258.

[13] Ibid., 235–276.

[14] *Columbia,* 102.

[15] Ibid., 103.

[16] Ibid., 104–105.

[17] Ibid., 104.

[18] Ibid.

[19] In the pre-*Challenger* period, levels 3 and 4 were responsible for the core elements of the shuttle, which meant that JSC was also a level 3 along with the other two space centers (MSC and KSC). For further information on this topic, see William Rogers, *Report of the Presidential Commission on the Space Shuttle* Challenger (Washington, D.C.: U.S. Government Printing Office, 1986), 101–103; Maureen Hogan Casamayou, *Bureaucracy in Crisis, Three Mile Island, the Shuttle* Challenger, *and Risk Assessment* (Boulder, CO: Westview Press, 1993), 23–26, 88–90. One of the most recent works on the *Challenger* accident is Diane Vaughan, *The* Challenger *Launch Decision: Risky Technology, Culture, and Deviance at NASA* (Chicago: University of Chicago Press, 1996).

[20] *Columbia,* 105.

[21] Ibid., 105–106.

[22] Ibid., 106.

[23] Ibid., 107.

[24] Ibid.

[25] Ibid., 107.

[26] William Langewiesche, "*Columbia*'s Last Flight," *Atlantic Monthly* (November 2002), 22.

[27] *Columbia,* 131.

[28] Ibid., 132.

[29] Ibid., 125.

[30] Ibid., 125, 131.

[31] Ibid., 131, 138.

[32] Ibid., 37.

[33] Ibid., 140.

[34] *Columbia,* 169.

[35] Ibid., 143.

[36] Langewiesche, 23.

[37] *Columbia,* 139.

[38] Ibid., 148.

[39] Ibid., 153–154.

[40] Ibid., 161–162.

[41] Ibid., 145.

[42] Ibid., 140.

[43] Langewiesche, 24.

[44] *Columbia,* 153.

[45] Ibid., 177.

[46] Ibid., 170.

[47] *Columbia,* 177–178.

[48] Ibid., 168.

[49] *Lost in Space,* 243.

[50] Ibid., 169.

[51] Ibid., 170.

[52] Ibid., 170.

[53] *Comm Check,* 202.

[54] Ibid., 208.

[55] Rogers, *Report of the Presidential Commission,* vol.1, 199.

[56] Ibid., 193

[57] Ibid.

[58] Ibid.

[59] Gilbert Y. Steiner, *The State of Welfare* (Washington, D.C.: The Brookings Institution, 1971), 31.

Chapter 4 Review Questions

1. On the basis of your reading of the Long essay and the case study, how would you define the term *administrative power?* Can it be measured? If so, how?
2. Based on the case study, how did the political environment influence the decision to launch the space shuttle *Columbia?* Particularly, who was involved and who was not?
3. What were the sources of these political pressures? Their points of view?
4. In your view, who was most responsible for the decision to launch the shuttle? How can one determine "responsible" or "irresponsible" use of administrative power? *And* ensure its "responsible" use?
5. Can you list the reasons why "the political dimensions" are repeatedly overlooked or ignored? Was this true in this case study? Or also in Cases No.1 and No. 2?
6. On the basis of Long's essay and your analysis of the case study, can you generalize about the most significant problems facing public administrators today in relating politics and administration? Does the Wilson essay in Chapter 1 offer any useful advice on this problem?

Key Terms

interest groups

organizational fragmentation

administrative rationality

balance of power

coordination of government

sources of conflict

sources of cohesion

maintaining political support

Suggestions for Further Reading

The classic works on interest groups and their influence on the governmental process are Arthur F. Bentley, *The Process of Government* (Cambridge, Mass.: Harvard University Press, 1908); E. Pendleton Herring, *Public Administration and the Public Interest* (New York: Russell and Russell, 1936); and David Truman, *The Governmental Process* (New York: Alfred A. Knopf, 1951). The influence of politics on public administration and the general power of politics within administrative processes were especially emphasized and popularized by the "new postwar realism" of authors such as Paul H. Appleby, *Big Democracy* (New York: Alfred A. Knopf, 1945) and *Policy and Administration* (Tuscaloosa, Ala.: University of Alabama Press, 1949); Robert A. Dahl and Charles E. Lindblom, *Politics, Economics, and Welfare* (New York: Harper and Brothers, 1953); and Her-

bert Simon et al., *Public Administration* (New York: Alfred A. Knopf, 1950). Of course, Long's numerous essays did much to explore as well as contribute to this topic and they are available in a single volume, *The Polity* (Chicago: Rand McNally and Co., 1962).

The last three decades have witnessed an enormous outpouring of books and articles on this subject. Perhaps some of the very best contemporary analyses of the aspects of power influencing administrative actions are found in Harold Seidman, *Politics, Position, and Power,* 5th ed. (New York: Oxford University Press, 1997); Sungham Im, *Bureaucratic Power, Democracy and Administrative Democracy* (Brookfield, Vt.: Ashgate, 2001); Allan J. Cigler and Bardett A. Loomis, eds., *Interest Group Politics,* 6th ed. (Washington, D.C.: Congressional Quarterly Press, 2002); Ronald Hrebenar, ed., *Inter-*

est Group Politics in America, 3rd ed. (Armonk, N.Y.: M.E. Sharpe, 1997); John F. Bibby, *Politics, Parties and Elections in America,* 5th ed. (Belmont, Calif.: Wadsworth, 2002); Jeffery Berry, *Interest Group Society,* 3rd ed. (Reading, MA: Addison-Wesley, 2001); Francis E. Rourke, *Bureaucracy, Politics and Public Policy,* 3rd ed. (Boston: Little, Brown, 1984); as well as Rourke's excellent edited collection entitled *Bureaucratic Power in National Policy Making,* 4th ed. (Boston: Little, Brown, 1986). Particularly good treatments of congressional oversight of administrative agencies are found in Joel D. Aberbach, *Keeping a Watchful Eye: The Politics of Congressional Oversight* (Washington, D.C.: The Brookings Institution, 1990); Morris P. Fiorina, *Congress: Keystone of the Washington Establishment,* 2nd ed. (New Haven: Yale University Press, 1989); and Christopher H. Foreman, Jr., *Signals from the Hill* (New Haven: Yale University Press, 1988). The rise of the power of "think tanks" in shaping policy agendas is well described by David M. Ricci, *The Transformation of American Politics: The New Washington and the Rise of Think Tanks* (New Haven: Yale University Press, 1993); and James A. Smith, *The Idea Brokers* (New York: Free Press, 1991).

For "overviews" of national political power, see Bradley H. Patterson, Jr., *White House Staff* (Washington, D.C.: Brookings, 2001); and Beryl A. Radin, *The Accountable Juggler* (Washington, D.C.: CQ Press, 2002), and at the local level, both Robert J. Waste, *Ecology of City Policy Making* (New York: Oxford University Press, 1989); and James H. Svara, *Official Leadership in the City: Patterns of Conflict and Cooperation* (New York: Oxford University Press, 1990). For an excellent general review of academic literature pertaining to this topic, see Herbert Kaufman, "Major Players: Bureaucracies in American Government," *Public Administration Review, 61* (January/February, 2001), pp. 18–42; and Chapter 3, "The Impact of Political Power and Public Policy," in Hal Rainey, *Understanding and Managing Public Organizations,* 2nd ed. (San Francisco: Jossey-Bass, 1996).

You should not overlook biographies and autobiographies as offering worthwhile insights, particularly Joseph A. Califano, Jr., *Governing America* (New York: Simon and Schuster, 1981); William Manchester, *American Caesar: Douglas MacArthur, 1880–1964* (Boston: Little, Brown, 1978); Norman Polmar and Thomas B. Allen, *Rickover: A Biography* (New York: Simon and Schuster, 1982); Robert Caro, *The Power Broker,* cited in Chapter 3, as well as others cited at the end of Chapter 3: Bob Woodward, *Maestro;* David Kessler, *A Question of Intent;* Wesley Clark, *Waging Modern War;* Norma Riccucci, *Unsung Heroes*; David Stockman, *The Triumph of Politics;* Deborah Shapley, *Promise and Power;* and Jameson W. Doig and Erwin C. Hargrove, *Leadership and Innovation.*

CHAPTER 5

Intergovernmental Relations (IGR): The Concept of IGR as Interdependence, Complexity, and Bargaining

The problems and tensions in the modern (intergovernmental) system are not primarily the product of ill will or ignorance, nor can they be traced to one level of government. Rather, the American intergovernmental system was founded on ambivalent principles and built to establish arenas for conflict and controversy.

Laurence J. O'Toole, Jr.

READING 5

Introduction

In some countries, the subject of intergovernmental relations (IGR) is not a frequent topic of conversation. Unitary forms of government, found in communist societies, Third World or developing nations, and even modernized traditional Western state regimes, allow for little or no semiautonomous local units of government. Within these unitary models, power flows from the top downward, and no competition with national sovereignty is tolerated from governmental subunits. Local autonomy is simply unknown.

By contrast, the central framing idea of the U.S. government was federalism. The federal structure, as designed by the U.S. Constitution, distributes authority among the various levels of federal, state, and local government. In part, federalism was a pragmatic requirement in 1787. The founders were faced with the difficult necessity of winning state support for ratification, and thus adopting a unitary form that would abolish or severely restrict state authority was clearly out of the question. However, ideological considerations were also important in opting for federalism. The founders had vivid memories of the dangers from top-down unitary government of George III's monarchy as well as the loose, extreme decentralization of the Articles of Confederation (in reality the U.S.'s first constitution). Neither had produced satisfactory government and so the founders chose a mixture of both, the novel federal format. Though it is and remains the central framing idea in the U.S. Constitution, the Constitution on the specifics of this subject, as in many others, was imprecise and unclear. The details of the wheres and whys of how the various functions of government would be parceled out among the levels and units are not addressed in the U.S. Constitution beyond the items listed in Article I, Section 8.

In the United States, public administrators, thus, work within an unusual, complex framework in which authority over agency and program activities is frequently shared by various levels, jurisdictions, and units of government. Because of this "scattering" of authority, administrative problems arise, leading in turn to the important study of IGR, which involves comprehending the complexities of the federal system based on mutual interdependence, shared functions, and intertwined influence. Morton Grodzins once aptly showed the confusion for public administrators who operate under this system. In the case of a county health officer, called "a sanitarian" in a rural county:

> The sanitarian is appointed by the state under merit standards established by the federal government. His base salary comes jointly from state and federal funds, the county provides him with an office and office amenities and pays a portion of his expenses, and the largest city in the county also contributes to his salary and office by virtue of his appointment as a city plumbing inspector. It is impossible from moment to moment to tell under which governmental hat the sanitarian operates. His work of inspecting the purity of food is carried out under federal standards; but he is enforcing state laws when inspecting commodities that have not been in interstate commerce; and somewhat perversely, he also acts under state authority when inspecting milk coming into the county from producing areas across the state border. He is a federal officer when impounding impure drugs shipped from a neighboring state; a federal-state officer when distributing typhoid immunization serum; a state officer when enforcing standards of industrial hygiene; a state-local officer when inspecting the city's water supply; and (to complete the circle) a local officer when insisting that the city butchers adopt more hygienic methods of handling their garbage. But he cannot and does not think of himself as acting in these separate capacities. All business in the county that concerns public health and sanitation he considers his business. Paid largely from federal funds, he does not find it strange to attend meetings of the city council to give expert advice on matters ranging from rotten apples to rabies control. He is even deputized as a member of both the city and county police forces.*

Morton Grodzins's example of the county health officer may be extreme, but it is not uncommon to find public administrators wearing several "governmental hats." Federalism confounds and confuses public administrators' roles and responsibilities to an extreme degree in the United States. Who's the boss? The federal government? State? Locals? Or . . . ? For many administrators, the answer, as that of the county health officer cited by Grodzins, is the ambiguous "It all depends."

Laurence J. O'Toole, Jr. (1948–), a professor of political science at the University of Georgia and author of numerous works on intergovernmental relations, federalism, and public administration, explores the current dimensions of IGR. This essay serves as an introduction to his own third-edition volume on the subject and provides readers with a unique broad-brush 200-year overview of the topic. In particular, O'Toole's study begins by carefully differentiating "federalism" from "intergovernmental relations" and demonstrates how these

---

*Morton Grodzins, "The Federal System," in The American Assembly, *Goals for Americans* (N.J.: Prentice-Hall, Inc., 1960), p. 265.

concepts are rooted in the framework of the U.S. Constitution. The author shows how the idea of "dual federalism" of the nineteenth century evolved into more complex interrelationships in the twentieth century. The essay outlines the diverse factors that have resulted in fundamentally changed IGR dynamics and how particularly in recent decades various presidents have advanced different reforms to cope with the apparent dilemmas and issues of the intergovernmental system. O'Toole's thesis is: Despite the subsequent repeated reform initiatives by presidents, the modern pattern of IGR since the 1960s has been marked by three persisting characteristics: interdependence, complexity, and bargaining.

As you read O'Toole's insightful article, you might reflect on:

What does O'Toole mean by those three terms, "interdependence," "complexity," and "bargaining"?

How did this IGR pattern emerge and why does it persist today, according to O'Toole?

What does this concept of IGR mean for practicing public administrators and how should they train themselves to deal with these problems? (Think about the case study "The Blast in Centralia No. 5" in order to help you draw some conclusions.)

What were the various reform agendas proposed by presidents to improve and strengthen IGR, and why is it so difficult to change this intergovernmental system?

How does "federalism" differ from "IGR," according to O'Toole?

American Intergovernmental Relations: An Overview

LAURENCE J. O'TOOLE, JR.

Who should determine the provisions of public policy regarding health, including support for health care for those who cannot afford it? Which authorities should act as the front line of defense in protecting the nation's environment? What does it mean when welfare is "reformed"? Who decides where the "safety net" is placed, and under whom? Should state governments be able to force localities to initiate new activities without providing the cash to

cover expenses? How about Washington doing the same to the states themselves? Should the nation adopt a common and upgraded school curriculum in an effort to improve education and, as a consequence, economic competitiveness with other nations? Or should local districts be permitted, even encouraged, to make their own decisions and create their own innovations?

Should states and the national government be involved in encouraging, or restricting, the economic development efforts of American cities? In creating or limiting the instruments available to them to advance themselves—such as development

Laurence J. O'Toole, Jr. (ed), American Intergovernmental Relations: An Overview, Third Edition, 1999. Copyright © 1999 Congressional Quarterly Inc. Reprinted by permission of the publisher, CQ Press.

authorities or municipal debt? When counties and states allow or encourage the construction of mega-malls and superhighways that contribute to sprawl, congestion, and the degradation of air quality and nat-ural resources, should the national authorities have any influence? How much? What is the best way for the federal government to be strongly involved in the enforcement of such important policies as ensuring citizens' civil rights and encouraging equal employ-ment opportunity? And how can local police and fire departments be protected against micromanagement from Washington?

How should the people handle problems that con-front one part of the United States but surpass that re-gion's ability to cope? When a huge oil spill devastates parts of the precious Alaskan wilderness, who should take action, and how? When a reform of national tax law creates unintended negative effects on the finances of the states, what should be done? When acid rain from industrial air pollution con-tributes to the deterioration of natural resources a thousand miles away, who should take responsibil-ity? All these and many more are topics of inter-governmental relations.

Intergovernmental relations is the subject of how our many and varied American governments deal with each other and what their relative roles, responsibili-ties, and levels of influence are and should be. This subject is no flash-in-the-pan concern; it has generated longstanding interest—indeed constant and pervasive controversy—throughout American political and ad-ministrative history.

In fact, the establishment of the United States was itself a sort of experiment in intergovernmental rela-tions, since an effort to create a federal system like this one had never before been attempted. Nearly every major matter of domestic policy debated and decided throughout the nation's existence has been imbued with important intergovernmental aspects. Intergov-ernmental issues have contributed to such significant events in American history as the Civil War, the es-tablishment of the social welfare state during the New Deal era, the attack on poverty in the 1960s, the at-tempt to shift responsibilities to the states during the Reagan years, and the enactment of "welfare reform" in the 1990s.

But the subject is more than a collection of isolated issues. Indeed, it would be difficult to make sense of the many policy disputes without first understanding the intergovernmental system—its historical devel-opment as well as its current structure. To prepare for an exploration of current issues and disputes and to provide a context for the readings that follow, this chapter offers a brief overview of the intergovern-mental system in the United States, with an empha-sis on the federal government's role in the system's development.

Federalism, as the term is understood today, means a system of authority constitutionally appor-tioned between central and regional governments.[1] In the American system, the central, or national, government is often called the federal government; the regional governments are the states. The federal-state relationship is interdependent: neither can abol-ish the other and each must deal with the other. Intergovernmental relations is the more comprehen-sive term, including the full range of federal-state-local relations.

As the new century dawns, there are approximately 85,000 American governments—one national, fifty state, and the rest local. The last-mentioned consist of several distinct types. *Counties,* numbering some 3,000 units, are general-purpose governments origi-nally created throughout most of the country to ad-minister state services at the local level. Today, counties are genuine local governments providing an array of services to their citizens, and many—especially the larger, more urban ones—are increasingly involved in complex intergovernmental arrangements with other local jurisdictions, states, and the national govern-ment. *Municipalities,* numbering about 19,000, are local governments established to serve people within an area of concentrated population. The nation's largest cities and smallest villages alike are munici-palities, although the types of powers they have and the services they offer may vary considerably. Mu-nicipalities are created to serve explicitly the interests of the local community. Through much of American history, municipalities have had extensive and often highly conflicting relationships with their "parent" states—relationships sometimes made all the more chal-lenging from the point of view of the municipalities since they are not granted constitutionally independent status by the states, as are the states in the U.S. framework. Since the New Deal era in the 1930s and the rapid expansion of the intergovernmental system in the 1960s, municipalities—especially large cities—have dealt directly with Washington on many matters. And as federal cutbacks to these governments took hold in certain important policy sectors in the 1980s and beyond, municipalities have often developed defensive and somewhat conflictual relations with both state and national authorities—as they have also sought to develop additional revenue sources and less one-sided dependence on the other levels.

Additional local governments include:

- Townships (approximately 17,000), which are usually subdivisions of rural counties and are relatively unimportant except in some parts of New England and the mid-Atlantic states.
- School districts (more than 14,000), which are separate governments established in many parts of the country to direct public school systems.
- Special districts (numbering 31,555 in a recent count), which are limited-purpose governments set up to handle one or perhaps a few public functions over a specially designated area.[2]

Special districts are currently responsible for managing public housing; building and maintaining bridges, tunnels, and roads; supplying water and sewage services to residents; assessing and regulating air quality; and caring for the district's mass transit needs. The creation of many of these districts over the years has been directly or indirectly encouraged by other governments—such as the states and Washington—which sought coordinated local action on one or another policy problem.

If given a chance to view their handiwork today, it is likely that the founders of the United States would find much to surprise them in the operations of American politics and government, especially in the intergovernmental workings. Yet intergovernmental developments over the past couple of centuries have been affected greatly by some fundamental choices consciously made by those early Americans.

The Founding and the Framework

The framers of the U.S. Constitution sought a way to combine the several states into a structure that would minimize "instability, injustice, and confusion," in the words of James Madison.[3] The founders were familiar with the arguments of earlier political thinkers who claimed that government protection of individual rights would have to be small-scale and cover a geographically limited jurisdiction. Yet their own experience suggested problems with such an arrangement. Under the Articles of Confederation, enacted after the Revolution, the thirteen American states had agreed on a formal arrangement that is now called a *confederation.*[4] The states were loosely joined for certain purposes, but their association fell far short of a real nation. The states retained almost all power, and the "united states" under the Articles found it virtually impossible to act with dispatch on matters of importance.

To solve this problem, the "federalists" of that period proposed to organize a nation able to act in a unified and central fashion for certain purposes. They argued that large republics, not small ones, were more likely to be able to prevent internal tyranny. They also suggested, however, that the states themselves remain independent governments with correspondingly independent jurisdictions. As a matter of fact, state autonomy was a political necessity at the time if widespread support of a new constitutional order were to be elicited. In the absence of any such historical arrangement, the new experiment in intergovernmental relations would have to develop out of the American experience.

The founders' construction of the new system virtually ensured continuing controversy about the respective roles of the national and state governments by creating sufficient ambiguity to leave many of the most important questions unresolved. As a result, later years were to see major changes in American intergovernmental relations under the influence of various political, economic, and social forces, while the basic framework remained in place.[5]

What does that framework actually stipulate? The Constitution seems to divide responsibilities between the two levels of government according to subject.

Certain functions (for example, interstate commerce and national defense) are assigned to the national authorities, while many others (such as selection of presidential electors) are left to the states. Furthermore, the Tenth Amendment in the Bill of Rights asserts that "the powers not delegated to the United States by the Constitution, nor prohibited by it to the States, are reserved to the States respectively, or to the people." The states appear to have been given an advantage.

Yet the explanation cannot end here, for the same Constitution provides conflicting cues, authorizing the national Congress to "provide for the . . . general Welfare" and to "make all Laws which shall be necessary and proper" for executing this and the other powers given to the legislature. What constitutes the "general welfare" and which laws are necessary and proper are inherently political questions. Thus, it should be no surprise that the answers adopted by different people and at different times have not been consistent. The founders established a framework in which American governments would have separate but not completely independent spheres. The different levels would find it both useful and necessary to engage in conflict and cooperation; neither would be willing or able to ignore the other.

The Idea of Dual Federalism

Even in the earliest decades of the nation's existence, this tension was evident between the idea of *dual federalism* (that is, each of the two levels of government operating independently within its separate jurisdiction without relying on the other for assistance or authorization) on the one hand and ambiguous overlap on the other.

The notion of dual federalism influenced the decisions of the Supreme Court at least until the early decades of the twentieth century. Furthermore, during the 1800s various presidents sometimes vetoed legislation that would have created a federal presence in policy fields such as public works construction on the grounds that the Constitution simply did not permit such national involvement in arenas reserved for the states.[6] In a number of fields, like education and social

policy, dual federalism was the predominant view of federal-state intergovernmental relations.

Conflict and Cooperation in Earlier Times

Yet neither sphere was completely independent, even in the early years. Throughout the nineteenth century, the national government and the states often disagreed about the limits of their own authority. The Civil War is perhaps the prime example, but conflict occurred on other matters as well, such as policy on labor, social welfare, and economic regulation. To resolve jurisdictional disputes, therefore, the federal and state governments found it necessary to recognize their interdependence.

Conflict was not the only stimulus, however, for interaction. As various policy problems captured the attention of the nation's officials and citizenry, federal and state governments were sometimes able to piece together intergovernmental mechanisms to address immediate concerns. For instance, if some early national and state leaders viewed direct federal aid for internal improvements (for example, road and canal construction) as a violation of constitutional restrictions on intergovernmental arrangements, the governments *were* able to agree to cooperate in the formation of *joint stock companies,* part public and part private entities created to surmount the restrictions on direct participation by the national government. (Governments and private businesses could buy stock in a company and appoint members to its board of directors, thus indirectly supporting and influencing its operations.)[7]

Another mechanism for cooperation during the nineteenth century, before the dramatically increased intergovernmental interdependence of recent years, was the *land grant.* Through this device, the federal government would offer some of its land (it owned plenty) to the states for specified purposes. The recipient government would be obliged to abide by certain federal requirements, but direct involvement by the national government was minimal. Land grants were intended to help achieve goals in the fields of education (thus the origins of today's nationwide set of land-grant colleges and universities), economic development, and (on a very limited scale) social welfare.

Other forms of intergovernmental cooperation, such as technical assistance from federal to state governments and informal exchanges and loans of personnel during peak or crisis periods, were relatively common occurrences even during the nation's first century. Nevertheless, it was not until the twentieth century that the dual federal perspective declined appreciably in significance and American intergovernmental relations developed into a system with sustained high levels of *interdependence* and consequent *complexity*. Several political, economic, and social events and trends fueled these developments.

Developments in the Early Twentieth Century

From early in the twentieth century until recent years, federal involvement, especially financial involvement, in intergovernmental relations escalated. The Progressive Era at the turn of the century brought an expanded role for government in general, as reformers argued that the society and the economy could not tolerate laissez-faire (that is, a completely unregulated free market). The concentration of power in large corporations, the reluctance of some state governments to enact regulatory and other social welfare legislation (although other states were leaders in enacting farsighted and sometimes tough policy on such subjects), and the dawning recognition that the nation's natural resources were limited and would have to be conserved encouraged an expanded domestic policy role for Washington. This shift was also encouraged in many cases by the newly developing and professionalizing state bureaucracies, which saw in federal involvement opportunities for upgrading and for expanded funding, and by some interest groups that had been pushing at the state level for public attention to one problem or another. (Then, as now, organized interests—whether concerned with expanded highway construction or social services—have recognized that

it is usually easier and more effective to deal with one central government on such matters than with scores of divergent ones throughout the states.)

The growing national will to attempt action in new arenas was followed by the central government's acquiring the practical wherewithal for action. The resources needed were money and clear authority; by the 1920s both had been generated.

Federal Financial Aid

In 1913 the U.S. Constitution was amended to permit the enactment of a federal income tax. Previously the national government had provided some limited financial support to the states, but the intergovernmental fiscal ties were few and far between. Until very recently the passage of the Sixteenth Amendment enabled the national government to raise revenue more easily than the subnational ones. The income tax, which was elastic (that is, its receipts increased faster than the economy during periods of growth), has been a more politically palatable revenue source than other sources typically emphasized by the states and by local governments.

This situation has changed in recent years. First, the income tax increased its bite in individuals' paychecks during the period of rapid inflation in the 1970s, resulting in a decline in its popularity and the enactment of an indexing provision to control the effects of inflation. Second, federal legislative changes during the 1980s reduced the progressiveness of the tax, that is, the extent to which it draws revenue from the affluent. Additional tax cuts in the 1990s created more tax breaks for the middle class and above, and other federal taxes, especially Social Security, began to assume a larger burden. Third, most states and even some local governments enacted income taxes of their own, with formulas tied in complicated ways to various provisions of the federal tax code. The development of intergovernmental finances in recent decades therefore documents one way in which the system has been linked via complexity. Thus, with the income tax the federal government created a source of money that could be tapped repeatedly to fill needs that had not yet received the states' wholehearted attention.

The obvious mechanism of intergovernmental co-operation in many such cases was the *grant-in-aid.* By 1920 there were eleven grants-in-aid operating in the United States. Land grants and other varieties of intergovernmental assistance were never again to outstrip cash grants in importance. In light of the significance of grants-in-aid since the early twentieth century, it would be useful to explain at this point some of the basic implications of this kind of program.

A grant-in-aid is a transfer of funds from one government to another for some specified purpose. Typically the recipient government is asked by the donor to abide by certain terms as conditions of the assistance.[8] These usually include a requirement that the recipient unit match the donor's financial contribution with one of its own, as well as a series of "strings," or stipulations, as to how the funds will be used, how the program will be managed, and how the recipient government will report to the donor.

Starting on a small scale early in the twentieth century, and then expanding rapidly during certain periods—especially the New Deal and Great Society eras—grants-in-aid from the federal government to the states and eventually local governments became extremely important features of the intergovernmental system in the United States. States, too, have provided financial support to their local governments. (In 1994 total state aid to other governments amounted to $225 billion. This total includes some federal aid passed to the local units through the states.)[9] But federal aid, because of its size, relative newness, and capacity to produce large-scale alterations in the intergovernmental system, may be considered an especially significant feature of America's fiscal federalism (see Table 1).

Validation of Grants-in-Aid

As the national government began to exercise influence through the use of grants-in-aid in the early 1900s, some observers wondered if the grant mechanism was an unconstitutional federal intrusion into the affairs of the states. Armed with the doctrine of dual federalism, critics of federal grants argued that Washington's offers were actually coercive inducements and violated the notion of separate spheres for these two levels of government. In a pair of landmark decisions in 1923 the Supreme Court paved the way for major expansions in the grant system—and for tremendously increased interdependence and complexity among levels of government—in succeeding years. The Court asserted that grants were voluntary arrangements and the federal government was therefore not violating the constitutionally established separation of functions in the federal system.[10] As the years elapsed, the grant framework became a dominant feature of the American intergovernmental network; it tied thousands of governments intricately together, for better or worse.

Basic Types of Assistance

Grants have offered the opportunity for substantially expanded federal influence over state and local governments, and a number of important political and administrative consequences flow from this fact. Yet it is essential to recognize that while grants create opportunities for national involvement, they do not vitiate the pluralism of the intergovernmental system—at least not necessarily. Grants have developed as the prime instruments used to promote bargaining and jockeying for advantage among governments; they have frequently stimulated both cooperation and conflict among donor and recipient governments. It should therefore surprise no one that the system of aid employed in the United States has elicited ambivalent evaluations from participants and citizens alike.

Grants come in many shapes and sizes. The donor government may structure the purpose quite narrowly, offering aid for the construction of certain kinds of highways within a state. Such *categorical grants* were typical in the early 1900s. The donor may also design an intergovernmental program for a variety of purposes within a broad field such as education, community development, or social services. This type of aid, called a *block grant,* gained some prominence in more recent decades. In the early 1970s a new form of aid, *revenue sharing,* was created to enable one government to offer financial aid to another with virtually no restrictions on its use.[11]

When enacted, all of these types of intergovernmental assistance required some rules and regulations

Table 1 Federal Aid to State and Local Governments, Selected Years

Year	Amount (Billions)[a]	Amount in Constant 1992 Dollars (Billions)	Number of Grants
1902	0.028		5
1912	—		7
1913	0.039		—
1920	—		11
1922	0.242		—
1932	0.593		12
1934	2.4		—
1937	—		26
1940	0.87	9.9	—
1946	0.82	6.9	28
1952	2.4	14.0	38
1960	7.0	33.4	132
1964	10.2	45.8	—
1967	15.2	64.8	379
1975	49.8	126.6	442
1978	77.9	159.5	—
1981	94.7	146.4	539
1982	88.1	127.4	441
1984	97.6	129.5	405
1987	108.4	130.4	435
1990	135.3	144.7	—
1992	178.1	178.1	—
1995	225.0	208.5	—
1998	246.1	215.2	—
2001 (est.)	300.7	246.7	—

[a]1961 dollars through 1937; otherwise, current dollars.

SOURCES: U.S. Advisory Commission on Intergovernmental Relations, *The Federal Role in the Federal System: The Dynamics of Growth—A Crisis of Confidence and Competence* (Washington, D.C.: ACIR, July 1980), 120–121; *Significant Features of Fiscal Federalism, 1990,* vol. 2, *Revenues and Expenditures* (Washington, D.C.: ACIR, August 1990), 42; American Council on Intergovernmental Relations, *Significant Features of Fiscal Federalism 1995,* vol. 2, *Revenues and Expenditures* (Albany, N.Y.: Nelson A. Rockefeller Institute of Government, February 1998), 38; and *Historical Tables, Budget of the United States Government, Fiscal Year 2000* (Washington, D.C.: Government Printing Office, 1999), Table 12.1, 203–204.

regarding the method of distributing the aid. How is a unit selected to receive assistance and how much is it entitled to? Some grants, including all federal block grants, specify a precise formula in the legislation creating the program. Such *formula grants* include quantifiable elements, such as size of population, amount of tax effort, proportion of population unemployed or below poverty level, density of housing, or rate of infant mortality. The specified formula is a rule that tells potential recipient governments precisely how they can calculate the quantity of aid to which they are entitled under the provisions of the law, as long as the recipient qualifies for such assistance under the other stipulations of the program. Usually, the elements in a formula are chosen to reflect characteristics related to the purpose of the aid (number of school-age children for an education grant, age and/or density of residential housing for housing assistance).

Some factors in the formula are also likely to have political significance since there is no such thing as a neutral formula—all formulas reward some states or localities more than others, depending on their relative standing given the formula specified.

However, another method of distributing aid is available. *Project grants* allocate funding on a competitive basis, and potential recipients have no advance knowledge about the size of the grant. Instead, the authorizing legislation typically indicates the sorts of jurisdictions that are eligible to apply for aid and the criteria that will be employed to judge the merit of a government's application. Whether or not a government then receives funding depends on how strong a case it can make in its own behalf. Bureaucrats in the federal departments that supply aid determine the relative worthiness of different proposals and different jurisdictions, often by means of a detailed decision-making and evaluation system.

Why bother to make these distinctions among types of aid? The answer is that different types of grants have tended to produce different types of relationships between and among the participating governments. Much of the intergovernmental system in the twentieth century can be rendered intelligible by analyzing the consequences of different types of aid, one of the subjects treated in the remainder of this chapter.

The Legacy of the New Deal

Most of the grant-in-aid programs developed by the national government in the early decades of the 1900s were relatively limited. They assisted other governments primarily in fields that commanded strong political support, such as agriculture and road construction. Federal assistance, and thus national influence, was directed almost entirely toward the states rather than local governments. During this period, and until the 1960s, the system of intergovernmental aid was dominated by categorical formula grants. For the first part of the century, these were accompanied by relatively few strings, required considerable matching on the part of the recipients, and were rare enough that they did not seem to impose much of an administrative or political burden on the states.

With the New Deal in the 1930s the federal government under the leadership of President Franklin D. Roosevelt tackled the challenging economic and social problems of the Depression era. Although it would have been technically possible to establish new national-level programs to cope with the difficulties of the period, the more politically palatable method of the grant-in-aid was repeatedly used instead. Thus, while the national government's role expanded, the states and local governments retained significant leverage. Within a two-year period, categorical grants were established in such a variety of fields—free school lunches, aid to dependent children, emergency work relief, and so on—that they became the foundation for the social welfare state in America. The first real forms of assistance to some of the nation's local governments, the cities, were initiated during this period as well. For the states and some of their local governments, then, national authorities were no longer distant or sporadically communicating entities. Instead, in many areas of domestic policy, two or three levels of government were tied together in intricate patterns of intergovernmental relations—more like a marble cake, than the layer cake of dual federalism.[12]

Thus, the New Deal period witnessed a permanent increase in the density and importance of intergovernmental relationships in the United States, and during the next couple of decades—even during the administration of Republican president Dwight D. Eisenhower—the number of federal programs and quantity of federal aid continued to grow. Eisenhower himself was uncomfortable with the apparently prominent role of the national government in domestic policy matters, and he established the Commission on Intergovernmental Relations with the explicit charge to identify areas of federal involvement that could feasibly be "returned" to the states. But even the very modest suggestions of this commission went unimplemented. During the 1950s it seemed, as it often has since then, that the idea of separating functions by level of government was supported in the abstract but was exceedingly difficult to execute. Concerted efforts to reduce the levels of interdependence and complexity in the intergovernmental system have been, for the most part, singularly unsuccessful. In later decades, occasional efforts to simplify had some limited impacts; yet even these were not without costs, and they introduced complicating changes as well, such as increased intergovernmental mandating in place of the grant mechanism in policy sectors from transportation to the environment. Mandates, in turn, have been a major issue during the most recent decade.

The difficulty experienced by American governments when they try to reduce their reliance on one another is not surprising. Since the New Deal, citizens and public officials have tried to harness the national government's tremendous resources in order to attack pressing problems and redress inequities. They have attempted at the same time to retain diversity and innovation through vital state and local governments wherever possible. Shifting to some form of dual federalism, with a much less intense pattern of relationships and dependencies, could affect federal commitments in a multitude of important policy areas, like environmental protection, civil rights, income security, and education. Furthermore, such a change might entail radical shifts in the nation's tax system. And even the most carefully considered plans would have to face bewildering dilemmas about how to reduce intergovernmental interdependence without inflicting serious inequities on some states and localities.

These days, when, as in the 1950s, one hears proposals to limit the federal role in the intergovernmental system and simplify the pattern of American governments, such caveats are useful to keep in mind. While many of the states are assuming newly resurgent roles in many policy sectors at the end of the century, Washington is certain to play a crucial part for the foreseeable future. It may even be asserted that creating a radically simplified intergovernmental arrangement by moving the national government out of a direct role in many important policy arenas is not a practical or responsible option. Why, then, the clamorous call for reform? Why have so many policy makers and intergovernmental experts complained about the "overloaded" pattern?[13] Later in this book, the considerable validity of a number of the criticisms will become clear. Focusing on the major developments affecting the intergovernmental system since the 1960s will be useful in understanding this controversy.

Creative Federalism and Its Implications

With Lyndon Johnson's presidency and the election of a heavily Democratic and activist Congress in 1964, a several-year period of tremendously expanded intergovernmental activities and initiatives began. Johnson proposed a "creative federalism" that would signify multiple new national commitments to assist states, localities, and private individuals and organizations in their efforts to solve many of the domestic difficulties of American society. These efforts of the Johnson era were directed primarily at problems of racial discrimination, poverty, and urban and rural development. The president and the Congress responded not just with rhetoric but with hundreds of intergovernmental programs.

Indeed, the number of federal programs of grant-in-aid tripled from the beginning of the 1960s to 1975 (Table 1). Almost all of the new programs from Washington were categorical grants, and—unlike earlier times—most of them were project grants. By the late 1960s most of the available grants were project grants, although many of these were relatively small and in toto constituted a minority of the aid dollars. In addition, the amount of support offered directly to local governments rose sharply. Many localities (especially the nation's older, larger, more fiscally strapped cities) came to consider the federal government more of an ally than their own state governments and became increasingly reliant on federal largesse. The results of these and other massive changes in the intergovernmental system enacted in such a compressed period were, as might be expected, mixed.

Intergovernmental Activism

In many respects the consequences of this major increase in intergovernmental activity were impressive. Although hampered by fiscal constraints, especially as the war in Southeast Asia drained its resources, the nation made measurable progress on a number of troubling problems.[14] The dramatic increase in federal support was especially welcome to many state and local governments, which had difficulty obtaining the resources to fund programs demanded by their citizenry; also, the emphasis on a variety of project grants meant that potential recipients could find appropriately targeted programs.

The explosion in the grant system had the further effect of encouraging or mandating the professionalization of personnel and the use of up-to-date financial procedures in the administrative agencies handling the programs in the recipient governments. Intergovernmental programs became increasingly influenced by functional specialists at all levels of government. The requirements attached to many of the new grants also forced states and localities to devote renewed attention to public problems they may have overlooked in the past.

Another trend fueled by creative federalism was the growth of interest groups in the nation's capital, especially intergovernmental groups. Those concerned with specific intergovernmental programs, whether on environmental pollution or juvenile delinquency, increasingly looked to Washington as they tried to influence legislation and the implementation of regulations, to monitor the actions of the federal agency involved, and to maintain contact with other interested parties. The tremendous expansion of the grant system in the 1960s was both a result of and a stimulus for a burgeoning number of interest groups operating at the national level in intergovernmental politics. These changes, too, contributed to the growing complexity of intergovernmental policy making and have served, since then, as a brake on any substantial efforts to disentangle the system.

These sorts of interest groups were not the only ones to achieve a heightened national presence. As the grants became ever more important and the system increasingly more complex, officials of state and local governments found it crucial to acquire information about the decision-making process in Washington. Furthermore, state and local officials began to realize that their own interests might deserve representation in the policy process at the national level. Accordingly, several groups of state or local general-purpose officials organized for the first time, moved their operations to Washington, or upgraded their staff and expanded their activities. These groups, including entities like the National Governors' Association, the

Council of State Governments, the National Association of Counties, and the U.S. Conference of Mayors, refer to themselves as public interest groups, or *PIGs* (really). By the 1960s they became increasingly recognized as leaders in the representation of state and local interests in national policy making. In addition to the individual state and local governments as well as associations of governments that began to locate offices and representatives in Washington, other more functionally specialized groups of state and local officials, such as highway officials, budget officers, and social workers, have organized into national groups and participate in the policy process. Nowadays, even in the midst of the financial constraints influencing intergovernmental decisions quite directly, any discussion of an intergovernmental issue in Congress or an administrative agency is likely to elicit concern, participation, lobbying, and debate involving many such organizations.

Thus, the Johnson era encouraged several salutary developments in intergovernmental relations and further elaborated other interesting trends. Yet, as might be expected when such massive changes are effected, difficulties and tensions also arose.

Emergent Frustrations and Tensions

Because the choices made available to state and local officials as a result of the tremendous increase in intergovernmental programs were almost limitless, potential recipients could afford to shop around and bargain for the most favorable deal. As a result of the interagency competition for clients, federal requirements would sometimes be loosely enforced. Recipients were more and more able to evade federal intent while absorbing federal dollars.

Conversely, the system, which now had huge numbers of partially overlapping (and often duplicating) grants, created vexing difficulties for officials at state and local levels. With several related programs available to assist a city in such tasks as rebuilding its sewers, a great deal of time, effort, and information went into deciding which program or programs to pursue. Grants established ostensibly for the same purpose might be housed in different federal agencies, require entirely different application and approval processes, stipulate very different matching requirements, and be implemented with conflicting schedules. Furthermore, as potential recipients of project grants scrambled to complete detailed applications for scores of grant requests on short notice, the winners were not necessarily the most competent or the most needy jurisdictions. Instead, the one who packaged proposals in the most salable fashion (exercising what came to be called grantsmanship), was often rewarded.

The systemic changes generated another set of tensions for state and local governments. With the multitude of programs, many of which were now funded by grants constructed with high matching ratios (that is, Washington would pay for most of the total expenses incurred under the program), state and local governments were finding it increasingly difficult either to abstain from commitments to federal aid or to make such commitments wholeheartedly. A program that can be subsidized by grant money becomes cheaper and therefore more attractive to the recipient government. However, a mushrooming number of appealing programs can significantly distort the recipient's budgeting process. Instead of spending its locally generated revenue on the public services judged most important by its own officials and citizens, a city can be encouraged to use its money as matching funds for programs that are, in essence, national priorities. The expansion of the aid system in the 1960s prompted complaints on this score from uneasy mayors, governors, and others who were concerned about their apparently declining ability to maintain some independence.

Such general-purpose officials had other concerns as well. Many of them believed the expanded system of categorical grants was composed of unduly narrow programs that were not readily adaptable to the needs in their own jurisdictions. Furthermore, the pattern, taken as a whole, had become so complex that it was all but impenetrable to generalists. These officials had a difficult time even figuring out how much aid was being received from federal sources. And many of the important, detailed decisions that are made as part of an intergovernmental grant bargain—for instance, determining the eligibility of clients for programs or establishing goals—were made far from the general-purpose officials. Increasingly important in

the intergovernmental policy process was a great number of specialists across governmental levels—especially in administrative agencies charged with executing the program, legislative committees with responsibility for the substantive area, and pressure groups with a strong interest in the program. Intergovernmental experts, particularly those concerned about the decreasing ability of general officials to oversee and direct activities in this maze, dubbed these policy networks *vertical functional autocracies.*

In these chains of influence, it became increasingly difficult for anyone, even major officials like governors or mayors or presidents, to decipher just *who* was causing *what* to happen intergovernmentally. When responsibility is so diffused, the mechanisms of democratic government cannot readily ensure that policy reflects the will of the people or their representatives. In other words, another possible cost of such an arrangement is a decline in political responsiveness.

In short, then, the era of creative federalism brought energy and inventiveness to intergovernmental questions; but the massive changes in the system meant a significant escalation in costs and frustrations as well. It should not be surprising, therefore, that interdependence and complexity emerged as major political features during the decades following the Johnson era. Despite manifold differences in emphasis, approach, and impact, intergovernmental actors during the most recent period have grappled with a structure exhibiting common characteristics and daunting demands. The following pages first characterize the modern intergovernmental pattern in general terms and then explore important events and efforts during several recent national administrations.

Interdependence, Complexity, and Intergovernmental Bargaining

In the pattern that emerged from the explosive growth of creative federalism it became difficult for actors in the system to make rational decisions to benefit the individuals or activities for which they held responsibility. It was also difficult to design any coherent change in the system itself. These problems stemmed directly from the dominant characteristics of the intergovernmental system: its interdependence and related complexity.

It would be helpful to define these two concepts more precisely here. *Interdependence* means that power is shared among branches and layers of government, even within policy sectors. Instead of one level consistently controlling decisions about policy, nearly any change requires mutual accommodation among several levels of government. No one is in control of the system itself, and unanticipated consequences are a fact of life. Complexity accompanies such interdependence. *Complexity* means that the intergovernmental network is large and differentiated; no one participating government can consistently possess enough information about its components and dynamics to make rational decisions on its own or to operate in isolation from the rest.

Especially since the era of creative federalism, but also as a consequence of the framework established by the founders, many participants in the intergovernmental system have plenty of opportunities to exercise influence—particularly to delay or frustrate action to which they are opposed. It is much more difficult, however, to generate and systematically execute *positive* action in a straightforwardly rational manner.

An important result of the system's grounding in interdependence and complexity (one that became obvious in the 1960s and endures in altered form) is that the typical style of decision making in the American intergovernmental system is one of bargaining under conditions of partial conflict among the participants. The actors in the system, including the various governments involved, have different interests to serve and objectives to seek; yet they cannot succeed by acting unilaterally. They may join together into one or more loose coalitions aimed at achieving some intergovernmental objective.[15] But they must perforce negotiate as a nearly ceaseless activity if they are to have any chance of defending themselves or achieving even some of their goals.

Of course, bargaining under conditions of partial conflict is a very abstract notion and encompasses many different types of situations. The bargaining between governments in a project grant structure differs in predictable and important ways from the bargaining activity likely with a formula grant: the former setting typically provides more influence to bureaucratic actors associated with the donor government, those who write the rules and evaluate the competitive applications from potential recipients. The fact of bargaining and its pervasiveness throughout the system, however, is important to keep in mind. Bargaining is typical even today, a time when many grant programs have not grown at nearly the pace of earlier periods and when other ties, ostensibly more controlling, unilateral, or regulatory ties have become prominent between levels. As readings in this book document, recent years have brought unfunded mandates (rather than grants) that have become increasingly used as a mechanism of coordination across governments. Yet these shifts do not unambiguously signify a new centralization. In some ways, also documented later in this volume, the states are now able to initiate more action, or to resist more, than in earlier periods. And federal officials may have fewer levers to enforce their own efforts at intergovernmental influence when the grant mechanism is absent from, or less prominent in, the bargaining arena. It may be concluded, therefore, that the shifts of the last two decades or more have altered the *types* of bargaining and the issues subject to negotiation. The fact of bargaining nevertheless remains crucial to an understanding of American intergovernmental dynamics.

Some of the tensions inherent in such an interdependent and complex system became visible in the 1960s and have escalated since. Red tape, which is the continuation of intergovernmental negotiation and conflict by other means, is one manifestation. The federal government has usually viewed the requirements it imposes on its grants as essential to ensure a program's integrity. Yet recipient units claim that the burdens have become excessive. (Localities also blame the states in part for their red-tape burden.) Federally created intergovernmental mandates have escalated sharply since 1975 and in the 1990s became the bête noire of state and local officials.

Two general points emerge. First, the problems and tensions in the modern system are not primarily the product of ill will or ignorance, nor can they be traced primarily to one level of government. Rather, the American intergovernmental system was founded on ambivalent principles and built to establish arenas for conflict and controversy. Second, changing the particular pattern of intergovernmental relationships or reforming certain aspects of the system—for example, through the enactment of spending and policy shifts like those the Republican congressional majority sought during the late 1990s—would have important consequences but could hardly resolve the value conflicts of a complex and interdependent system. At this point, accordingly, we should examine some of the developments in the American intergovernmental system since the period of creative federalism. Many of these are made comprehensible by an awareness of the difficulties just surveyed, and many, in turn, presage some of the topics of current interest and controversy.

Nixon's New Federalism

Richard Nixon reacted to the tensions in the changing system by proposing reforms ostensibly aimed at increasing the influence of general-purpose (especially elected) officials at all levels, shifting power away from Washington and toward federal field offices and state and local governments, reducing the control exercised by functional specialists, and trimming intergovernmental red tape. (This direction was maintained, though with somewhat diminished effort and effectiveness, by his successor, Gerald Ford.)

Of what, exactly, did Nixon's "new federalism" consist? He proposed a series of initiatives:

1. *Revenue sharing.* One of Nixon's most ambitious initiatives was to establish a program of revenue sharing from the federal level to state and local governments. Revenue sharing (also called general revenue sharing) seemed to meet the demands of state and local governments for more discretion, was attractive to the most financially hard-pressed jurisdictions, and could shift some influence to the general-purpose elected officials. In 1972 the State and Local Fiscal Assistance Act was passed with the support of much of the Democratic leadership in Congress as well as of the major PIGs of state and local officials. This law established a revenue-sharing program of approximately $6 billion per year for five years. All state governments and general-purpose local governments were eligible for aid, which was to be allocated on the basis of complicated formulas. The program was extended, with modifications, in 1976, and again in 1980. In 1984 revenue sharing was reenacted for localities alone, as the federal budget tightened. And in 1986, the program was ended because Congress found itself facing an increasingly severe national deficit. During its tenure, revenue sharing helped many governments. But even at its peak, it constituted only a small fraction of total federal assistance for the larger recipient governments.

2. *Block grants.* These began during the Johnson administration, but the idea is most closely identified with Nixon, who proposed a set of enactments in six policy fields along with the elimination of a series of closely related categorical grants. Defenders of these latter programs, including members of the vertical functional autocracies, resisted; their concerns would have no statutory protection once a block grant was put into place. Further, the Nixon proposals would have reduced the overall level of intergovernmental funding. Ultimately, only three of the additional block grants emerged from this period: in employment, social services, and community development. Yet some of these programs have had a major impact on intergovernmental affairs, and they were followed by additional block grants enacted during the Reagan years.

3. *Administrative initiatives.* Nixon encouraged the implementation of administrative reforms by supporting a series of efforts to simplify and expedite the grant application and review process.

Despite all these changes, the intergovernmental system was not radically altered. The more traditional categorical grant was by no means disused. Indeed, such programs and the amount of aid going to support them increased even through the Nixon years. And administrative and regulatory difficulties in the system proved to be more tenacious than many had anticipated. Impressively complex and interdependent, the system continued to face criticism from virtually all directions.

The Carter Period

President Jimmy Carter was not the activist in intergovernmental matters that Nixon was—or, for that matter, that his successor would be. But, as a former governor familiar with the concerns of general political executives and of state and local units, Carter worked at developing communication links with the PIGs and with state and local governments, tried to advance some administrative reforms, and paid special attention to economic problems facing the cities.

Yet Carter proposed no overall plan for reform of the system, nor did he recommend any major changes in the pattern of intergovernmental aid. Two developments during the late 1970s exacerbated some of the difficulties faced by policy makers and managers. First, a combination of sour economic conditions, federal budget difficulties, and Carter's fundamentally conservative fiscal instincts placed stringent limits on any efforts to increase federal aid. Federal spending increases slowed and in 1978 reversed direction: aid was being limited at a time when many units of government had come to depend on it. Second, during this period the federal government, especially Congress, did not easily loosen its hold on other units of government. Instead, Washington sought to accomplish its intergovernmental goals via direct requirements, frequently including some that were mandated across many different programs.

Reagan's Attempted Revolution

The first part of Ronald Reagan's time as president saw perhaps the most systematic, if not the most sustained, effort to remake the American intergovernmental system since the New Deal. Reagan ardently believed that the United States had been created as a system in which national powers and jurisdiction were severely limited, and in which the states had the strongest, most vital governments, with the broadest jurisdiction over domestic matters. Accordingly, he sought to reshape the intergovernmental pattern in a manner consistent with this understanding. Since his other priorities included tax reductions and significant defense spend-

ing increases, a related consequence was a renewed vulnerability of intergovernmental aid to sizable cuts. Since pressures by citizens and interest groups to address a whole set of policy issues at state and local levels did not abate, the stage was set for higher levels of tension and conflict in the system.

Reagan's major proposals, for which he adopted Nixon's term, the new federalism, were as follows:

1. *An additional series of block grants.* Reagan quickly proposed that more than 100 categoricals be combined into a handful of broadly based block grants with very few regulations. Congress complied with several of these initiatives.
2. *A dramatic simplification of the system of intergovernmental aid.* Program responsibilities were to be shifted to single levels of government and away from the "marble cake" configurations. Congress made no move to approve this plan, and Reagan's attention was diverted from this contentious issue.
3. *A devolution of responsibilities for many policies from the national level to the states.* Reagan suggested that scores of programs involving federal participation, including most of the remaining expensive ones, be turned over to the states in their entirety and that an appropriate quantity of revenue be shifted to the states as well. No action was taken on this proposal. Yet several years after Reagan had left office, some of the intent behind this idea was being fulfilled. By the 1990s new policy initiatives that might involve substantial new expenditures from Washington had become nearly impossible to enact in the political and budgetary climate of the time. Meanwhile, many states, which were being pressed by interest groups and the citizenry to address daunting problems like health care, infrastructure financing, education, and economic development, had become centers of more policy activism than had been seen in years outside of the nation's capital.
4. *Administrative simplification.* The president worked to trim red tape and lighten the putative burden of federal mandates. In this regard, Reagan scored his "successes," as did his prede-

cessors. Yet many complained about the abdication of federal responsibility for important national goals, and others felt the reforms did not go nearly far enough. Several years after Reagan's departure from the White House, the evidence accumulated that mandates from Washington had increased overall.

Reagan's efforts to restructure the intergovernmental system were challenged by many. By the second half of his first term, the most ambitious proposals had been set aside in favor of further grouping of categorical programs into block grants. Even these suggestions encountered hostility or indifference in Congress.

Nevertheless, the Reagan administration's efforts, and the complicated responses they stimulated, presaged a series of changes in the intergovernmental system as the century drew to a close.

Crosscurrents at Century's End: Struggles for Reform, Pressures toward Globalization

The administration of President George Bush did not signal a major departure from the intergovernmental trends of Reagan's second term, nor did President Bill Clinton seek to grab center stage with dramatic attempts to recraft the nature of the system. But by the middle of the 1990s events and influences from elsewhere had combined to place the American intergovernmental network in the midst of a variety of consequential forces. Most of the issues receiving attention during the Reagan years remained on the agenda, but shifts in political fortunes, economic conditions, and federalism jurisprudence combined during the 1990s to amplify the turbulence in the system. By the dawn of the twenty-first century the resolution of these influences is still uncertain, with forces pushing actively in quite different directions. But it is clear that a number of these recent developments will continue to be felt well into the new millennium. And it is equally clear that the prime characteristics of the system, complexity and interdependence, will continue to shape the details of intergovernmental bargaining and

frustrate the efforts of reformers to impose or craft a clear and coherent design.

For instance, and perhaps most prominently, by 1995 the Republican leadership in Congress had swept to victory. They had touted a "Contract with America" that offered a governmental future in which Washington would retreat from policy activism and leadership, taxes would be cut, and subnational governments would be freed from the shackles of irksome and expensive unfunded mandates imposed by the center. Meaningful steps were taken to convert the Contract into a reality. The Republicans in Congress sought to impose tight budgetary discipline, even to cut many programs dramatically, and passed an Unfunded Mandates Reform Act (UMRA) during their first year in power. But with resistance from the Democratic president Clinton, as well as the unpopularity of the apparent game of chicken between the branches culminating in the "shutdown" of government offices during 1995 and 1996, it became clear to the leadership in each branch that some accommodation with their counterpart institution would be necessary.

One result was a continuation, indeed increase, in intergovernmental assistance (see Table 1), even as politicians like Clinton announced that the era of big government was over. Leaders of both parties could find agreement on such aid useful as a means of acquiescing to the continuing realities of interdependence while also energizing and devolving discretion to other governments. The continuing appeal of block grants in this regard was obvious, with political leaders of both parties supporting these in principle even while disagreeing on many details. Significantly for the longer term, an important block grant, the program of Temporary Assistance to Needy Families, or TANF, was enacted in 1996, as part of the Personal Responsibility and Work Opportunity Reconciliation Act. This initiative ended the nationally supported Aid to Families with Dependent Children (AFDC) program, which had been the intergovernmental assistance effort at the core of the nation's social welfare protection for many of its poorest people.

AFDC as a categorical grant program had come to symbolize welfare, a program much maligned even if much less expensive than many had supposed. While Clinton and the Republican congressional leadership sought to glean advantage from the situation, they did agree to enact this major change in the nation's welfare policy—and major shift in responsibility "downward" to the states. TANF put an end to long-term welfare assistance, a frequent occurrence under the older program, and was designed to encourage welfare recipients to move permanently into the work force. The initiative also increased greatly the flexibility of states to shape their own approach—and their responsibility to fund the choices they made.

TANF symbolized, in a sense, one of the major currents in the turbulent intergovernmental maelstrom of the time: increased state discretion and innovation amid continuing intergovernmental ties. While some observers continue to worry that states will use their energies to benefit the most privileged interests, and that enhanced state fiscal responsibilities inevitably signal less redistribution and social protection in many of the nation's poorest states, others see this shift as emblematic of a healthy recognition that state governments have become more professional, competent, and energetic, and that the states are better equipped to meet the challenges of the new century than is Washington.

Furthermore, with fiscal pressures mounting in expensive policy sectors like health, Republican policy makers in particular advocated replicating the TANF action with block grants to replace costly intergovernmental programs like Medicaid. Here the politics, the stakes, and the concern on the part of PIGs that they not be buried under huge and escalating costs made taking radical action much more difficult. Stalemate characterized much of the intergovernmental debate on health policy during the 1990s.

More generally, as well, the 1990s produced evidence aplenty, amidst the partisanship and turbulence in Washington, that simple and dramatic shifts in the intergovernmental system would be unlikely—even as substantial efforts were mounted to make things happen in a big way. The complexity and interdependence of the system—and the fact of the public's mixed and ambivalent attitudes toward such major changes—continued to produce nuanced

and complicated results, even for all the attempts at systematization and "revolution."

A prime example has been the quixotic efforts at mandate reform. No one approves of unfunded mandates in principle, and yet their appearance escalated throughout the 1980s and into the 1990s. The Republican Contract with America called for their elimination. Meanwhile, the Democratic White House had initiated an administrative overhaul of the national government under the direction of Vice President Al Gore, the National Performance Review (NPR). NPR too called for a rationalizing of the nation's approach to intergovernmental relations; and, while avoiding the radical rhetoric of the Contract, the NPR trumpeted the need for an end to unfunded mandates imposed on the states and localities. The UMRA had been enacted quickly, and yet years later it became clear that, while not completely ineffective, the act has been unsuccessful in legislating an end to the kinds of nationally initiated regulatory ties that stimulated its passage. As Paul Posner shows, *both* political parties find reasons to support mandating, even if the mandates and policy sectors vary. And using legislation as a way of trying to prevent the intergovernmental regulation and associated (often acrimonious) bargaining does not address the more fun- damental sources of these ties in the first place.

In the meantime, the UMRA also required the U.S. Advisory Commission on Intergovernmental Relations, a respected governmentally established forum for analysis and improvement of the system active since the 1950s, to undertake an examination of the nation's mandates with a view toward recommending the elimination of the most onerous. The requirement resulted in a staff-produced, strongly argued critique of national mandates with several specific suggestions for mandate reduction. These proposals in turn ignited a firestorm of protest, as coalitions of groups mobilized to protect the national standards and regulations they had worked so hard to see enacted, on policy matters ranging from the rights of the disabled to emissions controls under the Clean Air Act. The Clinton administration, which had expressed general support for controlling mandates, was nonetheless responsive to this pressure from parts of its core constituencies and resisted the ACIR staff's recommendations. The full commission rejected its own staff's recommendation as this long-standing intergovernmental body was caught in the crossfire, and shortly thereafter the ACIR was defunded. The commission has ceased to function.

The death of the ACIR is a prime example of the perils of today's American intergovernmental relations: while virtually everyone favors "reform" and "simplification," at least as general principles, the reality is that the complexity and interdependence endemic in the system are no accidents. They have emerged as products of a long series of function-specific demands and political supports for cost sharing, standard setting, and cross-governmental bargaining. Remaking the system on behalf of goals like allocating functions to "appropriate" levels of government, clarifying the often obscure mechanisms of intergovernmental influence and administration, and reducing fiscal pressures imposed from Washington can be expected to run afoul of intense support for problem solving and bargaining in adaptation to the crosscurrents of policy change. The general desire for "reform," coupled with the considerable difficulty in building a coalition supportive of concrete and significant steps in that direction, is not confined to one political party or another, nor is the tendency unique to the environment of Washington, D.C. The states, for instance, are themselves heavy imposers of mandates on their own local governments. Rather, the tension between pragmatic problem solving for concrete and pressing issues, on the one hand, and worthy but rather abstract desires for systemwide reform, on the other, has been a hallmark of intergovernmental relations throughout the past several decades. This uncomfortable tension is likely to continue.

Meanwhile, neither the jurisprudence of federalism nor economic developments are likely to catalyze an easy reform or simplification of the system. Although both spheres witnessed important events during the 1990s, the impacts overall have been complicated and somewhat uncertain.

The Supreme Court, for instance, stirred the waters with potentially important decisions aimed, in part, at protecting or reclaiming some distinctive policy space for subnational authorities. Perhaps most significantly, the Court voided a national law in *United States v. Lopez* (1995) on the grounds that Washington had enacted a policy with no connection to interstate commerce. This limitation on national authority was the first since the 1930s decided on these grounds, and some observers have become hopeful—or fearful—that the federal judiciary might begin to establish national-state boundaries limiting the reach and interdependence in the system. The pattern nonetheless remains uncertain, with other precedents during the last two decades suggesting support for national authority.[16] Evidence on both tendencies is examined in some of the readings in this book.

Similarly, economic developments in recent years have had important effects on the system but have not constituted a force for reform or simplification. During his administration, for instance, President Clinton was not an ardent advocate for subnational governments—thus disappointing some who had hoped his experience as governor of Arkansas would make him especially sensitive to the needs and potential of the states, in particular. But this period did see significant increases in intergovernmental aid, as discussed above, despite a budget politics in Washington focused primarily on issues like tax reductions and "saving" Social Security. This more supportive fiscal development was a trend often neglected in the much more visible war over mandates.

Even this tendency, however, was complex. The growth in federal aid was concentrated in a few sectors and devoted primarily to big increases in spending for transfer payments. In many other spheres, the purse strings remained remarkably tight. And local governments have scrambled to replace national funding for some of their programs with state aid and alternative sources. The PIGs, which in earlier decades had organized into nationally important forces with the onset of large-scale federal assistance, struggled to define new roles of comparable influence in the lingering era of budgetary constraint. And the federal government continued to seek day-to-day influence through the channels of the hundreds of existing programs and the scattering of new ones enacted in recent years. All these participants continue to jockey for influence in the interdependent, complex, and fiscally strained system.

And as if this intricate pattern were not complex enough, increasing economic pressures toward globalization have now added another set of actors and considerations to the constraints and opportunities in the intergovernmental system. Business and market connections around the world—and, importantly, national governmental commitments to international agreements in a multitude of policy sectors—have pulled city managers, state economic development experts, local and state education specialists, and national environmental policy makers, among many others, into the ambit of forces and constraints emanating from abroad. In these crosscurrents of (primarily economic) influence, the bargaining has begun to include more parties and more options, for at least some of the decision makers. The overall system is, furthermore, even less transparent to citizens—with potential implications for responsiveness and the quality of democratic life. And potent pressures to extend and concentrate national influence to deal effectively with global forces have begun to penetrate domestic intergovernmental decision making.

The dizzying transformations at the end of the century, then, have resulted in an intergovernmental arrangement buffeted by a variety of shifts and shocks. Certainly the system differs in key respects from the one in place at the dawn of the Reagan period, for instance. And yet any vision of radical simplification—like that articulated by Reagan or, for that matter, by the congressional leadership during the 1990s—can be seen as chimerical. The notion of a dual federalism that could meet the challenges of the new century, of the nation's needs and aspirations in an increasingly interdependent world, seems increasingly remote, for all the apparent agreement on the attractiveness of reform and rationality. Despite the crosscurrents, regardless of the multiple developments of the last several years, the most fundamental aspects of American intergovernmental relations, including the strengths, weaknesses, frustrations, and dilemmas of the pattern, have remained prominent.

There is no denying that the form of the system has changed considerably since the nation's founding. Political, economic, and social forces have stimulated major changes in the overall scope of governmental activity, in the mix of values that intergovernmental arrangements are meant to serve, in the relative influence of the different governments, and in their degree of reliance on one another. Far from preserving a simple, stratified pattern, the choices made centuries ago created opportunities for dramatic shifts toward new forms of interdependence and complexity in the intergovernmental network.

Notes

1. Thus the term *federal* has two meanings in contemporary usage. One refers to a system of governance that employs a constitutional partitioning of authority between central and regional units. The other is as a synonym for the national government. Both notions are employed in this chapter and in various readings throughout the book. The meaning should be clear from the context.

2. U.S. Bureau of the Census, *1992 Census of Governments,* vol. 1, no. 1, *Governmental Organization* (Washington, D.C.: U.S. Government Printing Office, 1994), v.

3. Federalist No. 10, *The Federalist Papers,* ed. Clinton Rossiter (New York: New American Library, 1961), 77.

4. At the time, the term *federation* had a meaning close to that of *confederation* today. See Martin Diamond's essay in this book (no. 2). The meaning changed after the initiation of the American experiment in federated government.

5. The concepts of federalism (in the first sense mentioned in note 1) and intergovernmental relations are linked but not identical. The former refers to certain aspects of the dealings between national and regional governments, while the latter is meant to encompass relations among all governments within a nation. Intergovernmental relations are considerably affected but not completely determined by federalism. This book examines federalism but focuses broadly on intergovernmental relations. Nevertheless, interstate and interlocal

relations receive relatively less attention because of space limitations.

6. One example is Madison's veto of a bill to authorize construction of roads and canals in the states. See Daniel J. Elazar, *The American Partnership: Intergovernmental Cooperation in the Nineteenth Century* (Chicago: University of Chicago Press, 1962), 15.

7. Ibid.

8. The terms *recipient* and *donor* are borrowed from Jeffrey L. Pressman, *Federal Programs and City Politics* (Berkeley: University of California Press, 1975).

9. American Council on Intergovernmental Relations, *Significant Features of Fiscal Federalism 1995,* vol. 2, *Revenues and Expenditures* (Albany, N.Y.: Nelson A. Rockefeller Institute of Government, February 1998), 9.

10. The cases were *Massachusetts v. Mellon* and *Frothingham v. Mellon,* 262 U.S. 447 (1923).

11. As explained later in this chapter, this experiment proved temporary. Federal financial constraints during the Carter and Reagan administrations persuaded Congress to follow presidential recommendations; the program was ended for state and then local governments, respectively.

12. See Morton Grodzins's classic essay in Part I of this volume (no. 3).

13. For example, David B. Walker, *Toward a Functioning Federalism* (Cambridge, Mass.: Winthrop, 1981); and see Deil S. Wright, *Understanding Intergovernmental Relations,* 3rd ed. (Pacific Grove, Calif.: Brooks/Cole, 1988), 94.

14. See Norman Furniss and Timothy Tilton, *The Case for the Welfare State: From Social Security to Social Equality* (Bloomington: Indiana University Press, 1977); and John E. Schwarz, *America's Hidden Success: A Reassessment of Twenty Years of Public Policy* (New York: Norton, 1988).

15. Thomas Anton, *American Federalism and Public Policy: How the System Works* (Philadelphia: Temple University Press, 1989).

16. *United States v. Lopez,* 115 S.Ct. 1424 (1995).

☐ CASE STUDY 5

Introduction

In the foregoing essay, Professor O'Toole clearly and concisely presents an overview of the development of American intergovernmental relations as an important aspect of American government. He stresses that the contemporary nature of IGR particularly entails three characteristics: interdependency, complexity and bargaining among officials. How do these major features of IGR influence the practice of modern public administration? Shape the work of local government officials? Affect the outcomes of what they do?

The following case, "Wichita Confronts Contamination," by Susan Rosegrant of Harvard's John F. Kennedy School of Government, illustrates well several of the themes discussed in O'Toole's essay. In the summer of 1990, the Kansas Department of Health and Environment (KDHE), acting on behalf of the federal Environmental Protection Agency (EPA), reported that Wichita, Kansas, was sitting on a vast underground polluted lake of various commercial and industrial chemicals. It was located beneath the central downtown business district, called the Gilbert-Mosley site, and the hazardous chemicals were known to cause cancer and other health problems. The report said the contamination was spreading about a foot a day, and it was feared that serious community health problems and water quality deterioration would result if this underground pollution went unchecked. Besides the very vocal public outcry for government to "do something about the problem," the report also triggered an immediate reaction from the banking community which stopped making loans to downtown residential and commercial owners in the Gilbert-Mosley area, thereby causing serious economic repercussions. What should the city do to protect its environment and economy—indeed the very health of its citizens?

In the following case, the city manager, Chris Cherches, who is faced with the responsibility of drafting a plan of action to deal with this crisis, must work with various intergovernmental bodies such as the KDHE and EPA to frame options and devise a strategy to clean up the affected site. In the process, Cherches achieves a workable plan, but one that very much develops within—and depends on—an IGR framework, as described in the O'Toole essay.

As you read this case, try to think about:

How did IGR entities help to identify the problem, then frame the options for the city manager, and finally help him create a workable plan of action for the affected site?

Why were the environmental problems—*and* the IGR problems—so complex in this case?

Can you identify the negotiations among the various IGR actors in this story that occurred? Why were these negotiations so critical to dealing with Wichita's contamination?

In general what does this case tell us about the importance of IGR to the work of public administrators in the twenty-first century? And the IGR features of interdependency, complexity, and political bargaining?

Wichita Confronts Contamination

SUSAN ROSEGRANT

In the summer of 1990, the central business district of Wichita, Kansas, faced familiar problems of urban decline, along with the prospect of revitalization. The downturn in the regional oil and gas industry had exacerbated the nationwide real estate slump, leaving downtown Wichita stagnant. At the same time, local business leaders were pursuing a common formula for renewal: a project relying on substantial public improvements to

This case was written by Susan Rosegrant for Professor Alan Altshuler, director of the Taubman Center for State and Local Government at the John F. Kennedy School of Government, for use at the Program on Innovation in State and Local Government "CEO Symposium," September 24–26, 1992. Funding provided by the Ford Foundation. (1292)

Source: Case Program, John F. Kennedy School of Government, Harvard University, Parts A & B C16-92-1157.0 & C16-92-1158.0

leverage new private investment, a $375 million undertaking in all.

In downtown Wichita, however, a special problem was brewing. Hazardous chemicals known to cause cancer and other health problems had been detected in some private and industrial wells in Wichita's core area. Banks were growing more careful about requiring site inspections, and even soil and water sampling, before they would grant loans. And in June, local manufacturer Coleman Co., Inc., the venerable maker of camp stoves and other outdoor equipment, approached the city's legal department for advice about a contamination problem it had first discovered during routine tests in the fall of 1988.

In late August, the calm was shattered as the pieces of bad news suddenly fit together to form a frightening whole. The Kansas Department of Health and Environment (KDHE), acting on behalf of the Environmental Protection Agency (EPA), reported that

Wichita was sitting on an underground lake polluted by a variety of commercial and industrial chemicals. The area of contamination—dubbed the Gilbert and Mosley site after a street intersection near its center— was extensive, covering a plot about four miles long and one-and-one-half miles wide. Moreover, the polluted aquifer lay squarely beneath the city's central business district. The 8,000 parcels affected had an assessed value of about $86 million. Major banks, hotels, industrial headquarters, and homes all lay in the six-square-mile area. The worst pollution, consisting of high concentrations of trichloroethene, a chemical degreaser used to clean metal parts before painting, was found at Coleman's headquarters at the north end of the site.

Although KDHE had completed a preliminary study on Gilbert-Mosley the previous November, the August 1990 Listing Site Investigation was the first comprehensive contamination report that City Manager Chris Cherches had seen. According to his office's quick estimates, to clean the aquifer could cost as much as $20 million and take as long as 20 years. KDHE offered just two options in its report recommendations: either the companies responsible for the contamination could band together to clean up the area, or the state would rank the site for National Priority Listing, the first step toward activating Superfund.[1]

Contamination Fallout

The Wichita community did not view Gilbert-Mosley as a serious health risk. Although the contamination was moving south at the rate of about a foot a day, the polluted aquifer lay 15 feet below the surface and was not used for drinking water. "Kansas is not that concerned about water quality," explained William Cather, chair of the Sierra Club's small Kansas chapter. "We are concerned about water quantity."

But the potential economic impact of the contamination had the community up in arms. KDHE's report identified 508 area businesses as Potentially Responsible Parties (PRPs) under Superfund law. If Gilbert-Mosley became a Superfund site, all of these businesses would be potentially liable for cleanup costs regardless of whether they had contributed to the contamination. In the days following release of the Listing Site Investigation, KDHE received a barrage of phone calls from business owners anxious to understand the implications of their PRP status.

Even more threatening, however, was the response of the financial community. Just a few months earlier, in *US vs. Fleet Factors Corp.,* the US 11th Circuit Court in Atlanta had ruled that a lender may incur Superfund liability "by participating in financial management to a degree indicating a capacity to influence the corporation's treatment of hazardous wastes."[2]

Simply put, the ruling opened lenders to Superfund liability. Not only that, because of their relatively "deep pockets," financial institutions made ideal targets for Superfund cleanup cost recovery.

In the wake of the dramatic report, Wichita bankers took abrupt action, halting virtually all lending activity in Gilbert-Mosley, the heart of the city. "I don't think you could have hit a banker over the head with a two-by-four and gotten him to make a loan then," declared J.V. Lentell, chairman of the Kansas State Bank and Trust Co. "We already knew property values were plummeting in the downtown area. Downtown was drying up. It was the last thing we needed."

The banks' redlining had an immediate impact on both commercial and residential property owners. David C. Burk, for example, an architect turned developer, had formed an investment company to develop restaurant, retail, apartment, and office space in a few blocks of abandoned brick warehouses near Coleman's headquarters. Although he had drilled 20 test holes without finding contamination before launching his ill-timed venture, all three buildings he had contracts on, as well as those he had options to buy, fell within the contaminated zone. "As soon as Gilbert-Mosley came in, we lost our investors," he reported grimly. Residents were similarly affected, as they found it suddenly impossible to sell their homes. "There were hundreds of tragedies wrapped up here," declared Mayor Bob Knight. "I started getting calls from sons and daughters, trying to make provisions for a parent who was left alone and aged, who were unable to liquidate property."

As city government struggled in the days following the report's release to understand and respond to the crisis, it became clear that the twin threats of uncertain liability and the bank-imposed real estate freeze posed a substantial hazard to the city's tax base. Properties in the area had generated more than $12 million of the $203 million in local property taxes the previous year, but already, the county appraiser's office was receiving requests for reduced valuations. If all Gilbert-Mosley properties lost substantial value, or were frozen for months, or even years, not only would the redevelopment plan die, but the entire core area would be threatened. "When the groundwater problem came along," recalled city attorney Thomas R. Powell, "it looked like it was going to be the death knell."

The City Weighs Its Options

City Manager Cherches, who faced the immediate responsibility for drafting a plan, enlisted a cadre of staffers to study KDHE's two recommended options. In evaluating the possibilities, Cherches stressed that two priorities remained uppermost: to begin cleaning up the aquifer as soon as possible, and to preserve property values. The only way to do that: convince the banks to resume lending in the area.

1) *Let Companies Responsible for Contamination Clean Up the Site*

The first impulse on the part of some of Cherches's staff was to encourage Coleman and other polluters to take charge of the Gilbert-Mosley site. "In the very early stages, it was viewed as a business problem," recalled Mark Glaser, special assistant to the manager for management research. "The businesses contributed to the contamination. The businesses are basically responsible for cleaning up the contamination." Added city attorney Powell, "Our hope was that somehow Coleman would solve the problem."

But history argued strongly against this choice. Gilbert-Mosley was not the city's first experience with contaminated sites. Three years earlier, groundwater contamination had been discovered at a smaller site about two miles north of Gilbert-Mosley, known as 29th and Mead. There, also, the banks had stopped lending, and the county appraiser had lowered property values 40 percent. A group of about 100 potentially responsible parties at the site, including both the city and Coleman, had formed a PRP group to strike an agreement on how to pay for the initial EPA-required Remedial Investigation and Feasibility Study (RI/FS), which would identify sources and types of contamination along with remediation methods. But group negotiations had become divisive, then stalled, and the state had already placed the site on the National Priorities List (NPL). If the group fared no better in determining ultimate cleanup liability, it would face full implementation of Superfund and many years of real estate paralysis.

Given this experience, it seemed highly unlikely that the more than 500 PRPs at Gilbert-Mosley would be able to reach a timely agreement on liability. In addition, it was questionable whether Coleman would cooperate. Although the company had been a lead party at 29th and Mead, it had not pushed for a speedy resolution. Moreover, while Coleman acknowledged that it had found some pollution at its Gilbert-Mosley site, it was already discounting its responsibility for the overall contamination. Remarked city attorney Powell, "When they said they were going to pay for what they were responsible for, I didn't know if we would ever *agree* on what they were responsible for." If a PRP group at Gilbert-Mosley fared no better than the one at 29th and Mead, there would be no quick cleanup in sight, and no incentive for banks to resume lending until the threat of contamination had been removed.

2) *Rank the Site for Possible Superfund Status*

As unproductive as forming a PRP group might appear, Cherches and his staff soon concluded that KDHE's second option—to allow the site to be ranked for Superfund—was far less appealing.

If EPA became directly involved, Cherches learned, the cost of cleaning up Gilbert-Mosley would increase dramatically. The agency typically hired an oversight contractor, for example, to watch over the work of the regular contractor—a step that automatically added up to 40 percent to the cleanup bill. In addition, possible polluters faced the prospect of paying for the administrative oversight of EPA itself; the Superfund law called on EPA staffers to charge their time to the private firms. Moreover, EPA was allowed to overcharge as a means of replenishing its cleanup fund and punishing noncomplying businesses.

The threat of prolonged multi-party litigation was an even bigger deterrent to reliance on Superfund. Because any business in a contaminated area could be held responsible for cleanup costs, regardless of its contribution, lawyers played a major part in any Superfund resolution, as polluters sought to spread the blame, and faultless property owners struggled to avoid liability. In fact, Superfund law spread potential liability to such a broad number of parties, many of whom were wholly innocent, that any hope of quick resolution became mired in stalling tactics and litigation. This legal wrangling, along with third party lawsuits against polluters seeking damages due to contamination-related declines in property values, had given rise to Superfund's nickname as "The Lawyers' Full Employment Act of 1980." One city that Cherches talked to reported that its $30 million cleanup had sparked an estimated $700 million in civil law suits. A study commissioned by the American Insurance Association estimated that cleaning up 1,800 Superfund sites would generate $8 billion in legal fees.[3]

Finally, both litigation, and the oversight and administrative steps that EPA requires, add years to a typical Superfund cleanup. Of the average 10 years taken to clean up a site, seven are spent on study and assessment, legal proceedings, and crafting a remedy before the actual cleanup begins.[4] Judging from this track record, if Gilbert-Mosley became a Superfund site, it would be years before cleanup could even start.

According to Mayor Knight, who consulted a number of other mayors about Gilbert-Mosley, cities with major contamination problems faced a bleak prognosis. "I couldn't find any successful models," he recalled. "The only thing we found was failure: division, frustration, assigning blame, financial ruin, and, ultimately, the very worst thing that can happen to people who love cities, decline."

Special Assistant Glaser also placed successive phone calls in a desperate bid to find a new alternative:

What we kept hearing was, "I can't tell you what to do, but do something. Don't let it go Superfund. Once it goes Superfund, you're in trouble." We knew we had to do something, but nobody knew what that something would be.

A Third Option

Cherches rejected both of KDHE's options, and made up his mind fast. Within a week of the Listing Site Investigation's release, he decided to risk a major leap from existing precedents. Although no one had accused Wichita of being a polluter, and although the city had not even been listed as a PRP, Cherches proposed that the city take full responsibility for the Gilbert-Mosley cleanup. In doing so, Wichita would attempt to sidestep the time and resources normally spent on Superfund-related litigation, and to create some mechanism to get banks to start lending in the contaminated area again.

The most obvious and immediate barrier to a city-led cleanup was finding an acceptable way to finance it. Cherches was determined that Coleman and other contributors would pay as much as possible for the contamination they had caused. But the city could not

count on recouping all cleanup costs from responsible polluters. Some likely contributors were no longer in business, for example, and others lacked the resources to support their share of the cleanup. Moreover, in order to sell the idea to the state and EPA, the city would have to prove it had the funds available to support what could be a 20-year project without relying on uncertain corporate contributions.

Cherches's staff prepared a list of financing alternatives, and the most powerful argument against each, as follows:

- *Establish a special assessment district:* All property owners in the area would be charged an assessment to cover the cost of cleanup. Likely to create an uproar over the inequity of making a large group, comprised mostly of innocent property owners, pay for the pollution of a few.
- *Issue bonds:* Taxes would be raised throughout the city to help pay off the bonds. Could cause a property tax revolt, and would require a change in state statute to allow bonds to be used for ongoing maintenance of the cleanup program.
- *Create a tax increment finance district:* Would dedicate an increment of Gilbert-Mosley property taxes—bolstered by the cleanup—to pay for the program. An untried use of this concept, and, like the bond option, would require a change in state legislation.
- *County pay entire cost, with state assistance:* Based on rationale that the economic health of Wichita is important to the entire county. Would face certain opposition from the county, which believed polluters should pay the tab. The county might seek state reimbursement.
- *Impose a statewide tax:* Would spread the burden to the broadest number of constituents. Certain to provoke strong opposition from a rural state uninterested in solving Wichita's industrial problems.

In addition to the backing of the Wichita City Council, most of these plans would require the approval of the Sedgwick County Council, as well as the Wichita School Board, since their tax bases would be affected.

Even with a financing mechanism in place, though, a city-led plan would face a number of additional obstacles. Politically, the concept probably wouldn't fly unless Coleman and other contributors could be held at least partially accountable. "Some of the very early public response was, 'Why would the city get involved and commit our tax dollars?' " recalled Glaser. "We were thinking of signing on the dotted line to say we would be responsible for $20 million. Politically and fiscally, that doesn't wash. It's not even reasonable." Unfortunately, if the city wanted to take charge, it would have to make a commitment long before it knew the likelihood of getting major contributors other than Coleman to pay.

Cherches would also have to convince EPA, which had a reputation for being bureaucratic and inflexible, that the city had the resources and the commitment to take on such an unusual arrangement. There was no record of any city ever having stepped in to accept liability for a contamination problem it had not caused.

In addition, unless Wichita could come up with a way to revive lending in the contaminated district, it wouldn't make any difference who was responsible for the cleanup. The central business district could not afford to wait 20 years for life to return to normal.

Finally, a survey of the obstacles made it clear that the ultimate success of the plan would depend on a complex collaboration between multiple, and sometimes opposed, constituencies, including the city manager's office, the city council, the county commission, the school board, lenders, Coleman, KDHE, the state legislature, the governor, and EPA.

KDHE had already warned the city that it would have to report to EPA in January about progress at the Gilbert-Mosley site. Unless a cleanup plan had taken shape, the state would recommend that EPA take over. If Wichita was unable to solve any one of the obstacles it faced, it would have to confront the inevitability of Superfund, with all that could imply for the devastation of the city's core.

Developing the Plan

Wichita City Manager Chris Cherches moved fast to begin consolidating support for a city-led cleanup of the Gilbert-Mosley site. In order to present the plan to the various constituencies that would have to approve it, the city first had to decide how to pay for it. After weighing alternatives, Cherches concluded that creating a tax increment finance (TIF) district would be the most equitable and politically palatable way to raise funds. The city's approach, however, was a novel twist on the traditional TIF concept. Typically, a TIF district is set up in an area slated for redevelopment. After city-backed improvements are in place, the difference between the old, depressed property assessments and the new, higher values that have resulted from the improvements creates an increment that is then used to pay for the revitalization effort.

Wichita, by contrast, proposed what could be called a tax "decrement" plan: as a result of the contamination, the city would devalue all the property in the Gilbert-Mosley area—for example, by the 40 percent that property had dropped at the 29th and Mead contamination site—and then would immediately raise values back to their pre-contamination level, under the argument that the city plan would restore lost value. The difference would create the increment to be set aside each year to finance the cleanup. Although the city could find no examples of TIF being used to support environmental remediation, Glaser felt it was an ideal use of the concept. "This seemed like it really fit what the full intent of TIF was designed to do," he declared.

The city's initial talks with the Kansas Department of Health and Environment (KDHE) about assuming responsibility for Gilbert-Mosley had been encouraging. With the TIF proposal in place, KDHE became openly enthusiastic. Cherches began negotiating a plan for the state to oversee Wichita's cleanup in EPA's stead, thereby avoiding the agency's usual high oversight costs. After presenting the proposed plan to the public, and winning the unanimous approval of the city council, he next approached the local financial community.

Lenders, Cherches soon discovered, made eager allies. After all, they risked not only losing the value of their Gilbert-Mosley investments, but of being held liable for the actual cleanup. They also understood the importance to Wichita's economy—and to their own businesses—of returning real estate activity in the contaminated area to normal. But bankers would not resume lending until they had some sort of legal protection from cleanup liability in place.

The concept that the city and the lenders devised to satisfy this need was deceptively simple. Innocent property owners, including residents, businesses, and banks, could apply to the city for a document called the Certificate and Release for Environmental Conditions. If granted, the document would release the holder from any cleanup liability. With such a release in hand, properties could again be bought and sold without the specter of potential Superfund liability. But while the banking community overall embraced the plan, it would not implement it until the city had received EPA's assurance that it would not take over the site, negotiated firm agreements with KDHE and Coleman, and pushed through the changes in state law necessary to allow tax increment financing to be used for a long-term project.

Final Negotiations

Getting EPA's backing was easier than the city had expected. Cherches proposed that Wichita would follow all the usual EPA steps and requirements in cleaning up Gilbert-Mosley, but with KDHE acting as the primary oversight agency. Throughout the process, the city would report regularly to EPA on its progress. Although the city had expected some opposition, EPA actually had a great deal to gain and very little to lose: If the city succeeded, the agency could declare a victory with minimal expense or effort on its part. Conversely, if the plan failed, there was nothing to keep EPA from stepping in and implementing Superfund. After just one meeting in late November, Morris Kay, director of EPA's four-state Region VII, agreed in principle to support both the city-led plan and the state's offer to oversee the process. Although there was no written agreement guaranteeing that EPA would not intervene, Kay assured the city that as long as it was operating according to agency requirements, it would not intercede.

With EPA's support secure, the city still faced a major legislative challenge. A Kansas state law designed to ensure fiscal responsibility, the Cash Basis and Budget law, would not let local government commit operating revenues beyond one year. Wichita needed an exception to that law, and an amendment to TIF law, in order to be able to commit funds raised from a TIF district to a long-term environmental cleanup. Without the changes, the city would be unable to contract with KDHE to take on and finance what could be a 20-year effort.

Getting legislative approval of the TIF bill promised to be a struggle. The Cash Basis law was, in Cherches's words, a "sacred cow" that the legislature was loathe to touch. In addition, the traditional antagonism that existed between urban Wichita and the largely rural legislature was certain to complicate the bill's chances for passage. The city had to dispel the impression that its plan might be geared in Coleman's favor, a difficult task with the company's liability agreement still in negotiation. Moreover, because Kansas's part-time legislature met only from January through April, the city had a limited window of opportunity to prove the merits of its plan.

Wichita's credibility wasn't helped in March when both the county assessor and the state property valuation director declared unworkable the city's original proposal

to establish a tax increment by first lowering and then raising assessed property values. In its place, three Sedgwick County legislators responsible for reviewing the TIF bill worked with the city to craft a new amendment that allowed municipalities in the state that met narrowly defined requirements to earmark 20 percent of a specially created TIF district's base year property taxes, on an annual basis, for environmental cleanups. If the bill passed, Wichita would be able to reserve up to 20 percent of the first year's Gilbert-Mosley property tax revenues to use for groundwater cleanup each year, for the next 20 years.

On March 26, Wichita signed a consent decree with KDHE, spelling out the city's responsibilities, what KDHE's oversight obligations would be, and how the Certificate and Release program would work. But the major obstacle to legislative approval, the Coleman agreement, was not resolved until April 23, slightly more than a week before the legislature adjourned. The agreement divided the contaminated site into three zones: Coleman agreed to pay all cleanup costs for the area where it was the main polluter; it would split costs with the city in a second area where it was a contributor to contamination; and the city would be responsible for cleanup and cost recovery in the final area, where most of the pollution came from other sources. In addition, the camping equipment manufacturer agreed to pay $1 million for the initial Remedial Investigation/Feasibility Study required by EPA.

Although Special Assistant Glaser had expected the Coleman negotiations to be perhaps the biggest barrier to settlement, the manufacturer actually had good cause to settle. The agreement allowed Coleman to convey a responsible civic and environmental image, an important consideration for a maker of outdoor equipment. In addition, if Gilbert-Mosley had become a Superfund site, Coleman would have faced substantially higher costs, and would have been left vulnerable to almost endless third-party lawsuits. In fact, Coleman had already been sued by property owners seeking damages due to contamination-related declines in property values. "I feel we got a pretty good deal from Coleman," said city attorney Thomas Powell. "They needed it as badly as we did."

One week after the Coleman agreement was signed, the Kansas legislature approved the TIF bill, and Cherches began meeting again with the financial community the next day. On May 14, several major local banks signed an agreement not to refuse to lend on the security of real properties within Gilbert-Mosley if the owner had obtained a Certificate and Release for Environmental Conditions. With the start of the Certificate and Release program on August 2, there was no longer a reason for contamination, alone, to block real estate transactions in the Gilbert-Mosley site.

Epilogue

In August 1992, one year after the Certificate and Release program began, life had begun to return to normal in the Gilbert-Mosley area:

- The city of Wichita had granted more than 800 Certificate and Release forms. Some property owners just outside of the contaminated area had petitioned for inclusion, hoping to receive certificates that would remove all stigma of potential liability from their properties.
- Bank IV, one of Wichita's major lenders, had closed 11 loans in Gilbert-Mosley for a total of $6.4 million.
- Developer David Burk, who received the first Certificate and Release from the city, had wooed back investors to his redevelopment project, and had opened four restaurants and two retail stores in the contaminated area.
- The three plaintiffs in the first court case against Coleman received only $86,000, about one-fifth of what they had requested, after the jury ruled that as a result of the city-led cleanup plan, pollution-caused damage to downtown property values was temporary, not permanent. Thomas Powell, who had left his position as city attorney to enter private practice, appeared as an expert witness on Coleman's behalf to describe how the city plan had restored property values.
- Camp, Dresser & McKee, Inc., the environmental consultant hired by the city, was about to release the results of the Remedial Investigation/Feasibility Study, a site analysis that typically takes as long as five years to complete under Superfund.
- The business community had begun pushing forward on more modest plans for redevelopment. "The contamination is not even something that is widely discussed anymore," declared Mayor Bob Knight, "yet it could have been a total calamity for the city."

Gilbert-Mosley was still a depressed area, as it had been before the contamination was discovered. But with the city's plan in place, Knight once again had hope that the core downtown area might be rejuvenated. "If people are sufficiently committed to resolving complicated challenges, they can do extraordinary things," he declared. "I believe this is a moment in this community's history when we did something extraordinary."

Notes

1. Congress created Superfund, the Comprehensive Environmental Response, Compensation and Liability Act of 1980 (CERCLA), to give EPA the resources to clean up hazardous waste sites nationwide. Six years later, Congress passed the Superfund Amendments and Reauthorization Act of 1986 in an attempt to improve what critics had characterized as a sluggish and ineffective program.
2. David R. Tripp, "Wichita Strikes Back at the Blob," *Toxics Law Reporter,* June 25, 1991.
3. Marc K. Landy and Mary Hague, "Private Interests and Superfund," *The Public Interest,* No. 108, Summer 1992.
4. E. Donald Elliott, "Superfund: EPA Success, National Debacle?" *Natural Resources & Environment,* Vol. 6, No. 3, Winter 1992.

Chapter 5 Review Questions

1. Why are federalism and intergovernmental relations so critical to effective program performance in the public sector today? What is the difference between federalism and IGR? What was the founding fathers' rationale for establishing U.S. government in this federal manner?
2. What has been the recent practice of intergovernmental relations in the United States, according to Laurence J. O'Toole, Jr.? When and why did this IGR pattern emerge?

3. In what ways did the Wichita case study illustrate some of the characteristics and dilemmas of modern intergovernmental relations?

4. Who were the key IGR actors in this case, and how did they "calculate" to secure their own interests? Do you think that they successfully handled and resolved the complex issue? In particular, why was Cherches's role so critical?

5. What does the case study say about the role and importance of experts involved in IGR? Who were the experts in this case and how did they derive their professional standards? Is there a problem that their specialized expertise may not always be applied in the public interest? What safeguards are available to ensure that these experts will be guided by the broad public interest?

6. What does the case study say about the significance of political bargaining and coalition-building in IGR and its role in influencing outcomes? Can these political dimensions of IGR be pointed out in Case Study 5?

Key Terms

federalism	grants-in-aid	Tenth Amendment
PIGs	Sixteenth Amendment	policy sectors
intergovernmental relations	ACIR	creative federalism
state discretion	project grants	unfunded mandates
dual federalism	marble-cake federalism	vertical functional autocrats
Garcia Decision	land grants	interdependence
categorical grants	general revenue sharing	complexity
formula grants	performance standards	intergovernmental bargaining
block grants	crosscutting requirements	Reagan's atttempted IGR
intergovernmental network	The New Federalism	revolution

Suggestions for Further Reading

Some of the best up-to-date sources of information on the changing world of intergovernmental relations can be found in *The National Journal, Governing,* and *Publius.* Timothy Conlan, *New Federalism: Intergovernmental. Reform from Nixon to Reagan* (Washington, D.C.: Brookings, 1998) offers one of the best accounts of IGR during the past three decades, and for a fine analysis of the development of American federalism, read Samuel H. Beer, *To Make a Nation: The Rediscovery of American Federalism* (Cambridge, Mass.: Harvard University Press, 1993).

There are also a number of excellent "overviews" available, including Deil S. Wright, *Understanding*

Intergovernmental Relations, Fourth Edition (Monterey, Calif.: Brooks/Cole Publishing, 1995); Paul E. Peterson, *What Price Federalism?* (Washington, D.C.: The Brookings Institution, 1995); Robert Stoker, *Reluctant Partners* (Pittsburgh, Pa: Pittsburgh University Press, 1991); and David R. Berman, "Relating to Other Governments," in Charldean Newell, ed., *The Effective Local Government Manager,* 2nd ed. (Washington, D.C.: ICMA, 1993), pp. 167–198; and David B. Walker, *The Rebirth of Federalism* (Chatham, N.J.: Chatham House, 1995). For more current "overviews," see Russell L. Hanson, ed., *Governing Partners* (Boulder, Co.: Westview, 1998);

Robert F. Nagel, *The Implosion of American Federalism* (Oxford: Oxford University Press, 2002); John T. Noonan, *Narrowing the Nation's Power* (Berkeley: University of California Press, 2003); and Robert Agranoff and Michael McGuire, "American Federalism and the Search for Models of Management," *Public Administration Review* 61, (November/December 2001), pp. 671–681. Also two Web pages offer current IGR resources: The U.S. House of Representatives Committee on Government Reform (http://reform.house.gov/TIPRC/) and the Institute of Intergovernmental Relations (www.iigr.co/ publication_detail.php.publication=193).

Serious students of IGR also should begin by reading the U.S. Constitution and *The Federalist Papers.* The Kestnbaum Commission Report (June 1955), which contains information still helpful for understanding modern IGR, as well as other basic documents on IGR is contained in Richard J. Stillman, *Basic Documents of American Public Administration Since 1950* (New York: Holmes and Meier, 1982). Laurence J. O'Toole, Jr., ed., *American Intergovernmental Relations,* 3rd ed. (Washington, D.C.: Congressional Quarterly, 2000); Lewis G. Bender and James A. Stever, *Administering the New Federalism* (Boulder, Colo.: Westview Press, 1986); as well as Deil S. Wright and Harvey L. White, eds., *Federalism and Intergovernmental Relations* (Washington, D.C.: American Society for Public Administration, 1984) offer outstanding collections of classic IGR essays. For survey essays on federalism by distinguished scholars in this field, see the entire issue of *The Annals of the American Academy of Political and Social Science* (May 1990), edited by John Kincaid, and entitled "American Federalism: The Third Century." Where we are with the research in this field today is summarized by Vincent L. Marando and Patricia S. Florestano, "Intergovernmental Management: The State of the Discipline," in Naomi B. Lynn and Aaron Wildavsky, eds., *Public Administration: The State of the Discipline* (Chatham, N.J.: Chatham House, 1990).

For an outstanding model of academic research on federalism and IGR, see Martha Derthick, *The Influence of Federal Grants* (Cambridge, Mass.: Harvard University Press, 1970).

CHAPTER 6

Internal Dynamics: The Concept of the Informal Group

F or all of us the feeling of security and certainty derives always from assured membership of a group. If this is lost, no monetary gain, no job guarantee, can be sufficient compensation. Where groups change ceaselessly as jobs and mechanical processes change, the individual inevitably experiences a sense of void, of emptiness. . . .

Elton Mayo

READING 6

Introduction

Public administration was never the primary concern of Elton Mayo and Fritz Roethlisberger. Most of their research efforts centered around the study of business enterprises at the Harvard Business School, yet their impact on general administrative thought has been significant principally because from their investigations developed the *human relations* or *industrial sociological school* in organization theory. This school of thought emphasizes understanding and improving the dynamics of the internal human group within complex organizations; it was both a product of and a reaction to the scientific-management movement of the early part of this century. Frederick W. Taylor, an early founder of scientific management, had stressed that from the rational study of industrial organizations, "principles" of efficient, economical management could be derived.

Similarly, Elton Mayo, Fritz Roethlisberger, and a team of researchers from the Harvard Business School set out in 1927 at Western Electric's Hawthorne Electric Plant in Cicero, Illinois, near Chicago, to measure scientifically the effect of changes in the external environment on workers' output; they studied such matters as more or less lighting, shorter or longer lunch breaks, and increased or decreased hours in the work week. Their goal at first, like the goal of scientific management, was to discover the most efficient way to motivate workers. The Hawthorne Plant manufactured phones and telecommunications equipment for American Telephone and Telegraph (AT&T), employing at the time more than 40,000 workers. The company encouraged the Mayo-Roethlisberger experiments as part of its generally considered progressive management practices (progressive at least for that era).

While following the same methods as Taylor's scientific-management research, the Mayo-Roethlisberger team paradoxically arrived at different conclusions and insights from those of Taylor and his followers. The results of five years of intense study at the Hawthorne Plant revealed that the *primary work group* (that is, the relationships between workers and their supervisors and among workers themselves), had as much if not more impact on productivity as the formal physical surroundings and economic benefits derived from the job. For many, the Hawthorne experiment came "as the great illumination," or as Roethlisberger more modestly described it, "the systematic exploitation of the simple and obvious." It underscored a fundamental truth, obscured for some time by scientific-management theories, namely, that the employees of an organization constituted its basis, and that upon their attitudes, behavior, and morale within their primary groups ultimately depended industrial effectiveness and productivity. As Roethlisberger wrote:

> It is my simple thesis that a human problem requires a human solution. First, we have to learn to recognize a human problem when we see one; and second, upon recognizing it, we have to learn to deal with it as such and not as if it were something else.*

The Hawthorne investigators shifted the focus of management studies from simply the external elements of organizations to its internal and nonrational aspects. By interviewing techniques and by close observations of the dynamics of primary groups, that is, interrelations between workers, the investigators sought to understand the social codes and norms of behavior of informal work groups that were rarely displayed on the formal organization chart. "They studied the important social functions these groups perform for their members, the histories of these informal work groups, how they spontaneously appear, how they tend to perpetuate themselves, multiply, and disappear, how they are in constant jeopardy from technical change, and hence how they tend to resist innovation." In essence, like Freud and Jung in clinical psychology, they attempted to rationalize the irrational nature of human beings in the organizational context and find cures for the psychotic disorders of industrial institutions.

The Hawthorne experimenters also challenged the prevailing scientific management view of the individual employee, that is, that the greatest motivating factor for the worker was his or her paycheck. Rather, Roethlisberger argued, "Most of us want the satisfaction that comes from being accepted and recognized as people of worth by our friends and work associates. Money is only a small part of this social recognition. . . . We want the feeling of security that comes not so much from the amount of money we have in the bank as from being an accepted member of a group. A man whose job is without social function is like a man without a country; the activity to which he has to give the major portion of his life is robbed of all human meaning and significance."

After the termination of the Hawthorne Plant experiments, Mayo's writings led to broad speculations about administration and the problems of human society. In these later works, *The Human Problems of an Industrial Civilization* (1933), *The Social Problems of an Industrial Civilization* (1945), and *The Political Problems of Industrial Civilization* (1947), his central thesis emphasized that social skills have lagged behind technical skills. While the techniques of specialists, including engineers, chemists, and doctors, were important, it was by the leadership of administrators, in particular businesspeople, that human cooperation could be advanced and the problems of organization in society solved. In the deepest sense, Mayo became a social reformer who believed that improving the quality of administrative talent

*Fritz J. Roethlisberger, *Management and Morale* (Cambridge, Mass.: Harvard University Press, 1941), p. 7.

could help to build a better world. In his view, the administrator "becomes the guardian or preserver of the morale through the function of maintaining a condition of equilibrium, which will preserve the social values existing in the cooperative system."

To better understand the following selection by Mayo, it is helpful to know something about his background, which helped to shape the decidedly unique perspective of his writing. Mayo, the senior partner in the Hawthorne research effort, lived from 1880 to 1949 (his assistant, Roethlisberger, lived from 1898 to 1974). Born in Adelaide, Australia, Mayo was the second child in a large, impoverished family of seven. His life was unsettled—while growing up his family moved often, and in trying to find an occupation for himself, he drifted from one job to another. He went from business to publishing, to teaching, and then to medicine, but it was World War I that affected his life the most (as it did the lives of so many of his generation). While working as an interviewer of returning war veterans suffering from shell shock, Mayo learned firsthand about human suffering, dislocation, and tragedy.

Increasingly, thereafter, Mayo was drawn to the study of psychology—particularly the clinical writings of Janet and Freud, as well as the work of social systems theorists like Pareto and Henderson. It was Mayo's unique gift to be able to synthesize the ideas of clinical psychology and develop a grand systems theory into a way that would offer understanding and help for the problems of the worker in the industrial workplace. How were people to deal with and adapt to the traumatic upheavals caused by war, technology, and industrialization in the twentieth century? How could the suffering caused by these massive changes in the human condition be alleviated and possibly cured? How could human life for individuals and groups be improved? Mayo wrestled with these and other major philosophical and social issues for most of his life.

Grants from the Rockefeller and Carnegie Foundations brought Mayo to America in the 1920s, first to the University of Pennsylvania and then later to Harvard University to head the team of researchers at the Hawthorne Plant. There, with his probing mind and inspired personality, along with his emphasis on using rigorous, firsthand field investigations as a way to understand what really was happening inside American industrial life, he was able to give leadership to the overall direction of the Hawthorne experiments. The lasting fame of these experiments in social science and management literature is due in large measure to Mayo. He introduced the modern *team research* concept and indeed inspired other large-scale research efforts such as W. Lloyd Warner's *Yankee City.*

The following selection offers valuable insight into Mayo's views—his unique intuitiveness, his passionate concern for the betterment of human beings, his conviction that close, careful empirical-clinical analysis will yield "the facts" about human problems, and that this analysis can, in turn, lead to resolutions of these problems. Fundamental to all his beliefs is the idea that if only the informal nature of human organizations is recognized and properly dealt with (rather than the scientific, technological, and economic processes), then it is indeed possible to build a better world. This fundamental, reformist conviction spawned much of the human relations literature of post–World War II management thought by writers such as Maslow, Likert, McGregor, Herzberg, and many others who owe a debt to Mayo's writings and the Hawthorne experiments.

Mayo, however, was not without critics: labor unions attacked him for being anti-union, which he denied, and methodologists criticized his work for being unscientific and methodologically unsound, but he never admitted to being a statistician. Some suggest Mayo's values were too "pro-productivity," and not "pro-society" or "pro-human development," to which he would no doubt reply, "I was simply researching industrial productivity, not other factors." And some critics argue that Mayo's emphasis on small, blue-collar unskilled labor groups is outdated in an era of white-collar, educated professionals; but here again, Mayo might respond that he indeed studied a group that was representative of his own era. Furthermore, others would contend that he stressed cooperation and solidarity of the primary work group so much that he failed to appreciate the values of conflict and competition in assuring freedom of workers and progress for the overall organization. Mayo might respond to these criticisms by saying, "I merely reported on what our investigations uncovered at the time."

Most curiously, despite all his work at the Hawthorne Plant, not one of his recommendations was put into practice by the plant's management. Of what importance, then, were Mayo's work and the Hawthorne experiments? Perhaps Mayo's real genius was that he emphatically restated an old truth: human needs, values, and concerns of the basic informal group play a primary role in successful management practices.

As you read this selection, keep the following questions in mind:

Do the informal groups identified by Mayo's experiments in an industrial setting exist in public sector agencies? If so, do they operate in the same way in government as they do in business?

What do you think are the similarities, as well as differences, in the operation of an informal group in the public versus private settings?

Are Mayo's suggestions for dealing with the problems of securing the cooperation of individuals and human groups compatible with the goals and practices of public organizations? Where might there be problems in applying his ideas and techniques?

Referring back to Case Study No. 1, "The Blast in Centralia No. 5," or any prior case studies, identify the primary groups in these cases. Do Mayo's theories and prescriptions apply to them? If so, how?

Compare Weber's and Mayo's views. How do the two theorists compare in their conclusions and prescriptions for solving the bureaucratic problems of modern society? For instance, does Mayo emphasize material motives less than Weber does? If so, why?

Hawthorne and the Western Electric Company

ELTON MAYO

I shall make no attempt to describe at length that which has been already and fully described. The interested public is well acquainted with *Management*

From Elton Mayo, *The Social Problems of an Industrial Civilization.* Boston: Division of Research, Harvard Business School, 1945. Reprinted by permission of Harvard Business School Press.

and the Worker, the official account of the whole range of experiments, by my colleagues F. J. Roethlisberger of Harvard University and William J. Dickson of the Western Electric Company. The same public has not yet discovered *The Industrial Worker,*[1] by another colleague, T. North Whitehead. This is unfortunate, for the beginning of an answer to many problems significant for administration in the next decade is recorded in its pages. I refer to the problems involved in the making and adaptive re-making of working teams, the importance of which for collaboration in postwar years is still too little realized. Assuming that readers who wish to do so can consult these books, I have confined my remarks here to some comments upon the general development of the series of experiments.

A highly competent group of Western Electric engineers refused to accept defeat when experiments to demonstrate the effect of illumination on work seemed to lead nowhere. The conditions of scientific experiment had apparently been fulfilled—experimental room, control room; changes introduced one at a time; all other conditions held steady. And the results were perplexing: Roethlisberger gives two instances—lighting improved in the experimental room, production went up; but it rose also in the control room. The opposite of this: lighting diminished from 10 to 3 foot-candles in the experimental room and production again went up; simultaneously in the control room, with illumination constant, production also rose.[2] Many other experiments, and all inconclusive; yet it had seemed so easy to determine the effect of illumination on work.

In matters of mechanics or chemistry the modern engineer knows how to set about the improvement of process or the redress of error. But the determination of optimum working conditions for the human being is left largely to dogma and tradition, guess, or quasi-philosophical argument. In modern large-scale industry the three persistent problems of management are:

1. The application of science and technical skill to some material good or product.
2. The systematic ordering of operations.
3. The organization of teamwork—that is, of sustained cooperation.

The last must take account of the need for continual reorganization of teamwork as operating conditions are changed in an *adaptive* society.

The first of these holds enormous prestige and interest and is the subject of continuous experiment.

The second is well developed in practice. The third, by comparison with the other two, is almost wholly neglected. Yet it remains true that if these three are out of balance, the organization as a whole will not be successful. The first two operate to make an industry *effective,* in Chester Barnard's phrase,[3] the third, to make it *efficient.* For the larger and more complex the institution, the more dependent is it upon the wholehearted cooperation of every member of the group.

This was not altogether the attitude of Mr. G. A. Pennock and his colleagues when they set up the experimental "test room." But the illumination fiasco had made them alert to the need that very careful records should be kept of everything that happened in the room in addition to the obvious engineering and industrial devices.[4] Their observations therefore included not only records of industrial and engineering changes but also records of physiological or medical changes, and, in a sense, of social and anthropological. This last took the form of a "log" that gave as full an account as possible of the actual events of every day, a record that proved most useful to Whitehead when he was remeasuring the recording tapes and recalculating the changes in productive output. He was able to relate eccentricities of the output curve to the actual situation at a given time—that is to say, to the events of a specific day or week.

First Phase—The Test Room

The facts are by now well know. Briefly restated, the test room began its inquiry by, first, attempting to secure the active collaboration of the workers. This took some time but was gradually successful, especially after the retirement of the original first and second workers and after the new worker at the second bench had assumed informal leadership of the group. From this point on, the evidence presented by Whitehead or Roethlisberger and Dickson seems to show that the individual workers became a team, wholeheartedly committed to the project. Second, the conditions of work were changed one at a time: rest periods of different numbers and length, shorter working day, shorter working week, food with soup or coffee in the morning break. And the results seemed satisfactory: slowly at first, but later with increasing certainty, the output record (used as an index of well-being) mounted. Simultaneously the workers claimed that they felt less fatigued, felt that they were not making any special effort. Whether these claims were accurate or no, they at least indicated increased contentment with the general situation in the test room by comparison with the department outside. At every point in the program, the workers had been consulted with respect to proposed changes; they had arrived at the point of free expression of ideas and feelings to management. And it had been arranged thus that the twelfth experimental change should be a return to the original conditions of work—no rest periods, no midmorning lunch, no shortened day or week. It had also been arranged that, after 12 weeks of this, the group should return to the conditions of Period 7, a 15-minute midmorning break with lunch and a 10-minute midafternoon rest. The story is now well known: in Period 12 the daily and weekly output rose to a point higher than at any other time (the hourly rate adjusted itself downward by a small fraction), and in the whole 12 weeks "there was no downward trend." In the following period, the return to the conditions of work as in the seventh experimental change, the output curve soared to even greater heights: this thirteenth period lasted for 31 weeks.

These periods, 12 and 13, made it evident that increments of production could not be related point for point to the experimental changes introduced. Some major change was taking place that was chiefly responsible for the index of improved conditions—the steadily increasing output. Period 12—but for minor qualifications, such as "personal time out"—ignored the nominal return to original conditions of work and the output curve continued its upward passage. Put in other words, there was no actual return to original conditions. This served to bring another fact to the attention of the observers. Periods 7, 10, and 13 had nominally the same working conditions, as above described—15-minute rest and lunch in midmorning, 10-minute rest in the afternoon. But the average weekly output

for each worker was:

Period 7—2,500 units

Period 10—2,800 units

Period 13—3,000 units

Periods 3 and 12 resembled each other also in that both required a full day's work without rest periods. But here also the difference of average weekly output for each worker was:

Period 3—less than 2,500 units

Period 12—more than 2,900 units

Here then was a situation comparable perhaps with the illumination experiment, certainly suggestive of the Philadelphia experience where improved conditions for one team of mule spinners were reflected in improved morale not only in the experimental team but in the two other teams who had received no such benefit.

This interesting, and indeed amusing, result has been so often discussed that I need make no mystery of it now. I have often heard my colleague Roethlisberger declare that the major experimental change was introduced when those in charge sought to hold the situation humanly steady (in the interest of critical changes to be introduced) by getting the cooperation of the workers. What actually happened was that six individuals became a team and the team gave itself wholeheartedly and spontaneously to cooperation in the experiment. The consequence was that they felt themselves to be participating freely and without afterthought, and were happy in the knowledge that they were working without coercion from above or limitation from below. They were themselves astonished at the consequence, for they felt that they were working under less pressure than ever before: and in this, their feelings and performance echoed that of the mule spinners.

Here then are two topics which deserve the closest attention of all those engaged in administrative work—the organization of working teams and the free participation of such teams in the task and purpose of the organization as it directly affects them in their daily round.

Second Phase—The Interview Program

But such conclusions were not possible at the time: the major change, the question as to the exact difference between conditions of work in the test room and in the plant departments, remained something of a mystery. Officers of the company determined to "take another look" at departments outside the test room—this, with the idea that something quite important was there to be observed, something to which the experiment should have made them alert. So the interview program was introduced.

It was speedily discovered that the question-and-answer type of interview was useless in the situation. Workers wished to talk, and to talk freely under the seal of professional confidence (which was never abused) to someone who seemed representative of the company or who seemed, by his very attitude, to carry authority. The experience itself was unusual; there are few people in this world who have had the experience of finding someone intelligent, attentive, and eager to listen without interruption to all that he or she has to say. But to arrive at this point it became necessary to train interviewers how to listen, how to avoid interruption or the giving of advice, how generally to avoid anything that might put an end to free expression in an individual instance. Some approximate rules to guide the interviewer in his work were therefore set down. These were, more or less, as follows:[5]

1. Give your whole attention to the person interviewed, and make it evident that you are doing so.
2. Listen—don't talk.
3. Never argue; never give advice.
4. Listen to:
   (a) What he wants to say.
   (b) What he does not want to say.
   (c) What he cannot say without help.
5. As you listen, plot out tentatively and for subsequent correction the pattern (personal) that is being set before you. To test this, from time to time summarize what has been said and present

for comment (e.g., "Is this what you are telling me?"). Always do this with the greatest caution, that is, clarify but do not add or twist.
6. Remember that everything said must be considered a personal confidence and not divulged to anyone. (This does not prevent discussion of a situation between professional colleagues. Nor does it prevent some form of public report when due precaution has been taken.)

It must not be thought that this type of interviewing is easily learned. It is true that some persons, men and women alike, have a natural flair for the work, but, even with them, there tends to be an early period of discouragement, a feeling of futility, through which the experience and coaching of a senior interviewer must carry them. The important rules in the interview (important, that is, for the development of high skill) are two. First, Rule 4 that indicates the need to help the individual interviewed to articulate expression of an idea or attitude that he has not before expressed; and, second, Rule 5 which indicates the need from time to time to summarize what has been said and to present it for comment. Once equipped to do this effectively, interviewers develop very considerable skill. But, let me say again, this skill is not easily acquired. It demands of the interviewer a real capacity to follow the contours of another person's thinking, to understand the meaning for him of what he says.

I do not believe that any member of the research group or its associates had anticipated the immediate response that would be forthcoming to the introduction of such an interview program. Such comments as "This is the best thing the Company has ever done," or "The Company should have done this long ago," were frequently heard. It was as if workers had been awaiting an opportunity for expressing freely and without afterthought their feelings on a great variety of modern situations, not by any means limited to the various departments of the plant. To find an intelligent person who was not only eager to listen but also anxious to help to express ideas and feelings but dimly understood—this, for many thousand persons, was an experience without precedent in the modern world.

In a former statement I named two questions that inevitably presented themselves to the interviewing group in these early stages of the study:

1. Is some experience which might be described as an experience of personal futility a common incident of industrial organization for work?
2. Does life in a modern industrial city, in some unrealized way, predispose workers to obsessive response?[6]

And I said that these two questions "in some form" continued to preoccupy those in charge of the research until the conclusion of the study.[7]

After twelve years of further study (not yet concluded), there are certain developments that demand attention. For example, I had not fully realized in 1932, when the above was written, how profoundly the social structure of civilization has been shaken by scientific, engineering, and industrial development. This radical change—the passage from an established to an adaptive social order—has brought into being a host of new and unanticipated problems for management and for the individual worker. The management problem appears at its acutest in the work of the supervisor. No longer does the supervisor work with a team of persons that he has known for many years or perhaps a lifetime; he is leader of a group of individuals that forms and disappears almost as he watches it. Now it is difficult, if not impossible, to relate oneself to a working group one by one; it is relatively easy to do so if they are already a fully constituted team. A communication from the supervisor, for example, in the latter instance has to be made to one person only with the appropriate instructions; the individual will pass it on and work it out with the team. In the former instance, it has to be repeated to every individual and may often be misunderstood.

But for the individual worker the problem is really much more serious. He has suffered a profound loss of security and certainty in his actual living and in the background of his thinking. For all of us the feeling of security and certainty derives always from assured membership of a group. If this is lost, no monetary gain, no job guarantee, can be sufficient compensation. Where groups change ceaselessly as jobs and mechanical processes change, the individual inevitably experiences a sense of void, of emptiness, where his fathers knew the joy of comradeship and security. And in such a situation, his anxieties—many, no doubt, irrational or ill-founded—increase and he becomes more difficult both to fellow workers and to supervisor. The extreme of this is perhaps rarely encountered as yet, but increasingly we move in this direction as the tempo of industrial change is speeded by scientific and technical discovery.

In the first chapter of this book I have claimed that scientific method has a dual approach—represented in medicine by the clinic and the laboratory. In the clinic one studies the whole situation with two ends in view: first, to develop intimate knowledge of and skill in handling the facts, and, second, on the basis of such a skill to separate those aspects of the situation that skill has shown to be closely related for detailed laboratory study. When a study based upon laboratory method fails, or partially fails, because some essential factor has been unknowingly and arbitrarily excluded, the investigator, if he is wise, returns to clinical study of the entire situation to get some hint as to the nature of the excluded determinant. The members of the research division at Hawthorne, after the twelfth experimental period in the test room, were faced by just such a situation and knew it. The so-called interview program represented for them a return from the laboratory to clinical study. And, as in all clinical study, there was no immediate and welcome revelation of a single discarded determinant: there was rather a slow progress from one observation to another, all of them important—but only gradually building up into a single complex finding. This slow development has been elsewhere described, in *Management and the Worker;* one can however attempt a succinct résumé of the various observations, more or less as they occurred.

Officers of the company had prepared a short statement, a few sentences, to be repeated to the individual interviewed before the conversation began. This statement was designed to assure the worker that nothing he said would be repeated to his supervisors or to any company official outside the interviewing group. In many instances, the worker waved this aside and began to talk freely and at once. What doubts there were seemed to be resident in the interviewers rather than in those interviewed. Many workers, I cannot say the majority for we have no statistics, seemed to have something "on their minds," in ordinary phrase, about which they wished to talk freely to a competent listener. And these topics were by no means confined to matters affecting the company. This was, I think, the first observation that emerged from the mass of interviews reported daily. The research group began to talk about the need for *"emotional release"* and the great advantage that accrued to the individual when he had "talked off" his problem. The topics varied greatly. One worker two years before had been sharply reprimanded by his supervisor for not working as usual: in interview he wished to explain that on the night preceding the day of the incident his wife and child had both died, apparently unexpectedly. At the time he was unable to explain; afterwards he had no opportunity to do so. He told the story dramatically and in great detail; there was no doubt whatever that telling it thus benefited him greatly. But this story naturally was exceptional; more often a worker would speak of his family and domestic situation, of his church, of his relations with other members of the working group—quite usually the topic of which he spoke presented itself to him as a problem difficult for him to resolve. This led to the next successive illumination for the inquiry. It became manifest that, whatever the problem, it was partly, and sometimes wholly, determined by the attitude of the individual worker. And this defect or distortion of attitude was consequent on his past experience or his present situation, or, more usually, on both at once. One woman worker, for example, discovered for herself during an interview that her dislike of a certain supervisor was based upon a fancied resemblance to a detested stepfather. Small wonder that the same supervisor had warned the interviewer that she was "difficult to handle." But the discovery by the worker that her dislike was wholly irrational eased the situation considerably.[8] This type of case led the interviewing group to study carefully each worker's *personal situation* and attitude. These two phrases "emotional release" and "personal situation" became convenient titles for the first phases of observation and seemed to resume for the interviewers the effective work that they were doing. It was at this point that a change began to show itself in the study and in the conception of the study.

The original interviewers, in these days, after sixteen years of industrial experience, are emphatic on the point that the first cases singled out for report were special cases—individuals—and not representative either of the working group or of the interviews generally. It is estimated that such cases did not number more than an approximate two percent of the twenty thousand persons originally interviewed. Probably this error of emphasis was inevitable and for two reasons: first, the dramatic changes that occur in such instances seemed good evidence of the efficacy of the method, and, second, this type of interviewing had to be insisted upon as *necessary to the training of a skilled interviewer.* This last still holds good; a skilled interviewer must have passed through the stage of careful and observant listening to what an individual says and to all that he says. This stage of an interviewing program closely resembles the therapeutic method and its triumphs are apt to be therapeutic. And I do not believe that the study would have been equipped to advance further if it had failed to observe the great benefit of emotional release and the extent to which every individual's problems are conditioned by his personal history and situation. Indeed, even when one has advanced beyond the merely psychotherapeutic study of individuals to study of industrial groups, one has to beware of distortions similar in kind to those named; one has to know how to deal with such problems. The first phase of the interview program cannot therefore be discarded; it still retains its original importance. But industrial studies must nevertheless move beyond the individual in need of therapy. And this is the more true when the change from established routines to adaptive changes of routine seems generally to carry a consequence of loss of security for many persons.

A change of attitude in the research group came gradually. The close study of individuals continued, but in combination with an equally close study of groups. An early incident did much to set the new pattern for inquiry. One of the earliest questions proposed before the original test room experiment began was a question as to the fatigue involved in this or that type of work. Later a foreman of high reputation, no doubt with this in mind, came to the research group, now for the most part engaged in interviewing, and asserted that the workers in his department worked hard all day at their machines and must be considerably fatigued by the evening; he wanted an inquiry. Now the interviewers had discovered that this working group claimed a habit of doing most of their work in the morning period and "taking things easy" during the afternoon. The foreman obviously realized nothing of this, and it was therefore fortunate that the two possibilities could be directly tested. The officer in charge of the research made a quiet arrangement with the engineers to measure during a period the amount of electric current used by the group to operate its machines; this quantity indicated the over-all amount of work being done. The results of this test wholly supported the statements made by the workers in interview; far more current was used in the morning period than during the afternoon. And the attention of the research group was, by this and other incidents, thus redirected to a fact already known to them, namely, that the working group as a whole actually determined the output of individual workers by reference to a standard, predetermined but never clearly stated, that represented the group conception of a fair day's work. This standard was rarely, if ever, in accord with the standards of the efficiency engineers.

The final experiment, reported under the title of the Bank Wiring Observation Room, was set up to extend and confirm these observations.[9] Simultaneously it was realized that these facts did not in any way imply low working morale as suggested by such phrases as "restriction of output." On the contrary, the failure of free communication between management and workers in modern large-scale industry leads inevitably to the exercise of caution by the working group until such time as it knows clearly the range and meaning of changes imposed from above. The enthusiasm of the efficiency engineer for the organization of operations is excellent; his attempt to resume problems of cooperation under this heading is not. At the moment, he attempts to solve the many human difficulties involved in wholehearted cooperation by formally reorganizing the organization without any reference whatever to workers themselves. His procedure inevitably blocks communication and defeats his own admirable purpose.[10]

This observation, important as it is, was not however the leading point for the interviewers. The existence and influence of the group—those in active daily relationship with one another—became the important fact. The industrial interviewer must learn to distinguish and specify, as he listens to what a worker says, references to "personal" or group situations. More often than not, the special case, the individual who talks himself out of a gross distortion, is a solitary—one who has not "made the team." The usual interview, on the other hand, though not by any means free from distortion, is speaking as much for the working group as for the person. The influence of the communication in the interview, therefore, is not limited to the individual but extends to the group.

Two workers in a large industry were recently offered "upgrading"; to accept would mean leaving their group and taking a job in another department: they refused. Then representatives of the union put some pressure on them, claiming that, if they continued to refuse, the union organizers "might just as well give up" their efforts. With reluctance the workers reversed their decision and accepted the upgrading. Both girls at once needed the attention of an interviewer: they had liked the former group in which they had earned informal membership. Both felt adjustment to a new group and a novel situation as involving effort and private discontent. From both much was learned of the intimate organization and common practices of their groups, and their adjustments to their new groups were eased, thereby effectively helping reconstitute the teamwork in those groups.

In another recent interview a worker of eighteen protested to an interviewer that her mother was continually urging her to ask Mr. X, her supervisor, for a "raise." She had refused, but her loyalty to her mother and the pressure the latter exerted were affecting her work and her relations at work. She talked her situation out with an interviewer, and it became clear that to her a "raise" would mean departure from her daily companions and associates. Although not immediately relevant, it is interesting to note that, after explaining the situation at length to the interviewer, she was able to present her case dispassionately to her mother—without exaggeration or protest. The mother immediately understood and abandoned pressure for advancement, and the worker returned to effective work. This last instance illustrates one way in which the interview clears lines of communication of emotional blockage—within as without the plant. But this is not my immediate topic; my point is rather that the age-old human desire for persistence of human association will seriously complicate the development of an adaptive society if we cannot devise systematic methods of easing individuals from one group of associates into another.

But such an observation was not possible in the earliest inquiry. The important fact brought to the attention of the research division was that the ordinary conception of management-worker relation as existing between company officials, on the one hand, and an unspecified number of individuals, on the other, is utterly mistaken. Management, in any continuously successful plant, is not related to single workers but always to working groups. In every department that continues to operate, the workers have—whether aware of it or not—formed themselves into a group with appropriate customs, duties, routines, even rituals; and management succeeds (or fails) in proportion as it is accepted without reservation by the group as authority and leader. This, for example, occurred in the relay assembly test room at Hawthorne. Management, by consultation with the workers, by clear explanation of the proposed experiments and the reasons for them, by accepting the workers' verdict in special instances, unwittingly scored a success in two most important human matters—the workers became a self-governing team, and a team that cooperated wholeheartedly with management. The test room was responsible for many important findings—rest periods, hours of work, food, and the like: but the most important finding of all was unquestionably in the general area of teamwork and cooperation.

It was at this time that the research division published, for private circulation within the company, a monograph entitled "Complaints and Grievances." Careful description of many varied situations within the interviewers' experience showed that an articulate complaint only rarely, if ever, gave any logical clue to the grievance in which it had origin; this applied at least as strongly to groups as to individuals. Whereas economists and industry generally *tend to concentrate upon the complaint and upon logical inferences from its articulate statement* as an appropriate procedure, the interviewing group had learned almost to ignore, except as symptom, the—sometimes noisy—manifestation of discomfort and to study the situation anew to gain knowledge of its source. Diagnosis rather than argument became the proper method of procedure.

It is possible to quote an illustration from a recently published book, *China Enters the Machine Age.*[11] When industries had to be moved, during this war, from Shanghai and the Chinese coast to Kunming in the interior of China, the actual operation of an industry still depended for the most part on skilled workers who were refugees from Shanghai and elsewhere. These skilled workers knew their importance to the work and gained considerable prestige from it; nevertheless discontent was rife among them. Evidence of this was manifested by the continual, deliberate breaking of crockery in the company mess hall and complaints about the quality of the food provided. Yet this food was much better than could have been obtained outside the plant—especially at the prices charged. And in interview the individual workers admitted freely that the food was good and could not rightly be made the subject of complaint. But the relationship between the skilled workers as a group and the *Chih Yuan*—the executive and supervisory officers—was exceedingly unsatisfactory.

Many of these officers—the *Chih Yuan*—have been trained in the United States—enough at least to set a pattern for the whole group. Now in America we have learned in actual practice to accept the rabble hypothesis with reservations. But the logical Chinese student of engineering or economics, knowing nothing of these practical reservations, returns to his own country convinced that the workman who is not wholly responsive to the "financial incentive" is a troublemaker and a nuisance. And the Chinese worker lives up to this conviction by breaking plates.[12] Acceptance of the complaint about the food and collective bargaining of a logical type conducted at that level would surely have been useless.

Yet this is what industry, not only in China, does every day, with the high sanction of State authority and the alleged aid of lawyers and economists. In their behavior and their statements, economists indicate that they accept the rabble hypothesis and its dismal corollary of financial incentive as the only effective human motive. They substitute a logical hypothesis of small practical value for the actual facts.

The insight gained by the interviewing group, on the other hand, cannot be described as substituting irrational for rational motive, emotion for logic. On the contrary, it implies a need for competent study of complaints and the grievances that provoke them, a need for knowledge of the actual facts rather than acceptance of an outdated theory. It is amusing that certain industrialists, rigidly disciplined in economic theory, attempt to shrug off the Hawthorne studies as "theoretic." Actually the shoe is on the other foot; Hawthorne has restudied the facts without prejudice, whereas the critics have unquestioningly accepted that theory of man which had its vogue in the nineteenth century and has already outlived its usefulness.

The Hawthorne interview program has moved far since its beginning in 1929. Originally designed to study the comfort of workers in their work as a mass of individuals, it has come to clear specification of the relation of working groups to management as one of the fundamental problems of large-scale industry. It was indeed this study that first enabled us to assert that the third major preoccupation of management must be that of organizing teamwork, that is to say, of developing and sustaining cooperation.

In summary, certain entirely practical discoveries must be enumerated.

First, the early discovery that the interview aids the individual to get rid of useless emotional complications and to state his problem clearly. He is thus enabled to give himself good advice—a procedure far more effective than advice accepted from another. I have already given instances of this in discussing "emotional release" and the influence on individual attitude of personal history and personal situation.

Second, the interview has demonstrated its capacity to aid the individual to associate more easily, more satisfactorily, with other persons—fellow workers or supervisors—with whom he is in daily contact.

Third, the interview not only helps the individual to collaborate better with his own group of workers, it also develops his desire and capacity to work better with management. In this it resembles somewhat the action of the Philadelphia colonel.[13]

Someone, the interviewer, representing (for the worker) the plant organization outside his own group, has aided him to work better with his own group. This is the beginning of the necessary double loyalty—to his own group and to the larger organization. It remains only for management to make wise use of this beginning.

Fourth, beyond all this, interviewing possesses immense importance for the training of administrators in the difficult future that faces this continent and the world. It has been said that the interviewer has no authority and takes no action. Action can only be taken by the proper authority and through the formally constituted line of authority. The interviewer, however, contributes much to the facilitation of communication both up and down that line. He does this, first, by clearing away emotional distortion and exaggeration; second, his work manifestly aids to exact and objective statement the grievance that lies beyond the various complaints.

Work of this kind is immensely effective in the development of maturity of attitude and judgment in the intelligent and sensitive young men and women who give time to it. The subordination of oneself, of one's opinions and ideas, of the very human desire to give gratuitous advice, the subordination of all these to an intelligent effort to help another express ideas and feelings that he cannot easily express is, in itself, a most desirable education. As a preparation for the exercise of administrative responsibility, it is better than anything offered in a present university curriculum. It is no doubt necessary to train young men and women to present their knowledge and ideas with lucidity. But, if they are to be administrators, it is far more necessary to train them to listen carefully to what others say. Only he who knows how to help other persons to adequate expression can develop the many qualities demanded by a real maturity of judgment.

Finally, there remains the claim made above that the interview has proved to be the source of information of great objective value to management. The three persistent problems of modern large-scale industry have been stated as:

1. The application of science and technical skill to a material product.

2. The systematization of operations.
3. The organization of sustained cooperation.

When a representative of management claims that interview results are merely personal or subjective—and there are many who still echo this claim—he is actually telling us that he has himself been trained to give all his attention to the first and second problems, technical skill and the systematic ordering of operations; he does not realize that he has also been trained to ignore the third problem completely. For such persons, information on a problem, the existence of which they do not realize, is no information. It is no doubt in consequence of this ignorance or induced blindness that strikes or other difficulties so frequently occur in unexpected places. The interview method is the only method extant[14] that can contribute reasonably accurate information, or indeed any information, as to the extent of the actual cooperation between workers—teamwork—that obtains in a given department, and beyond this, the extent to which this cooperation includes management policy or is wary of it. The Hawthorne inquiry at least specified these most important industrial issues and made some tentative steps toward the development of a method of diagnosis and treatment in particular cases.

Notes

1. Cambridge, Harvard University Press, 1938, 2 vols.
2. *Management and Morale,* pp. 9–10.
3. Op. cit., p. 56.
4. For a full account of the experimental setup, see F. J. Roethlisberger and William J. Dickson, *Management and the Worker,* and T. North Whitehead, *The Industrial Worker,* Vol. 1.
5. For a full discussion of this type of interview, see F. J. Roethlisberger and William J. Dickson, op. cit., Chap. XIII. For a more complete summary and perhaps less technical discussion, see George C. Homans, *Fatigue of Workers* (New York, Reinhold Publishing Corporation, 1941).
6. Elton Mayo, *The Human Problems of an Industrial Civilization* (New York, The Macmillan Company, 1933; reprinted by Division of Research, Harvard Business School, 1946), p. 114.
7. Ibid.
8. F. J. Roethlisberger and William J. Dickson, op. cit., pp. 307–310.
9. F. J. Roethlisberger and William J. Dickson, op. cit., Part IV, pp. 379 ff.
10. For further evidence on this point, see Stanley B. Mathewson, *Restriction of Output among Unorganized Workers,* and also Elton Mayo, *The Human Problems of an Industrial Civilization,* pp. 119–121.
11. Shih Kuo-heng (Cambridge, Harvard University Press, 1944).
12. Ibid., Chap. VIII, pp. 111–127; also Chap. X, pp. 151–153.
13. Chap. III, supra.
14. We realize that there are at present in industry many individuals possessed of high skill in the actual handling of human situations. This skill usually derives from their own experience, is intuitive, and is not easily communicable.

⬛ CASE STUDY 6

Introduction

The concept of the informal group provides us with several critical insights into modern organizational life and the need for administrators to be realistic about what can and cannot be achieved, given the sentiments, feelings, values, and outlooks of men and women in any particular work setting. Clearly, as Mayo's essay points out, being realistic about the nature and workings of the human group is paramount in any successful administrative undertaking. Human groups present managers with both potentialities and pitfalls for achieving well-run internal operations. If managers are to lead organizations effectively, human groups need to be recognized, understood and well integrated within their operations.

The following story, "American Ground," may help shed further insight into the dynamics and influence of informal groups upon public administration. On September 11, 2001, at 9:59 a.m. a commercial jet hijacked by Al-Qaeda terrorists slammed into the South Tower of the World Trade Center. Twenty-nine minutes later, a second terrorist-commandeered jet hit the North Tower, killing 3000 civilians as well as many public safety personnel. For days the site seemed out of control as fires blazed, smoke belched from the ruins, and rescue workers haphazardly roamed the 1.5 trillion tons of debris, looking for survivors, all the time fearing further collapse of adjacent structures. But soon a crude management team under city direction emerged to run the demolition process and bring order to the chaotic rescue efforts. The Department of Design and Control (DDC), a relatively obscure New York City bureaucracy of 1300 employees, whose jobs normally involved oversight of city construction contracts for streets, sidewalks, jails, and the like, suddenly became responsible for the massive, billion-dollar World Trade Center cleanup. DDC's two top officials, Kenneth Holden and his lieutenant, Michael Burton, quickly turned into the most effective responders to this unprecedented emergency. However, as cleanup work progressed, they found themselves at the center of "a tribal dispute" between the several thousand construction workers attempting to clear the site as quickly as possible, firefighters who were slowly and methodically combing the rubble for remains of their 343 lost comrades and friends, and police who tried to keep order and control over demolition and rescue work. All three groups shared the same goal but wanted to accomplish it in radically different ways. Hostilities became intense (even physical), were publicized in the media, and stirred strong community reactions. The DDC managers as well as Mayor Rudolph Giuliani confronted a difficult dilemma—namely, how to get these powerful groups, linked together by a common goal yet each inflamed with highly charged personal emotions, to work as a team to accomplish the cleanup as quickly as possible.

William Langewiesche, *The Atlantic Monthly's* longtime correspondent, was the only journalist granted immediate, full access by officials to the World Trade Center demolition operations. His account unravels the human and technical complexity of the work. His story especially focuses upon how "the tribal dispute" came to a head and was resolved through the hard work of the mayor and DDC officials.

As you read this selection, try to keep in mind what possible lessons it may hold for public administrators; for example:

What causes informal groups—in this case, construction workers, firefighters, and police—to form such strong, emotional bonds? How can managers best identify their needs and wants?

Why do such groups exert enormous influence over public management? What are the specific sources of their disagreements as well as their support and methods of influence?

As the case unfolds, how did the mayor and DDC officials mediate this "tribal dispute"? What were the methods they used to defuse the conflict? Would you judge their interventions successful or not?

Does the foregoing reading by Elton Mayo offer any useful ideas for improving informal group cooperation that can be helpful for resolving this case?

American Ground: Unbuilding the World Trade Center

WILLIAM LANGEWIESCHE

On the morning of Friday, November 2, 2001, seven weeks and three days after the Twin Towers collapsed, tribal fighting broke out at the World Trade Center site. The battle was brief and inconclusive. It occurred near the northwest corner of the ruins, when an emotionally charged demonstration turned violent, and firemen attacked the police. Within that intense inner world it came as no surprise. Resentments and jealousies among the various groups had been mounting for weeks, as the initial rush to find survivors had transmuted into a grim search for the dead, and as territoriality and the embrace of tragedy had crept in. The catalyst for the confrontation was a decision made several days earlier by Mayor Rudolph Giuliani to rein in the firemen, who for nearly two months had basked in overwhelming public sympathy and enjoyed unaccustomed influence and unlimited access to the site. In the interest of returning the city to normal life, Giuliani declared that the firemen now would have to participate in a joint command, with the New York and Port Authority police and the civilian heavy-construction managers in the DDC. This did not sit well. Moreover, access would be restricted, new procedures would be imposed at the pile, and the number of searchers would be reduced by two thirds.

The reason given publicly for this new arrangement was "safety," a term so often used to mask other agendas in modern America that it caused an immediate, instinctive reaction of disbelief. Ordinary front-line fireman were the angriest. As many as 250 of their colleagues lay unaccounted for in the ruins, and they intended as a matter of honor to find every one of them. That week alone they had found fourteen. They were convinced that only they could sustain the necessary attention to detail on the pile, and that in his

eagerness to "clean up" the site (a term they despised), Giuliani was willing to risk overlooking some of the dead, scooping them up with the steel and concrete and relying on the sorting process at Fresh Kills* to separate their remains from the rubble.

To a degree the firemen's suspicions may have been well founded. Certainly the unbuilders themselves, operating under the direction of Mike Burton, were pursuing the most aggressive possible schedule of demolition and debris removal. Even Sam Melisi[†] had doubts about the city's motivations. To me he said, "If you do a good job, and you do it in record time—who knows what record time is, since nobody's ever dealt with this before—is there a bonus? Do you get to be a commissioner or something? I don't know. Burton's just hard to figure out. Sometimes he's very personable and human: 'Oh, geez, you found X amount of people. Oh, that's great.' And then other times: 'You're really taking way too much time to look at this stuff, and we've got to keep moving.' Putting his arm around me and winking. 'We really have to move on this.' But you know what? We're going to take as long as it has to take. We're not going to compromise on that. We just can't do it. I don't have an allegiance to any construction company, or even to the City of New York. My only allegiance is to the people who lost their lives—to their families. The best we can do is try to retrieve as many people as we can in the most humane fashion. And then when all this is over, I can just go back to doing what I do."

Melisi was the reasonable one, and the most broadly involved of any person at the Trade Center site. By comparison, the ordinary firemen were narrowly focused on the rubble underfoot, where the remains of civilians and police officers were regularly discovered, but only the recovery of their own people

*Crews hauled the Trade Center debris to the Fresh Kills landfill on Staten Island.

[†]Fireman Sam Melisi acted as the site's unofficial mediator.

seemed genuinely to interest them. Though their attitude was sometimes offensive to others working on the pile, it was not difficult to understand: the firemen were straightforward guys, initiates in a closed and fraternal society who lived and ate together at the station houses, and shared the drama of responding to emergencies. Some had lost family when the Trade Center fell, and nearly all had lost friends. Their bereavement was real. Still, for nearly two months they had let their collective emotions run unchecked, and had been indulged and encouraged in this by society at large, the presumption being something like, "It helps to cry." The effect had turned out to be quite the opposite: rather than serving a cathartic purpose, the emotionalism seemed to have heightened the firemen's sense of righteousness and loss. Now, with the city ordering cutbacks in the firemen's presence on the pile, the agitation among the rank and file was so great that the firefighters' unions warned the city that they had lost control, and would have to organize a protest to avoid a break with their own membership.

None of this was conducive to clear, calm thought. Two days before the fighting broke out, a fire captain and union trustee named Matty James presented the situation starkly to the *Daily News,* as if retrieval of the bodies were an all-or-nothing affair. He said, "The city may be ready to turn this into a construction job, but we're not. We want our brothers back. By doing this, the city is taking away from these families, these widows, these mothers and fathers, any chance for closure. What are we supposed to do? Go to the Fresh Kills landfill to look for our people?" In a similar style, the mother of a dead fireman whose body had been found said, "Our memorial Mass became a funeral. It gave me an opportunity to hug the casket and to say good-bye. It's just awful what they are trying to do . . . to deprive other women of that wonderful feeling."

Such was the rhetoric during the days leading up to that Friday morning, when hundreds of fireman began to assemble at the corner of Chambers and West Streets, by the red-brick walls of PS 89.* In the emergency command center on the second floor, most of the site-management team from the DDC made plans

to stay inside and out of sight. Mike Burton looked worriedly down at the scene in the street—at the slowly growing crowd, the opposing lines of blue-uniformed police officers, the television crews that were just then arriving. As if to himself he said, "These guys are not happy . . . not happy at all."

Earlier that morning Burton had led the first "combined" site-management meeting, at which the Fire Department, the police, and the DDC had been required to share the stage. It had taken place down the hallway, in the school auditorium. The various tribes had eyed one another with frank distrust, but had spoken in veiled terms to keep conflicts from breaking out into the open. Burton had said, "The DDC will have oversight [meaning: control] over all recovery efforts on the pile," in a tone that somehow implied that this was a decision imposed on him from far above. He had also said, "We're making a push for increased safety. There may be some negative consequences. The police will not let anyone in or out of this building after ten A.M." (Meaning: The firemen are being hysterical.) A fire chief in a white uniform shirt seemed not to have heard a word. He said, "We're trying to hammer out a plan for the removal of victims and uniformed personnel. We've just located fourteen Fire Department members near the South Tower." (Meaning: We're not going to make this easy.)

In the kindergarten room, Holden decided that he needed to go to the pile to keep a close watch on the situation himself. Peter Rinaldi[†] expressed concern for Holden's safety. Holden said, "I'm just going to wear a sign saying, 'I don't know Mike Burton.'" Burton smiled humorlessly. His relationship with Holden was increasingly strained. There was another Port Authority man in the room, a strapping ex-Marine named Tom O'Connor, whose wife had worked in a neighboring building. She had survived, but they had lost many friends in the attack. He said, "We are now viewed as monsters." His manner was matter-of-fact.

Becky Clough, a pugnacious DDC manager and one of the few women active on the ground at the heart of the site, said, "What are we afraid of? We're doing the right thing."

Burton said, "It had to happen sometime anyway. Maybe there are some positive sides."

---

*Officials used the Kindergarten room of the school as their base of operations.

[†]Peter Rinaldi worked for the Port Authority as an engineer.

O'Connor said, "So when are you losing your job?"

I slipped outside before the building was locked down, and walked through the demonstration. The crowd by then had grown to perhaps five hundred off-duty firemen, and it was continuing to expand as others streamed in from the subways and parking lots. Some were dressed in civilian clothes, but most wore the standard protective "turnout coats," black with yellow reflector strips and FDNY written in block letters across the back. Most were bareheaded. As protesters, they seemed awkward and self-conscious at first, and unsure of how to proceed, but they were also genuinely angry. Encouraged by a union official with a bullhorn, they raised their fists and chanted, "Bring our brothers home!" They waved a union banner and American flags. The TV crews moved in tightly, and found firemen for one-on-one interviews. A retired fire captain said, "My son Tommy is still in that building, and we haven't gotten to him yet." The firemen began shouting, "Bring Tommy home! Bring Tommy home!" The unions had promised City Hall that the demonstration would be orderly, and that it would remain outside the site's perimeter—that it would amount to little more than a show for the cameras. But the firemen proved difficult to control. As the crowd swelled to nearly a thousand, it grew louder and more confident, and suddenly surged south through the first police barricades toward the Trade Center ruins.

The TV crews followed eagerly. To the police the demonstrators shouted, "Walk with us!" and "Shut 'em down!" But the police were on duty, and after weeks of growing resentments on the pile they were not inclined to sympathize. As the demonstrators shoved through a second line of defense, the police shoved back, and some of the firemen started to swing. I saw one policeman go down with a roundhouse punch to the face; others responded, tackling and cuffing the offender. The crowd kept pushing through, with fights breaking out where the two groups met. These were big, physical guys on both sides, and they grappled in ungainly dances, straining hard, cursing each other, and toppling to the ground in aggressive embraces. Five policemen were injured. On the periphery the protesters who were arrested—twelve in all—were hustled into police vans. One was a tough-looking old man in a fireman's uniform, who kept bellowing, "My son's in there! My son's in there!" Firefighters shouted, "Let him go!" But like the others who had been arrested, the old man was hauled away.

The protesters gathered on West Street beside the ruins, where they were joined by a scattering of die-hard union sympathizers from the site—primarily a group of ironworkers who sauntered over out of curiosity, and got into the spirit of things. One in particular seemed to delight in showing the crowd how to go about making a TV appearance. He was the very image of a beefy construction worker, dressed in a hardhat and a soil-stained thermal undershirt. He climbed onto a diesel excavator and for several minutes mugged wordlessly for the cameras, waving an American flag and pumping his fist in the air. It was not clear that he knew or cared what the protest was about.

The same was obviously not true of the firefighters' union official, who climbed onto the excavator and used his bullhorn again, repeating his cry of "Bring our brothers home!" and threatening to find reinforcements by the thousands, including "brothers" from other cities, if Giuliani did not back down. Exhibiting more bravado than political sensitivity, he called on the police to release the men who had been arrested, and to march with the demonstrators on City Hall. But of course the police were angry at having been attacked—all the more so because they, too, had tribal allegiances, and had lost twenty-three colleagues in the Trade Center collapse. The firemen marched to City Hall, where they chanted, "Rudy must go!" This was somewhat gratuitous, since Giuliani was only two months from the end of his tenure. They also chanted for the ouster of their fire commissioner, Thomas Von Essen, who for years had been a well-liked New York fireman and union leader, but who now was going around quietly making the point that by far the greatest loss of life had been civilian, and that the Trade Center tragedy was larger than just a firefighters' or even a New Yorkers' affair.

Giuliani was infuriated by what he viewed as an assault on the city's all-important process of recovery, and he lashed out with the vindictiveness for which he was known. With the demonstration still going on, he called Holden on Holden's cell phone and demanded that he identify the ironworkers and fire them. This was only the second time in eight years that Holden had received a call from the mayor, and he was aghast at what he was hearing. Very few ironworkers had joined with the firemen, but the ones who had were likely to be union activists, and therefore just the sort of people who could rally sympathy across the pile. Any attempt to discipline them could easily backfire and lead to a full-scale rebellion. Moreover, for all he knew, the ironworkers were on their break (or could claim to be), and since they were not disrupting the work, they had every right to protest. This was the inner world of the Trade Center site, an emergency zone, yes, but not subject to martial law; if it was a turbulent and quarrelsome place, it was also courageous and creative, and an authentic piece of American ground. But Holden knew better than to argue with Giuliani, and he did not try. After ending the call, he dutifully had a DDC staffer at the scene take pictures of the ironworkers. It was a particularly unpleasant moment: the workers had no idea what the snapshots were about, and some posed for them festively, as if they were on a weekend outing. Holden looked disgusted by the whole affair. He was irritable in a way I had not seen before. As the demonstration drifted away from the pile, he came upon a New York tabloid-TV crew that was setting up to interview a man in an FDNY T-shirt—presumably about the depths of his sorrow. Holden told me he was tired of all the exploitation. He walked up to the reporter and demanded that he take his cameraman and leave. The reporter said, "We just want to . . ."

"Out!" Holden snapped, pointing north.

The reporter gave Holden a look of pure hatred. He said, "The man's got no heart."

"Out!"

By late afternoon Holden was sitting again in the kindergarten room of PS 89, thumbing glumly through pictures of the protesting ironworkers. He had no intention of following through with Giuliani's orders, but he knew that if he flaunted his disobedience, the repercussions would be swift and severe. He himself had told me earlier that the first lesson of "commissioner school" was "Don't contradict the mayor." The only alternative now was to procrastinate, and to hope that the idea would somehow go away. This was not the style of the Giuliani administration, in which the mayor's whims were treated as dictates. Indeed, dur-

ing several phone calls that followed, one of Giuliani's deputy mayors, Tony Coles, continued to demand punishment for the ironworkers long after it could conceivably have served a useful purpose. But Holden held the line, in this case for inaction, and with defensive skills unheralded even within PS 89, he managed to protect Giuliani from himself, and the nation from Giuliani, and to keep the recovery effort on track.

It was a troubled time anyway, that first half of November, the low point in New York's response to the Trade Center attack. The Yankees had lost the World Series—and to Arizona, of all teams. The various groups at the Trade Center site were turning into warring camps. To make matters worse, Giuliani seemed to have lost control of his emotions. After the demonstration (soon known as "the firemen's riot") he continued for several days to rage about the protesters' distortions, and what he saw as their betrayal of the city's well-being. He did not seek conciliation—for instance, by forgiving those who were involved in the demonstration. Rather, the police hunted down another six firemen identified as culprits, and booked them on charges of criminal trespassing. Among these men were the presidents of both firefighter's unions: Captain Peter L. Gorman, of the 2,500-member Uniformed Fire Officers Association, and Kevin E. Gallagher, the protester with the bullhorn, who headed the 9,000-member Uniformed Firefighters Association.

These were honest union officials, expressing the legitimate if misguided dissent of their membership, and their arrest was unusual, to say the least. It was also, of course, counterproductive. The firemen were outraged. Captain Gorman, who had worn the uniform for twenty-eight years, said, "They're putting me through the system like I'm a thug." He called the fire and police commissioners "Giuliani's goons," and Giuliani himself a "fascist." The unions threatened privately to hold a news conference and accuse the mayor of being "anti-American," but apparently thought better of going public with such a foolish claim. Instead, more accurately, a union spokesman said to *The New York Times,* "The mayor fails to realize that New York City is not a dictatorship, where if you don't like what a union is doing you can just go and lock up a union's president. The message being sent from City Hall is that if you don't agree with this administration, we will get you." Outside the Trade Center site America bloomed with bumper stickers proclaiming UNITED WE STAND, a strangely forlorn slogan in a country that so obviously draws strength from disagreement. Drawing strength from disagreement is a trick that the attacking terrorists must certainly have discounted. But of course there are also limits to the creative power of disunity—and the Trade Center response seemed to be veering toward just the sort of social implosion that the terrorists may have had in mind.

The tribalism that grew up on the pile had origins so primitive that they can only be understood as instinctual. At the core was an us-versus-them mentality brought on by the mere act of donning a uniform. Whether as firefighters or as the two sorts of police (city and Port Authority), the uniformed personnel at the site were generally drawn from the same white "ethnic" outer-borough neighborhoods and families, but as members of their respective organizations they had learned to distrust and resent the others. The hostility was historical, and because it was strongest on the lowest levels, among the rank and file, it had proved impossible to root out. People at the site referred to it alliteratively as the Battle of the Badges. Across the years it had led to frequent arguments over turf and occasional bouts of outright obstructionism at emergency scenes. At the Trade Center it had been a factor from the first moments after the attack, when the Police and Fire Departments had set up separate command posts several blocks apart, and without communication between them. There were consequences to this: after the South Tower fell, police helicopter pilots took a close-up look at the fire in the North Tower, and twenty-one minutes before the final collapse they urged their own command to evacuate the building. The warning was radioed to the policemen inside the North Tower, most of whom escaped, but it was not relayed to the fire commands, or to the firemen in the building, only some of whom were able to hear independently radioed orders to evacuate, and more than 120 of whom subsequently died. The lack of communication was certainly no more the fault of one side than of the other, but it aggravated the divisions between them. Even during the initial desperate search for survivors the police and firemen quar-

reled over turf, and asserted their differences. By the end of the first day the bucket brigades had separated according to uniform. Throughout the months that followed, individual friendships and family ties cut across the lines. Nonetheless, the tribalism festered and soon infected the construction crews, too, who did not quarrel much among themselves but generally distrusted the police as ordinary citizens do, and who probably hadn't given firemen much thought before, but came now to resent their claims to special privilege on the pile.

The firemen's claims were based on an unspoken tribal conceit: that the deaths of their own people were worthier than the deaths of others—and that they themselves, through association, were worthier too. This was difficult for the police and civilian workers at the site to accept. The collapse of the towers had been anything but certain. The firemen who had gone inside had been normally brave—as people are who are not cowards. They were not soldiers crossing the lip of a trench or assaulting a machine-gun nest in battle; they were men with a job that demanded mental willingness and hard physical labor, and on that day they were climbing endless stairwells one flight at a time in the company of friends, and with little obvious purpose in mind beyond perhaps finding the civilians who must have been injured by the twin attacks. The firemen in the South Tower were killed without warning. They were unintentional martyrs, noncombatants, typical casualties of war. Those in the North Tower felt the rumble of the South Tower's collapse, but as best as is known, most did not understand what had happened or conclude that their own building soon would come down. Later on, as the precariousness of the North Tower became clearer, there were firemen who committed acts of extraordinary heroism—for instance, by lingering to help civilians, or remaining in the lower lobbies, desperately working the radios and calling for an emergency retreat. But the Fire Department had no monopoly on altruism that day, and terrible though its casualties were, with 343 dead, it did not suffer the greatest losses. As the workers on the pile knew all too well, that sad distinction went to Cantor Fitzgerald,* where 658 people had died—some of them no doubt as altruists too. But what did such categories mean

*Brokerage firm Cantor Fitzgerald had offices in the Trade Center.

anyway? Nearly 3,000 people had been slaughtered here, nearly all of them on the job, and each of them at the last instant equally alone. Those who had not been vaporized lay scattered in the rubble's democratic embrace. The dead were dead now and didn't care. And it was absurd for the living to group and rank them.

Were it not for all the hype, this would hardly need saying. It's true that the United States was shaken, and that people in their insecurity felt the need for heroes. The dead firemen certainly fit the bill. They were seen as brawny, square-jawed men, with young wives and children—perfectly tragic figures, unreliant on microchips or machines, who seemed to have sprung from the American earth like valiant heroes from a simpler time. They had answered the call of history, rushed to the defense of the homeland, and unhesitatingly given their lives. They had died at the hands of barbarians, leaving behind widows who were helpless, or who were said to be. All this presented opportunities for image-making that neither the media nor the political system could resist. Progressives may have been shocked by the ease with which America slipped into patterns of the past—with women at the hearth, men as their protectors, and swarthy strangers at the gate. Rationalists may have worried about the wallowing in victimization, and the financial precedents being set by promises of payouts to the victims' families. As usual in America, there was reason for everyone to deplore the cynicism and crassness of the press. However, there would be time for refinements later. As an initial reaction to the first shock of war, the hero worship was probably a healthy thing, as long as it was confined to the dead.

But when it spilled over indiscriminately to the living, problems arose, and particularly at the center of attention, on the Trade Center pile. The firemen now on the scene were by definition those who either had escaped from the Twin Towers before the collapses or, more likely, had not been inside them to start with—in most cases because they had been somewhere else in the city at the time. They were not lesser men for this. But if the loss of the others was to mean anything beyond the waste of war, it had to be admitted that people on the pile since then, though ferociously dedicated to a grim and dangerous task, were simply not involved in heroics. Of course the situation was presented differently on the outside, where the public was led to be-

lieve that conditions on the pile were so difficult that merely by working there people were sacrificing themselves, and that the firemen in particular—anonymous figures who wore the same wide-brimmed helmets as their fallen brethren—deserved the nation's adoration. For many of the firemen, who tended to have led quiet lives until then, the sudden popularity became a disorienting thing. Even those with the strength to resist the publicity—who stayed off TV, and did not strut in public—seemed nonetheless to be influenced by this new external idea of themselves as tragic characters on a national stage. The image of "heroes" seeped through their ranks like a low-grade narcotic. It did not intoxicate them, but it skewed their view.

Strangely enough, it was this patriotic imagery that ultimately drove the disunity on the pile, and that by early November nearly caused the recovery effort to fall apart. The mechanisms were complex. On the one hand, there were some among the construction workers and the police who grew unreasonably impatient with the firemen, and became overeager to repeat the obvious—in polite terms, that these so-called heroes were just ordinary men. On the other hand, the firemen seemed to become steadily more self-absorbed and isolated from the larger cleanup efforts under way. . . .

Though the firemen who rioted on November 2 did not believe it, when Giuliani gave "safety" as the reason for reducing their presence on the pile, he was completely sincere. This was somewhat counterintuitive, since the safety record so far had been extraordinarily good: despite the fires, the instability of the ruins, and the crushing weight of the equipment and debris, not a single recovery worker had been killed, and only a few had been seriously injured. Indeed, discounting possible long-term respiratory problems, the injury rate was about half that of the construction-industry average. Some people claimed this as a sign of God's favor, but a more mundane explanation was that the inapplicability of ordinary rules and procedures to such a chaotic environment required workers there to think for themselves, which they proved very capable of doing. Nonetheless, the city had reason to be especially concerned about the firemen at the site, who formed maverick groups on the pile, prone to clustering too close to the diesel grapplers and to taking impetuous risks in the smoke and debris.

The lack of discipline was a well-known aspect of the firemen's culture. In some ways it was a necessary thing, hard to separate from their views of manliness and bravery and their eagerness to take on fires. It also, however, led to needless danger. After he left the service, in January of 2002, Commissioner Von Essen mentioned that as a longtime firefighter, he had often stood on floors among thirty others where only ten were needed. Indeed, on September 11 many of the firefighters who responded were off duty at the time, and many bypassed check-in procedures, or arrived by subway or car in violation of orders to stay away. Many also went into the towers unnecessarily and with little coordination, at a time when there were enough other firemen on duty to handle the evacuations, and when the Fire Department had decided that the fires were unfightable. Sixty off-duty firefighters died that day. "Courage is not enough," Von Essen later said. "The fact that the guys are so dedicated comes back to hurt them down the line." The police at the site were better disciplined—and, partly as a result, they suffered fewer casualties on the day of the attack. But nearly two months after the tragedy, with no conceivable justification for continuing to jump into voids or clamber across unstable cliffs, there were still firemen running wild.

Giuliani had good reason, therefore, to rein them in. Viewed from the outside, the plan seemed sensible: you scale back the searchers to three teams of twenty-five—one from each of the uniformed services; you allow only one spotter at a time to stand beside each diesel excavator on the pile; until human remains are found, you require the other team members to wait in designated "safe areas" nearby; you do not allow ordinary firemen to keep shutting down the site; you create a joint command to soothe people's egos but give practical control to the engineers and the construction types, who are businesslike and know how to finish the job; you shrink the perimeter, with the goal of returning even heavily damaged West Street as soon as possible to the city; you thin the crowds of hangers-on by requiring new badges for the inner and outer zones, and asking the Red Cross and the Salvation Army to con-

solidate and simplify their feeding operations; you scale back the public displays of mourning; you encourage people to get on with their lives.

The planners were not completely naive about the transition: they suspected that they might have some difficulty in getting the firemen to comply. Mike Burton decided that the best approach would be to start with strict enforcement of the new rules, and loosen up later for the sake of efficiency. I was surprised by his confidence that anything here could go according to plan. And indeed, little did.

Questions of personality and professional formation were at play. The construction crews, like the DDC itself, were made up of hard-driving people, accustomed to shaving minutes in a time-obsessed industry. Though they understood the desirability of finding the human remains at the Trade Center site, they were not going to slow the excavation of the ruins just to ensure that the final inspections at the Fresh Kills landfill did not turn up body parts. Mike Burton in particular was pushing for speed, and was determined to finish the job below cost and ahead of schedule—however arbitrary those targets may have been. He was climbing his mountain of success, and was not about to let a gang of irrational firemen get in his way. In public and during the morning meetings he was gracious and respectful toward them, but in private—in the confines of the kindergarten rooms, or during long walks with me on the pile—he let his impatience show. On the evening after the riot we came upon one of the new search-team "safe areas" (a ten-foot square of Jersey barriers spray-painted "FDNY"), and he shot me a hard little smile of victory. He used the firemen's term for it and said, "The penalty box." I assumed he was thinking about the attack on the police. He may have believed that the way forward was clear. He seemed not to notice that the penalty box was empty.

This was not a game. There were no rules. The firemen continued with their headstrong ways on the pile, refusing to submit to civilian authority. Five days after the riot, after the unions formally apologized to the police, Giuliani began a partial retreat. He said he would increase the size of the search teams to fifty. The firemen were unmollified. The place where their friends had been killed was still being turned into an unholy "construction site." Three days later, on November 10, charges were dropped against all but one of the arrested demonstrators. It did no good. The firemen pulled out the stops and demanded a meeting between the mayor and the dead firemen's families.

The meeting took place behind closed doors in a Sheraton hotel in midtown Manhattan, on the evening of November 12. It had been a rough day already: that morning an American Airlines flight departing for the Dominican Republic had crashed into a residential neighborhood in Queens, killing 265 people, and most of the officials at the meeting had visited the scene. Now they sat behind a table on a raised platform—the mayor, the medical examiner, the fire commissioner, and, from the Trade Center site, Mike Burton and Bill Cote.* The crowd they faced consisted mostly of widows—an increasingly organized group that spoke for mothers, fathers, and children as well, and that after two months of national sympathy was gaining significant political strength. Payouts to the victims' families hadn't yet begun, and firemen's widows, not without reason, felt neglected and put-upon. They believed that the city was essentially giving up on the search for the dead. And they were angry about it.

The medical examiner was the first to come under fire. He had begun to talk about the procedures in place for handling remains when he made the mistake of mentioning that full or even partially intact corpses had not recently been found, and that they were unlikely to be found in the future. A woman stood up and yelled, "You're a liar! We know what you're finding! You're a liar!" Others chimed in, shouting that their husbands' bodies had been recovered in good condition. One woman yelled that when her husband was found, the searchers on the pile could even see the dimple in his chin. It was as if an emotional dam had burst in the crowd. The medical examiner listened somberly. When the crowd briefly quieted, he tried to explain his reasoning: the excavation had moved into the mid-levels of the ruins, where the debris was severely compacted and the dead had been shattered or vaporized; furthermore, from what was known of the pile's composition, along with the processes of organic decay, there was little chance that whole bodies would be discovered in the future. The widows would have none of

this. They continued to shout "Liar!" until the medical examiner sat down. The months ahead would show that the medical examiner was wrong—that the ruins were riddled with unexpected cavities deep down, and that nearly whole corpses, particularly of heavily clad firemen, lay waiting to be found. However, this would have been impossible to predict at the time.

The mayor handled himself well that night. He was patient and compassionate, and he allowed the grieving crowd to rail, but he did not pander to it. About the medical examiner he simply said, "He's not lying. He's telling you what we know." Then it was Burton's turn to talk.

Burton started gamely into an explanation of the transition on the pile, including the new placement of spotters, the "safe areas," and the handling and inspection of the debris. The crowd listened sullenly for a while, until a woman stood up and yelled, "We don't even want to hear from you! You're Mr. Scoop and Dump!"

Burton was flustered. He said, "Listen, this will only be a few more minutes. Just let me explain our thinking, so we're all on the same page and can have a rational conversation."

The woman shouted, "No! You're not the sort of person I want to talk to! You're the problem!"

Burton tried a soothing tone. He said, "We'll get through this, if you'll just . . . "

"No! You're Mr. Scoop and Dump!"

Others joined in, shouting, "Scoop and Dump! Scoop and Dump! Scoop and Dump!" Burton allowed a small, nervous smile to flicker across his face. His tormentor saw it. She yelled, "You're smirking? You're smirking at me? You think this is funny? This isn't funny!" Someone else shouted, "Yeah, he's smirking!" and again the whole crowd started in. Burton was mortified. He made a few weak attempts to speak, but the widows were relentless, and they overwhelmed him. For minutes he stood miserably on the platform, absorbing the abuse, unable to advance or retreat. Bill Cote felt terrible for him, and wanted to go to his rescue, but could not. Finally the mayor stepped in and got the crowd to simmer down. He told a little story and made a quip that caused Burton's tormentor to smile. The mayor noticed and said, "You see, you just smirked. When people are nervous, they smirk. So can we please put this behind us now? Let's just stop."

But the widows were too angry for that, and they soon widened their attacks. They had some legitimate

*Bill Cote worked closely with Mike Burton and was also his good friend.

complaints—for instance, that the Fire Department had never gotten around to contacting some women about their husbands' deaths, or to clarifying the associated administrative and financial details. A few of those whose husbands had yet to be identified were still having a hard time accepting their demises. And what about their paychecks? If a fireman remained trapped somewhere inside the pile, wouldn't he still be on duty and earning overtime? Conversely, was it correct to assume that all those who had disappeared had stopped working at the moment of collapse? Unexpected though these questions seemed, they were obviously practical, and the fire commissioner admitted that the department had done a poor job of handling such things.

For the most part, though, the widows simply vented their emotions. They argued as much among themselves as with the officials at the head of the room. One woman kept insisting that her husband was still alive, because she could send signals to his beeper and it would respond. Others, who had accepted the reality of death, were infuriated by the possibility that any of the firemen's remains would not be found until they reached the landfill. Not surprisingly, this turned out to be the most difficult issue of the night. The crowd demanded to know why the final sifting operation could not be moved from Fresh Kills to the Trade Center site or the streets nearby. There were many reasons why—including dust, noise, neighborhood opposition, and, most important, the complete lack of space in Lower Manhattan—but neither Burton nor Cote was about to say that now. They promised to look into the possibility. Of course the crowd did not believe them. At one point a woman came forward with her son, a boy of about seven, and started screaming, "You tell him! You tell him!" Burton and Cote looked at her without understanding. Tell him what? She continued, "You tell him his father's going to be found at the dump!" The crowd broke into applause. The woman began to cry. "Tell him! Tell him!" Her son watched her in apparent confusion. Friends came up, put their arms around her, and led her and the boy gently away.

Burton and Cote were badly shaken. When the meeting ended, after more than three hours of emotional storms, the two of them got into Burton's Jeep and drove away through the quiet streets. At first they did not speak, except briefly to agree that the experience had been the worst of their lives. In the theater district they found a bar, and went in for a drink. The other customers there—tourists pioneering a return to the city, lovers hunched together before bed, late-night regulars of various kinds—could never have guessed the role of these nondescript men, or the utter seriousness of their talk.

The widows' meeting turned out to be a watershed in the Trade Center recovery. Burton and Cote were tough guys, accustomed to seeing life as a struggle, and they would not have been unjustified had they responded impatiently to the encounter. This was dangerous to admit out loud, but it was on many people's minds: the firemen's widows were victims of victimization itself, and in their agony and myopia they were starting to blunder around; moreover, they clearly did not represent the thousands of others who had lost family on September 11 and were coming to terms with the events more stoically. It would have been understandable, therefore, if Burton and Cote had mentally stiff-armed the widows, privately dismissing their emotions as overblown and rededicating themselves to the efficiency of the excavation. They had it within their power to do this—and had they been officials in many other parts of the world, they probably would have followed such a hard line. It was lucky for the ultimate success of the recovery effort that this was not the way they naturally reacted.

Instead, over a couple of beers they talked for the first time since September 11 about people's emotional reactions to the attack, and they questioned why they themselves had felt so little affected by the death and destruction at the site. Burton called Cote a "cold fish." Cote pointed out that neither of them had family or close friends who had died. It also had to be admitted that the project was going well, and that for both of them it was utterly consuming professionally, offering an emotional advantage that others did not have: they simply did not have time to dwell on the tragedy. Still, each had been moved that night by the suffering of the widows, and had been troubled by the realization that, though they had tried to do the best possible job, there were people who now believed that their actions were wrong, even wicked. It made them question the doggedness of their approach, and reminded them of a simple imperative that in the crush of daily decisions they were tending to forget; that the unbuilding was more than just a problem of deconstruction, and that for the final measure of success they would have to take emotions into account. They finished their beers, drove downtown, and walked through the site.

In practice the firemen had lost the fight, but the terms of the peace would have to be generous. Burton knew this now, and Giuliani did too. The mayor increased the search teams' numbers back to seventy-five per shift, though they would have to proceed on a less ambitious basis than before: it was understood that beyond being allowed to search for their dead, they would in fact have little say. The tensions never went away,

and indeed escalated toward the very end. But already on the morning after the widows' night, at the joint meeting at PS 89, one of the fire chiefs unintentionally made a show of his loss of power when his only contribution was to ask for a moment of silence for the dead of the Queens airline crash—a strangely irrelevant request that emphasized the changes under way by signaling that he had little to say about the work at hand. The widows would be heard from again—but increasingly through formal channels created for them. Mike Burton was now unchallenged as the Trade Center Czar. But he seemed to understand that to succeed he would have to keep his ambitions in check, and that America does not function as a dictatorship of rationalists.

Chapter 6 Review Questions

1. What is your definition of an informal group in organizations? How does it differ from the formal organization?
2. How are informal groups formed and how do they influence the activities of public organizations?
3. Do informal groups emerge and have an impact on *public* organizations in the same ways as they do upon *business* organizations?
4. In the case, "American Ground," what general lessons did you draw out specifically concerning *administrative* issues involving informal groups and the resolution of these issues?
5. Can you see any evidence of the influence of informal groups in organizations with which you are familiar? If so, how did these groups emerge and in what ways do they affect the policies and activities of those organizations?
6. Based on your personal observations of the workings of informal groups, would you modify Elton Mayo's concept in any way? For example, could you add more specifics about how to identify informal groups? Measure their strength? Identify their sources of influence on organizations? Reasons for their weakness? Methods for achieving the support of management? Ways of better communication? Means for improving their motivation? Resolving disputes between groups?

Key Terms

informal group

"great illumination"

social structure

Hawthorne experiments

interview program

scientific-technological change

Suggestions for Further Reading

The best book about the Hawthorne experiments is Fritz Roethlisberger and W.J. Dickson, *Management and the Worker* (Cambridge, Mass.: Harvard Univer-

sity Press, 1939). For a less complicated view, see Fritz Roethlisberger, *Management and Morale* (Cambridge, Mass.: Harvard University Press, 1941). Elton

Mayo's broad philosophic interpretations are contained in his "trilogy": *The Human Problems of an Industrial Organization* (New York: Macmillan Co., 1933); *The Social Problems of an Industrial Civilization* (Boston: Graduate School of Business Administration, Harvard University, 1945); and *The Political Problems of an Industrial Civilization* (same publisher, 1947). For an excellent retrospective on Hawthorne, refer to "An Interview with Fritz Roethlisberger," *Organizational Dynamics,* 1 (Autumn 1972), pp. 31–45; "Hawthorne Revisited: The Legend and the Legacy," *Organizational Dynamics,* 4 (Winter 1975), pp. 66–80; and Alfred A. Bolton, ed., "Special Issue: Relay Assembly Testroom Participants Remember: Hawthorne a Half Century Later," *International Journal of Public Administration,* Vol. 17, No. 2 (1994), entire issue. For a more recent history of Hawthorne, see Richard Gillespie, *Manufacturing Knowledge* (Cambridge: Cambridge University Press, 1991); as well as portions of P. F. Ballantyne, *Hawthorne Research* (London: Fitzory Dearborn, 2000); or the articles by Kevin T. Mahoney and David B. Baker, "Elton Mayo and Carl Rogers," *Journal of Vocational Behavior,* 60 (June 2002) pp. 437–450, Yeh Hsueh, "The Hawthorne Experiments," *History of Psychology*, 5 (May 2002), pp. 163–189; J. H. Smith, "The Enduring Legacy of Elton Mayo," 5 (March 1998), pp. 221–229; Ellen S. O'Connor, "The Politics of Management Thought," *Academy of Management Review,* 24 (January 1999), pp. 117–141; and Augustine Brannigan and William Zwerman, "The Real Hawthorne Effect," *Society,* 38 (January/February 2001), pp. 55–61.

Two classic interpretations of Hawthorne are George Homans, *The Human Group* (New York: Harcourt, Brace, 1950) and Henry Landsberger, *Hawthorne Revisited* (Ithaca, N.Y.: Cornell University Press, 1958). By contrast, to taste a small sampling of the scholarly arguments over Hawthorne, read Alex Carey, "The Hawthorne Studies: A Radical Criticism," *American Sociological Review,* 32 (June 1967), pp. 403–416; and more recently, Michael P. Bobic and Williams Eric Davis, "A Kind Word for Theory X," *Journal of Public Administration Research and Theory,*

121 (July 2003), pp. 239–263. For a review of small group theory applied to public administration, see Robert T. Golembiewski, "The Small Group and Public Administration," *Public Administration Review,* 19 (Summer 1959), pp. 149–156. For some interesting related perspectives on the psychological dimensions of public management, see Richard L. Schott, "The Psychological Development of Adults: Implications for Public Administration," *Public Administration Review,* 46 (November/December 1986), pp. 657–667; and Larry Hirshhorn, *The Workplace Within: Psychodynamics of Organizational Life* (Cambridge, Mass.: MIT Press, 1991). The legacy of Hawthorne can be found in numerous examples of the prolific postwar authors associated with the Human Relations School of Management: Chris Argyris, Warren Bennis, Frederick Herzberg, Daniel Katz, Robert Kahn, Rensis Likert, Douglas McGregor, Leonard Sayles, William Whyte, and many, many others who owe a tremendous debt to Hawthorne. In turn, their "spinoffs" and "impacts" on public administration have been profound and numerous but largely uncharted by scholars in the field, though for a useful compilation of many of their writings, refer to Frank J. Thompson, ed., *Classics of Public Personnel Policy,* Second Edition (Monterey, Calif.: Brooks/Cole, 1991). Much of the current thinking related to small groups inside organizations today can be found within organizational behavior studies—for example, in journals such as *The International Journal of Organization Theory and Behavior,* or personnel and organizational behavior in texts such as Michael L. Vasy et al., *Organizational Behavior and Public Management,* 3rd ed. (New York: Marcel Dekker, 1998). To witness the heavy influence of this ongoing emphasis upon developing human resources applied directly to modern public administration and its specific needs for improvement, read the Volcker Commission Report, entitled "The Report of the National Commission on the Public Service," *Leadership for America: Rebuilding the Public Service* (Lexington, Mass.: Lexington Books, 1990); and more recently, John D. Donahue and Joseph S. Nye, Jr., *For the People: Can We Fix Public Service?* (Washington, D.C.: Brookings, 2003).

CHAPTER 7

Key Decision Makers Inside Public Administration: The Concept of Competing Bureaucratic Subsystems

O ur public bureaucracy is composed of identifiable clusters of individuals who work and act in influential ways inside bureaucracy. Each of these subsystems shapes the broad outcomes of bureaucracy.

Richard J. Stillman II

READING 7

Introduction

Nearly 5 million people work for the federal government, and another roughly 15 million are employed by state and local governments in the United States. They may be highway engineers who maintain or build our roads; police who patrol neighborhoods; public school teachers who educate children; or forest rangers who run the national park system. America's public service is composed of many types of people who perform the vital and varied activities of modern government.

How can we generalize about these public servants? Their characteristics? The roles they play inside bureaucracy? The work they perform? Their influence on the policies and activities of public agencies? Why do *they* so significantly shape "the outcomes" of modern bureaucracy?

In the following selection by the author of this text, drawn from his book *The American Bureaucracy,* he gives us something of "an X-Ray" picture of the inside of modern public bureaucracy. He argues that government is not made up of simply *one* monolithic body of employees but rather distinctive clusters of five varieties of personnel: political appointees, professional careerists, civil servant generalists, unionized workers, and contract employees. The author outlines the attributes of each of these groups, which he labels "bureaucratic subsystems," the roles they play within public agencies, their origins and evolution, sources of recruitment, motivation(s), ladders for promotions, impacts on public policies, and issues or problems confronting each of these bureaucratic subsystems. The writer contends that the types of subsystems that make up the inside of any agency decisively influence the content of its work, direction of its policies, and decisions it makes—or fails to make. "The balance or imbalance of these groups within any agency," concludes Stillman, "is fundamental to its character, policies, and performance."

Rarely does just *one* subsystem compose any public organization, but rather several of these bureaucratic subsystems are normally found within most modern public bureaucracies. Which one is in charge and how they work out their relationships becomes critical to understanding what happens in public administration. As Stillman writes: "Most bureaucracies in the public sector are, however, dominated not by any one subsystem but by several; indeed, all these subsystems normally are found within their structures. Hence, policy outcomes frequently result from their jockeying for position, influence, and power over public bureaucratic actions. Conflicts between subsystems are common. Sometimes the competition for power and control over the policy-making apparatus can be quite severe and intense."

As you read this selection, keep the following questions in mind:

Why does the author conclude that contemporary public bureaucracy is *not* composed of only *one* variety of public officials but rather five types? How does this argument compare or contrast with that of Weber in Chapter 2?

According to the author, how did each distinctive subsystem begin, evolve, grow within government, and develop unique value-orientations?

In what ways does each one contribute to influencing decisively the public policy process as well as the implementation of public policy?

How does the size, composition, and relationships of groups in bureaucracy influence its work and "impacts" on society as a whole?

Inside Public Bureaucracy

RICHARD J. STILLMAN II

Once a young aide to President William Howard Taft kept repeating the phrase "machinery of government" while briefing the president. Taft, so the story goes, became exasperated and turned to a friend and whispered, "My God, the man actually *believes* government is a machine!"

Taft had it right. United States government, especially its bureaucracy, is not an automated assembly line, devoid of human beings, lifeless and machinelike. Quite to the contrary, our public bureaucracy is composed of identifiable clusters of individuals who work and act in influential ways inside the bureaucracy. Each of these subsystems shapes the broad outcomes of bureaucratic institutions. Each competes for power and influence over its particular bureaucracy. These human subsystems perform different tasks in government. Through diverse strategies they aim to achieve different goals with different stakes or outcomes for bureaucracy. Each serves vitally important functions within bureaucracy and significantly determines in various ways what bureaucracy does or does not do and how well it performs these functions. The size and influence of each of these human subgroups vary considerably from agency to agency and locale to locale. Yet many public organizations contain several of these subsystems. Some public operations have all five subsystems, which jockey with one another for influence and status.

The boundary between each of the subsystems is not always clear. They tend to overlap, with considerable gray areas between them. Subsystems in different agencies do not always exhibit the same exact dimensions, proportions, or precisely similar characteristics. Nor are all five groups necessarily found in every agency. Sometimes only one or two are represented. In other words, these subsystems are fairly open, fluid, and adaptive to differing organizational contexts and situations. They are also fundamentally *human and political, not machinelike in behavior.* Subsystems do have certain important similarities and differences in their roles, values, missions, power, status, functions, activities, and influence within public organizations. This chapter will examine the special characteristics of each subsystem within organizations and particularly how they affect the outputs of every agency from the inside. Brief descriptions of these five subsystems follow.

> *Political appointees* are those individuals who serve without tenure and whose appointments are based often, though not always, upon political ties or party loyalties.

> *Professional careerists* are various groups of personnel with specialized expertise in specific fields. Positions occupied by these groups are usually based on advanced professional training. This subsystem offers lifetime careers and stresses "rank-in-person" rather than "rank-in-job."

> The *general civil service* operates under "merit concepts." Characteristics of this subsystem are tenure, rank-in-position, and "classified" hierarchies of positions based upon the amount of tasks and responsibilities.

> *Unionized workers* are blue collar and, increasingly, white collar workers whose employment is based upon negotiated contracts between union representatives and management within the jurisdictions they serve.

> *Contractual employees* are untenured workers whose employment with government is directly or indirectly governed by various contractual agreements negotiated with individuals, private firms, nonprofit organizations, and universities for rendering specific services for a limited or specified time. They are not governed by civil service rules nor do they work under union contracts.

The Political Appointee Subsystem: The Birds of Passage

Most political appointees fill the top-level policy-making posts within federal, state, and local bureaucracies. These men and women serve in government without tenure, holding office at the pleasure of the chief elected official, who hires them, promotes them, or dismisses them. At the federal level, political appointees make up a fairly small group, with only 5,823 out of approximately 3 million federal civilian workers. Federal political appointees are divided into three categories: (1) PASs, or presidential appointments with the consent of the Senate (663); PAs, or presidential appointments not requiring Senate confirmation (1405); and agency appointments, those made by the agency chief (1725). The number of PASs has remained fairly stable over the past two decades (roughly 660), but the number of noncareer SES and schedule C political appointees has grown significantly. The number and categories of political appointees vary considerably in state and local jurisdictions. In some regions where there is no civil service system—particularly rural county governments or the machine-run cities—virtually all government jobs are handed out on the basis of party loyalty or political patronage. Today, however, most cities and states follow the federal pattern in reserving only top-level policy jobs for political appointees, who serve at the pleasure of a governor or mayor. Particularly in "reformed" or "clean" city and state governments, these posts are few and limited to only the very top levels. Colorado, for example, has only two dozen political appointees out of 5,000 manager-level posts. However, in Massachusetts all of the managers' positions in the state, some 3,500 jobs down to the supervisor's level, are considered "policy-making" positions and are available for the governor's appointees. Thus the "range" is quite wide, depending on the influence of "reformism" found within the local/regional politics.

Within federal bureaucracies, in particular, appointees' lack of tenure limits the length of their employment. The average federal political appointee serves only twenty-two months in office. Hugh Heclo has rightly observed that they are "birds of passage"[1] who recognize from the start that they will not be around for very long. The most they can look forward to is a four-year term, and if a president is reelected (and they are lucky) they *might* be reappointed for longer periods—though that is rare. Transience is their only common trademark. Most, therefore, set their sights and adapt their behavior for the short range by recognizing that if they are to accomplish *anything* in their jobs, they must move quickly. Short-term horizons, limited goals, and quick results tend to characterize their actions. This tendency among political appointees also probably characterizes state and local appointees within jurisdictions where there is a competitive party system. But elsewhere, if the top jobs have little or no turnover, political appointees can look forward to longer tenure in office, thus shifting their time horizons to somewhat longer perspectives.

Generally, though, appointees' job uncertainty means that they have to have another position, outside of government, to fall back on in case they fall out of favor or out of office (a good possibility given the hazards of these untenured posts today). Hence, many political appointees at the federal level are drawn from law firms or are on leave from big businesses, government, or universities. The pool from which they are drawn is thus quite small and tends to be, but is not always, confined to upperclass individuals who can afford a short time away from their regular lines of work. This qualification also tends to drastically limit the social characteristics of political appointees to white, urban, middle-aged males with advanced Ivy

League educations and ambitions for high-status careers.[2] While President Jimmy Carter attempted to recruit greater numbers of women and minorities into these posts, the bulk of political appointees even in his administration in the late 1970s, and of Ronald Reagan's in the 1980s, was largely drawn from this very small pool. However, in the 1990s President Bill Clinton drew his top appointees from a wider cross section of Americans. Historically, as law firms, businesses, and universities tended to become more representative, so too the "pool" of political appointees has tended to become more diverse and varied. Political appointees at the state and local levels, particularly as one moves closer to the grass roots, represent much more diversity in talent, training, income, and background. Generally, there is greater heterogeneity and better representation of social groups at lower governmental jurisdictions, though there is by no means a wide popular representation even there.[3]

While there are several prominent examples of political appointees whose faces reappear in government, usually at higher levels of bureaucracy when their party assumes office (George Shultz, James Baker, and Caspar Weinberger crop up repeatedly in Republican administrations, and William Perry and Warren Christopher in Democratic ones), most political appointees have limited backgrounds in government. Very few serve repeated spells in government; few work for more than one administration. Few survive election turnovers in the executive branch. Many simply do not want to stay more than a few years in office, nor can they, because of pressing outside professional or business commitments. Yet most are *drawn from and return to related fields of endeavor.* Western ranchers, businesspersons, and lawyers have tended to occupy the top slots at the Department of the Interior because of their prolonged involvement with western public lands; just as defense contractors, former military officers, and business executives have long been recruited to top political slots at DoD. And most return to these jobs afterwards. Thus different bureaucracies tend to draw their political appointees from different occupational-economic sectors of society as well as from different regions primarily because of these appointees' prior experience with the tasks and activities of the agency. An appropriate "track record" in the policy concerns of the agency, and the correct party identification, and especially policy positions that are in accord with the chief executive's, are important qualifications for such appointments.

Their specific policy roles in bureaucracy can be conceived of as loose-jointed, concentric rings that emanate outward from the office of the elected chief executive—a president, governor, or mayor. The most powerful appointees are those who occupy leadership roles within the major Cabinet-rank departments, sometimes referred to at the federal level as the inner Cabinet. The inner Cabinet is composed of the secretaries of Defense, State, and of the Office of Management and Budget, as well as senior noncareer or career ambassadors to major governments, such as Europe or China. These individuals are responsible for the operations of the largest public agencies (like DoD) and subsequently have powerful policy agenda-setting functions (like OMB). Similarly, inner Cabinets, made up of those closest to the governor or mayor and exercising major policy-organizational tasks, are found at state and local levels as well, though their titles differ. Inner Cabinet members at the federal level are often at the White House with the president or are representing their agencies before Congress. They are responsible for setting—and defending—the major policy priorities of the president and the agency they represent. They also exert the overall leadership within their particular organization, appoint numerous political personnel within the organization, and represent it before the media and special interest groups. Their most important function within government is to translate the campaign platforms and promises of the elected officials into administrative actions of major policy-administrative importance to the chief executive—the president, governor, or mayor. In short, they serve as linchpins between election-night rhetoric and actual institutional performance.

The next ring, or the outer Cabinet, is composed of men and women who see the president (or governor or mayor) less frequently but nevertheless hold Cabinet rank (also normally requiring Senate or legislative confirmation). They are frequently charged with running a major public agency such as the Department of Housing and Urban Development or the Department of Corrections at the state level. They are a rung below the inner Cabinet in *informal* power and status only, for their legal titles and prerogatives are normally much the same as those of their counterparts in the inner Cabinet. Indeed, they may have many of the same responsibilities, such as directing a large department, providing its leadership, setting its policy agenda, defending it before Congress, and so on.

The third level is generally termed the sub-Cabinet. It is composed of deputy secretaries, assistant secretaries, and administrative heads of major non-Cabinet agencies and bureaus. These individuals also occupy important policy-making posts, and sometimes highly sensitive and critical ones, such as that of deputy attorney general in the Department of Justice, who is normally responsible for the daily management of the department's activities, or of the assistant secretary for International Security Affairs in the Department of Defense, who is charged with shaping broad strategic policies within DoD. These men and women are generally more specialized in particular fields of expertise than the inner or outer Cabinet members. While they may have had a variety of experiences and backgrounds in government, business, law, or the professions, their training and work experiences tend to be more appropriate to the positions that they occupy. They have also usually had considerable experience handling political issues related to these offices and are expected to take positions on these issues in accordance with the president's overall priorities.

Given the increasing proliferation of special interest groups that watch closely these sub-Cabinet appointments and their pronouncements, key sub-Cabinet officials, at least during the last few years, are often drawn from the ranks of special interest groups and return to these after government service. Democrats tend to draw their appointees from left-leaning policy groups, while Republicans draw theirs from think tanks, legislative staffs, and policy-advocate groups on the right-wing.

Yet some scholars, such as Thomas P. Murphy, Donald E. Nuechterlein, and Ronald Stupak, have argued that the influence of this group of appointees over the policy-making process has declined in recent years because of its increase in numbers.[4] Though as a collective group their prominence and power has on the whole increased in recent years, a modified Gresham's law operates here; that is, increasing numbers of political appointees at this sub-Cabinet level drive down their individual influence over policy decisions. Put simply: a call from an assistant secretary does not mean what it once did.

The fourth group of appointees encompasses a wide variety of advisors to the secretary and directors of agencies and bureaus. Like the previous level of appointees, this level has expanded enormously in the past two decades as secretaries brought in their own people to help run their departments. At the federal level these assorted political appointees do not require Senate confirmation, so for the most part their ranks have grown without legislative oversight and control. Few, however, are active politicians or were closely involved with the election campaign of the chief executive. Most are more directly identified with the professional or policy issues of the agencies where they work. Many have had personal ties or friendships with their immediate supervisors. They are generally reputed to be experts in the field of law, business, or education and may have actually been drawn from the ranks of the civil service. Some have known or worked with each other before or fought the opposition party together over the very sets of policy issues they are now actively administering and formulating.

Compared with appointees at other levels, these men and women are the most expert and specialized, and they are often more willing to push forward the interests of their particular agencies and resist political intrusions from others. And yet as Frederick Mosher has observed of these appointees: "Some are eminent figures in their fields, often principal representatives and defenders of the services which they superintend. Yet their stance differs from that of the members of the permanent services below them. They *can* be replaced or their situations can be made so uncomfortable as to induce them to resign or at least alter their behavior."[5] Their lack of tenure is the heavy stick that ensures their ultimate responsiveness to higher circles of appointees.

Finally, there is an increasingly large group of individuals in public bureaucracy today who occupy a limbo-land between quasipolitical and non-political

territory. Their position at the federal level has been institutionalized through the creation of the Senior Executive Service (SES) in the 1978 Civil Service Reform Act.

SES developed a new category of upper-level administrators that is formed from supergrade officials in grades GS-16, 17, and 18 and in Executive Ranks IV and V, in which position assignments and pay are determined by political decision makers and yet are also protected by the civil service rules (career officials in SES have the option of retreating to GS-15 grades). The rationale for creating SES came mainly from the argument that improved management in government could result from greater mobility of its top executives. Drawn from senior career ranks, it was argued that like in business, the president and top executives should be able to shift senior managers from one post to another more easily than the hide-bound civil service rules allowed prior to 1978. Further, as in the case of business, bonus incentives were provided for rewarding outstanding performances in SES. On the other hand, unsatisfactory performances could cause removal or replacement in SES. By law, the bulk of these individuals must be drawn from the ranks of the civil service, since only 10 percent of SES members (or 703 of the current 8,130 SES employees) can be political appointees. About 40 percent of SES positions are designated as "career reserved" because of their sensitive positions. The number of SES positions has grown since 1980, but so has the number of noncareer or political-appointee positions.

While the jury is still out on whether or not the introduction of SES has proven successful, it remains a *potentially* important tool for improving federal management and control.

On the state level, twelve states have created SES systems. Four did so prior to the 1978 CSRA: California (1963), Minnesota (1969), Wisconsin (1973), and Oregon (1977). After the creation of the federal level SES, several states adopted their own SES systems shortly afterwards: Connecticut (1979), Florida (1980), Iowa (1980), Michigan (1980), Washington (1980), and Pennsylvania (1981). Both Tennessee and New Jersey passed their SES legislation in 1986, and Massachusetts gave the governor statutory authority to set up a senior career management system, which has not yet been implemented. While the state-level

SES systems, like the federal-level one, offer *potentially* enhanced career mobility, managerial control, and leadership flexibility, as Sherwood and Breyer suggest in their evaluation of state-level SES systems: "Little in the twenty-four-year history of executive personnel systems in the states suggests that they have come to occupy a highly significant role in the processes of governance."[6]

Why the disappointing performance of state-level SES systems? According to Deborah D. Roberts, "State SES systems contain too many lofty and contradictory goals that cannot all be satisfied. These contradictions revolve around incentives, membership quandaries, and diversity among the important players." Due to such challenging contradictions, according to Professor Roberts, existing state SES systems "are undergoing painful retrenchment and redirection, and few states appear willing to adopt new SES initiatives."[7]

To sum up the influence of the political appointee subsystem: First, these individuals occupy the highest, most prominent posts within public organizations. Thus, they serve as linchpins between campaign promises and bureaucratic performance. However, they are characterized overall as a highly diverse, fragmented, and transitory group with little cohesiveness.

Second, their influence within bureaucracy depends upon the policy positions they hold, the length of their government service, their connections with top elected officials, their own personalities, their support from outside groups, the immediate tasks at hand, and whether these lend themselves to imminent solutions. Generally, as one moves up the hierarchy of political officials to the inner Cabinet, these individuals have the most generalized backgrounds, and must deal with the broadest, most critical policy issues. They also exercise the widest, most influential policy roles inside public bureaucracy, if their tenure is long enough and their external support adequate to the performance of the tasks at hand. Here at the top the political winds blow the fiercest; the "turf battles" are the most intense, and the stakes are the highest.

Third, as one moves down the hierarchy of these political officials toward those of quasi-political status, greater degrees of specialization are found as well as more identification with the programmatic goals, tasks, and issues within the agencies they serve. They are less generalist in outlook and more concerned with pushing narrower policy agendas, which often means they are less interested in and responsive to their own chief's reelection priorities.

Fourth, sharp turf fights over policy issues therefore ensue frequently between these various levels of political appointees, largely because of the different perspectives built into their hierarchical roles. Here is where pitched policy battles frequently occur and are resolved. In the pecking order of appointees, those at or near the top push agendas that are broader and more responsive to the chief executive's agenda, while those lower down tend to be more programmatic and responsive to the priorities and issues of the particular agencies in which they work.

Fifth, while the subsystem of political appointees is highly fragmented, these tend to cluster into networks in which those near the top have close personal ties, even long friendships, with the chief elected official (though not necessarily with each other, nor are they necessarily active in his political campaigns). Those on the lower rungs tend to be experts in particular fields and to have personal networks that run downward into the agency and outward into various external support groups associated with an agency's mission.

Sixth, what draws all appointees together and keeps them loyal and responsible, at least to some degree, to the elected official's policy agenda (and makes them a distinct bureaucratic subsystem) is the fact that they can be removed or transferred at any time by a president, governor, or mayor. Fear of losing a job can be a powerful incentive to stay in line with the top-level agenda, or at least to refrain from stating opposing views in public.

However, in this constantly shifting world of personnel and goals, as Norton Long pointed out, determining to whom one is loyal and what one should accomplish become difficult if not impossible tasks. This level in bureaucracy is an ambiguous world in which appearances frequently count more than on-the-job practices. Participants thus spend enormous amounts of time posturing and posing in order to appear to do the correct things for the right people and taking readings and soundings to find information about their own status and about the intentions of others. The closed door, an invitation to the right party, the frequency of meetings with the superior, and the seating arrangement at the conference table often signal more than the untrained eye can perceive or the written document explain. Hard-driving, ambitious men and women, even with considerable experience and exposure, become quickly frustrated and disillusioned with the confusion and pretense inherent in this subsystem, as autobiographies of recent incumbents testify. Policy activity at this level of bureaucracy is very much like the greased pole competition at the old-fashioned county fair, where few, if any, climb to the top and reach the prize. The way up is slippery, uncertain, and treacherous, often crowded with many other frenzied competitors. There are no sure rules for success. And the prize, once reached, is often temporary, of little value, and hardly worth all that fierce competition and furiously expended energy. Many leave disillusioned and despairing about what they have done or failed to do. Good luck rather than personal skills often decides outcomes.

Seventh, political appointees, despite the highly ambiguous world in which they operate, ultimately are central to the governing processes at all levels of government. They are critical, individually and collectively, in the words of presidential scholar James P. Pfiffner, to assist chief executives in "hitting the ground running." But high job demands, family stress, extensive security checks, comparatively low pay (by contrast to other similarly responsible private-sector jobs), and detailed public and press scrutiny all combine to deter many from seeking such lines of work and to delay appointments. Indeed, President Clinton was slower than his recent predecessors in getting his own policy team in place, leading to criticism of Clinton's capacity to govern effectively.

The Professional Careerist Subsystem: Permanent Clusters of Powerful Experts

Professor Samuel H. Beer has said that U.S. society is governed by "technocratic politics" in which specialists with in-depth training and experience in different fields of government have assumed the duty of charting the course of various public organizations. As Beer argues:

> I would remark how rarely additions to the public agenda have been initiated by the demands of voters or the advocacy of pressure groups or the platforms of political parties. On the contrary, in the fields of health, housing, urban renewal, transportation, welfare, education, poverty and energy, it has been in very great measure, people in government service or closely associated with it acting on the basis of their specialties and technical knowledge who first perceived the problem, conceived the program, initially urged it on the President and Congress, went on to help lobby it through to enactment and then saw to its administration.[8]

Some scholars, including Zbigniew Brzezinski, have called the phenomenon "the technetronic age"; Don Price calls it "the scientific estate"; for Daniel Bell it is "the post-industrial age"; for Guy Benveniste, "the politics of expertise."[9] But whatever term is used to describe the role of experts within government, the professional strata, a subsystem below that of political appointees, is now recognized by many scholars as a significant influence over the activities of modern public organizations. As Frederick C. Mosher has perceptively written, "For better or worse—or better and worse—much of government is now in the hands of professionals (including scientists). The choice of these professionals, the determination of their skills and the content of their work are now principally determined not by the general government agencies, but by their own professional elites, professional organizations and the institutions and facilities of higher education. It is unlikely the trend toward professionalization in or outside government will be reversed or even slowed."[10]

Professionalization in government influenced not only the domestic agenda, as Beer suggests, but also how we viewed our broad global responsibilities in the post–World War II era. According to Robert D. Kaplan:

> The global responsibilities thrust upon the United States after World War II led to the creation of area experts in government, academia, and think tanks.

Their effect on policy and public opinion has been to splinter and compartmentalize what used to be geographic wholes. The academic and policy-making nomenklatura invented a new world based not on real borders so much as on the borders of their knowledge or lack thereof. As someone who has written extensively about Turkey and the Balkans, as well as the Middle East, I have seen how these areas constitute two entirely different subcultures of Washington society and workdom, with little or no cross-fertilization between the two.[11]

The development of professional control over the inner dynamics of U.S. bureaucracy came slowly and in piecemeal fashion, mostly in the twentieth century. Some agencies, such as DoJ, have since their inception been dominated by lawyers, but professionally trained lawyers with LL.B. degrees, steeped in learning, responsive to the American Bar Association's policy concerns. Specialists in highly diverse elements of the law did not appear at DoJ in any sizable numbers until the New Deal in the 1930s. Military officers held the top army posts from the time the War Department was established in 1789, but even throughout most of the nineteenth century officers were poorly trained and politically motivated amateurs with little or no technical competency (except for those trained as engineers at West Point).

The modern generalist-professional cadre of officers did not appear until after 1900, established largely through the reforms of secretary of war Elihu Root, who created the Army General Staff, a unified personnel system, as well as a series of advanced professional educational institutions for military officers. The Rogers Act of 1924 instituted what we now know as the professional foreign service, but the dominance of quality foreign service professionals such as George Kennan and Charles Bohlen throughout key State Department slots did not emerge until after World War II.

Likewise, the professional control of state and local agencies in many regions began at roughly the turn of the century with the formation of small, fledgling professional associations such as the International Association of Chiefs of Police (1893), the International Association of Fire Chiefs (1893), the

American Society of Municipal Engineers (1894), the Municipal Finance Officers Association (1906), the National Recreation Association (1906), the National Association of Public School Business Officials (1910), the National Organization for Public Health Nursing (1912), and the City Managers' Association (1914).

As Robert Wiebe observes of the process of grassroots professionalization in America:

Social workers . . . acted first to dissociate themselves from philanthropy and establish themselves as a distinct field within the new social sciences. Beginning with local leagues in Boston and New York, they had formed the National Federation of Settlements by 1911 and soon after captured the old National Conference of Charities and Corrections, renaming it the National Conference of Social Work. Also early in the century, they moved from ad hoc classes of special training to complete professional schools within such universities as Chicago and Harvard.[12]

The federal government also had an important hand in stimulating professionalism at the state and local levels. For example, again in the area of social work, Martha Derthick writes:

Congress in 1939 gave the Social Security Board authority to set personnel standards, perhaps because it was sympathetic to some degree of professionalism in the performance of public administration (on the assumption that it would lead to "efficiency") if not in the performance of social work. Even before this was done, the Board was demanding—on the basis of its authority to require efficient administration—that state plans include minimum standards for education, training, and experience (for local social workers).[13]

In many respects, at the local level and to a great extent at the federal level as well, professionalism was a means of battling "corruption as well as inefficiency," as Jeremy F. Plant and David S. Arnold point out: "Professionalism had to pervade the entire fabric of modern government," at least in the eyes of reformers who sought better government.[14] But, for the most part, until after World War II these professional groups were weak and ineffective voluntary associations exercising little control over the inner dynamics of local public bureaucracy. The postwar era, however, brought into grass-roots and higher-level government an influx of university-educated specialists with wide assortments of technical competence. The postwar era also brought about a new respect for and demand for these specialists to deal with a myriad of technical tasks from constructing highways, educating children, cleaning air and water, and administering complex regulatory machinery—often spawned by the professionals themselves—for certifying and controlling the application of skills inside and outside government. Today professional public official associations are extensive and varied, exercising hidden yet pervasive influence over government policy through certification, training, setting ethical standards, and playing policy advocacy roles within their specialized fields.

Professionals in government today, however, by no means make up a monolithic group or a homogeneous mass of experts; indeed, they differ considerably from one another. Directly under political appointees, *professional elites* comprise the core group of experts. These are the senior and most prestigious and respected members of the profession. They give not only internal direction to the profession but also to the entire agency by controlling the important positions and advancement to those positions and by setting recruitment and entrance requirements as well as overall personnel policies and priorities for the organization. Rising to these posts is achieved only through long-term career investment in the field, attendance at the "right" schools for basic and advanced training in the field, and advancement through progressive levels of responsibility and prominence in areas closely identified with the central concerns of the agency. Pilots in the air force, line officers in the navy, doctors in the U.S. Public Health Service, foresters in the U.S. Forest Service, senior staff lawyers at DoJ, and top-ranking educators in local school systems or in state departments of education tend to fill the elite slots within their respective agencies.

"Status" at times becomes an obsession with professionals. Knowing where one is or is not or how to advance "in the pecking order" of influence is important to most professionals. The registered nurse is considered an elite within that cluster of professionals. And not only is certification as an RN increasingly important to a nurse's elite status today, further certification within a very narrow specialized field within which she or he works, such as emergency room, orthopedic care, or surgery room practice, is also desirable. The continuous specialization of those who are already specialists within government is staggering.

The elites, in turn, within these various strata of professional clusters, provide the leadership as well as set the work standards, the qualifications for entrance and advancement, and the overall values for the profession. Much of the critical tensions and conflicts between clusters of professional elites are over policy questions and control of turf—between doctors and nurses in hospitals or between air force, army, navy, and marine corps top-ranking officers within DoD. Much of this conflict is hidden from public view. Rarely does it become public, because it can most often be settled between the competing parties or by political superiors. But at times internal dissent can become so strained that work production slows and the mission of the unit becomes jeopardized.

Line professionals, who fall just below the level of the senior elites, actually carry out the day-to-day functions of the public agency. Whereas a few dozen three- and four-star generals compose the army's top professional elite, more than 200,000 army officers from second lieutenants to generals direct much of the real work of the army in a wide variety of combat and noncombat jobs. Some, given their West Point training and combat duties in the infantry, armor, or artillery (combat sections that are considered "ideal" rungs in the ladder to the level of the elite) may become part of the professional elite; others in the line may have neither the interest nor the proper backgrounds to attain those high level assignments. The line officers are essentially the "doing" and "implementing" functionaries of bureaucracy and are most directly associated with the central missions of an agency.

Staff professionals in public agencies include a wide assortment of specialists and technical assistants who have unique and specialized expertise that may not be directly connected with the central tasks of the agency but are nonetheless critical to carrying out its assigned functions. Today almost every public bureaucracy employs a wide array of these individuals. They assume the critical advisory roles within an agency and in some government offices also frequently assume large and powerful policy roles, even though they are not directly in either the line or the elite ranks. In every federal department, the legal counsels, for example, not only can command high salaries, large staffs, exemptions from civil service hiring rules, and the ear of the top brass in the agency, but also frequently exercise enormous yet quiet influence over central policies of an agency through knowledge and expertise in the law (and often this advice is quite conservative in nature—more "don'ts" than "dos"). The top political and professional cadre yield to such legal policy advice on technical matters because no one else can supply this knowledge (or if the advice is purchased at high cost from outside law firms). One only need attend a city council or county board of supervisors' meeting to watch the frequency with which elected members turn to legal counsel for assistance or to view federal organization charts to discover the strategic positions legal counsels occupy in most departments.

Administrative professionals comprise an assortment of budget officials; program officers; planning personnel; and finance, purchasing, auditing, and supply officials found in every public organization (the G-1 through G-5 jobs in the U.S. military). These men and women are critical to the activities of the agency because they essentially serve as "the directing brain" of the organization ("the directing brain" is Elihu Root's name for this group in his 1902 proposal for the creation of a general staff in the U.S. Army, which was a pattern copied by other public agencies and business corporations). In larger organizations some of these slots are temporarily held by line professionals, but many are filled by permanent careerists from emerging professional groups, such as budgeting, personnel, and purchasing specialists. While these individuals do not as yet rank as full-fledged professionals, they are increasingly taking on all the trappings of professionals, having their own associations, journals, "ideal career tracks," and

educational requirements. Some even command higher salaries and status than their professional superiors. Municipal budget officers, for example, today are sometimes paid higher salaries than their bosses, city managers, or chief administrative officers, because of their critical budget and finance expertise in municipal decision-making processes.

In the uncertain environment within which agencies must operate, staff professionals must be adaptive and inventive in coping with the changing needs of their agencies. Much of their work is simply "fire-fighting" in order to maintain their structure amid turbulence, but much also is directed at thinking about the future of the organization, even if this planning is only incrementally achieved through short-term budgets, ad hoc personnel recruitment and selection, and partial programmatic design or redesign.

Finally, *paraprofessionals* make up another group increasingly seen within public agencies. These people receive substantially lower remunerative rewards for their work, although many units of government simply could not perform their assigned tasks without them. Many of these "paras" aspire to becoming full-fledged professionals in the field and use the experience as apprenticeship training. Others see this line of work as a rewarding lifetime career and seek no higher positions. From the standpoint of government, however, these workers are taking on increasing responsibility in various offices because of the rising costs of hiring fully qualified professionals. In other words, using paras is an effective governmental strategy for keeping down rapidly escalating personnel costs. In many cases paras perform the work as well as, if not better than, their highly paid counterparts. In this respect, their primary roles inside public organizations may well be an important economic function.

On the whole, what can be said about the influence of all the professional subsystems upon the activities and outputs of public bureaucratic institutions?

First and foremost, they are essential to the performance of the central missions of virtually every public agency. They define its mission, decide how it should be accomplished and who should accomplish it, as well as when it should be accomplished and where.

Second, by comparison with top-level political appointees, professionals by and large have longevity within agencies, thus giving them an enormous edge in the policy-making processes.

Third, professionals are not a single, unified group. They are part of a well-established pecking order, from elites down to "paras," that is based on education, skills, seniority, levels of responsibility, and general competence and experience. Elites occupy the highest level of policy-making roles; line professionals shape actions mainly through implementation practices; staff professionals fill advisory roles; administrative professionals prepare and plan tasks; and paraprofessionals carry out lower-level and lower-cost work.

Fourth, continuing political strength and popular support of professionals ultimately rest upon their recognized expertise and competence as well as on their ability to exercise these skills in a regular, uniform manner in the public interest. The widespread popularity of city-manager government rests fundamentally on its ability to apply systematic expertise to urban issues at the local level. Since expertise is professionals' stock in trade and is a source of authority and of legitimacy within government, a great deal of their efforts are directed at higher education and improving professionals' reputation for competence and application of knowledge. Professionals look to institutions of higher learning to sustain and enrich their knowledge base through training programs that give the professionals their credentials, and nurture the fundamental ethos and values of the profession. If political appointees draw support from their elected chiefs, professionals in government conversely derive their legitimacy from expertise acquired through higher education. The content and perspectives of these sources of learning influence the long-term priorities and fundamental value of professions. Hence, professions pay enormous attention to the shaping of professional education programs, examinations, accreditation, and licensing processes that help to determine the nature and content of professional work, as well as the knowledge and skill it requires.

Fifth, professionals influence policies not only by contributing a substantial share of the public work force and its top leadership cadre but also by moving upward and outward beyond the contours of their roles within agencies. As noted in the discussion of political appointees, they frequently assume temporary assignments at this level. Similarly, the influence of professionals is moving increasingly outward into legislative staff assignments or related nonprofit or business firms that directly and indirectly influence the course of bureaucratic policies.

Finally, the most serious tensions and conflicts within public organizations are generally hidden from view, since they arise mainly from policy disputes *between* clusters of key professionals and not as much from disputes between professional elites and political superiors. Many top political appointees today look highly professional, indeed *are drawn* from professional cadres, thus the tensions between political appointees and careerists are not as sharp and long-term compared to those *between* professional groups. Fights between the army, navy, and air force over defense appropriations and priorities are a permanent part of the Washington landscape, but it is within these professional service battles that defense policies for DoD develop. Likewise, the typical controversies that occur at the grass roots between police and firefighters over annual budget appropriations, length of work day, and salary increases figure equally prominently in determining the directions of local public safety policies.

The General Civil Service Subsystem: Ladders of Bureaucratic Specialists, Generalists, and Workers

While bits and pieces of the "ideal professional model" are being incorporated gradually into the general civil service, the bulk of government personnel are members of civil service and do not share in the professional model. Civil service is founded on the merit system, whereby positions are assigned on the basis of open, competitive examinations (written and/or oral) and candidates are evaluated and ranked in relationship to particular task requirements of a specific job. Generally, selection is made from among the top three scorers. Unlike the professional subsystem, civil service has no progressive job planning or control by elites but has, rather, a laissez-faire approach in which each individual seeks out and designs his or her own path within the system. Advanced training may or may not be essential. Rank is inherent in the job, not the person. Meeting the specific task requirements of the job is what counts most in landing a slot in civil service. Status, in turn, is derived from the specific job. A GS-9 civil servant, for instance, is a GS-9 because he or she holds that slot. If the employee leaves it, he or she is no longer a GS-9, unlike an air force colonel, who is a colonel wherever he or she serves. In the professional subsystem, conversely, rank inheres in the person, not the job.

The civil service subsystem was grafted onto U.S. bureaucracy somewhat haphazardly almost a century after the creation of the Republic. Even today its "fit" into government seems somewhat awkward and unsure. For the most part, this uncertainty about its place in U.S. public bureaucracy is caused by, as many scholars have noted, the growth of the general civil service out of a reaction to the excesses of the nineteenth-century spoils system, in which employment in public service was based largely, though not entirely, upon party loyalty and political patronage. In other words, it was built on a negative moral reaction to what was perceived as "evil" rather than on a positive and deliberate design.

The story of its growth is long and complex. To sum it up, in the late 1860s and throughout the 1870s a small band of reformers waged aggressive moral and political campaigns on behalf of civil service reform and against incompetence, graft, favoritism, and partisanship within the public service. Merit, they argued, should be the basis of appointment. Substantially modeled on the English civil service system, which had been in operation for nearly a half-century and was adapted to special pragmatic U.S. needs and concerns, the Civil Service Act (Pendleton Act) was enacted in 1883 mainly as a national reaction to the shooting of President James Garfield by a political supporter who had been refused a small patronage post.[15]

Pendleton became the classic model for "good personnel practices" throughout the nation. Extended gradually through executive order to cover increasing percentages of federal workers, it was also copied almost word for word by numerous states and localities. Localities borrowed from it their basic structural arrangements and concepts of merit processes, such as notions of a nonpartisan commission appointed by the chief executive to oversee the system, requirements of open, competitive examinations, probationary period prior to tenure, strict provision against political interference within civil service activities, classification of positions, and equal pay for equal work.

On the state level, New York passed a civil service law the same year as the federal government, and Massachusetts passed one the following year. Much of the civil service movement came in fits and starts. Some states, like Texas, never adopted a civil service system, and others like Virginia, recently abandoned the system entirely. Municipalities likewise moved to develop civil service systems, and most large cities by 1940 had some kind of merit system in place. Counties, though, have remained more backward; relatively few have merit systems in place.

The impetus for adoption of state/local merit systems came from essentially three forces. One was local and state reform groups that saw "merit" as a method of improving economy and efficiency in government and ridding government of corrupt political machines; another was the federal government, which played a major role in the adoption of grassroots civil service systems. The Social Security Act of 1935 and its 1940 amendments required state and local government employees administering health, welfare, and employment programs funded by the federal government to be covered by merit systems. The Intergovernmental Personnel Act (IPA) of 1970 further spurred local merit system development through its various programs to upgrade public personnel systems and employee skills. Finally, Supreme Court decisions played a major role, especially in limiting patronage systems. In such cases as *Elrod v. Burns* (1976) and *Branti v. Finkel* (1980), the Court struck down patronage practices involving the firing of nonpolicy-making, nonconfidential employees.

The federal civil service work force has stayed fairly constant in size over the past forty years, but the local and state work force has grown, nearly tripling during the same period. In fact, the federal share of the public work force fell from 27.7 percent of the total in 1961 to 16.2 percent in 1992. Also, the distribution of the federal work force shows certain regional biases; a higher percentage (32 percent) is located in the South, compared to 17 percent of the total civilian work force.

Today, 91 percent of the federal civilian work force, or approximately 3 million workers, are covered under civil service personnel rules. While several structural and procedural adaptations over time have been added, such as the Civil Service Reform Act of 1978, its essential concepts of "merit," "open, competitive examinations," and "equal pay for equal work" remain intact. Patricia W. Ingraham and David H. Rosenbloom summed up the current status of "merit" on the federal level: "While there continues to be strong support for the fundamental principles of merit, dissatisfaction with and confusion about the current system is high." They cited the complexity of regulations, the lack of training and trust of agency personnel dealing with civil service provisions, the absence of a clear definition of "merit" or of guidance for achieving a quality work force as critical problems.[16]

Even though a considerable diversity in civil service laws is found across the United States, in those areas of the public service covered by its practices scholars have discovered several common characteristics: First, the U.S. civil servant is largely representative of the general population. Repeated studies have indicated that civil service members—unlike political appointees or upper-level professionals—are broadly reflective of the American people's education, income, social status, age, and geographic backgrounds. Though these representational attributes appear in the aggregate—that is, when the entire public service is viewed statistically—they tend to break down in the various particular units or levels of government. Women are predominant in the bottom ranks as well as in certain fields such as nursing and teaching but are small minorities in police, fire, or other traditionally male occupational roles. Blacks and other minorities have made impressive gains in recent years in all areas of the public service, but the upper ranks still tend to be heavily representative of white males.

Members of the general civil service subsystem generally lack the cohesiveness and unity found among professionals. When asked what she or he does, the typical bureaucrat will say, "I work at the Office of Education" or "I'm with the County Sheriff's Department." Few are likely to see themselves in broader terms and to say, "I'm a bureaucrat" or "I work for the civil service." Whether because of the pejorative connotations attached to government work or the more personal attachment to a particular assigned task, most bureaucrats lack common ties with government as a whole or with the broad *public orientation* of their work. This phenomenon no doubt exists in the private sector as well, where few business people see themselves as dedicated to the free market, but rather perceive themselves as real estate agents, auto body repairmen, or retail sales clerks. Most are like civil servants, who identify with the agency or skill at which they work or with the people with whom they work. The grand design of the organization or the broad purposes of their occupation generally elude their interests or understanding.

This lack of common ties to the broad aspects and purposes of government may in large part be caused by the general lack of mobility within the civil service. In theory, the civil service subsystem provides for open, competitive exams that permit advancement into every level or part of government (though restricted to particular federal, state, or local jurisdictions). In practice, however, most civil servants spend their working lives within one agency. Eugene B. MacGregor, Jr., who studied the mobility of civil servants at the GS-14 level and above, discovered an average of seventeen to twenty-five years of service in the same agency or department.[17] Civil servants' depth of policy understanding, long-term views of issues, and particular expertise in an agency is therefore unmatched by comparison with those of transitory political appointees, who last in a post a mere twenty-two months at the federal level. Their longevity in an agency, expertise, sheer numbers, and longer time perspectives also make civil servants the core of modern bureaucracy.

So far, this discussion has pointed up several salient features of the civil service subsystem—its representational attributes as a whole, yet its uniquely unrepresentative elements in agencies or levels within the hierarchy: its lack of cohesiveness; its absence of mobility; its emphasis on rank inherent in the job; its diversity of jobs; the long-term career perspectives of its members; and its function as "the reservoir" of government expertise. Given these attributes, it is especially difficult to generalize about its influence on "bureaucratic outputs." As one veteran of government service says, "Civil servants don't really have mutual bonds or ties. There's nothing in particular in common except that these are people who know all the angles about how government works."[18]

Such seasoned cynicism, however, may obscure some of this subsystem's fundamental influences on bureaucratic activities. For one thing, as has already been emphasized, civil servants generally take the longer view of issues, problems, events, and actions, at least by comparison with political appointees (though they share this attribute with professional careerists). Their tenured positions make them somewhat more immune to the need for "quick fixes" or "instant results," compared with their politically driven bosses, who often see no further than the next election. For the most part, permanent bureaucrats realize that much that passes for "instant success" is ephemeral and that any real achievements in government come only in the long haul, after much struggle and persistence. Their view of what constitutes real, enduring change is therefore fundamentally different from the view of political appointees and leads to a much more realistic, conservative approach based upon recognition of the worth of incrementalism; namely that small steps taken over a long period of time will lead to permanent, solid achievements. This strategy of gradualism can be the source of exasperation and deep conflicts between civil servants and endless successions of political appointees, who normally want government to accomplish this or that task immediately, even yesterday. In particular, appointees in recent administrations who are fired up to make speedy changes and who have had little exposure to the realities of government find this philosophy of incrementalism frustrating. It quickly becomes the butt of their jokes about those "damn bureaucrats." These negative references symbolize the radically different time zones within which each subsystem operates. Their different "internal clocks" influence the basically different approaches to handling issues.

Also unlike political appointees, civil servants are restrained by the Hatch Act, and various "little Hatch Acts" that operate on state and local levels, from going public with their political opinions or policy views. Occasionally it may happen that dissent leaks out in the press, but active campaigning is expressly forbidden by law. Hence, civil servants generally must be discreet and work behind the scenes in dealing with the development, formulation, and implementation of policy questions. They realize that a head-on frontal assault on policy issues will only get them into needless political controversy. Experience over the years has taught them that those sorts of political firestorms are to be avoided at all costs; they waste time and energy and lead to few tangible results. As a result, on the whole they favor quiet discretion in handling problems.

This cautious attitude comes not merely from pragmatism in effecting programmatic change but also from fear about long-term personal survival. In a world of endlessly shifting political appointees, the civil servant, at least in the top ranks, knows quite well that job security depends on his or her not being too closely allied with any one political party, else he or she become "politically tainted" and shunned by the next group taking office. The desire to stay neutral from the political appointee subsystem and to work quietly from the inside, at least for most top-level civil servants, springs from a very fundamental interest in long-term survival.

Unlike the professional careerist, on the other hand, the general civil servant operates *without* the control of a professional elite and without an extensive mutual support network of peers with status in the subsystem. In the civil service subsystem, every employee charts his or her own way through the bureaucracy. The hazards are many and the minefields often hard to locate. Thus much of their time is spent networking outward and downward into the bureaucracy, building personal bridges and personal friendships inside and outside agencies in order to develop the myriad horizontal and vertical contacts that are necessary for gaining information, accurately assessing the landscape, and making alliances in this hazardous, uncertain, and lonely bureaucratic world.

These clusters of civil servants influence public policies through the social networks they have established over long periods, running in strange and uncharted pathways that run through an agency and outside into other unlikely agencies and even beyond government where information is swapped informally and ideas are traded within social contexts. When presidents complain about government leaking like a sieve, this is why. The informal group, as Elton Mayo and the Hawthorne researchers discovered long ago, operates with a similar potency in government and in business settings, though it is well hidden in the civil service.

What challenges are facing the civil service subsystem as a whole? Three significant task force reports have appeared in recent years examining civil service performance and making numerous recommendations for reform: *Civil Service 2000,*[19] a 1988 study prepared by the Hudson Institute on the federal public service; also at the federal level, *Leadership for America,*[20] a 1989 privately sponsored review, called "The Volcker Commission" in honor of its chair, former Federal Reserve chairman Paul A. Volcker; and at the state and local levels, *Hard Truths/Tough Choices,*[21] a 1993 "Winter Commission" report, named for its chair, former Governor William F. Winter. These studies drew upon some of the most talented expertise from a wide cross section of business, nonprofit, and government to analyze many of the present problems facing America's public service. Collectively, they offered numerous suggestions for improvement. While these reports are too complicated to be summarized in any concise way, overall they found no simple solutions for reforming civil service subsystems, but each one stressed important issues needing attention:

1. *Poor public image:* The Volcker Commission placed the first priority on dealing with the poor public image of the federal civil service. The report repeatedly cited data and examples of the low esteem that Americans had for public service. These negative perceptions led, in the Commission's thinking, to a general distrust of government and to its broader incapacity to function effectively and recruit capable candidates to serve in government. The Commission

surveyed, for example, 403 of the "best and brightest" college graduates who accepted employment and found only 16 percent chose positions in government (and half of those who selected public employment were graduates of public administration programs). Big businesses, small businesses, and academic institutions were preferred by a wide margin, leading to the conclusion that "the public service cannot compete for top graduates." Thus, this report laid stress upon targeting the recruitment of a better pool of candidates.

2. *Competence crisis:* Similarly, the Hudson Institute study's key findings and recommendations centered upon the "competency crisis" facing the federal public service. *Civil Service 2000* argued that there was a rising need for "a highly educated-skilled work force," yet attracting these workers in the 1990s "will become much more difficult." Recruitment is a problem, especially in high-wage locales such as New York City and in those top civil service grades, above GS-9, in which "the gap between top federal personnel civil service salaries and comparable private salaries was an average of 24 percent."[22]

3. *Removing barriers to a high performance work force:* On the state and local levels, the Winter Commission Report, by contrast, focused on the problems of "the highly fragmented local structures that impeded executive leadership and performance of the grassroots civil service systems." At the outset of the Winter Report, the priority was to give leaders the authority to act. Put them in charge of lean, responsive agencies. Hire and nurture knowledgeable, motivated employees and give them the freedom to innovate in accomplishing the agencies' missions. Engage citizens in the business of government, while at the same time encouraging them to be partners in problemsolving.

   The report emphasized that achieving such reforms will "hardly be painless or easy. Reforms may require constitutional amendments, new legislations, changes in rules and regulations, and restructuring many agencies and departments. Accomplishment of many of the changes may require political leaders and civic groups to mount aggressive campaigns."

The Unionized Subsystem: Cadres of Workers Inside Bureaucracy

Most texts on government or bureaucracy ignore an important policy-making subsystem of public agencies that over the past three decades has grown rapidly into one of the most potent forces determining the internal directions and external outputs of bureaucracy: namely, unionized public service workers. As David Stanley observes, "A whole new ball game has started since unions in the public sector have begun to operate"[23] Like the aforementioned subsystems, unionization has increasingly gained its own share of power and a role in shaping the inner dynamics of public bureaucracy—that is, its rules, regulations, operating procedures, and structural relationships. Unions also exercise external controls over bureaucratic performance and influence upon society—that is, its productivity, enforcement practices, political relationships, and policy agendas.

The formal institutional structure of public sector collective bargaining is essentially derived from the private sector, and Joel Douglas writes: "The present Public Service Labor Relations (PSLR) . . . legislative and legal framework is based on an adversarial relationship rooted in the National Labor Relations Act (NLRA) and is structured on private sector principles. These include narrow unit determination requirements, bargaining agent election procedures, exclusive union representation, a series of unfair labor and employment practices, and a decentralized bargaining structure. Reliance on the private sector model was successful in developing the (PSLR) legal framework in which employees, subject to restrictions, most notably the anti-strike ban, negotiate with government the terms and conditions of employment. Although the private and public sectors contain many similarities, distinct difference is noted in the public sector, since the government is both employer and regulator at the bargaining table. Other differences include the private

sector's reliance on market forces, distributive bargaining and the use of strikes and lockouts."[24]

Much like the professional careerist and civil service subsystems, the union subsystem was not a planned innovation. It just grew inside government, evolving particularly rapidly since the 1960s. As Frederick C. Mosher remarked, "The founders of the civil service did not bargain on collective bargaining."[25] If the Pendleton Act was the landmark piece of legislation creating the civil service, the explosion of union involvement within bureaucracy did not begin in earnest until John F. Kennedy signed Executive Orders 10987 and 10988 in 1962. These two orders for the first time gave unions the right to bargain collectively with federal management representatives on a limited range of items. They stimulated similar measures in numerous states and localities throughout the 1960s and 1970s. And while the unionization movement in government has slowed perceptibly during the 1980s because of cutbacks and the weakening of unions generally, the collective bargaining processes now in place are based largely upon legislation of the 1960s and 1970s and are accepted institutional practices within many jurisdictions throughout the United States.

Though the phenomenon of significant union influence over the activities of public bureaucracy is relatively new, some deep pockets of union activity date from the turn of the century. Indeed, in 1912 the Lloyd-La Follette Act gave federal workers the right to unionize, and for a number of years several large unions represented most of the U.S. postal employees as well as employees in certain fields of civilian defense and in several government corporations such as the Tennessee Valley Authority. States and localities with large urban and industrial populations, which had traditionally strong private sector unions, also saw unionization in limited areas of their public bureaucracies, such as in New York, Michigan, and California. Yet these public service unions were, for the most part, economically weak, poorly organized, and had few legal rights to bargain collectively with representatives from the agency's management.

Why did the 1960s usher in a new era of union influence inside government? The historical reasons are still not clear. Certainly the election of John F. Kennedy in 1960 was a critical factor. Throughout Kennedy's campaign he pledged union recognition and collective bargaining at the federal level. Shortly after his election, he appointed a task force headed by Arthur Goldberg to make recommendations on how to handle union-management relations within government. In turn, this task force study led to the two executive orders just cited. But other factors were also at work behind the scenes. Statistics show that private sector unionization reached it high point in 1955 with one-fourth of the national work force belonging to unions. This percentage of national union membership has been declining gradually ever since (now standing at 14.2 percent). With the "drying up," so to speak, of the private sector, major union leaders as early as the 1950s recognized that the public service was the last major untapped pool of nonunionized workers, and so they pressed their demands on Kennedy and subsequent administrations for the extension of union rights and prerogatives within this governmental sector. The American Federation of State, County and Municipal Employees (AFSCME) and other groups were instrumental in lobbying state legislatures for the right to organize and bargain collectively with state and local jurisdictions on behalf of public workers. Virtually all states permit some form of collective bargaining, yet today six states prohibit collective bargaining and public employees joining unions, and forbid recognition of unions in government.

Much of the union intrusion into the ranks of bureaucracy resulted from a more tolerant, even perhaps permissive, public attitude toward unions in government. By the 1960s unions were no longer considered entirely "evil" and antithetical to the public interest. No doubt, very real economic forces were at work as well. The promises of higher paychecks, shorter work weeks, and better working conditions lured many government workers, principally blue collar employees but increasing numbers of white collar employees as well, into public service unions. Certainly the postal strike of 1970 and the New York City transit strike of 1966—two early key disputes—stimulated union membership. Finally, union growth was fostered by legislation such as the Civil Service Reform Act of 1978, which formalized union-management collective bargaining procedures by federal statute.

Likewise, on the local level, in New York State, representatives of the Civil Service Employees Association had been meeting with management representatives since the early 1900s, but the Taylor Law was established by statute's formal collective bargaining arrangement for state and union representatives in 1967. In a few states, such as Massachusetts, union membership became a requirement for attaining a public job. In order for workers to have a job and a voice that would represent them at the bargaining table and involve them in the determination of their agency's activities, they joined public employee unions.

Whatever the causes of growth—and there are undoubtedly many—in contrast to the private sector, a sporadic but continuous climb in union strength has been apparent within public organizations. Today 35.9 percent of all federal civilian employees belong to unions (not including the 600,000 postal workers, 90 percent of whom are unionized); 34.3 percent of state and local workers are union members. Levels of unionization, however, range significantly from agency to agency and locale to locale. Thus, in practice the political clout of union members inside bureaucracy varies considerably. The postal service, made up largely of blue collar workers, is almost entirely unionized, whereas the employees of the Federal Reserve Board and the State Department are mainly white collar professionals, largely (though not altogether) untouched by unions. Urban industrial states and large metropolitan communities are heavily unionized, and public unions play major policy-making roles within their various public bureaucracies. On the other hand, rural, poorer, and less-industrialized regions contain fewer union members, who therefore have less policy involvement in their regions of the public sector. Some functional areas, such as education, transportation, and refuse collection, show a much higher level of union activity than other fields.

Today there are three prominent and powerful public service unions (and numerous lesser ones) that speak for many, though certainly not all, public employees: the American Federation of State, County and Municipal Employees, the American Federation of Government Employees (AFGE), and the American Federation of Teachers (AFT). The National Education Association is technically *not* a union but rather a professional association of primary and secondary schoolteachers, yet it looks and acts like a union, often aggressively by representing its rank and file in collective bargaining negotiations in various school districts across the country. NEA became especially active within the Democratic party, substantially assisting President Jimmy Carter's election in 1976 and his bid for reelection in 1980. AFSCME, AFT, and AFGE have grown rapidly in power and prominence within the AFL-CIO labor council over the last decades, extending their activism well beyond traditional union concerns into national political circles of the Democratic party by aiding the party financially as well as through considerable campaign manpower. Public service unions are active at the state and local levels as well, particularly where there are large concentrations of public workers (such as in state or county capitals) and strong Democratic party organizations.

However, the actual conduct of negotiations between unions and management within government—the principal source of union inputs into bureaucracy—remains a highly decentralized process, with local representatives of public employee unions conducting agency-by-agency or local jurisdiction-by-jurisdiction negotiated agreements. In other words, while the public employee unions have grown into the "big three" (or four, depending on how one counts NEA), no one person or group speaks for "the entire management side" of government. Separate bargains must be made with roughly 80,000 governmental jurisdictions in the United States and with many more "suborganizational" units within these separate governments that recognize the union right of negotiation. Not only is the process decentralized, but who actually speaks for the employers or management is also a highly complex and unsettled issue in many areas. Some governments use the civil service as spokescommission for management (Office of Personnel Management at the federal level); others have teams of top-level executives from *both* legislature and bureaucracy that speak for management. Highly diverse institutional arrangements for representation and the conducting of the actual negotiations are found across the United States, largely because the process still remains somewhat new, experimental, and undeveloped.

Equally unsettled is the scope of the bargaining that is allowed. In most jurisdictions, wages and hours—the two principal bargaining concerns in private industry—are legislatively determined and beyond the scope of public sector negotiations. These negotiations, therefore, mostly center on working conditions, grievance procedures, and other less major subjects. But even here, working conditions, grievance procedures, and "fringes" are often precisely prescribed by legislation, leaving little room for negotiations, even over these seemingly mundane matters. Further, laws on the books often stack the deck in management's favor. For example, according to the 1978 Civil Service Reform Act (CSR), management officials are authorized "to determine the mission, budget, organization, number of employees, and internal security practices of an agency . . . to hire, assign, direct, lay off and retain employees . . . or to suspend, remove, reduce in grade or pay, or take other disciplinary action."[26] In short, the CSR's tilt clearly favors management prerogatives over union rights, although through court decisions and legislative amendments unions have chipped away at these restrictions.

Another important condition of the union subsystem in government is that the actual means for enforcing their views at the bargaining table remain drastically restricted because of the ban on strikes by public employees at every level of government. The basic weapon used by private sector unions to enforce their demands in negotiations is illegal at the federal and many state and local settings, though thirteen states allow some or all public employees the right to strike. As Theodore Kheel writes, "The strike enables employees through their representatives to participate in the decisions setting wages, hours and working conditions. In the absence of the right to strike, an alternative system of determination is required when negotiating parties reach an impasse."[27] However, no such technique has yet been found for breaking public sector impasses. In reality, however, whether or not public employees are legally permitted to strike, strikes do occur in the public sector; sometimes they are called "the blue flu" or "sick-outs," or they are actual walk-outs. Public unions know very well how to play the inside political game. During negotiations they regularly make "end runs" around management to outside supporters, such as sympathetic legislators on city councils, in state assemblies, or in Congress. These potent friends of public unions frequently enable them to cut deals and achieve their priorities through the back door, thus undercutting management's position or dividing it so badly that its official bargaining position crumbles.

How then can the union subsystem's influence over policy outputs in bureaucracy be summarized vis-à-vis the other previously mentioned bureaucratic subsystems?

The first and perhaps the most significant aspect of union involvement with what happens inside U.S. bureaucracy is its variety. Some unions strive for nothing less than complete control from top to bottom of public bureaucracy. They want the options to select a public agency's top-ranking political cadre; to determine its internal structural arrangements, procedures, and rules as well as its methods of promotion, hiring, and firing; to specify its relations with other external groups; and most of all to call the shots as to what the agency will or will not do for the public. In general, those agencies are characterized by weak political executive oversight, an absence of a controlling professional elite, a strongly unionized rank and file, a degree of institutional autonomy, and traditions of union assertiveness, such as in the federal postal system and in large "weak-mayor" cities such as New York and San Francisco, where public service unions exert powerful long-term influence. At the other extreme, public sector unions are dormant or ineffective in right-to-work states, where public sector unions are outlawed entirely, and in agencies in the tight grip of professionals (strong city manager communities or the military) or under strong, united antiunion political executive leadership. Most situations in which unions operate, though, are at neither extreme, and so unions end up jockeying with other internal bureaucratic subsystems—political appointees, professionals, and civil servants—for varying degrees of autonomy and control over bureaucratic policies and outputs.

Second, the growth and intrusion of unions within bureaucracy have added new levels of complexities and complications to an already complex bureaucratic world. Whether such complexification of government has slowed down its institutional outputs or made it more productive is unclear and unmeasured, but it is apparent in many instances that new personnel and attendant rules and procedures have been added to administer this new subsystem and that relationships between labor and management have therefore become more formal and legalistic.

Third, in cases where the union subsystem has matured fully within public bureaucracies but has not become the dominant subsystem, it has brought with it new bipartisanship management practices. Collective bargaining forces management to sit down at regular intervals with union representatives to discuss grievances, working conditions, and other matters of concern to both parties.

Fourth, in many cases public service unions have won positive reforms that have long been advocated by public administration specialists to enhance, on the whole, the cause of "good government," such as better wages, working conditions, training programs and staffing levels, and organizational reforms promoting institutional productivity.

Finally, the real loser with the advent of public service unions into the internal dynamics of bureaucratic policy making has probably been the underlying philosophy and practices of the century-old civil service subsystem. Concepts such as merit selection, open competitive exams, non-partisan civil service boards, and "color blind" promotions based upon individual competence have yielded in many areas to union concerns about seniority, "closed shop" union membership, and neutral third-party mediation of disputes by those outside civil service. Indeed, in many instances the old neutral civil service commission has been replaced by highly partisan and political oversight agencies such as the Office of Personnel Management at the federal level. This is not to argue that the civil service subsystem will soon fade into a distant memory and its controlling procedures, rules, and personnel become history. To the contrary, it is alive and well today in many bureaucratic institutions, but it certainly has changed, or given ground to the influx of unionization over the last three decades inside the public service. In several cases as well, due to the fiscal constraints of recent years, we have witnessed considerable union cooperation with civil service managers for the self-interest of each party.[28]

Contract Employment: The Newest, Fastest-Growing Bureaucratic Subsystem

At the federal, state, and local levels, public agencies up to roughly 1950 did most, if not all, of the tasks assigned to them in-house, using their own personnel and resources and the facilities allocated by legislatures and political executives. Hence much of the theory of bureaucracy, as well as the managerial approaches to public enterprise put forward by public administration experts and scholars, were based upon assumptions, increasingly erroneous, that bureaucracies controlled their own operations, did their assigned work inside, with neat, clear lines of managerial control running from top political executives down to the workers who actually carried out the agency's assigned missions.

The reality of internal bureaucratic life today, however, is far different. In the 1990s the federal budget tells another story about how government agencies actually function. Roughly 14 percent of the national budget goes for its own internal personnel services and benefits (excluding pensions). This means that only slightly more than one-eighth of the total federal budget is spent on directing activities that the government performs itself, such as law enforcement, food and drug regulation, forestry service, air traffic control, and so on. However, the category of "other contractual services" indicates that roughly 16 percent of the total annual operating budget is spent for sundry activities performed by others who are contracted to render services from *outside* the federal bureaucracy.

In other words, close to 60 percent of the total obligation for goods and services produced by the federal government is contracted out (excluding funds for grants-in-aid to states and localities, direct transfer payments to individuals, debt servicing, and so on). The percentages run much higher for some agencies,

such as NASA and the Department of Energy, which have traditionally contracted out most of their work. The development of most major weapons systems is contracted out to private businesses, as is the construction of large capital projects such as dams, roads, bridges, and sewer systems. Three-fourths of research and development funding at the federal level is contracted out to universities, think tanks, consultants, and private industry.

At the state and local levels there are no comparable figures on the levels of contracting-out by governmental bureaucracy, though they probably mirror the federal pattern, with some communities going to extremes, such as Lakewood, California (originators of the Lakewood Plan), which contracts out all its municipal functions, including police protection. City Hall consists of little more than a city manager and a secretary, who principally act as contract-managers for the city council. While most localities do not go to that extreme degree of contracting for municipal services, most do draw upon private vendors and business enterprises in many ways for the construction of capital projects as well as for a variety of ongoing services, such as data collection, medical facilities, computer services, refuse disposal, as well as for accounting, auditing, and payroll functions. Today, most government agencies house varying mixes of full-time employees and temporary or long-term contract employees working side by side. The regular public employees and contractual employees are often difficult to differentiate from one another.

The story of the rise of contract labor inside bureaucracy is a complicated one. Early in the history of the U.S. government, mail delivery and canal projects were contracted out. However, until 1950 the use and application of contractual arrangements were drastically limited in most public agencies. All this changed, with the hot and cold war demands of the postwar era, when government increasingly needed highly skilled scientific and engineering talent from universities, private enterprises, and consulting firms to conceptualize, build, and implement numerous weapons programs. The Rand Corporation and the National Science Foundation were created by the federal government as outside sources for accomplishing in-house missions of DoD.

The growth of contracting-out for government services since then has been unprecedented in size, scope, and intensity. Government has been driven into contracting willy-nilly in so many fields because it has been asked to perform greater numbers of tasks of ever-greater complexity within shorter time frames, tasks for which it has neither the expertise nor the capacity to acquire it on a short-term basis. At the state and local levels, contractual employment accelerated in the 1970s, 1980s, and 1990s as a device for accomplishing programmatic goals while avoiding rising costs of hiring permanent civil servants (today a permanent civil servant costs government roughly twice the worker's *actual* salary, largely because of "hidden fringes" such as retirement programs and health and other benefit packages). Contracting-out is also a method of doing complex work in which states and localities have little expertise. But it has broad implications.

Some effects on public agencies and their outputs are fairly obvious. First, the growth of the contractual subsystem makes it increasingly hard to tell where government bureaucracy begins and ends. Is the permanent public agency that relies on the expertise of a single outside contractor *really* independent of that outside private enterprise? Or is the private contractor who relies on a public bureaucracy for all or most of his annual income *really* private, and not merely an extension of a public bureaucracy? Increasingly, the worlds separating government agencies and private sector businesses, universities, and consulting firms are dissolving into an area where boundaries overlap or are unclear and difficult to define.

What is clear, however, is that these "outside" groups perform much of the bureaucratic work of government. If their personnel were counted as government employees, the size of government bureaucracy would probably be twice as large as it is. Contracting-out, then, enables politicians to gain services for their constituents *and then* claim that they have "kept the lid on government personnel costs." Such a claim is clearly untrue and leads to further confusion—and deception—about the realities of the size and true nature of government.

Second, some sectors of government have clearly become "captives" of their contractors. The purveyors of many large DoD weapons systems, such as Hughes, Boeing, Rockwell, and McDonald Douglas, not only design and develop these multibillion dollar, multi-year systems but by proposing new weapons systems are also actively involved in establishing DoD and individual service priorities, budget requirements, personnel needs, and even the broad global strategic priorities of U.S. defense policy. And once the weapons are sold, these firms become the sole-source suppliers virtually dictating the costs—often overrun by huge amounts—to the contracting agency. Top executives move back and forth with ease between these firms and top policy-making posts within DoD. Harold Brown (DoD secretary under President Carter), William C. Foster (Brown's research and development specialist), Caspar Weinberger (a former DoD secretary under President Reagan), and John Lehmann (Weinberger's former secretary of the navy), and William J. Perry (President Clinton's secretary of defense) are all products of the contract world surrounding DoD. This is not meant to suggest that these individuals or others who serve "in-and-out" at high DoD policy-making levels have acted unethically or dishonestly; it simply means that their backgrounds and skills are utilized in *both* government and business at various managerial and staff levels and that they therefore significantly influence policies and administration in *both* sectors.

Another effect of the increasing rise and reliance upon the contractual subsystem within public bureaucracy is that there is less and less use for traditional bureaucratic techniques, such as standard in-house top-down rules, for direction and control of personnel and resources. More emphasis is now placed upon contract negotiations, formal agreements, legal sanctions, economic rewards and penalties for inducing compliance by contractors, and auditing and management information systems for "tracking" completion dates. All these procedures are essential for quality control and to make the contractors and subcontractors perform their services according to schedule. Bureaucrats at all levels increasingly are becoming contract managers as opposed to fulfilling their traditional line management roles.

Also, as suggested before, with the growing numbers of public personnel "off the books" because of their nontenured status, the traditional sorts of personnel work rules, personnel oversight controls, and procedures governing employee behavior have diminished in importance. Thus the problems of imposing public accountability on contract workers grow as the numbers of contract agents and subcontractors grow. Proper policy performance and implementation in regard to legality, honesty, competence, correctness of action, and effective completion of projects become increasingly difficult to ensure as the number of private businesses, universities, and others who perform the work of public agencies increases. Recent leaks of highly sensitive national security information by Hughes employees and the massive fraud cases of General Electric subcontractors working on various navy projects illustrate these enormous problems of public accountability and oversight. Indeed, *should* bureaucracy impose its public standards of accountability on such "private" groups and citizens? The difficult and uncharted ethical dimensions of the problems loom large. Finally, as the pressures of the contractual subsystem force new commitments and expenditures of funds years ahead of time, contractual arrangements become legally and politically "untouchable." As many scholars and budget experts now observe, not only is the federal budget out of control but also no one even knows how much is really being spent annually, largely because of the pressures of the growing contractual subsystem. Many contractors simply operate independently of the budget process—off the books and out of sight—developing independent accounting, auditing, and budgeting systems along with separate personnel rules, regulations, and procedures that are well beyond public scrutiny and oversight mechanisms.

Notes

1. Hugh Heclo, *A Government of Strangers* (Washington, DC: Brookings Institution, 1977), p. 103.
2. These characteristics of political appointees have been true for some time. See David T. Stanley, Dean E. Mann, and Jameson W. Doig, *Men Who Govern* (Washington, DC: Brookings Institution, 1967).
3. For data on the backgrounds of city managers that tend to show a high degree of heterogeneity, read Richard J. Stillman II, "Local Public Management in Transition," *The Municipal Year Book 1982* (Washington, DC: International City Management Assoc., 1982), pp. 161–173.
4. Thomas P. Murphy, Donald E. Nuechterlein, and Ronald Stupak, *Inside Bureaucracy: The View from the Assistant Secretary's Desk* (Boulder: Westview Press, 1978).
5. Frederick C. Mosher, *Democracy and the Public Service,* 2nd ed. (New York: Oxford University Press, 1982), p. 183.
6. Frank P. Sherwood and L. J. Breyer, "Executive Personnel Systems in States," *Public Administration Review* 47 (Sept./Oct. 1987): 410f.
7. Deborah D. Roberts, "The Governor as Leader: Strengthening Public Service Through Executive Leadership," in Frank J. Thompson (ed.), *Revitalizing State and Local Public Service: Strengthening Performance, Accountability, and Citizen Confidence* (San Francisco, CA: Jossey-Bass, 1993), pp. 51–52.
8. See Samuel H. Beer's presidential address before the American Political Science Association, "Federalism, Nationalism and Democracy in America," *American Political Science Review* 72(1) (March 1978).
9. Zbigniew Brzezinski, *Between Two Ages: America's Role in the Technetronic Era* (New York: Viking, 1970); Don Price, *The Scientific Estate* (Cambridge: Harvard University Press, 1965); Daniel Bell, "Notes on the Post-Industrial Society," *Public Interest,* 6 (Winter 1967): 24–35; and Guy Benveniste, *The Politics of Expertise,* 2nd ed. (San Francisco: Jossey-Bass, 1983).
10. Mosher, *Democracy,* p. 142.
11. Robert D. Kaplan, "There Is No 'Middle East,' " *New York Times Magazine,* Feb. 20, 1994, pp. 42–43.
12. Robert Wiebe, *The Search for Order: 1877–1920* (New York: Hill and Wang, 1967), pp. 120–121.
13. Martha Derthick, *The Influence of Federal Grants: Public Assistance in Massachusetts*

(Cambridge, MA: Harvard University Press, 1970), p. 159.

14. David S. Arnold and Jeremy F. Plant, *Public Official Associations and State and Local Government: A Bridge across One Hundred Years* (Fairfax, VA: George Mason University Press, 1994), p. 59.

15. The best account of the development of civil service remains Paul P. Van Riper's *History of the United States Civil Service* (Evanston, IL: Row Peterson, 1958).

16. Patricia W. Ingraham and Donald F. Kettl, *Agenda for Excellence: Public Service in America* (Chatham, NY: Chatham House, 1993).

17. Eugene B. MacGregor, "Politics and Career Mobility of Civil Servants," *American Political Science Review* 68 (1974): 24.

18. As cited in Heclo, *Government,* p. 142.

19. The Hudson Institute, *Civil Service 2000* (Washington, DC: U.S. Office of Personnel Management, 1988).

20. Paul A. Volcker, chair, *Leadership for America: Rebuilding the Public Service* (Lexington, MA: Lexington Books, 1990).

21. William A. Winter, chair, *Hard Truths, Tough Choices: Agenda for State and Local Reform,* Winter Commission Report, (San Francisco: Jossey-Bass, 1993).

22. Kaplan, pp. 42–43.

23. David T. Stanley, *Managing Local Government under Union Pressure* (Washington, DC: Brookings Institution, 1972), p. 136.

24. Joel M. Douglas, "Public Sector Collective Bargaining in the 1900s," in Frederick S. Lane (ed.), *Current Issues in Public Administration,* 5th ed. (New York: St. Martin's Press, 1994), p. 261.

25. Frederick C. Mosher, *Democracy and the Public Service* (New York: Oxford University Press, 1968), p. 178.

26. PL 95-45, October 13, 1978, Section 7106.

27. As quoted in Harry H. Wellington and Ralph K. Winter, Jr., *The Union and the Cities* (Washington, DC: Brookings Institution, 1971), p. 30.

28. As Joel M. Douglas concludes, "Bilateralism has replaced unilateralism in the decision-making processes." In Douglas, "Public Sector Collective Bargaining in the 1990s," *op. cit.,* pp. 271–72.

CASE STUDY 7

Introduction

The five critical personnel subsystems discussed in the foregoing essay, those of political appointees, professional careerists, general civil service, unionized workers, and contract employees, are some of the most influential, for the various reasons outlined by the author. Though they do not operate in a vacuum as groups or as individuals, they closely interact with each other and their degree of cooperation or conflict decisively determines the extent of their influence, the sorts of issues they handle, and what they achieve—or fail to achieve—in their work.

Perhaps the following case, "The Decision to Go to War with Iraq" by Professor James Pfiffner of George Mason University, is the most recent illustration of the enormously vital role that political appointees and professionals play within modern American government, both in setting policy and in carrying it out. Here we can vividly see how politically elected and appointed officials, especially so-called neocons (neoconservatives who held top defense policy positions in the Bush Administration), contended with the pros from the military, foreign service, and intelligence agencies in defining the war policy agenda and its implementation, yet their actions and interrelationships were hardly neat or clear-cut, or at least as neat and clear-cut as the foregoing conceptual essay outlines. Indeed, the complexities and difficulties of these working relationships—especially under such difficult, high-pressure controversies involving war and peace, life and death—are fraught with fundamental conflicts and ethical dilemmas.

As you read this case, try to reflect on issues raised in the foregoing conceptual reading, such as:

Who were the key political appointees involved? How did their ideas evolve? Why were some involved and others excluded from planning for the Iraq War? Did this affect the choices that were made—namely, by who was included? And by who was excluded?

How did professional careerists and political appointees who opposed the war attempt to exercise influence and try to shape the critical choices about going to war? Who were they? Why did they fail, in your opinion?

Can you generalize from this case study about the role of professionals versus appointees, their power and influence, and their working relationships within American government today? As well as how in the modern global context, they profoundly shape "public purposes"?

The Decision to Go to War with Iraq

JAMES P. PFIFFNER

To understand how the United States decided to go to war with Iraq, one must go back to the Gulf War of 1991. When Saddam Hussein invaded Kuwait in 1990, President George H. W. Bush assembled a broad international coalition to confront Saddam and throw his troops out of Kuwait. After a buildup of nearly half a million troops in the area and an extended bombing campaign, U.S. armed forces and their allies were able to defeat the Iraqis within 100 hours.[1] As U.S. troops drove the Iraqis out of Kuwait, Bush made the decision not to slaughter the retreating Iraqi troops on the "highway of death" from Kuwait City back to Basra in Iraq. More important, the president decided not to invade and occupy Iraq. To have done so would have exceeded the U.N. mandate and would have moved well beyond the coalition's support and the U.S. military mission. Bush

This case study is an original contribution prepared for the eighth edition of this text by Professor James P. Pfiffner, School of Public Policy, George Mason University, Fairfax, Virginia.

and his Assistant for National Security Affairs, Brent Scowcroft, put it this way:

Trying to eliminate Saddam, extending the ground war into an occupation of Iraq, would have violated our guideline about not changing objectives in midstream, engaging in "mission creep," . . . We would have been forced to occupy Baghdad and, in effect, rule Iraq. The coalition would instantly have collapsed, the Arabs deserting it in anger and other allies pulling out as well. Under those circumstances, there was no viable "exit strategy" we could see. . . . Had we gone the invasion route, the United States could conceivably still be an occupying power in a bitterly hostile land.[2]

President George H. W. Bush's restraint in limiting the coalition's military victory to driving the Iraqi army out of Kuwait without completely destroying it and invading Iraq was to come under considerable criticism from a group of public figures and defense intellectuals known as neoconservatives (neocons).[3]

This loosely connected group of critics of U.S. defense policy believed that the decision not to remove Saddam Hussein was a profound mistake. The neocons organized "The Project for the New American Century" and published a "Statement of Principles" in 1997. The statement noted that the United States was the sole remaining superpower and advocated an assertive U.S. foreign policy and increased defense spending to "accept responsibility for America's unique role in preserving and extending an international order friendly to our security, our prosperity, and our principles."[4] In 1998 the organization wrote an open letter to President Clinton arguing that Saddam's Iraq was a major threat to the United States as well as a destabilizing force in the Middle East. They stated that U.S. national security strategy "should aim, above all, at the removal of Saddam Hussein's regime from power," which "means a willingness to undertake military action as diplomacy is clearly failing."[5] The letter was signed by, among others, Donald Rumsfeld, Paul Wolfowitz, and Richard Perle.

When George W. Bush became president in 2001, he appointed Rumsfeld to be Secretary of Defense and Wolfowitz to be his deputy. Other neocons also joined the administration; Perle became Chair of the Defense Policy Board, advisory to the Secretary of Defense; Douglas Feith, Undersecretary of Defense for Policy; Lewis ("Scooter") Libby, Chief of Staff to Vice President Cheney; Stephen Hadley, Deputy to National Security Advisor Condoleezza Rice; John Bolton, Undersecretary of State for Arms Control and International Security Affairs. Vice President Cheney was a strong ally in their hostility toward Iraq and shared their desire to use U.S. military power to topple Saddam.

For the first six months of the Bush administration, however, their arguments did not persuade President Bush. During his presidential campaign, Bush tended to favor disengagement from the rest of the world, compared to the Clinton administration. Bush believed that the U.S. had been too involved in the Middle East peace process, and he thought that the U.S. should reconsider its commitment to peacekeeping in the Balkans. He also rejected the Clinton administration's attempt to foster a reconciliation between North and South Korea. In commenting on foreign relations during the presidential debates, Bush said, "It really depends on how our nation conducts itself in foreign policy. If we're an arrogant nation, they'll resent us. If we're a humble nation, but strong, they'll welcome us."[6] With his support of increased military spending and reservations about an active foreign policy, Bush seemed to echo Theodore Roosevelt's advice to "speak softly but carry a big stick." All of this changed, however, after the terrorist attacks on September 11, 2001.

The Public Debate over War with Iraq

Although the public campaign for war with Iraq did not begin until 2002, President Bush and part of his administration began considering it immediately after September 11, 2001. At the war cabinet meeting at Camp David on September 15, 2001, the issue of Iraq was raised by Deputy Secretary of Defense Paul Wolfowitz, who strongly favored going after Saddam Hussein and argued it might be easier than war in Afghanistan. Secretary of State Colin Powell, however, argued that the coalition backing the United States would not hold if the target was shifted to Iraq. Powell said, "If we go after Saddam Hussein, we lose our rightful place as good guy." CIA Director George Tenet and Chief of Staff Andrew Card agreed with those opposing the attack. The president finally decided not to pursue Iraq at that time and recalled, "If we tried to do too many things . . . the lack of focus would have been a huge risk."[7]

Nevertheless, on September 17, 2001, President Bush signed a top-secret plan for the war in Afghanistan that also directed the Defense Department to plan for a war with Iraq.[8] White House officials later said that Bush decided soon after the terrorist attacks that Iraq had to be confronted but that he did not make his decision public because "he didn't think the country could handle the shock of 9/11 and a lot of talk about dealing with states that had weapons of mass destruction."[9]

President Bush publicly signaled his decision to pursue war with Iraq in the State of the Union message on January 29, 2002, though his decision was somewhat obscure and stated at a high level of generality by including Iraq, Iran, and North Korea in what he termed an "axis of evil."[10] In the speech, Bush declared that the United States would "prevent regimes that sponsor terror from threatening America or our friends and allies with weapons of mass destruction. . . . The United States of America will not permit the world's most dangerous regimes to threaten us with the world's most destructive weapons. . . . History has called America and our allies to action. . . ."[11] According to the State Department Director of Policy and Planning, Richard Haas, by the summer of 2002, Bush had already made up his mind that war with Iraq was inevitable (barring capitulation by Saddam Hussein): "The president made a decision in the summer of 2002. We all saluted at that point. That is the way it works."[12] Haas said that he raised the issue of war with Iraq with Condoleezza Rice: "I raised this issue about were we really sure that we wanted to put Iraq front and center at this point, given the war on terrorism and other issues. And she said, essentially, that decision's been made, don't waste your breath."[13] The president may have made up his mind even earlier. In March 2002, the president told Rice, when she was in a meeting with several senators, "F____Saddam. We're taking him out."[14]

By spring 2002, military planning for Iraq had begun, and the administration started talking publicly about "regime change" in Iraq. The next major public pronouncement by the president on national security and Iraq came in the 2002 commencement address at the U.S. Military Academy at West Point, New York. The president asserted, "Containment is not possible when unbalanced dictators with weapons of mass destruction can deliver those weapons on missiles or secretly provide them to terrorist allies."[15]

Over the next three months, some professional military officers voiced reservations about U.S. plans to attack Iraq. Although it was not unusual for military professionals to disagree with White House decisions, it was unusual for their concerns to be voiced so openly to the press. *Washington Post* articles noted that "senior U.S. military officers" and "some top generals and admirals in the military establishment, including members of the Joint Chiefs of Staff," had argued for a cautious approach to Iraq. They were not convinced that Iraq had any connection to the 9/11 terrorist attacks; they felt that containment had worked up until then; they thought a military invasion would be costly; and they thought that a likely U.S. victory would entail a lengthy occupation of Iraq.[16] By August, members of President Bush's father's administration came out publicly against war with Iraq. Brent Scowcroft, George H.W. Bush's National Security Advisor and Rice's mentor, wrote in an op-ed piece entitled "Don't Attack Saddam" that "there is scant evidence to tie Saddam to terrorist organizations, and even less to the Sept. 11 attacks. . . . An attack on Iraq at this time would seriously jeopardize, if not destroy, the global counterterrorist campaign we have undertaken. . . . Worse, there is a virtual consensus in the world against an attack on Iraq at this time."[17]

James Baker, Secretary of State for Bush Senior, also expressed reservations about an attack on Iraq: "If we are to change the regime in Iraq, we will have to occupy the country militarily. The costs of doing so, politically, economically and in terms of casualties, could be great."[18] General Wesley Clark, former NATO Supreme Allied Commander, said, "We have not gone far enough in the war on terror. . . No evidence supports the Bush administration's assertion that the United States may need to invade Iraq soon, or else suffer terrorism at the hands of Iraqi dictator Saddam Hussein."[19] Combat veterans also expressed reservations about the wisdom of war with Iraq.[20] Vietnam veteran Chuck Hagel (R-NE) said, "It is interesting to me that many of those who want to rush this country into war don't know anything about war."[21] Retired General Anthony Zinni, senior advisor to Secretary of State Powell and former Chief of the U.S. Central Command (which includes the Middle East), stated: "We need to quit making enemies that we don't need to make enemies out of. . . . It's pretty interesting that all the generals see it the same way and all the others who have never fired a shot and are not to go to war see it another way."[22] James Webb, Vietnam Veteran and former Assistant Secretary of Defense and Secretary of the Navy in the Reagan Administration, argued that war with Iraq was ill-considered. Webb wrote:

American military leaders have been trying to bring a wider focus to the band of neoconservatives that began beating the war drums on Iraq before the dust had even settled on the World Trade Center. Despite the efforts of the neocons to shut them up or dismiss them as unqualified to deal in policy issues, these leaders, both active-duty and retired, have been nearly unanimous in their concerns. Is there an absolutely vital national interest that should lead us from containment to unilateral war and a long-term occupation of Iraq?[23]

General Norman Schwartzkopf, Commander of U.S. forces in the 1991 Gulf War, also expressed reservations about attacking Iraq in early 2003: "I don't know what intelligence the U.S. government has. . . . I guess I would like to have better information. . . . I think it is very important to wait and see what the inspectors come up with, and hopefully they come up with something conclusive."[24]

The Lead-up to War

On August 5, 2002, at Colin Powell's initiative, Condoleezza Rice arranged for him to spend two hours with the president in order to explain his own reservations about war with Iraq. He argued that it would destabilize the whole Middle East, that an American occupation would be seen as hostile by the Muslim world, and that war should not be undertaken unilaterally. If the president wanted to pursue a military attack, Powell urged him to recruit allies, preferably through the United Nations.[25] Although Bush was not persuaded by Powell's reservations about war with Iraq, by mid-August the administration decided that the President's scheduled speech of September 12 to the United Nations should be about Iraq.

Meanwhile, the Bush administration felt that opposition to war with Iraq was building and had to be countered. So after close consultation with President Bush and without informing Secretary of State Powell, Vice President Cheney took the occasion of an address to the Veterans of Foreign Wars Convention on August 26, 2002, to bluntly lay out the administration's case:[26] "Deliverable weapons of mass destruction in the hands of a terror network or a murderous dictator, or the two working together, constitutes as grave a threat as can be imagined. . . . The risks of inaction are far greater than the risk of action."[27] Cheney's public argument that a preemptive strike against Iraq was justified and that further U.N. inspections were useless undercut Powell's argument to seek further U.N. inspections and approval of U.S. action against Iraq.

At a meeting on September 7, the president reaffirmed his decision to go to the United Nations in early September, though Cheney and Rumsfeld pressed their argument that the United States should move against Saddam Hussein and that a new U.N. resolution to do it was not necessary. In his September 12 speech to the United Nations, the president framed the issue as one of credibility for the United Nations and stressed the urgent need for its many resolutions to be enforced. Citing Saddam's "flagrant violations" of U.N. resolutions, Bush declared that "we have been more than patient. . . . The conduct of the Iraqi regime is a threat to the authority of the United Nations and a threat to peace."[28] Shortly after Bush's U.N. speech,

the administration released a new national security doctrine for the United States that echoed the earlier neocon arguments and justified preemptive military strikes by the United States.[29]

Anticipating the congressional vote on a resolution authorizing war with Iraq, the president gave a speech to the nation from Cincinnati on October 7, 2002, in which he explained the need for authorizing military action:

> Some citizens wonder, "After 11 years of living with this problem, why do we need to confront it now?" And there's a reason. We have experienced the horror of September the 11th. We have seen that those who hate Americans are willing to crash airplanes into buildings full of innocent people. Our enemies would be no less willing, in fact they would be eager, to use biological or chemical or a nuclear weapon. Knowing these realities, America must not ignore the threat gathering against us. Facing clear evidence of peril, we cannot wait for the final proof, the smoking gun that could come in the form of a mushroom cloud.[30]

The president forcefully argued that America was vulnerable to terrorist attacks and that a hostile regime in Iraq might be willing to share its weapons of mass destruction (WMD: chemical, biological, nuclear) technology with terrorists. Thus, the United States had to act preemptively to prevent such a nightmare.

Although there was a debate in Congress and statements by those supporting and opposing the resolution to go to war with Iraq, there was never much doubt about the outcome. The deliberations lacked the drama of those in 1991 over the Gulf War Resolution. A number of Democrats voted for the resolution from fear that a negative vote could be used against them in the upcoming elections, and Majority Leader of the Senate Tom Daschle and House Minority Leader Richard Gephardt both voted for the measure. The resolution passed in the House by 296 to 133, with 6 Republicans and 126 Democrats (and 1 independent) voting against it. In the Senate, the resolution passed 77 to 23, with 21 Democrats, 1 Republican, and 1 independent voting against it. The final resolution, passed by the House on October 10 and by the Senate on October 11, stated: "The president is authorized to use the armed forces of the United States as he determines to be necessary and appropriate, in order to: (1) defend the national security of the United States against the continuing threat posed by Iraq; and (2) enforce all relevant United Nations Security Council resolutions regarding Iraq."[31]

After the administration convinced Congress to give the president the necessary authority to attack Iraq, Colin Powell, along with other U.S. diplomats, worked to build an international coalition to convince the U.N. Security Council to pass a new resolution on Iraq. After much negotiation within the Security Council on a strongly worded, unanimous resolution, Resolution 1441 was formed. It gave Iraq one week to promise to comply and until February 21, 2003 (at the latest), for the U.N. inspectors to report back on Iraq's compliance. U.N. weapons inspectors searched Iraq with seeming carte blanche and surprise visits to sites of possible weapons manufacture, but by late January, they had found no "smoking gun." Chief U.N. inspector, Hans Blix, said that he needed more time to do a thorough job. But as the initial reporting date for the U.N. inspectors (January 27, 2003) approached, President Bush became increasingly impatient with the inability of the U.N. inspection team to locate evidence of Iraq's WMD: "This business about, you know, more time—you know, how much time do we need to see clearly that he's not disarming?. . . . This looks like a rerun of a bad movie and I'm not interested in watching it."[32]

In his State of the Union address, January 28, 2003, President Bush said that the United Nations had given Saddam Hussein his "final chance to disarm" but "he has shown instead utter contempt for the United Nations and for the opinion of the world." Bush declared that "the course of [the United States] does not depend on the decisions of others" and that "we will consult, but let there be no misunderstanding. If Saddam Hussein does not fully disarm for the safety of our people, and for the peace of the world, we will lead a coalition to disarm him."[33]

The War in Iraq

Throughout February and early March, the United States and Britain continued to build up troop strength and military supplies in the Middle East in order to prepare for war. As various last-minute peace attempts failed, President Bush decided to attack. At 8 p.m., March 17, the president declared that "Saddam Hussein and his sons must leave Iraq within 48 hours" or the United States would commence military action against them.[34] Two days later, 130,000 U.S. and British troops began a land invasion of Iraq and a rush to Baghdad.

Within two weeks, U.S. forces were at the outskirts of Baghdad, but supply lines were overextended and had to be secured before further advances. After another week of combat, however, American troops overwhelmed the Iraqi Republican Guard. With only limited street fighting and relatively few American deaths (about 150 at that point), U.S. forces successfully occupied Baghdad. U.S. and British troops continued to mop up remaining resistance, and Iraqis began to realize that Saddam Hussein's rule was over. Jubilation marked the end of Saddam's reign for many, but looting along with general disorder and the destruction of government buildings also erupted. U.S. troops guarded parts of the infrastructure, but not before hospitals, libraries, and the Iraq National Museum were severely damaged by looters. As U.S. forces began to restore order throughout the country and sought to assist the Iraqis in establishing an interim government, President Bush declared the end of combat on May 1, 2003. In a national televised address from the deck of an aircraft carrier off the coast of California, the president proclaimed: "In the battle of Iraq, the United States and our allies have prevailed." He tied the war in Iraq to the war on terrorism by saying that "the battle of Iraq is one victory in a war on terror that began on September 11, 2001, and still goes on. . . . We have removed an ally of Al Qaeda, and cut off a source of terrorist funding."[35]

President Bush had been harshly critical of the U.N. weapons inspectors who had been unable to locate biological, chemical, or nuclear weapons in Iraq, but U.S. troops had not found them either. In his speech, the president said that "we have begun the search for hidden chemical and biological weapons." He did not mention the nuclear weapons that the United States had previously asserted that Saddam was developing.[36] The purpose of the speech, according to White House officials, was (1) to state that the role of U.S. forces in Iraq was shifting from war to a police function, (2) to signal that other countries could send humanitarian aid, and (3) to signal to American voters that the President was shifting his focus from war to domestic issues in preparation for the 2004 election.[37]

Failure to Find Weapons of Mass Destruction

After the initial failure of U.S. troops to find WMD in Iraq, the CIA sent in a search force of 1200 experts led by David Kay to locate the weapons. Kay's mission was to scour the country for WMD and report back to the president. As his search continued without success, critics of the administration began to charge that the president had misled the country about the presence of WMD in Iraq and their imminent threat to the United States. The Bush administration had claimed with some certainty that Iraq possessed chemical and biological weapons. President Bush on September 26, 2002, asserted that "the Iraqi regime possesses biological and chemical weapons. The Iraqi regime is building the facilities necessary to make more biological and chemical weapons."[38] That Iraq had chemical and biological weapons in the 1980s is certain, in part because some of the materials came from the United States and because Saddam used chemical weapons against Iran and against the Kurds in northern Iraq.[39] Nonetheless, serious questions about the administration's claims were raised when U.S. forces could not find evidence of Iraq's chemical and biological weapons immediately after the war, despite diligent searching by both U.S. military forces and the 1200 members of David Kay's Iraq Survey Group.[40]

Two other aspects of the president's claims turned out to be problematic: the implied connection between Saddam Hussein and the atrocities of 9/11 and the suggestion that Iraq had nuclear weapons. Two days after the 9/11 terrorist attacks, a Time/CNN poll found that 78 percent of respondents thought that Saddam Hussein was involved with the attacks on New York's twin Trade Towers and the Pentagon in Washington.[41] From 9/11 through the summer of 2003, President Bush and his administration strongly implied that there was a link between Saddam and the al Qaeda hijackers, despite Osama bin Laden's contempt for Saddam as the head of a secular state.[42]

The evidence connecting Saddam Hussein and al Qaeda was never very solid. Neither the FBI nor the CIA was able to establish that the 9/11 terrorist Mohamed Atta had been in Prague to meet with an Iraqi official, as the Bush administration had asserted.[43] Nor could a U.N. terrorism committee find a link between al Qaeda and Saddam.[44] Despite the lack of evidence, President Bush continued to link the war in Iraq with al Qaeda and 9/11. In his May 1, 2003, victory speech, he had said, "The battle of Iraq is one victory in a war on terror that began on September the 11th, 2001. . . . We've removed an ally of al Qaeda, and cut off a source of terrorist funding. . . . With those attacks [of 9/11], the terrorists and their supporters declared war on the United States. And war is what they got."[45] Yet on September 18, 2003, Bush conceded, "No, we've

had no evidence that Saddam Hussein was involved with September the 11th."[46] The president gave no explanation why he suddenly abandoned the previously implied connection.[47]

During 2002, President Bush and his administration had made a number of assertions about Saddam Hussein's potential nuclear capacity—for example, that Saddam had reconstituted his nuclear weapons program and was potentially less than a year away from possessing nuclear weapons. This was a powerful argument; even those who thought that Saddam could be deterred from using chemical and biological weapons (as he had been in 1991) might be persuaded that an attack was necessary if Saddam was close to creating nuclear weapons. The claim of Saddam's nuclear capacity turned out to be one of the strongest arguments that Bush made for initiating war with Iraq.

Prior to the president's campaign to convince Congress to grant him the authority to attack Iraq, the White House asked the CIA to prepare a National Intelligence Estimate (NIE) on Iraq—that is, an authoritative statement of the consensus of intelligence agencies about the potential threat from Iraq.[48] This NIE served as a basis for President Bush's speech in Cincinnati on October 7, 2002, to convince Congress to grant legal authorization for war with Iraq and, more broadly, to convince the nation of the clear, immediate threat from Saddam Hussein. In the speech, Bush said,

> We agree that the Iraqi dictator must not be permitted to threaten America and the world with horrible poisons and diseases and gasses and atomic weapons. . . . The evidence indicates that Iraq is reconstituting its nuclear weapons program. . . . He could have a nuclear weapon in less than a year. . . . Facing clear evidence of peril, we cannot wait for the final proof, the smoking gun that could come in the form of a mushroom cloud.[49]

Then in his State of the Union speech on January 28, 2003, President Bush said, "The British Government has learned that Saddam Hussein recently sought significant quantities of uranium from Africa."[50] The African country in question was Niger.

The problem with these statements again turned out to be lack of hard evidence upon which the president's claims were based. Two assertions about Saddam Hussein's nuclear capacity that the administration relied upon were of dubious authenticity. The first was the claim that Iraq sought uranium oxide ("yellowcake") from Niger. The British assertion that Saddam sought uranium oxide from Niger turned out to have been based (at least in part) on forged documents. The CIA had serious doubts about the accuracy of the claim and had even convinced NSC aides to take it out of the president's October 7, 2002, speech to the nation.[51] How the words got into the 2003 State of the Union address was not clear.

In addition to the Niger yellowcake claim, the administration also adduced as evidence for Iraq's reconstituting its nuclear program reports of large numbers of aluminum tubes purchased by Iraq. President Bush said in his September 12, 2002, speech to the United Nations, "Iraq has made several attempts to buy high-strength aluminum tubes used to enrich uranium for a nuclear weapon. Should Iraq acquire fissile material, it would be able to build a nuclear weapon within a year."[52] The evidence of the aluminum tubes was also featured in the National Intelligence Estimate issued in early October 2002, which had played an important role in convincing members of Congress to vote for the resolution giving the president the authority to go to war with Iraq. The State Department's Bureau of Intelligence and Research, however, dissented from the argument of the rest of the National Intelligence Estimate: "INR is not persuaded that the tubes in question are intended for use as centrifuge rotors. . . . INR considers it far more likely that the tubes are intended for another purpose, most likely the production of artillery rockets."[53] The physical characteristics of the tubes—diameter, length, composition, coating—matched closely the dimensions of aluminum tubes used in Medusa rockets but did not track as closely with the dimensions of centrifuge rotors.[54] The State Department concluded: "The activities we have detected do not, however, add up to a compelling case that Iraq is currently pursuing what INR would consider to be an integrated and comprehensive approach to acquire nuclear weapons."[55]

In his interim report to Congress in the fall of 2003, David Kay told Congress that Iraq's nuclear program was in "the very most rudimentary" state: "It clearly does not look like a massive, resurgent program, based on what we discovered."[56] According to Kay's report, Iraqi scientists said "to date we have not uncovered evidence that Iraq undertook significant post-1998 steps to actually build nuclear weapons or produce fissile material."[57] The administration's inference that Saddam Hussein was continuing his previous weapons programs was not unreasonable. Yet little evidence existed to support their conclusions about Saddam's

nuclear capacity, and they had used claims of dubious validity to make their case to the American people about nuclear weapons and a connection between Saddam and the atrocities of 9/11.

Was the Intelligence Process Politicized?

One possible explanation for the administration's inaccurate claims about Iraq's WMD was that the intelligence professionals of the government were pressured to suit their analyses to the policy goals of the administration. Allegations centered around the vice president's visits to CIA headquarters, the creation of the Office of Special Plans in the Office of the Secretary of Defense, and the use of the Defense Policy Board. Richard Cheney and his aide, Scooter Libby, made a number of personal visits to the CIA headquarters at Langley to question the CIA judgment that Iraq did not pose as immediate a threat as the administration was arguing. Although it is appropriate for the vice president and other high administration officials to challenge intelligence agencies, it is also possible that career civil servants may see this as unwarranted political pressure. Such intrusions during 2002 concerning Iraq seemed unusual within the intelligence community and were perceived by some CIA veterans as political pressure for the agency to come to the conclusions that the administration wanted.[58] Ray McGovern, who had been a CIA analyst from 1964 to 1990 and had briefed Vice President George H. W. Bush in the 1980s, said, "During my 27-year career at the Central Intelligence Agency, no vice president ever came to us for a working visit."[59]

In addition to close attention from the vice president, CIA analysis was also treated with suspicion in the Department of Defense because the CIA was not coming to the conclusions about Iraq's WMD capabilities that the secretary and deputy secretary of defense expected. A number of CIA analysts perceived this as political pressure.[60] In the Pentagon, according to a former official who attended the meetings, "They were the browbeaters. In interagency meetings Wolfowitz treated the analysts' work with contempt."[61] From the perspective of some CIA veterans, the administration was undermining the objectivity and professionalism of the intelligence process. Former Defense Intelligence Agency (DIA) analyst and specialist on Iraq, W. Patrick Lang, characterized the administration's efforts to influence intelligence as unprofessional: "What we have here is advocacy, not intelligence work."[62] One senior State Department analyst told a congressional committee that he felt pressured by the administration to shift his analysis to be more certain about the evidence on Iraq's activities. Other analysts told the Senate Intelligence Committee that the administration was disclosing only the worst-case scenario aspects of intelligence reports and not accurately representing the work of the professional analysts.[63]

Secretary Rumsfeld responded to his dissatisfaction with the analysis of the CIA by creating an Office of Special Plans headed by Deputy Undersecretary of Defense William Luti. This office was created to do intelligence analysis that brought a different perspective than the DIA and the CIA.[64] One important difference in their analysis was the weight they gave to claims provided by the Iraqi National Congress and its leader Ahmad Chalabi about Saddam Hussein's WMD. Chalabi, who left Iraq when he was young, and in the 1990s founded the Iraqi National Congress, was seen by the neocons as the best candidate to lead Iraq after Saddam's rule ended. The CIA had discounted Chalabi and the Iraqi exiles' claims because the exiles had a stake in the outcome of U.S. policy. Thus, the CIA did not consider them as credible as the Office of Special Plans judged.[65] According to Patrick Lang, former head of Middle East intelligence for the DIA, "The D.I.A. has been intimidated and beaten to a pulp. And there's no guts at all in the C.I.A."[66]

Another tactic Secretary Rumsfeld used to circumvent the established professional intelligence apparatus of the executive branch was his reliance upon the Defense Policy Board (DPB). The DPB was chaired by Richard Perle, a hawk on Iraq and former member of the Reagan administration. In Perle's opinion, the CIA's judgment about Iraq "isn't worth the paper it is written on."[67] The DPB also had as members other high visibility neocons and hawks on Iraq, such as James Woolsey and Newt Gingrich, as well as some other former defense officials not necessarily committed to war with Iraq. Interestingly, this board of outside advisors played a much more highly visible role in supporting the administration's war plans than the traditional outside advisory board to the president, the President's Foreign Intelligence Advisory Board (PFIAB). Perhaps that was because the PFIAB was chaired by Brent Scowcroft, National Security Advisor to President George H. W. Bush and critic of war with Iraq.

Although all executive branch agencies should take their guidance from the president and his appointees, it is dangerous for any administration to pressure intelli-

gence agencies to distort their professional judgments to support an administration's short-term policy goals. Once intelligence is politicized, presidents will find it difficult to distinguish the professionals' best judgment from what they think the president wants to hear. Evidence of undue pressure from the administration remains inconclusive and circumstantial at this time, insofar as the Bush administration put pressure on U.S. intelligence agencies to suit their analyses to its policy goals, but it jeopardized its own best sources of intelligence.

Conclusion

Disagreements in the international community and within the American public about the wisdom of war with Iraq were mirrored in divisions within the U.S. government. On the pro-war side were the neocons and the political leadership of the Bush administration: Vice President Cheney, Secretary of Defense Rumsfeld, and his deputy, Paul Wolfowitz, along with other officials on their staffs. The neocons were convinced that Saddam Hussein was an imminent threat to U.S. national security, and they were optimistic about the ability of U.S. military action to establish a democratic government in Iraq with beneficial consequences for the Middle East. After the 9/11 attacks, President Bush adopted the neocon vision of how national security policy should deal with the threat.

On the other side were the skeptics about the likelihood that war to depose Saddam Hussein would lead to democracy for Iraq as well as those who were dubious about some of the claims the administration made about Saddam's WMD. The skeptics included many (though not all) Democrats, members of George H. W. Bush's administration (particularly Scowcroft and Baker), some military leaders in the professional officer corps (active duty and retired), and some members of the career services in the Department of State and the Central Intelligence Agency. Members of the career services, however, are bound to follow the leadership of the president as head of the executive branch of government and commander in chief of the armed forces. Thus, their hesitation was generally confined to internal analysis, with some leaks to the press about their reservations. None of the doubters thought Saddam was good for Iraq, nor were they against democracy in Iraq. Their doubts sprang from their judgments that an invasion of Iraq would not achieve the goals sought by the president and might cause more harm to the United

States than good. They were particularly concerned that war in Iraq would divert resources from the war on terrorism, alienate other nations whose cooperation was needed in the war on terror, and spawn new terrorists among radical Muslims who might be mobilized by the U.S. occupation of an Arab country.

Possible justifications for war with Iraq ranged from the idealistic goal of bringing democracy to Iraqis and the humanitarian desire to rid them of a tyrant to geostrategic concerns about the future of the Middle East. That Saddam Hussein was a vicious tyrant who tortured his political enemies, gassed his own people, and invaded other countries was known long before the Bush administration decided to go to war to depose him. But the most compelling arguments to the American people were the assertions that the national security of the United States was at risk. Hence, claims that Saddam's WMD posed a direct threat to America were most effective in sustaining political support for war. After the war, when no WMD were found, the administration began to shift its justification for the war to the argument that if Iraq could become a democracy, it would foster democracy in other Middle East countries.

Whether the war with Iraq was in the best long-term national security interests of the United States depends on addressing the following questions about the future of Iraq which can only be answered with the passing of time.

1. Were Iraqis better off after the war than under Saddam Hussein? The removal of Saddam was certainly in the best interests of the people of Iraq. But internal security and a viable economy are also essential to any society, and their long-term absence could lead to questions about the efficacy of the war.
2. Will Iraq turn into a liberal democracy with religious tolerance, political parties, freedom of speech and the press, and other institutions of civil society central to democracies? If these liberal democratic characteristics flourish in Iraq, the war will be deemed successful. If Iraq descends into chronic civil war or a new dictatorship, the reasons for the war will be questioned.
3. Will the U.S. occupation be short, with few casualties, or long and drawn-out, with many casualties? If U.S. forces are seen as liberators and establish internal security through Iraqi sovereignty, the occupation will be considered successful. If U.S. troops come to be seen as a foreign occupying army under constant attack by guerilla raids, the occupation will be seen quite differ-

ently and will make the withdrawal of U.S. forces far more difficult.
4. Will the war in Iraq be taken by terrorists as a warning and thus discourage them from attacking the United States? Or will the U.S. occupation of an Arab country become a new rallying point and recruiting mechanism for terrorists who will make the war on terrorism that much more difficult for the United States?

President Bush has staked his historical reputation on positive answers to many of the questions posed above. His critics, however, contend that the administration overestimated the threat to the United States from Saddam Hussein and underestimated the difficulties of bringing democracy to Iraq. Answers to these difficult and divisive questions will not likely be settled soon.

Notes

1. For an analysis of the 1991 Gulf War, see "Presidential Policy Making and the Gulf War" in *The Presidency and the Persian Gulf War*, ed. Marcia Whicker, James Pfiffner, and Raymond Moore (Westport, CT: Praeger, 1993), 3–24.
2. George H. W. Bush and Brent Scowcroft, *A World Transformed* (New York: Knopf, 1998), 489.
3. The term *neoconservatives* originally referred to liberals, Democrats, and those on the left of American politics who became disillusioned with the liberal domestic policies of the Great Society and War on Poverty of the Johnson administration. In the 1990s, the focus of the neocons shifted to foreign policy and included many conservative Republicans. They favored an assertive foreign policy that was willing to use military power to undermine repressive regimes and replace them with democracies. They criticized the "realists" in foreign policy who believed that it is necessary to deal with repressive regimes when they support U.S. policies.
4. Project for the New American Century, "Statement of Principles" (June 3, 1997), posted on their Web site, http://www.newamericancentury.org. [Accessed December 4, 2003.]
5. Letter to the Honorable William J. Clinton (January 26, 1998) posted on their Web site, http://www. newamericancentury.org. [Accessed December 4, 2003.]

6. "The Second 2000 Gore-Bush Presidential Debate: October 11, 2000," Commission on Presidential Debates, p. 2 of transcript downloaded from www.debates.org. Bush also said, "I'm going to be judicious as to how to use the military. It needs to be in our vital interest, the mission needs to be clear, and the exit strategy obvious."

7. Bob Woodward, *Bush at War* (New York: Simon & Schuster, 2002), 84–91.

8. Glenn Kessler, "U.S. Decision on Iraq Has Puzzling Past," *Washington Post*, January 12, 2003.

9. Kessler, "U.S. Decision on Iraq."

10. David Frum, *The Right Man* (New York: Random House, 2003), 224, 238–240.

11. Weekly Compilation of Presidential Documents, *Administration of George W. Bush, 2002* (January 29, 2002), 133–139.

12. Richard Wolffe and Tamara Lipper, "Powell in the Bunker," *Newsweek* (March 24, 2003), 31. See also Jim Hoagland, "How He Got Here," *Washington Post*, March 21, 2003. See also Nicholas Lemann, "How It Came to War," *New Yorker* (March 31, 2003), 36. Haas said: "The moment was the first week of July [2002] when I had a meeting with Condi [Condoleezza Rice]."

13. Nicholas Lemann, "How It Came to War," *New Yorker* (March 31, 2003), 36.

14. Michael Elliot and James Carney, "First Stop Iraq," *Time* (March 31, 2003), 173.

15. Weekly Compilation of Presidential Documents, *Administration of George W. Bush, 2002*, "Commencement Address at the United States Military Academy in West Point, New York" (June 1, 2002), 944–948.

16. Thomas E. Ricks, "Some Top Military Brass Favor Status Quo in Iraq," *Washington Post*, (July 28, 2002). Also, Thomas E. Ricks, "Generals, Officials Are Split over Iraq," *Washington Post*, August 1, 2002, in which he says, "Much of the senior uniformed military, with the notable exception of some top Air Force and marine generals, opposes going to war anytime soon, a stance that is provoking frustration among civilian officials in the Pentagon and in the White House."

17. Brent Scowcroft, "Don't Attack Saddam," *Wall Street Journal*, August 15, 2002.

18. James A. Baker III, "The Right Way to Change a Regime," *New York Times*, August 25, 2002.

19. Tara Tuckwiller, "Don't Invade Yet, Ex-NATO Chief Says," *Charleston Gazette*, October 15, 2002.

20. Those who argued strongly for war with Iraq who did not have combat experience included President Bush, Vice President Cheney, National Security Advisor Condoleezza Rice, Secretary of Defense Rumsfeld (who flew Navy jets in 1953–54), Deputy Secretary of Defense Paul Wolfowitz, House Whip Tom DeLay, Chair of Defense Policy Board Richard Perle, Defense Policy Board member Newt Gingrich, and conservative commentator William Kristol. Combat veterans who were skeptical of the wisdom of war with Iraq included Secretary of State Colin Powell; Deputy Secretary of State Richard Armitage; some members of the Joint Chiefs of Staff (in the summer of 2002); many career military officers (in the summer of 2002); Senator Chuck Hagel (voted for the resolution on Iraq on 10/12/02); Senator John Kerry (voted for the resolution); retired General and former national Security Advisor Brent Scowcroft; James Webb (Vietnam veteran and former Secretary of the Navy); General Wesley Clark, former NATO Supreme Allied Commander; and Norman Schwartzkopf, commander of U.S. forces in the 1991 Gulf War. Retired General Anthony Zinni, former Chief of U.S. Central Command, said, "I just wish somebody in that chain of command would have seen combat at that time [during the Vietnam War]. They were my contemporaries. They should have been there, and they found a way not to serve. And where are their kids? Are their kids serving? My son is in the Marines." Thomas E. Ricks, "For Vietnam Vet Anthony Zinni Another War on Shaky Territory," *Washington Post*, December 23, 2003.

21. *Newsweek* (September 2, 2002), 28. See also Associated Press story in the *New York Times*, August 26, 2002.

22. *Washington Post*, "Powell Aide Disputes Views on Iraq," August 28, 2002.

23. James Webb, "Heading for Trouble," *Washington Post*, September 4, 2002. Former General Zinni agreed, "The more I saw, the more I thought that this was the product of the neocons who didn't understand the region and were going to create havoc there. These were dilettantes from Washington think tanks who never had an idea that worked on the ground." Thomas E. Ricks, "For Vietnam Vet Anthony Zinni Another War on Shaky Territory," *Washington Post*, December 23, 2003.

24. Thomas E. Ricks, "Desert Caution," *Washington Post*, January 28, 2003. Schwartzkopf prefaced the above remarks with, "The thought of Saddam Hussein with a sophisticated nuclear capability is a frightening thought, okay?"

25. Woodward, *Bush at War*, 333–334.

26. Nancy Gibbs, "Double-Edged Sword," *Time* (December 30, 2002, and January 6, 2003), 91.

27. Dana Milbank, "Cheney Says Iraqi Strike Is Justified," *Washington Post*, August 27, 2002.

28. The president's speech was printed in the *Washington Post*, September 13, 2002.

29. George W. Bush, *The National Security Strategy of the United States of America*, White House, 2002. [Available from whitehouse.gov/nsc/print/nssall.html].

30. George Bush, speech printed in the *Washington Post*, October 8, 2002.

31. U.S. Congress, "Authorization for the Use of Military Force Against Iraq," *New York Times*, October 12, 2002.

32. Karen DeYoung, "U.S. Escalates Iraq Rhetoric," *Washington Post*, January 22, 2003.

33. State of the Union address (January 28, 2003), printed in the *Washington Post*, January 29, 2003.

34. "President Says Saddam Hussein Must Leave Iraq within 48 Hours," Remarks by the President in Address to the Nation, transcript on White House Web site.

35. The speech was printed in the *New York Times*, May 2, 2003.

36. When asked about the failure up to that time of U.S. forces to find the weapons of mass destruction, government officials said, "We were not lying, but it was just a matter of emphasis." They played down the importance of WMD as the primary reasons for war with Iraq and emphasized the 9/11 attacks on the United States and the need to demonstrate that the United States was willing to project its force to fight terrorism. The officials were quoted by John Cochran, "Reason for War?" April 25, 2003, ABCNews.com. [Accessed April 29, 2003].

37. Elizabeth Bumiller, "Cold Truths behind Pomp," *New York Times*, May 2, 2003.

38. Dana Priest and Walter Pincus, "Bush Certainty on Iraq Arms Went beyond Analyst's Views," *Washington Post*, June 7, 2003.

39. In the 1980s, the U.S. Department of Commerce authorized the sale to Iraq of biological agents such as anthrax and bubonic plague. According to a memo to Secretary of State George Shultz in 1983, the Iraqis were using chemical weapons against the Iranians on an "almost daily basis." The Commerce Department also approved the sale by Dow Chemical of insecticides that were thought to be used for chemical weapons. Reported by Michael Dobbs, "U.S. Had Key Role in Iraq Buildup," *Washington Post*, December 30, 2002. See also Kenneth M. Pollack, *The Threatening Storm* (New York: Random House, 2002), 20–21, 170.

40. Walter Pincus and Dana Priest, "Iraq Weapons Report Won't Be Conclusive," *Washington Post*, September 25, 2003.

41. Dana Milbank and Claudia Deane, "Hussein Link to 9/11 Lingers in Many Minds," *Washington Post*, September 6, 2003.

42. In a tape urging Muslims to fight against the United States, Osama bin Laden said that the fighting should be for God, not for "pagan regimes in all the Arab countries, including Iraq. . . . Socialists are infidels wherever they are, either in Baghdad or Aden." Transcript posted on Web site www.indybay.org. [Accessed April 10, 2003.]

43. Dana Milbank and Walter Pincus, "Cheney Defends U.S. Actions in Bid to Revive Public Support," *Washington Post*, September 15, 2003. Milbank and Deane, "Hussein Link to 9/11 Lingers."

44. Associated Press, "U.N. Panel Finds No Evidence to Link Iraq, Al-Qaeda," online version at TruthOut.org, June 26, 2003.

45. Quoted in Milbank and Deane, "Hussein Link to 9/11 Lingers."

46. Dana Milbank, "Bush Disavows Hussein-Sept. 11 Link," *Washington Post*, September 18, 2003; David E. Sanger, "Bush Reports No Evidence of Hussein Tie to 9/11," *New York Times*, September 18, 2003.

47. For a full analysis on the misleading statements of President Bush on the link between Saddam and 9/11 and Saddam's nuclear capacity, see James P. Pfiffner, "Did President Bush Mislead the Country in His Arguments for War with Iraq?" *Presidential Studies Quarterly*, 34, no. 1 (2004).

48. Central Intelligence Agency, 2003, Key Judgments [from October 2002 NIE] Iraq's Continuing Programs for Weapons of Mass Destruction. Declassified excerpts published on the CIA Web site: www.odci.gov/nic/pubs/research, pp. 5–6. [Accessed October 10, 2003.]

49. George Bush, speech printed in the *Washington Post*, October 8, 2002.

50. State of the Union address (January 28, 2003), printed in the *Washington Post* (January 29, 2003).

51. Associated Press, "White House Official Apologizes for Role in Uranium Claim," *New York Times*, July 22, 2003, nytimes.com. [Accessed July 22, 2003.]

52. President Bush's address to United Nations, printed in the *New York Times*, September 13, 2003.

53. Central Intelligence Agency, 2003, Key Judgments [from October 2002 NIE] Iraq's Continuing Programs for Weapons of Mass Destruction. Declassified excerpts published on the CIA Web site www.odci.gov/nic/pubs/research, p. 9. [Accessed October 10, 2003.]

54. Barton Gellman and Walter Pincus, "Depiction of Threat Outgrew Supporting Evidence," *Washington Post*, August 10, 2003.

55. Central Intelligence Agency, 2003, Key Judgments [from October 2002 NIE] Iraq's Continuing Programs for Weapons of Mass Destruction. Declassified excerpts published on the CIA Web site www.odci.gov/nic/pubs/research, pp. 8–9 [Accessed October 10, 2003.]

56. Dana Priest and Walter Pincus, "Search in Iraq Finds No Banned Weapons," *Washington Post*, October 3, 2003.

57. David Kay, "Report on the Activities of the Iraq Survey Group to the House Permanent Select Committee on Intelligence and the House Committee on Appropriations, Subcommittee on Defense and the Senate Select Committee on Intelligence," p. 7. The page reference is to the unclassified report published on the CNN Web site http://cnn.allpolitics. [Accessed October 10, 2003.]

58. John B. Judis and Spencer Ackerman, "The Selling of the Iraq War: The First Casualty," *New Republic* (June 30, 2003), online version (tnr.com), p. 5.

59. Ray McGovern, "Cheney and the CIA: Not Business As Usual," online version at TruthOut.org, June 27, 2003.

60. James Risen, "C.I.A. Aides Feel Pressure in Preparing Iraqi Reports," *New York Times*, March 23, 2003.

61. Walter Pincus and Dana Priest, "Some Iraq Analysts Felt Pressure from Cheney Visits," *Washington Post*, June 5, 2003.

62. Bruce B. Auster, Mark Mazzetti, and Edward T. Pound, "Truth and Consequences," *U.S. News and World Report* (June 9, 2003), p. 17.

63. James Risen and Douglas Jehl, "Expert Said to Tell Legislators He Was Pressured to Distort Some Evidence," *New York Times*, June 25, 2003, *New York* Times Web site.

64. Judis and Ackerman, "The Selling of the Iraq War."

65. See Seymour M. Hersh, "Selective Intelligence," *New Yorker* (May 12, 2003), pp. 44–51.

66. Ibid.

67. Judis and Ackerman, "The Selling of the Iraq War."

Chapter 7 Review Questions

1. What are the five major subsystems in public agencies that decisively influence policy? Briefly describe the characteristics of each one.

2. Where are political appointees situated in the bureaucracy, and what functions do these individuals serve in U.S. government? Who were the political appointees in the case "The Decision to Go to War with Iraq," and what roles did they play? Why were they effective at developing their case for war and so significant in setting the policy agenda?

3. What are the essential differences between the professional careerists and the political appointees, as reflected in the case study? What are the sources of each one's influence and authority? In the case, how were these differences, outlooks, and sources of influence reflected? Generally, why are their roles so critical in shaping U.S. foreign policy?

4. Would you consider the professionals in the case to be among the professional elite? Why? Who were they, specifically?

5. Why were those presenting their case against war ineffective? How does information as well as timing of issues become so critical to their resolution? Specifically in the decision to go to war, what information and events turned out to be most critical in making that choice?

6. What does the case say generally about the ethical dilemmas of public professionals in government today? How can and should they behave in relationship to their political superiors? Can you draw out any clear rules of relationship based upon this case study?

Key Terms

political appointees

sub-cabinet officials

professional careerists

professional elites

SES

"inner" versus "outer" cabinet

Pendleton Act

GS rating

rank-in-person versus rank-in-job

Kennedy's Executive Orders
  10988 and 10987

public service unions

contract employment

line versus staff professionals

Suggestions for Further Reading

A number of excellent books deal with the origins, growth, and operations of the five types of bureaucratic subsystems discussed in this chapter. The best account of the rise of the U.S. civil service remains Paul Van Riper's *History of the U.S. Civil Service* (Evanston, Ill.: Row, Peterson, Co., 1958). For accounts of professionalism, read C. L. Gibb, *Hidden Hierarchies* (1966), Don Price, *Scientific Estate* (Cambridge: Harvard University Press, 1965), and Frederick C. Mosher, *Democracy and the Public Service,* 2nd ed. (New York: Oxford University Press, 1982). Studies advocating reforms in the civil service systems, such as the Volcker Commission Report, *Leadership for America* (1989), The Hudson Institute, *Civil Service 2000* (1988), and Frank J. Thompson (ed.), *Revitalizing State and Local Government: Strengthening Performance, Accountability, and Citizen Confidence* (1993), as well as several GAO studies such as *The Senior Executive Service* (1988), are some of the best guides to current public personnel practices and problems.

For a thoughtful look at the meaning of "merit" in relation to contemporary civil service, read Patricia W. Ingraham, *The Foundation of Merit* (Baltimore: Johns Hopkins Press, 1995). For accounts of the interplay between political appointees, professionals, and civil servants, read Frank J. Thompson, *Personnel Policy in the City* (Berkeley, Calif.: University of California Press, 1975); Norma M. Riccucci, *Unsung Heroes* (Washington, D.C.: Georgetown University Press, 1995); and Hugh Heclo, *A Government of Strangers* (Washington, D.C.: The Brookings Institution, 1977). Three books dealing with political appointees include John W. Macy, Bruce Adams, and J. Jackson Walter, eds., *America's Unelected Government: Appointing the President's Team* (Cambridge: Ballinger, 1983), G. Calvin MacKenzie, *The Politics of Presidential Appointments* (New York: Free Press, 1981), and by the same author, *The In and Outers* (Baltimore: Johns Hopkins Press, 1987). Excellent reviews of the impact of the 1978 Civil Service Reform Act are found in Patricia W. Ingraham and David H. Rosenbloom, eds., *The Promise and Paradox of Civil Service Reform* (San Francisco: Jossey-Bass, 1993). For the current operation of SES that was created by CSRA 1978, see OPM, *The Status of the Senior Executive Service* (1991); the Merit Protection Board, *The Senior Executive Service— Views of Former Federal Executives* (1989); Mark W. Huddleton and William A. Boyes, *The Higher Civil Services in the United States* (Pittsburgh: University of Pittsburgh Press, 1995); and the thoughtful essay by Norton Long, "SES and the Public Interest," *Public Administration Review* (May/June 1981). A helpful overview of key civil service issues is Patricia W. Ingraham and Don Kettl, *Agenda for Excellence* (Chatham, N.J.: Chatham Press, 1992), and for a general picture of civil service transformations today, see Paul Light, *The New Public Service* (Washington, D.C.: The Brookings Institution, 1999).

Useful perspectives on professional career systems are found in Frederick C. Mosher and Richard J. Stillman II, eds., *Professions in Government* (New Brunswick, N.J.: Transaction Books, 1982). For more recent analyses of professionalism, see Steven Brint, *In an Age of Experts* (Princeton, N.J.: Princeton University Press, 1994); James A. Smith, *The Idea Brokers* (New York: Free Press, 1991); and David S. Arnold and Jeremy F. Plant, *Public Official Associations and State and Local Government: A Bridge Across One Hundred Years* (Fairfax, Va.: George Mason University Press, 1994); and for unions, A. Lawrence Chickering, ed., *Public Employee Unions* (Washington, D.C.: The Brookings Institution, 1977), and David T. Stanley, *Managing Local Government under Union Pressure* (Washington, D.C.: The Brookings Institution, 1972). For more up-to-date studies of where we are today involving the problems of unions and the public service, read Joel M. Douglas's three essays: "Collective Bargaining and Public Sector Supervisors: A Trend Towards Exclusion?" *Public Administration Review* (Nov./Dec. 1987); "State Civil Service and Collective Bargaining Systems in Conflict," *Public Administration Review* (March/

April, 1992); and "Public Sector Labor Relations in the 21st Century: New Approaches, New Strategies," in Carolyn C. Ban and N. Riccucci, eds., *Public Personnel Management* (New York: Marcel Dekker, 1991).

Even though the contractual subsystem has emerged as a powerful and significant force within public bureaucracy today, relatively few scholars have examined the subject in much depth. This is both surprising and regrettable, though Clarence H. Danhof's *Government Contracting and Technological Change* (Washington, D.C.: The Brookings Institution, 1968), although somewhat dated, is still helpful for its history. Various recent books offer useful insights into portions of the contract subsystem: Ruth Hoogland De Hoog, *Partners in Public Service* (New York: SUNY Press, 1986); Don Kettl, *Sharing Power* (Washington, D.C.: The Brookings Institution, 1993); Phillip J. Cooper, *Governing by Contract* (Washington, D.C.: CQ Press, 2003); Susan R. Bernstein, *Managing Contracted Services in a Nonprofit Agency* (Philadelphia, Pa.: Temple University Press, 1991); as well as Chapters 9 and 10 in Lester M. Salamon, ed., *The Tools of Government* (New York: Oxford University Press, 2002).

One should not overlook six alternative perspectives for usefully exploring this complex topic: (1) recent autobiographies, such as Elliot Richardson, *Reflections of a Radical Moderate* (New York: Pantheon Books, 1996); (2) case studies of current policy issues, like Jacob S. Hacker, *The Road to Nowhere* (Princeton: Princeton University Press, 1997); (3) institutional studies, like Paul C. Light, *Monitoring Government* (Washington, D.C.: Brookings Institution, 1993); (4) analyses of specific influential groups like Robert Wood, ed., *Remedial Law* (Amherst: University of Massachusetts Press, 1990); (5) journals reporting on specific public service groups such as *PM* for city managers or *The Military Review* for army officers; and (6) empirical studies such as James L. Perry and Marie Thomson, *Civil Service: What Difference Does It Make?* (Armonk, N.Y.: M. E. Sharpe, 2004).

PART TWO

The Multiple Functions of Public Administrators: Their Major Activities, Responsibilities, and Roles

Public administrators must fulfill many functions, often simultaneously. Part Two focuses on several of the important activities performed by public administrators—decision making, administrative communications, management, personnel motivation, budgeting, and implementation. The extent, scope, and capability with which administrators perform these functions vary widely from administrator to administrator, from job to job, and from locale to locale. However, it is safe to say these six functions are considered some of the most critical activities that public administrators must perform if they are to succeed—indeed survive—in their jobs.

As in Part One of this book, in Part Two, chapter by chapter, a single concept is discussed in a reading and its relevance is illustrated in a case study. Although the six major roles of administrators are individually discussed in the following chapters, it should be emphasized that the reality of the administrative processes frequently forces public administrators to assume all these responsibilities at the same time; this makes their work much more complex, less neatly compartmentalized or clear-cut than these individual chapters may suggest. The significant functional concepts discussed in Part Two include:

CHAPTER 8

Decision Making: *The Concept of Incremental Choice* How are decisions made in the public sector and why do public administrators frequently feel as if they are "flying by the seat of their pants"?

CHAPTER 9

Administrative Communications: *The Concept of its Professional Centrality* How does the flow of communications inside and outside organizations influence the way decisions are made and how well (or how poorly) administrators perform their work? And what can be done to improve administrative communication?

CHAPTER 10

Executive Management: *The Concept of Effective Public Organizations* What is a successful management practice for public administrators to adopt? Why is public management often very different from business management?

CHAPTER 11

Public Personnel Motivation: *The Concept of The Public Service Culture* Why is personnel motivation so significant to organizational performance and productivity? How can public administrators most effectively motivate their employees?

CHAPTER 12

Public Budgeting: *The Concept of Budgeting as Political Choice* What is the nature of the budgetary process in government? Why is a knowledge of budgeting so fundamental to administrative survival?

CHAPTER 13

Implementation: *The Concept of an Ambiguity-Conflict Model* What is the best way for administrators to get their jobs done in a timely manner, efficiently, correctly, and responsibly? How can one best conceptualize this approach as a model?

CHAPTER **8**

Decision Making: The Concept of Incremental Choice

A wise policy-maker consequently expects that his policies will achieve only part of what he hopes and at the same time will produce unanticipated consequences he would have preferred to avoid. If he proceeds through a succession of incremental changes, he avoids serious lasting mistakes. . . .

Charles E. Lindblom

READING 8

Introduction

Few concepts are debated in administration more frequently than decision making—how decisions are made; whom they are made by; why they are decided on in the first place; and what impact they have once the choice is made. Gallons of ink have been spilled in academic journals debating whether decision making is an art or a science, how best to construct a decision-making model, or how to arrive at the most rational (or optimal) choice. One point emerges from these seemingly endless discussions: the process by which individuals and groups determine a correct course of action from various alternatives is one of the central functions of an administrator and thus deserves careful consideration by students of public administration.

What is the decision-making function? On one level, we all use decision making daily in confronting a myriad of personal choices, such as when to get up in the morning and what clothes to wear. On the larger and more complicated level of public administration, however, the decisional process involves vital community or societal choices—where to build a new school, when to negotiate an arms limitation treaty, or how to organize a new federal program for poverty relief. The process of choice runs the length and breadth of public administration and involves 4, 40, 400, or 4,000 steps, depending on the complexity and range of variables presented by the problem at hand.

Charles E. Lindblom (1917–   ), a Yale economist and long-time scholar of public policy issues, offers an important conceptual understanding of governmental decision making in his essay, "The Science of 'Muddling Through.'" Lindblom, unlike most economists, has seriously thought about the relationships between economics and politics for many years, an interest evident in his earliest writings with Robert A. Dahl in *Politics, Economics and*

Welfare (1953), as well as in his more recent book, *Politics and Markets* (1977). In an effort to realistically analyze the way governmental decisions are made, at the heart of Lindblom's brilliant studies is a model of decision making that he succinctly outlines in the following essay.

Based on earlier writings by Chester Barnard and Herbert Simon, Lindblom's central thesis is that there are two distinct varieties of decision making. One he calls the rational-comprehensive or root method, and the second, the successive limited comparisons or branch method. The first method is found in the classic texts on administration, and the latter is the "real" way decisions are arrived at in government. In the traditional *rational-comprehensive* or *root method* an administrator confronts a given objective, such as reducing poverty by a certain amount. The decision maker, in choosing the best policy to pursue, rationally ranks all the relevant values (or advantages) in attaining this objective, such as improving the health of the poor, reducing crime, improving property values, and eliminating illiteracy. He or she then formulates many possible alternatives to achieve the stated objective—for example, a guaranteed income plan, direct government subsidies, higher welfare payments, or work-relief programs—and selects from among the options the *best* alternative that serves to maximize the ranked list of values. This approach to decision making is *rational,* because the alternatives and values are logically selected and weighed in relative importance. It is also *comprehensive,* for all the alternatives and values are taken into account by the policy maker.

What *actually* occurs in administrative decision making, argues Lindblom, is quite another process, namely, the *successive limited comparisons* or *branch method.* An objective is established—reducing poverty by a set amount, for example—but in public discussions this objective quickly becomes compromised. It may soon be mixed up with other goals such as educating minority students or providing work relief for the jobless. Administrators tend to overlook or avoid many of the social values that could be derived from their program, concentrating instead on those that they consider immediately relevant. In selecting the appropriate course of action, administrators outline not a broad range of possibilities, but only a few incremental steps that experience tells them are feasible. Furthermore, in practice, policy makers do not rationally select the optimal program that satisfies a clearly delineated list of values. To the contrary, under the successive limited comparisons method, contends Lindblom, public administrators pragmatically select from among the immediate choices at hand the most suitable compromise that satisfies the groups and individuals concerned with the program.

Lindblom sees the first approach, the root method, as wrongly assuming that administrators making decisions have unlimited amounts of time and resources available to them. "It assumes intellectual capacities and sources of information that simply do not exist and it is even more absurd as an approach to policy when the time and money that can be allocated to a policy problem is limited, as is always the case." Second, the root method holds that there are always clear-cut values on which all interested parties agree. In fact, argues Lindblom, in a democratic society in which members of Congress, agencies, and interest groups are in continual disagreement over the relative importance of program objectives, policy makers cannot begin to rank explicitly the values derived from any program. There are simply too many groups with too many unknown values. The weight given to their relative importance depends ultimately on personal perspectives. "Even when an administrator resolves to follow his own values as a criterion for decisions, he will often not know how to rank them when they conflict with one another as they usually do." Third, the root method assumes that ends and means in policy choices are distinct, when in fact they are frequently intertwined. Selection of a goal to be accomplished often cannot easily be separated from the means by which it is achieved. For instance, the objective of slum clearance is intrinsically associated with the removal of residents from the neighborhood and the other methods used to achieve the goal, such as the clearing of buildings. Means and ends often become hopelessly confused in public policy choices. Finally, says Lindblom, the choice of a given course of action depends ultimately not on whether it maximizes the intended values (even if the values could be identified and ranked), but rather on whether it serves as a compromise acceptable to all parties concerned. "If agreement directly on policy as a test for the 'best' policy seems a poor substitute for testing the policy against its objectives, it ought to be remembered that objectives themselves have no ultimate validity other than they are agreed upon. . . . Agreement on policy thus becomes the only practicable test of the policy's correctness," argues Lindblom.

Lindblom's view of the reality of administrative decision making contains five characteristics. First, it is *incremental,* for small steps are always taken to achieve objectives, not broad leaps and bounds. Second, it is *noncomprehensive.* In other words, because policy makers' resources are always limited, they cannot take into consideration the full range of policy choices available to them at any given moment, nor can they possibly understand the full effects of their decisions or all of the values derived from any alternative they select. Third, the branch technique of decision making involves *successive comparisons* because policy is never made once and for all, but is made and remade endlessly by small chains of comparisons between narrow choices. Fourth, in practice, decision making *suffices* rather than maximizes from among the available options. "A wise policy maker completely expects that his policies will achieve only part of what he hopes and at the same time will produce unanticipated consequences he would have preferred to avoid." Finally, Lindblom's picture of governmental decision making rests on a *pluralist* conception of the public sector, in which many contending interest groups compete for influence over policy issues, continually forcing the administrator, as the person in the middle, to secure agreement among the competing parties. The political arts of compromise thus become a major part of decision-making methods.

There are two advantages of the branch method, asserts Lindblom. The first is that "if he proceeds through a succession of small incremental changes, the administrator therefore has the advantage of avoiding serious lasting mistakes" as well as permitting easy alterations should the wrong course be pursued. The second benefit of incrementalism is that it fits "hand and glove" with the American political system, which operates chiefly by means of gradual changes, rarely by dramatic shifts in public policies. "Non-incremental policy proposals are therefore typically not only politically irrelevant but also unpredictable in their policy consequences," writes Lindblom. The branch method allows for the art of compromise that American politics demands and produces the gradual changes that American tradition generally favors.

However, from the perspective of the "outside expert" or the academic problem solver, Lindblom points out, this approach seems "unscientific and unsystematic." Indeed, administrators may appear as if they were "flying by the seat of their pants," although in fact the outside theorists do not grasp that administrators are "often practicing a systematic method" of successive limited comparisons. Yet, as Lindblom says, ". . . sometimes decision makers are pursuing neither a theoretical approach nor successive comparisons nor any systematic method."

Lindblom's approach to governmental decision making, which for some may be too descriptive and not sufficiently prescriptive, debunks the classic view of how public choices are made, substituting an incremental model that is peculiarly a product and extension of economic theory of choice (subsequently, much of the language used in decisional theory—words like "optimizing" and "maximizing"—is derived from economics). Kenneth Arrow, Thomas Schelling, Herbert Simon, Edward Banfield, and Robert Dahl are among the major contemporary economists and political scientists who have pioneered the incremental view of decision making in the post–World War II era (refer to the numerous varieties of decision models outlined in the Suggestions for Further Reading at the end of this chapter). Lindblom has fully developed this idea into an elaborate working model in the following article, "The Science of 'Muddling Through.' "

As you read this selection, keep the following questions in mind:

Is Lindblom too pessimistic about the ability of administrators to make profound "big" choices that will significantly alter or reshape their external environment?

What do you see as the benefits and disadvantages of the branch method, and are there any remedies for its defects?

How does Lindblom's concept square with any of the previous case studies, such as Case Study 7, "The Decision to Go to War with Iraq"? Or was it a "root" or "branch" decision?

Does Lindblom's "muddling through" idea primarily apply in normal governmental decisions involving simple issues? How about catastrophes such as in Case Study 1, "The Blast in Centralia No. 5"? What decisional methods might have averted the unfortunate choices made in that case?

Do you agree with Lindblom that "the branch method compared to other decisional models often looks far superior," particularly from the perspective of the practitioner?

The Science of "Muddling Through"

CHARLES E. LINDBLOM

Suppose an administrator is given responsibility for formulating policy with respect to inflation. He might start by trying to list all related values in order

of importance, e.g., full employment, reasonable business profit, protection of small savings, prevention of a stock market crash. Then all possible policy outcomes could be rated as more or less efficient in attaining a maximum of these values. This would of course require a prodigious inquiry into values held by members of society and an equally prodigious set of calculations on how much of each value is equal to how much of each other value. He could then proceed to outline all possible policy alternatives. In a third step, he would undertake systematic comparison of his multitude of alternatives to determine which attains the greatest amount of values.

In comparing policies, he would take advantage of any theory available that generalized about classes of policies. In considering inflation, for example, he would compare all policies in the light of the theory of prices. Since no alternatives are beyond his investigation, he would consider strict central control and the abolition of all prices and markets on the one hand and elimination of all public controls with reliance completely on the free market on the other, both in the light of whatever theoretical generalizations he could find on such hypothetical economies.

Finally, he would try to make the choice that would in fact maximize his values.

An alternative line of attack would be to set as his principal objective, either explicitly or without conscious thought, the relatively simple goal of keeping prices level. This objective might be compromised or complicated by only a few other goals, such as full employment. He would in fact disregard most other social values as beyond his present interest, and he would for the moment not even attempt to rank the few values that he regarded as immediately relevant. Were he pressed, he would quickly admit that he was ignoring many related values and many possible important consequences of his policies.

As a second step, he would outline those relatively few policy alternatives that occurred to him. He would then compare them. In comparing his limited number of alternatives, most of them familiar from past controversies, he would not ordinarily find a body of theory precise enough to carry him through a comparison of their respective consequences. Instead he would rely heavily on the record of past experience with small policy steps to predict the consequences of similar steps extended into the future.

Moreover, he would find that the policy alternatives combined objectives or values in different ways. For example, one policy might offer price level stability at the cost of some risk of unemployment; another might offer less price stability but also less risk of unemployment. Hence, the next step in his approach—the

final selection—would combine into one the choice among values and the choice among instruments for reaching values. It would not, as in the first method of policy-making, approximate a more mechanical process of choosing the means that best satisfied goals that were previously clarified and ranked. Because practitioners of the second approach expect to achieve their goals only partially, they would expect to repeat endlessly the sequence just described, as conditions and aspirations changed and as accuracy of prediction improved.

By Root or by Branch

For complex problems, the first of these two approaches is of course impossible. Although such an approach can be described, it cannot be practiced except for relatively simple problems and even then only in a somewhat modified form. It assumes intellectual capacities and sources of information that men simply do not possess, and it is even more absurd as an approach to policy when the time and money that can be allocated to a policy problem is limited, as is always the case. Of particular importance to public administrators is the fact that public agencies are in effect usually instructed not to practice the first method. That is to say, their prescribed functions and constraints—the politically or legally possible—restrict their attention to relatively few values and relatively few alternative policies among the countless alternatives that might be imagined. It is the second method that is practiced.

Curiously, however, the literatures of decision making, policy formulation, planning, and public administration formalize the first approach rather than the second, leaving public administrators who handle complex decisions in the position of practicing what few preach. For emphasis I run some risk of overstatement. True enough, the literature is well aware of limits on man's capacities and of the inevitability that policies will be approached in some such style as the second. But attempts to formalize rational policy formulation—to lay out explicitly the necessary steps in the process—usually describe the first approach and not the second.[1]

The common tendency to describe policy formulation even for complex problems as though it followed the first approach has been strengthened by the attention given to, and successes enjoyed by, operations research, statistical decision theory, and systems analysis. The hallmarks of these procedures, typical of the first approach, are clarity of objective, explicitness of evaluation, a high degree of comprehensiveness of overview, and, wherever possible, quantification of values for mathematical analysis. But these advanced procedures remain largely the appropriate techniques of relatively small-scale problem-solving where the total number of variables to be considered is small and value problems restricted. Charles Hitch, head of the Economics Division of RAND Corporation, one of the leading centers for application of these techniques, has written:

> I would make the empirical generalization from my experience at RAND and elsewhere that operations research is the art of suboptimizing, i.e., of solving some lower-level problems, and that difficulties increase and our special competence diminishes by an order of magnitude with every level of decision making we attempt to ascend. The sort of simple explicit model which operations researchers are so proficient in using can certainly reflect most of the significant factors influencing traffic control on the George Washington Bridge, but the proportion of the relevant reality which we can represent by any such model or models in studying, say, a major foreign-policy decision, appears to be almost trivial.[2]

Accordingly, I propose in this paper to clarify and formalize the second method, much neglected in the literature. This might be described as the method of *successive limited comparisons.* I will contrast it with the first approach, which might be called the rational-comprehensive method.[3] More impressionistically and briefly—and therefore generally used in this article—they could be characterized as the branch method and root method, the former continually building out from the current situation, step-to-step and by small degrees; the latter starting from fundamentals anew each time, building on the past only as experience is embodied in a theory, and always prepared to start completely from the ground up.

Let us put the characteristics of the two methods side by side in simplest terms.

Rational-Comprehensive (Root)

1a. Clarification of values or objectives distinct from and usually prerequisite to empirical analysis of alternative policies.
2a. Policy formulation is therefore approached through means-end analysis: First the ends are isolated, then the means to achieve them are sought.
3a. The test of a "good" policy is that it can be shown to be the most appropriate means to desired ends.
4a. Analysis is comprehensive; every important relevant factor is taken into account.
5a. Theory is often heavily relied upon.

Successive Limited Comparisons (Branch)

1b. Selection of value goals and empirical analysis of the needed action are not distinct from one another but are closely intertwined.
2b. Since means and ends are not distinct, means-end analysis is often inappropriate or limited.
3b. The test of a "good" policy is typically that various analysts find themselves directly agreeing on a policy (without their agreeing that it is the most appropriate means to an agreed objective).
4b. Analysis is drastically limited:
  i) Important possible outcomes are neglected.
  ii) Important alternative potential policies are neglected.
  iii) Important affected values are neglected.
5b. A succession of comparisons greatly reduces or eliminates reliance on theory.

Assuming that the root method is familiar and understandable, we proceed directly to clarification of its alternative by contrast. In explaining the second, we shall be describing how most administrators do in fact approach complex questions, for the root method, the "best" way as a blueprint or model, is in fact not workable for complex policy questions, and administrators are forced to use the method of successive limited comparisons.

Intertwining Evaluation and Empirical Analysis (1b)

The quickest way to understand how values are handled in the method of successive limited comparisons is to see how the root method often breaks down in *its* handling of values or objectives. The idea that values should be clarified, and in advance of the examination of alternative policies, is appealing. But what happens when we attempt it for complex social problems? The first difficulty is that on many critical values or objectives, citizens disagree, congressmen disagree, and public administrators disagree. Even where a fairly specific objective is prescribed for the administrator, there remains considerable room for disagreement on sub-objectives. Consider, for example, the conflict with respect to locating public housing, described in Meyerson and Banfield's study of the Chicago Housing Authority[4]—disagreement which occurred despite the clear objective of providing a certain number of public housing units in the city. Similarly conflicting are objectives in highway location, traffic control, minimum wage administration, development of tourist facilities in national parks, or insect control.

Administrators cannot escape these conflicts by ascertaining the majority's preference, for preferences have not been registered on most issues; indeed, there often *are* no preferences in the absence of public discussion sufficient to bring an issue to the attention of the electorate. Furthermore, there is a question of whether intensity of feeling should be considered as well as the number of persons preferring each alternative. By the impossibility of doing otherwise, administrators often are reduced to deciding policy without clarifying objectives first.

Even when an administrator resolves to follow his own values as a criterion for decisions, he often will not know how to rank them when they conflict with

one another, as they usually do. Suppose, for example, that an administrator must relocate tenants living in tenements scheduled for destruction. One objective is to empty the buildings fairly promptly, another is to find suitable accommodation for persons displaced, another is to avoid friction with residents in other areas in which a large influx would be unwelcome, another is to deal with all concerned through persuasion if possible, and so on.

How does one state even to himself the relative importance of these partially conflicting values? A simple ranking of them is not enough; one needs ideally to know how much of one value is worth sacrificing for some of another value. The answer is that typically the administrator chooses—and must choose—directly among policies in which these values are combined in different ways. He cannot first clarify his values and then choose among policies.

A more subtle third point underlies both the first two. Social objectives do not always have the same relative values. One objective may be highly prized in one circumstance, another in another circumstance. If, for example, an administrator values highly both the dispatch with which his agency can carry through its projects *and* good public relations, it matters little which of the two possibly conflicting values he favors in some abstract or general sense. Policy questions arise in forms which put to administrators such a question as: Given the degree to which we are or are not already achieving the values of dispatch and the values of good public relations, is it worth sacrificing a little speed for a happier clientele, or is it better to risk offending the clientele so that we can get on with our work? The answer to such a question varies with circumstances.

The value problem is, as the example shows, always a problem of adjustments at a margin. But there is no practicable way to state marginal objectives or values except in terms of particular policies. That one value is preferred to another in one decision situation does not mean that it will be preferred in another decision situation in which it can be had only at great sacrifice of another value. Attempts to rank or order values in general and abstract terms so that they do not shift from decision to decision end up by ignoring the relevant marginal preferences. The significance of this third point thus goes very far. Even if all administrators had at hand an agreed set of values, objectives, and constraints, and an agreed ranking of these values, objectives, and constraints, their marginal values in actual choice situations would be impossible to formulate.

Unable consequently to formulate the relevant values first and then choose among policies to achieve them, administrators must choose directly among alternative policies that offer different marginal combinations of values. Somewhat paradoxically, the only practicable way to disclose one's relevant marginal values even to oneself is to describe the policy one chooses to achieve them. Except roughly and vaguely, I know of no way to describe—or even to understand—what my relative evaluations are for, say, freedom and security, speed and accuracy in governmental decisions, or low taxes and better schools than to describe my preferences among specific policy choices that might be made between the alternatives in each of the pairs.

In summary, two aspects of the process by which values are actually handled can be distinguished. The first is clear: evaluation and empirical analysis are intertwined; that is, one chooses among values and among policies at one and the same time. Put a little more elaborately, one simultaneously chooses a policy to attain certain objectives and chooses the objectives themselves. The second aspect is related but distinct: the administrator focuses his attention on marginal or incremental values. Whether he is aware of it or not, he does not find general formulations of objectives very helpful and in fact makes specific marginal or incremental comparisons. Two policies, X and Y, confront him. Both promise the same degree of attainment of objectives a, b, c, d, and e. But X promises him somewhat more of f than does Y, while Y promises him somewhat more of g than does X. In choosing between them, he is in fact offered the alternative of a marginal or incremental amount of f at the expense of a marginal or incremental amount of g. The only values that are relevant to his choice are these increments by which the two policies differ; and, when he finally chooses between the two marginal values, he does so by making a choice between policies.[5]

As to whether the attempt to clarify objectives in advance of policy selection is more or less rational than the close intertwining of marginal evaluation and empirical analysis, the principal difference established is that for complex problems the first is impossible and irrelevant, and the second is both possible and relevant. The second is possible because the administrator need not try to analyze any values except the values by which alternative policies differ and need not be concerned with them except as they differ marginally. His need for information on values or objectives is drastically reduced as compared with the root method; and his capacity for grasping, comprehending, and relating values to one another is not strained beyond the breaking point.

Relations Between Means and Ends (2b)

Decision-making is ordinarily formalized as a means-ends relationship: means are conceived to be evaluated and chosen in the light of ends finally selected independently of and prior to the choice of means. This is the means-ends relationship of the root method. But it follows from all that has just been said that such a means-ends relationship is possible only to the extent that values are agreed upon, are reconcilable, and are stable at the margin. Typically, therefore, such a means-ends relationship is absent from the branch method, where means and ends are simultaneously chosen.

Yet any departure from the means-ends relationship of the root method will strike some readers as inconceivable. For it will appear to them that only in such a relationship is it possible to determine whether one policy choice is better or worse than another. How can an administrator know whether he has made a wise or foolish decision if he is without prior values or objectives by which to judge his decisions? The answer to this question calls up the third distinctive difference between root and branch methods: how to decide the best policy.

The Test of "Good" Policy (3b)

In the root method, a decision is "correct," "good," or "rational" if it can be shown to attain some specified objective, where the objective can be specified without simply describing the decision itself. Where objectives are defined only through the marginal or incremental approach to values described above, it is still sometimes possible to test whether a policy does in fact attain the desired objectives; but a precise statement of the objectives takes the form of a description of the policy chosen or some alternative to it. To show that a policy is mistaken one cannot offer an abstract argument that important objectives are not achieved; one must instead argue that another policy is more to be preferred.

So far, the departure from customary ways of looking at problem-solving is not troublesome, for many administrators will be quick to agree that the most effective discussion of the correctness of policy does take the form of comparison with other policies that might have been chosen. But what of the situation in which administrators cannot agree on values or objectives, either abstractly or in marginal terms? What then is the test of "good" policy? For the root method, there is no test. Agreement on objectives failing, there is no standard of "correctness." For the method of successive limited comparisons, the test is agreement on policy itself, which remains possible even when agreement on values is not.

It has been suggested that continuing agreement in Congress on the desirability of extending old age insurance stems from liberal desires to strengthen the welfare programs of the federal government and from conservative desires to reduce union demands for private pension plans. If so, this is an excellent demonstration of the ease with which individuals of different ideologies often can agree on concrete policy. Labor mediators report a similar phenomenon: the contestants cannot agree on criteria for settling their disputes but can agree on specific proposals. Similarly, when one administrator's objective turns out to be another's means, they often can agree on policy.

Agreement on policy thus becomes the only practicable test of the policy's correctness. And for one administrator to seek to win the other over to agreement on ends as well would accomplish nothing and create quite unnecessary controversy.

If agreement directly on policy as a test for "best" policy seems a poor substitute for testing the policy

against its objectives, it ought to be remembered that objectives themselves have no ultimate validity other than they are agreed upon. Hence agreement is the test of "best" policy in both methods. But where the root method requires agreement on what elements in the decision constitute objectives and on which of these objectives should be sought, the branch method falls back on agreement wherever it can be found.

In an important sense, therefore, it is not irrational for an administrator to defend a policy as good without being able to specify what it is good for.

Non-Comprehensive Analysis (4b)

Ideally, rational-comprehensive analysis leaves out nothing important. But it is impossible to take everything important into consideration unless "important" is so narrowly defined that analysis is in fact quite limited. Limits on human intellectual capacities and on available information set definite limits to man's capacity to be comprehensive. In actual fact, therefore, no one can practice the rational-comprehensive method for really complex problems, and every administrator faced with a sufficiently complex problem must find ways drastically to simplify.

An administrator assisting in the formulation of agricultural economic policy cannot in the first place be competent on all possible policies. He cannot even comprehend one policy entirely. In planning a soil bank program, he cannot successfully anticipate the impact of higher or lower farm income on, say, urbanization—the possible consequent loosening of family ties, possible consequent eventual need for revisions in social security and further implications for tax problems arising out of new federal responsibilities for social security and municipal responsibilities for urban services. Nor, to follow another line of repercussions, can he work through the soil bank program's effects on prices for agricultural products in foreign markets and consequent implications for foreign relations, including those arising out of economic rivalry between the United States and the U.S.S.R.

In the method of successive limited comparisons, simplification is systematically achieved in two principal ways. First, it is achieved through limitation of policy comparisons to those policies that differ in relatively small degree from policies presently in effect. Such a limitation immediately reduces the number of alternatives to be investigated and also drastically simplifies the character of the investigation of each. For it is not necessary to undertake fundamental inquiry into an alternative and its consequences; it is necessary only to study those respects in which the proposed alternative and its consequences differ from the status quo. The empirical comparison of marginal differences among alternative policies that differ only marginally is, of course, a counterpart to the incremental or marginal comparison of values discussed above.[6]

Relevance as Well as Realism

It is a matter of common observation that in Western democracies public administrators and policy analysts in general do largely limit their analyses to incremental or marginal differences in policies that are chosen to differ only incrementally. They do not do so, however, solely because they desperately need some way to simplify their problems; they also do so in order to be relevant. Democracies change their policies almost entirely through incremental adjustments. Policy does not move in leaps and bounds.

The incremental character of political change in the United States has often been remarked. The two major political parties agree on fundamentals; they offer alternative policies to the voters only on relatively small points of difference. Both parties favor full employment, but they define it somewhat differently; both favor the development of water power resources, but in slightly different ways; and both favor unemployment compensation, but not the same level of benefits. Similarly, shifts of policy within a party take place largely through a series of relatively small changes, as can be seen in their only gradual acceptance of the idea of governmental responsibility for support of the unemployed, a change in party positions beginning in the early 30's and culminating in a sense in the Employment Act of 1946.

Party behavior is in turn rooted in public attitudes, and political theorists cannot conceive of democracy's surviving in the United States in the absence of fundamental agreement on potentially disruptive issues, with consequent limitation of policy debates to relatively small differences in policy.

Since the policies ignored by the administrator are politically impossible and so irrelevant, the simplification of analysis achieved by concentrating on policies that differ only incrementally is not a capricious kind of simplification. In addition, it can be argued that, given the limits on knowledge within which policy-makers are confined, simplifying by limiting the focus to small variations from present policy makes the most of available knowledge. Because policies being considered are like present and past policies, the administrator can obtain information and claim some insight. Non-incremental policy proposals are therefore typically not only politically irrelevant but also unpredictable in their consequences.

The second method of simplification of analysis is the practice of ignoring important possible consequences of possible policies, as well as the values attached to the neglected consequences. If this appears to disclose a shocking shortcoming of successive limited comparisons, it can be replied that, even if the exclusions are random, policies may nevertheless be more intelligently formulated than through futile attempts to achieve a comprehensiveness beyond human capacity. Actually, however, the exclusions, seeming arbitrary or random from one point of view, need be neither.

Achieving a Degree of Comprehensiveness

Suppose that each value neglected by one policy-making agency were a major concern of at least one other agency. In that case, a helpful division of labor would be achieved, and no agency need find its task beyond its capacities. The shortcomings of such a system would be that one agency might destroy a value either before another agency could be activated to safeguard it or in spite of another agency's efforts. But the possibility that important values may be lost is present in any form of organization, even where agencies attempt to comprehend in planning more than is humanly possible.

The virtue of such a hypothetical division of labor is that every important interest or value has its watchdog. And these watchdogs can protect the interests in their jurisdiction in two quite different ways: first, by redressing damages done by other agencies; and, second, by anticipating and heading off injury before it occurs.

In a society like that of the United States in which individuals are free to combine to pursue almost any possible common interest they might have and in which government agencies are sensitive to the pressures of these groups, the system described is approximated. Almost every interest has its watchdog. Without claiming that every interest has a sufficiently powerful watchdog, it can be argued that our system often can assure a more comprehensive regard for the values of the whole society than any attempt at intellectual comprehensiveness.

In the United States, for example, no part of government attempts a comprehensive overview of policy on income distribution. A policy nevertheless evolves, and one responding to a wide variety of interests. A process of mutual adjustment among farm groups, labor unions, municipalities and school boards, tax authorities, and government agencies with responsibilities in the fields of housing, health, highways, national parks, fire, and police accomplishes a distribution of income in which particular income problems neglected at one point in the decision processes become central at another point.

Mutual adjustment is more pervasive than the explicit forms it takes in negotiation between groups; it persists through the mutual impacts of groups upon each other even where they are not in communication. For all the imperfections and latent dangers in this ubiquitous process of mutual adjustment, it will often accomplish an adaptation of policies to a wider range of interests than could be done by one group centrally.

Note, too, how the incremental pattern of policy-making fits with the multiple pressure pattern. For when decisions are only incremental—closely related to known policies, it is easier for one group to anticipate the kind of moves another might make and easier

too for it to make correction for injury already accomplished.[7]

Even partisanship and narrowness, to use pejorative terms, will sometimes be assets to rational decision-making, for they can doubly insure that what one agency neglects, another will not; they specialize personnel to distinct points of view. The claim is valid that effective rational coordination of the federal administration, if possible to achieve at all, would require an agreed set of values[8]—if "rational" is defined as the practice of the root method of decision-making. But a high degree of administrative coordination occurs as each agency adjusts its policies to the concerns of the other agencies in the process of fragmented decision-making I have just described.

For all the apparent shortcomings of the incremental approach to policy alternatives with its arbitrary exclusion coupled with fragmentation, when compared to the root method, the branch method often looks far superior. In the root method, the inevitable exclusion of factors is accidental, unsystematic, and not defensible by any argument so far developed, while in the branch method the exclusions are deliberate, systematic, and defensible. Ideally, of course, the root method does not exclude; in practice it must.

Nor does the branch method necessarily neglect long-run considerations and objectives. It is clear that important values must be omitted in considering policy, and sometimes the only way long-run objectives can be given adequate attention is through the neglect of short-run consideration. But the values omitted can be either long-run or short-run.

Succession of Comparisons (5b)

The final distinctive element in the branch method is that the comparisons, together with the policy choice, proceed in a chronological series. Policy is not made once and for all; it is made and remade endlessly. Policy-making is a process of successive approximation to some desired objectives in which what is desired itself continues to change under reconsideration.

Making policy is at best a very rough process. Neither social scientists, nor politicians, nor public administrators yet know enough about the social world to avoid repeated error in predicting the consequences of policy moves. A wise policy-maker consequently expects that his policies will achieve only part of what he hopes and at the same time will produce unanticipated consequences he would have preferred to avoid. If he proceeds through a *succession* of incremental changes, he avoids serious lasting mistakes in several ways.

In the first place, past sequences of policy steps have given him knowledge about the probable consequences of further similar steps. Second, he need not attempt big jumps toward his goals that would require predictions beyond his or anyone else's knowledge, because he never expects his policy to be a final resolution of a problem. His decision is only one step, one that if successful can quickly be followed by another. Third, he is in effect able to test his previous predictions as he moves on to each further step. Lastly, he often can remedy a past error fairly quickly—more quickly than if policy proceeded through more distinct steps widely spaced in time.

Compare this comparative analysis of incremental changes with the aspiration to employ theory in the root method. Man cannot think without classifying, without subsuming one experience under a more general category of experiences. The attempt to push categorization as far as possible and to find general propositions which can be applied to specific situations is what I refer to with the word "theory." Where root analysis often leans heavily on theory in this sense, the branch method does not.

The assumption of root analysis is that theory is the most systematic and economical way to bring relevant knowledge to bear on a specific problem. Granting the assumption, an unhappy fact is that we do not have adequate theory to apply to problems in any policy area, although theory is more adequate in some areas— monetary policy, for example—than in others. Comparative analysis, as in the branch method, is sometimes a systematic alternative to theory.

Suppose an administrator must choose among a small group of policies that differ only incrementally from each other and from present policy. He might aspire to "understand" each of the alternatives—for example, to know all the consequences of each aspect of each policy. If so, he would indeed require theory.

In fact, however, he would usually decide that, *for policy-making purposes,* he need know, as explained above, only the consequences of each of those aspects of the policies in which they differed from one another. For this much more modest aspiration, he requires no theory (although it might be helpful, if available), for he can proceed to isolate probable differences by examining the differences in consequences associated with past differences in policies, a feasible program because he can take his observations from a long sequence of incremental changes.

For example, without a more comprehensive social theory about juvenile delinquency than scholars have yet produced, one cannot possibly understand the ways in which a variety of public policies—say on education, housing, recreation, employment, race relations, and policing—might encourage or discourage delinquency. And one needs such an understanding if he undertakes the comprehensive overview of the problem prescribed in the models of the root method. If, however, one merely wants to mobilize knowledge sufficient to assist in a choice among a small group of similar policies—alternative policies on juvenile court procedures, for example—he can do so by comparative analysis of the results of similar past policy moves.

Theorists and Practitioners

This difference explains—in some cases at least— why the administrator often feels that the outside expert or academic problem-solver is sometimes not helpful and why they in turn often urge more theory on him. And it explains why an administrator often feels more confident when "flying by the seat of his pants" than when following the advice of theorists. Theorists often ask the administrator to go the long way round to the solution of his problems, in effect ask him to follow the best canons of the scientific method, when the administrator knows the best available theory will work less well than more modest incremental comparisons. Theorists do not realize that the administrator is often in fact practicing a systematic method. It would be foolish to push this explanation too far, for sometimes practical decision-makers are pursuing neither a theoretical approach nor successive comparisons, nor any other systematic method.

It may be worth emphasizing that theory is sometimes of extremely limited helpfulness in policy-making for at least two rather different reasons. It is greedy for facts; it can be constructed only through a great collection of observations. And it is typically insufficiently precise for application to a policy process that moves through small changes. In contrast, the comparative method both economizes on the need for facts and directs the analyst's attention to just those facts that are relevant to the fine choices faced by the decision-maker.

With respect to precision of theory, economic theory serves as an example. It predicts that an economy without money or prices would in certain specified ways misallocate resources, but this finding pertains to an alternative far removed from the kind of policies on which administrators need help. On the other hand, it is not precise enough to predict the consequences of policies restricting business mergers, and this is the kind of issue on which the administrators need help. Only in relatively restricted areas does economic theory achieve sufficient precision to go far in resolving policy questions; its helpfulness in policy-making is always so limited that it requires supplementation through comparative analysis.

Successive Comparison as a System

Successive limited comparison is, then, indeed a method or system; it is not a failure of method for which administrators ought to apologize. None the less, its imperfections, which have not been explored in this paper, are many. For example, the method is without a built-in safeguard for all relevant values, and it also may lead the decision-maker to overlook excellent policies for no other reason than that they are not suggested by the chain of successive policy steps leading up to the present. Hence, it ought to be said that under this method, as well as under some of the most sophisticated variants of the root method—operations research, for example—policies will continue to be as foolish as they are wise.

Why then bother to describe the method in all the above detail? Because it is in fact a common method of policy formulation, and is, for complex problems, the principal reliance of administrators as well as of other policy analysts.[9] And because it will be superior to any other decision-making method available for complex problems in many circumstances, certainly superior to a futile attempt at super-human comprehensiveness. The reaction of the public administrator to the exposition of method doubtless will be less a discovery of a new method than a better acquaintance with an old. But by becoming more conscious of their practice of this method, administrators might practice it with more skill and know when to extend or constrict its use. (That they sometimes practice it effectively and sometimes not may explain the extremes of opinion on "muddling through," which is both praised as a highly sophisticated form of problem-solving and denounced as no method at all. For I suspect that in so far as there is a system in what is known as "muddling through," this method is it.)

One of the noteworthy incidental consequences of clarification of the method is the light it throws on the suspicion an administrator sometimes entertains that a consultant or adviser is not speaking relevantly and responsibly when in fact by all ordinary objective evidence he is. The trouble lies in the fact that most of us approach policy problems within a framework given by our view of a chain of successive policy choices made up to the present. One's thinking about appropriate policies with respect, say, to urban traffic control is greatly influenced by one's knowledge of the incremental steps taken up to the present. An administrator enjoys an intimate knowledge of his past sequences that "outsiders" do not share, and his thinking and that of the "outsider" will consequently be different in ways that may puzzle both. Both may appear to be talking intelligently, yet each may find the other unsatisfactory. The relevance of the policy chain of succession is even more clear when an American tries to discuss, say, antitrust policy with a Swiss, for the chains of policy in the two countries are strikingly different and the two individuals consequently have organized their knowledge in quite different ways.

If this phenomenon is a barrier to communication, an understanding of it promises an enrichment of intellectual interaction in policy formulation. Once the source of difference is understood, it will sometimes be stimulating for an administrator to seek out a policy analyst whose recent experience is with a policy chain different from his own.

This raises again a question only briefly discussed above on the merits of like-mindedness among government administrators. While much of organization theory argues the virtues of common values and agreed organizational objectives, for complex problems in which the root method is inapplicable, agencies will want among their own personnel two types of diversification: administrators whose thinking is organized by reference to policy chains other than those familiar to most members of the organization and, even more commonly, administrators whose professional or personal values or interests create diversity of view (perhaps coming from different specialties, social classes, geographical areas) so that, even within a single agency, decision-making can be fragmented and parts of the agency can serve as watchdogs for other parts.

Notes

1. James G. March and Herbert A. Simon similarly characterized the literature. They also take some important steps, as have Simon's recent articles, to describe a less heroic model of policy-making. See *Organizations* (John Wiley and Sons, 1958), p. 137.

2. "Operations Research and National Planning— A Dissent," 5 *Operations Research* 718 (October, 1957). Hitch's dissent is from particular points made in the article to which his paper is a reply; his claim that operations research is for low-level problems is widely accepted.

   For examples of the kind of problems to which operations research is applied, see C. W. Churchman, R. L. Ackoff and E. L. Arnoff, *Introduction to Operations Research* (John Wiley and Sons, 1957); and J. F. McCloskey and J. M. Coppinger (eds.), *Operations Research for Management,* Vol. II (The Johns Hopkins Press, 1956).

3. I am assuming that administrators often make policy and advise in the making of policy and

am treating decision-making and policy-making as synonymous for purposes of this paper.

4. Martin Meyerson and Edward C. Banfield, *Politics, Planning and the Public Interest* (The Free Press, 1955).

5. The line of argument is, of course, an extension of the theory of market choice, especially the theory of consumer choice, to public policy choices.

6. A more precise definition of incremental policies and a discussion of whether a change that appears "small" to one observer might be seen differently by another is to be found in my "Policy Analysis," 48 *American Economic Review* 298 (June, 1958).

7. The link between the practice of the method of successive limited comparisons and mutual adjustment of interests in a highly fragmented decision-making process adds a new facet to pluralist theories of government and administration.

8. Herbert Simon, Donald W. Smithburg, and Victor A. Thompson, *Public Administration* (Alfred A. Knopf, 1950), p. 434.

9. Elsewhere I have explored this same method of policy formulation as practiced by academic analysts of policy ("Policy Analysis," 48 *American Economic Review* 298 [June, 1958]). Although it has been here presented as a method for public administrators, it is no less necessary to analysts more removed from immediate policy questions, despite their tendencies to describe their own analytical efforts as though they were the rational-comprehensive method with an especially heavy use of theory. Similarly, this same method is inevitably resorted to in personal problem-solving, where means and ends are sometimes impossible to separate, where aspirations or objectives undergo constant development, and where drastic simplification of the complexity of the real world is urgent if problems are to be solved in the time that can be given to them. To an economist accustomed to dealing with the marginal or incremental concept in market processes, the central idea in the method is that both evaluation and empirical analysis are incremental. Accordingly I have referred to the method elsewhere as "the incremental method."

CASE STUDY 8

Introduction

One of the most explosive urban events of recent decades occurred in Philadelphia on May 13, 1985, when the Philadelphia police confronted the black activist cult MOVE. As the introduction to the following case, "The MOVE Disaster," recounts:

> After massive gunfire, deluges of water and explosive charges failed to dislodge the group from their fortified row house, police dropped plastic explosives from a helicopter onto a rooftop bunker. The bomb ignited an unexpected fire. Believing they could contain the fire, Police Commissioner Gregore Sambor and Fire Commissioner William Richmond decided to let the bunker burn. They miscalculated badly, and the fire raged out of control. Sweeping through three adjoining blocks, the inferno destroyed 61 homes and left 250 people homeless. Of the occupants of the MOVE house, one adult and one child fled through the flames into police custody. In the ashes were found the bodies of six adults and five children.

What caused this tragedy? Several investigative organizations and other observers attributed much of the blame to ineffective management by the city's mayor, W. Wilson Goode. Ironically, Goode previously had been viewed as a highly successful mayor, not only by those within the city but throughout the nation. This single event severely damaged his reputation as "an effective manager, a rising star in national politics, and a symbol of hope for his city," according to the author, Jack H. Nagel, a professor of political science and public policy and management at the University of Pennsylvania.

In the following case, Nagel focuses on how Goode made his choices related to the MOVE decision and explores the causes of why a previously well-regarded public manager should exhibit such an uncharacteristic breakdown in his performance, bordering on what some viewed as irresponsible behavior. The author first explains the background of MOVE as a controversial activist group within Philadelphia and the two central paradoxes of Mayor Goode's behavior in response to MOVE's actions. What makes Nagel's case study especially remarkable and insightful is how the author then goes on to probe beneath the surface of Goode's managerial actions related to MOVE. Nagel analyzes three particular psychological problems that the mayor exhibited and relates these mental difficulties to current theories of the psychology of decision making. From this case, the author generalizes important lessons and implications for government decision-making that relate directly and profoundly to the previous reading by Charles Lindblom.

As you review the following case, try to reflect on these questions:

How did Mayor Goode first decide to respond to MOVE's activities? What misconceptions did Goode implicitly hold about MOVE? What were the sources of these misconceptions, in your view?

Do you agree with the author that these misconceptions were ultimately rooted in the mayor's "unresolved decisional conflicts that impeded responsible and rational handling of the problem"? What were these "three decisional conflicts," according to the author? How does Nagel support his argument by drawing on the theory of decision making developed by Irving Janis and Leon Mann? What are the assumptions of the Janis/Mann thesis?

As opposed to the Lindblom incremental model, does Nagel's story suggest an entirely different understanding of decision making—one rooted in personal values? What are the implications for public managers and how they can or should improve their own decision-making capacities?

The MOVE Disaster

JACK H. NAGEL

On May 13, 1985, a confrontation between Philadelphia police and a cult called MOVE resulted in one of the most astounding debacles in the history of American municipal government. After massive gunfire, deluges of water, and explosive charges failed to dislodge the group from their fortified row house, police dropped plastic explosives from a helicopter onto a rooftop bunker. The bomb ignited an unexpected fire. Believing they could contain the fire, Police Commissioner Gregore Sambor and Fire Commissioner William Richmond decided to let the bunker burn. They miscalculated badly, and the fire raged out of control. Sweeping through three adjoining blocks, the inferno destroyed 61 homes and left 250 people homeless. Of the occupants of the MOVE house, one adult and one child fled through the flames into police custody. In the ashes were found the bodies of six adults and five children.

The MOVE tragedy severely damaged the reputation of Philadelphia Mayor W. Wilson Goode, who until then had been considered an effective manager, a rising star of national politics, and a symbol of hope for his city. In the aftermath of the disaster, a controversial grand jury decided not to bring criminal charges against the mayor and his chief aides, but condemned them for "morally reprehensible behavior" [Philadelphia Court of Common Pleas, 1988, p. 279]. The Philadelphia Special Investigation Commission (PSIC), appointed by the mayor himself, charged that "the Mayor abdi-cated his responsibilities as a leader," a condemnation shared by most informed observers.[1] With respect to the twelve values Charles Gilbert [1959] identifies with administrative responsibility, Goode and his key subordinates conspicuously failed to satisfy at least seven—responsiveness, consistency, stability, leadership, competence, efficacy, and prudence.

None of the many commentators ever satisfactorily explained why the previously impressive mayor was so irresponsible in this instance and in particular why his behavior contrasted so sharply with his reputation for hands-on management. Many observers subsequently avoided the incongruity by concluding that Goode had simply been "incompetent" all along. Whereas before MOVE he could do no wrong, after the disaster he seldom got credit for doing anything right. This paper will argue instead that, lamentable though it was, the mayor's performance exemplifies universal tendencies well understood by psychologists of decision making. Analysis of the MOVE case therefore can suggest insights that may enable other administrators to recognize and control situations in which they too might otherwise succumb to irresponsible patterns of action and inaction.

The presentation that follows is organized into five sections: (a) a brief history of MOVE and its conflict with the City of Philadelphia; (b) a description of two central paradoxes in Mayor Goode's response to MOVE; (c) an explanation of both paradoxes using a standard theory about the psychology of decision making; (d) a closer examination of three decisional conflicts that may explain why Goode had such difficulty dealing with this particular problem; and (e) reflections on lessons the MOVE disaster offers for the education of present and future public managers.

"The MOVE Disaster" (originally titled "Psychological Obstacles to Administrative Responsibility: Lessons of the MOVE Disaster"), by Jack H. Nagel, *Journal of Policy Analysis and Management*, Vol. 10, No. 1, pp. 1–23. Copyright © 1991 by John Wiley & Sons, Inc. Reprinted by permission of John Wiley & Sons, Inc.

MOVE Versus Philadelphia

The origins of MOVE can be traced to the early 1970s in the Powelton Village section of West Philadelphia, near the campuses of Drexel University and the University of Pennsylvania.[2] In this tolerant community, a haven for political and cultural rebels, a charismatic black handyman named Vincent Leaphart developed an anarchistic, back-to-nature philosophy, the main tenets of which were reverence for all animal life, rejection of "the [American] Lifestyle," and absolute refusal to cooperate with "the System." Aided by a white graduate in social work from Penn named Donald Glassey, who transcribed Leaphart's thoughts and taught them in a course at the Community College of Philadelphia, Leaphart attracted a "family" that eventually numbered at least forty members, most but not all of whom were black. At first they called themselves the American Christian Movement for Life, but they later shortened the name to MOVE. Following the example of Leaphart, who now referred to himself as John Africa, all the core members adopted the surname Africa, in honor of the continent where they believed life began.

As they put John Africa's philosophy into practice, MOVE generated frequent tension with landlords and neighbors, who complained about members' grossly unsanitary practices and their harboring of dogs, cats, rats, roaches, and flies. Beyond these spillovers of their peculiar lifestyle, MOVE members courted friction with authorities by confronting "the System" in all its manifestations, from the Philadelphia Zoo to Jimmy Carter. Using bullhorns to demonstrate and disrupt meetings, they perfected a vituperative rhetoric, profane and filled with sexual and racial provocation. When brought to trial, as they were literally hundreds of times, MOVE members acted as their own attorneys and clogged the courts by noncooperative, contemptuous tactics.

During the 1970s, a virtual feud developed between MOVE and the Philadelphia police. The mayor of Philadelphia was then Frank Rizzo, a former police commissioner famous for tough law enforcement. The majority of whites revered Mayor Rizzo's large and aggressive police department as a bulwark against crime and disorder, but political dissidents, blacks, and journalists accused the police of frequent brutality and disregard for civil liberties. As Anderson and Hevenor [1987, p. 11] observe, "MOVE demonstrators were frequently arrested, often harassed, and nearly always regarded with unconcealed disgust and contempt by

Philadelphia policemen. With their unwashed, garlic-reeking bodies, dreadlocks, and inpenetrable and obscene harangues, MOVE people were a constant affront to a police force that was (and is) largely white, ethnic . . . and Catholic."[3]

After a melee in March 1976, when MOVE accused the police of causing the death of a MOVE infant, John Africa apparently decided to turn to armed resistance. By this time, core members of MOVE occupied a house owned by Glassey on North 33rd Street. Using loudspeakers fixed in trees, they frequently harangued their neighbors. Responding to complaints, city officials attempted to investigate code violations but were refused admittance. In September 1975, the city began the protracted process of enforcing the code through the courts. A judgment mandating inspections was obtained in July 1976, whereupon MOVE constructed an eight-foot stockage around their compound. Heeding MOVE warnings that they would "cycle" (kill) their own children before submitting to inspections, the city refrained from enforcing the order. On May 20, 1977, mistakenly anticipating a city attempt to enter the premises, MOVE members brandished guns on the platform of their stockade. Shortly afterwards, Donald Glassey was arrested for filing false information when purchasing firearms. Turning informant to save himself, Glassey helped police seize MOVE guns and explosives at a location elsewhere in Philadelphia.

The stalemate in Powelton continued for nearly a year. On March 1, 1978, the city obtained court permission to blockade the MOVE headquarters for non-payment of utility bills and refusal to admit inspectors. Police cordoned off a four-block area around the house and shut off gas and water. The siege appeared to have succeeded when intermediaries helped negotiate a settlement that was announced on May 3. MOVE surrendered weapons, allowed officials to inspect the Powelton property, and promised to vacate the house by August 1. In return, the city relaxed its blockade, freed eighteen jailed MOVE members on their own recognizance, and promised to drop all charges once MOVE departed from Powelton.

When August 1 came, MOVE refused to leave, because no one had found a site for relocation they would accept. On August 8, Police Commissioner Joseph O'Neill directed a carefully planned operation to drive the occupants from the house. Announcing each action in advance in order to protect MOVE women and children, whom they regarded as hostages, the police used a bulldozer, ram, and armored truck to breach the walls of the compound. A crane began demolishing the upper stories. Believing that all MOVE weapons had been confiscated in May, authorities were careless about concealing themselves. Suddenly, police saw a gun muzzle protruding from a basement window. After deluge guns flooded the basement, gunfire erupted, killing Officer James Ramp and wounding eight other policemen and firefighters. Following the exchange of shots, police poured in more water and smoke to flush out the occupants. As the MOVE members surrendered, officers beat and kicked Delbert Africa while news photographers recorded the action.

During the next five years, MOVE was visible to most Philadelphians only through a series of trials. In 1980, nine members were sentenced to lengthy prison terms for the murder of Officer Ramp; a tenth followed in 1982. In 1981, three police officers were tried for the beating of Delbert Africa and acquitted.[4] On May 13, 1981, Federal agents arrested John Africa and eight followers in Rochester, New York, where MOVE had owned houses since 1977. (At various times, MOVE also had enclaves in Richmond, Virginia, and Chester, Pennsylvania.) Defending himself and Alphonso Robbins Africa against bombmaking charges, John Africa won acquittal from a jury in Philadelphia in July 1981, after which he dropped out of sight.

As it turned out, the MOVE leader had not gone far. With a group of about a dozen adults and children, he was living in a house owned by his sister, Louise James, at 6221 Osage Avenue in the Cobbs Creek section on the western edge of Philadelphia, three miles from the site of the demolished house in Powelton.

Whereas the 33rd Street house had been a freestanding structure surrounded by a yard and located on a busy street, the new MOVE headquarters was a row house on a narrow, quiet residential street. These physical differences were to prove tactically important during the 1985 confrontation, but events in the two years preceding that catastrophe pivoted around social and political differences between the two neighborhoods. Nonconformist, racially mixed Powelton was a bastion of opposition to Mayor Rizzo. Its residents divided bitterly over whether the cultists or the police were the more distasteful presence in their midst. One can easily imagine Frank Rizzo enjoying some amusement at their discomfort.

In 1980, barred by the City Charter from serving three consecutive terms, Rizzo was succeeded as mayor by the more liberal former Congressman, William J. Green, Jr. Fulfilling a campaign promise to

Philadelphia's increasingly powerful black voters, Green appointed W. Wilson Goode as Managing Director, the city's chief appointive official. Goode, a former civil-rights activist, had previously served as executive director of the nonprofit Philadelphia Council for Community Advancement—where he was credited with building more housing than all the city's housing agencies combined [Cohn, 1982, p. 27]—and as chair of the Pennsylvania Public Utilities Commission. As Managing Director, Goode was in charge of ten operating departments, including police and fire. Hardworking, accessible, and highly visible, he soon became hugely popular among blacks and many whites as well. When Green announced in late 1982 that he would not seek a second term, Goode resigned to campaign for the mayoralty. In May 1983, he defeated Frank Rizzo in the Democratic primary, winning the votes of 98% of blacks and 23% of whites. In the November general election, he would face two white opponents.

The Cobbs Creek neighborhood was typical of Wilson Goode's bedrock political base. Its residents, almost all black, were generally stable working- and middle-class families. Most owned their homes and took pride in keeping them pleasant and attractive. By the fall of 1983, MOVE had become an intolerable affliction to this peaceful community. The home of Lloyd and Lucretia Wilson next door was invaded by insects that had spread from 6221. When the Wilsons sought to fumigate, Conrad Africa went berserk. "The bugs are our brothers and sisters. If you exterminate the bugs, you exterminate us," he berated Lloyd Wilson [PSIC, 1985, 10/9 AM, pp. 89–90]. In September 1983, following a dispute over a parking space, a MOVE male struck a neighbor named Butch Marshall to the ground, and three MOVE women bit Marshall on the face, back, and groin. After another assault in October, the neighbors circulated to city authorities a petition that complained about attacks, garbage, rats, a pigeon coop, animals, and MOVE's blocking of a common driveway behind the row.

As the neighbors "were reaching the breaking point," they met with State Representative Peter Truman.[5] Truman implored them not to do anything that would endanger the election of the city's first black mayor. If they would endure a few months longer, he assured them, Goode would solve their problem. Aided by the arrival of cold weather, which lessened health hazards and reduced outdoor interaction with MOVE, the neighbors waited. In November 1983, Goode won a resounding victory with 55% of the vote.

If Goode's triumph held promise of deliverance for the 6200 block, John Africa saw it as a different sort of opportunity, one that would produce intensified torment for the Osage neighbors. Obsessed with freeing his followers from prison, the MOVE leader believed that the mayor had the power to obtain their release and that the residents of Osage Avenue could persuade him to use that power. MOVE therefore embarked upon a campaign of what Goode later would call "psychological warfare" against their neighbors, holding the block "hostage" in order to obtain as ransom the release of their ten convicted comrades. MOVE launched their campaign on Christmas morning, 1983. Beginning near dawn and continuing for eight hours, their rooftop loudspeakers blared an obscene diatribe that denounced the neighbors, the mayor-elect, and the System, and demanded freedom for MOVE prisoners. Eight days later, Wilson Goode became mayor of Philadelphia.

Two Paradoxes

Mayor Goode's response to MOVE's challenge can be characterized by describing two patterns, both of which seem paradoxical. First, for sixteen months he avoided any significant action; but when he finally decided to enforce the law, the city mobilized against MOVE in less than a week and tried to execute a hastily prepared plan in the span of twenty-four hours. Second, although he was widely perceived to be an energetic, detail-oriented administrator, when he decided the city should act against MOVE, Goode had minimal personal involvement in both the planning and the execution of the attack.

Delay Followed by Haste

MOVE's war against the System, by way of their neighbors, continued through 1984 and the spring of 1985. In December 1983, they began fortifying their house by nailing boards across the windows; the ramshackle effect contrasted starkly with the neat white trim and porches of the other houses. In October 1984 they started a rooftop construction that eventually became a bunker made of railroad ties, logs, and steel plates. Similar materials were placed against the interior walls of the house and basement. In May 1984, a hooded MOVE member brandished a shotgun on the roof, and

the cultists began the practice of running across the roofs of the row at night, waking frightened residents. Loudspeaker harangues were conducted daily for six to eight hours through the summer and fall of 1984. In these and other communications, MOVE members threatened the lives of President Reagan, Mayor Goode, judges, and any police officers who might try to enforce the law on Osage Avenue. A favorite tactic was to target a particular neighbor for a day, during which the unfortunate individual would be subjected to personal attacks filled with accusations of homosexuality, child molestation, promiscuity, or sexual inadequacy. As Bennie Swans of the Crisis Intervention Network later commented, "MOVE did not let up on those residents. They simply did not let up" [PSIC, 1985, 10/9 AM, p. 68].

Mayor Goode was aware of most of these developments. On March 9, 1984, Commissioner Sambor briefed him about the deteriorating situation on Osage Avenue. On May 28 and July 4, he met at their request with delegations of residents; they found the mayor knowledgeable about their plight and personally familiar with MOVE members, but unwilling to act. In June 1984, District Attorney Edward Rendell provided Goode with a memo outlining a legal strategy for disarming MOVE and abating the nuisance on Osage Avenue. Goode also received several phone calls from block captain Clifford Bond. On August 9, Lloyd Wilson came to City Hall to complain of an assault he had suffered the day before at the hands of Frank James Africa, while police officers watched from the corner. Goode "whisked" Wilson off to a side office, where he had a lengthy but unproductive conversation with Managing Director Leo Brooks and Commissioner Sambor. Subsequently, Wilson and his family abandoned their home, driven out by vermin, noise, and fear from which their government would not protect them.

During this time, city policy barred operating departments (including Health, Water, Human Services, Streets, and Licenses and Inspections) from carrying out their responsibilities with respect to MOVE, which they were told was "a police matter." For their part, the police maintained surveillance of the 6200 block, but refrained from intervention. They even discouraged state parole officials from serving outstanding fugitive warrants against two residents of the house, Frank James Africa and Larry Howard [Philadelphia Court of Common Pleas, 1988, p. 26]. In response to the neighbors' entreaties, Goode took only two tangible actions: He extended the hours of nearby city recreation centers so residents' children could escape the loudspeakers, and he arranged psychological counseling to help the children cope with chronic tension.

Five of the MOVE Commission's findings describe and condemn this protracted phase of inaction:

1. Mayor Goode's policy toward MOVE was one of appeasement, non-confrontation, and avoidance.
2. The Managing Director and the city's department heads failed to take any effective action on their own and, in fact, ordered their subordinates to refrain from taking action to deal meaningfully with the problem on Osage Avenue. . . .
3. In the first several months of his administration, the mayor was presented with compelling evidence that his policy of appeasement, non-confrontation, and avoidance was doomed to fail.
4. In the summer of 1984, the mayor was told that the legal basis existed at that time to act against certain MOVE members. Yet, the mayor held back, and continued to follow his policy of avoidance and non-confrontation.
5. From the fall of 1984 to the spring of 1985, the city's policy of appeasement conceded to the residents of 6221 Osage Ave. the continued right to exist above the law. [PSIC, 1986, pp. 11–13]

To this indictment should be added two more charges. First, by tolerating MOVE's abuses, the city government for two years abdicated its most basic responsibilities to the law-abiding residents of Osage Avenue. As Clifford Bond put it, "I was placed in a position of feeling not as a citizen" [PSIC, 1985, 10/9 AM, p. 4]. Second, by giving MOVE time to fortify their house, the policy of nonconfrontation made the task of dislodging the cult immensely more difficult when the mayor finally decided to act.

Sixteen months of delay abruptly gave way to fourteen days of hasty action in the spring of 1985. The shift in policy was precipitated by the neighbors. Unwilling to accept another summer of stench and harangues, they organized themselves as the United Residents of the 6200 Block of Osage Avenue and held a public protest meeting on April 25, during which several men announced they would respond to MOVE "in kind." At a May 1 press conference, the United Residents expressed their disgust with the city's inaction and requested intervention by Pennsylvania Governor Dick Thornburgh, a Republican. Coupled with new provocations by MOVE,

these actions got the attention of the media, and editorialists demanded that the city meet its responsibilities.

On May 3, Mayor Goode convened a high-level meeting at which he asked District Attorney Edward Rendell to establish a legal basis for city action against the occupants of 6221. On May 5 Rendell's staff interviewed Osage residents in order to prepare warrants. At a second high-level meeting on May 7, Goode directed Commissioner Sambor to develop a plan that was to be carried out under the supervision of Managing Director Leo Brooks, a former Army major general.

Having anticipated action, Sambor had set up a planning group a week earlier. Remarkably low in rank for such a major operation, it consisted of three men who had served under Sambor in his previous post as commander of the Police Academy: Lieutenant Frank Powell, head of the Bomb Disposal Unit; Sergeant Albert Revel, a pistol instructor; and Officer Michael Tursi, the Department's top sharpshooter.

On May 9, with Managing Director Brooks at his daughter's graduation in Virginia, Sambor briefed Goode on the plan the three officers had devised. He recommended that warrants be served on Sunday, May 12, which was Mother's Day. Out of concern for the holiday, Goode authorized Sambor to proceed on May 13. On May 11, a judge issued the warrants, and Sambor again briefed Goode. On the afternoon of May 12, police evacuated the neighborhood. Returning from Virginia that evening, Brooks heard on his car radio that the operation he was to head was underway. He arrived in Philadelphia in time to get a quick briefing from Sambor followed by a few hours' sleep.

At 5:35 a.m. on Monday, May 13, Sambor read an ultimatum to MOVE over a bullhorn, demanding that the four MOVE members named on the warrants surrender within fifteen minutes. MOVE used their own loudspeaker to reject the ultimatum in typical style, telling the police that their wives would be collecting insurance and sleeping with black men that night. When the fifteen minutes had expired, authorities directed water, tear gas, and smoke at the house and its roof. According to the police, MOVE responded with gunfire, and officers retaliated massively, firing many thousands of rounds in the next ninety minutes. The debacle was underway.

As the MOVE Commission and the grand jury pointed out, less hurried planning and execution might have prevented numerous errors and oversights. A full list would occupy many pages, so I shall mention just a few of the more egregious consequences of haste:

- Commissioner Sambor and his planners made little attempt to draw on the resources of other agencies, inside or outside the city government; consequently, they failed to consider alternative strategies and deprived themselves of expertise—such as the use of trained hostage negotiators—that might have resulted in better implementation of their plan.
- Goode, Sambor, and Brooks went ahead with the operation even though they knew that the mayor's directive to pick up the MOVE children before the assault had not been implemented. (MOVE adults usually took the children on daily outings to nearby Cobbs Creek Park, and as late as May 12, two of the children were observed outside the house.) Thus they "clearly risked the lives" of six innocent children, five of whom subsequently died in the conflagration [PSIC, 1986, p. 16].
- The quick, secretive, informal planning process deprived the tacticians of crucial knowledge possessed by others in city government, including surveillance officers. As a result, to take just one example, they did not appreciate the extent of the interior fortifications that foiled their initial strategy of attempting to insert tear gas through the walls.
- Contingency plans were not developed; the final, fatal decision to drop the bomb was the result of ill-considered improvisation. After the primary plan failed, officials were apparently determined to occupy the house before dark. When Brooks informed Goode of the bomb proposal by telephone at 5 p.m., the mayor paused only thirty seconds before approving the idea.
- Insufficient attention was given to communication systems, resulting in slow, incompatible, or non-existent communication channels between crucial actors—police and the occupants of the MOVE house, police and fire units, the mayor and managing director, and the managing director and police commissioner. Slow communications may have prevented Goode and Brooks from reversing in time Sambor's and Richmond's decision to let the bunker burn.

Arms-Length Action by a Hands-on Mayor

Until May 1985, both as Managing Director and as Mayor, Wilson Goode was perceived by the public as an incredibly hard-working, demanding, detail-oriented manager. Contemporary press descriptions give a vivid sense of his style: "He appears to be everywhere. . . . He annoys a lot of people because he continues to ask questions until he gets an answer that makes sense."[6] "He loves to come down hard on details" [Mallowe, 1980, p. 139]. "His zeal is prodigious, his double-digit days are legend . . ." [Javers, 1983]. "Today, in Philadelphia, in the first year of Wilson Goode's first term of office, there is absolutely no doubt about *who* is in charge" [Mallowe, 1984, p. 168]. Indeed, one of the few criticisms of Goode in this happy period was that he delegated too little: "He seeks near-absolute control over his operating departments" [Cohn, p. 21]. "He has an aversion to delegating authority. He tries to do too much on his own" [Mallowe, 1984, p. 226].

Goode's view of himself corresponded to the public image: "I want to know what the problems are in this city. . . . I can't do that sitting on the 16th floor here, I really can't" [Cohn, 1982, p. 13]. *"Someone* has to be in charge. People through the government must know that the mayor is there giving directions . . ." [Mallowe, 1984, p. 168]. "I'm a nuts-and-bolts person" [Mallowe, 1980, p. 139]. Perhaps his favorite term was "hands-on."

However, after he authorized an armed confrontation with MOVE, Goode was anything but hands-on. He held only two high-level meetings to plan the operation. The May 7 meeting focused on the legal basis for action, and the May 9 meeting lasted less than thirty minutes. On both occasions, Goode prevented detailed discussion of the police plan. The contrast in styles was pointed out to the MOVE Commission by District Attorney Rendell:

And I turned to the [Police] Commissioner and I said, "Are you going to use tear gas and water?" And he said yes and started to explain a little bit, and the Mayor said . . . , "Look, I will leave that up to you all. It's your plan and execute it." In other words, he cut off discussion. . . .

And I thought it was somewhat unusual. . . . I had known Wilson for the three years that he was Managing Director. I worked very closely with him . . . , and then while he was Mayor I had significant contact with him. Wilson's management style has always been one where he got involved in all—not in all of the details, but in certainly the significant details. And I thought that was . . . a little out of character. . . . [PSIC, 1985, 10/22 AM, pp. 71–72]

Rendell speculated that Goode wished to avoid leaks, that perhaps he "intended as soon as I walked out of the room to sit down and go over it blow by blow with the Police Commissioner" [PSIC, 1984, 10/22 AM, p. 95]. In fact, Sambor did brief Goode about the plan on May 11, but only because Brooks was out of town—at all other times, including May 13, Goode and Sambor strictly followed the chain of command, communicating with each other only through Brooks. Goode seems not to have been deeply engaged in the May 11 meeting, for he recalled it as occurring over the telephone, whereas Sambor testified in detail that he went to Goode's office. Goode's last briefing was by telephone on the evening of May 12, when Brooks called him to relay the discussion he had just had with the Police Commissioner.

On May 13 itself, Goode heeded the advice of his staff and Brooks by staying away not only from Osage Avenue, but also from Brooks' command post four blocks north at the Walnut Park Plaza, the tallest structure in the area. As the operation began, Goode followed developments together with four black elected officials whom he had invited to his home in Overbrook, about two miles from Osage Avenue. Later, in his office at City Hall, he was understandably preoccupied with MOVE. Although the mayor frequently conferred by phone with Brooks, Goode's distance from the scene and the clumsiness of his communication links prevented him from exercising effective control over the terrible events of that day.

In short, as the MOVE Commission concluded, "The mayor failed to perform his responsibility as the city's chief executive by not actively participating in the preparation, review and oversight of the plan" [PSIC, 1986, p. 16].

Irresponsibility and Decisional Conflict

In 1977, eight years before the MOVE disaster, the psychologists Irving Janis and Leon Mann published a treatise called *Decision Making*.[7] In it, they outlined a model based on psychological conflict that economically explains the two central paradoxes in Wilson Goode's actions, as well as many otherwise puzzling subsidiary aspects of his behavior during this tragic episode.

Janis and Mann premise their theory on the idea that decision making is not merely a cool intellectual process but also involves "hot" emotional influences. The need to make a decision is inherently stressful. Although moderate anxiety improves cognitive functioning, excessive stress can severely impair the quality of decision processes. The greatest stress occurs when all known options threaten to impose severe losses, especially if those losses are not merely "utilitarian" but include "highly ego-involving issues," such as severe social disapproval and/or self-disapproval [Janis and Mann, 1977, p. 46].

When a decision maker is faced with an emotionally consequential, no-win choice, how he or she copes with the problem depends crucially on two factors—hope and time. If the decision maker sees realistic hope of finding a solution superior to any of the risky options that are immediately apparent, then that person's efforts are likely to follow the desirable pattern Janis and Mann call *vigilance*, which is close kin to the familiar rational-comprehensive ideal. The vigilant decision maker canvasses a wide set of alternatives; considers the full range of goals and values involved; carefully weighs costs, risks, and benefits; intensively seeks and accurately assimilates new information; reexamines all alternatives before settling on a final choice; makes detailed provisions for implementing the chosen course; and devotes special attention to contingency plans [Janis and Mann, 1977, p. 11].

If, however, a decision maker loses hope of finding an acceptable option, he or she is likely to fall into either of two patterns of seriously defective search and appraisal. The first and more common syndrome, called *defensive avoidance*, typically occurs when there is no overwhelming pressure to change the existing policy even though its consequences are (like those of all other alternatives) highly unfavorable. The chief symptoms of defensive avoidance are procrastination, passing the buck and other ways of denying personal responsibility, and bolstering [Janis, 1989, p. 80]. "Bolstering" is a process of cognitive distortion in which one "spreads" or exaggerates the value of the chosen course compared to alternatives by avoiding exposure to disturbing information, selective attention and recall, wishful thinking, oversimplification, rationalization, and denial.

Defensive avoidance "satisfies a powerful emotional need—to avoid anticipatory fear, shame, and guilt" [Janis and Mann, 1977, p. 85]. Its emotional benefit is a state of "pseudocalm," resulting from the decision maker's suppression of troubling thoughts and avoidance of stimuli that might evoke the painful dilemma.

When external pressures impose a deadline or threaten an imminent disaster if the existing policy is maintained, the state of pseudocalm is shattered and the underlying conflict breaks through to the surface, arousing unbearable emotional stress. In such circumstances, the decision maker is likely to respond with the pattern of behavior Janis and Mann call *hypervigilance*.[8] Responding to "the strong desire to take action in order to alleviate emotional tension," the hypervigilant decision maker "superficially scans the most obvious alternatives open to him . . . , hastily choosing the first one that seems to hold the promise of escaping the worst danger" [Janis and Mann, 1977, pp. 47, 74]. Like defensive avoidance, hypervigilance involves severely defective search and appraisal:

A person in this state experiences so much cognitive constriction and perseveration that his thought processes are disrupted. The person's immediate memory span is reduced and his thinking becomes more simplistic. . . . [T]he person in a state of hypervigilance fails to recognize all the alternatives open to him and fails to use whatever remaining time is available to evaluate adequately those alternatives of which he is aware. He is likely to search frantically for a solution, persevere in his thinking about a limited number of alternatives, and then latch onto a hastily contrived solution that seems to promise immediate relief, often at the cost of considerable postdecisional regret. [Janis and Mann, 1977, p. 51]

An explanation for the first paradox of Wilson Goode's behavior toward MOVE should now be obvious. His delay/haste pattern is a textbook example of defensive avoidance followed by hypervigilance. The two stages are not really paradoxical, because they resulted from the same underlying decisional conflict. As Janis and Mann [1977, p. 66] observe, a "person's defensive avoidance pattern might abruptly change to hypervigilance if he encounters a new, dramatic danger signal." The mobilization of the Osage neighbors signaled to Goode that a continued policy of nonconfrontation would be fraught with new, unacceptable dangers—a certainty of severe political embarrassment and a high probability of unofficial violence against MOVE. The mayor was forced to act, and in his state of hypervigilance, he accepted the first option presented to him—the ill-fated proposal devised by Sambor's planners.

But why was the MOVE problem in particular so difficult for Wilson Goode to handle, when he had been able to deal effectively with many other issues in a distinguished career of public service? Janis and Mann [1977, p. 75] contend that both vigilant and defective patterns of problem solving are within the repertoire of every decision maker. Anyone, they believe, can fluctuate from one pattern to another depending not only on the objective circumstances of action, but also on the relation of those circumstances to personal values and affiliations, which determine whether actions and outcomes will be conducive to self-esteem and social approval for a particular individual. To explain the second paradox, it will therefore be necessary to look more closely at Wilson Goode, as well as at the finer details of his decision processes with respect to MOVE.

The Mayor's Decisional Conflicts

Goode's testimony to the MOVE Commission, coupled with other evidence about his personality and values, suggests that the drama on Osage Avenue aroused within the mayor severe conflicts that he was never able to resolve. Instead, he in effect fled from them, with the result that he virtually abdicated his responsibility as the city's chief administrator.[9] The mayor's conflicts may be summarized as three dilemmas: (1) MOVE's intransigence and irrationality appeared to necessitate the use of force that would almost surely end in bloodshed, but Goode saw himself as a peacemaker and a preserver of life; (2) to enforce the law against MOVE would require the mayor to depend on the Philadelphia Police Department, but the police might well be unreliable, among other reasons because his own relationship with them was uneasy and because many of them hated MOVE; (3) as a black committed to a policy of respecting civil rights, Goode felt dissonance about authorizing official coercion of a black group; but MOVE's bizarre behavior must also have aroused in him anger that he would have difficulty acknowledging, given his religious values and self-image as a controlled person.

Blood on the Hands of a Peacemaker

At first glance, Goode's desire to avoid action against MOVE appears readily understandable. In retrospect, everyone saw Osage Avenue as a no-win situation. If the city refrained from confronting MOVE, the cultists would make life intolerable for their neighbors. If the city attempted to enforce the laws, MOVE would respond violently, producing a high probability of death. District Attorney Rendell described the effect of this realization on the emotions of participants in the crucial meeting:

> I have attended a lot of meetings since I have been in public life, but I never ever had attended a meeting that had the impact on me that my meeting on Thursday, May 7, 1985 did, when in fact the plan of action was signed, sealed and delivered; when the arrest warrants and the search warrants were approved, signed by a judge; when we had picked a time and date to act; when we knew it was going to occur. There was almost a dread in that room so thick that you could have cut it with a knife. Because, understand, every one of us in that room knew that someone—there was an extraordinarily high likelihood that someone was going to die. [PSIC, 1985, 10/22 AM, p. 34]

Nevertheless, to some politicians the MOVE problem might have seemed a golden opportunity. Throughout history, leaders have won popularity by unleashing violence against unpopular enemies, foreign or domestic. By 1985, MOVE had alienated virtually everyone in Philadelphia. Confronting them would have cost Goode little if any support among his black political base, because the neighbors who were pleading for relief were not only black but also representative of his most reliable constituency. MOVE instead offered Goode an excellent chance to broaden his already impressive popularity, because forceful action against them in the name of law and order would have appealed most to those whites who were not yet part of his coalition.

Goode himself noted the political value of decisive leadership. Asked at the MOVE Commission hearings whether his staff's advice that he stay away from the scene of action was "substantive or political or both," he replied:

> I thought it was substantive. I don't think that it . . . had anything to do with politics. From my vantage point, both in foresight and hindsight, . . . it is far better for a Mayor to be perceived as being out there on the scene with hands-on than not to be and, therefore,

from a political point of view I think I lose points. . . . [PSIC, 1985 10/15 PM, p. 94]

In fact, despite the debacle, polls in the aftermath of May 13 showed strong public support for Goode's decision to act against MOVE. His approval ratings did not drop precipitously until the fall of 1985, when information revealed by the hearings made him appear inept, irresponsible, and evasive [Wilentz, 1985; Stevens, 1985].

True, as 1978 and the aftermath of 1985 showed, the public would be distressed at death to innocent parties—police, firefighters, or MOVE children. Police officers and firefighters do, however, accept mortal risks as part of their jobs; and, forewarned by MOVE's treachery in 1978, they could more carefully protect themselves from gunshots.[10] As for the children, if Goode had insisted on implementation of his explicit order to pick them up before commencing the operation, they probably could have been saved. Thus the people most likely to die in a properly planned and executed operation were MOVE adults. Most Philadelphians perceived them as dangerous, deranged, and incorrigible; their deaths in resisting legitimate authorities would have been mourned by few and welcomed by many.

Although the conclusion of this cold political logic might not have troubled most citizens, it appears to have been unacceptable for Wilson Goode. Perhaps the most revealing moment of his testimony to the MOVE Commission came when he was asked to describe his emotions as his office television showed the fire raging out of control:

> I went through very deep emotions at that time. I cried because I knew at that point that lives would be lost, and I knew that homes would be destroyed and I knew that despite all of our good intentions, that we had . . . an absolute disaster. And I can't explain to you or to anyone the kind of emotions that I went through, because everything about me is about preserving life and to know that any plan that I've had anything to do with would, in fact, bring about the cessation of life, was very tough. [PSIC, 1985, 10/15 PM, p. 95]

There are independent reasons for believing the sincerity of Goode's statement. Widely regarded as a deeply religious man, he has been a devoted and active member of the First Baptist Church of Paschall since 1955, serving during most of this time as a deacon and lay leader of the congregation. Well into adult life, he seriously considered entering the ministry. On his pastor's advice, he prayed for guidance. "I came away feeling strongly that I was called," he said later. "But it was a ministry of a different kind, a ministry of public service." An early profiler wrote, "His whole notion of public service is grounded in his faith, and he approaches his work at City Hall with almost an evangelical fervor" [Cohn, 1982, p. 13].

Indeed, most of Goode's career exhibits a marked inclination toward conciliation and peacemaking. As a community activist in the 1960s and early 1970s, "his low-key manner usually helped keep potentially explosive situations under control" [Cohn, p. 27]. As a politician, he first unified the previously divided black community, then established an effective alliance with white liberals in the Democratic primary, and finally in the 1983 general election, through a series of conciliatory gestures, won the support of Frank Rizzo. Consequently, he carried 27% of the white vote, and Philadelphia during the first year of his term rode a wave of elation, smugly comparing its newfound racial harmony to the bitter divisions in Chicago and other cities. As mayor, many of Goode's early string of triumphs depended on his ability to build consensus and placate opposition. The few criticisms of Goode during this period centered on claims that he was too willing to appease opponents and too reluctant to lead in the absence of consensus. His own view was more positive: "I've had a charmed life as mayor because I've learned the arts of compromise and negotiation" [Wilentz, 1985, p. 22].

A commitment to peacemaking is also consistent with the full pattern of Goode's dealings with MOVE. The disastrously little time and attention he devoted to planning the use of force contrasts strikingly with his extensive involvement in efforts to understand MOVE and to negotiate a solution [Marimow, 1985]. When Managing Director, he met about fifteen times with John Africa's sisters, Louise James and Laverne Sims, both of whom had been involved with MOVE and were also the mothers of MOVE members. "I always had a comfortable relationship with them, when we have shared together, where they have talked with me and I have listened a lot" [PSIC, 1985, 10/15 AM, p. 29]. The open door continued after he became mayor. On July 31, 1984, when city officials were anticipating a confrontation with MOVE on the August 8 anniversary of the Powelton shootout, the two sisters requested a meeting and were given almost instant access. Goode

told the MOVE Commission, "I literally jumped at that meeting because for the first time, I thought I had someone that I could talk to that could, in fact, avoid a conflict out there" [PSIC, 1985, 10/15 AM, p. 25]. (Note how the procrastination of defensive avoidance vanishes when hope appears.) As late as May 9, Goode sandwiched in his fateful meeting with Sambor between discussions with community activists, through whom he hoped to arrange a meeting with Gerald Ford Africa:

> I then asked them to go back, to indicate to Gerald Ford Africa that I was willing to meet at any point that he decided, that he decided that he wanted to meet. I would come to his house. I would go to a neutral house. . . . I would personally negotiate with him any type of release from the house that they were talking about, any movement they wanted to make at that time. . . . After the optimism on Thursday, about noon, they got back to me the next day and said that there was a 360 degrees turn in the attitude of Gerald Ford Africa when they went back, and that he became profane towards them and said he would not meet with me under any circumstances ever for anything. And it was at this point that that hope which I had of bringing about some negotiation in fact fell through. [PSIC, 1985, 10/15 AM, pp. 62–64]

In directing his personal effort concerning MOVE toward negotiation, Goode was clearly playing to the area where he "felt familiar, resourceful, and competent" [Marimow, 1985]. But such skills had probably developed precisely because they were so consistent with Goode's religious motivation and self-image. In contrast, to be "on the scene with hands-on" in managing a police operation against MOVE would be to risk coming away with blood on his hands—blood that might be politically advantageous but personally intolerable.

Unleashing on Unreliable Force

Thus, when the Osage neighbors precipitated Goode's final stage of hypervigilance, he kept the police operation at arms length, shielding himself from personal responsibility for the onslaught to come by entrusting the planning and execution to the police, whom he described time and again in the hearings as "experts" and "professionals." Goode's seemingly blind trust in his police force prompted this sarcastic interrogation by Commissioner Neil J. Welch, who had once directed the Philadelphia office of the FBI:

Welch: Now, we got a Mayor that's been a Mayor for a year or two and before that he was the Managing Director, and certainly isn't the first time he's seen the Philadelphia Police Department and its personnel perform. . . . [W]hat was your judgment as to the professional capability, the dependability, the quality and integrity of the Philadelphia Police Department to execute, to draft a plan and to execute it successfully?

Goode: My judgement was that Greg Sambor had the ability within the parameters which I set forth, to go out and to develop a plan. . . . It was my judgment that . . . being the kind of trained professional person and manager he is, that he, in fact, could do that. . . . That when he finished that plan, he was to discuss that with Leo Brooks, who I felt with his 30 years in the armed services, as a Major General, could evaluate appropriately and properly that overall plan. . . . So I left that meeting with full confidence that Greg Sambor and Leo Brooks could, in fact, carry out the assignment given to them.

Welch: Mayor, you displayed great confidence in your Police Department and your Police Commissioner, as you have just outlined. This is the same department that has been or would have been under almost continuous federal investigation, had it not, for a period of some time?

Goode: That's correct. [PSIC, 1985, 10/15 PM, pp. 119–121]

Having had responsibility for the Police Department during most of the past five years, to admit the department's faults would clearly arouse dissonance for Goode; but it is inconceivable that he did not know, at some level, that his police were an unreliable instrument for this task. The Federal investigations to which Welch referred were not only for corruption, but for brutality and civil rights violations; and the mutual hatred between the police and MOVE was obvious, especially after the death of Officer Ramp and the beating of Delbert Africa in 1978.

In his initial attempt to solve the MOVE problem, Goode in fact sought to bypass the Philadelphia police. On May 30, 1984, just two days after his first meeting with a delegation from Osage Avenue, the mayor led

ranking city officials to a session with U.S. Attorney Edward Dennis and representatives of the FBI and Secret Service. They rebuffed his argument that MOVE's threats against President Reagan and violations of their neighbors' rights constituted grounds for U.S. intervention. Although consistent with the buck-passing pattern typical of defensive avoidance, Goode's attempt to enlist Federal authorities can also be interpreted as a prudent effort to find an armed force more detached, disciplined, and reliable than his own police.

Worries about controlling the city police were also present, though not emphasized, in the days before the final confrontation. At the May 7 meeting, prompted by Councilman Lucien Blackwell's strong warning about officers who might seek vengeance for 1978, Goode instructed Sambor to "handpick" the men who would serve in the Osage Avenue confrontation. (Sambor later claimed not to have heard such an order and in any case did not implement it. One of the gas-insertion teams included two officers who had been accused of beating Delbert Africa [Anderson and Hevenor, 1987, p. 115].) Goode ultimately admitted to the MOVE Commission that he doubted police fire control so much that he feared their bullets might endanger his own life if he went to the scene:

Commissioner Audrey Bronson: I understand that you felt that your life would have been at risk—by whom?

Goode: Well, I have received a lot of information that simply people said to me, and I will share this candid discussion with you, that I should be careful of, first of all, of people who were MOVE sympathizers in the neighborhood, that with shots going on out there that a shot could easily go awry and hit me, that I should be— I should be—beware of even the potential for police shots going awry on the scene and therefore, there have been, as I was told, instances of the fact that commanders in the Army have, in fact, been mistakenly shot and I should be aware of those kinds of things and the people who talked with me simply persuaded me that, in fact, it would be a risk for me to be in the area. [PSIC, 1985, 11/6 PM, p. 54]

Although not explicit about who were "the people who talked with me," Goode's statement to the Commission is consistent with reports that telephoners purporting to be police officers warned the mayor he might be shot by police if he came to Osage Avenue.

In short, part of Goode's reluctance to act against MOVE must have resulted from doubts, whether conscious or suppressed, that he could sufficiently control the use of force by the police. In the end he made no real attempt to manage the violence he had authorized. Perhaps, as many in Philadelphia believe, Goode rationally calculated that any such effort might fail and therefore deliberately distanced himself from a potential disaster in order to avoid legal or political responsibility. Such motives cannot be ruled out, but they do not adequately explain the string of cognitive distortions by which the mayor apparently avoided appreciating the reality of what his forces were doing. He told his breakfast guests that police were only firing over the roof of the MOVE house; he interpreted explosions he heard from his home as stun grenades; he thought that the "explosive device" would be placed on MOVE's roof rather than dropped from a helicopter; and he mistook "snow" on his television screen for water from firefighters' squirts [PSIC, 1985, 10/15 AM, pp. 74, 97; 10/15 PM, p. 111; 11/6 AM, p. 111; 10/15 PM, p. 31]. Avowing these beliefs—all unsupported by others' testimony—would hardly help against criminal charges, and they only added to Goode's political vulnerability by subjecting him to ridicule. Such a consistent pattern of misperception seems more suited to deceive oneself than to deceive others, and better protection against self-condemnation than against the judgment of courts or voters. It therefore appears likely that deeper sources of ambivalence prevented the mayor from admitting to himself the full import of his decision to unleash official violence against MOVE.

Black Against Black: Identification and Anger

The foregoing analysis is not meant to portray Wilson Goode as a pacifist or as one whose values are entirely antithetical to those of the police. After completing ROTC at Morgan State University, he served in the U.S. Army from 1961 to 1963, rising to the rank of captain and commanding a unit of 223 military policemen. His military experience made a deep impression on Goode. He has said that he learned more about management in the army than he did earning a master's degree in governmental administration at the University of Pennsylvania.[11] As mayor, he has shown a marked penchant for appointing former military officers to high posts—including Leo Brooks, a major general in charge of the Philadelphia Defense Personnel Support Center

before Goode persuaded him to become Managing Director, and Gregore Sambor, a veteran and an officer in the reserves.

To Goode, however, the military seems to represent not so much legitimate violence as it does an organization that develops personal discipline and rewards it, regardless of race—in marked contrast to most of American society in his formative years. Early profiles of Brooks suggest the virtues that Goode most admires:

> [A mutual acquaintance described Brooks as] "made out of the same mold as Wilson." Goode and Brooks shared poor childhoods in the South, Army-officer training and strong religious underpinnings. Brooks' father is a Baptist minister . . . Brooks also is a black man who, like his new boss, has achieved success by making hard work his credo. [Cooke and Klibanoff, 1983]

> At heart a traditionalist, Brooks believes in the old-fashioned virtues of hard work, self-discipline . . . and taking responsibility for one's own actions. To him, nothing exceeds the importance of family. [Klibanoff, 1984]

To a black man with Wilson Goode's values, MOVE must have aroused deep and intense conflicts.[12] On the one hand, as a former civil rights activist who had himself been twice picked up by police for allegedly creating disturbances [Cohn, 1982, p. 21], Goode must have had some lingering identification with MOVE. In 1978, much of the black and liberal communities had seen the MOVE problem as a racially motivated attack by the Rizzo administration on the rights of a predominantly black group. On one occasion, five thousand demonstrators marched around City Hall to protest the siege in Powelton; their chants linked MOVE with South African blacks as fellow victims of racial oppression. In 1984, U.S. Attorney Dennis, himself black, strongly warned city officials against violating MOVE's civil rights [PSIC, 1985, 10/22 PM, p. 127]. Goode invoked his own concern for minority rights in explaining his reluctance to act:

> I think that if I was a different person, that perhaps I may have acted differently back in 1984. But I . . . do not feel that anyone who holds an office ought to use that office to infringe and violate other people's rights in order to achieve the overall good, and

I guess I feel that way because I know that for so long in this country that laws were, in fact, used to deprive blacks and women and Hispanics and others who were different, and therefore, I do not want, as mayor of this city to say to a group: Because you are different, because you don't comply with all the laws, therefore, I have the right, as the mayor, to simply go full speed and trample on you and all your rights. . . . [PSIC, 1985, 10/15 PM, pp. 97–98]

On the other hand, MOVE represented the antithesis of every standard by which Wilson Goode lived. They dwelt in filth; he was always well groomed. They lived communally; he had raised a family. They spewed profanity; he attended church every Sunday. They survived casually; he worked fifteen-hour days. They rejected the system; he aspired to run a major corporation. As they spurned his efforts to negotiate a peaceful solution, as they vilified him and threatened his life, the bizarre cultists must have aroused increasing anger in Goode. The impulse to vent this anger must have been strong, but his religious belief in preserving life and his self-image as a controlled person forbade yielding to it. "I've always felt that I have to be in control of me at all times," he once told an interviewer [Cohn, 1982, p. 27]; and another profiler got "the feeling that the emotion bottled up inside Wilson Goode is always close to eruption. You can see him almost counting to ten, thinking before he responds, calculating each sentence, crafting every phrase, then struggling mightily to rein in what might be rage" [Mallowe, 1984, p. 170].

For a time, the mayor hoped that MOVE itself would assume the moral burden of precipitating violence. After receiving Rendell's memo justifying urgent action in June 1984, Goode delayed until August 8, the anniversary of the Powelton shootout, because reports indicated that MOVE planned a major confrontation with "the System" on that date. At the mayor's direction, the police prepared a plan for capturing the MOVE house,[13] and three hundred officers were assembled near Osage Avenue. Goode's choice of language in describing this incident is revealing:

The August 8th 1984 plan was a reactive plan, was geared to go into effect only if certain types of aggressive behavior, aggressive steps were taken by MOVE members themselves. And therefore when they did not take any aggressive steps, nothing, in fact, was done at that time. [PSIC, 1985, 10/15 PM, p. 59]

The words "aggressive" and "aggression" recur frequently when Goode refers to the initiation of armed confrontation. It appears that he was willing in 1984 to do battle with MOVE, but only if MOVE were the aggressor, if MOVE bore the responsibility of having clearly initiated violence. To let deaths occur (or appear to occur) merely because of noise, stench, code violations, and unpaid utility bills was, to Goode, a morally unbalanced equation.[14]

On August 8, however, MOVE did nothing except take notes about the police preparations. After that day, Goode and other city officials entered a stage of full-blown defensive avoidance that lasted until May 1985. As the MOVE Commission observed about this period. "The policy of appeasement produced a rule of silence in City Hall, where information on the Osage Avenue situation was not disseminated and where city officials knowledgeable about the problems chose not to speak of them" [PSIC, 1986, p. 13]. Goode and his colleagues were thus able to entertain the wishful hope that the Osage Avenue problem "would disappear" by ignoring the readily available knowledge that MOVE members were vigorously and visibly fortifying their compound [PSIC, 1985, 10/15 PM, pp. 76–77]. Goode justified his policy of nonintervention on the grounds that no action should be taken "until such time as we worked out an overall plan that would be comprehensive in nature," but this argument was a rationalization for avoidance, as is shown by the fact that he did absolutely nothing to force the creation of such a plan [PSIC, 1985, 10/15 PM, pp. 75–80]. Indeed, the mayor had no contact with anyone concerning MOVE from August 9 until the end of April 1985 [PSIC, 10/15 AM, p. 40].

Goode's nine months of pseudocalm were then shattered by the United Residents' initiative, which revived what threatened to be an excruciating inner struggle. Rather than endure the tension during a protracted period of careful search and appraisal, the mayor sought to eliminate his conflict quickly by authorizing the police plan. Although he unleashed the violence of the police and perhaps in part vented his own anger through their vengeance, the use of force in this context was so dissonant with his self-image that he could not accept—psychologically at least as much as politically—the ownership that hands-on management would imply.

To shield himself from personal responsibility for violating crucial values, Wilson Goode thus abdicated his responsibility as an administrator. In so doing, he lost his best chance to control and minimize the inevitable violence. Because he was so reluctant to transgress his values, he permitted a series of events that in the end inflicted on them far greater damage than was necessary. The outcome has the irony of genuine tragedy. The preserver of life bore responsibility for eleven deaths; the builder of homes presided as sixty-one burned; the protector of rights permitted grotesquely excessive official violence.

Lessons for Present and Future Managers

Perhaps the only consolation we can take from so awful a disaster is the hope that its lessons will help prevent future catastrophes. Thus the MOVE Commission concluded their report with no fewer than thirty-eight recommendations covering such matters as communication systems, assignment of authority and responsibility, policies for controlling weapons and explosives, strategic planning processes, interdepartmental coordinating groups, and so forth. Though the Commission's proposals may be sensible and worthwhile, from the perspective of the analysis offered in this paper, such advice misses the most fundamental lessons of the MOVE debacle.

Organizational systems, policies, and procedures are ultimately controlled and implemented by human beings. Effective communication will not occur when subordinates believe that their superiors cannot bear to hear the truth. Clear allocation of authority will be wasted on executives who, succumbing to painful quandaries, rationalize evasion of responsibility.

Programs for educating public managers should therefore devote much more attention to the psychology of decision making, with a special focus on its prescriptive implications. For example, Janis [1989, ch. 10] concludes his recent book by suggesting twenty sets of leadership practices that might help policy makers avoid pitfalls that often result in defective decision making. As he observes, most of these recommendations will be costly to leaders and their support staffs in time, effort, and stress. Adjusting curricula to sensitize present and future decision makers to psychological factors will also demand new investments by schools, teachers, and students.

Dramatic examples like the MOVE disaster can help motivate such efforts, but in teaching the case during the past several years, I have found that students adopt their own avoidance strategies. Like the general public, their natural reaction is to debate, as one student put it, "whether moral bankruptcy or simple incompetence best explains this disaster." Whichever verdict is chosen, the effect is to distance oneself from the officials who are blamed for the debacle. The observer in effect is saying, "I would never be so evil, or so uncaring, or so inattentive, or so blundering as to permit such a horror!"

Interpreting the MOVE case in terms of a general theory such as the Janis and Mann conflict model elevates it from an idiosyncratic failure to a universal warning. Students can then move beyond emotional condemnation of a few officials to a sobering recognition of their own vulnerability to similar errors. The generality of the problem can be further emphasized by exploring parallel cases (though few will be so well documented as the MOVE incident). To take several recent examples, the delay/haste pattern appears to fit the British government's treatment of IRA strongholds in Belfast and Derry during the early 1970s, the Chinese government's response to the 1989 student demonstrations in Tienanmen Square, and the U.S. invasion of Panama to overthrow General Manuel Noriega.[15]

Once managers understand the dynamics of defensive avoidance and hypervigilance, what can they do to protect themselves? Because rationalization, denial, selective perception, and wishful thinking are so insidious, no one can be assured of immunity against defective decision processes. For this reason, Janis and Mann [1977, p. 396] recommend embedding preventive strategies in organizational standard operating procedures,[16] because "if the anti-defensive avoidance procedures are not institutionalized but are rather left to the discretion of the leader or the members, they will be more honored in the breach than in the observance."

Nevertheless, it is not unreasonable to hope that individual awareness will also help. Relying on face validity rather than any systematic evidence of effectiveness, I would suggest the following strategy to managers who wish to reduce their vulnerability.

First, learn to recognize the behavioral symptoms of defective decision making. For defensive avoidance, these include procrastinating, buck-passing, and downplaying danger signals. Symptoms of hypervigilance include grabbing the first available alternative, neglecting contingency plans, and believing that action must be taken under extreme time pressure whether or not compelling deadlines exist. Wise managers will not only monitor themselves for these symptoms, but will also encourage trusted advisors to fight the battle for their minds by calling such tendencies to their attention.

Second, when these symptoms are observed, identify the central no-win dilemma or dilemmas.[17] Conflicts that impede effective decision making are not always obvious and will vary from individual to individual. The desire to avoid responsibility and shield oneself from reality behind a screen of cognitive distortions becomes strongest when one's most central values are threatened, so the manager must heed the ancient injunction to "know thyself."

Third, learn to grasp problems firmly even when all options entail distasteful consequences for important values. The example of Wilson Goode shows that cherished virtues, if excessively protected, can be the source of tragic failure. Though vigilant problem solving and decisive management may induce stress, they are usually rewarded—if not with unequivocal triumph, then at least by controlled damage and the respect that strong leaders are accorded. In contrast, the inferno on Osage Avenue should burn into our memories the lesson that however bad available alternatives seem, potential outcomes can be far worse if avoidance and hasty action permit a tough situation to deteriorate into a nightmare.

References

Anderson, John, and Hilary Hevenor (1987), *Burning Down the House: MOVE and the Tragedy of Philadelphia* (New York: W.W. Norton and Co.).

Assefa, Hizkias, and Paul Wahrhaftig (1988), *Extremist Groups and Conflict Resolution: The MOVE Crisis in Philadelphia* (New York: Praeger).

Bowser, Charles W. (1989), *Let the Bunker Burn: The Final Battle with MOVE* (Philadelphia: Camino Books).

Boyette, Michael, with Randi Boyette (1989), *"Let It Burn!" The Philadelphia Tragedy* (Chicago: Contemporary Books).

Cohn, Roger (1982), "Wilson Goode Has Something to Prove," *Today Magazine, Philadelphia Inquirer* (July 25), pp. 10ff.

Cooke, Russell, and Hank Klibanoff (1983), "Work Is the Credo for New Managing Director," *Philadelphia Inquirer* (November 29), p. 12-A.

George, Alexander L. (1973), "The Case for Multiple Advocacy in Making Foreign Policy," *American Political Science Review* 66, pp. 751–785.

Gilbert, Charles E. (1959), "The Framework of Administrative Responsibility," *Journal of Politics* 21, pp. 373–407.

Goodman, Howard (1989), "Still Haunted by MOVE, Richmond Is Telling His Story," *Philadelphia Inquirer* (May 15), p. B-1.

Janis, Irving L. (1972), *Victims of Groupthink* (Boston: Houghton Mifflin).

Janis, Irving L. (1989), Crucial Decisions: Leadership in *Policymaking and Crisis Management* (New York: The Free Press).

Janis, Irving L., and Leon Mann (1977), *Decision Making: A Psychological Analysis of Conflict, Choice, and Commitment* (New York: The Free Press).

Javers, Ron (1983), "On the Run: Lunch with Wilson Goode," *Philadelphia Magazine* 74 (April), p. 8.

Klibanoff, Hank (1984), "The General," *Philadelphia Inquirer* (May 21), p. 4-B.

Mallowe, Mike (1980), "And Now, the Goode News," *Philadelphia Magazine* 71 (August), pp. 128ff.

Mallowe, Mike (1984), "The No-Frills Mayor," *Philadelphia Magazine* 75 (December), pp. 168ff.

Marimow, William K. (1985), "Two Images of Goode: Activism vs. Delegation," *Philadelphia Inquirer* (October 23), p. 1-A.

Philadelphia Court of Common Pleas (1988), *Report of the County Investigating Grand Jury of May 15, 1986*.

Philadelphia Special Investigation Commission (1985), *Hearings*.

Philadelphia Special Investigation Commission (1986), *Findings, Conclusions, and Recommendations*.

Sharifi, Jahan (1990), Unpublished student paper, University of Pennsylvania.

Stevens, William K. (1985), "Mayor Goode's Once-Solid Path Turns Rocky in Philadelphia," *New York Times* (October 23).

Wilentz, Amy (1985), "Goode's Intentions," *Time* 125 (May 27), p. 22.

Notes

1. PSIC, 1986, Finding 22; see also Findings 3, 15, 17, and 24, which use comparable language. The PSIC is generally known as "the MOVE Commission."

2. This account draws on the following sources, in addition to the author's knowledge as a resident

of West Philadelphia during the period described: PSIC [1986], which includes a chronology; Philadelphia Court of Common Pleas [1988], which includes a history of MOVE; Anderson and Hevenor [1987]; Assefa and Wahrhaftig [1988]; Bowser [1989]; and Boyette [1989]. Charles Bowser and Michael Boyette were, respectively, members of the MOVE Commission and the grand jury. The eighteen days of hearings the MOVE Commission conducted in October and November 1985 are my principal source [PSIC, 1985]. Transcripts are available in the Government Publications Department of the Philadelphia Free Library and the Urban Archives Center of Temple University. There is a volume for each day of hearings, with pages numbered separately within each volume for morning and afternoon sessions. I supplemented the transcripts by watching videotapes of key witnesses' testimony. (The hearings were televised live by WHYY-TV, the PBS station in Philadelphia.)

3. See also the testimony of Laverne Sims [PSIC, 1985, 10/10 AM, pp. 65–77].

4. District Attorney Edward Rendell later blamed the acquittal on the invective and curses that Delbert directed at the judge and jury [PSIC, 1985, 10/22 AM, pp. 119–120].

5. PSIC, 1985, 10/8 PM, p. 104. In Philadelphia there are 28 districts for the lower house of the state legislature compared with only 10 councilmanic districts; thus the state representative is often the elected official closest to the people of a neighborhood.

6. Cohn, 1982, p. 27. The second sentence is a quotation from Shirley Hamilton, Goode's chief of staff.

7. Janis is better known among students of politics, policy, and management for his earlier work on "groupthink" [Janis, 1972]. Elements of groupthink can be found in various official groups involved in the MOVE problem, but the full-blown syndrome does not appear, perhaps because the mayor's interpersonal style inhibited development of the requisite emotional cohesiveness. (Like other cults, MOVE itself exhibited a virulent form of groupthink.) Janis's work on organizational decisions has developed from the specific to the general. In *Decision Making,* he and Mann depict groupthink as a collective version of the broader phenomenon of defensive avoidance, which in turn is part of a "conflict model" based on psychological stress. In his latest book, *Crucial Decisions* [Janis, 1989], the conflict model becomes a component of a still more general "constraints model." The comprehensiveness of the constraints model is a virtue for some purposes, but I believe the paradoxical features of the MOVE case are explained best by the conflict model. Thus my account relies more on *Decision Making* than on *Crucial Decisions.*

8. The choice of words is unfortunate, because the authors use "vigilance" for their ideal problem-solving process; thus, "hypervigilance" suggests too much of a good thing. The hypervigilant actor exhibits too much emotional arousal and too much haste, but no true vigilance.

9. Although based as much as possible on published materials, the analysis that follows is necessarily inferential and speculative.

10. On May 13, only one police officer was struck by a MOVE bullet, and a bulletproof vest saved him from serious harm. A policy of protecting firefighters from possible MOVE gunfire was one reason the fire spread so fast and so far. Having vowed that no firefighter would face gunfire, Fire Commissioner William Richmond deliberately chose to sacrifice property in order to save lives [Goodman, 1989].

11. In a conversation with the author in February 1981.

12. Much the same argument can probably be made for Leo Brooks, which may help explain why he too failed to fulfill his responsibility in the MOVE operation. Despite the advantages of similarity in promoting trust and comfortable personal relations, leaders take a great risk in depending excessively on key subordinates who are too much like themselves.

13. This plan, prepared by Sergeant Herbert Kirk of the Police Academy, was the forerunner of the strategy employed the following May [PSIC, 1985, 10/11 PM].

14. Because some of his radical and civil libertarian supporters, both black and white, might have had the same attitude, Goode's calculation can be seen as both political and moral. As Sharifi [1990] observes, successful political leaders often mirror the potential reactions of key constituencies in their own concerns.

15. I owe these and other suggested parallels to an anonymous reviewer [of this article].

16. An example already well known in the policy-

making community is the system of multiple advocacy recommended by Alexander George [1973].

17. One device that might help raise conflicts to consciousness is the decisional balance sheet, a kind of expanded cost-benefit analysis that includes not only utilitarian gains and losses but also the approval and disapproval of reference groups and oneself [Janis and Mann, 1977, ch. 6]. Note that the purpose is to recognize consciously the role of emotional influences, not necessarily to eliminate them.

Chapter 8 Review Questions

1. What are the key differences between the *root* and *branch* methods of decision making? Summarize the advantages and disadvantages of each method.

2. Does the case study, "The MOVE Disaster," exemplify the root or branch method of decision making? Or another approach? Explain your reasons for your selection by citing examples from the case.

3. How does the case point up the influence of deeply held personal values or "unresolved decision conflicts" in the decisional process? Why did these hidden personal values in this case influence its outcome? In what ways did they impact on the decisional processes?

4. Compare this Case Study 8 involving MOVE with Case Study 4 dealing with "The Columbia Accident." Discuss the major differences in the way these two critical decisions were reached. In particular, consider the number and kinds of people who became involved in the decisional processes, their values, the care and manner by which the options for administrative action were presented and considered, the factors forcing the final decision, and the overall effectiveness of the decisional processes.

5. On the basis of your comparative appraisal of the two cases, can you generalize about how values and proper timing as well as the general political pressures play important roles in the way these or other public decisions are reached?

6. Also on the basis of your comparison of the two cases, why does who gets involved in the decisional process (or who is left out) play such a critical role in the quality and kind of decisions that are made in government?

Key Terms

incremental decision making
root method
branch method
clarification of objectives
intertwining ends and means
successive limited comparisons

rational comprehensive analysis
policy alternatives
maximization of values
empirical analysis
policy outcomes
ranking objectives

Suggestions for Further Reading

Making good, correct, and efficient decisions in the public interest has been a major concern of public administration literature since the early, "conscious" development of the field. In particular, the writings of Frederick Taylor and his followers about scientific management examined methods of rational decision making in organizations at the lower levels of industrial or business hierarchies. However, the post–World

War II writings of Herbert Simon, especially his *Administrative Behavior: The Study of Decision Making Processes in Administrative Organization* (New York: Macmillan, 1947), shifted the focus of administrative thinking to *the decision* as the central focus of study and analysis. The enormous impact of this book (for which Simon won the Nobel Prize in 1978), as well as his other writings on public administration, make it worthy of careful attention by students of the field even today. For useful background information on Simon's life and work, read his autobiography, Herbert A. Simon, *Models of My Life* (New York: Basic Books, 1991).

Other important writings on this topic include Charles E. Lindblom, *The Intelligence of Democracy: Decision Making Through Mutual Adjustment* (New York: Free Press, 1965), and his book co-authored with David Braybooke, *A Strategy of Decision* (New York: Free Press, 1963). For criticisms of the Simon-Lindblom incrementalist approach see Yehezkel Dror, "Muddling Through—Science or Inertia?" *Public Administration Review,* 24 (September 1964), pp. 154–157, and Amitai Etzioni, "Mixed Scanning: A Third Approach to Decision Making," *Public Administration Review,* 27 (December 1967), pp. 385–392. The debate over incrementalism is hardly over, for an entire symposium in the *Public Administration Review,* 39 (November/December 1979) was devoted to its pros and cons. Pay particular attention to the articles by Charles E. Lindblom, "Still Muddling, Not Yet Through" (pp. 511–516); Camille Cates, "Beyond Muddling" (pp. 527–531); and Bruce Adams, "The Limitations of Muddling Through" (pp. 545–552); plus Amitai Etzioni, "Mixed Scanning Revisited," *Public Administration Review,* 46 (January/February 1986), pp. 8–14. By contrast, Aaron Wildavsky, "Toward a Radical Incrementalism," in Alfred DeGrazia, *Congress: The First Branch of Government* (Washington, D.C.: American Enterprise Institute, 1966) pushes the incremental concept about as far as possible; whereas Paul R. Schulman, "Nonincremental Policy Making: Notes Toward an Alternative Paradigm," *American Political Science Review,* 69 (December 1975), presents possibly the most searching critique of the incremental model. James G. March, *A Primer on Decision-Making: How Decisions Happen* (New York: Free Press, 1994) offers a recent restatement of the incremental model as well as Herbert A. Simon, *Models of Bounded Rationality* (Cambridge: MIT Press, 1997).

Since the 1960s numerous decision models other than incrementalism have been proposed with various degrees of success. The most prominent include the *systems model* as represented in Fremont J. Lyden and Ernest G. Miller, eds., *Planning Programming-Budgeting: A Systems Approach to Management* (Chicago: Markham Publishing Co., 1968); *games theory* as outlined in Thomas C. Schelling, *The Strategy of Conflict* (Cambridge, Mass.: Harvard University Press, 1963); the *bureaucratic model* as represented in Graham T. Allison, *Essence of Decision: Explaining the Cuban Missile Crisis* (Boston: Little, Brown, 1971); *cost-benefit* as found in Edward M. Gramlich, *Benefit-Cost Analysis of Government Programs* (Englewood Cliffs, N.J.: Prentice-Hall, 1981); *personal judgment* approach of Harvey Sherman, *It All Depends* (Tuscaloosa, Ala.: University of Alabama Press, 1966); the *policy analysis method* as discussed in William N. Dunn, *Public Policy Analysis: An Introduction* (Englewood Cliffs, N.J.: Prentice-Hall, 1981). For a *chaos paradigm,* see L. Douglas Kiel, *Managing Chaos and Complexity in Government* (San Francisco, Calif.: Jossey-Bass, 1994); for a *psychological approach,* read Irving Janis and Leon Mann, *Decision-Making: A Psychological Analysis of Conflict, Choce, and Commitment* (New York: Free Press, 1977); for a collaborative approach, read *Collaborative Approaches: A Handbook for Public Policy Decision Making and Conflict Resolution* (Oregon, Public Policy Dispute Resolution Program, 2000); and for the *garbage can model,* read Michael D. Cohen et al., "A Garbage Can Model of Organizational Choice," *Administrative Science Quarterly,* 17 (1972), pp. 1–25. These only scratch the surface of a vast, complex area of decision-making research. You would be well advised to read the current issues of such journals as *Public Administration Review, Administrative Science Quarterly, Journal of Policy Analysis and Management, Public Management,* or *Harvard Business Review* for up-to-date perspectives on decision-making methodology.

For a fine scholarly critique of various decision-making approaches regarding their application to government, read George W. Downs and Patrick D. Larkey, *The Search for Government Efficiency: From Hubris to Helplessness* (New York: Random House, 1986); and for an excellent collection of applied cases involving local decision making, see James M. Banovetz, ed., *Managing Local Government: Cases in Decision Making,* 2nd ed. (Washington, D.C.: International City Management Assoc., 1998). The republished book, Geoffrey Vickers, *The Art of Judgment* (London: Sage, 1995 and first printed in 1965) offers one of the best arguments for practical judgment as the key to effective decision making.

Two recent books on decision-making that treat the topic in very different ways include Nikolaos Zahariadas, *Ambiguity and Choice in Public Policy: Political Decision Making in Modern Democracies* (Washington, D.C.: Georgetown University Press, 2003); and Giacomo Pignataro, ed., *Public Decision-Making Processes and Asymmetry of Information* (Boston: Kluwer, 2000).

CHAPTER 9

Administrative Communication: The Concept of Its Professional Centrality

P ublic Administration practitioners and scholars alike have generally failed to give communication the attention and respect it deserves. . . . For communication to reclaim its rightful place at the core of public administration, its rigor, complexity, salience, diversity, and richness need to be rediscovered.

—James L. Garnett

READING 9

Introduction

In arriving at even the most routine policy decisions, the typical public administrator is a prisoner of a seemingly endless communications network that defines the problem at hand and the possible alternatives. Administrators are normally pressed from many sides with informational and data sources flowing into their offices from their superiors, subordinates, other agencies, citizen groups, and the general public. Sometimes the information arrives through routine formal channels; at other times it wells up or trickles down to the administrator via unsolicited routes. Whatever the source, the public decision maker must selectively sort out this information, and, in turn, dispense a substantial quantity of information to people within and outside the organizational structure; this is done by memoranda, reports, conferences, phone conversations, and informal encounters that touch off a new chain of communications and decisions by others. Similar to a telephone switchboard, a policy maker's office acts as a nerve center where the lines of communications cross and are connected and where information is received, processed, stored, assembled, analyzed, and dispensed.

Our conceptual understanding of the importance and complexity of the communications links within public organizations and their critical role in administrative decisions begins to a large extent with the work of Herbert A. Simon (1916–2000). In collaboration with Donald Smithburg and Victor Thompson, Simon wrote the text *Public Administration* (1950); this work, drawing on Simon's earlier writing, *Administrative Behavior* (1947), for which Simon won the Nobel Prize for economics in 1978, offered one of the first integrated behavioral interpretations of public administration. By introducing ideas from sociology, psychology, and political science, Simon and his associates sought to discover "a realistic behavioral description of the process of administration," emphasizing its informal human dynamics.

At the root of public administration, according to Simon, Smithburg, and Thompson, were continual conflicts among contending groups that resulted from such internal pressures as empire-building tendencies, differing individual backgrounds, and varying group identifications, as well as such external pressures as competing interest groups, members of Congress, and other agency heads struggling for scarce resources and influence. Similar to Norton Long's conception of the political power contest surrounding administrative activities (discussed in Chapter 4), the authors envision administrators as people "in the middle of continual conflict" whose actions and activities demand a considerable effort directed toward conflict resolution and compromise. As they write, "public administrators, and particularly those responsible for directions of unitary organizations, are themselves initiators and transformers of policy, brokers, if you like, who seek to bring about agreement between the program goals of government agencies and the goals and values of groups that possess political power." In short, "the greatest distinction between public administration and other administration is . . . to be found in the political character of public administration."

Decisions within this political setting can never be wholly rational but rather, the authors contend, are of a "bounded rational" nature. Instead of insisting on an "optimal solution," the public policy maker must be satisfied with what is "good enough," or as Lindblom suggests more simply in Chapter 8, must "muddle through." The prime ends of a public administrator's efforts are decisions that are not "maximizing" but "sufficing," that have as their goals not efficiency but achieving agreement, compromise, and ultimately survival.

One of the major vehicles for achieving coordination and compromise, in the view of Simon, Smithburg, and Thompson, is the communications network, which they define as the "process whereby decisional premises are transmitted from one member of an organization to another." The communications network acts principally as an integrating device for bringing together frequently conflicting elements of an organization to secure cooperative group effort. Three steps are involved in the communications process: first, "someone must initiate the communication"; second, "the command must be transmitted from its source to its destination"; and third, "communications must make its impact on the recipient." The information travels in two ways: (1) the formal or planned channels such as memoranda, reports, and written communications; and (2) the unplanned or informal ways such as face-to-face contacts, conferences, or phone calls to friends. Simon, Smithburg, and Thompson place considerable emphasis on the informal lines of communications that many refer to as "the grapevine." "In most organizations, the greater part of the information that is used in decision-making is informally transmitted," they observe.

The central problems in communications are the blockages that occur: "Blockages in the communication system constitute one of the most serious problems in public administration. They may occur in any one of the three steps in the communications process: initiation, transmission, or reception. Those who have information may fail to tell those who need the information as a basis of action; those who should transmit the information may fail to do so; those who receive the information may be unwilling or unable to assimilate it."

Seven critical types of communications blockages in public organizations are enumerated by the authors, the first being, simply, *barriers of language.* Words are frequently misinterpreted or understood differently as messages pass from one individual to another within organizations. Second, *frames of reference* differ so that the perception of information varies among individuals. Personal "mental sets" thus often prevent accurate comprehension of the problem at hand. Third, *status distance* can block communications because as information moves upward or downward through the various hierarchical levels of an organization "a considerable filtering and distorting" occurs. Fourth, *geographical distance* impedes the communications process; a far-flung department with many field offices spread over the nation or the world has great difficulty in ensuring prompt and accurate information exchange among its component units. Fifth, *self-protection* of the individual who reports actions plays a role in the informational links. Often "information that will evoke a favorable reaction will be played up; the mistakes and the fumbles tend to be glossed over." Sometimes the deception is conscious and at other times unconscious, but this activity always serves to distort objective reality. Sixth, *the pressures of work* tend to leave important matters overlooked or unreported. Finally, the *censorship* inherent in many governmental activities such as foreign intelligence or military operations limits the accurate flow of information within many public agencies.

These characteristic psychological and institutional communication blockages, suggest Simon, Smithburg, and Thompson, raise the vital question of "where a particular decision can best be made." Selection of the appropriate place for decision making directly depends on how effectively and easily information can be transmitted from its source to a decisional center, and how effectively and easily the decision can be transmitted from the decision maker to the point where action will occur. For instance, a military hierarchy could grant to individual company commanders the authority for deciding on the use of tactical nuclear weapons. This action would reduce the "time costs" associated with communicating to higher headquarters in the event of possible enemy attack and thus would allow for extreme military flexibility at lower echelons, but "local option" in this case might very well increase other costs, such as the likelihood of a nuclear accident. On the other hand, if authority for using these weapons had to be cleared, say, by the president of the United States and by other major Allied powers, the risk of accident might very well be reduced, but the time costs of gaining consent to use these weapons from many sources might make a decision so cumbersome and lengthy that no opportunity for swift retaliatory response would exist. As Simon, Smithburg, and Thompson point out, "Ease or difficulty of communications may sometimes be a central consideration in determining how far down the administrative line the function of making a particular decision should be located." The authors thus view the communications process not only as determining the outcome of particular decisions but as a prime influence on the structure of decision making within organizations. Extreme decentralization may achieve flexibility and initiative at the local level but may exact costs in terms of uniformity and control of response; vice versa, extreme centralization may produce maximum oversight but may reduce organizational responsiveness. Ultimately, the costs associated with delegating such decisional authority within an organizational hierarchy are always relative and are determined by the values and objectives of the organization.

Simon, Smithburg, and Thompson's ideas on communications are now a half century old and tend to view the topic as akin to "a machine model"—structured, apolitical, and largely functionally oriented. So how is this subject conceptualized today by a modern theorist? The following selection, by Professor James Garnett at the Graduate Department of Public Policy and Administration, Rutgers University at Camden, author of the seminal book *Communicating for Results in Government* (1992), and considered the foremost scholar on this topic, paints a current overview of communication, stressing its professional centrality, ubiquity, *and* complexity for the field.

As you read this selection, keep the following questions in mind:

How does Professor Garnett's contemporary view of communication compare with the foregoing outline of Simon, Smithburg, and Thompson's? What's new in this field, according to Garnett? Reflect on any communications issues that might have been apparent to you in the previous cases, such as "The MOVE Disaster." Do they square with those outlined by Professor Garnett? Is it possible to trace the internal network of communications in an organization? The external network? What factors create or define the shape of internal *or* external informational network? For example, what impact have computers had in recent years?

Can you draw from this essay generalizations concerning the managing of the communication process as a means for enhancing effectiveness in public organizations? What suggestions does Professor Garnett recommend for managing more effectively?

Consider the following essay in relation to Norton Long's concept of administrative power. How does administrative communication influence issues of policy and power? Specifically, did communication influence the outcomes in the case study in Chapter 2, "How Kristin Died"?

Finally, why does Garnett argue that "communication ethics is not an oxymoron"? What does he mean by that comment?

Administrative Communication (Or How to Make All the Rest Work): The Concept of Its Professional Centrality

JAMES L. GARNETT

The first executive function is to develop and maintain a system of communication.

—*Chester Barnard,* The Functions of the Executive, *p. 226*

Note: This original essay was prepared by James L. Garnett especially for the eighth edition of this book.

A large part (perhaps all) of an executive's job has to do with giving and receiving communications. Managers are nerve centers in the organizational communication network. They receive all sorts of memoranda, letters, policy statements, instructions, reports, face-to-face communications and what not. Perhaps nothing is so important to successful administration as successful communication.

—*Robert S. Lorch,* Public Administration, *p. 174*

Since the time of Lorch's (1978) observation, above, public administrators continue to expend much of their time and effort on those communicative tasks *and* on the growing number and diversity of communications, including e-mail messages, contracts, service agreements, satisfaction surveys, and other forms. The pervasiveness of communication extends beyond the managerial workday. The actual administrative situations depicted by cases in this book testify to the centrality of communication in public service.

- In chapter 1, John Bartlow Martin's classic, vivid case "The Blast in Centralia No. 5: A Mine Disaster No One Stopped," numerous official and unofficial attempts to communicate the danger of Mine No. 5 failed to prompt sufficient action, contributing to the deaths of 111 miners. Leaders and members of UMWA Local 52, safety inspector Scanlon, and others attempting to safeguard mine conditions proved unable to overcome the multiple communication barriers of perception and hierarchy.
- In chapter 2, George Lardner Jr.'s plaintive account of his daughter's senseless murder by an unstable ex-boyfriend captures repeated occasions where one arm of Boston's criminal justice bureaucracy never received key reports from another arm that might have prevented the shooting. Two official complaints that would have triggered the ex-boyfriend Cartier's arrest and detention were still sitting on a clerk's desk when Kristin was killed.

Not all miscommunication leads to war, deadly explosions, or murder. More commonly, miscommunication has less drastic or immediate consequences but still affects administrative performance and government's ability to serve its citizens. Miscommunication among ethnic groups, public agencies, professional societies, and other organizations results frequently in losses of time, money, goodwill, and cooperation. This is more typical of the effects of communication in public service. As crucial as communication is in life-and-death situations, the larger consequences of miscommunication occur in the countless, daily interactions between public servants and citizens, between public servants and public officials, among public servants, and among the many public, private, and nonprofit actors in the increasingly complex delivery systems that provide public service. The collective consequences of miscommunication in these daily interactions—whether from intent or inadvertence, lack of skill or misuse of skill, overloading or boredom, inadequate technology or technology overkill—take an enormous toll on performance, credibility, trust and on what counts most, citizens' quality of life. Missing welfare checks, foregone medical treatment, cutoff of heat, and extra frustrations over obtaining help are all important to those we are called to serve.

As with the previously mentioned cases and other actual situations, communication is no panacea. Effective communication does not guarantee success, nor does miscommunication guarantee failure. Even if communication had been more prolific and accurate, various Centralia regulatory organizations had motives for furthering their perceived self-interest that often conflicted with motives and agendas of other organizations. In spite of prior warnings about the foam, strong political, economic, and administrative forces pushed for the Columbia to fly, making it difficult for warning messages to pierce the must-launch-now mindset. So, while communication is hardly a panacea, it does play a crucial role in administrative success or failure. Sound communication contributes to performance and increases the chances for success, and faulty communication contributes to the likelihood of failure. Perhaps what these cases and other slices of real life demonstrate is that communication is an extremely complex process typically undertaken in complicated political, social, economic, and technological contexts. These factors compound the need for communicating with as much knowledge, skill, and effort as possible instead of assuming that communication is routine because it is so common. Foltz (1973, 1) sensed this contradiction when he wrote, "Let's get rid of the thought that there's nothing to communications. Let's recognize that communications is tough, hard, demanding. It's one of the most damned and least understood skills in existence. It's at the core of every problem facing us as individuals, families, groups, nations." Chester Barnard, one of the seminal writers on administration, also understood the centrality of communication when he emphasized that "developing and maintaining a system of communication" (1938, 226) ranked as the first executive principle.

This chapter aims to raise the salience of communication within Public Administration by emphasizing communication's centrality to almost everything public administrators do. Other aims are to place the various types of public sector communication in context, address some key issues concerning communication, and provide guidance on sound communication practice. Because all the rich cases in this book provide insights about communication, a number of them (along with other events) will be used to illustrate key issues and concepts.

Communication Processes and Players

This section describes key public sector communication processes and roles. These are hardly the only ones, but they are the central ones. Overlap and interaction among these processes and roles is unavoidable—and important. The newsmaking process, although predominantly aimed at external publics, fuels intraorganizational communication within government agencies. While interorganizational communication within the public sector occurs most frequently among service provider organizations, it increasingly involves stakeholder client/customer groups.

Public Officials and the News Media: The Newsmaking Process

The concept of administrative communication typically centers on the newsmaking process. Traditional press relations, now termed *media relations* to reflect the broader efforts to report news through television, radio, the Internet, and other channels, has dominated both the practice and scholarship on government communication—to the detriment of our understanding of other key communication processes. Because of its historically central role, however, newsmaking provides a good point of departure. Most government agencies of any size and financial resources have a staff or person who fields questions from reporters and who proactively attempts to get news coverage (typically favorable) about their agency. Business companies and nonprofit organizations engaged in providing or advocating public services also generally have such a function, whether called public relations, media relations, public information, public affairs, communication, or some other name. In the past, former news reporters or editors typically staffed such units because they knew the newsmaking process and they held strong contacts with fellow reporters and editors. Public information or public affairs specialists disseminated news to newspapers and to radio and television stations by means of news releases, interviews, and news conferences. According to extensive research conducted by Grunig and Grunig (1992), media relations (what they call the *public information model*) is still the predominant model of government (and business) communication, although releases may now be distributed by electronic mail and news conferences be broadcast by satellite.

Several trends have begun to revolutionize the newsmaking process. The public increasingly demands direct communication with public officials rather than have interactions filter through reporters, editors, commentators, and others. Growing audiences for C-SPAN, public radio, and other live, direct broadcasts of agency hearings, legislative debates, and even a presidential impeachment trial attest to this trend. To their credit, many elected and appointed officials have actively pursued more direct contact with constituents rather than rely solely on getting messages conveyed by news sources, however important those sources remain. President Bill Clinton, for one, showed extraordinary talent at using direct televised presidential addresses and nationally televised "town meetings" to reach citizens in the studio audience and nationwide audiences who witnessed and identified with this direct interaction. To underscore the constant need to combine communication skill with ethics, some commentators have observed that part of President Clinton's skill in influencing (and some would say misleading) public opinion about his sexual affairs later aggravated his legal and constitutional problems—and as with his State of the Union address during his trial, helped him survive those challenges. Many federal, state, and local government agencies have increased their direct contact with citizens by using telephone hotlines, interactive cable television, Web sites, neighborhood meetings, and other channels to send information about government policies, programs, and actions and to receive information from citizens about program impact, citizen satisfaction, or consumer preferences.

Even though Osborne and Gabler's influential book *Reinventing Government* said surprisingly little about the role of communication in a more entrepreneurial public sector, its discussion of consumer feedback and the consumer orientation it helped spawn has been another trend that has made governments and others conducting the public's business more attuned to the role as communication *receiver* and less preoccupied with *sending*—traditionally through the news media. Make no mistake: the role of news organizations and their reporters, editors, commentators, and others in the newsmaking process continues to thrive as our individual and professional scholarly fascination with proliferating numbers and formats of news sources will attest. Increasingly, however, public sector actors will pursue the need to diversify their ability to communicate with important stakeholders and other publics.

Just as the demands of citizen consumers have expanded the functions of public sector communication, administrators are increasingly demanding a more managerial focus from their communication function.

Professional Managers and Professional Communicators: The Managerial Communication Process

While all public servants at every level have an essential role as communicators, our specialization-oriented society has singled out some as professional communicators, whether called press secretary, public information officer, public affairs specialist, or some other title. Such specialists, as indicated earlier, have traditionally had backgrounds in journalism and were principally involved in the media-relations role. The first expansion of the communication function involved producing, or helping produce, other forms of information reports, internal and external newsletters, videos, and the like. This required professional communicators to possess a broader set of knowledge and skill but still primarily involved sending information, although to more diverse audiences than news reporters and editors. While savvy officials and administrators appreciated the importance of sound media relations and the broader set of information "products," many public executives and administrators in the last two decades began demanding more of their communication unit. In particular, administrators wanted their communication function to provide help with management tasks and problems. And many professional communicators, wanting to play a more central role, actively sought and prepared for such management-related tasks, including paying attention to what tangible results their efforts were producing. These progressive communication professionals realized that when the communication function in organizations pays no attention to communication effects or to measuring them, it is "relegated to the status of an output function that executives systematically exclude from decision making and strategic planning" (Broom and Dozier 1983, 5). Best practice communication units in the public sector now provide substantial expertise and support to their organizations and, in turn, need administrative support to be most effective, as Table 9.1 conveys.

The relationship between public administrators and public communicators can be far more productive and satisfying if both regard each other as professionals, see the needs and constraints of the other, and actively

Table 9.1 Mutual Reliance Between Public Administrators and Professional Communicators

Communication Professionals Can Help Public Administrators with:

Strategic Planning Gathering and organizing information about internal strengths and weaknesses and external opportunities and threats and helping craft a Communication Strategic Plan that supports and helps implement the overall Strategic Plan by identifying key issues, audiences, resource potentials, messages, and outcomes.

Policy and Program Implementation Assisting with implementation by identifying existing and potential stakeholders for an existing or proposed program or policy, learning stakeholder opinions about such programs or policies, as well as stakeholders' likely response, program or policy revisions, or mutual interests that could facilitate implementation.

Boundary Scanning/Environmental Scanning Detecting changes in the agency's environment that can affect agency decisions, actions, and results. Training in public opinion and media relations gives many communication professionals the capability to help agencies gather information about trends, actions, perceptions, and so on, beyond their boundaries. Scanning can be done informally through contacts or through systematic surveys, focus groups, interviews, content analyses, and other methods.

Stakeholder Analysis Regular or special analysis of key agency stakeholders (clients, customers, special interests, other public agencies, and so on) to determine their policy positions, program agendas, organizational strategy, resource needs, posture toward an agency, and specific initiatives.

Issue Marketing Finding out what clients, constituents, customers, and other key stakeholders regard to be important issues, how they stand on these issues, how likely they are to become actively involved in these issues, and what kinds of messages would best be able to reach them. Issue marketing can also test various stakeholder positions on a predetermined set of issues.

Agenda Setting Shaping the agency's agenda by discovering what agency stakeholders want to happen and by directly influencing the policy agenda. Communication professionals can utilize opinion research and scanning skills to detect and present stakeholder preferences for the agency's agenda. Communication professionals can also help affect the news media agenda that shapes public and political agendas that, in turn, influence the agency's agenda. This can give an organization more self-control over its policy and management agendas.

Conflict Management/Dispute Resolution Identifying conflicts or potential conflicts among agencies, stakeholders, interest groups, and others; and helping manage these conflicts constructively by identifying interests and solutions as well as conflicts.

Communication/Information Auditing Comparing information/communication flows in an agency with actual information/communication needs; assessing the quantity and quality of information; and identifying information overloads, bottlenecks, and gaps.

Outcomes Assessment Evaluating outcomes—the more fundamental results of policy and programs. Communication professionals can assist in soliciting opinions about customer satisfaction and working with program and policy analysts to craft sound and user-friendly surveys, interviews, focus groups, or other assessment instruments.

Public Administrators Can Help Communicators

- See the broader organizational/managerial picture
- Stay focused on issues of administrative/performance significance rather than be caught up with brochures, videos, or other "products" of public information
- Tap into managerial influence networks so that communicators can get the information and support needed to get the job done
- Become involved in the formative stages of a program, project, or issue to facilitate early advice and minimize the need for damage control later
- Get the support needed to appropriately evaluate the results of communication
- Obtain the training needed to provide broader, more managerial, and strategic capabilities

work to make the other more effective in serving the public. Even though the relationship with professional communicators is crucial, effective public administrators understand that they are often their organization's most important communicator and act accordingly. The next two sections examine this role, first with internal and then with external communication.

Public Executives, Administrators, and Employees: The Internal Communication Process

Just as politics is too crucial to administration to be left entirely to politicians, communication is too critical to managerial success to be left solely to the professional communicators. Public executives, first-line supervisors, and all administrators in between must interact daily with managerial superiors, subordinates, peers, staff professionals, and other audiences inside the organization.

Internal communication can be thought of as downward, upward, or lateral. Downward communication has historically received the most emphasis in organization and management theory—and probably also in management practice (Garnett 1997b). Katz and Kahn (1966) identify the functions of downward communication as issuing task directives, giving task-related information, giving feedback on job performance, and conveying an overall sense of mission. Directives and task-related information tend to dominate downward channels in public-sector agencies, leaving performance feedback and mission-related information underused and undervalued. "If this imbalance occurs, public employees can become desensitized to task-related messages and starved for communication about their performance and about agency direction. Imbalance in downward communication often causes other organizational dysfunctions such as depressed morale, preoccupations with routine tasks, and indifference to overall agency performance" (Garnett 1992a, 103). One of the many factors contributing to the MOVE disaster (see Nagel, chapter 8 of this volume) was the lack of downward communication about an overall emergency plan for how each participating department (police, fire, emergency services) fit into the overall plan and feedback on how each phase was progressing. In this case there may not have been enough task-oriented communication either, and upward and lateral communication were also critically deficient.

Upward communication can carry a number of vital messages: feedback on whether downward messages are received, understood, and acted upon; warnings about problems needing attention; intelligence gleaned by subordinates about key stakeholders; soundings about organizational morale and performance. This book is full of cases where inattention to upward messages—both internal and external—lost performance, money, political support, and even lives. As reflected in Case Study 1 in this text, repeated attempts by UMWA Local 52 and Illinois Mine Inspector Driscoll Scanlan to alert state, coal company, union, and other officials of dangerous conditions in Mine No. 5 failed to prompt action. They failed due to economic and political predisposition against their message, and to their inability to convey a greater sense of urgency and to use a broader range of communication channels. Research on public-sector communication shows the tendency for upward communication to be distorted or lost because of reluctance to send or receive bad news and the tendency for subordinates to bear self-serving messages up the ranks (Tullock 1965; Downs 1967; Kaufman and Couzens 1973). Garnett (1992a) describes a number of techniques for improving upward communication. Reducing administrative layers that can delay and distort messages might have saved time and lives in situations like the Centralia mine. One of the National Performance Review's justifications for eliminating layers of federal middle management is to make interactions between top and lower organizational levels more direct, efficient, and accurate. Some evidence of this exists (Garnett 1997c), but the full record is still out. Bypassing routine channels to get messages more quickly and directly into the hands of those who need to know can aid upward communication but can also damage accountability and information dissemination if abused. Even though the foam conditions and its vulnerability were communicated, NASA could not prevent all miscommunication before the Columbia liftoff, but using predetermined codes, signals, language, and other means to make messages more distortion-resistant generally helps.

Important communication within public-sector organizations is increasingly lateral—among organizational peers in the same or different unit. Key functions of lateral communication include task coordination, information sharing, multidisciplinary problem solving, and mutual emotional support. Research summarized in Garnett (1992a) shows that openness, trust, and satisfaction over the level of emotional support relates to the quality of interpersonal communication, especially lateral communication. Because they are shared among status equals, lateral messages tend to be more honest and accurate than are messages up or down the hierarchy. Lateral communication also typically follows *subformal* networks (carrying informal, unofficial messages through formal channels) that tend to be more accurate and honest than *formal* networks that carry official messages through formal channels (Downs 1967). Unlike subformal communication networks used by public servants in their official capacity but not for the official record, *personal* communication networks carry unofficial messages by public servants acting apart from their official capacity. Expressions of personal interest and emotional support are examples of personal communication, as are gossip and rumors. Because rumors are typically conveyed unofficially and laterally, they often are surprisingly accurate. Whether rumors are accurate or misleading, coping with rumors and grapevines is an essential skill for public administrators (Garnett 1992b).

As crucial as it is to organizational health and performance, lateral communication has historically been undervalued, receiving less scholarly attention than have upward, and particularly downward, communication (Garnett 1997b). Research by Walton (1962) showed that interaction among navy engineers and scientists was penalized by superiors who were suspicious of subordinates communicating with each other and who wanted communication to come through them. The increasing need to use multidisciplinary teams to solve increasingly complex public-sector problems and to compensate for reduced staffing heightens the importance of lateral communication. In light of smaller, more professionalized workforces, reduced bureaucratic layering, enhanced communication technologies, heightened attention to assessing performance, and other changes, there are indications of greater attention to upward communication and to downward communication about mission and performance feedback (Garnett 1997c).

Boundary Spanners and External Audiences: The Interorganizational Communication Process

Just when this planet evolved from being primarily dominated by *organizational* dynamics to one characterized by *interorganizational* dynamics is not clear. What *is* clear is that we now live in a world where virtually every policy decision, virtually every business or government transaction, and even virtually every decision about personal lifestyle involves more than one organization or has implications for multiple organizations. Massive public-private partnerships such as space missions like Columbia and emergency responses like MOVE, or even international, multiorganizational efforts like the first and second Gulf Wars or intervention in Bosnia, most visibly demonstrate the need for orchestrated cooperation among multiple organizations. But communication between or among public-service providers, regulators, customers, interest groups, or others also characterizes dynamics in more microlevel situations as well. Communication gaps among various parts of Boston's criminal justice system contributed to Kristin Lardner's murder, for example.

Three factors contribute to the rise of the interorganizational dimension in public management: (1) Economic interdependence, both globally and locally, stimulates interaction among organizations. (2) Issue or policy networks through which political policy decisions are made have tended to become larger and more diverse (see Heclo, in chapter 14 of this volume). The shift from primarily direct government provision of public services to provision by more complex, more diverse networks of public, private, and nonprofit organizations has profound implications for communication as well as governance

(Osborne and Gaebler 1992). Since this trend is so powerful and will likely continue, the term *public sector* or *public interest,* rather than *government service,* is used to refer to these diverse networks of service providers. (3) Greater access to information/communication technology and the liberalizing of many political economic, and service institutions have enabled looser coupling among traditional hierarchies and recoupling in various ways, many of them interorganizational.

Because of the enhanced importance of external environments and relationships with stakeholder organizations in the environment that supply resources, purchase services, or monitor behavior, boundary spanning and external communication take on added significance. Boundary spanners are those public executives, communication professionals, or even operating-level employees who systematically or sporadically communicate with their counterparts or with other actors in the external environment and share information and observations both ways. Some boundary spanners, such as community-relations specialists or legislative liaisons, have this assigned role. Others take this on because they recognize its importance. This explains why military base commanders, hospital executives, and city managers, among others, typically maintain active civic and social ties with their communities. Boundary spanning can be informal, relying on the greater accuracy of subformal and lateral communication, or it can be highly formal and systematized, such as with environmental scanning (Garnett 1992a; Harris 1997), issue management (Harris 1997), or regular opinion sampling of stakeholders (Garnett 1992a). Organizations with turbulent environments need effective boundary spanning to learn and adapt.

Interorganizational communication has yet to be explored as much as other facets of public-sector communication, but some salient concepts have emerged (O'Toole 1997). Various interorganizational structures exist, each influencing communication patterns. With a *hierarchical* structure, one agency has authority over others, and channels typically run from that agency to subordinate agencies. The National Institutes of Health reporting to the Office of Secretary of Health and Human Services portrays this structure.

A variation of this is the *lead agency* pattern, with a number of agencies reporting to the lead agency for a particular project or assignment. NASA played this role for the Columbia mission. Another variant is the *wheel* pattern, with communication typically flowing to and from one central organization. By having a central clearinghouse for information, coordination can often be achieved without formal authority. In the broken channel structure, "direct links exist among some agencies, but no agency is linked directly to all others with control over the others" (Garnett, 1992a, 162).

Public administrators who discover they need to communicate externally within a broken channel pattern need to make extra effort to identify and compensate for the gaps that exist. Understanding the particular dynamics of the other interorganizational patterns is also helpful. For example, O'Toole (1997, p. 64) has observed that "those [organizations] located most centrally in the structure of interdependence also sit at the nexus of more interaction and communication links. A unit's location within an organizational structure can thus determine information flows and information can be a source of power." In general, communicating with people in a different organization from our own requires greater planning and effort. Communication preferences of the intended audience, the organizational culture they work in, the management system and routines into which your message will enter, and other factors are likely to be less familiar than for internal interaction and will require more analysis and planning (Garnett 1992a).

Crucial Issues in Public Sector Communication

Understanding public-sector communication involves more than knowing the players and processes. A number of issues overlap or even transcend players and processes. Addressing all salient issues in an overview chapter like this one is impossible. However, we can address several of the most crucial communication issues facing public administrators at the dawn of the twenty-first century.

Gaining and Maintaining Credibility with Citizens: Conventional Government Communication Is Likely to Fail!

In another work (Garnett 1997a), I pose *The Credibility Conundrum* that: *"at a time when government communication most needs credibility to help restore public confidence, it has the least"*. According to the National Commission on Civic Renewal (1998, 29), 77 percent of Americans in 1964 trusted their national government to do the right thing usually or most of the time, but only 37 percent held that opinion in 1994. In 1999, immediately after the United States Senate acquitted President Clinton of charges of perjury and obstruction of justice, public trust in government had been further damaged in the United States. Don Eberly, Director of the Civil Society Project that monitors and promotes citizen participation in governance, assessed that "this scandal will rank with Vietnam and Watergate as a source of lasting scars. . . . It will strengthen the cancers that are already rampant in our body politic. Trust in our national institutions has almost evaporated" (Polman 1999, A1). Thus, at a time when government credibility is most needed to break the cycle of distrust, its lack becomes a barrier to improving trust. Campaigns to restore public confidence through media blitzes face difficulties, because media institutions themselves face a credibility crisis and because many citizens have become skeptical of government public relations. The *Propaganda Paradox* (Garnett 1997a, 8) holds that *"the more zealous government's efforts to persuade citizens, the less they are persuaded."* Related to the *Credibility Conundrum,* this paradox reflects historic skepticism in many nations that governments are communicating honestly and openly (Heise 1985; Garnett 1992a; Carnevale 1995). Whether they regard government communication as propaganda, public relations, or "spin doctoring," citizens have become conditioned to expect the "spin" from their governments and to consciously or subconsciously discount these messages through counterbias (Downs 1967; Garnett 1992a).

Another reason for what Heise (1985) calls "the confidence gap" between government and the governed arises because governments have traditionally employed communication practices that have been either unilateral or, if bilateral, more oriented to government's sending messages than to receiving them. Historically, government communication in the United States (and in other developed and developing nations) tends to fit three of Grunig and Hunt's (1984) stages of public relations. The first stage, the press agentry/publicity model, was practiced to promote early celebrities such as Andrew Jackson, Buffalo Bill, P.T. Barnum, and the like. This model is characterized by unabashed, one-sided promotion of a person, product, or cause and can still be found in electoral campaigns and promotions of star athletes and entertainers. At the turn of the twentieth century, according to Grunig and Hunt (1984) and Grunig and Grunig (1992, 288), ". . . a second model of public relations, the public information model, developed as a reaction to attacks on large corporations and government agencies by muckraking journalists. Leaders of these organizations realized they needed more than the propaganda of press agents to counter the attacks on them in the media. Instead, they hired their own journalists as public relations practitioners to write 'press handouts' explaining their actions. Although practitioners of the public information model generally chose to write only good things about their organizations, the information they did report generally was truthful and accurate."

Both the press-agentry and public information models constitute basically one-way sending to publics, primarily through the news media. Behavioral and social science knowledge that exploded during and after World War I enabled the use of what Grunig and Grunig (1992) typed the two-way asymmetrical model. In this model, information was sought as well as sent to external publics, but the emphasis was clearly on getting publics to accept government's or other sender's position by using scientific theories that enabled persuasion, propaganda, and the "engineering of consent" (Grunig and Grunig 1992, 288). This model, what Garnett (1997a) calls the public affairs model, is more proactive in outreach but still treats publics more as audiences to be enlightened and convinced than partners to be involved. This model too has widespread use in governments worldwide.

According to a growing body of scholarship, these traditional models of public relations that have relied on sending messages and manipulating consent have generally been unsuccessful in both promoting the organizational agenda and in promoting a broader sense of the public interest (Grunig 1997). Such research includes that on the U.S. Nuclear Regulatory Commission (Childers 1989), higher education (Kelly 1989), various government organizations (Heise 1985; Garnett 1992a), and a wide range of business, nonprofit, and government organizations (Grunig and Grunig 1992; Grunig 1997). The general sense of such research is that basically one-way "tell and sell" approaches fail to improve the image of those organizations that use them either in terms of media coverage or direct stakeholder perception. Thus these approaches tend to fail in achieving the very purpose for which they were designed: influencing public opinion, not to mention achieving more fundamental aims of improving public-sector performance.

Four reasons exist for the general failure of these basically unilateral communication approaches: First, the track record of most governments (and businesses) for generally communicating messages favorable to them and playing down or ignoring unfavorable messages has conditioned citizens to reject or discount what they regard as the same old propaganda (Heise 1985).

Second, governments' publics, usually without thinking about it, reflect a general finding of communication research that shows people, especially more educated people, tend to reject messages they perceive to be extreme or implausible (Zimbardo, Ebbeson, and Maslach 1977; Garnett 1989). People therefore tend to be suspicious of one-sided arguments or claims they think are beyond the realm of plausibility. "When government communications convey the message that 'no problem exists' or 'everything is under control,' such skewed messages tend to trigger cynicism and counterbias" (Garnett 1997a, 8). Governments serious about improving their public image concentrate on improving their performance, product, and responsiveness, not on preoccupation with spin-doctoring their image. Well-regarded governments recognize the difference between marketing and promotion. *Promotion*

concentrates on getting people to like the existing product. *Marketing* attempts to discover what product people want, what features it should have, and how to get people to use that product. Without improving product and performance the best-conceived promotions have a "tough sell."

Third, often lacking true reciprocity in communicating with their governments to voice their preferences or to raise questions, many citizens have taken the most cautious course or the only course open to them—disbelieving the government's message or discounting it. And fourth, in an era of "call-in" or "talkback" radio, interactive television, and interactive computer communication, where citizens are accustomed to taking an active role, many resent the passive role relegated to them by basically one-way communication from government and other public-sector organizations that maintain a press agentry or public information model. Despite the demonstrated lack of effectiveness of the public information and press agentry models, they are the most numerous public relations models applied in government (Grunig 1997).

If these predominantly one-way "tell and sell" approaches to communicating tend to fail, particularly in the long run, what does work? Part of the answer comes from research on the effectiveness of the various communication models and part from examples of new approaches for facilitating involvement. "The fourth model, the 'two-way symmetrical,' describes a model of public relations that is based on research and that uses communication to manage conflict and improve understanding with strategic publics. Because the two-way symmetrical model bases public relations on negotiation and compromise, it does not force the organization to choose whether it is right on particular issues. Rather, two-way symmetrical public relations allows the question of what is right to be settled by negotiation, since nearly every side to a conflict—such as nuclear power, abortion, or gun control—believes its position to be right" (Grunig 1997, 264). "The IABC [International Association of Business Communicators] research provided strong evidence that excellent public relations departments use the two-way symmetrical model and that as a result they more often meet the objectives of their communication and make the organization more effective" (Grunig

1997, 265). The IABC research program that studied a number of government as well as business organizations found that in actuality effective public relations departments use both the two-way symmetrical (what I call the communication model) and the two-way asymmetrical (public affairs) model to negotiate with stakeholders or to persuade them, as appropriate.

One example of the two-way symmetrical communication model at work involves the highly controversial issue of cleaning up nuclear waste. Fernald, Ohio, near Cincinnati, is the site of a former nuclear weapons uranium refinery now operated by the U.S. Department of Energy. In an effort to improve public participation in making decisions about nuclear cleanup at environmental Superfund sites like Fernald, the Department of Energy created advisory boards for each major nuclear waste site. These boards were comprised of public officials, environmentalists, neighbors of the nuclear site, local activists, health professionals, businesspeople, academics, labor representatives, and as non-voting members, representatives of DOE and federal and state environmental protection agencies. Basic options for these advisory boards were to reject any local disposal of nuclear waste (not-in-my-backyard [NIMBY] response), "accepting its political, technical and financial costs; it could accept on-site disposal of all contaminated soil, and lose the use of some land while incurring some local political fallout; or it could find an acceptable middle ground, avoiding or minimizing the worst drawbacks to either extreme" (Applegate and Sarno 1996, 1).

The last course of action was pursued and involved extensive two-way give-and-take negotiation among those represented. A game simulation was created to help participants, both experts and novices, see the trade-offs involved in various removal or cleanup alternatives (Applegate and Sarno 1997). This facilitated communication and decision making. The consensus reached provided for cleanup in less than half the time originally projected and at a savings of over $2 billion.

The chief lessons here are that instead of ignoring the problem and complaints about it or relying on persuading citizens that no problem existed or that they could learn to live with it, the government actively involved citizens in a mutual process of communicating and problem solving. This involved more risk in some ways, because the government had to be willing to also be persuaded by the arguments of others, making the necessary adjustments in policy or practice. But it was a more productive and more ethical process, because it avoided unilaterally trying to pass off ideological or technical positions onto citizens. The government in this case started with the assumption that the public had a right to know and to be heard. This attitude was reflected in the wide range of communication mechanisms established, including regular public meetings, educational programs, direct contacts with key stakeholders, a liaison program, and an extensive public reading room, among others (Applegate and Sarno 1997). This genuine spirit of reciprocity and partnership and the extra communication effort involved has resulted in improved performance (quicker cleanup at lower cost) and a deeper sense of mutual trust and credibility.

This approach to communicating and problem solving is also practiced in many other contexts. "In Santa Monica, California, the Public Electronic Network, . . . a pioneering community network set up by the city, has allowed city residents from all walks of life to share ideas, debate issues, and seek common solutions to local problems. In an effort to address Santa Monica's growing problems with homelessness, homeowners and homeless people who logged on from public terminals joined with city council members and other city staff in an electronic discussion that led directly to the creation of a new program that provided public services that the homeless needed and that homeowners could support" (*Communication as Engagement,* prologue). Such efforts at two-way communication that attempt to negotiate meaning rather than solely transmit it will become more common in the next century if public administrators and communication professionals can rise to the challenge of changing their perspective and practice. Another example of the government recognizing that the receiving, listening role is at least as important as the sending role is the U.S. Internal Revenue Service's use of in-person and electronic forums to get feedback from taxpayers. This parallels efforts made by many governments and other public service organizations at all levels to tap citizen/customer feedback using multiple channels, a practice discussed in the next section.

Linking Diverse Audiences Using Diverse Media: Making the Most of Cyberspace and the Coffee Klatch

We tend to think of communication/information technologies as high-tech (computer communication, satellite television, remote-sensing systems, and the like). Technology, broadly defined as a means to achieving an end, can also be low-tech (for example, drama, flyer distribution, and neighborhood coffee klatches). The challenges for public administrators include being knowledgeable about the communication technologies range (both high-tech and low-tech) currently available, as well as about emerging technologies. Knowing the current range of communication technologies helps administrators and professional communicators use appropriate media to reach particular target audiences. Public officials in Los Angeles were able to address a number of social and legal issues relevant to their Spanish-speaking citizens by incorporating these issues into plots for a popular soap opera, "Cancion de la Raza." Public administrators also need to know what technologies are emerging or are likely to emerge, so that they don't fall behind the technology curve. Some populations in India, for example, have no reliable telephone service but can be reached by satellite television. This is only one example of communication technologies leap-frogging a generation or more.

In making decisions about which technologies to utilize, the inherent strengths and weaknesses of various media need to be considered along with the compensating advantages of using multiple media (Garnett 1996). Oral messages typically are more vulnerable to misinterpretation than are written messages. Renovations of the U.S. Air Traffic Control System scheduled for 2000 included installing the capability for using e-mail to communicate between airport control towers and airplane cockpits. The Federal Aviation Administration expected that adding the capability to report or verify flight instructions in writing would reduce misinterpretations that caused airplane accidents. In the Centralia mine case, however, the overreliance on written reports and letters (a slower, less dramatic medium) reduced the capacity of miners and mine inspectors to vividly convey mine dangers.

Reaching hard-to-reach audiences is another issue that deserves—and is getting—more attention. For the 2000 census, the U.S. Bureau of the Census made efforts on an unprecedented scale to identify and reach stakeholder groups and audiences that are historically underrepresented in census counts (such as urban Hispanic Americans) and other hard-to-reach groups more recently identified (such as survivalist communes). Bureau communication specialists and consultants traveled to target areas, finding group members knowledgeable about the communication behaviors and preferences of that group, and obtaining and following their advice about how best to reach that audience. This constitutes one of the largest efforts at targeted, communication strategic planning (Garnett 1992a) ever practiced by the United States government.

Radio is another medium that governments, public interest groups, and others have used effectively to air emergency warnings and information and to engage citizens in dialogue through call-in interactive radio and through regular broadcasts from officials. Savvy public officials know which radio stations Spanish-speaking, Hebrew-speaking, sports-minded, or other kinds of groups would likely listen to in their geographic area and can utilize these stations to listen to and talk to such target audiences. Today, however, through the technology of Internet radio, the number and range of stations that citizens can tune in to are multiplying rapidly. Most standard computers today can be used to tune in to stations in all parts of the United States, Canada, Europe, Asia, Australia, and other continents, typically for free at this stage (Ahrens 1999). This allows Hebrew-speaking stakeholder groups in Los Angeles, for example, to access radio programs in New York or even Jerusalem, thus diversifying the news, cultural programming, and other programming they get. It has also become cheaper and easier for citizens to start their own station by means of computer, further multiplying and diversifying the messages and agendas carried by radio. Public-sector officials will need to become aware of changing radio-use patterns of key stakeholder groups in their regions and communicate accordingly.

Access constitutes another critical issue for determining appropriate communication technologies. The widespread availability of public information on government World Wide Web sites has increased access for numerous organizations and individuals, making it easier, cheaper, and faster to acquire information or to do business with government. Despite the creation of Internet labs in many public libraries and public schools, access to this communication technology is limited by factors such as geography, income, and educational level. Public librarians in Muncie, Indiana thought that people in the library's service area needed the access that their bookmobiles provided, but a higher-tech version. They therefore added seven computer terminals and converted a bookmobile into a CyberMobile that travels throughout their district, including rural areas, so that citizens had access and instruction for using the Internet. Efforts such as these hardly guarantee access to communication technologies, but they help. Utilizing a number of various communication technologies—low-tech as well as high-tech—for both sending and receiving increases the likelihood of access with various publics.

When utilizing communication technologies, public administrators also need to recognize the ways that people obtain and process information. Because of their potential for richness and interest, stories have always been an integral means to transmit values and heritage in a society. Thinking perhaps that stories were more trivial and subjective than survey results or other forms of information, governments and other public-sector actors have only rarely used the potential of stories to convey or receive messages on many levels. Because stories have the capability of capturing the emotional as well as the informational level, stories typically are often superior in terms of message impact, retention, and motivating people. Preachers recognize this when they include stories in sermons. Parents tell children about their own childhood in order to teach lessons but also to establish emotional bonds. "The potential power of stories as communication forms will increasingly be rediscovered. Sagas, legends, proverbs, myths, folklore, and other types of the story form have

influenced values and behavior regarding government and administration. The influence of stories and folklore can be positive, as with attempts to help families understand policy changes affecting them in rural areas (Thompson 1982), or invidious, as with Nazi uses of legend to stir nationalism and feelings of racial superiority (Lixfeld 1994)" (Garnett 1997c, 756).

Part of the impact of the excellence movement (Peters and Waterman 1982) and reinvention movement (Osborne and Gaebler 1992) is that their lessons of best practice are conveyed by stories about actual companies, government organizations, and people—and that they are told in a more compelling way than dry case accounts. Reports of the National Performance Review are full of stories of reinvention successes, often told by actual managers or stakeholders themselves, and increasingly by means of the more visual media of video or CD-ROM. In the rush toward high-tech, stories, drama, poetry, humor, and other creative forms can provide the "high-touch" that is equally necessary (Holzer 1997; Lundberg 1997).

The power of thinking and communicating spatially is also becoming better understood. Every Thursday morning Philadelphia Police Chief John Timony hosts a meeting of top brass and district commanders. The first part of the meeting consists of using Geographic Information Systems crime-mapping to view the types of crime that have occurred by location. Patterns of crime can then be detected that would go unnoticed with a less visual analysis. District commanders are then grilled about how their forces will respond to these crime patterns. The power of crime mapping has been given substantial credit for reducing crime in Philadelphia and in New York City, where Chief Timony learned the technique. Creative use of the many technologies for communicating, including simulations and electronic networks described earlier, deserves greater attention among public administrators.

The Concept of Communication Ethics Is Not an Oxymoron

An earlier discussion (Garnett 1992a) maintained that ethical communication requires the qualities of *accuracy, usefulness, openness,* and *fairness.* Violations of communication ethics tend to damage individual or collective credibility and produce other destructive consequences. Disinformation (deliberate distortion) in relations between Iraq and the United States contributed to misunderstanding and ultimately to war. If information is deliberately or inadvertently inaccurate, negotiations or other relations become problematic, because the parties cannot depend on that information for basing their actions. *Usefulness* in communicating means avoiding bombarding stakeholders with messages they cannot use because of faulty content or inappropriate media. It also means supplying stakeholders with information they need for acting responsibly, whether as citizens or as public servants. Case Study 2 in this text, "How Kristin Died," for example, involved too many instances of her friends or public servants failing, because of inertia or not wanting to become involved, to relate information that might have made a difference. Too often, actors in this tragedy lament, "If only I had known." A decided challenge in today's public service (with an increasing number and complexity of issues and more numerous and more diverse sets of stakeholders) is to provide sufficient useful information while avoiding overload. In a classic research study on administrative feedback between federal agency headquarters and field offices, Kaufman and Couzens (1973) discovered that employees rarely think they have too much information to do their jobs properly. Even with the prodigious information technologies available today, we tend to err on the side of disseminating too little information. If public administrators fail to supply others with adequate information for acting competently, then ethically they share responsibility for performance failures.

Another quality of ethical communicating is *responsiveness*. Stakeholders have a right to know that their messages will be acted on responsibly and responsively. This means, among other things, making sure that those public servants who are complained about are not the primary or only ones to respond to complaints. In Case Study 1 in this book, "The Blast in Centralia No. 5," Local 52 was unable to effectively bypass the formal chain of command within the governor's office to get Governor Green's attention. Staff member Chapman short-circuited the miners' Save Our Lives letter by routing it to the Department of Mines and

Minerals for reply even though that department's inaction was the chief object of the miners' complaints. This pattern of bureaucratic pigeon-holing is still common. Where feasible, more independent, neutral parties should also be involved in investigating complaints and responding to them. The widespread use of centrally staffed complaint hotlines; ombudsmen, public advocates, or system navigators; inspectors general and other mechanisms, often with response tracking and deadlines for responding, has helped to improve responsiveness in many jurisdictions.

• • •

A related ethical issue that deserves far more attention than could be devoted here is groupthink, "a mode of thinking that people engage in when they are deeply involved in a cohesive in-group, when the members' strivings for unanimity override their motivation to realistically appraise alternative courses of action" (Janis 1972, as cited in 't Hart and Kroon 1997, 104). The irony with groupthink is that the characteristics of good groups or teams—loyalty, camaraderie, homogeneity of purpose and training, strong unimpartial leadership, and group cohesion—can discourage independent thinking and promote groupthink to avoid conflict. External pressure to decide, whether real or perceived, also increases the tendency for groupthink. The strong sense within NASA and Morton Thiokol that in 1986 the Challenger had to be launched "this time" to avoid further economic and political costs of delay muted isolated cautions about weather hazards. Some experts might even suggest that because the Challenger episode involved multiple organizations and multiple teams, it is a less obvious example of "groupthink," perhaps more of *"systemthink."* According to Nagel (in chapter 8 of this volume) failure to seek and factor in opposing views and insufficient objections to illconceived operational "plans" in the MOVE confrontation contributed to those situations getting out of control. To avoid groupthink and its dangers, public executives and administrators need to learn to recognize its symptoms and correct them, or better yet, build mechanisms for accountability, impartial leadership, links to sound information, vigilance over process, heterogeneity of membership, and other factors that minimize groupthink. Groupthink does not always result in policy fiascoes, and policy fiascoes can occur for other reasons ('t Hart and Kroon 1997), but certainly groupthink should be discouraged in most cases. To knowingly foster conditions that tend to produce faulty decision making would be irresponsible and unethical.

Raising the Salience of Communication in Public Administration

For reasons discussed here and elsewhere (Garnett 1997a, b), public administration practitioners and scholars alike have generally failed to recognize the centrality of communication in their profession and to give communication attention. Administrative communication that was mostly "tell and sell" was often manipulative and rarely linked to organizational performance and, thus, did not deserve much attention or respect. In the realm of public administration scholarship, administrative communication, after being more valued in the heyday of the field (Garnett 1997b), has too often been perceived as "soft" or "too applied." Ironically, these are labels the field of public administration itself has fought to overcome. For communication to reclaim its rightful place at the core of public administration, its rigor, complexity, salience, diversity, richness, and, above all, centrality, will need to be rediscovered.

References

Ahrens, F. 1999. The Radio Waves of the Future: Internet Stations Give Listeners a New Way to Tune In. *Washington Post* online edition, 21 January.

Applegate, J. S., and D. J. Sarno. 1996. "Coping with Complex Facts and Multiple Parties in Public Disputes." *Consensus: Helping Public Officials Resolve Stubborn Policy Disputes* 21 (July): MIT-Harvard Public Disputes Program.

———. 1997. "FUTURESITE: An Environmental Remediation Game-Simulation." *Simulation & Gaming* 28, (1): 13–27.

Barnard, C. I. 1938. *The Functions of the Executive.* Cambridge, Mass: Harvard University Press.

Broom, G. M., and D. M. Dozier. 1983. "An Overview: Evaluation Research in Public Relations." *Public Relations Quarterly* 28 (3): 5–8.

Carnevale, D. G. 1995. *Trustworthy Government: Leadership and Management Strategies for Building Trust and High Performance.* San Francisco: Jossey-Bass.

Childers, L. 1989. "Credibility of Public Relations at the NRC." In Public Relations Research *Annual,* ed. J. E. Grunig, and L. A. Grunig. Vol. 1, pp. 97–114.

Downs, A. 1967. *Inside Bureaucracy.* Boston: Little, Brown.

Foltz, R. G. 1973. *Management by Communication.* Philadelphia: Thomas Nelson and Sons.

Garnett, J. L. 1989. "Effective Communication." In *Handbook of Public Administration,* ed. J. L. Perry. pp. 554–558 San Francisco: Jossey-Bass.

———. 1992a. *Communicating for Results in Government: A Strategic Approach for Public Managers.* San Francisco: Jossey-Bass.

———. 1992b. "Coping with Rumors and Grapevines: Practical Lessons for Public Personnel Administration." *Review of Public Personnel Administration* 12 (3): 42–49.

———. 1996. "Communicating Effectively." In *Handbook of Public Administration,* 2nd ed., ed. J. L. Perry. 665–681 San Francisco: Jossey-Bass.

———. 1997a. "Administrative Communication: Domain, Threats, and Legitimacy." In *Handbook of Administrative Communication,* ed. J. L. Garnett and A. Kouzmin, pp. 1–20. New York: Marcel Dekker.

———. 1997b. "Trends and Gaps in the Treatment of Communication in Organization and Management Theory." In *Handbook of Administrative Communication,* ed. J. L. Garnett, and A. Kouzmin, pp. 21–60. New York: Marcel Dekker.

———. 1997c. "Epilog: Directions and Agendas for Administrative Communication." In *Handbook of Administrative Communication,* ed. J. L. Garnett and A. Kouzmin, pp. 747–770. New York: Marcel Dekker.

Grunig, J. E. 1997. "Public Relations Management in Business and Government." In *Handbook of Administrative Communication,* ed. J. L. Garnett, and A. Kouzmin, pp. 241–283. New York: Marcel Dekker.

Grunig, J. E., and L. A. Grunig. 1992. "Models of Public Relations and Communication." In *Excellence in Public Relations and Communication Management,* ed. J. E. Grunig. Hillsdale, IL: Lawrence Erlbaum Associates.

Grunig, J. E., and T. Hunt. 1984. *Managing Public Relations.* New York: Holt, Rinehart & Winston.

Harris, Richard. 1997. "Boundary Spanners, Legitimacy, and Corporate Communications." In *Handbook of Administrative Communication,* ed. J. L. Garnett and A. Kouzmin, pp. 309–328 New York: Marcel Dekker.

't Hart, Paul, and Marceline Kroon. 1997. "Groupthink in Government: Pathologies of Small-Group Decision Making." *Handbook of Administrative Communication,* ed. J. L. Gannett and A. Kouzmin, pp. 101–139 New York: Marcel Dekker.

Heise, A. 1985. "Toward Closing the Confidence Gap: An Alternative Approach to Communication Between Public and Government." *Public Administration Quarterly* (Summer): 196–217.

Holzer, M. 1997. "Communicating Through Forms." In *Handbook of Administrative Communication,* ed. J. L. Garnett and A. Kouzmin, pp. 203–225. New York: Marcel Dekker.

Katz, D., and R. L. Kahn. 1966. *The Social Psychology of Organizations.* New York: John Wiley & Sons.

Kaufman, H., with M. Couzens. 1973. *Administrative Feedback: Monitoring Subordinates' Behavior.* Washington, D.C.: The Brookings Institution.

Kelly, K. S. 1989. Shifting the Public Relations Paradigm: A Theory of Donor Relations Developed Through a Critical Analysis of Fund Raising and its Effect on Organizational Autonomy. Ph.D. diss., University of Maryland, College Park.

Lorch, R. S. 1978. *Public Administration.* St. Paul: West.

Lundberg, E. 1997. "Communicating Through Humor in the Workplace: Looking for Laughs in All the Work Places." In *Handbook of Administrative Communication,* ed. J. L. Garnett and A. Kouzmin. pp. 227–240. New York: Marcel Dekker.

National Commission on Civic Renewal. 1998. *A Nation of Spectators: How Civic Disengagement Weakens America and What We Can Do About It.* College Park, Md.: The National Commission on Civic Renewal.

Osborne, D., and T. Gøebler. 1992. *Reinventing Government: How the Entrepreneurial Spirit is Transforming the Public Sector from Schoolhouse to Statehouse, City Hall to the Pentagon.* Reading, Mass.: Addison-Wesley.

O'Toole, L. 1997. "Interorganizational Communication: Opportunities and Challenges for Public Administration." In *Handbook of Administrative Communication,* ed. J. L. Garnett and A. Kouzmin. New York: Marcel Dekker.

Peters, T., and A. Waterman. 1982. *In Search of Excellence.* New York: Warner Books.

Polman, D. 1999. Echoes of Scandal May Go Past 2000. *The Philadelphia Inquirer,* 14 February.

Tullock, G. 1965. *The Politics of Bureaucracy.* Washington, D.C.: Public Affairs Press.

Walton, E. 1962. A Magnetic Theory of Organizational Communication. China Lake, Calif. U.S. Naval Ordnance Test Station.

Zimbardo, P. G., E. B. Ebbesen, and C. Maslach. 1977. *Influencing Attitudes and Changing Behavior.* Reading, Mass.: Addison-Wesley.

Acknowledgment

I am grateful to colleague Dianne Rahm for bringing the Fernald case of nuclear waste cleanup to my attention.

☐ CASE STUDY 9

Introduction

As Dr. Garnett's essay stresses, for public administrators today, internal and external communications are central to influencing their work, both in terms of helping to set the agenda for what they do and then decisively shaping public opinion about how well or poorly they perform their roles. External media such as radio, TV and newspaper coverage, its volume and content, as well as various "internal players," help to create the issues public agencies address, how they perform or fail to perform their tasks, and then largely determine public perceptions of what they accomplish. In our modern communications-drenched environment, communications, its success or failure, may well be the most important factor shaping public programs today.

Possibly the most glaring recent instance of communications breakdown at the local level occurred during the tragic shootings at Columbine High School, Littleton, Colorado, on April 20, 1999. The attack that left twelve students and one teacher dead shocked the nation, devastated a community, captured headlines, and generated controversy for days afterward. For many, the inconceivable happened: Two heavily armed teenagers, Eric Harris and Dylan Klebold, from quiet, upper–middle class suburbia, deliberately prepared and executed the mass killings. Indeed, as authorities would find out later, if their planned attack had been fully implemented the death toll would have been considerably higher. The shooters had scattered seventy-six bombs through the school, two in nearby fields, and thirteen in two cars inside the parking lot, for a total of ninety-nine bombs. If the two twenty-pound propane tank bombs they set to detonate at 11:17 a.m. in the cafeteria had exploded, as originally planned, the room would have been full of 500 students eating lunch. As one sheriff's deputy observed afterward, "Bad bomb makers made for a lot of live kids. . . ."

Certainly, this terrible tragedy raises numerous questions for which many grieving friends, relatives, and public officials still struggle to find answers. However, from an administrative perspective, at the heart of law enforcement's combined response to this new sort of homegrown terrorism lay a crucial problem of poor communication. From the first Jefferson County sheriff dispatcher's call "female down" at Columbine at 11:23 a.m., a series of administrative communications flaws unfold. The following story by Susan Rosegrant, written for the Kennedy School of Government Case Program, focuses upon many of the communication breakdowns that took place throughout all phases of the emergency response to the shootings.

As you read this thoughtful, retrospective study, try to look specifically at how ineffective communications influenced the decisions that the responders made.

What effect did the unavailability of up-to-date floor plans for Columbine High School have on police choices? Why were current maps not readily on hand?

Why did ultimately a thousand law enforcement officers arrive at Columbine from surrounding metro-Denver jurisdictions? What were the effects upon those already there attempting to cope with the emergency? What accounted for such ineffective coordination among various units?

How did the perceptions of each type of emergency responders—for example, SWAT teams, bomb experts, and medical crews—shape their communications, both what they saw and how they related what they saw to others at the scene? Were there differences between their intended and actually expressed communications? If so, can you cite examples?

What caused the delay in setting up a central command post, and how did that add to the confusion of operational communications and decision making among law enforcement personnel?

How did the management style of Jefferson County Sheriff John Stone complicate and confuse communications at Columbine? What assumptions did Stone make about the situation, and what would you recommend that he should have said or done differently during the crisis?

In what ways did the media add to the difficulties of the emergency responders? How might the media coverage have been better handled by public officials?

Overall, who were the major sources of miscommunications throughout this case? Can you generalize about the overall impacts of flawed information upon the effectiveness of law enforcement during the emergency? And what can be done in the future to prevent the repetition of such mistakes?

The Shootings at Columbine High School: The Law Enforcement Response

SUSAN ROSEGRANT

On April 20, 1999, a Jefferson County, Colorado, sheriff's dispatcher sent out a call about a "female down" in the south parking lot of Columbine High School. The radio message at 11:23 a.m. that Tuesday morning was the first official word alerting area law enforcement to the fact that something had gone very wrong at the large suburban school about eight miles southwest of Denver. By 11:32, a deputy on the scene had called for mutual aid, and within a half hour, hundreds of emergency responders were arriving to help stop a bloody siege at the school by an unknown number of gunmen—gunmen who were said to be armed with automatic weapons, bombs, and grenades.

The chaotic scene that law enforcement and emergency medical personnel faced, however, seemed designed to frustrate their best efforts. Witnesses were providing conflicting reports about the number of armed attackers, their location in the building, and their ages. The commanders who had rushed to the scene didn't have and couldn't find an up-to-date map of the school's sprawling maze of rooms and corridors. By the time the first Special Weapons and Tactics (SWAT) team entered the school shortly after noon, the gunmen had grown quiet—removing the clear objective of an active target. As SWAT members moved cautiously through the school, the piercing sirens of fire alarms triggered by bombs made it almost impossible to communicate. Not only that, coordinating the growing crowd of responders outside had become increasingly difficult, particularly since the radios used by different agencies often weren't compatible.

Over the next few hours, the Jefferson County Sheriff's Office and other law enforcement agencies first secured the perimeter of the building so that the shooters could not escape, then struggled to evacuate students, teachers, and staff—particularly those who had been wounded—and to apprehend the killers. Not until almost 4:00 p.m. would SWAT members discover that two student gunmen,

Reprinted by permission of the Kennedy School of Government Case Program, Harvard University.

Eric Harris and Dylan Klebold, were already dead, having committed suicide in the library just minutes after the first SWAT team entered the building. Horrified SWAT members also discovered the ten students that Harris and Klebold had executed in the library about a half hour before killing themselves. In all, the two had killed or fatally wounded 12 students and one teacher and injured 24 others in the span of 16 terrifying minutes.[1]

Before the week was out, the deadliest school shooting in US history would spark impassioned debates across the nation about such issues as school safety, gun control, the impact of violent video games, and the pressures of suburban life. Within the emergency response community, the attack also spurred a crucial question: Could law enforcement and emergency medical personnel in the Columbine area have done anything better in responding to the terrorist act or in reducing its grave toll?

The Jefferson County Sheriff's Office

Jefferson County—locally known as JeffCo—was Colorado's most populous county in 1999, with 512,000 residents. Twelve police departments operated within the county's towns and cities, but the JeffCo Sheriff's Office provided law enforcement for the 173,000 residents in unincorporated areas of the county, including Columbine High School, where a JeffCo deputy was on duty every day as the school community resource officer.[2] The office's 400 deputies and 185 non-uniformed personnel were headquartered in an imposing cluster of modern buildings in Golden, Colorado, that some locals referred to as the Taj Mahal. JeffCo had its own bomb squad and a part-time SWAT team, whose 12 members worked as regular members of the force unless called in for a tactical emergency.[3]

In April 1999, the JeffCo Sheriff's Office was in a period of transition. John P. Stone, who had served as a county commissioner for 12 years, had been elected to

Exhibit A: Cast of Characters

Jefferson County Sheriff's Office
John P. Stone—Sheriff
John Dunaway—Undersheriff
Dave Walcher—Lieutenant
Terry Manwaring—Lieutenant and SWAT
    commander
John Kiekbusch—Lieutenant
Steve Davis—Public information officer
Phil Hy—Sergeant
Barry Williams—Sergeant and SWAT team leader
Allen Simmons—Deputy and SWAT team leader
Neil Gardner—Deputy and school community
    resource officer
Paul Magor—Deputy
Scott Taborsky—Deputy
Paul Smoker—Deputy

Littleton Fire Department
William Pessemier—Chief
Ray Rahne—Battalion Chief
Chuck Burdick—Division Chief
James Olsen—Paramedic Captain
Wayne Zygowicz—Division Chief for emergency
    medical services

Arapahoe County Sheriff's Office
Patrick Sullivan—Sheriff
Robert Armstrong—Captain
Mark Campbell—Captain
Bruce Williamson—Lieutenant and SWAT
    commander
Louis Perea—SWAT team leader
Joe Dempsey—Deputy Inspector and bomb
    squad team leader
Dan Davis—Deputy and bomb squad member

Littleton Police Department
Bob Brandt—Commander
Bill Black—Sergeant

Arvada Police Department
Ron Sloan—Chief
Daryl Hoffman—Sergeant and member of the
    Jefferson County Regional SWAT Team
A.J. DeAndrea—Officer and member of the
    Jefferson County Regional SWAT Team

Denver Police Department
Gerry Whitman—Division Chief
Vincent DiManna—Captain and SWAT commander

Golden Police Department
Russell Cook—Chief

Columbine High School
Frank DeAngelis—Principal
Chris Mikesell—Dean of students
Peter Horvath—Dean of students

a four-year term as sheriff the previous November, and had assumed office in January, at the same time bringing on board a new undersheriff, John Dunaway (see Exhibit A for a partial list of individuals involved in the response to or aftermath of the Columbine High School shootings). Although Stone had been out of law enforcement for more than a decade, earlier in their careers both men had been patrolmen for the Lakewood Police Department—the county's largest police department—and Dunaway, who had risen to police captain at Lake-

wood, had most recently served as director of the JeffCo Public School District's Risk Management Department, responsible, in part, for physical security in the schools.

While Stone was new to the Sheriff's Office, though, he was well acquainted with the county's overall emergency response capabilities. Outside of routine SWAT team training, the Sheriff's Office hadn't invested significant time or resources over the years in pre-incident planning—for example, for hostage situations in major public buildings. But both the Sheriff's Office and the county had extensive experience in coordinating disaster and emergency responses because of the regular incidence in the region of major brush and forest fires, often in difficult and mountainous terrain. In addition, in 1997, while still a commissioner, Stone had helped organize a trip to Emmitsburg, Maryland, for county representatives and local organization leaders to attend a Federal Emergency Management Agency (FEMA) disaster training course.

The four-day session, which FEMA designed specially to address the needs of Jefferson County, Stone says, included training and "tabletop" exercises that had improved the county's implementation of "incident command"—a clearly defined incident management structure designating, among other things, command roles, tasks to be accomplished, and a system to assign responsibility for each task. According to some law enforcement officials, the county's focus had paid off. "JeffCo is one of the most interactive places I've ever worked, in terms of people working together," says Ron Sloan, chief of the Arvada Police Department, "and that's not only the law enforcement agencies, but all the human services agencies."

Nevertheless, like most other law enforcement agencies in the area, the JeffCo Sheriff's Office rarely held inter-jurisdictional exercises with the police or fire departments in the county, other than an occasional natural disaster response exercise. Joint exercises were even rarer with agencies outside of the county. In addition, while the Sheriff's Office often helped out police departments within JeffCo, it had not often had to call on other agencies for mutual aid. Criminal responses and investigations, in particular, Stone says, were almost always handled with the county's own internal resources.

The Initial Attack: The JeffCo Sheriff's Office Responds

On Tuesday morning, April 20, 1999, JeffCo Sheriff's Deputy Neil Gardner, the school community resource officer assigned to Columbine High School, was eating lunch in his car near an area northwest of the school known as the Smokers' Pit. Just minutes earlier, a sheriff's dispatcher had reported a brushfire and explosion in a field about three miles south of Columbine, but that wasn't Gardner's concern. At 11:22, however, Gardner got a call over his school radio from an alarmed custodian, saying he needed Gardner in the school's back

parking lot. One minute later, a sheriff's dispatcher, responding to a 911 report of a "paralyzed" girl in the south lower parking lot of the school, radioed Deputy Paul Magor, who had been heading towards the brushfire, and directed him instead toward Columbine, saying, "Female down in the south lot of Columbine High School." Gardner, who was already driving toward the school, heard the message and turned on his lights and siren (for a chronology of events, see Exhibit B).[4]

Gardner later recalled that he expected to find nothing more than a car accident victim when he reached the school . . . . But the reality was far grimmer. Two Columbine seniors, Eric Harris and Dylan Klebold, had just launched a brutal armed attack on their fellow students. When students and staff first heard shots at 11:19 that morning, many assumed it was part of Senior Prank Day, or that the two, who were toting guns and wearing long black dusters, were filming a video. By the time Gardner arrived five minutes after the shooting began, however, Harris and Klebold had already shot at 11 students on the west and southwest side of the building, killing two and injuring six.[5]

As Garder pulled to a stop at 11:24, he saw students running from the school and smoke rising from the south parking lot's west end, and heard explosions and gunfire. The next several minutes would seem horribly unreal. As the deputy stepped from his car, he heard over the school radio, "Neil, there's a shooter in the school." Almost at the same moment, a gunman, who had been firing into the west entrance of the school along with a second shooter, turned and shot at Gardner from about 60 yards away with a semi-automatic rifle. Gardner, armed only with a 45 semi-automatic handgun, returned fire. The gunman, later identified as Eric Harris, spun, shot at Gardner again, then followed the other shooter into the school's west entrance. The two would never emerge from the school again alive.

Inside Columbine, the chaos worsened. At 11:25, Patti Nielson, a teacher hiding in the library who had been sprayed with glass and metal fragments when Klebold and Harris shot at the west doors, called 911 on a cell phone to report shooting outside the library. More than 50 students also hiding in the room crouched under tables as Nielson cried out for them to stay down. A minute later, William "Dave" Sanders, a teacher who had run upstairs after heroically warning students in the cafeteria to escape, was shot in the hallway outside the library and critically wounded. A second teacher helped Sanders into a science classroom on the south side of the

Exhibit B: Chronology of Events

April 20, 1999

11:19 a.m.   Eric Harris and Dylan Klebold begin shooting at fellow Columbine High School students after bombs planted inside the school fail to explode.

11:21   A Jefferson County Sheriff's deputy heads towards a reported explosion in a field about three miles from Columbine High School.

11:22   A Columbine custodian radios Deputy Neil Gardner, the school community resource officer, for help.

11:23   A JeffCo dispatcher sends an alert about a "female down" at Columbine High School.

11:24   Deputy Gardner exchanges gunfire with Eric Harris outside the school.

11:26   Deputy Gardner calls for reinforcements.

Deputies exchange shots with Eric Harris, who is just inside the school.

Teacher Dave Sanders is shot and critically wounded.

11:29   Eric Harris and Dylan Klebold enter the library and during the next seven minutes kill ten students, wound 12 more, and shoot out the windows at students and deputies. Deputy Gardner calls for emergency medical help.

11:32   A JeffCo Sheriff's Office deputy broadcasts a call for mutual aid.

11:52   JeffCo Undersheriff John Dunaway appoints JeffCo Lieutenant Dave Walcher as incident commander.

12:00 p.m.   Local television stations begin full-time live coverage of shootings at Columbine.

12:02   Littleton Fire Department paramedics rescue three student shooting victims from behind the school.

12:06   A first SWAT team led by JeffCo Deputy Allen Simmons enters the east side of Columbine as JeffCo Lieutenant Terry Manwaring leads a second group around the school.

12:08   Eric Harris and Dylan Klebold commit suicide in the library.

12:10   Littleton Fire sets up the first of four medical triage sites.

12:25   Leawood Elementary is established as the primary debriefing site.

12:34   Lieutenant Manwaring's SWAT team rescues one shooting victim outside west end of school.

12:40   Incident command post begins operating out of JeffCo's mobile command bus.

1:09   JeffCo Sergeant Barry Williams leads SWAT team into west side of school.

1:26   SWAT team led by Williams evacuates large group of students from kitchen area.

1:30   JeffCo Public Information Officer Steve Davis holds his first hourly news conference in Clement Park.

1:57   SWAT leader Sergeant Williams hears first accounts alluding to critically injured teacher Dave Sanders.

Exhibit B: (continued)

2:15	Rooftop sniper radios SWAT leader Williams about "1 bleeding to death" sign in window.
2:17	SWAT leader Williams splits his team, putting one half under Deputy A.J. DeAndrea.
2:24	Deputy DeAndrea and his team locate and evacuate some 60 students. Soon after, they evacuate an additional 60 students.
2:42	SWAT leader Williams and his team reach Dave Sanders and 60 students and call for medical help.
3:07–3:17	A Denver paramedic declares Dave Sanders dead.
3:22	Williams's SWAT team enters the library and finds twelve students dead, including Eric Harris and Dylan Klebold. SWAT members call paramedics to rescue one injured student.
4:45	SWAT teams complete a second search of the school and bomb technicians begin their search.
10:30	New SWAT teams launch a third sweep of the high school as bomb technicians continue their search.
11:30	Parents of missing children are told to go home for the night after bomb experts suspend search until morning.
April 21	
7:30 a.m.	Investigators return to Columbine and identify the victims.

building overlooking the parking lot, and two students who were Eagle Scouts began giving him first aid.

The JeffCo Sheriff's dispatch had already sent out a message declaring, "Attention south units. Possible shots fired at Columbine High School." At 11:26, Gardner called for reinforcements. Panic-stricken students were running from different sides of the building, and two JeffCo deputies, Scott Taborsky and Paul Smoker, arriving from the northwest discovered a student who had been shot in the first phase of the attack lying behind an athletic shed on the west side of the school. Another badly wounded student lay nearby. As the two deputies went to help the second student, Gardner, who was just down the hill from them, spotted a gunman inside the west doors and shouted, "There he is!" The gunman, Harris again, shot through the opening of a broken window at Gardner as first Gardner, and then Deputy Smoker, returned fire. As the gunman retreated, and Gardner radioed in a "Code 33" for emergency assistance, the deputies heard more gunfire from within the school.

Over the next few minutes, the already desperate scene degenerated. Teacher Patti Nielson, who was under a counter just inside the library, reported over her cell phone that there was smoke drifting in and shots right outside the door. Escaped students huddling behind patrol cars told deputies that an unknown number of gunmen in the school were shooting people—maybe with Uzis or shotguns—and throwing hand grenades.[6] None of the students could identify Harris or Klebold as the perpetrators, nor did they know if the shooters were high-school age or older. Gardner, who could see four victims lying injured, including the girl originally reported as "down" in the parking lot, radioed for emergency medical assistance. Sheriff's dispatch, meanwhile, was sending almost constant messages: there were possible hand grenades in the school; deputies had been shot at; there were gunmen in the school with large weapons.

At about 11:30, the gunmen shot out some of the west windows of the library, aiming at escaping students and the handful of deputies who had arrived. Although teacher Patti Nielson had stopped talking on her cell phone when the gunmen entered the library, over the next several minutes, the dispatcher could hear numerous gunshots, and a person shouting,

"Yahoo!" Investigators would later discover that Harris and Klebold had killed ten people and wounded 12 in the seven-and-a-half minutes they spent in the library.[7]

Outside, meanwhile, a deputy began loading students hiding behind a patrol car into a separate sheriff's car and driving them to safety, three or four at a time. The dispatch center called in off-duty dispatchers, and switched to 12-hour shifts to increase available personnel. At the same time, the media, which had heard of a shooting incident at Columbine, began calling the JeffCo Sheriff's Office for information. Less than ten minutes had passed since the first dispatch alert about an injured student in the parking lot of Columbine High School. At 11:32, Deputy Paul Magor, who was guarding the entrance to the south parking lot, radioed for mutual aid.

The Growing Response: Reinforcements Arrive

Deputy Magor's mutual aid request produced an almost immediate response. In fact, since agencies in the area had been monitoring the JeffCo dispatches, dozens of responders were already on the way, and would soon transform Columbine into a major multi-jurisdictional response. This kind of "self-dispatching" to a large incident was not uncommon. Moreover, because Columbine lay near several law enforcement jurisdictions, a number of responders had personal reasons for wanting to arrive quickly. . . . A student hiding in the school kitchen with 17 others had already called the Denver Police Department, hoping to speak with his police officer father, and several of the first Denver and Littleton police officers to arrive had children in the school.

When Lieutenant Terry Manwaring, JeffCo's SWAT commander, arrived at 11:36, law enforcement representatives had already begun to congregate a couple of blocks north of the school on Pierce Street, the north-south access road that ran along Columbine's east side . . . . Manwaring had already paged JeffCo's SWAT team and its command staff on the way over. Now, as JeffCo's first command level representative present, Manwaring told dispatch that the command post and SWAT staging area would be placed at the point where officers were already gathering, the intersection of Pierce and Leawood.

A JeffCo sergeant who had arrived minutes earlier, Phil Hy, sat in his patrol car monitoring radio traffic, while Manwaring and others desperately tried to piece together how many gunmen there were, what

they looked like, and where they all were located. The information coming over the radio was sketchy and often inconsistent. Dispatch had reported a possible suspect on the football field, as many as six to eight gunmen in the school, shooters in paramilitary garb, and the possibility of hostages being held inside. Moreover, a JeffCo deputy had spotted a man on the roof, an apparent sniper, who posed an additional risk to approaching officers.[8]

Most of this information, though, was dead wrong. As Manwaring arrived, Harris and Klebold—still in the library—had just shot the last person they would kill other than themselves. The two gunmen would spend the next half hour, investigators later concluded, wandering through the school, firing at random targets, and throwing bombs. The two returned to the cafeteria, at one point, and shot at two large bombs in duffel bags they had placed there earlier that had failed to explode, hoping—but failing—to trigger an explosion. They wandered back upstairs to the main office area and fired shots into ceilings and walls. Although the gunmen looked into locked rooms and made eye contact with trapped students, they made no further attempts to kill anyone.

Outside, though, none of this was clear. At 11:38, a pipe bomb thrown by the shooters blew out windows near the cafeteria, and students hidden inside ran to a nearby deputy in the parking lot, and ducked behind cars. The student holed up in the kitchen with a cell phone told the Denver police officer on the line that he could hear a gunman nearby with school keys and a walkie talkie.[9] At 11:40, four minutes after Harris and Klebold left the library, some 30 students ran out from the school's west side, including many who had survived the shooting spree in the library. Based on student accounts, a deputy reported that one of the gunmen might be a student named "Ned Harris," and that he might be wearing bulletproof armor.[10]

Meanwhile, law enforcement personnel continued to arrive. According to Captain Mark Campbell, commander of the patrol division of the Arapahoe Sheriff's Office, the corner of Pierce and Leawood was already congested with patrol cars and emergency response vehicles by the time he got to Columbine at 11:45. "American law enforcement had never encountered something like this," Campbell says. "I'd seen a lot of stuff, and when I turned the corner, I was flabbergasted. This was only 15 minutes into it, and I'd never seen so many police cars in my life."

Amidst growing fears that the gunmen might take advantage of the confusion to sneak out of the school, at least eight JeffCo deputies—who already had been assisting escaping students, driving injured students to medical attention, and blocking access roads—stationed themselves around Columbine, forming an inner perimeter to watch the building's 25 exterior doors. Captain Robert Armstrong, the on-call commander for the Arapahoe County Sheriff's Office, and perhaps the most experienced commander on scene, stepped in and directed Denver police and the Colorado State Patrol to form a second perimeter away from the school to further secure the area, limit traffic access, and keep press and parents from approaching.[11] Anxiety that the shooters might have associates outside the school, or plans to launch attacks elsewhere, increased when firefighters reported that the brushfire a few miles south of the school that morning had been triggered by bombs, and could be related to the attack on Columbine. Bomb squads from the JeffCo and Arapahoe County Sheriff's Offices already had been told to report to the school.

At 11:45, JeffCo Lieutenant Dave Walcher drove up, followed soon after by five members of Denver's Metro SWAT team, including SWAT Commander Captain Vincent DiManna, who had a son and niece at Columbine.[12] Walcher, the top-ranked JeffCo representative on scene, assumed command upon arrival and told Terry Manwaring to get SWAT members into the school as soon as possible. A few minutes later, JeffCo Undersheriff John Dunaway arrived. Dunaway officially appointed Lieutenant Walcher as incident commander, and authorized an ad hoc SWAT team comprised of Denver, JeffCo, and Littleton Police members to enter the building as soon as it could.

Inside the school's science wing, meanwhile, the teacher who had helped Dave Sanders into a room had placed a hurriedly written sign in the window reading, "1 bleeding to death." A second teacher in the classroom contacted a dispatcher by cell phone, and tried to describe how to reach the room where Sanders lay, an area which was in the most isolated part of the building with no exterior door nearby. When a dispatcher contacted Sergeant Phil Hy just before noon to ask whether someone could get to the injured teacher, however, Hy replied that there was not yet a secure entry point for attempting such a rescue. Soon after, the dispatcher warned those in the room with Sanders not to break out a window because it might alert the shooters to their location.

The number of gunmen in the school was still unknown. Minutes before noon, though, dispatch radioed the command post with its first suspect description: "Eric Harris, 5'10", thin build, shaved blond hair, black pants and white T-shirt, light blue gym backpack."[13]

The Emergency Medical Response

As law enforcement struggled to make sense of what was happening at Columbine, fire and emergency medical resources had also arrived, and faced a similarly disorienting scene.

Littleton Fire Department Battalion Chief Ray Rahne, the shift commander, had driven over to Columbine on a whim after hearing the first report of a female down, thinking that—unlikely as it seemed in that area—there might have been a drive-by shooting. Littleton Fire's eight stations in the Littleton area handled fire fighting and emergency medical services for about 190,000 people, and although the high school wasn't in Littleton, the fire department's service area included Columbine. When Rahne pulled up at the school's main entrance on Pierce Street at 11:34, though, he had heard nothing beyond the initial report. Although Littleton Fire and the JeffCo Sheriff's Office both had VHF radio systems, JeffCo was just one of 16 different law enforcement agencies in Littleton Fire's service area, and the two agencies rarely worked together and weren't using the same channels. As a result, Rahne was completely unaware that deputies had had firefights with gunmen on the other side of the school, and he had not heard about Neil Gardner's 11:29 call for medical help.

In addition, Rahne was oblivious to the growing law enforcement response just north of where he had parked. Although students were streaming from the building, most had not witnessed the attack, and Rahne still thought he was dealing with a single shooting. "We did not realize for about the first 20 minutes that an exchange of gunfire had taken place between the school resource officer and Harris and Klebold at the back of the school," says Littleton Fire Chief William Pessemier, who arrived about 20 minutes after Rahne. "We didn't have JeffCo's channels on our radios, and they didn't have ours."

According to Rahne, he soon spotted a girl sitting on the corner across the street from the school who had been shot in the ankle, and took her to a private ambulance.[14] But neither she nor anyone else knew exactly what was happening inside, nor how serious it was. "I stayed in front of the school, set up command, and said, 'I need police officers for command in front of the school,'" Rahne recalls, "and nobody came."

Shortly before noon, Rahne finally heard that there were victims down behind the southwest side of the school, and sent two Littleton rescue units that had been waiting nearby to respond. As paramedics approached the back of the school, however, they hit an impasse. While some police officers and deputies who were crouched behind cars were waving them on, others motioned for them to stop. Despite the mixed signals, the paramedics parked as close as they could to four students lying on the ground outside the cafeteria, and rushed out to examine them. The first student they checked was already dead.[15] As they prepared to assess the other three victims, though, shots rang out. Gunmen in the school were firing down from the second floor—from what officers would later learn was the library—and police officers and deputies on the ground, including Neil Gardner, returned fire. "They just literally took two bodies and threw them in one rescue, basically right on top of each other, and then took another one and put it in another rescue and just got out of there," reports Rahne. The student who was already dead was left behind.

Rahne, meanwhile, had been summoned to the JeffCo command post about two blocks north on Pierce from where he had been waiting. Arriving at about the same time as Fire Chief Pessemier, the two men discovered a scene of turmoil as fire engines, ambulances, and police cars converged at the intersection.[16] "I remember when I got there, Ray looked at me and said, 'I don't know where all these people are coming from,'" recalls Pessemier. "'I didn't call them.'" Adds Rahne: "I finally just started screaming, 'Who's in charge? Who's in charge?' But nobody would say. We had no staging, we had no base, because I hadn't called for anything, and we were getting all these self-dispatched people coming to the scene."[17]

As Rahne began to transfer command of the incident to Pessemier, the ambulances that had sped out from behind the school pulled up, and the paramedics jumped out screaming for help. "They opened up the back of the ambulance and the blood was just running out of it," Rahne says. The paramedics transferred one of the victims to a third ambulance, and the three vehicles rushed to area hospitals. Anne Marie Hochhalter, one of the first people shot, was estimated to have been just minutes away from death when she reached the emergency department. "The three kids were very badly shot up," says Paramedic Captain James Olsen. "One was barely alive, and another had half of his face shot off." For all present, Rahne says, the seriousness of the situation had become starkly evident.

Once Fire Chief Pessemier had assumed incident command for the agency, he appointed Rahne operations chief for fire and emergency medical operations. At 12:10, Pessemier and Rahne set up two medical triage sites; one on the east side near the school's main entrance, and a second a few blocks west of the school at the intersection of two small residential streets, Yukon and Caley. Yukon/Caley had already become a de facto triage site, since deputies who had evacuated students from the grounds west of Columbine early on had brought injured students to the intersection and laid them down for treatment in one homeowner's front yard. When Rahne sent a lieutenant to Yukon/Caley to investigate, the lieutenant promptly called for ten more ambulances and a helicopter to transport eleven shooting victims, four of them critical.

The fire command staff also established two medical staging areas near the command post, and a fire staging area a few blocks south of Columbine on Pierce. . . . With staging and triage in place, the fire and emergency medical operation began to flow more smoothly. Littleton Fire still couldn't communicate directly with the JeffCo Sheriff's Office, however, nor could it communicate with most of the engines and ambulances reporting from other jurisdictions because of radio system incompatibilities. In order to ensure the ability to talk, Rahne says, he sent at least one Littleton Fire representative with a radio on all emergency medical or fire teams that he dispatched.

Chief Pessemier and JeffCo Lieutenant Dave Walcher, meanwhile, set up a unified command—incorporating both the medical and the law enforcement response. "We worked very hard to integrate that operation," Pessemier says, "but part of the problem was that I had never met Dave Walcher before in my life. We didn't have a real strong relationship with many of the law enforcement agencies in the local area." Despite limited experience in coordinating or participating in such a complex multi-agency response, however, personnel from all agencies strove to cooperate, according to those at the scene. "Maybe it was Lance [Kirklin]," one of the critically wounded students whose ambulance had briefly stopped at the command post on the way to the hospital, explains Littleton Fire Department Division Chief Chuck Burdick, who served as the department's law enforcement liaison. "A lot of people saw Lance come through, and the magnitude of it was such that people realized this is too big to have petty issues between us. We've got to get through this, and the only way we're going to get through this is with the support of each other. I think we all knew that."

SWAT's First Entrance

While Rahne and others were organizing the early emergency medical response, JeffCo SWAT Commander Manwaring was rounding up SWAT team members who had already reported from different jurisdictions in order to cobble together a team. Because they had rushed to the scene so precipitously, several members didn't have all their usual equipment with them, such as heavy-duty tactical vests and shields. Just after noon, as the rescue units raced from the back of the school with the three student shooting victims, Manwaring asked to borrow a Littleton fire engine to use as a shield, and 12 SWAT members from the JeffCo Sheriff's Office and the Denver and Littleton police departments approached the east side of Columbine, sheltered by the slow-moving truck with a SWAT member at the wheel.

When they reached the school, Manwaring broke the group in two. One half, led by Manwaring and Denver Commander Vincent DiManna, continued around the north of the building—still crouching behind the fire truck—towards the west side, where the shootouts had occurred. The other half, led by JeffCo SWAT Deputy Allen Simmons, prepared to enter the east side just south of the main doors.

What the SWAT teams would confront was a sprawling 250,000-square-foot building on two levels, containing 75 classrooms, many smaller rooms and closets, and such large gathering areas as the gymnasium, cafeteria, and auditorium. The school had been significantly updated and expanded in 1995, including the addition of a new cafeteria and library. Unfortunately, the SWAT teams didn't have an updated map of the school among the emergency resources they kept on hand. Although Littleton Fire had begun running off copies of its Columbine "pre-plan," a simplified room plan that showed where to go for alarm and sprinkler shutoffs, for example, Manwaring hadn't received a copy. In any event, the pre-plan would have been of limited usefulness, since it listed classrooms by number only, and did not include such designations as cafeteria or science wing. Instead, Manwaring had only a sketch drawn hastily by a student. In fact, when he sent the first team in, the SWAT commander thought the school's cafeteria was still on the east side, its location before the remodeling four years earlier.

At 12:06, slightly more than a half hour after Manwaring first paged the JeffCo SWAT team, Simmons's group entered the east side of Columbine. According to many observers, forming an ad hoc, multi-jurisdictional SWAT team and sending it into a critical tactical situation that quickly was almost unprecedented. Normal operating procedure, by contrast, was for a team to wait until all its members had arrived, to deploy as a team, and to receive a detailed explanation of what was happening before entering. "It was very, very fast for everything up to that point," says Lieutenant Bruce Williamson, SWAT commander for the Arapahoe Sheriff's Office, who would arrive about 40 minutes later. "Columbine High School broke all the molds."

Inside the building, beneath wailing fire alarms, the six SWAT team members began to move slowly from room to room. The team, which split in two to cover more territory, soon found one teacher and two staff members as it advanced carefully through the warren of classrooms. Arvada Police Department Chief Ron Sloan, whose department had two officers on JeffCo's SWAT team, says members were undoubtedly trying to figure out what kind of situation they were facing: hostage-taking, barricaded suspects, a mental health situation, or some type of terrorist act. "I'm sure it was in the minds of people, 'Are they going to flee the scene now that the police are here, or are they going to secrete themselves somewhere and level some kind of demand?'" Sloan says. "For it to continue on after the initial police presence, and for homicides to be taking place indiscriminately after that, particularly by young people in a school, was almost unheard of."

SWAT members were also straining their senses to try to detect a sound or motion that would reveal the presence of one or more shooters. In fact, however, almost from the moment the first SWAT team entered, the actual targets were gone. Reports from inside the school and from escaping students of shooting and of bombs exploding dropped off sharply after noon—though such accounts did not stop entirely. Investigators later determined that Harris and Klebold had killed themselves in the library at 12:08, shortly after firing at the paramedics rescuing victims below. Responders, however, had no such information at the time to guide their actions. "You cannot assume anything, yet you have to assume something, so what you assume is the worst," explains Chief Sloan of Arvada. "And the worst case scenario is that the bad guys are secreting themselves, they're taking hostages, and they'll shoot you as soon as the door opens." He adds: "You can't assume that they've committed suicide. You can't assume that this room does not have suspects in it. You have to assume the worst."

With the first SWAT team inside, those in charge outside continued to try to organize the flood of incoming information into a coherent account. At 12:14, although in reality Harris and Klebold were already dead, students on a cell phone in the school reported to 911 that the shooters were nearby. A few minutes later, police detained a young man approaching the school carrying an unloaded rifle and a knife who was dressed in clothes similar to those reportedly worn by the gunmen.[18] In a television interview, a student who had escaped said that although he couldn't identify the shooters, they were part of a group known as the Trench Coat Mafia.[19]

Troubling news had also come in from the site of the earlier brushfire. Sixteen bomb experts who had assembled from Jefferson and Arapahoe counties, Denver, and the Federal Bureau of Investigation had spread out to advise SWAT teams before they entered the school; search the house of Eric Harris, who had been formally identified as a likely suspect; and evaluate the bombs that had sparked the fire earlier that morning. The two bomb technicians examining the refuse from the fire had quickly discovered the remains of an alarm clock— evidence not only that the gunmen had probably planted the bombs as diversionary devices to draw responders away from the school before the attack, but, even more disturbingly, that the shooters were capable of making timed devices.[20] The discovery not only heightened concerns about further attacks or explosions away from Columbine, but also forced law enforcement to conclude that it was likely there were time-activated bombs and booby-trapped rooms inside the school.

Establishing Incident Command

By 12:40, JeffCo's mobile command bus had arrived, and instead of grouping around Sgt. Phil Hy's patrol car, the command post operation moved inside the bus.[21] In addition to JeffCo's incident commander, Lieutenant Dave Walcher—who was often joined by Undersheriff Dunaway, and sometimes by Sheriff Stone—command level representatives included Captain Robert Armstrong from Arapahoe; Division Chief Gerry Whitman from the Denver Police; Major John Wise from the Colorado State Patrol; Commander Bob Brandt from the Littleton Police; and either Chief Pessemier or Division Chief Chuck Burdick representing Littleton Fire.

According to Sheriff Stone, JeffCo established incident command using the same basic management model that the JeffCo representatives had studied and trained on during the four-day FEMA workshop a year-and-a-half earlier. "My position in this thing was almost

like a symphony director," Stone says. "You're watching every one of these things going on, but you have to make sure every instrument's playing properly." With Walcher handling incident command, Stone says, Dunaway took charge of operations, while he, himself, was "trying to do all the support stuff, get the investigation going, get the county involved, the media, and all these other support things that you have to do."

But for some others on the scene, the division of responsibilities wasn't always obvious. Virtually all law enforcement officials involved with the Columbine response say it was the kind of emergency that would have been difficult for any single agency to coordinate. Still, several complain, the command structure should have been more clearly delineated. "Everybody asked questions like, 'Who's actually in charge?'" recalls one command level officer. "Well, quite frankly, I couldn't tell you. If I had to guess from being around the command post, I would say it was a combination of Gerry Whitman, Robert Armstrong, John Dunaway, and Walcher. Those would be the key four." Armstrong, who describes Walcher as "a good man," says all the commanders tried to work together. "What we did is we'd say, 'What about this? What about that?' So we could play off each other. So you had more than one mind making those decisions."

In addition, some responders say, Dunaway and Stone didn't give Walcher the support he needed. Walcher, who had previously spent seven years with the JeffCo SWAT team, had only recently been promoted to lieutenant, and had no experience managing a major incident. While it wasn't necessarily preferable for a sheriff or undersheriff to be the incident commander during such an event, the top law enforcement officials— presumably the agency's most experienced people at managing an emergency response—would generally remain available to serve as sounding boards, ask questions, and make suggestions. Dunaway, however, spent a lot of time outside of the command post talking with school administrators, law enforcement and county officials, and others who had come to the vehicle. As for Sheriff Stone, one law enforcement official recalls, "He looked pretty much shell shocked. If I was a brand new sheriff and was going through some administrative changes, trying to reorganize my department, and this thing hit me a few months into my term, I probably would have looked just like him."

Walcher, however, says he had all the support he needed, particularly given the collaborative effort that quickly coalesced among the experienced command staff at the post. "No one agency by itself could handle this," he contends. "With all those agencies there, we had the people that we could immediately task to do the things that had to be done. People that day stepped up to the plate and tried to make a difference." And although Dunaway confirms that he frequently went outside the command vehicle to talk, he says the conversations served the dual purpose of helping coordinate the broader operation and shielding those inside from unnecessary interference. "As people came to the command post, the last thing I was going to have any of them believing was that I was disinterested in their presence or in their offers of assistance," Dunaway explains.

Still, some claimed the response to the shootings was more disorganized than it needed to be. "Even with full incident command in place, it'll look chaotic," says Arapahoe Sheriff Patrick Sullivan. "But at least you're getting things done better, and people are communicating, and those who need to get information are getting information." At Columbine, though, incident command seemed to have slipped. There was no formal staging area for law enforcement, for example, which added to the confusion in the streets around the school and near the command post. And although Dunaway was in charge of operations for the incident, neither he nor anyone else appeared to have assumed full responsibility for assigning jobs such as traffic control, logistics, communications, and officer relief—all key pieces of incident command.

While Walcher and Dunaway both readily concede that the response did not meet a textbook case of incident command, however, they question whether a more formalized structure would have been appropriate. The fast-evolving demands of the situation, the number of responding officers, and the need to hand off tasks to individuals from many agencies and jurisdictions argued against imposing a rigid structure under one lead agency, they say. "I don't think incident command was ever intended to be used for combat operations," says Dunaway, "and that is basically what we were dealing with there." Moreover, given the enormity of the undertaking, says Walcher, some tasks necessarily fell to the wayside. "The last thing on my mind was, 'Gee, where's our staging area going to be?'" he recalls. "The street was filling up so fast with cop cars that I had no clue where we could have a staging area, whether we could even have access to it, nor did I care, because I was too busy worrying about kids who had been shot and getting a SWAT team in there that could end the situation." He adds: "It wasn't a traditional incident command, but the system in place accomplished what really needed to get done."

As Walcher and the other commanders prioritized and delegated jobs, some agencies simply tackled tasks that needed doing, rather than seeking direction from the command post. Captain Mark Campbell, for example, who was deploying officers from the Arapahoe Sheriff's Office as they arrived, had noticed that the northbound lanes of Pierce Street were clogged with haphazardly parked patrol cars, blocking the passage of emergency vehicles. To free the lanes, Campbell called on several early-arriving members of the Arapahoe SWAT team, who either contacted the vehicles' owners, Campbell says, or simply lifted the cars out of the way.[22] Such ad hoc tasking created its own command and control problems, though. One suburban SWAT team, for example, never even checked in with the command post, but simply deployed itself around the school.

Communication Breakdown

While the somewhat haphazard command approach may have complicated the Columbine response, though, a far bigger impediment was the inability of different agencies to talk. Indeed, responders say, the absence of linked communication systems greatly increased the difficulty of establishing and maintaining effective incident command—particularly given the many departments and jurisdictions on scene. Had all responding agencies been using compatible systems with a databank of channels to choose from, for example, the command post could have allotted a channel for each major task or area of responsibility, such as traffic control, SWAT, logistics, emergency medical, and perimeter control. Such a system, a regular feature of incident command, would have simplified both the division of the response into manageable pieces, and the management of each of those pieces. "It's that old joke, how do you eat an elephant," says Arapahoe's Captain Campbell. "In little bitty bits. You kind of break things down."

As it was, as additional agencies continued to arrive, the ability of all those involved to communicate deteriorated significantly. While the JeffCo Sheriff's office still used a VHF radio, for example, many other responding agencies, such as Denver and Arapahoe, had either analog or digital 800 megahertz (MHz) systems, neither of which could communicate directly with a VHF system, nor with each other. "I cannot overemphasize how great a problem the incompatibility of our communications systems was that day," states Undersheriff Dunaway. "What that presented was almost unmanageable."

Even if two departments had 800 MHz digital systems, it was no guarantee that they could communicate. Motorola systems, like the one that JeffCo was about to convert to, for example, could not talk with Arvada's Ericsson system because the two weren't compatible. Similarly, although the JeffCo Sheriff's Office and Littleton Fire both had VHF systems, they couldn't communicate during the early hours of the incident because they were using different channels. "If the officer doesn't ever flip that switch and practice talking to that agency," notes Littleton Paramedic Captain James Olsen, "he's not going to know how to do it when the incident comes down."[23]

Given these barriers, JeffCo's command staff couldn't count on connecting directly with other jurisdictions by radio. Instead, it pieced together informal links, placing a JeffCo Sheriff's Office representative with a radio on every team, or passing messages through its own dispatch center to a different center, and then back to the field. Even this last method, however, often broke down. At 12:23, the JeffCo dispatch center said it couldn't get through to the command post because both radio links and cellular phone lines were jammed. Indeed, the center was so overloaded that calls were going instead to dispatchers in Littleton, Denver, and other municipalities, who then had to relay messages back to JeffCo. "Radios and cell phones and everything were absolutely useless," declares Steve Davis, public information officer for the JeffCo Sheriff's Office, "they were so overwhelmed with the amount of traffic in the air."

Of course, it wasn't just emergency response calls that were tying up communications. At 11:47, a local television station ran the first report of possible shootings at Columbine High School. By noon, area TV stations had switched to full-time live coverage, and parents and relatives were besieging school, law enforcement, and county officials for information about their children and loved ones.

Lieutenant John Kiekbusch of the JeffCo Sheriff's investigation division had established four debriefing areas where officers could question students and staff about what they had seen. By 12:25, the JeffCo Sheriff's Office and school administrators had settled on Leawood Elementary School, less than a mile from Columbine, as the primary debriefing site. Counselors from the Victim Services Unit of the JeffCo Sheriff's Office had already been sent to the elementary school to talk with students and parents, and the dispatch center began specifically directing parents there. "Where the media was very helpful was in continually broadcasting that information very early on so we wouldn't have a mass of parents

running down to Columbine looking for their kids," says Sheriff Stone.

Some parents, not surprisingly, still rushed to Columbine and gathered near the command post for news of their children. For their part, many students and staff who had escaped the school never went to Leawood Elementary for questioning, and did not reunite with parents or relatives until hours later. Although JeffCo assigned officers trained in crowd control to escort students from safe areas near Columbine to buses that would take them to the elementary school, scores of students simply headed home or to the houses of friends. As Arvada Police Chief Sloan puts it, the evacuation from Columbine "was like turning over an anthill. Whoosh . . . they were out of there."

SWAT Approaches the West Side

As the command staff struggled to bring order and efficiency to the overall response, SWAT Commander Lieutenant Terry Manwaring continued his efforts to insert teams into Columbine and apprehend the killers. Almost a half hour after leaving Deputy Allen Simmons and his team on the east side of Columbine, Manwaring and his group of five finally worked their way around to the upper west entrance of the school at 12:34, still using the fire truck as a shield.[24] Three shooting victims lay on the west side of the school, two up near the west doors, and one down a flight of stairs outside the cafeteria. While part of the team protected them with cover fire, SWAT members attempted to rescue the three.[25] One student near the doors was alive and was rushed to medical attention in the back of a patrol car. The other two, however, were already dead.[26]

After dealing with the victims, Manwaring had hoped to send a SWAT team directly into the building through the upper entrance. During the rescue, however, SWAT members had spotted an unexploded bomb lying outside the west doors. Manwaring had heard there could be time- or motion-activated bombs in the school, and he didn't want to risk sending SWAT members past a device that might be triggered at any point. Instead, the SWAT commander decided to drive the fire truck over the bomb and straight through the doors into the school—assuming that the vehicle would absorb any blast. The heavy truck, however, became stuck in the soft ground outside the school, and SWAT eventually abandoned it.

As Manwaring's group was struggling with the fire truck, ten members of the JeffCo SWAT team, headed by Sgt. Barry Williams, arrived at the command post. Over the next 20 minutes, Williams led the team around to the school's west end—using a front end loader they had commandeered as a cover—while two SWAT snipers broke off from the group and stationed themselves on roofs south of the school and opposite the library windows and science wing.

A. J. DeAndrea, an officer with the Arvada Police Department and member of the JeffCo SWAT team, had been having a family picnic with his wife, who was nine months pregnant, when he was paged and told there had been a shooting at Columbine. DeAndrea, who approached the school's west end behind the front end loader, recalls the scene at Columbine as "surreal." First, he saw one of JeffCo's SWAT members driving a fire truck. Then he noticed one of the early students to be shot and killed, Rachel Scott, on the ground nearby—his first realization that there had been fatalities. Farther down the hill was the body of Daniel Rohrbough.

Manwaring gave the newly arrived team a terse summary. It still wasn't known how many suspects were inside, although there were estimates of as many as eight gunmen in the building—conceivably some kind of terrorist group. Because of the bomb outside the west doors, the SWAT team didn't enter there. Nor did it go through the open emergency exit door leading straight to the library, out of which a number of distraught students had escaped about an hour-and-a-half earlier, because there was a bomb visible there. Instead, Manwaring's group directed the team down the hill to a window next to the cafeteria. Although the entry point was a floor below where deputies had last spotted the gunmen, shooting from the library windows, Manwaring had no reason to believe the two had stayed in that area, says Lieutenant Bruce Williamson, SWAT commander for the Arapahoe Sheriff's Office. "The team going into the school had no idea where the last known location of these guys was," explains Williamson. "They were shooting all over."

Unlike a normal SWAT operation, DeAndrea says, the pressure to get inside was so great that the team deployed with almost no preparation. "As we entered, we were told all kinds of things," DeAndrea recalls. "We were told, 'Last seen in the business area. Last seen in the science area. They are possibly in the air ducts moving around. We've got somebody on the roof.' I remember the Channel Four news helicopter coming in real low trying to see what they had up there." The team did not know there had been a massacre in the library, though, nor was it told that there was a report of

a badly injured person in the science wing. Neither Manwaring nor DiManna, apparently, had been given that information. In addition, Manwaring still didn't have a map of the school, and most SWAT members had never been in the building.

On the other side of the school, meanwhile, SWAT Deputy Allen Simmons had called for assistance with the grueling and time-consuming process of breaking down doors and searching rooms for suspects and victims. Although Harris and Klebold had been dead for more than a half hour, the command post was still receiving regular cell phone reports of gunshots and explosions from students and staff hidden throughout the school, which further complicated the search.[27] Shortly before 1:00, a SWAT team from the Arapahoe Sheriff's Office joined Simmons in the east side search, while other members of the Arapahoe team, along with JeffCo, Lakewood, Denver, and Littleton, established a tactical command post on Pierce Street right outside the main school entrance.

In Manwaring's absence, JeffCo had named Commander Bob Brandt and Sergeant Bill Black of the Littleton Police to coordinate the SWAT deployment. Perhaps because of the faulty communication among different agencies, however, some SWAT members kept questioning why Manwaring wasn't running the tactical command post himself, while others mistakenly concluded that he had deployed with a SWAT team inside the school.[28] "We kept asking where he was, because all the commanders need to get together and formulate a tactical plan together," says Arapahoe SWAT team leader Louis Perea. "That wasn't happening."

At about 1:00, a school staff member gave an Arapahoe deputy a Columbine yearbook from the previous year with the photos of Eric Harris and Dylan Klebold circled. Captain Campbell sent plainclothes officers to make copies of the pictures and distributed them to the command and tactical posts. By 1:15, investigators had gone to both students' houses.

West Side SWAT Enters

The eight members of the JeffCo SWAT team led by Barry Williams, along with a few Denver SWAT members, broke a window and climbed into the school at about 1:09. Had shots been fired shortly before or as the west side SWAT team arrived, DeAndrea says, the team's goal would have been simple: respond to the shots and stop the threat. Absent an active shooter, however,

SWAT's mission was to carefully search the building—rescuing students and teachers while trying to apprehend the shooters, who most likely were in hiding or holding hostages. "With shots fired, we're going to do a rapid and immediate deployment with an assault team, and we're going to take care of the shots being fired," DeAndrea explains. "Without that, we're not going to run haphazardly anywhere."

Once through the window, team members found themselves in a teachers lounge, standing in about three inches of water that had accumulated from the cafeteria sprinkler system, activated by bombs thrown earlier by Harris and Klebold. The group was immediately bombarded with sounds and smells. "You've got the school bell going off, you've got the fire alarm going off, you can smell gun powder in the air, and there's an overwhelming noise from the sprinklers made by the water coming down," DeAndrea recalls. While some members were particularly disconcerted by the alarms, DeAndrea says, what bothered him most were the alarm system's flashing strobe lights, which chillingly mimicked the flash of a gun, and which also created sudden shadows that forced him to recheck areas repeatedly to ensure there was no one hiding or preparing to attack.

Looking into the cafeteria, DeAndrea recounts, was an otherworldly experience. "We don't hear shots fired," he says. "We don't see kids running around. There's nothing. It's like this place is locked down. It's eerie. First thing in my mind, I'm thinking ambush. Where are they? They've got hostages. We're going to find them here somewhere, and they're hunkered down." Carefully picking their way past exploded and unexploded bombs, the team scanned the cafeteria and headed into the kitchen area.

Almost immediately, DeAndrea says, the team heard movement behind a door. "We'd shout, 'Police department, open the door! Police department, open the door!' Expecting for that door to open, and we're going to engage in gunfire," he recalls. No one, however, opened the doors. There were no gunmen hidden in the school's rooms, and students, traumatized by what they had already witnessed or heard, would not undo the locks.

DeAndrea, the designated breacher for his team, had made a conscious decision not to bring his usual 55-pound ram into the building, because carrying it would hinder his ability to wield a gun. Instead, he used a tool that resembled a specialized crowbar, allowing him to break off door handles and pop doors

open. A number of doors in Columbine were difficult to breach, though, since students hiding inside had piled furniture or other objects against them for further protection. "We're busting down doors wholeheartedly thinking we're going to go through that door and we're going to engage somebody," DeAndrea says. "Do we think that we might get shot? Absolutely. Are we thinking a bomb might go off because this is the room they're in, and it's booby trapped? Absolutely. But we still have to get through the door."

Instead of gunmen, the team found 20 to 30 students hidden in the kitchen area, as well as two male staff members hiding in the walk-in freezers. The team began to evacuate students and staff, even as Williams passed on a report that the shooters might be in the library or the science area. JeffCo had been joined by more SWAT members from Denver, and the team passed small groups of students from one member to another and then out the same window through which they had entered. Once outside, students were directed up the outside stairs to be driven to safety. Since the path took them past the bodies of both Daniel Rohrbough and Rachel Scott, officers told students to focus only on the person immediately in front of them.

Away from the building at last, SWAT members took students to the east side, where law enforcement personnel quickly searched them, not only looking for injuries, but trying to ascertain that the attackers were not among the escaping students. To help, deputies had recruited Columbine's two deans of students, Chris Mikesell and Peter Horvath, stationing them near the tactical command post on the east side of the school. Mikesell and Horvath scanned passing students, searching not only for Harris and Klebold, but also for students who were thought to be associates of the two, and who might be accomplices in the attack. Once checked, students were supposed to duck through a hole cut in the fence and board buses waiting on an adjacent residential street. Because of a lack of communication, though, Arapahoe's Captain Campbell says, a Denver officer down the street was stopping buses at first and wouldn't let them pass. "By the time the buses came down to pick these kids up and transport them over to Leawood, the kids had already said, 'Screw this, I'm out of here,'" says Campbell.

With the two SWAT teams in the building, meanwhile, SWAT commanders Manwaring and DiManna had returned to the tactical command post on the east side of the building. Manwaring, who finally had gotten a current floor plan for the school from school administrators, sent in some additional SWAT members after the original two teams to help secure the evacuation routes. He did not, however, send new teams into other parts of the school, fearing that too many SWAT teams inside would add to the confusion and unacceptably increase the risk of friendly fire.

Managing Information

Although communications at Columbine were patchy and unreliable on April 20, due to overloaded cell phone systems and incompatible radios, information continued to pour into the JeffCo Sheriff's command post. Despite periodic breakdowns, the three dispatchers in the mobile command bus were receiving messages from the JeffCo dispatch center, other regional dispatchers, county officials, school officials, the tactical command post, and officers responsible for the different aspects of the response. In addition, messages were being relayed in regarding cell phone calls made to families, police, and even television and radio stations by students trapped in the school. Finally, there was a constant stream of reports, queries, and requests from people—official and otherwise—who had gathered around the command post. "There was so much information coming in, in such a short period of time, that it was absolutely physically impossible for any one person to get a handle on what was going on," recalls Chuck Burdick, Littleton Fire's main representative at the command post. "At one point in time, I remember very vividly my brain just saying, 'Absolute overload.' I got to the point where I didn't hear anything. Not even gray noise—it was no noise at all. It was the strangest experience I've ever had."

The volume of information wasn't the only problem, Burdick says. Because it sometimes took a long time for messages to get through, he says, many accounts were outdated, leading to a skewed understanding of what was happening inside the school. Early on, for example, reports of gunfire in one area of the building were sometimes received along with later accounts of shots and explosions in other parts of the building, leading responders to assume that there were more than two gunmen at work. "That's what led law enforcement to think there were six or more shooters in the school," Burdick explains.

SWAT member DeAndrea, who recalls being peppered with information as he was first working his way through the high school, says he had great sympathy for those on the outside trying to unravel conflicting accounts. "Go back and look at the hundreds of people who are around that command post with information," he says, "on top of the hundreds of phone calls that are coming in to a very small number of people. If I call in and tell you one thing, and somebody else calls in and tells you another thing, who knows whose information is more correct? We're not computers to process all this information and get it all out accurately." He adds: "I'll tell you, I was happier to be inside the school than to be at the command post."

Much of the crush of information was unavoidable. But, according to some responders on scene, commanders could have eliminated a portion of the extraneous input. Although it was standard practice among law enforcement to cordon off a command post during a major incident, JeffCo had not stationed officers around the mobile command trucks, and didn't isolate the vehicles with crime scene tape until later in the afternoon. As a result, people came and went relatively freely. "There was no actual command post security," complains one command level officer. "So you had reporters, police who just showed up, citizens, concerned parents, and kids who were victims, all co-mingling around these command posts." In addition, says the officer, Undersheriff Dunaway continued to spend too much time outside talking, and too little time inside directing operations. "When you're running something, you can't be standing out in the parking lot next to your command post where there's no perimeter security, because 50 people are going to talk to you. He needed to be in somewhere, sitting down, getting fed information, and he didn't do that."

Dunaway and some others, though, dismiss the charge that students or parents came close to the command posts. Moreover, the Undersheriff says, his conversations outside the post, which included periodic meetings with Sheriff Stone and chief investigator Lieutenant Kiekbusch, were a necessary part of the effort to learn more about Harris and Klebold, to search for additional suspects, and to ascertain whether the attack was going to spread beyond the high school. "I needed to retain a certain distance from the operational aspects of it in order to contemplate the policy-level issues that we might face that day," Dunaway says.

Managing the Media

Just as Columbine was the biggest and most complex incident that most local emergency responders had ever confronted, so it was the biggest event most local media had ever covered, and quickly became a leading national and international story as well. When Steve Davis, public information officer (PIO) for the JeffCo Sheriff's Office, first left for Columbine at about 11:30 that morning, though, he had no idea how important the event would become.[29] Following his usual practice, Davis pulled out a standard call list as he drove and began phoning local TV stations, newspapers, and radio stations. "I told them I've got a report of shots fired, explosions at the school, I'm on my way down there, and I'll try to pick a place to meet," Davis recalls.

By the time he got to Columbine at about 11:45, Davis says, there were at least two television crews and a radio station on scene, as well as a few PIOs from other jurisdictions who had reported in case Davis needed help. Already it was clear that the incident was going to be too large to handle by simply traveling from one media representative to another. Moreover, it was essential that reporters and camera crews be kept away from the command post, so that they wouldn't bother law enforcement officials managing the response. Accordingly, Davis, with the help of the other PIOs, told reporters that all interviews would take place at a designated media center in the parking lot at the northeast corner of Clement Park— a recreational area which abutted the high school's north side. Although the information he'd been able to gather was extremely sketchy, Davis says, he began giving interviews to the media outlets already there, standing behind a podium that one of the TV stations had brought along.

As the seriousness of the attack at Columbine began to emerge, however, and as news operations flocked to the scene, Davis soon realized he could not satisfy the barrage of requests for individual interviews. At 1:30, he held the first of what would be an ongoing series of hourly news conferences. Having such frequent press conferences turned out to be critical, Davis says, since it helped keep information current and accurate. "There were so many rumors and myths getting started, it gave me a chance to confirm stories or chop them off right at the root immediately, instead of letting them fester all day," he explains.

On the other hand, the hourly updates made it almost impossible for Davis to stay abreast of the latest developments himself. "Most of the news conferences would run 30 to 40 minutes with questions and answers," he recounts. "When I ended that, I would start to walk out and was just mobbed by media wanting an individual interview. By the time I got done doing that, it was time for the next news conference. I would literally have to run over to the command post, stick my head in, and say, 'OK, what's new? What's changed?' Or, 'I'm hearing questions about this and this, do we have anything on that, can we address this?' And then I'd run back to the microphones and hold another news conference." Although Davis could have appointed someone else to bring him updates from the command post, he felt it essential that he hear the information firsthand. "There were so many concerns about what was going out and the accuracy of what was going out," he notes, "that I wanted to hear it straight from those people before I turned around and went to the microphones."[30]

Despite his efforts to keep the press cloistered in one area, Davis says, some media representatives sought out more dramatic stories and footage. Several journalists got near to the command post, and a TV reporter at the Yukon/Caley triage area interviewed wounded students, even though families had not yet been notified of the students' injuries. Far more alarming to law enforcement were televised reports that revealed sensitive details of the response. Helicopter news footage early on, for example, showed Manwaring's SWAT team making its slow approach to the school behind the cover of the fire truck. "Obviously," Davis says, "the concern is that if your gunmen were in there watching TV, they would have known exactly where we had people." Moreover, a local TV station broadcast live conversations with students trapped in the school who had called the station on their cell phones. "The kids are saying, 'I'm holed up in the science room with 23 other kids and we've got the door barricaded,'" recalls Davis. "And we're thinking, 'Get that off the air!' Now we're telling the gunmen exactly which room to go to in order to find 23 more hostages." Even the helicopters, themselves, posed a problem, kicking up dirt that in some cases temporarily blinded the rooftop snipers, and making it harder for responders outside the building to hear.[31]

Members of the JeffCo Sheriff's Office also had to be vigilant in restricting the press to a media area outside of Leawood Elementary. As the afternoon wore on, more and more panic-stricken students and parents were gathering. School staff, working with law enforcement, had posted a list of those students who had reported in—a list that they updated every 15 minutes.

The SWAT Response Continues

The efforts by the command staff and by Steve Davis to digest and act upon incoming information were mirrored inside Columbine by the intensive efforts of the SWAT teams to understand what they were seeing and hearing and to make appropriate decisions. At 2:17, JeffCo SWAT leader Barry Williams, in charge of the west side team, divided his group in half in order to move more quickly through the lower level of the school. The sense of urgency driving the team had only increased. Shortly before 2:00, Williams had received the first reports from dispatch alluding to the critically injured Dave Sanders, one alerting him to an injured teacher in the science area, while another—later found to have identified the wrong room—said a male was doing CPR on a victim in the library, and that a blue and white shirt was hanging from the door knob to signal the victim's presence. In addition, one of the two snipers on the roof radioed Williams at 2:15 to report the sign in the second-story window reading, "1 bleeding to death." Although Williams had asked dispatch for directions to reach the victim, though, his connection with dispatch was erratic, and he apparently was never given a clear description of where the science wing or the library were located. From the reports he had received, it wasn't even clear whether there was just one victim, or a few in different parts of the school.

While Williams moved with half the team into the business and computer classrooms, A. J. DeAndrea took a team of three JeffCo deputies and a Denver officer and headed into the auditorium, where they had been warned shooters might be concealed on the catwalk. Alarms and strobe lights were still assaulting their senses, DeAndrea says, making it extremely difficult for members of even the same team to talk. "You can't hear anything," he remembers. "Basically, everything is hand signals, because unless I'm in your face yelling, you're not going to be able to communicate." DeAndrea also had trouble hearing dispatch reports, he says, and couldn't communicate well with the other half of the JeffCo SWAT team, let alone Simmons's SWAT team on the other side of the school, because the line-of-sight radios didn't receive well within the core of the building. "Barry [Williams] and I communicated very rarely," he says. "I was getting some transmissions, but I'm sure that I missed a lot."

After checking the auditorium, which was empty, DeAndrea's group emerged on the upper level of the school, where a dispatch report had indicated there might be students hidden nearby. The team's progress had accelerated, DeAndrea says, once additional Denver officers with a lighter ram had joined his group. In fact, one of the few encouraging aspects of the response was the ease with which members of the two teams interacted, despite the fact that SWAT teams rarely worked with other jurisdictions.[32] "There was not

a glitch," DeAndrea says. "There were no egos that day. There was no posturing. It was a total team effort."

In addition, although there were now a couple dozen SWAT members working their way through the school—including some who had become separated from their teams, and who had only irregular radio contact with other officers—no SWAT members mistakenly shot at each other. "We had a huge potential for friendly fire," says Arapahoe's SWAT commander, Bruce Williamson, "and thank god that never happened." Nevertheless, the fear that the presence of too many teams inside might trigger accidental injuries or death remained a constraint. According to one report, the Lakewood SWAT team, which had positioned itself south of the school, volunteered to try to rescue the bleeding victim upstairs, having seen the sign in the window. But incident commander Walcher vetoed the attempt, claiming there would be too much risk of surprising teams already inside and precipitating dangerous crossfire.[33]

Upstairs at last, DeAndrea says, SWAT members could see motion in a room close by, off of the choir room in the music section. When the team breached the door of the room at 2:24, DeAndrea says, they found 60 students crammed into one small space. "They're terrified," he says. "I've never seen fear like this before. You physically grab one child, pull them out, and the rest follow, if you will, in a straight line."

DeAndrea had been told there could be a shooting victim nearby, he says. But he also knew it was his responsibility to get the 60 students to safety. "Now we have a problem," he says. "We've got 60 kids. It's negligent for us to leave them in there knowing that there are bombs inside this school. Do we know if any bombs are on a timer? Is the whole school going to blow up? We stop everything, and we need to get these 60 out, and we're in the dead center of the school."

DeAndrea's team set to work, hurrying students in groups of ten out the west side of the school along the exact route SWAT had used to enter, with a SWAT member at the head, middle, and end of each cluster. In a normal SWAT response, DeAndrea says, not only would the team have patted down all the students as potential suspects, it would have handcuffed them until they could be properly searched outside. But given the pressure to get the students out of the building safely, DeAndrea simply ordered them to keep their hands on their heads until an officer told them to take them down. The news helicopter footage of students existing the school with their hands on top of their heads became an enduring image of the Columbine tragedy.

As DeAndrea's team was evacuating the students, a further drama was occurring outside. A deputy who had spent the previous two hours conducting air surveillance from a news helicopter radioed dispatch that someone was trying to climb out a broken window on the school's southwest side.[34] The Lakewood SWAT team, which had been checking the parking lot for vehicles belonging to Harris and Klebold, convinced an armored car company to loan them a bulletproof car. Just after they drove the armored car to the side of the school, SWAT members managed to catch the seriously injured student, Patrick Ireland, as he fell from the library window.[35]

The Final Discoveries

Between 2:30 and 2:45 that afternoon, the three main SWAT teams searching and clearing Columbine High School began to converge. After removing the 60 students from the choir room, DeAndrea's team found two more groups of about 30 students each in two nearby rooms and handed them to Simmons's team, which had just worked its way down the southern east-west hallway, to escort out the east side of the building. The group led by Barry Williams, meanwhile, had finished its search of the business wing downstairs, and had mounted the stairs by the cafeteria—coming up just down the hall from the other two teams and heading into the science wing. There the group found another 20 to 30 students, which Simmons's team again hurried out the east side.

At 2:42, Williams's team finally reached the critically injured teacher, Dave Sanders, as well as about 60 students in that and an adjoining classroom. Williams radioed for medical help and a member of the team stayed behind as the others escorted the traumatized students from the building. Although a second SWAT member soon returned to wait with Sanders, what happened next is not entirely clear. Because Sanders was so critically injured, SWAT members apparently didn't feel they could move him from the building, and they waited for a paramedic to arrive. At the same time, however, paramedics continued to hover outside the east entrance, expecting that the injured party would be carried out to them. Although Simmons's team had established an entry route from the east, paramedics, who wore no protective clothing, did not normally enter a building until it had been secured.[36] After the two SWAT members waited for about 20 to 30 minutes, a Denver paramedic finally arrived from the west side of the building. Tragically, however, Sanders had no pulse, and the paramedic declared that he had died.[37]

The horror of the day had not yet ended, though. Williams's SWAT team finally entered the library at 3:22, the last area of the school to be searched. Immediately, Williams radioed to dispatch. "Barry Williams is a very calm, cool, collected man," DeAndrea says. "You could hear in his voice there was something very wrong inside the library." The scene inside, DeAndrea says, was shocking and terribly sad. Although one girl with several gunshot wounds was still alive, twelve other students in the room were dead, most huddled under tables where they had tried to hide. Two, however, surrounded by weapons and bombs, matched the description of the gunmen, and appeared to have committed suicide with gunshot wounds to the head. Despite the apparent suicides, law enforcement still had to operate under the assumption that there might be accomplices in the building or already outside.

Given the many bombs visible in the room, SWAT moved as quickly as possible, radioing for paramedics, and evacuating four staff members found hiding in rooms off the library, including teacher Patti Nielson, who had climbed into a cupboard following the shooting spree almost four hours earlier. As two paramedics removed the wounded student via the library's emergency exit—walking around bombs in the hallway—the SWAT team called for the bomb squad to take over.[38]

Back in the hall outside the library, DeAndrea says, the three SWAT teams studied a map that Williams's group had torn from the wall, and concluded they had searched the whole school. Even now, though, they didn't quit. The teams returned to the main lobby on the east side of the building, regrouped with reinforcements along normal jurisdictional lines, and went back through the building for a rapid second sweep—this time, finding no one alive.[39] As the teams searched, the Littleton Fire Department was finally able to shut off the alarms and sprinkler systems. Outside, meanwhile, Sheriff Stone and Steve Davis held a news briefing at which Stone announced the possibility of "up to 25 dead" as the result of the attack.[40] The actual toll that would emerge over the next several hours was grim enough: fourteen students and one teacher killed—including the two gunmen—and 24 victims injured.

The JeffCo Sheriff's Office, in its final report, declared the "deadly shootings and massacre" at Columbine over after the SWAT teams completed their second search at

4:45. More than 160 victims had been treated at four triage sites for maladies ranging from shock to gunshot wounds, and 24 students had been transported to area hospitals. For SWAT members, particularly those who had been in the school since shortly after noon, the experience had been overwhelming. "Typically when we do a tactical operation and we make an entry into a high-risk situation, two minutes is a very long time," notes Williamson, the Arapahoe SWAT commander. "This went on for hours. So the adrenaline dump and the noise and the screaming kids and the dead children and the blood and the carnage and the signs of the explosions from the devices that went off in the school— they were dealing with that for a long time." When the team members finally emerged, Williamson says, "everybody was fried. That's emotionally the worst day I've ever dealt with. I've got four kids of my own. I went home and hugged them all."

By the end of the first day, almost 1,000 representatives of area law enforcement and emergency response agencies had reported to Columbine. While the Denver Police had provided the most aid to JeffCo during the shootings, followed by the Arapahoe Sheriff's Office and the Littleton Police, responders came from half a dozen sheriff's offices; 12 fire and EMS agencies, employing 46 ambulances and two helicopters; 20 area police departments; the Bureau of Alcohol, Tobacco and Firearms; the Colorado Bureau of Investigation; the FBI, and the Colorado National Guard.

The Bomb Squad and Investigators Take Over

If Eric Harris and Dylan Klebold hadn't scattered explosive devices around Columbine High School, investigators would have been able to conduct an immediate crime scene analysis, which in all probability would have allowed the coroner to identify the victims and remove their bodies from the school the night of the attack. As it was, the location and removal of bombs forced a delay in the identification of victims that was a final cruel twist for both families and responders.

Although the 16 bomb technicians originally assembled, joined by evidence collection experts from the FBI and the Bureau of Alcohol, Tobacco and Firearms, worked quickly after the SWAT teams finished, they faced a monumental task. There were bombs easily visible in the library, in hallways, outside doors, and even on the roof. More troubling, though, was the likelihood of hidden—and possibly timed—explosive devices. In the cafeteria alone there were more than 400 unsearched backpacks, and the school had 1,952 lockers, any one of which could contain a bomb.

Technicians first disposed of all the bombs from the library that they could retrieve without moving any of the bodies, including those of Klebold and Harris, since the victims had to remain undisturbed until investigators had completed their initial crime scene analysis. Late that afternoon, as bomb experts discussed which part of the school to clear next, though, Deputy Inspector Joe Dempsey, team leader of the Arapahoe County Sheriff's bomb squad, along with a Denver bomb squad detective, spotted the top of an alarm clock poking out from a large, blanket-covered mound in the back seat of a car identified as Klebold's. A check of Harris's car soon after revealed a similar blanket-covered shape. Given the danger posed by the large bombs, experts had to clear the cars before returning to the building. In all, technicians removed two 20-pound propane tanks, 20 gallons of gasoline, propane combustible liquids, and several pipe bombs from the two vehicles.

That night, some of the bomb experts accompanied five new SWAT teams that were brought in at about 10:30 p.m. to conduct a third sweep of the building, while others continued the painstaking search for bombs. Bomb squad commanders called off the clearing process, though, after an overly tired technician lowering a pipe bomb into a special disposal trailer at about 10:40 p.m. bumped the device into the side, setting off an explosion that threw 15 live bombs out of the trailer. "We were getting a lot of pressure because the evidence people and the command staff and the families—everybody wanted into that school," explains Deputy Dan Davis, a member of the Arapahoe bomb team. "But we couldn't say that it was safe for them to go there." Parents who were still waiting at Leawood Elementary for word of their missing children were advised by 11:30 p.m. to go home for the night.

At 7:30 a.m. the following morning, April 21, the coroner and a team from the JeffCo Sheriff's Office returned to the library, followed by two forensic teams, to collect evidence, identify the deceased, and take videos and photographs of the crime scene. Investigators, relying primarily on physical descriptions provided by waiting parents the previous night, identified all the victims by noon, and officials notified the families soon after.[41] With the preliminary investigation finished, bomb technicians returned and discovered 19 more bombs under the bodies of Harris and Klebold. The bodies were finally removed from Columbine late that afternoon. "If it ever happens to anybody again, I would hope that they make a contingency plan to photograph everybody and move the bodies the first night so you can look for devices, because having to go back in there again was very traumatic for those guys," says Joe Dempsey. "We would have felt better had we known that we were able to take the kids out of the library that first night."

Before a full-fledged investigation of the incident could begin, the bomb squads still had to clear the rest of the school, including the backpack-strewn cafeteria, where technicians had already found a large propane tank bomb that had failed to explode. Given the enormity of the task, and the desire to move forward quickly, the Bureau of Alcohol, Tobacco and Firearms brought in dogs trained to sniff out explosives, and took them through as the experts in the library were finishing. That afternoon, after the dogs completed their work, officials declared the building safe enough for investigators to enter. But perhaps due to sensory overload from all of the ammunition, detonated bombs, and other explosive materials in the building, the dogs missed one of the two largest bombs in the school—a second 20-pound propane bomb with a timer hidden in a duffel bag in the cafeteria. After a technician spotted the bomb Thursday, he ordered everyone from the building, and bomb squad members returned for a meticulous backpack-by-backpack search.

According to plans and homemade videotapes later uncovered by investigators, Harris and Klebold had timed the two propane bombs to explode in the cafeteria at 11:17, when the room was likely to be teeming with almost 500 students. The two then planned to shoot those students who tried to escape.[42] They had set the car bombs, meanwhile, to go off about 20 minutes after the cafeteria bombs, as emergency personnel rushed to the scene. Had the plan worked as envisioned, bomb experts say, the exploding tanks and ensuing giant fireballs probably would have killed or injured many of the students in the area, and might have caused parts of the library to collapse into the cafeteria. "The good Lord was looking after this school and all those kids because neither one of those bombs went off in the cafeteria," says Robert Armstrong of Arapahoe. "That's a big thing. Bad bomb makers made for a lot of live kids. We've got to be thankful for that."

In all, bomb technicians found 76 explosive devices at the school, as well as two bombs in the field, 13 in the two cars, and eight more at the two students' houses, for a total of 99. "Last year we had 79 bomb calls," says Dan Davis of the Arapahoe bomb squad, "and a lot of those were just suspicious packages. This was well over a year's worth of devices in one

night." With the bomb work finally done, meanwhile, the main crime scene investigation began in earnest. When completed in mid-June, seven teams had collected more than 10,000 pieces of evidence, taken some 10,000 photographs, and conducted about 5,000 interviews. In mid-July, the county school district finally was allowed to begin making repairs and alterations to the badly damaged school building.[43]

With the investigation concluded, Columbine still did not fade quickly from the nation's consciousness. Over the following months, commentators, politicians, and others—backing a range of causes from gun control, to curtailed violence in movies, to increased parental involvement—pointed to the shootings at the high school as a poignant and powerful symbol of the need for change in American society. While residents in the Columbine area also mulled these issues, for many, an examination of the emergency response, itself, became the primary focus. Newspaper articles critical of law enforcement actions appeared within days of the shootings, and several months later, the families of victims brought lawsuits against emergency responders, the school, and even the parents of Eric Harris and Dylan Klebold.

Even without this outside scrutiny, though, the shootings at Columbine would remain etched in the minds of all those who were there on April 20, 1999, whether students, teachers, or SWAT members. And for many, the questions raised by the experience would never be easily answered. "I think about this thing every day of my life," says JeffCo SWAT member A.J. DeAndrea. "I have to read about it every day in the newspaper. I see those kids lying there every day. I've soul searched, what could I have done differently? What could I have done better?" He adds: "The only way I could have changed it is to have been right there, to know it was going to go down, and to have been able to engage them the second that they started. And lives still would have been lost."

Notes

1. It would be months more before some investigators accepted that the carnage unleashed that day had been the work of just those two.
2. Though the school had a Littleton address, it actually lay about two-and-a-half miles outside the city border.
3. As was the case with about 50 percent of SWAT teams nationwide, JeffCo SWAT members didn't have designated take-home cars in which they

could keep their tactical equipment. As a result, when paged for a SWAT response, most members headed first to the Sheriff's Office to gather their equipment and then drove together to the scene. Full-time urban SWAT teams, by contrast, typically kept their equipment with them at all times, and could report directly to a developing incident.

4. In addition to original interviews, this account relies heavily on the Jefferson County Sheriff's Office Report in CD-ROM format, titled, "Columbine High School Shootings: April 20, 1999." Due to legal proceedings related to the shootings at Columbine, many law enforcement responders declined to be interviewed for this case study.

5. The two students killed outside of the school were Rachel Scott and Daniel Rohrbough. The student first reported as injured in the parking lot, meanwhile, was Anne Marie Hochhalter, who survived the attack, but whose injuries left her paralyzed.

6. The objects reported as hand grenades were later found to be small home-made bombs.

7. Thirty-four students who were also in the library were uninjured.

8. The man was later discovered to be a heating and air conditioning repairman who was there to fix a leak. He was removed from the roof shortly after noon.

9. According to the JeffCo Sheriff's Report, instead of a gunman, the students were hearing custodians with keys and school radios.

10. Harris's nickname was "Reb," which may have aggravated confusion over his first name.

11. Although Columbine wasn't in Arapahoe County, several members of the Arapahoe Sheriff's Office command staff reported before JeffCo because their headquarters was only a few miles away, while it was about 15 miles to JeffCo's headquarters in Golden.

12. DiManna was off duty when the shooting broke out, but drove directly to Columbine when he heard the report on his radio.

13. Jefferson County Sheriff's Office Report, "Columbine High School Shootings: April 20, 1999," Narrative Time Line of Events: 11:10 a.m. to 11:59 a.m.

14. Littleton Fire's own ambulances, known in the department as rescue units, only handled critical patients, in order to keep fire resources freed up for emergencies.

15. The victim was Daniel Rohrbough, one of the first students to be killed by the shooters.

16. The congestion was worse than it might have been, Rahne says, because Denver police didn't trust the capabilities of outlying agencies and had called for their own fire department and paramedics to report. "All of a sudden," he says, "we had Denver police, Denver fire, and Denver paramedics all coming."

17. Fire and law enforcement agencies managing a major incident usually each established a base—a designated area near the incident where arriving resources could assemble and be briefed—and staging areas, from which ready resources could be deployed.

18. The individual was questioned and later released. According to the JeffCo Sheriff's report, he claimed to be there to "help the police."

19. Although law enforcement and the media initially seized on the Trench Coat Mafia angle, students identified with this set were later found to be so loosely organized that they didn't constitute a real group, and Harris and Klebold weren't even members of that crowd.

20. The bomb that initially exploded in the field was inside a backpack, and detonated after a road worker picked up the bag and tossed it aside. A bomb in a second backpack nearby exploded soon after, probably ignited by the fire. Bomb technicians were never able to determine whether the device functioned as planned, or was simply triggered when thrown.

21. Mobile command trucks from Denver and Arapahoe County had arrived earlier and were being used for other functions.

22. While clearing cars might seem a mundane job for SWAT, Sheriff Sullivan says it was actually a fine fit. "Number one, they're a team. Number two, they're very healthy, very strong individuals."

23. Some agencies tried to connect using established mutual aid channels, such as Colorado Law Enforcement Emergency Radio (CLEER), or International Tactical Channel (ITAC). Even these, however, had frequency constraints, with CLEER being a UHF channel, and ITAC only available to users of 800 MHz systems.

24. The group had to move slowly, observers say, because the fastest and most direct route to the west entrance went right by the school, within easy shooting range of any gunmen who might be inside.

25. After shots were exchanged during the initial medical rescues on the south side of the school,

Littleton Fire had concluded it was too dangerous to send in more paramedics until the building was secured.

26. The deceased students were Rachel Scott and
Daniel Rohrbough, the latter being the student
already pronounced dead by the paramedics
more than a half hour before.

27. Investigators later speculated that those hidden
were actually hearing the sounds of SWAT
teams breaking down doors.

28. Unlike many SWAT commanders, Manwaring
often deployed to the site with the team instead
of remaining at a tactical command post, although he didn't enter the building.

29. Davis had been with the Sheriff's Office for 20
years, eighteen-and-a-half of them in uniform
before becoming the PIO.

30. Among the breaking stories Davis had to deal
with early that afternoon was the apprehension by officers of three young men dressed in
black who were walking near the school. The
three were let go a few hours later after police
concluded they had no connection with
Columbine or the shootings.

31. The JeffCo Sheriff's Office eventually asked the
Federal Aviation Administration to impose temporary flight restrictions over the school to clear the
airspace.

32. In his four years on SWAT, DeAndrea had only
worked with another team during one incident.

33. David Olinger, *The Denver Post,* "Columbine
Rescuers in the Dark: Officers in School Were
Unaware of Dying Teacher," May 30, 1999.

34. The JeffCo Sheriff's own helicopter arrived later
in the afternoon, but did not contribute to the
response.

35. Ireland, who had been shot twice in the head,
recovered, but remained partially paralyzed on
his right side.

36. By this time, Littleton Fire had established two
additional triage sites to treat the injured, including one right outside the main east entrance.

37. Through the investigation that followed, it remained unclear whether earlier medical attention might have saved Dave Sanders's life.

38. The injured student, Lisa Kreutz, survived her injuries.

39. Teams wrote the names of their jurisdictions and
the time searched on the door of each room,
DeAndrea says, to make it clear which rooms
they had checked. The only untoward occurrence of the second sweep was when a SWAT
team used frangible slugs fired from a shotgun
to blow the hinges off a locked door without
warning the other teams in advance, sparking a
short-lived armed response.

40. Stone was roundly criticized for releasing such
an inaccurate figure. According to Davis,
though, the number was not far out of line,
given the conflicting reports they'd received
from inside the school, and the number of critically injured students already rushed to hospitals who were not expected to survive.

41. Although the coroner wanted to withhold noti-
fications until after a formal identification, District Attorney David Thomas and a few
associates broke the news to families still waiting at Leawood, as well as to those who had returned to their homes.

42. Although Joe Dempsey says one of the timed
pipe bombs intended to trigger a propane tank
did go off, either because the timer worked or
because a pipe bomb tossed near it set it off, it
didn't detonate with the force necessary to
puncture and ignite the propane tank.

43. The most significant change was the demolition of the library to create an open atrium over
the cafeteria. The school also added an emergency exit door to the science wing.

Chapter 9 Review Questions

1. According to James Garnett, why do public administrators need to keep in mind the centrality of communications? How does one find out about the key players and processes
influencing communications both inside and outside an organization and learn to deal with
them effectively? Do you concur with Garnett's thesis about the professional centrality
of information networks? Why or why not?

2. What problems of communications are illustrated in the Columbine shooting case? Which were the most important ones in creating the dilemmas that officials faced?

3. What types of communications issues discussed in the Garnett reading are illustrated in the Columbine case? How in retrospect would Garnett advise local law enforcement to deal with those issues?

4. What does the case study tell us especially about the communications between governmental jurisdictions, as well as between the media and public agencies today? Are there any enduring lessons for public administrators?

5. How do communications systems make or break an administrator's ability to control and direct the policies of his or her organization? As an administrator, what techniques would you utilize to ensure that the information you receive is accurate, timely, and *not* distorted by preconceived personal or institutional biases?

6. Can you generalize about the ethical dilemmas created by communications processes for those who work for a public organization, especially for those who value truthfulness and open communications in performing their work? What risks are apparent within the organization when people are not able to communicate *everything* or are not *told* everything necessary to perform their work? Can you identify your own ethical standards concerning communications in a public agency?

Key Terms

internal versus external communications processes

communications players

government communication

newsmaking process

managerial communication process

interorganizational communications

the credibility conundrum

the propaganda paradox

"tell and sell" communications methods

the two-way symmetrical model

ethical communication

Suggestions for Further Reading

The importance placed on communications processes in shaping governmental and organizational decisions was largely the result of several seminal works. These writings of the following key theorists should be studied with some care: Chester Barnard, *The Functions of the Executive* (Cambridge, Mass.: Harvard University Press, 1938); Herbert Simon, *Administrative Behavior: A Study of Decision-Making Processes in Administrative Organization,* 4th ed. (New York: Free Press 1997); Karl W. Deutsch, *The Nerves of Government* (New York: Free Press, 1950); Norbert Weiner, *Cybernetics: Or Control and Communication in the Animal and the Machine* (New York: John Wiley & Sons, 1948). For a useful study of Herbert Simon and

his contributions not only to this area but the entire field of public administration, see the whole issue *Public Administration Quarterly* (Fall 1988), especially the opening interview with Simon. One should also read Simon's autobiography, *Models of My Life* (New York: Basic Books, 1991). For an evaluation of Barnard's contributions, see the entire issue of Jack Rabin and Thomas Vocino, eds., "Special Issue: Papers in Honor of Chester I. Barnard," *International Journal of Public Administration,* 17 (1994) as well as William G. Scott, *Chester I. Barnard and the Guardians of the Managerial State* (Lawrence, Kans.: University Press of Kansas, 1994). Harlan Cleveland, *The Knowledge Executive: Leadership in an Information Society* (New

York: E. P. Dutton, 1985), presents a lively study of this topic from a leadership perspective.

For more pragmatic works on the subject, review Herbert Kaufman in collaboration with Michael Couzens, *Administrative Feedback: Monitoring Subordinates' Behavior* (Washington, D.C.: The Brookings Institution, 1973); Hindy Schachter, *Public Agency Communication* (Chicago: Nelson-Hall, 1983); and Doris Graber, *Public Sector Communications* (Washington, D.C.: CQ Press, 1992). The best practical textbooks on this topic are David S. Arnold, Christine S. Becker, and Elizabeth K. Kellar, *Effective Communication: Getting the Message Across* (Washington, D.C.: International City Management Association, 1983); James L. Garnett, *Communicating for Results in Government: A Strategic Approach for Public Managers* (San Francisco, Calif.: Jossey-Bass, 1992); and P. V. Lewis, *Organizational Communications: The Essence of Effective Management,* 3rd ed. (New York: Wiley, 1987).

General handbooks provide useful overviews of this topic. See C. C. Arnold and J. W. Bowers, eds., *Handbook of Rhetorical and Communication Theory* (Needham Heights, Mass.: Allyn & Bacon, 1984); C. R. Berger and S. H. Chafee, eds., *Handbook of Communication Science* (Newbury Park, Calif.: Sage, 1987); and James

L. Garnett and Alexander Kouzmin, eds., *Handbook of Administrative Communication* (New York: Marcel Dekker, 1997). For a recent synthesis of this literature, read Janet D. Weiss, "Public Information," in Lester M. Salamon, ed., *The Tools of Government* (New York: Oxford University Press 2002), pp. 217–254.

The crisis of war can illuminate problems of administrative communications with unusual clarity. For some excellent examples, see Gordon W. Prange, *At Dawn We Slept: The Untold Story of Pearl Harbor* (New York: McGraw-Hill, 1981); E. B. Potter, *Battle for Leyte Gulf: Command and Communications* (Syracuse, N.Y.: Inter-University Case No. 126); John W. Spanier, *The Truman-MacArthur Controversy and the Korean War* (Cambridge, Mass.: Harvard University Press, 1959); Sam Adams, "Vietnam Cover-up: Playing War with Numbers," *Harper's Magazine* (May 1975); Deborah Shapley, *Promise and Power: The Life and Times of Robert McNamara* (Boston: Little, Brown, 1993); and from the Gulf War, in Bob Woodward, *The Commanders* (New York: Simon and Schuster, 1991). Perhaps the best of such military studies are Douglas S. Freeman, *Lee's Lieutenants,* 3 volumes (New York: Scribner's, 1944) and John Keegan, *The Face of Battle* (New York: Viking, 1976).

CHAPTER 10

Executive Management: The Concept of Effective Public Organizations

The discussion here . . . can proceed using a relatively straightforward definition of agency effectiveness: the agency performs well in discharging the administrative and operational functions pursuant to the mission. It achieves the mission as conceived by the organization and its stakeholders or pursues achievement of it in an evidently successful way.

—Hal G. Rainey and Paula Steinbauer

Introduction

Writings on public management are a comparatively new phenomenon; in fact, they are peculiarly products of this century because large-scale formal organizations, both public and private, are modern in origin and existence. Humanity's dependence on massive organizations that span the continent and the globe is therefore recent; hence, the comprehensive, detailed analysis of these institutions is also new to scholarly interest. The flood of modern literature analyzing the nature, behavior, and ideal methods for constructing viable human institutions and internal personal relationships has been prompted in part by the need to establish and construct these organizations in ways that effectively cope with problems of the present age.

One critical dilemma in studying modern organizations and their management lies in the proper theoretical perspective. As Dwight Waldo reminds us, studying organization is akin to the fable of the blind men and the elephant. "Each of the blind men . . . touched with his hands a different part of the elephant, and as a result there was among them a radical difference of opinion as to the nature of the beast."*

A principal cause of the considerable divergence of opinion about organizations thus stems from the specialized vantage points from which observers come to examine human institutions. The economist has a different view from the philosopher, so also the insider versus the outsider and the worker versus the manager. These ideas are not right or wrong; rather, a number of approaches exist for reaching the truth about complex formal organizations.

---

*Dwight Waldo, *Ideas and Issues in Public Administration* (New York: McGraw-Hill, 1953), p. 64.

In studying organizations, material that is valid or useful to one individual may not seem so to another.

For one reason or another, very often *one* theoretical perspective in America tends to dominate our understanding of what constitutes good or appropriate public sector organizational practices, namely business perspectives. Not infrequently do we read about political candidates or their appointees promising, "I can make government more businesslike!" or citing as their reason for holding high public office "a successful track-record as a manager in private enterprise." Editorial writers, civic association speakers, and media pundits often echo these refrains in favor of applying entrepreneurial talent to public enterprises. Popular opinion generally supports the viewpoint that if only public administrators would simply manage their affairs like business, government—and maybe even the entire country—would run a lot better.

The tendency to identify good management in government with good business management is common even in serious public administration literature. Indeed, discussions of business management methods dominated much of the early development of the conscious study of public administration at the beginning of the twentieth century. Frederick W. Taylor and his business-oriented scientific management concepts served as the core of much of the field of public administration prior to World War II. The Brownlow Committee Report (1937), which some scholars believe was the highwater mark of the influence of public administration thinking on government, largely mirrored the business organization practices of the day. In many respects, this strong influence of business practices on government continues today through application of such private sector techniques as performance budgets, cost-benefit analysis, cost-accounting procedures, performance appraisals, management by objective, zero-based budgeting, and so on. Indeed, you only need to think about the names of major governmental processes and institutions to appreciate the enormous influence of what Waldo calls "our business civilization"—via government corporations, city managers, efficiency ratings, contracting out for services, chief administrative officers, and county executives.

At the conceptual root of making government run more like a business is a belief in the "Three *E*'s," or the values of efficiency, economy, and effectiveness. "If only government could be more efficient, economical, and effective, our worries would be over!" So the popular view goes. During the last decade or so, thanks to the "reinventing government" movement, which drew heavily on the work of business guru Peter Drucker, whose writings focus on effective business managers, the third *E, effectiveness,* emerged prominently and pervasively throughout the public sector as an important, if not *the* important value for managers to strive toward. Yet, despite the recent renewed enthusiasm on both scholarly and popular levels to "reinvent government" in order to run it more effectively just like business, the fundamental issue remains unanswered: What is an effective government enterprise? What does the term mean and how is it practiced by public managers? How can it be applied to the public sector? What are its theoretical elements and their implications for government executives? What are its utility and its limitations?

In the following essay, "Galloping Elephants," Professor Hal G. Rainey, a distinguished scholar in the field of public management, and his doctoral student Paula Steinbauer, both currently at the University of Georgia, thoughtfully examine the considerable evidence surrounding the contemporary literature and research on effective government organizations. Their goal, as they indicate at the outset, is to develop the elements of a conceptual framework, or a theory, to explain public agency effectiveness. The authors begin by citing examples of government effectiveness that stand in stark contrast to popular notions about its incompetence and wastefulness. Drawing on current scholarship, the authors next create a list of propositions about effective public agencies. What they discover from the available research is a conceptual framework that includes the following basic components: supportive behaviors from external stakeholders, such as political authorities; agency autonomy in refining and implementing its mission; high mission "valence" or an attractive mission; a strong, mission-oriented culture; and certain leadership behaviors. Combined, these factors enhance several forms of motivation for people in any agency—task motivation, mission motivation, and public service motivation—that can be linked together to promote effective public agency management.

Note how the authors at the beginning of their article define *effectiveness* as: "whether the agency does well that which it is supposed to do, whether people in the agency work hard and well, whether the actions and procedures of the agency and its members are well suited to achieving its mission, and whether the agency actually achieves its mission."

As you review this thought-provoking article that maps out the vast intellectual landscape of current research on this subject in a readable and concise way, you might think about the following issues:

> Do you concur with how the authors define *effectiveness,* which serves as the basis for their argument? Is it a workable and useful definition? Are there any elements you would add—or delete?

> How does the authors' understanding of effective public agencies relate to other values that are basic to government, such as economy, efficiency, rule of law, and equity? Can such values be related to or included easily within the "effectiveness" framework, or are they fundamentally different? Why or why not?

> On a practical level, based upon your own experiences and readings, do the authors' arguments make good sense for public managers and supervisors to pay attention to as well as practice? If so, how? Or if not, why not?

Galloping Elephants: Developing Elements of a Theory of Effective Government Organizations

HAL G. RAINEY AND PAULA STEINBAUER

A corollary of this fact is the falsity of an equally common claim: that public and nonprofit organizations cannot, and on average do not, operate as efficiently as private businesses. . . . (Simon 1998, 11)

The elephant serves as a virtually archetypical symbol of a large, cumbersome, lumbering being. Yet an elephant can run *very* fast. Pachyderm means thick-skinned, yet elephants display sensitivity in acts of altruism and nurturance beyond those that are instinctively parental in many animals. Government organizations, or bureaucracies, have virtually an archetypical status as cumbersome, bungling entities, yet many of them perform *very* well. Impugned for centuries as insensitive, they also commonly display sensitivity and responsiveness to the needs of clients and others (e.g., Goodsell 1994; Gore 1995, 49). This article develops and advances concepts and propositions, summarized in Exhibit 10.1, about why government agencies perform well, when they do. In its present form, this set of propositions will evoke comparisons to the parable of the blind men trying to describe the elephant, because the propositions need much more articulation, justification, and specification of relations among them. They do, however, consider and develop some fundamental issues such as: What provides the basic incentive for effective performance of government agencies, in the absence of economic markets for their outputs? Is it a form of public service motivation or a motivation to

achieve the mission of the agency, or is it more specific task-related incentives such as interest in the work tasks themselves, or is it pay or other benefits? The propositions hold that all these forms of motivation contribute to the performance of effective agencies, especially when members of the agency see them as linked together. The propositions also hold that characteristics of the external oversight and political influence on the agency relate to its effectiveness, as do characteristics of the agency's mission, culture, leadership, and tasks, and that these factors in turn enhance the three forms of motivation just mentioned.

This article develops such propositions as a step toward development of a theory of effective government agencies on the argument that we need more theoretical development of that topic.[1] That public and academic discourse on bureaucracy tends to be negative will be considered here to be obvious and will not be elaborated, even though this mostly negative orientation involves many important issues and nuances. Much of the literature treats the government bureaucracy as a social problem and liability, rather than as an asset. Many authors focus on the problem that public bureaucracies are too bureaucratic, with too much hierarchy, too little innovativeness and energy, too much red tape, too much spending, too little efficiency, too little responsiveness to almost everyone and everything outside their boundaries and most of what is inside them, too much of a lot of other bad things, and too little of a lot of other good things (e.g., Barton 1980; A. Downs 1967; Niskanen 1971; Warwick 1975).[2] If this list seems long, it is rather brief compared to Caiden's (1991) listing of 175 bureaucratic pathologies (cited in Bozeman forthcoming).[3]

On the other hand, all along in academic and public discussion of the government bureaucracy, one can detect more ambivalence than rigid antipathy, even in predominantly negative treatments. Recently, too, more

Exhibit 10.1   Propositions About Effective Public Agencies

Public agencies are more likely to perform effectively when there are higher levels of the following conditions.

Relations with oversight authorities (legislative, executive, judicial) that are:
- Attentive to agency mission accomplishment
- Supportive
- Delegative

Relations with other stakeholders characterized by:
- Favorable public opinion and general public support
- Multiple, influential, mobilizable constituent and client groups
- Effective relations with partners and suppliers
  - Effective management of contracting and contractors
  - Effective utilization of technology and other resources
  - Effective negotiation of networks

Autonomy in operationalization and pursuit of agency mission, but not extremely high levels of autonomy (a curvilinear relationship between autonomy and agency effectiveness)

Mission valence (the attractiveness of the mission):
- Difficult but feasible
- Reasonably clear and understandable
- Worthy/worthwhile/legitimate
- Interesting/exciting
- Important/influential
- Distinctive

Strong organizational culture, linked to mission

Leadership characterized by:
- Stability (a curvilinear relationship between leadership stability and agency effectiveness)
- Multiplicity—a cadre of leaders, teams of leaders at multiple levels
- Commitment to mission
- Effective goal setting in relation to task and mission accomplishment
- Effective coping with political and administrative constraints

Task design characterized by:
- Intrinsic motivation (interest, growth, responsibility, service, and mission accomplishment)
- Extrinsic rewards (pay, benefits, promotions, working conditions)

Utilization of technology

Development of human resources:
- Effective recruitment, selection, placement, training, and development
- Values and preferences among recruits and members that support task and mission motivation

Professionalism among members:
- Special knowledge and skills related to task and mission accomplishment
- Commitment to task and mission accomplishment

Motivation among members:
- Public service motivation
- Mission motivation
- Task motivation

and more authors defend the public bureaucracy or debunk stereotypes and negative allegations about it (e.g., G.W. Downs and Larkey 1986; Goodsell 1994; Milward and Rainey 1983; Stillman 1996; Wamsley et al. 1990), while others describe and analyze excellent leadership and management in government agencies (Ban 1995; Barzelay 1992; Behn 1991; Cohen and Eimicke 1995; Cooper and Wright 1992; Denhardt 1993; Doig and Hargrove 1987; Hargrove and Glidewell 1990; Holzer and Callahan 1998; Osborne and Gaebler 1992; Riccucci 1995; Thompson and Jones 1994). Recent empirical research further undercuts some academic assertions about public bureaucracies, indicating that they are not as evasive of external control and oversight as is often alleged (Rubin 1985; Wood and Waterman 1994) and that people in them show more effort and motivation, and less shirking and slacking, than sometimes is alleged (Brehm and Gates 1997; H.G. Rainey 1983). Recent research also shows evidence of the historical inaccuracy of some current reformers' depictions of public bureaucracies as traditionally hidebound hierarchies that resisted innovation and entrepreneurial behaviors; rather, the evidence indicates frequent instances of entrepreneurial, innovative, and generally effective performance (Wolf 1997).

Examples of Agency Effectiveness

In addition, numerous specific examples of agency accomplishments provide evidence that government agencies often carry out their tasks and missions very competently. About the Social Security Administration (SSA), for example, one can point out the following:

- The agency operates the social security program efficiently in an administrative sense. An economist discussing reforms of the system in 1998 pointed out that one reason to save the system is that it is very efficient, with administrative costs running at 0.8 percent of benefits (Eisner 1998). This is lower than comparable figures for private annuity companies, even considering that they must pay taxes and provide payouts to shareholders. The figure for SSA represents increased efficiency over the last decade. A Roper survey in the early 1980s asked a representative sample of Americans to estimate the percent of each dollar in the Social Security program that goes to administrative expenses. The median estimate was fifty dollars out of every one hundred. The actual figure at that time was $1.30 out of every one hundred.

- The efficiency gain reflects ongoing efforts to control costs. During the 1980s, SSA carried out Project 17,000, which reduced employment in the agency by 17,000 employees.

- Outside Kansas City, large caves have been developed as industrial storage facilities, and one can drive underground on roads that run through the caves, accompanied by large trucks that deliver and receive materials at the storage facilities. The SSA Public Service Center (PSC) in Kansas City operates a file storage facility in one of these caves, containing millions of file folders. SSA employees work in this facility, communicating information from the files to other employees in the PSC offices downtown, who need information from the files to process client claims and requests. The PSC operates this storage facility to hold down costs. It is much less expensive to store the files in this remote site than to store them in office space in downtown Kansas City.

- SSA has proficiently advanced the computerization of claims processing, with computers now performing many of the functions that employees once performed.

- In 1995, the rankings of a major national survey of customer satisfaction with telephone service found that the SSA ranked number one in the nation. Others high in the ratings included Southwest Airlines; L.L. Bean; Nordstrom; Xerox; Disney; Saturn; Federal Express; and AT&T Universal Credit. Mutual fund companies ranked 8th, and variable annuity providers ranked 11th; these rankings are noteworthy because these companies provide services roughly similar to those of the Social Security Administration (Gore 1995, 49–51).

- In the 1970s, SSA reorganized the structure for claims processing in their large public service centers (Rainey and Rainey 1986). To solve a problem of excessive delays in processing the claims, SSA created work modules of about forty people each, that included all the specialists necessary to process a claim from beginning to end. The work modules were essentially teams that worked on a particular set of cases—much like having work teams build automobiles rather than manufacturing them on assembly lines. The change to these modules was painful, difficult, innovative, well-led, well-managed, and very successful. This provides an excellent example of effective leadership of major organizational change (H.G. Rainey 1997, 344–48).

Significantly, one can also point to an example about a very distinct agency, the U.S. Department of Defense. In the Gulf War, the military performed so well in certain ways that one could call the results virtually miraculous. In the years after Vietnam, authors made national reputations and became talk show celebrities by criticizing the poor management and leadership of the U.S. military. Whether or not one approved of the Gulf War, and in spite of many controversies and criticisms related to it, the success in actually carrying out the operations (including related functions such as logistic support) was so evident, with such a low number of casualties on the part of the U.S. and allied forces, that it has to be striking to anyone at all familiar with military operations.

One can point to other examples as well—such as the Centers for Disease Control—that typically receive favorable assessments of their general performance and professionalism, and still others such as those described by authors cited in this article (e.g., Denhardt 1993; Holzer and Callahan 1998; Wolf 1993 and 1997). Gold (1982), for example, identifies as well-managed, successful organizations the U.S. Forest Service, the U.S. Customs Service, the U.S. Passport Office, and the governments of Sunnyvale, California, and Charlotte, North Carolina. Wolf (1997) identifies the Bureau of Standards in the Com-

merce Department between 1917 and 1924 as the agency most highly rated for effectiveness in his large sample of agencies, thus suggesting that effective public agencies have been around for a long time. Significantly, also, Osborne and Gaebler's (1992) very influential proposals for reforms of public management draw almost exclusively on examples of practices that already exist in governmental organizations. The examples illustrate the point that in spite of immensely complex issues over what performance means and how one assesses it, public agencies often perform very well.

Mixed Results of Privatization

Another indication of effective performance by public agencies comes from the limited success of privatization initiatives. Assessments of the privatization of public services generally tend to report savings that result from privatization, but the results also show a mixed pattern with many instances where no savings were achieved, and with few findings of the very large savings projected by some proponents of privatization. The more carefully designed the study, the smaller the reported savings (e.g., Gill and Rainey 1997). Similarly, evaluation of the privatization of state-owned enterprises is much more complicated than its aggressive proponents have projected (Durant, Legge, and Moussios 1998). These limited successes of privatization support Simon's assertion, quoted at the beginning of this article, that public organizations can and often do perform as well as private firms.

Lowery (1997), among others, helps to explain why one should expect mixed results from certain types of privatization when he analyzes quasi market failures, such as the failure of a market to develop for the contract (i.e., there may be little competition for the contract). As Lowery points out, the aggressive proponents of privatization implicitly rely on the dubious assumption that the bureaucrats who could not manage effectively before contracting-out suddenly become transformed into highly efficient and effective managers of the development and monitoring of contracts. The mixed results suggest that the success of privatization initiatives depends heavily on sound management by government employees, and they return us to the questions: When and how do government agencies and the people in them perform well? Why would bureaucrats who otherwise have weak incentives for efficiency, or who otherwise face dysfunctional incentives and information patterns, be motivated to have a successful contracting process?

Power Sharing and the Hollow State

In addition, the extension of privatization arrangements, and the increasingly *networked* or *hollow state* character of many public programs, strains the depiction of the public bureaucracy as a centralized, retentive, monolithic entity. If so centralized and retentive, why has the bureaucracy allowed all this privatization, and how could it remain so centralized and retentive if it is sharing power with so many entities (Kettl 1993; Milward, Provan, and Else 1993)? These developments, then, indicate the need to rethink the more negative depictions of public bureaucracy and to consider theories that explain effective government agencies.

Business Blunders and Generic Theories of Management

Business firms produce abundant examples of waste, inefficiency, blundering, and fraud, even in the most reputable and admired firms. This raises the issue of whether market exposure actually causes business firms to perform more effectively than nonmarket government agencies. A rich tradition in organization and management theory involves a generic perspective on those topics. This tradition is the idea that distinctions between public and private, and for-profit and nonprofit organizations amount to stereotypes and oversimplifications (H.G. Rainey 1997, 55ff). Many scholars who study organizations emphasize the commonalities among organizations, especially among those that purportedly differ by location in the public and private sectors. Simon (1998, 11), in the assertion mentioned above and quoted at the

outset, provides an example of this perspective. Significantly, in relation to the later sections of this article, he attributes the prospects for effective public organizations to, among other factors, the presence of dedicated public servants who are motivated not by narrow economic self-interest but by organizational loyalty and identification (and by implication, an ideal of public service). Simon also argues that effective public administration is essential to democracy. He thus quite dramatically implies the need to seek explanations and theories of effective government organizations.

Models of Excellence in Government Organizations

To develop a theory of effective government agencies, one obviously has to decide how to proceed. Lowery (1997), while not directly pursuing models of effective agencies, suggests employing concepts and methods from economics-based and public choice theory to analyze some of the oversimplifications of those same approaches. His analysis of quasi market failures develops useful concepts for elaborating that discussion. The approach in this article, however, focuses more on government agencies and their general effectiveness, and it draws more on case studies and empirical research in public administration and public bureaucracy as well as concepts from organization and management theory. The propositions advanced later will draw on conclusions from many of the authors on successful leadership and management who are cited above. Some of those authors concentrate on one part of the elephant such as leadership, mission, or culture, and some draw only implicit conclusions about linkages to organizational effectiveness. The full group of references is not easily summarized here.

One subset of the references, however, includes efforts to characterize government agencies that perform efficiently. These profiles represent efforts to develop models of excellent organizations and to specify their attributes. Exhibit 10.2 summarizes some of these profiles. An elaborate review and cri-

Exhibit 10.2   Characteristics of High Performance Government Agencies

	Gold (1982)	STEP (1985)	Wilson (1989)
Mission/public orientation	Emphasize clear mission and objectives	Closer contact with customers to better understand their needs	Mission is clear and reflects a widely shared and warmly endorsed organizational culture External political support
Leadership/ managing employees	Employees take pride in the organization and its product Focus on treating employees fairly and respectfully through honest and open communication Emphasize delegation of responsibility and authority as widely as possible Management aims at challenging and encouraging people Management emphasizes innovative ways of managing	Increased discretionary authority for managers and employees for greater control over accountability Increased employee participation taps their knowledge, skills, and commitment	Executives command loyalty, define and instill a clear sense of mission, attract talented workers, and make exacting demands of subordinates Leaders make peer expectations serve the organization Maximize discretionary authority for operators Executive takes resposibility for organizational maintenance Bottom-up implementation perspective
Task design/ work environment	Places great value on the people in the organization Job tasks and goals are clear	Partnerships to allow the sharing of knowledge, expertise, and other resources State-of-the-art productivity improvement techniques Improved work measurements to provide a base for planning and implementing service improvements and worker evaluation	Clearly defined goals Widespread agreement on how critical tasks are performed Agency autonomy to develop operational goals from which tasks are designed Ability to control or keep contextual goals in proper perspective.

Note: Portions of this exhibit are adapted from Rainey (1997, 359) and from Hale (1996, 139), with portions using Hale's terminology and summary.

Denhardt (1993)	Alliance (1994)	Hale (1996)	Holzer and Callahan (1998)
Dedication to public service and understanding public intent Serving the public, which represents democratic values	Mission clarity and understanding Maintain open and productive communication among stakeholders	Focused mission that is clarified and communicated to organization members	Customer focused Build partnerships with public and private organizations and citizens
Leader demonstrates commitment to mission Manager builds sense of community in organization Manager clearly articulates values Managers insist on high ethical standards Empowered and shared leadership Employees accept responsibility and performance accountability	Empowered employees Organizations allocate resources for continual learning Employees accept accountability to achieve results with rewards and consequences Motivate and inspire people to succeed	Enabling leadership that emphasizes learning, communication, flexibility, sharing, and vision development	Manage for quality using long-term strategic planning with support from top leadership Develop human resources and empower employees through team building, systematic training, recognition, and balancing employee and organizational needs
Pragmatic incrementalism (change is natural, appropriate) Approach to change is creative and humane Commitment to values	Define outcomes and focus on results (performance measures) Institute new work processes as necessary Flexible, adjust nimbly to new conditions Competitive in terms of performance Restructure work processes to meet customer needs	Emphasize learning and carefully support learning, risk taking, training, communication, and work measurement Nurturing-community culture that is supportive and emphasizes teamwork, participation, flexible authority, and effective reward and recognition	Adapt technologies that include open access to data, automation for productivity, cost-effective applications, and cross-cutting techniques that deliver on public demands Measure for performance by establishing goals and measuring results, justifying and allocating as necessary resource requirements, and developing organizational improvement strategies

tique of these efforts is beyond the scope of this article, but the row headings on the left of the exhibit indicate common topics in the profiles, including aspects of the agency mission and public orientation (including public service), leadership and primary means of managing employees, and task design and work environment. Especially as summarized in the exhibit, in ways that cannot do full justice to the analyses, the profiles need much more specification and articulation to move in the direction of a theory. Yet some of their implications are clear, and they show up in the propositions in Exhibit 10.1 and in the discussion of them that follows.

Also of significance are some omissions in the implicit models in Exhibit 10.2. (In the parlance of organizational effectiveness researchers, they mostly represent *internal process models*.) Additional factors receive emphasis in other research on agency effectiveness. Wolf (1993) analyzed forty-four case studies of federal agencies to construct measures of the agencies' characteristics and their relationships to the organization's effectiveness. As do most of the profiles in Exhibit 10.2, his findings indicated the importance of leadership and sense of mission. In addition, however, he found important a variable representing political autonomy (that included *universal political support* and/or freedom from direction by political authorities). This variable indicates the importance of relations with oversight authorities and other external stakeholders, a topic that receives little or no emphasis in the profiles in Exhibit 10.2. It also suggests the need for a supportive and delegative role by those authorities that allows the agency reasonable autonomy to develop and pursue its mission (cf. Wilson 1989; Meier 1993a).

Propositions and a Framework

As we indicated earlier, Exhibit 10.1 states propositions about effective agencies that draw on the references just cited and on additional references and examples that are described below. Figure 10.1 provides a diagram that suggests a framework linking these propositions and their component concepts. While Exhibit 10.1 does not clearly posit all the rela-

tionships, it bears the implication that all the components in Exhibit 10.1 should be positively related in the more effective agencies. Also, in Figure 10.1 and in the discussion to follow, some of the relationships are hypothesized so clearly that they have sharp and challenging implications for research, theory, and practice.

The Meaning of Effectiveness

In the literature on organization theory, the topic of organizational effectiveness is complex and inconclusive in certain ways, and it involves an unresolved diversity of models, including goal models, internal process models, stakeholder models, resource dependence models, participant satisfaction models, and competing values models (Daft 1998, ch. 2; H.G. Rainey 1997, ch. 6). The discussion here cannot resolve these variations, but it can proceed using a relatively straightforward definition of agency effectiveness: The agency performs well in discharging the administrative and operational functions pursuant to the mission. It achieves the mission as conceived by the organization and its stakeholders, or pursues achievement of it in an evidently successful way. While it skirts some of the controversies over the concept of organizational performance, this approach to effectiveness bears similarities to conceptions some researchers and authors use (Collins and Porras 1994; Gold 1982; Peters and Waterman 1982; Wolf 1997).

This concept of effectiveness refers to whether the agency does well that which it is supposed to do, whether people in the agency work hard and well, whether the actions and procedures of the agency and its members are well suited to achieving its mission, and whether the agency actually achieves its mission. Does it produce the actions and outputs pursuant to the mission or the institutional mandate (Osborne and Gaebler 1992, 351; Wolf 1997), and does it appear to contribute to outcomes indicated by the mission? Did the U.S. military win the Gulf War, does the CDC reduce health risks, and does the Social Security Administration pay benefits expeditiously, accurately, and appropriately, and do all these

Figure 10.1 Characteristics of Effective Government Agencies

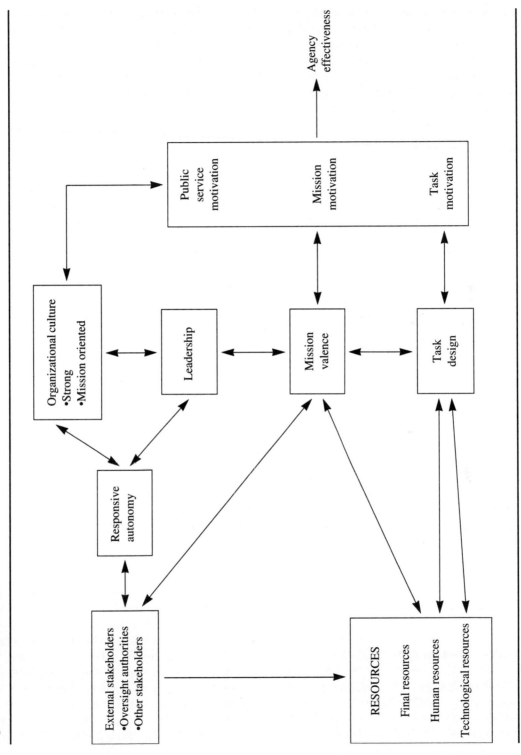

results come in significant part from the activities of the agencies and their members? As additional examples, the Coast Guard has stated as one of its central goals the reduction of accidental deaths and injuries from maritime casualties (U.S. Coast Guard 1996). The National Highway Traffic Safety Administration (1996) includes in its mission the goals of saving lives, preventing injuries, and reducing traffic-related health care problems. Evidence that the agencies' operations have contributed substantially to the achievement of these goals provides evidence of agency effectiveness.

This concept of effectiveness concerns the organization's administrative and operational effectiveness, and not necessarily the effectiveness of the general policy design in which the agency operates. For example, the Social Security Administration may operate the Old Age and Survivors Insurance program very effectively, in the sense that claimants' benefits are expeditiously and accurately authorized, calculated, and paid in ways that provide income security for the clients. The program, however, still may need reform through some form of privatization or some other adjustment because of the fiscal and financial implications of the benefits and benefit schedules that Congress mandated for the program. As another example, the U.S. military performed well in the Gulf War, but critics can dispute or lament the policy decision to proceed with military force. In addition, declaring that the Forest Service is an effective organization does not resolve controversies over the use of public forests for timbering by private firms.

Numerous other conceptual and methodological complexities can be discussed at length. The most important objective of this article, however, is to advance concepts and generalizations useful to theorizing about agency performance, so it is best simply to move to the propositions themselves.

Relations with Stakeholders

The propositions use the term *stakeholders* from the organization theory literature to refer to persons, groups, and institutions that have an interest in the activities and outcomes of the organization sufficient to draw their participation and attention to the agency. Oversight authorities such as legislative, executive, and judicial authorities are one obvious component of this part of the framework. Other stakeholders, such as constituent and client groups, the general public, and various partners and suppliers such as contractors, exert less legally formal influences on government agencies.

Effective agencies will have oversight authorities that are supportive, delegative, and attentive to agency mission accomplishment. The authorities will devote attention to the agency, in a demanding way that emphasizes effective performance. Yet the authorities also will tend to be supportive in the sense of providing resources and authorization necessary to support good performance. They will be delegative in that they will refrain from micromanagement and extensive intervention in decisions about the management of the agency.

As an example of these conditions of oversight, one can point to the response of congressional leaders such as Wilbur Mills when the Social Security Administration was having serious problems with backlogs in claims processing during the 1970s. Congress had expanded the types of coverage and benefits of the social security program, and the population of entitled persons had grown rapidly. Decisions about claims became more complicated, more varied, and simply more voluminous. More claims took longer to process, and citizens complained to their congressmen about delays in receiving a response about their claims and inquiries. To oversimplify for brevity, Mills and other congressional leaders essentially told Commissioner Robert Ball to fix the problem and accepted Ball's assurances that such efforts were underway. SSA actually took some time to adopt reforms, while devoting considerable attention to diagnosis and planning. The ultimate solution, which involved reorganizing the major payment centers (public service centers) into work modules where teams worked together to process claims, proved highly successful. While demanding a solution, congressional leaders delegated the selection and management of the solution to the agency's leaders. By contrast, in more recent years observers have expressed concern that rapid turnover in the top executives at SSA, due to efforts by presidential administrations to increase their control over the agency, has damaged effective management within the agency (Rainey and Rainey 1986; U.S. GAO 1986). As a roughly similar example, the highly effective Gulf War operations were conducted relatively autonomously by commanders there, without extensive control or intervention from Washington. As an example of the failure of oversight officials to focus on mission accomplishment, the Federal Emergency Management Agency (FEMA) had a reputation for weak performance at one point, frequently attributed to oversight officials' use of the agency as a haven for political cronies.

Other Stakeholders

Summarizing research on the influence of interest groups on public bureaucracies, Meier (1993a) concludes that *an agency is better able to obtain resources and autonomy of operations when it has interest groups that, in addition to being attentive and interested, are geographically dispersed, diverse along various dimensions (such as demographic makeup), mobilizable, and multiple.* That is, an agency loses autonomy if it is captured by an interest group, and it gains autonomy and influence if it has supporters that are diverse but mobilizable. The agency can play diffcrent groups off against each other but, as is elaborately discussed in the literature on public bureaucracy and public management, it usually needs the support of interest groups to gain resources. In addition, as is implied in the discussion of issue networks, policy subsystems, and subgovernments, other actors, such as experts, play a part in this process.

Agencies will also tend to be more effective when they have favorable public support. This includes generally favorable public opinion and media coverage.

More effective agencies also will manage well their relations with allies and partners (Holzer and Callahan 1998) *such as contractors and other public, private, and nonprofit entities with which they interact in carrying out their work.* For example, a growing literature now details the requirements for effective management of contracts and privatization initiatives (e.g., Globerman and Vining 1996; Donahue 1990; Gill and Rainey 1997; Kettl 1993; Lowery 1997; H.G. Rainey 1997; Rehfuss 1989) as well as the effective management of networks of actors and organizations more generally (Provan and Milward 1995; O'Toole 1997). Agencies that have in place systems that meet these requirements should more effectively manage such relations and thereby enhance their own effectiveness.

Autonomy

Government agencies will be more effective when they have higher levels of autonomy in relation to external stakeholders, but not extremely high levels of autonomy. (The relationship between autonomy and effectiveness is curvilinear.)

When oversight authorities are supportive and delegative, as we have described above, they grant autonomy to the agency. Autonomy to manage its mission and tasks tends to enhance an agency's performance of the mission and tasks. Yet the following discussion of organizational culture describes examples of agencies that became too insular. The SSA example above illustrate the responsiveness of the agency and its leaders to the demands of stakeholders. An effective agency's autonomy does not imply extreme isolation from communication and exchange with external stakeholders; it should be conceived as a responsive autonomy. Wolf (1998) concludes from his data that agency leaders earn grants of autonomy from oversight officials through skillful management of relations with external stakeholders.

Mission Valence

The higher the mission valence of the government agency, the more effectively the agency will perform. The concept of mission valence draws on the concept of *valence* from the expectancy theory of work motivation. Formulations of that theory use the concept of valence from chemistry (the positive or negative charges of atomic particles) to refer to the positive or negative attractiveness of an outcome of behavior—

to how good or bad, attractive or unattractive, a person considers an outcome to be (H.G. Rainey 1997, 229–32). An agency's mission can be attractive or abhorrent (e.g., combat, war) to individuals. The more engaging, attractive, and worthwhile the mission is to people, the more the agency will be able to attract support from those people, to attract some of them to join the agency, and to motivate them to perform well in the agency (depending on some other conditions we will discuss).

The external stakeholders and the members of the organization interactively establish the organization's mission. The mission is the general social contribution and purpose of the agency and its related general goals. The military services must defend the nation, be prepared for combat engagements and, when necessary, to win them. The Social Security Administration provides income security for retired persons and their survivors. The Centers for Disease Control must defend the populace against diseases and other dangers to health. Any organization has a mission, in this general sense, whether or not the organization has joined the herd of organizations issuing mission statements. The mission has higher valence when it has higher levels of the dimensions listed in Exhibit 10.1 (cf. Behn 1991, 67–69; DiIulio 1994; Hargrove and Glidewell 1990; Wilson 1989).

Organizational Culture

Effective government agencies have a strong organizational culture, effectively linked to mission accomplishment.

Organizational culture is probably the most overused and loosely used term in contemporary management discourse. Journalists regularly use it to interpret developments in business firms and other organizations. In any brainstorming or planning session of government employees that is concerned with organizational improvement, leadership, or related matters, participants will repeatedly refer to the need to change the cultures of agencies. These casual uses of the term typically refer to a subdimension of culture, such as employees' attitudes toward risk taking, but their common usage suggests the need for a concept such as culture. Scholars, of course, have devoted much attention to culture and regularly assert its importance to organizational analysis (Schein 1992; Trice and Beyer 1993), including the analysis of government agencies (Wilson 1989; H.G. Rainey 1997, 273–81).

Culture refers to patterns of shared meaning in organizations, including shared values and beliefs about appropriate behaviors and actions. It also refers to such matters as the nature of the organization and its relation to other entities or to the basis for authority in the organization. Culture can be manifest in, and influenced by, symbols, ceremonies, statements, and actions of leaders. The proposition above asserts that a strong organizational culture will be related positively to agency effectiveness when the culture is effectively linked to mission accomplishment. The literature now contains numerous examples of strong or salient cultures in agencies that promote the agencies' effectiveness in accomplishing their missions and the roles of leaders in shaping such cultures (e.g., Doig and Hargrove 1987; Lewis 1980 and 1987; Maynard-Moody, Stull, and Mitchell 1986; Mashaw 1983, 216; Meier 1993a; Rainey 1997, 273–81; Wilson 1989). In addition, authors suggest guidelines for leaders in their efforts to influence and develop culture (Schein 1992; Trice and Beyer 1993; Yukl 1998).

Like other propositions advanced here, this proposition about strong agency culture runs into complexities and potential controversy, since a strong culture could make an agency impervious to external oversight and control, resistant to innovation, or otherwise poorly adapted to imperatives of its environment. Examples of such a problem include Hoover and the FBI, and the case of a public health agency in Kansas that became so focused on professional autonomy that the legislature ultimately intervened to assert authority over the agency (Maynard-Moody et al. 1986). Strong culture does not need to imply insularity or arrogance. Values strongly espoused in a strong culture can include adaptiveness, surveillance of the environment, and responsiveness. The two examples above can be interpreted as illustrations of ineffective linkages to agency mission that in the long run damaged the agencies' effectiveness.

Leadership

The more effective the leadership of the agency, the more effective the agency. More effective leadership is characterized by more stability, multiplicity, commitment to mission, effective goal setting, and effective administrative and political coping.

Scholars regularly cite leadership as an essential element in the success of public agencies. Leadership has long been treated as an important determinant of an agency's power and influence (Meier 1993a, 75–77; Rourke 1984). More recently, numerous authors describe and analyze effective, innovative, and exemplary leaders in government agencies (Behn 1991; Cooper and Wright 1992; Doig and Hargrove 1987; Hargrove and Glidewell 1990; Riccucci 1995; Terry 1995). As we noted earlier, Wolf (1993) reports empirical evidence of a significant role of leadership in achieving agency effectiveness. Holzer and Callahan (1998, 160) report results of a survey of winners of an award for exemplary state and local public service initiatives, in which the respondents rate the support of top agency executives as the most important factor in the success of agency innovations.

Like most fundamental topics in the social sciences, the topic of leadership is vast, richly elaborated, and inconclusive (Yukl 1998). Enough listings of desirable leadership skills and qualities could be gathered to build another great pyramid. They vary widely, and none of them can claim conclusive validation. One could choose any of a number of such listings, but one can reasonably choose, as a general conception of leadership skills for government agencies, the *Executive Core Competencies* of the Senior Executive Service (U.S. OPM 1998). The competencies include the following: leading change (including leadership competencies of creativity and innovation and service motivation, among others); leading people (e.g., conflict management, team building); results driven [sic] (e.g., accountability, customer service); business acumen (financial, human resources, and technology management); and building coalitions and communication (e.g., interpersonal skills, partnering, political savvy). From many sources in the leadership literature, one can add that leaders need a basic motivation for the role, along with a drive to take responsibility, to lead others, and to make a difference.

In addition to such general conceptions, however, the subdimensions of leadership cited in the proposition above and in Exhibit 10.1 seem particularly important to leadership in government agencies. First, scholars and experts emphasize the problems that result from rapid turnover of top executives in public agencies (e.g., Warwick 1975; Heclo 1978; U.S. GAO 1986). Conversely, various researchers have reported an apparent linkage between stable, long-term leadership—often from career civil servants—and effective performance of public agencies (Behn 1991; DiIulio 1994; Doig and Hargrove 1987; G.W. Rainey 1990; Rainey and Rainey 1986; Riccucci 1995). Excessive stability of leadership can build a harmful insularity, of course, and there are also important examples of generalist leaders such as Eliot Richardson who earned reputations as excellent government executives through a variety of relatively short-term posts in different agencies. Riccucci (1995) provides additional examples of effective leaders without long-term governmental experience. Leadership stability, then, needs to be considered in association with other dimensions in Exhibit 10.1, which hypothesizes a curvilinear relationship between leadership stability and agency effectiveness.

Shared leadership, for example, can make a short-term leader more influential on agency effectiveness. The literature on management in both the public and private sectors increasingly emphasizes the importance of sharing leadership roles among teams or cadres of leaders, as well as the empowerment of individuals to assume roles in the leadership of various parts of the work (e.g., Behn 1991; Denhardt 1993; Huber and Glick 1993; Sims and Lorenzi 1992; Terry 1995, ch. 4). As an example of a skillful approach to shared leadership, one can cite James Webb's creation of a leadership triad at NASA and his emphasis on maximal leadership continuity in the agency (Lambright 1987). Although he did not possess scientific skills, he established a strong relationship with assistant administrators who did have those skills, and he thereby enhanced his own legitimacy, and more importantly the quality and legitimacy of the decisions of the leadership team. Somewhat similarly, Nancy Hanks, as the early and influential chair of the National

Endowment for the Arts, empowered her deputy chairman to serve as the chief spokesperson for the agency, to complement her own abilities and her preference for working in small, informal settings (Wyszomirski 1987). Such skillful exercises in empowerment and team leadership can help even short-term political appointees to ensure that their influences on the agency endure (Ingraham 1988).

The problem of turnover at the top of many agencies also makes a strong commitment to an agency's mission an important aspect of leadership. The most effective agency executives, such as Robert Ball, Hyman Rickover, Nancy Hanks, James Webb, and Gifford Pinchot, all embody such a commitment. Analysts of their careers conclude that they displayed a desire to "make a difference" (Doig and Hargrove 1987, 11) coupled with an ability to see new possibilities, which led them to focus on the agency and its mission as an avenue for exerting influence on the development and pursuit of new possibilities.

The most frequently repeated observation about the distinctive characteristics of public agencies concerns the vagueness, multiplicity, and mutual conflict among agency goals. Therefore, skillful leadership through mission development and through goal setting in relation to the mission contribute significantly to agency effectiveness. The literature now offers numerous examples of such leadership practices (e.g., Behn 1991; Denhardt 1993; Riccucci 1995; Wilson 1989).

Finally, it seems to be obvious that leaders of effective public agencies will display skills in coping with the political and administrative pressures and constraints of their roles. Yet the importance of this dimension of leadership is reflected in frequent expressions of concern that these constraints penalize effective leadership and make it scarce in public agencies (e.g., National Academy of Public Administration 1986; Thompson 1993, 18–22). Significantly, accounts of the most influential and innovative agency leaders emphasize their ability to turn into opportunities the constraints that supposedly impede many executives and to cope with the pressures and complexities of their roles (Ban 1995; Doig and Hargrove 1987; Hargrove and Glidewell 1990; Lewis 1980 and 1987; Riccucci 1995).

Task Design

The more the task design in the agency provides extrinsic and intrinsic rewards to individuals and groups, the more effective the agency.

In addition to the general mission, there are more specific characteristics of the work people do, and in the framework these are included in a broad conception of *task*. Included in this conception of task are those factors associated with an individual's relatively specific ongoing activities that provide extrinsic and intrinsic rewards for work. Organizational behavior researchers commonly define extrinsic rewards as those mediated externally to the individual and provided by the organization, such as pay, promotion, and physical conditions of work. Intrinsic rewards are mediated internally to the individual and include psychological rewards such as interest in the work, enjoyment of the work, a sense of growth and development, and a sense of worthwhile accomplishment. Organizational psychologists have developed measures of the motivating potential of jobs, which assess the degree to which the job provides autonomy, task significance, task identity, feedback from the work, and skill variety. These factors tend to increase intrinsic work motivation (Hackman and Oldham 1980). This conception of task design is intended to include conditions mentioned in the profiles of excellent public organizations described in earlier sections, such as whether the members are empowered, whether they are organized into teams and have a teamwork orientation, and whether decisions are participative.

Included in this conception of task and task design are extrinsic rewards associated with the more specific, day to day work of the individual, such as those that are mentioned above. These rewards will also depend, of course, on organizational structures and policies such as human resource management/personnel policies.

The distinction between task and mission is useful in analyzing whether they are two distinct sources of incentive and motivation in government agencies that are separable but that need to be linked together. For example, consider a professor who is excited about her work for the day. How much is she motivated by the overall mission or general societal contribution of the university, and how much by the intrinsic rewards from her enjoyment of the more specific activities of teaching and research? A NASA employee may enjoy his job designing and implementing training procedures for space shuttle astronauts. How much additional motivation does he derive from the overall mission of advancing space exploration and travel?

Utilization of Technology and Development of Human Resources

Exhibit 10.1 hypothesizes that utilization of technology and development of human resources relate to agency effectiveness, because Holzer and Callahan (1998) emphasize the importance of these processes in innovative government agencies and because of the obvious importance of such processes in building the internal capacity of an agency. Holzer and Callahan provide elaboration on effective utilization of technology and human resources; other examples and case studies abound. SSA, for example, has used computerization to improve markedly the efficiency and accuracy of case processing. Herbert Kaufman's classic study, *The Forest Ranger,* provides case illustrations of the effective development of human resources.

Professionalism

Various authors attribute agency effectiveness to professionalism among the members of the agency (Brehm and Gates 1997; Wilson 1989; Wolf 1993 and 1998). Authors in public administration have analyzed professionalism in that field, and an elaborate literature examines the topic of professionalism in sociology and organization theory. This latter material develops the concept more elaborately than do some of the authors who write about professionalism in public agencies. For example, sociologists define professions as occupations with the following characteristics: they apply advanced skills based on theoretical knowledge; they require advanced training; they require testing of competence through examinations and other means; they are organized into professional associations; they emphasize adherence to a code of conduct;

they espouse altruistic service. Members of such professionalized occupations tend to have values and beliefs that accord with the occupational characteristics, such as belief in collegial maintenance of standards among professionals, identification with other professionals, and commitment to professional norms. Authors on professionalism in public agencies tend to define it less elaborately—as involving specialized skills that require advanced education or training, membership in professional groups outside the agency (Wilson 1989), or simply a commitment to professional norms of performance and behavior and to do the work right and well (Brehm and Gates 1997).

Professionalism can enhance an agency's performance by increasing its autonomy, due to the social status and intellectual authority and independence of professionals in the agency (Wolf 1998). In addition, professional norms and technical training provide incentives and guidelines for individuals in the agencies (Wilson 1989; Brehm and Gates 1997).

Motivation

Effective government agencies have high levels of motivation among their members, including high levels of public service motivation, mission motivation, and task motivation.

The preceding propositions lead to this one. The framework and propositions generally assert the important role of motivation that stimulates effort and effective behaviors among people in the organization. The proposition refers to all of the several forms of motivation to emphasize the important questions: Can we actually conceive and validate these three separate forms? Is there a general motive to serve the public? Is it stimulated in government agencies, stimulated to higher levels in some than others, and in turn translated into motivation, effort, and effective behavior?

Public Service Motivation

Public service motivation can be defined as a general altruistic motivation to serve the interests of a community of people, a state, a nation, or humankind.

Major social scientists recently have referred to evolutionary developments that have fostered in human beings motives and attitudes conducive to communal and collective behaviors, including trust, reciprocity, and identification with organizations (Ostrom 1998; Simon 1998). Since animals display altruistic behaviors, behaviors that involve self-sacrifice on the part of their groups, these motives should be considered fundamental in humans as well, and in some persons as strong as the more extrinsic motives for money or other material gain. Such forms of motivation have been part of human discourse since classic times, when, for example, Athenians pledged to leave their city better than they found it.

A form of public service motivation has been part of discourse in public administration for a long time. Frederickson and Hart (1985), for example, discuss a "patriotism of benevolence" that involves benevolent impulses and behaviors toward a broad community. They define it as an affection for all people in the nation and a devotion to defending their basic rights, as granted by enabling documents such as the Constitution. Frederickson (1997) treats such a motive, and associated ethical and equitable behaviors, as a central theme in public administration.

Interestingly, however, this topic has attracted not nearly as much systematic research as one might have expected. Various surveys have found that government executives and managers tend to express a motive to serve the public or society in a worthwhile way (e.g., Sikula 1973). Kilpatrick, Cummings, and Jennings (1964) found that federal executives, scientists, and engineers gave higher ratings than did their counterparts in business to work-related values such as the importance of doing your best, even if you dislike your work, the importance of doing work that is worthwhile to society, and the importance of helping others. H.G. Rainey (1983) found that state agency managers rated the "opportunity to engage in meaningful public service" as a more important work reward than did managers in large business firms. Among the very large sample of executives and managers in the *Federal Employee Attitude Surveys,* high percentages of the respondents who enter the federal government rate public service and having an impact on public affairs as the most important reasons to

enter federal service; very low percentages of these groups rate salary and job security as important attractions (Crewson 1995, 94). Analyzing other large social surveys such as the *General Social Survey,* Crewson (1997) also finds that public sector respondents, as compared to private sector respondents, place a higher value on work that is useful to society and that helps others. These results and other findings within such surveys suggest the form that general service motives in government may take—placing a high value on work that helps others and benefits society as a whole, on a degree of self-sacrifice, and on responsibility and integrity. Public managers often mention such motives (Hartman and Weber 1980; Lasko 1980; Kelman 1989; Sandeep 1989).

Seeking to refine the conception of public service motives, Perry and Wise (1990) suggest that public service motives can fall into three categories: *instrumental motives,* including participation in policy formulation, commitment to a public program because of personal identification, and advocacy for a special or private interest; *norm-based motives,* including a desire to serve the public interest, loyalty to duty and to government, and social equity; and *affective motives,* including commitment to a program based on a conviction about its social importance and the patriotism of benevolence (Frederickson and Hart 1985; Frederickson 1997).

Perry (1996a and 1997) provides more recent evidence of the dimensions of a general public service motive and ways to assess it. He analyzed survey questionnaire responses from about four hundred people, including managers and employees in various government and business organizations, and graduate and undergraduate students. He developed scales for four dimensions of public service motivation: attraction to public policy making, commitment to the public interest and civic duty, compassion, and self-sacrifice. He found higher levels of some of these factors associated with religious involvement and family background.

These findings and those cited above show that public service motivation is a complex concept that deserves more attention. The evidence, however, strongly supports the existence of a general form of public service motivation that tends to be more prevalent among government employees than private sector employees. The evidence also suggests that this form of motivation involves a general motive to provide significant service that benefits the community, the public, or society in dutiful, compassionate, and self-sacrificing ways.

Mission Motivation

The above proposition about motivation also holds that high levels of mission motivation contribute significantly to the effectiveness of public agencies. Why coin a term such as *mission motivation* and propose it as a new concept? Wilson (1989) describes the existence of a *sense of mission* in such agencies as the Army Corps of Engineers and the Forestry Service. Various authors describe how leaders develop a sense of mission for their agencies and inculcate it into the culture of the agency through goal setting, symbolic actions, and other techniques (e.g., Behn 1991; Cooper 1987; Denhardt 1993). The proposition about mission motivation asserts that members have perceptions of the mission of the agency and may be highly motivated to contribute to the achievement of the mission. When so motivated, an individual will extend effort and seek to perform well in ways that he or she perceives to be related to accomplishing the mission.[4]

This pattern of motivation differs from public service motivation, although the propositions and framework assert that they have a strong relation to each other in effective agencies. While public service motivation focuses on altruistic service that benefits a community or a larger population, mission motivation has as its target or objective the mission of the agency. For example, this distinction raises the issue of how much of a person's motivation is accounted for by a sense that her actions contribute to a general public service, and how much is accounted for by this sense of mission? When a tank commander in the Desert Storm operation works hard to contribute to an effective combat initiative by his unit, how much is he motivated by a perception or belief that he is contributing a valuable service to the nation or to hu-

mankind, and how much by a perception or belief that his actions contribute to the mission of winning combat engagements in defense of the nation? How much is a module manager in a public service center of the Social Security Administration motivated by a belief that her actions contribute to something worthwhile and important to the nation as a whole, and how much is motivated by a belief that sound management of her module will contribute to the mission of providing income security for the retired people who have earned it through their contributions to the program?

An earlier section introduced the concept of mission valence because of its relevance to the role of mission motivation. A mission can have a high valence for an individual and attract that person to an agency. Members of NASA, for example, observe that many people came to NASA and remained there because of interest in and excitement about the mission of space exploration, when they could have worked in the private sector for higher pay. Motivation in organizations always involves at least two general steps—first, joining and staying; second, working hard and well. One can take the first step without taking the second (March and Simon 1958). High levels of mission valence will tend to attract certain individuals who will self-select into the organization on the basis of the valence of the mission for them, but then their levels of mission motivation will further depend on their perceptions about the linkage of their work to the mission. Buchanan (1974 and 1975) some years ago reported evidence that idealistic people may enter the public service and later become discouraged because they cannot see the linkage of their work activities to their ideals. Through leadership practices such as those described earlier, the agency must sharpen and make salient the relations of individuals' work to the mission. In turn, the perceived linkage of the mission to public service values can enhance both mission valence and mission motivation, such that in the government agencies that perform the best, members will show both high levels of mission motivation and high levels of public service motivation and will feel that the mission of the agency contributes to general worthwhile public service.

Task Motivation

The distinction made earlier in this article between the general concept of task motivation and the concepts of public service motivation and mission motivation serves a purpose of distinguishing among patterns of motivation. Returning to the example of the highly motivated professor, consider how much of that person's motivation might derive from a sense of contributing a valuable public service; how much from a sense of contributing to the university's mission of advancing teaching, research, and public service; and how much from enjoyment of the specific work itself? Other examples of the task motivation at issue here include a NASA employee who finds it fun and exciting to develop and implement safety and emergency drills for training astronauts. Also, a district office manager for the Social Security Administration enjoys the tasks of managing the office, supervising personnel, and engaging in public relations activities such as appearing on a local radio show to answer questions about the social security programs.

These examples illustrate the broad concept of task motivation advanced here. They reflect the influence of the relatively specific and immediate extrinsic and intrinsic rewards available through the person's role in the organization, as described earlier in the discussion of task design. These factors can be independent of, or weakly related to, public service motivation and mission motivation. For example, agency employees may express high levels of motivation in spite of low levels of some of these rewards, such as favorable physical surroundings at work. Ultimately, however, the framework and the proposals hold that agency effectiveness will be highest where organizational design, task design, leadership, and other factors produce desirable levels of extrinsic and intrinsic rewards through tasks and where members of the agency perceive that task activities and accomplishments contribute to mission accomplishment, which in turn contributes to the provision of a worthwhile and valuable public service.

Ultimately, too, the propositions and framework hypothesize that the several forms of motivation play a significant role in determining agency effectiveness, as do the other factors such as leadership and culture. These actually posit very debatable and researchable concepts and relations that might be opposed by other interpretations. For example, one might argue that external forces, such as technological and economic factors, drive the performance of public agencies by providing new technologies and human and financial resources, such that the espoused motives of bureaucrats and the dramaturgy of leadership provide merely a superficial, self-justificatory labeling for developments that are essentially out of the control of the people in the organizations. Such alternative interpretations, along with the general importance of the performance of government agencies, provide all the more reason to continue to develop theories to explain their performance.

Direction for Further Development and the Problem of Parsimony

The concepts and relations in the propositions advanced here need more development in a variety of ways. In particular, however, many related concepts and topics that are not discussed here need further consideration in relation to the propositions and agency effectiveness. These include typologies of agencies and differences by type of agency; organizational socialization processes; organizational commitment or identification; performance measures and their availability and adequacy; and numerous others.

The lengthy list of variables in Exhibit 10.1 raises the question of whether the list can and should be pared down to a more parsimonious set. In a sense, the set of variables is not so vast if one conceives it as basis for a LISREL analysis or a similar analysis that would treat the subdimensions under the more general variables as indicators of the more general variable that would factor together in measures of it. As a hypothetical statement about the most important variables, however, based on the literature reviewed and cited in this article, one can posit that the variables for the following concepts will emerge as the most important: relations with external authorities and stakeholders, autonomy, leadership, professionalism, and motivation among members.

A Symbiosis of Freedom?

As we noted earlier, Simon (1998) emphasizes the essential role of effective public administration in maintaining the strength of democracy. Other social scientists have remarked on the interesting tendency of democratic systems to coincide with free market systems, and conservative economists often have mentioned the need for an effective, albeit limited, government in a prosperous economy. Analysis of effective government agencies should be part of a new dialogue on the role of government and public administration (e.g., Durant 1998) that recognizes that effective organizations in business, government, and the nonprofit sector benefit each other. Pursuit of systematic explanations and theories about effective government agencies should continue as part of the effort to enhance these mutual benefits.

References

Ban, C. 1995. *How Do Public Managers Manage?* San Francisco: Jossey-Bass.

Barton, A.H. 1980. "A Diagnosis of Bureaucratic Maladies." In *Making Bureaucracies Work,* C. H. Weiss and A. H. Barton, eds. Thousand Oaks, Calif.: Sage.

Barzelay, M. 1992. *Breaking Through Bureaucracy.* Berkeley: University of California Press.

Behn, R.D. 1991. *Leadership Counts.* Cambridge, Mass.: Harvard University Press.

Bozeman, B. 1999. *Bureaucracy and Red Tape.* Upper Saddle River, N.J.: Prentice-Hall.

Brehm, J., and Gates, S. 1997. *Working, Shirking, and Sabotage: Bureaucratic Response to a Democratic Public.* Ann Arbor: University of Michigan Press.

Buchanan, B. 1974. "Government Managers, Business Executives, and Organizational Commitment." *Public Administration Review* 35: 339–47.

———. 1975. "Red Tape and the Service Ethic: Some Unexpected Differences Between Public and Private Managers." *Administration and Society* 6: 423–38.

Caiden, G. 1991. "What Really Is Public Maladministration?" *Public Administration Review* 51(6): 486–93.

Cohen, S., and W. Eimicke. 1995. *The New Effective Public Manager.* San Francisco: Jossey-Bass.

Collins, J.C., and J.I. Porras. 1994. *Built to Last: Successful Habits of Visionary Companies.* New York: Harper Business.

Cooper, J.M. 1987. "Gifford Pinchot Creates a Forest Service." In Doig and Hargrove, eds., 63–95.

Cooper, T.L., and N.D. Wright. 1992. *Exemplary Public Administrators.* San Francisco: Jossey-Bass.

Crewson, P.E. 1995. "A Comparative Analysis of Public and Private Sector Entrant Quality." *American Journal of Political Science* 39: 628–39.

———. 1997. "Public-Service Motivation: Building Empirical Evidence of Incidence and Effect." *Journal of Public Administration Research and Theory* 7(4): 499–518.

Daft, R.L. 1998. *Organization Theory and Design,* 6th ed. Cincinnati, Ohio: South-Western College Publishing.

Denhardt, R.B. 1993. *The Pursuit of Significance.* Belmont, Calif.: Wadsworth.

DiIulio, J.D. 1994. "Principled Agents: The Cultural Bases of Behavior in a Federal Government Bureaucracy." *Journal of Public Administration Research and Theory* 4(3): 277–318.

Doig, J.W., and E.C. Hargrove, eds. 1987. *Leadership and Innovation: A Biographical Perspective on Entrepreneurs in Government.* Baltimore: Johns Hopkins University Press.

Donahue, J.D. 1990. *The Privatization Decision.* New York: Basic Books.

Downs, A. 1967. *Inside Bureaucracy.* Boston: Little, Brown.

Downs, G.W., and P. Larkey. 1986. *The Search for Government Efficiency: From Hubris to Helplessness.* New York: Random House.

Durant, R.F. 1992. *The Administrative Presidency Revisited: Public Lands, the BLM, and the Reagan Revolution.* Albany: State University of New York Press.

———. 1998. "Agenda Setting, the 'Third Wave,' and the Administrative State." *Administration & Society* 30: 211–47.

Durant, R.F., J.S. Legge, and A. Moussios. 1998. "People, Profits, and Service Delivery: Lessons from the Privatization of British Telecom." *American Journal of Political Science* 42(1): 1:97–117.

Eisner, R. 1998. "Cut Social Security? No, Expand It." *Wall Street Journal,* 16 Dec., p. 22.

Frederickson, H.G. 1997. *The Spirit of Public Administration.* San Francisco: Jossey-Bass.

Frederickson, H.G., and D.K. Hart. 1985. "The Public Service and the Patriotism of Benevolence." *Public Administration Review* 45: 547–53.

Gill, J., and H.G. Rainey. 1997. "The Relationship Between Privatization and Public Management in Georgia State Government." Paper presented at the Southeastern Conference on Public Administration, Knoxville, Tenn., Sept. 25.

Globerman, S., and A.R. Vining. 1996. "A Framework for Evaluating the Government Contracting-Out Decision with an Application to Information Technology." *Public Administration Review* 56(6): 577–86.

Gold, K.A. 1982. "Managing for Success: A Comparison of the Public and Private Sectors." *Public Administration Review* 42: 568–75.

Goodsell, C. 1994. *The Case for Bureaucracy,* 3rd ed. Chatham, N.J.: Chatham House.

Gore, A. 1993. *From Red Tape to Results: Creating a Government That Works Better and Costs Less. Report of the National Performance Review.* Washington, D.C.: U.S. Government Printing Office.

———. 1995. *Common Sense Government: Works Better and Costs Less. Third Report of the National Performance Review.* Washington, D.C.: U.S. Government Printing Office.

Hackman, J.R., and G.R. Oldham. 1980. *Work Redesign.* Reading, Mass.: Addison-Wesley.

Hale, S.J. 1996. "Achieving High Performance in Public Organizations." In *Handbook of Public Administration,* J. L. Perry, ed., 151–66. San Francisco: Jossey-Bass.

Hargrove, E.C., and J.C. Glidewell, eds. 1990. *Impossible Jobs in Public Management.* Lawrence: University Press of Kansas.

Hartman, R., and A. Weber. 1980. *The Rewards of Public Service.* Washington, D.C.: Brookings.

Heclo, H. 1978. "Issue Networks and the Executive Establishment." In A. King, ed. *The New American Political System.* Washington, D.C.: American Enterprise Institute.

Hill, L.B. 1991. "Who Governs the American Administrative State? A Bureaucratic-Centered Image of Governance." *Journal of Public Administration Research and Theory* 1(3): 261–94.

———1992. "Introduction: Public Bureaucracy and the American State," and "Taking Bureaucracy Seriously." In *The State of Public Bureaucracy,* Larry B. Hill, ed., 1–57. Armonk, N.Y.: Sharpe.

Holzer, M., and K. Callahan. 1998. *Government at Work: Best Practices and Model Programs.* Thousand Oaks, Calif.: Sage.

Huber, G.P., and W.H. Glick, eds. 1993. *Organizational Change and Redesign.* New York: Oxford University Press.

Ingraham, P.W. 1998. "Transition and Policy Change in Washington." *Public Productivity Review* 12: 61–72.

Kelman, S. 1989. "The Making of Government Good Guys." *New York Times,* 2 July, business section, 1.

Kettl, D.F. 1993. *Sharing Power.* Washington, D.C.: Brookings.

Kilpatrick, F.P., M.C. Cummings and M.K. Jennings. 1964. *The Image of the Federal Service.* Washington, D.C.: Brookings.

Lambright, W.H. 1987. "James Webb and the Uses of Administrative Power." In Doig and Hargrove, eds., 174–203.

Lasko, W. 1980. "Executive Accountability: Will SES Make a Difference?" *Bureaucrat* 9: 6–7.

Lewis, E.B. 1980. *Public Entrepreneurship.* Bloomington: Indiana University Press.

———. 1987. "Admiral Hyman Rickover: Technological Entrepreneurship in the U.S. Navy." In Doig and Hargrove, eds.

Lowery, D. 1997. "Consumer Sovereignty and Quasimarket Failure." Department of Political Science, University of North Carolina at Chapel Hill.

March, J.G., and H. A. Simon. 1958. *Organizations.* New York: Wiley.

Mashaw, J.L. 1983. *Bureaucratic Justice.* New Haven, Conn.: Yale University Press.

Maynard-Moody, S., D.D. Stull, and J. Mitchell. 1986. "Reorganization as Status Drama: Building, Maintaining, and Displacing Dominant Subcultures." *Public Administration Review* 46:301–10.

Meier, K.J. 1993a. *Politics and the Bureaucracy.* Pacific Grove, Calif.: Brooks/Cole.

———. 1993b. "Representative Bureaucracy: A Theoretical and Empirical Exposition." In James L. Perry, ed. *Research in Public Administration,* vol. 2, 1–36. Greenwich, Conn.: JAI Press.

Milward, H.B., K.G. Provan, and B.A. Else. 1993. "What Does the 'Hollow State' Look Like?" In B. Bozeman, ed. *Public Management: State of the Art,* 309–22. San Francisco: Jossey-Bass.

Milward, H.B., and H.G. Rainey. 1983. "Don't Blame the Bureaucracy." *Journal of Public Policy* 3:149–68.

National Academy of Public Administration. 1986. *Revitalizing Federal Management.* Washington, D.C.: National Academy of Public Administration.

National Highway Traffic Safety Administration. 1996. *The National Highway Traffic Safety Administration Case Study: Strategic Planning and Performance Measurement.* Washington, D.C.: National Highway Traffic Safety Administration.

Niskanen, W.A. 1971. *Bureaucracy and Representative Government.* Chicago: Aldine.

Osborne, D., and T. Gaebler. 1992. *Reinventing Government.* Reading, Mass.: Addison-Wesley.

Ostrom, E. 1998. "A Behavioral Approach to the Rational Choice Theory of Collective Action." *American Political Science Review* 92(1): 1–22.

O'Toole, L.J. 1997. "Treating Networks Seriously: Practical and Research-Based Agendas in Public Administration." *Public Administration Review* 57(1): 45–52.

Perry, J.L. 1996a. "Measuring Public Service Motivation: An Assessment of Construct Reliability and Validity." *Journal of Public Administration Research and Theory* 6: 5–24.

———. 1996b. *Handbook of Public Administration,* 2nd ed. San Francisco: Jossey-Bass.

———. 1997. "Antecedents of Public Service Motivation." *Journal of Public Administration Research and Theory* 7(2): 181–98.

Perry, J.L., and L.R. Wise. 1990. "The Motivational Bases of Public Service." *Public Administration Review* 50: 367–73.

Peters, T.J., and R.H. Waterman. 1982. *In Search of Excellence: Lessons from America's Best-Run Companies.* New York: Harper & Row.

Provan, K.G., and H.B. Milward. 1995. "A Preliminary Theory of Interorganizational Network Effectiveness: A Comparative Study of Four Community Mental Health Systems." *Administrative Science Quarterly* 40: 1–33.

Rainey, G.W. 1990. "Implementation and Managerial Creativity: A Study of the Development of Client-Centered Units in Human Service Programs." In D.J. Palumbo and D.J. Calista, eds. *Implementation and the Policy Process.* New York: Greenwood.

Rainey, G.W., and H.G. Rainey. 1986. "Breaching the Hierarchical Imperative: The Modularization of the Social Security Claims Process." In D.J. Calista, ed., *Bureaucratic and Governmental Reform.* JAI Research Annual in Public Policy Analysis and Management. Greenwich, Conn.: JAI Press.

Rainey, H.G. 1983. "Public Agencies and Private Firms: Incentive Structures, Goals, and Individual Roles." *Administration and Society* 15: 207–42.

———. 1997. *Understanding and Managing Public Organizations,* 2nd ed. San Francisco: Jossey-Bass.

Rehfuss, J. 1989. *The Job of the Public Manager.* Homewood, Ill.: Dorsey.

Riccucci, N.M. 1995. *Unsung Heroes: Federal Executives Making a Difference.* Washington, D.C.: Georgetown University Press.

Rourke, F.E. 1984. *Bureaucracy, Politics, and Public Policy.* Boston: Little, Brown.

Rubin, I.S. 1985. *Shrinking the Federal Government: The Effect of Cutbacks on Five Federal Agencies.* New York: Longman.

Sandeep, P. 1989. "Why Government Can't Always Get the Best." *Government Executive* (March): 64.

Schein, E.H. 1992. *Organizational Culture and Leadership: A Dynamic View.* San Francisco: Jossey-Bass.

Sikula, A.F. 1973. "The Values and Value Systems of Governmental Executives." *Public Personnel Management* 2: 16–22.

Simon, H.A. 1998. "Why Public Administration?" *Journal of Public Administration Research and Theory* 8(1): 1–12.

Sims, H.P., and P. Lorenzi. 1992. *The New Leadership Paradigm.* Newbury Park, Calif.: Sage.

Stillman, R. 1996. *The American Bureaucracy,* 2nd ed. Chicago: Nelson-Hall.

Terry, L.D. 1995. *Leadership of Public Bureaucracies: The Administrator as Conservator.* Thousand Oaks, California: Sage.

Thompson, F.J., ed. 1993. *Revitalizing State and Local Public Service.* San Francisco: Jossey-Bass.

Thompson, F., and L.R. Jones. 1994. *Reinventing the Pentagon.* San Francisco: Jossey-Bass.

Trice, H.M., and J. M. Beyer. 1993. *The Cultures of Work Organizations.* Englewood Cliffs, N.J.: Prentice-Hall.

U.S. Coast Guard. 1996. *Using Outcome Information to Redirect Programs: A Case Study of the Coast Guard's Pilot Project under the Government Performance and Results Act.* Washington, D.C.: American Society for Public Administration.

U.S. General Accounting Office (GAO). 1986. *Social Security: Actions and Plans to Reduce Agency Staff.* GAO/HRD-86-76BR. Washington, D.C.: U.S. General Accounting Office.

U.S. Office of Personnel Management (OPM). 1998. *OPM Message to the Senior Executive Service.* Washington, D.C.: U.S. Office of Personnel Management (Winter): SES-98-02.

Wamsley, G.L., et al. 1990. *Refounding Public Administration.* Newbury Park, Calif.: Sage.

Warwick, D.P. 1975. *A Theory of Public Bureaucracy.* Cambridge, Mass.: Harvard University Press.

Wilson, J.Q. 1989. *Bureaucracy.* New York: Basic Books.

Wolf, P.J. 1993. "A Case Survey of Bureaucratic Effectiveness in U.S. Cabinet Agencies: Preliminary Results." *Journal of Public Administration Research and Theory* 3(2): 161–81.

———. 1997. "Why Must We Reinvent the Federal Government? Putting Historical Developmental Claims to the Test." *Journal of Public Administration Research and Theory* 7(3): 353–88.

———. 1998. "Explaining Political Autonomy in U.S. Federal Agencies: The Relative Importance of Leadership, Professionalism, and Specialization." Paper presented at the annual meeting of the American Political Science Association, Boston, Sept. 3–6.

Wood, B.D., and R. W. Waterman. 1994. *Bureaucratic Dynamics.* Boulder, Colo.: Westview.

Wyszomirski, M.J. 1987. "The Politics of Art: Nancy Hanks and the National Endowment for the Arts." In Doig and Hargrove, eds., 207–45.

Yukl, G. 1998. *Leadership in Organizations.* Upper Saddle River, N.J.: Prentice-Hall.

Notes

1. Wolf (1993) tests seven theories of bureaucratic effectiveness and argues that we do not need new theories, we need tests of existing theory. The propositions and discussion in this article draw on Wolf's analysis as valuable, but also proceed on the argument that such theories as we have need much more articulation.
2. This observation overstates the case in an effort at lively discourse. In fairness one should acknowledge that the references cited provide a more balanced and subtle analysis than depicted in this sentence.
3. While not necessarily negative in its assessment of bureaucratic performance, much of the academic literature on public bureaucracy concentrates on the problem of bureaucratic power, whether there is too much of it, and how it can be controlled (see Hill 1991 and 1992; Durant 1992), rather than on when and why it performs effectively.
4. A reason to use a term such as *mission motivation* is that it implies a different concept from a sense of mission. It includes not just the perception of a mission but the extension of effort toward achieving it.

☐ CASE STUDY 10

Introduction

From the standpoint of modern public managers, the demands of running government organizations are heavy, complicated, *and* certainly not as neat, tidy, or simple as many management theorists suggest or have us believe. Indeed, today the reality of much of government sector activities is accomplished in partnership with a maze of for-profit, nonprofit, and other government entities. There is little left today of "solo in-house" public management enterprise. To do the public's work requires instead that chief executives manage numerous complicated systems involving multiple organizations often crossing national borders, even spanning the globe, relying upon sophisticated technologies and professional expertise to make them operate, as well as on numerous other organizations for support to achieve their mission(s).

The following case, "The Lessons of Valujet 592," ably demonstrates that very point, namely, the complexities of modern management systems and, even with the best management practices, why they can sometimes fail, with disastrous consequences.

The author, William Langewiesche, himself a commercial pilot, got to the recovery site nineteen hours after the well-publicized crash of Valujet 592, which killed all aboard, 110 people, on May 11, 1996. He carefully recounts what happened and thoughtfully probes its causes. Beyond the immediate fire in the cargo-hold resulting from an accidentally triggered oxygen-generating canister onboard Flight 592, the author reveals a highly complex managerial system that had been set up to prevent such accidents, but failed to function properly through a series of mistakes.

As you read the following story, try to reflect on these questions:

What was the sequence of failures in the management system that led to the crash of Valujet 592? Where did the FAA regulatory management system break down, and why?

What does the author mean when he refers to "engineer speak" and how did it contribute to the accident? What can be done about it?

Why does Langewiesche argue that the ValuJet case "represents a nearly perfect system accident"?

How does this case compare with "The Blast in Centralia"? Were the same "system failures" readily apparent there as well?

Do you agree with the author that in complex systems like this one, some accidents are "normal" and bound to occur *and* that trying to prevent them *all* could even make operations more dangerous? Upon what theory and assumptions does Langewiesche base his thesis?

Does this case ultimately support the effectiveness thesis of the previous essay, namely, that elements of effectiveness are identifiable and, if attended to properly by government managers, can prevent such tragedies from occurring? If so, explain what a public manager at the FAA *should* have done to have prevented this crash. Or do you concur with the author of this case study that indeed there are real limits on details that any public manager reasonably can or should pay attention to, which means that accidents like this one are bound to occur periodically?

The Lessons of ValuJet 592

WILLIAM LANGEWIESCHE

On a muggy May afternoon in 1996 an emergency dispatcher in southern Florida got a call from a man on a cellular phone. The caller said, "Yes. I am fishing at Everglades Holiday Park, and a large jet aircraft has just crashed out here. Large. Like airliner-size."

The dispatcher said, "Wait a minute. Everglades Park?"

"Everglades Holiday Park, along canal L-sixty-seven. You need to get your choppers in the air. I'm a pilot. I have a GPS. I'll give you coordinates."

"Okay, sir. What kind of plane did you say? Is it a large plane?"

"A large aircraft similar to a seven-twenty-seven or a umm . . . I can't think of it."

This lapse was unimportant. The caller was a born accident observer—a computer engineer and a private pilot with pride in his technical competence and a passion for detail. His name was Walton Little. When he

William Langewiesche, "The Lessons of ValuJet 592," as appeared in *The Atlantic Monthly* (March 1998), pp. 81–98. Reprinted with permission.

first saw the airplane, it was banked steeply to the right and flying low, just above the swamp. Later he filed an official report, in which he stated,

> There was no smoke, no strange engine noise, no debris in the air, no dangling materials or control surfaces, no apparent deformation of the airframe, and no areas that appeared to have missing panels or surfaces. . . . Sunlight was shining on the aircraft, and some surfaces were more reflective and some less reflective. I saw a difference in reflection of the wing skin in the area where I would expect the ailerons to be, as though they were not neutral. In particular, the lower (outboard) portion of the right wing appeared less reflective as though the aileron was deflected upward.

Nearby fishermen ducked into their boat for cover—but not Walton Little, who stood on his deck, facing "about 115 degrees," and watched the airplane hit the water. The shock wave passed through his body.

I was in disbelief that the crash had occurred. I stood there for just a moment to consider that it really did happen. I was already thinking that I needed to get my cellular phone out of the storage compartment and call 911, but I wanted to assure myself of what I was doing because it is against the law to make false calls to 911.

He called within a minute. After telling the dispatcher about the crash and reading off his latitude and longitude, he said, "I'm in a bass boat on the canal. I thought it was an aircraft from an air show or something, and . . ."

The dispatcher interrupted. "What did you . . . Did you see flames and stuff come up, sir?"

"I heard the impact, and I saw dirt and mud fly in the air. The plane was sideways before it went out of my sight on the horizon about a mile from me."

"Yes, sir. Okay. You said it looked like a seven-twenty-seven that went down?"

"Uh, it's that type aircraft. It has twin engines in the rear. It is larger than an executive jet, like a Learjet."

"Yes, sir."

"It's much bigger than that. I won't tell you it's a seven-twenty-seven, but it's that type aircraft. No engines on the wing, two engines in the rear. I do not see any smoke, but I saw a tremendous cloud of mud and dirt go into the sky when it hit."

"Okay, sir."

"It was white with blue trim."

"White with blue trim, sir?"

"It will not be in one piece."

Walton Little was right. The airplane was a twin-engine DC-9 painted the colors of ValuJet, an aggressive young discount airline based in Atlanta. When it hit the Everglades, it was banked vertically to the right and pointed nearly straight down. The airplane did not sink mysteriously into the swamp, as reports later suggested, but shattered as it hit the surface with the furious force of a fast dive.

By the time Walton Little felt the shock wave, everyone aboard was dead—two pilots, three flight attendants, and 105 passengers. Their remains lay in a shallow, watery crater filled with liquid mud and grass. All that marked the surface was a fractured engine, a few dead fish, some jet fuel, and a scattering of personal papers, clothes, and twisted pieces of aluminum—the stuff of tragedy. During those first few days some officials worried aloud about the accident's effect on nature, but the swamp was not so fragile as that, and quickly resumed

its usual life. The families of those who died have proved less resilient. Most will feel the poison forever.

For the rest of us, though, the accident should be finished business. The official investigation is over, a "cause" has been found, contributing factors have been acknowledged, and the Federal Aviation Administration has written new regulations. Editorialists have expressed their outrage, and individuals have been held responsible. After a long suspension ValuJet has returned to the air with a renewed commitment to safety. Other airlines, too, have promised to be more careful. And even the FAA has gone through a housecleaning. So by conventional standards the reaction to the tragedy has been admirable. And yes, we know anyway that flying is almost always safe. After years as a working pilot, I have a poetic idea of why: airplanes are fundamentally at home in the sky. Certainly my own experience is that passengers do not need to cower around the exit rows, or carry emergency "smoke hoods," or fear bad weather, or worry about some impending collapse of airline safety. Those are ideas promoted by aviation illiterates—overly cautious people who can always find an audience, and who would smother us in their fear of violent death. The public has the sense in the long run to ignore them. Nonetheless, the ValuJet accident continues to raise troubling questions—no longer about what happened but about why it happened, and what is to keep something similar from happening in the future. As these questions lead into the complicated and human core of flight safety, they become increasingly difficult to answer.

Consider, for simplicity, that there are three kinds of airplane accidents. The most common ones might be called "procedural." They are those old-fashioned accidents that result from single obvious mistakes, that can immediately be understood in simple terms, and that have simple resolutions. To avoid such accidents pilots must not fly into violent thunderstorms, or take off with ice on their wings, or descend prematurely, or let fear or boredom gain the upper hand. Mechanics, ramp agents, and air-traffic controllers must observe equally simple rules. As practitioners, we have together learned many painful lessons.

The second kind of accident could be called "engineered." It consists of those surprising materials failures that should have been predicted by designers or discovered by test pilots but were not. Such failures at first defy understanding, but ultimately they yield to examination and result in tangible solutions. An American Eagle ATR turboprop dives into a frozen field in

Roselawn, Indiana, because its deicing boots did not protect its wings from freezing rain—and as a result new boots are designed, and the entire testing process undergoes review. A USAir Boeing 737 crashes near Pittsburgh because of a rare hard-over rudder movement—and as a result a redesigned rudder-control mechanism will be installed on the whole fleet. A TWA Boeing 747 blows apart off New York because, whatever the source of ignition, its nearly empty center tank contained an explosive mixture of fuel and air—and as a result explosive mixtures may in the future be avoided. Such tragic failures seem all too familiar, but in fact they are rare, and they will grow rarer still as aeronautical engineering improves. One can regret the lives lost and deplore the slowness with which officials respond, but in the long run there is reason to be optimistic. The Wright brothers were products of the Enlightenment. Our science will prevail.

The ValuJet accident is different. I would argue that it represents the third and most elusive kind of disaster, a "system accident," which may lie beyond the reach of conventional solution, and which a small group of thinkers, inspired by the Yale sociologist Charles Perrow, has been exploring elsewhere—for example, in power generation, chemical manufacturing, nuclear-weapons control, and space flight. Perrow has coined the more loaded term "normal accident" for such disasters, because he believes that they are normal for our time. His point is that these accidents are science's illegitimate children, bastards born of the confusion that lies within the complex organizations with which we manage our dangerous technologies. Perrow is not an expert on commercial flying, but his thinking applies to it nonetheless. In this case the organization includes not only ValuJet, the archetype of new-style airlines, but also the contractors that serve it and the government entities that, despite economic deregulation, are expected to oversee it. Taken as a whole, the airline system is complex indeed.

Keep in mind that it is also competitive, and that if one of its purposes is to make money, the other is to move the public through thin air cheaply and at high speed. Safety is never first, and it never will be, but for obvious reasons it is a necessary part of the venture. Risk is a part too, but on the everyday level of practical compromises and small decisions—the building blocks of this ambitious enterprise—the view of risk is usually obscured. The people involved do not consciously trade safety for money or convenience, but they inevitably make a lot of bad little choices. They get away with

those choices because, as Perrow says, Murphy's Law is wrong—what *can* go wrong usually goes *right*. But then one day a few of the bad little choices come together, and circumstances take an airplane down. Who, then, is really to blame?

We can find fault among those directly involved—and we probably need to. But if our purpose is to attack the roots of such an accident, we may find them so entwined with the system that they are impossible to extract without toppling the whole structure. In the case of ValuJet the study of system accidents presents us with the possibility that we have come to depend on flight, that unless we are willing to end our affordable airline system as we know it, we cannot stop the occasional sacrifice. Beyond the questions of blame, it requires us to consider that our solutions, by adding to the complexity and obscurity of the airline business, may actually increase the risk of accidents. System-accident thinking does not demand that we accept our fate without a struggle, but it serves as an important caution.

Smoke in the Cockpit

The distinction among procedural, engineered, and system accidents is of course not absolute. Most accidents are a bit of each. And even in the most extreme cases of system failure the post-crash investigation must work its way forward conventionally, usefully identifying those problems that can be fixed, before the remaining questions begin to force a still-deeper examination. That was certainly the way with ValuJet Flight 592.

It was headed from Miami to Atlanta, flown by Captain Candalyn Kubeck, age thirty-five, and her copilot Richard Hazen, age fifty-two. They represented a new kind of commercial pilot, experienced not only in the cockpit but in the rough-and-tumble of the deregulated airline industry, where both had held a number of low-paid flying jobs before settling on ValuJet. It would have been no shock to them that ValuJet pilots were non-unionized, or that the company required them to pay for their own training. With 9,000 flight hours behind her, more than 2,000 of them in a DC-9, Kubeck earned what the free market said she was worth—about $43,000 a year, plus bonuses. Hazen, formerly in the Air Force and with similar experience, earned a bit more than half as much.

Pilots were not the only low-paid employees at ValuJet—flight attendants, ramp agents, and mechanics made a lot less there than they would have at a more traditional airline. So much work was farmed out to temporary employees and independent contractors that ValuJet was sometimes called a "virtual airline." FAA regulators had begun to worry that the company was moving too fast, and not keeping up with its paperwork, but there was no evidence that the people involved were inadequate. Many of the pilots were refugees from the labor wars at the old Eastern Airlines, and they were generally as competent and experienced as their higher-paid friends at United, American, and Delta. ValuJet was helping the entire industry to understand just how far cost-cutting could be pushed. Its flights were cheap and full, and its stock was strong on Wall Street.

But six minutes out of Miami, while climbing northwest through 11,000 feet, Richard Hazen radioed, "Ah, five-ninety-two needs an immediate return to Miami." In the deliberate calm of pilot talk this was strong language. The time was thirty-one seconds after 2:10 P.M., and the sun was shining. Something had gone wrong with the airplane.

The radar controller at Miami Departure answered immediately. Using ValuJet's radio name "Critter" (for the company's cartoonish logo—a smiling airplane), he gave the flight clearance to turn initially toward the west, away from Miami and conflicting traffic flows, and to begin a descent to the airport. "Critter five-ninety-two, ah roger, turn left heading two-seven-zero, descend and maintain seven thousand."

Hazen said, "Two-seven-zero, seven thousand, five-ninety-two."

The controller was Jesse Fisher, age thirty-six, a seven-year veteran, who had twice handled the successful return of an airliner that had lost cabin pressurization. He had worked the night before, and had gone home, fed his cat, and slept well. He felt alert and rested. He said, "What kind of problem are you having?"

Hazen said, "Ah, smoke in the cockpit. Smoke in the cabin." His tone was urgent.

Fisher kept his own tone flat. He said, "Roger." Over his shoulder he called, "I need a supervisor here!"

The supervisor plugged in beside him. On Fisher's radar screen Flight 592 appeared as a little oval and an associated group of numbers, including a readout of its altitude. Fisher noticed that the airplane had not yet started to turn. He gave the pilots another heading, farther to the left, and cleared them down to 5,000 feet.

Aboard the airplane Hazen acknowledged the new heading but misheard the altitude assignment. It didn't matter. Flight 592 was burning, and the situation in the cockpit was rapidly getting out of hand. One minute into the emergency the pilots were still tracking away from Miami, and had not begun their return. Hazen said, "Critter five-ninety-two, we need the, ah, closest airport available."

The transmission was garbled or blocked, or Fisher was distracted by competing voices within the radar room. For whatever reason, he did not hear Hazen's request. When investigators later asked him if in retrospect he would have done anything differently, he admitted that he kept asking himself the same question. Even without hearing Hazen's request he might have suggested some slightly closer airport. But given that the flight's position was only twenty-five miles to the northwest, Miami still seemed like the best choice, because of the emergency equipment there. In any case "Miami" was the request he *had* heard, and he intended to deliver it.

To Hazen he said, "Critter five-ninety-two, they're gonna be standing, standing by for you." He meant the crash crews at Miami. "You can plan Runway One-two. When able, direct to Dolphin now."

Hazen said, ". . . need radar vectors." His transmission was garbled by loud background noises. Fisher thought he sounded "shaky."

Fisher answered, "Critter five-ninety-two, turn left heading one-four-zero."

Hazen said, "One-four-zero." It was his last coherent response.

The flight had only now begun to move through a gradual left turn. Fisher watched the target on his screen as it tracked through the heading changes: the turn tightened and then slowed again. With each sweep of the radar beam the altitude readouts showed a gradual descent—8,800, 8,500, 8,100. Two minutes into the crisis Fisher said, "Critter five-ninety-two, keep the turn around, heading ah one-two-zero."

Flight 592 may have tried to respond—someone keyed a microphone without talking.

Fisher said, "Critter five-ninety-two, contact Miami Approach on—correction, no, you just keep on my frequency."

Two and a half minutes had gone by. It was 2:13 P.M. The airplane was passing through 7,500 feet when suddenly it tightened the left turn and entered a steep dive. Fisher's radar showed the turn and an altitude readout of XXX—code for such a rapid altitude change that the computer cannot keep up. Investigators later calculated that the airplane rolled to a sixty-degree left bank and dove 6,400 feet in thirty-two seconds. During that loss of control Fisher radioed mechanically, "Critter five-ninety-two, you can, ah, turn left, heading one-zero-zero, and join the Runway One-two localizer at Miami." He also radioed, "Critter five-ninety-two, descend and maintain three thousand."

Then the incredible happened. The airplane rolled wings-level again and pulled sharply out of its dive. It is highly unlikely that the airplane would have done this on its own. It is possible that the autopilot kicked in, or that one of the pilots, having been incapacitated by smoke or defeated by melting control cables, somehow momentarily regained control. Fisher watched the radar target straighten toward the southeast, and again read out a nearly level altitude—now, however, merely a thousand feet. The airplane's speed was almost 500 miles an hour.

The frequency crackled with another unintelligible transmission. Shocked into the realization that the airplane would be unable to make Miami, Fisher said, "Critter five-ninety-two, Opa-Locka Airport's about ah twelve o'clock at fifteen miles."

Walton Little, in his bass boat, spotted the airplane then, as it rolled steeply to the right. The radar, too, noticed that last quick turn toward the south, just before the final nose-over. On the next sweep of the radar the flight's data block went into "coast" on Fisher's screen, indicating that contact had been lost. The supervisor marked the spot electronically and launched rescue procedures.

Fisher continued to work the other airplanes in his sector. Five minutes after the impact another low-paid pilot, this one for American Eagle, radioed, "Ah, how did Critter make out?" Fisher didn't answer.

The Recovery Operation

It was known from the start that fire took the airplane down. The federal investigation began within hours, with the arrival that evening of a National Transportation Safety Board team from Washington. The investigators set up shop in an airport hotel, which they began to refer to as the "command post." The language is important. As we will see, similar forms of linguistic stiffness, specifically engineerspeak, ultimately proved to have been involved in the downing of Flight 592—and this is a factor that the NTSB investigators, because of their own verbal awkwardness, have been unable quite to recognize.

It is not reasonable to blame them for this, though. The NTSB is a technical agency, staffed by technicians, which occupies a central position in the stilted world of aviation. Its job is to examine important accidents and to issue nonbinding safety recommendations—opinions, really—to industry and government. Because the investigators have no regulatory authority and must rely on persuasion to influence events, it may at times be necessary for them to use official-sounding language. Even among its opponents, who often feel that its recommendations are impractical, the NTSB has a reputation for technical competence. The NTSB is a piece of engineering done right. In a world built on compromise, it manages to play the old-fashioned, unambiguous role of the public's defender.

The press plays a more difficult role, though one equally important to the public's safety. It has a classically symbiotic relationship with the NTSB, relying on the investigators for information while providing them with their only effective voice. Nonetheless, in the time of crisis immediately after an accident, a tension exists between the two. Working under pressure to get the story out, reporters resent the caution of the investigators and their reluctance to speculate anonymously. Working under pressure to get the story right, investigators, for their part, resent the reporters' incessant demands during the difficult first days of an accident probe—the recovery of human remains and airplane parts. By the time I got to Miami, nineteen hours after Flight 592 hit the swamp, the two camps had assumed their habitual positions and were passing each other warily in the hotel lobby.

Twenty miles to the northwest, deep in the Everglades, the recovery operation was already under way. The NTSB had set up a staging area—a "forward ops base," one official called it—beside the Tamiami Trail, a two-lane highway that traverses the watery grasslands of southern Florida. Within two days this staging area blossomed into a chaotic encampment of excited officials—local, state, and federal—with their tents and air-conditioned trailers, their helicopters, their cars and flashing lights. I quit counting the agencies. The NTSB had politely excluded most of them from the actual accident site, which lay seven miles north, along a narrow levee road.

The press was excluded even from the staging area, but was provided with two news conferences a day, during which investigators cautiously doled out tidbits of information. One NTSB official said to me, "We've got to feed them or we'll lose control." But the reporters were well behaved, and if anything a bit overcivilized. Near the staging area they settled into their own little town of television trucks, tents, and lawn chairs. The location gave them good Everglades backdrops and shots of alligators swimming by; the viewing public could not have guessed that they stood so far from the action. They acted impatient, but in truth this was not a bad assignment; at its peak their little town boasted pay phones and pizza delivery.

Maybe it was because of my obvious lack of deadline that the investigators made an exception in my case. They slipped me into the front seat of a Florida Game and Fish helicopter whose pilot, in a fraternal gesture, invited me to take the controls for the run out to the crash site. From the staging area we skimmed north across the swamped grasslands, loosely following the levee road, before swinging wide to circle over the impact zone—a new pond defined by a ring of turned mud and surrounded by a larger area of grass and water and accident debris. Searchers in white protective suits waded side by side through the muck, piling pieces of people and airplane into flat-bottomed boats. It was hot and unpleasant work performed in a contained little hell, a place that one investigator later described to me as reeking of fuel, earth, and rotting flesh—the special smell of an airplane accident. We descended onto the levee, about 300 yards away from the crash site, where an American flag and a few tents and trucks constituted the recovery base.

The mood there was quiet and purposeful, with no sign among the workers of the emotional trauma that officials had been worriedly predicting since the operation began. The workers on break sat in the shade of an awning, sipping cold drinks and chatting. They were policemen and firemen, not heroes but straightforward guys accustomed to confronting death. Not knowing who I was, they spoke to me frankly about the gruesome details of their work, and made indelicate jokes, but they seemed more worried about dehydration than about "taking the job home" or losing sleep. I relaxed in their company, relieved to have escaped for a while the expectation of grief.

It was, of course, a somber place to be. Human remains lay bagged in a refrigerated truck for later transport to the morgue. A decontamination crew washed down torn and twisted pieces of airplane, none longer than several feet. Investigators tagged the most promising wreckage, to be trucked immediately to a hangar at an outlying Miami airport, where specialists could study it. Farther down the levee I came upon a soiled photograph of a young woman with a small-town face and a head of teased hair. A white-suited crew arrived on an airboat and clambered up the embankment to be

washed down. Another crew set off. A boatload of muddy wreckage arrived. The next day the families of the dead came on buses, and laid flowers and cried. Pieces of the airplane kept being hauled up for nearly another month.

Much was made of this recovery, which—prior to the offshore retrieval of TWA's Flight 800—the NTSB called the most challenging in its history. It is true that the swamp made the search slow and difficult, and that the violence of the impact meant that meticulous work was required to reconstruct the critical forward cargo hold. However, it is also true that the physical part of the investigation served to confirm what a look at a shipping ticket had already suggested—that ValuJet Flight 592 burned and crashed not because the airplane failed but, in large part, because the airline did.

To me as a pilot, the most impressive aspect of the investigation was the speed with which it worked through the false pursuit of an electrical fire—an explanation supported by my own experiences in flight, and all the more plausible here because the ValuJet DC-9 was old and had experienced a variety of electrical failures earlier the same day, including a tripped circuit breaker that had resisted the attentions of a mechanic in Atlanta, and then mysteriously had fixed itself. I was impressed also by the instincts of the reporters, who for all their technical ignorance seized on the news that Flight 592 had been loaded with a potentially dangerous cargo of chemical oxygen generators—more than a hundred little firebombs that could have caused this accident, and that indeed did.

Flight 592 crashed on a Saturday afternoon. By Sunday the recovery teams were pulling up scorched and soot-stained pieces. On Monday a searcher happened to step on the flight-data recorder, one of two required black boxes meant to help with accident investigations. The NTSB took the recorder to its Washington laboratory and found that a blip in the flight data six minutes after Flight 592's takeoff seemed to indicate a momentary rise in air pressure. Immediately afterward the recorder began to fail intermittently, apparently because of electrical-power interruptions. On Tuesday night, at a press conference at the hotel, Robert Francis, the vice-chairman of the NTSB and the senior official on the scene, announced in a monotone, "There could have been an explosion." A hazardous-materials team would be joining the investigation. The investigation was focusing on the airplane's forward cargo hold, which was located just below and behind the cockpit, and was unequipped with fire detection and extinguishing systems. Routine paperwork indicated that the Miami ground crew had loaded the hold with homeward-bound ValuJet "company material," a witch's brew of three tires—at least two of them mounted—and five cardboard boxes of old oxygen generators.

Inferno in the Air

Oxygen generators are safety devices. They are small steel canisters mounted in airplane ceilings and seatbacks and linked to the flimsy oxygen masks that dangle in front of passengers when a cabin loses pressurization. To activate oxygen flow the passenger pulls a lanyard, which slides a retaining pin from a spring-loaded hammer, which falls on a minute explosive charge, which sparks a chemical reaction that liberates the oxygen within the sodium-chlorate core. This reaction produces heat, which may cause the surface temperature of the canister to rise to 500° Fahrenheit if the canister is mounted correctly in a ventilated bracket, and much higher if it is sealed in a box with other canisters, which may themselves be heating up. If there is a good source of fuel nearby, such as tires and cardboard boxes, the presence of pure oxygen will cause the canisters to burn ferociously. Was there an explosion on Flight 592? Perhaps. But in any event the airplane was blowtorched into the ground.

It is ironic that the airplane's own emergency-oxygen system was different—a set of simple oxygen tanks, similar to those used in hospitals, that do not emit heat during use. The oxygen generators in Flight 592's forward cargo hold came from three MD-80s, a more modern kind of twin jet, which ValuJet had recently bought and was having refurbished at a hangar across the airport in Miami. As was its practice for most maintenance, ValuJet had hired an outside company to do the job—in this case a large firm called SabreTech, owned by Sabreliner, of St. Louis, and licensed by the FAA to perform the often critical work. SabreTech, in turn, hired contract mechanics from other companies on an as-needed basis. It later turned out that three-fourths of the people on the project were just such temporary outsiders. The vulnerability of American wageworkers could be sensed in their testimony after the accident. They inhabited a world of boss men and sudden firings, with few protections or guarantees for the future. As the ValuJet deadline approached, they worked in shifts, day and night, and sometimes through the weekend as well. It was their contribution to our cheap flying.

We will never know everyone at fault in this story. ValuJet gave the order to replace oxygen generators on the MD-80s, most of which had come to the end of their licensed lifetimes. It provided SabreTech with explicit removal procedures and general warnings about the dangers of fire. Over several weeks SabreTech workers extracted the generators and taped or cut off their lanyards before stacking most of them in five cardboard boxes that happened to be lying around the hangar. Apparently they believed that securing the lanyards would keep the generators from being fired inadvertently. What they did not do was place the required plastic safety caps over the firing pins—a precaution spelled out on the second line of ValuJet's written work order. The problem for SabreTech was that no one had such caps, or cared much about finding them. Ultimately the caps were forgotten or ignored. At the end of the job, in the rush to complete batches of paperwork on all three MD-80s, two mechanics routinely "pencil-whipped" the problem by signing off on the safety-cap line as well as on the others, certifying that the work had been done. SabreTech inspectors and supervisors signed off on the work too, apparently without giving the caps much thought.

The timing is not clear. For weeks the five boxes stood on a parts rack beside the airplanes. Eventually mechanics lugged them over to SabreTech's shipping-and-receiving department, where they sat on the floor in the area designated for ValuJet property. A few days before the accident a SabreTech manager told the shipping clerk to clean up the area and get all the boxes off the floor in preparation for an upcoming inspection by Continental Airlines, a potential customer. The boxes were unmarked, and the manager did not care what was in them.

The shipping clerk then did what shipping clerks do, and prepared to send the oxygen generators home to ValuJet headquarters, in Atlanta. He redistributed them equally among the five boxes, laying the canisters horizontally end to end, and packing bubble wrap on top. After sealing the boxes he applied address labels and ValuJet company-material stickers, and wrote "aircraft parts." As part of the load he included two large main tires and a smaller nose tire—at least two of which were mounted on wheels. The next day he asked a co-worker, the receiving clerk, to make out a shipping ticket, and to write "oxygen canisters—empty" on it. The receiving clerk wrote "Oxy Canisters" and then put "Empty" between quotation marks, as if he did not believe it. He also listed the tires.

The cargo stood for another day or two, until May 11, when the SabreTech driver had time to deliver the boxes across the airport to Flight 592. There the ValuJet ramp agent accepted the material, though federal regulations forbade him to, even if the generators were empty, since canisters that have been discharged contain a toxic residue, and ValuJet was not licensed to carry any such officially designated hazardous materials. He discussed the cargo's weight with the copilot, Richard Hazen, who also should have known better. Together they decided to place the load in the forward hold, where ValuJet workers laid one of the big main tires flat, placed the nose tire at the center of it, and stacked the five boxes on top of it around the outer edge, in a loose ring. They leaned the other main tire against a bulkhead. It was an unstable arrangement. No one knows exactly what happened then, but it seems likely that the first oxygen generator ignited during the loading or during taxiing or on takeoff, as the airplane climbed skyward.

Two weeks later and halfway through the recovery of the scorched and shattered parts a worker finally found the airplane's cockpit voice recorder, the second black box sought by the investigators. It had recorded normal sounds and conversation up to the moment—six minutes after takeoff—when the flight-data recorder indicated a pulse of high pressure. The pulse may have been one of the tires exploding. In the cockpit it sounded like a chirp and a simultaneous beep on the public-address system. The captain, Candalyn Kubeck, asked, "What was that?"

Hazen said, "I don't know." They scanned the airplane's instruments and found sudden indications of electrical failure. It was not the cause but a symptom of the inferno in the hold—the wires and electrical panels were probably melting and burning along with other, more crucial parts of the airplane—but the pilots' first thought was that the airplane was merely up to its circuit-breaking tricks again. The recording here is garbled. Kubeck seems to have asked, "About to lose a bus?" Then, more clearly, she said, "We've got some electrical problem."

Hazen said, "Yeah. That battery charger's kickin' in. Oooh, we gotta . . ."

"We're losing everything," Kubeck said. "We need, we need to go back to Miami."

Twenty seconds had passed since the strange chirp in the cockpit. A total electrical failure, though serious, was not in those sunny conditions a life-threatening emergency. But suddenly there was incoherent shouting from the passenger cabin, and women and men screaming, "Fire!" The shouting continued for thirteen seconds and then subsided.

Kubeck said, "To Miami," and Hazen put in the call to Jesse Fisher, the air-traffic controller. When Fisher asked, "What kind of problem are you having?" Kubeck answered, off-radio, "Fire," and Hazen transmitted his urgent "Smoke in the cockpit. Smoke in the cabin."

Investigators now presume that the smoke was black and thick, and perhaps poisonous. The recorder picked up the sound of the cockpit door opening, and the voice of the chief flight attendant, who said, "Okay, we need oxygen. We can't get oxygen back there." Did she mean that the airplane's cabin masks had not dropped, or that they had dropped but were not working? If the smoke was poisonous, the masks might not have helped much, since by design they mix cabin air into the oxygen flow. The pilots were equipped with better, isolating-type masks and with goggles, but may not have had time to put them on. Only a minute had passed since the first strange chirp. Now the voice recorder captured the sound of renewed shouting from the cabin. In the cockpit the flight attendant said, "Completely on fire."

The recording was of little use to the NTSB's technical investigation, but because it showed that the passengers had died in agony, it added emotional weight to a political reaction that was already spreading beyond the details of the accident and that had begun to call the entire airline industry into question. The public, it seemed, would not be placated this time by standard reassurances and the discovery of a culprit or two. The press and the NTSB had put aside their on-site antagonism and had joined forces in a natural coalition with Congress. The questioning was motivated not by an immediate fear of unsafe skies (despite the warnings of Mary Schiavo, a federal whistle-blower who claimed special insight) but rather by a more nuanced suspicion that competition in the open sky had gone too far, and that the FAA, the agency charged with protecting the flying public, had fallen into the hands of industry insiders.

The Hunt for Blame

The FAA's administrator then was a onetime airline boss named David Hinson—the sort of glib and self-assured executive who does well in closed circles of like-minded men. Now, however, he would have to address a diverse and skeptical audience. The day after the ValuJet accident he had flown to Miami and made the incredible assertion that ValuJet was a safe airline—when for 110 people lying dead in a nearby swamp it very obviously was not. He also said, "I would fly on it," as if he believed that he had to reassure a nation of children. It was an insulting performance, and it was taken as evidence of the FAA's isolation and of its betrayal of the public's trust.

After a good night's sleep Hinson might have tried to repair the damage. Instead he appeared two days later at a Senate hearing in Washington sounding like an unrepentant Prussian: "We have a very professional, highly dedicated, organized, and efficient inspector work force that do their job day in and day out. And when we say an airline is safe to fly, it is safe to fly. There is no gray area."

His colleagues must have winced. Aviation safety is nothing but a gray area, and the regulation of it is an indirect process of negotiation and maneuver. Consider the size of the airline business, the scale of the sky, and the loneliness of an airplane in flight. The FAA can affect safety by establishing standards and enforcing them through inspections and paperwork, but it cannot throw the switches or turn the wrenches, or in this case supervise the disposal of old oxygen generators. Safety is ultimately in the hands of the operators, the mechanics and pilots and their managers, because it involves a blizzard of small judgments. Hinson might have admitted this reality to the American public, which is certainly capable of understanding such subtleties, but instead, inexplicably, he chose to link the FAA's reputation to that of ValuJet. This placed the agency in an impossible position. Whether for incompetence or for cronyism, the FAA would now inevitably be blamed.

Within days it came out that certain inspectors at the FAA had been worried about ValuJet for some time and had described their concerns in their reports. Their consensus was that the airline was expanding too fast (from two to fifty-two airplanes over its two-and-a-half-year life) and that it had neither the procedures nor the people in place to maintain standards of safety. The FAA tried to keep pace, but because of its other commitments—including countering the threat of terrorism—it could assign only three inspectors to the airline. At the time of the accident they had run 1,471 routine checks on the operation and made two additional eleven-day inspections, in 1994 and 1995. This level of scrutiny was about normal. But by early 1996 concern had grown within the FAA about the disproportionate number of infractions committed by ValuJet and the string of small bang-ups it had had. The agency began to move more aggressively. An aircraft-maintenance group found such serious problems in both the FAA's surveillance and the airline's operations that it wrote an internal report recommending that ValuJet be "recertified" immediately—meaning that it be grounded and started all over again. The report was apparently sent to Washington, where for reasons that remain unexplained it lay buried until after the accident. Meanwhile, on February 22, 1996, headquarters launched a 120-day "special emphasis" inspection, a preliminary report on which was issued after the first week. This suggested a wide range of problems. The special-emphasis inspection was ongoing when, on May 11, Flight 592 went down.

As this record of official concern emerged, the question changed from why Hinson had insisted on calling ValuJet "safe" after the accident to why he had not shut down the airline before the accident. Trapped by his own simplistic formulations, he could provide no convincing answer. The press and Congress were sharply critical. The FAA launched an exhaustive thirty-day review of ValuJet, perhaps the most concentrated airline inspection in history, assigning sixty inspectors to perform in one month the equivalent of four years' work. Lewis Jordan, a founder and the president of ValuJet, complained that Hinson was, in effect, conducting a witch hunt that no airline could withstand. Jordan had been trying shamelessly to shift the blame for the deaths onto his own contractor, SabreTech, and he received little sympathy now. No one was surprised when ValuJet was grounded indefinitely five weeks after the accident.

Here now was proof that the FAA had earlier neglected its duties. The agency's chief regulator, Anthony Broderick, was the first to lose his job. Broderick was an expert technocrat, disliked by safety crusaders because of his conservative approach to instituting and applying regulations, and respected by aviation insiders for the same reason. Hinson let him take the fall: Broderick was a man of integrity and would accept responsibility for the FAA's poor performance. But if Hinson thought that he himself could escape with this sacrifice, he was wrong. Broderick's airline friends now joined the critics in disgust. Hinson announced his upcoming resignation.

In a sense, the system worked. The tragedy did have some positive consequences—primarily because the NTSB did an even better job than usual, not only pinpointing the source and history of the fire but also recognizing some of its larger implications. With a well-timed series of press feedings and public hearings the accident team kept the difficult organizational issues alive and managed to stretch the soul-searching through the end of the year and beyond. By shaking up the FAA, the team reminded the agency of its mandate to oversee the safety of the airlines—perhaps prodding the FAA into a renewed commitment to inspections and a resolution to hold airlines responsible for their actions and for the performance of outside shops.

For the airlines, the investigation served as a necessary reminder of the possible consequences of cost-cutting and complacency. Among airline executives smart enough to notice, it may also have served as a warning about the public's growing distrust of their motives and about widespread anger with the whole industry—anger that may have as much to do with the way passengers are handled as with their fears of dying. However one wants to read it, the ValuJet turmoil marked the limits of the public's tolerance. The airlines were cowed, and they submitted eagerly to the banning of oxygen generators as cargo on passenger flights. They then rushed ahead of the FAA with a $400 million promise (not yet fulfilled) to install fire detectors and extinguishers in all cargo holds. The desire to find hidden hazards runs up against the practical difficulties of inspecting cargo. Nonetheless, ground crews can be counted on for a while to watch what they load into airplanes and what they take out and throw away.

And the guilty companies? They lost money and were sued, of course. After firing the two mechanics who had falsely signed the work orders, SabreTech tried to put its house in order. Nonetheless, its customers fled and did not return. The Miami operation shrank from 650 to 135 employees, and in January of 1997 was forced to close its doors. Soon afterward, as the result of a two-month FAA investigation, SabreTech's new Orlando facility was forced to close as well. ValuJet survived its grounding, and under intense FAA scrutiny returned to the sky later in 1996, with a reduced and standardized fleet of DC-9s; it ultimately changed its name to AirTran. For a while it was probably the safest airline in the country. What, then, explains the feeling, particular to this case, that so little has in reality been achieved?

A "Normal Accident"

Pilots are safety practitioners, steeped in a can-do attitude toward survival and confident in their own skills. We tend to think that man-made accidents must lie within human control. This idea has been encouraged to some extent by the work of a group of Berkeley professors—notably the political scientist Todd La Porte—who study "high-reliability organizations,"

meaning those with good track records at handling apparently hazardous technologies: aircraft carriers, air-traffic-control centers, certain power companies. They believe that organizations can learn from past mistakes and can tailor themselves to achieve new objectives, and that if the right, albeit difficult, steps are taken, many accidents can be avoided.

Charles Perrow's thinking is more difficult for pilots like me to accept. Perrow came unintentionally to his theory about normal accidents after studying the failings of large organizations. His point is not that some technologies are riskier than others, which is obvious, but that the control and operation of some of the riskiest technologies require organizations so complex that serious failures are virtually guaranteed to occur. Those failures will occasionally combine in unforeseeable ways, and if they induce further failures in an operating environment of tightly interrelated processes, the failures will spin out of control, defeating all interventions. The resulting accidents are inevitable, Perrow asserts, because they emerge from the venture itself. You cannot eliminate one without killing the other.

Perrow's seminal book *Normal Accidents: Living With High-Risk Technologies* (1984) is an unusual work—a hodgepodge of storytelling and exhortation, out of which this new way of thinking has risen. His central device is an organizational chart on which to plot the likelihood of serious system accidents. He does not append numerical values to the chart but uses a set of general risk indicators. In one quadrant stand the processes—like those of most manufacturing—that are simple, slow, linear, and visible, and in which the operators experience failures as isolated and containable events. In the opposite one stand the opaque and tangled processes characterized by a combination of what Perrow calls "interactive complexity" and "tight coupling." By "interactive complexity" he means not simply that there are many elements involved but that those elements are linked in multiple and often unpredictable ways. The failure of one part—whether material, psychological, or organizational—may coincide with the failure of an entirely different part, and this unforeseeable combination will cause the failure of other parts, and so on. If the system is large, the possible combinations of failures are practically infinite. Such unravelings seem to have an intelligence of their own: they expose hidden connections, neutralize redundancies, bypass "firewalls," and exploit chance circumstances that no engineer could have planned for. When the operating system is inherently quick and inflexible (like a chemical process, an automated response to missile attack, or a jet airliner in flight), the cascading failures can accelerate out of control, confounding the human operators and denying them a chance to jury-rig a recovery. That lack of slack is Perrow's tight coupling. Then the only difference between a harmless accident and a human tragedy may be a question, as in chemical plants, of which way the wind blows.

I ran across this thinking by chance, a year before the ValuJet crash, when I picked up a copy of Scott D. Sagan's book *The Limits of Safety: Organizations, Accidents, and Nuclear Weapons* (1993). Sagan, a Stanford political scientist who is a generation younger than Perrow, is the most persuasive of Perrow's interpreters, and with *The Limits of Safety* he has solidified system-accident thinking, focusing it more clearly than Perrow was able to. *The Limits of Safety* starts by placing high-reliability and normal-accident theories in opposition and then tests them against a laboriously researched and previously secret history of failures within U.S. nuclear-weapons programs. The test is a transparent artifice, but it serves to define the two theories. Sagan's obvious bias does not diminish his work.

Strategic nuclear weapons pose an especially difficult problem for system-accident thinking, for two reasons: first, there has never been an accidental nuclear detonation, let alone an accidental nuclear war; and second, if a real possibility of such an apocalyptic failure exists, it threatens the very logic of nuclear deterrence—the expectation of rational behavior on which we continue to base our arsenals. Once again the pursuit of system accidents leads to uncomfortable ends. Sagan is not a man to advocate disarmament, and he shies away from doing so in his book, observing realistically that nuclear weapons are here to stay. Nonetheless, once he has defined "accidents" as less than nuclear explosions (as false warnings, near launches, and other unanticipated breakdowns in this ultimate "high-reliability" system), Sagan discovers a pattern of accidents, some of which were contained only by chance. The reader is hardly surprised when Sagan concludes that such accidents are inevitable.

The book interested me not because of the accidents themselves but because of their pattern, which seemed strangely familiar. Though the pattern represented possibilities that I as a pilot had categorically rejected, this new perspective required me to face the unpredictable side of my own experience with the sky. I had to admit that some of my friends had died in crazy and unlucky ways, that some flights had gone uncontrollably wrong, and that perhaps not even the pilots were to blame. What is more, I had to admit that no matter how carefully I checked my own airplanes, and how cautiously I flew them, the same could happen to me.

That is where we stand now as a society with ValuJet Flight 592, and it may explain our continuing discomfort with the accident. The ValuJet case represents a nearly perfect system accident. It arose from a process that fits most of Perrow's technical requirements of unpredictability and interactive complexity and some of those of tight coupling. More important, it fits the most basic definitions of an accident caused by the very functioning of the system or industry within which it occurred. Flight 592 burned because of its cargo of oxygen generators, yes, but more fundamentally because of a tangle of confusions that will take some entirely different form next time. It is frustrating to fight such a thing, and wrongdoing is difficult to assign.

ValuJet's Pretend Reality

Take, for example, the case of the two SabreTech mechanics who helped to remove the oxygen canisters from the ValuJet MD-80s, ignored the written work orders to install safety caps, stacked the dangerous canisters improperly in cardboard boxes, and finished by falsely signing off on the job. They will probably suffer for the rest of their lives for their negligence, as perhaps they should. But here is what really happened: Nearly 600 people logged time working on the three ValuJet airplanes in SabreTech's Miami hangar, and of them seventy-two logged 910 hours over several weeks for replacing oxygen generators, in most cases because they had "expired"—reached the end of their approved lives. According to ValuJet work card No. 0069, which was supplied to investigators, the second step of the seven-step removal process was *If generator has not been expended, install shipping cap on firing pin.*

This required a gang of hard-pressed mechanics to draw a verbal distinction between canisters that *were* "expired," meaning most of the ones they were removing, and canisters that were *not* "expended," meaning many of the same ones, loaded and ready to fire, on which they were expected to put nonexistent caps. Also involved were canisters that were expired and expended, and others that were not expired but were expended. And then, of course, there was the set of new replacement canisters, which were both unexpended and unexpired. If this seems confusing, do not waste your time trying to figure it out—the SabreTech mechanics did not, nor should they have been expected to. The NTSB suggested that one problem at SabreTech's Miami facility may have been the presence of Spanish-speaking immigrants on the work force, but quite obviously the language problem lay on the other side—with Valu-Jet and the English-speaking engineers, literalists, who wrote the orders and technical manuals as if they were writing to themselves. The real problem, in other words, was engineerspeak.

Before the accident the worry was not about old parts but about new ones—the safe refurbishing of the MD-80s in time to meet the ValuJet deadline. The mechanics quickly removed the oxygen canisters from their brackets and wired green tags to most of them. The green tags meant "repairable," which these canisters were not. It is not clear how many of the seventy-two workers were aware that these canisters couldn't be used again, since the replacement of oxygen generators is a rare operation, though of the people questioned after the accident most claimed to have known at least why the canisters had to be removed. But here, too, there is evidence of confusion. After the accident two tagged canisters were found still lying in the SabreTech hangar. On one of the tags, under "Reason for Removal," someone had written, "out of date." On the other tag someone had written, "generators have been fired."

Yes, a mechanic might have found his way past the ValuJet work card and into the huge MD-80 maintenance manual, to chapter 35-22-01, within which line "h" would have instructed him to "store or dispose of oxygen generator." By diligently pursuing his options, the mechanic could have found his way to a different part of the manual and learned that "all serviceable and unserviceable (unexpended) oxygen generators (canisters) are to be stored in an area that ensures that each unit is not exposed to high temperatures or possible damage." By pondering the implications of the parentheses he might have deduced that the "unexpended" canisters were also "unserviceable" canisters and that because he had no shipping cap, he should perhaps take such canisters to a safe area and "initiate" them, according to the procedures described in section 2.D. To initiate an oxygen generator is of course to fire it off, triggering the chemical reaction that produces oxygen

and leaves a mildly toxic residue within the canister, which is then classified as hazardous waste. Section 2.D contains the admonition "An expended oxygen generator (canister) contains both barium oxide and asbestos fibers and must be disposed of in accordance with local regulatory compliances and using authorized procedures." No wonder the mechanics stuck the old generators in boxes.

The supervisors and inspectors failed miserably here, though after the accident they proved clever at ducking responsibility. At the least they should have supplied the required safety caps and verified that those caps were being used. If they had—despite all the other errors that were made—Flight 592 would not have burned. For larger reasons, too, their failure is an essential part of this story. It represents not the avarice of profit takers but rather something more insidious—the sort of collective relaxation of technical standards that the Boston College sociologist Diane Vaughan has called "the normalization of deviance," and that she believes existed at NASA in the years leading up to the 1986 explosion of the space shuttle *Challenger*. The leaking O-rings that caused the catastrophic blow-by of rocket fuel were a well-known design weakness, and had been the subject of worried memos and conferences up to the eve of the launch. Vaughan's book *The Challenger Launch Decision* (1996) is a 575-page exercise in system-accident thinking. After a long immersion in NASA's technical culture, Vaughan concludes that the O-ring worries were put aside in part because the agency had gotten away with launching the O-rings before. As Perrow has argued, what can go wrong usually goes right—and then people draw the wrong conclusions. In a general way this is what happened at SabreTech. Some mechanics now claim to have expressed their concerns about the safety caps, but if they did, they were not heard. The operation had grown used to taking shortcuts.

But let us be honest—mechanics who are too careful will never get the job done. The airline system as it stands today requires people, in flight or on the ground, to compromise, to make choices, and sometimes even to gamble. The SabreTech crews went astray—but not far astray—by allowing themselves quite naturally not to worry about discarded parts. A fire hazard? Sure. The mechanics taped off the lanyards and may have shoved the canisters a little farther away from the airplanes they were working on. The canisters had no warnings about heat on them and none of the standard hazardous-materials placards. It probably would not have mattered anyway, because the work area was crowded with placards and officially designated hazardous materials, and people had learned not to take them too seriously. Out of curiosity a few of the mechanics fired off some canisters and listened to the oxygen come out—it went *pssst*. No one seems to have considered the possibility that the canisters might accidentally be shipped. The mechanics did finally carry the five cardboard boxes over to the shipping department, but only because that was where ValuJet property was stored—an arrangement that itself made sense.

When the shipping clerk got to work the next morning, he found the boxes without explanation on the floor of the ValuJet area. The boxes were innocent-looking, and he left them alone until he was told to tidy up. Sending them to Atlanta seemed like the best way to do that. He had shipped off "company material" before without ValuJet's specific approval, and he had heard no complaints. He knew he was dealing with oxygen canisters, but apparently did not understand the difference between oxygen storage tanks and generators designed to fire off. When he prepared the boxes for shipping, he noticed the green "repairable" tags mistakenly placed on the canisters by the mechanics, and misunderstood them to signify "unserviceable" or "out of service," as he variably said after the accident. He also drew the unpredictable conclusion that the canisters were therefore empty. He asked the receiving clerk to fill out a shipping ticket. The receiving clerk did as he was asked, listing the tires and canisters, and put quotation marks around the word "Empty." Later, when asked why, he replied, "No reason. I always put like, when I put my check, I put 'Carlos' in quotations. No reason I put that." The reason was that it was his habit. On the shipping ticket he also put "5 boxes" between quotation marks.

But a day or so later, over by Flight 592, the ValuJet ramp agent who signed for the cargo didn't care about such subtleties. ValuJet was not authorized to carry hazardous cargoes of any sort, and it seems obvious now that a shipping ticket listing tires on wheel assemblies and oxygen canisters (whether or not they were empty) should have aroused the ramp agent's suspicions. No one would have complained had he opened the boxes, or summarily rejected the load. There was no hazardous-materials paperwork associated with it, but he had been formally trained in the recognition of unmarked hazards. His ValuJet station-operations manual specifically warned, "Cargo may be declared under a general description that may have hazards which are not apparent, that the shipper may not be aware of this. You must be conscious of the fact that these items have caused serious incidents, and in fact, endangered the safety of the aircraft and personnel involved." It also said,

> Your responsibility in recognizing hazardous materials is dependent on your ability to: 1. Be Alert! 2. Take the time to ask questions! 3. Look for labels! . . . Ramp agents should be alert whenever handling luggage or boxes. Any item that might be considered hazardous should be brought to the attention of your supervisor or pilot, and brought to the immediate attention of Flight Control and, if required, the FAA. REMEMBER: SAFETY OF PASSENGERS AND FELLOW EMPLOYEES DEPENDS ON YOU!

It is possible that the ramp agent was lulled by the company-material labels. Would the SabreTech workers ship hazardous cargo without letting him know? His conversation with the copilot, Richard Hazen, about the weight of the load may have lulled him as well. Hazen, too, had been formally trained to spot hazardous materials, and he would have understood better than the ramp agent the dangerous nature of oxygen canisters, but he said nothing. It was a routine moment in a routine day. The morning's pesky electrical problems had perhaps been resolved. The crew was calmly and rationally preparing the airplane for the next flight, a procedure that had always worked for them before. As a result the passengers' last line of defense folded. They were unlucky, and the system killed them.

Giving Up on a Zero-Accident Future

What are we to make of this tangle of circumstance and error? One suspicion is that its causes may lie in the market forces of a deregulated airline industry, and that in order to keep such catastrophes from happening in the future we might need to consider the possibility of re-regulation—a return to the old system of limited competition, union work forces, higher salaries, and expensive tickets. There are calls now for just that. The improvement in safety would come from slowing things down, and allowing a few anointed airlines the leisure to discover their mistakes and act on them. The effects on society, however, would be costly and anti-egalitarian—a return to a constricted system that many fewer people could afford to use. Moreover, technical trends would argue against it. Despite the obvious chaos of the business and the apparent frequency of airline accidents, air travel has become safer under deregulation. Reductions in "procedural" and "engineered" accidents have more than compensated for any increase in system accidents—which in any case must have occurred in the past as well.

The other way to regulate the airline industry is not economic but operational—detailed governmental oversight of all the technical aspects of flight. This is an approach we have taken since the birth of the airlines, in the 1920s, and it is what we expect of the FAA today. Strictly applied standards are all the more important in a free market, in which unchecked competition would eventually require airlines to cut costs to the point of operating unsafely, until accidents forced them out of business one by one. A company should not overload its airplanes or fly them with worn-out parts, but it also cannot compete effectively against other companies that do. Day to day, airline executives may resent the intrusion of government, but in their more reflective moments they must also realize that they need this regulation in order to survive. The friendship that has grown up between the two sides—between the regulators and the regulated—is an expression of this fact, which no amount of self-reform at the FAA can change. When after the ValuJet crash David Hinson, of the FAA, reacted to accusations of cronyism by going to Congress and humbly requesting that his agency's "dual mandate" be eliminated, so that it would no longer be required by law to promote the airlines, he and Congress (which did as he requested) were engaged in a particularly hollow form of political theater.

The FAA's critics had real points to make. The agency had become too worried about the reactions of its allies in the airline industry, and it needed to try harder to enforce existing regulations. Perhaps it needed even to write some new regulations. Like NASA before the *Challenger* accident, the FAA needed to listen to the opinions and worries of its own lower-level employees. But there are limits to all this, too. When, at a post-crash press conference in Miami, a reporter asked Robert Francis, of the NTSB, "Shouldn't the government protect us against this kind of thing?" the best answer would have been "It cannot, and never will."

The truth helps, because in our frustration with such system accidents we may be tempted to invent solutions that, by adding to the obscurity and complexity of the system, may aggravate just those characteristics that led to the accidents in the first place. This argument for a theoretical point of *diminishing* safety is a central part of Perrow's thinking, and it seems to be borne out in practice. In his exploration of the North American early-warning system Sagan found that the failures of safety devices and backup systems gave the most dangerous false indications of missile attack—the kind that could have triggered a response. The radiation accidents at Chernobyl and Three Mile Island were both induced by failures in the safety systems. Remember also that the ValuJet oxygen generators were safety devices, that they were backup systems, and that they were removed from the MD-80s because of regulations limiting their useful lives. This is not an argument against such devices but a reminder that elaboration comes at a price.

Human reactions add to the problem. Administrators can think up impressive chains of command and control, and impose complex double checks and procedures on an operating system, and they can load the structure with redundancies, but on the receiving end there comes a point—in the privacy of a hangar or a cockpit—beyond which people rebel. These rebellions are now common throughout the airline business—and, indeed, throughout society. They result in unpredictable and arbitrary actions, all the more so because in the modern, insecure workplace they remain undeclared. The one thing that always gets done is the required paperwork.

Paperwork is a necessary and inevitable part of the system, but it, too, introduces dangers. The problem is not just the burden that it places on practical operations but also the deception that it breeds. The two unfortunate mechanics who signed off on the nonexistent safety caps just happened to be the slowest to slip away when the supervisors needed signatures. The other mechanics almost certainly would have signed too, as did the inspectors. Their good old-fashioned pencil-whipping is perhaps the most widespread form of Vaughan's "normalization of deviance." The falsification they committed was part of a larger deception—the creation of an entire pretend reality that includes unworkable chains of command, unlearnable training programs, unreadable manuals, and the fiction of regulations, checks, and controls. Such pretend realities extend even into the most self-consciously progressive large organizations, with their attempts to formalize informality, to deregulate the workplace, to share profits and responsibilities, to respect the integrity and initiative of the individual. The systems work in principle, and usually in practice as well, but the two may have little to do with each other. Paperwork floats free of the ground and obscures the murky workplaces where, in the confusion of real life, system accidents are born.

It would be wrong to conclude that we should join the alarmists in their prophesies of doom. Flying will remain safe, and for conventional reasons, including the admirable reaction we have seen to the ValuJet crash. But it should also be clear that there are struc-

tural limits to flight safety, and that any dream of a zero-accident future is probably about as realistic as the old ValuJet promise to put safety first. If that is true, we had better get used to it. Conventional accidents— those I call procedural or engineered—will submit to our solutions, but as air travel continues to expand, we can expect capricious system accidents to blossom. Understanding why might keep us from making the system even more complex, and therefore perhaps more dangerous, too.

Chapter 10 Review Questions

1. Briefly, how do Rainey and Steinbauer develop a concept of effective government performance? In your view, do they make their case? Why or why not?

2. Despite their thesis, there is a repeated public assertion—evidenced in the popular press and in political campaigns—that government is ineffective, inefficient, and uneconomical, and thus needs to become more businesslike. In your opinion, what are the sources and causes of this repeated public outcry? According to the authors, why is it an inaccurate perception? Or why is it only partly correct?

3. From your own experiences, how can citizens become more informed about the realities of government performance? And support its improvement?

4. If you were charged with constructing a better FAA management system that would prevent such problems as the ValuJet disaster from recurring in the future, what would you recommend? Or, as the author of the ValuJet case argues, do we simply have to accept that such accidents will happen periodically and recognize that preventing all these from occurring is impossible, even counterproductive?

5. Does the case, "The Lessons of ValuJet 592," ultimately support or contradict the Rainey and Steinbauer argument? On the other hand, does the case offer a different, even a more convincing model?

6. What is meant by Diane Vaughan's phrase "the normalization of deviance" (as cited in this case study)? How can organizations keep it from happening?

Key Terms

oversight authorities
stakeholders
autonomy
mission valence
mission-oriented culture
task motivation
mission motivation
public service motivation
task design

intrinsic motivation
extrinsic rewards
agency effectiveness
privatization
the hollow state
generic theories of management
empowerment of leadership
work environment
professionalism

Suggestions for Further Reading

Much of the earliest literature on management in this century focused on the role of line managers in business—for example, Henri Fayol, *General and Industrial Management,* translated by Constance Storrs (London: Pitman, 1949); or Frederick W. Taylor, *Scientific Management* (New York: Harper & Row, 1911). Their emphasis on the values of efficiency, rationality, and clear lines of hierarchy was carried over into the public sector by such authors as Henry Bruere, W. F. Willoughby, Frederick Cleveland, Luther Gulick, and others, who pioneered the development of management techniques in the public sector prior to World War II. For a good collection of the works of these writers, see Frederick C. Mosher, *Basic Literature of American Public Administration, 1787–1950* (New York: Holmes and Meier, 1981); and for several excellent summary essays on the lives of key management theorists, read Brian R. Fry, *Mastering Public Administration* (Chatham, N.J.: Chatham House, 1989).

A book that should be read in its entirety is Chester I. Barnard, *The Functions of the Executive* (Cambridge, Mass.: Harvard University Press, 1938), because Barnard stands in marked contrast to the pre–World War II scientific management theorists and because he made an enormous impact on other postwar writers, like Herbert Simon, who decisively reshaped our whole view of this field. William B. Wolf, *The Basic Barnard* (Ithaca, N.Y.: Institute of Labor Relations, Cornell University, 1974) offers the best available commentary on Barnard's life and work. A good summary of the work of another important figure, Henry Mintzberg, can be found in Henry Mintzberg, *Mintzberg on Management: Inside Our Strange World of Organizations* (New York: Free Press, 1989).

Post–World War Two management thought was aptly described by Harold Koontz as "the management theory jungle," i.e., it is divided into multiple schools and perspectives. To sample some of these diverse points of view, read C. West Churchman, *The Systems Approach* (New York: Dell Publishing, 1968), or Bertram M. Gross, *The Managing of Organizations* (New York: Free Press, 1964), for the *systems approach;* read Harry Levinson, *The Exceptional Executive: A Psychological Conception* (Cambridge, Mass.: Harvard University Press, 1968), or Rensis Likert, *The Human Organization: Its Management and Value* (New York: McGraw-Hill, 1967), for the *human behavioral school;* refer to the several hundred cases available through the Harvard Business School that were instrumental in pioneering the methodology of the *case method;* for the *policy emphasis,* see Paul Appleby, *Policy and Administration* (Tuscaloosa, Ala.: University of Alabama Press, 1949); and the *decision school* of management is well represented in books by Charles E. Lindblom and Herbert A. Simon (discussed in "Further Readings" at the end of Chapters 8 and 9).

Where are we today in public management thought? Again, no consensus prevails, as described in the excellent overview essays by Hal G. Rainey, "Public Management: Recent Developments and Current Prospects," in Naomi B. Lynn and Aaron Wildavsky, eds., *Public Administration: The State of the Discipline* (Chatham, N.J.: Chatham House, 1990); as well as Eugene B. McGregor Jr., "Public Management," *JPAM,* 16, no. 1, 153–61 (1997). The older schools are still very influential, but unquestionably economic pressures have brought about a new outpouring of ideas on economy, efficiency and effectiveness, which are reflected in various "how to" *practical efficiency-oriented managerial writings,* such as Stephen Cohen, *The Effective Public Manager,* 3rd ed. (New York: Wiley, 2002), and his *Tools for Innovators* (New York: Wiley, 1998). For the best and largest current collection of these writings that apply to local government, contact the International City/County Management Association, Washington, D.C. There are numerous, more specialized books that focus also on peculiar management problems associated with various levels of government as well as on many specialized policy fields like defense, law enforcement, health care, and others. The *leadership* perspective remains popular, as reflected by John W. Gardner, *On Leadership* (New York: Free Press, 1990); and Jameson W. Doig and Erwin C. Hargrove, eds., *Leadership and Innovation: Entrepreneurs in Government* (Baltimore: Johns Hopkins University Press, 1990).

For two excellent textbooks that provide an up-to-date, realistic picture of the recent problems and trends in public management, see Hal G. Rainey, *Understanding and Managing Public Organizations,* 2nd ed., (San Francisco: Jossey-Bass, 1997); and Charldean Newell, ed., *The Effective Local Government Manager,* 2nd ed. (Washington, D.C.: ICMA, 1993). Useful readers on this topic are J. Steven Ott et al., eds., *Public Management* (Chicago: Nelson-Hall, 1991); Patricia W. Ingraham et al., eds., *New Paradigms for Government* (San Francisco: Jossey-Bass, 1994); Marc Holzer, ed., *The Public Productivity Handbook* (New York: Dekker, 1991); and Jeffrey L. Brudney et al., eds., *Advancing Public Management* (Washington, D.C.: Georgetown University Press, 2000). Many outstanding cases on public management can be obtained through the case program, John F. Kennedy School of Government, Harvard University, 79 JFK Street, Cambridge, Massachusetts 02138; for the best case collection related to local government management, see James M. Banovetz, ed., *Local Government: Cases in Decision Making* 2nd ed., (Washington, D.C.: ICMA, 1998); and for "best practice" cases, see Marc Holzer and Kathy Callahan, *Government at Work* (Thousand Oaks, CA: Sage, 1997).

In the 1990s, public management practices were dominated by the "reinventing government movement" and so the two critical works that are "must" reading on this topic are David Osborne and Ted Gaebler, *Reinventing Government* (Reading, Mass.: Addison-Wesley, 1992); and Al Gore, *Creating a Government That Works Better and Costs Less* (Washington, D.C.: USGPO, 1993). For a critical appraisal of the application of reinventing ideas within the federal government, see Donald F. Kettl and John J. DiIulio, Jr., eds., *Inside the Reinvention Machine* (Washington, D.C.: The Brookings Institution, 1995).

Some of the best treatments of public management by leading scholars include: Mark H. Moore, *Creating Public Value* (Cambridge: Harvard University Press, 1995); Paul C. Light, *Thickening Government* (Washington, D.C.: The Brookings Institution, 1995); Donald F. Kettl, *Sharing Power* (Washington, D.C.: The Brookings Institution, 1993); Norma Riccucci, *Unsung Heroes* (Washington, D.C.: Georgetown University Press, 1995); Laurence E. Lynn, Jr., *Public Management As Art, Science, and Profession* (Chatham, N.J.: Chatham Publishers, 1996); Walter J. M. Kickert et al., eds., *Managing Complex Networks for the Public Sector* (Thousand Oaks, CA: Sage, 1997); and Lester M. Salamon, ed., *The Tools of Government* (New York: Oxford University Press, 2002). For contemporary managerial research studies, several excellent journals are worth sampling, such as the *Harvard Business Review, Public Administration Review, Governing,* and the *Journal of Public Administration Research and Theory.*

CHAPTER 11

Public Personnel Motivation: The Concept of the Public Service Culture

. . . W*e must wonder why the nurturing of a public service culture has received so little attention in government organizations, society, or the research community. Public service motives are the underpinnings for the uniqueness that defines the public service culture. They provide the basis for activities that educate and empower the citizens as members of a democratic state. They are the platform from which public servants bring values and engagement to their work. They fortify public servants to overcome self-serving interests, moral inertia, and risk avoidance.*

—Lois Recascino Wise

READING 11

Introduction

The emphasis on contemporary research in personnel motivation has resulted in an impressive subfield of public administration that deals with the many ramifications of the individual in public organizations. Today, most scholars and practitioners of public administration are aware that the handling of personnel motivational issues can be one critical key to the successful management of any public agency.

Chapter 6 explored how our important understanding of the role of the informal group within organizations began. Though concerned primarily with business organizations, Elton Mayo's discoveries in the field of human relations at Western Electric in the 1920s expanded the traditional theories of public administration by showing how critical an impact the human group had on the management process.

However, early researchers in the personnel field tended to accept the basic goals of increased efficiency in organizational activities and actually sought ways by which management could obtain greater productivity from workers. Initially, monotony, alienation, and worker fatigue frequently were problems focused upon in personnel studies. These studies often recommended a restructuring of the formal or procedural aspects of the institution to achieve greater or improved efficiency.

The second-generation personnel specialists like Chris Argyris, Warren Bennis, Rensis Likert, and Douglas McGregor have continued to stress the significance of the problems of the individual in organizations, but frequently with less concern about organizational performance and more careful attention toward helping to achieve worker satisfaction and personal growth on the job. Such writers de-emphasized traditional administrative goals such as efficiency and, instead, stressed support of individual values and a humanistic environment within organizations.

In the following essay, "The Public Service Culture," written especially for this text, Lois Recascino Wise offers a unique assessment of the current state of motivational research as it pertains to the public service. She begins her essay with a review of the current research literature in this field, but as Dr. Wise suggests, her aim more involves conceptualizing and "enriching understanding of the construct of public service motives, the process of public service motivation, and its implications for democratic governance." Her argument is premised on the assumption that "a public service motive is a type of human need" that is "stronger for some people than others." Professor Wise defines "public motives" as "the process that causes individuals to perform acts that contribute to the public good as a way of satisfying their personal needs." Substantively, such motives entail "affective, norm-based and rational attributes" that the author discusses in some depth. Not everyone in government, of course, is disposed toward public service motivations, nor are they necessarily absent in other organizations, even in McDonald's, argues Dr. Wise. She says, however, that "public service motivation is more prevalent in government than in business or industry" because of "the nature and mission (of) government organizations."

Above all, Dr. Wise believes, "Public service motives are significant because they provide a value basis for governance," especially in three ways: by (1) fostering "citizenry educated in the issues and processes of government"; (2) incorporating values, and not merely facts or analytical techniques, into administrative decision-making; and (3) encouraging commitment and responsibility for the work of government and its consequences. Professor Wise concludes by suggesting that public managers should make a conscious effort to develop a culture of public service throughout the workplace, for "if managers do nothing to promote and reward people who display public service motives, we should not expect those motives to be important in the organizations they lead."

Briefly, a word about Dr. Wise's academic background. Her research interests center on the broad areas of employment and management, with special focus on the public sector, especially civil service systems, administrative reforms, attitudes toward change and innovation, performance motivation in the public and private sectors, and systems for distributing organizational rewards and determining status in the bureaucracy. Dr. Wise teaches primarily in the areas of public management and human resource management, and her works have appeared in the major scholarly and professional journals. She is the author of *Labor Market Policies and Employment Policies in the United States* and is one of the most respected international scholars in this field of study. Dr. Wise serves as a consultant to public- and private-sector organizations in the United States and Europe and was recently awarded one of the highest prizes in Sweden for her research contributions to that nation's public administration development.

As you review her thoughtful exploratory essay on the "state of the art" of this subject, you might consider the following questions:

How does Dr. Wise define the term "public service motivation"?

Where does the author argue that most of our understanding of personnel motivation derives from?

Do you agree with her fundamental idea that public service motivation is more prevalent in government?

What does the author mean by the terms "rational," "norm-based," and "affective"? How do these concepts shape public service motivation?

How can "the public service culture" concept specifically help practicing public administrators in motivating their employees? Is it a pragmatic *and* valid conceptual framework, in your view, that can apply to all levels of public service—local, state, and federal? If so, explain how you would use her concept to motivate employees in the public sector.

The Public Service Culture

LOIS RECASCINO WISE

In 1961 President Kennedy issued the challenge "Ask not what your country can do for you but what you can do for your country." The call inspired a generation of Americans to government service. Thousands joined the newly created Peace Corps and its domestic counterpart, Volunteers in Service to America, but interest in working for the state overall was also high during the 1960s and 1970s. This was a generation that not only believed it could make the world a better place to live but also believed that it had a responsibility to shoulder the burden. In those days, college graduates who chose their first full-time job based on the size of the salary offered were seen as odd and were perhaps even stigmatized by their peers (Orloff 1978; Johnson and Prieve 1975).

Times have changed. In response to flight from government by officials who converted their knowledge into private sector expertise for higher pay, President Bush asserted, "Government should be an opportunity for public service, not private gain" (Waldman 1989: 16). More recent evidence suggests that high pay lures graduates from programs in public affairs into private

"The Public Service Culture," by Lois Recascino Wise. This essay was written especially for this volume.

sector consulting (Barrett and Greene 1998). Graduates are more likely to look with a jaundiced eye at the notion of employment as a form of personal sacrifice. At the same time, public management practices seem to be increasingly grounded in the assumption that monetary rewards, rather than purposive or social rewards, are the principal incentives for organizational membership and job performance among government employees. We can see this underlying belief in the use of special salary allowances for recruiting certain occupational groups, for example, and in continuing efforts to find an effective way to link performance to pay.

It was in this context that at the beginning of the 1990s Perry and Wise (1990) called for a renewed interest in studying and testing the propositions of public service motivation. Drawing on previous research, including work focused on voluntary organizations (Knoke and Wright-Isak 1982), they attempted to identify a theoretical framework for public service motivation. They identified three categories of public service motives and put forward a set of research propositions about the process of public service motivation. They called for research examining the behavioral implications of those propositions, for research developing new methods to operationalize and measure public service motivation, and for research that would refine the theoretical framework and research hypotheses pertaining to the motivational bases of public service.

Over the last two decades, using various definitions of the construct, a number of researchers have examined public service motivation. These empirical studies can be mainly placed in two different categories. The first set focuses on finding evidence of whether or not a public service motivation exists (Rainey 1982; 1976, 1991; Crewson 1995, 1997, Jurkiewicz et al. 1998; Gabris and Simo 1995; Brewer 1998; Vinzant 1998). The second set attempts to develop more sophisticated measurements for operationalizing the public service motivation construct (Perry 1996, 1997). Research is still limited, however, regarding the development of a theoretical framework for how public service motives affect behavior or for exploring the implications of public service motivation for bureaucratic outputs.

The contributions that contemporary studies have made to our ability to measure and compile evidence of public service motivation, however, are not the focus of this essay. Our interest lies more in elaborating and enriching understanding of the construct of public service motives, the process of public service motivation, and its implications for democratic governance. To this end the essay turns to a discussion of public service motives and the operating conditions of public service motivation. It then considers the linkages and tensions between public service motives and attributes of bureaucracy in a democracy. Some management implications for developing a public service work culture are discussed in the conclusions.

What Do We Know?

In this section we review literature regarding public service motivation and address four key questions. The first asks what public service motives are, and the second, what the operating conditions of public service motivation are. Under the second question we consider whether public service motives are constant and exclusive to the public sector. The third question pertains to whether public service motivation is more prevalent in the public sector, and the fourth seeks to explore the significance of public service motives.

What Are Public Service Motives?

A public service motive is a type of human need. The desire to fulfill human needs influences behavior. People have many different competing needs. Both theorists and empirical researchers have attempted to define human need structures and explain the way they affect behavior in various situations, including the workplace. Not all motives for work are identified by these content theories of human needs (Georgiou 1973; Perrow 1978). None of these theories, for example, identifies human spiritual needs as having implications for work motivation, but there are many people whose spiritual needs are so strong that they choose a career in a church, synagogue, or other religious organization. By the same token, individuals may have such strong needs to perform acts of public service and to contribute to the advancement of the quality of life in society that they may choose a career of public service. Like spiritual needs, public service motives will be stronger for some people than they are for others.

Behavior that contributes to the public good fulfills a human need among those with public service needs or motives. We believe that these motives are primarily addressed in the public sector because government work focuses on public service, because it is in the interest of public sector organizations to promote and cultivate these values and motives, and because the public sector is larger than the nonprofit sector. This is not to say that everyone working in the public sector is predisposed to public service motives, nor is it to say that people who are stimulated by public service motives do not have other needs that are responsive to the incentives that their organizations offer. In the same way, people working for the church, temple, or mosque are not motivated by their spiritual needs alone.

Public service motivation pertains to the process that causes individuals to perform acts that contribute to the public good as a way of satisfying their personal needs. Acts rooted in the desire to fulfill a public service need can involve the decision to pursue public administration as a field of study, and the decision to join an organization that provides opportunities to fulfill public service needs, as well as the performance of a set of responsibilities and tasks related to one's status as an employee or volunteer in an organization. As a form of intrinsic motivation, the potential gain from public service motivation is a function of how individuals expect to feel as a consequence of performing acts of public service.

Based on previous theoretical work, Perry and Wise (1990) organized public service motives into three broad categories. These are affective, norm-based, and rational motives. The same act can be motivated by various public service needs. For example, one individual may join the military service based on a love of country, while another joins because of a sense of duty and responsibility.

Normative orientations are based on social values and norms of what is proper and appropriate and include a desire to serve the public interest; to fulfill a sense of duty to the community; and to express a unique sense of loyalty to the government (Downs 1967; Karl 1979; Buchanan 1975; Knoke and Wright-Isak 1982). Frederickson (1970) argues that the pursuit of social equity is a primary obligation of public servants.

Affective motives are rooted in an individual's emotions. Affective motives would include a deep belief in the importance of a particular program to society. Gulick referred to this sort of commitment as anchored in a nobility of the great objectives of public service (Blumberg 1981), distinguishing it from public service acts based on a personal identification with a public program. For example, person A is motivated to join public service to advance the goals of the War on Poverty because she experienced poverty and deprivation as a child. Person B is motivated to join the War on Poverty because he abhors starvation in a rich society. Person A's behavior is rooted in rational motives while Person B's behavior is affective. An affective love of nature and a desire to protect the environment draws individuals into public sector employment. Frederickson and Hart (1985) contend that a primary motive for public servants is a patriotism of benevolence, which they define as an encompassing

love of and desire to protect the people within a political jurisdiction. This love of humanity provides opportunities for moral heroism and personal sacrifice for others.

Perry and Wise (1990) include rational motives as a basis for public service behavior. The underlying premise is that individual choice among a set of possible alternatives is motivated by an assessment of the potential utility maximization from each option. Rational motives would include a desire to represent some special interest and a personal identification with a program or policy goal, as well as desires for personal gain and personal need fulfillment (Downs 1967). The opportunity to participate in policy formulation or program implementation may be anchored in needs for power, esteem from others, and self-esteem. According to Rawls (1971:84), public service enables individuals to experience ". . . the realization of self which comes from a skillful and devoted exercise of social duties."

This third category of public service motives is not universally accepted. Some argue that public service can be rooted only in prosocial behavior (Rainey 1982). According to this school of thought, rational, self-serving motives by definition are not public service motives regardless of the social or public good they produce. We take the perspective here that human beings are complex and contradictory and indeed may embark on public service careers or perform acts of significant public service primarily based on their own human needs and self-interest. These motives may mature and develop into normative or affective bases for behavior. If this is so, then how members of a society prioritize their needs and interests becomes increasingly important for the furtherance of the public good.

What Are the Operating Conditions of Public Service Motivation?

Are Public Service Motives Constant?

Human behavior is based on a mix of motives, and motives vary over time in their salience to single individuals and to society as a whole. By extension, the motives for public service employment should vary among countries and geographic regions and also among units of government that have separate purposes and client groups. Not only can individuals switch among the categories of public service motives that they identify as important, but individuals may also turn away from these motives altogether as their needs are fulfilled, as their beliefs are proven wrong, or as other needs become more dominant (Homans 1961; Clark and Wilson 1961; Opsahl and Dunnette 1970; Deci and Ryan 1987). If the underlying assumptions for management practice and administrative policy in an organization change, we should expect shifts in the priority attached to different motivational bases for work (March and Simon 1958).

Individuals with public service motives are not by definition devoid of other motives and human needs. Concerns for basic human needs may be central for a Peace Corps worker in a primitive setting. Worries about job security may preoccupy public service–oriented workers during a reduction in force. Concerns for personal safety and career advancement are also important motivators for individuals dedicated to law enforcement, for example. In the same vein, persons pursuing religious careers have needs for personal development and growth that motivate their job-related behavior.

Contextual factors may also be significant in explaining trends in public sector employment. For example, the availability of government jobs affects the likelihood that a particular individual will find employment in the public sector regardless of the strength of her public service needs. If government jobs are clustered in some distant central location, such as a capital city, or if government imposes a hiring freeze, individuals will turn to other sectors. When government organizations undergo a reduction in force or pay cuts, human needs for job security and monetary reward may gain importance over public service motives for incumbent employees. If bureaucratic red tape prevents action or change for the public good, the strength of public service motivation among individuals will be negatively affected (Buchanan 1975). The perception that effort exerted

to create change inside the bureaucracy amounts to "pushing Jell-O" reduces the likelihood that individuals will be motivated to participate in innovation and reform activities in the future. The rational person acts under the belief that effort produces some result. When environmental forces inhibit goal achievement, motivation is reduced (Luthans and Kreitner 1975; Pfeffner and Salancik 1978).

Situational factors play a role in explaining when public service motives surface and dominate individual behavior and when behavior occurs as a consequence of other motives. Public service motives may be dominant, for example, when an individual embarks on a career or makes similar life choices. Public service motives may dominate in certain situational contexts on the job that trigger deeply held values and beliefs and call for acts of moral heroism. For example, Brewer (1998) reports that fraud and abuse account for whistle-blowing behavior among individuals with public service motives. Public service motives may anchor individual discretion and judgment and decisions to depart from established practice. The strength of public service motives may give individuals the courage to resist organizational norms and peer pressure that are in conflict with the way they interpret the public good. These tensions between self-serving interests and interests that serve the public good may occur in the daily performance of their work. They may develop into a habitual behavior in which public servants increasingly lean toward the end of the continuum that represents their own interests rather than the end that represents the public good (Gawthrop 1998b: 134).

As Gawthrop (1998b: 139) notes:

Public managers must recover the truly authentic and creative freedom to decide what they should do ethically in resolving the daily conflicts and challenges that confront them. Until they are capable of freeing themselves from the bondage of habit, any attempt to define professional behavior as truly ethical is an exercise in futility that can only result in a pathetic self-deception. The habits of the self-serving good allow public servants to pursue procedural quasi-ethical life. The net result, to paraphrase H. Richard Niebuhr, is a government of persons without fault, operating in a society without judgment, through the ministrations of a Constitution without purpose.

Are Public Service Motives Exclusive to the Public Sector?

We know by deduction that that public service motives cannot be found exclusively in the public sector. There is no mechanism to test and sort individuals in the labor market to identify and steer those with certain motives into one sector or another. Many people do not consciously choose a sector of employment and may not be fully aware of their own motives for joining a particular organization (Oldham 1976; Orloff 1978; Soelberg 1967; Wanous 1972, 1979, 1980). Individuals in the labor market rely on imperfect information and assumptions about employers in choosing organizations. Public sector employers may send conflicting signals to potential employees by emphasizing high pay and monetary benefits in their recruitment programs, thereby attracting and recruiting individuals whose motives for work are met by monetary rewards rather than the intrinsic returns from acts of public service. By the same token, we know that individuals with strong spiritual motives for work can fulfill these needs in other sectors. A priest or rabbi, for example, can work in the military as a chaplain. A deeply religious person can find rewarding secular employment in health care, counseling, or the arts, for example.

Another reason that public service motives cannot be exclusive to the public sector is that boundaries between sectors of employment are vague and organizational purposes and tasks overlap between sectors. The health care industry in the United States, for example, is found in the public, private, and nonprofit sectors. The opportunity to serve the public interest or to advance the public good is not exclusively limited to public sector employment. This is not to say that there are not unique motives that pertain to public service, but rather to acknowledge that public service can occur in many forums. Many corporations have public policy programs. An individual working for the McDonald's Corporation, for example, could fulfill

strong affective needs for public service by being involved in the Ronald McDonald House Program.

Is Public Service Motivation More Prevalent in the Public Sector?

If public service motives are not exclusively found in the public sector, is public service motivation prevalent in government organizations (Brewer 1998)? The question has two meanings. One is whether public service motivation is more prevalent than other types of motivation in government. To grant this premise, we would have to assume that public service motives are so strong that they always dominate human needs for growth, social contact, and physical and security-related needs, for example. Those public servants that Downs (1967) refers to as zealots may meet this assumption, but it does not seem a reasonable expectation for most.

The other interpretation is whether public service motivation is *more prevalent* in government than it is in other sectors of employment. There is a logic for thinking that public service motivation is less prevalent in business and industry, as Brewer (1998) demonstrates. One reason would be that by the nature of their mission and purpose, government organizations overall provide more opportunities for individuals to fulfill public service needs and thus would attract more of those individuals who prioritize their public service motives than would business or industry. Further, if government employers value public service motivation, then it should be expected that the work culture in public sector organizations cultivates and reinforces public service motives more than organizations in business or industry, as some research suggests (Romzek 1990).

If we posit that public service motivation is more prevalent in government than in business or industry, we acknowledge that systemic and organizational factors contribute to an organization's value orientation, and in turn, that public organizations must have separate value orientations. Consequently, the extent to which agencies or firms are able to recruit people with public service motives and are able to maintain and strengthen those human needs should also vary. We should also expect variations within organizations in the extent to which public service motivation accounts for behavior. Individuals will adapt to the operating incentive structure (Deci 1975; Wanous 1972; Clary and Miller 1986). For different reasons, certain branches or divisions might be less likely to recruit or nurture public service motives. Individuals working in certain occupational groups or professional areas may be more or less likely to be motivated by public service needs than others. Vinzant (1998), for example, contends that public service motivation enables protective services workers to cope with the particularly difficult stresses of their occupation.

In defining public service motivation, we have given examples of various categories of public service motives, identified factors in the public service motivation process, and identified some contextual factors important in the process of public service motivation. Public service motives are at the root of the behaviors and actions taken to achieve outcomes that serve the public good. The performance of public service acts and the attainment of public good outcomes are both dependent upon the strength and nature of an individual's public service motives and needs. But the public service motivation process is affected by individual and contextual factors, as motivation theories indicate. For example, an individual may have a strong desire to work for the state but believe that some personal attribute or characteristic makes such employment unlikely. The expectancy theory of motivation would posit that such an individual would have low motivation to apply for a government job, despite the high value she or he attaches to it as a vehicle of public service. Recruitment agents of the state could reinforce or counter the belief of low probability. The mission, policies, administrative structure, and culture of organizations can promote or dampen an individual's belief that the workplace provides an opportunity to fulfill public service needs. At the same time, an individual might think that even if the public service act were performed, factors affecting political, economic, or social capital would make goal achievement unlikely, and this in turn can reduce the amount of motivation an individual would have. These expectations might vary at times, depending on factors such as leadership support or available resources.

Of What Significance Are Public Service Motives?

If public service motives can exist in any sector and may appear in varying degrees of strength within public organizations, what significance does the construct have for public administration or more generally for the advancement of democratic and social values? Public service motives are significant because they provide a value basis for governance.

In developing the notion of the human side of public administration, Gawthrop (1998a) argues that members of the public service must act from a personal commitment to a public problem and an allegiance to the community. Public service motives anchor bureaucratic behavior and action, a connection that becomes increasingly significant as prevailing ideas about the role and status of public servants are rejected, and calls for responsibility, courage, flexibility, and proactive behavior are continually heard. Three ideas are central to these writings. These are the responsibility for educating the public in democratic issues and processes, the importance of individual values in administrative life, and the responsibility for engaging the citizenry in the administrative process.

Education

An important output of bureaucracy is a citizenry educated in the issues and processes of government (Gaus 1947; Gawthrop 1998a). Gaus (1947) sees education as a way of enhancing human growth and the value of human worth. Gawthrop (1998a) describes the responsibility for educating the citizenry as rooted in affective motives and based on a love of humanity. Education of the citizenry contributes to the bureaucracy's responsibility for engaging the public in the democratic and administrative process and achievement of an enriched sense of community. Education empowers the citizenry. It balances bureaucratic values and engagement as inputs in the administrative process because an educated citizenry is an empowered partner in governance.

Educating the public is in tension with both the tenets of efficiency and professionalism. The norm of professionalism means that individuals should use their professional expertise to make the best judgment based on the facts of the case (Mosher 1978). The tenet of efficiency means that tasks should be performed with the least use of resources and in the least amount of time. Educating the public would slow down the process, increase costs related to educational activities themselves, and occupy greater numbers of public servants in the education process itself.

Values

Gawthrop (1998a) contends that there is an integral relationship between administration and democratic values. In arguing for the appropriateness of values in public administration, he contends that an emphasis on facts and evidence in decision making does not mean that values must be excluded from the equation. Both facts and values contribute to solutions of public administration questions, but the public servant must weigh the consequences of both in making a decision. Frederickson (1971) also makes a strong case for incorporating values into public administration when he asserts "Administrators are not neutral, they should be committed to both good management and social equity as values. . . ." If we are concerned about justice and equity in the outcomes of government, value judgments are an integral part of the administrative process.

Shared values may be the cornerstone of a cohesive public organization (Meier 1997: 73, 74). To the extent that shared values facilitate achieving a common goal among members of an organization, they may be associated with greater commitment to organizational purposes, and consequently to higher levels of motivation and performance related to achieving those goals (Meier 1997). Individuals with congruent values are more able to anticipate each other's actions and are more likely to have the same assessments regarding which workplace behavior is important (Schein 1985; Kluckhohn 1951). Empirical studies show that especially when an individual public servant's values are like those held by the work group or organization, personal values are more likely

to be reflected in decisions involving discretion (Meier 1997:74). But at the same time, shared values may limit the range of problem solutions considered and may function as a form of peer pressure. The strength of individual public service motives may counter the possibility of "group think" and other conformist behavior when they challenge the public interest.

In direct conflict with the notion of introducing individual values to administrative behavior is the prevailing administrative norm of neutrality. The norm of neutrality means that bureaucrats should remain emotionally disaffected by the problems they face and detached from the clients they serve. Thompson (1985) captures the kernel of the neutrality ethic:

> The use of discretion . . . can never be the occasion for applying any moral principles other than those implicit in the orders and policies of the superiors to whom one is responsible in the organization. The ethic of neutrality portrays the ideal administrator as a completely reliable instrument of the goals of the organization, never injecting personal values into the process of furthering these goals.

Many years ago Herbert Simon (1945: 2) posited and Blau's (1955: 30) pioneering work demonstrated that even lower-level public servants make discretionary decisions that modify public policy outcomes and have significant consequences for agency clientele—for example, in determining eligibility for benefits or opportunities for employment. Neiderhoffer (1967: 10) similarly found that police officers may decide if and how the law should be applied. These decisions may be turning points in the lives of young offenders, for example. Some research suggests that police discretion is bounded by organizational norms and values (Jones 1977: 300–301; 200). Vinzant (1998) argues that public servants who clearly articulate value conflicts in their work demonstrate higher job satisfaction and greater motivation even in a highly stressful work situation.

Engagement

A concern for engagement focuses on securing greater personal involvement from public servants for their work and its consequences. Many scholars think that bureaucrats mainly try to limit their responsibility and risk in discretionary situations and that this behavior reduces the quality of government outputs for target citizens and undermines an organization's ability to achieve its primary mission (Jones 1977: 301; Blau 1955: 50).

Engagement means that public servants should not take a passive role in the policy implementation process, for example, but should be fully engaged in the event and able to identify pitfalls and problems that can undermine program success. In defining the philosophy of a New Public Administration, Frederickson (1971), for example, calls for public servants to become engaged in change. New Public Administration means "changing those policies and structures that inhibit social equity."

Engagement also means that public servants should "... think of what ought to be done instead of merely doing that which must be done" (Gawthrop 1998a). They cannot seek refuge within the boundaries of their job description and assigned responsibilities when presented with professional dilemmas. Gawthrop (1998a) submits that both moral inertia and unimaginative performance on the part of public servants are unacceptable. In this sense, the demand for engagement challenges the morality of rule-following behavior. A religious leader may perform the forms and rituals of the sacrament without engaging an internal spiritual emotion that creates an affective bond with the congregation. Similarly, a bureaucrat may go through the routines and motions of a job following the forms and rules prescribed but never engaging an affective emotion for the citizen clients he or she is positioned to serve, or in turn, feeling any concern for the outcome of their interaction.

The call for greater engagement is similar to what Carnevale (1995: 38) calls "working beyond contract." Working beyond contract means that job performance includes moral involvement, innovative behavior, spontaneity, and prosocial behavior. Working beyond contract means doing more than meeting minimum job performance standards or even meeting satisfactory standards. Similarly, Wise (1999) describes as outmoded the notion that a civil servant's tasks and responsibilities can be defined and contained

in a box, arguing that civil servants must step outside the box and anticipate the work that needs to be done, contributing their creativity and problem-solving ability to the organization.

This call for engagement is in tension with what Thompson (1985) refers to as the tenet of structure. That is the notion that a person's position and status in an organization determines his or her responsibility.

> The ethic of structure asserts that, even if administrators may have some scope for independent moral judgment, they cannot be held morally responsible for most of the decisions and policies of government. Their personal moral responsibility extends only to the specific duties of their own office for which they are legally liable.

This means that the policies of an organization can be morally wrong, but individual employees can be held harmless if they perform the duties and routines of their jobs and follow existing rules and regulations. Such thinking inhibits democratic accountability (Thompson 1985). Public servants must assume the moral responsibility for their work. By engaging in questions of public administration, we require public servants to accept accountability for the full consequences of public administration activities. Good intention does not absolve public servants of responsibility for their actions; administrators must demonstrate that they were fully engaged in the issue and that they attempted to foresee possible negative consequences (Thompson 1985). Individuals need to bring imagination and creativity to their work (Gawthrop 1998a).

Conclusions

Public service motives have the potential for advancing the democratic state, but they also are at the heart of a fundamental tension with key tenets of administrative behavior. These ideas run counter to a large body of work and thinking in public administration that rests on a different set of notions about what should be prioritized in bureaucratic conduct. If "good" public administration means rule-based, efficient, economical, and professional management, then it is incompatible with an emphasis on values, education, and engagement. Efficiency, for example, is clearly at odds with the slow task of engaging and educating the citizenry so that people can participate in the administrative process. Similarly, if professional management means reliance on expert advice and knowledge, it too is at odds with education and engagement. Likewise, rule-following behavior is in tension with the tenets of moral responsibility and individual courage. It may fail to deliver socially equitable public outcomes and may cloak acts of moral cowardice.

Public service motivation does not occur in a vacuum. We have argued that contextual factors related to individual actors, situations, events, and the organizations in which behavior occurs influence the strength of public service motivation. This means that to some significant degree both organizations and societies can enhance or reduce the prevalence of public service motivation, and in turn, the performance of acts that serve the public good and represent the public interest.

Organizational policies and practices may account for variations within the public sector in the strength of public service motives. If managers do nothing to promote and reward people who display public service motives, we should not expect those motives to be important in the organizations they lead. Without evidence that the administrative policies and management practices of a particular organization reward and promote public service motivation, we cannot expect to find public service the motivational basis for behavior.

Steven Kelman (1987: 94) remarked that "if the norm of public spirit dies, our society would look bleaker and our lives as individuals would be more impoverished." In that spirit we must wonder why the nurturing of a public service culture has received so little attention in government organizations, society, or the research community. Public service motives are the underpinning for the uniqueness that defines the public service culture. They provide the basis for activities that educate and empower the citizens as members of a democratic state. They are the platform from which public servants bring values and

engagement to their work. They fortify public servants to overcome self-serving interests, moral inertia, and risk avoidance. They anchor acts of judgment and discretion in a concern for the common good. It is for these reasons that public service motives are significant.

References

Adler, N. J. 1997. *International Dimensions of Organizational Behavior.* 3rd ed. Cincinnati, Ohio: South-Western College Publishing.

Barnard, C. I. 1938. *The Functions of the Executive.* Cambridge: Harvard University.

Barrett, K., and R. Greene. 1998. "A Managerial Brain Drain." *Governing* 11 (November): 72.

Blau, P. M. 1955. *The Dynamics of Bureaucracy.* New York: John Wiley & Sons.

Blumberg, S. K. 1981. "Seven Decades of Public Administration: A Tribute to Luther Gulick." *Public Administration Review* 41(2): 245–248.

Brewer, G. 1998. "Whistleblowers in the Federal Civil Service: New Evidence of the Public Service Ethic." *Journal of Public Administration Research and Theory* 8(3): 413–430.

Buchanan, B. 1975. "Red Tape and the Service Ethic." *Administration and Society* 6(4): 423–444.

Carnevale, D. G. 1995. *Trustworthy Government.* San Francisco: Jossey-Bass.

Clark, P. B., and J. Q. Wilson. 1961. "Incentive Systems: A Theory of Organizations." *Administrative Science Quarterly* 6: 129–165.

Clary, E.G., and J. Miller. 1986. "Socialization and Situational Influences on Sustained Altruism." *Child Development* 57: 1358–69.

Crewson, P. E. 1995. The Public Service Ethic. Ph.D. diss., American University, Washington, D.C.

———. 1997. "Public Service Motivation: Building Empirical Evidence of Incidence and Effect." *Journal of Public Administration Research and Theory* 7(4): 499–519.

Deci, E. 1975. *Intrinsic Motivation.* New York: Plenum Press.

Deci, E., and R. M. Ryan. 1987. "The Support of Autonomy and the Control of Behavior." *Journal of Personality and Social Psychology* 53: 1024–37.

Downs, A. 1967. *Inside Democracy.* Boston: Little, Brown.

Frederickson, H. G. 1970. *Toward a New Public Administration.* Scranton, Penn.: Chandler.

Frederickson, H. G., and D. K. Hart. 1985. "The Public Service and Patriotism of Benevolence." *Public Administration Review* 45(5): 547–53.

Gabris, G. T., and G. Simo. 1995. "Public Sector Motivation as an Independent Variable Affecting Career Decisions." *Public Personnel Management* 24(1): 33–51.

Gaus, J. 1947. *Reflections on Public Administration.* Tuscaloosa, Ala: University of Alabama Press.

Gawthrop, L. C. 1998a. "The Human Side of Public Administration." *PS Politics and Society* 31: 4 (December): 763–769. (See also www.apsanet.org/PS/dec98)

———. 1998b. *Public Service and Democracy: Ethical Imperatives of the 21st Century.* New York: Chatham House.

Georgiou, P. 1973. "The Goal-Paradigm and Notes towards a Counter Paradigm." *Administrative Science Quarterly* 18: 291–340.

Hofstede, G. 1980. *Culture's Consequences: International Differences in Work-Related Values.* London: Sage.

Homans, G. 1961. *Social Behavior: Its Elementary Forms.* New York: Harcourt, Brace.

Hyneman. 1950. *Bureaucracy in a Democracy.* New York: Harper & Brothers.

Johnson, A.C., and E.A. Prieve. 1975. "Changing Perspectives of College Students toward Salary Offers." *Personnel Journal* 54: 156–161.

Jones, B. D. 1977. "Distributional Considerations in Models of Government Services Provision." *Urban Affairs Quarterly* 12: 291–312.

Jurkiewicz, C. L., T. K. Massey, and R. G. Brown. 1998. "Motivation in Organizations." *Public Productivity and Management Review* 21(3) 230–250.

Karl, B. D. 1979. "Louis Brownlow." *Public Administration Review* 39(6): 511–516.

Kelman, S. 1987. "Public Choice and the Public Spirit." *The Public Interest* 87 (Spring): 80–94.

Kluckhohn, C. 1951. "Values and Value-Orientations in the Theory of Action." In *Toward a General Theory of Action,* ed. T. Parsons and E. Schils. Cambridge, Mass.: Harvard University Press.

Knoke, D., and C. Wright-Isak. 1982. "Individual Motives and Organizational Incentive Systems." *Research in the Sociology of Organizations* 1: 209–254.

Luthans, F., and R. Kreitner. 1975. *Organizational Behavior Modification.* Glenview, Ill.: Scott, Foresman.

Macy, J. W. Jr. 1971. *Public Service: The Human Side of Government.* New York: Harper & Row.

March, J. G., and H. Simon. 1958. *Organizations.* New York: John Wiley & Sons.

Meier, K. J. 1992. *Politics and the Bureaucracy: Policy Making in the Fourth Branch of Government.* 3rd ed. Pacific Grove, Calif.: Brooks/Cole.

———. 1997. "Bureaucracy and Democracy: The Case for More Bureaucracy and Less Democracy." *Public Administration Review* 57(3): 193–199.

Mosher, F. C. 1978. "Professions in the Public Service." *Public Administration Review* 368: 144–50.

Neiderhoffer, A. 1967. *Behind the Blue Shield.* Garden City, N.Y.: Anchor Books.

Oldham, G. 1976. "Organizational Choice and Some Correlates of Individuals' Expectancies." *Decision Sciences* 7: 873–884.

Opsahl, R.L., and M.D. Dunnette. 1970. "The Role of Financial Compensation in Industrial Motivation." In *Management and Motivation,* ed. V. H. Vroom and E. L. Deci, pp. 127–159. New York: Penguin Books.

Orloff, J. K. 1978. "Public or Private Sector Bound?" *Civil Service Journal* 19: 14–17.

Perrow, C. 1978. "Demystifying Organizations." In *The Management of Human Services Organizations,* ed. E. Hansfield and R. Saari, pp. 105–120. New York: Columbia University Press.

Perry, J. L. 1996. "Measuring Public Service Motivation: An Assessment of Construct Reliability and Validity." *Journal of Public Administration Research and Theory* 6(1): 5–22.

———. 1997. "Antecedents of Public Service Motivation." *Journal of Public Administration Research and Theory* 7(2): 181–197.

Perry, J. L., and L. R. Wise. 1990. "The Motivational Bases of Public Service." *Public Administration Review* 50(3): 367–373.

Pfeffner, J., and G. R. Salancik. 1978. *The External Control of Organizations: A Resource Dependence Perspective.* New York: Harper & Row.

Rainey, H. 1976. "Perceptions of Incentives in Business and Government." *Public Administration Review* 36: 233–244.

———. 1982. "Reward Preferences among Public and Private Managers: In Search of the Service Ethic." *American Review of Public Administration* 50(3): 374–382.

———. 1991. *Understanding and Managing Public Organizations.* San Francisco: Jossey-Bass.

Rawls, J. 1971. *A Theory of Justice.* Cambridge, Mass.: Belknap Press.

Romzek, B. 1990. "Employee Investment and Commitment." *Public Administration Review* 50 (May/June): 374–382.

Schein, E. H. 1985. *Organizational Culture and Leadership.* San Francisco: Jossey-Bass.

Simon, H. 1945. *Administrative Behavior.* New York: Free Press.

Soelberg, P.O. 1967. "Unprogrammed Decision Making." *Industrial Management Review* 8: 19–29.

Thompson, D. F. 1985. "The Possibility of Administrative Ethics." *Public Administration Review* 45(5): 555–561.

Vinzant, J.C. 1998. "Where Values Collide: Motivation and Role Conflict in Child and Adult Protective Services." *American Review of Public Administration* 28(4): 347–366.

Waldman, S. 1989. The Revolving Door. *Newsweek,* 6 February.

Wamsley, G. L., et al. 1990. *Refounding Public Administration.* Newbury Park, Calif.: Sage.

Wanous, J. 1972. "Occupational Preferences." *Journal of Applied Psychology* 56: 152–55.

———. 1976. "Organizational Entry: From Naïve Expectations to Realistic Beliefs." *Journal of Applied Psychology* 61: 22–29.

———. 1979. T. Keon and J. C. Latack. *Choosing an Organization.* Lansing, Mich.: Dept. of Management, Michigan State University.

———. 1980. *Organizational Entry.* Reading, Mass.: Addison-Wesley.

Wise, L. R. 1999. "Job Evaluation: White Elephant on the Path to Reform." *Review of Public Administration Research.* In press.

⬚ CASE STUDY 11

Introduction

The Red Cross was founded in 1881 by Clara Barton, as described in her own words, "to afford ready succor and assistance to sufferers of national or widespread calamities." Over the next century the Red Cross became America's premier, nonprofit disaster-relief organization with much of its work accomplished through volunteers in its 1034 local chapters across the United States. Today as a huge $3 billion, quasi-governmental agency, it operates under a congressionally mandated charter and is governed by a fifty-person board made up of several appointed senior federal officials.

In 1999, after an extensive national search, the Red Cross selected Dr. Bernadine Healy to succeed Elizabeth Dole as its president. Publicly at least, Healy was chosen because she "knew blood." Though, as one board member added, we hired "a change agent for a culture resistant to change." After eight years of listening to the Red Cross promise to reform and upgrade the safety of its blood-testing procedures, the Federal Drug Administration (FDA) obtained a court-ordered supervision decree over the Red Cross's blood-testing processes in 1993. Under Dole's presidency, significant progress at improving its blood testing had been achieved. Nonetheless, by 1999 the Red Cross still remained under FDA court-ordered supervision, and its Atlanta chapter had recently been cited for a number of testing violations.

In many ways, Healy was an ideal candidate to assume the Red Cross presidency at that particular moment. As a Harvard Medical School Graduate, she "knew blood," and as a former head of the National Institutes of Health and dean of the Ohio Medical School, she possessed impressive administrative credentials for managing large, complicated health-related facilities. Moreover, she had just survived a life-threatening brain tumor operation and therefore wanted badly to serve as Red Cross president in order "to do good" and make a positive difference for society. Yet, despite all these "pluses" that she brought to the job, within two years Healy was forced to resign.

As you read the following story by *New York Times Magazine* writer Deborah Sontag, try to think about how it relates to Lois Wise's foregoing conceptual essay on public service motivation.

What motivated Healy to accept the Red Cross presidency? Would you judge these motives to be in line with "public service motives" as described by Wise?

How would you characterize "the traditional" Red Cross organizational culture? Its values? Outlook? Do you think this culture also "squared" with the "public service values" outlined by Wise? What were the essential sources of differences between the public service ideals professed by Healy vs. the Red Cross volunteers?

In your view, was Healy well enough informed about the Red Cross culture prior to accepting the presidency? Likewise, was the Red Cross knowledgeable enough about Healy's managerial style prior to hiring her? What would you recommend both the potential employee (Healy) and employer (the Red Cross) do to ensure "a better fit" during the recruitment and selection process?

Ultimately, what were the chief causes of Healy's forced resignation? In retrospect, might you suggest some specific strategies that Healy could have used to better "read" and then "accommodate to" the traditional Red Cross culture? If she accepted your recommended strategies, what personal behavioral as well as value changes would Healy have had to adopt?

Generally do you think the notion of "public service culture" as advanced by Wise has relevance to this case study? Does it offer practical advice for resolving conflicts apparent in this case? If so, how and in what ways? If not, where would you amend or revise that concept?

Who Brought Bernadine Healy Down?

DEBORAH SONTAG

The vast, empty foyer of the American Red Cross's stately headquarters in Washington seemed as remote from ground zero as white marble from rubble. That was my inescapable, if facile, thought as I glided up the Tara-like central staircase one morning in early November. The holy hush was misleading, though. It gave no hint of the passionate, even viperous intrigue that was playing out behind closed doors. At a moment

when the Red Cross was supposed to be absorbed with ministering to a nation in crisis, it was confronting an internal crisis of its own making.

It had been just over a week since Dr. Bernadine Healy, 57, had announced her resignation under pressure as Red Cross president. I sat waiting for her in the president's office wing, which was still her domain but increasingly provided her little sanctuary. Healy, baldly showcasing her impatience toward Red Cross sanctities about tradition, had long displayed a saying attributed to Clara Barton above the mantle: "It irritates me to be told how things have always been done. . . . I defy the tyranny of precedent."

Sweeping into the room, Healy sank into a cranberry-colored chair and exhaled. Healy is a fine-boned, exquisitely tailored woman who, with her crisp blond coif and colorful blazers, looked more like the Republican senator she once aspired to be than a cardiologist who ran a humanitarian organization. That day, she was showing the jittery strain of the previous two months, in which she first commanded a huge disaster-relief effort and then suffered the humiliation of rejection by the Red Cross's 50-member board of governors. Under her severance agreement, Healy was supposed to stay on through year's end while the general counsel, Harold J. Decker, took over as acting C.E.O. But it was already getting pretty uncomfortable.

"I can't believe it," she said, a great sigh collapsing her small frame. "They've just fired my chief of staff. Poor Kate. They gave her a few hours to pack up and be gone. They want to get rid of us that badly?" Over the next couple of hours, there were many knocks at the door and sniffles outside it as Healy's assistants were reassigned, a first step toward their eventual firing. Healy, who had spent the previous day at a grueling Congressional subcommittee hearing, was agitated. She believed that the Red Cross might be seeking to deflect criticism—and avoid self-criticism—by scapegoating her. She could feel it coming, she said. The board was going to reverse course and blame unpopular decisions on her. Healy decided that day to pack up her office and return to her Ohio home as soon as possible.

It was a terribly intimate moment to observe, and Healy later said that she regretted I had been there. Her eyes watery, Healy had stared at a portrait of Barton, her heroine, who founded the American Red Cross in 1881. "You know Clara Barton was fired, too," she said, coughing up a dry laugh. "The difference is, she lasted 20 some years and I only lasted two. They got her on a trumped-up charge that she used lumber left over from a disaster recovery program in her home. It tarnished her reputation, although history ultimately redeemed her." Healy paused, hearing herself. "Not that I'm Clara Barton." She shook her head and rolled her eyes. "Far from it."

The Red Cross has come a long way since Barton established it "to afford ready succor and assistance to sufferers in time of national or widespread calamities." It now generates about $3 billion in revenues a year as a quasi-governmental bureaucracy with a split personality. On the one hand, it is what Barton intended, a nonprofit disaster-relief organization, and that chapter-based service side gives the Red Cross its identity as an icon

of volunteerism. But the Red Cross is also a blood business, which after a history of indebtedness and regulatory troubles has come to operate like a centralized corporation. Tensions between the two sides are echoed in other turf battles: between the 1,034 local chapters and the national headquarters, between veterans who believe their "mission" is good deeds and newcomers who believe theirs is good management and between the president and a board so big that Decker said his first impression was "politburo."

In a confidential memo to the board in late October, Healy bitterly described how the organization's internecine dynamic was summed up for her by another executive when she arrived in September 1999: "Red Crossers will give you the shirt off their back, but will as easily put a knife in your back."

All this makes the Red Cross a difficult, unwieldy institution to head. Since 1989, there have been three leaders and four interim leaders, counting Decker. Healy succeeded Elizabeth Dole, the first female president since Clara Barton. Dole spent much of the 1990's at the helm, taking a year off when her husband ran for president, then returning and eventually leaving to prepare her own presidential bid. The Red Cross board chairman, David T. McLaughlin, said that Dole's departure was "not terribly dissimilar" from Healy's. Dole "got out ahead of the game and stepped down," he said, "but she, too, left under some pressure," the result of combustible internal politics. Unlike Dole, McLaughlin said, Healy "more than brought on" her own departure, but both women were "fighting a culture, a culture that had grown up over a long period of time."

In two years on the job, the biggest disasters under Healy's watch as Red Cross president were Hurricane Floyd and Tropical Storm Allison. On Sept. 11, she stood outside on the headquarters' marble steps as snipers positioned themselves on the White House roof and, in the distance, smoke rose in blankets from the Pentagon. She knew in her gut that the day would have serious consequences for the organization that she commanded and for her personally.

McLaughlin would say later that Healy, the first physician-president of the organization, went at the initial Sept. 11 response "very clinically, and I have to say not emotionally. She was totally in action, on point." That intensity of focus, however, was not a quality of Healy's that was roundly admired within the Red Cross. Some thought her too driven and steely for an organization that they considered an affair of the heart. The previous Red Cross president, they say, had more of a politician's human touch. "Elizabeth Dole would notice the pin you were wearing, and Dr. Healy would notice the stain on your jacket," the director of one chapter said. "Dr. Healy was not people-oriented, and the Red Cross is all about people."

That day, however, the Red Cross had to be all about performance. And Healy found what she considered a serious wrinkle in an operation otherwise shifting into high gear efficiently. At noon, Healy's office received a call from the Pentagon: "Where the hell are you guys? Where's the Red Cross?" The Pentagon requested "water, food and other things we typically provide," according to an internal memo. Charles DeVita, the organization's security chief, placed a puzzled call of inquiry on Healy's behalf to the Disaster Operations Center, a corporate-style bunker known as the DOC, which is the Virginia-based command center for all disasters. The DOC was run by two women with 60 years of experience between them. They resented DeVita's phone call, a colleague of theirs told me: DeVita was a former assistant Secret Service director whom Healy had recruited just last year. What did the two of them know about activating the DOC?

That evening, Healy, believing the problem resolved, took a police escort to the site. She arrived at a scene of breathtaking devastation, with an army of firefighters "doing everything possible" to battle the blazing building. She saw "the Sallies," as the Salvation Army is called in charity circles, out in full force. But, to echo the caller from the Pentagon, where the hell was the Red Cross?

Healy expected to find the specialized teams usually dispatched by the DOC after plane crashes. Instead she found only four volunteers from the small, local Arlington County chapter—"bless their hearts"—earnestly trying to provide assistance to hundreds of emergency workers. There was no E.R.V., or emergency response vehicle, because Arlington's was in the shop. They didn't have any cots, so some firefighters were stretched out on the ground. Stunned, Healy punched out the phone number of a senior administrator who oversaw the two women at the DOC. She suggested the administrator report immediately to the scene, "get down on his knees and pray to God for forgiveness that we're not here."

Over the next week, Healy also stumbled on other serious problems that originated in the DOC—a failure to dispatch chaplains to the Pennsylvania crash site and a failure to realize that a confidential database of hospitalized victims existed. And by the professional standards of Healy and her executive team, the problems

demanded a swift, sure response: the two women had to go. Although it was not Healy who actually fired the women, she was held responsible by many for what was seen as a coldhearted, ill-timed attack on two women who meant well. Adding a touch of melodrama, one of the women collapsed after she was dismissed and ended up in an intensive-care unit. All told, the incidents served to accelerate opposition to Healy.

Some of the reaction was anxiety. "We're all afraid for our jobs," one senior official at the DOC wrote in an e-mail message that ended up circulating widely through the Red Cross's quite gossipy e-mail system. Some of it was resentment. "We have been silent up to now, but the deeply disturbing news of Dr. Healy firing two of our top people in Disaster Services is just too much," one couple, former co-chairpeople of the volunteer system, wrote in another e-mail message. Referring to themselves as previous victims of Healy's, they asked: "Why isn't the board of governors doing something about her?"

Well before Sept. 11, some Red Cross governors were growing uncomfortable with what they told Healy in her July evaluation was her hard-charging style. She had been encountering mounting resistance from the chapters too. The chapters had always operated pretty autonomously. They did not like it when Healy, who was aghast to learn how much of their financial reporting to headquarters was voluntary, sought to oversee them more closely. Although the Red Cross is effectively a public trust, it has never been a particularly transparent organization, not even internally.

Some chapter directors opposed her oversight for philosophical reasons; they feared that it represented the first steps toward centralization in an organization that should belong to the grass roots. Others didn't want Big Brother peering into their affairs. Or streamlining the chapter system in a way that would reduce their power or cut jobs. And then there were those with something to hide, like the administrator in Jersey City.

Healy thinks that her downfall probably began, improbably, right there in Jersey City when all these tensions exploded. An audit of the small, poor Hudson County, N.J., chapter had uncovered irregularities, suggesting embezzlement by the director; he was a longtime Red Crosser who apparently had treated his fief as a personal charity ward. Healy was horrified, suspended the man and his bookkeeper without pay and hired an outside firm to do a forensic audit. The auditors found what appeared to be significant theft, and the Red Cross turned the matter over to the local prosecutor's office.

In mid-December, a grand jury handed up indictments of Joseph Lecowich, the director, and Catalina Escoto, the bookkeeper, on charges of stealing $1 million in Red Cross funds.

The fact that Healy's suspicions were proved right in the end did not matter. Several board members and veteran administrators thought that she should have suspended the employees *with* pay, and they objected to involving external auditors. During her July evaluation, some members criticized her for being "too fast and too tough" in Jersey City. She asked them, "What should I have been, too soft and too slow?" And they said, "See, you're too defensive."

When the Red Cross board hired Healy, a Harvard Medical School graduate and mother of two daughters, ages 15 and 22, it understood exactly whom it was getting. From her stints as the first female director of the National Institutes of Health and as dean of the Ohio State University medical school, she had an established track record. A blunt-talking New Yorker born and bred in working-class Queens, she was not known as a diplomat. Rather, she was known as a driven professional who ruffled feathers but made things happen.

Dimon R. McFerson, then the C.E.O. of Nationwide, was the Red Cross governor who oversaw the 1999 search. He said that Healy was selected because she was the best candidate and that he would make the same choice again now. The board was unconcerned about Healy's "head-on style," he said, although in retrospect it seems inevitable that the board and Healy would end up on a collision course. "We hired a change agent for a culture resistant to change," one board member said.

Under the Red Cross's Congressionally established charter, seven of its 50 board members are senior government officials, like cabinet secretaries, who almost never participate. Another 12 are corporate, business and academic leaders who are not Red Cross lifers. Neither is McLaughlin; he is a former chairman of CBS, president of Dartmouth College and president of the Aspen Institute who, like his predecessors, was appointed Red Cross chairman by the president of the United States.

The remaining 30 governors, who are selected by local Red Cross chapters through a competitive nomination process, really control the organization. They tend to be lifelong Red Crossers who have worked their way up from local to national prominence within the organization; they also tend to be protective of traditions—and of veteran employees with whom they have longstanding relationships. Not all of them, McLaughlin said, straining to be diplomatic, "possess strong governmental or financial or programmatic experience on top of their incredible loyalty to the Red Cross." But because they are willing to give so much of their time, many of them end up presiding over the board's internal committees—for as long as six years—and those committee chairmen dominate the executive committee whose decisions tend to be rubber-stamped by the full board.

During the year that Dole took a sabbatical, the executive committee started playing a more hands-on role, and quickly took to it. When Dole returned, according to many Red Crossers, she did not exercise the same strong leadership she had previously. (Dole did not return several calls to her Washington office.) Then, during the year between Dole and Healy, there was another interim president. And so by the time Healy arrived, the board was acting like a hydra-headed C.E.O., "overstepping its role and authority," McLaughlin, who took over last May, said.

"I tried to pull them back," he added. "I tried to help her."

The board hired Healy at the hefty salary of $400,000, twice what Dole made, because that was Healy's value in the marketplace. According to McFerson, the board was attracted to Healy's medical background and the fact that she "knew blood," since "blood was the area that needed the most attention." The board's sole concern was that Healy was coming off "a medical challenge," as McFerson put it. She had just recovered from a brain tumor.

When the tumor was diagnosed, Healy told me, she had, in true medical-drama style, been given three months to live. Her unexpected recovery played a role in her decision to take the Red Cross job. In her grateful, post-illness state of mind, she was drawn to the chance to "do good." And in a way, some Red Cross veterans were a bit taken aback by Healy's insta-passion about the Red Cross itself. She was an outsider with the zeal of an insider; she came on so strong and fast with designs for the organization's "greatness" that some grew suspicious that Healy, who had waged a failed campaign for the United States Senate in Ohio, was motivated more by personal ambition.

It wasn't long after Healy moved to Washington from her home in Ohio, where her husband, Dr. Floyd Loop, runs the Cleveland Clinic Foundation, that she realized she would be butting heads with the board.

"She was an entrepreneur, and entrepreneurs don't like boards or controls," McLaughlin said. "She kept getting out ahead of the board, and the board was chasing after her. In hindsight, her decisions were right. But her personal style was uneven."

Healy, in turn, did not like what she found organizationally. In a confidential memo that she sent the board shortly before her resignation, Healy laid out a withering analysis of the Red Cross that she had inherited. She described "a corporate culture steeped in silos, turf battles, gossip and very little teamwork. Management structure was almost militaristic . . . [but] unlike the military, there were few commonly understood performance measures, and almost no system of reward or consequences for performance."

On the "blood side" of the Red Cross, which outsiders know so little about, such a corporate culture was not only costly but also potentially dangerous. The Red Cross began "sticking" people on a large scale during World War II, when it was called on to provide blood for soldiers. Now, the Red Cross collects blood donations at thousands of sites, tests and processes the blood at its regional plants and then sells the blood products—red blood cells, platelets and plasma—to hospitals. It is an almost $2 billion a year industry. But for years, Red Cross officials say, they underpriced their blood, thinking of themselves as a charity. With that mind-set, they went deeper and deeper into debt, underpaying employees and ignoring infrastructure and quality controls.

Food and Drug Administration inspectors found egregious problems: some Red Cross blood centers would keep testing blood until the tests delivered the desired results; for instance, blood that tested borderline-positive for a given virus would be retested five or six times until the numbers came out negative. "That was a huge issue," said Dr. Jerry E. Squires, the chief scientific officer of the Red Cross.

In 1993, after eight years of listening to the Red Cross promise to reform, the F.D.A. obtained a court-supervised consent decree, forcing the organization to improve its practices to ensure the safety of the national blood supply—45 percent of which is provided by the Red Cross.

Dole oversaw an administrative and financial "divorce" of blood from the chapters and centralized it so that it would operate more like a business. It was such a radical overhaul that the Red Cross was "declaring victory long before we should have," McLaughlin said. Even though the Atlanta blood center had just been cited for multiple violations, the violations did not seem to Red Cross executives as "critical or dangerous" as the

ones from previous years, a senior official said. So when Healy took over, the board told her that the organization's battle with the F.D.A. was nearing resolution and that Atlanta was an isolated case.

After Healy had been on the job five months, however, F.D.A. inspectors paid an unexpected visit to national headquarters. They stayed almost two months. In the end, they delivered a 21-page notice listing all the violations at headquarters itself. These included inadequate "tracking of inventory": pints of blood that were supposed to be quarantined because of their donors' medical histories ended up released for distribution. There were also labeling problems: blood testing positive for cytomegalovirus (CMV), for instance, was labeled negative.

Healy was "stunned," she told a senior F.D.A. official. Subsequently, in a meeting with F.D.A. officials, Healy candidly acknowledged widespread "infrastructure, quality and auditor problems," including a headquarters computer system that periodically "lost functionality," according to an affidavit in the court file. Healy also said that some Red Cross staff members treated the F.D.A.'s demands with a "willful lack of urgency."

In her meeting with the F.D.A., Healy said she found that some Red Cross officials possessed a startling "lack of concern for patients." The F.D.A. wanted the Red Cross to move from an "ear stick" to a "finger stick" method of drawing blood for testing, for instance; the ear-stick method often overestimated the blood count, deeming some with low blood counts eligible for donation. "In one instance in the past, this caused a perfectly healthy donor to require an emergency blood transfusion hours later," Healy wrote in a memo, adding that the reason the Red Cross was resisting the change was that it would decrease blood collections by 5 to 6 percent.

"Although the blood supply was safe," Healy wrote in her memo, "the near misses that had occurred presented a clear risk for the future." The gravity of the findings propelled the board to set aside $100 million to upgrade the blood business. Healy hired several high-profile executives to oversee the process. One new executive was Decker, who had been associate general counsel at Pharmacia. He and others moved quickly into positions of power within the organization, which some veteran Red Crossers found threatening, although in fairness, Healy was promoting insiders too. Would the Red Cross be overtaken by bloodless professionalism?

McLaughlin said that he considered Healy's "brilliant" hires to be her legacy, ensuring a solid future for the American Red Cross—if the individuals stay. The F.D.A., however, is dubious about the Red Cross's ability to follow through on its intended reforms. Despite Healy's concern and investment of time, money and personnel, the F.D.A. also found serious problems under her watch, citing the troubled Salt Lake City blood center for multiple violations last spring. In mid-December, the F.D.A. for the first time asked a judge to hold the Red Cross in contempt of the 1993 consent decree and to authorize serious financial penalties—$10,000 a day per violation, which could amount to more than $10 million a year.

In the days after Sept. 11, Healy oversaw the transformation of the Red Cross's austere headquarters into what looked like the stage set for a field hospital. Medical technicians were stationed at gurneys beneath stained-glass windows, drawing blood in assembly-line fashion. Outside in the garden, the Red Cross choir performed "God Bless America" and received a standing ovation from hundreds of phlebotomists and donors. Healy found it moving. "It was like a temple of healing and grieving," she said.

At first, the Red Cross sought to impose a system on would-be donors, urging them to make appointments to return as needs arose. But people would not be turned away. They wanted to wait in long lines and give of their vital fluids. It was a spiritual thing, Healy said, and her intuition told her to respect those feelings, even if it wasn't the most logical way to proceed.

Over the following two weeks, the Red Cross's three-day reserve of blood built to a 10-day reserve because the demand was less than expected: there were relatively few wounded. Nonetheless, the Red Cross continued to collect blood, having decided it should stockpile in anticipation of another attack or a military deployment. Eventually, some red blood cells, which expire after 42 days, had to be thrown away, which engendered considerable criticism of the Red Cross for being overzealous in its collections. Healy shrugs this off: "Look, the plasma was saved and frozen. People don't realize that red blood cells are perishable commodities. They expire. It happens. Better to have had too much than too little."

It is that kind of crisp logic that Healy's critics found off-putting—even when she was right and especially when she displayed a certainty that she was right. It bothered the board again and again. She would not walk them through the paces of her decision making; she didn't like stupid questions; she wanted action—yesterday. Then Healy, after taking insufficient time to explain herself, would end up feeling misunderstood. It happened with her subordinates too.

On Sept. 13, for instance, Healy boarded an Amtrak train for New York. The head of Amtrak had lent five mail cars to the Red Cross to transport supplies to the World Trade Center relief effort. Healy pushed her subordinates to load up the cars by 11 a.m., which required working through the night. Some of the workers thought her haste was excessive and that she simply wanted the glory of personally delivering the goods. But she was unaware. She was elated as she watched the Red Cross executives on the train working their cellphones, like Ramesh Thadani, her new "C.E.O. of blood," who was trying to line up freezers for plasma. "I was thinking, 'Hey, we did it guys,'" she told me wistfully. "I didn't know they were irritated."

That same week, Healy taped a first batch of solicitations for donations. Many Americans believed that she was asking them to use the Red Cross as a conduit for cash assistance to the Sept. 11 victims themselves. But she never said any such thing. Her appeals were vague, the essence of which was that Americans should give of their blood and their dollars to help the American Red Cross provide "lifesaving assistance." "Together, we can save a life," each public service announcement ended.

Healy's appeals were purposely general because the American Red Cross sees its role in a disaster as broad. It is not a charity per se but a disaster-relief organization that sets up mess halls and respite centers for emergency workers while providing food, comfort, counseling and safe haven for survivors and their families. The Red Cross never solicits funds just for individual victims.

In fact, until Sept. 11, it had never solicited donations for individual disasters, either, but rather—and this is mandated language—"for this and other disasters." Since the Red Cross can raise serious money only in the wake of a high-profile disaster, it uses the high-profile disasters to beef up general disaster-relief funds. That way, there is money in the pot to assist, as Decker puts it, "the little old lady in Philadelphia who loses her home to fire"—and to cover some of the operating expenses of the DOC.

This practice of the Red Cross has come under fire many times—after the San Francisco earthquake of 1989, the Oklahoma City bombing of 1995, the Red River floods of 1997, the wildfires in the San Diego area last January. Some communities just didn't like the idea that the money being raised because they suffered an earthquake, say, was going to be used elsewhere or tucked into the Red Cross's coffers. In several instances, the Red Cross ended up having to redirect funds back to disaster-struck communities because the pressure grew too intense.

But the Red Cross stuck by its approach until Healy declared Sept. 11 an extraordinary disaster that belonged in a class of its own. It didn't make sense to her to treat Sept. 11 as if it were an earthquake. Americans were responding quite specifically to the enormity of a terrorist attack. They were donating buckets of money, over $600 million in the end, because she believed they were heartbroken and scared. She thought that to commingle those emotions and those funds with the money set aside for more plebeian disasters would never stand up to public scrutiny. Besides, she did not want huge sums of money deposited in a general disaster-relief fund that is sometimes used as a "piggy bank" for the chapters. So she created a stand-alone fund for Sept. 11 and whatever might follow it. The Liberty Fund, with its own team of 800 outside auditors, was born.

This set off alarms throughout the Red Cross system. What about the little old lady in Philadelphia? Was Healy single-handedly changing a Red Cross commitment to equity for all victims? Was she making Sept. 11 victims into a special class whose treatment would raise difficult demands from other disaster victims down the road? Was she unwittingly creating public expectations that all money raised would go to Sept. 11 victims?

Healy didn't think she was creating such expectations, not among reasonable people. She didn't call it the Sept. 11 Fund, after all. And Healy said she felt that the Red Cross needed to plan ahead at the same time as it dealt with the crisis of the moment creatively. So while she set up a cash gift program for victims' families, which was novel for the Red Cross, she also seized the opportunity to beef up some expensive pet projects that had gained new urgency—like the weapons-of-mass-destruction-preparedness program and the creation of a strategic reserve of frozen blood. She thought this was logical, but she didn't initially bother to explain herself to the American public. She didn't even bother to explain herself to the board, which turned out to be a fatal lapse. For while the governors ended up endorsing the Liberty Fund, they were forced to do so after Healy had already made it a *fait accompli*. And they would never forget that.

On Oct. 3, as if the Red Cross didn't have enough to deal with, a board member from Louisiana placed a big thorny issue on the table: Israel, or specifically the Israeli Red Shield of David, Israel's disaster-relief organization. The executive committee asked Healy to leave the room so that they could discuss the matter freely. Members were concerned that she would stifle open discussion because of her intense, domineering views on the subject.

The American Red Cross has long opposed the exclusion of Israel's Red Shield of David, called Magen David Adom (M.D.A.), from the international federation of Red Cross and Red Crescent societies. But Healy decided to give teeth to that quiet opposition. She believed that the international movement needed to be prodded to clear the legal and diplomatic hurdles preventing it from accepting the Star of David as an emblem. If the Geneva Convention—which recognizes only the cross and the crescent as internationally protected symbols of humanitarian aid societies—needed to be amended, then amend it, she believed. If not, then skirt it.

Two months after assuming command of the American Red Cross in September 1999, Healy flew to Geneva to address a large assembly of the International Red Cross movement. And, in the eyes of international officials, she charged in like a bull in a china shop.

"She comes in and makes a speech in which she harangues the assembled membership about the inequity of the exclusion of M.D.A. and how the American Red Cross is going to make inclusion happen now, whether we liked it or not," said Christopher Lamb, an executive of the international federation. "She spoke about the movement, describing everyone as cowards and failures and people who didn't understand."

Healy nominated Lawrence Eagleburger, the former secretary of state, to the commission that governs the international movement. After her speech, he lost the election. Officials in Geneva postulated that Healy felt humiliated, which in turn fueled a redoubling of her commitment to Israel. But Eagleburger, who went on to serve as her ambassador on the Israel issue, wrote in a *Washington Post* op-ed column recently that Healy simply refused to turn "a blind eye on a moral wrong." And persuaded by her passion, the American Red Cross board went right along with her. It agreed to start withholding its $4.5 million annual dues to the international federation; that money is 25 percent of the federation headquarters' budget.

Officials in Geneva contend that they had been proceeding quietly, on a diplomatic track, to include Israel since 1995. Yet just two months after the Americans began withholding their dues, there was progress. An international working group decided the world needed a neutral emblem to stand alongside the cross or crescent. Switzerland was laying the groundwork for a diplomatic conference when the latest wave of Israeli-Palestinian violence broke out in September 2000, stalling things.

After Sept. 11 this year, a high-ranking official from Geneva flew to the United States to try to persuade the American Red Cross to resume dues payments before the federation's fall assembly. The American policy was counterproductive, causing unhealthy tensions within the international movement, he said. The board member from Louisiana was persuaded to reconsider, and so were others. They didn't like the idea that Healy was forcing the American Red Cross to take a strong political stance, because one of its credos was neutrality.

In an Oct. 3 closed-door meeting, the executive committee voted 9 to 1 to second the Louisiana board member's motion to stop withholding dues. The vote was tentative, pending future discussions. But Healy found out about the vote as the board members emerged from their session, considered it decisive and exploded.

"I said, 'This is not the time to do this,' she told me. "I said, 'You can't overturn this principle in a secret proposal in a secret session. Deserting Israel right now—what's the signal that you're sending?' They got mad at me. Later, they said I was insubordinate. It was all downhill from there."

At about that time, Terry J. Sicilia, a chapter director in Denver, wrote a letter to a senior vice president at headquarters to express his disappointment in Healy's leadership since Sept. 11. He asked, "Do you really feel the need to raise more money and blood?" He was concerned in part that the Sept. 11 fund-raising drive would make it more difficult for local chapters to raise money for their own needs.

Sicilia's letter was leaked to the Chronicle of Philanthropy Web site, which is checked daily by those in the charity world. It opened up the internal drama of the Red Cross to the public eye, and it helped create a drumbeat against Healy.

Healy, however, was getting mixed signals from within the Red Cross. In mid-October, she received a huge bouquet of flowers from the Watergate Florist with a card that read, "Thank you for being a truly great boss." It was signed by 11 senior Red Cross executives,

including Decker, "and our 1.6 million colleagues." She placed the card on her mantel—and later gave it to me, saying, "I don't want this anymore." Shortly after getting the flowers, Healy received a standing ovation from Red Cross executives who traveled to Washington to attend a weapons-of-mass-destruction-preparedness seminar. "I could have gotten a sunburn from all that warmth," she said.

Nonetheless, after the firing of the DOC women, the creation of the Liberty Fund by fiat and the blowup over the Israel issue, Healy's departure was becoming inevitable. "Bernadine brought discipline, authority and accountability to the American Red Cross," McLaughlin said. "But every time she took a strong position, a little more of her capital with the board was spent. At a certain point, you can't recoup."

On Tuesday, Oct. 23, the governors met to vote on whether they had confidence in Healy's leadership. Some sat in the board room in D.C.; others were piped in by speakerphone. In the end, six members voted for Healy, three abstained and about 27 voted against her, according to McLaughlin. By that count, 14 of the board members did not participate in the vote. Gloria White, a retired vice chancellor at Washington University, was one of very few board members who spoke on the record about the decision. She gave me a succinct statement about Healy: "She was one of the finest leaders the Red Cross has ever had." Then she said: "It will have to rest there. There's nothing to be served by going beyond that. They have made their decisions."

McLaughlin said that he recommended that Healy's departure be put off for six months, but that he did not prevail. Three days later, McLaughlin and Healy appeared together publicly to announce her resignation. Healy told me that McLaughlin wanted her to say that she was exhausted; as someone who prides herself on her stamina, she bristled at the very notion. So instead, she and McLaughlin gave *no* reason for her departure. Reporters were puzzled; they pushed Healy to explain why she was "abandoning" the Red Cross. Healy, growing teary-eyed, said that she had no choice; she was forced out. McLaughlin, sticking to the original script in which they were going to keep this fact hidden for the sake of her dignity, then denied this. It was, she said later, the "press conference from hell."

A few days later, she wrote a letter to the board: "Maybe you wanted more of a Mary Poppins and less of a Jack Welch."

Shortly after Healy's resignation, hundreds of Red Cross executives from around the country gathered in an all-white ballroom on E Street NW in Washington for another "W.M.D.," or weapons-of-mass-destruction workshop. This time, Healy was not invited. But her face stared up from the cover of *The Humanitarian* magazine at every place setting. "If they were trying to disappear her, they should have lost the magazine," one woman in a red jacket whispered. Her colleague pointed to a faux balcony hanging over the ballroom, saying that he kept expecting Healy to appear. "Don't cry for me, disaster relief workers," someone joked.

The workshop did not impart a tremendous amount of new information. But it did serve unofficially as a kind of pep rally for those who felt, in a nondenominational way, that they had been doing God's work since Sept. 11 and did not deserve to have their good intentions maligned. The public questioning of the Red Cross had intensified in the wake of Healy's departure, and while some in the room resented her for that, most resented the "negativity of the media" instead.

Barry White from South Carolina passed around a cartoon from *The Oregonian* that elicited groans and "darns!" The cartoon showed the Statue of Liberty lying on a cot waiting for blood as Dracula, on the next bed, sucked from the donations. The blood bag was labeled "Sept. 11th Aid," and the vampire wore the Red Cross logo on his chest.

There was an air of defiance—and denial—in the ballroom that day as national officials set out to pump up spirits. Some sounded almost like preachers. "Since Sept. 11, the network has been working in miraculous ways," an executive vice president told the crowd. He intoned a sacred tenet: "As we all know, we're the first on the scene and the last to leave." A Philadelphia chapter executive told a story about a volunteer who "forever changed" the life of a little boy, as "Red Cross volunteers do again and again and again."

Only at the end of the day did some rise to interrupt the cheerleading, like a New Jersey executive who began by suggesting that his colleagues realize the Red Cross is not "omnipotent." At this point, I was hustled out of the room by a senior public-relations executive (who later left the Red Cross) so that the assembled could have a "free and open discussion."

It had taken me weeks to penetrate the Red Cross, which seemed excessively skittish of observation, much less of scrutiny. Eventually, McLaughlin intervened and got me into the ballroom that day and later inside the Red Cross's new, post-Sept. 11 call-in center outside Washington. In its nervousness about media scrutiny of its troubles, the Red Cross had been hiding its assets too—people like Cyndi Sadler, a volunteer from Louisiana who was, weirdly, sitting in a converted Levitz furniture store in suburban Virginia fielding calls from World Trade Center widows.

As I approached, Sadler was signing off a call to New Jersey. "I couldn't get you off my mind all weekend," she said into the phone. "It just breaks my heart for y'all." Hanging up, Sadler shook her frosted blond mane. "She ended with 'God bless you,'" Sadler said. "Now that's some progress."

"This case I'm working?" she continued, taking a swig of Diet Dr Pepper. "The woman called Saturday irate, and I mean, iiii-rate. She was going to call the press. She had lost her sister in the World Trade Center, and she'd been trying to get benefits for her nephew. But somehow her paperwork got lost. Just plain fell through the cracks. So I let her vent; I took her lashes. And before long, she was eating out of my hands."

Sadler has a big heart and an easy laugh, and she was like many of the Red Cross volunteers I met: earnest and industrious and Middle American. The kind of person who will follow you into the ladies' room to continue a conversation and talk right through the stall door. "I think it's awesome that we live in a country like this, with a Red Cross to reach out," she said. It was hard not to be touched by her and by the massive display of volunteerism that she is part of, the people who didn't know much of anything about Healy or McLaughlin or the F.D.A. or the Liberty Fund. They just knew about giving three weeks of their time when disaster struck and about how it made them feel queasy when the goodness of an institution like the Red Cross was questioned.

I talked to Sadler the day after a grueling hearing in November, during which congressmen suggested to Healy that the Red Cross was punch-drunk with donations and pig-headedly ignoring its donors' desires for all their money to go directly to the victims. Representative Peter Deutsch, Democrat of Florida, told Healy, "I don't think anybody who wrote a check for the Red Cross expected it would be used for frozen blood."

At that point, the Red Cross was already doing a pretty good job of getting money directly to the victims' families—it had handed out emergency cash grants averaging $14,500 to 2,700 families—but it was making mistakes, and the mistakes were highlighted during the hearing. Russa Steiner of New Hope, Pa., the widow of a World Trade Center victim, had received only $1,244 for incidentals until her name was put on the witness list for the hearing. That listing prompted the Red Cross to discover that Steiner had "fallen through the cracks." Luis Garcia, manager of the gift program, told me later that Steiner's application had been approved but that a

Red Cross worker had accidentally left the requisition for her check inside her case file and closed it up. So just before the hearing began, the Red Cross hurriedly handed her $27,000, which made the organization look bungling.

Healy's testimony, a lame duck's defense of an institution that had just thrown her out, was almost painful to watch. Smiling through clenched teeth, she tried to explain why the Liberty Fund was never meant solely for victims of Sept. 11. She talked about why she thought the Red Cross needed to be girding itself for future terrorist acts. But her logic did not pierce the emotion in the room.

During the hearing, the Red Cross began receiving an onslaught of angry e-mail messages. Some 1,500 arrived between 6:30 p.m. and 8 a.m. the following day. A man named Philip wrote: "I am thoroughly disgusted and disappointed over your failing the families of victims from Sept. 11. I'll never contribute another penny or drop of blood."

To McLaughlin and Decker, it was becoming clearer by the day that the Red Cross had to do something. It could not simply lament that it was being misunderstood. It could not just say: "Trust us. We're the disaster professionals." That trust was shattered.

So the Red Cross backpedaled away from controversy as fast as it could. In a stunning reversal, McLaughlin and Decker held a news conference in Washington on Nov. 14—carried live by CNN—to say that it would spend the entire Liberty Fund to care for the victims of the Sept. 11 attacks, their families and the rescue workers. "With this action, we hope to restore the faith of our donors and the trust of the American public," McLaughlin declared.

Two weeks earlier, McLaughlin had told me that Healy's concept for the fund was "just right." In fact, the Red Cross could have stuck by it, if it were not for its desire to repent. A senior official explained it to me rather crudely, insisting it was "moronic" to use the whole Liberty Fund as "an A.T.M. machine for the victims' families." Almost half of the fund was pledged by corporations, he said, and the corporations may well have agreed to redirect their money toward, say, a blood reserve. This would have allowed the Red Cross to respect the public's desire to support the victims, and only the victims, while sticking to its plan.

But the Red Cross needed to quell the furor and so chose a concrete, sentimental response rather than what might well have been a wiser policy.

It also decided—after many angry e-mail messages from American Jews—to continue to withhold its dues from the international federation and reaffirm its commitment to Israel's equivalent of the Red Cross. ("They didn't want to make Healy a martyr is what we heard," an official in Geneva said.)

Those actions took the public pressure off the American Red Cross, and as McLaughlin and Decker had hoped, the organization faded from the spotlight. What will happen inside remains to be seen. Clearly, the American Red Cross's problems transcend Healy and will outlive her unless the stresses of Sept. 11 succeed in shocking the organization through a real transformation.

McLaughlin and Decker are ambitious about reform, along the same lines that Healy was, although they hope to accomplish more by using gentler tactics. Still, Decker, who expects to serve from six months to a year as interim C.E.O., is talking tough. "People will be held accountable for performing," Decker says. "If we have to change some culture here, that's what's going to have to happen. People can vote with their feet if they don't like it."

McLaughlin, for his part, said he does not want to recruit a replacement for Healy until he restructures the governance system that keeps undermining Red Cross presidents. He cannot slim down the board unless he goes to Congress and asks it to revise the Red Cross charter, which is cumbersome. So he will seek to make the powerful executive committee more representative of the board at large—that is, to reduce its dominance by Red Cross insiders. He also wants to establish qualifications for board members so that loyalty to the Red Cross alone, while honorable, is not enough.

Inside the Red Cross, these are fighting words. And McLaughlin and Decker are not Red Cross lifers. There is no telling what kind of resistance they will encounter and how they will handle it.

Back in Ohio, Healy's moods shift as she tries to understand how she went from commanding a historic relief effort to overseeing her suburban household. When she is her usual confident self, she declares that it is common for boards and presidents to clash. But when she is blue, an uncharacteristic state for Bernadine Healy, she laments that she was all wrong for the Red Cross and that she failed at something very important. "So much potential for greatness," she says, her voice trailing off. And though she is talking about the organization, it sounds for one moment as if she is talking about herself.

Chapter 11 Review Questions

1. In your own words, can you describe the Wise concept of "public service culture"? What does the author mean by that term? What assumptions about human nature does her motivational concept rest on? Do you believe these are valid assumptions?

2. Why does Wise argue that public service motivation is found more often in government than business or elsewhere? Do you agree or disagree? Why or why not?

3. Regarding the foregoing case study, "Who Brought Bernadine Healy Down?", describe the various cross-pressures and multiple responsibilities that Healy faced. Why do these persisting cross-pressures and responsibilities make it so difficult to frame a clear, consistent motivational system in government or nonprofits?

4. Are public sector motives rooted in rational, norm-based, affective categories, as Wise's essay theorizes? Why or why not?

5. Given the difficult realities of the contemporary working environment of public administration today, how would you develop and implement an effective "public service culture" for a government agency? Assess some of the strengths and weaknesses of this system that you envisioned, as well as the difficulties in establishing it.

6. Select any one of the prior cases in this text and examine carefully the motivations of one or more of the public officials. How do these motives compare and contrast with those discussed in Case 11—are they the same or fundamentally different? Explain why.

Key Terms

public service motives
public service culture
rational motives
norm-based motives
affective motives
normative orientation

rule-following behavior
self-interested motives
normative values
engagement
professional management

Suggestions for Further Reading

Public personnel administration is a field of enormous complexity, specialization, and rapid change, and, therefore, looking at current basic introductory texts offers a good overview: N. Joseph Cayer, *Public Personnel Administration in the U.S.,* 3rd ed. (New York: St. Martin's, 1995); Dennis Dresang, *Public Personnel Management and Public Policy,* 3rd ed. (Reading, Mass.: Addison-Wesley, 2000); Steven W. Hays and Richard C. Kearney, *Public Personnel Administration,* 4th ed. (Englewood Cliffs, N.J.: Prentice-Hall, 2002); Lloyd G. Nigro and Felix A. Nigro, *The New Public Personnel Administration,* 5th ed. (Itasca, Ill.: F. E. Peacock Publishers, Inc., 2000); Carolyn Ban, *Public Personnel Management,* 3rd ed. (New York: Longman, 2001); Evan M. Berman, James Bowman, and Jonathan West, *Human Resource Management in Public Service* (Thousand Oaks, Calif.: Sage, 2000); Donald Klinger and John Nalbandian, *Public Personnel Management,* 5th ed. (Englewood Cliffs, N.J.: Prentice-Hall, 2002); and

Dennis D. Riley, *Public Personnel Administration,* 2nd ed. (New York: HarperCollins, 2001). To supplement these introductions, students should further examine the basic *framing* documents of public personnel, such as the Civil Service Act of 1883, the Hatch Act, the Civil Service Reform Act of 1978, as well as several others contained in Frederick C. Mosher, ed., *Basic Documents of American Public Administration: 1776–1950* (New York: Holmes and Meier, 1976), and Richard J. Stillman II, ed., *Basic Documents of American Public Administration: Since 1950* (New York: Holmes and Meier, 1982).

For the best history of the American civil service system, see Paul Van Riper, *History of U.S. Civil Service* (New York: Harper & Row, 1958). For an insightful view of personnel practices at the local level, read Frank J. Thompson, *Personnel Policy in the City: The Politics of Jobs in Oakland* (Berkeley: University of California Press, 1975); and for a view of its operation at the federal level, see Frederick C. Mosher, *Democracy and the Public Service,* 2nd ed. (New York: Oxford University Press, 1982); Patricia W. Ingraham, *The Foundation of Merit: Service in American Democracy* (Baltimore: Johns Hopkins Press, 1995); Paul Light, *The New Public Service* (Washington, D.C.: The Brookings Institution, 1999); or Hugh Heclo, *A Government of Strangers: Executive Politics in Washington* (Washington, D.C.: The Brookings Institution, 1977). Articles contained in the "classics" series on personnel give readers a useful overview of the scope, diversity, and complexity of this field, especially in Frank J. Thompson, ed., *Classics of Public Personnel Policy,* 2nd ed. (Monterey, Calif.: Brooks/Cole, 1990) as well as other contemporary sets of readings in Patricia W. Ingraham and Barbara Romzek, eds. *Rethinking Public Personnel Systems* (San Francisco: Jossey-Bass, 1994); Jack Rabin, et al., eds., *Handbook of Public Personnel Administration* (New York: Dekker, 1995); Stephen E. Coudrey, *Handbook of Human Resource Management* (San Francisco: Jossey-Bass, 1998) and part 6 of James L. Perry, *Handbook of Public Administration,* 2nd ed. (San Francisco: Jossey-Bass, 1996). "Further Readings" in chapter 9 of this text offers useful additional references. Excellent sources for further readings on personnel motivation are also found in chapters 6 and 7 in Hal G. Rainey, *Understanding and Managing Public Organizations,* 2nd ed. (San Francisco: Jossey-Bass, 1996). For three recent thoughtful essays, read Gene Brewer et al., "Individual Conceptions of Public Service," *Public Administration Review* (May/June 2000); Sue Frank and Gregory Lewis, "Who Wants to Work for the Government?" *Public Administration Review* (July/August 2002); and Laurance O'Toole and Kenneth Meier, "Public Management, Personnel Stability, and Organizational Performance" *Journal of Public Administration Research and Theory* (January 2003).

Other current writings on personnel motivation include Linda Holbeche, *Motivating People in Lean Organizations* (Woburn, Mass.: Butterworth-Heineman, 1998); Barbara Glanz, *Handle with Care: Motivating and Retaining Employees* (New York.: McGraw-Hill, 2002); Janet and Robert Denhardt, *Creating a Culture of Innovation* (Arlington, VA.: Pricewaterhouse Coopers Endowment for the Business of Government, 2001).

At the federal level, the Volcker Commission Report for a federal review of this topic, *Leadership for America* (Lexington, Mass.: Lexington Books, 1990), or for the local level, Frank J. Thompson, ed., *Revitalizing State and Local Government* (San Francisco: Jossey-Bass, 1993), provide numerous specific ideas for improving public service motivation throughout government. Norma M. Riccucci's *Unsung Heroes* (Washington, D.C.: Georgetown University Press, 1995) offers good examples of what motivates outstanding federal executives.

One would also do well to skim current issues of *Public Administration Review, Harvard Business Review, Public Personnel Management, The Bureaucrat,* and *Public Management* for recent and fast-changing trends in the field of personnel. One should also visit the government management Web site at www.govleaders.org to sample the numerous problems.

CHAPTER 12

Public Budgeting: The Concept of Budgeting as Political Choice

The essence of budgeting is that it allocates scarce resources and hence implies choice between potential objects of expenditure. Budgeting implies balance and it requires some kind of decision-making process.

Irene S. Rubin

Introduction

Budgets serve many important functions in government. In one sense, budgets are contracts annually agreed on by the executive and legislative branches that allow executive agencies and departments to raise and spend public funds in specified ways for the coming fiscal year (normally running in state and local governments from July 1 to June 30; changed at the federal level by the Congressional Budget Act of 1974 to end on September 30 and to begin October 1 each year). A budget imposes a mutual set of legal obligations between the elected and appointed officers of public organizations with regard to taxation and expenditure policies. A budget is, therefore, a legal contract that provides a vehicle for fiscal controls over subordinate units of government by the politically elected representatives of the people.

Budgets have other purposes as well: they can be planning devices used to translate presently scarce fiscal and human resources in the public sector into future governmental goals and programs. In this respect, budgets are vital instruments for directing what tasks government will perform and how human talent in society and public monies will be used.

In addition, budgets are forces for internal coordination and efficiency in public administration. Budget formulations annually impose choices concerning how public programs should be undertaken, interrelated, and measured in terms of their value, effectiveness, and worth to the general public. Related to the concept of budgets as a coordinating device is the idea that budgets are economic documents. In this role federal budgets are tools of fiscal policy, for they stimulate or slow down national economic growth through increased or decreased taxation or revenue expenditures. Finally, budgets can also be viewed as political documents, reflecting through the allocation of funds the ultimate desires, interests, and power of various groups within the body politic as expressed by elected legislative bodies. In setting up an annual budget, various political participants engage in log rolling, compromises, and bargains to create a document that by and large mirrors the current priorities of the locality, state, or nation. The quality and quantity of government that the citizenry desires and will support at any given time is expressed by the budget.

Our conceptual understanding of these roles of the budget in modern government is comparatively new, being chiefly a twentieth-century phenomenon. In large part, our instituting formal budget documents began in the Progressive Era, when public budgets were developed as vehicles for governmental reform to produce improved economy and efficiency in the public sector and as instruments for imposing greater control over public spending. Many of these ideas and concepts were borrowed from the experience and practices of business management.

Although there remains a strong emphasis on the earlier notions of budgets as vehicles for imposing control, economy, and efficiency in government, a prominent current view of the role of budgets—and a perspective frequently held by political scientists, budgeting specialists, and public administration practitioners—is a political one: budgets are principally governed by considerations of compromise, strategy, and bargaining. Irene S. Rubin, a political scientist and prominent authority on public budgeting at Northern Illinois University, presents the political view of budget making in the opening chapter of her book *The Politics of Public Budgeting*. Rubin envisions government budgets as "not merely technical managerial documents" but rather "they are also intrinsically and irreducibly political." Her thesis is that although public budgets share many features of budgeting in general, such as presenting choices over possible expenditures and problems of balancing revenues with expenditures, they differ in fundamental ways. The open environments within which budgets are developed, the variety of actors involved, the constraints imposed as well as the emphasis on public accountability, give budgets special and distinctive features in the public sector. These aspects add complexity and unique dilemmas to their formulation, operation, and conceptualization.

Professor Rubin's essay at the outset defines "what is budgeting" and the distinctive features of government budgets. From a local case of budget making in Dekalb, Illinois, she underscores the critical political dynamics of public budgeting processes and the variety of participants that are involved, even within the local setting. The elements of budgetary politics concern, in her view, "separate but linked" decision clusters, specifically five clusters dealing with the revenue process (How much income will be available and from where?); budget process (How will the budget choices be made?); expenditure process (Which programs will get what?); the balance cluster (How will revenues and expenditures be balanced?); and budget implementation issues (How will the budget be put into operation?). Her essay concludes with an important distinction between understanding "macrobudgeting," or top-down budget viewpoints, versus "microbudgeting," which focuses on the specific actors and their strategies in putting together budgets.

As you read the following selection, keep in mind such questions as:

Why does Rubin stress throughout her writing the political over the technical or managerial aspects of public budgeting?

From her perspective, what differences are apparent between government and business budget-making? Do you agree with her conclusions about these fundamental differences?

How do "macro" and "micro" views of budgets differ and yet why are *both* essential for a complete understanding of the budgetary process? What are the advantages and disadvantages of both ways of conceptualizing budgets? Do these perspectives on budgets relate to any of our earlier readings such as Charles Lindblom's "incremental decision-making model"?

Why does Rubin focus on understanding modern budgetary processes as "separate but linked decision clusters"? What are the major clusters of issues apparent in each?

The Politics of Public Budgets

IRENE S. RUBIN

Public budgets describe what governments do by listing how governments spend money. A budget links tasks to be performed with the amount of resources necessary to accomplish those tasks, ensuring that money will be available to wage war, provide housing, or maintain streets. Budgets limit expenditures to the revenues available, to ensure balance and prevent overspending. Most of the work in drawing up a budget is technical, estimating how much it will cost to feed a thousand shut-ins with a Meals on Wheels program or how much revenue will be produced from a 1 percent tax on retail sales. But public budgets are not merely technical managerial documents; they are also intrinsically and irreducibly political.

- Budgets reflect choices about what government will and will not do. They reflect general public consensus about what kinds of services governments should provide and what citizens are entitled to as members of society. Should government provide services that the private sector could provide, such as water, electricity, transportation, and housing? Do all citizens have a guarantee of health care, regardless of ability to pay? Are all insured against hunger? Are they entitled to some kind of housing?
- Budgets reflect priorities—between police and

flood control, day care and defense, the Northeast and the Southwest. The budget process mediates between groups and individuals who want different things from government and determines who gets what. These decisions may influence whether the poor get job training or the police get riot training, both as a response to an increased number of unemployed.

- Budgets reflect the relative proportion of decisions made for local and constituency purposes, and for efficiency, effectiveness, and broader public goals. Budgets reflect the degree of importance legislators put on satisfying their constituents and the legislators' willingness to listen to interest-group demands. For example, the Defense Department may decide to spend more money to keep a military base open because the local economy depends on it and to spend less money to improve combat readiness.
- Budgets provide a powerful tool of accountability to citizens who want to know how the government is spending their money and if government has generally followed their preferences. Budgeting links citizen preferences and governmental outcomes.
- Budgets reflect citizens' preferences for different forms of taxation and different levels of taxation, as well as the ability of specific groups of taxpayers to shift tax burdens to others. The budget reflects the degree to which the government redistributes wealth upward or downward through the tax system.

From *The Politics of Public Budgeting* by Irene B. Rubin (Chatham, N.J.: Chatham House Publishers, 1990), pp. 1–28. Reprinted by permission of Chatham House Publishers.

- At the national level, the budget influences the economy, so fiscal policy affects the level of employment—how many people are out of work at any time.
- Budgets reflect the relative power of different individuals and organizations to influence budget outcomes. Budgetary decision making provides a picture of the relative power of budget actors within and between branches of government, as well as the importance of citizens in general and specific interest groups.

In all these ways, public budgeting is political. But budgeting is not typical of other political processes and hence one example among many. It is both an important and a unique arena of politics. It is important because of the specific policy issues reflected in the budget: the scope of government, the distribution of wealth, the openness of government to interest groups, and the accountability of government to the public at large. It is unique because these decisions have to take place in the context of budgeting, with its need for balance, its openness to the environment, and its requirements for timely decisions so that government can carry on without interruption.

Public budgets clearly have political implications, but what does it mean to say that key political decisions are made in the context of budgeting? The answer has several parts. First, what is budgeting? Second, what is public budgeting, as opposed to individual or family budgeting or the budgeting of private organizations? Third, what does *political* mean in the context of public budgeting?

What Is Budgeting?

The essence of budgeting is that it allocates scarce resources and hence implies choice between potential objects of expenditure. Budgeting implies balance, and it requires some kind of decision-making process.

Making Budgetary Choices

All budgeting, whether public or private, individual or organizational, involves choices between possible expenditures. Since no one has unlimited resources, people budget all the time. A young child makes a budget (a plan for spending, balancing revenues and expenditures) when she decides to spend money on a marshmallow rabbit rather than a chocolate one, assuming she has money enough for only one rabbit. The air force may choose between two different airplanes to replace current bombers. These examples illustrate the simplest form of budgeting because they involve only one actor, one resource, one time, and two straightforward and comparable choices.

Normally, budgeting does not take place by comparing only two reasonably similar items. There may be a nearly unlimited number of choices. Budgeting usually limits the options to consider by grouping together similar things that can be reasonably compared. When I go to the supermarket, I do not compare all the possible things I could buy, not only because I cannot absorb that number of comparisons, but because the comparisons would be meaningless and a waste of time. I do not go to the supermarket and decide to get either a turkey or a bottle of soda pop. I compare main dishes with main dishes, beverages with beverages, desserts with desserts. Then I have a common denominator for comparison. For example, I may look at the main course and ask about the amount of protein for the dollar. I may compare the desserts in terms of the amount of cholesterol or the calories.

There is a tendency, then, to make comparisons within categories where the comparison is meaningful. This is as true for governmental budgeting as it is for shoppers. For example, weapons might be compared with weapons or automobiles with automobiles. They could be compared in terms of speed, reliability, availability of spare parts, and so on, and the one that did the most of what you wanted it to do at the least cost would be the best choice. As long as there is agreement on the goals to be achieved, the choice should be straightforward.

Sometimes, budgeting requires comparison of different, and seemingly incomparable things. If I do not have enough money to buy a whole balanced meal, I may have to make choices between main dishes and desserts. How do I compare the satisfaction of a sweet tooth to the nourishment of a turkey?

Or, in the public sector, how do I compare the benefits of providing shelters for the homeless with buying more helicopters for the navy? I may then move to more general comparisons, such as how clearly were the requests made and the benefits spelled out; who got the benefits last time and whose turn is it this time; are there any specific contingencies that make one choice more likely than the other? For example, will we be embarrassed to show our treatment of the homeless in front of a visiting dignitary? Or, are disarmament negotiations coming up in which we need to display strength or make a symbolic gesture of restraint? Comparing dissimilar items may require a list of priorities. It may be possible to do two or more important things if they are sequenced properly.

Budgeting often allocates money, but it can allocate any scarce resource, for example, time. A student may choose between studying for an exam or playing softball and drinking beer afterward. In this example, it is time that is at a premium, not money. Or it could be medical skills that are in short supply, or expensive equipment, or apartment space, or water.

Government programs often involve a choice of resources and sometimes involve combinations of resources, each of which has different characteristics. For example, some federal farm programs involve direct cash payments plus loans at below-market interest rates, and welfare programs often involve dollar payments plus food stamps, which allow recipients to pay less for food. Federal budgets often assign agencies money, personnel, and sometimes borrowing authority, three different kinds of resources.

Balancing and Borrowing

Budgets have to balance. A plan for expenditures that pays no attention to ensuring that revenues cover expenditures is not a budget. That may sound odd in view of huge federal deficits, but a budget may technically be balanced by borrowing. Balance means only that outgo is matched or exceeded by income. The borrowing, of course, has to be paid off. Borrowing means spending more now and paying more in the future in order to maintain balance. It is a balance over time.

To illustrate the nature of budget balance, consider me as shopper again. Suppose I spend all my weekly shopping money before I buy my dessert. I have the option of treating my dollar limit as if it were more flexible, by adding the dimension of time. I can buy the dessert and everything else in the basket, going over my budget, and then eat less at the end of the month. Or I can pay the bill with a credit card, assuming I will have more money in the future with which to pay off the bill when it comes due. The possibility of borrowing against the future is part of most budget choices.

Process

Budgeting cannot proceed without some kind of decision process. Even in the simplest cases of budgeting, there has to be some limit set to spending, some order of decision making, some way to structure comparisons among alternatives, and some way to compare choices. Budget processes also regulate the flow of decisions so they are made in a timely manner.

Back to my shopping example: If I shop for the main course first, and spend more money than I intended on it because I found some fresh fish, there will be less money left for purchasing the dessert. Hence, unless I set a firm limit on the amount of money to spend for each segment of the meal, the order in which I do the purchasing counts. Of course, if I get to the end of my shopping and do not have enough money left for dessert, I can put back some of the items already in the cart and squeeze out enough money for dessert.

Governmental budgeting is also concerned with procedures for managing tradeoffs between large categories of spending. Budgeters may determine the relative importance of each category first, attaching a dollar level in proportion to the assigned importance, or they may allow purchasing in each area to go on independently, later reworking the choices until the balance between the parts is acceptable.

The order of decisions is important in another sense. I can determine how much money I am likely to have first and then set that as an absolute limit on expenditures, or I can determine what I must have, what I wish to have, and what I need to set aside for emergencies and then go out and try to find enough money to cover some or all of those expenditures.

Especially in emergencies, such as accidents or other health emergencies, people are likely to obligate the money first and worry about where it will come from later. Governmental budgeting, too, may concentrate first on revenues and later on expenditures, or first on expenditures and later on income. Like individuals or families, during emergencies such as floods or hurricanes or wars, governments will commit the expenditures first and worry about where the money will come from later.

Governmental Budgeting

Public budgeting shares the characteristics of budgeting in general but differs from household and business budgeting in some key ways. First, in public budgeting, there are always people and organizations with different perspectives and different goals trying to get what they want out of the budget. In individual budgets, there may be only one person involved; and in family and business budgets, there may be only a limited number of actors and they may have similar views of what they want to achieve through the budget.

Second, public budgets are more open to the environment than budgets of families or businesses are. Not only are public budgets open to the economy but also to other levels of government, to citizens, to interest groups, to the press, and to politicians.

Third, budgets form a crucial link between citizen taxpayers and government officials. The document itself may be a key form of accountability. This function does not apply to businesses, families, or individuals.

Fourth, public budgeting is characterized by a variety of constraints, legal limits, perceived limits imposed by public opinion, rules and regulations about how to carry out the budget, and many more. Public budgeting is far more constrained in this sense than budgets of individuals or businesses.

Public budgeting has five particular characteristics that differentiate it from other kinds of budgeting. First, public budgeting is characterized by a variety of budgetary actors who often have different priorities and different levels of power over budget outcomes.

These actors have to be regulated and orchestrated by the budget process. Second, in government there is a distinction between those who pay taxes and those who decide how money will be spent—the citizens and the elected politicians. Public officials can force citizens to pay taxes for expenditures they do not want, but citizens can vote politicians out of office. Third, the budget document is important as a means of public accountability. Fourth, public budgets are very vulnerable to the environment—to the economy, to changes in public opinion, to elections, to local contingencies such as natural disasters like floods, or political disasters such as the police bombing of MOVE headquarters in Philadelphia, which burned down part of a neighborhood. Fifth, public budgets are incredibly constrained. Although there is a built-in necessity to make budgets adaptable to contingencies, there are many elements of public budgets that are beyond the immediate control of those who draw up budgets.

A Variety of Actors

The first characteristic of public budgeting was the variety of actors involved in the budget and their frequently clashing motivations and goals. On a regular basis, bureau chiefs, executive budget officers, and chief executives are involved in the budget process, as are legislators, both on committees and as a whole group. Interest groups may be involved at intervals, sometimes for relatively long stretches of time, sometimes briefly. Sometimes citizens play a direct or indirect role in the budget process. Courts may play a role in budgets at any level of government at unpredictable intervals. When they do play a role in budgetary decisions, what are these actors trying to achieve?

Bureau Chiefs.   Many students of budgeting assume that agency heads always want to expand their agencies, that their demands are almost limitless, and that it is up to other budget actors to curtail and limit their demands. The reasons given for that desire for expansion include prestige, more subordinates, more space, larger desks, more secretaries, and not incidentally, more salary. The argument presumes that agency heads judge their bureaucratic skills in terms of the satisfaction of their budget requests. Successful bureaucrats bring back the budget. Agency expansion is the measure of success.

Recent research has suggested that while some bureaucrats may be motivated by salaries, many feel that one of their major rewards is the opportunity to do good for people—to house the homeless, feed the hungry, find jobs for the unemployed, and send out checks to the disabled.[1] For these bureaucrats, efforts to expand agency budgets are the result of their belief in the programs they work for.

Recent research has also suggested that the bureaucracy has become more professional, which introduces the possibility of another motivation, the desire to do a good job, to do it right, to put in the best machinery that exists or build the biggest, toughest engineering project or the most complicated weapons.

The generalization that bureaucrats always press for budget increases appears to be too strong. Some agencies are much more aggressive in pushing for growth than others. Some are downright moribund. Sometimes agency heads refuse to expand when given the opportunity,[2] suggesting there are some countervailing values to growth. One of these countervailing values is agency autonomy. Administrators may prefer to maintain autonomy rather than increase the budget if it comes down to a choice between the two. A second countervailing value to growth is professionalism, the desire to get the job done, and do it quickly and right. Administrators generally prefer to hire employees who have the ability to get the job done, plus a little, spare amount of intelligence, motivation, and energy just in case they need to get some extra work done or do it fast in response to a political request.[3] Administrators may refuse to add employees if the proposed employees do not add to the agency's capacity to get things done.

A third countervailing value is program loyalty. Expansion may be seen as undesirable if the new mission swamps the existing mission, if it appears contradictory to the existing mission, or if the program requires more money to carry out than is provided, forcing the agency to spend money designated for existing programs on new ones or do a poor job.

A fourth countervailing value is belief in the chain of command. Many, if not all, bureaucrats believe that their role is to carry out the policies of the chief executive and the legislature. If those policies mean cutting back budgets, agency heads cut back the agencies. Agency heads may be appointed precisely because they are willing to make cuts in their agencies.[4]

Bureaucrats, then, do not always try to expand their agencies' budgets. They have other, competing goals, which sometimes dominate. Also, their achievements can be measured by other than expanded budgets. They may go for some specific items in the budget without raising totals, or may try for changes in the wording of legislation. They may strive to get a statutory basis for the agency and security of funding. They may take as a goal providing more efficient and effective service, rather than expanded or more expensive service.

The Executive Budget Office.   The traditional role of the budget office has been to scrutinize requests coming up from the agencies, to find waste and eliminate it, and to discourage most requests for new money. The executive budget office has been perceived as the naysayer, the protector of the public purse. Most staff members in the budget office are very conscious of the need to balance the budget, to avoid deficits, and to manage cash flow so that there is money on hand to pay bills. Hence they tend to be skeptical of requests for new money.

In recent years, however, there has been a change in the role of budget office. At the national level under President Ronald Reagan, budgeting became much more top-down, with the director of the Office of Management and Budget (OMB) proposing specific cuts and negotiating them directly with Congress, without much scrutiny of requests coming up from departments or bureaus. OMB became more involved in trying to accomplish the policy goals of the President through the budget.[5] At state levels too, there has been an evolution of budget staff from more technical to more political and more policy-related goals. When the governor is looking for new spending proposals these may come from his budget office.

Chief Executive Officers.   The role of chief executive officers (the mayor or city manager, the governor, the President) is highly variable, and hence these executives' goals in the budget process cannot be predicted without knowledge of the individuals. Some chief executives have been expansive, proposing new programs; others have been economy minded, cutting back proposals generated by the legislatures. Some have been efficiency oriented, reorganizing staffs and trying to maintain service levels without increases in taxes or expenditures.

Legislators.   Legislators have sometimes been described as always trying to increase expenditures.[6] Their motivation is viewed as getting reelected, which depends on their ability to provide constituents services and deliver "pork"—jobs and capital projects—to their districts. Norms of reciprocity magnify the effects of these spending demands because legislators are reluctant to cut others' pork lest their own be cut in return. At the city level, a council member described this norm of reciprocity, "There is an unwritten rule that if something is in a councilman's district, we'll go along and scratch each other's back."[7]

For some legislators, however, getting reelected is not a high priority. They view elected office as a service they perform for the community rather than a career, and while they may be responsive to constituents' needs, they are simply not motivated to start new projects or give public employees a raise in order to get reelected. Also, some legislators feel secure about the possibility of reelection, and hence have no urgent need to deliver pork in order to increase their chances of reelections.[8]

Even assuming the motivation to get reelected, holding down taxes may be as important to reelection as spending on programs and projects. The consequence of tax reduction is usually curtailed expenditures. Legislators are bound to try to balance the budget, which puts some constraints on the desire to spend.

The tendency to provide pork is real, but there are counterbalancing factors. Some legislators are more immune to pressures from constituents because they are secure electorally, and legislators can organize themselves in such a way as to insulate themselves somewhat from these pressures. They can, for example,

select more electorally secure representatives for key positions on appropriations committees; they can separate committees that deal extensively with interest groups from those that deal with expenditures; they can set up buffer groups to deal with interest groups; they can structure the budget process so that revenue limits precede and guide spending proposals.

Moreover, legislators have interests other than providing pork. Some legislators are deeply concerned about solving social problems, designing and funding defense and foreign aid systems, and monitoring the executive branch. The proportion of federal budget spent on pork-type projects has declined in recent years, despite reforms in Congress that decentralized control and allowed pressure for pork to increase.[9] "Congressmen are not single-minded seekers of local benefits, struggling feverishly to win every last dollar for their districts. However important the quest for local benefits may be, it is always tempered by other competing concerns."[10] The pull for local benefits depends on the program. Some, like water projects, are oriented to local payoffs; others, like entitlements programs for large numbers of people, are not. Programs with local pull account for smaller and smaller proportions of the budget,[11] and the trend has accelerated since 1978.[12]

Interest Groups.   Interest groups, too, have often been singled out as the driving force behind budget increases. They are said to want more benefits for their members and to be undeterred by concerns for overall budget balance or the negative effects of tax increases. Moreover, their power has been depicted as great. Well-funded interest groups reportedly wine and dine legislators and provide campaign funding for candidates who agree with their positions.

There is some truth to this picture, but it is oversimplified. Interest groups have other policy goals besides budget levels. In fact, most probably deal with the budget only when a crisis occurs, such as a threat to funding levels. Because they can be counted on to come to the defense of a threatened program, they reduce the flexibility of budget decision makers, who find it difficult to cut programs with strong interest-group backing. But many areas of the budget do not have strong interest-group backing. For example, foreign aid programs have few domestic constituencies. Agencies may even have negative constituencies, that is, interest groups that want to reduce their funding and terminate their programs. The American Medical Association sought for years to eliminate the Health Planning Program.

Often when there are interest groups, there are many rather than one, and these interest groups may have conflicting styles or conflicting goals, canceling one another out or absorbing energy in battles among themselves. A coalition of interest groups representing broad geographic areas and a variety of constituencies is likely to be more effective at lobbying.

Hence coalitions may form, but individual members of the coalition may not go along with measures supported by others, so the range of items lobbied for as a unified group may be narrow. Extensive negotiations and continual efforts are required to get two or more independent groups together for a lobbying effort, and the arrangement can then fall apart. In short, interest groups are often interested in maintaining their autonomy.

Individuals.   Individuals seldom have a direct role in the budget process, as they did in the DeKalb case, but they often have an indirect role. They may vote on referenda to limit revenues, forbid some forms of taxation, or require budgetary balance. They voice their opinions also in public opinion polls, and more informally by calling or writing their elected representatives and giving their opinions. Their knowledge of the budget is not usually detailed, but their feelings about the acceptability of taxation are an important part of the constraints of public budgeting. Their preferences for less visible taxes and for taxes earmarked for specific approved expenditures have been an important factor in public budgeting.

The Courts.   Another budget actor that plays an intermittent role in determining expenditures is the courts.[13] The courts get involved when other actors, often interest groups, bring a case against the government. Suits that affect the budget may involve service levels or the legality of particular forms of taxation. If a particular tax is judged unconstitutional,

the result is usually lost revenues. If there are suits concerning levels of service, governments may be forced to spend more money on that service. There can also be damage suits against governments that affect expenditures. These suits are usually settled without regard to the government agencies' ability to pay. The result may be forced cuts in other areas of the budget, tax increases, or even bankruptcy. When the courts get involved, they may determine budget priorities. They introduce a kind of rigidity into the budget that says do this, or pay this, first.

Typical areas in which courts have gotten involved and mandated expenditures for state and local governments are prison overcrowding (declared cruel and unusual punishment) and deinstitutionalization of mentally ill and mentally handicapped patients. In each case, the rights of the institutionalized population required more services or more space, often involving expenditures of additional funds. From the perspective of the courts, the priority of rights outweighs immediate concerns for budget balances, autonomy of governmental units, and local priorities.

Power Differentials.   These various actors not only have different and potentially clashing budgetary goals, but they typically have different levels of power. Thus, at times, the budget office may completely dominate the agencies; at times, the Congress may differ from the President on budgetary policy and pass its own preferences. The courts may preempt the decision making of the executive and the legislature. Some particular interest groups may always be able to get tax breaks for themselves.

The combination of different preferences and different levels of power has to be orchestrated by the budget process in such a way that agreement is reached, and the players stay in the game, continuing to abide by the rules. If some actors feel too powerless over the budget, they may cease to participate or become obstructionist, blocking any agreements or imposing rigid, nonnegotiable solutions. Why participate in negotiations and discussions if the decision will go against you regardless of what you do? If some actors lose on important issues, they may try to influence budget implementation to favor themselves.

Or the actors with less budget power may try to change the budget process so that they have a better chance of influencing the outcomes.

The Separation of Payer and Decider

The second feature of public budgeting is that decisions about how money will be spent are made not by those providing the money but by their representatives. The payers and the deciders are two distinct groups. The payers are not given a choice about whether they want to pay or how much they want to pay. The power of the state may force them to pay. They may protest if they do not like how their money is being spent, and elect new representatives. They cannot, generally, take their money and do something else with it.

The distinction between the payers and the deciders leads to two crucial characteristics of public budgeting: public *accountability* and political *acceptability*. *Accountability* means to make sure that every penny of public money is spent as agreed, and to report accurately to the public on how money was spent. *Acceptability* means that public officials who make budget decisions are constrained by what the public wants. Sometimes they will do precisely what they think the public wants, even if the results are inefficient or inequitable, and sometimes they will present the budget so that it will be accepted by the public, even if they have not precisely followed public will. This effort may involve persuasion or deception.

Since public demands may not be clearly expressed, and since different segments of the public may make different and competing demands, and since public officials themselves may have priorities, officials may not be able or willing to be bound tightly to public opinion. Nevertheless, if politicians knowingly make decisions that differ from what the public wants, there is pressure to present the budget in a way that makes it appear acceptable. That pressure creates a tension between accountability, which requires nearly complete openness, and acceptability, which sometimes involves hiding or distorting information or presenting it in an unclear fashion.

The Budget Document and Accountability

Because of the separation of payer and decider, the budget document itself becomes an important means of public accountability. How did the public's representatives actually decide to spend taxpayer money? Did they waste it? Did they spend it on defense or police or on social services? The streets are in terrible shape—how much money did they spend on street repair? Citizens do not typically watch the decision making, but they and the press have access to the budget document and can look for the answers. They can hold the government accountable through the budget, to see that what officials promised them was actually delivered.

But budgets do not always present a complete and accurate picture. One example of how budgets can lose information happened recently in a state university. A university president decided to expand the big-time sports program, in an environment of overall financial scarcity. While some faculty members undoubtedly favored the action, many would have opposed it if they had been asked. The president did not ask their opinions, however; instead, the full costs of the program were disguised to make the budget appear acceptable. Because of progressive underestimates of costs in the sports program, some pundits labeled the sports program the case of the disappearing budget.

To obscure the real costs, the president broke up the costs for the program and scattered them among different portions of the budget. To complicate the picture further, he drew on different pockets of revenue, including student athletic fees, bond revenues, and voluntary donations. When asked, he said money going to the athletic programs was earmarked and could not be spent on other programs, so that professors trying to get more money to teach history or biology would look elsewhere than to sports. The amount of money showing as costs in the athletic program remained constant every year, although the program costs were expanding. Fearing conflict and disapproval, the president hid the costs in the budget.

The more complicated the budget, the more different activities and accounts, the greater the discretion of the administrators. As one university president offered, "Not a day goes by when we do not wish we had a more complex budget." The complexity allows for choice of where to report expenditures, and which revenues to use, to highlight some expenditures and gloss over others.

It would be misleading to suggest that the tension between accountability and acceptability always leads to more distortion or more secrecy. Sometimes the balance tends toward more accountability and budgets become clearer and more representative of true costs. The federal budget, for example, has moved toward clearer and more comprehensive portraits of public expenditures in recent years. But the tension is always present, and each budget represents some degree of selectivity about what it will present and how. The art of selective revelation is part of public budgeting.

Openness to the Environment

Public budgets are open to the environment. The environment for budgeting includes a number of different factors including the over-all level of resources available (the amount of taxable wealth, the existing tax structure, current economic conditions); the degree of certainty of revenues; and a variety of emergencies such as very heavy snowfall, tornadoes, wars, bridge collapses, droughts, chemical explosions, and water pollution. The environment also includes rigidities resulting from earlier decisions, which may now be embodied in law. For example, rapid inflation in housing prices in California resulted in a citizen referendum to protect themselves from rapidly rising property taxes. The result of the referendum was incorporated in the state constitution, limiting the taxing options of local government. Constitutional restrictions to maintain a balanced budget or limit expenditures or put a ceiling on borrowing operate in a similar manner. Prior borrowing creates a legal obligation for future budgets, an obligation that may press other possible expenditures out of consideration or require higher levels of taxation. The environment in this sense may frame policy issues and limit alternatives. Public opinion is also part of the budgetary environment, and the perception of change in public opinion will be reflected in changing budgets.

The intergovernmental system is also a key part of the environment for budget actors. The legal sources of revenues, limits on borrowing, strings attached to grants, and mandated costs are but a few of the budgetary implications of the intergovernmental system. The requirement that some grants be spent on particular items or that a recipient match expenditures on grants may result in a pattern of spending different from what the state or local government would have preferred.

Budget Constraints

Openness to the environment creates the need for budgets to be flexible. Public officials have to be able to adapt quickly, reallocating funds to meet emergencies, spending more now and making up the difference later, cutting back expenditures during the year to meet sudden declines in revenues or increases in expenditures. But the same openness to the environment that creates the need for flexibility may simultaneously subject budgeting to numerous constraints.

For example, in California, a statewide referendum limited the rate of growth of local assessments, restraining the growth of property tax revenues. Federal grants provide budgetary constraints when they can be spent only on particular programs. The courts may create budgetary constraints by declaring programs inadequate or taxes illegal. Legal obligations to repay debt and maintain public businesses separate from the rest of the budget also create constraints.

The need for flexibility and the number of budgetary constraints contest with one another, creating patterns typical of public budgeting. For example, local officials may press for home rule, which gives more independence and autonomy to local governments to manage their own affairs and adapt to changing conditions. But state officials may erode home rule through continually mandating local costs. State universities may try to squirrel away contingency funds outside those appropriated by the legislature so that they can respond to emergencies; the legislature may then try to appropriate and hence control this new local source of revenues.

The Meaning of Politics in Public Budgeting

Public budgets have a number of special characteristics. These characteristics suggest some of the ways that the budget is political. Political is a word that covers a number of meanings, even when narrowed to the context of budgetary decision making. The purpose of this book is to clarify the meaning of politics in the context of budgeting by sorting out some key meanings and showing how these meanings apply to different parts of budgetary decision making.

Concepts of Politics in the Budget

The literature suggests at least five major ways of viewing politics in the budget: reformism, incrementalist bargaining, interest group determinism, process, and policy making.

- The first is a reform orientation, which argues that politics and budgeting are or should be antithetical, that budgeting should be primarily or exclusively technical, and that comparison between items should be technical and efficiency based. Politics in the sense of the opinions and priorities of elected officials and interest groups is an unwanted intrusion that reduces efficiency and makes decision making less rational. The politics of reform involves a clash of views between professional staff and elected officials over the boundary between technical budget decisions and properly political ones.

- The second perspective is the incrementalist view, which sees budgeting as negotiations among a group of routine actors, bureaucrats, budget officers, chief executives, and legislators, who meet each year and bargain to resolution. To the extent that interest groups are included at all in this view, they are conceived of in the pluralist model. The process is open, anyone can play and win, and the overall outcome is good; conflict is held down because everyone wins something and no one wins too much.

- The third view is that interest groups are dominant actors in the budget process. In its extreme form this argument posits that richer and more powerful interest groups determine the budget. Some interests are represented by interest groups and others are not, or are represented by weaker interest groups; the outcome does not approximate democracy. There may be big winners and big losers in this model. Conflict is more extensive than in the incrementalist model. This view of politics in budgeting raises the questions of whether these interest groups represent narrow or broad coalitions, or possibly even class interest. To what extent do these interest groups represent oil or banking or the homeless, and to what extent do they represent business and labor more broadly?

- The fourth view of politics in the budget is that the budget process itself is the center and focus of budget politics. Those with particular budget goals try to change the budget process to favor their goals. Branches of government struggle with one another over budgetary power through the budget process; the budget process becomes the means of achieving or denying separation and balance between the branches of government. The degree of examination of budget requests, and the degree to which review is technical or political, cursory or detailed, is regulated by the budget process. The ability of interest groups to influence the budget, the role of the public in budget decisions, the openness of budget decision making—all these are part of the politics of process. In this view of politics, the individual actors and their strategies and goals may or may not be important, depending on the role assigned to individual actors in the budget process, and depending on whether the external environment allows any flexibility.

- The fifth view is that the politics of budgeting centers in policy debates, including debates about the role of the budget. Spending levels, taxing policies, and willingness to borrow to sustain spending during recessions are all major policy issues that have to be resolved one way or another during budget deliberations. Budgets may reflect a policy of moderating economic cycles or they may express a policy of allowing the economy to run its course. Each is a policy. Similarly, budgets must allocate funding to particular programs, and in the course of doing so, decide priorities for federal, state, and local governments. This view of politics in the budget emphasizes tradeoffs, especially those that occur between major areas of the budget, such as social services and defense or police. This view also emphasizes the role of the budget office in making policy and the format of the budget in encouraging comparisons between programs.

These five views of politics have been developed over time, and like an ancient document, the messages have been written over one another. Surely they are not all equally true, and certainly they often contradict each other. Parts of each may still be true, and they may be true of different parts of budgetary decision making, or true of budgetary decision making at different times or at different levels of government.

Budgetary Decision Making

The focus . . . is to explore the kind of politics that occurs in budgetary decision making. What is budgetary decision making like? We have already discovered that public budgeting is open to environmental changes and deals with policy conflicts. Policy conflicts can delay particular decisions or prevent them from being made at all; other budget decisions must be independent enough to be made without the missing pieces. They can be corrected later when missing pieces fall into place. Environmental emergencies can reorder priorities and alter targets that have already been determined. As a result, public budgeting must be segmental and interruptible. The need for segmentation and interruptibility is satisfied by dividing budgeting into separate but linked decision clusters: revenues, process, expenditures, balance, and implementation.

Decision making in each cluster proceeds somewhat independently while referring to decisions made in the other clusters, or in anticipation of decisions likely to be made in other clusters. These decision clusters are ultimately interdependent, but do not occur in a fixed sequence. The decision one needs to have in one decision cluster may not be made by an-

other decision cluster in time to use. Then one may guess, or use an old figure, and then change when the new figure is determined. Sometimes decision-making cycles between estimates of revenues, estimates of expenditures, new estimates of revenues and new estimates of expenditures, in an iterative process.

The Revenue Cluster

Revenue decisions include technical estimates of how much income will be available for the following year, assuming no change in the tax structures, and policy decisions about changes in the level or type of taxation. Will taxes be raised or lowered? Will tax breaks be granted, and if so, to whom, for what purpose? Which tax sources will be emphasized, and which deemphasized, with what effect on regions, and economic classes, or on age groups? How visible will the tax burden be? Interest groups are intensely involved in the revenue cluster. The revenue cluster emphasizes the scarcity of resources that is an essential element in budgeting and illustrates the tension between accountability and acceptability that is a characteristic of public budgets. Revenues are also extremely sensitive to the environment because changes in the economy influence revenue levels and because the perception of public opinion influences the public officials' willingness to increase taxes.

The Budget Process

The process cluster concerns how to make budget decisions. Who should participate in the budget deliberations? Should the agency heads have power independent of the central budget office? How influential should interest groups be? How much power should the legislature have? How should the work be divided, and when should particular decisions be made? Normally the legislature takes a key role in establishing budget process, although the chief executive may propose desired changes. Interest groups play a minor role, if any role at all. The politics of process may revolve around individuals or groups trying to maximize their power through rearranging the budget process. This jockeying for power rises to importance when the competing parties represent the executive and legislative branches and involve the definition of the separation and balance between the branches of government. The politics of process may revolve around the policy issues of the level of spending and the ability of government to balance its budget.

The Expenditure Cluster

The expenditure cluster involves some technical estimates of likely expenditures, such as for grants that are dependent on formulas and benefit programs whose costs depend on the level of unemployment. But many expenditure decisions are policy relevant—which programs will be funded at what level, who will benefit from public programs and who will not, where and how cuts will be made, and whose interests will be protected. Agency heads are more involved in these decisions than in taxation or process decisions, and interest groups are also often active. This portion of the budget emphasizes the element of choice between items of expenditures in the definition of budgeting and illustrates the nature of the constraints on choices that is characteristic of public budgeting in particular.

The Balance Cluster

The balance cluster concerns the basic budgetary question whether the budget has to be balanced each year with each year's revenues, or whether borrowing is allowed to balance the budget, and if so, how much, for how long, and for what purposes. The politics of balance deals with questions whether balance should be achieved by increasing revenues, decreasing expenditures, or both, and hence reflects policies about the desirable scope of government. Sometimes the politics of balance emphasizes definitions, as the group in power seeks to make its deficits look smaller by defining them away. The balance cluster also deals with questions of how deficits should be eliminated once they occur and their amounts are pinned down. At the national level, because deficits may be incurred during recessions in an effort to help the economy recover, the ability to run a deficit is linked to policies

favoring or opposing the role of the budget in controlling the economy and, in particular, the use of the budget to moderate unemployment. These issues—whether budgets should balance, the proper scope of government and level of taxation, and the role of government in moderating unemployment—are issues that the general public cares about. Citizens may participate in this decision cluster through referenda and opinion polls; broad groups of taxpayers and interest-group coalitions representing broad segments of society may be involved in lobbying on this issue. Political parties may even include their policies toward deficits in their election platforms.

Budget Implementation

Finally, there is a cluster of decisions around budget implementation. How close should actual expenditures be to the ones planned in the budget? How can one justify variation from the budget plan? Can the budget be remade after it is approved, during the budget year? The key issues here revolve around the need to implement decisions exactly as made and the need to make changes during the year because of changes in the environment. The potential conflict is usually resolved by treating implementation as technical rather than policy related. Executive branch staff play the major role in implementation, with much smaller and more occasional roles for the legislature. Interest groups play virtually no role in implementation. The allowance of technical changes does open the door to policy changes during the year, but these are normally carefully monitored and may cause open conflict when they occur.

Microbudgeting and Macrobudgeting

The five clusters of decision making outline the nature of the decisions actually being made, but tell little about how and why the decisions are made. On the one hand there are a number of budget actors, who all have individual motivations, who strategize to get what they want from the budget. The focus on the actors and their strategies is called *microbudgeting*. But the actors do not simply bargain with one another or with whomever they meet in the corridor. The actors are assigned budget roles by the budget process, the issues they examine are often framed by the budget process, and the timing and coordination of their decisions are often regulated by the budget process. The budget actors are not totally free to come to budget agreements in any way they choose. Individual actors are bound by environmental constraints. There are choices they are not free to make because they are against the law, or because the courts decree it, or because previous decision makers have bound their hands. The total amount of revenue available is a kind of constraint, as is popular demand for some programs and popular dislike of others. Budgetary decision making has to account not just for budgetary actors but also for budget processes and the environment. This more top-down and systemic perspective on budgeting is called *macrobudgeting*. Contemporary budgeting gives more emphasis to macrobudgeting than exclusively to microbudgeting.

One way of viewing the determinants of budgetary outcomes is as a causal model, depicted in Figure 12.1. In this schema, the environment, budget processes, and individuals' strategies all affect outcomes.

The environment influences budgetary outcomes directly and indirectly, through process and through individual strategies. The environment influences outcomes directly, without going through either budget process or individual strategies, when it imposes emergencies that reorder priorities. Thus a war or a natural disaster preempts normal budgetary decision making.

The environment influences the budget process in several ways. The level of resources available—both the actual level of wealth and the willingness of the citizens to pay their taxes—influences the degree of centralization of budgeting. When resources are especially scarce and there is apparent need to either cut back according to a given set of policies

or make each dollar count toward specific economic goals, there is no room for bottom-up demands that result in compromises and a little bit of gain for everyone regardless of need. When resources are abundant, a more decentralized model of process may hold, with less emphasis on comparing policies and less competition between supporters of different policies.

The environment may influence the format of budget as well as the degree of centralization of decision making. When revenues are growing, there may be more emphasis on planning and on linking the budget to future community goals, to stimulate public demands for new spending. When there is little new money, the idea of planning may seem superfluous. Changing direction, or setting new goals, may seem impossible in the face of declining revenues that make current goals difficult to sustain.

Environment in the sense of the results of prior decisions may also influence process. If there is a huge accumulation of debt and little apparent way to control it, or if the budget has been growing very rapidly for reasons other than war, there may be attempts to change the budget process in an effort to control spending and debt. In contrast, if the environment suggests the need for additional spending, and the current budget process is delivering very slow growth, the process may be changed to make spending decisions quicker and easier.

The level of certainty of funding influences strategies as well. If whatever an agency was promised may never arrive, agency heads are likely to engage in continuous lobbying for their money, and continual rebudgeting internally every time circumstances change. Long-term or future agreements will be perceived as worthless; the possibility of toning down conflict by stretching out budget allocation times will disappear. Attention will focus on what is available now, and going after whatever it is, whether it is what you want or not, because what you really want may never show up and hence is not worth waiting for.

The intergovernmental grant structure is part of the environment that may influence strategies. Because some grant money may seem free, state and local governments may focus their energies on getting

Figure 12.1   Decision Making: Environment, Process, and Strategies

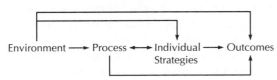

grants instead of raising local revenues. Or they may seek to decrease the amount of match required for a grant or increase their authority over how the money can be spent. Intergovernmental grants may make some expenditures relatively cheap, and some cutbacks relatively expensive, and hence frame constraints and choices for state and local budget officials.

The legal environment also influences strategies. For example, if public school teachers want tax raises to fund education and there is a provision in the state constitution forbidding income taxes, the teachers must either campaign for a constitutional revision (a time consuming and difficult task) or support a tax they know to be more burdensome to the poor. Thus the environment frames choices and influences strategies.

In Figure 12.1, the budget process influences strategies directly, and to a lesser extent, outcomes directly. But there is a double-headed arrow on the linkage between budget processes and strategies, suggesting that individuals' strategies also influence budget processes.

Budget processes influence strategies in some fairly obvious ways. If the budget structure allows for lengthy detailed budget hearings, open to the public and interest groups, at which decisions are often made, then various actors are likely to concentrate their efforts on making a good impression at these hearings. If the chief executive prepares the budget, which is subject to only superficial scrutiny and pro forma hearings before being approved by the legislature, anyone who wants to influence the budget—including the legislators themselves—must make their opinions heard earlier in the process, before the final executive proposal is put together. Informal discussion with department heads, or even telephone calls to the budget office, may be the route to influence. If the budget is made two or three times, with only the last one effective, then strategies may be to play out the first time or two with grandstanding—extreme positions to attract media attention—and more detailed and moderate positions later when the final decisions are made. The budget process orders the decisions in such a way that some of them are critical and determine or influence those that come afterward. Budget strategies naturally gravitate to those key decisions no matter where they are located.

When budget outcomes contradict some group's preference, the group may try to change the budget process to help it get the outcomes it prefers. When coalitions of the dissatisfied can agree on particular changes, fairly substantial changes in process may result. A change in process will bring about a change in outcome if the change in process shifts power from one group of individuals who want to accomplish one goal to another group with different goals.

The final link in the figure is between the strategies of budget actors and outcomes. The effect of different strategies on the outcomes is hard to gauge. It seems obvious, however, that strategies that ignore the process or the environment are doomed to failure. Budget actors have to figure out where the flexibility is before they can influence how that flexibility will be used. Strategies that try to bypass superiors or fool legislators generally do not work; strategies that involve careful documentation of need and appear to save money are generally more successful.

Summary and Conclusions

Public budgeting shares the characteristics of all budgeting. It makes choices between possible expenditures, it has to balance, and it has a decision-making process. But public budgeting has a number of additional features peculiar to itself, such as its openness to the environment; the variety of actors involved in budgeting, all of whom come to it with different goals; the separation of taxpayers from budget decision makers; the use of the budget document as a means of public accountability; and the numerous constraints typical of public budgeting.

Public budgeting is both technical and political. Politics takes on some special meanings in the context of budgetary decision making. Budgetary decision making must be flexible, adaptive, and interruptible, which leads to a structure of five semi-independent strands of decision making, revenues, process, expenditures, balance, and implementation. Each such strand generates its own political characteristics.

Budget outcomes are not solely the result of budget actors negotiating with one another in a free-for-all;

outcomes depend on the environment, and on the budget process as well as individual strategies. Individual strategies have to be framed in a broader context than simply perceived self-interest.

Budgeting is not well described as an annual process with little change from year to year. Budgetary decision making changes over time: interest group power waxes and wanes, competition in the budget increases and decreases, and the budget process itself varies over time. Changes in process take place in response to individuals, committees, and branches of government jockeying for power; in response to changes in the environment from rich to lean, or vice versa; in response to changes in the power of interest groups; and in response to scandals or excesses of various kinds.

Notes

1. Patricia Ingraham and Charles Barilleaux, "Motivating Government Managers for Retrenchment: Some Possible Lessons from the Senior Executive Service," *Public Administration Review* 43, no. 3 (1983): 393–402. They cite the Office of Personnel Management Federal Employee Attitude Surveys of 1979 and 1980, extracting responses from those in the Senior Executive Service, the upper ranks of the civil service and appointed administrators. In 1979, 99 percent of the senior executives said that they considered accomplishing something worthwhile to be very important; 97 percent said the same in 1980. By contrast, in response to the question "How much would you be motivated by a cash award," only 45 percent said either to a great extent or a very great extent.

2. Twelve percent of LeLoup and Moreland's Department of Agriculture requests between 1946 and 1971 were for decreases. See Lance LeLoup, *Budgetary Politics,* 3rd ed. (Brunswick, Ohio: King's Court, 1986), 83. For a more recent case study of an agency requesting decreases, see the case study of the Office of Personnel Management, in Irene Rubin, *Shrinking the Federal Government* (White Plains: Longman, 1985). See Irene Rubin,

Running in the Red: The Political Dynamics of Urban Fiscal Stress (Albany: State University of New York Press, 1982) for an example of a department refusing additional employees.

3. For a good discussion of this phenomenon, see Frank Thompson, *The Politics of Personnel in the City* (Berkeley: University of California Press, 1975).

4. See Rubin, *Shrinking the Federal Government,* for examples during the Reagan administration.

5. U.S. Senate, Committee on Governmental Affairs, *Office of Management and Budget: Evolving Roles and Future Issues,* Committee Print 99–134, 99th Cong., 2nd sess., prepared by the Congressional Research Service of the Library of Congress, February 1986.

6. See, for example, Kenneth Shepsle and Barry Weingast, "Legislative Politics and Budget Outcomes," in *Federal Budget Policy in the 1980s,* Gregory Mills and John Palmer, eds. (Washington, D.C.: Urban Institute Press, 1984), 343–367.

7. Rubin, *Running in the Red,* 56.

8. For a vivid account of the relationship between pork-barrel spending and building political coalitions, see Martin Shefter, "New York City's Fiscal Crisis: The Politics of Inflation and Retrenchment," *Public Interest* 48 (Summer 1977): 99–127.

9. See John Ellwood, "Comments," in Mills and Palmer, *Federal Budget Policy in the 1980s,* 368–378.

10. Douglas Arnold, "The Local Roots of Domestic Policy," in *The New Congress,* Thomas Mann and Norman Ornstein, eds. (Washington, D.C.: American Enterprise Institute, 1981), 252, quoted by Ellwood, in Mills and Palmer.

11. Arnold, "Local Roots," 282.

12. Ellwood, in Mills and Palmer, 370.

13. Linda Harriman and Jeffrey Straussman, "Do Judges Determine Budget Decisions? Federal Court Decisions in Prison Reform and State Spending for Corrections," *Public Administration Review* 43, no. 4 (1983): 343–351.

☐ **CASE STUDY 12**

Introduction

Perhaps nothing is more vital to our understanding of public administration than how monies are budgeted to achieve public purposes. This subject, many believe, directly and decisively influences what policies are pursued and how management of public programs is achieved. For some, budgets in reality are what public administration is all about, namely the translation of public purposes into practical actions through the raising and expenditures of government monies. Rubin's foregoing essay therefore offers several stimulating insights into this critical process. It especially shows why this subject should not be viewed as merely a dry, technical document but as something that affects the central fabric of modern democratic society and the choices it faces.

Let's next turn to an actual example of the ideas expressed in Dr. Rubin's selection by studying the following case, "Wisconsin's Budget Deficit," authored by James K. Conant, who is a professor of government and politics at George Mason University and specializes in public budgeting and financial management. A bit of background is useful before reading his case. In the wake of the dot-com industry's collapse, the steep stock market drop, the rise of the dollar against foreign currencies, increased unemployment, and other economic factors, March 2001 officially began a serious nationwide recession that in turn triggered critical budget problems in at least forty-five states due to what the National Conference of State Legislatures (NCSL) termed "anemic revenues." At least half of the states in fiscal year (FY) 2002 had to revise their revenue targets downward, and in half of these states, their actual revenues failed to meet the revised lower targets. At the same time, all states after 9/11 experienced increased pressures for higher expenditures and twenty-eight states reported significantly above average estimated expenditure levels for FY 2002.

Of course, economic booms and busts were nothing new for state and local budgets to experience. Indeed, FY 2001 was the fourth recession in thirty years; the three prior ones occurred during the mid-1970s, the early 1980s, and early 1990s. In past fiscal downturns, budget experts recommended more legislative self-discipline, as well as establishing "rainy-day funds" (saving funds during boom times in order to cushion the shocks of economic busts). Wisconsin had indeed created a rainy-day fund but never put money into it, and so when several factors coincided to bring about the sharp recession in FY 2001, Wisconsin like most states was unprepared. Professor Conant carefully recounts how Wisconsin responded to this serious fiscal crisis and analyzes its causes, remedies, and consequences generally for public budgeting.

As you read his detailed study, you might reflect on the following questions:

Does the Wisconsin case demonstrate any of the unique characteristics of public budgeting that Rubin's foregoing essay outlines? If so, which ones, and why are these so crucial to formulating government budgets as opposed to personal or business budgets?

Who were the chief actors in the Wisconsin case? Why were some more influential than others? What strategies did they employ? Were some of their strategies more effective than others? Which strategies and why?

What budget constraints were most critical to shaping the final outcome of the case? Did they correspond with those outlined by Rubin or were others important that she did not mention?

Were the five budget decision-making processes described in the Rubin essay evident within the Wisconsin case? Or, were they so entangled with one another that each was hard to delineate clearly?

In your view, is the case an example of what Rubin describes as "macro-" or "microbudgeting"? Or both? Can you define each term and cite examples from the case?

Why does the case author, Professor Conant, at the end suggest "An Iron Law of Incrementalism" to explain what happened? What does he mean by this "law"? Do you concur?

Wisconsin's Budget Deficit

JAMES K. CONANT

During the 1990–1991 recession, Wisconsin experienced a relatively mild degree of fiscal stress.[1] In one study of that recession, Wisconsin's fiscal stress was ranked lowest among the 50 states.[2] In a remarkable turn of fortune, however, Wisconsin was among the states experiencing the highest levels of fiscal stress in the early stages of the current recession.[3] Wisconsin's fiscal year (FY) 2002 budget woes were a function of both structural and cyclical causes. The structural problem was created by budget and policy decisions made during the 1990s. These decisions substantially increased expenditures and reduced tax revenues, throwing the state budget out of balance. The economic recession that officially began in March of 2001 not only unmasked the underlying structural problem but also contributed significantly to the size of Wisconsin's FY 2002 budget deficit.

In this article, both the structural and cyclical factors associated with the high level of fiscal stress Wisconsin experienced during FY 2002 are examined, the size of the budget deficit is defined, the remedies elected officials proposed and enacted to "fix" the deficit are identified, and some of the costs and consequences of Wisconsin's budget deficit will be examined. This study is concluded with some general reflections on the state's financial problems that may serve as "lessons learned." Some of these lessons may be applicable beyond the boundaries of Wisconsin.

From James K. Conant, "Wisconsin's Budget Deficit." *Public Budgeting and Finance* (Summer 2003), pp. 5–25. Reprinted by permission of Blackwell Publishing Ltd.

Wisconsin's Budget and Balanced Budget Requirements

Wisconsin's budget is a biennial, or two-year, budget. Thus, the data and decision making for FY 2002 (July 1, 2001–June 30, 2002) must be considered within the context of the FY 2001–2003 budget and budgetary process. Wisconsin's biennial budget is passed in odd-numbered years. For example, the FY 2001–2003 budget was passed in calendar year 2001, and it includes fiscal years 2001–2002 (FY 2002) and 2002–2003 (FY 2003). During even-numbered years, the legislature holds a "budget review" or "budget adjustment" session to make technical and substantive adjustments to the biennial budget.[4] The FY 2001–2003 biennial budget bill, the budget adjustment bill, and state documents produced as part of both budget processes serve as important resources for this analysis.

Total state expenditures during the 1999–2001 biennium were $54.4 billion, General Fund Expenditures were $37.5 billion, and General Purpose Revenue Expenditures were $21.7 billion.[5] Because state officials, reporters, and agencies outside the state may use any or all of these figures for various purposes, it is important to define the fund sources that support each type of expenditure category. General Purpose Revenues consist primarily (97 percent) of state taxes that are not earmarked, such as the individual income tax, corporate income tax, and sales tax. General Fund Revenues consist of General Purpose Revenues (54 percent), Program Revenues (mostly fees; 17.6 percent), and Federal

Revenue (28.4 percent).[6] Special Revenue Funds are added to General Fund Revenues to support total state spending.[7] It is worth noting that General Purpose Tax Revenues and General Fund Tax Revenues are virtually identical (99 percent), and thus the terms may be used interchangeably.[8]

Wisconsin's General Fund budget must be balanced each year. The balanced budget requirement is contained in state statutes, rather than in the state's constitution. In fact, language in Article VIII section 5 of Wisconsin's 1848 constitution allows the state to run a deficit in a given year, as long as a tax is levied "for the ensuing year, sufficient, with other sources of income, to pay the deficiency as well as the estimated expenses of the ensuing year."[9] Statutory language, however, requires an end of year General Fund surplus of no less than one percent of General Fund appropriations.[10] The required surplus, however, is not intended to be a tool for reducing anticipated or known General Fund budget deficits.[11]

Wisconsin's budget bill is the state's central policy document, as well as the document through which the state appropriates funds and raises revenues. All legislation with an estimated cost of more than $100,000 must be included in the budget bill, and the legislature must take up the budget bill in its first session. After the budget bill is passed, the legislature must adjourn. During the budgetary process, Wisconsin's state lawmakers focus their attention on General Purpose Revenues (and the expenditures supported by these revenues) because General Purpose Revenues are "discretionary" funds. For this reason, General Purpose Revenues and Expenditures will be highlighted when appropriate.

Coping with Fiscal Stress: The FY 2001–2003 Budget (Act 16)

As Wisconsin's governor and legislators began the process of putting together the 2001–2003 biennial budget, they had to deal with a budget gap or predicted deficit that had both cyclical and structural causes. For this reason alone, Wisconsin's lawmakers might have had a more difficult time fixing their fiscal problems than their counterparts in many other states. Several other factors, however, magnified the problem Wisconsin's lawmakers faced.

First, at the beginning of the 2001–2003 biennial budget process, Republican Governor McCallum ruled

out income and sales tax increases as a means of addressing the state's budgetary problems, and Democrats in the legislature did not challenge the anti-tax presumption.[12] Second, the size of the budget problem kept on growing, even as lawmakers attempted to find remedies. Third, Wisconsin's Rainy Day Fund existed in name only; there was no money in it.

In retrospect, of course, the uncertainty associated with emerging budget gaps and budget deficits fades from view, and what "should have been done" may seem very clear. Yet, for some Wisconsin lawmakers and others close to the budget process, the true size of the state's budget problem was apparently hard to pin down, and decisions had to be made in a context of a relatively high degree of uncertainty. The difficult circumstances lawmakers faced were reflected in part by the ways in which data on Wisconsin's budget circumstances changed over time in various state documents and newspaper reports.[13]

In any case, with the benefit of hindsight, it appears that state lawmakers had estimates in January of 2001 indicating the need to address a $2.4 billion budget gap. Of that $2.4 billion, $1.1 billion was described in state budget documents as a "mismatch between ongoing revenues and ongoing expenditures (a structural deficit) from the 1999–2001 biennium."[14] The remaining $1.3 billion was described as a "revenue shortfall."[15]

To put the size of the budget gap in perspective, we can compare it to the state's biennial budget for FY 1999–2001. The $2.4 billion budget gap was 6.3 percent of Wisconsin's General Fund Expenditures for FY 1999–2001, and it was 11.1 percent of the General Purpose Revenue Expenditures.[16]

As might be expected, the size of the budget gap made the process of putting together the 2001–2003 budget bill highly contentious. Because Republicans controlled the governorship and Assembly and Democrats controlled the Senate, partisan differences contributed to the conflict. On August 30, 2001, more than seven months after it was introduced and two months into the new fiscal year, the legislature passed a biennial budget, Act 16, which presumably eliminated the $2.4 billion gap. Act 16, the FY 2001–2003 budget bill, contained a total of $46 billion of estimated revenues and expenditures.[17] Of this total, $22.5 billion was (estimated) General Purpose Revenues and Expenditures.[18]

With the passage of the budget bill, Governor McCallum claimed credit for fixing the state's huge biennial budget problem. In state documents published under his name, the following appears: the "$2.4 billion budget gap was closed without an increase in general taxes."[19] Given the size of the problem McCallum and the state's legislators had to address, claiming credit for "fixing" the deficit problem seems unsurprising.

Yet, less than six months after Act 16 was passed, lawmakers were engaged in another attempt to solve the state's budget problems. This time, the stakes were even higher. Wisconsin's elected officials had already made significant reductions in state expenditures and, in order to secure the revenue needed to avoid further cuts, they had borrowed heavily from the state's future Tobacco Fund revenues. Elected officials now found it necessary, in the beginning of calendar year 2002, however, to respond to a growing deficit in a fiscal year that was already half over (FY 2002).

A Growing Deficit, the "Budget Reform" Bill, and Act 109

In January of 2002, Governor McCallum had a "Budget Reform Bill" introduced in the legislature. In the "Budget Reform Bill Summary," which accompanied the proposed legislation, McCallum seemed to acknowledge that the state's fiscal problems were worse than had previously been thought. Specifically, the "Budget Reform Bill Summary" contains a table showing a "Total Shortfall from Act 16" of nearly $1.3 billion. The table also contains McCallum's proposed remedies for addressing this shortfall.[20]

The legislative process through which the "Budget Reform Bill" became law was even more tortuous and more contentious than that of Act 16, the 2001–2003 biennial budget bill. Nevertheless, seven months after it was introduced, the Budget Reform Act, Act 109, was signed into law July 26, 2002. It is worth noting, however, that the language in the 2002 annual review bill shows that it was designed to address a $1.1 billion deficit, rather than the $1.3 billion figure reported in Governor McCallum's "Budget Reform Summary." If the smaller deficit figure ($1.1 billion) is added to the $2.4 billion budget gap identified in January of 2001, the combined budget gap/deficit for the 2001–2003 budget was $3.5 billion.

Assuming the latter number represents the full scale of the biennial deficit, it would be nearly 9.3 percent of 1999–2001 General Fund Expenditures and 15.6 percent of General Purpose Revenue Expenditures. Additionally, the $3.5 billion figure would be approximately 7.1 percent of all revenues and approximately 14.2 percent of all estimated General Purpose Revenues for the 2001–2003 biennium. In comparative terms, looking backward to the 1990–1991 recession, the scale of Wisconsin's FY 2001–2003 budget problems approaches that of the states that had the largest budget problems during the 1990–1991 recession.[21]

To complicate matters further for Wisconsin's lawmakers, even the most optimistic forecasts available in July of 2002 showed an estimated deficit for the upcoming biennium of FY 2003–2005 of at least $1.3 billion, unless taxes were raised or additional cuts in spending were made.[22] Later estimates put the figure as high as $3.5 billion.[23] Thus, there were good reasons for state lawmakers to believe that budget deficits would remain the number one item on Wisconsin's legislative agenda for the foreseeable future.

Causes of the State Budget Gap and Deficit

As already noted, the causes of Wisconsin's 2001–2003 budget deficit are both structural and cyclical. Some additional background on both the structural and cyclical dimensions of the deficit will be provided in the sections that follow.

Structural Factors: Expenditure Decisions

Like lawmakers in many states, Wisconsin's governor, Republican Tommy Thompson, and the state's legislators increased spending and cut taxes during the period from 1992 through 2000. The spending increases were many and continuous, with the four most visible areas being corrections (prisons), Medicaid, welfare to work programs, and K–12 education. Of these four, the K–12 expenditure increase was the largest and thus the most important.

Specifically, new statutory provisions included in the 1994 budget adjustment bill (Act 437) required that state support to K–12 schools be increased from 48.4 percent to 66.6 percent by fiscal year 1996–1997.[24] The change required by the 1994 legislation was remarkable in its scale and for its fiscal requirements. At the time this commitment was formalized into law in 1994, state aid to K–12 schools was the state's largest expenditure of General Purpose Revenue, with a cost of approximately $2.2 billion.[25] Those costs would grow, of course, in the two fiscal years before the 66.6 percent requirement took effect.

At the time the expanded level of support was approved, Governor Thompson acknowledged that the costs of the initiative would be very high. Specifically, Thompson estimated in 1994 that "the state would have to pick up $1.2 billion in new spending in the next budget."[26] The size or significance of this figure becomes clear when it is compared to the General Purpose Tax Revenues collected during the fiscal year (1994–1995) in which the legislation was passed. In that year, General Purpose Tax Revenues totaled $7.8 billion.[27] If the school aid commitment were to be financed from new tax revenues, those revenues would have to grow by at least 15.4 percent.[28]

The story of how this huge increase in state education aid came about has many dimensions, including extended historical roots. The most interesting factor in this story, however, may be raw, partisan competition. The stakes in this competition between Republicans and Democrats had been rising in Wisconsin for more than a decade, and the school aid decision can be viewed as just one part of it. From the time he took office in 1987, Governor Thompson aggressively employed and continuously worked to expand the powers of the executive office. In the minds of many, the growth in the governor's power came at the expense of the legislature.

Democrats in the legislature, however, did not passively accept Thompson's attempt to expand his control over state policy and administration. Indeed, party leaders were searching for ways to contain the governor's growing power, his influence on state policy and administration, and Republican electoral fortunes. In a move that was probably motivated by a mixture of good intentions (in public policy terms) and an effort to put Thompson in a difficult position, Democrats made a proposal in 1994 to remove the costs of K–12 schools from the property tax.

Ironically, the Democrats used Republican Governor John Engler and the neighboring state of Michigan as their models. Specifically, Engler was mounting an initiative to remove K–12 funding from the property tax in Michigan. The thrust of the Wisconsin Democrats' policy argument was that rising property tax burdens and the inequities that result from using the property tax for K–12 education had to be addressed with bold action. Like Engler, they proposed to fix these problems by eliminating the property tax as a source for K–12 financing.

Not to be overlooked were two key elements of the Democratic proposal. First, no specific source for funding the new initiative was defined. Second, the proposal was placed on the table in a very public way about six months before the upcoming election. Democrats knew, of course, that Thompson planned to run for reelection.

Never one to shrink from a challenge, Tommy Thompson took on this Democratic gambit with gusto. In his reelection campaign, he not only promised to dramatically increase state aid for K–12 schools, he also promised to do so without raising state general taxes. Although he acknowledged that his approach entailed financial risks and would require significant reductions in funding for state agencies,[29] he was soon off and running with his new initiative. In the 1995–1997 biennial budget, he succeeded in putting his plan into law.

For veteran observers of the state budget, who had watched the state's lawmakers repeatedly raise state taxes during the 1960s, 1970s, and 1980s to fund ever larger amounts of aid to local governments, the school aid initiative might have seemed risky indeed. Yet, as often happens in politics, the exigencies of the moment seemed to push lessons from the past out of sight.

Structural Factors: Tax Cuts

In addition to making decisions that expanded state expenditures, Wisconsin's lawmakers also made decisions that substantially reduced its General Fund Tax Revenues. It is worth noting that commitments to large new expenditures occurred primarily during the first half of the 1990s, whereas the tax law changes with big, negative fiscal impacts were made during the latter half of the decade. Specifically, the key tax law changes were enacted in 1997 and 1999, with the big effects occurring in FY 1999–2000, 2000–2001, 2001–2002, and 2002–2003.

The effects these tax law changes had on the state's General Fund (or General Purpose) Tax Revenues are summarized by type of tax in Table 12.1.

The data in Table 12.1 show that tax law changes reduced Wisconsin's General Fund Revenues by $197.6 million in FY 1998–1999, $622.3 million in FY 1999–2000, $991.8 million in FY 2000–2001, and $978.9 billion in FY 2001–2002. Additionally, tax law changes were expected to reduce FY 2002–2003 revenue by $1.069 billion.

In four of the five fiscal years in which substantial tax cuts were made, statutory changes affecting the income tax were the principal source of General Fund

Table 12.1 Tax Law Changes Beginning in 1995

($ in millions)

	1995–96	1996–97	1997–98	1998–99	1999–00	2000–01	2001–02	2002–03	Eight-Year Total
Individual Income	$ 0.06	$ (0.84)	$ (9.92)	$(327.51)	$ (29.66)	$(1,059.70)	$(1,113.61)	$(1,211.41)	$(3,752.59)
Sales and Use	$14.30	$25.86	$ 28.11	$ 33.24	$(654.62)	$ 33.91	$ 35.32	$ 37.69	$ (446.19)
Corp. Income & Franchise	$ 0.00	$ 0.90	$ 6.05	$ 7.25	$ 17.85	$ 14.28	$ 21.78	$ 19.28	$ 87.39
Excise	$22.30	$22.30	$ 69.80	$ 82.40	$ 81.88	$ 81.20	$ 143.95	$ 153.05	$ 656.88
Utility	$ 3.00	$41.80	$ 26.30	$ 7.00	$ (37.73)	$ (61.51)	$ (66.29)	$ (67.75)	$ (155.18)
Subtotal/Yearly Change	$ 9.66	$90.02	$120.34	$(197.62)	$ 622.28)	$ (991.82)	$ (978.85)	$(1,069.14)	$(3,609.69)

Source: Legislative Fiscal Bureau, "Tax Law Changes Beginning in 1995," November 2002.

Tax Revenue reductions. In FY 1999–2000, however, the principal source of the lost tax revenue was a sales tax rebate of $654.6 million. The decision to take this action was made in 1999, and it was included in 1999 Act 10, the 1999–2001 biennial budget bill.

Press stories at the time noted that there were differences of opinion about the appropriate size for a one-time tax rebate, with preferences ranging from about $700 million to $950 million.[30] Additionally, there was debate about whether the rebate should be paid as an income or sales tax rebate. What seems most striking about these stories, however, is that no opposition to the tax cut is reported. A couple of legislators did express concern about making a tax cut of this size a permanent cut, but they strongly supported the one-time rebate.[31]

Yet, at the time these concerns were expressed, large, permanent income tax reductions had already been made. Specifically, in 1997 Act 27, the biennial budget bill, Wisconsin's governor and legislators had made tax law changes that lowered income tax rates, adjusted percentages for indexing, increased the married couple credit, and expanded the credit for working families. Then, later in 1997, as part of 1997 Act 237, the budget adjustment bill, the governor and legislature reduced income tax rates again, increased higher education deductions, and made several other changes that lowered income taxes.

On top of the tax cuts made in 1997, larger income tax reductions were added in 1999. As part of 1999 Acts 9, 10, and 198, an "Additional Income Tax Reduction Package" was put through that (further) reduced Personal Income Tax Revenue by $653 million in 2000–2001 and $691 million in 2001–2002. The changes were also expected to reduce 2002–2003 tax revenue by $721 million, for a three-year total of $1.828 billion.[32]

Whatever one might think of the merits of the individual tax cut decisions in Wisconsin, the aggregate costs make those tax cut decisions seem surprising, or even irresponsible, particularly when they are considered in light of large new expenditure commitments elected officials made during the first half of the 1990s. Ironically, the way in which these tax cuts were packaged and the way in which their effects ballooned over time is reminiscent of proposals that have been made and enacted in recent years at the national level.

To be fair to Wisconsin's elected officials, however, it is important to acknowledge that their decisions were made within a particular context. That context, the

1990s, included rapid economic growth and strong growth in state tax revenues. The context also included intense partisan competition.

Two other, less visible elements were part of the context during the 1990s. The first was the echoes of a fundamental political lesson, learned from the 1978 election, that running budget surpluses was bad politics. In the 1978 gubernatorial election, Republican challenger Lee Sherman Dreyfus upset heavily favored Acting Governor Martin Schreiber, a Democrat. The key factor in the election campaign was the Dreyfus promise to return all of the state's rapidly growing surplus to the voters. Schreiber was slow to respond to the Dreyfus pledge, in part because, as lieutenant governor, he had first-hand experience with the way in which economic fluctuations created the boom circumstances for the 1973–1975 budget and the budget for 1975–1977.

A second invisible element of the political context of the 1990s was, perhaps, an implicit acceptance of the fiscal strategy developed by the Dreyfus Administration (1978–1982) called "Fiscal Brinksmanship."[33] The key presumption of the strategy was that revenue should be cut during good times and expenditures cut during recessions. The long-term objective of the strategy was to reduce the size of government.[34]

It is worth noting that the strategy of Fiscal Brinksmanship led to huge budget deficits during the deep recession of the early 1980s. Thus, in one respect, the FY 2002 budget problems have an eerily familiar ring. In any case, the deficit left by the Dreyfus Administration was cleaned up by Democratic Governor Anthony Earl and state legislators during the 1983–1985 budget. The deficit was "fixed" by raising taxes and cutting expenditures.

Cyclical Factors

With respect to the cyclical dimensions of Wisconsin's current budget deficit, two factors help to explain what was happening to the state's economy during the recession that officially began in March of 2001. The first factor was that, despite its self-proclaimed identity as "America's Dairyland,"[35] Wisconsin's economy has, since the early 1900s, been heavily based on manufacturing. Indeed, Wisconsin's economic performance has traditionally been heavily dependent on the sale of machinery and electrical equipment overseas. The second factor is that the European and some of the Far East economies were growing slowly or were in recession even before the U.S. recession started. These global economic problems had weakened demand for Wisconsin's exports even before the U.S. recession began.

Wisconsin's budgetary experience during the early stages of the current recession can also be understood by reviewing studies that have examined the relationship between economic performance and Wisconsin state revenues. These studies have consistently shown that only a small slowdown in economic growth can have a significant negative effect on the state's revenues. For example, a study of the 1991 recession conducted by University of Wisconsin–Madison economist Don Nichols showed that the recession cost the state between $400 million and $900 million in General Purpose Revenues for the 1991–1993 biennium.[36] This key finding was one of the factors that led Nichols to complete his study with a call for a "budget stabilization" fund that could be used to protect the state from the effects of these cyclical fluctuations.[37]

Nichols's study not only made a persuasive case for the urgent need to have a budget stabilization fund but also contained a warning sign for the future. That is to say, Nichols repeatedly emphasized the fact that the 1991–1992 national recession's effect was only "mild" in Wisconsin. The recession, he noted, only slowed the rate of economic and employment growth in the state. According to Nichols, "it is easy to see from these estimates that a severe recession would place the state in a very difficult fiscal position."[38] Unfortunately, what Nichols forecast in 1991 was playing out in very real terms in 2001 and 2002.

The effects of the current recession on Wisconsin's General Fund (or General Purpose) Tax Revenues[39] are shown in Table 12.2. The January 2001 estimates for the 2001–2003 biennium (produced by the Legislative Fiscal Bureau) were $667 million less than the estimates presented by the Department of Administration just two months earlier (November of 2000). To this figure must be added $389.9 million. This was the size of the drop in expected surplus for the FY 1999–2001 budget that could be carried forward into the 2001–2003 budget. When these two numbers are added together, they make up most of the $1.2 billion "revenue shortfall" state lawmakers knew about in January of 2001 as they began to put together the FY 2001–2003 budget.[40]

The data in Table 12.2 also show that after Act 16 was passed in August of 2001, additional General Fund (or General Purpose) Tax Revenue estimates were made. The January 16, 2002, estimate showed an additional $892.9 million drop from the May 2001 estimate. It appears that this large estimated revenue loss has to be

piled on top of another figure. Specifically, the May 2001 estimates produced by the Legislative Fiscal Bureau were $491.1 million less than the estimates this legislative agency produced in January of 2001.[41] By adding these totals together, we get the $1.3 billion General Fund Revenue shortfall Governor McCallum reported in his January 2002 "Budget Reform Bill Summary."

Remedies Proposed and Implemented

Whenever state lawmakers find themselves facing a budget deficit, they have four options. They can raise taxes, cut spending, employ some combination of both tax increases and spending cuts, or employ some method of "creative bookkeeping."[42] In historical terms, published records from the states show that they have often employed some combination of both tax increases and spending cuts, because it is a relatively balanced approach. As noted earlier in this article, however, Scott McCallum, who became governor in January of 2001 after Tommy Thompson left Wisconsin to join the Bush Administration as Secretary of Health and Social Services, ruled out any increases in the income and sales taxes at the start of the FY 2001–2003 budget process.

Even with this choice, the size of the required spending cuts might have been reduced if Wisconsin's lawmakers could have drawn upon a Rainy Day Fund, but the state's Rainy Day Fund existed in name only. Legislation setting up such a fund was passed in 1986, but money was never appropriated for it.[43] Thus, one of the most convenient remedies the state might have had to deal with the cyclical dimensions of the state deficit was not available.

Wisconsin was a latecomer among states in getting Rainy Day Fund legislation on the books, and, as already noted, partisan political competition and the "lesson" of the 1978 gubernatorial election were the principal reasons for this circumstance. These two factors, particularly the partisan competition between Republican Governor Tommy Thompson and Democrats in the state legislature, were key reasons the Rainy Day Fund's coffers remained empty even after it was statutorily established.

There was one other source of money, however, that Wisconsin's lawmakers could tap to reduce, at least temporarily, the size of the spending cuts required to balance the 2001–2003 biennial budget. This source of funds was the tobacco settlement money the state was due to

Table 12.2 General Fund Tax Revenue Estimates for the 2001–2003 Biennium

			($ in millions)			
	FY 2001–02	$ Change from Previous Estimate	FY 2002–03	$ Change from Previous Estimate	FY 2001–03	$ Change from Previous Estimate
Nov. 20, 2000	11,000.8		11,802.9		22,803.7	
Jan. 5, 2001	10,754.9	(245.9)	11,381.8	(421.1)	22,136.7	(667.0)
May 15, 2001	10,575.0	(179.9)	11,070.6	(311.2)	21,645.6	(491.1)
Jan. 16, 2002	10,218.2	(356.8)	10,534.7	(535.9)	20,752.9	(892.7)
July 2002	10,209.7	(8.5)	10,515.5	(19.2)	20,725.2	(27.7)
Sept. 3, 2002 (actual)	10,020.2	(189.5)				(189.5)
Net Change 11/00–9/02		(980.6)		(1,287.4)		(2,268.0)

Sources: Department of Administration, "Agency Budget Requests and Revenue Estimates: FY 2002, FY 2003," Division of Executive Budget and Finance, Nov. 2000; Legislative Fiscal Bureau, "General Fund Expenditures and Revenue Projections," Jan. 25, 2001; Legislative Fiscal Bureau, "Estimates of General Fund Tax Collections," May 15, 2001; Legislative Fiscal Bureau, Preliminary 2000–01 General Fund Tax Collection, Sept. 6, 2001; Legislative Fiscal Bureau, "Review of Status of the State's General Fund," Jan. 16, 2002.

get over a 30-year period. Perhaps not surprisingly, state lawmakers found it expedient to draw heavily on this source of funds.

First-Round Remedies (2001)

Act 16, the 2001–2003 biennial budget bill passed by the legislature in August of 2001, contained five major initiatives designed to fix the state's $2.4 billion budget deficit: (1) 5 percent cuts to state agency budgets, (2) delays in staffing new prisons, (3) use of the proceeds from the sale of tobacco settlement agreement revenue bonds, (4) reallocation of federal intergovernmental transfer revenues to support state medical assistance funding, and (5) "extraordinary accounting devices . . . employed to ensure a positive budget balance."[44]

Governor McCallum reported that he fixed (eliminated) the "extraordinary accounting devices" with item vetoes. He also maintained that the other remedies were sufficient to fix the $2.4 billion problem. Yet, even using the numbers in the governor's Budget Reform Bill Summary, it appears that the $2.4 billion gap did not include all relevant expenditure requirements. For example, the document shows that the full cost of schools aids was not included in Act 16. Thus, even if actions taken in Act 16 covered the estimated gap of $2.4 billion, the estimate itself may have understated the problem.

A more detailed review of Act 16 and its consequences may be useful, but it is beyond the scope of this study. Consequently, the focus will shift to the second round of budget reduction proposals recommended in the Governor's budget repair bill of January 2002.

Second-Round Remedies (Proposed in January of 2002)

Although the struggle to complete the 2001–2003 budget did not come to fruition until Act 16 was passed and signed in August of 2001, a second round of remedies to the 2001–2003 budget deficit was begun less than six months later, in January of 2002. The need for the second round was apparently created by the emergence of an additional $1.3 billion gap between revenues and expenditures. As might be expected, the already painful expenditure cuts incorporated into Act 16 were expanded. So too, was the use of tobacco settlement funds.

Governor McCallum's January 2002 budget adjustment bill was built on the premise that "high-priority programs" were exempt from "any budget reductions."[45]

These programs were defined as "direct assistance to Wisconsin's most vulnerable citizens—the poor, disabled, and elderly," and the two-thirds commitment to state funding of K–12 school costs, including the additional $115 million needed to meet the commitment for FY 2002–2003.[46] Also included in the high-priority list were medical assistance, the court system, and the public defender.[47]

What remained for the budget cutters' ax in the biennial budget adjustment bill was just over one half of the General Purpose Revenue Expenditures, or $6.1 billion.[48] The three largest elements of this total were the University of Wisconsin System, at $2.1 billion, the Shared Revenue Fund (state aid to cities, villages, towns, and counties), at just over $2.0 billion, and corrections, at $1.5 billion.[49]

The governor proposed a reduction for the UW System of 1 percent in FY 2001–2002 and 4.5 percent in FY 2002–2003, for a total reduction of more than $50 million.[50] He proposed a reduction of 6 percent in the corrections budget for FY 2002–2003, or approximately $40 million.[51] The most dramatic proposal, however, fell on the Shared Revenue Fund; McCallum recommended eliminating the fund over a two-year period.[52] The proposed expenditure reduction (or savings) for FY 2002–2003 was $730 million, and for 2003–2004 it was an additional $574 million.[53]

To soften the burden of the dramatic reduction in and elimination of the Shared Revenue Fund monies for local governments, McCallum proposed using $380 million from the tobacco settlement funds in FY 2002–2003 and $214 million in FY 2003–2004. For local governments, however, the net result was a reduction of $350 million in FY 2002–2003 and another $360 million in FY 2003–2004. Thereafter, there would be no state support, which amounts to another $350 million reduction. It is also worth noting that McCallum's budget repair bill also included a wide range of cuts in other areas, including a 3.5 percent cut in the appropriations for all state agencies in 2001–2002 and a 5 percent cut in 2002–2003.

Second-Round Remedies Adopted (July of 2002)

Ultimately, the Budget Reform Act passed by the legislature and signed by the governor included $163.4 million in new spending and $1.282 billion in decreases to the deficit (i.e., budget reductions and increases in revenue).[54] The single largest element of the deficit reduction efforts was $829 million in revenues from tobacco settlement funds. Funding to education was indeed protected from major cuts, as was, surprisingly, the Shared Revenue Fund. Also, the UW System was spared all but a $6.7 million funding reduction. The greatest cuts came in the form of a $104.4 million across-the-board state operations reduction. The rest of the budget remedies came in the form of reductions for nonpriority programs, increased fees, and accounting gimmicks.

Consequences

Given the close proximity of the cuts contained in Act 16 (the biennial budget bill) and the budget adjustment bill that was presented by the governor less than six months later, a description of the consequences or effects of the state deficit and remedies for it will be melded together. No attempt here is made to be comprehensive in reporting consequences. Instead, only a small number of consequences will be identified. What might be considered the "positive" consequences of the current budget crisis and events leading to it will be discussed first, followed by the alternative perspectives.

"Positive" View

It seems useful to begin this section of the article with reference to two groups that might have supported, rather than objected to, at least some of the consequences of the state's budget deficit, the remedies selected to deal with that deficit, or both. For example, anti-tax groups, especially the anti-tax elements of the business community, must have been happy that certain remedies were not employed. Specifically, the majority of the tax cuts passed in the 1990s went to upper-income individuals. Consequently, if General Fund tax increases had been proposed to balance the FY 2001–2003 budget, they very likely would have come at this group's expense.

Second, at least some members of the education lobby or establishment, including some local school board members, administrators, and teachers, must have been relieved that the new level of state support for K–12 did not fall victim to the budget ax in Act 16 or the biennial budget repair bill. Indeed, from an outsider's perspective, it seems as though this commitment by Thompson and the 1993 legislature had somehow acquired the status of a holy object.

One cannot help but wonder, however, whether Thompson and the 1993 legislature would have chosen the path they did if they had known, or even suspected, that the result of their bold new initiative would be the elimination of the Shared Revenue Fund. It also seems strange that the influence of local governments somehow collapsed between 1993 and 2001. This circumstance certainly deserves additional scrutiny.

Negative Consequences

One interesting consequence of Governor McCallum's January 2002 proposed budget reductions was that the Regents of the University of Wisconsin System announced a halt to undergraduate admissions in March of 2002.[55] By doing so, the Regents were not only playing a high-stakes game but also flexing their political muscle. University of Wisconsin campuses, both four-year and two-year, are widely distributed in the state. Consequently, a large percentage of legislators had a direct stake in this "admissions crisis."

Apparently, the University Regents and administrators were banking on more favorable budget treatment from state legislators after they were "softened up" by parents of graduating high school seniors, who wanted their children to go to a state college or university and thus secure the benefit of low-cost, in-state tuition. The fact that almost all of the proposed reductions in the UW System budget were dropped shows that their gamble paid off.

A second consequence of the budget deficits was the creation of an upheaval in state-local relations. The proposed elimination of the Shared Revenue Fund seems almost unimaginable to long-time observers and students of Wisconsin state government. The Shared Tax Fund, as it was called in 1911 when it was established as part of Wisconsin's Progressive revolution, was created at the same time the state income tax was established. Indeed, the income tax was the source for this fund, and the purpose of the fund was to provide property tax relief and a more equitable form of financing local governments.[56]

From the 1960s through the end of the 1990s, the Shared Tax or Shared Revenue Fund, as it was renamed, was expanded and changed by a variety of governors and legislatures.[57] Indeed, this fund, along with the School Aid Fund, has been one of the hallmarks of the close connection between the state government and local governments for most of the past 100 years.[58] Because the Shared Revenue Fund has had an "equalization" component in it for more than

30 years, the fund not only provided state aid to almost all local governments but also some extra state aid to local governments that were "property poor."

Along with proposing to eliminate the Shared Revenue account, Governor McCallum proposed strict property tax controls. The combination of the two changes would essentially have left local governments with little choice but to make significant cuts in their programs and activities. This "new order" of things would have been a remarkable reversal of a 100-year tradition and an intensive 40-year effort on the part of state lawmakers to ensure strong local governments and high levels of local government services. By using tobacco settlement funds to offset the majority of the 2001–2003 deficit, a "new order" of things was postponed, at least for a short time.

A third consequence of Wisconsin's budget deficit was that Wisconsin's governor and legislators assigned the rights to $5.4 billion worth of tobacco settlement money the state would have been paid over a 30-year period.[59] In exchange for this $5.4 billion, Wisconsin's lawmakers will have recovered (for short-term use) approximately $1.3 billion.[60] This figure represents about 20 percent of the value of the tobacco proceeds. By almost any account, this is an extraordinarily poor short-term trade, and it will doubtless have a wide range of long-term consequences for the state.

A fourth consequence of the budget deficit was a dramatic deterioration of the state's bond rating. The lowered rating will significantly raise the cost of state borrowing for the foreseeable future. The added costs of borrowing will, in turn, put more pressure on the state's General Fund budget. Higher interest rates may crowd out spending for programs that are important to many state constituents, and higher interest rates may require a scaling back of state building projects.

Finally, among the most interesting consequences that seem to have emerged from the budget fiasco in the state is a sense of shock, disbelief, and even betrayal on the part of some of the state's citizens. In conversations this author had with state residents about the budget deficit, the question that came up repeatedly was: how could this have happened to us? In particular, it seemed very odd to people that in the summer of 2000 they were getting refund checks from Governor Thompson and state legislators who wanted to return the state surplus to the taxpayers, and suddenly, only months later, the state was plunged into a fiscal crisis.

Interestingly, the skepticism or cynicism these citizens voiced about their state government and state of-

ficials was echoed by some current and former government officials. For example, the former long-serving mayor of Madison, Paul Soglin, articulated what others seemed to be feeling. As reported in *The Capital Times,* the former mayor argued that the budget crisis was partly a function of having "too many legislators selling our state government."[61] He went on to say that "too many legislators for $10,000 campaign contributions are prepared to add millions of dollars of spending for special interests."[62]

Undoubtedly, the ripple effects of the tremendous reductions in state spending that have been or are now being put into law will continue for some years. Furthermore, even larger spending cuts will be needed in the 2003–2005 biennial budget, and these cuts will undoubtedly create more ripples. It is worth noting that one scholarly analysis shows that most of the budget gap for 2003–2005 is the result of a structural, not a cyclical, imbalance between anticipated revenues and expenditures.[63]

The mental images of this unfolding budget fiasco clash in a most dramatic way with newspaper articles and pictures from 1998, when the state's economy was booming and state officials and citizens were celebrating Wisconsin's 150th anniversary. At that time, state officials and citizens not only looked forward to the future with self-confidence but also seemed justified in doing so.

Yet, the structural imbalance between revenues and expenditures was already in place by 1998, and the economic downturn that would unmask and exacerbate this "legacy" of 1990s policy and budget decision making was not far away. Sobering as these facts are, the worst may yet be in store for the state. There is no more tobacco settlement money to paper over the structural imbalance or the revenue shortfalls caused by an ongoing recession.

Reflections

A number of lessons emerge as one traverses the news about Wisconsin's budget situation and reflects upon the budgeting literature. First, the Wisconsin case seems to suggest the need for a budget/policy parallel to Michels' "Iron Law of Oligarchy."[64] Perhaps we need, for elected officials and academics, a more forceful statement of the "wisdom" of incrementalism as articulated in "The Science of Muddling Through" and other articles and books by Charles Lindblom.[65] Perhaps we also need to alert state budget makers to the "Iron Law of Incrementalism"; to wit, elected officials who break the boundaries of incrementalism in budget and policy decision making do so at their peril and may put the state's budget and citizens at risk.

Second, a governor who plans to embark on a campaign for large-scale policy and budgetary change might want to enter office with a preformulated exit strategy. The Wisconsin case seems to show that Tommy Thompson got "out of town" just in time—just before the budget crisis came into full bloom. At least at some point in his term, Thompson apparently developed an exit strategy, and that strategy involved doing everything he could to help George Bush win the election in 2000. The strategy worked, and Thompson's reward was an invitation to join the new president's cabinet.

Third, despite Thompson's shrewd (or lucky) exit strategy, the facts show that he left the state with a large budget problem. Indeed, the tax rebate conceived at the end of his term may have been designed to endear himself to the state's voters, but it also served to exacerbate underlying fiscal problems. Even his long-time lieutenant governor and loyal subordinate, Scott McCallum, openly acknowledged in his 2001 budget summary that a large "structural deficit" was passed forward to him from the 1999–2001 (Thompson's last) budget. As expected, however, McCallum did not explicitly blame Thompson or the 1999–2001 legislature for the problem.

Fourth, the state's legislators must share part of the blame for the current budget crisis. In retrospect, it appears that they let too much institutional power slip out of their hands and into the governor's. A more independent legislature might have provided a more effective, and, in retrospect, essential check on an activist and extraordinarily powerful governor.

Fifth, the fact that the partisan political game was played with such vigor in the state during the 1980s and 1990s appears to have had significant negative consequences for the state and its people. Competition between political parties has usually been considered a hallmark of democracy in the academic literature on the states, and thus viewed positively. At least in the Wisconsin case, it also seems clear that unbridled partisan competition can have powerful negative consequences. Indeed, state officials' tardiness in establishing a Rainy Day Fund, and even more importantly their unwillingness to put money into the fund once it was established, can be largely explained by two decades of partisan competition.

Sixth, resonating with and exacerbating that partisan competition was an apparent implicit acceptance of the strategy known in Wisconsin as "Fiscal Brinksmanship." This strategy was a key causal factor of Wisconsin's deep budget crisis during the early 1980s, and it appears to have been a significant contributing factor in the current budget crisis.

Seventh, if Wisconsin's lawmakers had taken steps to fund their Rainy Day Fund, the state's 1999–2001 structural budget deficit might not have emerged in the first place. Contribution requirements for the fund might have snagged a large part of the new revenues generated during the 1990s that were ultimately put to use to expand spending.

Eighth, if the state had put money into its Rainy Day Fund, some of the large cuts made in the 2001–2003 budget bill (Act 16) and the budget repair bill might have been avoided. Alternatively, the Rainy Day Fund might have been used in place of the tobacco funds, which then would have been available for health-related programs and other purposes in future years. One can only hope that, after the current budget crisis is over, the state's lawmakers will do the prudent thing and put money into the Rainy Day Fund.

Finally, the Wisconsin case study illustrates once again that imperatives that drive budgeting in good economic times can create hardships during recessions. Specifically, during good times, governors and legislators often feel compelled to cut taxes and increase spending. Such actions can push the underlying relationship between taxes and spending out of balance and thus create a structural deficit. When cyclical deficits are added to structural deficits, as was the case in Wisconsin, dramatic remedies are required. In sum, particularly for Wisconsin, the 2001–2002 bust part of the boom-and-bust cycle has demonstrated once again, and in a most dramatic way, the power of economic cycles and the risks of structural deficits.

Notes

1. Among the reasons for this circumstance is that state general purpose tax revenue continued to grow during the recession, but the growth rate was slower than in prerecession years.

2. Russell S. Sobel and Randall G. Holcombe, "The Impact of State Rainy Day Funds in Easing State Fiscal Crises during the 1990–1991 Recession," *Public Budgeting and Finance* 19, no. 3 (Fall 1999): 28–48. According to Sobel and Holcombe's measure of fiscal stress during the 1990–1991 recession, Wisconsin experienced the least amount of fiscal stress of all the states, with only a $37.3 million cumulative shortfall for fiscal years 1989–1992, less than one half of one percent of the state's FY 1988 budget.

3. National Conference of State Legislatures, *State Fiscal Outlook for FY 2002: January Update.*

4. From 1972 through 1980, the operative term employed for the session and the bill was "budget review." Since 1982, however, the term "budget adjustment" has been used during most of these sessions. For details, see Richard Roe, "Executive Budget Bills Enacted by the Wisconsin Legislature, 1931–1997," Legislative Reference Bureau, Brief 99-3 (January 1999).

5. Wisconsin Department of Administration, *2000 Annual Fiscal Report* (October 2000); Wisconsin Department of Administration, *2001 Annual Fiscal Report* (October 2001).

6. The percentages are calculated from data for FY 2001. See Wisconsin Department of Administration, *2001 Annual Fiscal Report* (October 2001).

7. The term "special funds" employed in the "Annual Fiscal Report" includes transportation and conservation funds, (some) federal funds, fees, etc. A more complete list of fund sources that are not part of the general fund includes debt service, capital projects, pension and retirement funds, trust and agency funds, and others. For more detail, see Department of Administration, *2001 Annual Fiscal Report,* or see notes for "Wisconsin State Revenues and Expenditures: Fiscal Years 1970-1971—1999-2000," *Wisconsin Blue Book, 2001–2002* (Madison: Joint Committee on Legislative Organization, 2002), 816.

8. Ibid.

9. "Wisconsin Constitution," *Wisconsin Blue Book 1999–2000* (Madison: Joint Committee on Legislative Organization, 2000), 175.

10. The 1 percent requirement took effect for the first time in the 1983–1985 biennium. The specific language can be found in *Wisconsin Statutes,* chapter 20.003, section 4. In 1999, the statutory requirement was modified. The General Fund balance required was increased from 1 percent in FY 1999–2000 to 2 percent by FY 2005–2006, rising gradually over the years. For some reason, however, no surplus was formally required for FY 2001–2002. For more discussion of these matters, see Legislative Reference Bureau, "Budget Stabilization and Appropriation Limits," Brief 01–12 (November 2001).

11. The surplus can be viewed as a tool designed to cover modest errors or changes in estimated revenues or other required technical changes.

12. It is interesting to note that David Broder, along with several other journalists, has criticized Democrats in Congress for the same reticence.

13. For state citizens concerned about the deficit, the story must have been difficult to follow. The size of the deficit kept growing, and newspaper columnists and, from time to time, state budget officials did not consistently identify the fiscal year or years or the fund basis for which deficit figures were given or discussed.

14. Scott McCallum, Governor, "Budget Reform Bill Summary," Division of Executive Budget and Finance, Department of Administration (January 2002), 1.

15. Ibid.

16. These calculations are made from data supplied from Legislative Fiscal Bureau, *1999–01 Wisconsin State Budget: Comparative Summary of Budget Provisions Enacted as 1999 Acts 9 and 10* (January 2000), 25.

17. Legislative Fiscal Bureau, "Comparative Summary of Budget Priorities: Senate, Assembly, and Conference Committee," 25 July 2001.

18. Ibid.

19. McCallum, "Budget Reform Bill Summary," 1.

20. Ibid., 2. Missing from the "Budget Reform Bill Summary," however, is documentation showing that the remedies contained in Act 16 actually fixed the deficit problem. In short, perhaps because of the way it was crafted, the "Budget Reform Bill Summary" leaves some doubt about whether the original $2.4 billion fiscal problem was solved by Act 16.

21. Data released by the National Conference of State Legislatures showed that the five states that had the most serious budget problems had deficits that were 10 to 15 percent of their General Fund budget. See National Conference of State Legislatures, *Revised State Deficit Projections for FY 1991 and FY 1992* (May 1991).

22. Bob Lang, "Structural Balance of the State's General Fund Budget," Wisconsin Legislative Fiscal Bureau, 15 March 2002.

23. Dennis Chapman, "Campaign Notebook," *Milwaukee Journal Sentinel,* 2 November 2002, p. 10A.

24. "Summary of Significant Legislation Enacted by the 1993 Legislature," *Wisconsin Blue Book 1995–1996* (Madison: Joint Committee on Legislative Organization, 1996), 312.

25. Department of Administration, Division of Executive Budget and Finance, *State of Wisconsin Budget in Brief 1997–1999* (February 1997).

26. Tommy Thompson, *Power to the People: An American State at Work* (New York: Harper Collins, 1996), 139.

27. "State Government Revenues—All Funds: Fiscal Years 1993–94, 1994–95, and 1995–96," *Wisconsin Blue Book 1997–1998* (Madison: Joint Committee on Legislative Organization, 1998), 793.

28. In his book, Thompson reports that he made dramatic reductions in state agency spending to pay for part of the costs. He also notes that he had $400 million in new revenue to help pay for the $1.2 billion in new school aid costs. See Tommy Thompson, *Power to the People: An American State at Work,* 140–143.

29. Tommy Thompson, *Power to the People: An American State at Work,* 140–143.

30. See Steven Walters, "Sales Tax Rebate Picks Up Support, Governor Backs Refund, Up to $350 a Couple," *Milwaukee Journal Sentinel,* 27 August 1999, p. 1; Dennis Chapman, "Tax Rebate Fever Hits Minnesota—Under Proposal, Wisconsin Could Follow Suit," *Milwaukee Journal Sentinel,* 29 August 1999, p. 1; Lori Holly, "Deal on State Taxes Can't Come Too Soon, Finely Says Rebate Could Settle Budget, Giving County More Information on 2000 Funds," *Milwaukee Journal Sentinel,* 30 August 1999, p. 1.

31. Richard P. Jones, "Tax Rebate Plan Grows, but Cuts Are Challenged: Two Senators Warn that Slashing Revenue Could Lead to a Fiscal Crisis in Two Years," *Milwaukee Journal Sentinel,* 1 September 1999, p. 1.

32. Legislative Fiscal Bureau, "Tax Law Changes Beginning in 1995" (November 2002).

33. Don Nichols, "The Effect of Economic Recession on the Budget," in *Dollars and Sense: Policy Choices and the Wisconsin Budget,* ed. James K. Conant, Robert H. Haveman, and Jack Huddleston, vol. II (Madison: La Follette Institute of Public Affairs, 1991), 74–76.

34. Ibid.

35. This description appears on state license plates and thus serves as a good barometer of self-image and image to be projected to others outside the state.

36. Don Nichols, "The Effect of Economic Recession on the Budget," 71.

37. Steve Schultze, "Recession Gnaws at State Revenues," *The Milwaukee Journal,* 3 March 1992, p. A5.

38. Don Nichols, "The Effect of Economic Recession on the Budget," 71.

39. The General Purpose Tax Revenues make up 99% of the General Fund Tax Revenues.

40. In the Governors Reform Bill Summary, "fading revenue estimates" is given as the reason for the entire amount. See Scott McCallum, Governor, 1.

41. Ibid.

42. Creative bookkeeping could include, for example, pushing payments due in the current fiscal year into the next fiscal year; it can also include budget "redefinition," in which what constitutes the General Purpose Revenue or General Fund budget is redefined.

43. Dan Ritsche and Richard Roe, "State Budget Stabilization—The 'Rainy-Day' Fund," Wisconsin Legislative Reference Bureau (14 June 2002).

44. Scott McCallum, Governor, "Budget Reform Bill Summary," 1.

45. Ibid., 5.

46. Ibid.

47. Ibid.

48. Wisconsin Legislative Fiscal Bureau, *Wisconsin 2001–2003 Budget: Comparative Summary of Budget Provisions* (December 2001), 65.

49. Ibid.

50. Scott McCallum, Governor, "Budget Reform Bill Summary."

51. Ibid., 3, 41.

52. Ibid., 3, 38.

53. These calculations are made from data supplied on p. 24 of the "Budget Reform Bill Summary."

54. Legislative Fiscal Bureau, "2001–03 Budget Adjustment Bill, Comparative Summary of Budget Recommendations, 2001 Wisconsin Act 109" (September 2002).

55. *The Capital Times,* "Undergrad Admission Suspended," 9 March 2002, p. 1. It is worth noting that the University of Wisconsin System was given the opportunity to use tuition increases (up to 7 percent) as a means to offset a substantial part of its General Fund reduction.

56. James K. Conant, draft volume of *Wisconsin Government Politics* (under review), chapter 10.

57. Ibid.

58. Ibid.

59. Estimates vary as to the exact expected value of Wisconsin's tobacco settlement, but senior officials at Wisconsin's Legislative Finance Bureau use the $5.4 billion figure.

60. *Milwaukee Journal Sentinel,* "Sale of Tobacco Assets Exceeds Projections," 3 May 2002.
61. Matt Pommer, "Soglin Ties Caucuses to Budget Problems," *The Capital Times,* 27 March 2002, p. 1.
62. Ibid.
63. Andrew Rechovsky, "Wisconsin's Structural Deficit: Our Fiscal Future at the Crossroads," La Follette Institute of Public Affairs, University of Wisconsin–Madison (May 2002).
64. Robert Michels, *Political Parties: A Sociological Study of Oligarchic Tendencies in Modern Democracy* (Glencoe, IL: Free Press, 1949).
65. See Charles Lindblom, "The Science of Muddling Through," *Public Administration Review* 19 (1959): 79–88; Charles Lindblom, "Contexts for Change and Strategy: A Reply," *Public Administration Review* 24 (1964): 157–158; Charles Lindblom, *The Intelligence of Democracy* (New York: Free Press, 1965); and Charles Lindblom, "Still Muddling, Not Yet Through," *Public Administration Review* 39 (1979): 517–526.

Chapter 12 Review Questions

1. Why does Irene Rubin at the outset argue that "public budgets are not merely technical managerial documents; they are also intrinsically and irreducibly political"? Do you agree or disagree based on your reading of the case "Wisconsin's Budget Deficit"?

2. In two or three sentences, summarize how Rubin defines "a public budget." How does it differ from the budget of a private firm?

3. Why does Rubin stress that the chief tension in public budgeting is between public accountability and public acceptability? What does she mean by those terms? Was that tension illustrated in the case study "Wisconsin's Budget Deficit"?

4. Who are the major participants that Rubin believes are most involved in the public budgetary processes? What are they trying to achieve? Who was involved in the "Wisconsin's Budget Deficit" case? What were their roles as well as the strategies they used to achieve their goals?

5. List the five basic "budgetary decision-making clusters" that Rubin's essay outlines. Who are the key actors involved in each cluster? The special pattern of politics in each cluster? Did "Wisconsin's Budget Deficit" represent any one (or more) cluster? Does it "fit" Rubin's "cluster model" and if so, why? Or if not, why not?

6. What are the essential differences between microbudgeting and macrobudgeting according to Rubin? Why is it important to distinguish between the two? Did the case "Wisconsin's Budget Deficit" represent either or both?

Key Terms

bureau chiefs

chief executive officers

power differentials

separation of payer and decider

open environment

budget constraints

reform orientation

incrementalist view

revenue cluster

expenditure cluster

balance cluster

budget implementation

microbudgeting

macrobudgeting

legal environment

intergovernmental grant structure

individual strategies

budget outcomes

fiscal year

policy choices

Suggestions for Further Reading

An excellent way to increase your understanding of budgets is to obtain a current city, county, state, or federal budget (usually the summary document provides all the important information) and read it carefully. Most summaries are written so that the layperson can understand their major contents and proposals. Also, now that public budgets are frequently the subjects of front-page headlines, read the major news coverage devoted to them, particularly in leading newspapers like the *New York Times, Washington Post, Christian Science Monitor, Los Angeles Times, St. Louis Post Dispatch,* and *Wall Street Journal* as well as in news magazines like *Time, The Economist,* and *Newsweek.* The best up-to-date, scholarly survey of budgetary subjects is found in a thoughtfully edited journal, *Public Budgeting and Finance.* Each issue contains insightful articles by some of the leading experts in the field. Also do not neglect studying current issues of the *Public Administration Review, The National Journal,* or *Governing,* as well as the annual volumes of *Setting National Priorities* published by the Brookings Institution in Washington, D.C.

Although they become dated quickly, introductory texts also offer a useful overview. For the best recent ones, see Robert D. Lee, Jr., and Ronald W. Johnson, *Public Budgeting Systems,* 6th ed. (Gaithersburg: Aspen Publishing, 1998); David Nice, *Public Budgeting* (Belmont, Calif.: Wadsworth, 2001); Irene S. Rubin, *The Politics of Public Budgeting,* 4th ed. (New York: Seven Bridges, 2000); Albert C. Hyde, *Government Budgeting: Theory, Process, Politics,* 2nd ed. (Pacific Grove, Calif.: Brooks/Cole, 1993); Robert W. Kweit, *Public Budgeting* (New York: Longman, 1995); John L. Mikeskill, *Fiscal Administration,* 6th ed. (Belmont, Calif.: Wadsworth, 2002); and James J. Gosling, *Budgetary Politics in American Government,* 2nd ed. (New York: Garland, 1997). For an outstanding historic collection of several of the best essays written on public budgeting, see Allen Schick, *Perspectives on Budgeting,* Revised Edition (Washington, D.C.: American Society for Public Administration, 1987). A handy, free guide-

book that explains the difficult and arcane jargon of budgeting is *A Glossary of Terms Used in the Federal Budget Process* (Washington, D.C.: General Accounting Office, 1977). For a useful handbook synthesizing our knowledge on various aspects of budgeting, see Allen Schick, *The Capacity to Budget* (Washington, D.C.: Urban Institute, 1990). Current cases can be found in Aman Khan and W. Bartley Hildreth, *Case Studies in Public Budgeting and Financial Management,* 2nd ed. (Dubuque, Iowa: Kendall/Hunt, 1996).

Undoubtedly, a profound impact on federal budgetary practices was made by the enactment of the 1974 Congressional Budget Reform Act, which is examined in several scholarly books, including Allen Schick, *Congress and Money* (Washington, D.C.: The Urban Institute, 1980); Dennis S. Ippolito, *Congressional Spending* (Ithaca, N.Y.: Cornell University Press, 1981); Lance T. LeLoup, *The Fiscal Congress* (Westport, Conn.: Greenwood Press, 1980); Rudolph G. Penner, ed., *The Congressional Budget Process After Five Years* (Washington, D.C.: American Enterprise Institute, 1981); and James P. Pfiffner, *The President, the Budget, and Congress* (Boulder, Colo.: Westview Press, 1979). For two thoughtful case studies of federal budgetary politics, read Paul Light, *Artful Work: The Politics of Social Security Reform* (New York: Random House, 1985); and Irene S. Rubin, *Shrinking the Federal Government* (New York: Longman, 1985); and for an excellent critical look at the application of various budgetary systems, see George W. Downs and Patrick D. Larkey, *The Search for Government Efficiency* (New York: Random House, 1986), especially Chapters 4 and 5; and Roy T. Meyers, *Strategic Budgeting* (Ann Arbor: University of Michigan Press, 1997); as well as two insightful essays in the *Public Administration Review* 44 (March/April 1984): Hardy Wickwar, "Budgets One and Many," pp. 99–102, and Naomi Caiden, "The New Rules of the Federal Budget Game," pp. 109–117.

For practical, "how-to" books on budgeting, refer to Edward A. Leham, *Simplified Government Budgeting*

(Chicago: Municipal Finance Officers Association, 1981); Richard J. Stillman II, *Results-oriented Budgeting for Local Public Managers* (Columbia: Institute of Governmental Research, University of South Carolina, 1982); Garasimos A. Gianakis and Clifford P. McCue, *Local Government Budgeting: A Managerial Approach,* (Westport, Conn.: Praeger, 1999); and Dall W. Forsythe, *Memos to the Governor* (Washington, D.C.: Georgetown University Press, 1997). Part five of James L. Perry, ed., *Handbook of Public Administration,* 2nd ed. (San Francisco: Jossey-Bass, 1996), offers several applied essays on public budgeting.

A remarkable inside look at federal budgeting is William Greider, *The Education of David Stockman and Other Americans* (New York: Dutton, 1981). Also read David Stockman's autobiography, *The Triumph of Politics: The Inside Story of the Reagan Revolution* (New York: Harper & Row, 1986).

Three handbooks published by Marcel Dekker are also worth consulting: *Handbook of Public Finance,* (New York: 1998) edited by Fred Thompson and Mark T. Green; *Handbook of Debt Management,* New York: 1996) edited by Gerald J. Miller, and *Public Budgeting and Finance,* 4th ed., (New York: 1997) by Robert T. Golembiewski and Jack Rabin.

For more theoretical texts, see Aman Khan and W. Bartley Hildreth, eds., *Budgetory Theory in the Public Sector* (Westport, Conn: Greenwood, 2002); Aron Wildavsky, *Budgeting and Governing* (New Brunswick, N.J.: Transaction Books, 2001) and John R. Bartle, *Research in Public Administration: Evolving Theories of Public Budgeting,* volume 6 (Amsterdam: JAI, 2001).

CHAPTER 13

Implementation: The Concept of an Ambiguity-Conflict Model

A s implementation research evolved, two schools of thought developed as to the most effective method for studying and describing implementation: top-down and bottom-up. Top-down theorists see policy designers as central actors and concentrate their attention on factors that can be manipulated at the central level. Bottom-up theorists emphasize target groups and service deliverers, arguing policy really is made at the local level. Most reviewers now agree that some convergence of these two perspectives . . . is necessary for the field to develop.

Richard E. Matland

READING 13

Introduction

From the very beginning of its conscious development as a field of study, public administration has stressed the importance of "good," "correct," "timely," and "efficient" execution of public objectives. Sound implementation was and perhaps still is "the bottom line" of what the administrative enterprise is all about. As Woodrow Wilson wrote in "The Study of Administration," the first American essay on public administration in 1887, "The broad plans of government action are not administration; the detailed execution of such plans is administration."[1]

Although "detailed execution" may well have always been the central preoccupation of public administrators, the last three decades have witnessed an impressive emergence and growth of scholarship directed specifically at exploring this subject. Indeed, by the 1980s implementation scholarship had become a distinct and separate subfield of public administration, political science, and policy studies. Implementation scholarship now boasts its own considerable array of professional journals and dedicated scholars, as well as sizable conferences oriented toward discussing various intellectual viewpoints and new methodologies related to this subject.

[1]Woodrow Wilson, "The Study of Administration," *Political Science Quarterly,* 2 (June 1887), p. 197.

Much of the original impetus to develop a conscious subfield of study concerning implementation came from what many perceived as the apparent failure of the Great Society Programs. In the mid-1960s President Lyndon B. Johnson succeeded in pushing through Congress in a relatively short period a vast range of new types of social programs designed to alleviate major social problems (such as hunger, delinquency, poverty, unemployment, racial discrimination, and urban decay) as well as other prominent social concerns of the day and aimed at building "The Great Society." As Robert T. Nakamura and Frank Smallwood write, "It was not long before disillusionment began to set in as it became apparent that it might be easier to 'legitimize' social policy by passing ambiguous legislation than to carry out such policy by means of effective program implementation."[2]

By the late 1960s and early 1970s students of public affairs began questioning the value of passing so many laws creating new social programs without paying adequate attention to whether these laws were effectively implemented or carried out at all. Theodore Lowi, in his *The End of Liberalism* (1969), popularized this attack on the broad expansion of governmental activities, which, he argued, had eroded clear standards for administrative accountability and consequently had led to a crisis of public authority over the role and purposes of government in society. As public programs grew into more and more abstract and complex activities, according to Lowi, "it became more difficult to set precise legislative guidelines for execution of public policy."[3] It also opened up government programs to chaotic pluralistic competition. Lowi termed this phenomenon *interest group liberalism.* His solution was to return to a more simplified structure in which Congress and the president make precise laws and the courts formulate strict judicial standards to guide administrative actions, thereby reducing administrative discretion to a minimum. Hence, implementation would become little if any problem for administrators because their choices would be restricted and their direction from policy makers would be well defined and specific.

Meanwhile, other scholars were by then also busily pointing out that the Great Society Programs were not working as planned. Several case studies appeared at this time making much the same point—namely, that the Great Society Social Programs, for various reasons, were not or could not be effectively implemented—such as Martha Derthick's *New Towns In-Town*[4] and Daniel P. Moynihan's *Maximum Feasible Misunderstanding.*[5] Jeffrey Pressman and Aaron Wildavsky's *Implementation* (1973)[6] especially sparked much of the serious academic interest in this topic. Pressman and Wildavsky wrote what was essentially a case study of the Economic Development Administration's effort in the late 1960s to provide jobs for the "hard-core" unemployed in Oakland, California. Their case turned out to be a study in how not to get things done in government. At the end of their book they offered a prescriptive list of warnings about what should *not* be done to accomplish public policy objectives: "Implementation should not be divorced from policy"; "Designers of policy [should] consider the direct means for achieving their ends"; "Continuity of leadership is important"; "Simplicity in policies is much to be desired"; and so on.

---

[2]Robert T. Nakamura and Frank Smallwood, *The Politics of Policy Implementation* (New York: St. Martin's Press, 1980), p. 11.

[3]Theodore J. Lowi, *The End of Liberalism* (New York: W. W. Norton, 1969), p. 127.

[4]Martha Derthick, *New Towns In-Town* (Washington, D.C.: Urban Institute, 1972).

[5]Daniel P. Moynihan, *Maximum Feasible Misunderstanding* (New York: Free Press, 1970).

[6]Jeffrey L. Pressman and Aaron B. Wildavsky, *Implementation* (Berkeley: University of California Press, 1973).

After the appearance of the Pressman and Wildavsky book, Edwin C. Hargrove of the Urban Institute called implementation "the missing link" in social theory, and soon an impressive array of new methodological approaches began to search for "the missing link."[7] Several of the more prominent implementation theories that have been put forward during the past three decades include the following:

Implementation as a linear process: Donald S. Van Meter and Carl E. Van Horn, in an essay entitled "The Policy Implementation Process: A Conceptual Framework," which appeared in *Administration and Society* (1975), argue that implementation involves a linear process composed of six variables that link policy with performance: standards and objectives; resources; interorganizational communications and enforcement activities; characteristics of the implementing agencies; economic, social, and political conditions; and the disposition of the implementers.[8] Presumably relationships or changes in any one of these inputs ultimately, according to the authors, can influence the successful performance of the policy objectives.

Implementation as politics of mutual adaptation: In a study of several federal programs by Milbrey McLaughlin in 1975 for the Rand Corporation, the writer concludes, "The amount of interest, commitment and support evidenced by the principal actors had a major influence on the prospects for success."[9] In other words, the political support from the top, according to McLaughlin, was the key to success or failure of program implementation.

Implementation as gamesmanship: Eugene Bardach's *Implementation Game* (1977), as the book's title indicates, sees the subject essentially as a "game," "where bargaining, persuasion, and maneuvering under conditions of uncertainty occur"[10] to exercise control of outcomes. For Bardach, implementation therefore involves all the arts of gamesmanship: learning the rules of the game, devising tactics and strategy, controlling the flow of communications, and dealing with crises and uncertain situations as they arise.

Implementation as conditions for effectively accomplishing objectives: Paul Sabatier and Daniel Mazmanian in "The Conditions of Effective Implementation: A Guide to Accomplishing Policy Objectives" (1979)[11] attempt to forecast what conditions promote or prevent policy implementation. They argue that the likelihood of implementation is enhanced by the existence of a favorable or "optimal" set of conditions. Conversely, in their view, implementation is impeded or altogether prevented when some or all of these conditions do not exist. Much of their essay is devoted to elaborating on the five conditions they consider necessary "that can go a long way toward assuring effective policy implementation if they are met."

[7]Edwin C. Hargrove, *The Missing Link* (Washington, D.C.: Urban Institute, 1975).

[8]Donald S. Van Meter and Carl E. Van Horn, "The Policy Implementation Process: A Conceptual Framework," *Administration and Society,* 6, no. 4 (February 1975), p. 449.

[9]Milbrey McLaughlin, "Implementation as Mutual Adaptation," in Walter Williams and Richard Elmore (eds.), *Social Program Implementation* (New York: Academic Press, 1976), pp. 167–180.

[10]Eugene Bardach, *The Implementation Game* (Cambridge, Mass.: M.I.T. Press, 1977), p. 56.

[11]Paul Sabatier and Daniel Mazmanian, "The Conditions of Effective Implementation: A Guide to Accomplishing Policy Objectives," *Policy Analysis,* 5, no. 4 (Fall 1979), pp. 481–504.

Implementation as a circular policy leadership process: By comparison, Robert T. Nakamura and Frank Smallwood perceive implementation as a circular process intricately involved within the entire public policy-making process. In their book *The Politics of Policy
Implementation* (1980), the authors argue, "Implementation is but one part of this [pol-
icy] process and is inextricably related to, and interdependent with, the other parts."[12]
For Nakamura and Smallwood the critical element linking implementation to the rest
of the policy process is leadership, which, in their words, is necessary "to coordinate
activities in all three environments" (policy formulation, implementation, and evaluation) to achieve program goals.

Implementation as contingency theory: Ernest R. Alexander, by contrast, in "From Idea
to Action," in *Administration and Society* (1985), develops a contingency model of policy implementation.[13] He views implementation as a complex "continuing interactive
process," one that involves interactions with the environment, stimulus, policy, programs, and outcomes—all very much depending on the specific content, elements, and
timing of these interactions.

Implementation as case analysis: As with the Pressman and Wildavsky book, case studies
of a single implementation situation remain a popular approach to understanding this subject. They seek to draw specific "lessons" about right—or wrong—approaches to accomplishing public policies within a specialized policy field. Charles S. Bullock III and Charles
M. Lamb's *Implementation of Civil Rights Policy* (1986) presents a highly sophisticated
case analysis of this sort.[14] It analyzes in depth five cases in the civil rights field and draws
conclusions about the significance of ten specific variables involving the effective implementation of civil rights policies. The authors conclude that five variables in particular are
critical for successful policy implementation: federal involvement, specific agency standards, agency commitment, support from superiors, and favorable cost/benefit ratios.

Today the debate among scholars continues over what constitutes the appropriate conceptual framework to best comprehend the implementation of public policy. It remains hardly a
settled matter, with theories and counter-theories being put forward at a brisk pace. Certainly,
as yet, scholars have not agreed on any *one* model to explain public implementation processes
or how models work in government. Nevertheless, it would be worthwhile to look closely at
one of the more recent approaches to this topic to help clarify and understand this topic more
thoroughly. The following current conceptual framework is presented by Richard E. Matland
of the University of Houston. The author begins with "a dragnet review" of the vast implementation literature over the past three decades. He synthesizes and reconceptualizes the previous studies into two major schools that he terms "top-down" and "bottom-up" approaches.
His new model attempts to reconcile both approaches by offering another conceptual framework, one that builds upon prior thinking, or what he refers to as "The Ambiguity-Conflict
Model." The author describes carefully how he develops his model, which essentially sees

[12]Nakamura and Smallwood, *The Politics of Policy Implementation,* p. 21.

[13]Ernest R. Alexander, "From Idea to Action: Notes for a Contingency Theory of the Policy Implementation
Process," *Administration and Society,* 16, no. 4 (February 1985), pp. 403–425.

[14]Charles S. Bullock III and Charles M. Lamb, *Implementation of Civil Rights Policy* (Monterey, Calif.: Brooks/Cole
Publishing, 1986).

implementation processes, their success or failure, as dependent upon the degree of a policy's ambiguity as well as upon its degree of inherent conflict. His thinking leads, in turn, to four paradigms that he discusses in some detail as a way to clarify our contemporary understanding of implementation processes.

As you read this selection, keep the following questions in mind:

What assumptions does the author make in building his conceptual model of ambiguity-conflict for implementation? Did he assume, for example, that implementation activities take place in an open, democratic, and pluralistic society? One governed by laws? Or what? How do such assumptions shape the concept he puts forward?

What implications does this model have for practicing public administrators? Can they use it successfully to predict when conditions are "ripe" for implementing programs or *how* to implement programs? Indeed, how does Matland define "successful implementation"? Do you concur with him?

Is the author optimistic about the possibilities of predicting conditions to allow for successful implementation of public policies? Explain the "pros/cons" of his ambiguity/conflict model as a predictor of success.

Would this model have proved useful for the policy makers and administrators designing a program in any of the previous case studies you have read in this text? If so, how? Or if not, why not?

Synthesizing the Implementation Literature: The Ambiguity-Conflict Model of Policy Implementation

RICHARD E. MATLAND

Several recent articles and books have reviewed the policy implementation literature, summarizing what has been learned and identifying obstacles standing in the way of further knowledge (O'Toole 1986; Sabatier 1986; McLaughlin 1987; Van Horn 1987; Goggin et al. 1990). The extent of agreement is surprising; most of these authors paint a similar picture of past work and suggest similar paths for future work. These reviews emphasize the need for closure and coherence in our

theoretical models. Perhaps most telling is O'Toole's (1986) review of more than one hundred implementation studies, in which he finds these studies referring to over three hundred key variables. A literature with three hundred critical variables doesn't need more variables: It needs *structure*.

As implementation research evolved, two schools of thought developed as to the most effective method for studying and describing implementation: top-down and bottom-up. Top-down theorists see policy designers as the central actors and concentrate their attention on factors that can be manipulated at the central level. Bottom-up theorists emphasize target groups and service deliverers, arguing policy really is made at the local level. Most reviewers now agree that some convergence of these two perspectives, tying the macrolevel variables of the top-down models to the microlevel variables "bottom-uppers" consider, is necessary for the field to develop. This article reviews the two major implementation schools and previous attempts to synthesize the literature. The ambiguity-conflict model then is presented as an alternative model for reconciling the existing findings on implementation.

Top-down, Bottom-up, and Attempts to Combine Them

Top-down Models

Top-down models (Van Meter and Van Horn 1975; Mazmanian and Sabatier 1981, 1983, 1989) see implementation as concern with the degree to which the actions of implementing officials and target groups coincide with the goals embodied in an authoritative decision. Mazmanian and Sabatier (1983, 20) define implementation as "The carrying out of a basic policy decision, usually incorporated in a statute but which can also take the form of important executive orders or court decisions . . ." The starting point is the authoritative decision; as the name implies, centrally located actors are seen as most relevant to producing the desired effects.

In the most fully developed top-down model, Mazmanian and Sabatier (1989) present three general sets of factors (tractability of the problem, ability of statute to structure implementation, and nonstatutory variables affecting implementation) which they argue determine the probability of successful implementation. These factors then are developed into a set of sixteen independent variables that are hypothesized to influence goal compliance. The complexity of their model points to one of the more striking problems and recurrent criticisms of implementation research—the lack of parsimony.

Top-downers have exhibited a strong desire to develop generalizable policy advice. This requires finding consistent, recognizable patterns in behavior across different policy areas. Belief that such patterns

exist and the desire to give advice has given the top-down view a highly prescriptive bent and has led to a concentration on variables that can be manipulated at the central level. Common top-down advice is: Make policy goals clear and consistent (Van Meter and Van Horn 1975; Mazmanian and Sabatier 1983); minimize the number of actors (Pressman and Wildavsky 1973); limit the extent of change necessary (Van Meter and Van Horn 1975; Mazmanian and Sabatier 1983); and place implementation responsibility in an agency sympathetic with the policy's goals (Van Meter and Van Horn 1975; Sabatier 1986).

Top-downers meet three sets of criticisms. First, top-down models take the statutory language as their starting point. This fails to consider the significance of actions taken earlier in the policy-making process. Winter (1985 and 1986) notes that many implementation barriers are found in the initial stages of the policy-making process and to understand policy implementation these processes must be studied carefully. Nakamura and Smallwood (1980) argue that the policy-formation process gives implementers important cues about intensity of demands, and about the size, stability, and degree of consensus among those pushing for change. An analysis that takes policy as given and does not consider its past history might miss vital connections. By concentrating on the statutory language, top-downers may fail to consider broader public objectives. O'Toole (1989) argues that a top-down analysis of wastewater treatment would find that privately managed facilities are superior because they are built more quickly, they are less expensive to build, and they provide approximately the same quality of waste treatment as publicly owned facilities. When broader issues such as affirmative action, compliance with Davis-Bacon labor laws, use and development of innovative technology, and local government autonomy and accountability are considered, publicly owned and operated facilities score much higher.

Second, top-downers have been accused of seeing implementation as a purely administrative process and either ignoring the political aspects or trying to eliminate them (Berman 1978; Hoppe, van de Graaf, and van Dijk 1985; Baier, March, and Saetren 1986). For example, the call for clear, explicit, and consistent goals contradicts much of what is known about how legislation is passed. Passage of legislation often requires ambiguous language and contradictory goals to hold together a passing coalition. The top-down emphasis on clarity, rule promulgation, and monitoring brings to mind the Weberian bureaucrat making independent decisions based on merit and technical criteria, free from political influence. It is, however, rarely possible to separate politics from administration. Attempts to insulate an inherently political subject matter from politics do not necessarily lead to apolitical actions. They instead may lead directly to policy failure.

Finally, top-down models have been criticized for their exclusive emphasis on the statute framers as key actors. This criticism has two primary variants. One argues from a normative perspective that local service deliverers have expertise and knowledge of the true problems; therefore, they are in a better position to propose purposeful policy. Top-down models, however, see local actors as impediments to successful implementation, agents whose shirking behavior needs to be controlled. The second variant argues from a positive perspective that discretion for street-level bureaucrats is inevitably so great that it is simply unrealistic to expect policy designers to be able to control the actions of these agents. That service deliverers ultimately determine policy is a major tenet of bottom-up models.

Bottom-up Models

Bottom-uppers, such as Berman (1978 and 1980); Hjern and Porter (1981); Hjern (1982); Hjern and Hull (1982); Hull and Hjern (1987); and Lipsky (1978) argue that a more realistic understanding of implementation can be gained by looking at a policy from the view of the target population and the service deliverers. Policy implementation occurs on two levels (Berman 1978). At the macroimplementation level, centrally located actors devise a government program; at the microimplementation level, local organizations react to the macrolevel plans, develop their own programs, and implement them. Berman argues that most implementation problems stem from the interaction of a policy with the microlevel institutional setting. Central planners only indirectly can influence microlevel factors. Therefore, there is wide variation in how the same national policy is implemented at the local level. Contextual factors within the implementing environment can completely dominate rules created at the top of the implementing pyramid, and policy designers will be unable to control the process. Under these conditions, according to the bottom-uppers, if local level implementers are not given the freedom to adapt the program to local conditions, it is likely to fail (Palumbo, Maynard-Moody, and Wright 1984).

Bottom-uppers argue that the goals, strategies, activities, and contacts of the actors involved in the microimplementation process must be understood in order to understand implementation. It is at the microlevel that policy directly affects people. The influence of policy on the action of street-level bureaucrats must be evaluated in order to predict that policy's effect (Weatherley and Lipsky 1977). Because implementation arises from the interaction of policy and setting, it is unrealistic to expect the development of a simple or single theory of implementation that is "context free" (Maynard-Moody, Musheno, and Palumbo 1990).

The most extensive empirical work within the bottom-up tradition has been that of Benny Hjern (1982) and his colleagues (Hjern and Hull 1985; Hull and Hjern 1987). Hjern's strategy is to study a policy problem, asking microlevel actors about their goals, activities, problems, and contacts. This technique enables Hjern to map a network that identifies the relevant implementation structure for a specific policy at the local, regional, and national levels, and allows him to evaluate the significance of government programs vis-à-vis other influences such as markets. It also enables him to see strategic coalitions as well as unintended effects of policy and the dynamic nature of policy implementation. Hjern finds that central initiatives are poorly adapted to local conditions. Program success depends in large part on the skills of individuals in the local implementation structure who can adapt policy to local conditions; it depends only to a limited degree on central activities.

While top-downers have a strong desire to present prescriptive advice, bottom-uppers have placed more emphasis on describing what factors have caused difficulty in reaching stated goals. The strongly inductive nature of this research combined with results finding most of the relevant factors varying from site to site has led to few explicit policy recommendations. The primary policy recommendation from researchers within this tradition is for a flexible strategy that allows for adaptation to local difficulties and contextual factors (Maynard-Moody, Musheno, and Palumbo 1990). Some researchers have suggested that policy changes should be consonant with the values of implementing agents (Berman 1978).

Two criticisms of bottom-up models appear with some consistency—one normative, one methodological. The normative criticism is that, in a democratic system, policy control should be exercised by actors whose power derives from their accountability to sovereign voters through their elected representatives. The authority of local service deliverers does not derive from this base of power. Decentralization should occur within a context of central control. Street-level bureaucrats *do* have great discretion in their interactions with clients. To proceed from this fact to theorize that because such flexibility exists it should serve as the basis for designing policy, however, is to turn the role of theory on its head (Linder and Peters 1987). It effectively equates description with prescription. Flexibility and autonomy might be appropriate when the goals of the policy formulators and implementers are the same, but if they differ greatly, flexibility and autonomy may lead to policies which result in lower performance on official goals. Classic organizational theory is rife with examples of agents subordinating the goals of their principals and concentrating on their own subgoals (March and Simon 1958; Merton 1957; Michels 1949; Selznick 1949).

The second criticism is that the bottom-up methodology overemphasizes the level of local autonomy. Hjern's methodology relies on perceptions; therefore, indirect effects and the effects actors are unconscious of are not registered. Variations in actions can be explained largely by local level differences, yet all actions may fall within a limited range where the borders are set by centrally determined policy. While central actors do not act in detail or intervene in specific cases, they can structure the goals and strategies of those participants who are active. The institutional structure, the available resources, and the access to an implementing arena may be determined centrally and substantially can affect policy outcomes. Sabatier (1986) notes that a bottom-up analysis of environmental regulations in the United States would find that central government authorities play only a limited role. Most suits are brought by environmental interest organizations on behalf of individuals. Yet the decision to give individuals standing and the right to sue for collective damages under class-action suits is a crucial factor that was decided by policy designers when they framed the policy. By giving these actors access, the central policy designers structured the actions that occurred later.

Combinations of the Two Perspectives: Previous Attempts

Limited number of attempts have been made to combine these two major perspectives and other perspectives on implementation. One group of researchers has proposed different ways of combining the two formats within the same model and another group has searched for conditions under which one approach is more appropriate than the other.

Elmore's concept of forward and backward mapping (1982 and 1985) is an early attempt to combine top-down and bottom-up perspectives. Elmore argues that policy designers should choose policy instruments based on the incentive structure of target groups. Forward mapping consists of stating precise policy objectives, elaborating detailed means-ends schemes, and specifying explicit outcome criteria by which to judge policy at each stage. Backward mapping consists of stating precisely the behavior to be changed at the lowest level, describing a set of operations that can insure the change, and repeating the procedure upwards by steps until the central level is reached. By using backward mapping, policy designers may find more appropriate tools than those initially chosen. This process insures consideration of the microimplementers' and target groups' interpretations of the policy problem and possible solutions.

Elmore's approach is a useful suggestion for policy designers; micro implementers' and target groups' views must be considered in planning an implementation strategy. On the other hand, it is not a theoretical model in the traditional sense. Sellitz, Wrightsman, and Cook (1976, 16) define theory as a "set of concepts plus the interrelationships that are assumed to exist among those concepts." The consequences that logically follow from the relationships posed in the theory should be testable hypotheses. Elmore's model has no predictions as to generalized behavior. No specific interrelationships are hypothesized; effectively there are no hypotheses to test. As a tool, Elmore's discussion is useful; as a theory, however, it lacks explanatory power.

Sabatier (1986; 1988; 1991; Sabatier and Pelkey 1987) has moved away from the top-down perspective, which he helped develop, and toward a combined perspective. He now argues that policy needs to be analyzed in cycles of more than ten years. The longer time allows for an opportunity to consider policy learning, a concept emphasized by Sabatier. Policies operate within parameters most easily identified by using a top-down approach. These parameters include socioeconomic conditions, legal instruments, and the basic government structure. These remain relatively stable over long periods of time. Within this structure, however, substantial actions occur. Sabatier argues that advocacy coalitions should be the main unit of analysis in the study of these actions. Advocacy coalitions are groups of policy advocates from differing organizations, both public and private, who share the same set of beliefs and goals. These groups attempt to have their views of policy problems, solutions, and legitimate actors accepted. Sabatier urges the use of Hjern's networking methodology to develop a mapping of these advocacy coalitions.

Sabatier's proposal represents a legitimate method for studying public policy. When examining a broad policy area over a long period of time, however, the question of whether this is actually studying implementation becomes a relevant concern. Sabatier's definition of implementation does not appear to be about the same process. A policy field followed over many years can change so radically that it bears little resemblance to its initial form. If implementation research is to retain a meaningful definition, it should be tied to a specific policy rather than to all actions in a policy field.

Goggin et al. (1990) present a communications model of intergovernmental policy implementation that sees state implementers at the nexus of a series of communication channels. They describe three clusters of variables that affect state implementation: inducements and constraints from the top (the federal level), inducements and constraints from the bottom (state and local levels), and state-specific factors defined as decisional outcomes and state capacity. Elements of the two major models are considered by including signals from both the top and the bottom. The communication model also emphasizes that signals are perceived differently, distortions occur, and contextual conditions can affect the interpretation of signals.

Some authors prefer to discuss when a model is appropriately applied rather than to try to build a combined model. Dunshire (1978) and Saetren (1983) argue that the two perspectives should apply to different times in the implementation process. Top-down perspectives are more appropriate in the early planning stages, but a bottom-up view is more appropriate in later evaluation stages.

Berman (1980) argues that an implementation plan should be developed using either the top-down or bottom-up approach depending on a set of parameters that describes the policy context. He argues that these situational parameters are dimensions that the implementation designer cannot influence. They include scope of change, validity of technology, goal conflict, institutional setting, and environmental stability. Berman suggests that when change is incremental, technology is certain, environment is stable, goal conflict is low, and institutional setting is tightly coupled, an implementation plan should follow the tenets of the top-down model. He convincingly argues that when a viable solution already exists, efforts should be concentrated on making sure that solution is used. Therefore a top-down strategy is appropriate. Berman suggests further that major policy changes involving uncertain technology—with goal conflicts and an unstable and loosely coupled environment—should be built around a bottom-up framework. This argument is less convincing. Part of the confusion lies in the distinction between a descriptive and a prescriptive model. It virtually is certain that when major policy changes are implemented where technology is uncertain and goal conflict high, bargaining *necessarily* occurs and adjustments are made. As a description of the process, many factors emphasized in bottom-up models are relevant. A prescription that suggests these conditions should lead to the delegation of autonomy to microlevel implementers, however, makes implementation feasibility the sole criterion on which to evaluate implementation plans. Linder and Peters (1987) argue that while feasibility is an important consideration, other political, economic, or ethical criteria may lead to a desire for a more centrally directed policy. For example, instituting or expanding civil rights to a new sector of the populace is a policy that probably exhibits most of the conditions in which Berman recommends a bottom-up strategy. Nevertheless, a policy with strong central steering may be preferred as the most effective way to assure actions consistent with policy objectives. Berman argues that choosing a top-down strategy can lead to resistance, disregard, and pro forma compliance. Such dangers certainly do exist. Choosing a bottom-up strategy, however, may lead to cooptation and pursuit of individual goals that run contrary to the policy objectives, and these are often more objectionable.

In synthesizing the two implementation models I have chosen to develop a model that explains when the two approaches are most appropriate rather than to develop a model that combines both simultaneously. I believe this is the most fruitful approach to synthesis for both theoreticians and practitioners. Until now, implementation studies have tended to present long lists of variables that may affect implementation. The conditions under which these variables are important and the reasons we should expect them to be important have been ignored to a large degree or have been treated superficially. This has given us a field overflowing with diagrams and flow charts with a prodigious number of variables. Synthesis that merely combines ten variables considered by the top-downers with ten variables considered by the bottom-uppers, without exploring the theoretical relationship between them, is likely to exacerbate the problem. I have chosen, therefore, to concentrate on a more limited set of variables and to explore their theoretical implications more fully.

Structuring implementation research and bringing some closure to the topic is likely to be even more important for policy designers. While many factors may be relevant and more accurate decisions could be made if all factors were considered, even readily available information isn't considered when decisions are made (Feldman and March 1981). Therefore, while it is proper to remind policy designers to consider all relevant factors, a much greater service is rendered if policy designers are given an adequate description of the implementation process that directs them to the variables of greatest importance and to the factors on which to focus their scarce resources should their search processes be limited, as they inevitably are.

What Is Successful Implementation?

Before turning to model exposition, a proper definition of *successful implementation* should be discussed. Policy can be defined as the programmatic activities formulated in response to an authoritative decision. These activities are the policy designer's plans for carrying out the wishes expressed by a legitimating organization, be it a legislature, a judicial agent, or an executive body. The pivotal question is whether attention should be focused on fidelity to the designer's plan or on the general consequences of the implementation actions when determining success. Disagreements between top-down and bottom-up theorists have at their very base disagreements over this question. Top-down theorists desire to measure success in terms of specific outcomes tied directly to the statutes that are the source of a program. Bottom-up theorists prefer a much broader evaluation, in which a program leading to "positive effects" can be labeled a success (Palumbo, Maynard-Moody, and Wright 1984).

The failure to specify what is meant by *successful implementation* causes considerable confusion. Ingram and Schneider (1990) note several plausible definitions of successful implementation. Among these are: agencies comply with the directives of the statues; agencies are held accountable for reaching specific indicators of success; goals of the statute are achieved; local goals are achieved, or there is an improvement in the political climate around the program. In determining which of these definitions is appropriate, the decision hinges on whether the statutory designer's values should be accorded a normative value greater than those of other actors, especially local actors. If the policy designers' desires do have a superior value, then the bottom-uppers' measure of success is inappropriate. This assertion is grounded in democratic theory. Statutory designers derive their power by being elected or by receiving a mandate from duly elected officials. This mandate can be revoked through electoral disapproval by sovereign voters. The street-level bureaucrat has no such base of power. Clearly, discretionary power exists at the local level, but this power is based on the inability to control actions. Street-level bureaucrats do have legitimate claims to power based on their expertise, but this power claim does not have the same moral quality as claims based on powers bestowed by a sovereign citizenry. It is therefore legitimate to measure implementation success in terms of its ability to execute faithfully the goals and means present in the statutory mandate.

This proposal quickly runs into difficulties, however, when specific policies are considered. Statutory mandates often are exceedingly vague. They do not incorporate specific goals and they fail to provide reasonable yardsticks with which to measure policy results. Broader evaluation standards need to be used when significant ambiguity exists regarding the specific goals of a policy. These can range over a broad set of plausible measures. For example, efficiency gains and economic growth may be used in one case, whereas enhanced support of the political system may be valid in another. Increased understanding and alleviation of local problems are two measures of success that frequently are likely to be relevant.

To recapitulate, when policy goals explicitly have been stated, then, based on democratic theory, the statutory designers' values have a superior value. In such instances the correct standard of implementation success is loyalty to the prescribed goals. When a policy does not have explicitly stated goals, the choice of a standard becomes more difficult, and more general societal norms and values come into play.

A Comprehensive Model of Implementation: Theoretical Bases

In reviewing the implementation literature it becomes apparent that top-downers and bottom-uppers choose to study different types of policies. Top-downers tend to choose relatively clear policies. Bottom-uppers study policies with greater uncertainty inherent in the policy. Because so many of the studies are single case studies, few consider how implementation varies when a different type of policy is considered. Building a more effective model of implementation requires a much more careful evaluation of a policy's characteristics. The ambiguity/conflict model presented below is a contingency model that attempts to provide this more comprehensive and coherent basis for understanding implementation.

Four implementation perspectives are developed in the ambiguity/conflict model, based on a policy's ambiguity and conflict level. Organizational theorists and decision-making scholars have invested substantial effort in showing how conflict and ambiguity affect decision making. The ambiguity/conflict model draws extensively on that work. Through analysis of a policy's level of ambiguity and conflict this model provides an analytical tool for identifying which of several differing models in the literature best describes the implementation process. Before considering the four perspectives individually, the attributes by which policies are to be differentiated—ambiguity and conflict—need to be described thoroughly.

Policy Conflict

Conflict plays a central role in distinguishing between decision-making models; it is just as relevant when distinguishing between descriptions of the implementation process. Both rational and bureaucratic politics models of decision making assume that individual actors are rationally self-interested. They differ, however, on the degree of goal congruence that exists. Rational models assume goals are agreed upon and therefore one can maximize individual or social welfare functions, subject to a set of situational constraints. The problem is defined as finding the one best way to attain an agreed-upon goal (Luce and Raiffa 1957; Raiffa 1970; Lave and March 1975). Bureaucratic politics models (Allison 1971; Halperin 1974), on the other hand, posit that a utility function cannot be written, because there is no agreed-upon set of goals. While the rational model defines decision making so that conflict does not exist, the bureaucratic politics model makes conflict its primary emphasis. When conflict exists, actions change and actors resort to bargaining mechanisms such as side payments, log rolling, and oversight to reach agreements and hold coalitions together. Coercive methods of insuring compliance are used. Actions tend to be the results of a long bargaining process. The bargaining process does not lead to an agreement on goals; rather, it focuses entirely on reaching an agreement on actions (means). Often the process culminates in no action, because actors are unable to reach agreement.

For conflict to exist there must be an interdependence of actors, an incompatibility of objectives, and a perceived zero-sum element to the interactions (Dahrendorf 1958). Policy conflict will exist when more than one organization sees a policy as directly relevant to its interests and when the organizations have incongruous views. Such differences can arise regarding either the professed goals of a policy or the programmatic activities that are planned to carry out a policy. Disputes over policy means can develop over jurisdictional issues or over the substance of the proposed means for reaching the goals. For example, pollution reduction may be an agreed-upon goal. Nevertheless, an engineer, an economist, and a lawyer may prefer very different means to carry out the agreed-upon policy. The intensity of conflict increases with an increase in incompatibility of concerns, and with an increase in the perceived stakes for each actor. The more important a decision is, the more aggressive behavior will be.

Many top-down authors have treated conflict as an endogenous variable that policy designers can influence and should minimize. Virtually all have emphasized the importance of delegating policy to a sympathetic agency. Placing a policy in an agency where it conflicts with existing policies and goals leads to few resources, little support, and almost certain failure. Top-downers also recommend scaling back a project to engender less opposition and limit interdependence. The hope is that by decreasing the conflict level the implementation process will move toward the rational decision-making model and away from the bureaucratic politics model. While top-downers have seen conflict as manipulable, bottom-uppers have argued that the policy's conflict level is not manipulable and is given, because of subject matter (Berman 1980).

Certain types of conflict are manipulable. It is possible to make policies more palatable by limiting the changes they bring about, by means such as hold-harmless clauses, or by providing remunerative incentives for essential actors to join. On the other hand, there are clear limits to this. Some policies are inevitably controversial and it is not possible to adjust them to avoid conflict. Often a conflict is based on an incompatibility of values and it is not possible to placate the involved parties by providing resources or other side payments. The level of policy conflict has a number of important effects. Policy conflict directly affects the ease of access to the implementation process. At low levels of conflict access is relatively easy; at high levels of conflict barriers to entry are higher. Intensity also rises with conflict levels. The types of conflict resolution mechanisms also change: analytical methods such as persuasion or problem solving are most common at low levels of conflict and bargaining and coercion are most common at high levels of conflict.

Policy Ambiguity

Policy ambiguity in implementation arises from a number of sources but can be characterized broadly as falling into two categories: ambiguity of goals and ambiguity of means. In top-down models goal clarity is an important independent variable that directly affects policy success. Goal ambiguity is seen as leading to misunderstanding and uncertainty and therefore often is culpable in implementation failure. The position of top-downers is quite explicit—policies should be pushed in the direction of greater goal clarity.

This recommendation fails to consider the dysfunctional effects of clarity and the positive effects of ambiguity. In designing a policy, goal conflict and ambiguity often are negatively correlated. One of the ways to limit conflict is through ambiguity. The clearer goals are, the more likely they are to lead to conflict. In a study of personnel information policy in the United States and the United Kingdom, Regan (1984) argues that considering implementation in the policy formulation phase led to the sacrifice of programmatic goals. As the policy became more explicit, existing actors became aware of threats to their turf and acted to limit the scope and range of proposed policy changes to maintain existing patterns of bureaucratic power and structure. Under other conditions, ambiguity is often a prerequisite for getting new policies passed at the legitimation stage. Many legislative compromises depend on language sufficiently ambiguous that diverse actors can interpret the same act in different ways. This is a natural and inevitable result of the working of political process (Berman 1978; Baier, March, and Saetren 1986).

Ambiguity is not limited to goals; it also affects policy means. Ambiguity of means appears in many ways, perhaps most obviously in cases where the technology needed to reach a policy's goals does not exist. Policy means also are ambiguous when there are uncertainties about what roles various organizations are to play in the implementation process, or when a complex environment makes it difficult to know which tools to use, how to use them, and what the effects of their use will be.

There have been calls to avoid ambiguity in policy means by limiting policy to those areas with an understanding of how actions occur and those areas with known instrumental means to attain desired goals. If actions were thus limited, however, many important but difficult questions would remain unanswered. As Tukey (1962) has noted, "Far better an approximate answer to the *right* question, which is often very vague, than an exact answer to the wrong question, which can always be made precise." Finding an answer often requires a learning and experimenting process. The implementation process not only provides an opportunity to learn new methods, it also provides an opportunity to reach new goals (Offerdal 1984). Offerdal suggests implementation should be a phase where principles and visions as well as technological knowledge are tested.

While several top-down models recommend eliminating ambiguity, it is unclear whether policy ambiguity can be manipulated easily when designing policy. At times, ambiguity more appropriately is seen as a fixed parameter. Even when it is not completely fixed, it is likely to be resistant to substantial movement. This may be due to a fragile political coalition, but it also may be due to poor understanding of a problem. Especially when prescribing means, policy designers rightly may believe they lack the technical knowledge to produce a programmed implementation package.

Leaving aside the normative aspect of whether ambiguous policies should be enacted, it is sufficient to note that such policies *are* enacted. Politicians react to demand for action by producing action. They do not pause to consider the feasibility of policy implementation (Jones 1975). The system routinely produces policies with ambiguous goals and exceedingly ambiguous means (Lowi 1979). It is therefore reasonable to expect that public policy will have a wide range of ambiguity.

The degree of ambiguity inherent in a policy directly affects the implementation process in significant ways. It influences the ability of superiors to monitor activities, the likelihood that the policy is uniformly understood across the many implementation sites, the probability that local contextual factors play a significant role, and the degree to which relevant actors vary sharply across implementation sites.

A Comprehensive Implementation Model: Exposition of the Four Perspectives

In reviewing proposals for remedying implementation failure, O'Toole (1986) found that the literature makes contradictory recommendations. I believe this occurs because the underlying antecedent characteristics of a policy are analyzed insufficiently. The factors that help implement policy under one set of conditions exacerbate already existing problems under another. Previous theoretical work has failed to identify the conditions under which policy recommendations will be effective. The conflict-ambiguity matrix presented in Exhibit 13.1 is an initial step toward sorting out various useful recommendations in the literature.

Each box in Exhibit 13.1 presents the type of implementation process, the central principle determining outcomes for this type of implementation, and an example of a policy that fits this category. The four cells in the conflict-ambiguity matrix are reviewed below. The following aspects are discussed for each perspective: the central principle describing the factor expected to have the greatest influence on the implementation outcome; a description of the implementation process with special emphasis on the implications of policy ambiguity and conflict; a discussion of the expected pitfalls; and the appropriateness of top-down or bottom-up approaches as a description of the process.

Administrative Implementation: Low Policy Ambiguity and Low Policy Conflict

In decision-making theory, choice opportunities where ambiguity and conflict are low provide the prerequisite

Exhibit 13.1 Ambiguity-Conflict Matrix: Policy Implementation Processes

| | | CONFLICT | |
		Low	**High**
AMBIGUITY	**Low**	*Administrative Implementation* Resources Example: Smallpox eradication	*Political Implementation* Power Example: Busing
	High	*Experimental Implementation* Contextual Conditions Example: Headstart	*Symbolic Implementation* Coalition Strength Example: Community action agencies

conditions for a rational decision-making process. Goals are given and a technology (means) for solving the existing problem is known. Simon (1960) called decisions of this type "programmed decisions." The central principle in administrative implementation is *outcomes are determined by resources.* The desired outcome is virtually assured, given that *sufficient resources* are appropriated for the program.

The implementation process can be compared to a machine. At the top of the machine is a central authority. This authority has information, resources, and sanction capabilities to help enact the desired policy. Information flows from the top down. Implementation is ordered in a hierarchical manner with each underlying link receiving orders from the level above. The policy is spelled out explicitly at each level, and at each link in the chain actors have a clear idea of their responsibilities and tasks. The paradigm invoked is Weberian bureaucrats loyally carrying out their appointed duties.

Low levels of ambiguity mean it is clear which actors are to be active in implementation. As the actors are stable over time, they develop standard operating procedures to expedite their work. The transparency of the technology makes clear which resources are required, and resource procurement is built into the implementation process. The system therefore is relatively closed to outside influence. The isolation from environmental factors, along with the programmed nature of policy, results in relatively uniform outcomes at the microlevel across many settings.

Etzioni (1961) describes three types of mechanisms for gaining compliance from an actor: normative, coercive, and remunerative. A normative mechanism induces compliance through reference to a mutually held goal or to the legitimacy of the person requesting action (for example, a superior in a hierarchy). A coercive mechanism threatens sanctions for failing to comply with a request for action. A remunerative mechanism includes sufficient incentives, often additional resources, to make the desired course of action attractive to the agent. For administrative implementation, where levels of conflict are low, normative compliance mechanisms are generally sufficient. The orders given are perceived as legitimate, and there is little controversy that might lead to subversion.

Remunerative mechanisms may be used, especially for pulling in outside resources, but most actions are induced through normative mechanisms. In those few cases where coercive mechanisms are needed, they can be expected to be effective since means are clear and easily monitored.

Since a technology for dealing with the problem exists, implementation activities are concerned primarily with getting the technology in place and functioning. They often consist of a set of rules that structures discretion so as to insure the preferred outcomes. Implementation failure occurs because of technical problems: the machine sputters. Problems occur because of misunderstanding, poor coordination, insufficient resources, insufficient time to use the correct technology, or lack of an effective monitoring strategy to control and sanction deviant behavior.

As messages pass through a communication network, they tend to get distorted. Even when the message appears clear to the sender, it may fail to be comprehended fully due to cognitive limitations of the receiver. In addition, cognitive dissonance may lead to selective perception. Pressman and Wildavsky (1973) calculate the probability of successful implementation as less than 50 percent if an order is followed with 90 percent accuracy after going through six hierarchical levels. If orders are comprehended with less than 90 percent accuracy, the probability of success will fall even faster.

This description of the implementation process closely parallels those found in traditional top-down approaches. Top-down models are descended from old public administration models, and the Wilsonian tradition, which defined administration as separate from politics, is effective in these cases. When a policy is characterized by a high degree of consensus and the means for reaching the policy goal are known, the implementation process becomes dominated by technocratic questions of compliance and follow-up. An example of such a policy is the World Health Organization's (WHO) program to eliminate smallpox. The means—mass vaccination and quarantine—and goals—eradication of smallpox—were clear. As the program developed, standard operating procedures were established to decrease discretion and increase efficiency. Success was determined largely by the level of resources available and the efficiency of the program developed

to implement the policy. The differences between WHO's program to eradicate smallpox and the U.S. program to contain tuberculosis show strikingly the crucial role that resources play for administrative policies. In the case of smallpox, there were sufficient resources to continue active implementation until the disease was eliminated completely. In the case of tuberculosis, existing policy led to a decreasing number of cases and appeared to have effective control over tuberculosis into the early 1980s. At that time federal funding was cut off. The consequence of that action has been both a resurgence of tuberculosis in the 1990s and the appearance of a drug-resistant strain of tuberculosis.

Kelman (1984) describes how he developed an implementation plan for the Emergency Energy Assistance program. This program was to take effect in case of a new energy crisis. The policy theory was to allow market prices on energy, tax the windfall profits of energy companies, and recycle the money back to citizens via an emergency energy rebate. The rebate portion of the program was both clear and nonconflictual, and therefore it fit the administrative implementation paradigm. Nevertheless, difficulties existed with implementation. This program required substantial new capacity; virtually all adult citizens in the United States would need to be identified and to have checks mailed to them, all in a short time. There were many obstacles: finding an agency with the expertise and capacity to process tremendous numbers of cases quickly (i.e., a problem of sufficient resources); combining several different lists to develop one complete list of eligible recipients (coordination problems); and providing citizens access throughout the country to file complaints in case of oversight (resource problems). Kelman, using the implementation literature as a guide, revised the initial plans, which called for state agencies to provide lists of recipients. Noting the great difficulties involved in getting 150 different agencies to provide data on short notice, he devised a plan that gave full responsibility to the Internal Revenue Service (IRS) and based the identification of recipients on IRS records. Placing the primary responsibility for the program with the IRS helped to minimize possible coordination problems and enabled policy designers to take advantage of IRS's capacity to train large numbers of employees quickly. IRS also had the necessary expertise to quickly process applications and to deal with consumer complaints. According to Kelman, IRS support was relatively easy to enlist because of its loyalty to the congressional mandate, a promise of resources, and an opportunity for the IRS to improve its image by giving people money rather than taking money away from them. Kelman's discussion is instructive: it indicates that the problems that arise under conditions of low ambiguity and low conflict are primarily technical, and it shows that, even for policies with low levels of conflict and ambiguity, an implementation plan can require substantial effort.

Political Implementation: Low Policy Ambiguity and High Policy Conflict

Low ambiguity and high conflict are typical of political models of decision making (Allison 1971; Halperin 1974; Elmore 1978). Actors have clearly defined goals, but dissension occurs because these clearly defined goals are incompatible. Equally conflictual battles can occur over means. It is often precisely in the designing of the implementation policy that conflicts develop and vigorous battles erupt. The central principle in political implementation is that *implementation outcomes are decided by power.* In some cases one actor or a coalition of actors have sufficient power to force their will on other participants. In other cases actors resort to bargaining to reach an agreement.

For policies of this type, compliance is not automatically forthcoming. While there is an explicit policy, essential resources are controlled by skeptical actors outside the implementing organization or by actors actively opposed to the proposed policy. Often both conditions exist. Such a system is more open to influences from the environment than from administrative implementation. The implementation program consists of securing the compliance of actors whose resources are vital to policy success and ensuring that the process is not thwarted by opponents of the policy. Since some of the actors whose cooperation is required may disagree with the policy goals, successful implementation depends on either having sufficient power to force one's will on the other participants or having sufficient resources to be able to bargain an agreement on means. Coercive and remunerative mechanisms will predominate.

Coercive mechanisms are most effective when the desired outcomes are easily monitored and the coercing principal controls a resource essential to the agent. This point is made convincingly by Durant (1984) in his study of two controversies involving the Tennessee Valley Authority (TVA) and the Environmental Protection Agency (EPA). He found that where the sanctions available to the EPA threatened the central mission of the TVA, compliance was quickly forthcoming. In the case where the controversy did not threaten the central mission of the TVA and the sanctions seemed less onerous, several years were spent arguing and litigating before the TVA finally complied.

The greater the implementer's authority to require agent action, the more likely it is that agents will comply with the principal's requests. Agents, however, often are not in a direct line relationship with the implementer, and coercive mechanisms fail to bring about compliance. Many actors have independent bases of power and can refuse to participate without having their own missions threatened. Even where there are relatively strong sanction opportunities (such as federal grants to states and local entities) states and municipalities exhibit a surprising degree of independence (Ingram 1977). Under these conditions, activities are directed toward reaching a negotiated agreement on actions. Agreement on goals is unnecessary, agreement on actions is sufficient. Many bargaining techniques commonly found in the legislative forum reappear. Disputes are resolved through side payments, logrolling, oversight, or ambiguity. Questions that cannot be resolved can be buried in ambiguous text and left for later resolution.

The opposing sides of a policy question previously may have done battle at the policy adoption stage. The shift of forum, however, can result in a change in the balance of power. A legislative coalition often consists of actors whose support is fleeting. Supporters agree to vote for a policy on the basis of logrolling, in response to political pressure, or simply because it appears to be a sensible policy. Many of these supporters have little interest in the implementation stage. Even among those with an active interest the rewards from oversight are limited and likely to lead to only sporadic activities (Mayhew 1974; Ogul 1976). This venue shift can result in the nonimplementation of policy. This view is borne out by the regulation literature, which finds industries more successful at influencing the implementation phase than the legislative phase of policy (Stigler 1971; Joskow and Noll 1985).

The description of the policy process proposed by the newer top-down models comes closest to capturing the essence of the implementation process under these conditions. The traditional public administration models and the earliest top-down models took an administrative view of what is essentially a political problem; they failed to identify the sources of implementation barriers. The more sophisticated top-down models, which were developed partially in response to the failings of standard public administration teachings, emphasize political factors. Among the political factors built into Mazmanian and Sabatier's model (1989) are general public support, support from upper-level political leaders, resources and support from relevant constituency groups, and the commitment of implementing officials.

The bottom-up argument, that policies are decided at the microlevel, fails because it does not take account of the considerable forces and power that can be brought to bear upon an issue when it is unambiguously and explicitly formulated. School integration through busing is an example of a highly contentious yet unambiguous issue implemented by central authorities, with local officials looking on with little power to halt actions. While local authorities may disagree, sometimes vehemently, with the means that are used, the central authorities (i.e., the courts) have sufficient power to force their plan on the other participants. Low ambiguity insures that monitoring of compliance is relatively easy; attempts at subversion are likely to be caught and swiftly punished.

Experimental Implementation: High Policy Ambiguity and Low Policy Conflict

If a policy exhibits a high level of ambiguity and low level of conflict, outcomes will depend largely on which actors are active and most involved. The central principle driving this type of implementation is that *contextual conditions dominate the process.* Outcomes depend heavily on the resources and actors present in the microimplementing environment. These

are likely to vary strongly from site to site; therefore broad variations in outcomes will occur. In decision-making terms, this type of implementation condition closely parallels a "garbage can" process with streams of actors, problems, solutions, and choice opportunities combining to produce outcomes that are hard to predict. The conditions that are required for a choice opportunity to develop into a garbage can are problematic preferences (ambiguous goals); uncertain technology (no predefined correct behavior); and fluid participation (actors vary over time) (Cohen, March, and Olsen 1972; March and Olsen 1976 and 1986). By definition, experimental implementation defines cases where preferences are problematic and technology is uncertain. The crucial element is: Which participants are active and what is their intensity of participation? Participants' level of activity in a choice situation depends on the intensity of their feelings, the number of other demands on their time, their physical proximity to the place where decisions are made, and a host of other variables.

As a result of policy ambiguity, the implemented program differs from site to site. The constellation of actors participating, the pressures on the actors, the perceptions of what the policy is, the available resources, and possible programmatic activities vary widely across policy settings. The lack of conflict is likely to open the arena for a large number of actors to participate and to provide those who have intense interests, or substantial slack resources, with an opportunity to mold policy significantly. The opportunities are excellent for bureaucratic entrepreneurs to create policies to deal with local needs.

This process is more open to environmental influences than are other forms of implementation. Program mutations arise as different organizations implement different policies in different environments. These mutations can be seen as natural experiments, and it is important for policy designers to actively use them to enhance their knowledge of change processes within the policy area, with a strong emphasis on formative evaluations (Mohr 1988). For policies that have clear goals, it is possible to carry out and use summative evaluations that explicitly state whether the policy has reached its appointed goal. For policies with unclear goals, it is far more useful to use formative evaluations that describe the process and describe the way outcomes are arrived at without an explicit stamp of approval or disapproval.

Policies where both goals and means are unclear naturally fall into the category of experimental implementation. In addition, policies with clear and widely supported goals but with unclear means of implementation take on experimental characteristics. For many policies the goals are agreed upon and known, yet the means of reaching these goals is unknown. Implementing policies of this type can be technology-forcing and can lead to the development of entirely new capabilities. Nakamura and Smallwood (1980) point to the Clean Air Act of 1970 as a prime example of a case where the technology did not exist before the policy was passed; it developed quickly in response to the Act. Biomedical research is another example where technology doesn't exist but policy is widely supported. On the other hand, ambiguous policies can breed limited accountability and can lead to the creation of minifiefdoms with leaders pursuing their own interests. These may have little, if any, connection to the public interest.

The emphasis on seeing each iteration of a policy as an experiment is important when one evaluates possible pitfalls to the implementation process. More important than a *successful* outcome is one that produces learning. Policies operate in areas where there is insufficient knowledge to institute programmed implementation or of how elements in the policy environment are causally connected. Ambiguity should be seen as an opportunity to learn both new means and new goals. Two pitfalls must be avoided. First, the process should not be forced into an artificially constrained form. Programs demanding conformity are likely to meet with superficial compliance efforts from local implementers. In addition, demanding uniformity when processes are poorly understood robs us of vital information and limits the street-level bureaucrats' use of their knowledge as a resource. Since uniformity is to be discouraged, development of effective compliance monitoring mechanisms is of limited relevance. Second, the process requires a conscious realization that learning is the goal. If there are fifty sites with fifty

differing results, but the information is neither gathered nor compared, then learning is likely to occur in a random pattern. Evaluation and feedback are vital components of effective learning.

The bottom-up description of the policy implementation process is superior to the top-down in describing conditions in this category. The emphasis on the opportunities available to local-level actors appears most appropriate. Tolerance for ambiguity is much greater in bottom-up than in top-down models. The top-down models emphasize command, control, and uniformity and fail to take into account the diversity inherent in much implementation that occurs.

Headstart is an excellent example of experimental implementation. It officially was approved in March 1965 and was to begin in the summer of 1965. The Office of Economic Opportunity (OEO) had barely three months to prepare, far too short a time to develop any type of comprehensive plan. The central administration had only the most general notion of what the goals of a preschool program for disadvantaged children should be. At the same time, Sargent Shriver III, the director of the OEO, had a serious problem in that he was unable to spend all of his budget. These factors combined to produce a situation in which virtually all proposals for summer school programs were approved. There was a cornucopia of proposals, and Headstart meant many different things for its first several iterations. Over time, as information was gathered, the program became more structured, but at the start few attempts were made to steer it from the top. The meaning of Headstart in those early stages was dependent almost exclusively on which actors were involved at the microlevel and what resources they had at their disposal.

Symbolic Implementation: High Policy Ambiguity and High Policy Conflict

It may seem implausible that a policy can have high levels of ambiguity and yet be conflictual. As was noted earlier, many scholars suggest making a policy more ambiguous to diminish conflict. Nevertheless, policies do exist that appropriately are characterized as having both high levels of ambiguity and high levels of conflict. Policies that invoke highly salient symbols often produce high levels of conflict even when the policy is vague. Symbolic policies play an important role in confirming new goals, in reaffirming a commitment to old goals, or in emphasizing important values and principles (Olsen 1970). The high level of conflict is important, because it structures the way resolutions are developed. The high level of ambiguity results in outcomes that vary across sites. The central principle is that local level *coalitional strength* determines the outcome. The policy course is determined by the coalition of actors at the local level who control the available resources.

For policy with only a referential goal, differing perspectives will develop as to how to translate the abstract goal into instrumental actions. The inherent ambiguity leads to a proliferation of interpretations. Competition ensues over the correct "vision." Actors see their interests tied to a specific policy definition, and therefore similar competing coalitions are likely to form at differing sites. The strength of these actors will vary across the possible sites. Contextual conditions at the local level affect outcomes through their effect on coalition strength. Variations in coalition strength and dominant coalition make-up manifest themselves in differing programs in different localities. Outcomes are bounded and less differentiated than for cases of experimental implementation, because opposition coalitions are able to put effective limits on policy even when they cannot determine its content. Nevertheless, substantial variation is expected, with coalition strength at the local level being of central importance in determining the policy outcome.

Professions are likely to play an especially important role for symbolic policies. Professional training provides a strong set of norms as to legitimate activities and effective problem-solving actions. When faced with a vague referential goal and an ambiguous program of action, actors with professional training are likely to step in quickly with proposals grounded in their professions. Professions with competing claims over an area and different standard programs for attacking problems often form the core of competing coalitions. For example, a youth employment program may have an official goal of improving opportunities for disadvantaged youths. This policy has a referential goal that may include any of the following subgoals: decreased crime, increased educational opportunities, increased income, and provision of on-the-job training. Among actors with different training, there are substantially different proposals for implementing this policy. Their implementation battles are likely to be long and bitter.

Policies aimed at redistributing power or goods are perhaps the most obvious examples of programs that fall under this category. Policy goals often provide little information to a policy designer about how to proceed, yet the symbols are sufficient to create significant opposition before any plans are promulgated. The Community Action Agencies (CAA) established as part of the War on Poverty are a prime example of a symbolic policy. The stated goal of the CAA was to facilitate local citizenry empowerment. What this meant was unclear to virtually all participants. Despite great ambiguity, the CAA generated considerable controversy and animosity, often precisely because the policy was ambiguous and there was a fear of what the policy implied for existing relationships.

Symbolic implementation policies are conflictual, therefore they exhibit similarities to political implementation. Actors are intensely involved, and disagreements are resolved through coercion or bargaining; problem solving or persuasion are used to a limited degree only. Any actor's influence is tied to the strength of the coalition of which she is part. Symbolic implementation *differs* from political implementation in that coalitional strength at the microlevel, not at the macrolevel, determines the implementation outcome. This difference occurs because of a high ambiguity level. When a policy has a referent goal and ambiguous means it is solidly in the symbolic quadrant. As the ambiguity level decreases the policy moves upward, toward the political implementation quadrant. A decrease in ambiguity, either through explicit goals or a crystallization of discussion around a limited number of possible means, would provide central level actors an increased opportunity to assert some control and influence. When the policy is very clear, the macrolevel actors are able to exert considerable control, and this becomes a case of political implementation.

When dealing with cases of symbolic implementation, identifying the competing factions at the local level, along with the microlevel contextual factors that affect the strengths of the competing factions, is central to accurate explanations of policy outcomes. Neither the top-down nor bottom-up models appear entirely appropriate in describing the implementation process when there is substantial conflict and an ambiguous policy. The macroimplementers who are so prominent in the top-down models see their powers diminish. Policy ambiguity makes it difficult for the macroimplementers to monitor activities, and it is much more difficult to structure actions at the local level. Nevertheless, centrally located actors do constitute an important influence through provision of resources and incentives and through focusing attention on an issue area. Because of the higher level of conflict, the process is likely to be highly political, but it will be dominated by local actors. The bottom-uppers are correct in that the local actors are paramount, but their models do not emphasize the strongly political nature of the interactions.

Conclusion

I noted at the outset that the implementation literature suffers from a lack of theoretical structure. By drawing on the organizational theory literature, considering how ambiguity and conflict affect policy implementation, and combining these factors into the ambiguity/conflict model, this article provides a more theoretically grounded approach to implementation. By studying a policy's level of conflict and ambiguity, testable predictions can be made as to how the implementation process will unfold.

Traditional top-down models, based on the public administration tradition, present an accurate description of the implementation process when policy is clear and conflict is low. The recommendations found in this literature provide a useful set of heuristics in promulgating an implementation plan. Because there is a clear policy, macroimplementation planners wield considerable influence. Bottom-up models provide an accurate description of the implementation process when policy is ambiguous and conflict is low. The expectation is that conditions at the microimplementation level dominate and should be encouraged to vary. Under conditions identified as political implementation, where conflict is high and ambiguity is low, the newer top-down models—which emphasize the importance of structuring access and providing resources with a conscious concern for the heavily politicized atmosphere that attends such policies—provide an important starting point. When there is substantial conflict and an ambiguous policy, both models have some relevancy. Microlevel actors dominate the process, but actions are highly political as emphasized by top-down models.

One implicit concern underlying this model is that ambiguity should not be seen as a flaw in a policy. Despite its being blamed often for implementation failure, ambiguity can be useful. Ambiguity can ease agreement both at the legitimation and the formulation stage. It provides an opportunity to learn new methods, technologies, and goals. Widespread variation provides an abundance of knowledge which should be actively nurtured. Ambiguity should be viewed neither as an evil nor as a good. It should be seen as a characteristic of a policy, without imbuing it with any normative value.

Finally, while I have argued that under certain conditions it is most appropriate to hold either a top-down or a bottom-up perspective, it is important to recognize that both schools contain kernels of truth relevant in any implementation situation. For example, central authorities inevitably influence policy implementation through decisions on funding and jurisdiction, even when policies are vague and conflict is low. It is also clear that policies are almost never self-executing. A microimplementation process occurs, even for purely technical questions with all the characteristics of administrative implementation. This model provides a description for the policy designer pondering where the most important problems are likely to lie. For the researcher it provides a map to those elements expected to most greatly influence policy outcomes.

References

Allison, Graham. 1971. *Essence of Decision: Explaining the Cuban Missile Crisis.* Boston: Little, Brown.

Baier, Vicki, J. G. March, and H. Saetren. 1986. "Implementation and Ambiguity." *Scandinavian Journal of Management Studies* 2:197–212.

Berman, Paul. 1978. "The Study of Macro- and Micro-Implementation." *Public Policy* 26:2:157–84.

———. 1980. "Thinking about Programmed and Adaptive Implementation: Matching Strategies to Situations." In H. Ingram and D. Mann, eds. *Why Policies Succeed or Fail.* Beverly Hills, Calif.: Sage.

Cohen, Michael D., James March, and Johan P. Olsen. 1972. "A Garbage Can Model of Organizational Choice." *Administrative Science Quarterly* 17:1–25.

Dahrendorf, Ralf. 1958. "Towards a Theory of Social Conflict." *Journal of Conflict Resolution* 2(2): 170–83.

Dunshire, Andrew. 1978. *Implementation in a Bureaucracy.* Oxford: Martin Robertson.

Durant, Robert F. 1984. "EPA, TVA and Pollution Control: Implications for a Theory of Regulatory Policy Implementation." *Public Administration Review* 44(3): 305–15.

Edelman, Murray S. 1964. *The Symbolic Use of Politics.* Champaign: University of Illinois Press.

———. 1977. *Political Language: Words That Succeed and Policies That Fail.* New York: Academic Press.

Elmore, Richard F. 1978. "Organizational Models of Social Program Implementation." *Public Policy* 26(2): 185–226.

———. 1982. "Backward Mapping: Implementation Research and Policy Decisions." In Walter L. Williams, ed. *Studying Implementation: Methodological and Administrative Issues.* Chatham, N.J.: Chatham Publishing.

———. 1985. "Forward and Backward Mapping." In K. Hanf and T. Toonen, eds. *Policy Implementation in Federal and Unitary Systems.* Derdrecht: Martinus Nijhoff.

Etzioni, Amitai. 1961. *Complex Organizations: A Sociological Reader.* New York: Holt, Rinehart and Winston.

Feldman, Martha S., and James G. March. 1981. "Information in Organizations as Signal and Symbols." *Administrative Science Quarterly* 26: 171–86.

Goggin, Malcolm L., Ann Bowman, Lester, James P. Lester, and Laurence J. O'Toole, Jr. 1990. *Implementation Theory and Practice: Toward a Third Generation.* Glenview, Ill.: Scott, Foresman/Little, Brown.

Gormley, William T., Jr. 1986. "Regulatory Issue Networks in a Federal System." *Polity* 17(2): 595–620.

Halperin, Morten H. 1974. *Bureaucratic Politics and Foreign Policy.* Washington, D.C.: Brookings.

Hjern, Benny. 1982. Implementation Research—The Link Gone Missing." *Journal of Public Policy* 2(3): 301–08.

Hjern, Benny, and Chris Hull. 1982. "Implementation Research as Empirical Constitutionalism." *European Journal of Political Research* 10(2): 105–16.

———. 1985. "Small Firm Employment Creation: An Assistance Structure Explanation." In K. Hanf and T. Toonen, eds. *Policy Implementation in Federal and Unitary Systems.* Dordrecht: Martinus Nijhoff.

Hjern, Benny, and David Porter. 1981. "Implementation Structures: A New Unit of Administrative Analysis." *Organization Studies* 2: 211–27.

Hoppe, Robert, Henk van de Graaf, and Asje van Dijk. 1985. "Implementation as Design Problem: Problem Tractability, Policy Theory, and Feasibility Testing." Paper presented at meeting of the International Political Science Association, Paris, July.

Hull, Chris, and Benny Hjern. 1987. *Helping Small Firms Grow: An Implementation Approach.* London: Croom Helm.

Ingram, Helen. 1977. "Policy Implementation through Bargaining: Federal Grants in Aid." *Public Policy* 25(4): 499–526.

Ingram, Helen, and Anne Schneider. 1990. "Improving Implementation Through Framing Smarter Statutes." *Journal of Public Policy* 10(1): 67–88.

Jones, Charles. 1975. *Clean Air: The Politics and Unpolitics of Air Pollution Control.* Pittsburgh: University of Pittsburgh Press.

Joskow, Paul L., and Roger C. Noll. 1985. "Regulation in Theory and Practice: An Overview." In G. Fromm, ed. *Studies in Public Regulation.* Cambridge, Mass.: MIT Press.

Kelman, Steven. 1984. "Using Implementation Research to Solve Implementation Problems: The Case of Energy Emergency Assistance." *Journal of Policy Analysis and Management* 4(1): 75–91.

Lave, Charles A., and James G. March. 1975. *An Introduction to Models in the Social Sciences.* New York: Harper & Row.

Linder, Stephen H., and B. Guy Peters. 1987. "A Design Perspective on Policy Implementation: The Fallacies of Misplaced Prescription." *Policy Studies Review* 6(3): 459–75.

Lipsky, Michael. 1978. "Standing the Study of Policy Implementation on Its Head." In Walter D. Burnham and Martha Weinberg, eds., *American Politics and Public Policy.* Cambridge, Mass.: MIT Press.

Lowi, Theodore J., 1979. *The End of Liberalism.* New York: Norton.

Luce, Duncan R., and Howard Raiffa. 1957. *Games and Decisions.* New York: Wiley.

McLaughlin, Milbrey Wallin. 1987. "Learning From Experience: Lessons From Policy Implementation." *Educational Evaluation and Policy Analysis* 9(2): 171–78.

March, James G., and Johan P. Olsen. 1976. *Ambiguity and Choice in Organizations.* Oslo: Universitetsforlaget.

———.1986. "Garbage Can Models of Decision Making in Organizations." In James G. March and Roger Weissinger-Baylon, eds., *Ambiguity and Command: Organizational Perspectives on Military Decision Making.* Cambridge, Mass.: Ballinger.

March, James G., and Herbert A. Simon. 1958. *Organizations.* New York: Wiley.

Mayhew, David R. 1974. *Congress: The Electoral Connection.* New Haven, Conn.: Yale University Press.

Maynard-Moody, Steven; Michael Musheno, and Dennis Palumbo. 1990. "Street-wise Social Policy: Resolving the Dilemma of Street-Level Influence and Successful Implementation." *Western Political Quarterly* 43(4): 833–48.

Mazmanian, Daniel, and Paul A. Sabatier. 1983. *Implementation and Public Policy.* Glenview, Ill.: Scott, Foresman.

———. 1989. *Implementation and Public Policy.* rev. ed. Latham, Md.: University Press of America.

Mazmanian, Daniel, and Sabatier, Paul A., eds. 1981. *Effective Policy Implementation.* Lexington, Mass.: Lexington Books.

Merton, Robert K. 1957. *Social Theory and Social Structure,* 2nd ed. Glencoe, Ill.: Free Press.

Michels, Robert. 1949. *Political Parties.* Glencoe, Ill.: Free Press.

Mohr, Lawrence B. 1988. *Impact Analysis for Program Evaluation.* Chicago: Dorsey.

Nakamura, Robert T., and Frank Smallwood. 1980. *The Politics of Policy Implementation.* New York: St. Martin's.

Offerdal, Audun. 1984. "Implementation and Politics, or: Whether It Is a Success or a Failure." (in Norwegian) *Statsviteren,* Nr. 2–3.

Ogul, Morris S. 1976. *Congress Oversees The Executive.* Pittsburgh: University of Pittsburgh Press.

Olsen, Johan P. 1970. "Local Budgeting—Decision-Making or Ritual Act?" *Scandinavian Political Studies* 5: 85–118.

O'Toole, Laurence, Jr. 1986. "Policy Recommendations for Multi-Actor Implementation: An Assessment of the Field." *Journal of Public Policy* 6(2): 181–210.

———. 1989. "Goal Multiplicity in the Implementation Setting: Subtle Impacts and The Case of Waste-water Treatment Privatization." *Policy Studies Journal* 18(1): 1–20.

Palumbo, Dennis J., Steven Maynard-Moody, and Paula Wright. 1984. "Measuring Degrees of Successful Implementation." *Evaluation Review* 8(1): 45–74.

Pressman, Jeffrey, and Aaron Wildavsky. 1973. *Implementation.* Berkeley: University of California Press.

Raiffa, Howard. 1970. *Decision Analysis.* Reading, Mass.: Addison-Wesley.

Regan, Priscilla M. 1984. "Personal Information Policies in the United States and Britain: The Dilemma of Implementation Considerations." *Journal of Public Policy* 4(1): 19–38.

Sabatier, Paul A. 1986. "Top-Down and Bottom-Up Approaches to Implementation Research: A Critical Analysis and Suggested Synthesis." *Journal of Public Policy* 6(1): 21–48.

———. 1988. "An Advocacy Coalition Framework of Policy Change and the Role of Policy-Oriented Learning Therein." *Policy Sciences* 21(3): 129–68.

———. 1991. "Towards Better Theories of the Policy Process." *PS: Political Science and Politics* 24(2): 147–56.

Sabatier, Paul A., and Neil Pelkey. 1987. "Incorporating Multiple Actors and Guidance Instruments into Models of Regulatory Policymaking: An Advocacy Coalition Framework." *Administration and Society* 19(2): 236–63.

Saetren, Harald. 1983. *The Implementation of Public Policy.* (in Norwegian) Oslo: Universitetsforlaget.

Sellite, Claire, Lawrence S. Wrightsman, and Stuart W. Cook. 1990. *Research Methods in Social Relations,* 3rd ed. New York: Holt, Rinehart and Winston.

Selznick, Philip. 1949. *TVA and the Grassroots.* Berkeley: University of California Press.

Simon, Herbert A. 1960. *The New Science of Management Decision.* New York: Harper.

Stigler, George. 1971. "The Economics of Regulation." *Bell Journal of Regulation* 2: 3–21.

Tukey, John. 1962. "The Future of Data Analysis." *Annals of Mathematical Statistics* 33(1): 13–14.

Van Horn, Carl E. 1987. "Applied Implementation Research." Paper presented at Midwest Political Science Association Meeting, Chicago.

Van Meter, Donald S., and Carl E. Van Horn. 1975. "The Policy Implementation Process: A Conceptual Framework." *Administration and Society* 6(4): 445–88.

Weatherley, Richard, and Michael Lipsky. 1977. "Street-Level Bureaucrats and Institutional Innovation: Implementing Special Education Reform." *Harvard Educational Review* 47: 170–96.

Winter, Soeren. 1985. "Implementation Barriers." (in Danish) *Politica* 17(4): 467–87.

———. 1986. "How Policy-Making Affects Implementation: The Decentralization of the Danish Disablement Pension Administration." *Scandinavian Political Studies* 9(4): 361–85.

⌐▭ CASE STUDY 13

Introduction

As the foregoing essay by Richard E. Matland indicates, serious scholars are spilling a lot of ink over the problems of public sector implementation. Theories about bureaucratic implementation, as a consequence, now abound in books and journals. But from the standpoint of the practicing public administrator on the firing line, how does a new program develop, find support, and ultimately become implemented? How are governmental objectives achieved in practice? What are successful methods used for implementation and what are the real-life problems administrators encounter in the implementation process? Does the theory of successful implementation "square" with its actual practice from the standpoint of the flesh-and-blood public administrator?

The following case, "They Had A Plan," by *Time* magazine correspondent Michael Elliott recounts how a strategic plan was forged by the White House to fight al-Qaeda terrorism prior to 9/11 but never implemented. Here is a fascinating tale of a lost opportunity to prevent the attack that killed 3000 Americans. The proposal was originally conceived several years prior to 9/11 and was extensively debated within the intelligence community and White House, but by the time it was approved for action, it was too late. The following case lays out the elements of planning, the key players, the obstacles they faced, and the chief sources of delay. This gripping, behind-the-scenes sage of a failed attempt at preemptive strike against al-Qaeda demonstrates particularly well how complicated undertaking government action becomes when so many players are involved, the threat is unknown, and a presidential transition occurs.

As you read the following case study, reflect on several issues influencing the failure of the plan's implementation:

Who were the key players in developing the proposal, and why was it so difficult for them to reach closure on the idea?

What chief rationale(s) did they put forward to support their plan? Do you think these were the most effective arguments to advance their idea?

What approval processes did the supporters go through to "clear" their concept? Why were these so critical yet time-consuming?

How did a presidential transition further complicate implementation? Were there other significant roadblocks that caused delays?

Do you think the foregoing reading by Richard Matland adequately addresses the problems posed by such complicated roadblocks as represented by this case?

They Had a Plan

MICHAEL ELLIOTT

Sometimes history is made by the force of arms on battlefields, sometimes by the fall of an exhausted empire. But often when historians set about figuring why a nation took one course rather than another, they are most interested in who said what to whom at a meeting far from the public eye whose true significance may have been missed even by those who took part in it.

One such meeting took place in the White House situation room during the first week of January 2001. The session was part of a program designed by Bill Clinton's National Security Advisor, Sandy Berger, who wanted the transition between the Clinton and George W. Bush administrations to run as smoothly as possible. With some bitterness, Berger remembered how little he and his colleagues had been helped by the first Bush Administration in 1992–93. Eager to avoid a repeat of that experience, he had set up a series of 10 briefings by his team for his successor, Condoleezza Rice, and her deputy, Stephen Hadley.

Berger attended only one of the briefings—the session that dealt with the threat posed to the U.S. by international terrorism, and especially by al-Qaeda. "I'm coming to this briefing," he says he told Rice, "to underscore how important I think this subject is." Later, alone in his office with Rice, Berger says he told her, "I believe that the Bush Administration will spend more time on terrorism generally, and on al-Qaeda specifically, than any other subject."

The terrorism briefing was delivered by Richard Clarke, a career bureaucrat who had served in the first Bush Administration and risen during the Clinton years to become the White House's point man on terrorism. As chair of the interagency Counter-Terrorism Security Group (CSG), Clarke was known as a bit of an obsessive—just the sort of person you want in a job of that kind. Since the bombing of the U.S.S. *Cole* in Yemen on Oct. 12, 2000—an attack that left 17 Americans dead—he had been working on an aggressive plan to take the fight to al-Qaeda. The result was a strategy paper that he had

From Michael Elliott, "They Had a Plan." *Time Magazine* (August 12, 2002), pp. 28–43. © 2002 Time Inc. Reprinted with permission.

presented to Berger and the other national security "principals" on Dec. 20. But Berger and the principals decided to shelve the plan and let the next Administration take it up. With less than a month left in office, they did not think it appropriate to launch a major initiative against Osama bin Laden. "We would be handing [the Bush Administration] a war when they took office on Jan. 20," says a former senior Clinton aide. "That wasn't going to happen." Now it was up to Rice's team to consider what Clarke had put together.

Berger had left the room by the time Clarke, using a Powerpoint presentation, outlined his thinking to Rice. A senior Bush Administration official denies being handed a formal plan to take the offensive against al-Qaeda, and says Clarke's materials merely dealt with whether the new Administration should take "a more active approach" to the terrorist group. (Rice declined to comment, but through a spokeswoman said she recalled no briefing at which Berger was present.) Other senior officials from both the Clinton and Bush administrations, however, say that Clarke had a set of proposals to "roll back" al-Qaeda. In fact, the heading on Slide 14 of the Powerpoint presentation reads, "Response to al-Qaeda: Roll back." Clarke's proposals called for the "breakup" of al-Qaeda cells and the arrest of their personnel. The financial support for its terrorist activities would be systematically attacked, its assets frozen, its funding from fake charities stopped. Nations where al-Qaeda was causing trouble—Uzbekistan, the Philippines, Yemen—would be given aid to fight the terrorists. Most important, Clarke wanted to see a dramatic increase in covert action in Afghanistan to "eliminate the sanctuary" where al-Qaeda had its terrorist training camps and bin Laden was being protected by the radical Islamic Taliban regime. The Taliban had come to power in 1996, bringing a sort of order to a nation that had been riven by bloody feuds between ethnic warlords since the Soviets had pulled out. Clarke supported a substantial increase in American support for the Northern Alliance, the last remaining resistance to the Taliban. That way, terrorists graduating from the training camps would have been forced to stay in Afghanistan, fighting (and dying) for the Taliban on the front lines. At the same time, the U.S. military would start planning for air strikes on the camps and for the introduction of special-operations forces into Afghanistan. The plan was estimated to cost "several hundreds of millions of dollars." In the words of a senior Bush Administration official, the proposals amounted to "everything we've done since 9/11."

And that's the point. The proposals Clarke developed in the winter of 2000–01 were not given another hearing by top decision makers until late April, and then spent another four months making their laborious way through the bureaucracy before they were readied for approval by President Bush. It is quite true that nobody predicted Sept. 11—that nobody guessed in advance how and when the attacks would come. But other things are true too. By last summer, many of those in the know—the spooks, the buttoned-down bureaucrats, the law-enforcement professionals in a dozen countries—were almost frantic with worry that a major terrorist attack against American interests was imminent. It wasn't averted because 2001 saw a systematic collapse in the ability of Washington's national security apparatus to handle the terrorist threat.

The winter proposals became a victim of the transition process, turf wars and time spent on the pet policies of new top officials. The Bush Administration chose to institute its own "policy review process" on the terrorist threat. Clarke told TIME that the review moved "as fast as could be expected." And Administration officials insist that by the time the review was endorsed by the Bush principals on Sept. 4, it was more aggressive than anything contemplated the previous winter. The final plan, they say, was designed not to "roll back" al-Qaeda but to "eliminate" it. But that delay came at a cost. The Northern Alliance was desperate for help but got little of it. And in a bureaucratic squabble that would be far-fetched on *The West Wing,* nobody in Washington could decide whether a Predator drone—an unmanned aerial vehicle (UAV) and the best possible source of real intelligence on what was happening in the terror camps—should be sent to fly over Afghanistan. So the Predator sat idle from October 2000 until after Sept. 11. No single person was responsible for all this. But "Washington"—that organic compound of officials and politicians, in uniform and out, with faces both familiar and unknown—failed horribly.

Could al-Qaeda's plot have been foiled if the U.S. had taken the fight to the terrorists in January 2001? Perhaps not. The thrust of the winter plan was to attack al-Qaeda outside the U.S. Yet by the beginning of that year,

Mohamed Atta and Marwan Al-Shehhi, two Arabs who had been leaders of a terrorist cell in Hamburg, Germany, were already living in Florida, honing their skills in flight schools. Nawaf Alhazmi and Khalid Almihdhar had been doing the same in Southern California. The hijackers maintained tight security, generally avoided cell phones, rented apartments under false names and used cash—not wire transfers—wherever possible. If every plan to attack al-Qaeda had been executed and every lead explored, Atta's team might still never have been caught.

But there's another possibility. An aggressive campaign to degrade the terrorist network worldwide—to shut down the conveyor belt of recruits coming out of the Afghan camps, to attack the financial and logistical support on which the hijackers depended—just might have rendered it incapable of carrying out the Sept. 11 attacks. Perhaps some of those who had to approve the operation might have been killed, or the money trail to Florida disrupted. We will never know, because we never tried. This is the secret history of that failure.

Unfinished Business

Berger was determined that when he left office, Rice should have a full understanding of the terrorist threat. In a sense, this was an admission of failure. For the Clinton years had been marked by a drumbeat of terror attacks against American targets, and they didn't seem to be stopping. In 1993 the World Trade Center had been bombed for the first time; in 1996 19 American servicemen had been killed when the Khobar Towers, in Dhahran, Saudi Arabia, was bombed; two years later, American embassies in Kenya and Tanzania were attacked. As the millennium celebrations at the end of 1999 approached, the CIA warned that it expected five to 15 attacks against American targets over the New Year's weekend. But three times, the U.S. got lucky. The Jordanians broke up an al-Qaeda cell in Amman; Ahmed Ressam, an Algerian based in Montreal, panicked when stopped at a border crossing from Canada while carrying explosives intended for Los Angeles International Airport; and on Jan. 3, 2000, an al-Qaeda attack on the U.S.S. *The Sullivans* in Yemen foundered after terrorists overloaded their small boat.

From the start of the Clinton Administration, the job of thwarting terror had fallen to Clarke. A bureaucratic survivor who now leads the Bush Administration's office on cyberterrorism, he has served four Presidents from both parties—staff members joke that the framed photos in his office have two sides, one for a Republican President to admire, the other for a Democrat. Aggressive and legendarily abrasive, Clarke was desperate to persuade skeptics to take the terror threat as seriously as he did. "Clarke is unbelievably determined, high-energy, focused and imaginative," says a senior Clinton Administration official." But he's totally insensitive to rolling over others who are in his way." By the end of 2000, Clarke didn't need to roll over his boss; Berger was just as sure of the danger.

The two men had an ally in George Tenet, who had been appointed Director of Central Intelligence in 1997. "He wasn't sleeping on the job on this," says a senior Clinton aide of Tenet, "whatever inherent problems there were in the agency." Those problems were immense. Although the CIA claims it had penetrated al-Qaeda, Republican Congressman Saxby Chambliss of Georgia, chairman of the House Intelligence Subcommittee on Terrorism and Homeland Security, doubts that it ever got anywhere near the top of the organization. "The CIA," he says, "were not able to recruit human assets to penetrate al-Qaeda and the al-Qaeda leadership." Nobody pretends that such an exercise would have been easy. Says a counterterrorism official: "Where are you going to find a person loyal to the U.S. who's willing to eat dung beetles and sleep on the ground in a cave for two or three years? You don't find people willing to do that who also speak fluent Pashtu or Arabic."

In the absence of men sleeping with the beetles, the CIA had to depend on less reliable allies. The agency attempted to recruit tribal leaders in Afghanistan who might be persuaded to take on bin Laden; contingency plans had been made for the CIA to fly one of its planes to a desert landing strip in Afghanistan if he was ever captured. (Clinton had signed presidential "findings" that were ambiguous on the question of whether bin Laden could be killed in such an attack.) But the tribal groups' loyalty was always in doubt. Despite the occasional abortive raid, they never seemed to get close to bin Laden. That meant that the Clinton team had to fall back on a second strategy: taking out bin Laden by cruise missile, which had been tried after the embassy bombings in 1998. For all of 2000, sources tell TIME, Clinton ordered two U.S. Navy submarines to stay on station in the northern Arabian Sea, ready to attack if bin Laden's coordinates could be determined.

But the plan was twice flawed. First, the missiles could be used only if bin Laden's whereabouts were known, and the CIA never definitively delivered that information. By early 2000, Clinton was becoming infuriated by the lack of intelligence on bin Laden's movements. "We've got to do better than this," he scribbled on one memo. "This is unsatisfactory." Second, even if a target could ever be found, the missiles might take too long to hit it. The Pentagon thought it could dump a Tomahawk missile on bin Laden's camp within six hours of a decision to attack, but the experts in the White House thought that was impossibly long. Any missiles fired at Afghanistan would have to fly over Pakistan, and Pakistan's Inter-Services Intelligence agency (ISI) was close to the Taliban. White House aides were sure bin Laden would be tipped off as soon as the Pakistanis detected the missiles.

Berger and Clarke wanted something more robust. On Nov. 7, Berger met with William Cohen, then Secretary of Defense, in the Pentagon. The time had come, said Berger, for the Pentagon to rethink its approach to operations against bin Laden. "We've been hit many times, and we'll be hit again," Berger said. "Yet we have no option beyond cruise missiles." He wanted "boots on the ground"—U.S. special-ops forces deployed inside Afghanistan on a search-and-destroy mission targeting bin Laden. Cohen said he would look at the idea, but he and General Hugh Shelton, Chairman of the Joint Chiefs of Staff, were dead set against it. They feared a repeat of Desert One, the 1980 fiasco in which special-ops commandos crashed in Iran during an abortive mission to rescue American hostages.

It wasn't just Pentagon nerves that got in the way of a more aggressive counterterrorism policy. So did politics. After the U.S.S. *Cole* was bombed, the secretive Joint Special Operations Command at Fort Bragg, N.C., drew up plans to have Delta Force members swoop into Afghanistan and grab bin Laden. But the warriors were never given the go-ahead; the Clinton Administration did not order an American retaliation for the attack. "We didn't do diddly," gripes a counterterrorism official. "We didn't even blow up a baby-milk factory." In fact, despite strong suspicion that bin Laden was behind the attack in Yemen, the CIA and FBI had not officially concluded that he was, and would be unable to do so before Clinton left office. That made it politically impossible for Clinton to strike—especially given the upcoming election and his own lack of credibility on national security. "If we had done anything, say, two weeks before the election," says a former senior Clinton aide, "we'd be accused of helping Al Gore."

For Clarke, the bombing of the *Cole* was final proof that the old policy hadn't worked. It was time for something more aggressive—a plan to make war against al-Qaeda. One element was vital. The Taliban's control of Afghanistan was not yet complete; in the northeast of the country, Northern Alliance forces led by Ahmed Shah Massoud, a legendary guerrilla leader who had fought against the Soviet invaders of Afghanistan in the 1980s, were still resisting Taliban rule. Clarke argued that Massoud should be given the resources to develop a viable fighting force. That way, terrorists leaving al-Qaeda's training camps in Afghanistan would have been forced to join the Taliban forces fighting in the north. "You keep them on the front lines in Afghanistan," says a counter terrorism official. "Hopefully you're killing them in the process, and they're not leaving Afghanistan to plot terrorist operations. That was the general approach." But the approach meant that Americans had to engage directly in the snake pit of Afghan politics.

The Last Man Standing

In the spring of 2001, Afghanistan was as rough a place as it ever is. Four sets of forces battled for position. Most of the country was under the authority of the Taliban, but it was not a homogeneous group. Some of its leaders, like Mullah Mohammed Omar, the self-styled emir of Afghanistan were dyed-in-the-wool Islamic radicals; others were fierce Afghan nationalists. The Taliban's principal support had come from Pakistan—another interested party, which wanted a reasonably peaceful border to its west—and in particular from the hard men of the ISI. But Pakistan's policy was not all of a piece either. Since General Pervez Musharraf had taken power in a 1999 coup, some Pakistan officials desperate to curry favor with the U.S.—which had cut off aid to Pakistan after it tested a nuclear device in 1998—had seen the wisdom of distancing themselves from the Taliban, or at the least attempting to moderate its more radical behavior.

The third element was the Northern Alliance, a resistance movement whose stronghold was in northeast Afghanistan. Most of the Alliance's forces and leaders were, like Massoud, ethnic Tajiks—a minority in Afghanistan. Massoud controlled less than 10% of the country and had been beaten back by the Taliban in 2000. Nonetheless, by dint of his personality and reputation, Massoud was "the only military threat to the Taliban," says

Francesc Vendrell, who was then the special representative in Afghanistan of the U.N. Secretary-General.

And then there was al-Qaeda. The group had been born in Afghanistan when Islamic radicals began flocking there in 1979, after the Soviets invaded. Bin Laden and his closest associates had returned in 1996, when they were expelled from Sudan. Al-Qaeda's terrorist training camps were in Afghanistan, and bin-Laden's forces and money were vital to sustaining the Taliban's offensives against Massoud.

By last spring, the uneasy equilibrium among the four forces was beginning to break down. "Moderates" in the Taliban—those who tried to keep lines open to intermediaries in the U.N. and the U.S.—were losing ground. In 2000, Mullah Mohammed Rabbani, thought to be the second most powerful member of the Taliban, had reached out clandestinely to Massoud. "He understood that our country had been sold out to al-Qaeda and Pakistan," says Ahmad Jamsheed, Massoud's secretary. But in April 2001, Rabbani died of liver cancer. By that month, says the U.N.'s Vendrell, "it was al-Qaeda that was running the Taliban, not vice versa."

A few weeks before Rabbani's death, Musharraf's government had started to come to the same conclusion: the Pakistanis were no longer able to moderate Taliban behavior. To worldwide condemnation, the Taliban had announced its intention to blow up the 1,700-year-old stone statues of the Buddha in the Bamiyan Valley, Musharraf dispatched his right-hand man, Interior Minister Moinuddin Haider, to plead with Mullah Omar for the Buddhas to be saved. The Taliban's Foreign Minister and its ambassador to Pakistan, says a Pakistani official close to the talks, were in favor of saving the Buddhas. But Mullah Omar, says a member of the Pakistani delegation, listened to what Haider had to say and replied, "If on Judgment Day I stand before Allah, I'll see those two statues floating before me, and I know that Allah will ask me why, when I had the power, I did not destroy them." A few days later, the Buddhas were blown up.

By summer, Pakistan had a deeper grievance. The country had suffered a wave of sectarian assassinations, with gangs throwing grenades into mosques and murdering clerics. The authorities in Islamabad knew that the murderers had fled to Afghanistan (one of them was openly running a store in Kabul) and sent a delegation to ask for their return. "We gave them lists of names, photos and the locations of training camps where these fellows could be found," says Brigadier Javid Iqbal

Cheema, director of Pakistan's National Crisis Management Cell, "but not a single individual was ever handed over to us." The Pakistanis were furious.

As the snows cleared for the annual spring military campaign, a joint offensive against Massoud by the Taliban and al-Qaeda seemed likely. But the influence of al-Qaeda on the Taliban was proving deeply unpopular among ordinary Afghans, especially in the urban centers. "I thought at most 20% of the population supported the Taliban by early summer," says Vendrell. And bin Laden's power made Massoud's plea for outside assistance more urgent. "We told the Americans—we told everyone—that al-Qaeda was set upon a transnational program," says Abdullah Abdullah, once a close aide to Massoud and now the Afghan Foreign Minister. In April, Massoud addressed the European Parliament in Strasbourg, France, seeking support for the Northern Alliance. "If President Bush doesn't help us," he told a reporter, "these terrorists will damage the U.S. and Europe very soon."

But Massoud never got the help that he needed—or that Clarke's plan had deemed necessary. Most of the time, Northern Alliance delegates to Washington had to be satisfied with meeting low-level bureaucrats. The Alliance craved recognition by the U.S. as a "legitimate resistance movement" but never got it, though on a visit in July, Abdullah did finally get to meet some top National Security Council (NSC) and State Department officials for the first time. The best the Americans seemed prepared to do was turn a blind eye to the trickle of aid from Iran, Russia and India. Vendrell remembers much talk that spring of increased support from the Americans. But in truth Massoud's best help came from Iran, which persuaded all supporters of the Northern Alliance to channel their aid through Massoud alone.

Only once did something happen that might have given Massoud hope that the U.S. would help. In late June, he was joined in Dushanbe, Tajikistan, by Abdul Haq, a leading Pashtun, based in Dubai, who was opposed to the Taliban. Haq was accompanied by someone Massoud knew well: Peter Tomsen, a retired ambassador who from 1989 to '92 had been the U.S. State Department's special envoy to the Afghan resistance. Also present was James Ritchie, a successful Chicago options trader who had spent part of his childhood in Afghanistan and was helping bankroll the groups opposed to the Taliban. (Haq was captured and executed by the Taliban last October while on a quixotic mission to Afghanistan.) Tomsen insists that the June 2001 trip was a private one, though he had told State

Department officials of it in advance. Their message, he says, was limited to a noncommittal "good luck and be careful."

The purpose of the meeting, according to Tomsen, was to see if Massoud and Haq could forge a joint strategy against the Taliban. "The idea," says Sayeed Hussain Anwari, now the Afghan Minister of Agriculture, who was present at the meeting, "was to bring Abdul Haq inside the country to begin an armed struggle in the southeast." Still hoping for direct assistance from Washington, Massoud gave Tomsen all the intelligence he had on al-Qaeda and asked Tomsen to take it back to Washington. But when he briefed State Department officials after his trip, their reaction was muted. The American position was clear. If anything was to be done to change the realities in Afghanistan, it would have to be done not by the U.S. but by Pakistan. Massoud was on his own.

Clarke: Crying Wolf

In Washington, Dick Clarke didn't seem to have a lot of friends either. His proposals were still grinding away. No other great power handles the transition from one government to another in so shambolic a way as the U.S.—new appointments take months to be confirmed by the Senate; incoming Administrations tinker with even the most sensible of existing policies. The fight against terrorism was one of the casualties of the transition, as Washington spent eight months going over and over a document whose outline had long been clear. "If we hadn't had a transition," says a senior Clinton Administration official, "probably in late October or early November 2000, we would have had [the plan to go on the offensive] as a presidential directive."

As the new Administration took office, Rice kept Clarke in his job as counterterrorism czar. In early February he repeated to Vice President Dick Cheney the briefing he had given to Rice and Hadley. There are differing opinions on how seriously the Bush team took Clarke's warnings. Some members of the outgoing Administration got the sense that the Bush team thought the Clintonites had become obsessed with terrorism. "It was clear," says one, "that this was not the same priority to them that it was to us."

For other observers, however, the real point was not that the new Administration dismissed the terrorist theat. On the contrary, Rice, Hadley and Cheney, says an official, "all got that it was important." The question is,

How high a priority did terrorism get? Clarke says that dealing with al-Qaeda "was in the top tier of issues reviewed by the Bush Administration." But other topics got far more attention. The whole Bush national security team was obsessed with setting up a national system of missile defense. Secretary of Defense Donald Rumsfeld was absorbed by a long review of the military's force structure. Attorney General John Ashcroft had come into office as a dedicated crime buster. Rice was desperately trying to keep in line a national-security team—including Rumsfeld, Cheney and Secretary of State Colin Powell—whose members had wildly different agendas and styles. "Terrorism," says a former Clinton White House official, speaking of the new Administration, "wasn't on their plate of key issues." Al-Qaeda had not been a feature of the landscape when the Republicans left office in 1993. The Bush team, says an official, "had to learn about [al-Qaeda] and figure out where it fit into their broader foreign policy." But doing so meant delay.

Some counterterrorism officials think there is another reason for the Bush Administration's dilatory response. Clarke's paper, says an official, "was a Clinton proposal." Keeping Clarke around was one thing; buying into the analysis of an Administration that the Bush team considered feckless and naive was quite another. So Rice instructed Clarke to initiate a new "policy review process" on the terrorism threat. Clarke dived into yet another round of meetings. And his proposals were nibbled nearly to death.

This was, after all, a White House plan, which means it was resented from the moment of conception. "When you look at the Pentagon and the CIA," says a former senior Clinton aide, "it's not their plan. The military will never accept the White House staff doing military planning." Terrorism, officials from the State Department suggested, needed to be put in the broader context of American policy in South Asia. The rollback plan was becoming the victim of a classic Washington power play between those with "functional" responsibilities—like terrorism—and those with "regional" ones—like relations with India and Pakistan. The State Department's South Asia bureau, according to a participant in the meetings, argued that a fistful of other issues—Kashmir, nuclear proliferation, Musharraf's dictatorship—were just as pressing as terrorism. By now, Clarke's famously short fuse was giving off sparks. A participant at one of the meetings paraphrases Clarke's attitude this way: "These people are trying to kill us. I could give a f—— if Musharraf was democratically elected. What I do care about is Pakistan's support for the Taliban and turning a blind eye to this terrorist cancer growing in their neighbor's backyard."

It was Bush who broke the deadlock. Each morning the CIA gives the Chief Executive a top-secret Presidential Daily Brief (PDB) on pressing issues of national security. One day in early spring, Tenet briefed Bush on the hunt for Abu Zubaydah, al-Qaeda's head of international operations, who was suspected of having been involved in the planning of the attack on the U.S.S. *Cole*. After the PDB, Bush told Rice that the approach to al-Qaeda was too scattershot. He was tired of "swatting at flies" and asked for a comprehensive plan for attacking terrorism. According to an official, Rice came back to the NSC and said, "The President wants a plan to eliminate al-Qaeda." Clarke reminded her that he already had one.

But having a plan isn't the same as executing it. Clarke's paper now had to go through three more stages: the Deputies' Committee, made up of the No. 2s to the main national-security officials; the Principals' Committee, which included Cheney, Rice, Tenet, Powell and Rumsfeld; and finally, the President. Only when Bush had signed off would the plan become what the Bush team called a national-security presidential directive.

On April 30, nearly six weeks after the Administration started holding deputies' meetings, Clarke presented a new plan to them. In addition to Hadley, who chaired the hour-long meeting, the gathering included Cheney's chief of staff, Lewis Libby; Richard Armitage, the barrel-chested Deputy Secretary of State; Paul Wolfowitz, the scholarly hawk from the Pentagon; and John McLaughlin from the CIA. Armitage was enthusiastic about Clarke's plan, according to a senior official. But the CIA was gun-shy. Tenet was a Clinton holdover and thus vulnerable if anything went wrong. His agency was unwilling to take risks; it wanted "top cover" from the White House. The deputies, says a senior official, decided to have "three parallel reviews—one on al-Qaeda, one on the Pakistani political situation and the third on Indo-Pakistani relations." The issues, the deputies thought, were interrelated. "They wanted to view them holistically," says the senior official, "and not until they'd had three separate meetings on each of these were they able to hold a fourth integrating them all."

There was more. Throughout the spring, one bureaucratic wrangle in particular rumbled on, poisoning the atmosphere. At issue: the Predator.

The Predator had first been used in Bosnia in 1995. Later, the CIA and the Pentagon began a highly classified program designed to produce pictures—viewable in real time—that would be fine-grained enough to identify individuals. The new, improved Predator was finally ready in September 2000, and the CIA flew it over Afghanistan in a two-week "test of concept." First results were promising; one video sent to the White House showed a man who might have been bin Laden. For the first time, the CIA now had a way to check out a tip by one of its agents among the Afghan tribes. If there was a report that bin Laden was in the vicinity, says a former aide to Clinton, "we could put the Predator over the location and have eyes on the target."

But in October 2000, the Predator crashed when landing at its base in a country bordering Afghanistan. The unmanned aerial vehicle needed repairs, and in any event, the CIA and the Pentagon decided that the winter weather over Afghanistan would make it difficult to take good pictures. The Clinton team left office assuming that the Predator would be back in the skies by March 2001.

In fact, the Predator wouldn't fly again until after Sept. 11. In early 2001 it was decided to develop a new version that would not just take photos but also be armed with Hellfire missiles. To the frustration of Clarke and other White House aides, the CIA and the Pentagon couldn't decide who controlled the new program or who should pay for it—though each craft cost only $1 million. While the new UAV was being rapidly developed at a site in the southwestern U.S., the CIA opposed using the old one for pure surveillance because it feared al-Qaeda might see it. "Once we were going to arm the thing," says a senior U.S. intelligence official, "we didn't want to expose the capability by just having it fly overhead and spot a bunch of guys we couldn't do anything about." Clarke and his supporters were livid. "Dick Clarke insisted that it be kept in the air," says a Bush Administration official. The counterterrorism team argued that the Taliban had shot at the UAV during the Clinton test, so its existence was hardly a secret. Besides, combined with on-the-ground intelligence, a Predator might just gather enough information in time to get a Tomahawk off to the target. But when the deputies held their fourth and final meeting on July 16, they still hadn't sorted out what to do with the Predator. Squabbles over who would pay for it continued into August.

Administration sources insist that they were not idle in the spring. They set up, for example, a new center in the Treasury to track suspicious foreign assets and reviewed Clinton's "findings" on whether the CIA could kill bin Laden. But by the summer, policy reviews were hardly what was needed.

Intelligence services were picking up enough chatter about a terrorist attack to scare the pants off top officials. On June 22, the Defense Department put its troops on full alert and ordered six ships from the Fifth Fleet, based in Bahrain, to steam out to sea, for fear that they might be attacked in port. U.S. officials thought an attack might be mounted on American forces at the NATO base at Incirlik, Turkey, or maybe in Rome or Belgium, Germany or Southeast Asia, perhaps the Philippines—anywhere, it seems, but in the U.S. When Independence Day passed without incident, Clarke called a meeting and asked Ben Bonk, deputy director of the CIA's counterterrorism center, to brief on bin Laden's plans. Bonk's evidence that al-Qaeda was planning "something spectacular," says an official who was in the room, "was very gripping." But nobody knew what or when or where the spectacular would be. As if to crystallize how much and how little anyone in the know actually knew, the counterterrorism center released a report titled "Threat of Impending al-Qaeda Attack to Continue Indefinitely."

Predictably, nerves frayed. Clarke, who was widely loathed in the CIA, where he was accused of self-aggrandizement, began to lose credibility. He cried wolf, said his detractors; he had been in the job too long. "The guy was reading way too many fiction novels," says a counterterrorism official. "He turned into a Chicken Little. The sky was always falling for Dick Clarke. We had our strings jerked by him so many times, he was simply not taken seriously." Clarke wasn't the only one living on the edge. So, say senior officials, was Tenet. Every few days, the CIA director would call Tom Pickard, who had become acting director of the FBI in June, asking, "What do you hear? Do you have anything?" Pickard never had to ask what the topic was.

In mid-July, Tenet sat down for a special meeting with Rice and aides. "George briefed Condi that there was going to be a major attack," says an official; another, who was present at the meeting, says Tenet broke out a huge wall chart ("They always have wall charts") with dozens of threats. Tenet couldn't rule out a domestic attack but thought it more likely that al-Qaeda would strike overseas. One date already worrying the Secret Service was July 20, when Bush would arrive in Genoa for the G-8 summit. Tenet had intelligence that al-Qaeda was planning to attack Bush there. The Italians, who had heard the same report (the way European intelligence sources tell it, everyone but the President's dog "knew" an attack was coming) put frogmen in the harbor, closed airspace around the town and ringed it with antiaircraft guns.

But nothing happened. After Genoa, says a senior intelligence official, there was a collective sigh of relief: "A lot of folks started letting their guard down." After the final deputies' meeting on Clarke's draft of a presidential directive, on July 16, it wasn't easy to find a date for the Principals' Committee to look at the plan—the last stage before the paper went to Bush. "There was one meeting scheduled for August," says a senior official, "but too many principals were out of town." Eventually a date was picked: the principals would look at the draft on Sept. 4. That was about nine months after Clarke first put his plan on paper.

A Burned-Out Case

Clarke wasn't the only person having a bad year. In New York City, John O'Neill led the FBI's National Security Division, commanding more than 100 experienced agents. By spring they were all overloaded. O'Neill's boss, Assistant FBI Director Barry Mawn, spent part of his time pleading with Washington for more agents, more linguists, more clerical help. He got nowhere. O'Neill was a legend both in New York, where he hung out at famous watering holes like Elaine's, and in the counterterrorism world. Since 1995, when he helped coordinate the arrest in Pakistan of Ramzi Yousef, the man responsible for the 1993 bombing of the World Trade Center, O'Neill had been one of the FBI's leading figures in the fight against terrorism. Brash, slick and ambitious, he had spent the late 1990s working closely with Clarke and the handful of other top officials for whom bin Laden had become an obsession.

Now O'Neill was having a lousy few months. The New York City field office had primary responsibility for the investigation of the attack on the U.S.S. *Cole.* But the case had gone badly from the start. The Yemeni authorities had been lethargic and uncooperative, and O'Neill, who led the team in Aden, had run afoul of Barbara Bodine, then the U.S. ambassador to Yemen, who believed the FBI's large presence was causing political problems for the Yemeni regime. When O'Neill left Yemen on a trip home for Thanksgiving, Bodine barred his return. Seething, O'Neill tried to supervise the investigation from afar. At the same time, his team in New York City was working double time preparing for the trial in January 2001 of four co-conspirators in the case of the 1998 African embassy bombings. That involved agents shuttling between Nairobi, Dar es Salaam and New York, escorting witnesses, ferrying documents

and guarding al-Qaeda turncoats who would give evidence for the prosecution.

Yet the FBI as a whole was ill equipped to deal with the terrorist threat. It had neither the language skills nor the analytical savvy to understand al-Qaeda. The bureau's information-technology capability dated to pre-Internet days. Chambliss says the counterterrorism investigations were decentralized at the bureau's 56 field offices, which were actually discouraged from sharing information with one another or with headquarters.

That was if the cases ever got started. An investigation by Chambliss's subcommittee found that the FBI paid "insufficient attention" to tracking terrorists' finances. Most agents in the field were assigned to criminal units; few field squads were dedicated to gathering intelligence on radical fundamentalists. During the Clinton Administration, says a former senior aide, Clarke became so frustrated with the bureau that he began touring its field offices, giving agents "al-Qaeda 101" classes. The bureau was, in fact, wiretapping some suspected Islamic radicals and debriefing a few al-Qaeda hands who had flipped. But at the end of the Clinton years, the aide says, the FBI told the White House that "there's not a substantial al-Qaeda presence in the U.S., and to the extent there was a presence, they had it covered."

The FBI didn't, and O'Neill must have known that it didn't. So, as it happens, did some of his key allies, who were not in the U.S. at all but overseas. In Europe and especially in France the threat of Islamic terrorism had been particularly sharp ever since the Algerian Armed Islamic Group launched a bombing campaign in Paris in 1995. By 2000, counterterrorism experts in Europe knew the Islamic diaspora communities in Europe were seeded with cells of terrorists. And after the arrest of Ressam, European officials were convinced that terrorists would soon attack targets in the U.S. Jean-Louis Bruguière, a French magistrate who has led many of the most prominent terrorist cases, says Ressam's arrest signaled that the U.S. "had to join the rest of the world in considering itself at acute risk of attack."

Throughout the winter and spring of 2001, European law-enforcement agencies scored a series of dramatic hits against al-Qaeda and associated radical Islamic cells, with some help from the CIA. The day after Christmas 2000, German authorities in Frankfurt arrested four Algerians on suspicion of plotting to bomb targets in Strasbourg. Two months later, the British arrested six Algerians on terrorism charges. In April, Italian police busted a cell whose members were suspected of plotting to bomb the American embassy in Rome. Two months later, the Spanish arrested Mohammed Bensakhria, an Algerian who had been in Afghanistan and had links to top al-Qaeda officials, including bin Laden. Bensakhria, the French alleged, had directed the Frankfurt cell involved in the Strasbourg plot. And in the most stunning coup of all, on July 28, Djamel Beghal, a Frenchman of Algerian descent who had been on France's terrorist watch list since 1997, was arrested in Dubai on his way back from Afghanistan. After being persuaded of terrorism's evil by Islamic scholars, Beghal told of a plot to attack the American embassy in Paris and gave investigators new details on al-Qaeda's top leadership, including the international-operations role of Abu Zabaydah. (Now back in France, he has tried to recant his confession.) French sources tell TIME they believe U.S. authorities knew about Beghal's testimony.

This action by cops in Europe was meat and drink to O'Neill. The problem was that it convinced some U.S. antiterrorism officials that if there was going to be an attack on American interests that summer, it would take place outside the U.S. In early June, for example, the FBI was so concerned about threats to investigators left in Yemen that it moved the agents from Aden to the American embassy in Sana'a. Then came a second, very specific warning about the team's safety, and Washington decided to pull out of Yemen entirely. "John [O'Neill] would say, 'There's a lot of traffic,'" recalls Mawn. "Everybody was saying, 'The drumbeats are going; something's going to happen.' I said, 'Where and what?' And they'd say, 'We don't know, but it seems to be overseas, probably.'"

Some didn't lose sight of the threat at home. On Aug. 6, while on vacation in Crawford, Texas, Bush was given a PDB, this one on the possibility of al-Qaeda attacks in the U.S. And not one but two FBI field offices had inklings of al-Qaeda activity in the U.S. that, had they been aggressively pursued, might have fleshed out the intelligence chatter about an upcoming attack. But the systemic weaknesses in the FBI's bureaucracy prevented anything from being done.

The first warning came from Phoenix, Ariz. On July 10, agent Kenneth Williams wrote a paper detailing his suspicions about some suspected Islamic radicals who had been taking flying lessons in Arizona. Williams proposed an investigation to see if al-Qaeda was using flight schools nationwide. He spoke with the voice of experience; he had been working on international terrorism cases for years. The Phoenix office, according to

former FBI agent James Hauswirth, had been investigating men with possible Islamic terrorist links since 1994, though without much support from the FBI's local bosses. Williams had started work on his probe of flight schools in early 2001 but had spent much of the next months on nonterrorist cases. Once he was back on terrorism, it took only a few weeks for alarm bells to ring. He submitted his memo to headquarters and to two FBI field offices, including New York City. In all three places it died.

Five weeks after Williams wrote his memo, a second warning came in from another FBI field office, and once again, headquarters bungled the case. On Aug. 13, Zacarias Moussaoui, a 30-year-old Frenchman of Moroccan ancestry, arrived at Pan Am International Flight Academy in Minnesota for simulator training on a Boeing 747. Moussaoui, who had been in the U.S. since February and had already taken flying lessons at a school in Norman, Okla., was in a hurry. John Rosengren, who was director of operations at Pan Am until February this year, says Moussaoui wanted to learn how to fly the 747 in "four or five days." After just two days of training, Moussaoui's flight instructor expressed concern that his student didn't want it known that he was a Muslim. One of Pan Am's managers had a contact in the FBI, should the manager call him? "I said, 'No problem,'" says Rosengren. "The next day I got a call from a Minneapolis agent telling me Moussaoui had been detained at the Residence Inn in Eagan."

Though Moussaoui is the only person to be indicted in connection with the Sept. 11 attacks, his role in them is as clear as mud. (He is detained in Alexandria, Va., awaiting trial in federal district court.) German authorities have confirmed to TIME that—as alleged in the indictment—Ramzi Binalshibh, a Hamburg friend of Atta and Al-Shehhi, wired two money transfers to Moussaoui in August. Binalshibh, who was denied a visa to visit the U.S. four times in 2000, is thought to have been one of the conduits for funds to the hijackers, relaying cash that originated in the Persian Gulf. But no known telephone calls or other evidence links the hijackers directly to Moussaoui.

Whatever Moussaoui's true tale may be, the Minnesota field office was convinced he was worth checking out. Agents spent much of the next two weeks in an increasingly frantic—and ultimately fruitless—effort to persuade FBI headquarters to authorize a national-security warrant to search Moussaoui's computer. From Washington, requests were sent to authorities in Paris for background details on the suspect. Like most things having to do with Moussaoui, the contents of the dossier sent over from Paris are in dispute. One senior French law-enforcement source told TIME the Americans were given "everything they needed" to understand that Moussaoui was associated with Islamic terrorist groups. "Even a neophyte," says this source, "working in some remote corner of Florida, would have understood the threat based on what was sent." But several officials in FBI headquarters say that before Sept. 11 the French sent only a three-page document, which portrayed Moussaoui as a radical but was too sketchy to justify a search warrant for his computer.

The precise wording of the French letter isn't the issue. The extraordinary thing about Moussaoui's case—like the Phoenix memo—is that it was never brought to the attention of top officials in Washington who were, almost literally, sleepless with worry about an imminent terrorist attack. Nobody in the FBI or CIA ever informed anybody in the White House of Moussaoui's detention. That was unforgivable. "Do you think," says a White House antiterrorism official, "that if Dick Clarke had known the FBI had in custody a foreigner who was learning to fly a plane in midair," he wouldn't have done something?"

In blissless ignorance, Clarke and Tenet waited for the meeting of the Principals. But the odd little ways of Washington had one more trick to play. Heeding the pleas from the FBI's New York City office where Mawn and O'Neill were desperate for new linguists and analysts, acting FBI director Pickard asked the Justice Department for some $50 million for the bureau's counterterrorism program. He was turned down. In August, a bureau source says, he appealed to Attorney General Ashcroft. The reply was a flat no.

Pickard got Ashcroft's letter on Sept. 10. A few days before, O'Neill had started a new job. He was burned out, and he knew it. Over the summer, he had come to realize that he had made too many enemies ever to succeed Mawn. O'Neill handed in his papers, left the FBI and began a new life as head of security at the World Trade Center.

The Two Visitors

As the first cool nights of fall settled on northeast Afghanistan, Ahmed Shah Massoud was barely hanging on. His summer offensive had been a bust. An attempt to capture the city of Taloqan, which he had lost to the Taliban in 2000, ended in failure. But old allies, like the brutal Uzbek warlord Abdul Rashid Dostum, had returned to the field, and Massoud still thought the unpopularity of the Taliban might yet make them vulnerable. "He was telling us not to worry, that we'd soon capture Kabul," says Shah Pacha, an infantry commander in the Northern Alliance.

Around Sept. 1, Massoud summoned his top men to his command post in Khoja Bahauddin. The intention was to plan an attack, but Zahir Akbar, one of Massoud's generals, remembers a phone call after which Massoud changed his plans. "He'd been told al-Qaeda and the Pakistanis were deploying five combat units to the front line," says Akbar. Northern Alliance soldiers reported a buildup of Taliban and al-Qaeda forces; there was no big push from the south, although there were a number of skirmishes in the first week in September. "We were puzzled and confused when they didn't attack," says a senior Afghan intelligence source. "And Taliban communications showed the units had been ordered to wait."

What were they waiting for? Some of Massoud's closest aides think they know. For about three weeks two Arab journalists had been waiting in Khoja Bahauddin to interview Massoud. The men said they represented the Islamic Observation Center in London and had a letter of introduction from its head, Yasser al-Siri. The men, who had been given safe passage through the Taliban front lines, "said they'd like to document Islam in Afghanistan," recalls Faheem Dashty, who made films with the Northern Alliance and is editor in chief of the Kabul *Weekly* newspaper. By the night of Sept. 8, the visitors were getting antsy, pestering Massoud's officials to firm up the meeting with him and threatening to return to Kabul if they could not see Massoud in the next 24 hours. "They were so worried and excitable they were begging us," says Jamsheed, Massoud's secretary.

The interview was finally granted just before lunch on Sunday, Sept. 9. Dashty was asked to record it on his camera. Massoud sat next to his friend Masood Khalili, now Afghanistan's ambassador to India. "The commander said he wanted to sit with me and translate," says Khalili. "Then he and I would go and have lunch together by the Oxus River." The Arabs entered and set up a TV camera in front of Massoud; the guests, says Khalili, were "very calm, very quiet." Khalili asked them which newspaper they represented. When they replied that they were acting for "Islamic Centers," says Khalili, he became reluctant to continue, but Massoud said they should all go ahead.

Khalili says Massoud asked to know the Arabs' questions before they started recording. "I remember that out of 15 questions, eight were about bin Laden," says Khalili. "I looked over at Massoud. He looked uncomfortable; there were five worry lines on his forehead instead of the one he usually had. But he said, 'O.K, Let's film.'" Khalili started translating the first question into Dari; Dashty was fiddling with the lighting on his camera. "Then," says Dashty, "I felt the explosion." The bomb was in the camera, and it killed one of the Arabs; the second was shot dead by Massoud's guards while trying to escape. Khalili believes he was saved by his passport, which was in his left breast pocket—eight pieces of shrapnel were found embedded in it. Dashty remembers being rushed to a helicopter with Massoud, who had terrible wounds. The chopper flew them both to a hospital in Tajikistan. By the time they arrived, Massoud was dead.

The killers had come from Europe, and they were members of a group allied with al-Qaeda. Massoud's enemies had been waiting for the news. Within hours, Taliban radio began to crackle: "Your father is dead. Now you can't resist us." "They were clever," says a member of Massoud's staff. "Their offensive was primed to begin after the assassination." That night the Taliban attacked Massoud's front lines. One last time, his forces held out on their own.

As the battle raged, Clarke's plan awaited Bush's signature. Soon enough, the Northern Alliance would get all the aid it had been seeking—U.S. special forces, money, B-52 bombers, and of course, as many Predators as the CIA and Pentagon could get into the sky. The decision that had been put off for so long had suddenly become easy because a little more than 50 hours after Massoud's death, Atta, sitting on American Airlines Flight 11 on the runway at Boston's Logan Airport, had used his mobile phone to speak for the last time to his friend Al-Shehhi, on United Flight 175. Their plot was a go.

That morning, O'Neill, Clarke's former partner in the fight against international terrorism, arrived at his new place of work. He had been on the job just two weeks. After Atta and Al-Shehhi crashed their planes into the World Trade Center, O'Neill called his son and a girlfriend from outside the Towers to say he was safe. Then he rushed back in. His body was identified 10 days later.

Chapter 13 Review Questions

1. How do you define the word "implementation"? In what ways does "implementation" differ from "management" or "administration"? What are the similarities and differences among these terms?

2. Can you outline how the concept of implementation draws on other ideas concerning decision making, communications, politics, budgeting, intergovernmental relations, public professional expertise, and the general environment that have been discussed earlier in this text? How does the concept of implementation both use and build on these other concepts?

3. Why has implementation become such a major concern for students and practitioners of public administration and public policy in recent decades? What was responsible for its development as a recent focus of scholarly research? Do you think there is a valid need for studying implementation in the public sector and, if so, why?

4. What are the essential elements of the implementation model that Richard T. Matland proposes? How did he develop his "new" model? What are its basic assumptions and utility for practicing public administrators? Can you define in your own words its basic processes? Is it applicable to all situations, such as in foreign affairs? Or, just within America? Do you see any limitations to this model?

5. From your reading of this case, "They Had a Plan," in what part of the four-cell matrix of Matland's model would you categorize it that best predicts its possible implementation failure? Did Matland's model, in your view, adequately address political factors for influencing nonimplementation?

6. Consider the key policy makers in the case study and evaluate why they were unsuccessful at implementing their plan. By what standards, according to Matland, can we judge "success" or "failure" of program implementation? In your opinion, what was the *most critical* ingredient for turning the outcome of this case study into a success story of implementation?

Key Terms

top-down approaches
policy conflict
target population
statutory language
key actors
conflicting policy priorities
veto points
policy feedback

bottom-up approaches
policy ambiguity
prescriptive policy advice
descriptive causal factors
street-level bureaucrats
fixers
performance evaluation
constituency intervention points

Suggestions for Further Reading

The book that started much of the contemporary theorizing about this subject is now in its second edition and is still well worth reading: Jeffrey L. Pressman and Aaron B. Wildavsky, *Implementation,* 2nd ed. (Berkeley, Calif.: University of California Press, 1978) as well as several of the case studies that criticized the implementation of Great Society programs and also stimulated early research in this field, especially Martha Derthick, *New Towns In-Town* (Washington, D.C.: Urban Institute, 1972); Daniel P. Moynihan, *Maximum Feasible Misunderstanding* (New York: Free Press, 1969); Stephan K. Bailey and Edith K. Mosher, *ESEA: The Office of Education Administers a Law* (Syracuse: Syracuse University Press, 1968), as well as Beryl A. Radin, *Implementation, Change and the Federal Bureaucracy* (New York: Teachers College Press, 1977).

Serious students of implementation theory should review carefully the major conceptual approaches cited in the introduction to this chapter as well as other important contributions, such as Martin Rein and Francine F. Rabinovitz, "Implementation: A Theoretical Perspective," in Walter D. Burnham and Martha W. Weinberg, eds., *American Politics and Public Policy* (Cambridge, Mass.: MIT Press, 1978); and also in the same book, Michael M. Lipsky, "Implementation on Its Head"; Carl E. Van Horn, *Policy Implementation in the Federal System* (Lexington, Mass.: Lexington Books, 1979); A. Dunsire, *Implementation in Bureaucracy* (New York: St. Martin's Press, 1979); Walter Williams, *The Implementation Perspective* (Berkeley, Calif.: University of California Press, 1980); J. S. Larson, *Why Government Programs Fail* (1980); Helen M. Ingram and Dean E. Mann, eds., *Why Policies Succeed or Fail* (Los Angeles: Sage, 1980); R. D. Behn, "Why Murphy Was Right," *Policy Analysis* (Summer 1980); G. C. Edwards, *Implementing Public Policy* (Washington, D.C.: Congressional Quarterly Press, 1980); Susan Barrett and Colin Fudge, eds., *Policy and Action: Essays on Implementation of Public Policy* (London: Methuen, Inc., 1981); Dennis J. Palumbo and Marvin A. Harder, eds., *Implementing Public Policy* (Lexington, Mass.: Lexington Books, 1981); Daniel A. Mazmanian and Paul A. Sabatier, eds., *Effective Public Policy Implementation* (Lexington, Mass.: Lexington Books, 1982); B. Hjern and D. O. Porter, "Implementation Structure," *Organization Studies* (1981); Randall B. Ripley and Grace A. Franklin, *Bureaucracy and Policy Implementation* (Homewood, Ill.: Dorsey Press, 1982); Walter Williams et al., *Studying Implementation: Methodological and Administrative Issues* (Chatham, N.J.: Chatham House, 1982); and B. Hjern and C. Hull, eds., "Implementation Beyond Hierarchy," Special Issue, *European Journal of Political Research.* For a helpful reader, see George C. Edwards III, ed., *Public Policy Implementation* (Greenwich, Conn.: JAI Press, 1989). For two reviews of techniques, strategies, and directions for further research, read David L. Weimer, "The Current Data of Design Craft: Borrowing, Tinkering and Problem Solving," *Public Administration Review,* 53 (March/April 1993), pp. 110–120, as well as Helen Ingram, "Implementation: A Review and Suggested Framework," Naomi B. Lynn and Aaron Wildavsky, eds., *Public Administration: The State of the Discipline* (Chatham, N.J.: Chatham House, 1990).

Several recent articles in the *Journal of Public Administration Research and Theory* are well worth revewing: Robert Blair, "Policy Tools Theory and Implementation Networks" 12, no. 1 (2002), pp. 161–190, Robert Chackerian and Paul Marima,

"Comprehensive Administrative Reform Implementation," 11, no. 3 (2001), pp. 353–377; Peter and Linda de Leon, "Whatever Happened to Policy Implementation?" 12, no. 4 (2002), pp. 467–492; and Heather Hill, "Understanding Implementation," 13, no. 3 (2002), pp. 265–282.

Four important book-length, scholarly implementation studies are Lester M. Salamon, ed., *Beyond Privatization: The Tools of Government Action* (Washington, D.C.: The Urban Institute, 1989), or his more recent book, *The Tools of Government* (New York: Oxford University Press, 2002); Malcolm L. Goggin, Ann O'M. Bowman, James P. Lester, and Laurence J. O'Toole, Jr., *Implementation Theory and Practice: Toward a Third Generation* (Glenview, Ill.: Scott, Foresman and Co., 1990); see especially its excellent bibliography, as well as Robert Stoker, *Reluctant Partners* (Pittsburgh: University of Pittsburgh Press, 1991). For recent books that address specific sectors of policy implementation, see Daniel Ellsberg, *Risk, Ambiguity and Decision* (New York: Garland, 2001); Martha Gibson, *Conflict Amid Consensus* (Washington, D.C.: Georgetown University Press, 2000); Amihai Glazer, *Why Government Succeeds and Why It Fails* (Cambridge, Mass.: Harvard University Press, 2001); Lawrence Jones et al., eds., *Learning from International Public Management Reform,* 2 volumes (Oxford: JAI/Elsevier Science, 2001); A.C. Lin, *Reform in the Making* (Princeton, N.J.: Princeton University Press, 2000); Stuart Nagel, *Super-Optimizing Examples* (New York: Nova Science, 1999); Miroslav Nincic and Joseph Lepgold, eds., *Being Useful* (Ann Arbor: University of Michigan Press, 2000); Vito Tanzi, *Policies, Institutions and the Dark Side of Economics* (Northhampton, Mass: Edward Elgar, 2000); and for a how-to-do-it-practical guidebook, read Peter Pande et al., *The Six Sigma Way Team Field Book* (New York: McGraw Hill, 2001).

PART THREE

Enduring and Unresolved Relationships: Central Value Questions, Issues, and Dilemmas of Contemporary Public Administration

Part Three focuses on three key persistent and pressing relationships in the field of public administration today: the problems of political-administrative relationships; the bureaucracy and the public interest; and ethics and the public service. All of these relational issues are new in the sense that they have come to the forefront of recent discussions and controversies in public administration. Yet, these issues have certainly been part of the problems and perplexities of public administration since its inception as an identifiable field of study after the dawn of the twentieth century. Indeed, the topics of political-administrative relationships, the problems of ethics, and relationships between bureaucracy and the public interest were central themes of the writings of many early administrative theorists, such as Woodrow Wilson, Frederick Taylor, Luther Gulick, Louis Brownlow, and Leonard White. No doubt one could even trace the origins of these topics back to the classic writings of Plato, Aristotle, Moses, and Pericles. But for a variety of reasons, we are witnessing the reemergence of these older issues as very real dilemmas for public administrators today. Readings and cases in Part Three therefore address these critical issues:

CHAPTER 14
The Relationship Between Politics and Administration: *The Concept of Issue Networks* What are the current trends and practices in political oversight and control of administration? What are the implications for public administration and the governance of America?

CHAPTER 15
The Relationship Between Bureaucracy and the Public Interest: *The Concept of Public Sector Deregulation* What is the "public interest"? Is there such a thing that can serve as a guide to public administrators' work? How can it be applied as a meaningful concept to influence the direction and activities of government bureaucracies?

CHAPTER 16
The Relationship Between Ethics and Public Administration: *The Concept of Competing Ethical Obligations* How are ethical choices involved in contemporary decisions facing public servants? What is an appropriate conceptual model for understanding how ethics influences public administrators' choices? How can these choices be made in a more responsible manner?

CHAPTER 14

The Relationship Between Politics and Administration: The Concept of Issue Networks

The iron triangle concept is not so much wrong as it is disastrously incomplete. And the conventional view is especially inappropriate for understanding changes in politics and administration during recent years. . . . Looking for the closed triangles of control, we tend to miss the fairly open networks of people that increasingly impinge upon government.

Hugh Heclo

READING 14

Introduction

Perhaps no issue has been more controversial or more discussed in public administration since its inception as a self-conscious field of study than the appropriate relationship between the politically elected representatives of the legislature and the permanent bureaucracy of the executive branch. Indeed, as was pointed out in Chapter 1, the first essay on the subject of public administration written in the United States, "The Study of Administration," prepared by a young political scientist named Woodrow Wilson in 1887, essentially wrestled with the problem of the proper relationship between these two spheres of government: politics and administration.[1] Wilson wrote his essay at a time when civil service reform had recently been instituted in the federal government (the Pendleton Act had been passed in 1883). Wilson sought to encourage the development of the newly established merit system and the emergence of a field of academic study—public administration—because in his words, "It is getting to be harder to run a constitution than to frame one." The new complexities of government—both in terms of widening popular participation of the citizenry in democratic government and the rising technological problems of organizing public programs—created, in Wilson's view, the urgent need for developing effective administrative services free from congressional "meddling."

[1]Woodrow Wilson, "The Study of Administration," *Political Science Quarterly,* 2 (June 1887), pp. 197–222. Reprinted with permission from *Political Science Quarterly.*

Generally, the drift—both in terms of intellectual thought and institutional reform in the United States during the century after Wilson's writing—until the 1970s was toward a realization of the Wilsonian argument in favor of greater administrative independence from legislative oversight. War, international involvements, economic crises, and a host of other influences (including public administration theorists) supported the claims for administrative independence from detailed legislative control. In particular, as political scientist Allen Schick notes, three factors led to congressional acquiescence. The first factor was the massive growth in the size of government. "Big government weakened the ability of Congress to govern by controlling the details and it vested administration with more details over which to govern. In the face of bigness Congress could master the small things only by losing sight of the important issues." This was bolstered as the message of public administration theorists "that a legislature should not trespass on administrative matters inevitably registered on Congressional thinking about its appropriate role, especially because the theme was so attractively laced with the promise of order and efficiency in the public service and carried the warning that legislative intrusion would be injurious to good government."[2]

Nonpartisanship in foreign affairs also played a powerful role in checking congressional intrusion in executive affairs by conveying "the assurance that unchecked executive power would be applied benevolently in the national interest of the United States." Pluralism, a third factor in fostering congressional retreat, according to Schick, furthered administrative independence by the convincing certainty that wider administrative discretion over executive agencies would be in fact used "to provide benefits to powerful interests in society to the benefit of everyone."

In retrospect, perhaps these assumptions were naive, but they were generally accepted as truths until the early 1970s. Suddenly the abuses of Watergate, the disastrous consequences of Vietnam, the failure of numerous Great Society social programs, combined with an unusually high turnover of congressional seats, brought about a dramatic revival of congressional interest in the problems of Congress' control over executive activities. A variety of new laws were enacted to achieve more control: for example, widening the requirement of Senate approval of presidential appointees to executive offices; creation of the Congressional Budget Office to act as a legislative fiscal watchdog; the passage of the Freedom of Information Act to provide Congress and the general public with greater access to executive activities; and the War Powers Resolution, which restricted presidential initiative in foreign military involvements.

Concomitant with the rise of congressional oversight in the 1960s and 1970s, it became fashionable to argue that governmental policies emerged from *iron triangles*—three-way interactions involving elected members of Congress, particularly key committee and subcommittee chairpersons; career bureaucrats, particularly agency heads or senior staffers; and special interest lobbies, particularly powerful lobbies in specialized fields such as health, welfare, education, and defense. From this closed triad of interests, so the theory goes, governmental policies emerge by means of members of Congress writing and passing favorable legislation, bureaucrats implementing these congressional mandates in return for bigger budgets, and special-interest groups backing (with re-election monies and other support) the helpful members of Congress: in all, a tidy and closed relationship.

[2]Allen Schick, "Congress and the 'Details' of Administration," *Public Administration Review*, 36 (September/October 1976), pp. 516–528.

Is this how the political-administrative relationships in government actually work today? In the following essay, Hugh Heclo (1944–   ), currently distinguished Robinson University professor at George Mason University, takes issue with the iron triangle conception of modern political-administrative relationships. He emphasizes, "The iron triangle concept is not so much wrong as it is disastrously incomplete." "Unfortunately," writes Heclo, "our standard political conceptions of power and control are not very well suited to the loose-jointed play of influence that is emerging in political administration. We tend to look for one group exerting dominance over another, for subgovernments that are strongly insulated from other outside forces in the environment, for policies that get 'produced' by a few 'makers.'" Instead, says Heclo, in "looking for the few who are powerful, we tend to overlook the many whose webs of influence provoke and guide the exercise of power. These webs, or what I will call 'issue networks,' are particularly relevant to the highly intricate and confusing welfare policies that have been undertaken in recent years."

Note that in Heclo's view of the *issue networks,* unlike the iron triangle concept, which assumed a small identifiable circle of participants, the participants are largely shifting, fluid, and anonymous. In fact, he writes, "it is almost impossible to say where a network leaves off and its environment begins." Whereas iron triangles are seen as relatively stable groups that coalesce around narrow policy issues, Heclo's issue networks are dispersed and numerous players move in and out of the transitory networks, without anyone being clearly in control over programs or policies. Although the "iron triangles at their roots had economic gain as an interest of all parties concerned," Heclo believes "any direct material interest is often secondary to intellectual or emotional commitment involving issue networks." Passion, ideas, and moral dedication replace, to a significant degree, material and economic gain from policy involvement.

The profound influence of the rise of these issue networks on government is manifold, Heclo thinks, especially in adding new layers of complexity to government. First, networks keep issues, potentially simple to solve, complex instead, primarily to gain power and influence by virtue of their own specialized expertise. Second, rather than fostering knowledge and consensus, issue networks push for argument, division, and contention to "maintain the purity of their viewpoints," which in turn sustain support from their natural but narrow public constituencies. Third, issue networks spawn true believers who become zealots for narrow interests rather than seekers of broad mandates of consensus, support, and confidence for public programs. Finally, rather than pushing for closure of debate, issue networks thrive by keeping arguments boiling and disagreements brewing. They survive by talking, debating, and arguing the alternatives, and not by finding common grounds for agreement and getting down to making things happen.

As you read this selection, keep the following questions in mind:

How does Heclo's issue network concept differ from the notion of iron triangles as the basis for political-administrative relationships?

What examples does Heclo give to support his new conceptualization of this relationship?

Do you find his arguments reasonable and correct on the basis of your experience or your reading of the case studies in this text?

What impact does the rise of issue networks have on democratic government in general and public administration in particular?

What new roles must public administrators assume, given the growth of issue networks today? Specifically, in your opinion, how can an administrator prepare or be trained for assuming these new roles?

Issue Networks and the Executive Establishment

HUGH HECLO

The connection between politics and administration arouses remarkably little interest in the United States. The presidency is considered more glamorous, Congress more intriguing, elections more exciting, and interest groups more troublesome. General levels of public interest can be gauged by the burst of indifference that usually greets the announcement of a new President's cabinet or rumors of a political appointee's resignation. Unless there is some White House "tie-in" or scandal (preferably both), news stories about presidential appointments are usually treated by the media as routine filler material.

This lack of interest in political administration is rarely found in other democratic countries, and it has not always prevailed in the United States. In most nations the ups and downs of political executives are taken as vital signs of the health of a government, indeed of its survival. In the United States, the nineteenth-century turmoil over one type of connection between politics and administration—party spoils—frequently overwhelmed any notion of presidential leadership. Anyone reading the history of those troubled decades is likely to be struck by the way in which political administration in Washington registered many of the deeper strains in American society at large. It is a curious switch that appointments to the bureaucracy should loom so large in the history of the nineteenth century, when the federal government did little, and be so completely discounted in the

twentieth century, when government tries to do so much.

Political administration in Washington continues to register strains in American politics and society, although in ways more subtle than the nineteenth-century spoils scramble between Federalists and Democrats, Pro- and Anti-tariff forces, Nationalists and States-Righters, and so on. Unlike many other countries, the United States has never created a high level, government-wide civil service. Neither has it been favored with a political structure that automatically produces a stock of experienced political manpower for top executive positions in government.[1] How then does political administration in Washington work? More to the point, how might the expanding role of government be changing the connection between administration and politics?

Received opinion on this subject suggests that we already know the answers. Control is said to be vested in an informal but enduring series of "iron triangles" linking executive bureaus, congressional committees, and interest group clienteles with a stake in particular programs. A President or presidential appointee may occasionally try to muscle in, but few people doubt the capacity of these governments to thwart outsiders in the long run.

Based largely on early studies of agricultural, water, and public works policies, the iron triangle concept is not so much wrong as it is disastrously incomplete.[2] And the conventional view is especially inappropriate for understanding changes in politics and administration during recent years. Preoccupied with trying to find the few truly powerful actors, observers tend to overlook the power and influence that arise out

"Issue Networks and the Executive Establishment" by Hugh Heclo from *The Political System,* edited by Anthony King, 1978, pp. 87–124. Reprinted with permission of The American Enterprise Institute for Public Policy Research, Washington, D.C.

of the configurations through which leading policy makers move and do business with each other. Looking for the closed triangles of control, we tend to miss the fairly open networks of people that increasingly impinge upon government.

To do justice to the subject would require a major study of the Washington community and the combined inspiration of a Leonard White and a James Young. Tolerating a fair bit of injustice, one can sketch a few of the factors that seem to be at work. The first is growth in the sheer mass of government activity and associated expectations. The second is the peculiar, loose-jointed play of influence that is accompanying this growth. Related to these two is the third: the layering and specialization that have overtaken the government work force, not least the political leadership of the bureaucracy.

All of this vastly complicates the job of presidential appointees both in controlling their own actions and in managing the bureaucracy. But there is much more at stake than the troubles faced by people in government. There is the deeper problem of connecting what politicians, officials, and their fellow travelers are doing in Washington with what the public at large can understand and accept. It is on this point that political administration registers some of the larger strains of American politics and society, much as it did in the nineteenth century. For what it shows is a dissolving of organized politics and a politicizing of organizational life throughout the nation. . . .

Unfortunately, our standard political conceptions of power and control are not very well suited to the loose-jointed play of influence that is emerging in political administration. We tend to look for one group exerting dominance over another, for subgovernments that are strongly insulated from other outside forces in the environment, for policies that get "produced" by a few "makers." Seeing former government officials opening law firms or joining a new trade association, we naturally think of ways in which they are trying to conquer and control particular pieces of government machinery.

Obviously questions of power are still important. But for a host of policy initiatives undertaken in the last twenty years it is all but impossible to identify clearly who the dominant actors are. Who is controlling those actions that go to make up our national policy on abortions, or on income redistribution, or consumer protection, or energy? Looking for the few who are powerful, we tend to overlook the many whose webs of influence provoke and guide the exercise of power. These webs, or what I will call "issue networks," are particularly relevant to the highly intricate and confusing welfare policies that have been undertaken in recent years.

The notion of iron triangles and subgovernments presumes small circles of participants who have succeeded in becoming largely autonomous. Issue networks, on the other hand, comprise a large number of participants with quite variable degrees of mutual commitment or of dependence on others in their environment; in fact it is almost impossible to say where a network leaves off and its environment begins. Iron triangles and subgovernments suggest a stable set of participants coalesced to control fairly narrow public programs which are in the direct economic interest of each party to the alliance. Issue networks are almost the reverse image in each respect. Participants move in and out of the networks constantly. Rather than groups united in dominance over a program, no one, as far as one can tell, is in control of the policies and issues. Any direct material interest is often secondary to intellectual or emotional commitment. Network members reinforce each other's sense of issues as their interests, rather than (as standard political or economic models would have it) interests defining positions on issues.

Issue networks operate at many levels, from the vocal minority who turn up at local planning commission hearings to the renowned professor who is quietly telephoned by the White House to give a quick "reading" on some participant or policy. The price of buying into one or another issue network is watching, reading, talking about, and trying to act on particular policy problems. Powerful interest groups can be found represented in networks but so too can individuals in or out of government who have a reputation for being knowledgeable. Particular professions may be prominent, but the true experts in the networks are those who are issue-skilled (that is, well informed about the ins and outs of a particular policy debate) regardless of formal professional training. More than mere technical experts, network people are policy activists who know each other through the issues. Those who emerge to positions of wider leadership are policy politicians—experts in using experts, victuallers of knowledge in a world hungry for right decisions.

In the old days—when the primary problem of government was assumed to be doing what was right, rather than knowing what was right—policy knowledge could be contained in the slim adages of public administration. Public executives, it was thought, needed to know how to execute. They needed power commensurate with their responsibility. Nowadays, of course, political administrators do not execute but are involved in making highly important decisions on society's behalf, and they must mobilize policy intermediaries to deliver the goods. Knowing what is right becomes crucial, and since no one knows that for sure, going through the process of dealing with those who are judged knowledgeable (or at least continuously concerned) becomes even more crucial. Instead of power commensurate with responsibility, issue networks seek influence commensurate with their understanding of the various, complex social choices being made. Of course some participants would like nothing better than complete power over the issues in question. Others seem to want little more than the security that comes with being well informed. As the executive of one new group moving to Washington put it, "We didn't come here to change the world; we came to minimize our surprises."[3]

Whatever the participants' motivation, it is the issue network that ties together what would otherwise be the contradictory tendencies of, on the one hand, more widespread organizational participation in public policy and, on the other, more narrow technocratic specialization in complex modern policies. Such networks need to be distinguished from three other more familiar terms used in connection with political administration. An issue network is a shared-knowledge group having to do with some aspect (or, as defined by the network, some problem) of public policy. It is therefore more well-defined

than, first, a shared-attention group or "public"; those in the networks are likely to have a common base of information and understanding of how one knows about policy and identifies its problems. But knowledge does not necessarily produce agreement. Issue networks may or may not, therefore, be mobilized into, second, a shared-action group (creating a coalition) or, third, a shared-belief group (becoming a conventional interest organization). Increasingly, it is through networks of people who regard each other as knowledgeable, or at least as needing to be answered, that public policy issues tend to be refined, evidence debated, and alternative options worked out—though rarely in any controlled, well-organized way.

What does an issue network look like? It is difficult to say precisely, for at any given time only one part of a network may be active and through time the various connections may intensify or fade among the policy intermediaries and the executive and congressional bureaucracies. For example, there is no single health policy network but various sets of people knowledgeable and concerned about cost-control mechanisms, insurance techniques, nutritional programs, prepaid plans, and so on. At one time, those expert in designing a nationwide insurance system may seem to be operating in relative isolation, until it becomes clear that previous efforts to control costs have already created precedents that have to be accommodated in any new system, or that the issue of federal funding for abortions has laid land mines in the path of any workable plan.

The debate on energy policy is rich in examples of the kaleidoscopic interaction of changing issue networks. The Carter administration's initial proposal was worked out among experts who were closely tied in to conservation-minded networks. Soon it became clear that those concerned with macroeconomic policies had been largely bypassed in the planning, and last-minute amendments were made in the proposal presented to Congress, a fact that was not lost on the networks of leading economists and economic correspondents. Once congressional consideration began, it quickly became evident that attempts to define the energy debate in terms of a classic confrontation between big oil companies and consumer interests were doomed. More and more policy watchers joined in the debate, bringing to it their own concerns and analyses: tax reformers, nuclear power specialists, civil rights groups interested in more jobs; the list soon grew beyond the wildest dreams of the original energy policy planners. The problem, it became clear, was that no one could quickly turn the many networks of knowledgeable people into a shared-action coalition, much less into a single, shared-attitude group believing it faced the moral equivalent of war. Or, if it was a war, it was a Vietnam-type quagmire.

It would be foolish to suggest that the clouds of issue networks that have accompanied expanding national policies are set to replace the more familiar politics of subgovernments in Washington. What they are doing is to overlay the once stable political reference points with new forces that complicate calculations, decrease predictability, and impose considerable strains on those charged with government leadership. The overlay of networks and issue politics not only confronts but also seeps down into the formerly well-established politics of particular policies and programs. Social security, which for a generation had been quietly managed by a small circle of insiders, becomes controversial and politicized. The Army Corps of Engineers, once the picturebook example of control by subgovernments, is dragged into the brawl on environmental politics. The once quiet "traffic safety establishment" finds its own safety permanently endangered by the consumer movement. Confrontation between networks and iron triangles in the Social and Rehabilitation Service, the disintegration of the mighty politics of the Public Health Service and its corps—the list could be extended into a chronicle of American national government during the last generation. The point is that a somewhat new and difficult dynamic is being played out in the world of politics and administration. It is not what has been feared for so long: that technocrats and other people in white coats will expropriate the policy process. If there is to be any expropriation, it is likely to be by the policy activists, those who care deeply about a set of issues and are determined to shape the fabric of public policy accordingly. . . .

The Executive Leadership Problem

Washington has always relied on informal means of producing political leaders in government. This is no less true now than in the days when party spoils ruled presidential appointments. It is the informal mechanisms that have changed. No doubt some of the increasing emphasis on educational credentials, professional specialization, and technical facility merely reflects changes in society at large. But it is also important to recognize that government activity has itself been changing the informal mechanisms that produce political administrators. Accumulating policy commitments have become crucial forces affecting the kind of executive leadership that emerges. E. E. Schattschneider put it better when he observed that "new policies create new politics."[4]

For many years now the list of issues on the public agenda has grown more dense as new policy concerns have been added and few dropped. Administratively, this has proliferated the number of policy intermediaries. Politically, it has mobilized more and more groups of people who feel they have a stake, a determined stake, in this or that issue of public policy. These changes are in turn encouraging further specialization of the government's work force and bureaucratic layering in its political leadership. However, the term "political" needs to be used carefully. Modern officials responsible for making the connection between politics and administration bear little resemblance to the party politicians who once filled patronage jobs. Rather, today's political executive is likely to be a person knowledgeable about the substance of particular issues and adept at moving among the networks of people who are intensely concerned about them.

What are the implications for American government and politics? The verdict cannot be one-sided, if only because political management of the bureaucracy serves a number of diverse purposes. At least three important advantages can be found in the emerging system.

First, the reliance on issue networks and policy politicians is obviously consistent with some of the larger changes in society. Ordinary voters are apparently less constrained by party identification and more attracted to an issue-based style of politics. Party organizations are said to have fallen into a state of decay and to have become less capable of supplying enough highly qualified executive manpower. If government is committed to intervening in more complex, specialized areas, it is useful to draw upon the experts and policy specialists for the public management of these programs. Moreover, the congruence between an executive leadership and an electorate that are both uninterested in party politics may help stabilize a rapidly changing society. Since no one really knows how to solve the policy puzzles, policy politicians have the important quality of being disposable without any serious political ramifications (unless of course there are major symbolic implications, as in President Nixon's firing of Attorney General Elliot Richardson).

Within government, the operation of issue networks may have a second advantage in that they link Congress and the executive branch in ways that political parties no longer can. For many years, reformers have sought to revive the idea of party discipline as a means of spanning the distance between the two branches and turning their natural competition to useful purposes. But as the troubled dealings of recent Democratic Presidents with their majorities in Congress have indicated, political parties tend to be a weak bridge.

Meanwhile, the linkages of technocracy between the branches are indeliberately growing. The congressional bureaucracy that has blossomed in Washington during the last generation is in many ways like the political bureaucracy in the executive branch. In general, the new breed of congressional staffer is not a legislative crony or beneficiary of patronage favors. Personal loyalty to the congressman is still paramount, but the new-style legislative bureaucrat is likely to be someone skilled in dealing with certain complex policy issues, possibly with credentials as a policy analyst, but certainly an expert in using other experts and their networks.

None of this means an absence of conflict between President and Congress. Policy technicians in the two branches are still working for different sets of clients with different interests. The point is that the growth of specialized policy networks tends to perform the same useful services that it was once hoped a disciplined national party system would perform. Sharing policy knowledge, the networks provide a minimum common framework for political debate and decision in the two branches. For example, on energy policy, regardless of one's position on gas deregulation or incentives to producers, the policy technocracy has established a common language for discussing the issues, a shared grammar for identifying the major points of contention, a mutually familiar rhetoric of argumentation. Whether in Congress or the executive branch or somewhere outside, the "movers and shakers" in energy policy (as in health insurance, welfare reform, strategic arms limitation, occupational safety, and a host of other policy areas) tend to share an analytic repertoire for coping with the issues. Like experienced party politicians of earlier times, policy politicians in the knowledge networks may not agree; but they understand each other's way of looking at the world and arguing about policy choices.

A third advantage is the increased maneuvering room offered to political executives by the loose-jointed play of influence. If appointees were ambassadors from clearly defined interest groups and professions, or if policy were monopolized in iron triangles, then the chances for executive leadership in the bureaucracy would be small. In fact, however, the proliferation of administrative middlemen and networks of policy watchers offers new strategic resources for public managers. These are mainly opportunities to split and recombine the many sources of support and opposition that exist on policy issues. Of course, there are limits on how far a political executive can go in shopping for a constituency, but the general tendency over time has been to extend those limits. A secretary of labor will obviously pay close attention to what the AFL-CIO has to say, but there are many other voices to hear, not only in the union movement but also minority groups interested in jobs, state and local officials administering the department's programs, consumer groups worried about wage-push inflation, employees faced with unsafe working conditions, and so on. By the same token, former Secretary of Transportation William Coleman found new room for maneuver on the problem of landings by supersonic planes when he opened up the setpiece debate between pro- and anti-Concorde groups to a wider play of influence through public hearings. Clearly the richness of issue politics demands a high degree of skill to contain expectations and manage the natural dissatisfaction that comes from courting some groups rather than others. But at least it is a game that can be affected by skill, rather than one that is predetermined by immutable forces.

These three advantages are substantial. But before we embrace the rule of policy politicians and their networks, it is worth considering the threats they pose for American government. Issue networks may be good at influencing policy, but can they govern? Should they?

The first and foremost problem is the old one of democratic legitimacy. Weaknesses in executive leadership below the level of the President have never really been due to interest groups, party politics, or Congress. The primary problem has always been the lack of any democratically based power. Political executives get their popular mandate to do anything in the bureaucracy secondhand, from either an elected chief executive or Congress. The emerging system of political technocrats makes this democratic weakness much more severe. The more closely political administrators become identified with the various specialized policy networks, the farther they become separated from the ordinary citizen. Political executives can maneuver among the already mobilized issue networks and may occasionally do a little mobilizing of their own. But this is not the same thing as creating a broad base of public understanding and support for national policies. The typical presidential appointee will travel to any number of conferences, make speeches to the membership of one association after another, but almost never will he or she have to see or listen to an ordinary member of the public. The trouble is that only a small minority of citizens, even of those who are seriously attentive to public affairs, are likely to be mobilized in the various networks.[5] Those who are not policy activists depend

on the ability of government institutions to act on their behalf.

If the problem were merely an information gap between policy experts and the bulk of the population, then more communication might help. Yet instead of garnering support for policy choices, more communication from the issue networks tends to produce an "everything causes cancer" syndrome among ordinary citizens. Policy forensics among the networks yield more experts making more sophisticated claims and counterclaims to the point that the nonspecialist becomes inclined to concede everything and believe nothing that he hears. The ongoing debates on energy policy, health crises, or arms limitation are rich in examples of public skepticism about what "they," the abstruse policy experts, are doing and saying. While the highly knowledgeable have been playing a larger role in government, the proportion of the general public concluding that those running the government don't seem to know what they are doing has risen rather steadily.[6] Likewise, the more government has tried to help, the more feelings of public helplessness have grown.

No doubt many factors and events are linked to these changing public attitudes. The point is that the increasing prominence of issue networks is bound to aggravate problems of legitimacy and public disenchantment. Policy activists have little desire to recognize an unpleasant fact: that their influential systems for knowledgeable policy making tend to make democratic politics more difficult. There are at least four reasons.

Complexity

Democratic political competition is based on the idea of trying to simplify complexity into a few, broadly intelligible choices. The various issue networks, on the other hand, have a stake in searching out complexity in what might seem simple. Those who deal with particular policy issues over the years recognize that policy objectives are usually vague and results difficult to measure. Actions relevant to one policy goal can frequently be shown to be inconsistent with others. To gain a reputation as a knowledgeable participant, one must juggle all of these complexities and demand that other technocrats in the issue networks do the same.

Consensus

A major aim in democratic politics is, after open argument, to arrive at some workable consensus of views. Whether by trading off one issue against another or by combining related issues, the goal is agreement. Policy activists may commend this democratic purpose in theory, but what their issue networks actually provide is a way of processing dissension. The aim is good policy—the right outcome on the issue. Since what that means is disputable among knowledgeable people, the desire for agreement must often take second place to one's understanding of the issue. Trade-offs or combinations—say, right-to-life groups with nuclear-arms-control people; environmentalists and consumerists; civil liberties groups and anti-gun controllers—represent a kind of impurity for many of the newly proliferating groups. In general there are few imperatives pushing for political consensus among the issue networks and many rewards for those who become practiced in the techniques of informed skepticism about different positions.

Confidence

Democratic politics presumes a kind of psychological asymmetry between leaders and followers. Those competing for leadership positions are expected to be sure of themselves and of what is to be done, while those led are expected to have a certain amount of detachment and dubiety in choosing how to give their consent to be governed. Politicians are supposed to take credit for successes, to avoid any appearance of failure, and to fix blame clearly on their opponents; voters weight these claims and come to tentative judgments, pending the next competition among the leaders.

The emerging policy networks tend to reverse the situation. Activists mobilized around the policy issues are the true believers. To survive, the newer breed of leaders, or policy politicians, must become well versed in the complex, highly disputed substance of the issues. A certain tentativeness comes naturally as ostensible leaders try to spread themselves across the issues. Taking credit shows a lack of understanding of how intricate policies work and may antagonize those who really have been zealously pushing the issue. Spreading blame threatens others in the established networks and may raise expectations that new leadership can guarantee a better policy result. Vagueness about what is to be done allows policy problems to be dealt with as they develop and in accord with the intensity of opinion among policy specialists at that time. None of this is likely to warm the average citizen's confidence in his leaders. The new breed of policy politicians are cool precisely because the issue networks are hot.

Closure

Part of the genius of democratic politics is its ability to find a nonviolent decision-rule (by voting) for ending debate in favor of action. All the incentives in the policy technocracy work against such decisive closure. New studies and findings can always be brought to bear. The biggest rewards in these highly intellectual groups go to those who successfully challenge accepted wisdom. The networks thrive by continuously weighing alternative courses of action on particular policies, not by suspending disbelief and accepting that something must be done.

For all of these reasons, what is good for policy making (in the sense of involving well-informed people and rigorous analysts) may be bad for democratic politics. The emerging policy technocracy tends, as Henry Aaron has said of social science research, to "corrode any simple faiths around which political coalitions ordinarily are built."[7] Should we be content with simple faiths? Perhaps not; but the great danger is that the emerging world of issue politics and policy experts will turn John Stuart Mill's argument about the connection between liberty and popular government on its head. More informed argument about policy choices may produce more incomprehensibility. More policy intermediaries may widen participation among activists but deepen suspicions among unorganized nonspecialists. There may be more group involvement and less democratic legiti- macy, more knowledge and more Know-Nothingism. Activists are likely to remain unsatisfied with, and nonactivists uncommitted to, what government is doing. Superficially this canceling of forces might seem to assure a conservative tilt away from new, ex- pansionary government policies. However, in terms of undermining a democratic identification of ordi- nary citizens with their government, the tendencies are profoundly radical.

A second difficulty with the issue networks is the problem that they create for the President as ostensi- ble chief of the executive establishment. The emerg- ing policy technocracy puts presidential appointees outside of the chief executive's reach in a way that narrowly focused iron triangles rarely can. At the end of the day, constituents of these triangles can at least be bought off by giving them some of the ma- terial advantages that they crave. But for issue ac- tivists it is likely to be a question of policy choices that are right or wrong. In this situation, more analy- sis and staff expertise—far from helping—may only hinder the President in playing an independent po- litical leadership role. The influence of the policy technicians and their networks permeates every- thing the White House may want to do. Without their expertise there are no option papers, no de- tailed data and elaborate assessments to stand up against the onslaught of the issue experts in Con- gress and outside. Of course a President can replace a political executive, but that is probably merely to substitute one incumbent of the relevant policy net- work for another.

It is, therefore, no accident that President Carter found himself with a cabinet almost none of whom were either his longstanding political backers or lead- ers of his party. Few if any of his personal retinue could have passed through the reputational screens of the networks to be named, for example, a secretary of labor or defense. Moreover, anyone known to be close to the President and placed in an operating po- sition in the bureaucracy puts himself, and through him the President, in an extremely vulnerable posi- tion. Of the three cabinet members who were Presi- dent Carter's own men, one, Andrew Young, was under extreme pressure to resign in the first several

months. Another Carter associate, Bert Lance, was successfully forced to resign after six months, and the third, Griffin Bell, was given particularly tough treat- ment during his confirmation hearings and was being pressured to resign after only a year in office. The emerging system of political administration tends to produce executive arrangements in which the Presi- dent's power stakes are on the line almost every- where in terms of policy, whereas almost nowhere is anyone on the line for him personally.

Where does all this leave the President as a politi- cian and as an executive of executives? In an impos- sible position. The problem of connecting politics and administration currently places any President in a classic no-win predicament. If he attempts to use per- sonal loyalists as agency and department heads, he will be accused of politicizing the bureaucracy and will most likely put his executives in an untenable po- sition for dealing with their organizations and the re- lated networks. If he tries to create a countervailing source of policy expertise at the center, he will be ac- cused of aggrandizing the Imperial Presidency and may hopelessly bureaucratize the White House's op- erations. If he relies on some benighted idea of col- lective cabinet government and on departmental executives for leadership in the bureaucracy (as Carter did in his first term), then the President does more than risk abdicating his own leadership responsibilities as the only elected executive in the national government; he is bound to become a creature of the issue networks and the policy specialists. It would be pleasant to think that there is a neat way out of this trilemma, but there is not.

Finally, there are disturbing questions surrounding the accountability of a political technocracy. The real problem is not that policy specialists specialize but that, by the nature of public office, they must gener- alize. Whatever an influential political executive does is done with all the collective authority of government and in the name of the public at large. It is not diffi- cult to imagine situations in which policies make ex- cellent sense within the cloisters of the expert issue watchers and yet are nonsense or worse seen from the viewpoint of ordinary people, the kinds of people po- litical executives rarely meet. Since political execu- tives themselves never need to pass muster with the electorate, the main source of democratic accountability must lie with the President and Congress. Given the President's problems and Congress's own burgeoning bureaucracy of policy specialists, the prospects for a democratically responsible executive establishment are poor at best.

Perhaps we need not worry. A case could be made that all we are seeing is a temporary commotion stirred up by a generation of reformist policies. In time the policy process may reenter a period of detumescence as the new groups and networks subside into the familiar triangulations of power.

However, a stronger case can be made that the changes will endure. In the first place, sufficient policy-making forces have now converged in Washington that it is unlikely that we will see a return to the familiar cycle of federal quiescence and policy experimentation by state governments. The central government, surrounded by networks of policy specialists, probably now has the capacity for taking continual policy initiatives. In the second place, there seems to be no way of braking, much less reversing, policy expectations generated by the compensatory mentality. To cut back on commitments undertaken in the last generation would itself be a major act of redistribution and could be expected to yield even more turmoil in the policy process. Once it becomes accepted that relative rather than absolute deprivation is what matters, the crusaders can always be counted upon to be in business.

A third reason why our politics and administration may never be the same lies in the very fact that so many policies have already been accumulated. Having to make policy in an environment already crowded with public commitments and programs increases the odds of multiple, indirect impacts of one policy on another, of one perspective set in tension with another, of one group and then another being mobilized. This sort of complexity and unpredictability creates a hostile setting for any return to traditional interest group politics.

Imagine trying to govern in a situation where the short-term political resources you need are stacked around a changing series of discrete issues, and where people overseeing these issues have nothing to prevent their pressing claims beyond any resources that they can offer in return. Imagine too that the more they do so, the more you lose understanding and support from public backers who have the long-term resources that you need. Whipsawed between cynics and true believers, policy would always tend to evolve to levels of insolubility. It is not easy for a society to politicize itself and at the same time depoliticize government leadership. But we in the United States may be managing to do just this.

Notes

1. Hugh Heclo, *A Government of Strangers: Executive Politics in Washington* (Washington, D.C.: Brookings Institution, 1977).
2. Perhaps the most widely cited interpretations are J. Leiper Freeman, *The Political Process* (New York: Random House, 1965); and Douglass Cater, *Power in Washington* (New York: Vintage, 1964)
3. Steven V. Roberts, "Trade Associations Flocking to Capital as U.S. Role Rises," *New York Times,* March 4, 1978, p. 44.
4. E. E. Schattschneider, *Politics, Pressures and the Tariff* (Hamden: Archon, 1963), p. 288 (originally published 1935).
5. An interesting recent case study showing the complexity of trying to generalize about who is "mobilizable" is James N. Rosenau, *Citizenship Between Elections* (New York: The Free Press, 1974).
6. Since 1964 the Institute for Social Research at the University of Michigan has asked the question, "Do you feel that almost all of the people running the government are smart people, or do you think that quite a few of them don't seem to know what they are doing?" The proportions choosing the latter view have been 28 percent (1964), 38 percent (1968), 45 percent (1970), 42 percent (1972), 47 percent (1974), and 52 percent (1976). For similar findings on public feelings of lack of control over the policy process, see U.S. Congress, Senate, Subcommittee on Intergovernmental Relations of the Committee on

Government Operations, *Confidence and Concern: Citizens View American Government,* committee print, 93d Cong., 1st sess., 1973, pt. 1, p. 30. For a more complete discussion of recent trends see the two articles by Arthur H.

Miller and Jack Citrin in the *American Political Science Review* (September 1974).

7. Henry J. Aaron, *Politics and the Professors* (Washington, D.C.: Brookings Institution, 1978), p. 159.

☐ CASE STUDY 14

Introduction

Professor Heclo in the foregoing reading advances an important conceptualization, or rather reconceptualization, of political-administrative relationships, which some scholars suggest are central to the problems confronting modern public administration. However, from the standpoint of the practitioner of public administration, what skills and attributes are most critical for individuals working within high-level policy making arenas? What characteristics are evident in those civil servants who perform well in top political-administrative positions? Are there special human abilities to be found in public officials who effectively do their jobs where politics and administration intersect?

The following case study is from a recent book, *The Politics of Fat,* by Laura Sims, Professor of Human Nutrition at the University of Maryland, College Park and a former administrator of the U.S. Department of Agriculture's Human Nutrition Information Service. Her case recounts how the half-century-old National School Lunch Program, which had as its original goal to feed malnourished school children while supporting farmers, was transformed in the 1990s into a new kind of program promoting sound nutrition for youth. By exploring the process of this program's "reinvention," Dr. Sims affords us a rare insider glimpse behind the scenes, showing how various health and consumer advocates came into play to support this change, along with those who wanted to keep the program running the way it was originally set up, especially the American School Food Service Association and other local school administration groups. The author calls these groups "advocacy coalitions," which is different terminology but means much the same thing that Hugh Heclo refers to in the foregoing essay on "issue networks." Dr. Sims not only gives excellent insights into how these networks actually operate within this particular policy arena, but also emphasizes the central role of a "policy entrepreneur," Ellen Haas, the USDA's Undersecretary for Food, Nutrition, and Consumer Services, as well as the broader changing external political environment for creating this new agenda issue, building support for its adoption, and making the policy change ultimately happen.

As you read "Reinventing School Lunch," try to think about the following questions:

Who was specifically involved, pro *and* con, within this issue network? And why?

What most influenced the policy reform—the political strength of its advocates? Weakness of the opposition? The effective leadership of Ellen Haas? The broad changes in the external political environment? Or what?

After carefully studying this case, do you think that it supports Heclo's thesis, or not, concerning the way that public policy is developed within American government today?

Reinventing School Lunch: Transforming a Food Policy into a Nutrition Policy

LAURA S. SIMS

The largest and the oldest of all child nutrition and food assistance programs is the National School Lunch Program, permanently authorized in 1946 through the National School Lunch Act and created by Congress as "a measure of national security, to safeguard the health and well-being of the Nation's children and to encourage the domestic consumption of nutritious agricultural commodities and other food." That same premise—feeding schoolchildren while supporting agriculture—remains a grounding principle for the National School Lunch Program today but also has served as the basis for rancorous disputes and conflicting policies regarding its operation.

Administered at the federal level by the U.S. Department of Agriculture's (USDA's) Food and Consumer Service (FCS) (formerly named the Food and Nutrition Service [FNS]), the National School Lunch Program is administered at the state level by the state department of education and usually at the local level by the school district administration. All public schools are automatically eligible to participate in the program, and it is voluntary in private schools. Almost all public schools (99 percent) and the majority of private schools (83 percent) in the nation do participate in the National School Lunch Program— over 93,000 schools in fiscal year 1996, according to the USDA.

Even though the NSLP is available to about 92 percent of all students, only 56 percent actually participate, and participation is much greater in elementary schools than in secondary schools. In 1992, 25 million children participated in the NSLP each day, at a cost to the government of $4.1 billion.

Schools that elect to participate in the NSLP get both federal cash subsidies and donated agricultural commodities from the USDA for each meal served. The NSLP currently operates as an "entitlement,"

"Reinventing School Lunch: Transforming a Food Policy into a Nutrition Policy," by Laura S. Sims from *The Politics of Fat: Food and Nutrition Policy in America* (Armonk, NY: M. E. Sharpe, 1998) pp. 67–89. Reprinted by permission of M. E. Sharpe.

meaning that federal funds must be provided to all schools that apply and meet the program's eligibility criteria. A three-tiered reimbursement system is used to calculate benefits the school district receives, as follows: children from households with incomes at or below 130 percent of poverty receive free meals; those between 130 percent and 185 percent of poverty receive reduced-price meals; and those above 185 percent of poverty pay for a "full-price" meal. Federal subsidies to each school district are based on the number of children from each of the above groups (even those who are paying full price) who participate in the school feeding program. In 1993, free, reduced-price, and full-price meal subsidies to school districts were $1.695, $1.295, and $0.1625, respectively. Average full prices for lunches ranged from $1.11 in elementary schools to $1.22 in middle and high schools. Severe-need schools (defined as those providing at least 40 percent free meals, with higher costs than the regular rate) are eligible to receive additional assistance of $0.02 per meal served. Current estimates show that over half of all participating children receive either free or reduced-price lunches.

The original 1946 legislation that created the National School Lunch Program set the standard for the kinds of foods that were to be offered to schoolchildren participating in the program. Until recently, these requirements were based on a standard "meal pattern" for all school lunches. The traditional school lunch, offered to children for half a century, was required to include the following foods:

1/2 pint fluid milk

2 ounces protein (meat, fish, 2 eggs, 4 tablespoons peanut butter, or 1 cup dry beans or peas)

3/4-cup serving consisting of two or more vegetables or fruits or both (juice can meet half of this requirement)

8 servings of bread, pasta, or grain per week

This meal pattern reflects a goal that, over the period of one week, children will receive at least one-third of the recommended dietary allowances (RDA) (a standard set to meet the amounts of nutrients needed by groups of healthy people) for basic nutrients, such as protein, vitamins, and minerals. USDA studies show that low-income children depend upon the NSLP to provide up to one-third to one-half of their total daily nutrient intake.

Policy Issues at Work in the National School Lunch Program

When the National School Lunch Program was established in the mid-1940s, the dietary concerns were not the same as they are today. Formulators of that original bill were worried about nutrient deficiencies and making sure that young people received *enough* food to be well nourished. Today, however, concerns are in the opposite direction: obesity among schoolchildren has reached an all-time high. The Dietary Guidelines for Americans, a document first released by both the U.S. Departments of Agriculture and Health and Human Services in 1980, serves as the basis for all nutrition policy. The third edition of that document (published in 1990) was the first to quantify the recommendation for dietary fat; its text suggested that healthy people (over the age of 2) should consume no more than 30 percent of their calories as fat. As explained in more depth later, studies had indicated that school lunches were failing to meet this criterion. Thus, a policy dilemma arises when a major USDA program—such as the NSLP—is not following policy guidelines issued by the same federal department!

Another major policy issue emanates from the initial two-pronged policy objectives for the National School Lunch Program—providing nutritious lunches for children while at the same time providing a ready outlet for agricultural commodities. Can the USDA be friend to both farmer and health professional? Can a food program also be a nutrition and health program? (Those who answer in the affirmative cite the phenomenal success of the "WIC" Program [the Supplemental Nutrition Program for *W*omen, *I*nfants, and *C*hildren], where targeted supplemental food has been shown to produce documented health benefits.)

This policy dilemma is captured directly in the controversy over using agricultural commodities in the National School Lunch Program. Those who favor their use cite economic reasons—that it is simply good business not to be wasteful but to use any surplus foods to feed hungry children. (In fact, according to one USDA estimate, if donated food commodities had not been used in 1987, the costs of the NSLP would have been $880 million higher than its actual cash costs.) Those who oppose the use of commodity products in school meals cite the fact that a number of these products (notably, processed cheese, peanut butter, processed meat, and the like) provide higher levels of dietary fat, cholesterol, sugar, and sodium than are suitable for children.

To receive federal benefits for running the National School Lunch Program, the school district agrees to abide by the rules and follow the requirements for participation. This means that in order to accept cash subsidies to run the NSLP, the school district must also agree to accept various donated agricultural commodities, the value of which is estimated to be between 15 percent to 20 percent of the cash outlay for the NSLP. Both "entitlement commodities," valued at about 14 cents a meal, and "bonus" commodities are available to school food service managers. These donated foods are essentially "free" to the school food authority; the other 80 percent of the food must be purchased locally. Therein lies the dilemma—local school food service managers often feel that if they choose not to accept the donated commodities, they run the risk of pricing themselves out of an ability to provide free and reduced-price lunches to the children who need them.

Recognizing that some products are especially high in fat (and particularly saturated fat), the USDA has recently made a concerted effort to cut back on the amount of dietary fat in surplus commodities donated to schools. Low-fat beef patties are a good example of this initiative. In the early 1990s (the first years these alternative low-fat products were offered), they made up only 5 percent of the total ground beef used in the program. School lunch managers, already operating under tight financial constraints and recognizing that children will eat only those foods with which they are familiar, are reluctant to use the new lower-fat products for fear of operating at a deficit. This aspect of running the NSLP was dramatically captured in the title of an article that appeared in the *Washington Post,* "Dissing the Salmon: Schools Can't Sell USDA's Delicacies," which described a situation in which the USDA had been able to purchase millions of pounds of flaked salmon and over a million pounds of frozen asparagus for distribution to schools, only to learn that the children refused to eat the food!

Advocacy Coalitions at Work in the National School Lunch Program

The policy subsystems at work in the National School Lunch Program are vast. The web of interest groups, consumer advocacy groups, and professional associations interested in the National School Lunch Program is as complex as it is dedicated. Those systems starting with the legislative and regulatory aspects of the program as well as those dealing with the implementation of the NSLP span the range from those who produce, process, and deliver the food to school administrators and school food service personnel, to cafeteria workers who prepare and serve the food, to advocacy groups and professional organizations that are interested in the delivery of government-sponsored food assistance programs, to parents and caregivers, and finally to the children who actually participate in the program. With a program that has existed for fifty years and is so prominently remembered by most adults in this country, it is no surprise that an entire industry has built up over the years to lobby for and to implement the NSLP.

The variety and array of agencies, legislative committees, media, interest groups, consumer advocacy groups, and professional associations that have built up around the issue of the National School Lunch Program are vast indeed. In the executive branch of government, the U.S. Department of Agriculture has had primary responsibility for the administration of this program since its creation in 1946. More recently, the School Lunch Program has been given a more prominent role as a key domestic policy area by the White House—i.e., the Executive Office of the President—both in welfare reform and in agriculture policy.

Within the Congress, two major types of committees exist that influence both the reauthorization of the program and its operation: the authorizing committees and the appropriations committees. The authorizing committee responsible for the NSLP in the House of Representatives was the Education and Labor Committee, reconfigured and renamed for the 104th Congress as the Economic and Educational Opportunities Committee. In addition, the House Committee on Agriculture—with its Subcommittee on Departmental Operations, Nutrition, and Foreign Agriculture—has played a key role in oversight of the operation of the NSLP. In the Senate, the Agriculture, Nutrition, and Forestry Committee has retained authorizing responsibility for the National School Lunch Program. Appropriations committees in each house of Congress—the Agriculture Appropriations Subcommittee in the House and the Agriculture, Rural Development, and Related Agencies Appropriations Subcommittee in the Senate—have final authority to approve the amount of money appropriated for the operation of the program. Thus, while an "education" committee in the House authorizes the program, an "agriculture" subcommittee actually approves the funding.

In November 1994, Republicans assumed control of both houses of Congress after a hiatus of forty years. The committee structure and leadership changed dramatically, resulting in changing roles and responsibilities for numerous legislators. A number of Republican legislators found themselves cast in the role of downsizing or even eliminating those very programs of which they were once personally very supportive. One example of this dilemma was William F. Goodling (R-Pennsylvania), whose personal story was chronicled in a detailed *Washington Post* article. Representative Goodling, chairman of the House Economic and Educational Opportunities Committee, was quoted as saying, "I have long defended some of these programs, especially the school lunch program. But, that doesn't mean that school lunch or any of the other food and nutrition programs cannot be improved. And we are under the mandate from the Republican Caucus and in the Contract with America, to make some changes." Other GOP members in the House publicly described their ideological dilemma—while they remained supportive of nutrition programs, they were committed to giving state governments greater flexibility and less paperwork in the administration of the programs.

A vast network of groups in the private sector exists to actively influence the operation of the NSLP. A group's interest in the program stems primarily from the base concern of the organization. If an organization mainly represents food or agricultural commodity interests, it will be far more concerned about commodity specifications, cost considerations, transportation, food storage and safety issues, and other matters related to the food offered to children in schools. These organizations range from agriculture production groups such as the Farmers Union to commodity-specific organizations, such as the National Cattlemen's Beef Association, the National Dairy Council, the United Fresh Fruit and Vegetable Association, and the National Wholesale Grocers' Association.

If the organization represents health and nutrition professionals, it will more likely be concerned with issues such as the nutritional quality of the meals served, whether the children are learning good nutritional and health practices, and personnel issues such as whether credentialed professionals are providing the needed services. Professional associations—such as the American Dietetic Association (ADA) (with nearly 70,000 members), the American Public Health Association (APHA), and smaller groups of professionals such as the Society for Nutrition Education (SNE) and the National Association of State Nutrition Education and Training Program Coordinators (NASNET)—are active in monitoring changes to the NSLP. Most active, however, in representing its members' vested interests regarding the administration of the NSLP is the American School Food Service Association (ASFSA), which has over 65,000 members.

Large organizations with specific targeted purposes such as the ASFSA have the resources to mount effective lobbying efforts, being able both to operate at the "grassroots" level and to hire well-trained, well-connected lobbyists in Washington. In this regard, the ASFSA has long retained the services of a well-known lobbyist in Washington circles, Marshall Matz, a lawyer who boasts a long record of key bipartisan accomplishments with various food and nutrition programs. In addition, the ASFSA has a "government relations" manager on its own staff to organize and coordinate the organization's lobbying efforts (incidentally, the person who most recently held this position was a key staff member for a member of Congress who was on the NSLP authorizing committee). The approaches and effectiveness of the American School Food Service Association's lobbying efforts as the organization has sought to influence key regulatory and legislative changes proposed for the National School Lunch Program are key to this case study.

Consumer advocacy organizations certainly are concerned about many similar issues, but their focus is usually on the recipients of program services—that is, whether entitled children are receiving access to the program and whether the program is meeting the needs of poor and disadvantaged groups. Other consumer groups have focused on the internal, "qualitative" aspects of the menus served in the NSLP,

concerned primarily with the nutritional value of the food served. An example of the first type of organization is the Food Research and Action Center (FRAC), which has focused its efforts on the "access" issue for low-income children, while groups such as Public Voice for Food and Health Policy and the Center for Science in the Public Interest (CSPI) have mounted an extensive effort (primarily via the media) to inform the public about the nutritional quality of the meals offered in the School Lunch Program.

A number of coalitions have also been formed whose activities focus on the NSLP. The Child Nutrition Forum, organized and administered by the FRAC, consists of a number of child advocacy organizations, public interest groups, and professional associations; its focus is to bring these various groups together to draw legislative and media attention to access issues involving participation of low-income children in child nutrition programs, including school lunch, school breakfast, and other child care feeding programs. A more recently formed, but short-lived, coalition was Advocates for Better Children's Diets (A-B-C-D). Included among its members were many of the same organizations that are in the Child Nutrition Forum, but the group also included trade associations, such as the American Soy Association. Those unfamiliar with this issue may question why such a group would want to be involved in a coalition that seeks to influence the operation of the School Lunch Program. Texturized vegetable protein (made from soy) is a key ingredient of ground beef patties served to schoolchildren as one measure to reduce the dietary fat in the School Lunch Program. Therefore, this product can be promoted in efforts to improve the "quality" (i.e., reduce the fat content) of the school lunch meals.

Specialized media also play a role in the web of groups that comprise the School Lunch Program's policy subsystem by informing both the internal and external groups about the activities going on in Washington related to the program. For example, the American School Food Service Association publishes two periodicals, the *School Lunch Journal* and the *School Food Service Research Review*. Published twice annually, the latter publication, which is designed primarily for the academic reader, contains articles that feature evaluation and research conducted on the School Lunch Program. Coalitions and advocacy groups also use publications as a means of disseminating their message and often develop "media kits" to inform the public via the print and visual media.

Documenting the Need for Policy Changes in the National School Lunch Program

A substantive factual research base is often required to define the nature of policy changes that may be needed. Older program evaluation reports, authorized and funded by the USDA, had focused on the nutritional content of the school meals but had limited their analysis to those nutrients identified in the original 1946 legislation. Times were much different at the close of World War II, and the goals of the School Lunch Program were aimed primarily at assuring that undernourished children would receive adequate food with sufficient calories, vitamins, and minerals. Using data from the Survey of Food Consumption in Low-Income Households, 1977–78, researchers in the early 1980s gave high grades to the NSLP. Students participating in the School Lunch Program had higher nutrient intakes than nonparticipants, especially for protein and most vitamins and minerals, but not for calories, iron, magnesium, and vitamin B-6.

Using data collected between 1979 and 1983, the USDA's Food and Nutrition Service, under contract with the System Development Corporation in Santa Monica, California, conducted the National Evaluation of School Nutrition Programs. The study concluded that children who participated in the School Lunch Program received more of almost all nutrients examined than nonparticipants. The positive impact of school lunch on energy intakes as well as vitamins A and B-6 were noted, although the program did not improve children's intakes of iron and vitamin C. It must be noted that these evaluations focused mainly on assessing calories, vitamins, and minerals, according to the criterion for meeting one-third of the RDA for those nutrients as specified in the 1946 legislation that established the program.

What was needed, of course, was a current analysis of the nutritional content of school meals reflective of the macronutrient content, such as fat. No longer were micronutrients, such as most vitamins and minerals, of major health concern, and the older evaluations did not provide much usable data on those nutrients shown to be associated with the development of debilitating chronic diseases, such as fat, cholesterol, and sodium. In the late 1980s and early 1990s, the only data available on the fat content of school lunches were those collected by consumer advocacy organizations as a result of conducting their own surveys. The Center for Science in the Public Interest in its "White Paper on School Lunch Nutrition" showcased the results of its analyses of lunches from three school programs. In two of the programs, they found an average of 42 percent of calories from fat, and lunches from the third program contained 41 percent of calories from fat when whole milk was served and 35 percent when skim milk was served.

Another organization that was prominent in showcasing problems with the National School Lunch Program was Public Voice for Food and Health Policy, founded by Ellen Haas in 1983. In 1988, after reviewing menus from fifty school districts nationwide, Public Voice asserted that "many schools have pumped their menus with high-fat commodities contributed from farm surpluses, such as butter, cheese, eggs, and processed foods—[thus] cutting food costs but also cutting dietary value." At a press conference, Ellen Haas publicly went on record as suggesting that "the program is run more as an agricultural support program than a nutritional program."

These first efforts to publicly expose the types of meals fed to schoolchildren as part of the National School Lunch Program were followed by a series of four reports issued by Public Voice—"What's for Lunch? A Progress Report on Reducing Fat in the School Lunch Program," in 1989; "What's for Lunch? II: A 1990 Survey of Options in the School Lunch Program"; "Heading for a Health Crisis: Eating Patterns of America's School Children," in 1991; and "Agriculture First: Nutrition, Commodities and the National School Lunch Program," in 1992. Most of these reports carried a common theme—that USDA administrators were placing higher priority on distributing agricultural commodities than on providing nutritious school lunches. Recommendations were usually targeted both to Congress to reform dairy policies and to the USDA to reform its commodity distribution practices to encourage the purchase of lower-fat dairy, meat, and poultry products and to expand the availability of fresh fruits and vegetables. The 1991 report, in particular, was notable because it was followed by a response from then USDA Secretary Edward Madigan, who publicly "pledged to take steps to reduce the fat content of meals provided by the National School Lunch Program, [thus] bringing their nutritive content into compliance with federal dietary guidelines by 1994."

The data needed to reform the National School Lunch Program were actually collected as part of a study initiated during the George Bush administration by former USDA Secretary Madigan, who was also personally committed to improving the nutritional quality of the meals served in the School Lunch Program. This study, the School Nutrition Dietary Assessment Study, was conducted by Mathematica Policy Research, under contract with the USDA's Food and Nutrition Service. The study collected meal information from a nationally representative sample of 545 schools and 3,350 students in May 1992. A most significant finding was that for the first time, the amount of dietary fat in school lunches was documented, and the results showed just how different the amounts of macronutrients were in school lunches compared to the amounts recommended in the Dietary Guidelines. School lunches provided much more dietary fat (38 percent, compared to the Dietary Guidelines' recommendation of 30 percent), saturated fat (15 percent, compared to 10 percent), and sodium (1,479 mg, compared to 800 mg). Further, less than 5 percent of the 515 schools sampled offered school lunches that were close to the Dietary Guidelines' recommendation for fat. On the positive side, however, school lunches were providing one-third or more of the daily recommended dietary allowances for calories; protein; vitamins A, C, and B-6; and the minerals iron, zinc, and calcium. Thus, this study confirmed what many health professionals and nutritionists had long suspected—the NSLP does a good job of providing at least one-third of the RDA for many nutrients, but the meals contained far too much fat, saturated fat, cholesterol, and sodium.

One of the concerns reported was that those schools that offered low-fat (32 percent or less of calories) meals showed a 6 percent lower participation rate than other schools. The report noted, however, that NSLP participation rates in schools offering meals that were in the range of 32 to 35 percent of calories from fat were similar to participation rates in schools where the average meal's fat content was 35 percent or higher. According to the authors of the report, "these findings suggest that schools can make some modifications to reduce the fat content of lunches without adversely affecting participation; if, however, the fat content is reduced to levels below 32 percent of calories, participation falls substantially."

Regulatory and Legislative Reform Efforts

In most traditional analyses, regulatory actions follow legislative changes. However, in the case of reform of the National School Lunch Program, this sequence of policy changes did not apply. The NSLP was permanently authorized, but related programs that were carried under the same legislation were due to expire in 1994. Thus, congressional action was needed to reauthorize these programs, and Congress used this forum as a vehicle to make changes in the NSLP as well. The changes proposed to the NSLP—both legislative and regulatory—will be discussed in chronological sequence in this section of the case study. (To highlight these various policy activities, accounts of the legislative endeavors will be in *italics,* while those initiatives taking place in the regulatory arena will be in "regular" font.)

Building on her success as a consumer activist and media specialist and fresh from her appointment as the USDA's assistant secretary (later, the position was elevated to the title of undersecretary) for Food, Nutrition, and Consumer Services, Ellen Haas decided to take her school lunch reform message directly to both the public and to the health professionals and consumer advocates who had supported her activities in the past. The School Nutrition Dietary Assessment Study had provided ample evidence for the kind of reforms in the quality of the school meals that she had long envisioned. This report, released in October 1993, was the first study of the school meals program in ten years and provided important documentation of the nutritional performance of the program. Disturbing—but a clear mandate for Haas—was the finding that virtually none of the schools offered meals that conformed to the Dietary Guidelines recommendations. The study had shown that school lunches exceeded dietary guidelines for fat by 25 percent, saturated fat by 50 percent, and sodium by nearly 100 percent. The report also stated that children who ate school lunch consumed significantly higher amounts of calories from fat than children who got their lunch elsewhere. Especially troubling was the finding that nearly half of the more than 25 million school meals served were to needy students, for whom this may be their only nourishing meal of the day.

This message was taken to the public in a series of public hearings focusing on "Nutrition Objectives for School Meals." These regional hearings were held in four cities—Atlanta; Los Angeles; Flint, Michigan; and Washington, D.C.—in late fall 1993. Originally announced in the *Federal Register* (58 FR 47853 September 13, 1993), the hearings were staged "to provide an opportunity for public dialogue before policy changes are proposed for the National School Lunch Program."

The response exceeded everyone's expectations. There were 350 witnesses at the four hearings—including children, parents, teachers, nutritionists and dietitians, school food service personnel, farmers, physicians, the food industry, and community leaders—and 2,500 additional comments were filed afterward by the public. Over 90 percent of these comments supported changes in the National School Lunch Program and applauded the USDA's efforts to improve the nutritional quality of the meals served. In addition to these "public" hearings, Haas provided a forum for interested professionals by meeting regularly with a small group of representatives from consumer, health, and professional groups. In addition, she was a popular "keynote" speaker at meetings of these professional and consumer groups. She continued to court the media, especially those reporters with whom she had developed friendships from her days at Public Voice—Marian Burros from the *New York Times* and Laura Shapiro of *Newsweek*. Clearly, the objective of "creating a positive political climate" for reform of the National School Lunch Program had been initiated.

On November 2, 1993, Senator Patrick Leahy (D-Vermont), chair of the Senate Agriculture, Nutrition, and Forestry Committee, introduced S. 1614, the Better Nutrition and Health for Children Act. Designed to add health-promotion aspects to current child nutrition programs that were up for congressional reauthorization in 1994, the bill was designed to improve child nutrition programs by making school meals conform to the Dietary Guidelines. It also provided for increased funding for nutrition education and increased access to meals for children during the summer.

Representative Kildee (D-Michigan) introduced a related bill in the House (H.R. 8) on January 5, 1993, and it was referred to the House Committee on Education and Labor (the name of the committee before it was changed by the 104th Congress). Hearings were held before the Subcommittee on Elementary, Secondary, and Vocational Education on April 12 and 14, 1994, some sixteen months after the bill was introduced. The bill, known at this point as the Healthy Meals for Healthy Americans Act of 1994, received voice vote approval on May 18, 1994, from the full House Education and Labor Committee.

During markup of the bill, several amendments were approved by voice vote, including one proposed by Representative George Miller (D-California) that would permit some schools to drop whole milk from their menus if it accounted for less than 1 percent of *the total milk consumed at the school in the previous year. Miller's amendment initially was opposed by Representative Steven Gunderson (R-Wisconsin), whose dairy state had long supported the School Lunch Program's requirement that schools must offer whole milk along with other types. Gunderson offered a substitute that would have allowed milk purchases to be based on a survey of students' preferences. He later withdrew his amendment, saying that he thought the Miller amendment would have little effect in most school districts.*

The action line of the story now shifts back to the regulatory arena. Following on the heels of the widely publicized School Nutrition Dietary Assessment Study and personal stories gleaned from hearings and reported in popular media stories, the USDA's Ellen Haas clearly had the tools she required—along with a formidable arsenal of departmental regulatory tools and legislative connections—to bring about changes to the National School Lunch Program. The approach used in making the announcement was Haas's trademark press announcement plus public relations effort, tied this time to regulatory reform.

On June 8, 1994, then Secretary of Agriculture Mike Espy and Undersecretary Ellen Haas announced the USDA's School Meals Initiative for Healthy Children. In regulatory parlance, these changes were formulated as "proposed rules," a form of enforceable policy initiated by the executive branch that does not require congressional action. The complete text of the preamble and proposed rules appeared in the June 10, 1994, edition of the *Federal Register,* allowing for a ninety-day comment period, ending on September 8, 1994.

The USDA's School Meals Initiative for Healthy Children was based on four strategies to update and improve the quality of school meals:

1. *Eating for health:* Using the power of regulatory reform to ensure that school meals would meet standards for fat and saturated fat content as well as for key nutrients and calories, thus meeting the 1990 Dietary Guidelines for Americans' recommendations
2. *Making food choices:* Launching a nutrition education initiative for children as well as working with professional chefs and other members of the food and agricultural community to offer training and technical assistance to local meal providers
3. *Maximizing resources:* Improving the nutritional profile of commodities by putting nutri-

tion labels on commodities, working more closely with federal partners at the Department of Health and Human Services (DHHS) and the Department of Education (DOE), as well as establishing links to local farmers to enhance access to locally grown commodities

4. *Managing for the future:* Streamlining administration of the NSLP by using technology, reducing paperwork and procedures, and emphasizing flexibility

In order to ensure that schools met the Dietary Guidelines recommendations, a new plan was designed to replace the "meal pattern" system, which school lunch directors had followed since 1946 (i.e., planning meals by incorporating a USDA-specified number of servings of certain foods, such as meat/meat alternative, fruit and/or vegetables, bread, and milk), and use instead a "flexible system of menu planning" called "nutrient standard menu planning" or NuMenus. The USDA-proposed rule mandated that schools use a "nutrient standard" to ensure that the meals offered to children complied with the Dietary Guidelines. The plan required school food services to determine the nutritional content of the school meals by using a computer analysis program, or alternatively, schools could use an "assisted" version of the nutrient analysis by receiving help from outside groups, like state agencies or consultants.

The American School Food Service Association, the major professional organization concerned with the administration of school lunch programs, initially applauded the USDA (at least in public statements) for the "high priority [it] has given to the National School Lunch . . . program" and for giving the 92,000 schools participating in the program four years to comply with the regulations. But its campaign to overturn the regulations was just beginning. ASFSA members complained about the "paperwork burden" associated with compliance, the cost of the new foods in the program, and the level of technical competence required to use computers to determine the nutrient content of school meals. So the association took its cause—and its lobbyist—instead to the Congress, where program reauthorization debates were in progress.

On July 19, 1994, the House passed H.R. 8, and on August 25, 1994, the Senate passed S. 1614 by voice vote. Although the two bills had similar goals, a House-Senate conference committee was needed to work out differences between the measures. The amended legislation was finally approved by the House on October 5 by voice vote and agreed to by the Senate on October 6, 1994. The resulting bill, the Healthy Meals for Healthy Americans Act, was signed into law by President Bill Clinton on November 2, 1994, as Public Law 103-448.

The final legislation reauthorized child nutrition programs as expected but also contained some important policy changes. The USDA's proposed regulations had called for schools to adopt a "nutrient standard menu-planning" system by 1996, a method that would use computers to track the nutrient content of a meal offered in the School Lunch Program. This measure, in particular, was quite unpopular with many school food service directors, who voiced their opposition through the ASFSA's lobbying efforts. In response to this pressure, Congress offered a loophole—the final legislation included language that gave schools an additional option of using a "food-based menu-planning" system, which would allow school lunch directors to meet the Dietary Guidelines in their menus by tracking foods rather than nutrients—the way they were used to doing it.

After years of debate, Congress also settled the issue of whether schools must offer students whole milk as one of their beverage options. Nutritionists have long argued that the requirement adds unnecessary fat to children's diets. But under a carefully crafted provision in the law, the whole-milk requirement was replaced with language that requires schools to "offer students a variety of fluid milk [whole, chocolate, 1 percent, etc.] consistent with prior year preferences." In other words, if students didn't drink whole milk one year, it didn't have to be served the next. To placate the dairy lobby, which strenuously fought the removal of the whole-milk language, the bill required the USDA to provide schools with an amount of low-fat cheese that is the "milkfat equivalent" of the "lost" whole milk.

The final bill also excluded a provision in the House version that would have required the USDA to engage in a formal process known as "negotiated rule making," making it mandatory that the agency meet with interest groups before it issued certain proposed regulations. This provision was sought by groups such as the American School Food Service Association that strenuously opposed the USDA's June 1994 proposed regulations and wished to be able to change any contentious language before such regulations were issued. (Those close to the situation felt that "neg-reg," as it is colloquially called, is just a way of letting a special-interest group write the regulations it wants to implement.)

The chapter on regulatory reform was not closed until June 13, 1995, when the *final* rule on the Schools Meals Initiative for Healthy Children was published as 7CFR Parts 210 and 220, "Child Nutrition Programs: School Meal Initiatives for Healthy Children; Final Rule." The USDA called this final rule "the most comprehensive and integrated reform of school meals in the 50 year history of these programs." (Much more than just new rules for menu planning, the School Meals Initiative included support for innovative nutrition education, improved opportunities for technical assistance and training for school lunch personnel, and reformulation of donated commodities.) The USDA's final rule was similar to that which the department had proposed a year earlier, except that it included a new menu-planning approach: a food-based menu plan, which, while reminiscent of the plan currently in use, suggested alternatives for reducing the fat content of the meal by adding foods such as grains, fruits, and vegetables. Thus, the final rules accepted three menu planning approaches—the nutrient-based, the assisted nutrient-based, and the newly added food-based.

In addition to these regulatory changes, the USDA initiated "Team Nutrition," a nationwide integrated program designed to help implement the School Meals Initiative for Healthy Children. The mission of Team Nutrition was "to improve the health and education of children by creating innovative public and private partnerships that promote food choices for a healthful diet through the media, school, families and the community."

The Team Nutrition initiative was announced publicly on June 12, 1995, at a media extravaganza attended by first lady Hillary Rodham Clinton and USDA Secretary Dan Glickman. In addition to the regulatory changes previously discussed, Team Nutrition included several other initiatives—a nutrition education initiative designed to motivate children to make food choices for a healthy diet; a training and technical assistance initiative to provide support to school food service personnel; and changes to reduce the fat content of agricultural commodities used in the NSLP.

Nutrition Education

This initiative clearly has received the lion's share of public attention and resources. Moving away from the "typical" sources of nutrition education materials and techniques, USDA Undersecretary Ellen Haas clearly wanted something different and reached out to popular media channels. In less than two years, partnership agreements were reached with the Walt Disney Company to use two characters, "Timon" and "Pumbaa," from its movie *The Lion King* as "spokestoons" to promote the importance of a healthy diet to children; with Scholastic, Inc., to develop nutrition education materials for use in schools; with the national PTA organization for distribution of materials promoting parent involvement in the effort; with the USDA's Cooperative State Research, Education, and Extension Service to develop and distribute a community action kit; and with the California Department of Education to serve as models and evaluation projects for Team Nutrition's community-based nutrition promotion efforts.

Technical Assistance and Training

The technical assistance component of Team Nutrition has included the development of "tasty, low-fat, low-cost" recipes with chefs working with local school food service directors (another source of great consternation for the ASFSA); the development of a training plan and standards; the participation of volunteer chefs at local school cafeterias; as well as the development of a national nutrient database and software to implement the NuMenus system in schools.

Commodity Improvement

As described earlier in this case study, the use of donated commodities has long been a source of frustration for those seeking to reduce the dietary fat content of School Lunch Program menus. One direct way of reducing the fat content of school lunches is to change the nature of the agricultural commodities offered free to school lunch administrators or to offer more "low-fat" commodities.

Staff at the USDA's Food and Consumer Service unit work with staff at other USDA agencies, the Agricultural Marketing Service (AMS) and the Farm Service Agency (FSA), in developing the specifications for commodities that are used in the NSLP. The AMS handles "Group A Commodities," such as livestock, poultry, dairy, and fruits and vegetables; while the FSA has its own dairy division and a domestic program that handles grains, peanuts, and other miscellaneous items. Unlike menu standards for the NSLP, commodity specifications are not published in the *Federal Register* or codified in the

Code of Federal Regulations (CFR). Rather, they are distributed to the industries that bid to supply these foods. When specifications are developed, the requesting organization—in this case, the FCS—works with the AMS and the food industry to develop them. Issues that are considered in developing these specifications include technical feasibility of supplying the products, flavor and acceptability, body and texture, color, and nutrient quality.

To support the USDA's School Meals Initiative for Healthy Children and meet the concerns about agricultural commodities in the NSLP, the USDA established the Commodities Improvement Council in May 1994, early in the process of school lunch reform. Composed of USDA undersecretaries of Food, Nutrition, and Consumer Services and Farm and Foreign Agriculture Services and the assistant secretary for Marketing and Regulatory Programs, the council was charged with developing policy for improving the nutritional profile of USDA commodity offerings while maintaining the department's support for domestic agriculture markets.

The council established a Tri-Agency Task Force to conduct a comprehensive review of the specifications for all commodity products. The charge to the task force was to identify commodities that could be improved by modifying their fat, sodium, or sugar levels while making sure that the products were acceptable to schoolchildren. As a result of this review, more than two-thirds of the 142 distributed commodities (such as fruits, vegetables, grain products, and most unprocessed poultry products such as turkey and chicken) were excluded from further modification because they are typically purchased in their simplest, most natural or unprocessed form. Of the remaining 46 commodities considered for improvement, the council approved half for modification. Meat, cheese, and peanut butter were among the products targeted for fat reduction from their current levels. Canned meat will be reduced from 22–25 percent fat to 19–22 percent, fresh ground beef and pork from 20–21 percent to 17–18 percent fat content, and frozen ground beef and pork from 17–19 percent to 15–17 percent fat content. The task force also recommended that the USDA work with the food industry to develop some new products, including "lite" butter, low-fat macaroni and cheese, meatless spaghetti sauce, reduced-fat cheese, boneless turkey ham, and prune puree (to be used as a fat substitute).

In addition to these low- or reduced-fat products, the USDA is also seeking to provide schools with additional quantities of fruits, vegetables, and grain products that contain virtually no fat. It is also pilot-testing a program in which fresh produce is purchased for the USDA by the Department of Defense and delivered directly to schools. While the American School Food Service Association supported the commodity initiative, many school food service directors were skeptical of its effect, questioning whether children would accept the taste of reduced-fat, -sugar, and -sodium products.

The legislative story had not ended, however. Shortly after the final rules for the School Meals Initiative for Healthy Children were announced by the USDA, Representative William Goodling (R-Pennsylvania) introduced H.R. 2066, the Healthy Meals for Children Act. On July 19, 1995, the proposed bill was referred to the House Committee on Economic and Educational Opportunities, and on August 4, 1995, it was referred to the Subcommittee on Early Childhood, Youth, and Families. After languishing in legislative limbo for nine months, the bill was discharged from subcommittee action by the full committee on May 1, 1996, and on the same day, the committee considered H.R. 2066, amended it in markup, and passed it by voice vote, ordering it to be reported. After being reported to the House (as amended) by the full committee on May 7, it was called up by the House under suspension of the rules on May 14 and passed by voice vote. For many who were not following these developments closely, the bill is quite innocuous. It simply "amend[s] the National School Lunch Act to provide greater flexibility to schools to meet the Dietary Guidelines for Americans under the school lunch and school breakfast programs, as amended."

On March 14, 1996, Senator Thad Cochran (R-Mississippi) introduced a similar bill (S. 1613) into the Senate. Described by Senator Cochran as "virtually the same as H.R. 2066," the bill passed the Senate on May 16, 1996, without amendment by unanimous consent. The bill, which passed by voice vote in both houses, met with bipartisan support in Congress.

Critics of the bill had argued that its wording was too vague and did not provide for accountability for schools to follow nutrient-based standards in the NSLP. Before the bill was signed by President Clinton, an important clause was added at the "eleventh hour" to alleviate administration concerns. (A spokesperson for the ASFSA said that the decision apparently came directly from the Office of Management and Budget [OMB] in the White House, with Agriculture Secretary Dan Glickman's support.) The OMB's suggested amendment gave the secretary of agriculture the final decision-making authority to determine whether submitted menu plans met the nutrient standards for the NSLP; the official wording of the legislation now reads that schools can use any method "within guidelines established by the Secretary." On May 29, 1996, President Clinton signed into law the enrolled version of the bill, which became Public Law 104–149.

Looking Back . . .

Why was such legislation needed when new regulations governing the implementation of the NSLP had just been promulgated? Several reasons may be offered. The first has to do with the larger political environment under which changes to the NSLP were made. The 104th Congress, which took office in January 1995, had originally attempted to "block-grant" the School Lunch Program as one of its first actions in the Contract with America legislative proposals. The rationale was to improve decision making and implementation at the local level and decrease the level of federal involvement. After vigorous lobbying by the ASFSA and others, the NSLP was not included in any "block-grant" legislation. However, it was appealing to Republicans to offer a bill later that appeared to decrease the level of federal involvement in the School Lunch Program.

Legislation that permits "maximum flexibility" in planning school lunch menus certainly sounds as though it would decrease federal involvement in how the program would be operated at the local level. As Representative William Goodling was quoted as saying, "The bottom line is that the basic responsibility for developing reasonable approaches to meeting the dietary guidelines is with the school food authorities, with Federal guidance and oversight, but not a panoply of prescriptive rules or preset options."

Democrats and Republicans alike say this episode vividly "illustrates how a well-meaning federal agency carrying out a long-overdue change in nutritional standards barged into an area where local school districts know best." Even the *Congressional Record* contains the following statement: "We are moving this bipartisan legislation because the USDA Food and Consumer Service under the direction of Ellen Haas is out of control. In the name of advancing good nutrition for children, the USDA is burying our schools in bureaucratic paperwork and regulatory micromanagement."

The bill was backed by an intense lobbying effort by the American School Food Service Association, which used all its power—strong, effective lobbying coupled with an intensive grassroots letter-writing campaign from its 65,000 members—to ensure passage of the bill. It also enlisted the support of the American Association of School Administrators, the National School Boards Association, and the Association of School Business Officials by publishing estimates of increased costs associated with implementing the USDA regulations and by raising fears of increased "Washington involvement" in local affairs. Former House Speaker Tip O'Neill's maxim that "all politics is local" certainly held true in this case.

A second reason for the legislative activity is that school food service officials were quite unhappy with the new USDA regulations; in fact, after the proposed rules were announced in June 1994, the USDA received over 14,000 comments, 12,000 of those reportedly coming from disgruntled ASFSA members. Feeling that their comments had not been attended to in writing the regulations, fearing increased costs associated with implementing the new regulations, and desiring more flexibility in implementing them, the group sought the only way to offset regulations to which it was opposed—new legislation. This new act allowed school food service authorities to use "any reasonable approach" to meet the Dietary Guidelines for Americans under the National School Lunch Act. (Presumably this language also permits the very same meal pattern that the USDA, in the School Nutrition Dietary Assessment Study, had found to be high in fat and saturated fat, and had found not to meet Dietary Guidelines recommendations.) Further, the bill states, "The Secretary [of the USDA] may not *require* a school to conduct or use a nutrient analysis to meet the requirements," the clause to which school food service managers were most opposed.

While the USDA and the ASFSA membership share many common goals and say they have never disagreed on the ultimate outcome of improving the nutritional quality of the NSLP, the "devil," as they say, "is in the details." The USDA regulations can specify the nutrient standards on which the NSLP is based, but the overriding legislation now stipulates how and when those nutrient standards can be met. The USDA's goals of having school meals meet the recommendations of the 1990 Dietary Guidelines for Americans can be met mainly by serving more grains and breads in school lunches and increasing the amount of fruits and vegetables offered, options that school food service managers maintain are too expensive. Further, in order to ensure that these requirements were met, the USDA wanted school food service administrators to keep track of the nutrient content of school meals by using computer-based nutrient analyses. School food service administrators balked, much preferring to continue using their current system and not wanting to implement new technology that was highly dependent on computers and personnel trained to use them.

The third, and perhaps most telling, reason is the "feud" that developed between Ellen Haas and the American School Food Service Association, the primary professional organization supporting the lobbying effort behind the National School Lunch Program. Appointed as USDA assistant secretary in 1993 (over one of ASFSA's former presidents), Ellen Haas had one of the most powerful jobs in the federal bureaucracy and control over nearly 60 percent of the entire USDA budget (roughly $40 billion), the third largest nondefense department in the federal government.

During her professional rise in visibility and influence from local consumer activist to prominence at the national level, Ellen Haas became known as a clear, strong voice for consumers. She developed an enviable record of being able to court the media, policy makers, and "regular citizens advocates" with equal fervor and convince them of the validity of her views. In her role as executive director and founder of the consumer advocacy and research group Public Voice for Food and Health Policy, Haas demonstrated an ability to strongly and ardently advocate for changes in the quality of the foods served in the School Lunch Program. Since 1990, the series of reports issued by Public Voice had publicly—and personally—identified her with concerns about the quality of the food served in the School Lunch Program and had pitted her against the program's most powerful political ally, the American School Food Service Association. Now as the bureaucrat "in charge" of this vast and important program, how could she bring about the various changes that she had so long and so staunchly advocated?

The American School Food Service Association was already piqued by the Haas appointment. Then, as one of her first public acts as assistant secretary at the USDA, the ASFSA was the target of criticism for participation figures in the NSLP and for the nutritional quality of the meals served to schoolchildren, criticisms it felt were unfair and undeserved. In announcing what needed to be done to improve school meals, the ASFSA felt Haas had overlooked the "good news" in the School Nutrition Dietary Assessment Study—that NSLP meals offered more than the recommended amounts of protein and selected vitamins and minerals, and that a statistically significant proportion of the schools surveyed were already meeting the Dietary Guidelines using the current meal plan.

Further insult came when the NSLP came under attack by the legislative proposals of the 104th Congress to block-grant the program. Many closely associated with the process felt that Haas had not been a true "advocate" for the NSLP when her personal dynamism and contacts were most needed on Capitol Hill. They felt she had taken personal ownership of the Team Nutrition project to such a degree that she had no time or interest in working with them to fend off the block-grant proposals.

The disaffection between the USDA's undersecretary and the primary professional organization for school food service managers was clearly a public embarrassment for the Clinton administration. The AFSFA accused Haas of writing "heavy-handed" regulations by proposing that criminal penalties would be imposed if school food service personnel refused to change the meal patterns that did not meet the Dietary Guidelines. Former officers of the ASFSA publicly criticized Haas's administration of the NSLP, saying, "Ever since Haas started in the administration, the Under Secretary has discredited the school lunch program . . . she has humiliated [school food service] people . . . maligned and discredited them."

The "feud" between Haas and the ASFSA has manifested itself in a variety of rather subtle, but devastatingly personal ways; she was snubbed as a speaker at the ASFSA's annual meeting, a veritable "command performance" for the USDA undersecretary with responsibility for the NSLP. And when it came to Team Nutrition, the school food service group felt it had been insulted and bypassed. She was accused of snubbing old-timers at the ASFSA by bringing in executive chefs from high-class restaurants to "show them how to cook," and rather than reinforcing the efforts of local "experts," they felt that educational efforts had been turned over to Disney "spokestoons" and outside consultants. The relationship was never "healthy"—for either the undersecretary or the ASFSA—and probably irreparably harmed the effort to reform the NSLP.

Analysis and Comment

Reform of the National School Lunch Program is a perfect example of the importance of the agenda-setting stage of the policy-making process. The reauthorization of the National School Lunch Program was due in 1994.

This action was usually pro forma; no one seriously challenged the existence of the program after fifty years, and serious modifications to the content of the program were felt to be within the realm of USDA bureaucrats. Therefore, any major changes to the program would need to take place in the regulatory arena.

Nutrition and health professionals had clamored for change in the nutritional standards of the NSLP for years. All knew perfectly well that while school meals were meeting the recommended amounts of vitamins, minerals, and protein, they provided too much fat, saturated fat, sodium, and cholesterol. It took the power of a USDA-financed study, the School Nutrition Dietary Assessment Study, to bring this to the attention

of policy makers who were in a position to remedy the problem.

The other key to putting reform of the NSLP on the public agenda was the appointment in 1993 of Ellen Haas as assistant secretary of Food, Nutrition, and Consumer Services. She served as a "policy entrepreneur" in this matter. Without her energy and attention focused on the matter of the *quality* of school meals offered to children in the NSLP, any reform efforts would certainly have been much milder and less riveting. In bringing the matter to the attention of professionals and the public (who usually are only mildly interested, at best, in these issues), the results might have been more successful in the long run and certainly would have exacted less personal cost to Haas.

Chapter 14 Review Questions

1. How does Heclo conceptualize the current relationship between politics and administration? What are the basic elements of his *issue network* idea and how does the idea differ from the *iron triangle* notion of political-administrative relations?
2. Heclo primarily applied the issue network notion to the federal level of government. Is it possible to apply it to state and local levels as well? Describe why or why not.
3. In what ways does the issue network concept pose serious dilemmas for democratic government in general and public administration in particular? Does the case offer "answers" to this issue?
4. What implications does the issue network theory hold for the practical functions and training of public administrators? Does it essentially alter the types of jobs, tasks, and roles they perform? Think about what the case study tells us about preparing students for these kinds of jobs.
5. Did you find this issue network concept evident in the "Reinventing School Lunch" case study? If so, in what ways? If not, how would you conceptualize the political-administrative relationships as reflected in the case study?
6. On the basis of your analysis of the foregoing reading and case study, what general recommendations would you make to improve the relationships between administration and politics in America? Be sure to think carefully about the *value implications* of any new reform measures you may advocate.

Key Terms

politics-administration dichotomy

issue networks

proliferation of interests

think tanks

technopols

trade and professional associations

public policy processes

iron triangles

policy makers

issue specialization

issue watchers

single-issue organizations

presidential appointees

professional-bureaucratic complex

Suggestions for Further Reading

You would do well to compare and contrast Heclo's ideas with those of earlier theorists who argued for a clearer, more distinct separation of politics and administration (what is termed the political-administrative dichotomy), especially Woodrow Wilson, "The Study of Administration," *Political Science Quarterly,* 2 (June 1887), pp. 197–222; Frank J. Goodnow, *Politics and Administration* (New York: Macmillan, 1900); or the later writers who discovered the interest groups involved with administrative processes and gave roots to the iron triangle concept, particularly Paul H. Appleby, *Policy and Administration* (Tuscaloosa, Ala.: University of Alabama Press, 1949); E. Pendleton Herring, *Public Administration and the Public Interest* (New York: Russell and Russell, 1936); and David B. Truman, *The Governmental Process* (New York: Alfred A. Knopf, 1951).

Of course, because of the sheer size, complexity, and power of American government, more complicated political-administrative relationships have arisen in the last three decades, described by several astute observers, including Hugh Heclo, *A Government of Strangers: Executive Politics in Washington* (Washington, D.C.: The Brookings Institution, 1977); Don K. Price, *The Scientific Estate* (Cambridge, Mass.: Harvard University Press, 1965); Frederick C. Mosher, *Democracy and the Public Service,* 2nd ed. (New York: Oxford University Press, 1982); Christopher H. Foreman, Jr., *Signals from the Hill* (New Haven, Conn.: Yale University Press, 1988); Emmette S. Redford, *Democracy in the Administrative State* (New York: Oxford University Press, 1969); Francis E. Rourke, *Bureaucracy, Politics and Public Policy,* 3rd ed. (Boston: Little, Brown, 1984); Harold Seidman and Robert Gilmour, *Politics, Position and Power,* 5th ed. (New York: Oxford University Press, 1986); Lawrence C. Dodd and Richard L. Schott, *Congress and the Administrative State* (New York: John Wiley & Sons, 1979); Louis Fisher, *The Politics of Shared Power: Congress and the Executive* (Washington, D.C.: Congressional Quarterly Press, 1981); and Herbert Kaufman, *The Administrative Behavior of Federal Bureau Chiefs* (Washington, D.C.: The Brookings Institution, 1981).

The *National Journal, Governing,* and *Congressional Quarterly* provide timely insiders' views of this topic. You should give particular attention to the writers who discuss the changes during the last decade or so that have decisively altered political-administrative relationships: see David M. Ricci, *The Transformation of American Politics* (New Haven, Conn.: Yale University Press, 1993); Donald F. Kettl, *Sharing Power* (Washington, D.C.: The Brookings Institution, 1993); James Q. Wilson, *Bureaucracy* (New York: Basic Books, 1989); Paul C. Light, *Thickening Government* (Washington, D.C.: The Brookings Institution, 1995); and James H. Svara, *Official Leadership in the City* (New York: Oxford University Press, 1990).

The federal health-care reform attempts in the 1990s point out well the influence of issue networks, and the two best books so far on this topic are Jacob S. Hacker, *The Road to Nowhere* (Princeton, N.J.: Princeton University Press, 1997) and Mark E. Rushefsky and Kant Patel, *Politics, Power and Policy Making* (Armonk, N.Y.: M. E. Sharpe, 1998). For where we are today with issue network theory, see Lawrence J. O'Toole Jr., "Treating Networks Seriously," *Public Administration Review* 57 (Jan./Feb. 1997), pp. 45–52; and R.A.W. Rhodes, *Understanding Governance* (Buckingham, U.K.: Open University Press, 1997).

As could be expected, the debate rages on with regard to the relationship between politics and public administration. Within the context of water, health-care reform, and most recently foreign policy, scholars and career administrative executives alike continue to search for the right formula for a productive relationship. Compare Linda Wines Smith and Sujata Millick, "Partnering for the People: Alliances Between Career Administrators and Political Appointees in Federal Agencies; Topic: Leadership Balance Between Professional Administrators and Elected Officials," *ASPA Report* 25, no. 9 (September 2002), with Joel D. Aberbach and Bert A. Rockman, *In the Web of Politics: Three Decades of the U.S. Federal Executive* (Washington, D.C.: The *Brookings Institution,*

2000). These authors present contrasting theories that, on the one hand, suggest the historical conflicts between politics and administration can be resolved through an acceptance and meshing of skills and, on the other hand, assert the problem is not with the current relationship but rather the inability of elected officials to decide what government ought to do.

Other resources focus on one of three commonly identified results of the ongoing conflict. These common threads include the decline in quality and morale of federal executives, the relative responsiveness of the bureaucracy to political authority, and the insatiable appetite for "reinvention." The quality and morale of federal executives is discussed in a number of sources, including: "Sharing Isn't Easy: When Separate Institutions Clash," *Governance* 11 (April 1998), pp. 137–152; "The Results Act: Playing Chicken," (www.goveexec.com/features/0198mgmt.html), pp. 1–2; "The New Public Management and the Future of Public Service: Push, Pull, Balance and Beyond," *Canadian Public Administration* (Summer 1998), pp. 370–386; Martin Dyckman, "Civil Service Workers Deserve More Than They're Getting," *St. Petersburg Times* (January 28, 2002); Paul C. Light, *The New Public Service* (Washington, D.C.: The Brookings Institution, 1999); and Donald C. Menzel, "Images of Public Administration" (www.aspanet.org/ethicscommunity/documents).

The responsiveness of the bureaucracy to political authority is discussed within the context of the absence of accountability and repercussion of failed decisions. These topics are analyzed by Rebecca K.C. Hersman, *Friends and Foes: How Congress and the President Really Make Foreign Policy* (Washington, D.C.: The Brookings Institution, 2000); and "The New Faces of Foreign Policy," *Congressional Quarterly Weekly Report* (November 28, 1998), p. 3203.

The "iron triangle" continues to be assessed, often in an expanded dialogue about "reinvention." Reinvention is considered with regard to budgeting, representation, and other issues of interest to us all. See "What Price New Public Management?" *Political Quarterly* 69 (July/September 1998), pp. 271–274; "A New Zealand Tragedy: Problems of Political Responsibility," *Governance* 11 (April 1998), pp. 231–240; Rita Mae Kelly, "An Inclusive Democratic Polity, Representative Bureaucracies and the New Public Management," *Public Administration Review* 58 (May/June 1998), pp. 201–208; "What Drives the Machinery of Government Change? Australia, Canada and the United Kingdom 1950–1977," *Public Administration* 77 (1999), p. 7; *Taking Stock: Assessing Public Sector Reforms* (Montreal: McGill-Queens University Press, 1998), p. 252. In some cases, such as in *A Reinvented Government or the Same Old Government? The Clinton Legacy* (Washington, D.C.: The Brookings Institution, 2000), pp. 118–139, authors question whether or not, given the basic form of government in the United States, reinvention is really necessary or even possible.

The Relationship Between Bureaucracy and the Public Interest: The Concept of Public Sector Deregulation

*T*o do better, we have to deregulate the government. If deregulation of a market makes sense because it liberates the entrepreneurial energies of its members, then it is possible that deregulating the public sector may also help energize it.

James Q. Wilson

Introduction

Since the advent of public administration as an identifiable field, considerable scholarly debate has ensued over the question of public interest. Is there such a thing? How can it serve to guide the work of practicing public administrators? From where does the concept of public interest derive? How can it be applied as a meaningful concept in public agencies to influence the direction of administrative decisions?

Thoughtful administrative theorists have wrestled with these questions throughout the twentieth century but have arrived at very different "answers." Much of the dialogue on this subject turns ultimately on what "image" or "identity" theorists support for the field or how they define its substance and boundaries as an academic and applied field of practice. Three major perspectives have been put forward by scholars.

First, there are those administrative scientists who identify public administration essentially as a "tool" or "technique" in order to produce this or that most "efficient," "economical," or "effective" result. These writers tend to be highly positivist and rational in their thinking about the field. They view the emergence of "the public interest" from the application of the "right value-free tool of analysis" that will automatically achieve "correct results" for the general welfare. Writings by Frederick Taylor, the father of scientific management, or Herbert Simon, one of the founders of the behavioral movement within contemporary administrative sciences, advance such points of view. Listen to Herbert Simon's perspective on this topic:

The theory of administration is concerned with how an organization should be constructed and operated in order to accomplish its work efficiently. A fundamental principle of administration, which follows almost immediately from the rational character of "good" administration, is that among several alternatives involving the same expenditure, the one should always be selected which leads to the greatest accomplishment of administrative objectives; and among several alternatives that lead to the same accomplishment the one should be selected which involves the least expenditure.[1]

By contrast to this "rational machine model," whereby administrators become like "cogs" or "robots," the field of public administration is seen by other writers as central to the governance of America's constitutional democracy. They give public administrators key, creative leadership role(s) in promoting "the public interest." There is a long tradition of reformist literature in the field, dating from Woodrow Wilson's classic 1887 essay (refer to Chapter 1), which advance this viewpoint, namely that public administration is essential in order "to run the constitution." By placing public administration at the center of constitutional governance, administrative discretion and influence are enhanced, and "the public interest" consequently becomes equated with trained, enlightened public administration that advances broad community interests through the wise application of expertise and problem-solving skills. Influential authors such as Paul Appleby, Norton Long, Emmette Redford, and Merle Fainsod have advocated this perspective, but perhaps Carl Friedrich most forcefully articulated it:

> A modern administrator is in many cases dealing with problems so novel and complex that they call for the highest creative ability. This need for creative solutions effectively focuses attention upon the need for action. The pious formulas about the will of the people are all very well, but when it comes to these issues of social maladjustment, the popular will has little content. . . .
> . . . Throughout the length and breadth of our technical civilization there is arising a type of responsibility on the part of the permanent administrator, the man who is called upon to seek and find the creative solutions for our crying technical needs, which cannot be effectively enforced except by fellow-technicians who are capable of judging his policy in terms of the scientific knowledge bearing upon it.[2]

If Friedrich's view sees "good government" derived from the professionalism, expertise, training, ethical standards as well as the creativity of the public service, a third set of influential writers such as Arthur Bentley, David Truman, and Robert Dahl view the "public interest" as mainly the product of the pulling and hauling of various group interests in society. For these political scientists, there is no such "absolute" as "the public interest," but rather "it" is merely a "process" or the resultant of the contest among special interests as codified in law, rules, and informal agreements. Public administrators thus become much

---

[1]Herbert A. Simon, *Administrative Behavior: A Study of Decision-Making Processes in Administrative Organization* (New York: Free Press, 1947), p. 38.

[2]Carl J. Friedrich, "Public Policy and the Nature of Administrative Responsibility," in Friedrich and Mason, eds., *Public Policy* (Cambridge: Harvard University Press, 1940), p. 12.

less important figures in shaping "the public interest." Among group theorists' writings, public administrators are viewed as "people-in-the-middle" for resolving competing interests or as catalysts through which varied interests are transmuted and represented. David Truman describes the administrator's mediatory role as follows:

> The administrator is called upon to resolve the difficulties that were too thorny for the legislature to solve, and he must do so in face of the very forces that were acting in the legislature, though their relative strength may have changed. Note that it is not the ambiguities in the law that make difficult the question of what groups shall have privileged access to an administrator. Almost all legislative declarations are ambiguous in part. It is rather the causes of the ambiguity that make the difference. If the administrator holds out for an interpretation of these controverted ambiguous provisions that is not in itself a compromise, he invites the affected groups either to denounce his "dictatorial" methods and his "unscrupulous assumption of powers not granted to him" or to expose his "sell-out" of the "public interest."[3]

In the following selection from his recent book, *Bureaucracy,* James Q. Wilson, (1930–) the James Collins Professor of Management Emeritus at the University of California, Los Angeles, and 1990 recipient of the James Madison Award of the American Political Science Association, examines this subject in light of the operations of public agencies in the late twentieth century. His book drew upon a wide range of contemporary studies of the U.S. Army, FBI, DEA, CIA, Social Security, and other public entities and tried to provide a comprehensive analysis, as the book's subtitle suggests, of "what government agencies do and why they do it." In his last chapter, Wilson offers his appraisal of how public agencies can be made more responsible and responsive to "the public interest." While he does not define what the "public interest" is, Wilson begins by making the assumption that "the daily incentives operating in the political work encourage a very different course of action" by bureaucrats which often is contradictory to achievement of their own "public purposes." In other words, the incentive structures within which bureaucrats must operate often confound or prevent attainment of "the public interest." Wilson outlines why this happens and what, in his view, can be done about it. His reforms are modest, but they are argued compellingly.

As you read Wilson's essay, you should think about:

What assumptions does he make about the nature of public administration which in turn shape his understanding about "what is the public interest"?

How do you evaluate his proposed reforms? Their pluses? Negatives?

In what ways does Wilson's thinking compare and contrast with the three historic perspectives on the public interest and public administration which were outlined in this introduction? Does Wilson offer us a fourth alternative model? Since most of Wilson's argument is derived from federal examples, do his ideas also apply to state/local levels?

---

[3]David B. Truman, *The Governmental Process* (New York: Alfred A. Knopf, 1951), p. 443.

Bureaucracy and the Public Interest

JAMES Q. WILSON

The German army beat the French army in 1940; the Texas prisons for many years did a better job than did the Michigan prisons; Carver High School in Atlanta became a better school under Norris Hogans. These successes were the result of skilled executives who correctly identified the critical tasks of their organizations, distributed authority in a way appropriate to those tasks, infused their subordinates with a sense of mission, and acquired sufficient autonomy to permit them to get on with the job. The critical tasks were different in each case, and so the organizations differed in culture and patterns of authority, but all three were alike in one sense: incentives, culture, and authority were combined in a way that suited the task at hand. . . . [But] the daily incentives operating in the political world encourage a very different course of action.

Armies

Though the leadership and initiative of field officers and noncoms is of critical importance, the Pentagon is filled with generals who want to control combat from headquarters or from helicopters, using radios to gather information and computers to process it. Though the skill of the infantryman almost always has been a key to military success, the U.S. Army traditionally has put its best people in specialized units (intelligence, engineering, communications), leaving the leftovers for the infantry.[1] Though it has fought wars since 1945 everywhere except in Europe, the army continues to devote most of its planning to big-tank battles on the West German plains.

From *Bureaucracy: What Government Agencies Do & Why They Do It* by James Q. Wilson. Copyright © 1989 by Basic Books, Inc. Reprinted by permission of Basic Books, a member of Perseus Books, L.L.C.

Prisons

. . . Many observers gave the most favorable attention to prison executives who seemed to voice the best intentions (rehabilitation, prisoner self-governance) rather than the best accomplishments (safe, decent facilities).

Schools

Especially in big cities, many administrators keep principals weak and teachers busy filling out reports, all with an eye toward minimizing complaints from parents, auditors, interest groups, and the press. Teachers individually grumble that they are treated as robots instead of professionals, but collectively they usually oppose any steps—vouchers, merit pay, open enrollment, strengthened principals—that in fact have given teachers a larger role in designing curricula and managing their classrooms. . . . politically, extra resources . . . go to all schools "equally" rather than disproportionately to those schools that were improving the most.

These generals, wardens, administrators, and teachers have not been behaving irrationally; rather, they have been responding to the incentives and constraints that they encounter on a daily basis. Those incentives include the need to manage situations over which they have little control on the basis of a poorly defined or nonexistent sense of mission and in the face of a complex array of constraints that seems always to grow, never to shrink. Outside groups—elected officials, interest groups, professional associations, the media—demand a voice in the running of these agencies and make that demand effective by imposing rules on the agencies and demanding that all these rules be enforced all of the time. Moreover, habitual patterns of action—the lessons of the past, the memories of earlier struggles, the expectations of one's co-workers—narrow the area within which new courses of action are sought.

Bureaucrats often complain of "legislative micromanagement," and indeed it exists. . . . with respect to the armed forces, there has been a dramatic increase in the number of hearings, reports, investigations, statutory amendments, and budgetary adjustments with which the Pentagon must deal.[2] But there also has been a sharp increase in presidential micromanagement. Herbert Kaufman notes that for a half century or more the White House has feared agency independence more than agency paralysis, and so it has multiplied the number of presidential staffers, central management offices, and requirements for higher-level reviews. Once you start along the path of congressional or White House control, the process acquires a momentum of its own. "As more constraints are imposed, rigidities fixing agencies in their established ways intensify. As a result, complaints that they do not respond to controls also intensify. Further controls, checkpoints, and clearances are therefore introduced."[3] Much the same story can be told with respect to the growing involvement of the courts in agency affairs.

With some conspicuous exceptions the result of this process has been to deflect the attention of agency executives away from how the tasks of their agencies get defined and toward the constraints that must be observed no matter what the tasks may be. Who then decides what tasks shall be performed? In a production agency with observable outputs and routinized work processes, the answer is relatively simple: The laws and regulations that created the agency also define its job. But in procedural, coping, and craft agencies, the answer seems to be nobody in particular and everybody in general. The operating-level workers define the tasks, occasionally by design, as in those cases where operator ideology makes a difference, but more commonly by accident, as in those instances where prior experiences, professional norms, situational and technological imperatives, and peer-group expectations shape the nature of the work.

From time to time a gifted executive appears at a politically propitious time and makes things happen differently. He or she creates a new institution that acquires a distinctive competence, a strong sense of mission, and an ability to achieve socially valued goals. The Army Corps of Engineers, the Social Security Administration, the Marine Corps, the Forest Service, the FBI: For many years after they were created, and in many instances still today, these agencies, along with a few others that could be mentioned, were a kind of elite service that stood as a living refutation of the proposition that "all bureaucrats are dim-witted paper-shufflers." And these are only the federal examples; at the local level one can find many school systems and police departments that have acquired a praiseworthy organizational character.

But one must ask whether today one could create from scratch the Marine Corps, or the FBI, or the Forest Service; possibly, but probably not. Who would dare suggest that a new agency come into being with its own personnel system (and thus with fewer opportunities for civil servants to get tenure), with a single dominant mission (and thus with little organizational deference to the myriad other goals outsiders would want it to serve), and with an arduous training regime designed to instill *esprit de corps* (and thus with less regard for those niceties and conveniences that sedentary people believe to be important)? Or how optimistic should we be that today we could organize a Social Security Administration in a way that would bring to Washington men and women of exceptional talent? Might not many of those people decide today that they do not want to risk running afoul of the conflict-of-interest laws, that they have no stomach for close media and congressional scrutiny, and that they would not accept the federal pay levels pegged to the salaries of members of Congress fearful of raising their own compensation?

It would be a folly of historical romanticism to imagine that great agencies were created in a golden age that is destined never to return, but it would be shortsighted to deny that we have paid a price for having emphasized rules and constraints to the neglect of tasks and mission. At the end of her careful review of the problems the SSA has had in managing disability insurance and supplemental security income, Martha Derthick makes the same point this way: "If the agencies repeatedly fall short, one ought at least to consider the possibility that there is a systematic mismatch between what they are instructed to do and their capacity to do it."[4] In recent years, when Congress has been creating new programs and modifying old ones at a dizzying rate, often on the basis of perfunctory hearings (or, as with the Senate's consideration of the 1988 drug bill, no hearings at all), a government agency capable of responding adequately to these endless changes would have to be versatile and adaptable, "capable of devising new routines or altering old ones very quickly." These qualities, she concludes, "are rarely found in large formal organizations."[5] I would only add that government agencies are far less flexible than formal organizations generally.

Things are not made much better by our national tendency to engage in bureaucrat-bashing. One has to have some perspective on this. It is true that bureaucracies prefer the present to the future, the known to the unknown, and the dominant mission to rival missions; many agencies in fact are skeptical of things that were "NIH"—Not Invented Here. Every social grouping, whether a neighborhood, a nation, or an organization, acquires a culture; changing that culture is like moving a cemetery: it is always difficult and some believe it is sacrilegious. It is also true, as many conservatives argue, that the government tries to do things that it is incapable of doing well, just as it is true, as many liberals allege, that the government in fact does many things well enough. As Charles Wolf has argued, both markets and governments have their imperfections; many things we might want to do collectively require us to choose between unsatisfactory alternatives.[6]

A Few Modest Suggestions That May Make a Small Difference

To do better we have to deregulate the government.* If deregulation of a market makes sense because it liberates the entrepreneurial energies of its members,

*I first saw this phrase in an essay by Constance Horner, then director of the federal Office of Personnel Management: "Beyond Mr. Gradgrind: The Case for Deregulating the Public Sector," *Policy Review* 44 (Spring 1988): 34–38. It also appears in Gary C. Bryner, *Bureaucratic Discretion* (New York: Pergamon Press, 1987), 215.

then it is possible that deregulating the public sector also may help energize it. The difference, of course, is that both the price system and the profit motive provide a discipline in markets that is absent in non-markets. Whether any useful substitutes for this discipline can be found for public-sector workers is not clear, though I will offer some suggestions. But even if we cannot expect the same results from deregulation in the two sectors we can agree at a minimum that detailed regulation, even of public employees, rarely is compatible with energy, pride in workmanship, and the exercise of initiative. The best evidence for this proposition, if any is needed, is that most people do not like working in an environment in which every action is second-guessed, every initiative viewed with suspicion, and every controversial decision denounced as malfeasance.

James Colvard, for many years a senior civilian manager in the navy, suggests that the government needs to emulate methods that work in the better parts of the private sector: "a bias toward action, small staffs, and a high level of delegation which is based on trust."[7] A panel of the National Academy of Public Administration (NAPA), consisting of sixteen senior government executives holding the rank of assistant secretary, issued a report making the same point:

> Over many years, government has become entwined in elaborate management control systems and the accretion of progressively more detailed administrative procedures. This development has not produced superior management. Instead, it has produced managerial overburden. . . . Procedures overwhelm substance. Organizations become discredited, along with their employees. . . . The critical elements of leadership in management appear to wither in the face of a preoccupation with process. The tools are endlessly "perfected"; the manager who is expected to use these tools believes himself to be ignored. . . . Management systems are not management. . . . The attitude of those who design and administer the rules . . . must be reoriented from a "control mentality" to one of "how can I help get the mission of this agency accomplished."[8]

But how can government "delegate" and "trust" and still maintain accountability? If it is a mistake to foster an ethos that encourages every bureaucrat to "go by the book," is it not an equally serious problem to allow zealots to engage in "mission madness," charging off to implement their private versions of some ambiguous public goal? (Steven Emerson has written a useful account of mission madness in some highly secret military intelligence and covert-action agencies.[9]) Given everything we know about the bureaucratic desire for autonomy and the political rewards of rule making, is there any reason to suppose that anybody will find it in his or her interest to abandon the "control mentality" and adopt the "mission accomplishment" mentality?

Possibly not. But it may be worth thinking about what a modestly deregulated government might look like. It might look as it once did, when some of the better federal agencies were created. At the time the Corps of Engineers, the Forest Service, and the FBI were founded, much of the federal government was awash in political patronage, petty cabals, and episodic corruption. Organizing an elite service in those days may have been easier than doing so today, when the problems are less patronage and corruption than they are officiousness and complexity. But the keys to organizational success have not changed. The agencies were started by strong leaders who were able to command personal loyalty, define and instill a clear and powerful sense of mission, attract talented workers who believed they were joining something special, and make exacting demands on subordinates.

Today there is not much chance to create a new agency; almost every agency one can imagine already has been created. Even so, the lessons one learns from changing agencies confirm what can be inferred from studying their founding.

First: Executives should understand the culture of their organizations—that is, what their subordinates believe constitute the core tasks of the agency—and the strengths and limitations of that culture. If members widely share and warmly endorse that culture the agency has a sense of mission. This permits the executive to economize on scarce incentives (people want to do certain tasks even when there are no special rewards for doing it); to state general objectives confident that subordinates will understand the appropriate ways of achieving them; and to delegate responsibility knowing that lower-level decisions probably will conform to higher-level expectations.

A good executive realizes that workers can make subtle, precise, and realistic judgments, but only if those judgments refer to a related, coherent set of behaviors. People cannot easily keep in mind many quite different things or strike reasonable balances among competing tasks. People want to know what is expected of them; they do not want to be told, in answer to this question, that "on the one hand this, but on the other hand that."

In defining a core mission and sorting out tasks that either fit or do not fit with this mission, executives must be aware of their many rivals for the right to define it. Operators with professional backgrounds will bring to the agency their skills but also their biases: Lawyers, economists, and engineers see the world in very different ways. You cannot hire them as if they were tools that in your skilled hands will perform exactly the task you set for them. Black and Decker may make tools like that, but Harvard and MIT do not. Worker peer groups also set expectations to which operators conform, especially when the operators work in a threatening, unpredictable, or confrontational environment. You may design the ideal patrol officer or schoolteacher, but unless you understand the demands made by the street and the classroom, your design will remain an artistic expression destined for the walls of some organizational museum.

These advantages of infusing an agency with a sense of mission are purchased at a price. An agency with a strong mission will give perfunctory attention, if any at all, to tasks that are not central to that mission. Diplomats in the State Department will have little interest in embassy security; intelligence officers in the CIA will not worry as much as they should about counterintelligence; narcotics agents in the DEA will minimize the importance of improper prescriptions written by physicians; power engineers in the TVA will not think as hard about environmental protection or conservation as about maximizing the efficiency of generating units; fighter pilots in the USAF will look at air transport as a homely stepchild; and navy admirals who earned their flag serving on aircraft carriers will not press zealously to expand the role of minesweepers.

If the organization must perform a diverse set of tasks, those tasks that are not part of the core mission will need special protection. This requires giving autonomy to the subordinate tasks subunit (for example, by providing for them a special organizational niche) and creating a career track so that talented people performing non-mission tasks can rise to high rank in the agency. No single organization, however, can perform well a wide variety of tasks; inevitably some will be neglected. In this case, the wise executive will arrange to devolve the slighted tasks onto another agency, or to a wholly new organization created for the purpose. Running multitask conglomerates is as risky in the public as in the private sector. There are limits to the number of different jobs managers can manage. Moreover, conglomerate agencies rarely can develop a sense of mission; the cost of trying to do everything is that few things are done well. The turf-conscious executive who stoutly refuses to surrender any tasks, no matter how neglected, to another agency is courting disaster; in time the failure of his or her agency to perform some orphan task will lead to a political or organizational crisis. Long ago the State Department should have got out of the business of building embassies. Diplomats are good at many things, but supervising carpenters and plumbers is not one of them. Let agencies whose mission is construction—the Army Corps of Engineers or the navy's Seabees—build buildings.

Second: Negotiate with one's political superiors to get some agreement as to which are the *essential* constraints that must be observed by your agency and which the marginal constraints. This, frankly, may be impossible. The decentralization of authority in Congress (and in some state legislatures) and the unreliability of most expressions of presidential or gubernatorial backing are such that in most cases you will discover, by experience if not by precept, that all constraints are essential all of the time. But perhaps with effort some maneuvering room may be won. A few agencies obtained the right to use more flexible, less cumbersome personnel systems modeled on the China Lake experiment, and Congress has the power to broaden those opportunities. Perhaps

some enlightened member of Congress will be able to get statutory authority for the equivalent of China Lake with respect to procurement regulations. An executive is well advised to spend time showing that member how to do it.

Third: Match the distribution of authority and the control over resources to the tasks your organization is performing. In general, authority should be placed at the lowest level at which all essential elements of information are available. Bureaucracies will differ greatly in what level that may be. At one extreme are agencies such as the Internal Revenue Service or maximum-security prisons, in which uniformity of treatment and precision of control are so important as to make it necessary for there to be exacting, centrally determined rules for most tasks. At the other extreme are public schools, police departments, and armies, organizations in which operational uncertainties are so great that discretion must be given to (or if not given will be taken by) lower-level workers.

A good place in which to think through these matters is the area of weapons procurement. The over-centralization of design control is one of the many criticisms of such procurement on which all commentators seem agreed. Buying a new aircraft may be likened to remodeling one's home: You never know how much it will cost until you are done; you quickly find out that changing your mind midway through the work costs a lot of money; and you soon realize that decisions have to be made by people on the spot who can look at the pipes, wires, and joists. The Pentagon procures aircraft as if none of its members had ever built or remodeled a house. It does so because both it and its legislative superiors refuse to allow authority to flow down to the point where decisions rationally can be made.

The same analysis can be applied to public schools. As John Chubb and Terry Moe have shown, public and private schools differ in the locus of effective control.[10] At least in big cities, decisions in private schools that are made by headmasters or in Catholic schools that are made by small archdiocesan staffs are made in public schools by massive, cumbersome headquarters bureaucracies. Of course, there are perfectly understandable political reasons for this difference, but not very many good reasons for it. Many sympathetic critics of the public schools believe that the single most useful organizational change that could be made would be to have educational management decisions—on personnel, scheduling, and instructional matters—made at the school level.[11]

Fourth: Judge organizations by results. This [essay] has made it clear that what constitutes a valued result in government usually is a matter of dispute. But even when fairly clear performance standards exist, legislatures and executives often ignore them with unhappy results. William E. Turcotte compared how two state governments oversaw their state liquor monopolies. The state that applied clear standards to its liquor bureaucrats produced significantly more profit and lower administrative costs than did the state with unclear or conflicting standards.[12]

Even when results are hard to assess, more can be done than is often the case. If someone set out to evaluate the output of a private school, hospital, or security service, he or she would have at least as much trouble as would someone trying to measure the output of a public school, hospital, or police department. Governments are not the only institutions with ambiguous products.

There are two ways to cope with the problem in government. One is to supply the service or product in a marketlike environment. Shift the burden of evaluation off the shoulders of professional evaluators and onto the shoulders of clients and customers, and let the latter vote with their feet. The "client" in these cases can be individual citizens or government agencies; what is important is that the client be able to choose from among rival suppliers.

But some public services cannot be supplied, or are never going to be supplied, by a market. We can imagine allowing parents to choose among schools, but we cannot imagine letting them choose (at least for most purposes) among police departments or armies. In that case one should adopt the second way of evaluating a public service: carry out a demonstration project or conduct a field experiment. (I will use the two ideas interchangeably, though some scholars distinguish between them.[13]) An experiment is a planned alteration in a state of affairs designed to measure the effect of the intervention. It involves asking the

question, "if I change X, what will happen to Y, having first made certain that everything else stays the same?" It sounds easy, but it is not.

A good experiment (bad ones are worse than no experiment at all) requires that one do the following: First, identify a course of action to be tested; call it the treatment. A "treatment" can be a police tactic, a school curriculum, or a welfare program. Second, decide what impact the treatment is intended to have; call this the outcome. The outcome can be a crime rate, an achievement score, a work effort, a housing condition, or an income level. Third, give the treatment to one group (the experimental group) and withhold it from another (the control group). A group might be a police precinct, a class of students, the tenants in a housing project, or people who meet some eligibility requirement (say, having low incomes). It is quite important how the membership in these groups is determined. It should be done randomly; that is, all eligible precincts, schools, tenants, or people should be randomly sorted into experimental and control groups. Random assignment means that all the characteristics of the members of the experimental and control groups are likely to be identical. Fourth, assess the condition of each group before and after the treatment. The first assessment describes the baseline condition, the second the outcome condition. This outcome assessment should continue for some time after the end of the treatment, because experience has shown that many treatments seem to have a short-term effect that quickly disappears. Fifth, make certain that the evaluation is done by people other than those providing the treatment. People like to believe that their efforts are worthwhile, so much so that perhaps unwittingly they will gather data in ways that make it look like the treatment worked even when it did not.*

---

*Matters are, of course, a bit more complicated than this summary might suggest. There is a small library of books on evaluative research that go into these matters in more detail; a good place to begin is Richard P. Nathan, *Social Science in Government* (New York: Basic Books, 1988). On the political aspects of evaluation, see Henry J. Aaron, *Politics and the Professors* (Washington, D.C.: The Brookings Institution, 1978). On the technical side see Thomas D. Cook and Donald T. Campbell, *Quasi-Experimentation* (Chicago: Rand McNally, 1979). There is even a journal, *Evaluation Review*, specializing in these issues.

The object of all this is to find out what works. Using this method we have discovered that tripling the number of patrol cars on a beat does not lower the crime rate; that foot patrol reduces the fear of crime but not (ordinarily) its incidence; and that arresting spouse-beaters reduces (for a while) future assaults more than does counseling the assaulters.[14] We have learned that giving people an income supplement (akin to the negative income tax) reduces work effort and in some cases encourages families to break up.[15] We have learned that giving special job training and support to welfare mothers, ex-offenders, and school drop-outs produces sizable gains in the employment records of the welfare recipients but no gain for the ex-offenders and school drop-outs.[16] We have learned that a housing allowance program increases the welfare of poor families even though it does not improve the stock of housing.[17] We have learned that more flexible pay and classification systems greatly benefit the managers of navy research centers and improve the work atmosphere at the centers.[18]

There also have been many failed or flawed management experiments. In the 1930s, Herbert Simon carried out what may have been the first serious such experiment when he tried to find out how to improve the performance of welfare workers in the California State Relief Administration. Though elegantly designed, the experimental changes proved so controversial and the political environment of the agency so unstable that it is not clear that any useful inferences can be drawn from the project.[19] The attempt to evaluate educational vouchers at Alum Rock was undercut by the political need to restrict participation by private schools. There are countless other "studies" that are evaluations in name only; in reality they are self-congratulatory conclusions written by program administrators. The administrative world is a political world, not a scientific laboratory, and evaluators of administration must come to terms with that fact. Often there are no mutually acceptable terms. But where reasonable terms can be struck, it is possible to learn more than untutored experience can tell us about what works.

Such dry and dusty research projects probably seem thin fare to people who want Big Answers to Big Questions such as "How can we curb rampant bureaucracy?" or "How can we unleash the creative talents of our dedicated public servants?" But public management is not an arena in which to find Big Answers; it is a world of settled institutions designed to allow imperfect people to use flawed procedures to cope with insoluble problems.

The fifth and final bit of advice flows directly from the limits on judging agencies by their results. All organizations seek the stability and comfort that comes from relying on standard operating procedures— "SOPs." When results are unknown or equivocal, bureaus will have no incentive to alter those SOPs so as better to achieve their goals, only an incentive to modify them to conform to externally imposed constraints. The SOPs will represent an internally defined equilibrium that reconciles the situational imperatives, professional norms, bureaucratic ideologies, peer-group expectations, and (if present) leadership demands unique to that agency. The only way to minimize the adverse effect of allowing human affairs to be managed by organizations driven by their autonomous SOPs is to keep the number, size, and authority of such organizations as small as possible. If none of the four preceding bits of advice work, the reader must confront the realization that there are no solutions for the bureaucracy problem that are not also "solutions" to the government problem. More precisely: All complex organizations display bureaucratic problems of confusion, red tape, and the avoidance of responsibility. Those problems are much greater in government bureaucracies because government itself is the institutionalization of confusion (arising out of the need to moderate competing demands); of red tape (arising out of the need to satisfy demands that cannot be moderated); and of avoided responsibility (arising out of the desire to retain power by minimizing criticism).

In short, you can have less bureaucracy only if you have less government. Many, if not most, of the difficulties we experience in dealing with government agencies arise from the agencies being part of a fragmented and open political system. If an agency is to have a sense of mission, if constraints are to be minimized, if authority is to be decentralized, if officials are to be judged on the basis of the outputs they produce rather than the inputs they consume, then legislators, judges, and lobbyists will have to act against their own interests. They will have to say "no" to influential constituents, forgo the opportunity to expand their own influence, and take seriously the task of judging the organizational feasibility as well as the political popularity of a proposed new program. It is hard to imagine this happening, partly because politicians and judges have no incentive to make it happen and partly because there are certain tasks a democratic government must undertake even if they cannot be performed efficiently. The greatest mistake citizens can make when they complain of "the bureaucracy" is to suppose that their frustrations arise simply out of management problems; they do not—they arise out of governance problems.

Bureaucracy and the American Regime

The central feature of the American constitutional system—the separation of powers—exacerbates many of these problems. The governments of the United States were not designed to be efficient or powerful, but to be tolerable and malleable. Those who devised these arrangements always assumed that the federal government would exercise few and limited powers. As long as that assumption was correct (which it was for a century and a half) the quality of public administration was not a serious problem except in the minds of those reformers (Woodrow Wilson was probably the first) who desired to rationalize government in order to rationalize society. The founders knew that the separation of powers would make it so difficult to start a new program or to create a new agency that it was hardly necessary to think about how those agencies would be administered. As a result, the Constitution is virtually silent on what kind of administration we should have. At least until the Civil War thrust the problem on us, scarcely anyone in the country would have known what you were talking about if you spoke of the "problem of administration."

Matters were very different in much of Europe. Kings and princes long had ruled; when their authority was captured by parliaments, the tradition of ruling was already well established. From the first the ministers of the parliamentary regimes thought about the problems of administration because in those countries there was something to administer. The centralization of executive authority in the hands of a prime minister and the exclusion (by and large) of parliament from much say in executive affairs facilitated the process of controlling the administrative agencies and bending them to some central will. The constitutions of many European states easily could have been written by a school of management.

Today, the United States at every level has big and active governments. Some people worry that a constitutional system well-designed to preserve liberty when governments were small is poorly designed to implement policy now that governments are large. The contrast between how the United States and the nations of Western Europe manage environmental and industrial regulation is illuminating: Here the separation of powers insures, if not causes, clumsy and adversarial regulation; there the unification of powers permits, if not causes, smooth and consensual regulation.

I am not convinced that the choice is that simple, however. It would take another book to judge the advantages and disadvantages of the separation of powers. The balance sheet on both sides of the ledger would contain many more entries than those that derive from a discussion of public administration. But even confining our attention to administration, there is more to be said for the American system than many of its critics admit.

America has a paradoxical bureaucracy unlike that found in almost any other advanced nation. The paradox is the existence in one set of institutions of two qualities ordinarily quite separate: the multiplication of rules and the opportunity for access. We have a system laden with rules; elsewhere that is a sure sign that the bureaucracy is aloof from the people, distant from their concerns, and preoccupied with the power and privileges of the bureaucrats—an elaborate, grinding machine that can crush the spirit of any who dare oppose it. We also have a system suffused with participation: advisory boards, citizen groups, neighborhood councils, congressional investigators, crusading journalists, and lawyers serving writs; elsewhere this popular involvement would be taken as evidence that the administrative system is no system at all, but a bungling, jerry-built contraption wallowing in inefficiency and shot through with corruption and favoritism.

That these two traits, rules and openness, could coexist would have astonished Max Weber and continues to astonish (or elude) many contemporary students of the subject. Public bureaucracy in this country is neither as rational and predictable as Weber hoped nor as crushing and mechanistic as he feared. It is rule-bound without being overpowering, participatory without being corrupt. This paradox exists partly because of the character and mores of the American people: They are too informal, spontaneous, and other-directed to be either neutral arbiters or passionless Grad-grinds. And partly it exists because of the nature of the regime: Our constitutional system, and above all the exceptional power enjoyed by the legislative branch, makes it impossible for us to have anything like a government by appointed experts but easy for individual citizens to obtain redress from the abuses of power. Anyone who wishes it otherwise would have to produce a wholly different regime, and curing the mischiefs of bureaucracy seems an inadequate reason for that. Parliamentary regimes that supply more consistent direction to their bureaucracies also supply more bureaucracy to their citizens. The fragmented American regime may produce chaotic government, but the coherent European regimes produce bigger governments.

In the meantime we live in a country that despite its baffling array of rules and regulations and the insatiable desire of some people to use government to rationalize society still makes it possible to get drinkable water instantly, put through a telephone call in seconds, deliver a letter in a day, and obtain a passport in a week. Our Social Security checks arrive on time. Some state prisons, and most of the federal ones, are reasonably decent and humane institutions. The great majority of Americans, cursing all the while, pay their taxes. One can stand on the deck of an aircraft carrier during night flight operations and watch two thousand nineteen-year-old boys faultlessly operate one of the most complex organizational systems ever created. There are not many places where all this happens. It is astonishing it can be made to happen at all.

Notes

1. Arthur T. Hadley, *The Straw Giant* (New York: Random House, 1986), 53–57, 249–52.
2. CSIS, *U.S. Defense Acquisition: A Process in Trouble* (Washington, D.C.: Center for Strategic and International Studies, March 1987), 13–16.
3. Herbert Kaufman, *The Administrative Behavior of Federal Bureau Chiefs* (Washington, D.C.: The Brookings Institution, 1981), 192.
4. Martha Derthick, *Agency Under Stress: The Social Security Administration and American Government* (Washington, D.C.: Brookings Institution, 1990).
5. Ibid., chap. 3.
6. Charles Wolf, Jr., *Markets or Governments: Choosing Between Imperfect Alternatives* (Cambridge, Mass.: MIT Press, 1988).
7. James Colvard, "Procurement: What Price Mistrust?" *Government Executive* (March 1985): 21.
8. NAPA, *Revitalizing Federal Management: Managers and Their Overburdened Systems* (Washington, D.C.: National Academy of Public Administration, November 1983), vii, viii, 8.
9. Steven Emerson, *Secret Warriors* (New York: G. P. Putnam's Sons, 1988).
10. John E. Chubb and Terry M. Moe, "Politics, Markets, and the Organization of Schools," *American Political Science Review* 82 (1988): 1065–87.
11. Chester E. Finn, Jr., "Decentralize, Deregulate, Empower," *Policy Review* (Summer 1986): 60; Edward A. Wynne, *A Year in the Life of an Excellent Elementary School* (1993, out of print).
12. William E. Turcotte, "Control Systems, Performance, and Satisfaction in Two State Agencies," *Administrative Science Quarterly* 19 (1974): 60–73.
13. Richard P. Nathan, *Social Science in Government: Uses and Misuses* (New York: Basic Books, 1988), chap. 3.
14. These projects were all done by the Police Foundation and are described in James Q.

Wilson, *Thinking About Crime*, rev. ed. (New York: Basic Books, 1983).

15. See Joseph A. Pechman and P. Michael Timpane, eds., *Work Incentives and Income Guarantees* (Washington, D.C.: Brookings Institution, 1975); and R. Thayne Robson, ed., *Employment and Training R&D* (Kalamazoo, Mich.: Upjohn Institute for Employment Research, 1984).

16. Nathan, *Social Science*, chap. 5; and Manpower Demonstration Research Corporation,

Summary and Findings of the National Supported Work Demonstration (Cambridge, Mass.: Ballinger, 1980).

17. See studies cited in chap. 19.

18. See references to China Lake research cited in chap. 8.

19. Clarence E. Ridley and Herbert A. Simon, *Measuring Municipal Activities* (Chicago: International City Managers' Association, 1938).

☐ CASE STUDY 15

Introduction

One of the largest, most complex as well as successful government projects recently completed is the Human Genome Project (HGP). Stretching over two decades, costing more than 3 billion, and involving two American plus one English public agency and scientists from six nations, HGP discovered the sequence of chemical letters making up the human genome, our basic DNA blueprint, with revolutionary significance for science, medicine, and public and private enterprises. First conceptualized in the early 1980s and finished by 2003, HGP possibly rivals winning World War II or building the interstate highway system as one of the U.S. government's most remarkable achievements during its two-century-plus history. Yet, ironically, few Americans know much about it, let alone realize it is a one-of-a-kind public administration success story. Possibly, the vastness, technical-scientific complexity, as well as lack of much media attention throughout its development, meant relatively few people could comprehend its public policy importance or its administrative accomplishments. Only after the announcement of its DNA discovery did the general public begin to recognize HGP's existence, though still very few think of its scientific achievement as resulting from effective public administration.

The following case study, "The Human Genome Project," by Professor W. Henry Lambright, director of the Center for Environmental Policy and Administration at the Maxwell School, Syracuse University, vividly recounts the HGP story and explores the reasons why it carried out its mission so effectively. Dr. Lambright thoughtfully concludes that five factors especially worked in its favor: (1) possessing a clear-cut goal, (2) maintaining a flexible organizational structure, (3) sustaining strong political support, (4) facing competition from the private sector, and (5) enjoying dedicated project leadership throughout its lifespan. In Lambright's words, HGP created a successful "partnership model of R&D. . . . Partnerships across agencies, sectors and nations are likely to be the wave of the future for large-scale public efforts at the frontier of knowledge."

As you read this fascinating case about one of the most amazing scientific-technological breakthroughs, try to keep in mind what "lessons" we can learn in relationship to Wilson's conceptual essay about the key factors necessary for enabling bureaucracy to promote the public interest:

Specifically compare Wilson's recommended factors for bureaucratic success at achieving "the public interest" with Lambright's five factors that led to HGP's success. Were they the same or different? If different, why?

How did the overall context of HGP's development lead to achieving its goal effectively? Would you credit this to good luck or design?

Why did the general HGP "incentive structures" foster its success? Did these evolve over time or were they put in place from the project's start?

Are HGP's "best practices" transferable to other public activities? Or were they a one-of-a kind event?

Ultimately, does this case's thesis argue that "the public interest" is achieved best through that program which is administered best?

The Human Genome Project

W. HENRY LAMBRIGHT

On May 10, 1998, J. Craig Venter, a former NIH scientist turned biotech entrepreneur, announced he was setting up a new company, Celera, that would sequence the human genome within three years for $300 million. This was four years ahead of the target date for the publicly funded, $3 billion Human Genome Project. The announcement was taken by virtually everyone as a direct challenge to the government effort and the bioscience establishment.

The media called it a race for the Holy Grail of biology, the complete description of the human genome. James Watson, Nobel Prize-winning biologist, co-discoverer of the double helical structure of DNA, and first director of the Human Genome Project, saw the struggle as one of good versus evil, public versus private interests. He likened Venter's assault on the genome project to Hitler's annexation of Poland. He asked his successor as project director, Francis Collins, whether he was up to the challenge. Would he be a Churchill or a Chamberlain?

Two years later, in 2000, at a White House ceremony led by President Clinton, in which British Prime Minister Tony Blair participated by teleconference, a draw was declared. Although the public and private projects were still not finished, they had reached a climactic point where

From W. Henry Lambright, "Managing 'Big Science': A Case Study of the Human Genome Project." New Ways to Manage Series, The IBM Center for The Business of Government (March 2002), pp. 10–31. Reprinted by permission of the IBM Center for The Business of Government.

the human genome could be almost fully sequenced in a preliminary way. In 2001, scientific papers were published by HGP and Celera, and biology's own "Project Apollo" was heralded a resounding success.

How did this huge project—involving thousands of researchers, costing billions, and extending well over a decade—get started? How did it get organized? What was its scientific strategy and how was it implemented? What were the factors that affected its pace and direction? What lessons can be learned about leadership and management of large-scale technical ventures from this particular experience?

To answer these questions, it is necessary to review HGP's history. The present period is one of transition, as the HGP finishes and polishes the human genome draft and initiates new research paths. A number of these activities involve partnerships with the private industrial sector, in contrast to earlier experience. HGP is moving from development of a tool to its uses.

In getting to this transition period, HGP has gone through five previous phases. The following study of the project tracks events through these eras, which include:

1. Conceptualization—when HGP was developed, 1980–86.
2. Adoption—when HGP began, first as a DOE project, then as a national effort, involving NIH and DOE, 1986–90.
3. Initial implementation—when James Watson gave shape to the effort, 1990–93.

Human Genome Project Milestones

1953	Watson and Crick discover the helical structure of DNA.
September 1986	DOE reallocates $5.3 million to initiate a human genome initiative.
1987	DOE establishes three genome research centers among its national labs.
1988	National Research Council of the National Academy of Sciences panel of prominent genetics researchers publishes report endorsing the HGP. Recommends incremental approach: first mapping and then sequencing.
1988	NIH Director Wyngaarden establishes new Office of Human Genome Research and appoints James Watson as its director. NIH and DOE sign memorandum of understanding to collaborate on HGP.
1990	Watson develops strategic plan for the project of 15 years, endorsing phased approach of mapping and then sequencing. Six centers established in the U.S. to do the HGP work.
April 1992	Watson resigns over conflict with Bernadine Healy, NIH's director.
July 1992	Venter resigns from NIH to accept offer to proceed with gene sequencing at a new non-profit, The Institute for Genomic Research (TIGR).
January 1, 1993	Healy appoints Francis Collins of the University of Michigan to direct HGP, effective in April.
1993	The Wellcome Trust opens new sequencing lab, the Sanger Centre, headed by John Sulston, near Cambridge, England.
August 1993	Clinton appoints Harold Varmus to be NIH director.
October 1993	NIH and DOE agree on revised plan for 1993–98. GenBank shifts to NIH.
1994	NIH rejects proposal from Venter's nonprofit, TIGR, to speed up gene sequencing with "shotgun" method.
May 1995	Venter announces TIGR has sequenced first entire genome of a living organism, *H. Influenzae.*
	Collins makes new grants to pilot projects at HGP centers to test new strategies and techniques aimed at speeding pace of HGP.
February 1996	Wellcome Trust organizes first International Strategy Meeting on Human Genome Sequencing in Bermuda. Forty leaders in genome research agree to make available all results within 24 hours.
January 1998	Applied Biosystems produces "next generation" sequencing technology, greatly accelerating the process of sequencing. Partners with Venter to form new profit-making company, Celera. Venter leaves TIGR to become president of Celera.
May 9, 1998	Venter announces Celera will sequence entire human genome in three years.
May 12, 1998	Collins meets with senior HGP staff, center directors, and key advisors and discusses response to Venter's challenge.
1998	Collins shifts to crash program with a 2000 interim goal deadline.
Summer 1999	Celera announces successful sequencing of Drosophila in just four months.
December 21, 1999	Meeting between HGP team and Venter's group.
March 14, 2000	Clinton and Blair issue joint statement on human genome issues.
June 26, 2000	Clinton and Blair proclaim a "tie" in completion of the first survey of the entire human genome.
February 15 & 16, 2001	HGP and Celera publish separately their genomic findings.
January 2002	Tony White, head of parent company, reorients Celera to develop new drugs rather than to pursue Venter's interest in research and sales of genetic information. Venter resigns.
2003	Projected completion of HGP.

4. Maintaining momentum and growing—when Francis Collins succeeded Watson and sought to speed the venture, 1993–98.
5. Reorientation—when HGP shifted dramatically to a crash project, 1998–2001—and achieved its reorientation goal.
6. The present transitional phase, 2001–2003, when HGP is being fully completed as the post-genome sequencing projects are begun.

HGP is often called the most significant federal science and technology undertaking since Project Apollo. It certainly has been a historic milestone for biomedical research, not just technically, but managerially. It has been controversial throughout its history.

Conceptualization, 1980–86

In 1953, James Watson and Francis Crick discovered the double helical structure of DNA, later winning Nobel prizes for their achievement. In succeeding years, biologists all over the world continued advances, probing deeper and deeper into the mysteries of life, particularly the basic building blocks of heredity: genes.

By the beginning of the 1980s, biologists were deciphering the human genetic code, one gene at a time. Some individuals speculated that it might someday be possible to sequence the entire human genome (i.e., the full complement of DNA in human cells). This was a technological vision that leapfrogged existing knowledge and technical capabilities. It entailed unraveling 3.1 billion base molecules making up DNA, a project whose scale was far beyond the mainstream of human genetics research.

The first major meeting to discuss the feasibility of sequencing the human genome took place in 1985. Robert Sinsheimer, president of the University of California, Santa Cruz, invited a group of leading life scientists to his campus to discuss such a project's feasibility. Sinsheimer was looking for a large initiative he could promote to build his institution into a major center for genomic research. The meeting stimulated discussion, with plenty of views, most of which opposed the HGP idea. Big Science—research costing billions and organized as a project with milestones, expensive equipment, and a managerial hierarchy—was not in the tradition of biology. It had been pioneered in physics, sparked by the Manhattan Project, and in space with the Apollo experience, but had not

penetrated biology to a significant extent. Sinsheimer also ran into bureaucratic obstacles within the University of California system and abandoned the idea.

However, the notion of a human genome project continued to percolate within the scientific community. In early 1986, Sydney Brenner of the Medical Research Council (MRC) laboratory in Cambridge, England, urged the European Union to undertake a concerted program to map and sequence the human genome. What enhanced the technical feasibility of the project was the rapid advance of a range of relevant technologies. What might otherwise require thousands of scientists doing extremely difficult and dull tasks over decades could be expedited by the first automated sequencing machines, invented in 1986 by Leroy Hood and Lloyd Smith of the California Institute of Technology.

There was another issue that made for conflict. Even if feasible, was deciphering the human genome really the best way to spend limited research money? The work was more like developing a technology, or (worse) data gathering, than conducting basic research experiments driven by theory. It was more industrial than academic in style—not what a good academic scientist was supposed to do. The money and talent would detract from smaller, less expensive, "better" science, in the view of many researchers. Also, it would take money from many scientists and give it to a relative few willing to prostitute themselves, said critics. The principal agency supporting biomedical research, the National Institutes of Health, was responsive to the scientific community in setting its agenda. While scientists debated, NIH waited.

Adoption, 1986–90

The trigger for moving beyond talk to action for NIH was the decision by the Department of Energy in September 1986 to reallocate $5.3 million from its budget to initiate a human genome initiative. The principal decision maker was Charles DeLisi, a cancer biologist who headed DOE's Office of Health and Environmental Research.

To DeLisi, a human genome project was a logical outgrowth of DOE's long-term research mission to study the effects of radiation on human health. Also, it was Big Science, the staple of DOE's national laboratories, which faced a diminishing demand for nuclear work. To the extent Big Science had established any foothold

U.S. Human Genome Project Funding* ($Millions)

The Human Genome Project is sometimes reported to have a cost of $3 billion. However, this figure refers to the total projected funding over a 15-year period (1990–2005) for a wide range of scientific activities related to genomics. These include studies of human diseases, experimental organisms (such as bacteria, yeast, worms, flies, and mice); development of new technologies for biological and medical research; computational methods to analyze genomes; and ethical, legal, and social issues related to genetics. Human genome sequencing represents only a small fraction of the overall 15-year budget.

The DOE and NIH genome programs set aside 3% to 5% of their respective total annual budgets for the study of the project's ethical, legal, and social issues (ELSI). For an in-depth look at the ELSI surrounding the project, see the ELSI website.**

For explanation of the NIH budget, contact the Office of Human Genome Communications, National Human Genome Research Institute, National Institutes of Health.***

FY	Wellcome Trust	DOE	NIH	Total
1992-2000	306			306
1988		10.7	17.2	27.9
1989		18.5	28.2	46.7
1990		27.2	59.5	86.7
1991		47.4	87.4	134.8
1992		59.4	104.8	164.2
1993		63.0	106.1	169.1
1994		63.3	127.0	190.3
1995		68.7	153.8	222.5
1996		73.9	169.3	243.2
1997		77.9	188.9	266.8
1998		85.5	218.3	303.8
1999		89.9	225.7	315.6
2000		88.9	271.7	360.6
2001		86.4	308.4	394.8
2002		87.8	346.7	434.3
Total	306	948.5	2066.3	3320.8

*   These numbers do not include construction funds, which are a very small part of the budget.

**   www.ornl.gov/hgmis/elsi/elsi.html

*** This information is from: www.ornl.gov/hgmis/project/budget.html

in biology, it had been at DOE in connection with radiation experiments. The DOE move caused great chagrin among many academic bioscientists, one of whom denounced the effort as "a scheme for unemployed bomb makers." It was clearly seen as a threat. Many non-DOE observers held that if there was to be a Human Genome Project, NIH and the academic scientists who performed research under its purview had to be in charge.

Formulating a Plan

In 1987, as DOE established three genome research centers among its national labs, the National Research Council (NRC) of the National Academy of Sciences convened a panel that included many of the most prominent genetics researchers of the day, including both advocates and skeptics of a human genome project.

The NRC report came out in 1988. It endorsed the HGP. The skeptics and optimists united, but in doing so emphasized the need for a comprehensive, scientifically sound effort to generate maximum knowledge and create as perfect a picture as possible of the genetic makeup of any individual. If the Human Genome Project could be likened, metaphorically, to producing a "book of life," there was a first stage called mapping, which was the stage of defining the chapters. This meant identifying milestones or markers along the enormous length of a DNA molecule.

Once these chapters were delineated, the second stage of sequencing could commence. Sequencing meant going deeper, decoding the material in chapters and giving order to the letters within chapters, between the markers. This steady, incremental approach was geared to a total understanding, irrespective of whether some chapters might be more potentially valuable in terms of health or economic benefit than others. It aimed at as complete and accurate a product as was possible. Because the human genome was seen as a giant puzzle, decoding and arranging more than 3 billion chemical letters, it was viewed as a task that would necessarily have to be divided among many investigators.

NRC recommended spending $200 million a year in new money (meaning the funds would not be taken away from other NIH research). It estimated that HGP would take between 10 and 15 years to complete, and cost as much as $3 billion. This figure included expenses for infrastructure, as well as the sequencing of simpler organisms for purposes of comparison with the much more complex human genome. NRC recognized there could be more than one agency involved in the HGP, but called for a "lead" agency. It did not specifically name which agency should play that role, but its view in favor of NIH was obvious. This was a project with a goal, but a relatively uncertain timetable. It was not a top-down, managed "crash project" like Manhattan or Apollo. The NRC declared:

> A large-scale, massive effort to ascertain the sequence of the entire genome cannot be adequately justified at the present time. . . . the Council wants to state in the clearest possible terms our opposition to any current proposal that envisions the establishment of one or a few large centers that are designed to map and/or sequence the human genome. . . . it is of the utmost importance that traditions of peer-reviewed research, of the sort currently funded by the National Institutes of Health, not be adversely affected by efforts to map or sequence the human genome.

Not everyone on the NRC went along with the recommended incremental approach. Significantly, one of the members of the panel, Walter Gilbert, a Harvard University Nobel Prize-winning biologist, resigned from the NRC committee before it issued its report. He announced plans to start a private company, the Genome Corporation, that would move much more quickly than NRC recommended, employing a different scientific strategy than the one NRC favored. His new company could potentially gain a proprietary advantage and sell genome data for profit.

Gilbert's venture never got off the ground because he could not raise venture capital. However, his action raised many alarms among bioscientists who wanted knowledge to flow freely so they could have access to it for research. Also, some scientists saw the human genome in symbolic terms. It was a gift of God. To make a profit from something so intrinsic to humanity was immoral. If many academic scientists and their allies in NIH looked askance at DOE and its national labs, they were even more wary of business.

Getting a Director

Armed with the NRC report, James Wyngaarden, NIH director, now made his move. Obtaining a small appropriation from Congress, he established a new Office of Human Genome Research, which reported to him. As director of the office, he appointed, in September 1988, James Watson, who had been one of HGP's strongest proponents in advising him. The appointment of Watson was extraordinarily important. He was the most famous biologist in the world. His appointment brought immediate scientific legitimacy to HGP. Scientific carping diminished quickly. In addition, the Watson appointment to NIH immediately put DOE's program in the shadows. Watson said he had no choice in accepting the appointment: "I would only once have the opportunity to let my scientific life encompass a path from double helix to these billion steps of the human genome."

NIH and DOE signed a memorandum of understanding and agreed to collaborate on HGP. HGP thus became a national program. In form, the two agencies might be equal. In reality, NIH was dominant. Watson was not only a great scientist, he was a flamboyant showman. DeLisi soon left DOE, replaced by leaders unknown in comparison to Watson. Also, Congress proved far more generous in funding NIH than DOE. DOE had little choice but to be the junior partner. For better or worse, HGP became associated primarily with NIH, an agency that had little experience in managing large-scale science and technology projects. Big Science and NIH had to adapt to one another.

In 1989, NIH elevated HGP from an office to the National Center for Human Genome Research (NCHGR). Congress appropriated funds directly to this new entity and gave Watson authority to award grants through an extramural program. He was now in a position to put some of his ideas into action.

Initial Implementation, 1990–93

Keeping his position as director of the Cold Spring Harbor Laboratory on Long Island, New York, Watson commuted regularly to Washington, D.C., and NIH's Bethesda campus. He started with just two employees, with staff gradually expanding. In a move unusual for NIH, Watson developed a strategic plan stretching 15 years. He began with an initial five-year plan. In a move that made it abundantly clear who was in charge of this national program, he declared that the HGP would start "officially" in 1990—thus peremptorily dismissing the four years of effort DOE had expended, as well as NIH's own previous work. Watson said the project would run until 2005, by which time the entire human genome would be sequenced as accurately as possible. He endorsed the phased approach espoused by NRC—mapping, then sequencing. In an unprecedented and bold action, Watson also announced that 3 percent of his budget (later raised to 5 percent) would go to social, legal, and ethical studies of the impacts of the research. He said that there would be societal impacts from HGP, and he wanted them studied so that the technology—and he regarded HGP as developing a new technology or capability—could be used wisely.

Watson was extremely effective with Congress. "My name was good," he recalled. Leslie Roberts wrote in *Science*:

> . . . members of Congress were spellbound when the eccentric Nobel Laureate swept in to testify. Watson was eloquent in touting the project's goal: "to find out what being human is." He also had the refreshing quality of saying what he thought, no matter how politically incorrect—an unusual quality in Washington, D.C.

There were debates within Watson's advisory panel about scientific strategy. Instead of the steady, phased, comprehensive approach of Watson, some advisers favored targeting and understanding disease genes. This was the real payoff, they said. It was what Congress cared about. Watson, however, held his ground. He likened the human genome to a particle accelerator. There was a proper way to build such a machine if it was to work effectively.

Watson pushed the first stage of the project, which was to chart maps of human chromosomes. With chromosome maps in hand, he believed the genes within could be better found and sequenced, and the disease genes would be a byproduct.

Administrative Strategy

To achieve his purposes, however, Watson could not go along with NIH's traditional single investigator approach. This approach mainly involved grants to individual academic investigators who submitted ideas through peer-reviewed proposals to NIH. It was a basic research model that had served NIH well. However, Watson adopted a "center" strategy, which had been previously used primarily for clinical research, relying on universities. He did not build up an intramural laboratory within NIH. While he allowed university and other research institutions creative freedom to compete for center awards and go through peer review, it was clear that they had to gear their pursuits to HGP goals and fit into a pattern of his design. This was mission-oriented research in a basic science NIH setting. There

were six initial centers established to do the work of HGP in the United States, all six at universities. These were the Whitehead Institute for Biomedical Research, affiliated with MIT; the University of Michigan; Baylor College of Medicine; University of Utah; University of California, San Francisco; and Washington University in St. Louis.

In addition to the initial centers, Watson expanded the project to other research institutions in the United States and other countries. He wanted broad involvement, as he insisted the human genome belonged to the world, not just the United States. Soon researchers from England, France, Israel, Germany, Canada, and Japan were involved, usually supported by their own governments. The linkages of U.S. centers with partners abroad placed NIH at the hub of a consortium of institutions. Watson imposed certain rules through force of his personality. In particular, he was emphatic that researchers in the United States and other countries share information toward a common goal.

While Watson saw HGP in technological terms, he was not really building a machine but aggregating information into a blueprint. The work of HGP was distributed widely, among individuals, institutions, and countries that were in some respects competitors. But, ultimately, information had to be brought together so the blueprint would make sense. What made this "large-scale approach" to science different from other life-science research at NIH was that there was less emphasis on theory and hypothesis as in the traditional model of science. This was a project focused on technical capacity to gather huge data sets of a particular type and assemble them in a meaningful pattern.

This Big Science approach was new to NIH and biology, but had some precursors at DOE. However, the model of organization Watson adopted was one of "distributed" or decentralized Big Science. He built up to perhaps a dozen major academic centers as HGP evolved. Each had its own procedures and quality controls. They coordinated with one another and through Watson's office to divide the labor of HGP. Watson was "directive" and sometimes abrasive, but, as one former center head recalled, he was so able and such a towering figure in biology, "you forgave him." Nevertheless, the consortium model was an unwieldy structure for HGP.

Whatever its scientific merit (or limits), this spreading of the project had political dividends in that it meant many institutions (and, in the United States, congressional districts) had stakes in the project. Such support was especially important in the early days of HGP, when it was getting off the ground. This was a period of budget deficit and cost-cutting in government. Other Big Science projects at the time—the Superconducting Supercollider and the Space Station—were under heavy fire. The Space Station barely survived, and the Collider project was terminated by Congress in 1993.

One of the key technical decisions Watson made was to support Robert Waterston of Washington University in St. Louis, and John Sulston, then with the Medical Research Council laboratory in England, on a pilot project, the sequencing of the roundworm. This partnership ultimately became a backbone of HGP in some ways—a "transatlantic alliance."

Conflict at NIH

While Watson coordinated various elements of the international consortium of organizations he had established, he ran into increasing problems with his own NIH organization. Watson did not have an intramural research program, but there was genome work under way at NIH. J. Craig Venter was a scientist who ran a large lab at NIH's National Institute for Neurological Disorders and Stroke, an entity over which Watson had no control. Venter not only had biomedical ability, but also was attracted to the applications to his science of information technology. He had been among the first scientists at NIH to acquire sequencing machines. Initially, Watson and Venter saw common purpose, but after a while began to contend. Venter had developed with a colleague, Mark Adams, "a new technique, called expressed sequence tags, which enabled them to find genes at unprecedented speed." Venter was an outspoken individual, and he said his approach "was a bargain in comparison to the genome project." He boasted that his approach would allow him to find 80 percent to 90 percent of the genes within a few years, for a fraction of the HGP cost. Watson dismissed Venter's "cream-skimming approach."

Venter, however, had the backing of NIH's new director, Bernadine Healy, an M.D. who had been appointed in 1991 by President George H. W. Bush following her stint at the White House Office of Science and Technology Policy (OSTP). She and Watson had crossed swords earlier when she was at OSTP. Watson had disparaged her ability and suggested she had her job only because she was a woman. Now she was his boss. Moreover, she was actively promoting NIH's patenting inventions from its employees as part of a technology transfer strategy she espoused. Venter was her poster child. Watson argued that if NIH patented genes, it would undermine the policy of openness and information sharing he had established for HGP participants.

The dispute became public in the summer of 1991, when both Venter and Watson appeared before a congressional hearing. Venter noted that NIH liked what he was doing, so much so that it was filing patent applications on the partial genes he was identifying—at the rate of 1,000 a month. Venter's bravado caused Watson to blow up. He called Venter's patenting "sheer lunacy," and declared "virtually any monkey" could do what Venter was doing. Aside from his concern about communication within the project, Watson's approach was to identify whole genes and determine what they did. He explained that if the patents on sequencing tags held, then anyone could lay claim to a gene without knowing its function. "I am horrified," Watson told Congress.

The Watson-Healy feud worsened. In April 1992, Healy backed an examination by NIH of Watson's personal shareholdings in biotechnology companies for possible conflict of interest. Outraged, Watson resigned—via a fax from his Cold Spring Harbor lab. He declared that no one could work with that woman. Ironically, Venter, who apparently could work with Healy, resigned in July from NIH to accept an offer of $70 million from a venture capital company. He intended to demonstrate his gene identification strategy at a new nonprofit, The Institute for Genomic Research (TIGR). Venter was utterly determined to proceed with gene sequencing with the approach he chose, and felt the need for an organizational setting that gave him more freedom than NIH. A nonprofit model seemed to make sense, although he felt at the time he was taking a huge personal risk.

Maintaining Momentum and Growing, 1993–98

A New Leader

The Human Genome Project was in trouble. Unless a new leader of great ability could be found soon, the project would founder. The centrifugal forces operating in the consortium Watson had established were immense. Healy knew she had to find a replacement, fast.

While she may not have wanted Watson, she did want NIH to lead HGP. On January 1, 1993, NIH announced that Francis Collins of the University of Michigan had agreed to direct the NIH genome program, effective in April. Collins had achieved renown for co-discovering the genes associated with several dreaded maladies— cystic fibrosis, neurofibromatosis, and Huntington's disease. He was a medical doctor/scientist and headed a laboratory that had a secure base of funding from several sources. His laboratory was one of the original genome centers Watson had established. He had to take a cut in pay to become director of HGP. If Watson was a superstar in bioscience, Collins was a very bright star on the rise.

Why did he take the job? One reason was that many other scientists in the program believed he had the right blend of technical and administrative skills, and they pressed him hard. Another was that he wanted it, he said, "because there is only one human genome program. It will happen only once, and this is that moment in history. The chance to stand at the helm of that project and put my own personal stamp on it is more than I could imagine." He also stated, "My whole career has been spent training for this job—this is more important than putting a man on the moon or splitting the atom." He recounted that it was Healy who made him realize this was his calling. She asked him to imagine a time in the future when they met as old people in a nursing home. He would say to her: "Damn it, Bernie, you should have made me take the job."

The Collins appointment was regarded as a major coup for Healy and allowed her to show her own commitment to HGP. With Clinton taking office January 20, she was on the way out, and hiring Collins to bolster HGP might well be seen as her principal NIH legacy. If Watson was universally regarded as the ideal man to get HGP off the ground, Collins was seen by many as the right choice to bring it to fruition.

Collins had a very different leadership style from Watson. Watson was a scientific celebrity and loved the limelight. Collins was relatively unknown, quiet, and did not particularly enjoy the goldfish bowl aspect of heading HGP. Watson was a "big picture" leader, a scientific visionary who would delegate a lot of work. Collins was much more into the nitty-gritty and hands-on details of management. Watson worked hard, but maintained his Cold Spring Harbor lab. Collins was totally absorbed in HGP and left the University of Michigan. Watson was a biologist and Collins a doctor and researcher. As a scientist, Watson always spoke of HGP as creating a technology that would advance the scientific frontier. Collins spoke about the health impacts of the technology. Watson assumed he was always "number one," an attitude that brought his ego into conflict with that of Healy. Collins was more consensual, more comfortable in a team concept of leadership.

In coming to NIH, Collins extracted two promises from Healy. First, he wanted laboratory space at NIH, so he could continue his research even while serving as an administrator and also build an intramural research program staffed by NIH researchers reporting to him. Second, he wanted the organization he headed to have institute status, the major designation at NIH. The Watson office had been established administratively, with minimal congressional authority. With Watson in charge, it had a high status in spite of its bureaucratic base. But without a stronger mandate and position, it was extremely vulnerable to NIH directors and their whims. NIH legislation was thus approved at the beginning of the Clinton administration, and this gave Collins' operation "permanent" status—meaning an NIH director or HHS secretary could not arbitrarily reorganize it out of existence. This action also meant the HGP ultimately would have the same bureaucratic status as the institutes with a research focus on the heart, cancer, and other diseases. Eventually, HGP's organizational home was renamed the National Human Genome Research Institute (NHGRI).

Healy set in motion the machinery to provide Collins what he wanted and she left June 30. Ruth Kirschstein, a long-time NIH career administrator, served as interim director. President Clinton announced in August that his appointee as NIH director would be Harold Varmus, a Nobel Laureate cancer researcher from the University of California, San Francisco. As it turned out, Varmus and Collins got along well and formed a cohesive team. Varmus removed an issue by ending his predecessor's drive to patent partial genes. Moreover, Varmus, unlike Healy, worked easily with Congress, and before too long the NIH budget, HGP included, rose substantially. This internal top-level support aided Collins enormously in managing HGP.

Taking Stock

When Collins took command, he found HGP making progress, but not quickly enough. Most positive was the discovery of disease genes. As Watson had predicted, they were coming as "spinoffs" from the mapping work. These gave Collins ammunition in testifying before

Congress. Every week, it seemed, the discovery of another deadly disease gene could be announced. "The reason the public pays and is excited—well, disease genes are at the top of the list," said Collins. Also, the consortium was growing. Particularly important was an infusion of new funds from Great Britain's Wellcome Trust, possibly the world's largest medical philanthropy, which in 1993 opened a major new sequencing lab, the Sanger Centre, near Cambridge, England. The lab was headed by John Sulston. This meant that the Waterston-Sulston transatlantic connection Watson had funded became potentially more significant in the Collins era.

On the negative side, the mapping was not phasing into sequencing as fast as Collins believed was necessary if the 2005 deadline was to be met. With President Clinton anxious to hold the line on federal expenditures and much of HGP's money still concentrated on mapping, Collins was worried that "we have mortgaged part of our future."

Nevertheless, he maintained the general approach he inherited. It was an approach he was sure would work, but it was slow, and the various academic laboratories made for a cumbersome structure. Collins' initial change was not in Watson's scientific strategy or organizational approach, but in trying to speed the execution of the project. In October, NIH and DOE agreed on a revised plan for 1993–1998. The plan was to accelerate work toward the goal of completing the human genome by 2005. The database for HGP information, called GenBank, which had been under DOE during the tenure of former Secretary James D. Watkins, now was shifted to NIH, a move that further underlined the NIH leadership role in the project. Moreover, to bolster that role even more and help in project acceleration, Collins continued to add staff and start the building of HGP's intramural research. He achieved a major coup when he enticed a former colleague at Michigan to leave the university to head the intramural laboratory, which Collins wanted to look ahead to applications.

The Shotgun Alternative

In 1994, NIH received a proposal from Craig Venter's nonprofit institute, TIGR. It involved a dramatic bacterial gene sequencing method called "shotgun." It had been devised by Hamilton Smith, a Johns Hopkins biochemist, Nobel Prize winner, and member of TIGR's advisory board. Instead of spending months, possibly years, mapping, Smith proposed to Venter a much more brute-force approach. The initial step was to shear DNA into thousands of random pieces. The second step was to sequence the DNA of each fragment. The third step was to use a computer program to align the overlapping fragments to produce a single, contiguous DNA sequence of an entire organism. The boldness of the strategy appealed to Venter virtually from the start. It was compatible with his own methods, going back to his work at NIH. It could help him forward his dream of decoding the human genome. Venter soon had Smith developing his shotgun strategy under TIGR auspices. Venter deployed eight TIGR personnel and 14 of the most advanced DNA sequencing machines available to the activity. To help pay for this work, TIGR submitted its 1994 proposal to NIH. NIH rejected the proposal, saying the shotgun method would not work effectively. Venter called Collins to argue his case, to no avail.

In May 1995, after 13 months of effort, Venter and Smith announced their TIGR team had sequenced the first entire genome of a living organism, *H. Influenzae*, at 1.8 million letters of DNA. They published an article describing their work in *Science* two months later. Their announcement sent a shockwave through the HGP community. Even Watson, who had little regard for Venter, said it was "a great moment in science." What Venter and Smith had shown was that their particular approach, propelled by new computer programs and sequencing machines, could produce results. Nevertheless, most bioscience researchers were skeptical that the technique would work on more complex organisms and certainly not on the most complex of all, the human genome. It was too much akin to relying on a computer to put together a giant jigsaw puzzle. It would force certain pieces together simply because they appeared a fit and would omit others, contended the skeptics.

Collins made clear that HGP would stay on its present course. His goal, he asserted, was to assemble the definitive "book of life." In other words, the HGP approach would yield a complete, high-quality product. The shotgun approach would err and leave gaps. Accuracy was critical where the human genome was concerned, said Collins. He saw two requirements for achieving the quality product by 2005. The first was "construction of a complete physical map for each chromosome, consisting of a series of purified overlapping fragments of DNA that would provide the raw materials for DNA sequencing. The second was for major improvements in the speed and efficiency of DNA sequencing. Unfortunately, he worried that neither requirement was progressing as he hoped."

Efforts to Speed HGP

Collins was not alone in worrying about HGP's pace. Maynard Olson, who headed the HGP center at the University of Washington, Seattle, wrote a commentary in *Science* entitled "Time to Sequence." While not necessarily subscribing to Venter's approach, he said HGP should get on with the sequencing task, and do so "on time, and under budget." Also, Waterston and Sulston paid Collins a visit. They were well into their research on *C. elegans*, the roundworm, an organism far more complex than the one Venter and Smith had sequenced. They "were chomping at the bit, urging Collins to let them plunge into all-out sequencing. In the right hands, they argued, the technology was good enough; the only stumbling block was money." "Just do it," Sulston urged. The result might not be as accurate as originally wished, but it would be adequate, they said. It would be a difference between 99.99 percent and 99.9 percent accuracy.

Collins was not ready for such a decision that entailed a major change not favored by many HGP participants. His cautious approach earned him praise in some quarters and criticism in others. What he did do was make several new grants to HGP centers, testing novel techniques and strategies. He said he wanted to see what these pilot projects produced before shifting direction.

One strategy that could be employed fairly easily to speed HGP was to get information from HGP out quicker, and seek more communication and cooperation among centers. In February 1996, the Wellcome Trust organized the first International Strategy Meeting on Human Genome Sequencing in Bermuda. In December 1992, NIH and DOE had established guidelines on sharing data and resources, which allowed researchers to keep data private for six months. The question was whether this policy had to be changed. The answer was yes. A "Bermuda Accord" was struck that stated: "All human genome sequencing information should be freely available and in the public domain in order to encourage research and development and to maximize its benefit to society." HGP participants agreed to release data in 24 hours.

At the Bermuda meeting, attended by 40 leaders in the genome research community, attention was also given to other aspects of HGP scientific strategy. James Weber, director of the Marshfield Medical Research Foundation in Wisconsin, spoke, touting the shotgun approach. Most of those attending criticized the technique. "They trounced him," a Weber associate stated. "They said [the sequence] would be full of holes, a 'Swiss cheese genome.'" Weber believed the major centers did not want to change from what they were doing to an entirely different strategy. It meant, he said, "overturning their labs." Venter, the foremost advocate of the shotgun approach, was at the meeting, but said nothing.

Reorientation, 1998–2001

Venter's Challenge

In January 1998, the firm Applied Biosystems, a leading manufacturer of sequencing machines, completed work on its "next generation" technology. The firm believed the advance made was so prodigious that it could assure the 2005 deadline would be met. The new machines sped the process of sequencing enormously. The company knew it could make money selling the machines to HGP and its university centers. It could do even better financially by gaining control of genome data itself and then selling the genomic information. Mike Hunkapiller, president of Applied Biosystems, sought to partner with Venter, who had the scientific expertise Applied Biosystems did not have. Venter seized the opportunity. With his shotgun scientific approach and the bioinformatic technology of Applied Biosystems, he saw his longtime goal, the human genome, now within reach. Soon, Tony White, president of Perkin-Elmer Corporation (PE), parent company of Applied Biosystems, became the third party in the alliance. He provided additional money for the venture. A new profit-making company was formed, called Celera (from the Latin for "swift"). Venter left TIGR to become president of Celera. Critics noted that the entrepreneurial Venter had become wealthier with his successive moves: from NIH to TIGR, from TIGR to Celera. Venter, however, recalled he made each move reluctantly, especially the one to Celera. "I didn't want to be in business," he said. "I wanted to do science, but I wanted even more to sequence the human genome."

On May 8, Venter and Hunkapiller met with NIH Director Harold Varmus, and then traveled to Washington Dulles Airport to catch Collins. They informed both men that they had a new technology and the organization to exploit it. Venter said his company would take a limited number of patents and work out license arrangements with pharmaceutical corporations and others interested in the data. He also said he would release sequence data free of charge where appropriate. Venter remembers the meeting as one in which he stressed a desire for private-public cooperation toward a common goal. He recalls Varmus, at least, as intrigued. Collins, however, has a totally different recollection of what transpired, maintaining that he and Varmus were united, and that Venter's notion of cooperation was on his terms alone.

The next day, the *New York Times* broke the story. HGP now had a private sector rival, it announced. The article declared that the business "venture would outstrip and to some extent make redundant" the $3 billion public HGP. It suggested that HGP might have troubles with Congress as a consequence. Varmus quickly rebutted these statements in a letter to the *Times*, protesting that the success of Venter's new entity was not a "fait accompli" and that the feasibility of his approach would "not be known for at least 18 months."

From the outset, the media treated the Celera-HGP situation as a race between the private and public sectors. On May 9, Venter certainly acted as if he were in a race. He publicly threw down the gauntlet to HGP, announcing Celera would sequence the entire human genome in three years, at a cost of $300 million.

Collins' Response

On May 12, Collins held a breakfast meeting with senior HGP staffers, center directors, and key advisers, such as James Watson. The meeting had been planned for several months and just happened to occur at this tumultuous moment. It was at Watson's Cold Spring Harbor Laboratory and there was an emergency atmosphere. The *New York Times* of that morning carried an article implying the takeover of the Human Genome Project by Venter and suggested that the public enterprise might have to be satisfied with sequencing a mouse instead of a human.

The individuals at the meeting were upset and angry, outraged by what they had read in the newspapers about Venter's challenge. HGP had spent $1 billion and completed only 4 percent of the human genome at this point owing to the fact very little of HGP had been focused on human sequencing by then. Most of those present had spent years on the project. How could an upstart like Venter steal their glory? He had the benefit of all the results and technology that came from the public money spent and all the public data HGP had

released. But he was holding his own information to himself. What if Congress fell for Venter's claims? Would it kill the public HGP? Of course, the group believed Venter's approach would never work. It was one matter to sequence *H. Influenzae* and entirely another to sequence the 3 billion base of a human being. But Venter was resourceful and could not be underestimated. He was seen as the potential "Bill Gates of Biotech."

Venter now had a gigantic bankroll from Perkin Elmer and would be getting 300 $300,000 sequencing machines that were more sophisticated than those HGP had. He would also be getting one of the world's fastest supercomputers to help him reassemble sequenced fragments. The group worried that he would not really share data, in spite of what he was saying to the media, and would seek commercially to exploit what was rightfully free to all. Watson compared Venter's assault on HGP to Hitler's march on Poland. He asked Collins: Are you going to be a Churchill or a Chamberlain?

Within three days of Venter's challenge, the Wellcome Trust declared it would double its support for HGP at the Sanger Center, to $330 million, saying Sanger would take responsibility for one-third of the sequencing. Sulston, the director of Sanger, and Dr. Michael Morgan, the Wellcome Trust's program officer, stated that if NIH pulled out of the race to sequence the genome, they would lead the public effort. Speaking before a packed auditorium at the Sanger facility, Morgan declared the Trust would not only double the Sanger budget, but would challenge any patent applications on DNA sequences it regarded as contrary to the public interest. "To leave this to a private company which has to make money," he declared, "seems to me to be completely and utterly stupid." His audience gave him a standing ovation.

Soon after the Wellcome Trust action, Collins brought some of the principals in HGP together for a meeting near NIH. This meeting marked the point at which Collins articulated a radical change in policy. He had been building toward this altered course for some time. In December 1997, Collins had met with some of the key center directors who were engaged in the pilot projects he had funded the year before. He had discussed concerns about the way HGP was organized, the fact that there needed to be greater coordination in order to accelerate the project. From work deriving from the pilots, he had a good idea who his top performers were. The issue for him was whether/when to make a move toward a different organizational strategy. Venter helped push him over the edge of decision in 1998. This was no longer a decision on how to meet the 2005 goal Watson had set. It was now a decision to compete with Venter. That would mean a goal of 2001.

Hence, at the 1998 meeting, Collins proposed a possible reorientation in program strategy. He urged that HGP go for an early "rough draft" of the human genome. He emphasized he was not trying to change the ultimate goal, which was still to produce a near-letter-perfect assembly of all 3 billion bases in the human genome. He argued this rough draft not be seen as "a substitute." His aim was to get 90 percent of the sequence completed and made public by the end of 2001, and then fill in the gaps later. The rough draft would be useful to researchers hunting for disease genes. It would also undercut any patent position Venter or some other company might claim. Collins' new position was greeted with dismay by some HGP participants and with enthusiasm by others. In September, his NIH advisory committee gave him formal approval. Collins declared that "this was not a time to be conservative, cautious, or coast along."

HGP had sequenced 5 percent of the human genome by this time. But both NIH and the Wellcome Trust were about to pump more money into the project, as the public project acquired the same machines as Celera. "The day we announced Celera," said Tony White, "we set off an arms race and we were in the arms business. Everyone, including the government, had to retool, and that meant buying our equipment." Venter got the new sequencing machines first. HGP soon followed.

As HGP acquired state-of-the-art equipment, it reorganized. Up to this time, Collins had presided over a loosely coupled consortium of laboratories across the United States, which were coordinated even more loosely with a number of foreign entities. He had maintained that organizational scheme and enlarged upon it. There were now 16 major genome centers capable of sequencing, known as the G-16. The time had come to centralize, he concluded, with the support of his Advisory Council.

Thus, he soon began funneling additional funds to just three centers—Washington University in St. Louis, Baylor College of Medicine in Houston, and the Whitehead Institute. The Wellcome Trust again increased funding for Sanger. DOE did what it could to strengthen its Joint Genome Institute (as its aggregate of three national labs was now called). What emerged in 1998 was a new management model for HGP that would rely mainly on five genome centers, the ones willing to "sign up" to the demanding requirements he set. This group came to be known as the G-5. This more centralized approach meant that 85 percent of the work would be performed by the G-5, the rest by the remaining 11 centers, which continued in the program. But money was distributed differently, as was power to make decisions.

Collins offered Celera the chance to join the alliance, but Venter rebuffed the offer and said Collins' new schedule had little to do with reality. Venter accused Collins "of putting humanity in a Waring blender and coming up with a patchwork quilt." Collins responded by saying Venter's program was the "Cliff Notes version of the genome."

Collins also changed HGP's scientific strategy. He halted mapping and went fully to sequencing. HGP was converted from an academic-style research effort into an industrial-like crash program, with laboratories operating day and night. As competition heightened, the deadline for HGP was moved up again to spring 2000, 18 months earlier than the previous aim. As the new deadline was again moved closer, the information to be attained became less complete. HGP leaders played down the competition and justified the change in terms of good science. "The best service to the scientific community," explained Eric Lander, director of the Whitehead Institute, who emerged as one of the most influential directors of the G-5, "is to deliver the draft sequence rapidly and then to circle back and perform in the course of another year-and-a-half, at most, the finishing of that sequence."

Collins billed himself as the "operating manager and field marshal" of "team sequence," as he called the reshaped alliance. About half of the sequence would be produced by Washington University in St. Louis, and Sanger, working in tandem. The team at Houston would concentrate on three particular chromosomes. The Whitehead Institute would focus on one chromosome and "whatever [else] needs to be done." That turned out to be a great deal, and Lander's center grew particularly rapidly and took on an assembly-line machine appearance.

Collins told his immediate staff to concentrate solely on managing closely the HGP effort. They drew up charts with milestones and interim deadlines, and monitored performance. Collins had weekly conference calls every Friday at 11:00 a.m. with G-5 directors. "Signing up" meant the directors agreed to allow others in the team access to their work, virtually as they did it. It was a "checks and balances" scheme to make sure what was done under the accelerated schedule was accurate. Going directly to sequencing put tremendous pressure on the group at Washington University to assemble a usable genome-wide map at unprecedented speed and scale. To Collins' relief, Waterston and his team "delivered."

The center directors involved chafed initially at some of the oversight procedures, and Collins took some of them "to the woodshed," as he put it, to obviate resistance and gain cooperation. But if HGP was to compete with Celera, which had the efficiency of doing all its work in one facility—where hierarchy prevailed, and money and technology were available and focused—HGP had to change in a big way. Center directors, who normally competed with one another for grants and glory, had to operate like division directors within a "virtual organization." The G-5 group had to subordinate individual egos to the larger goal of meeting an external challenge. Otherwise, they would fail together. Fortunately for Collins, he was backed strongly by Varmus as he reoriented HGP strategy. The centralization and leadership aspects of this strategy went against the grain of NIH culture, which was very much "bottom up." The crash project approach was precisely what the NRC had warned against in its 1988 report. But it was now 10 years later, and circumstances had changed. Varmus made sure Collins got the additional money and other support he needed to scale up and redirect his operation.

Keeping Cohesion

Collins' decision to concentrate effort and push for an expedited rough draft sequence initially angered some of those earlier collaborators who felt excluded, but after private meetings with Collins, most parties concerned with HGP coalesced. Not all. Sydney Brenner, of the Medical Research Council in England, didn't like the new policy. "Once the genome initiative got consolidated into this managed project, it became a bit like Stalinist Russia," he complained. "If you're not with us, you must be against us." The key to getting agreement among various participants was the common fear that if Celera "won," they would have to go through Celera and its patent controls and expensive subscription rates to get access to genomic information. Venter said the fears of academic researchers were groundless. Trust, however, was lacking between the two sides. Whitehead/MIT's Lander had industry connections, but he made it clear that his loyalty in the genome race lay firmly behind the public genome project—what he called "the Forces of Good."

One who left the HGP camp was Gerry Rubin of the University of California at Berkeley. Both HGP and Celera had projects to sequence the fruit fly (*Drosophila melanogaster*). For Venter, sequencing the fruit fly before HGP was a way to show his critics how well his shotgun sequencing technique worked. With "an offer I could not refuse," Rubin was enticed to Venter's fruit fly team. In the summer of 1999, Celera announced *Drosophila* had been successfully sequenced—in just four months, one-tenth the time it had taken to sequence the previous largest genome, which had been much less complex than the fly. Rubin's defection appalled many associated with HGP, but it showed that Celera had more than a scientific strategy and hardware. It had and could get top technical talent. Ironically, Collins had brought Rubin and Venter together at a scientific conference.

By fall, the radical overhaul of HGP was an accomplished fact. With tens of millions of additional dollars that Varmus helped acquire from the NIH budget, the G-5 centers were being equipped with hundreds of new automated DNA sequencers. They were also adding new personnel to man these machines. Ph.D. students, who had been a large part of the HGP workforce and who found genome sequencing tedious, were increasingly complemented by scores of technicians more suitable for the work. The major university centers changed dramatically in style and appearance. Waterston's lab at Washington University in St. Louis employed 200 people working in shifts and operated 19 hours a day.

However, a serious problem surfaced when DOE signaled a possible agreement with Celera to help it sequence the three human chromosomes for which it was responsible. NIH could not order a sister agency to stay in the fold, but did make its disagreement clear. Moreover, the Wellcome Trust contacted Lord Sainsbury, the British science minister, who held talks with Neal Lane, President Clinton's science advisor. In September 1999, Prime Minister Blair also became involved, presumably asking Clinton to intervene. Whether DOE succumbed to pressure from the White House or from NIH, the fact was that DOE dropped its potential Celera relationship before it was consummated.

The entry of Blair into genome policy reflected the degree to which the issue of control of genome data was escalating to summit-level politics. There were those in both the United States and Great Britain who believed the Bermuda Accord on prompt release of DNA sequence data should become a formal international agreement. That did not happen, but the fact that the move was advocated suggests the degree to which many felt the stakes in the HGP-Celera dispute were exceptionally high. It also shows how different were the political atmospherics surrounding HGP at the end of the 1990s from what they had been at the outset of the decade.

HGP had emerged relatively quietly from the scientific community and bureaucracy. It was Big Science, but took a while to become high-visibility Big Science. Similarly, Walter Gilbert had in the early days tried and failed to get venture capital for a private genomics company. Now politicians and business executives were hyper-attentive to the implications of genome policy. The media, focusing on "the race," followed developments as an ongoing story. Venter proved highly skilled in using the media to make his case. The discoveries of disease genes along the way had added to the sense that serious issues were involved with this research. Policy makers were increasingly aware that biotechnology could well be the dominant technology of the twenty-first century, and who controlled that technology mattered not only in health, but also in economic competitiveness. They might not fully understand where the genome project fit in, but they assumed it was at the cutting edge. In short, the genome project was now politicized.

Efforts at Compromise

The obvious political heat and visibility of the contest, the bitter words that appeared frequently in the media, issued by both sides, led some participants to seek compromise. In late 1999, urgent discussions took place. Among those involved were Lander, for the public program, and Rockefeller University President Arnold Levine, a member of Celera's advisory board. There was the view that the approaches were complementary. Also, some Celera supporters worried that if HGP "lost," it might cause Congress to cut NIH's budget for genome research in general, an outcome regarded as negative. There was definitely a threat there, as the debate took on ideological tones of government versus business. The more the debate was framed in that way, the more politicians would take sides, and there could be damage, especially to NIH. Venter seemed to be getting the better of the contest in the media. He came across as David versus Goliath, the outsider versus the establishment. Collins wished to manage science, not a public relations campaign, and he had to learn the political aspects of HGP on the job.

On December 21, 1999, the two sides met. HGP was represented by Collins, Waterston, Varmus, and Martin Bobrow, head of clinical genetics at Addenbrooke's

Hospital in Cambridge, England. Venter's group included Tony White, Celera executive Paul Gilman, and Levine. Collins brought to the meeting a draft statement of "shared principles," which he hoped to release if the meeting went well.

But the meeting soured. Venter insisted on exclusive commercial distribution rights for joint data for up to five years, whereas Collins considered six to 12 months appropriate (by which time HGP would have essentially completed its sequence and made its data available to everyone). Celera also insisted on rights to various applications of the sequence, including being exclusive distributor over the Internet.

In February 2000, Collins faxed a "confidential" letter addressed to Venter, White, Levine, and Gilman and signed by Collins, Varmus, Waterston, and Bobrow, reiterating the major disagreements between HGP and Celera. Collins wrote: "While establishing a monopoly on commercial uses of the human genome sequence may be in Celera's business interest, it is not in the best interests of science or the general public." Questioning whether Celera really wanted to budge from its position, Collins gave Venter one week to resume negotiations. Failing that, he stated, "We will conclude that the initial proposal whereby the data from the public HGP and Celera are collaboratively merged is no longer workable." On the eve of Collins' March 6 deadline, the Wellcome Trust released the letter to the media, presumably to pressure Celera. Instead, Celera used the letter to denounce its competitor's "slimy" and "dumb" tactics. The leak provided the media a field day and embarrassed Collins, who denied he had anything to do with the leak. It also showed that Collins could not control the actions of his British partner.

In addition to many public comments condemning HGP, Celera's formal response to Collins on March 7 was that " . . . we continue to be interested in pursuing good-faith discussions toward collaboration," provided the company's commercial interests were protected. It saw no problem in releasing data intended "for pure research applications."

The President and Prime Minister Speak Out

On March 14, Clinton and Blair issued a statement on human genome issues, including this paragraph:

We applaud the decision by scientists working on the Human Genome Project to release raw fundamental information about the human DNA sequence and its variants rapidly into the public domain, and we commend other scientists around the world to adopt this policy.

The statement was obviously not only aimed at Celera, but other firms that were interested in taking out patents on genes. Another company, Incyte, was increasingly active. It was not pursuing the human genome as a whole, like Celera; rather, it was targeting a search for specific disease genes it saw as potentially valuable commercially. Clinton and Blair saw a possible problem in the future. However, their remarks caused another problem: a huge dip in stock price for Celera, and the biotech industry generally. That was not what was intended, and it made Venter look even more like a symbol of small private enterprise being pressed by big government. The *Wall Street Journal* gave him op-ed space to plead his case as a victim.

Success

Having become part of the controversy, Clinton now sought to lead in a solution. He told Lane, his science advisor, to "fix it . . . make these guys work together." Unaware of the president's action, Collins spoke to Ari Patrinos, the senior administrator of DOE responsible for that department's part of the genome project. He asked Patrinos if he could do anything to defuse the enlarging conflict. For years, DOE, which began HGP, had been the junior partner in the government enterprise. Now its leadership was needed as a broker. Patrinos had a series of meetings with Collins and Venter, searching for points of agreement. It was critical that the one-upsmanship cease, he made clear. The reality was that each side had certain advantages. Venter had the benefit of access to all the genome discoveries which HGP made public. On the other hand, HGP had started earlier and had much more money. However they started, they were now in a dead heat for the "finish line." Indeed, they were racing for a finish line everyone understood was artificially constructed, in the sense that a rough draft would leave more work to do. At the same time, that finish line was probably good enough to be useful scientifically and politically.

Collins chafed at being in a "race" in which the rules were such that every 24 hours he was giving away data that benefited his competitor. The concepts of "winning" or "losing" did not fit under those circumstances, he felt. Nevertheless, the politics were such he had little choice but to seek "victory" if a compromise proved impossible. Venter was urged by his business associates to avoid a truce and win the race. The benefits from being first were clear from a business perspective. But Venter saw himself as more a scientist than a business executive, and did not want to hurt NIH. Moreover, while he was confident he was ahead, he knew better than anyone the risks in his approach. Nothing was certain. Under the terms Patrinos was discussing, Venter and the public project would get equal credit. The first public signs that an accord was within reach came in June when Venter and Collins appeared together without incident at an NIH cancer conference. As the final preparations were hastily laid for a White House ceremony to make the official announcement, Venter and Collins, clothed in ceremonial lab coats, appeared on the cover of *Time magazine.*

On June 26, at a White House ceremony, Clinton announced that the rough drafts of the HGP and Celera human genomes were ready. Tony Blair attended via teleconference. James Watson was there in a seat of honor. Collins and Venter made a joint announcement, evincing pleasure with their share of the prize. Neither could claim a complete book of life was attained. That would take more time. According to HGP, it would be 2003 when the ultimate goal was attained. But the basic structure—this was now known, and all that remained was to publish the formal scientific papers.

Unfortunately, the truce broke down in December over plans to jointly publish. On February 16, 2001, Venter published his paper on the human genome in *Science*, and at essentially the same time Collins' group published its report in *Nature*. The debate over who "really" won would go on for years, but was already fading in early 2001. The consensus on the part of most observers at this point in time was that history would say both sides won, with humanity the ultimate winner.

Conclusions

The Human Genome Project is generally viewed as a governmental success. It is also seen as having had frustrations along the way, been intensely controversial, and overcome or resolved the issues that came up. These were hurdles that were technical, organizational, and political. What factors were critical in shaping and influencing the course of the program? There are probably a hundred that could be mentioned. Many are scientific or technological, such as the development of new sequencing machines. The emphasis here is on the managerial factors.

Goals

Large-scale, public, technical projects need clear, unmistakable, specific goals. The larger the projects are, the more important it is that these goals be defined and communicated to all constituencies. What a clear goal provides is a constant point of reference against which to measure, direct, prioritize, and modify actions by various individuals and organizations involved.

The major goal of HGP was clear—to sequence the more than 3 billion letters of the human genetic code. The goal was bold—it represented not an incremental decision but a discontinuous change, a leap forward in science and technology. It was estimated that it would take 15 years and $3 billion to realize the goal. While there are caveats that might be raised about timing and money, the widespread perception today is that HGP is a federal project that has worked, on time and within budget.

While the ultimate goal did not change, HGP did insert an interim goal, the "rough draft" of 2000. The interim goal may well have been good science strategy; it was surely good political strategy, needed to compete with Celera. It had the positive impact of accelerating HGP's movement toward the final goal. The interim goal became as important as the final goal in achieving success, since it established HGP's credibility at a time HGP was under attack in the media and Congress. Significantly, HGP spent approximately the same amount of money to sequence the interim human genome that Celera did in the 1998–2001 period. Achieving the interim goal diffused the conflict between the public and private sectors. It was a consensus goal—an arranged finish line. Once met, HGP could continue its work, in a less contested setting, toward the final goal.

Organization

Organization has to do with "who does what," the formal and informal division of labor. It pertains to the allocation of tasks and whether the parts add up to an organizational machine that helps accomplish the overall mission. Sometimes organizational arrangements stand in the way of mission success. Government bureaucracy is viewed as subject to inefficiency, because it is accountable to many constituencies and embodies values other than pure efficiency.

Venter felt that he had to leave NIH to accomplish the human genome mission. He moved from NIH to a nonprofit organization (TIGR), and then to a profit-making entity, Celera, to find the best possible base from which to accomplish the sequencing of the human genome. His own success in this respect shows that there are alternatives to government under certain conditions.

One of those conditions is timing. An earlier scientist-turned-entrepreneur, Walter Gilbert, could not attract business venture capital when he tried to set up a company to sequence the human genome in the late 1980s. When a goal is very distant, its attainment problematic, and its costs enormous, government may be the only instrument able and willing to make the huge front-end research investment necessary. When the multiple, initial technical and financial hurdles of a new field are surmounted, the private sector may enter, as it did in the human genome case.

The way government was organized to pursue HGP was not a result of careful strategic planning. Governmental involvement started through DOE; then came NIH, which quickly asserted itself as "lead agency." While NIH was in charge, DOE retained its autonomy, and at one point almost made an arrangement to work with Celera. Keeping what became an interagency international consortium cohesive and pointing in the same direction was critical to HGP success. There were limits to what NIH, as the lead agency, could do, however, as indicated not only by the DOE possible defection, but also by the independent actions of the Wellcome Trust in England in leaking the Collins letter/ultimatum.

The organizational model of HGP for most of its project life was that of a loosely coupled international consortium. Located in six countries, this consortium had multiple sponsors and performers. There were various players engaged and they often moved in accord with individual rather than project-wide goals. However, in the early days of HGP, the mapping and sequencing tasks were viewed as so vast and technically complex as to require a large number of performers, primarily in the academic community. These performers were structured as centers—groups of researchers and technicians working with sophisticated equipment. Moreover, the first director of HGP wanted to maximize geographical spread and participation as values in themselves. He also involved social scientists, ethicists, and legal scholars, asking them to look beyond the science to its impacts.

However, the downside of HGP's structure was sensed by Collins as early as 1995 and became abundantly clear when Celera came into the picture. Venter's scientific approach and brash style made him controversial to HGP leadership and the scientific establishment generally. But his record showed that a single organization, backed by requisite money and technology, could move fast if led by the right person. Confronted by Celera, the second HGP director, Collins, concluded that HGP's organization was too loose and too uncoupled, a barrier to competing with Celera. He went from the pluralistic model he inherited and on which he built, to a more centralized model, relying on the G-5 centers. Efficiency and speed took precedence over participation. The original organizational strategy might well have made sense in the early years of HGP, when it was getting established. However, later, when much of the scientific groundwork was laid and it was confronted by an external competitor, HGP needed a very different organizational approach.

Political Support

HGP has had political support throughout its history. Had the interim goal not been set and achieved, that support might well have eroded. Goals, organization, and political support go together in government programs, one influencing the other. Politicians may understand little about the technical details of HGP, but they do think they know something about schedules and money. They react negatively to what they perceive as mismanagement, as seen in schedule slippage and cost overruns. Hence, what HGP had to do was to show results to keep the confidence of elected officials.

Luckily, HGP drew on a vast reservoir of political support that is virtually unique to NIH. Had DOE been lead agency, HGP might not have fared as well in getting needed resources. But NIH is among the most favored of government agencies, because Congress and the White House see health research as a priority. NIH, like the Department of Defense, wages war—in its case on disease, and politicians tend to worry about their own infirmities as well as those of their families. If national security helps Defense budgets, so personal security helps get money for NIH.

HGP benefited from this situation. Moreover, NIH Director Varmus proved exceptionally adept in working with the White House and, especially, Congress. Since Varmus also favored HGP within NIH priorities, he helped to shore up HGP's political support.

It should be emphasized that while NIH—and HGP particularly—had considerable goodwill in Congress and the White House, it still had to perform. The HGP spinoffs of disease gene discoveries over the years helped in this respect. The attainment of the interim goal helped even more.

Competition

Competition was a critical factor in HGP's success, but could have been its undoing. It was bureaucratic competition with DOE that induced NIH to get started with HGP. Subsequently, HGP faced internal and external competition.

The internal competition reflected the NIH bureaucratic strategy up to 1998. As noted earlier, when the goal of the HGP was announced and NIH became lead agency, NIH decided to use university-based centers as the prime mechanism by which to accomplish the sequencing goal. Universities are notoriously hard to manage, given their emphasis on freedom of inquiry. On the other hand, NIH believed the top researchers it needed were in the universities. The question was how to enlist them in mission-oriented research of this kind and get their maximum output. One answer was organization (centers) and the other was competition. The centers competed for the money in the HGP budget. The competition was important in getting the universities to maximize their effort and deliver on their promises.

NIH used peer review in managing the competition. That is, those centers that participated had to prove to reviewers, as well as NIH, that they were better than others, or would perform a specific task others could not. This enabled HGP to get academic talent working on the project that was top flight, or at least perceived as such by the scientific community. Center directors, particularly, were members of the academic elite, individuals who had established credentials and were competitive for themselves and their institutions. HGP used such competitive drives to get the most from extramural research. Non-performing centers could be dropped from the project. This system emphasizing many university centers is probably sound for a project at a scientific frontier, when technical uncertainties are limiting factors, and there is a need to explore more than one route to success. Yet internal competition can also slow down a project that has severe deadlines. There comes a point where what is a valuable form of competition early in a project can be a barrier to achievement later in its life. This is especially so where external competition becomes a dominating factor in decision making.

The external competition came from Celera. It was formidable scientifically and politically. Venter was a strong and determined rival, and the evidence suggests

HGP—and the biomedical research establishment—erred for a long time in not taking him seriously. He was tenacious, skilled, and outspoken in his challenge to HGP. His shotgun approach was not valued by NIH and its peer reviewers, but one has to wonder whether it was his approach or Venter himself who was at issue prior to his sequencing *H. Influenzae* in 1995. After that event, he had to be taken seriously. Moreover, in 1998, when he got an edge through new advanced sequencing machines, he forced HGP to realize how capable a rival he was. From 1998 to 2001, HGP moved into a crash project mode and Venter became the enemy. He became the measure against which HGP performance was to be judged, for better or worse. Whether or not HGP wished to be in a race, it was in one.

Leadership

Circumstances affecting large-scale technical projects change over time. The ultimate goal may be a constant, an overall destiny. Getting there entails shifting strategies that are scientific, organizational, and political. Leadership is utterly critical—probably the single most critical factor in success. It took a certain leadership to launch HGP, and another kind to make the changes that are bringing it to a successful conclusion.

HGP had had two very different leaders. Watson was a charismatic leader, a man who will go down in the history of science for co-discovery of the double helical structure of DNA in 1953. He was the best possible person to launch HGP at a time when it was highly controversial among scientists. Few others could, by sheer personal force, have made HGP not only legitimate, but also "where the action was" in bioscience. Great projects that promise breakthroughs require recruitment of extremely able people. It is almost impossible to quantify this human dimension of projects, but there are certain projects that draw the very top people in a field to them. Having Watson at the helm made a difference in this respect. Watson was also an exceptional "scientific salesman" for HGP before Congress. The spreading of centers around the country was no doubt good science in Watson's mind, but it was also good politics, building a legislative base for HGP at the outset, when it needed it. Internationalizing HGP may have also made sense scientifically, but it additionally served Watson's purpose to make HGP a project for the world, not just the United States. Moreover, it supplemented funding of HGP. Early support of the U.S.-British Waterston-Sulston team turned out to be especially significant.

But it is not at all clear that the volatile, often abrasive Watson was the right man to implement HGP over the long haul. There are charismatic and institutional leaders, the latter following the former. Collins appears to have fulfilled the role of institutional leader well. Less flashy, much more consensual in style, Collins was able to strike an alliance with Varmus, his superior at NIH, nurture congressional relations, and develop a team approach to management that became increasingly critical as time went on.

Collins might have initially operated primarily as a "maintainer" and "augmenter" of the Watson approach during his tenure. But circumstances were such that his greatest contribution to HGP's success was his later decision to reorient the project. The process that led to this decision started before Venter's 1998 challenge, perhaps as early as 1995, when Waterston and Sulston paid him a visit and argued for a rough draft strategy that moved more rapidly from mapping to sequencing. His thinking evolved in 1996 with pilot projects to find ways to speed the project. Then came a meeting in 1997 with HGP principals in which he discussed the need to restructure HGP to meet the 2005 deadline Watson had set. Within months, Collins shifted to a crash program with a 2000 deadline for an interim goal. Perhaps he should have moved sooner toward the crash project mode, but would such a move have been possible in the NIH culture without the sense of crisis that Venter posed? What Celera did was present an external threat that empowered Collins to make big changes. Collins moved from the role of a project manager to a project leader. The bold changes he made affected science, organization, and politics.

Forces internal and external to HGP converged, and Collins acted. He did so in the nick of time and in such a way as to save HGP's credibility. It is ironic that Venter helped Collins reorient HGP. Venter created a crisis that affected not only NIH but also the bioscience establishment generally, putting into sharp question the basic government-university strategy for getting the research done. Collins transformed the loose consortium into a tight alliance with a small circle of performers and decision makers. Had Collins and others not responded, the public HGP might well have "lost"—or appeared to have done so. Appearances can be as important as reality in government, and public ridicule could have been HGP's fate.

Instead, HGP is today acknowledged a success, even as it completes the full decoding of the human genome. If Collins was empowered by external competition, Venter received vindication for his effort when he stood together with Collins at the White House victory cere-mony. A negotiated finish line made both sides winners and allowed science to move ahead toward the ultimate goal, a complete genome in 2003.

Ironically, the continuing progress of HGP, and its policy of early release of data, may have contributed to the decision by Celera's parent company to change Celera's course from selling new genomic information to developing drugs. This decision forced Venter to resign as Celera's president and scientific leader in early 2002.

In conclusion, the Human Genome Project shows that relationships among government, national labora-tories, industry, universities, and foreign partners are changing dramatically at the frontier of science. The Human Genome Project may well be a harbinger of the future in more ways than one. It is likely a model for large-scale technical projects in the 21st century. The implications of this case for science, policy, and ad-ministration are therefore profound.

HGP is both like and unlike the Manhattan and Apollo projects. It is alike in being a mega project that is also a breakthrough project. It is different in being transnational and involving the private industry sector as an autonomous (possibly adversarial) actor, rather than strictly as a contractor. HGP, in the present transition phase, is now consciously partnering with the private sector in looking to genomic applications in health. In some cases, joint funding is involved. There is evidence that other institutes at NIH are looking at HGP as an ex-ample of an approach they might emulate. The next phase in the human genome revolution has already begun.

Chapter 15 Review Questions

1. Sum up in a few sentences James Q. Wilson's approach to improving bureaucratic re-sponsiveness to the public interest. How does his perspective compare and contrast to the three approaches outlined in the introduction to this chapter?
2. What are some of the basic unstated assumptions about public bureacracy and public in-terest implicit in Wilson's argument? Are these assumptions valid, in your view?
3. Would you propose any other administrative reforms for securing "the public interest," other than those outlined by Wilson? If so, explain your reasons.
4. In the human genome case study, list the central factors that you found led to its success. Rank those you see as most important. Which ones were least important? What criteria did you use to rank order these factors?
5. Given your list, does it differ from James Q. Wilson's prescriptions for achieving the public interest by bureaucracy? If so, why?
6. Think about ideas for securing the "public interest" discussed in this chapter related to earlier ones such as chapter 3, "ecology of administration," chapter 4, "politics and ad-ministration" or chapter 13, "implementation." Would other theorists approach the prob-lem securing the "public interest" differently? If so how?

Key Terms

deregulate government
culture of the organization
control mentality
mission accomplishment
balancing distribution of
    authority with program tasks
overcentralization of control

judging agencies by results
separation of powers
paradoxical bureaucracy
legislative micromanagement
presidential micromanagement
turf-conscious administrator

Suggestions for Further Reading

The proper role of government in serving the public interest is one that has been considered and debated for decades. Certainly with the founding of the United States, one need only turn to the Federalist papers to read about the concerns for the role of government. Specifically, "Publius" [James Madison], *The Federalist* No. 10, (New York Packet, November 23, 1787) serves as a starting point for understanding the interests and intensity of the citizen's desires for assuring a "public voice" in government matters. Readings that continue this debate concerning government's relationship with the public can be found in John Stuart Mill's *On Liberty* (London: J.W. Parker and Son, 1859) and *Consideration on Representative Government* (London: Parker, Son and Bourn, 1861) and Georg Wilhelm Friedrich Hegel, *The Philosophy of Right* (Berlin: In der Kicolaischen Buchhandlung, 1821). For a good introductory discussion of democratic administration, one should read Paul H. Appleby's *Big Democracy* (New York: Alfred A. Knopf, 1945), as well as *Policy and Administration* (Tuscaloosa, Ala.: University of Alabama Press, 1949) and *Morality and Administration in Democratic Government* (Baton Rouge: LSU Press, 1952). Appleby clearly is one of the most influential American authors on the subject of administrative democracy. For further interpretations of his essays, a helpful compilation is included in Roscoe C. Martin's (ed.) *Public Administration and Democracy: Essays in Honor of Paul H. Appleby* (Syracuse, N.Y.: Syracuse University Press, 1965).

The discussion involving bureaucracy and the public interest is further outlined when one explores the literature on political bureaucracy. For an overview of the requirements for serving the public interest from a bureaucratic standpoint, one should read Lewis C. Mainzer, *Political Bureaucracy* (Glenview, Ill.: Scott, Foresman and Co., 1973), and Peter Woll, *American Bureaucracy* (New York: W. W. Norton and Co., 1963). Additionally, for several essays in defense of the "administrative machinery's" ability to respond to the public interest, see Norton Long, *The Polity* (Chicago: Rand McNally and Co., 1962). On the other hand, Peter Blau, *The Dynamics of Bureaucracy* (Chicago: University of Chicago Press, 1955), argues that bureaucracy and democracy are incompatible and are incapable of successfully co-existing.

Another level of discussion on bureaucracy and the public interest can be found within debates over representative bureaucracy. Much of this literature argues for its importance as a democratic ideal. Steven G. Koven's chapter, "The Bureaucratic-Democratic Conundrum: A Contemporary Inquiry into the Labyrinth," in *Handbook of Bureaucracy,* Ali Farazmand, ed. (New York: Marcel Dekker, Inc., 1994), pp. 79–96; and Brian J. Cook, "The Representative Function of Bureaucracy: Public Administration in Constitutive Perspective," *Administration & Society,* 23, 4 (February 1992), pp. 403–429, provide a valuable "first-look" at the significance of representative bureaucracy. Further, Charles M. Wiltse, "The Representative Function of Bureaucracy," *American Political Science Review,* 35 (June 1941), pp. 510–516 should be reviewed for discussion on bureaucracy's role in assisting Congress in fulfilling its constitutional obligation of providing representation. Students of public administration should also be familiar with Norton E. Long, "Bureaucracy and Constitutionalism," *American Political Science Review,* 46 (September 1952), pp. 808–818, and Charles Merriam, *Political Power* (New York: McGraw-Hill, 1934). A more recent theoretical exploration is offered by Samuel P. Krislov, *Representative Bureaucracy* (Englewood Cliffs, N.J.: Prentice-Hall, 1974), and Harry Kranz, *The Participatory Bureaucracy* (Lexington, Mass.: Lexington Books, 1976). Further readings should include Morris Janowitz, Deil Wright, and William Delany, *Public Administration and the Public—Perspectives Toward Government in a Metropolitan Community,* no. 36 in University of Michigan, Michigan Governmental Studies (Ann Arbor: Bureau of Government, Institute of Government Administration, University of Michigan, 1958).

The challenge to representative bureaucracy in practice involves how to hold it institutionally accountable to the public. Bernard Rosen's *Holding*

Government Bureaucracies Accountable, 3rd ed., (New York: Praeger Publishers, 1999) and Anthony M. Bertelli and Laurence E. Lynn, Jr., "Managerial Responsibility," *Public Administration Review*, 63 (May/June 2003), pp. 259–268 offer basic overviews of these accountability issues. The difficulties in doing so, however, are defined in M. Shamsul Haque's chapter, "The Emerging Challenges to Bureaucratic Accountability: A Critical Perspective," in *The Handbook of Bureaucracy,* Ali Farazmand, ed. (New York: Marcel Dekker, 1994), pp. 265–286.

Further, J. Donald Kingsley, *Representative Bureaucracy: An Interpretation of the British Civil Service* (Yellow Springs, Ohio: Antioch Press, 1944), introduced representative bureaucracy as class and racial issues. One should, as counterpoint to this book, also examine the role of public personnel in a democratic regime, and thus read Frederick C. Mosher's *Democracy and the Public Service* 2nd ed. (New York: Oxford University Press, 1982). More specifically, it would be helpful to examine the public administrator as a link with the public interest. Peter deLeon calls for "participatory policy analysis" in "The Democratization of the Policy Sciences," *Public Administration Review,* 52, 2 (March/April 1992), pp. 125–129. Other excellent readings include Richard C. Box, "The Administrator as Trustee of the Public Interest: Normative Ideals and Daily Practice," *Administration & Society,* 24, 3 (November 1992), pp. 323–345; John Clayton Thomas, "Public Involvement and Governmental Effectiveness: A Decision-Making Model for Public Managers," *Administration & Society,* 24, 4 (February 1993), pp. 444–469, and Philip Selznick, *TVA and the Grass Roots* (New York: Harper & Row, 1949). Norton E. Long provides a standard for evaluating the outcomes, management structures, and processes, programs, and policies in "Conceptual Notes on the Public Interest for Public Administration and Policy Analysts," *Administration & Society,* 22, 2 (August 1990), pp. 170–181; Steven J. Balla and John R. Wright, "Interest Groups Advisory Committees and Congressional Control of the Bureaucracy," *American Journal of Political Science,* 45, 4 (October 2001), pp. 799–812. Finally, the argument that public administration is the "mechanism" whereby decisions are made in compatibility with the

basic tenets of democracy is found in Emmette S. Redford, *Democracy in the Administrative State* (New York: Oxford University Press, 1969).

"The public" is defined in numerous ways: first, the so-called "active citizen" is often characterized as being on the receiving end of public goods. For a useful essay on the active citizenship, read Camilla Stivers, "The Public Agency as Policy: Active Citizenship in the Administrative State," *Administration & Society,* 22, 1 (May 1990), pp. 86–105, and also worthwhile is Norton E. Long's "Seeking the Polity's Bottom Line: A Conceptual Note," *Administration & Society,* 24, 2 (August 1992), pp. 107–114. One of the most famous evaluations of how the public interest is defined at the local level as an interplay of pluralist forces is Robert A. Dahl's *Who Governs? Democracy and Power in an American City* (New Haven: Yale University Press, 1961).

No discussion is complete without examining the role of interest groups in the American bureaucratic regime. A "must-read" on this topic is E. Pendleton Herring, *Group Representation before Congress* (Baltimore: Johns Hopkins Press, 1929) and his *Public Administration and the Public Interest* (New York: McGraw Hill, 1936). Others worth scanning include Allan J. Cigler and Burdett A. Loomis, eds., *Interest Group Politics,* 6th ed. (Washington, D.C.: Congressional Quarterly Press, 2002); V.O. Key, Jr., *Politics, Parties, and Pressure Groups* (New York: Thomas Y. Crowell Co., 1942); and David B. Truman, *The Governmental Process* (New York: Alfred A. Knopf, 1951). For the best book outlining the problems associated with pressure groups, read Theodore Lowi's *The End of Liberalism* (New York: W. W. Norton and Co., 1969); yet, by contrast, an examination of the usefulness of special interests to shaping the public good can be found in Grant McConnell's *Private Power and American Democracy* (New York: Alfred A. Knopf, 1966).

Public opinion is also another important aspect for developing the public interest. For a discussion on public opinion and the means for directing it toward advancing the public interest, read Harold D. Lasswell, *Democracy Through Public Opinion* (Menasha, Wisc.: George Banta Publishing Co., 1941). Other books include: V. O. Key, Jr., *Public Opinion and*

American Democracy (New York: Alfred A. Knopf, 1961); Water Lippmann, *Public Opinion* (New York: Harcourt, Brace, and Co., 1922); Angus Campbell, Philip E. Converse, Warren E. Miller, and Donald Stokes, *The American Voter* (New York: John Wiley and Sons, 1960); and more recently, Thomas E. Patterson, *The Vanishing Voter* (New York: Vintage, 2003).

Recent books addressing important aspects of bureaucracy/public interest interrelationships include: Richard C. Box, *Citizen Governance* (Thousand Oaks, Calif.: Sage, 1998); Peter deLeon, *Democracy and the Policy Sciences* (New York: SUNY Press, 1997); Louis C. Gawthrop, *Public Service and Democracy* (Chatham, N.J.: Chatham House, 1998); Patricia W. Ingraham, *The Foundation of Merit: Public Service in American Democracy* (Baltimore, Md.: Johns Hopkins, 1995); Peter A. Lawler, et al. (eds.), *Active Duty* (Landam, Md.: Roman and Littlefield, 1998); William D. Richardson, *Democracy, Bureaucracy and Character* (Lawrence, Kans.: University Press of Kansas, 1997); Gary C. Wamsley, et al. (eds.), *Refounding Democractic Public Administration* (Thousand Oaks, Calif.: Sage, 1996); Donald F. Kettl, *The Transformation of Governance* (Baltimore, Md.: Johns Hopkins University Press, 2002); and Theda Skocpal, *Diminished Democracy* (Norman: University of Oklahoma Press, 2003). For a recent excellent case study of the practical issues involving these problems, see Anne Khademian, "The Securities Exchange Commission," *Public Administration Review*, 62 (September/October 2002), pp. 515–527.

CHAPTER 16

The Relationship Between Ethics and Public Administration: The Concept of Competing Ethical Obligations

*T*he twentieth century has hardly been distinguished either by its observance of agreed moral codes or by its concentration on ethical inquiry. On the contrary, it has been distinguished by a "decay" of traditional moral codes, a widespread feeling that morality is "relative" if not utterly meaningless, and a disposition to regard ethical inquiry as frivolous, irrelevant. These currents of thought and feeling have been associated with a "falling away" from religious belief and a concomitant rise of "belief" in science and its philosophical—or anti-philosophical—aura.

Dwight Waldo

READING 16

Introduction

Leading thinkers in public administration long ago recognized that the critical issues of government ultimately involved moral choices. The definitive policy decisions made by public officials often have at their base conflicting ethical issues, such as whether to give precedence to the public interest or to the narrower demands of profession, department, bureau, or clientele. The ambivalent position in which public officials often find themselves has led some sensitive administrative theorists like Chester Barnard to say that the chief qualification of an executive is the ability to resolve these competing ethical codes—legal, technical, personal, professional, and organizational codes. In Barnard's view, the strength and quality of an administrator lies in his or her capacity to deal effectively with the moral complexities of organizations without being broken by the imposed problems of choice: ". . . neither men of weak responsibility nor those of limited capability," writes Barnard, "can endure or carry the burden of many simultaneous obligations of different types. If they are 'overloaded,' either ability, responsibility, or morality or all three will be destroyed. Conversely, a condition of complex morality, great activity, and high responsibility cannot endure without commensurate ability."[1]

For Paul Appleby, another administrative theorist, the institutional arrangements in government provide the most effective safeguards for ensuring ethical administrative behavior. Appleby, in his book *Morality and Administration in Democratic Government,*[2] contends, however, that the traditional constitutional arrangements, such as checks and balances, federalism, or the Bill of Rights, do not supply this protection against immorality. Rather, two institutional safeguards are the best guarantees of administrative morality: (1) the ballot box and (2) hierarchy. By means of the *ballot box* the electorate judges direct the performance of government at periodic intervals. Through *hierarchy* important decisions are forced upward in the administrative structure where they can receive broader, less technical, and more political review. Appleby equates the application of broad, disinterested, and political judgment with responsible and ethical administration.

In another selection written as a memorial essay to Appleby, "Ethics and the Public Service," Stephen K. Bailey draws on Appleby's writings to develop some further insights into the essential qualities of moral behavior in the public service. At the core of Bailey's essay is his emphasis on three moral qualities in public administration: "optimism, courage, and fairness tempered by charity." Optimism, in the author's view, is the ability of a public servant to deal with morally ambiguous situations confidently and purposefully. Courage is the capacity to decide and act in the face of situations when inaction, indecision, or agreement with the popular trend would provide the easy solution. Fairness tempered by charity allows for the maintenance of standards of justice in decisions affecting the public interest.[3]

Bailey emphasizes the high ethical content of most important public questions. He points out how the varied complexities of public service add enormous complications to moral behavior so that the resolution of public issues can never be black or white. The "best solution," writes Bailey, "rarely is without its costs. . . . And one mark of moral maturity is in the appreciation of the inevitability of untoward and often malignant effects of benign moral choices." A strain of pessimism appears in Bailey's writing, for he observes that public policies rarely lead to a total victory for the "right" and a total defeat for the "wrong." Indeed, policy solutions themselves often create new policy problems.

Is ethical conduct in the public service the result of Barnard's thesis of an administrator's creative ability to resolve "competing ethical codes"? Or Appleby's "institutional safeguards"? Or Bailey's essential "moral qualities"?

In the following selection by Dwight Waldo, "Public Administration and Ethics," the author attempts to "map" the difficult and complicated terrain of the relationship between public administration and ethics. As Waldo asserts at the beginning: ". . . moral or ethical behavior in public administration is a complicated matter, indeed *chaotic.*" In order to elaborate on the reasons for this current complexity, he proceeds to sketch briefly the historical backdrop of how the distinction between "public" and "private" morality evolved and the

---

[1]Chester I. Barnard, *The Functions of the Executive* (Cambridge, Mass.: Harvard University Press, 1938), p. 272.

[2]Paul H. Appleby, *Morality and Administration in Democratic Government* (Baton Rouge, La.: Louisiana State University Press, 1952).

[3]Stephen K. Bailey, "Ethics and the Public Service," in Roscoe C. Martin, ed., *Public Administration and Democracy* (Syracuse, N.Y.: Syracuse University Press, 1965).

relationship between "the state and higher law." Here we are treated to a concise 2000-year overview of political theories that brought us to our present twenty-first-century dilemmas. He thus provides us with a thoughtful intellectual background for comprehending our contemporary confused scene. Waldo then develops further perspectives on the present by what he calls "a map—of sorts" or an outline "of the sources and types of ethical obligations to which the public administrator is expected to respond." He identifies a dozen ethical obligations, ranging from the broadest "Obligations to the Constitution" and "To Religion and to God" to the narrowest, "To Self" and "To Family and Friends." He defends this "mapping project" in the subsequent sections on "A Need for Maps" and "A Need for Navigation Instruments" because "If we are going to talk about ethics in public life, it would be useful to know what we are talking about." In the end, Waldo offers no easy answers but rather concludes with six thought-provoking "observations and reflections" on this topic concerning "some of the matters that would be worthy of attention in a more serious and systematic way."

A word about Dwight Waldo (1913–2000): This selection you are about to read came from one of eleven out-of-course lectures that he delivered before he retired as the Albert Schweitzer Distinguished Service Professor from the Maxwell School of Citizenship and Public Affairs, Syracuse University. Together these lectures were published as a book, *The Enterprise of Public Administration: A Summary View,* in which Waldo attempted to sum up his four decades of involvement both as a practitioner and as an academic within the field. Waldo served in the Bureau of the Budget during World War II, as director of the Institute of Governmental Studies at the University of California at Berkeley in the 1950s, as editor-in-chief of the *Public Administration Review* for twelve years in the 1960s and 1970s, and as president of the National Association of Schools of Public Affairs and Administration in the 1970s. However, he made his lasting mark on the field by his seminal writings, such as *The Administrative State, The Study of Public Administration, Perspectives on Administration, The Novelist on Organization and Administration,* and many others. Waldo's contributions were deemed so important to the advancement of the field by his peers that the American Society for Public Administration named its annual prize for lifetime academic achievement The Dwight Waldo Award.

When you read his essay, you will no doubt gain an appreciation of why Waldo's contributions are regarded so highly by administrative scholars. Few others write with such stylistic grace, raise such profound questions, and provide the historical context to present-day issues in public administration. In particular, try to think about these questions as you read the essay:

Why does Waldo argue we need "maps" and "navigation instruments" to guide us through this subject? What does he mean by those terms, and do you concur with his rationale for advancing this thesis?

Do you agree with his list of twelve "ethical obligations"? Would you add to or delete from his list?

Why does he contend that "the twentieth century has hardly been distinguished either by its observance on agreed moral codes or by its concentration on ethical inquiry"? What does he view as the sources for this decay of morality?

From your reading of Waldo, what practical advice does his essay offer the public administrator on the firing line in sorting out the ethical dilemmas that he or she faces?

Public Administration and Ethics:
A Prologue to a Preface

DWIGHT WALDO

"No process has been discovered by which promotion to a position of public responsibility will do away with a man's interest in his own welfare, his partialities, race, and prejudices."—James Harvey Robinson

"You are welcome to my house; you are welcome to my heart . . . my personal feelings have nothing to do with the present case. . . . As George Washington, I would do anything in my power for you. As President, I can do nothing."—George Washington, to a friend seeking an appointment

"There is not a moral vice which cannot be made into relative good by context. There is not a moral virtue which cannot in peculiar circumstances have patently evil results."—Stephen Bailey

"The big organization dehumanizes the individual by turning him into a functionary. In doing so it makes everything possible by creating a new kind of man, one who is morally unbounded in his role as functionary. . . . His ethic is the ethic of the good soldier: take the order, do the job, do it the best way you know how, because that is your honor, your virtue, your pride-in-work."—F. William Howton

"It seems to be inevitable that the struggle to maintain cooperation among men should destroy some men morally as battle destroys some physically."—Chester Barnard

"The raising of moral considerations in any discussion on organizations usually causes discomfort. . . . Nonetheless, if morality is about what is right and wrong, then behavior in organizations is largely determined by such considerations."—David Bradley and Roy Wilkie

"The first duty of a civil servant is to give his undivided allegiance to the State at all times and on all occasions when the State has a claim on his service."—Board of Inquiry, United Kingdom, 1928

The subtitle of this presentation and the several heterogeneous epigraphs are directed toward emphasizing the central theme of this presentation, namely, that moral or ethical* behavior in public administration is a complicated matter, indeed, *chaotic*. While some facets of the matter have been treated with insight and clarity, nothing in the way of a comprehensive and systematic treatise exists—or if so I am unaware of it.[1] This situation may not reflect just accident or lack of interest. What may be reflected is the fact that a systematic treatise is impossible, given the scope, complexity, and intractability of the material from which it would have to be constructed and given an inability to find acceptable or defensible foundations of ideas and beliefs on which it could be grounded.

In this discussion I hope to indicate some of the subjects that might be given attention in a systematic treatise. I appreciate that even this hope may represent pretentiousness.

*Strictly speaking, *moral* signifies right behavior in an immediate and customary sense; *ethical* signifies right behavior as examined and reflected upon. But no warranty is given that this distinction is always made in what follows.

Public Morality and Private Morality

An appropriate beginning is to note a distinction between public and private morality and the possibility of a conflict between them.[2] This is a very elementary distinction, but much evidence indicates that it is little understood. As presented in the media, including the columns of the pundits, morality in public office is a simple matter of obeying the law, being honest, and telling the truth. *Not so.*

Public morality concerns decisions made and action taken directed toward the good of a collectivity which is seen or conceptualized as "the public," that is, as an entity or group larger than immediate social groups such as family and clan. Conventionally, "the public" in the modern West is equated with "the nation," or "the country." Thus when decisions are made and actions taken vis-à-vis other nations or countries a public interest is presumed to be in view. Similarly, when the decision or action is directed inward toward the affairs of the nation-state, a public or general interest is presumed to come before private or group interests.

In either case a decision or action justified as moral because it is judged to be in the interest of the public may be immoral from the standpoint of all, or nearly all, interpretations of moral behavior for individuals. The most common example is killing. When done by an individual it is, commonly, the crime of homicide. When done in warfare or law enforcement on behalf of the public it is an act of duty and honor, perhaps of heroism—presuming the "correct" circumstances. All important governments have committed what would be "sins" if done by individuals, what would be "crimes" if done under their own laws by individuals acting privately.

Those in government who decide and act on behalf of the public will from time to time, of *necessity* as I see it, be lying, stealing, cheating, killing. What must be faced is that all decision and action in the public interest is inevitably morally complex, and that the price of any good characteristically entails some bad. Usually the bad is not as simple and stark as the terms just listed signify; but sometimes it *is,* and honesty and insight on our part can begin with so acknowledging.

Ironically, the concept of "the public" is regarded, and I believe properly, as a good and even precious thing. It is a heritage from Greek and Roman antiquity. Its projection, elaboration, nurture, and defense are generally represented as the work of inspired thinkers, virtuous statesmen, and brave warriors. How can this be, when sins and crimes are committed in the name of the public? The answer is twofold. First, my favorite question: Compared to what? Assuming government is desirable, or at least inevitable, what legitimating concept is better? At least the idea of government in the name of a public advances that enterprise beyond purely personal and often tyrannical rule. Second, once in motion, so to speak, the concept of the public becomes invested with, a shelter for, and even a source of, goods that we identify with words such as citizenship, security, justice, and liberty.

The State and Higher Law

To see the matter of public and private morality in perspective it is necessary to understand the complicated relationship of both moralities to the concept of *higher law.* The concept of higher law, simply put for our purposes, holds that there is a source and measure of rightness that is above and beyond both individual and government. In our own history it is represented prominently in the justification of the Revolution against the government of George III, and it inspired the Declaration of Independence.

The classical Greek philosophers, from whom much of our tradition of political thought derives, sought a moral unity. Are the good man and the good citizen the same? Both Plato and Aristotle answered the question affirmatively, though Plato more certainly than Aristotle. In the comparatively simple world of the city-state this answer could be made plausible, given the Greek conviction of superiority and the elitist nature of citizenship: the polity creates citizens in its admirable image and is thus the source of man's morality; there can be no legitimate appeal from what it holds to be right.

But as Sophocles' *Antigone* signifies, the idea of a higher law—in this case the laws of Zeus as against those of the king, Creon—existed even in Athens. During the Hellenistic period, after the decline of the city-state, the idea of a natural law above and beyond the mundane world was elaborated, especially by the Stoics. A sense of personhood apart from the polity, and of the essential equality of humans *as* humans was developing, and this was accompanied by a growing belief that right and wrong rested on foundations beyond the polity. As Sabine put it in his history of political theory: "Men were slowly making souls for themselves." With Christianity these ideas were of course broadened and deepened. The idea of God's law, or natural law—and characteristically the two became conflated—was to become a powerful force in relation to both private and public morality.

For more than a millennium after the fall of Rome, during a period in which government all but disappeared in the West, the relationship of the two powers, the sacred and the secular—for most purposes to be equated with Church and secular authority—was at the center of political philosophy and political controversy; but the theoretical and logical supremacy of the higher law was seldom questioned. With the emergence of the modern state a new era opened. The authority of a state, even a secular state, to determine right and wrong for its citizens was powerfully asserted by political theorists, notably Machiavelli and Hobbes. On the other hand, the long era of higher-law thinking had left an indelible imprint on thought and attitude. That there is something to which one's conscience gives access and which provides guidance on right and wrong remains a strong feeling even among those who regard themselves as completely secular.

The discussion of higher law has indicated that the initial duality of public morality and private morality was simplistic. There *is* an important, and insufficiently appreciated, distinction between the two, as I hope was demonstrated. But two important matters are now apparent. One is that higher law does not equate with or relate only to private morality as against public. Its sanction can be claimed by the polity if the polity represents the sacred as well as the secular, that is, if there is no separation of church and state—or perhaps even if there is.

The other matter is that the public-private distinction is but one example, albeit a crucial one for our purposes, of a class of relationships that can be designated *collectivity-person*. The biological person is

of course distinguishable from any collectivity: nation, party, union, family, whatever. But whether the person can have or should have moral standing apart from the collectivities that have created him and given him meaning is a large part of what ethics is about; for all collectivities of any durability and significance will claim, explicitly or implicitly, to be the source of moral authority. While the state may well, and in some cases inevitably will, claim moral supremacy, the individual will have to weigh its claims against his or her interpretations of competing claims of other collectivities *and* the claims of higher law and "conscience."

Plainly, the ethical landscape is becoming very cluttered and complex. More to this shortly. But first a few words on *reason of state*. Reason of state is public morality at its extreme reach. Plainly put, it is conduct that violates all or nearly all standards of right conduct for individuals; this in the interests of the creating, preserving, or enhancing state power, and rationalized by "the ends justify the means" logic. A few years ago I had occasion to review the literature on this subject in Political Science in the United States. Significantly, what I found was very little, and this mostly by émigré scholars. Unbelievably, there is no entry for this important subject in the seventeen-volume *International Encyclopedia of the Social Sciences,* even though it was planned and executed during the moral-ethical hurricane of the Vietnam War. A number of historical factors, beyond exploring here, have led us to gloss over and even deny the complexities and contradictions that exist when public and private morality conflict, as inevitably they sometimes will.

A Map—of Sorts

A few years ago, attempting to address the subject "Ethical Obligations and the Public Service," I made a rough sketch of the ethical obligations of the public administrator as seen from one point of view. Later, this sketch was somewhat elaborated and refined in collaboration with Patrick Hennigan in a yet unpublished essay. It will serve present purposes to indicate the nature of this endeavor.

The sketch, or "map," as we called it, is of ethical obligations of the public administrator with special reference to the United States. The perspective taken is that of the *sources* and *types* of ethical obligations to which the public administrator is expected to respond. We identify a dozen, but as we indicate, the list is capable of indefinite expansion and does not lend itself to logical ordering.

First. Obligation to the Constitution.   This is a legal obligation of course, but it is also a source of ethical obligations, which may be symbolized and solemnized by an oath to uphold and defend the Constitution. The upholding of regime and of regime values is a normal source of public-service obligation, and the Constitution is the foundation of regime and of regime values for the United States. But note: not an unambiguous foundation. A great deal of our history, including a civil war, can be written in terms of different interpretations of the Constitution.

Second. Obligation to Law.   Laws made under the Constitution are a source not just of legal obligation but also of ethical obligations, as public-service codes of ethics normally underscore. Note again the ambiguities and puzzles. What if the law is unclear? What if laws conflict? What if a law seems unconstitutional, or violates a tenet of higher law? What is the ethical status of regulations made under the law?

Third. Obligation to Nation or Country.   By most interpretations, a nation or country or people is separable from regime, and plainly this sense of identity with a nation, country, or people creates ethical obligations. Indeed, in many situations the obligation to country—Fatherland, Motherland, Homeland, however it may be put—overrides the obligation to regime. Lincoln, justifying his actions in 1864: "Was it possible to lose the nation, and yet preserve the constitution?"

Fourth. Obligation to Democracy.   As indicated in previous discussions, this is separable from obligation to Constitution, granted that the relationship is complicated and arguable. Whatever the intent of the Framers—and I do not expect agreement on that, ever—democracy happened: it came to be accepted

as an ideology or ethic and as a set of practices that somewhat overlie and somewhat intertwine with the Constitution. The emotional and intellectual acceptance of democracy creates obligations that are acknowledged and usually felt by the public administrator. But again, note the ambiguities: Is the will of the people *always* and *only* expressed in law? If in other ways, how? And how legitimated? Is the *will* of the people, however expressed, to be put ahead of the *welfare* of the people as seen by a public official with information not available to the people?

Fifth. Obligation to Organizational-Bureaucratic Norms.   These may be logically divided between those that are *generic* and those that are *specific*. The generic obligations are deeply rooted, perhaps in human nature, certainly in history and culture. They are associated with such terms as loyalty, duty, and order, as well as, perhaps, productivity, economy, efficiency. Specific obligations will depend upon circumstance: the function, the clientele, the technology.

Sixth. Obligation to Profession and Professionalism.   The disagreements among sociologists as to what precisely *profession* entails may be disregarded here. All would agree that a profession, indeed a well-developed occupation, has an ethos that acts to shape the values and behavior of members. This ethos concerns actions pertaining to fellow professionals, clients, patients, employers, and perhaps humanity in general. We have become much more aware of the strength and effects of professional values and behavior in public administration since the publication of Frederick Mosher's *Democracy and the Public Service*.

Seventh. Obligation to Family and Friends. Obligation to family is bedrock in most if not all morality. But in countries shaped by the Western political tradition it is formally accepted that *in principle* obligation to country and/or regime as well as to the public is higher than that to family. While the newspaper on almost any day will indicate that the principle is often breached, we are very clear and insistent on the *principle,* and on the whole we believe that the principle prevails. But in countries in which the concept of public is recent and inchoate and in which family or other social group remains the center of loyalty and values, the principle is breached massively, so much so that the creation of an effective government may be impossible.

Friendship is less than family, but shares with it the immediate, personal bond; and friendship as well as family is honored in moral tradition. To indicate the ethical problems that may arise from this source one has only to set forth a name: Bert Lance.

Eighth. Obligation to Self.

Yes, to self: this is a respectable part of our moral tradition, best epitomized in the Shakespearean "This above all, to thine own self be true." Selfishness and egocentrism are by general agreement bad. The argument for *self* is that self-regard is the basis for other-regard, that proper conduct toward others, doing one's duty, must be based on personal strength and integrity. But, granting the principle, how does one draw the line in practice between proper self-regard and a public interest?

Ninth. Obligation to Middle-Range Collectivities.

In view here is a large and heterogeneous lot: party, class, race, union, church, interest group, and others. That these are capable of creating obligations felt as moral is quite clear, and that these obligations are carried into public administration is also quite clear. When, and how, is it proper for such obligations to affect administrative behavior, to influence public decisions?

Tenth. Obligation to the Public Interest or General Welfare.

This obligation is related to Constitution, to nation, to democracy. But it is analytically distinct. It is often explicitly embodied in law, but also has something of a separate existence. The concept is notoriously difficult to operationalize, and has been repeatedly subject to critical demolition. But presumably anyone in public administration must take it seriously, if only as a myth that must be honored in certain procedural and symbolic ways.

Eleventh. Obligation to Humanity or the World.

It is an old idea, and perhaps despite all a growing idea, that an obligation is owed to humanity in general, to the world as a total entity, to the future as the symbol and summation of all that can be hoped. All "higher" religions trend in this direction, however vaguely and imperfectly. It is certainly an ingredient in various forms of one-world consciousness, and it figures prominently in the environmental ethic and in ecological politics.

Twelfth. Obligation to Religion, or to God.

Immediately one must ask, are these two things or the same thing? The answer is not simple. But that obligations are seen as imposed by religion or God is not doubted even by atheists. One could quickly point to areas of public administration in which these felt obligations are at the center of "what's happening"—or possibly not happening.

A Need for Maps

Obviously, this listing of sources and types of ethical obligations involved in public administration is rough. The number, twelve, is plainly arbitrary. Perhaps some of the items were wrongly included, or should be combined. Perhaps some should be further divided and refined. Certainly other items might be included: *science,* for example, since science is interpreted not just to require a set of proper procedures but to be an ethos with accompanying ethical imperatives. As we know, *face-to-face groups* develop their own norms and powerfully influence behavior, but were not even mentioned. And what of *conscience?* Is it to be regarded as only a passive transmitter of signals or as in part at least an autonomous source of moral conduct?

You will have noticed that I did not attempt to order the twelve types of obligations, that is, list them in order of importance or ethical imperative. This was neither an oversight nor—I believe—a lack of intelligence on my part, but rather reflected the untidiness of the ethical universe. Perhaps the list included incommensurables. In any event, we lack the agreed beliefs which would enable us to construct an order of priority, one to twelve, with the higher obligation always superior to the lower.

How are we to proceed? How can we achieve enough clarity so that we can at least discuss our differences with minimum confusion, the least heat and the most light? My own view is that a desirable, perhaps necessary, preliminary activity is to construct more and better maps of the realm we propose to understand. Granted that this expectation may reflect only the habits of academia; professors are prone to extensive preparation for intellectual journeys never undertaken. But I do not see how we can move beyond a confused disagreement until there is more agreement on what we are talking about.

If I am essentially correct, then what would be useful would be a serious and sizable mapmaking program. We need various types of maps, analogous to maps that show physical features, climatic factors, demographic data, economic activity, and so forth. We need maps of differing scale, some indicating the main features of a large part of the organizational world, some detailing particular levels, functions, and activities. Despite common elements, presumably—no, certainly—the ethical problems of a legislator are significantly different from those of a military officer, those of a regulatory commissioner different from those of a police chief, those of a first-line supervisor from those of a department head.

Simply put: If we are going to talk about ethics in public life it would be useful to know what we are talking about.

A Need for Navigation Instruments

The metaphor of maps may not have been the most apt, but I now use one that may be less felicitous, that of navigation instruments. But at least the second metaphor is complementary: given maps, how do we navigate? How do we find our way through what the maps show us? Let me indicate the nature of some navigation equipment that would be of use.

First, it would be useful to have an instrument to guide us through the historical dimensions of our ethical problems in public administration. Above all, it would be useful to have an explication of the implications and consequences of the disjunction, noted in earlier discussions, between the rise of political self-awareness and the rise of administrative self-awareness. Both as a part of that inquiry and independently, what do we know about the rise and

growth of administrative morality, of notions of stewardship, duty and obligations, reciprocal or unilateral? With respect to estate management, which has been so large a part of administrative history, have rules of proper conduct been widely divergent, or has the nature of the function disposed toward uniformity? Since estate management has been centrally involved in royal governance, from Sumer to the Sun King—and beyond—what effect has this had on bureaucratic morality? Perhaps it is worth more than mere mention that *estate* and *state* are cognates, both derived from the Latin *stare:* "to be *or* stand"; the essential notion in both cases is of substance, firmness, an organizing center.

Second, it would be useful to have instruments provided by the social sciences or derived from a survey of them. Immediately, we face the fact indicated in the epigraph from Bradley and Wilkie at the head of this chapter: "The raising of moral considerations in any discussion on organizations usually causes discomfort." In addressing organizational behavior as in contemporary social science generally, ethics is not just a neglected interest, it is a rejected interest. I shall return to this point; but what I have in mind presently need not cause serious discomfort, though it no doubt would strike many as a peculiar interest and a waste of energy. What I have in view is not an addressing of ethical issues as such, but rather a survey to determine what the several social sciences have to say about ethical matters, either directly or indirectly. For example, are ethical issues present in disguise—morality pretending to be science? We can see that the *yes* answer has often been true in the past, and not a few claim it is true now. What would the most honest, nonideological view reveal? Aside from this question, do the paradigms and tools of the several social sciences offer any handles for ethical inquiry?

Political Science, presumably, would be most centrally involved. And that brings me, inevitably, back to the theme of disjunction: what are the consequences for both Political Science and Public Administration, more broadly, *politics* and *administration,* of the fact that politics reached self-awareness in classical Greece and administration not until the late nineteenth century—this despite the fact that, even (especially?) in small and simple polities, politics and administration were inevitably intermingled.

The other social sciences, even Anthropology, need also to be surveyed. "Even Anthropology?"—an argument could be made that its determined lack of normativeness plus its comparativeness make it particularly germane. Sociology—beginning with its ancestry in Montesquieu and others, and certainly decisively in Comte, Spencer, Durkheim, Weber, Parsons, and other major figures—is rich with relevant material; whether in spite of or because of its scientific stance is hard to say. And Economics? One should not, of course, be put off with its scientific aura and impressive technical apparatus. Adam Smith, in his own view and that of his contemporaries, was a moral philosopher; and Irving Kristol has recently reminded us that Smith's *An Inquiry into the Nature and Causes of the Wealth of Nations* was not intended as a defense of the *morality* of free enterprise. Economics, both in what it attends to and in what it refuses to attend to, in the behavior it licenses and in the behavior it forbids, is very central to any inquiry into ethical conduct in administration: As a random illustration, the recent realization that noxious waste chemicals simply have been dumped in tens of thousands of locations. What sins are committed in the name of externalities and exogenous variables?

Third, ethics as a self-aware enterprise, together with the philosophic matrices from which differing ethical theories are derived, needs to be searched and ordered for the purposes of ethical analysis and judgment in public administration. It may be thought peculiar, to say the least of it, that only well into this discussion ethical theory as such is brought to the fore. But as I view the matter it deserves no high priority. For ethics has little attended to proper behavior in large-scale organization. Its central interests have been elsewhere, tending to oscillate between the probing of traditional relationships such as those of family and friendships and rather abstract and bloodless general principles of conduct. While there is to be sure a great deal in the literature that is relevant, its relevance becomes clear only by extrapolation and application.

Fourth, religion also needs to be surveyed with the object of determining what instruments of navigation it can provide. For our purposes attention should be centered on the Judeo-Christian stream of religious thought and practice, but all major religions should be included. Among the many subjects on which I am not expert are theology and religious history. However, it takes only a little knowledge and understanding to appreciate three things. The first is that theology as such, like ethics to which it is linked in many ways, has attended very little to proper conduct in formal organizations, at least those not religious. Second, as with ethics, there is in theology a great deal that can be made relevant by extrapolation and application. In fact, the writings of Reinhold Niebuhr moved vigorously in this direction; and perhaps I do less than justice to others of whose work I may be unaware. Third, the history and effect of religious institutions and the second, third and X-order effects of religious thought and practice are of so great import for organizational life that one could devote a career to the matter without doing more than explore a few areas. The point is made simply by referring to the work under the heading of Protestant Ethic.

The Pyramid Puzzle

Not surprisingly, many of the most interesting and significant questions concerning administration and ethics concern the theory and practice of hierarchy. Some of these questions are generic, in the sense that they apply to business and nonprofit private organizations as well as to public administration. But some have a special relevance to public administration, as they concern governmental institutions and political ideology. It will be instructive to focus briefly on this pyramid puzzle in the public context.

Central, at least to my own interest, is the fact that hierarchy is represented both as a force for morality and a source of immorality. Both cases are familiar to us, though perhaps not in the context of ethics.

The affirmative case has it that hierarchy is a force that works both for the soft values of democracy and the hard values of effectiveness, efficiency, and economy; indeed, that the achievement of the soft and hard values is complementary, not two things but a single thing. This is a central theme of old-line Public Administration, and the reasoning and conclusions are familiar: Democracy is, realistically, achievable only if power is concentrated so that it can be held accountable, and this is possible only through hierarchy. Otherwise, responsibility bleeds into the social surround. The devices for focusing citizen attention so that it could be made effective—devices such as the short ballot and party reform—were part of the old-line package. Responsibility was viewed as owed upward, subordinate to superordinate, to the top of the pyramid, then bridged over by the electoral principle to the people. Authority was viewed as moving the other direction, upward from the people through their elected representative, then bridged over to the top of the pyramid and descending, echelon by echelon, to every officer and employee.

That this way of viewing things has considerable logic and force strikes me as self-evident. It is plausibly, though hardly unarguably, based on Constitution and history, and can be bolstered with much evidence. It can be, and has been, buttressed by arguments from foreign experience and from business practice. Able and honorable persons have supported the main tenets of the argument. Thus Paul Appleby in his *Morality and Administration in Democratic Government:*[3] The hierarchical principle forwards effective government, but above all it is necessary to democratic government, insuring through its operation the triumph of the general interest over special interests. Thus Marver Bernstein in "Ethics in Government: The Problems in Perspective,"[4] arguing that serious ethical irregularities as well as inefficiencies are all but assured through the absence of hierarchical control in the arrangements for some regulatory agencies, which create conflicts of interest or in effect make the regulatory agencies captives of the interests to be regulated. Thus Victor Thompson in his *Without Sympathy or Enthusiasm: The Problem of Administrative Compassion,*[5] where he argues that the prescriptions for participation equal an invitation for the unauthorized to steal the "tool" of administration from its "owners," the public.

The case against hierarchy in turn has considerable logic and force. It also has roots in Constitution and history, and can be bolstered with much evidence. In this case persons who are able and honorable have stressed the contradictions involved in using hierarchy as a means of promoting democracy,

the limitations of hierarchy as a means of achieving effectiveness and efficiency, and its complicity in forwarding immorality. Thus Vincent Ostrom in his *The Intellectual Crisis in American Public Administration,*[6] arguing the spuriousness of the case for centralization, and the greater democracy achievable by organizing public administration into smaller units more in accord with "consumer" will and control. Thus the advocates of a New Public Administration,[7] who take social equity as guiding principle and seek to achieve it "proactively," through client-oriented and client-involving devices. Thus F. William Howton—quoted in one of the epigraphs[8]—who speaks for many who believe that hierarchy with its accustomed corollaries creates deformed humans with deadened consciences. Thus Frederick Thayer in his *An End to Hierarchy! An End to Competition!*[9] who finds hierarchy implicated in immorality as well as promoting inefficiency, and necessarily to be abolished if there is to be a tolerable future—indeed, perhaps, a *future.*

My aim is not to weigh the arguments, much less render a verdict, but rather to emphasize the tangle of ethical problems in and related to the principle and practice of hierarchy; this by way of illustrating the central position of ethical concerns in our professional business—whether or not we care to attend to them *as* ethical questions. But before passing on, let me pose one question that many would regard as the paramount one: What difference does democracy make with respect to the morality of actions taken by government? Rousseau, if I understand him correctly, argued that while the people can be *mistaken,* they cannot be *wrong.* Two examples to ponder, the first from history, the second hypothetical. (1) If the bombing of Haiphong was "immoral," was the firebombing of Hamburg and Dresden—which was massively greater—also immoral? If not, why not? (2) If the Holocaust had been carried out under a democratic government rather than a dictatorship, would an Eichmann have been any more or less immoral? In reflecting on this, bear in mind Herman Finer's notable essay on "Administrative Responsibility in Government,"[10] in which he holds with regard to the public servant: "The first commandment is subservience."

Observations and Reflections

The spirit and nature of this discussion was indicated by the [essay] subtitle, A Prologue to a Preface. At most I can hope to point to some of the matters that would be worthy of attention in a more serious and systematic inquiry. In conclusion, the following further observations and reflections. I shall proceed discontinuously, serially.

First   The twentieth century has hardly been distinguished either by its observance of agreed moral codes or by its concentration on ethical inquiry. On the contrary, it has been distinguished by a "decay" of traditional moral codes, a widespread feeling that morality is "relative" if not utterly meaningless, and a disposition to regard ethical inquiry as frivolous, irrelevant. These currents of thought and feeling have been associated with a "falling away" from religious belief and a concomitant rise of "belief" in science and its philosophical—or anti-philosophical—aura.

These developments have coincided with the Organizational Revolution: an unprecedented increase in the variety, number, size, and power of organizations, at the center of which is government, public administration. It has coincided also, and relatedly, with the arrival of administrative self-awareness, with a new type of "scientific" interest in administrative study and a resulting increase in administrative technology.

So we confront this historical situation: Just at the time the organizational world is thickening and thus the need for ethical guidance increasing, not only does old morality erode but no serious effort is made to create new codes of conduct appropriate to the new situation; and the scientific mentality that is largely responsible for the Organizational Revolution simultaneously makes it difficult to take ethical matters seriously.

Second   In no country does the level of conscious ethical conduct in government reach the level of complex reality, but the United States may have one problem to an unusual degree. It has often been observed that Americans tend to view morality very heavily if not exclusively in sexual and pecuniary terms: in the public area, Elizabeth Rays on payrolls and Tongsun Parks passing envelopes of currency behind closed doors.

As I see it, a concern for *public* morality must indeed include a concern with the ordinary garden varieties of sexual and pecuniary misconduct within or affecting public life; we would have to be ignorant of history and oblivious to contemporary political life to think otherwise. However, as even my few shallow probes indicate, the matter of ethically proper conduct reaches far, far beyond the popular images of sex and money. It presents problems of conduct for which traditional morality, growing in and shaped to simpler times, provides little guidance. Or worse, it provides *mis*guidance.

Third   Some of the better writings bearing on our subject emphasize the prevalence, perhaps even the necessity, of "moral ambiguity" in organizational life. Thus Stephen Bailey in his "Ethics and the Public Service";[11] I refer back to the epigraph from this essay emphasizing the "contextuality" of good and evil. Thus Melville Dalton in his *Men Who Manage,*[12] who concluded that persons from a middle-class background are more likely to become successful managers than persons from a working-class background, not because of superior ability or technical skill but because of a socialization that better prepares them to cope with moral ambiguity.

If we cannot *clarify* the ethics of the organizational world, perhaps it will help if we can advance *understanding* of the complexity and confusion. If ambiguity cannot be eliminated, then a "tolerance for ambiguity" becomes an essential operating skill. A *moral* quality as well as an operating skill? I shall not try to answer that.

Fourth   The following seems to be true, almost axiomatically: Moral complexity increases as memberships in organizations increase; persons in formal organizations in addition to traditional/nonformal organizations face greater moral complexity than those only in the latter; those in formal *public* organizations face more moral complexity than those in nonpublic organizations; and moral complexity increases as responsibilities in an administrative hierarchy increase.

If this is a correct view, then high-placed administrators (managers, executives) in public organizations are at the very center of ethical complexity. In this connection I refer you to the probing of morality in relation to administration in Chester Barnard's *The Functions of the Executive*[13]—from which comes the epigraph at the head of this chapter. *The Functions* is of course widely and correctly viewed as a seminal work. But it is a commentary on the interests of the past generation that this discussion of morality has been generally ignored.

Barnard believed that "moral creativeness" was an essential executive function. As the quoted sentence indicates, he believed also that the burden assumed could lead to moral breakdown. In a similar vein Stephen Bailey, in the essay cited in observation Third above, uses the metaphor "above the timber line" to signify the severe moral climate in which the high executive must operate and the dangers to which he is exposed.

Fifth We have recently seen, and we presently see, the growth of a gray area, an area in which any clear distinction between the categories of *public* and *private* disappears, disappears in a complex and subtle blending of new organizational modes and legal arrangements. In this gray area, hierarchy is diminished, but does not disappear; new lateral and diagonal relationships grow up and operate along with it, making it formally and operationally difficult to answer the question: Who's in charge here?

As I view it, our ethical problems are compounded in this growing gray world. Who will be responsible for what to whom? In what will duty consist and by what can honesty be judged? One view is that, with hierarchy relaxed and freedom increased, the way is open for the development of authentic *personal* morality. Harlan Cleveland seeks a solution in the hope and prescription that managers in the "horizontal"[14] world that is emerging will regard themselves as "public managers"—because in fact they will be. I confess that on most days I find it hard to share either of these two varieties of optimism.

Sixth As the epigraph from David Bradley and Roy Wilkie indicates, "the raising of moral considerations" in the study of organizations has not been popular. Indeed, the chapter on Morality and Organizations in their *The Concept of Organization*[15] is, to my knowledge, without a parallel in the scores of general treatments of organizational behavior or theory.

A number of factors, some pertaining to American public affairs and without need of mention, and some pertaining to the general climate of our intellectual life that are beyond explicating here, suggest that there may be a change in the situation, that we will begin to address seriously the ethical dimensions of our organizational world—here I allow myself a bit of optimism. This may be best done—perhaps it can be done only—by working from the empirical base legitimated in recent social science. It might begin, for example, with mapmaking, along the lines suggested earlier. Later, just possibly, we may be able to address the ethical as such.

One point of view has it that ethical inquiry is dangerous. Samuel Butler put it this way: "The foundations of morality are like all other foundations: if you dig too much about them, the superstructure will come tumbling down." But in our case, the digging has been done; the superstructure is already down. But then, the old superstructure was not to our purpose anyway. Perhaps on a new foundation we can use some of the fallen materials to build a superstructure that *is* to our purpose?

Notes

1. Certainly Robert T. Golembiewski's *Men, Management, and Morality: Towards a New Organizational Ethic* (New York: 1965) is an able and useful work, and I do not wish to demean it. But the picture in my mind is of a work even broader in scope, one taking into account developments of the past decade. Neither do I mean to slight the useful work of Wayne A. R. Leys, done when ethics was *really* unfashionable: *Ethics and Social Policy* (New York: 1946), and *Ethics for Policy Decisions: The Art of Asking Deliberative Questions* (New York: 1952).

2. The analysis set forth in this section is a brief version of that in my "Reflections on

Public Morality" (*6 Administration and Society* [November 1974], pp. 267–282).

3. Paul Appleby, *Morality and Administration in Democratic Government* (Baton Rouge, La.: 1952).

4. Marver Bernstein, "Ethics in Government: The Problems in Perspective" (*61 National Civic Review* [July 1972], pp. 341–347).

5. Victor Thompson, *Without Sympathy or Enthusiasm: The Problem of Administrative Compassion* (Tuscaloosa, Ala.: University of Alabama Press, 1975).

6. Vincent Ostrom, *The Intellectual Crisis in American Public Administration* (Tuscaloosa, Ala.: University of Alabama Press, 1973).

7. See the symposium, H. George Frederickson, ed., "Social Equity and Public Administration" (*34 Public Administration Review* [January/February 1974], pp. 1–51).

8. F. William Howton, *Functionaries* (Chicago: 1969).

9. Frederick C. Thayer, *An End to Hierarchy! An End to Competition! Organizing the Politics and Economics of Survival* (New York: New Viewpoints, 1973).

10. Herman Finer, "Administrative Responsibility in Democratic Government" (*1 Public Administration Review* [Summer 1941], pp. 335–350).

11. Stephen Bailey, "Ethics and the Public Service" (*23 Public Administration Review* [December 1964], pp. 234–243).

12. Melville Dalton, *Men Who Manage* (New York: 1959).

13. Chester Barnard, *The Functions of the Executive* (Cambridge, Mass.: 1947). See especially chapter 17, The Nature of Executive Responsibility.

14. Harlan Cleveland, *The Future Executive: A Guide for Tomorrow's Managers* (New York: 1972).

15. David Bradley and Roy Wilkie, *The Concept of Organization: An Introduction to Organizations* (Glasgow: 1974).

☐ CASE STUDY 16

Introduction

Dwight Waldo's foregoing essay treated readers to a broad-brush overview of the modern complicated ethical terrain confronting public administrators. Rather than *one* code, he "maps" a dozen (or more) competing ethical obligations which administrators must recognize. How in fact does an administrator choose among these codes and decide which one or several to adhere to? How do administrators juggle these competing demands? Prioritize them? Decide which one or several that they owe their ultimate allegiance to? Especially when "the answers" are not clear-cut, nor even the "questions," as is true in many difficult administrative problems?

In the following selection, "The Case of the Butterfly Ballot," by Robert S. Montjoy and Christa Daryl Slaton, both political science professors at Auburn University, we can begin to comprehend in a more concrete way why ethical decisions within public administration are so complicated, as Waldo's essay emphasized. The case focuses on the well-publicized controversy of the 2000 presidential election, specifically the decision by election officials to use the famous butterfly ballot in Palm Beach, Florida. The authors not only describe carefully the circumstances that led to its adoption but also probe the related factors of voter error, choice of voting equipment, polling place organization, adequacy of voter information, and complexities of local election laws. Altogether, such factors, as Montjoy and Slaton stress, fostered an extreme degree of widely shared administrative responsibilities that in turn enhanced ethical complexity well beyond the abilities of local election officials to cope effectively. Rather than "scapegoating" or assigning blame to a single individual or group, the authors argue that this problem must be addressed systemically by understanding how elections work as an administrative whole as well as how the parts must effectively operate together. Election officials, rather than focusing upon just specifically assigned tasks, need to recognize their shared public responsibilities for making the entire complex system run. The authors ultimately recommend "the necessity for sustained dialogue among all parties who share responsibility for election administration and the challenges caused by their different interests and values."

As you read this case, try to relate its central message to some of the themes of the preceding essay by Dwight Waldo:

Why is it so much easier for the public and the media to assign blame or "scapegoat" rather than seeing such problems systemically as the authors suggest?

What do the authors mean by "objective" vs. "subjective" responsibility? Which one do they favor and why? Do you concur?

Why does the American electoral system foster widely shared administrative responsibilities that in turn create such a high degree of ethical complexity? What are some of the major roadblocks or impediments for effectively dealing with this dilemma? Do you find the authors' solution the most reasonable answer? If so, why? If not, why not?

How were some of Waldo's conceptual ideas related to problems posed by this case? Did his essay offer any useful ideas for coping with issues of ethical complexity for practicing public administrators like those in this case study?

The Case of the Butterfly Ballot

ROBERT S. MONTJOY AND CHRISTA DARYL SLATON

Theresa LePore, the supervisor of elections for Palm Beach County, Florida, designed a ballot that listed candidates on two facing pages with a column of holes for voters to punch their choice running down the middle. The Gore ticket was listed second on the left page, but the voter was required to punch the third hole in the center in order to vote for it. After the election a number of voters said they had mistakenly punched the second hole and voted for the Buchanan ticket, which was listed first on the right-hand page. Subsequent statistical analysis showed unexpectedly high returns for Buchanan, lending further credence to the claim that he had been the accidental recipient of Gore votes (Wand et al. 2001).

From Robert S. Montjoy and Christa Daryl Slaton, "The Case of the Butterfly Ballot." *Public Integrity* (Summer 2002), pp. 195–210. Reprinted by permission of the American Society for Public Administration.

There was also an unusually high incidence of ballots with undervotes or overvotes in the presidential race.

With the presidential election hanging on Florida's electoral vote, many citizens and some newspapers pilloried LePore, an elected Democrat, for stealing votes from Gore. No fewer than twenty-five lawsuits were filed against her, asserting that the butterfly ballot design confused voters and cost Al Gore the presidential election ("Defending" 2000, 1). Some newspapers referred to her as "Madame Butterfly" and described the flaws in her design without ever mentioning that registered voters were mailed sample ballots prior to the election (Lopez 2000). She has been the target of protests and harassment by voters who called her "Racist" and shouted "Give truth a chance" as well as extensive hate mail (Tuchman 2001). Long-time Democratic friends have accused LePore of being a "closet Republican or being 'paid off' as part of a conspiracy to elect Bush" ("Defending" 2000, 2).

The Decision to Use the Butterfly Ballot

Is it reasonable to blame the problem on an individual? To answer this question one has to examine the situation as it existed when the decision was made. The precipitating factor was the number of candidates to be placed on the ballot. A 1998 constitutional amendment had liberalized ballot access rules. The result was that ten presidential candidates qualified for the 2000 election. In contrast, the 1996 election had only four candidates on the ballot. Since each candidate had a running mate, twenty names had to fit on the ballot in 2000. There was also a requirement for a write-in position.

The VotoMatic punch card system used in Palm Beach County presents the ballot as a series of pages on which the names of candidates are printed. The voter is given a blank card to insert in a holding device under the pages. Each page, when turned, exposes a different column of holes. The voter pushes a stylus through the hole to record a vote on the card. Thus the need to line up the candidates with the holes in the card constrains the options for laying out the ballot.

The usual layout was to list the candidates down a single page with the punch holes to the right. This was the pattern that Palm Beach County followed for the rest of the races on the November ballot. However, fitting ten pairs of presidential candidates plus a write-in position on a single page would have required a reduction in font size. With a large elderly population, LePore was concerned that many voters would have difficulty reading the small type. As a member of the Election Center's National Task Force on Voting Accessibility (for blind, visually impaired, and disabled voters), she had been sensitized to the special needs of different populations.

The voting equipment allowed two alternatives to the single-page, columnar layout. One was to continue the column of names onto the next page. The concern with this layout was that voters, accustomed to seeing all candidates in a single view, would treat the second page as a separate race and overvote. The other alternative was to print names on the facing page, thereby producing the famous butterfly ballot. LePore thought the latter option would not be confusing because the county had used it in 1988.

It is now evident that the ballot did confuse some voters. LePore herself acknowledges the ballot design was a "mistake" ("Newspaper" 2001). But ethics does not require omniscience. It requires reasonable decisions based on appropriate goals, values, and available information. Making the ballot legible for all voters is an appropriate goal. The relevant question is what means were available to anticipate or avoid voting problems. There are at least four factors likely to affect voting errors: ballot design, voting equipment, polling place operations, and voter information and responsibility.

Factors Related to Voting Errors

Ballot Design

Design specialists have pointed out problems in the layout of the butterfly ballot and the need for user testing ("Human Factors" 2001). The implication is that user tests should be standard practice for new ballot designs. Such tests have not been standard in the past, but it is certainly reasonable to consider them now.

While user testing can be a valuable aid, it should not be considered a panacea. Don Norman, an authority on user testing, commented in an interview:

> In fact, it's not easy to user-test, because the error rate is like one percent. And so you're going to have to make sure you test 500 people in order to make sure you've really tested it. Second, you've got to be careful how you test it. . . . You can't just show the ballot, you have to show it in context, inside the voting booth. . . . It's not like a menu—I go and I read it and I study it and I think about it and try to evaluate which candidate I want. Instead, I go in already knowing which candidate I want. . . . You go in for Gore and it's the second name on the ballot so you punch the second hole. (Johnson 2000)

The Palm Beach County error rate was higher than one percent, but the point remains that serious user testing, like voter education programs, requires time and resources. The fact that seventy-four Georgia second graders all successfully completed a butterfly ballot in a classroom exercise makes the point that user testing will not necessarily identify a problem, especially if conditions do not match those in the polling place ("Ballot" 2000).

There has been very little attention to user testing for voting equipment and ballot design. Susan King Roth (1998) conducted studies of the human-machine interface for Franklin County, Ohio, in 1993 and 1996. She arranged polling place-like tests with nineteen and thirty-two subjects respectively to compare different types of voting systems. The methods involved videotaping the subjects while they voted, administering a questionnaire afterward, and then engaging in verbal discussion. Issues that emerged included type size—a particular problem for older voters—and ballot design. The layout on the DRE (direct recording, electronic) equipment confused some voters trying to associate the names of presidential candidates (George Bush and Bill Clinton) with the proper square to press. This work was reported in a design journal (Roth 1998) and was not widely known among elections officials.

It illustrates what can be done with a small number of subjects, though still not an insignificant effort. Although such testing can show user preferences, it will not necessarily predict actual error rates for small groups of voters or tell in a single test how to resolve tradeoffs between problems, such as type size and ballot organization. It shows promise for generic testing of equipment and ballot types and for the development of standards and instructions.

In determining the utility of testing, one should avoid too simple an analogy with consumer testing in industry. Elections have to encompass the full range of citizens; government cannot niche market to homogeneous groups. The product life of each ballot is one election and the costs of production (including tests) are not borne directly by the user. The costs and benefits of testing methods must be compared with other uses of public funds. Before Election 2000, the return on a realistic test would probably not have seemed worth the investment. Perhaps now it will, at least in cases of major changes, but the issue needs to be decided in the context of constraints on ballot preparation time (usually a function of state nomination procedures) and available resources (usually a function of local government budgets).

In the Palm Beach County case the idea of user testing was not considered because there had not been a noticeable problem with ballot confusion in the past, even with a butterfly ballot. No state- or association-sponsored program had advocated or provided training in ballot design or user testing for elections officials. A 1984 review panel on equipment standards assembled by the National Clearinghouse on Election Administration had expressed concern with the lack of attention paid by manufacturers or officials to the human-machine interface and advocated attention to ballot design and

format (Roth 1998). However, the subsequent standards did not deal with these issues.

Blaming an individual ignores the lack of the supportive professional infrastructure that will be needed if similar problems are to be avoided in the future. User testing of individual ballots may be impractical for most jurisdictions. Yet governments and foundations could sponsor generic testing of ballot types; professional organizations of elections officials could disseminate the results and incorporate ballot design in training programs; and states could revise their reporting requirements to routinely collect information that could be used to improve system performance.

Voting Equipment

Studies conducted after Election 2000 have found more indications of voting errors (defined as the difference between the total number of ballots cast and the total votes for president) in punch card equipment than in other types, although there is some disagreement about the relative advantage of DRE equipment over punch cards (Caltech/MIT 2001; Brady, Buchler, Jarvis, and McNulty 2001). Of the new equipment now on the market, both optical scan and DRE systems give the designer a larger ballot face on which to position candidates' names. Some optical scan equipment and the very latest punch card systems read ballots and tabulate votes at the polling place, as opposed to a central location. These systems can be set to return ballots that contain overvotes or undervotes, giving the voter a chance to correct any errors (National Commission 2001).

The time for Palm Beach County to have changed voting equipment would have been before the problem of the long presidential ballot. LePore had been researching voting equipment for several years and had been concerned about levels of undervoting and overvoting. There were no systematic, objective studies of the relationship between voting equipment and voting errors before Election 2000. Using vendor-supplied information and reports from other jurisdictions, she had concluded that DRE equipment would be best for her county, but she estimated the cost of equipping the county at approximately $14 million.

She did not ask for the equipment purchase before the 2000 election because she believed that the commission would not divert funds from other needs to replace a system that seemed to be working satisfactorily and because DRE equipment had not yet been certified by the state of Florida. In the aftermath of Election 2000 the state of Florida has moved to replace punch cards in all counties, but the decision was not so clear before.

Polling Place Operations

A third line of defense against voting error is the operation of the polling place. In particular, the number of voting stations and the number and quality of poll workers affect how long a voter has to stand in line, the availability of help, and how much trouble is involved in correcting an error. The number of stations is more likely to be an important factor where lever and DRE machines are used because the voter is occupying relatively expensive (and therefore scarce) equipment while completing the ballot. Paper ballots, punch cards (the system used in Palm Beach County), and optical scan systems are less likely to have problems with the number of voting stations.

The number and quality of poll workers have a major effect on polling place operations. They substantially set the tone of the polling place, greet voters, check registration, provide special instructions for voters, answer questions, and help voters correct errors (e.g., by replacing spoiled ballots). They are the only representatives of the system with whom most voters interact directly election after election, but they are not regular employees of the election office or even of the county. Instead, they are temporary workers who may or may not have experience from previous elections. Palm Beach County recruited, trained, and deployed about four thousand poll workers for the general election. Theresa LePore prepared and presented a PowerPoint presentation on the ballot and the rules for voting and told the poll workers to remind voters to check for incomplete punches.

Poll workers are an extreme case of street-level bureaucracy as defined by Michael Lipsky (1980). In this case the normal problems of control—physical separation, extreme time pressure, frequent demand overloads—are exacerbated by the temporary nature of employment and by constraints on recruiting and training. Although there is no systematic data on this point, anecdotal evidence from jurisdictions around the country indicates that many poll workers behave like street-level bureaucrats coping with an overflow of demands. Often tired and harried, they may not take time to answer questions fully, and long lines may discourage voters from asking questions in the first place.

Critics have called for better training of poll workers, but many of the conditions that determine the quality of the workforce are beyond the control of election officials. Palm Beach County pays a total of $90 to $120 for workers to attend mandatory training and then staff the polls from 6:00 A.M. to around 8:30 P.M. The scheduling of elections on workdays eliminates essentially the entire working population from the eligible pool. As a result, poll workers throughout the nation are mostly retirees, a fact that actually helps recruiting in Palm Beach County with its large retired population. Elections officials around the country struggle to field an adequate poll worker force (National Commission 2001; National Task Force 2001; U.S. General Accounting Office 2001, 158–159).

Voter Information and Voter Responsibility

The task of informing voters is a daunting one for elections officials. Typically, they rely on newspaper notices, public service announcements on broadcast media, direct mailings (as in the case of sample ballots), and instructions posted in polling places. Other actors, such as campaigns and interest groups, also provide information—and sometimes misinformation or misleading information, as the broadcast media's calling Florida for Gore before the polls closed in the panhandle illustrates. As election day approaches, the public is bombarded with messages. Getting technical information on where, when, and how to vote through to prospective voters is difficult.

In Palm Beach County the election office sent out over 655,000 sample ballots to all registered voters with copies to the political parties and the news media. (Rarely was this fact mentioned in news media stories on the butterfly ballot.) The office received no complaints. At the time, no one anticipated that the layout would be a problem. And if they had, it would have been too late to redesign the ballot. At that point the best that could have been done would have been to publicize warnings and instruct poll workers to caution voters.

The samples did not show the holes that would later prove confusing to some voters. They did show that there were ten presidential candidates spread over two pages, that the punch holes would be in the center of the spread, and that the names were staggered. There is, of course, no data on the comparative error rates of voters who read the sample ballot and those who did not, but one would expect a much lower rate among the former.

Critics have pointed out a number of ways in which the ballot was confusing and have stressed the impact of time pressure on the voter's ability to respond adequately. For example:

They [voters] had to go back and forth from one column to another as they deciphered and marked their ballot, and they had to look for punch holes on the left or the right depending on the column they were in. Consequently, voters were confronted with a very difficult cognitive task given the short time that they have to complete their ballot. (Brady 2000, 2)

While this and other comments contain much useful information about design, the assumption seems to be that the voter encounters all of these challenges for the first time in the polling place. Many states, including Florida, have relied, instead, on sample ballots to provide an opportunity for advance study and preparation. There is certainly no way to compel people to read the sample, just as there is no way to compel them to pay attention to campaigns or to vote. Yet in a discussion of ethics, it seems reasonable to ask what responsibility the voter has.

Most of the national reform commissions have recommended increased voter education without specifying what form it should take. A critical issue in any such effort is the assumed role of the learner. Are voters to be regarded as passive clients or "coproducers," active participants in the production of a public service (Ostrom 1996)?

The concept of voter responsibility can be contentious. A list of voters' rights and responsibilities included in Florida reform legislation was challenged as intimidating to voters. The fear of intimidation and discrimination is not trivial. The past requirement in some states that voters present poll tax receipts for the previous two years is an example. Yet avoidance of the issue will only hinder the development of education efforts and lead to finger-pointing in the event of future problems.

In summary, several factors affected the Florida ballot problem, directly or indirectly. These include the number of candidates, the voting equipment, the population in Palm Beach County, LePore's focus on the problem of eyesight, the lack of professional training for or emphasis on user testing, a situation in at least some polling places that made voter assistance difficult or time consuming to obtain, and the fact that the sample ballots did not accomplish their intended purpose in all cases. This case supports three conclusions: (1) Elections officials do exercise discretion that can have a substantial impact on outcomes; (2) nevertheless, they do not have unilateral control; the decisions of numerous parties affect the electoral process; (3) many of the actions necessary to avoid an election problem would have to be undertaken well before the election by actors who have no direct responsibility for the conduct of the elections.

Analysis

What constitutes ethical behavior under such circumstances? In *The Responsible Administrator* Cooper (1998) argues that ethical behavior is necessarily responsible behavior but that traditional notions of responsibility are not sufficient guidance for the complex world of public administration. To make this point he distinguishes two aspects of responsibility: objective and subjective.

Objective and Subjective Responsibility

Objective responsibility is responsibility *to* someone *for* certain tasks, for example, a poll worker responsible to her supervisor for properly checking voters' names against the registration list. Cooper contends that this type is the basis of much traditional public administration thought. Objective responsibility relies on two assumptions—certainty and hierarchical control—which rarely obtain in complex situations like the butterfly ballot case.

The assumption of certainty is that the scientific method reveals a natural order which allows us to apply technical rationality in complex human endeavors and achieve predictability in human behavior. L. Douglas Kiel argues, however, that "the new scientific paradigm teaches us that uncertainty, instability, and unpredictability are essential to the creative processes of nature" and "chaos is not unusual or exceptional. It is a normal part of reality" (1994, 4). As the television networks discovered on election night, voters do not always behave according to predictions. Even when knowledge exists, it may not be available to decision-makers or they may not recognize its utility in advance of problems. The implication for ethical evaluation is that one cannot impose a standard of certainty. Responsibility does require, instead, "an ongoing process of developing the best course for action for specific structures we face within constraints of time and information" (Cooper 1998, 7).

The assumption of hierarchy is that a clear chain of command assigns specified individual responsibility and appropriate conduct at each level so that ultimate accountability can be pinpointed with precision. Kiel argues that Max Weber's "machinelike ideal of bureaucracy" is an "attempt to obtain certainty and order in an increasingly complex world . . . a world that we know intuitively is uncertain" (1994, 12).

Most elections officials do not operate in large hierarchies. They work in local (county, township, and some city) offices, some of which are headed by independently elected officials, while others are part of the local government's staff under the general governing body. Statutory law and court decisions play major roles in elections administration. Some, but not all, states have central offices or commissions with rulemaking authority. Although legal authority attempts to provide guidance and coordination, the Florida examples—both the issue of ballot design and that of recount procedures—demonstrate what public administrators have long recognized: the complete elimination of discretion is impossible.

In fact, a plethora of detailed statutes passed at different times for different purposes can create discretion for the administrator who must decide which ones to obey, especially when resources are scarce (Montjoy and O'Toole 1979). Unfunded federal and state mandates (e.g., motor voter, multilingual ballot requirements) serve useful purposes but typically add to costs, often forcing choices among desirable activities. Similarly, a county official in New Jersey commented to one of us regarding a state-mandated training program for poll workers: "It's a great program. My only choice is whether to obey the law or put on an election."

The inadequacy of objective responsibility in situations such as these leads us to Cooper's concept of subjective responsibility, which is based in individual feelings and beliefs. It is a personal, moral compass that is rooted in one's "own belief about loyalty, conscience, and identification" (Cooper 1998, 78). Subjective responsibility is not a justification for each individual to do whatever he or she thinks. Rather, it is a call to look beyond the objective requirements of one's job. It is important to achieve consistency between objective responsibility and the values and principles that guide one's own conscience. The degree to which these responsibilities are in conflict can affect the manner in which ethical conduct is consistent and avoids idiosyncratic behavior. Both entail the articulation of values, principles, and reflection on one's conduct.

The Need for Continuous Dialogue

The most important point for present purposes is Cooper's emphasis on reflection and dialogue, not only by individuals but among professionals and other participants, as they work to resolve the recurring friction between objective and subjective responsibility. The basic argument is that there is no quick fix or simple answer. In a complex and interdependent system ethics requires more than simply doing one's job. It requires engaging others to define and work out the implications of values, roles, and responsibilities. This is a relatively new role for many elections officials. Further, this admonition for dialogue and reflection applies not only to elections officials but to others—voters, the news media, political parties, interest groups—who regularly participate.

The Election Center, a national nonprofit organization of election officials, provides an example of professional development and reflective dialogue. Since 1994 it has operated a professional education program in partnership with the Master of Public Administration faculty from Auburn University. In 1997 it assembled a group of program graduates to develop a statement of principles and standards of conduct. They were asked to first articulate the *values* that they embraced as elections administrators in a representative democracy and then to translate their values into statements of principle that would guide those in the voter registration and elections field. After an intense three-day discussion of values and principles, the group reached unanimous agreement on the two documents.

Throughout the discussion of the standards of conduct, the emphasis was on "we"—referring to all those employed in voter registration and elections. In the final minutes of approval of the standards of conduct, one participant proposed that all the references to "we" be changed to "I." It was her belief that those who work in the elections field recognized their special role in preserving democracy and faith in the democratic process and that each person should adhere to a code of ethics that places emphasis on *individual* responsibility. Her proposal, which was unanimously accepted, was a reflection of a dialogue among elections officials seeking to meld their subjective responsibility with objective responsibility and to express the standards of conduct by which their values would be expressed to fulfill their "sacred honor to protect and promote public trust and confidence by [their] conduct of accurate and fair elections."

This example illustrates that reflection and dialogue among people who play the same basic role in the elections process can help define individual responsibility. This is a necessary and extraordinarily helpful step, but it is not, alone, sufficient. One reason is that conditions and expectations change, so the process has to continue. The other is that the interdependence of the system requires additional parties to be involved at some point. It is important to recognize that different players have different interests or at least different visions of the public interest.

Players and Interests

Dialogue among different parties can inform the sense of purpose and obligation that each brings to the electoral process, and it can lead to changes in the formal rules and procedures. This call for dialogue differs from the usual admonition for an inclusive policy process. One normally expects participants to pursue their own interests in policymaking. In fact, some views of ethics expect the greater public good to emerge from an aggregation of competing interests (Heineman, Bluhm, Peterson, and Kearny 1997). Electoral policy is different in that it deals with the aggregation rules themselves or their application. Narrowly self-interested and competitive behavior is less likely to serve the public interest when the object is to design or refine the decision rules and practices for the electoral system itself.

John Rawls makes this point in his *Theory of Justice* (1971). He defines justice as the result of a fair game and a fair game as one designed by people who do not know what their positions will be in the actual play of the game. People intuitively recognize the distinction between the design of the game and the play of the game as well as the admonition not to change the rules in the middle of the game. Thus many people questioned the Florida recount and contest because the counting rules were being decided with supposed knowledge of their immediate consequences for the interested parties, even though subsequent analysis suggested that the parties may have been mistaken about who would benefit from which rules (Cauchon and Drinkard 2001). Recognizing that even the perception of favoritism was damaging to the electoral process, the National Commission on Elections Standards and Reform (2001) recommended abandoning the "intent of the voter" standard used for recounts by Florida and some other states in favor of defining a vote for each type of equipment (e.g., count chad hanging by one corner but not by two).

There is an inherent tension between the need to avoid decisions that may affect the outcome in the midst of a contest and the practical impossibility of eliminating discretion. Although an ultimate resolution to this tension is not likely to be found, it would seem helpful to regularly review procedures between major elections and to adjust them if necessary. The difficulty of legislative action and the need for equal protection statewide as enunciated in *Bush v. Gore* both suggest a greater reliance on administrative rule making than is now the case in many states. Such action would require enabling legislation in some states and a culling of extremely detailed mandates from the codes in many of them.

It is, of course, impossible to completely avoid knowledge of self-interested implications in the making of electoral policy. Yet it should be possible to take steps that promote a holistic view and a focus on the public interest. Practical steps could include discussion within and among groups during periods of relative calm between major elections and the collection and sharing of comparative state and even cross-national information on problems and solutions. For example, the newly created Election Reform Information Project (www.electionline.org) funded by the Pew Charitable Trusts collects, digests, and disseminates information and ideas for all interested parties with the goals of keeping reform on the public agenda and enhancing the informational basis for decisions. That the right forum can encourage participants to transcend narrow self-interest has been demonstrated by researchers in the United States, Europe, and Australia (Slaton 2001; Coote and Lanaghan 1997; Delap 1998; Slaton 1992).

Unfortunately, political incentives often run counter to ethical obligations. Election law is made at the state and federal levels. In most states virtually all funds for election administration come from local budgets. At no level do policymakers have much incentive to focus on the detailed needs of the system. No economic interest group routinely pushes an election reform agenda. Certainly, there have been movements—women's suffrage, civil rights, and the National Voter Registration Act of 1993, for example—but not sustained attention to the overall mechanics of the system. Furthermore, the normal inertia of the policy process may be reinforced by the fact that a change in the electoral system has the potential to directly affect all members of a legislative body, and that the old system was good enough to get them there in the first place.

Election 2000 has created an exception to this generalization. Numerous commissions have studied electoral problems, several bills have been introduced into Congress, and a number of states have enacted reform legislation. In Florida the various parties got together to draft and pass legislation addressing many aspects of the electoral system. At the election supervisors' summer meeting in June 2001 a state senator who had sponsored the reform bill said, "If there is something wrong with the law, it's the legislature's fault." It is not only important that the legislature took responsibility but also that it recognized and drew on the expertise of elections officials and other participants.

Will broad interest in the elections process be sustained? The interdependence of the system makes this an important question. Policymakers tend to respond to demands articulated by organized interests. The task of figuring out all the consequences of a proposal are often ignored, particularly if no important party is raising objections or offering free information. Two parties that might help to focus attention on the whole system are the press and elections officials.

The press plays very important roles in elections. Ideally, they contribute to the public good by providing an objective source of information that helps voters pursue their own interests through the electoral process. But various press organizations compete with each other for market share. Competition places a premium on speed that can have negative consequences, as in the premature projection of winners or pressure on election officials to emphasize speed over accuracy in releasing results. Similarly, the need to attract audience may draw press attention away from the electoral process if public interest wanes. Certainly, past experience and economic incentives would suggest this outcome.

The press has a public responsibility, not only to follow election campaigns, but also to educate itself and the public on the workings of the system. An attentive and responsible press can help direct attention to issues of public interest in election decisions and push these issues onto the policy agenda. Doing so effectively requires a holistic focus—some knowledge of the whole system and its interdependencies. There is probably very little economic interest in playing this role; it is a matter of ethics. At a minimum the press should recognize its own role in and responsibility for flaws in the system.

The most logical advocates for a holistic view of the system are elections officials themselves. One normally thinks of public managers as a primary source of expertise on the systems that they administer. Elections officials have not routinely played this role. There appear to be a number of reasons for this situation, including the need for a strictly neutral posture in the *conduct* of elections and a lack of professional development among elections officials.

Frank Goodnow (1900) has been inaccurately characterized as advocating a strict dichotomy of policy and administration, but he did warn against political activities of administrators that would interfere with the expression of the public will (Montjoy and Watson 1995). His point applies particularly to the need for strict neutrality by elections officials in the *conduct* of elections. Pressures for neutrality and strict adherence to rules do not, however, preclude policy advice any more than prohibitions on partisanship have prevented the partisan election of elections officials, although the combinations do pose some finely crafted role differentiations. In fact, they should be the subjects of continuing ethical analysis among elections officials, who until very recently had little identity or organization to promote such interaction. And except for the attention following the 2000 presidential election, they have had little ability to influence policy.

Historically, these officials have not been well organized to develop or articulate positions on electoral policy. They share no common preservice education to provide a sense of professional identity. As noted, the vast majority work at the local levels, while most policy is made at the state and federal level. Some officials, such as Florida's supervisors of elections, concentrate solely on elections while others, such as many county clerks, share elections with other responsibilities. Some states have effective organizations of elections officials that monitor and try to influence electoral policy; others do not, or did not before Election 2000.

There are movements to increase professional development. Anecdotal evidence indicates that state associations are becoming more active. The Election Center is working to increase professionalism among elections officials through conferences, the creation of a code of ethics, and a national certification program in partnership with Auburn University. Various reform commissions and public administration scholars are advocating human resource development (Wise 2001; Montjoy 2001; National Commission 2001; National Task Force 2001). Professional development, too, is a matter of interdependence because it requires financial support.

Elections officials are a weak constituency for policymakers. Their role in the policy process is not well defined or universally accepted by other players, such as legislators. Furthermore, the implication of continual shifts in roles between neutrality in the conduct of elections and advocacy in policymaking requires careful thought. This is prime material for ethical analysis, and elections officials must engage each other in order to do it. Continuing professional development is a necessary condition.

Conclusion

The U.S. election system is complex and interdependent. Most analysts of the 2000 presidential election have failed to recognize or understand the multiple actors and responsibilities in this multilayered, interdependent system. The Palm Beach County case demonstrates how a failure to recognize the complexity of the system can lead to unjust and unproductive ethical analysis. This examination has identified multiple actors who share responsibility for the conduct of fair and open elections.

Subjective responsibility requires individuals to transcend formal job definitions and narrow self interest. Because responsibilities are shared, disparate groups with different values and interests will have to work together to effect systemic improvements. Policymakers need the knowledge and holistic views that elections officials should be able to provide. Elections officials must deal with the challenges of playing a more proactive role in the policy process as it affects election rules, practices, and resources while maintaining political neutrality. All parties must deal with the challenge of sustaining energy and focus through the peaks and troughs of the electoral cycle.

The call here is not for a specific set of guidelines, which could hardly be expected to address the myriad situations in the thousands of electoral jurisdictions of the United States and which would quickly become dated in any case. The call is for sustained reflection and dialogue on the public interest in the electoral process and the roles and interdependencies of the various players in it. There are few incentives for such a dialogue, but there is a clear ethical obligation.

References

"Ballot Child's Play for 8-year-olds." 2000. *JSOnline: Milwaukee Journal Sentinel.* www.jsonline.com/election2000/ap/nov00/ap-ballot-quiz (November 10).

Brady, Henry E. 2000. "Report on Voting and Ballot Form in Palm Beach County." http://elections.fas.harvard.edu/statement/hbrady/.

Brady, Henry E., Justin Buchler, Matt Jarvis, and John McNulty. 2001. "Counting All the Votes: The Performance of Voting Technology in the United States." Survey Research Center and Institute of Governmental Studies, University of California, Berkeley. http://www.electionline.org/news.jsp?s'reports.

Caltech/MIT Voting Technology Project 2001. "Voting: What Is, What Could Be." California Institute of Technology and Massachusetts Institute of Technology Corporation. http://www.electionline.org/news.jsp?s'reports.

Cauchon, Dennis, and Jim Drinkard. 2001. "Florida Voter Errors Cost Gore the Election." *USA Today,* May 11–13, 1.

Cooper, Terry L. 1998. *The Responsible Administrator: An Approach to Ethics for the Administrative Role.* San Francisco: Jossey-Bass.

Coote, Anna, and Jo Lanaghan. 1997. *Citizen Juries.* London: Institute of Public Policy Research.

"Defending the Ballot." 2000. ABCNEWS.com. http://more.abcnews.go.com/sections/politics/dailynews/lepore001221.html (December 21).

Delap, Clare. 1998. *Making Better Decisions.* London: Institute of Public Policy Research.

Goodnow, Frank. 1900. *Politics and Administration.* New York: Macmillan.

Heineman, Robert A., William T. Bluhm, Steven A. Peterson, and Edward N. Kearny. 1997. *The World of the Policy Analyst.* Chatham, N.J.: Chatham House.

Human Factors for Better Ballots. 2001. *IIE Solutions* 33, 9 (January).

Johnson, Steven. 2000. "The Butterfly Effect." *FEED Magazine,* November 17. http://www.feedmag.com/dialog/di423.shtml.

Kiel, L. Douglas. 1994. *Managing Chaos and Complexity in Government: A New Paradigm for Managing Change, Innovation, and Organizational Renewal.* San Francisco: Jossey-Bass.

Lipsky, Michael. 1980. *Street-level Bureaucracy.* New York: Russell Sage.

Lopez, Steve. 2000. "Madame Butterfly Follies." TIME.com, www.time.com/mag . . . e/article/0,9171,1101001127–88803,00.html (November 27).

Montjoy, Robert S. 2001. "Considering a National Concentration in Election Administration." *Journal of Public Affairs Education* 7 (January): 53–55.

Montjoy, Robert S., and Lawrence J. O'Toole Jr. 1979. "Toward a Theory of Policy Implementation: An Organizational Perspective." *Public Administration Review,* September-October, 465–476.

Montjoy, Robert S., and Douglas J. Watson. 1995. "A Case for a Reinterpreted Dichotomy of Politics and Administration in Council-Manager Government." *Public Administration Review,* May–June, 231–239.

Mosher, Frederick. 1968. *Democracy and the Public Service.* New York: Oxford University Press.

National Commission on Election Standards and Reform. 2001. "Report and Recommendations to Improve America's Election System." Washington, D.C.: National Association of Counties.

National Task Force on Election Reform. 2001. "Election 2000: Review and Recommendations by the Nation's Election Administrators." The Election Center, 12543 Westella Drive, Suite 100, Houston, Texas.

"Newspaper: Butterfly Ballot Cost Gore White House." 2001. CNN.com. http://www.cnn.com/20 . . . 03/11/palmbeach.recount/index.html (March 11).

Ostrom, Eleanor. 1996. "Crossing the Great Divide: Coproduction, Synergy, and Development." *World Development,* June, 1073–1087.

Rawls, John. 1971. *A Theory of Justice.* Cambridge: Belknap Press of Harvard University Press.

Roth, Susan K. 1998. "Disenfranchised by Design: Voting Systems and the Election Process." *Information Design Journal* 9: 1–5. http://www.informationdesign.org/pubs/roth1998.html.

Slaton, Christa D. 2001. "New Models of Citizen Deliberation." *Futures* 33: 356–360.

———. 1992. *Televote.* New York: Praeger.

Tuchman, Gary. 2001. "Ballot Nightmare Lingers for Palm Beach Election Chief." CNN.com. www.cnn.com (January 5).

U.S. General Accounting Office. 2001. "Elections: Perspectives on Activities and Challenges Across the Nation," GAO–02–03. http//www.gao.gov/new.items/d023.pdf.

Wand, Jonathan, N., Kenneth W. Shotts, Jasjeet S. Sekhon, Walter R. Mebane Jr., Michael C. Herron, and Henry E. Brady. 2001. "The Butterfly Ballot Did It: The Aberrant Vote for Buchanan in Palm Beach County, Florida." *American Political Science Review,* December, 793–810.

Wise, Charles R. 2001. "Election Administration in Crisis: An Early Look at Bush Versus Gore." *Public Administration Review,* March-April, 131–139.

Chapter 16 Review Questions

1. In brief, can you concisely sum up the advice about ethical behavior in the public office suggested by Waldo's essay? How do his views on the subject differ from those of Chester Barnard, Stephen Bailey, or Paul Appleby, to which the introduction of this chapter refers? Whose approach to ethics in government do you find the more persuasive? Explain your answer.

2. What factors in "The Butterfly Ballot Case" created so many difficult ethical dilemmas for election officials? Why were they unprepared to deal with these problems? Did objective or subjective responsibilities most influence their actions? What is meant by both terms? Which one is more influential in actions of elections officials and why?

3. On the basis of your reading of the case study, would you add any points to Waldo's essay regarding other obligations as well as criteria or standards for ethical behavior by public officials?

4. Why do issues that arise in government always contain at least some degree of ethical or moral choice? In your opinion, are similar moral choices apparent in decision making in the private sector?

5. Some observers argue that it is impossible to teach individuals who are preparing for public service careers to be moral and ethical—in other words, family background, religion, personal attitudes, and upbringing have more to do with a person's ethical orientation

than does formal educational training. Do you agree? Or are there ways formal class-room training can inculcate ethical behavior in those persons who may someday fill government posts?

6. Compare and contrast Case Study 1, "The Blast in Centralia No. 5," with Case Study 16 from the standpoint of ethical lessons for public administrators. Can you extract from the two cases a specific list of important lessons for practicing public administrators?

Key Terms

public versus private morality

higher law

ethical obligations

moral complexity

reason of state

the pyramid puzzle

metaphor of maps

ethical theory

Suggestions for Further Reading

Despite the enormous concern expressed about this topic in recent years, perhaps the most sensitive treatments remain those by earlier theorists: Chester Barnard, *The Functions of the Executive* (Cambridge, Mass.: Harvard University Press, 1938)—especially chapter 17; Paul H. Appleby, *Morality and Administration in Democratic Government* (Baton Rouge, La.: Louisiana State University Press, 1952); and Frederick C. Mosher, *Democracy and the Public Service,* 2nd ed. (New York: Oxford University Press, 1982)—especially chapter 8.

The classic scholarly debate over this subject (though it is couched in terms of responsibility instead of ethics) is between Carl J. Friedrich, "Public Policy and the Nature of Administrative Responsibility," *Public Policy,* 1 (Cambridge, Mass.: Harvard University Press, 1940), pp. 3–24; and Herman Finer, "Administrative Responsibility in Democratic Government," *Public Administration Review,* 1 (Summer 1941), pp. 335–350. Along with the Friedrich-Finer arguments, which remain highly germane even today, you should also read John M. Gaus, "The Responsibility of Public Administration," in Leonard D. White, *The Frontiers of Public Administration* (Chicago: University of Chicago Press, 1936), pp. 26–44, as well as Arthur A. Maass and Laurence I. Radway, "Gauging Administrative Responsibility," *Public Administration Review,* 9 (Summer 1949), pp. 182–192.

For other important writings that have addressed this subject with varying degrees of success or failure, see John Rohr, *Ethics for Bureaucrats,* 2nd ed. (New York: Marcel Dekker, 1988); Sissela E. Bok, *Lying* (New York: Random House, 1979), and *Secrets* (New York: Pantheon, 1983); John P. Burke, *Bureaucratic Responsibility* (Baltimore: The Johns Hopkins Press, 1986). Terry L. Cooper, *An Ethic of Citizenship for Public Administration* (Englewood Cliffs, N.J.: Prentice Hall, 1991); William L. Richter et al., *Combating Corruption/Encouraging Ethics: A Sourcebook for Public Service* (Washington, D.C.: American Society for Public Administration, 1990); Terry L. Cooper, *The Responsible Administrator: An Approach to Ethics for the Administrative Role,* 3rd ed. (San Francisco: Jossey-Bass, 1990); Gerald M. Pops and Thomas J. Paulak, *The Case for Justice* (San Francisco: Jossey-Bass, 1991); David H. Rosenbloom and James D. Carroll, eds., *Towards Constitutional Competence: A Casebook for Public Administrators* (Englewood Cliffs, N.J.: Prentice Hall, 1990); Kathryn G. Denhardt, *The Ethics of Public Service: Resolving Moral Dilemmas in Public Organizations* (New York: Greenwood, 1988); James Q. Wilson, *The Moral Sense* (New York: Free Press, 1993); and Louis C. Gawthrop, *Public Service and Democracy: Ethical Imperatives for the 21st century* (Chatham, N.J.: Chatham House, 1999).

In addition, there are several excellent essays, such as Mark T. Lilla, "Ethos, 'Ethics' and Public

Service," *The Public Interest,* 63 (Spring 1981), pp. 3–17, or, in the same issue, Thomas C. Schelling, "Economic Reasoning and the Ethics of Policy," pp. 37–61. For other essays, see York Wilbern, "Types and Levels of Public Morality," *Public Administration Review,* 44 (March/April 1984), pp. 102–108; Barbara S. Romzek and Melvin J. Dubnik, "Accountability in the Public Sector: Lessons from the Challenger Tragedy," *Public Administration Review,* 47 (May/June 1987), pp. 227–238; Terry L. Cooper, "Hierarchy, Virtue, and the Practice of Public Administration: A Perspective for Normative Ethics" *Public Administration Review,* 47 (July/August, 1987), pp. 320–328; Dennis F. Thompson, "The Possibility of Administrative Ethics," *Public Administration Review,* 45 (September/October 1985), pp. 555–561; James S. Bowman, "Ethics in Government, A National Survey of Public Administration," *Public Administration Review,* 50 (May/June 1990), pp. 345–353; J. Patrick Dobel, "Integrity in the Public Service," *Public Administration Review,* 50 (May/June 1990) pp. 354–366; Lloyd G. Nigro and William D. Richardson, "Between Citizen and Administration: Administrative Ethics and *PAR,"* *Public Administration Review,* 50 (November/December 1990), pp. 623–635; Richard T. Green, "Character Ethics and Public Administration," *International Journal of Public Administration,* 17 (1994), pp. 2137–2164; Debra Stewart, "Theoretical Foundations of Ethics in Public Administration: Approaches to Understanding Moral Action," *Administration and Society,* 23 (November 1991), pp. 357–373; Philip H. Jos and Samuel M. Hines, Jr., "Care, Justice and Public Administration," *Administration and Society,* 25 (November 1993), pp. 373–392; Lewis Mainzer, "Vulgar Ethics for Public Administration," *Administration and Society,* 23 (May 1991), pp. 3–28; Louis C. Gawthrop, "The Ethical Foundations of American Public Administration," *International Journal of Public Administration,* 16 (1993), pp. 139–163; Dennis Wittmer, "Ethical Sensitivity and Managerial Decision-Making: An Experiment," *Journal of Public Administration Research and Theory,* 2 (1992), pp. 443–462; Frank Marini, "The Use of Literature in the Exploration of Public Administration Ethics: The Example of Antigone," *Public Administration*

Review, 52 (September/October 1992), pp. 420–426; as well as the entire issue of *The Annals* (January 1995) devoted to essays on "Ethics in American Public Service." For an unusual counterargument that ethical conduct is a result of our biological make-up and thus there is little we can do about it, see Edward O. Wilson, "The Biological Basis of Morality," *The Atlantic Monthly,* 281, 4 (April, 1998), pp. 53–70.

Any in-depth review of this subject should include study of the Ethics in Government Act of 1978, as well as the enabling legislation and debates over such seminal oversight mechanisms as the War Powers Resolution of 1973, Freedom of Information Act 1967 (with 1974 amendments), Privacy Act (1974), the Inspector General's Office (1976), and the various ombudsman offices instituted within state and local governments. For many of these recent documents, see Richard J. Stillman II, ed., *Basic Documents of American Public Administration Since 1950* (New York: Holmes and Meier, 1982). Additionally, one should not overlook various professional association codes of conduct, such as the Code of Ethics of the American Society for Public Administration in *Applying Standards and Ethics in the 21st Century,* 4th ed. (Washington, D.C., ASPA, 1998).

Further reading that examines the practice of public administration through the mutiple lens of values includes the following recent texts: Montgomery, Van Wart, *Changing Public Sector Values* (New York and London: Garland, 1998); Guy B. Adams and Danny L. Balfour, *Unmasking Administrative Evil* (London: Sage, 1998); Arthur Isak Applebaum, *Ethics for Adversaries: The Morality of Roles in Public and Professional Life* (Princeton, N.J.: Princeton University Press, 1999); Michael Hunt, *Reform, Ethics and Leadership in Public Service: A Festschrift in Honour of Richard A. Chapman* (Aldershot, N.H.: Ashgate, 1998); John A. Rohr, *Civil Servants and Their Constitutions.* (Lawrence: University Press of Kansas, 2002); and John A. Rohr, *Public Service, Ethics, and Constitutional Practice* (Lawrence: University Press of Kansas, 1999). For specific ethical issues involving networks, see Peter L. Cruise, "A Brave New Networked World," *Public Administration and Management,* 7, 1 (2002), pp. 1–7; and in the same issue, an essay on globalization, Charles Garafalo, "Globalization, Moral Justification, and the Public Service," pp. 56–70.

For useful, up-to-date essays concerning ethics education, read James Bowman and Donald Menzel (eds.), *Teaching Ethics and Values in Public Administration Programs* (New York: SUNY Press, 1998).

Also, it is helpful to consider six alternative routes for studying this topic. First, many novels focus on the role of ethics in public life. For an excellent discussion of how they contribute to our understanding of the subject, see Dwight Waldo, *The Novelist on Organization and Administration: An Inquiry into the Relationship Between Two Worlds* (Berkeley, Calif.: Institute of Governmental Studies, June 1968), or Marc Holzer, Kenneth Morris, and William Ludwin, *Literature in Bureaucracy* (Wayne, N.J.: Avery Publishing, 1979). Second, autobiographies of distinguished public servants are worth reading, such as Elliot Richardson, *Reflections of a Radical Moderate* (New York: Pantheon Books, 1996). Third, insightful films on important leadership issues are very helpful. For the application of films to study these issues, see Hartwick Classic Leadership Cases, available from Hartwick Humanities in Management Institute, Hartwick College, Oneonta, New York 13820. Fourth, the new journal, *Public Integrity*, which began with the Winter 1999 issue, contains numerous, thoughtful essays, commentaries, reports, and book reviews on contemporary public ethics. Fifth, biographers remain rich sources for ethical insight; for example, see Gary Wills, *Certain Trumpets* (New York: Simon & Schuster, 1994).

Finally, Web sites dealing with ethics and public administration are also well worth looking at, especially http://www.aspanet.org/ethics/index.html as well as http://plsc.uark.edu/book/books/ethics/.

Name Index

Subject Index